Footprint

Syria & Lebanon Handbook

The travel guide

Ivan Mannheim

"You are not enclosed within your bodies,
nor confined to houses or fields.
That which is you dwells above the
mountain and roves with the wind."

Syria and Lebanon Handbook
First edition
© Footprint Handbooks Ltd 2001

Published by Footprint Handbooks
6 Riverside Court
Lower Bristol Road
Bath BA2 3DZ. England
T +44 (0)1225 469141
F +44 (0)1225 469461
Email discover@footprintbooks.com
Web www.footprintbooks.com

ISBN 1 900949 90 3
CIP DATA: A catalogue record for this
book is available from the British Library

Distributed in the USA by
Publishers Group West

Credits

Series editors
Patrick Dawson and Rachel Fielding

Editorial
Editor: Sarah Thorowgood
Maps: Sarah Sorensen

Production
Typesetting: Richard Ponsford and
Leona Bailey
Maps: Robert Lunn and Claire Benison
Colour maps: Kevin Feeney

Cover: Camilla Ford

Design
Mytton Williams

Photography
Front cover: Impact Photos
Back cover: Robert Harding
Picture Library
Inside colour section: Impact Photos,
James Davis Travel Photography,
Pictures Colour Library, Art Directors
and TRIP.

Print
Manufactured in Italy by LEGOPRINT

Every effort has been made to ensure
that the facts in this Handbook are
accurate. However, travellers should still
obtain advice from consulates, airlines
etc about current travel and visa
requirements before travelling. The
authors and publishers cannot accept
responsibility for any loss, injury or
inconvenience however caused.

Syria & Lebanon

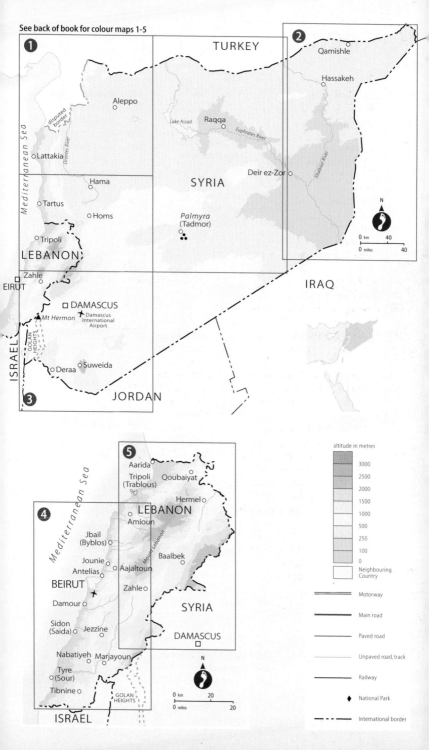

See back of book for colour maps 1-5

1

TURKEY

2

Qamishle

Hassakeh

Aleppo

Lake Assad

Raqqa

Euphrates River

Khabour River

Lattakia

Orontes River

disputed border

Mediterranean Sea

SYRIA

Deir ez-Zor

Hama

Tartus

Homs

Palmyra
(Tadmor)

Tripoli

LEBANON

Zahle

BEIRUT

DAMASCUS

Mt Hermon

Damascus International Airport

GOLAN HEIGHTS

ISRAEL

Deraa

Suweida

IRAQ

3

JORDAN

N

0 km 40
0 miles 40

5

Aarida

Tripoli
(Trablous)

Qoubaiyat

Hermel

LEBANON

Amioun

4

Mediterranean Sea

Jbail
(Byblos)

Jounie

Antelias

Aajaltoun

Mount Lebanon

Baalbek

BEIRUT

Zahle

Damour

SYRIA

Sidon
(Saida)

Jezzine

DAMASCUS

Nabatiyeh

Marjayoun

Tyre
(Sour)

Tibnine

GOLAN HEIGHTS

ISRAEL

N

0 km 20
0 miles 20

altitude in metres	
	3000
	2500
	2000
	1500
	1000
	500
	250
	100
	0
	Neighbouring Country

══════ Motorway

────── Main road

────── Paved road

────── Unpaved road, track

────── Railway

◆ National Park

─·─·─ International border

2

Contents

Right: *Aleppo's famous covered souk, which dates from the 13th-16th centuries, though it is believed to be based on the grid pattern of streets established by the Greeks in the third century BC.*

A foot in the door

4

Right: the picturesque village of Maaloula, near Damascus, where Aramaic, the language of Christ, is still spoken.
Below: Palmyra's monumental arch, with the Arab castle behind. This caravan city in the midst of the Syrian desert was ruled by a force to be reckoned with, Queen Zenobia, who challenged the might of the Roman Empire.

Right: the mighty Crusader castle of Krak des Chevaliers, in Syria's Jebel Ansariye mountains, is the largest and best preserved in the Middle East.
Above: Bedouin children near Ebla (Tell Mardikh), in Syria.

Highlights

Both Syria and Lebanon still labour under their media stereotypes as places of religious fanaticism, terrorism and intractable conflict. True, the region has had more than its fair share of wars, atrocities and suffering. Indeed, conflict here goes right back to the dawn of history, resonating through the Old Testament stories of the Exodus, when Moses led his people from exile in Egypt back to the Promised Land. But it is these same twists of religion, history and geography that make this such a fascinating region to visit. Forget your preconceptions and go see for yourself – you will find yourself stepping into a wonderful world of breathtakingly beautiful and well preserved historic monuments, stunning scenery, delicious food and diverse peoples. *Ahlan wa sahlan!*, 'You are welcome!' is a refrain you will hear over and over again, said almost as a matter of course, and yet with the heartfelt warmth, sincerity and instinctive hospitality so typical of both the Syrians and Lebanese.

Layers of history

This is an ancient land. Working your way backwards through the Islamic, Crusader, Byzantine and Roman periods, by the time you get to the birth of Christ there are another half a dozen civilizations still to go, taking you right back to the earliest origins of settlement and agriculture. The remnants left by these civilizations are no mere 'piles of old stones', but dramatically impressive monuments, some still in use today. The lavishly decorated Umayyad Mosque in Damascus still throngs with worshippers and reverberates with the daily calls to prayer. The formidable Crusader castle of Krak des Chevaliers, towering impressively on its hilltop, looks for all the world as if a contingent of heavily armoured knights might still be holding out inside. The delicate ruins of the Byzantine church of St Simeon would only need a new roof to make it perfectly serviceable. The world famous Roman temples, theatres and colonnaded streets of Palmyra and Baalbek continue to reflect their former Imperial grandeur and indeed are still being used to host annual cultural festivals.

Height, heat & dust

The towering peaks of Mount Lebanon present an awesome sight, rising abruptly from the shores of the Mediterranean and climbing steeply to their snowy heights. Equally spectacular are the views looking down: to the west on the shimmering azure of the Mediterranean, with the seemingly endless sprawl of coastal development reduced to Legoland proportions; to the east on the rich patchwork of the Bekaa Valley's fertile agricultural lands. Deep in the bowels of these mountains, meanwhile, the Jeita Grotto boasts a huge network of caverns dripping with enormous, gnarled stalactites and stalagmites, as well as all manner of other weird rock formations. Syria, too, has attractive mountain scenery in its little explored Jebel Ansariye range. Gently rolling hills and olive groves merge eventually into more rugged, forest-clad peaks and valleys. Then there are the vast expanses of the desolate yet eerily beautiful Syrian desert, home of the Bedouin and setting for the oasis which spawned Palmyra. One of the great rivers of the world, the mighty Euphrates, also flows through Syria, marking a line between the parched desert and the rain fed plains of the Jezira.

Everyone under the sun

The label 'Arab' can be broadly applied to all the peoples of Syria and Lebanon, though some Lebanese prefer, however tenuously, to claim descent from the Phoenicians instead! Whether or not they accept the Arab label, most would agree that within this there are also distinct 'Syrian' and 'Lebanese' identities, and much more importantly, a vast and complex web of different religious and ethnic groups. At its simplest, the religious division is between Muslim and Christian. However, within Islam there are several different branches: Sunni, Shi'ite, Ismaili, Alawi and Druze.

Likewise, Christianity is represented by the Eastern Orthodox (Greek, Armenian, Syrian), Catholic (Greek, Armenian, Chaldean) and Maronite churches. The Bekaa Valley, a stronghold of the radical Hezbollah, is also the setting for numerous Christian monasteries (not to mention a couple of internationally acclaimed vineyards). It takes less than an hour to drive from the staunchly Maronite Qadisha Valley to the Sunni Muslim old city of Tripoli; likewise from the Druze villages of the Chouf mountains to the Shi'ite ones of southern Lebanon. And, as often as not, there is an untold story of peaceful coexistence and common purpose amongst all the much reported conflict: ordinary people with lots of goodwill and good humour, working hard to make the best of their lives.

Bird's eye view: of salopettes & bikinis It's not something which most people would associate with Lebanon, but should you visit in the winter or early spring months, you could indulge in some skiing at one of several excellently equipped mountain resorts. If you really want to show off, you can always nip down to the coast in the afternoon for a spot of sunbathing on the beach. During the summer, you can also try your hand at paragliding. Whether you're an expert or a complete novice on a tandem flight with a qualified instructor, you will soar like an eagle from upper slopes of Mount Lebanon slowly down to land at the coast. Or if you prefer a less hectic scene, the Al Shouf Cedar Reserve has numerous beautiful and tranquil walks through the best of what's left of Lebanon's truly majestic cedar forests. Famous as the national emblem, some of these trees are more than a thousand years old, their trunks several metres in circumference and their branches spreading gracefully to form a thick, dark canopy.

Back to the future Both Damascus and Aleppo lay claim to being the oldest continuously inhabited cities in the world, and exploring the narrow alleyways, crowded souks and ancient monuments of their excellently preserved 'old city' areas you really do get a sense of historical continuity. Donkeys jostle for space with Suzuki minivans, lavish silk brocades compete for your attention with the latest lingerie, while around the corner from a graceful 14th-century mosque you might find a newly opened bar or club.

Monaco meets Paris Beirut's origins also go back at least as far as Phoenician times and here and there you can see small traces of its ancient past. However, this is overwhelmingly a modern city. In the 1960s Beirut was dubbed the 'Paris of the Middle East', drawing the rich and the famous into its high society world of wining and dining, gambling casinos, cabaret extravaganzas and beach resorts. Today the city is working hard to recapture this reputation, and if the determination, flair and joie de vivre of the Lebanese is anything to go by, it looks likely to succeed. In what is billed as the biggest urban redevelopment project in the world, the heart of Beirut has been almost completely rebuilt in recent years. The result is a unique blending of the ultra-modern with the graceful lines of restored 1920s French Mandate period architecture.

Feasts fit for kings - or merchants Middle Eastern cuisine is famous the world over and no visit would be complete without sampling what is undoubtedly some of the finest food that the region has to offer. A traditional Arabic meal, complete with a bewildering array of delicious mezze dishes, juicy chicken, meat or fish grills and outrageously sweet sweets, not to mention a good supply of arak to wash it all down with, is an experience not to be missed. Done properly, an Arabic meal can last for hours and amount to a major social event in itself. The Lebanese in particular are gourmets par excellence, and here you will find a huge selection of restaurants; not just serving Arabic food, but also every other imaginable cuisine under the sun. Syria does not have quite the same range, though both Damascus and Aleppo are starting to make a name for themselves. Already they boast quite a collection of excellent restaurants set in beautifully restored 17th- and 18th-century palaces and merchants' houses.

Clockwise from top: the new Cafe d'Orient and La Plage complex, on the Corniche in Beirut's Ain el-Mreisse district; the delicate remains of the Umayyad Palace at Aanjar, in Lebanon's Bekaa Valley; the ancient 'cedars of the Lord' have been logged since Phoenician times and are mentioned repeatedly in the Bible, today they are Lebanon's national emblem; the courtyard of Mir Amin Palace in Beit ed-Dine, today a luxurious hotel; Beirut old and new; graceful columns and arches of an Ottoman period building contrasts with the glass and steel of a modern office block.

Next page: never a place to do things by halves, Beirut actually has two Hard Rock Cafés!

Essentials

2

Essentials

Planning your trip

Both Syria and Lebanon easily justify separate visits in their own right, but, together, these two countries lend themselves ideally to a journey which will give you a broad and varied insight into the Arab world. Indeed, they have so much to offer that it's hard to know where to begin. Ask yourself what you want from your visit. Do you have a specific focus of interest, or are you happy simply travelling around, meeting people and exploring on a more or less random basis?

Be realistic: with such a wealth of possibilities it is easy to bite off more than you can chew. While it is possible to cover a surprising amount within a comparatively short period of time, if you are forever rushing between places and worrying about getting behind schedule, you are going to miss out. It is far better to see a few places properly and travel at a leisurely pace, allowing you to really enjoy both the sightseeing and travelling.

Be flexible: however well you plan in advance, there are any number of unexpected things that can happen. Be prepared to modify your plans according to the circumstances (be it the weather, new acquaintances or whatever). Once you get there you will soon start meeting people, hearing about or discovering unexpected places and perhaps going off on a completely different tangent.

Where to go

Greek, Roman and Byzantine monuments In the vast expanses of the desert-steppe which covers much of western Syria, the spectacular ruins of the ancient caravan city of **Palmyra**, the 'bride of the desert', rise majestically out of the wilderness. The differing influences of the Greeks, Parthians and Romans, along with Palmyra's own indigenous culture, combined to produce some truly distinctive artistic and architectural styles and today the ruins of Palmyra are undoubtedly amongst the most impressive in the Middle East.

The fertile plains of the Orontes valley near Hama provide an altogether different setting for the ruins of the Roman city of **Apamea** (known as Aphamia or Qalat Mudiq in Arabic). The most striking feature of these ruins is the long line of columns marking the main colonnaded street.

In the sombre black basalt landscape of the Hauran region in the far south of Syria, the town of **Bosra** boasts one of the largest and best preserved Roman theatres in the Middle East. In addition to the theatre/citadel, there are the ruins of an extensive Roman city, and some later Byzantine and Islamic monuments.

Half-way between Aleppo and Deir ez-Zor, on the edges of the desert, the crumbling walls of **Rasafeh** loom up, providing a dramatic prelude to this huge and awesome fortified caravan city. Built by the Roman emperor Diocletian in the third century AD, it became known as Sergiopolis during the Byzantine era in honour of the Roman soldier Sergius executed for converting to Christianity. By the sixth century it had developed into a flourishing pilgrimage centre with at least three churches.

To the northeast of Hama, on the edge of the Syrian desert, the setting for **Qasr Ibn Warden** is every bit as dramatic as that of Rasafeh. The use of wide bands of large, square black basalt blocks alternating with narrow bands of thin clay brickwork is elegant, striking and an architectural style found nowhere else in Syria.

Directly overlooking the mighty Euphrates river to the southeast of Deir ez-Zor, the city of **Dura Europos**, originally established by the Seleucids and dubbed the "Pompeii of the Syrian Desert", is famous for the frescos which were discovered here, most notably those of a synagogue which were miraculously preserved and are now on display in Damascus museum.

Syria
See also under 'Sports and special interest travel', page 62

Essentials

Museums of Syria and Lebanon

As you might expect of a region so rich in history, both countries have several fascinating museums well worth visiting.

*In Syria, the **Damascus National museum** and the **Aleppo National museum** have a wealth of really stunning artefacts from all over the country. Unfortunately, however, the presentation at both is little changed since the 1950s, and looks distinctly dated. In contrast, the new **Hama Archaeological museum**, opened in 2000, is excellently presented, with clear, well written interpretation boards, imaginative displays and equally impressive artefacts. Likewise, the small but excellent **Deir ez-Zor museum**, opened in 1996, adopts a modern format incorporating reconstructions and clear, informative explanations which help to bring the fascinating and often remarkably beautiful ancient artefacts of the Euphrates and Jezira regions to life. Some of Syria's museums are housed in buildings which are important historic monuments in their own right. The best example of this is perhaps the **Azem Palace** in Damascus. Also noteworthy is the **Maarat al-Numan museum**, set in a huge 16th-century Ottoman khan and containing a superb collection of Byzantine mosaics gathered from various sites around the central plains and Orontes Valley. Although entirely a modern affair, the **Suweida museum** likewise houses a remarkable collection of mosaics from nearby Shahba.*

*The only major museum in Lebanon, and justifiably a source of great pride amongst Lebanese, is the newly reopened **Beirut National museum**. Before the civil war, this was one of the finest in the Middle East. During the war, it stood on the infamous 'Green Line' separating the warring factions of East and West Beirut and suffered heavy damage. Now fully restored to its former glory, it is truly inspiring – a fitting symbol of the country's regeneration. On a rather different tack, the **Gibran museum** in Bcharre, at the head of the Qadisha valley, displays the paintings of the poet and artist Khalil Gibran, best known in the west for The Prophet. Many of Lebanon's historical and arhaeological sites include small museums, perhaps the most notable of these being the recently opened museum at **Baalbek**, in one of the vaulted tunnels beneath the huge Temple of Jupiter. Elsewhere, the Lebanese flair for enterprise has spawned some interesting museums. In Deir el-Qamar, in the Chouf mountains to the southeast of Beirut, the **Marie Baz museum**, housed in a 17th-century palace, contains a striking collection of expertly sculpted waxwork models chronicling all the major historical and politcal figures of the country. Around the corner, in another 17th-century palace, is a small, thoroughly enjoyable **holograms museum**!*

The 'Dead Cities' Scattered around the beautiful and rugged limestone hills to the northwest, west and southwest of Aleppo are literally hundreds of so-called 'Dead Cities', the ruins of settlements dating from the Byzantine era. These give a fascinating insight into the important role played by Syria in the early development of Christianity. Far and away the most famous of these is the remarkably well preserved church and pilgrimage complex of **St Simeon (Qalat Samaan)**, built around the hermitage of this famous saint who spent much of his life perched on top of a tall pillar. Of the other Dead City sites in the region, some (**Mushabbak**, **Qalb Lozeh** and **Bara** for example) are equally well preserved. Others consist only of tumbled ruins, yet even these retain a highly atmospheric, almost magical beauty, particularly when bathed in the rich golden light of the setting sun, or in spring when the olive groves and wild flowers are in full blossom.

Crusader and Arab Castles   When TE Lawrence undertook a walking tour of the Crusader and Arab castles of the Holy Land, he managed to visit no less than 36, the majority located in present-day Syria. Today there are still numerous castles to be found in the coastal Jebel Ansariye mountains, some remarkably intact, others crumbling ruins.

Standing proudly on a hilltop in the coastal mountains half-way between Homs and Tartus, **Krak des Chevaliers** is the largest and most imposing of the Crusader castles to be found anywhere in the Middle East. The whole castle is immaculately preserved, its mighty and complex fortifications a testimony to the engineering skills and determination of the Crusaders.

Qalat Saladin, to the east of Lattakia, was known to the Crusaders as Saône and only given its present name in the 1950s in commemoration of Saladin's capture of it in the 12th century. Though not as well preserved as Krak des Chevaliers, it is certainly on a par with it, and all the more impressive for its romantic location.

Perched high up on a spur within sight of the coast roughly half-way between Tartus and Lattakia, **Qalat Marqab** cuts an imposing silhouette against the skyline. Built of black basalt rock, even from a distance its huge size and sombre, brooding appearance are striking, while the views out over the Mediterranean are equally memorable.

Qalat al-Kahf was one of the headquarters of the Syrian leader of the much feared Assassins, a radical sect which was active in Syria during the 12th-13th centuries. Finding Qalat al-Kahf, deep in the Jebel Ansariye mountains, is a challenge in itself, and while not much of the castle remains, the setting is stunningly beautiful.

Islamic monuments   Justifiably ranked as one of the most important in the Islamic world, the **Umayyad Mosque** in Damascus is a truly awe-inspiring feast for the eyes, with its lavish mosaic decoration, towering minarets and huge dome. The elegant **Tekkiyeh as-Suleimaniyeh Mosque** also in Damascus was built in honour of the Ottoman sultan Suleiman the Magnificent in the 16th century. The complex also includes a *madrassa* (religious school) which now serves as a handicrafts market, while housed somewhat incongruously in the grounds of the mosque itself is a military museum.

Built in the 18th century as a royal residence by the Ottoman governor of Damascus, Assad Pasha al-Azem, the **Azem Palace**, with its tranquil, shaded courtyards and bubbling fountains surrounded by lavishly decorated rooms, is the largest and most opulent of many such palaces to be found in Syria.

The formidable **Ayyubid Citadel**, perched atop its conical mound, dominates the centre of the ancient city of Aleppo. Built by the son of Saladin, its massive fortifications represent the greatest masterpiece of Arab military architecture in Syria.

The town of Hama is famous primarily for its huge wooden water-wheels, or *norias*. In their present form these were built by the Ayyubids in the 13th century to harness the Orontes river, lifting its waters to a level where they could be used to irrigate the surrounding countryside. Today many of these *norias* still survive, and during the summer their distinctive groaning noise can be heard as the waters of the river push them round.

Baalbek   Set in the arresting beauty of the Bekaa Valley, the enormous Roman temple complex at Baalbek is Lebanon's prime historic attraction, awesome for its sheer size, elaborate decoration and excellent state of preservation. Built on the site of an ancient Phoenician temple and known to the Romans as Heliopolis, the 'City of the Sun', this became one of the empire's great cultic centres for the worship of Jupiter, a massive and elaborate monument to Rome's imperial might in a region which never fully submitted to its power.

Aanjar   The Bekaa valley also provides the setting for the remains of an eighth-century Umayyad settlement at Aanjar, within which stand the ruins of a graceful palace built by

Essentials

Lebanon

☞ *Taking it easy*

*At one time, practically every town in the Middle East supported at least one Turkish bath (or hammam). This luxury was first introduced to the region by the Romans, and enthusiastically embraced by every civilization which followed. Today, there are still plenty to be found around Syria. Some of them (notably the **Hammam Nur** ud-Din in Damascus and the **Hammam Yalbogha al-Nasri** in Aleppo) are beautiful, lavishly decorated historic monuments. As well as admiring their architecture, you can step inside for a gloriously soothing steam bath, scrub down and massage; the ideal way to unwind after a hard day's sightseeing or shopping.*

the Caliph Walid I, under whose rule the great Umayyad Mosque of Damascus was erected. The delicate columns and arches of the palace silhouetted against the Lebanon mountains provide a vivid image of this little-represented period in Lebanon's history.

Beit ed-Dine The palace of Beit ed-Dine was the seat of government of the powerful Shihab family which ruled much of present-day Lebanon as the Ottoman-appointed governors of what was in effect a mountain principality. Built in the early 19th century, the palace served as the summer residence of the president after independence. It suffered heavy damage during the civil war but has now been immaculately restored, standing today as a gem of Ottoman architecture, delightfully situated overlooking a deep, fertile valley in the Chouf mountains to the southeast of Beirut.

Jbail (Byblos) Excavations at Byblos, on the Mediterranean coast to the north of Beirut, have revealed it to be one of the oldest cities in the world. This was one of the great city-ports of the ancient Phoenician era, a wealthy centre of commerce from where ships traded throughout the Mediterranean and beyond, and also an important religious centre where the cult worship of Adonis and Astarte drew the attention of even the Egyptians. Today, the imposing ruins of a Crusader castle overlook the excavated remains of the ancient city, while the carefully restored Ottoman souks are full of shops selling antiques, souvenirs and handicrafts. The tiny fishing harbour, meanwhile, exudes an almost timeless atmosphere of Mediterranean charm, and is the setting for several delightful restaurants, the most famous of them being the Byblos Fishing Club, founded by the legendary Pepe Abed.

Tripoli Unlike Beirut, the northern coastal city of Tripoli has managed to preserve much of its old character and quiet, friendly atmosphere. The medieval core of the city is still intact, with a maze of narrow *souks* where life seems to have changed little over the centuries, and a wealth of Mameluke and Ottoman period monuments providing a testament to its importance as a cultural and commercial centre. Standing over the medieval city is the imposing St Gilles Citadel, built by Raymond St Gilles in the course of his attempts to wrest the coastal part of the city from Muslim rule.

Sidon (Saida) A short drive south of Beirut, Sidon was once one of the great Phoenician city-states of the region but is famous today for its picturesque Crusader 'Sea Castle' and charming medieval town arranged around a small harbour. Like Tripoli, the old parts of the town have changed little over the centuries and provide an unique insight into what Lebanese towns were like before the onslaught of 20th century development.

Tyre (Sour) In the far south of the country, Tyre was another of the great Phoenician city-states, though what has been preserved here are the extensive ruins of the city during Greek and Roman times, including two sections of the main colonnaded

Festivals

When planning your trip, take into account the major festivals in the region. If any coincide with your visit, it is well worth making an effort to catch them.

In Syria, the **Palmyra Desert Festival**, from 2-5 May is a major annual event. In the day there is a full programme of horse and camel racing (if you've never seen a camel race before, its highly entertaining; often the challenge seems to be as much to do with getting the animals to run – if that's the right word – in the right direction, let alone actually win). During the evenings there are perfomances of folk dancing, music etc in the restored Roman theatre in the midst of the ruins. The **Bosra Festival** is held every other year (on odd-numbered years), usually starting on the 1 September and lasting for around 15 days. Again, this festival uses the huge Roman theatre here as a venue for a lively programme of music, singing, dancing and drama, with many visiting acts from abroad. For further details of both these festivals you could try

contacting the Ministry of Tourism (see page 80), though whether or not they will actually be able to help is another question, or else try their website: www.syriatourism.org

The **Baalbek Festival**, held from early July through to mid-August each year, is perhaps the most prestigious in the Middle East. Before the civil war it enjoyed worldwide renown and boasted a line-up of big names from the Bolshoi Ballet to The Who. Re-started once again in 1997, it is well on its way to regaining its former reputation, presenting a dazzling spectacle of sight and sound amongst the awesome ruins. For full details, check the festival website; www.baalbeck.org.lb A couple of other regional festivals have also been re-instated at important sites in Lebanon; the **Beit ed-Dine Festival** (held in July/ August; try www.beiteddine.org.lb for details) and the **Byblos Festival** (held in August/September; contact the Ministry of Tourism – see page 404 – for details, and for details of any other new festivals).

street, a triumphal arch, a necropolis and a huge hippodrome. The small fishing harbour, surrounded by the town's Christian quarter and Ottoman-period souks, are also very picturesque.

Itineraries

It is possible to get round most of the major sites in either country within the space of one or two weeks, but you must be prepared to do a lot of travelling and willing to spend only a minimum of time at each place. The list of highlights above, though by no means comprehensive, will help you prioritize, while the suggested itineraries below will give you some idea of what is feasible in a given amount of time.

Given that there is so much to see, unless you have unlimited time you will have to be selective

Most visitors to Syria arrive by air in Damascus, although if you are coming overland from Turkey, Aleppo will probably be your first port of call. In either case, the country lends itself fairly logically to a triangular circuit; Damascus-Homs-Hama-Aleppo-Raqqa-Deir ez-Zor-Palmyra-Damascus (whatever the starting point or direction), with detours to the southern Hauran, the coastal mountains and Mediterranean coast, and the northeastern Jezira. If your time is limited, concentrate on the main corridor between Damascus and Aleppo, and make excursions to Palmyra, the southern Hauran and the coastal mountains. As a general rule it makes most sense to base yourself for a time in each of the major towns and cities and then organize excursions to the places of interest in the vicinity.

There are two approaches to planning an itinerary for Lebanon. The country's small size means that it is perfectly possible to base yourself in Beirut (or Jounieh, or anywhere else that is reasonably centrally located) and make excursions all over Lebanon from there. Alternatively you can travel around the country, staying at different places along the way. The main advantage of basing yourself in Beirut is the vast choice of hotels there (at least in the mid-range to luxury bracket); elsewhere in the country accommodation is more limited (particularly in the south). The main disadvantage is that you have to negotiate miles of chaotic traffic jams every time you enter or leave the capital.

Syria: 1 week

Day 1: Fly to Damascus; sightseeing.

Day 2: Full day sightseeing/shopping in Damascus.

Day 3: Early morning departure to Palmyra; rest of day sightseeing, including sunset.

Day 4: Sunrise in Palmyra; travel to Hama (via Homs); rest of day sightseeing in Hama.

Day 5: Full day excursion from Hama to Apamea, Masyaf and Krak des Chevaliers.

Day 6: Early morning travel to Aleppo; rest of day sightseeing/shopping.

Day 7: Morning excursion to St Simeon; afternoon return to Damascus; night flight home.

Syria: 2 weeks

Day 1: Fly to Damascus.

Day 2: Full day sightseeing/shopping in Damascus.

Day 3: Full day excursion to Bosra, Suweida and Qanawat.

Day 4: Early morning departure to Palmyra; rest of day sightseeing, including sunset.

Day 5: Sunrise in Palmyra; travel to Deir ez-Zor; visit museum; excursion to Dura Europos (and Mari if time).

Day 6: Travel to Aleppo, visiting Rasafeh, Ath Thawra Dam and Qalat Jaber en route.

Day 7: Full day sightseeing/shopping in Aleppo.

Day 8: Full day excursion to Mushabbak, St Simeon, Ain Dara and Cyrrhus.

Day 9: Full day excursion to Qalb Lozeh, Bara and around, Maarat al-Numan and Ebla (or a selection of these).

Day 10: Travel to Hama; visit *norias* and museum; excursion to Apamea and Masyaf.

Day 11: Travel to Tartus, spending most of day visiting Krak des Chevaliers en route (and Safita if time).

Day 12: Full day sightseeing Tartus and Arwad Island.

Day 13: Travel to Lattakia, visiting Qalat Marqab and Qalat Saladin en route.

Day 14: Return to Damascus (visiting Maaloula en route if time); night flight home.

Syria: 3 weeks

Days 1-4: Damascus, Bosra, Suweida, Qanawat, Quneitra and Maaloula (using Damascus as a base).

Days 5-6: Palmyra, with excursion to Qasr al-Heir al-Sharki.

Days 7-8: Deir ez-Zor, Dura Europos, Mari (Tell Hariri), Halabiye/Zalabiye (using Deir ez-Zor as a base).

Day 9: Travel to Aleppo, visiting Rasafeh, Ath Thawra Dam and Qalat Jaber en route.

Days 10-11: Shopping/sightseeing in Aleppo.

Day 12: Full day excursion to Mushabbak, St Simeon, Ain Dara and Cyrrhus.

Day 13: Full day excursion to Qalb Lozeh, Bara and around, Maarat al-Numan and Ebla (or a selection of these).

Day 14: Train through mountains to Lattakia; excursion to Ugarit (Ras Shamra) and Kassab etc if time.

Day 15: Half day excursion to Qalat Saladin; travel to Tartus, visiting Qalat Marqab en route.

Day 16: Full day sightseeing Tartus and Arwad Island.

Day 17: Full day excursion to Dreikish, Hosn Suleiman and Qalat al-Kahf.

Day 18: Drive via Safita to Krak des Chevaliers; sightseeing; stay overnight in area.

Day 19: Travel to Hama via Masyaf and Apamea.

Day 20: Sightseeing in Hama; half day excursion to Qasr Ibn Warden and beehive houses, visiting Salamiyeh and Qalat Shmemis on way back if time.

Day 21: Return Damascus; fly home.

Day 1: Arrive Beirut (by air or from Syria); sightseeing/shopping.

Day 2: Full day excursion Nahr el-Kalb, Jeita Grotto Jounieh/Harissa (télépherique).

Day 3: Full day excursion Deir el-Qamar, Beit ed-Dine and Al Shouf Cedar Reserve.

Day 4: Travel to Tripoli, visiting Byblos (Jbail) en route.

Day 5: Half day sightseeing Tripoli; travel to Bcharre; sightseeing Qadisha valley.

Day 6: Half day sightseeing Qadisha valley; travel via the Cedars (Al Arz) to Baalbek.

Day 7: Half day sightseeing Baalbek; return Beirut; fly home/cross to Syria.

Lebanon: 1 week

Day 1: Arrive Beirut (by air or from Syria); sightseeing/shopping.

Day 2: Full day sightseeing/shopping in Beirut.

Day 3: Full day excursion Nahr el-Kalb, Jeita Grotto Jounieh/Harissa (télépherique).

Day 4: Full day excursion Deir el-Qamar, Beit ed-Dine and Al Shouf Cedar Reserve.

Day 5: Full day excursion Sidon (Saida) and Tyre (Sour).

Day 6: Travel to Byblos (Jbail); rest of day sightseeing plus relaxing on beach.

Day 7: Full day excursion up Adonis valley (Nahr Ibrahim) to Afqa, visiting La Reserve en route and returning via Aaqoura, Laqlouq and St Charbel's monastery.

Day 8: Travel to Tripoli; rest of day sightseeing.

Day 9: Half day sightseeing/shopping; travel to Bcharre; sightseeing Qadisha valley.

Day 10: Full day sightseeing Qadisha valley.

Day 11: Travel via the Cedars (Al Arz) to Zahle; visit Ksara vinyard plus around Zahle.

Day 12: Full day sightseeing Baalbek and Aajar (overnight Zahle or Baalbek)

Day 13: Return Beirut, going via Zahle-Bikfaya road, and then through Broummana and Beit Meri.

Day 14: Fly home/cross to Syria.

Lebanon: 2 weeks

Day 1: Arrive Damascus; sightseeing/shopping.

Day 2: Full day excursion Palmyra.

Day 3: Full day excursion Maaloula and Krak des Chevaliers.

Day 4: Cross Jdaide border into Lebanon; travel via Aanjar to Baalbek; rest of day sightseeing; overnight Baalbek or Zahle.

Day 5: Travel to Beirut; rest of day sightseeing/shopping.

Day 6: Full day excursion to Deir el-Qamar, Beit ed-Dine and Al Shouf Cedar Reserve.

Day 7: Return Damascus/fly home, or half day excursion to Byblos; fly home from Beirut.

Syria & Lebanon: 1 week

When to go

As a general rule, Syria is at its best during the spring (late March to early June) and autumn (early September to early November). During both these seasons temperatures are on the whole pleasantly mild (15-20°C). Spring is when the country is at its greenest, the wild flowers and olive groves are in full blossom and the showers and cooler air mean that the atmosphere is free from haze, so you get the best views. During the summer (early June to early September) it is generally very hot and dry, with temperatures averaging 30°C and sometimes reaching above 40°C, particularly from mid-July to mid-August. Sightseeing in such conditions can be very hard work. Winter (mid-November to mid-March) by contrast can be bitterly cold, temperatures often fall close to freezing and this is also when the majority of the rainfall comes.

Syria

These generalizations apply most accurately to the most densely populated central spine of the country between Damascus and Aleppo (ie the Orontes valley and central plains). There are considerable regional variations according to the altitude and local geography. The coastal Jebel Ansariye mountains, the limestone hills around Aleppo, the northeastern Jezira region and the Hauran plateau in the south of the country are colder and there is a higher chance of rain here during the early spring (until the end of April) and late autumn (from late October). They are also less unbearably hot during the summer, particularly in the case of the coastal mountains.

Essentials

Essentials

Conversely, sites such as Palmyra in the Syrian desert can be very pleasant during the daytime even during the depths of winter (providing it is sunny). Remember that temperatures drop dramatically at night in the desert during winter, and even in summer there is a significant drop. The Mediterranean coastal strip gets extremely humid during the summer months, but otherwise conforms to the norm.

Lebanon Very loosely, Lebanon's climate is at its most attractive during spring and autumn, though its unique topography and long Mediterranean sea board mean that there are enormous local variations in any given season. Choosing a 'best time' depends entirely on where you are planning to go and what you are planning to do.

The coast gets very hot and humid during the summer months (mid-May to mid-September), and particularly so during July and August. Visiting Beirut or any of the towns and cities along the coast is hard work in these conditions and this is also when the beach resorts are at their busiest. Both spring and autumn are short-lived, but during March, April and October there are usually spells of pleasantly warm and reasonably dry weather. Note, however, that March/April is also the time of the so-called *khamsin*, when hot, dry, sand-laden winds sometimes blow in from the Sahara. Winters on the coast are cool and rainy, with frequent heavy thunderstorms and rough seas.

The mountains enjoy an essentially alpine climate. The summer months see the Lebanese decamping to the mountains in droves, exchanging the heat and humidity on the coast for blissfully cool mountain breezes and warm sunny days. The cooling effects of the breezes do not reduce the burning power of the sun, however, and proper protection is essential. Higher up, it gets quite chilly at night, even in July and August. Though temperatures get steadily cooler, the weather generally stays pleasantly dry and sunny right through to November. By December it is cold and the winter rains and snows begin in earnest, usually lasting through to around May, when it begins to warm up again.

The Bekaa Valley experiences hot dry summers (early June to mid-September) and cold dry winters (mid-November to mid-March). Spring is the ideal time in the Bekaa, with cool, crisp, sunny days and an abundance of flowering and blossoming against a backdrop of snow-capped mountains. The autumn climate is equally pleasant and with its changing colours, fruit-laden orchards and harvests, is also a time of beauty and abundance.

Tours and tour operators

For details of local tour operators in Syria & Lebanon, see the Essentials sections of the Damascus & Beirut chapters. For details of sports & special interest tour operators in Syria & Lebanon, see page 62

There are plenty of foreign tour operators offering fairly detailed tours of Syria and Lebanon, though they tend to be extremely expensive. Organized tours run by local tour operators are readily available and are considerably cheaper. Many of these local tour operators can arrange tours covering both countries. Most of the foreign package tours which visit Lebanon do so as part of a tour of the wider region. Many of them do just a quick dash into Lebanon from Syria to visit Baalbek, sometimes even returning to Syria the same day. If you are travelling independently but your time is limited, it might make sense to join a tour organized by a local tour operator in Beirut; these are reasonably good value and allow you to get round the major sights fairly quickly. However, by far the most rewarding way to visit Syria and Lebanon is on your own initiative. These are fascinating and rewarding countries in which to travel, and if you do it yourself you will have far more contact with people and gain more of an insight into them and their countries.

Abercrombie & Kent Travel Sloane Square House, Holbein Pl, London SW1 8NS, T020-77309600, F020-77309376, www.abercrombiekent.com *Ancient World Tours*, PO Box 12950, London W6 8GY, T07071-222950, F01328-823293, www.ancient.

co.uk *The British Museum Traveller*, 46 Bloomsbury St, London WC1B 3QQ, T020-74367575, F020-75808677. *Cricketer Holidays*, 4 The White House, Beacon Rd, Crowborough, East Sussex, TN6 1AB, T01892-667459, F01892-662355. *Cox & Kings*, 4th floor, Gordon House, 10 Greencoat Pl, London SW1P 1PH, T020-78735000, F020-76306038, www.coxandkings.co.uk *Eastern Approaches*, 5 Mill Rd, Stow, Selkirkshire, TD1 2SD, Scotland, T01578-730361, F01578-730714, w.ball@easynet. co.uk *Egyptian Encounter*, Longcroft House, Arnewood Bridge Rd, Sway, Nr Lymington, Hants SO41 6DA, T01590-683364. *Exodus*, 9 Weir Rd, London, SW12 0LT, T020-86755550, F020-86730779, www.exodus.co.uk *Explore Worldwide*, 1 Fredrick St, Aldershot, Hants, GU11 1LQ, T01252-319448, F01252-343170, www. exploreworldwide.com *Fellowship Tours*, PO Box 29, Chard, Somerset, TA20 2YY, F01460-221406. *Inter Church Travel*, Saga Building, Middelburg Square, Folkestone, Kent CT20 1BL, T0800-300444. *Martin Randall Travel*, 10 Barley Mow Passage, Chiswick, London W4 4PH, T020-87423355, F020-87421066, www.martinrandall.com *McCabe Travel*, 53-55 Balham Hill, London SW12 9DR, T020-86756828. *Orientours Pilgrimages*, Sovereign House, 11 Ballards Lane, Finchley, London, T020-83469114, www.traveleshop.com/operators/otpop.html *Page & Moy*, 136-40 London Rd, Leicester LE2 1EN, T08700-106212, www.pagemoy.com *Prospect Music & Art Tours*, 36 Manchester St, London, W1U 7LH, T020-74865704, F020-74865868. *Sunvil Holidays* Sunvil House, Upper Square, Old Isleworth, Middx TW7 7BJ, T020-85684499, F020-85688330, www.sunvil.co.uk *Swan Hellenic Tours*, 77 New Oxford St, London WC1A 1PP, T020-78002200, F020-78002723, www.swan-hellenic.co.uk *The Imaginative Traveller*, 1 Betts Avenue, Martlesham Heath, Suffolk IP5 3RHW4, T020-87428612, F0208-7423045 www.imaginative-traveller.com *Voyages Jules Verne*, 21 Dorset Square, London NW1 6QG, T020-77235066, F020-77238629, www.vjv.co.uk

Essentials

Finding out more

For a full list of websites relating to Syria & Lebanon, & the Middle East region in general, see page 71

Syria does not have any dedicated tourist offices abroad, although their embassies will provide you with a selection of the Ministry of Tourism's free maps/pamphlets. At most Syrian embassies this is all you will get, and nothing more (other than a visa).

Lebanon has only two Ministry of Tourism offices abroad, in Paris and Cairo. *Office du Tourisme du Liban*, 124 Rue du Faubourg, Honore, 75008 Paris, France, T01-43591036, F01-43591199. *Lebanon Tourist Office*, 1 Talaat Harb St, Midan al-Tahrir, Cairo, Egypt, T/F202-3937529. Elsewhere, you should contact the Lebanese embassy. These tend to be a little more helpful than the Syrian embassies, with at least one member of staff assigned to dealing with tourism-related queries.

By far the best source of information on Lebanon is the internet, with a range of websites covering everything from details of visa requirements to hotels, restaurants, shopping etc. Websites giving information on Syria are not quite so developed but still more useful than the stonewalling you will encounter at most of their embassies.

Language

For a list of useful Arabic words & phrases, see page 659

Arabic is the national language in both Syria and Lebanon. In Syria, even in very remote areas, you will usually be able to find someone who speaks at least a little **English**, while in the major towns and cities and at important tourist sites, English is fairly widely spoken. Many older generation Syrians also speak a little French.

The great premium placed on education in Lebanon is reflected in the high levels of fluency in both English and French, even in remote, rural areas. Due to its colonial history **French** remains the most widely spoken language after Arabic. However, amongst the younger generations, English is increasingly seen as the more desirable second language. In short, you are much more likely to find someone who can help you out in either French or English in Lebanon than you are in Syria.

Disabled travellers

Despite the considerable obstacles to disabled travel in Syria & Lebanon, if you do go, you can be sure that people everywhere will be extremely accommodating & helpful

Provisions for disabled travellers are largely non-existent in Syria. In Lebanon, some of the luxury hotels have facilities for disabled people, but it is getting around the country which is the problem. In both countries, urban areas generally have uneven, cracked and pot-holed pavements, with ridiculously high kerbs. Visiting historic sites often involves traversing rough, uneven ground unsuitable for wheelchairs.

The following organizations can provide you with further advice and put you in touch with travel agents and tour operators specializing in travel for the disabled. *RADAR* (*Royal Association for Disability and Rehabilitation*), 12 City Forum, 250 City Rd, London EC1V 8AF, UK, T020-72503222, minicom T020-72504119, www.radar. org.uk *Irish Wheelchair Association*, Blackheath Drive, Clontarf, Dublin 3, Republic of Ireland, T01-8338241, F01-8333873, iwa@iol.ie *Mobility International*, 25 Rue de Manchester, Bruxelles B-1070, Belgium, T02-4106297. *Mobility International USA*, PO Box 10767, Eugene, OR 97440, T541-3431284, www.miusa.org *Society for the Advancement of Travel for the Handicapped* (*SATH*), 347 5th Ave, Suite 610, New York, NY 10016, USA, T212-4477284, www.sath.org *ACROD* (*Austalian Council for the Rehabilitation of the Disabled*), PO Box 60, Curtin, Canberrra, ACT 2605, Australia, T02-62824333. *Disabled Persons Assembly*, 173-175 Victoria St, Wellington, New Zealand, T04-8119100.

Gay and lesbian travellers

Homosexuality is officially illegal in Syria and Lebanon, and very much frowned on. A gay scene does exist in Beirut, but you really need some sort of introduction to it.

Premarriage homosexuality amongst men is probably far more widespread than most Syrians and Lebanese would admit, but it remains a taboo subject. The idea of women engaging in lesbian relationships is something which Syrian and Lebanese men seem totally unable to come to terms with, and most would deny that it occurs at all. Gay and lesbian travellers are therefore advised to be discreet about their sexuality. Paradoxically, the carefully segregated nature of society means that public behaviour which would be seen as inappropriate between members of the opposite sex (eg holding hands, kissing on the cheek etc) is acceptable between members of the same sex.

Student travellers

Anyone in full-time education is entitled to an **International Student Identity Card (ISIC)**. These are issued by student travel offices and travel agencies across the world. In Syria an ISIC card is enormously valuable since it entitles you to massive discounts on entry fees to museums and historic sites etc. For example, the entry fee for most museums and sites is a hefty S£300 (a little over £4.50/US$6.50 at the official bank rate), while with a student card it is usually only S£15. Not surprisingly, a lively market in fake ISIC cards has sprung up (Aleppo and Palmyra are the easiest places to get them) and at some sites your card will be very carefully scrutinized. In Lebanon, an ISIC card entitles you to a discount entry fee at the National Museum in Beirut, but elsewhere you still have to pay the full fee. There is one travel agent in Beirut (*Campus Travel*, see 'Essentials' in the Beirut chapter) which can offer heavily discounted student fares on international flights. To qualify you must either have an ISIC card and be under 31 years old, or have a 'GO 25' card and be under 25.

Travel with children

Children are positively doted on throughout the Middle East. "Do you have children?", or, more commonly, "How many children do you have?" is a standard question asked of foreigners. Unlike in Europe or North America, children are warmly welcomed in restaurants, and most hotels will go out of their way to accommodate them. Indeed, if you are travelling with children, you will constantly find yourself receiving offers of help and hospitality. There are of course important health considerations specific to children (see page 66), but facilities are reasonably good in all but the most out-of-the-way places in Syria, and excellent throughout Lebanon. With a little bit of planning, it is easy to travel safely and comfortably with children in both countries.

Women travellers

Generally, women travelling alone in Syria experience no more harassment than is the norm in most European countries; the majority report it to be amongst the most relaxed in the Middle East in this respect. While it can be more demanding, there are also distinct advantages. In the vast majority of situations women are treated with great respect. Seasoned female travellers in Syria argue that they get the best of both worlds. As a foreigner they are generally accorded the status of 'honorary males' in public, while in private they have access to female society, from which men are excluded. When invited to a Muslim Syrian household, male guests are usually confined to the guest room while women are whisked away behind the scenes into the 'real' household, where they can meet wives, mothers, sisters and other members of the extended family.

Amongst Syria's Christians (and amongst wealthier Syrians of any background), social etiquette and codes of dress are much more relaxed. Nevertheless, women travellers should make an effort to dress modestly, particularly away from the big towns and cities, where conservative Muslim values tend to prevail. Skimpy,

Essentials

Syria

tight-fitting or revealing clothes cause great offence to Muslims. Much more acceptable are loose-fitting clothes that do not highlight the lines of your body and do not expose anything more than your head, hands and feet. A scarf is useful for covering up further if you begin to feel exposed or uncomfortable in a given situation; it is also very good protection against the sun. Some women argue that it makes absolutely no difference to a determined male what you are wearing. However, given that actual harassment is relatively rare, the main object of dressing modestly is to show respect for Islamic values and not cause offence. Wearing a wedding ring may help to classify you as 'respectably married', while photos of a husband and children (whether real or imaginary) will further raise your status.

Remember that most Syrian women do not travel alone, and in more remote areas are rarely seen in public. The widely held perception of western women is based on the images in western magazines, films and satellite TV which portray them as having 'loose' sexual morals which can lead to problems of sexual harassment. Cases of violent sexual assault are, however, extremely rare and a firm, unambiguous response will deal with most situations. In public, the best approach is to make a scene; someone is bound to come to your aid, while the perpetrator will quickly vanish in a cloud of shame. Predictably enough, many women travellers report receiving far more unwanted attention after dark in the 'red light' districts of Damascus (Martyrs' Square) and Aleppo (the area of cheap hotels bounded by Baron St, Al Maari St, Al Kouwatly St and Bab al-Faraj St).

Lebanon On the surface, Lebanon is much more relaxed than Syria, and arguably the most liberal of all the Middle Eastern countries. Lebanese women love to dress in all the latest fashions. Indeed, the 'body-beautiful' concept is deeply rooted in the Lebanese psyche, and showing off their bodies appears to be a major preoccupation amongst Lebanese women. The glossy magazine image of the ideal Lebanese woman is one who divides her time between fitness/body toning activities, hair and beauty treatments, designer shopping and a high society world of wining and dining and dancing and romancing. In reality, however, the unspoken rules governing relationships and sexual behaviour remain very conservative indeed (amongst both Muslims and Christians). The majority of women live with their families until they are married and however much they may appear to indulge in a 'high society' lifestyle, they are in fact carefully chaperoned and protected from any possibility of bringing 'dishonour' to the family. As a foreign women travelling alone in Lebanon, you are likely to attract a considerable amount of attention from young Lebanese males in certain situations, but on the whole it tends to be reasonably good natured and polite. The Lebanese love to charm, and you can either play the game or make it clear that you are not interested. If the come-ons are threatening or unpleasant, make your feelings known clearly and firmly. It is very important to remember that however liberal attitudes may appear to be towards women's dress in Beirut and Jounieh and other cosmopolitan areas, as soon as you head inland into remoter rural (and particularly Muslim) areas, attitudes are much more conservative. Loose-fitting clothing that covers the arms and legs and a headscarf are preferable in such areas, and obligatory if visiting mosques.

Before you travel

Passport A full passport valid for at least six months beyond your intended period of stay is required to visit both Syria and Lebanon. Make sure that there is plenty of space in your passport for entry/exit stamps, visa extensions and any other visas you intend to buy while travelling. A supply of passport photos is very useful for any visas or visa extensions you might want to apply for while travelling. You should always carry your passport with you when travelling in Syria and Lebanon. Make photocopies of all your

Syrian embassies and consulates abroad

Australia *(Consulate) 57 Cardigan St, Carlton, Victoria 3053, T03-93478445, F03-93478447, or 10 Belmore St, Arncliffe, NSW 2205, T02-95977714, F02-95972226.*

Belgium *Ave Franklin Roosevelt 3, Brussels 1050, T02-6480135.*

Egypt *Sharia Abd ar-Rahim Sabri 18, Doqqi, Cairo, T02-3777020, F03-3358232.*

France *20 Rue Vaneau, 75007 Paris, T01-45518235.*

Germany *Otto Grotewohl Str 2, Berlin, T030-2202046; Consulate, Andreas Hermes Str 5, Bonn 2, T0228-819920.*

Italy *Piazza Coeli 1, Rome, T06-6797791.*

Jordan *Tawfiq Abu al-Huda St, between 3rd-4th Circle, Amman, T06-4641935, F06-4641945.*

Spain *Plaza de Plateria de Martinez 1, Madrid, T91-4201602.*

Switzerland *72 Rue de Lausanne, 1202 Geneva, T22-326522.*

Turkey *Abdullah Cevdet Sokak No 7, Cankaya, Ankara, T312-4409657.*

UK *8 Belgrave Square, London SW1 8PH, T020-72459012, F020-72354621, visa info line T0891-600171.*

USA *2215 Wyoming Av NW, Washington DC 20008, T202-2326313.*

Essentials

documents and keep them separate from the originals. Ideally, you should leave a set of photocopies with someone at home whom you can contact easily.

All foreign nationals require a valid tourist visa, which **must be obtained before arriving in Syria**; they are rarely, if ever, issued at the point of entry. The only exceptions to this are for nationalities who do not have a Syrian embassy in their home country (eg Australians, New Zealanders and Dutch). Officially, these nationalities are entitled to a visa at the point of entry, although in practice you may find that it takes a great deal of dogged persistence to persuade the immigration officials that this is the case. Many travellers have been unsuccessful. If you are travelling via the UK or Europe, you are much better off applying at an embassy there, although you may be asked to provide proof of residence in the UK, which creates a further set of hurdles.

Rather bizarrely, **it is currently impossible to get a Syrian visa in Lebanon**, since there is no Syrian embassy there. It is also almost impossible for foreign tourists to get a Syrian visa in Jordan, since the only people officially being issued with them are Jordanians, or those with permanent Jordanian residency. As with obtaining visas at the border, the only possible exception to this rule is if there is no Syrian embassy in your home country. However, the Syrian embassy is far from consistent on this point and, even assuming that they do concede, you will have to do battle with their Kafkaesque bureaucracy in order to get the visa. Be safe and get your visa before coming to Jordan (Syrian visas are available in Cairo and Ankara, although they are much easier to obtain in your home country).

Single entry visas must be used within three months of the date of issue, and multiple entry visas within six months of the date of issue. If you are planning to go from Syria into Lebanon and then back to Syria, be sure to obtain a multiple entry Syrian visa. It is in fact possible to re-enter on a single entry visa (see page 132), but it will cost you the equivalent of another visa, and involve hours of extra bureaucracy. Visa applications must include a letter from your employer to the effect that you have a job to come back to, the application form in duplicate, two passport photos and the relevant fee. Visas applied for in person at the London embassy are usually issued within four working days. Visa fees at the Syrian embassy in London vary greatly according to your nationality (see box). It is usually (though not always) slightly cheaper to apply for a Syrian visa in your home country.

All tourist visas are initially only valid for a period of 15 days. If you wish to stay for more than 15 days you must apply for a visa extension at a Passport and Immigration office. There are branches of these offices in most major towns and cities (see under

Syrian visas
You will not be issued with a visa, or allowed entry into Syria even with a visa, if there is any evidence in your passport of a visit to Israel (see 'Entry/Exit Stamp Game' box, page 26)

Prices for Syrian Tourist Visas issued in London

	Single entry (UK£)	Multiple entry (UK£)
Belgium	23	29
Canada	33	68
France	17.50	33
Germany	20	33
Ireland	35	63
Italy	13	18
Japan	15	31
Netherlands	22	25.50
Norway	19	19
Spain	17.50	23
Switzerland	13	13
UK	33	51
USA	51	51

'Directory' in the relevant 'Essentials' sections). The application generally has to be made on the 14th or 15th day of your stay, but if you tell the official concerned that you are heading to a place where there is no office (eg Palmyra), they may give you your extension earlier. The period for which your visa will be extended appears to vary from place to place. The norm is a further 15 days, but one month is also usually possible if you insist, while some travellers have been given as much as three months. You need to provide anywhere between two and six passport photos, and there is a fee of not more than S£50 (usually S£25). In most places you can get your visa extension on the same day if you arrive early. In Damascus you must come back the next day, and quite a few travellers complain of rude, unhelpful officials. The Homs office is rather inefficient and chaotic. The Aleppo office is fairly efficient providing you get there early. The Tartus office is efficient and quick; if you can time it right, this is a good place to get it done.

Lebanese visas

As with Syria, the Lebanese authorities will not issue you with a visa, or allow you entry into the country even with a visa, if there is any evidence in your passport of a visit to Israel

Nationals of the following countries are able to obtain a tourist entry or transit visa on arrival at any official point of entry (land, sea or air) into Lebanon: Andorra; Australia; Austria; Belgium; Canada; Denmark; Finland; France; Germany; Greece; Holland; Ireland; Italy; Japan; Luxemburg; Norway; Portugal; South Korea; Spain; Sweden; Switzerland; UK; USA; Gulf Cooperation Council (GCC) countries. If you get your visa at the point of entry, the following visa fees apply (irrespective of nationality). A transit visa valid for 48 hours is free. A transit visa valid for up to two weeks costs LL25,000. A single entry tourist visa valid for up to three months costs LL50,000. A multiple entry tourist visa valid for up to six months costs LL100,000. Note that visas obtained on the point of entry must be paid for in Lebanese Lira, though this is not a problem as the Lebanese never miss an opportunity to offer currency exchange facilities, whether in the form of banks or moneychangers.

The US-imposed ban on US citizens travelling to Lebanon has now been lifted, although the US travel advisory service still warns against going there. In practice, US citizens face no greater risk than anyone else; see under 'Safety' below

You can also obtain tourist visas in advance from Lebanese embassies abroad. These are slightly more expensive. In London they cost (irrespective of nationality) £25 for a single entry valid for three months, and £50 for a multiple entry valid for six months. Visas must be used within three months of the date of issue. You will need two passport photos, two copies of the application form, an employer's letter stating that you have a job to come back to (or else a letter of invitation from someone resident in Lebanon) and the relevant fee. If you are of Lebanese descent, or married/related to a Lebanese national you must provide proof of identity. Visa applications made in London are usually processed within 24-48 hours. For details of how to extend your visa, see page 442.

Travel insurance

You are strongly advised to take out travel insurance before setting off. The medical component of such insurance is the most important. Check exactly what the level of

Lebanese embassies and consulates abroad

Australia 27 Endeavour St, Red Hill, ACT 2603, T02-62957378, F02-62397024.

Belgium 2 Rue Guillaume Stocq, Brusssels 1050, T02-6457760, F02-6457769.

Canada 640 Lyon St, Ottawa, KIS 3Z5, T613-2365825, F613-23211609.

Cyprus 1 Queen Olga Street-1101, P.O. Box 1924-1515, Nicosia, T02-780866, F02-776662.

Egypt 22 Rue el Mansour Mohamed, Zamalek, Cairo, T02-3322823, F02-3322818.

France 3 Villa Copernic, Paris 750016, T01-40677575, F01-40671642.

Germany Berlinerstrasse 126-127, Berlin 13187, T030-4749860, F030-47498666.

Greece 6, 25th Martiou St, Paleo Psychico 154, 52, Athens, T01-6755873, F01-6755612

Italy Via Giacomo Carissimi 38, Rome 00198, T06-8537211, F06-8411794.

Japan Chiyoda House, 5th Floor, 2-17-8 Nagata-Cho Chiyoda-Ku, Tokyo 100-0014, T03-35801227, F03-35802281.

Jordan 17 Mohammad Ali Bdeir St, Abdoun, T/F06-5929111.

Netherlands Frederick Straat 2, 2514 LK La, Haye, The Hague, T070-3658906, F070-3620779.

Spain 178 Paseo de la Castellana, 3 izqueirda, Madrid 16, T091-3451368, F091-3455631.

Sweden Kommendorsgatan 35-II, 11458 Stockholm, T08-6651965, F08-6626824.

Switzerland 10 Thunstrasse, 3074 Muri bei berne-BP 463, Berne, T031-9506565, F031-9506566.

Turkey Kizkulesi Sok No 44, Gaziosmanpasa, Ankara, T312-4467487, F312-4461023.

UK Consular Section (for visas), 15 Palace Garden Mews, London W8 4RA, T020-72297265.

USA 2560 28th St NW, Washington DC 20008, T202-9396300, F202-939-6324.

NB For a full list of all Lebanese embassies and consulates around the world, check the official Lebanese embassy website: www.lebanonembassy.org

Essentials

cover is for specific eventualities: in particular whether a flight home is covered in case of an emergency; whether the insurance company will pay any medical expenses directly or whether you must pay in advance and claim back afterwards; and whether specific activities such as skiing are covered (if not you can often get the policy extended to cover such activities). Most policies have very low ceilings on the value of individual items covered in the event of theft; if you have something of great value, the cheapest way of covering it is often through household insurance.

In theory, anyone arriving from a country where yellow fever or cholera occurs frequently must present the immigration authorities with up-to-date certificates of vaccination. In practice this is rarely enforced, but if you are arriving by the overland route through Africa, for example, it is worth having these certificates just in case. Other than these, no vaccinations are required for either Syria or Lebanon, but see the 'Health' section on page 66 for full details of recommended inoculations.

Vaccination certificates

Most travellers take far too much. The only essentials are your passport, money and ticket. Everything else is a matter of personal choice, and it's all readily available once you get there anyway. We have not included a comprehensive list of what to take (if you can't pack your own bag, perhaps you should stay at home), but here are a few points worth bearing in mind.

Appropriate **clothing** is perhaps the most vital consideration (see also page 21 for some pointers on what is, and what is not, culturally acceptable for women travellers). In the summer months, and for much of the spring and autumn, the daytime heat (and, more importantly, the extremely high humidity all along the coast) makes light-weight, loose-fitting cotton clothes a must. A hat, high factor sun block and

What to take

If you are a full-time student, an ISIC card will entitle you to massive savings on entry fees to historic sites & museums in Syria (see page 21), so be sure to bring one with you

Essentials

👉 *The entry/exit stamp game*

Currently both Syria and Lebanon will not issue you with a visa, or allow you entry into the country, even with a visa, if there is any evidence of a visit to Israel in your passport. (Jordan and Egypt do not apply any such restrictions with regard to visiting Israel). If you do have any Israeli stamps in your passport, it is usually possible, at least for British passport holders, to obtain a new passport before leaving if you explain the situation.

The Israeli authorities are willing to stamp a separate piece of paper rather than your passport (provided you ask), but nowadays the Syrian and Lebanese authorities have cottoned on to this fact. In their quest to prohibit people who have visited Israel coming to their countries they will scrutinize your passport for any evidence of an entry/exit stamp to/from a country neighbouring Israel. Thus if you enter or leave Israel via the Rafah or Taba border crossings with Egypt, the Egyptian entry/exit stamp (complete with the name of the border in Arabic) will alert the Syrian/Lebanese authorities to the fact that you have been in Israel. Likewise for the Wadi Arabah/Arava and Jisr Sheikh Hussein/Jordan River border crossings

between Israel and Jordan. If you wish to visit Israel as well as Syria and/or Lebanon, the safest option is to leave Israel till last.

However, there are two other options. If you fly from Tel Aviv to Amman, your Jordanian entry stamp will simply be for Queen Alia International Airport and therefore will not provide any conclusive evidence that you have been in Israel, allowing you to continue on to Syria and Lebanon (make sure your flight is into Queen Alia International Airport, and not Marka). The second option is to visit Israel from Jordan via the King Hussein (Allenby) Bridge border crossing, and return the same way. At this border crossing (and only this one), the Jordanian authorities are willing to put your exit/entry stamps on a separate sheet of paper, so leaving no evidence of a visit to Israel in your passport. Note that this will only work if you do a roundtrip from Jordan to Israel and back again. If you fly to Israel and then enter Jordan by the King Hussein (Allenby) Bridge border crossing and ask to have your entry stamp on a separate piece of paper, when you try to enter Syria, the absence of a Jordanian entry stamp will be enough to alert the authorities.

---

sunglasses are also essential. Bear in mind, however, that even in the height of summer night time temperatures can drop dramatically in desert settings such as Palmyra, and in the higher reaches of the Lebanese mountains. During winter, it can get extremely cold throughout both Syria and Lebanon. This is particularly true up in the mountains, where you can expect heavy snowfall, but at the same time, down on the plains around Damascus and Aleppo, biting winds, driving rain and even snow are not uncommon, so warm clothing and protection against the wind and rain is important. Early spring and late autumn can also be surprisingly cold, even at lower altitudes. Strong walking boots with firm ankle support are a must if you plan to do any hiking. On the other hand, comfortable, open sandals are best for less strenuous town and city walking in summer.

Toiletries, including tampons, sanitary towels, condoms and contact lens cleaning equipment, can be easily obtained throughout Lebanon. In Syria, you can find them in major cities such as Damascus, Aleppo and Lattakia, but outside these centres the range and availability of such goods is less reliable. If you are on medication, bring adequate supplies with you. Locally available insect repellents are generally less effective than the stronger western varieties. Photographic products are widely available, but tend to be more expensive than at home, and film stock is not always as fresh as it could be.

If you are planning to stay in cheaper hotels and dormitories, a sheet sleeping bag is useful, as are earplugs and an airline-type eye mask. If you will be camping, you need to bring all your own equipment (a good sleeping bag is recommended in any case for late autumn through to early spring). Other useful items include a torch/flash-light for exploring the dark nooks and crannies of Crusader castles and other historic sites, a penknife (the Swiss Army range, or similar, with their various accessories are best) and a universal sink plug (with a wide flange to fit any waste-pipe).

Syria The standard duty free allowance is 200 cigarettes and 1 litre of wine or spirits (official Syrian regulations also list 1 litre of Eau de Cologne and 2 used packs of play-ing cards!). Video camera equipment must be declared to customs on arrival. If you bring more than US$5,000 into the country or take out more than US$2,000, you are officially supposed to declare it. In practice this is very rarely enforced, but if you want to be absolutely sure of avoiding potential problems, stick to the rules.

Duty free

Lebanon The standard duty free allowance is 400 cigarettes and 1 litre of spirits, or 200 cigarettes and 2 litres of spirits. You may have to declare video and computer equip-ment on arrival, although in practice restrictions on such items are rarely enforced. There are no restrictions on the import or export of foreign or Lebanese currency.

Money

Syria

The basic unit of currency is the Syrian Pound (S£) or Lira. Notes come in denomina-tions of S£500, S£100, S£50, S£25, S£10 and S£5. Coins come in denominations of S£25, S£10, S£5 and S£1. The division of the S£ into 100 piastres is largely redundant.

Currency

All foreign exchange transactions are handled (officially at least) by the state-owned *Commercial Bank of Syria (CBS)*, which has a complete monopoly over the financial sector. The only exception to this is the *Cham Palace* chain of hotels, which are autho-rized to change cash and traveller's cheques (TCs) at the official bank rate. There is talk of this monopoly being gradually lifted and the financial sector being opened up to private competition. Initially, the plan is to allow a few Lebanese banks to open within a 'Free Zone' near the *Sheraton* hotel in Damascus. When or whether this will actually happen (and what degree of freedom these banks will be given if it does) is anybody's guess, though most observers agree that change is in the air.

Changing money

Cash All major foreign currencies can be changed without problem at the *CBS*, and there is no commission for cash. US dollars are the most widely recognized, and in all except the cheaper budget hotels (**E-G** category, see below), rooms must be paid for in US dollars, making this the most practical currency.

Travellers' cheques (TCs) The great advantage of TCs is that if they are lost or sto-len you can get them replaced. The difference in the bank exchange rate as compared with cash is minimal, although there is a flat fee of S£25 per transaction. Take *Ameri-can Express* or *Thomas Cook* TCs, as both have offices in Damascus. Note that these offices cannot cash TCs themselves, and replacing lost/stolen TCs can be a lengthy process. In theory you should be able to change US$ traveller cheques into 50% S£ cash and 50% US$ cash at all branches of the *CBS*. In practice, however, at the time of writing you could only do this at the branch on Yousuf Azmeh Square in Damascus.

Credit cards Most major credit cards (Visa, Mastercard, American Express, Diners Club International etc) are accepted at the more expensive hotels (**LL-C** category) and res-taurants, and at larger tourist souvenir and handicraft shops in the main cities. They can also be used to pay for airline tickets and, in some cases, car hire. **However, officially at**

Essentials

Exchange rates for the Syrian Pound (May 2001)

US $	45.00
Euro	40.05
Canadian $	29.25
£ Sterling	64.30
French Franc	6.11
German Mark	20.48
Swiss Franc	25.95
Italian Lira (1000)	20.68
Japanese Yen (100)	36.75
Jordanian Dinar	62.99
Australian Dollar	23.29
Egyptian Pound	11.54
Lebanese Lira (1000)	29.62

NB The above rates are the official Commercial Bank of Syria rates for changing cash. Rates for changing traveller's cheques are either identical (as is the case with US$ and UK£), or else just a fraction higher (eg 5.95 French Francs).

least, it is impossible to get cash advances against credit cards in Syria. That said, the situation is becoming much more relaxed. Some of the luxury hotels will give small cash advances against a credit card, providing you are a guest, though you should ask discreetly. Similarly, there are several private companies that are willing to do the same (the tourist information office in Damascus will even point you in the right direction in this respect). Even so, obtaining cash advances remains difficult (and impossible outside Damascus and Aleppo), and you will have to pay a hefty fee for the service.

Black market Officially, dealing in the currency black market in Syria is strictly illegal and subject to severe penalties, but in practice it appears to be increasingly tolerated. Nevertheless, a good deal of discretion is advised. The souks of Damascus and Aleppo are the best places to change money, or else try asking (discreetly) in jewellery or souvenir shops, or at your hotel. Outside of Damascus and Aleppo, it is either impossible to change money on the black market, or rates are significantly lower (one exception to this is Qamishle on the Turkish border). US dollars in cash are the most easily changed (and for the best rates), followed by UK pounds sterling. TCs can be changed on the black market in a few places in Damascus and Aleppo for a few S£s less than the cash rate. The rates being offered on the black market have fallen over the last few years and at the time of writing were artificially low, being only slightly better than the official bank rates. However, if the deregulation of the financial sector goes ahead, and assuming that the government prevents a wholesale devaluation of the S£, black market rates are likely to improve significantly.

Buying Syrian Pounds abroad Although officially it is illegal to export or import S£s, in practice they can be bought fairly easily in most neighbouring countries. In Lebanon they are readily available from practically every moneychanger in Beirut or else at the border, and can be bought at roughly the equivalent of the black market rate within Syria. In Jordan, they can also be bought at money changers in Amman, while in Turkey the best place to buy S£s is on the border.

Reconverting currency Changing S£s back into hard currency is very difficult in Syria. In theory, if you have your receipts from changing money at the CBS, you should be able to change up to the same amount back into hard currency, but in practice bank managers are extremely reluctant to part with their precious US$ currency and will generally flatly refuse. If you are continuing on to Jordan or Lebanon, you will have no problem changing your S£s there; otherwise it's really a case of trying not to end up with too many S£s left over.

Having money sent to you in Syria is in theory possible through the *CBS*. In practice, however, it is an extremely lengthy and frustrating process.

Transferring
money

The cost of living and travelling in Syria is dramatically cheaper than in Europe or North America. Indeed, Syria is one of the cheapest countries in the Middle East, and is much cheaper than Lebanon (see below). How much you spend will depend not only on the degree of comfort you want to travel in, but also on how much you want to do in a given amount of time.

Cost of living
& travelling

Accommodation ranges from the cheapest of budget hotels, where a dormitory bed will cost from around S£150 (a little over US$3 or UK£2 at the official bank rate), through to luxury 5-star establishments charging rates comparable with those in Europe and North America. Restaurants are remarkably cheap, with even the most expensive ones generally not working out at much more than US$10-15 per head, while a meal in a cheap restaurant (or else a meal of snacks from food stalls) can be had for as little as S£150 or less. Entry fees to major sites and museums are relatively high at S£300 (equivalent to a little over US$6.50 or UK£4.50 at the official bank rate), which soon adds up if you are packing a lot in (although if you have a valid ISIC card entry fees are just S£15 in most cases). Transport costs are extremely low (the 4-5 hour journey between Damascus and Aleppo on a luxury a/c coach, for example, costs just S£150, equivalent to just over US$3 or UK£2), but again they soon add up if you are moving around a lot.

The tightest of budget travel (dormitory accommodation, a diet of cheap staples, only the occasional drink and travel by the cheapest local transport) will allow you to survive off the equivalent of around US$10 per day, but this involves keeping a very strict eye on exactly what you spend at all times. A more realistic figure, allowing a little leeway to treat yourself now and again, would be more like US$15 per day, or perhaps even US$20 if you are planning to do a lot in a short space of time. A mid-range budget (more comfortable hotel accommodation, generally with a/c rooms, reasonable restaurant meals, a/c coaches and taxis wherever needed) will mean spending in the region of US$50 per day. Luxury travel (international class hotels, the best restaurants and a private vehicle, perhaps with driver and guide), means moving into the equivalent price ranges as for luxury travel in Europe and North America; basically from US$150-200 per day upwards.

Lebanon

The basic unit of currency is the Lebanese Lira (LL), also referred to as the Lebanese Pound. In the aftermath of the rollercoaster inflation which gripped Lebanon during the civil war, the smaller denomination banknotes (LL1, LL10, LL50, LL100, LL250) became something of a rarity, and in the case of LL1 and LL10 banknotes, collectors items. The banknotes you come across in everyday life are LL500, LL1000, LL5000, LL10,000, LL20,000, LL50,000 and LL100,000. Newly minted LL50, 100, 250 and 500 coins are now also in circulation. In addition, the US$ operates as a parallel currency, being completely interchangeable with the LL. You can pay for anything in either currency, and you will often be given change in a combination of the two.

Currency

With Lebanon fast rebuilding its reputation as the financial centre of the Middle East, changing or accessing money is generally very easy, though one exception to this is with changing travellers' cheques). There are numerous banks in all the major towns and cities, and in the major cities they are even more numerous money changers.

Changing
money

Essentials

Exchange rates for the Lebanese Lira (May 2001)

US $	1,507.50
Euro	1,337.44
Canadian $	966.13
£ Sterling	2,161.21
French Franc	203.04
German Mark	682.92
Swiss Franc	875.04
Italian Lira (1000)	622.70
Japanese Yen (100)	1,210.00
Jordanian Dinar	2,120.25
Australian Dollar	754.29
Egyptian Pound	388.48
Syrian Pound	322.59

NB *Exchange rates for all foreign currencies are calculated according to the US$ exchange rate. In recent years the Bank of Lebanon has held the US$-LL exchange rate fairly stable, at around LL1,500 for US$1. For the latest exchange rates, check the* Daily Star's *website (listed under the 'Cambio' link); www.dailystar.com.lb*

Cash All major currencies can be exchanged at most banks and at all money changers (the latter will change just about anything, provided they can find out the going rates). The US$ is the most convenient currency.

Travellers' Cheques (TCs) Changing TCs is surprisingly difficult in Lebanon. If you are intending to carry your money in this form, make sure that you have US$ TCs, as TCs in any other currency can only be changed at one bank in Beirut (see page 440). All banks charge a hefty commission for changing US$ TCs; though the fee is usually only around 1%, they all apply a minimum charge of US$5, and in some cases an additional US$2 'handling' fee. You will also be asked to produce the original purchase slip (even though this is supposed to be kept separate from the TCs). Most money changers charge around 4-5% commission for changing US$ TCs, and are extremely reluctant to deal with TCs in any other currency.

Credit Cards All the major credit cards are recognized in Lebanon. As well as being accepted in most hotels, restaurants, shops etc, nearly all the banks in Lebanon will allow you to draw money against major credit (or debit) cards, making them a much more convenient alternative to TCs. Most banks also have ATMs (cash-point machines) which can be used in the same way. *HSBC* and *Credit Libanais* both have lots of branches with ATMs accepting Visa, Mastercard, Cirrus, +Plus, Global Access etc, or there are plenty of other banks offering the same services. You can draw your money in either LL or US$.

Black market With the financial sector completely free from government regulation, there is no black market (nor any need for one).

Reconverting currency This is absolutely no problem, although you will obviously lose out on the difference between the buying and selling rates. The money changers in Beirut have supplies of most major foreign currencies.

Transferring money *Western Union Money Transfer* is represented in Beirut through *Byblos Bank*, *Khalaf Trading* and the *Lebanese-Canadian Bank* (amongst others), which between them have branches all over the capital. The head office contact number is T01-601315. Note, however, that this is an expensive way of transferring money. A better bet may be to have money transferred to Lebanon through one of the banks with branches in Europe or North America. These include *HSBC*, *Bank Audi*, *Byblos Bank* and *Banque du Liban et d'Outre Mer*. It is also possible to set up a bank account with these banks before leaving home, and then draw money from them once you are in Lebanon.

The cost of living and travelling in Lebanon is more in line with that in Europe and North America. The major difference with Syria is in terms of the cost of accommodation and eating. The vast majority of hotels in Lebanon fall into the mid-range and luxury categories (ie from around US$40-50 for a double room upwards), with the luxury end of the market being heavily over-represented. That said, there are a limited number of cheaper hotels to be found, as well as a few genuine budget places where you can get a bed in a dormitory for around US$4-6. Eating out is also comparatively expensive; a meal in a restaurant will generally cost a minimum of US$10 per head, and around US$15 will be closer to the norm, while in the more expensive restaurants, the sky's the limit. To eat cheaply, you have to restrict yourself for the most part to a diet of takeaway food and give Lebanon's extensive restaurant scene a miss. Likewise, if you plan to indulge in Lebanon's vibrant nightlife, you have to be prepared to shell out a lot, though if you buy alcohol from a shop it is considerably cheaper. Transport is one thing which is fairly cheap in Lebanon. The journey between Beirut and Tripoli for example costs just LL1,500-2,000 (US$1-1.33).

Cost of living & travelling

Sticking to the very strictest of budgets, it is possible to survive in Lebanon on around US$15-20 per day, though as soon as you start to treat yourself a little, this will quickly rise. A mid-range budget (a/c hotels, restaurant meals and perhaps a hire car) involves a big step up to around US$80-100 per day. At the luxury end of the scale, you are looking at a minimum of around US$200 per day, or whatever extravagant sum you wish to part with.

Getting there

Syria

From Europe London is the cheapest place from which to buy flights to Syria, although very good deals can also be found in other European cities such as Paris, Amsterdam, Berlin and Frankfurt. For discounted fares from London's so-called 'bucket shops', look through the travel advertisements of magazines such as *Time Out* and *TNT*, the latter being available free outside most Tube stations every Tuesday. The broadsheet newspapers all feature weekly travel supplements on Saturdays and Sundays which also contain many adverts for cheap flights. Shop around.

Air
The majority of international flights arrive at Damascus International Airport, although a few go direct to Aleppo

Bear in mind that the cheapest flights generally involve a lengthy stopover along the way. Prices vary according to the season and the period for which flights are valid. Be sure to check other details, such as penalties for changing the date of the return flight, and the frequency of flights; if you plan to set your return date while you are in Syria and are flying with an airline which has a limited number of flights each week, you may run into problems with availability of seats during busy times. Some of the airlines offering cheap flights to Syria (anywhere between £280-350 depending on the airline, validity and season) include *Turkish Airlines* www.turkishairlines.com, *Lufthansa* www.lufthansa.com, *Czech* www.csa.cz, *Malev* (Hungarian) www.malev.hu, *Olympic* (Greece) www.olympic-airways.gr, *Air Malta* www.airmalta.com and *Air France* www.airfrance.com

British Mediterranean (a subsidiary of *British Airways*) offers direct flights to Damascus, though these are comparatively expensive (usually around the £400 mark). Also well worth checking out is the Syrian national carrier, *Syrian Air*. Their

Discount flight agents in the UK & Ireland

Usit Campus, 52 Grosvener Gardens, London SW1W 0AG, T08702-401010, www.usitworld.com; 53 Forest Rd, Edinburgh EH1 2QP, T0131-225 6111; Fountain Centre, College St, Belfast BT1 6ET, T01232-324073; 19 Aston Quay, Dublin 2, T01-602 1777. Student/youth travel specialists with branches also in Birmingham, Brighton, Bristol, Cambridge, Glasgow and Manchester.

Council Travel, 28a Poland St, London W1V 3DB, T020-7437 7767, www.destinations-group.com

The London Flight Centre, 131 Earl's Court Rd, London SW5 9RH, T020-7244 6411; 47 Notting Hill Gate, London W11 3JS, T020-7727 4290.

STA Travel, 86 Old Brompton Rd, London SW7 3LH, T020-7437 6262, www.statravel.co.uk Also have other branches in London, as well as in Brighton, Bristol, Cambridge, Leeds, Manchester, Newcastle and Oxford and on many University campuses. Specialists in cheap student/youth flights and tours, and also good for student Ids and insurance.

Trailfinders, 194 Kensington High St, London W8 7RG, T020-7983 3939.

office in London is at 27 Albermarle Street, W1, T020-74932851, F020-74932199. They operate direct flights between London (and also several other European capitals) and Damascus (just 4-5 hours), with departure and arrival times at reasonable hours of the day in both directions (most other airlines arrive at or depart from Damascus at odd hours of the night/early morning). Fares, meanwhile, are generally only slightly more expensive than the cheapest airlines. The only disadvantages are that getting through to their office on the phone can be ridiculously difficult (try faxing them with your phone number; hopefully they will phone you back), and for some obscure reason they do not accept credit cards.

From North America *Syrian Air* does not operate direct flights to North America. *Gulf Air* operates direct flights to Damascus from both New York and Montreal, but the cheapest option is to buy a cheap return flight to London and then shop around for deals there.

From Australia & New Zealand *Emirates* www.emirates.com, *Gulf Air* www.gulfairco.com and *MEA* (Middle East Airlines) www.mea.com.lb (the Lebanese national carrier) offer good value return flights from Australia to Damascus for around A$1,700. From New Zealand it is much more expensive, costing around NZ$2,500 for a return.

From the Middle East Lebanon: Though possible by air, the journey by road between Beirut and Damascus takes only around 3-4 hours, making this a much quicker and cheaper option. **Jordan**: *Royal Jordanian* www.rja.com.jo, *Syrian Air*, *British Mediterranean* and a number of other airlines operate daily flights between Amman and Damascus. However, these are expensive (around US$60 one way) compared with the cost of a coach ticket (US$6) and, given that the journey by road only takes around 4-5 hours depending on border formalities, by the time you take into account getting to and from the airports and checking-in etc, flying is certainly no quicker. **Egypt**: Both *Syrian Air* and *Egypt Air* have daily flights between Cairo and Damascus (US$160/241 single/return), while the latter also has one flight weekly (Tue) between Alexandria and Damascus.

Land Syria has land borders with Turkey, Lebanon and Jordan (and of course Iraq and Israel; although the only way to enter Iraq as a tourist at present is as part of an organized group at a cost of around US$500 per day, while the Syrian-Israeli border is not an option, unless you want to get shot).

Discount flight agents in North America

Air Brokers International, 323 Geary St, Suite 411, San Francisco, CA94102, T01-800-883 3273, www.airbrokers.com Consolidator and specialist on RTW and Circle Pacific tickets.
Council Travel, 205 E 42nd St, New York, NY 10017, T1-888-COUNCIL, www. counciltravel.com Student/budget agency with branches in many other US cities.
Discount Airfares Worldwide On-Line, www.etn.nl/discount.htm A hub of consolidator and discount agent links.

International Travel Network/Airlines of the Web, www.itn.net/airlines Online air travel information and reservations.
STA Travel, 5900 Wilshire Blvd, Suite 2110, Los Angeles, CA 90036, T1-800-777 0112, www.sta-travel.com Also branches in New York, San Francisco, Boston, Miami, Chicago, Seattle and Washington DC.
Travel CUTS, 187 College St, Toronto, ON, M5T 1P7, T1-800-667 2887, www.travelcuts.com Specialist in student discount fares, Ids and other travel services. Branches in other Canadian cities.

From Turkey There are several border posts between Turkey and Syria. The most important and frequently used crossing is **Cilvegözü/Bab al-Hawa**, linking Antakya and Aleppo. All public transport comes this way. It can get quite busy, but the officials here are more used to dealing with tourists. An interesting alternative is the **Yayladgi/Kassab** crossing, linking Antakya with Lattakia. This is a minor border post, though tourists seem to have no problems crossing here, and the road between the two cities is very beautiful. Way to the east is the **Nusaybin/Qamishle**, linking southeast Turkey with the northeastern Jezira region of Syria, although with the ongoing conflict between Turkish government troops and the PKK, this is not really an advisable option. In addition, there are a series of minor border posts along the northern border between the two countries (Kilis/Azaz; Barak/Jarablus; Mursitpinar/Ain al-Arab; Akçakale/Tell Aybad), but tourists may have problems crossing at these borders.

As a rule, it is impossible to obtain Syrian visas at the border (see under 'Syrian visas', above), although Turkish visas are issued to most nationalities without any problems. There are regular **luxury coach** services connecting Turkey with Syria. Note that while coach companies in Istanbul/Ankara and Aleppo/Damascus will offer you tickets for the whole journey between these cities (and indeed beyond), they all involve a change of coach (and often a lengthy wait) at Antakya. Usually it is quicker (and sometimes considerably cheaper) to buy a ticket only as far as Antakya and then pick up an onward coach from there. There is also a once-weekly **train** service between Istanbul and Damascus/Aleppo, departing Istanbul on Thu and departing Damascus/Aleppo on Tue.

From Jordan There are two land borders between Jordan and Syria. The one most commonly used by coaches and service taxis running between Amman and Damascus is the **Jabir/Nasib** border, for the simple reason that the whole route via this border is on a fast motorway. If you are travelling by your own transport, the **Ramtha/Deraa** border is probably a better bet, if only because it is not so busy. Both borders are open 24 hours, and each has currency exchange facilities on both sides. As a rule, it is impossible to obtain a Syrian visa at these border crossings, although Jordanian visas can be obtained without any problem. Leaving Jordan there is a JD4 departure tax. Leaving Syria there is no departure tax. There are regular *JETT* and *Karnak* (the Jordanian and Syrian state-owned transport companies) **a/c coaches** operating between Amman and Damascus for JD5/US$7 one way. The journey takes around 4-5 hours including border formalities. In addition there are regular **service taxis** which are slightly more expensive, but also slightly quicker (in theory) as there are fewer people to get through the border formalities. There is also a twice-weekly **train** which runs between Amman and

☛ *Discount flight agents in Australia and New Zealand*

Flight Centres, *82 Elizabeth St, Sydney,* *Ultimo, Sydney, and 256 Flinders St,*
T13-1600; 205 Queen St, Auckland, *Melbourne. In NZ: 10 High St, Auckland,*
T09-309 6171. Also branches in other *T09-366 6673. Also in major towns and*
towns and cities. *university campuses.*
STA Travel, *T1300-360960,* ***Travel.com.au***, *80 Clarence St, Sydney,*
www.statravelaus.com.au; 702 Harris St, *T02-929 01500, www.travel.com.au*

Damascus (departing on a Mon and Thu in either direction) on the old narrow-gauge Hejaz railway which TE Lawrence spent so much time trying to blow up during the First World War. However, this really is a trip for enthusiasts only, being just about the slowest way of going short of crawling on your hands and knees: the journey takes in the region of 11 hours, if you are lucky, but can take *much* longer.

From Lebanon There are four border crossings between Lebanon and Syria. The main one is **Jdaide** on the Beirut-Damascus highway. The second is at **El Qaa**, on the road between Baalbek and Homs. The third is at **Aarida**, on the road between Tripoli and Tartus. The fourth is **Dabousiyeh**, which links Tripoli with the motorway running between Homs and Tartus. There are regular luxury coaches, buses, microbuses and ser-vice taxis plying between Beirut and Damascus (3-4 hours depending on border formal-ities), and also between Beirut/Tripoli and most other cities in Syria, though the majority of the public transport runs to Damascus or Aleppo. Luxury coaches are strongly recom-mended as the best means of travelling between Lebanon and Syria, particularly for the journey between Beirut and Damascus via the Jdaide border. They are much more com-fortable, and much safer, than the service taxis. As a rule, it is impossible to get Syrian visas on the border, but the Lebanese will issue most nationalities with a tourist visa on the border (see under 'Lebanese visas', above). Going in either direction, there are no departure taxes. Changing money is not a problem at any of the borders. On border areas of Lebanon, S£s are just as readily accepted as LL or US$, and can easily be exchanged in Beirut. The same is not true, however, of LL in Syria.

Sea At the time of writing there were no passenger ferries operating into or out of Syria, though in the past irregular passenger/vehicle ferries used to operate between Izmir (Turkey) and Lattakia. Likewise, all passenger services between Alexandria (Egypt) and Lattakia have now been suspended.

Lebanon

Air **From Europe** London is the cheapest place from which to buy flights to Lebanon,
All international although very good deals can nowadays also be found in other European cities such as
flights arrive at Beirut Paris, Amsterdam, Berlin and Frankfurt. See under 'Syria', above for general comments
International Airport, about finding discounted fares, and what to look out for. In Lebanon, the 'high season' is
some 10 km to the south from May to September, and around Christmas; airlines with a limited number of flights
of the city centre each week may fully booked up during these periods (this is particularly true around
Christmas). *MEA* (the Lebanese national carrier) and *British Mediterranean* offer direct flights between London and Beirut, although there are plenty of other airlines offering indirect flights. A direct return flight from London during the high season will cost in the region of £450. Much cheaper deals are available on airlines which do not fly direct, such as *Olympic* www.olympic-airways.gr (via Athens), *Air France* www.airfrance.com (via Paris), *Turkish Airlines* www.turkishairlines.com (via Istanbul), and *TAROM* www.tarom.digiro.net (via Bucharest), all of which will cost in the region of £280-350 depending on the season and validity of the ticket. Both *Olympic* and *British*

Mediterranean offer the option of an 'open jaws' ticket which allows you to fly into Beirut and out of Damascus or Amman (or viceversa) which is very useful if you are planning to visit Syria and Jordan as well as Lebanon. Most European national carriers have direct flights from their respective capital cities (as do *MEA* www.mea.com.lb). The most frequent flights are from Paris (at least twice daily with *Air France* and *MEA*), while the cheapest flights are generally from Amsterdam with *KLM* www.klm.com

From North America   All *MEA* flights from North America go via Europe, as do those with other airlines. The cheapest option is to buy a flight to London and then shop around for cheap deals there.

From Australia/New Zealand   Because of the large numbers of Lebanese people living in Australia, there are several airlines which fly to Beirut from Melbourne and Sydney, including *Emirates* www.emirates.com, *Gulf Air* www.gulfairco.com, *Malaysia Airlines* www.malaysiaairlines.com.my/ and *MEA*. A return high season flight will cost in the region of A$1800. There are no direct flights from New Zealand; either go first to Australia, or else head for Europe and pick up a flight from there.

From the Middle East   Jordan: *Royal Jordanian* www.rja.com.jo, *MEA*, *Olympic* and *British Mediterranean* between them offer regular daily flights daily between Amman and Beirut. It is much cheaper and more interesting (though not quicker) to travel overland. **Egypt**: *MEA* operates daily flights between Cairo and Beirut.

Lebanon's only land border is with Syria (leaving aside the Israeli-Lebanese border **Land** which, despite what some more enthusiastic Christian Lebanese may tell you, is firmly closed). See above, under Syria, for details of the border crossings between the two countries. For information on bringing a private vehicle into Lebanon, see below.

From Cyprus   A hydrofoil ferry service (passenger only) operates between Larnaka in **Sea** Cyprus and Jounieh. At the time of writing, services were somewhat erratic, with once-weekly departures (in theory) during the summer months only (May to September). There is talk of a more regular service being established in the future, perhaps from Beirut itself, though no one seems very sure as to exactly when this might happen.

Overland from Europe

The overland route from Europe though the Middle East is alive and well and travelling overland to this region is an enormously rewarding option. It's certainly not the cheapest or quickest way to get there, but if you have the time and resources, the advantages far outweigh the extra cost and effort involved.

Although Libya is starting to open up to tourists, the continuing danger of violent attacks against foreigners in Algeria means that a complete circuit of the Mediterranean remains impractical for the time being. However, by combining the overland route from Europe through Turkey to Syria, Lebanon, Jordan and Egypt with sea routes across the Mediterranean from Israel, you can still make a very interesting circuit without having to double back the way you came. There is also the option of continuing down into Africa.

AA Overseas Assistance, Copenhagen Court, New St, Basingstoke, Hants, RG21 7DT, **Further** T01256-493819, F01256-460750, for information on applying for a Carnet. *Viamare* **information** *Travel Ltd*, Graphic House, 2 Sumatra Rd, London, NW6 1PU, T020-74314560, F020-74315456, for details of Mediterranean passenger/vehicle ferries (Italy, Greece, Albania, Turkey, Cyprus, Israel). *Thomas Cook*, PO Box 227, Thorpe Wood, Peterborough, PE3 6PU, T01733-503571, F01733-503596, publishing@thomascook.

tmailuk.sprint.com (or any local branch of Thomas Cook), for its European and overseas timetables for rail and bus services, and for its *Greek Island Hopping* guidebook/timetable (published annually February/March). It covers the entire Greek ferry system, including the lines used by Inter-railers and Eurailers to cross the Adriatic from Italy to Greece, all international scheduled shipping across the eastern Mediterranean, and many Turkish ferries. *Automobile Club de Syrie*, Rue 29 Mai (in same blding as *French Towers* hotel), PO Box 3364, Damascus, T2317745, F2317744, member of FIA. *Automobile et Touring Club de Syrie*, Zuhair bin abi Selmah St, Wafk al-Ajem blding, near Italian Embassy, PO Box 1175, Aleppo, T247272, member of AIT. *Automobile et Touring Club du Liban*, PO Box 115, Jounieh, T09-917570, F09-917580. *Royal Automobile Club of Jordan*, Al Ameerah Sarvath al-Ibrahimi Shuhada St, near 8th Circle, Amman, T5850640.

Touching down

Airport information

Syria   Damascus International Airport, 25 km to the southeast of Damascus, handles the vast majority of international flights arriving in Syria (a small number go to Aleppo). Although considerably more streamlined than in the past, if it is busy you may still have to queue for some time to get through immigration. Note that the **yellow Entry/Exit card** which you must fill in on arrival is an important piece of documentation which you will need to submit when you leave the country, or when you extend your visa.

  Once through immigration and customs (foreign tourists are rarely detained by customs), there is a branch of the *Commercial Bank of Syria (CBS)* in the main arrivals hall, open 24 hours, 7 days, where you can change cash and TCs (rates are identical to CBS rates throughout Syria, though below the black market rate). The **tourist information** counter (T2248437) is open in theory 24 hours (though often unattended). They can provide you with Ministry of Tourism maps/pamphlets but otherwise are of little use. There is a **hotel reservations** desk which will make bookings for you in the mid-range to luxury hotels (**C** category or above). The *Cham*, *Meridien* and *Sheraton* hotel chains all have desks here, as do the *Europcar* and *Hertz/Chamcar* car hire companies. There are also several desks for companies offering **taxis** into Damascus. During the day they charge around S£400-500/US$10, but late at night this rises to around S£1000/US$20. Between 0600-2400 there is a **bus service** which runs into the centre of Damascus, departing every 30 minutes from just outside the arrivals hall. The journey takes 30-45 minutes and costs S£10 (if you have a large amount of luggage you may have to pay an extra S£10 for it).

  Other facilities in the arrivals hall include a rather expensive **cafeteria**. Arriving passengers are also allowed access to the airport's fancy new **duty free** shop where you can buy a wide range of cigarettes, wines, spirits, confectionery, cosmetics, electrical goods etc. The cigarettes and spirits in particular are amongst the cheapest you will find anywhere.

Lebanon   For airport information, T628000. Lebanon's only airport, Beirut International Airport, is 10 km to the south of central Beirut. A fast new dual carriageway runs between the centre of town and the airport, sparing visitors the unsightly sprawl of the Southern Suburbs and all the billboards bearing Hizbollah propaganda. The airport itself has been completely rebuilt and expanded, and is now a gleaming, modern, state-of-the-art (if over-optimistically large) complex.

  Tourist and transit **visas** are available on arrival for most nationalities (see page 24 for full details). They must be paid for in Lebanese Lira (LL), but there is a branch of the

Touching down: Syria

Official time Syria is two hours ahead of GMT Oct-Apr, and three hours ahead May-Sep.

International Direct Dialing (IDD) The IDD code to telephone Syria from abroad is +963 (the 963 must be preceded by the relevant international access code; 00 in the case of the UK), followed by the area code minus the initial 0, followed by the phone number (eg to phone Damascus from the UK you should dial 00-963-11-XXXXXXX.

Emergency services Ambulance T110, Police T112, Fire T113, Traffic police T115.

Directory enquiries National T141/142, International T143/144.

Electricity 220 volts, 50 AC. European two-pin sockets are the norm. Electricity supply is on the whole reliable, although power cuts do occur (particularly in Aleppo).

Weights and measures The metric system is used in Syria (kilogrammes, litres, kilometres etc).

Business hours NB All government offices and Muslim shops/businesses close in the afternoon during Ramadan, though many shops reopen after sunset. **Banks** are generally open Sat-Thu 0830-1230 (and occasionally 0800-1330), closed Fri. In Damascus and Aleppo there are also exchange booths which open later and, in the case of Damascus, on Fri also. Branches of the Cham Palace chain of hotels throughout the country can change cash and TCs at any time of the day or night. **Post Offices** vary considerably in their opening times: in Damascus the central post office is open Sat-Thu 0800-1900, Fri 0900-1200 (for stamps only); in Aleppo it is open seven days 0800-1700; in smaller towns the norm is Sat-Thu 0800-1400, closed Fri, although there is lots of variation from place to place. **Government offices** are almost always open Sat-Thu 0800-1400, closed Fri. **Airline offices/travel agents** are generally open Sat-Thu 0830-1330 and 1600-1800 (or sometimes 1930), closed Fri. **Shops** in most towns and cities are generally open Sat-Thu 0830-1330 and 1630-2000, closed Fri (though some shops stay open on Fri). In the souks of Aleppo and Damascus, shops are open Sat-Thu 0800-2000 (and sometimes 2200 in summer), but always closed Fri.

Lebanese-Canadian Bank in immigration (open daily, 24 hours) where you can change money. Once through immigration and customs, you emerge into the arrivals hall. There are more than half a dozen car hire firms with desks here, including *Hertz*, *Avis*, *Budget*, *Europcar*, *Hala*, *Best* and *Thrifty*. There is also a **tourist information** office (open daily 0900-2400), with a full range of Ministry of Tourism pamphlets, magazines, hotel guides etc. The staff here are friendly and obliging, but only of limited help (they are unable to make hotel reservations for you, for example). The only food outlet is a *House of Donuts* café/snack bar.

Upstairs on the first floor is the departures hall. There is another branch of the *Lebanese-Canadian Bank* here (also open daily, 24 hours), which can change cash (but not TCs) and also has an ATM (accepting Visa, Mastercard, Cirrus and +Plus), as well offering Western Union Money Transfer. Both *Air France* and *MEA* have offices here. There is also a small bookshop/newsagent and a **post office** and, up on the mezzanine floor, a coffee shop/snack bar. Whether you are departing from or arriving at Beirut airport, you can take advantage of the enormous **duty free shopping** complex. Run by the same company that runs the duty free shop at Damascus airport, this one is much bigger, and has a vast range of goods on offer. Boasting features such as the largest cigar shop in the world (complete with Cuban girls rolling cigars), it is an unashamedly glitzy and ostentatious affair, on a par with Dubai airport's duty free shop. Cigarettes and alcohol are as cheap as in Damascus, and there are frequent special offers and promotions on most other goods.

Touching down: Lebanon

Official time Lebanon is two hours ahead of GMT Oct-Apr, and three hours ahead May-Sep.

International Direct Dialing (IDD) The IDD code to telephone Lebanon from abroad is +961 (follow the same procedure as for Syria).

Emergency services Red Cross T140, Police T160, Fire T175.

Directory enquiries National T120/113, International T100.

Electricity 220 volts, 50 AC. European two-pin sockets are the norm. The electricity supply is on the whole reliable in Beirut, but in other parts of the country power cuts remain a feature of everyday life. Throughout the country, many hotels and businesses are equipped with their own generators. Repeated Israeli attacks in recent years on Lebanese electricity relay stations have done nothing to help the situation.

Weights and measures The metric system is used in Lebanon (kilogrammes, litres, kilometres etc).

Business hours NB All Muslim-run shops and businesses (but not government offices) close in the afternoon during Ramadan, though many shops reopen after sunset. **Banks** are open Mon-Fri 0830-1230, Sat 0830-1200, closed Sun. Note that banks are not able to change US$ (cash or TCs) into LL (or give cash advances against credit cards in LL) on Saturdays, though they can carry out all these transactions in US$. **Post offices** are open Mon-Fri 0800-1700, Sat 0800-1200, closed Sun. **Government offices** are open Mon-Fri 0800-1700, Sat 0800-1200, closed Sun. **Shops and commercial offices** are generally open Mon-Sat 0900-1830, closed Sun, though during the hottest summer months many close around 1500 each day. It is nearly always possible to find at least one grocery store which stays open as late as 23-2400, and on Sundays.

The easiest way to get to and from the airport is by **taxi**. The price of a taxi into the centre of town varies enormously, depending on your bargaining skills and the time of day or night. During the day, you can expect offers to start at around US$30, though they will rapidly fall to around US$7-10 with a bit of bargaining (walking determinedly out of the arrivals lounge into the parking area invariably gets things moving a bit more quickly). At night, or in the early hours of the morning, it is considerably harder to get prices down. To catch a **bus**, you must walk for just over 1 km to the round-about at the entrance to the airport complex. From here you can catch an LCC bus No 5 all the way to Ain el-Mreisse (on the Corniche opposite McDonalds), going via Cola bus stand, Raouche and along the sea front. However, these buses only run between around 0630-1730 (if going to the airport by No 5 bus, bear in mind that the journey takes 40 minutes-1 hour). There are also **microbuses** and **service taxis** which run between roundabout outside the airport complex and the road junction known as Balbirs (near the Hippodrome, from where there are buses and service taxis into the centre), but again, these only run during the day. Late at night your only options are to bargain with the taxi drivers or sit it out until the buses start running.

Airport/ departure tax **Syria** There is a departure tax of S£200 on all international flights from Syria. There is no departure tax if leaving by land or sea. **Lebanon** There is an airport tax of US$42 on all flights from Beirut International Airport. This should be included in the cost of your ticket, but be sure to check in any case. There is no departure tax if leaving by land or sea.

Tourist information **Syria** There are two tourist information offices in Damascus, as well as a counter at the airport. Most other towns in Syria also have a tourist information office. Although very willing to help, none of them are really able to do much more than offer you a free Ministry of Tourism pamphlet/map of the relevant town/region. **Lebanon** The main tourist information office, in the centre of West Beirut, is well stocked with Ministry of Tourism pamphlets and maps, as is the branch at Beirut International Airport. There are also small branch offices in Tripoli, Zahle and Byblos. The Tripoli office can put you in touch with official guides as well as offering the usual free pamphlets/maps.

Rules, customs and etiquette

Although there are plenty of exceptions, as a rule just about everything, including the **Bargaining** price of hotel rooms etc, can be bargained over. For some things such as souvenirs and handicrafts it is almost expected, particularly in the souks of Damascus and Aleppo (on the other hand, some souvenir/handicraft shops are fixed price). Where bargaining is the norm, shop owners will quote you a starting price well above what they actually expect to receive. Successful bargaining is something of an art. Trying to hurry things along never helps. Give yourself plenty of time and be prepared to sit around drinking cups of tea and exchanging small talk: it is all part of the process. It is always worth shopping around to compare prices and quality. Try also to establish in your own mind what you think the item you are after is worth, and use this as a basis for your negotiations. At the end of the day, if you think the final price is too high, be prepared to walk away empty handed (as often as not you will be called back to hear one 'final, last, lowest possible' price, at which point you can begin bargaining all over again). Conversely, try to avoid relentlessly driving down the price just for the sake of it; if you stop to consider the amount you are offering and compare it with prices back home, you may realize that you are being downright mean.

You will be judged to a large extent by your appearance. Both Syrians and Lebanese **Clothing** place a lot of importance on smartness and cleanliness and making the effort to be presentable in public will earn you greater respect. Rather confusingly for women, however, depending on the context there is a great deal of variation in both Syria and Lebanon as to what types of clothing are socially acceptable. See above, under 'Women Travellers'. Bear in mind also the comments below under 'Visiting mosques'.

In **Syria**, except in more cosmopolitan centres such as Damascus, Aleppo or Lattakia, **Conduct** it is not usually acceptable for foreign men (or indeed any unrelated male) to talk to *Syrians & Lebanese are* women on their own. Nor is it usual for men and women to shake hands. Do not take *generally very open &* pictures of women without their consent, or more importantly that of their male *welcoming & will often* escort. Female tourists are more likely to be given permission, but you should never *go out of their way to* take this for granted. Open displays of affection between couples can also cause *help foreigners. Return* offence and are not acceptable in public. *the gesture by being* *equally polite & friendly*

One thing which you will soon get used to in Syria are the Big Brother-type portraits of former President Hafez al-Assad, and now his son, President Bashar Assad, staring down at you from every conceivable vantage point. You will soon realize that attempts to engage in political conversations are generally met by a rather repetitious stock of `acceptable' opinions. Remember that although the country is starting to open up a little there is still a massive secret police apparatus in place and for all intents and purposes the walls really do have ears. For the sake of sparing local acquaintances embarrassment and potential trouble, steer clear of delicate topics.

In **Lebanon** by contrast everyone is more than happy to talk endlessly about all aspects of local and regional politics. If you find yourself on the receiving end of particularly extreme views, bear in mind that there are many people who have lived through some pretty horrific experiences and feelings often run very deep. In both Syria and Lebanon, a great deal of discretion (or better still outright silence) is in order on the subject of visiting Israel.

Drugs Possession of narcotics is illegal in Syria and Lebanon. Those caught in possession risk a long prison sentence and/or deportation. Although the Bekaa valley used to be famed for its cannabis production, these days it is not readily available in Lebanon or Syria and you are very unlikely to be offered it on the street. Indeed, there is a marked intolerance to drug taking in both countries and the drugs scene is distinctly seedy (not to mention paranoid) and best avoided.

Photography Avoid taking pictures of military installations, or anything which might be construed as 'sensitive'. In Syria, the definition of 'sensitive' can include very unimportant public buildings which may boast an armed guard at the entrance.

Tipping The standard 10% is acceptable in more expensive restaurants; otherwise it is really down to your own discretion. Remember that the more expensive restaurants often add a service charge in any case.

Visiting mosques Non-Muslims are welcome in most mosques in Syria and Lebanon, although in some Shi'ite mosques they are only allowed into the courtyard of the mosque and not the prayer hall itself. In any case, always seek permission before entering a mosque. Remember that shoes must be removed before entering the prayer hall, although socks can be left on. It is very important that both men and women dress modestly, covering arms and legs (shorts are not acceptable) and in the case of women wearing a headscarf. At larger, more important mosques, such as the Umayyad Mosque in Damascus, women are required to hire a full-length black hooded robe at the entrance (and men also if they attempt to enter in shorts).

Safety

Syria Syria is probably the safest of all the Middle Eastern countries in which to travel. Theft and violent crime are virtually unheard of and you are safe wandering around the big cities at any time of the day or night (notwithstanding the inevitable offers of help if you are looking lost). Nevertheless, the usual precautions are advisable with regard to valuables: never leave them unattended in hotel rooms, and keep your money and important documents (passport etc) on your person, preferably in a moneybelt or something similar. There are occasional stories of tourists falling foul of the Syrian secret police, but such occurrences are rare and so long as you don't do anything to antagonize them or arouse their suspicion you will be fine.

Lebanon Having been emblazoned on everyone's mind as a place of brutal and interminable civil war, suicide bombings and hostage taking, Lebanon is still trying to shake off its media image. In fact, today's Lebanon is essentially a perfectly safe place in which to travel. Ordinary crime is perhaps more of a problem than in Syria, but no worse (and in many cases much better) than in Europe or North America. Provided you take the usual pre-cautions (never leave valuables unattended in hotel rooms, keep your money and important documents on your person, preferably in a money belt or something similar), you should have no problem. Likewise, the threat of personal violence is minimal, pro-vided you use your common sense and do not put yourself in any obviously dangerous situations. (Wandering around the poorer areas of the Palestinian refugee camps in Bei-rut's Southern Suburbs without a local escort, for example, might be asking for trouble).

Most people's concerns centre around the situation in southern Lebanon. Although the Israelis have now withdrawn from their so-called 'security zone' in southern Lebanon, at the time of writing this region had yet to return to normality. The most serious problem is of landmines; in the area formerly occupied by Israel there are known to be at least 130,000, and in all likelihood there are many more. Although it is perfectly possible to visit places such as Beaufort Castle, El Khiam prison and Bent Jbail, it is essential that you stick to the roads and avoid walking through open countryside. The other problem is that at the time of writing Hizbollah were still active in these areas and carrying out occasional cross-border attacks against Israel, which in turn was carrying out counter-offensives. Likewise, Israeli air strikes on suspected Hizbollah bases in the Bekaa Valley, both in the southern Bekaa and further north around Baalbek, remain a possibility.

It is important to keep yourself informed of events in these areas; these days only the more dramatic flare-ups make it into the Western media, but even the smallest incidents are reported on in detail by the press in Lebanon. Ultimately, it is really a question using your common sense and weighing up the risks for yourself. Bear in mind that even when there has been a flare-up of fighting in southern Lebanon, the rest of the country is still perfectly safe to visit. In southern Lebanon, Beit ed-Dine and the surrounding areas, Sidon and Tyre are perfectly safe. Inland of Tyre, more care needs to be taken. In the Bekaa Valley, Baalbek, the Bekaa Valley to the north of Baalbek, Aanjar, Zahle and surrounding areas are generally perfectly safe. The southern Bekaa Valley, however, is less so. See also the specific warnings given in the relevant sections of this book. Ultimately, however, the only real advice one can give is to keep yourself well informed of the current situation and make up your own mind.

Where to stay

Syria

There is a reasonable selection of top-end (**LL-A** category) hotels in Damascus, with a few international chains complementing the national luxury *Cham Palace* hotel chain, though there is nothing like the same selection as you will find in Beirut. In Aleppo, the selection of top-end hotels is now augmented by a couple of excellent independent establishments occupying beautifully restored 17th/18th century palaces. In other major towns/cities (or at important tourist sites) you will generally only find only one top-end hotel, usually a branch of the *Cham Palace* chain, with perhaps one other providing some sort of competition. **B** category hotels are very limited throughout Syria. **C/D** category hotels are plentiful in the major cities, as are **E/F/G** category hotels. There are an increasing number of cheap budget hotels offering dormitory accommodation for backpackers. These are usually very basic, with the main variation being in the level of cleanliness. It is striking how often even quite sizeable towns in Syria have no hotel at all.

While the lower mid-range and budget hotels (**D-G** category) generally accept payment in S£s, practically all hotels from **C** category upwards will accept payment only in US$ cash. Most luxury hotels also accept major credit cards, and a few will accept US$ TCs, but where this is not the case you really need to have a fairly large supply of US$ cash with you, which can be a pain. Nearly all hotels above **C** category also charge an extra 10% government tax; be sure to check whether this is included in the price you are quoted.

Hotels in some places, most notably Palmyra and to a lesser extent Hama, show marked variations in prices between the low and high seasons. In the case of Palmyra, the high season is March-April and August-December, while in Hama it is April/May and July-October. Elsewhere, prices generally stay stable throughout the year, although there are small variations in some categories in Damascus, where the high season is during the summer months (July-October).

There is only one so-called 'hostel' in Syria, at Bosra in the south of the country. It's essentially just a budget dormitory place, but its location inside the Roman theatre/Arab citadel there makes for a highly atmospheric and unusual place to stay.

Hotels

Hostels

Essentials

☞ Hotel price categories

*The price categories used in this book are based on the cost of a double room, including all service and taxes, during the high season. They are **not** star ratings.*

LL US$201+ *Really prestigious international-class luxury hotels and resorts, generally part of a multinational chain. All facilities for the business and leisure traveller to the highest international standard. Major credit cards accepted. There are only a handful of hotels in this category in Syria, while in Lebanon there are lots.*

L US$151-200 *International class luxury hotels and resorts, often part of a luxury chain. They offer all the usual facilities, including 24 hour room service, a/c, TV/dish, IDD, minibar, attached bath, choice of restaurants/bars, swimming pool and other sports such as tennis, health centre, conference/banquet hall, shopping, bank, car hire etc. Major credit cards accepted. Again, hotels in this category are thin on the ground in Syria, but plentiful in Lebanon.*

AL US$101-150 *Luxury hotels, generally offering very comfortable, fully equipped*

rooms, but without the same range of other facilities to be found in LL/L category hotels, and without that feeling of international luxury. Generally with only one restaurant and bar, although a choice of cuisines.

A US$76-100 *In Syria, hotels in this category are generally overpriced for what you get, offering facilities rather more in keeping with a B or C category hotel. In Lebanon it tends to work the other way, with hotels in this category often matching AL category hotels in terms of the facilities on offer.*

B US$51-75 *Comfortable hotels offering rooms with a/c, TV/dish, phone (usually IDD in Lebanon) and attached bath. Restaurant and bar. Often very good value for money (particularly in Syria).*

C US$31-50 *Rooms generally have a/c, TV (and perhaps dish), phone, fridge and attached bath. There is usually a restaurant. Hotels in this category are reasonably comfortable, though there can be a lot of variation in the quality of facilities.*

D US$21-30 *In Syria, rooms may have*

Camping There are very few official campsites in Syria. Beside the Damascus-Aleppo motorway just outside Damascus, the government-run *Harasta* campsite is a thoroughly unappealing place: noisy, with little natural shade and very basic toilet/shower facilities. By contrast, the privately run *Camping Kaddour* to the west of Aleppo is very pleasant. It is ideal for overlanders arriving from Turkey, and also makes a great base from which to explore the Dead Cities. In Aleppo, campervans are allowed to park up outside the tourist information office in the centre of the city. In Palmyra, the *Garden* restaurant offers very pleasant camping amidst date palms and olive trees, while the *Zenobia* hotel allows campervans to park up in its yard, though being rough gravel, it is not really suitable for pitching a tent.

Providing you have your own equipment, there are plenty of opportunities for 'unofficial' camping. The coastal Jebel Ansariye mountains are probably the most beautiful area, with plenty of attractive woodlands complete with streams and waterfalls offering idyllic sites. Camping at some of the more remote historic monuments and archaeological sites is also an option, although you should ask permission first. In more populated areas, camping will certainly generate a great deal of curiosity amongst local people, and in all likelihood you will be invited to stay in someone's house; trying to persuade them that you actually want to camp may be difficult.

Lebanon

Hotels There are numerous luxury (**LL-AL** category) and top-end (**A** category) hotels in and around Beirut. Nearly all of them are of a very high standard, having undergone major

a/c, or else just a fan, as well as TV, phone, fridge attached bath. Good value when clean (notably in Damascus), but in the vast majority of cases hotels in this category in Syria are rather shabby and essentially overpriced. In Lebanon, rooms rarely have a/c and are invariably shabby. Hotels in this category are very thin on the ground in Beirut, and not very appealing (in some cases they are downright seedy; take care). They are more common (and slightly better) outside the capital.

E US$16-20 In Syria, you can expect rather basic rooms with fan, TV, phone, fridge and attached bath. Hotels in this category tend to be rather shabby, though there are some notable exceptions. Rarely with a restaurant. In Lebanon, there is very little in the way of accommodation in this category.

F US$11-15 In Syria, rooms generally have a fan, phone and attached bath only, though occasionally you will find a TV and perhaps even a/c. Check to see if there is hot water (you may have to pay for hot showers). This is the cheapest accommodation you will find without

resorting to dormitories or very basic G category rooms. In Lebanon, hotels in this category are more or less non-existent; where you do find them, there is usually little to distinguish them from G category hotels.

G US$10 or less The very simplest of hotels. In Syria they offer very basic rooms (or more commonly dormitories), usually with a fan and shared toilet/shower facilities. Cleanliness and hygiene varies greatly. There are some real bargains, clean, friendly and well run, but also some really squalid places. In Lebanon, hotels in this category invariably consist of dormitories and tend to be very basic indeed, though there are a couple of exceptions.

Abbreviations The following abbreviations are used in the Sleeping sections; a/c = air conditioning; TV = television; dish = satellite television; IDD = international direct dialing; T = telephone; F = fax; bath = bathroom (which may include a bathtub in the more expensive hotels, but otherwise simply indicates a shower, sink and toilet).

refurbishments since the end of the civil war. As confidence in the stability of the country grows, new ones are opening all the time. **C/D** category hotels are somewhat thin on the ground, however, while **E/F/G** category hotels are very few in number. Outside of Beirut, other than in surrounding areas such as Jounieh and the Metn mountains to the east of Beirut, or popular winter resorts such as the Cedars above Bcharre, the choice of accommodation is much more limited. In the south of the country it is extremely sparse. Although hotels are now required by law to display their prices in LL, all accept payment in US$. Due to the abundance of top-end and luxury hotels in Beirut, many of them offer huge discounts (sometimes as much as 50% off the quoted price). On the other hand, be sure to check whether the 16% service charge and 5% government tax is included in the quoted price (if not, the additional 21% will make a major difference to your bill).

For budget travellers the accommodation situation in Lebanon is extremely limited. However, it is still possible to spend no more than US$4-6 per night on a bed if you are willing to stay in very basic places providing accommodation on a dormitory basis for Syrian workers. With a couple of notable exceptions (one in Beirut and the other in Tripoli), these are not really suitable for women travelling alone due to the dorm set up, although if there are a few of you, you can always just pay for the whole room. There are around half a dozen such places in Beirut. Outside of the capital, the only places with similar deals are Amchit (campsite near Byblos, see below), Tripoli (a couple of really good budget places here), Baalbek and Sidon (very basic indeed). These provide a sufficient number of bases from which to visit the whole of Lebanon (it is in fact easily possible to visit the whole country in a series of day-trips from Beirut).

Budget accommodation

Long-term accommodation	If you are going to be in Lebanon for a month or more, it is worth considering renting an apartment on a long-term basis. In Beirut there are quite a few such apartments, usually consisting of one or two bedrooms, a lounge, shower/toilet and kitchenette. Shared among two or four people, these can work out very good value for the level of facilities. For a list of furnished apartments in Beirut, ask at the tourist information centre in Beirut for a copy of the Ministry of Tourism's Hotel Guide. Along the coast to the north of Beirut there are plenty of beach resorts which also offer long-term accommodation in chalets. These are usually rented for the whole of the summer season (although they can also sometimes be taken for a week or a month at a time), and during this period it is necessary to book well in advance.
Hostels & youth hostels	There is an **E/F** category *YWCA* hostel in Beirut which offers excellent value, clean and accommodation for women. However, during term time, it is generally fully booked up with students, and even during the holidays it is essential that you book in advance. The *Lebanese Youth Hostels Federation* has recently published details of eight youth hostels and 'partner lodging centres' around Lebanon. At the time of writing, most of these were not yet fully operational. At those which are already up and running (namely the 'partner lodging centres'), the main emphasis appears to be on organised visits for youth groups, rather than providing accommodation for independent travellers. For more information, try emailing the Ministry of Tourism (mot@lebanon-tourism.gov.lb), which publishes a pamphlet listing the youth hostels, or else contact the Federation directly (T01-366099, F01-369760, media999@dm.net.lb
Camping	There is a good campsite at Amchit, *Camping Amchit Les Colombres*, a couple of km to the north of Jbail (Byblos). It's a well run, friendly place which offers chalets and 'tungalows' (tent-like bungalows), as well as camping (see page 463). In the Lebanon mountains, above Afqa, *La Reserve* offers full camping facilities as well as a wide range of outdoor activities (see page 504). Camping is also possible in the *Al Shouf Cedar Reserve*, in the Chouf mountains to the south of Barouk (see page 572). Some of the hotels at The Cedars (Al Arz), above Bcharre, will allow you to pitch a tent. Throughout the Lebanon mountains there are plenty of idyllic places for camping, although you are strongly advised to ask for permission before setting up camp. The Bekaa Valley is equally idyllic, though camping is not really advisable as the military are likely to be rather touchy.

Getting around

Syria

Air	*Syrian Air* operates domestic flights between Damascus and Aleppo, Lattakia, Qamishle and Deir ez-Zor (though flights to and from Deir ez-Zor were suspended at the time of writing). See page 126 for details. **NB** If you want to buy tickets with *Syrian Air* to international destinations, you must first go to the *Commercial Bank of Syria* (CBS) and change the relevant amount of hard currency into Syrian pounds at what is known as the 'Aviation rate' (tell the bank that you are buying an air ticket).
Train	The main backbone of Syria's railway system runs north-south between Damascus and Aleppo (via Homs and Hama), east-west between Aleppo and Deir ez-Zor, and then north-south again between Deir ez-Zor and Qamishle in the far northeast of the country. A branch line connects Aleppo with Lattakia on the Mediterranean coast, while another one connects Homs with Tartus and Lattakia. There is also a narrow-gauge line which runs from Damascus to Zabadani and Serghaya. In addition, there are two international lines: the first linking Damascus/Aleppo with Istanbul, and the second linking Damascus with Amman.

Unfortunately, the railway system is largely ignored by most Syrians in favour of the extensive road transport network. As a result, services have been drastically cut; for example, nowadays there is just one train daily in each direction between Damascus and Aleppo and between Aleppo and Qamishle. A major disadvantage of the railway system is that the majority of stations are inconveniently situated a long way from the centre of towns. In addition, you will more often than not find that trains arrive and depart at some ungodly hour of the night/morning. Moreover, while you can usually count on trains leaving on time from their starting point, if you try to join them en route there is a strong likelihood that they will be delayed.

Overall, our advice is to follow the Syrian example and stick to the roads. One exception to this is the railway line between Aleppo and Lattakia which winds its way spectacularly through the beautiful coastal mountains, often carried on high viaducts across valleys and gorges. There are convenient departure/arrival times at both ends, and in both Aleppo and Lattakia the train station is not overly far from the centre of town.

Road (public transport)

Public road transport is by far the most popular means of travel in Syria, with choices ranging from modern luxury a/c coaches to buses, microbuses, service taxis and private taxis. Coach services in particular have undergone radical improvements in recent years.

Karnak The state-owned coach company *Karnak* at one time had a monopoly on coach travel. Today, however, it is complemented by numerous other private luxury coach companies. *Karnak* currently operates a steadily dwindling network of services between the major cities (over the last few years it has reduced its fleet of coaches from 90 to just 21). Prices are slightly cheaper than those of private companies, reflecting the often rather battered state of its aging fleet of a/c coaches. It does have a few new coaches, but these tend to be used for its international services to Amman and Beirut. One advantage of *Karnak* is that in Aleppo, Homs and Palmyra their ticket offices/coach stations are closer to the centre of town (in the case of Aleppo and Palmyra they are right in the centre).

Luxury Coach There is a bewildering array of private luxury coach companies offering services between all the major towns and cities. These operate modern luxury a/c coaches which provide the most comfortable and fastest means of intercity travel. Although they are the most expensive, they are still extremely good value, particularly given the level of comfort; the 4-5 hour, 355 km trip from Damascus to Aleppo, for example, costs just S£150 (just over US$3, or UK£2 at the official bank rate). There are generally only minor variations in price between companies. With so many different companies, services on all the major routes are very frequent, so advance booking is rarely necessary, though it is perfectly possible to book a couple of days ahead if you prefer. **NB** Both *Karnak* and the private luxury coaches will not usually drop you off en route; if they do, they will charge you the full fare to the final destination. They will only ever pick up passengers at designated stops, so don't bother trying to flag them down by the roadside. **NB** During the annual *Hajj*, many private coach companies lease out their coaches to groups making the pilgrimage to Mecca, with the result that services within Syria are greatly reduced.

Bus Buses operate on all major and many minor routes. There is a good deal of variation in bus types. At one end of the scale there are large, relatively comfortable buses comparable with the private coaches, though without a/c, while at the other end of the scale there are small, rickety and fairly cramped 20-seater buses. The larger buses are sometimes referred to as Pullmans, although the term is very loosely applied; it is not uncommon to see small, rickety buses with 'Pullman' – or 'Poulman' or some other misspelling – written on the side. The smaller buses are often referred to as 'hob-hob' buses, translating roughly as 'stop-stop' in reference to the fact that they will stop anywhere en route to pick up and drop off passengers. Prices are significantly cheaper than *Karnak* or private luxury coaches, the main disadvantage (apart from the discomfort) being that the frequent stops en route means that journey times are much slower. However, this can also be an advantage if you want to get off en route without paying the full fare to the final destination. The majority of buses do not run to a fixed timetable, simply leaving when full.

Microbus Microbuses (usually Hiace minivans or similar) are becoming increasingly popular in Syria. They complement bus services, generally operating on minor routes or shorter intercity routes. Like the buses they are cheaper than coaches and simply leave when full. Microbuses tend to travel faster than regular buses and, being smaller, have to stop less frequently. They are also more cramped, although if you can get the front seats, they are relatively comfortable. In Damascus, microbuses form an important part of the local transport system.

Service taxi Intercity service taxis ('serveece') are fairly limited in Syria, and becoming increasingly redundant in the face of competition from luxury coaches and microbuses. They operate only on major intercity routes within the country, as well to and from Amman in Jordan and Beirut in Lebanon. They take a total of five passengers and leave when full. Fares are significantly more expensive than with the other forms of public transport, yet they offer no real advantages (indeed, they tend to be more cramped and uncomfortable, and are often driven by seemingly suicidal maniacs).

Private taxi Private taxis can be found in all the major cities and towns. They provide a convenient and relatively cheap means of getting around. In larger cities you will find some with working meters, but if not you should always agree a price before getting in. You can also negotiate with private taxis to take you on longer intercity journeys or to visit specific places of interest.

Car hire

See page 125 for details of car hire companies based in Damascus, & the prices they charge

Although relatively expensive, hiring a car is an attractive option in Syria, particularly if you intend to visit remoter areas where public transport can be erratic or non-existent. The number of car hire firms in Syria has mushroomed in recent years, with numerous local companies now competing with the large international firms. The vast majority are based in Damascus, with a few also represented in Aleppo. While the local companies are sometimes significantly cheaper than the international ones (some offer cars for as little as US$30 per day, as opposed to an average of around US$60 per day), it is very important to check the rental conditions carefully.

In particular, the smaller local companies often do not offer any insurance cover (other than third party) with their vehicles (insurance arrangements in Syria are both extremely expensive and notoriously unreliable). In such cases, if you have an accident, you will usually be liable for the full cost of the repairs. Even where insurance cover is provided, some companies require you to pay the full rental fee for the period that the car is being repaired. In some cases, you may be required to pay for both. You are strongly advised to clarify exactly what your liability is in case of an accident. If you are involved in an accident, make sure that you obtain a police report; without one, any insurance arrangement that you do have may be invalidated.

The minimum age for car hire varies between 21 and 25. Most companies require that you have held a full licence for at least one year. An international driving licence is not compulsory, although it is useful to have one in any case. Most companies have a minimum rental period of three days. There is usually a choice between limited mileage (usually up to 125 km) and unlimited mileage; unless you are sure that you are not going to be covering any great distances in the end it generally works out cheaper in the end to go for unlimited mileage. Most companies require either a credit card or else a cash deposit, usually in the region of US$500-1000.

Bear in mind that many of the smaller companies only have half a dozen or so vehicles at their disposal and so are often fully booked up. During the summer in particular you are advised to book in advance if you want to be sure of getting a car.

Vehicles drive on the right in Syria. Official speed limits do exist, although these are never enforced and certainly never adhered to. Note that the tow-away zones in big cities *are* enforced, and if you park in one of these (usually fairly clearly indicated by a picture of a car being towed within a red-bordered triangle) you may well return to find that your car has been removed. There are plenty of traffic police around in all the major towns and cities, whose main job is to direct traffic, even where there are traffic lights. Rumour has it that they are forbidden to stop vehicles with foreign plates, although obviously this does not apply to hire cars. Make sure you always have all your documents with you, including your passport. Note that motorcycles are forbidden in parts of the Abou Roumaneh and Al Charkasiye districts of Damascus (close to the Presidential Palace). If you're on a motorbike, you'll soon know if you've strayed into these areas as you'll be stopped by smartly dressed individuals with dark glasses and sub-machine guns: it's probably best not to argue.

Road rules

There is a great deal of variation in the quality of roads and you have to be prepared for some pretty erratic behaviour from other road users. The backbone of Syria's road network is the Damascus-Aleppo highway running north-south between the two cities. Although this is a good quality motorway for most of its length, with 2-3 lanes in each direction separated by a central reservation, great care still needs to be taken when driving on it. As well as fast new cars hurtling up and down it at speeds well in excess of 150 kph, you have to watch out for tractors bumbling along at maybe 20 kph, buses stopping suddenly to pick up passengers, people doing U-turns across the central reservation and sometimes driving in the wrong direction down the hard shoulder. From Damascus there are also good motorways heading south towards the Jordanian border and west towards the Lebanese border, while another motorway runs west from Homs and then north along the Mediterranean coast via Tartus to Lattakia. The highway along the Euphrates River between Aleppo and Dier ez-Zor and other important highways such as those linking Damascus, Homs and Deir ez-Zor with Palmyra are normal roads, in some places fairly wide and in others surprisingly narrow, though generally in good condition.

Driving conditions

A huge amount of work has been carried out in recent years widening and resurfacing roads throughout the country. Nevertheless, there are still plenty of very narrow minor roads, often heavily pot-holed or poorly surfaced. Particular care needs to be taken in the coastal Jebel Ansariye mountains (see page 246). One of the great joys of driving in Syria is that as soon as you get out of the major cities (where heavy congestion and chaotic driving are the norms) the amount of traffic on the roads is minimal. One exception to this is the highway between Aleppo and Lattakia which is always full of heavy lorry traffic along the whole of its length. If at all possible, driving at night anywhere in Syria (except in well-lit urban areas) should be avoided altogether; the twin hazards of some vehicles having faulty lights or no lights at all, and others leaving their main beams permanently on, makes for a potentially lethal combination.

Major routes generally have **signposts** in English as well as Arabic, although there are plenty of exceptions to this. Minor routes are generally less well signposted. In the district of Idlib on the other hand, even the tiniest village or cluster of houses is indicated on road signs. Sometimes it takes a while to figure out the meaning of road signs – even when written in English. My favourite, to be seen approaching towns and villages on the Damascus-Aleppo highway, reads: "Make light speed, a place full of inhabitants".

Essentials

Essentials

Bicycle There is an ever-growing contingent of intrepid travellers to be seen exploring Syria by bicycle. Those considering cycling in Syria should bear in mind the substantial distances involved, coupled with the fact that even fairly large towns often do not have any hotels. Although the terrain is not as hilly as in Lebanon, the heat during summer is fierce, and head winds and cross-winds can be a real problem (good tail winds always seem to be remarkably elusive). Given the distances involved, it is worth considering putting your bike on a bus for the longer journeys (slogging across the Syrian desert to Palmyra, for example, is only really for those interested in testing their endurance to the limit). The large luxury coaches have enough room to stow bicycles in their luggage compartments, while older buses generally have a large rack on the roof.

If you bring your own hi-tech mountain or touring bike, bear in mind that spares will be difficult to find in Syria. Some shops in Damascus and Aleppo now stock imported mountain bikes, though a lot of these come from China and are actually pretty basic. It is perhaps worth considering buying a bike in Syria; although it will be heavier, slower and without the same range of gear ratios, you will at least be able to find spares for it. You will find workshops where you can get most repairs carried out in almost every town, but you should still carry your own basic tool kit and a supply of spares. Probably the most attractive areas to cyclists are the coastal Jebel Ansariye mountains and the so-called 'Dead City' region around Aleppo; here traffic is minimal and the scenery very beautiful, even if the terrain is hilly.

Hitching Hitching is not a widely accepted concept in Syria, except in more remote areas where there is no regular public transport. Some sort of payment is often expected. Women are strongly advised not to hitch unless accompanied by a male companion.

Lebanon

Air There are no internal commercial air services in Lebanon (nor any need for them in a country of this size.

Train Lebanon's railway system, which once consisted of a narrow-gauge line running along the whole length of the coast, and another running inland from Beirut to Damascus and to Homs (via Baalbek), is now completely defunct. There is talk of restoring the coastal line as a tourist attraction, but as yet nothing has been done about it.

Road (public transport) **Coach, bus and microbus** Other than the international connections with Syria (see 'Getting there', above), bus and coach services within Lebanon are still very limited. There are regular coaches and buses between Beirut and Tripoli, between Beirut and Sidon (Saida), and between Sidon (Saida) and Tyre (Sour). Microbuses provide connections between Beirut and the main destinations in the Bekaa valley. They are also starting to compete with service taxis on some routes, for example between Tripoli and Bcharre. There are an increasing number of bus services operating within Greater Beirut and as far north as Jbail (Byblos).

Service taxi Generally referred to as 'servees', service taxis (shared taxis), are an important form of public transport throughout the country and within larger cities such as Beirut and Tripoli. They are essentially a normal taxi (almost always a Mercedes) which is shared between five passengers. Within Beirut they usually operate along more or less fixed routes, picking up and dropping off passengers along the way, although they will sometimes just head off in the direction of the destination of their first passenger, hoping to pick up more along the way. Most service taxi journeys within Beirut cost LL1000 (LL1500 for longer trips). All the major towns and cities in Lebanon are connected by service taxi, with the most frequent services being along the coast to the north and south of Beirut, and inland to Zahle and Baalbek. In the mountains, service taxis are less

Lebanese car culture

Perhaps the most striking first impression for those arriving in Lebanon from Syria is the sheer volume of traffic. While cities such as Damascus may be congested, as soon as you are out in the countryside, traffic falls away to practically nil. In Lebanon, however, the whole country appears at times to be choked with cars. And not the usual beaten-up old jalopies that you find elsewhere in the Middle East, but brand new, top-of-the-range Mercedes, BMWs and the like. The more time you spend in Lebanon, the more you realize the full depth of the obsession that the Lebanese have with their cars.

Consider, for example, the solid traffic to be found crawling at a snail's pace in each direction along the fashionable Manara/Ras Beirut stretch of the Corniche on an average summer's evening. At first you might be tempted to feel sorry for all those people stuck in such a massive traffic jam, until, that is, you realize that the majority of them are simply cruising up and down the Corniche again and again for entertainment! The same scene can be found in almost every town up and down the coast, with open-topped sports cars driving round and round in circles, music blaring. If anything, you get the impression that the slow-moving pace of the traffic suits them just fine; that way everyone gets a good chance to see and be seen, and perhaps to lean over and chat with their friends crawling along in the opposite direction in this self-made lunacy of a traffic-jam.

The defining moment for me came late one evening while sitting on the balcony of a hotel near the port in East Beirut. Down below a car came cruising past, stereo thumping, and driver with his elbow sticking out of the window. Nothing particularly noteworthy for Lebanon, except for the lead hanging off the driver's arm and the dog trotting along beside the car! The concept of 'walking the dog' suddenly took on a whole new meaning.

Essentials

---

frequent, only really operating on a regular basis to a few more important centres; to reach very remote places you really need your own transport or a private taxi. Always establish in advance whether a taxi is operating as a service taxi or not: the sight of a tourist may tempt service taxi drivers to take you as a private fare.

Private taxi Private taxis are plentiful in all the major towns and cities. They are equally willing to take you for short local trips or longer inter-city journeys, or you can easily hire them for a whole day's sightseeing (or more). Always agree a price before setting off, and be prepared to bargain hard before getting a reasonable price.

Car hire in Lebanon is comparatively cheap, with rates starting from as little as US$20 **Car hire** per day for the smallest cars. During peak periods (May, Aug-Sep, Dec), it is extremely difficult to lay your hands on the cheapest hire cars; if possible, bookings should be made at least two weeks in advance. Even outside these times, you are advised to book at least a week ahead. On all but the cheapest deals, you can usually get discounts for periods of a week or more. If you want to be able to visit more remote areas of the country at will, particularly in the mountains, this is the only really viable option (short of hitching or hiring a taxi for the day) unless you have your own vehicle. Beirut is the main centre for car hire, with numerous companies offering everything from small hatchbacks to luxury Mercedes and four-wheel drives.

Conditions vary from company to company. A full driving licence held for at least two years is required by all (though not an international licence). Minimum ages vary from 21-25. All require a deposit, either in the form of a credit card imprint, or else cash in the region of US$500. Be sure to check whether the quoted rates include unlimited mileage (this is usually the case for all rentals of three days or more, or in some cases one week or more). Insurance arrangements are much more reliable in Lebanon than in Syria, although policies in Lebanon carry a somewhat alarming clause along the lines of "war, invasion and hold-up are not covered". However, being involved in an accident (even if it is only a low-speed knock in heavy traffic), or having your car stolen are infinitely more likely scenarios. In either case, you are liable for an excess of anywhere between US$300 (for minor damage to a small car) and US$2,500 (for theft or a total write-off of a luxury car). Most companies offer CDW (Crash Damage Waiver) as an optional extra (usually between US$5-10 per day depending on the type of car); this reduces (but does not completely remove) the excess payable in the event of an accident. Also worth considering is PAI (Personal Accident Insurance), usually costing an additional US$3 per day. Whatever you do, make sure you read the small print before hiring a car. However carefully you drive, there is always the risk of an accident given the driving conditions in Lebanon (see below), but the risk of theft can be greatly reduced by always engaging the steering lock and by making use of supervised parking lots in towns and cities.

Road rules

In a country where a whole generation has grown up against a background of lawlessness & random & senseless death, driving dangerously has perhaps become a substitute for that once pervasive atmosphere of fear

Road rules? What road rules? The only road rule I've ever come across in Lebanon is the one which says that whoever has the biggest, fastest, flashiest car rules the road. In theory, one drives on the right; in practice the Lebanese will aim their cars wherever they see a gap (and pedestrians do *not* constitute an obstacle). Road junctions often seem to be designed with a view to encouraging four-way head-on collisions, and that seems to be just fine with the Lebanese. Overtaking, meanwhile, is only really a worthy manoeuvre on blind corners. Traffic lights are not popular and only seem to be respected when there are contingents of traffic police controlling every approach. Indeed, the reappearance of traffic police on the roads of Lebanon is comparatively recent. And as if to say "Yeah, but it's more to do with image than enforcement", the traffic police have been issued with utterly impractical but highly poseworthy Harley Davidson motorcycles. Whether the Rayban shades are also standard issue is not clear. Essentially, the Lebanese approach to driving is all about machismo; driving fast, recklessly and aggressively whenever possible, and just posing whenever the traffic is too heavy to allow for speed.

Driving conditions

As has already been implied, of all the countries in the Middle East, Lebanon is far and away the most chaotic and terrifying place to drive. That being said, if you are a competent and confident driver, provided you are not stupid enough to take on the Lebanese at their own game, it is perfectly possible to drive all over Lebanon (reasonably) safely. The main problem is the sheer volume of traffic; for such a small country there are massive numbers of cars; indeed, the automobile can be said to be something of a national obsession. Beirut is a pain, because it is so big and you therefore spend so much of your time inching your way through the chaos every time you enter or leave. If you are touring the country by car or motorbike, this is a major argument in favour of actually travelling around the country and making the extra effort to find accommodation along the way, rather than using Beirut as a base for day-trips to places of interest. The coastal motorway which runs north from Beirut as far as Tripoli is hopelessly congested along the first stretch as it runs through the unbroken urban sprawl between Beirut and Jounieh. North of Jounieh it is generally fairly fast and free-flowing. If getting from point to point quickly is not your priority, the old coast road from Jounieh all the way up to Tripoli runs parallel, hugging the actual coastline for much of the way and taking you through the smaller towns along the coast. It's much slower and actually quite congested in places, but more interesting. The coastal motorway now also runs south from Beirut as far as Sidon (once you are clear of Beirut's hopelessly congested Southern Suburbs, it's reasonably fast), while the stretch to the south of Sidon should be open by the time this book is published. The other major highway in terms of volume of traffic is the Beirut-Damascus highway. This is an average width, two-lane road (with section which have been widened to four lanes), but being the main artery connecting coastal Lebanon with the Bekaa valley and Syria beyond, it is always busy with heavy lorries as well as cars. Driving on it is never pleasant. A new motorway is under construction along this route, though it will be quite some time before it is completed. As soon as you head off on the minor roads running through the mountains, there is very little traffic. The roads themselves are narrow, twisting and often in poor condition, but the scenery is stunning. Bear in mind that the higher roads get blocked by snow during winter (the Beirut-Damascus highway and the main routes up to the ski resorts are kept open). The roads in the Bekaa valley (with the exception of the main road to Baalbek and this section of the Beirut-Damascus highway) are also generally small and relatively traffic free.

Bicycle

Cycling in Lebanon is certainly a possibility, although it's one that generally meets with total incredulity from the Lebanese ('But what happened to your car? You poor thing. Hey, look, you can borrow mine,'). The main problem is traffic. The coastal and Beirut-Damascus corridors are best avoided altogether (this is fairly easily, since a bicycle with its front wheel off will go no problem in the boot of a service taxi for an extra fare), but the mountains offer plenty of very beautiful and quiet roads for those willing to take on the gradients. The Bekaa valley is flatter, the roads are on the whole quiet and it is also stunningly beautiful. You will find fairly good bicycle shops in Beirut and most repairs should be possible without too much problem.

Hitching

On any of the major transport routes, hitching is more or less impossible simply because as soon as you stick your thumb out you will attract the attention of any passing service taxi driver. However, on quiet roads in remoter areas hitching is perfectly possible. You should be equally prepared for paying the equivalent of a service taxi fare for the ride, or being invited to someone's house, lavished with hospitality and probably taken round the rest of the country. Women travelling alone are not advised to hitch.

Keeping in touch

Syria

Points of contact

All European and North American countries (and the vast majority of other countries from around the world) have **embassies** in Damascus. If your passport is lost or stolen, your embassy should be able to help you obtain a replacement. However, except in the case of extreme emergencies (in the event of serious civil unrest, or a regional war breaking out, for example), foreign embassies are very reluctant to do anything else for their nationals. Several European countries, and the USA, also have **cultural centres** in Damascus (there are also branches of the Centre Culturel Français and the British Council in Aleppo). These are generally geared primarily towards providing Syrians with details of educational opportunities in their respective countries, and organizing/hosting cultural events (the Centre Culturel Français in Damascus is by far the most active in terms of its programme of cultural events). They can also be a useful source of information and contacts, particularly for long-term residents in Syria.

For listings of all foreign embassies & cultural centres in Damascus, see the Directory in the Essentials section of the Damascus chapter

Internet

Until recently the internet was viewed as a threat to security in Syria, providing as it does a means of communication and an information source which the state is essentially unable to monitor and control. However, the new president, Bashar Assad, is an enthusiastic advocate and under him access to the internet is gradually spreading. Indeed, Bashar Assad's only official position prior to becoming president was as head of the Syrian Computer Society, and he is said to have been directly responsible for introducing the internet in Syria. At the time of writing there were a handful of private internet cafés in Damascus and Aleppo (and one in Tartus) as well as government-run

Note that access to both Hotmail & Yahoomail are currently blocked in Syria. You are advised to get an alternative address: both Excite & Talk21 work fine

access centres in the telephone offices of major cities. Opinion is divided as to whether this is one area in which the pace of change will be rapid, or whether it will be subject to the same cautious, steady approach being applied to other modernizing programmes. Given the great pressure coming from the business community to be allowed to harness the commercial potential of the internet, and the fact that neighbouring countries (notably Jordan and Lebanon) are forging ahead on this front, there is at least a chance that the pace of change will be faster rather than slower.

There are currently only two servers in the whole country, both of them state-controlled; s.c.s-net.org, serving the scientific community, and net.sy, which is the most widely used. Already, however, they are unable to keep up with demand. The other major constraint is the telephone network, which is currently being upgraded. At the time of writing the new system had been installed in Damascus and Aleppo only.

Costs for internet use are relatively expensive, though if internet cafés begin to proliferate in the same way as they have in Lebanon and Jordan, prices will certainly come down quickly. At the time of writing the government-run access centres in the telephone offices were charging S£2 per minute (S£120 per hour; roughly US$2.60 or UK£1.85 per hour at the official exchange rate). Private internet cafés were generally charging S£5 per minute, or else around S£2.5 per minute for longer periods of use.

Post Airmail **letters** (up to 20 g) cost S£17, and **postcards** S£10 (whether to Europe, North America or Australia/NZ). Postal services are very erratic; when posted in Damascus, mail to Europe generally takes only 4-5 days, whereas from other towns and cities it can take as long as 2-3 weeks. To North America and Australia/NZ you are looking at a minimum of two weeks and anything up to one month.

To send a **parcel**, you should take it unwrapped to the post office, where its contents will be inspected. It must then be sewn up in cotton. Parcels to the UK/Europe cost S£170 per kilogram, to North America S£285 per kilogram, and to Australia/NZ S£350 per kilogram.

There is a **poste restante** counter at the central post office in Damascus (open Sat-Thu 0800-1700, closed Fri). To collect mail you must present your passport as ID and pay S£10 per item of mail. Mail sent here should have your surname in capital letters and underlined to avoid it being filed under your first name. It should be addressed to: c/o Poste Restante, Central Post Office, Said al-Jabri Ave, Damascus, Syria. Alternatively, American Express in Damascus offer a poste restante service (c/o Client's Mail, Al Moutanabi Place, PO Box 1373, Damascus, Syria).

There is a branch of *DHL* in Damascus. Sending packages from Syria by courier works out significantly cheaper than from Lebanon or Jordan.

Telephone The cheapest and most convenient way of making international (and national) calls is
To call Syria from by cardphone. There are currently two cardphone systems operating in Syria. The
Lebanon you simply dial more modern one is a public-private partnership between the state-owned *Syrian*
02 followed by the city *Telephone Exchange (STE)* and *Easycomm*. At the time of writing, STE/Easycomm
code, less the initial zero cardphones had been installed in Damascus (and some surrounding districts) and
(eg to call Damascus Aleppo only (bear in mind, therefore, that phonecards bought in Damascus and Alep-
from Lebanon, dial 0211 po cannot be used elsewhere in the country, and vice versa). The cards are credit card
followed by the number) size and made of thick plastic, with photos of various historic monuments on one side. They come in denominations of S£100, S£200 (for local/national calls only), S£500 and S£1000 (local, national and international calls), though at the time of writing only the S£500 card appeared to be available. STE/Easycomm cardphone booths can be found dotted all over Damascus and Aleppo (see in the Directory of the relevant Essentials sections for pointers as to the quieter locations). The cards themselves are sold at shops near the booths (often from late-opening juice bars and the like; just ask around), or else from the main telephone office. The STE/Easycomm cardphones also take coins, making them convenient for local and national calls; if you arm yourself

with enough change (S£25 is the largest denomination coin) you can even make international calls in this way.

The older cardphone system is operated by STE and found throughout the rest of the country. The cards are made of very thin plastic (they are easily damaged, so handle them carefully). They come in values of S£250 (domestic/national), S£500 and S£1000, though often only the latter is available. STE cardphones are located at the main telephone offices *only* (either inside or just outside), where you can also buy the cards (either over the counter, or else from semi-official touts outside). Here you will also find some coin-operated phone booths, good for local and national calls only.

Note that it is no longer possible to place calls through the operator at main telephone offices (these offices now only deal with bill payments for domestic/commercial phone lines and mobile phone accounts, as well as offering telegram/fax services, and internet access in some cases).

Telegrams and **faxes** can be sent from the main telephone offices of larger towns. All but the most basic hotels now have fax machines as well, making this a more convenient way to send and receive faxes. Bear in mind, however, that making international calls (and sending faxes) from hotels is considerably more expensive. Take particular care with the luxury hotels, which generally charge exhorbitant rates. It is not possible to make collect (reverse charges) calls from Syria. If you want to minimize expenditure on phone calls, your best bet is to phone through the number of your hotel and get people to phone you back.

Newspapers and magazines Although there are plenty of Arabic language newspapers in Syria, there is only one English language newspaper, the *Syria Times*. Unfortunately, it is something of a joke in terms of news coverage, being almost entirely devoted to blatantly anti-Israeli and pro-Arab propaganda. It's also atrociously written. Its only saving grace is a small 'What's On' section with listings of exhibitions, lectures and films etc, as well as emergency numbers and exchange rates. An increasingly wide range of international newspapers and magazines are available from news stands around Damascus, as well as from the bookshops of luxury hotels. In Aleppo, you only find them in the luxury hotels, while in the rest of Syria they are rarely seen at all.

Media

For details of websites relating to Syria, Lebanon & the Middle East in general, see page 73

Radio At the time of writing, the *Syrian Broadcasting Company*'s foreign language broadcasts had been suspended. Close to Lebanon (eg in Tartus) it is often possible to pick up Lebanese music channels. The best frequency for receiving the *BBC World Service* is 1323 kHz (MW), although it is also available in SW bands. *Voice of America* can be heard on 1260 kHz (AM).

Television Channel 2 of *Syrian TV* broadcasts in French and English. The English news is at 2200, and the French news at 2000. Many hotels now have satellite TV (even cheap budget hotels often have one in the lobby).

Lebanon

All European and North American countries (and the vast majority of other countries from around the world) have **embassies** in or around Beirut. If you passport is lost or stolen, your embassy should be able to help you obtain a replacement. However, except in the case of extreme emergencies (in the event of serious civil unrest, or a regional war breaking out, for example), foreign embassies are very reluctant to do anything else for their nationals. Several European countries have **cultural centres** in Beirut. These are generally geared primarily towards providing Lebanese with details of educational opportunities in their respective countries, and organizing or hosting cultural events (the *Centre Culturel Français* is by far the most active in terms of its

Points of contact

For listings of all foreign embassies & cultural centres, see the Directory in the Essentials section of the Beirut chapter

programme of cultural events). They can also be a useful source of information and contacts, particularly for long-term residents in Lebanon.

Internet
There are no restrictions on internet access in Lebanon

There is a thriving internet café scene in Beirut, ranging from very simple internet 'offices' with nothing more than desks and computer terminals, through to very pleasant cafés, where the emphasis is as much on providing good tea, coffee, snacks and meals etc in comfortable surroundings. Many internet places also offer computer games, which often represent a significant portion of their business. All other major towns and cities (and even a few larger villages) have at least one internet café. The cost of internet access in Lebanon varies between LL3,000 (US$2) and LL5,000 (US$3.33). With ever more competition, rates are likely to fall over time.

Post
Postal services in Lebanon are now run by the private *Liban Post* company, whose distinctive blue and yellow logo is prominently displayed outside post offices in all towns and cities. **Postcards** to Europe cost LL900, while to USA, Canada, Australia etc they cost LL1,300. **Letters** (up to 20 g) to Europe cost LL1,100, to USA, Canada, Australia etc LL1,500. Beirut is the best place to have mail sent to you **poste restante** (see page 440 for details). You can send **parcels** weighing up to 10 kg through the Lebanese postal system. A parcel of 1, 5 or 10 kg to the UK costs LL29,400, LL65,500 or LL110,750 respectively (other European destinations vary slightly, but are comparable), to the USA/Canada LL24,800, LL102,700 or LL189,250 respectively, and to Australia LL24,800, LL99,500 or LL182,400.

Telephone
At the time of writing there were no cardphones in operation in Lebanon. International calls can be made either from a government-run telephone office (known as a *Centrale*) in any of the major towns and cities, or from private telephone offices, of which there are plenty in Beirut, and usually at least one in smaller towns. Government-run telephone offices apply a three minute minimum period for international calls. The private telephone offices have shorter minimum periods for international calls (usually two minutes) and are significantly cheaper. For details of government and private telephone rates, see page 441. Local and national calls can be made from practically any shop. **Faxes** can be sent and received at most of the private telephone offices, and from nearly all hotels. Bear in mind that making international calls (and sending faxes) from hotels is considerably more expensive. Take particular care with the luxury hotels, which generally charge exhorbitant rates.

Media
Newspapers The censorship which is so prevalent in Syria is almost completely absent in Lebanon. There is one English-language daily newspaper, the *Daily Star*, relaunched in 1996, and a weekly magazine, *Monday Morning*, which includes interesting features on national and regional issues alongside plenty of features on Lebanon's high society social scene. The French-language daily is *L'Orient le Jour*, which is a condensed version of the Arabic-language daily *Al Nahar*. It includes useful listings of events in Lebanon. There are in addition numerous Arabic-language papers, some of them independent, others propaganda organs for various political parties and religious groups. All the major foreign newspapers and magazines are readily available in Beirut, though they are extremely expensive (eg *The Times* LL4,500/US$3, *Sunday Times* LL12,500/just over US$8). There is a huge range of magazines and glossies, though again, prices are high.

Radio *Radio Liban*, which is controlled by the Ministry of Information, broadcasts on 96.2 MHz (FM). It has daily French-language broadcasts at 1800. There are numerous other radio stations within Lebanon, many of which can only be picked up over a relatively small area. Explore the radio waves for yourself. On the whole they broadcast a diet of either Arabic or Western pop music (or sometimes a mixture of the two), along with various chat shows and phone-ins. *Radio One* broadcasts on 105.5 MHz (FM) and can be picked up over most of the country. It is styled on the BBC's Radio One in the UK and often has visiting DJs from there. The best frequency for receiving *BBC World Service* is 1323 kHz (MW), although it is also available on 720 kHz (MW) and in various SW bands. *Voice of America* is on 1260 kHz (AM).

Television There are numerous TV stations in Lebanon, nearly all of which represent a political or religious faction. *Télé Liban* is the only government-controlled TV station. It broadcasts on three channels and has programmes in Arabic, French and English. Of the private TV stations, the four most popular ones are; the *Lebanese Broadcasting Company (LBC)*, established in 1985 by the 'Lebanese Forces' Christian militia of Samir Geagae but now has broad popular appeal and shows plenty of foreign programmes; *Future TV*, owned by the Prime Minister, Rafiq Hariri; *MTV* (no relation to its American counterpart), an Orthodox Christian station owned by the former vice prime minister, Michel Murr; and *MBN*, owned by Nabih Berri, the Shi'ite speaker of parliament. In addition, most hotels have satellite TV, and generally subscribe to all the major international channels.

Food and drink

Syria and Lebanon both share the same, essentially Arabic, cuisine. **Meat**, in the form of lamb or chicken, features fairly prominently in the Arab diet, along with **staples** such as chick peas (in the form of falafels or hummus), other vegetables, and of course bread (*khubz*). Despite the prominence of meat, **vegetarians** can be sure of a nutritious and reasonably varied diet (hummus, falafels, baba ganoush and other mezze dishes, as well as fuul, fatteh, salads, rice, vegetable stews and bread). All kinds of **international** cuisine and **fast food** are widely available throughout Lebanon, and to a much lesser extent in Syria.

Many visitors are surprised at how readily available **alcohol** is in what is a predominantly Muslim region. This reflects the diverse nature of society in the Middle East (in Lebanon Christians represent nearly 50% of the population, in Syria they account for around 10%, which is numerically significant) and also its essentially tolerant nature. Locally brewed and imported beers are readily available, some good wines are grown (notably in Lebanon), while the much loved Arab contribution to the liqueur cabinet, *arak*, is ubiquitous.

Syria

On the whole, the range of Arabic food on offer in Syria is somewhat limited, although in Damascus and Aleppo there is an ever increasing number of excellent restaurants where the selection is more varied and imaginative. Elsewhere, you will find yourself confronted by a rather predictable choice of roast chicken, meat kebabs, hummus, salads, chips etc. Those travelling on a tight budget will find themselves living off a diet of falafels, shawarmas, hummus, fuul, fatteh etc, and the occasional half roast chicken or plate of kebabs. Damascus, Aleppo and Lattakia have a fairly large selection of restaurants serving various types of international cuisine, as well as Western-style fast food places serving burgers, pizzas etc.

Tea and **coffee** compete as the national drinks. Both are served in the usual Arabic way (see glossary below) and Syria has numerous traditional-style cafés where people come to drink tea and coffee, enjoy a *nargileh* (see glossary below), play cards or backgammon, gossip and socialize. You can get excellent freshly squeezed **fruit juices**, with dedicated juice bars being a common feature of all larger towns and cities.

Essentials

What's on offer depends very much on the season. It may be oranges, apples, pears, bananas, pomegranates or melons. Lemonade made from fresh lemon and fizzy mineral water is another one to look out for. *Laban* and *Ayran* are common **dairy**-based drinks, although straightforward milk (*haleeb*) is something of a rarity. Usually if you ask for milk, you will be given powdered or UHT milk. **Fizzy drinks** of all kinds are widely available, both international brands such as *Coca Cola, Seven Up* etc, and local lookalikes. **Mineral water** is widely available.

Bars are not that common. There are a few independent ones in Damascus, and all the luxury hotels also have their own bars, but otherwise the choice is limited to those restaurants which serve alcohol. Alternatively, there are off-licences in the Christian areas of most towns and cities where you can buy alcohol directly and more cheaply. Locally brewed beers include *Al Shark* (or *Al Chark*, from Aleppo) and *Barada* (from Damascus). Neither are particularly good and you have to watch out for out-of-date bottles, but when fresh and properly chilled, they are certainly drinkable. Imported beers include *Heineken* and *Carlsberg*, though these are at least double the price of local varieties. As throughout the Middle East, the local liqueur, *arak* is found everywhere and is very popular. Other imported spirits (particularly whisky) are also fairly widely available.

Lebanon

Lebanon has a well deserved reputation for the best cooking in the region, and it's here that you'll get a true taste of what Arabic cuisine is really about. The fusing of Arabic and Mediterranean influences combined with the Lebanese love of food has ensured that eating is always something of a gourmet experience. Indeed, as well as Arabic food, in Lebanon you can sample the very best of practically any cuisine from around the world, whether it be European, Asian, Far Eastern or Latin American. Beirut and its environs have the highest concentration of restaurants, with everything from cheap snack places and Western-style fast-food joints to sumptuously elegant gourmet establishments, with prices to match. Elsewhere, along the coast, and in the mountains inland, there are also many excellent restaurants. Up in the mountains you can often find more traditional places serving excellent mezzes at very good prices, although just because a restaurant is remote doesn't mean it's cheaper. One place particularly famous for its mezzes is Zahle, in the Bekaa valley. Sea food is considered a particular speciality in Lebanon, probably at least partly because it is so scarce; during the civil war many people took to dynamiting the fish out of the sea and stocks are still seriously depleted.

If you are on a tight budget you will be very limited as to what you can eat, and where. Sit-down meals at proper restaurants are more or less out of the question. Instead you will have to content yourself with snacks of falafels and shawarmas, bowls of fuul or hummus with bread, half roast chickens, salads etc. Note that in addition to the usual falafel/shawarma sandwiches, you can get a wide range of other fillings from many snack bars (the choice is much wider than that usually available in Syria). In the mountains, even general grocery stores will often put together a sandwich for you.

Western **fast food** features prominently in Lebanon, with *KFC, Baskin Robbins, Pizza Hut* and dozens of others all making a showing. Even *McDonalds*, previously banned for its Jewish connections, now has a branch in Beirut. Alongside these there are plenty of local versions. However, Western-style fast food is more expensive than in the West, and really a middle class preserve.

Coffee, in its traditional Arabic form, is more widely drunk than **tea**, although in the traditional cafés of Tripoli or Sidon both are equally popular (the latter usually being brewed from a *Lipton's* tea bag and served in the Arabic way, black and sweet). In the classy and fashionable cafés of Beirut (and indeed most towns), you'll find the very best expresso and probably every conceivable blend of tea. **Fizzy soft drinks** (*Coca Cola*,

Pepsi, Seven Up, Miranda etc) are widely available, as is mineral water. Freshly-squeezed **fruit juice** (particularly orange) and fresh fruit milkshakes are also popular.

Lebanon is more famous, however, for its **alcohol**. The Bekaa valley vineyards of Ksara, Kefraya and Chateau Musar produce some excellent **wines**, as well as the powerful spirit *arak*. Other spirits, in particular whiskey, are also popular, with just about every major brand being imported. *Al Maaza* and *Lazziza* are both good quality, light lagers brewed locally under licence from *Amstel*, alongside which there are plenty of other imported brands. Many places now have draught beers on tap, while a few British-style 'pubs' even have draught *Guinness* on tap.

A glossary of Arabic cuisine

Bread

Bread, known Arabic as *khubz* or *eish* (literally 'life'), is the mainstay of the Arabic diet. It is baked unleavened (without yeast) in flat round discs and accompanies just about every meal or snack. Often it serves as an eating implement, or is rolled up with a filling inside to make a 'sandwich' snack. When it is fresh it is delicious although surprisingly for a region where so much of it is consumed, it has often been standing about for the best part of a day by the time it reaches your plate.

Mezze dishes

Perhaps the most attractive feature of Arabic cuisine is the mezze. When done properly, this consists of a spread of numerous small dips, salads and nibbles of fresh raw vegetables, olive etc, which are served as an extended starter course and, if the company is not teetotal, usually washed down with plenty of beer or arak. To fully appreciate a proper mezze spread you really need to be in a group of several people or you'll never get round the array of dishes; it also works out very reasonably when divided amongst several people. For smaller numbers you can just ask for a selection. If you do not want a full meal, you can always do away with the main courses and just concentrate on the mezze. Many of the items listed below are also served individually as a side dish in snack places and simple restaurants, or indeed as snacks in themselves. A selection of the more popular mezze dishes is given here.

Baba Ganoush (Moutabbal) Chargrilled eggplant (aubergine), tahini, olive oil, lemon juice and garlic blended into a smooth paste and served as a dip.
Falafel Small deep-fried balls of ground, spiced chick-peas. Very popular, both as part of a mezze, and as the basis of one of Syria and Lebanon's most ubiquitous snacks (see below).
Fattoush Salad of toasted croutons, cucumbers, tomatoes, onion and mint.
Hummus Purée of chick-peas, tahini, lemon and garlic, served as a dip with bread. Probably the most common mezze dish, often also eaten along with salad as a side dish to a plate of meat in simpler restaurants, or as a light snack in its own right.
Kibbeh Ground lamb and burghul (bulghur/bulgar/cracked) wheat meatballs stuffed with olives and pine nuts and fried or baked. Something of a national dish in Lebanon.
Kibbeh Nayeh Raw kibbeh, eaten like steak tartare.
Loubieh (fasulya) Cooked French beans with tomatoes onion and garlic, served hot as a stew or cold as a kind of salad.
Mouhammara Mixture of ground nuts, olive oil, cumin and chillis, eaten with bread.
Rocca Rocket salad.
Tabouleh Finely chopped salad of burghul wheat, tomatoes, onions, mint and parsley.
Taratour Thick mayonnaise of puréed pine nuts, garlic and lemon, used as a dip.
Warak Enab (warak dawali) Vine leaves stuffed with rice and vegetables.

Essentials

'Main' meat dishes So-called 'main' courses are more limited and consist primarily of meat dishes (usually lamb or chicken), or else fish (see below). Note that many listed below are also often served as snacks.

Bamia Baby okra and lamb in a tomato stew.

Bukhari rice Lamb and rice stir-fried with onion, lemon, carrot and tomato.

Kebab In Syria at least, if you ask for 'kebab', you will most likely be offered *kofte kebab*, though strictly speaking *kebab* is just chunks of meat chargrilled on a skewer.

Kofte kebab Minced meat and finely chopped onions, herbs and spices pressed onto a skewer and chargrilled. You order by weight.

Kouzi Whole lamb baked over rice so that it soaks up the juice of the meat.

Mensaf A traditional Bedouin dish, consisting of lamb cooked with herbs in a yoghurt sauce and served on a bed of rice with pine nuts. You are most likely to come across this dish at Palmyra in Syria.

Saleek Lamb and rice dish cooked in milk.

Shish taouk Fillets of chicken breast chargrilled on a skewer. Extremely popular throughout Syria and Lebanon, on offer in practically every restaurant.

Fish The price of fish in Lebanon is pretty astronomical. In Syria it is also expensive, but nothing like the price it is in Lebanon. From mid-October to mid-November supplies are more plentiful and prices fall correspondingly. It is most commonly either grilled or fried and served with lemon, salad and chips.

Gambari Prawns.

Hamour Red Sea fish of the grouper family.

Najil Saddle-back grouper.

Samak nahri Trout.

Sayyadiya Delicately spiced fish (usually red mullet or bass) served with rice.

Shaour Red Sea fish of the emperor family.

Sultan Ibrahim (literally 'King Abraham', ie the king of fishes) Red mullet.

Snacks Traditional snack bars (and indeed many restaurants) serve a wide range of snacks. If you are on a tight budget, or are a vegetarian, many of these will become staples.

Ejje Omelette, usually with chopped onion and herbs. Makes a good breakfast dish.

Falafel The falafel sandwich must be the most ubiquitous snack throughout Syria; you will find snack bars serving this (and often only this) everywhere you go. In Lebanon it is also popular, though nowhere near as ubiquitous. Several falafel balls (see under mezze dishes) are crushed on an open piece of Arabic bread, garnished with salad and pickled vegetables (usually tomatoes, beetroot, onion and lettuce), topped by a yoghurt and *tahini* sauce and then rolled up into a 'sandwich'. They are very cheap and filling, though if you are on a tight budget and relying on them as a staple, they can get pretty monotonous. The freshness of the bread, as well as the filling, is what makes or breaks them.

Farouj Roast chicken. Although this should really appear under 'main' meat dishes, roast chicken is such a common form of light meal or snack (especially in Syria) that we have included it here. Everywhere you go throughout Syria you will find simple restaurants, snack places and shops with roasting ovens outside containing several spits of roasting chickens. The standard portion is a half chicken ('*nuss farouj*'), sometimes served with a small portion of garlic dip and a few pickled vegetables and chips. As often as not, roast chickens are bought as takeaways to be eaten at home.

Fatayer Triangular pastry pockets filled with spinnach (*sbanikh*), meat or cheese. These make great snacks. Usually sold from bakeries specializing in these and other items, including *mannoushi*, see below.

Fatteh An excellent, very filling snack consisting of fuul and laban mixed together with small pieces of bread and topped with pine nuts and melted butter. Also sometimes served with fried minced meat mixed in.

Fuul Slow-cooked mash of fava beans and red lentils, dressed with lemon, olive oil and cumin, and sometimes a little yoghurt and *tahini* sauce. An excellent, filling and nutritious snack, traditionally a breakfast dish, though available any time of day.

Kushary Staple of pasta, rice and lentils mixed with onions, chilli and tomato paste. More common in Egypt, but found also in Syria and Lebanon.

Mannoushi Thin, crusty 'pizzas' topped with a thin layer of meat (*Lahmeh*), cheese (*Jebneh*), or *Zaatar*, a seasoning with thyme and *sumak*. A good breakfast snack.

'Sandweech' Both falafels and shawarmas are commonly referred to simply as 'sandwiches' (or *sandweech*). In addition, there are numerous other fillings available in many snack bars. *Shish taouk* and *kofte* can be ordered in sandwich form, or it's a case of looking to see what's on offer.

Shawarma This is essentially a meat version of a falafel sandwich, and an equally ubiquitous snack bar favourite. Layers of lamb or chicken roasted on a vertical spit are sliced off into small flat breads and rolled up with salad, pickled vegetables and a garlic sauce into a sandwich which is then steeped in extra fat as a special favour. Again they are cheap and filling, and if you are on a tight budget and not a vegetarian you will no doubt be eating plenty of them.

Some of these make an appearance in other dishes listed here, or else are popular as drinks in their own right. **Dairy products**

Ayran Salty yoghurt drink, good refreshing rehydration material.

Haleeb Milk.

Jebneh (Jibni) Fairly hard and stringy white cheese.

Laban Slightly sour yoghurt drink, also widely used in cooking as a milk substitute.

Labneh Thick creamy cheese, often spiced and used as a dip, for example *Labneh Maa Toum*, with garlic and olive oil.

The Arab tooth is certainly very sweet. The range of sweets, pastries, biscuits and puddings on offer is enormous, but they all share one thing in common: copious amounts of sugar in one form or another. Most are served at restaurants, but to see the full range of what's on offer you should go to a pâtisserie, where you will be confronted by a bewildering selection. Many pâtisseries also have an area where you can sit and eat, and some also serve tea, coffee, soft drinks etc. **Sweets**

Asabeeh Rolled filo pastry filled with pistachios, pine nuts and cashews and honey. Often referred to as 'lady's finger'.

Atait Small pancakes stuffed with nuts or cheese and doused with syrup.

Baklawa Layered pastry filled with nuts and steeped in honey and lemon syrup. Probably the most common and best known Arabic sweet.

Barazak Crisp, light biscuits sprinkled with sesame seeds.

Basboosa Semolina tart soaked in syrup.

Booza Ice cream.

Borma Crushed pine nuts or pistachios wrapped in shredded pastry and sliced into segments.

Halawat al-Jebneh Soft thick pastry stuffed with *labneh* cheese and steeped in syrup and ice cream.

Halwa A sweet made from sesame paste, usually studded with fruit and nuts and made in a slab.

Kamar ed-Dine Apricot nectar, often served as a break of fast during Ramadan.

Kunafi Pastry stuffed with sweet white cheese, nuts and syrup.

Ma'amul Biscuits stuffed with date, pistachio or walnut paste.

Muhalabiyyeh Fine, smooth textured semolina and milk pudding, sometimes with pistachios, pine nuts and almonds, served cold.

Sanioura Dry, crumbly macaroon-like biscuit. A speciality of Sidon in Lebanon.

Um Ali Literally 'Ali's mother', a pastry pudding with raisin and coconut, steeped in milk.

Essentials

Tea & coffee Tea and coffee are widely drunk throughout the Middle East, though they are made very differently from in the West. Arabic coffee (or Turkish or Greek, depending on where you are) is known in the Middle East as *Kahweh* (or *Ah'weh*). The Arab attitude to coffee is basically the stronger the better. The coffee is boiled up in tiny pots and served very strong in equally tiny cups, complete with a thick sludge of coffee grounds at the bottom. It is served without sugar (*balasekir* or *sadah*), with medium sugar (*wassad*), or with lots of sugar (*helweh*). Cardamom is sometimes added to give a delicate aromatic flavour. You can also get excellent expresso coffee (especially in Lebanon), just as strong but without the thick sludge at the bottom. Instant coffee is referred to everywhere as 'Nescafe' and is available on request in more expensive restaurants and hotels. The Arabic word for tea is *Shai* (or *chai*), which is generally drunk strong and black, and with copious amounts of sugar. Mint tea and green tea are also available, though not so popular.

Arak Arak is an Arabic equivalent of the Greek *oozo* or Turkish *raki*, a potent liqueur made from grapes (in fact the left-overs of wine pressing) and flavoured with aniseed. It is very popular and is usually drunk with ice and/or cold water which makes the otherwise clear alcohol go a cloudy white. The cheapest brands cost as little as US$2 for a litre, while the best ones cost as much as US$20. Only the most experienced drinkers, however, can actually detect any difference, except perhaps in the quality of their hangover the next day.

Nargileh Not exactly an item of 'cuisine', the nargileh nevertheless goes hand in hand with eating and drinking. It consists of a large waterpipe, known also as a *shish* or 'hubbly bubbly', through which tobacco, often flavoured with apple or strawberry, is smoked. Nargilehs are enjoyed at great length in cafés throughout Syria and Lebanon alongside tea and coffee and endless games of cards and backgammon, or else after a meal.

Shopping

Syria

Syria is something of a paradise for souvenir, handicraft and antique hunters. The most interesting and rewarding places to go exploring are the souks of Damascus and Aleppo. The luxury hotels also have their own shops where you can find most the things on offer in the souks; the prices are generally higher, though in some cases so is the quality.

Handicrafts, Things to look out for include: wooden chess sets and backgammon boards; wooden
souvenirs & boxes etc inlaid with mother-of-pearl; carpets and rugs; jewellery; gold and silver-
antiques ware; brassware; Damascene swords; musical instruments; nargilehs; fabrics and silk brocades (for which Damascus is famous); antique coins etc. For details of where to find all these, see the relevant Essentials sections.

Books The range of books available in Syria is predictably limited, and anything remotely political is censored. You can, however, find a reasonable selection of books on Syrian history and architecture etc. Damascus is the best place for English-language books. There are a number of good independent bookshops, as well as those attached to the luxury hotels (the latter offer the best choice in terms of fiction). The selection in Aleppo is more limited, while elsewhere you will be lucky to find anything in English.

Photography Colour negative film is widely available, although colour transparency (slide) film can generally only be found in Damascus and Aleppo. The shops inside luxury hotels are good places to go as they have a fairly brisk turnover and the film is therefore usually fairly fresh. Black and white film is rarer.

Lebanon

You can buy more or less anything in Lebanon, but prices tend to be on a level with those of Europe and North America.

The selection of handicrafts and souvenirs on offer in Lebanon is actually reasonably good, although if you are visiting Syria as well you will find many of the same items there at cheaper prices. Things to look out for in Lebanon include woven reed and palm-leaf baskets, hats and mats etc, handmade pottery, hand-blown glass, copper ware (plates, trays, coffee pots etc), nargilehs, hand-woven tapestries, rugs and carpets, wooden and inlaid-wood items (boxes, chess sets, backgammon boards etc), gold and silver jewellery and embroidered cloth. There are plenty of tourist-orientated shops in Beirut which sell these goods. Although not specifically for tourists, you can often find interesting handicrafts and souvenirs in the souks of Tripoli and Sidon. Tripoli is famous for its gold souk, and the prices here are reported to be lower than in Damascus or Aleppo. For antiques, particularly archaeological artefacts, Jbail (Byblos) is a good place to look, although you should bear in mind that many of the artefacts on sale are probably fakes. Those that are not are on sale illegally, since officially all artefacts of any archaeological significance should be handed over to the Department of Antiquities. There is, however, open and widespread flouting of this law.

Handicrafts, souvenirs & antiques

Beirut has an excellent selection of bookshops and the range of books on offer is equally impressive. In Tripoli the range is more limited, while elsewhere English-language books are fairly rare.

Books

Colour negative film is widely available, although colour transparency (slide) film can generally only be found in Beirut and Tripoli. The shops inside luxury hotels are good places to go as they have a fairly brisk turnover and the film is therefore usually fairly fresh. Black and white film is rarer.

Photography

Entertainment

Syria

The nightlife scene in Syria is on the whole pretty dire. For nightclubs, the luxury hotels in Damascus and Aleppo are about your best bet, although they generally lack atmosphere. The nightclubs in the centre of Damascus and Aleppo are for the most part very seedy places with close connections to the prostitution business, and best avoided. There are a few pleasant bars in Damascus, but elsewhere, apart from the bars in the luxury hotels which are very expensive and also lack atmosphere, the best you can expect is a drink with your meal at a restaurant, providing they serve alcohol.

Bars & nightclubs

The traditional Arabic cafés are where most Syrians come to relax, play cards or backgammon, smoke a nargileh, drink tea or coffee, and meet friends and socialize. This is where you will get an insight into the real Syrian 'scene'.

Cafés

There are plenty of cinemas in Damascus and Aleppo, though with the odd exception they tend to show a predictable selection of cheap kung-fu/action movies. The billboards outside give a good idea of what to expect. The cinema attached to the *Cham Palace* hotel in Damascus is one venue which does show reasonable films. Otherwise,

Cinemas

your best bet is to check out what is showing at the various cultural centres; the *Centre Culturel Français* in Damascus has the most extensive programme.

Theatres Again, there is a limited amount on offer in Syria in this respect. The various cultural centres in Damascus and Aleppo all publish programmes of events, which also include concerts, exhibitions, lectures etc.

Lebanon

Bars & Of all the Middle Eastern countries, Lebanon has far and away the best nightlife scene.
nightclubs The best nightclubs are in Beirut, many of them easily competing with anything you'll find in Europe or North America in terms of atmosphere and trendiness. There are also plenty of bars, many of which offer live music in the evenings. As with most things in Lebanon, visiting bars and nightclubs is a very expensive business. For a detailed selection of bars and nightclubs in Beirut, see page 431.

Cinemas The Lebanese are keen cinema-goers and you can generally see the latest European and American releases soon after they come out. Beirut has several large multiplexes as well as numerous smaller cinemas, and there are a couple more large multiplexes heading north along the coast between Beirut and Jounieh. See the relevant 'Essentials' sections for more details.

Theatres There are quite a few theatres in Beirut, the majority of which put out a steady diet of cabarets and musicals. There are a couple of more serious theatres with excellent reputations, although most of the plays they stage are in Arabic. See page 433 for more details.

Sport and special interest travel

These areas of the tourist industry are rather poorly represented in Syria. In Lebanon, by contrast, activities such as skiing are well developed, while the potential for other 'adventure tourism' activities is also being exploited.

Syria

Hiking There are certainly plenty of opportunities for hiking, most notably in the coastal **Jebel Ansariye** mountains and the limestone hills **around Aleppo**, though this is not really recognized as an activity in Syria. If you want to do it you will have to bring all your own equipment for camping etc, and be prepared for the fact that there are no maps of a sufficiently small scale for hiking, nor any official guides.

Camel & This has yet to be properly developed as an activity in Syria, despite the ample poten-
4-wheel tial for it. However, if you are interested in making a trip into the desert, whether by
drive safaris camel or four-wheel drive, it is worth making enquiries with one of the major local tour operators in Damascus. They may be able to arrange something.

Watersports & The two luxury hotels-cum-beach resorts at **Blue Beach** near Lattakia, the *Meridien*
beach resorts and the *Cote d'Azur de Cham*, both offer the usual range of watersports, including water-skiing, wind surfing, sailing etc.

Lebanon

Hiking, nature Lebanon's mountains offer some excellent opportunities for hiking, and are at last start-
& wildlife ing to benefit from the establishment of Nature Reserves designed to protect the

country's unique flora and fauna. There are numerous short walks and longer hikes you can make through the **Al Shouf Cedar Reserve**, in the Chouf mountains to the southeast of Beirut. All hikes in the reserve must be organized in advance. Fully trained guides are available to lead hikes. Camping is also possible in one part of the reserve. For more information, see page 572. The **Horsh Ehden Nature Reserve** (see page 521), above the town of Ehden in the Qadisha valley, is less well established, though it likewise offers the potential for some beautiful hiking, and is home to a wide variety of plants and animals. There are also some beautiful walks along the floor of the **Qadisha valley**, as well as more strenuous hikes to the 3,083 m summit of **Qornet es-Saouda**, above The Cedars (Al Arz). The owner of the *Chbat* hotel in Bcharre (see page 514) can provide detailed information on these walks and hikes, and can also arrange for guides etc. Above the ancient Afqa spring at the head of the Adonis Valley (Nahr Ibrahim), **La Reserve** is a recently established camping-cum-activity centre with a beautiful setting and stunning views (see page 504). As well as hiking, pony trekking and mountain biking, they also organize pot-holing, abseiling, archery, canoeing and rafting.

Essentials

Four-wheel drive 'Safaris'

Visitors to the Al Shouf Cedar Reserve can make a short tour of the reserve by four-wheel drive. It is also possible to reach the summit of Qornet es-Saouda by four-wheel drive. For those interested in exploring the country more systematically by four-wheel drive, there is a small independent Lebanese tour operator which specializes in such tours; *TLB*, PO Box 197, Antelias, Lebanon, T04-419848, F04-402634, contact@tlb.com.lb, www.lbctt.com.lb

Skiing

For up-to-date info on all Lebanon's ski resorts, try the following website: www.skileb.com

'Ski in the morning and sunbathe on the beach in the afternoon'. Thus goes the old cliche about Lebanon. As a day's programme it might be stretching it a bit, but Lebanon's mountains certainly offer excellent opportunities for skiing, and large-scale ongoing investments in the skiing infrastructure are making Lebanon an increasingly appealing venue. The skiing season generally runs from around mid-December to mid-April. All the resorts have ski equipment available for hire, instructors and medical/rescue facilities.

To the northeast of Beirut, on the slopes of Jebel Sannine, the largest and best-equipped resort is **Faraya Mazaar** (see page 496), next door to which is the luxury private resort of **Faqra** (see page 498). Nearby, on another face of the same mountain, but reached by a different road, is the tiny resort of **Qanat Bakich** (see page 493). To the southeast of Tripoli, on the slopes of Qornet es-Saouda, the next most popular resort after Faraya Mazaar is the **Cedars** (see page 523). Finally, to the east of Jbail (Byblos), on the slopes of Jebel Tannourine, **Laqlouq** (see page 507) has recently received considerable investment and is now a close contender with the Cedars.

Paragliding

The slopes of Mount Lebanon lend themselves ideally to the sport of paragliding, something which has not gone unnoticed in Lebanon. A small paragliding school has been established, the *Thermique* School of Paragliding, affiliated to the CERPP (Centre Ecole Regionale de Parapente des Pyrenees) in France. Run by Raja Saoude, the club offers courses lasting around seven days (depending on weather conditions) which include full training and five solo flights ($500-600 including insurance and accommodation). Alternatively, if you just want to experience the sensation, you can go on a tandem flight with a qualified instructor, for which no experience is necessary ($45). The main venues for paragliding are the Cedars, Faraya Mazaar, Harissa, Qanat Bakich and Miziara. Courses run from May to October (tandem flights only outside these months, weather permitting). During this period Raja divides his time between the Cedars (currently based in the *Alpine* hotel, T06-671057, or 03-213102, and the school's main base in Aajaltoun; *Le Magasin de Parapente*, T/F09-953756, or T03-288193, www.thermique.com.lb

Watersports & beach resorts The numerous beach resorts along Lebanon's Mediterranean coast offer the full range of watersports, including water-skiing, jet-skiing, wind surfing, sailing etc. The choice of such activities is much wider than Syria, and the equipment is usually in better condition. Unfortunately, however, the beach resorts themselves (and the coast in general) are on the whole a major disappointment. Indeed, the term 'beach resort' is something of a misnomer given that very few of them actually have sand beaches; in Beirut most of them consist simply of concrete sunbathing areas by the sea, complete with freshwater swimming pools and all the other paraphernalia of restaurants, bars etc. Anywhere you go, they are almost without exception relentlessly ugly affairs which have reduced much of Lebanon's coastline to something of an eyesore.

Diving
For details of dive centres based in Beirut, see page 435 Most of the diving in Lebanon is in the form of boat dives, with wreck diving being popular (for example at the wreck of a French submarine which sank near the airport during the Second World War), though there are also some opportunities for shore dives. Other possibilities include cave diving and altitude diving. Marine life off Lebanon's coast has suffered from the effects of pollution, as well as indiscriminate fishing during the war, but is now slowly starting to recover. Nevertheless, it is no match for that to be found in the Red Sea for example, prompting the dive companies to organize occasional trips to the Red Sea or Cyprus.

Holidays and festivals

Public holidays

Syria Note that the following are fixed public holidays; many of the major Muslim and Christian holidays are also public holidays, although their precise dates vary from year to year.

1 Jan	New Year's Day*
22 Feb	Union Day
8 Mar	Revolution Day/Women's Day*
22 Mar	Arab League Day
17 Apr	Independence Day*
1 May	Workers' Day*
6 May	Martyrs' Day*
29 May	Marine's Day
6 Oct	Veteran's Day
16 Oct	Flight Day
16 Nov	Correctionist Movement Day
14 Dec	Peasants' Day
25 Dec	Christmas Day*

Only those holidays marked * are celebrated nationally. The remainder are celebrated in a limited way, perhaps with a cultural event and certain government offices closing, or in the case of something like Marine's Day, with that section of the armed forces having a holiday.

Islamic Holidays

*The precise dates of Islamic holidays are determined by the appearance of the moon
and are not known until shortly beforehand. As a general rule, however, they occur
around 11 days earlier each year.*

	2001	*2002*	*2003*	*2004*
Eid al-Fitr (end of Ramadan)	16 Dec	5 Dec	24 Nov	13 Nov
Eid al-Adha	6 Mar	23 Feb	12 Feb	1 Feb
Ras as-Sana (New Year)	26 Mar	15 Mar	4 Mar	23 Feb
Moulid an-Nabi (Prophet's Birthday)	3 Jun	23 May	12 May	1 May
Leilat al-Meiraj	12 Oct	1 Oct	20 Sep	9 Sep
Ramadan (start of)	16 Nov	5 Nov	25 Oct	14 Oct

Note that the following are fixed public holidays; many of the major Muslim and Christian holidays are also public holidays, but their precise dates change from year to year
(see below).

Lebanon

1 January	New Year's Day
9 February	Feast of St Maroun
1 May	Labour Day
6 May	Martyrs' Day
15 August	Assumption
1 November	All Saints Day
22 November	Independence Day
25 December	Christmas Day

Islamic holidays

Islamic holidays are calculated according to the lunar calendar and therefore fall on
different dates each year (see box for projected dates from 2001-2004).

Ras as-Sana (Islamic New Year) 1st Muharram. The first 10 days of the year are
regarded as holy, especially the 10th.

Ashoura 9th and 10th Muharram. Anniversary of the killing of Hussein, commemorated by Shi'ite Muslims (Shi'ites are a small minority in Jordan and Syria, so this event
is not widely celebrated in these two countries; in Lebanon it plays a much more
important role, though mainly in the south of the country). Ashoura also celebrates
the meeting of Adam and Eve after leaving Paradise, and the end of the Flood.

Moulid an-Nabi The Prophet Mohammad's birthday. 12th Rabi al-Awwal.

Leilat al-Meiraj Ascension of Mohammad from Haram al-Sharif (Temple Mount) in
Jerusalem. 27th Rajab.

Ramadan The Islamic month of fasting. The most important event in the Islamic cal-
ender. 21st Ramadan is the *Shab-e-Qadr* or 'Night of Prayer'.

Eid al-Fitr Literally 'the small feast'. Three days of celebration, beginning 1st
Shawwal, to mark the end of Ramadan.

Essentials

Eid al-Adha Literally 'the great feast'. Begins on 10th Zilhaj and lasts for four days. Commemorates Ibrahim's (Abraham's) near sacrifice of his son Ismail (though in Christian and Judaic tradition it is Isaac who is nearly sacrificed), and coincides with the *Hajj*, or pilgrimage to Mecca. Marked by the sacrifice of a sheep, feasting and donations to the poor.

Christian holidays

In addition to the fixed-date Christian holidays listed above under Public holidays, Good Friday and Easter Sunday are both public as well as religious holidays; each are celebrated on different dates every year, in the case of both the Western (Latin) and Eastern (Orthodox) churches.

Health

On the whole, standards of hygiene are good in Syria and excellent in Lebanon, and the health risks generally much lower than in Africa or Asia for example. Vaccinations are not absolutely necessary, but all the same you are advised to make sure that you are up to date with your polio, tetanus and typhoid shots. A hepatitis jab is also worth considering. Malaria is not a problem. As a rule, the worst you can expect is an upset stomach, though more serious food poisoning or gastric infections are not unknown. Tap water is generally safe to drink but if you prefer to be ultra-safe, bottled mineral water is widely available. Raw fruit and vegetables are a potential hazard unless you have washed or peeled them yourself. On the other hand, salads are an integral part of Middle Eastern cuisine and avoiding eating them in some form or other is not entirely practical. Perhaps the greatest health hazard is from heatstroke and/or dehydration. Proper protection against the sun and an adequate intake of water and salt are essential.

The standards of private medical facilities are high in both Syria and Lebanon. There are plenty of international standard hospitals in Damascus and Beirut and good medical facilities in most other major cities. Note that good medical insurance is absolutely vital as private healthcare is extremely expensive, particularly in Lebanon.

Before travelling

Take out good medical insurance. Check exactly what the level of cover is for specific eventualities, in particular whether a flight home is covered in case of an emergency, whether the insurance company will pay any medical expenses directly or whether you must pay and then claim it back, and whether specific activities such as diving are covered. You should have a dental check up. If you suffer from a chronic illness (such as diabetes, high blood pressure, ear or sinus troubles, cardio-pulmonary disease or nervous disorder) arrange for a check up with your doctor, who can at the same time provide you with a letter explaining the details of your disability. If you are on regular medication, make sure you have enough to cover the period of your travel.

Children

More preparation is necessary for babies and children than for an adult and perhaps a more care should be taken. Children can become more rapidly ill than adults (on the other hand they often recover more quickly). Diarrhoea and vomiting are the most common problems, so take the usual precautions. Breastfeeding is best and most convenient for babies, but powdered milk and baby foods are widely available. The treatment of diarrhoea is the same for adults, except that it should start earlier and be continued with more persistence. Children get dehydrated very quickly in hot countries and can become drowsy and uncooperative unless cajoled to drink water or juice plus salts. Upper respiratory infections, such as colds, catarrh and middle ear infections are also common and if your child suffers from these normally take some antibiotics against the possibility. Outer ear infections after swimming are also common and antibiotic eardrops will help.

Vaccination

Vaccination for **smallpox** is no longer required anywhere in the world. Neither is **cholera** vaccination recognized as necessary for international travel by the *World Health Organisation* – it is not very effective either. You may be asked for a **Yellow Fever** certificate if you have been travelling in a country affected by the disease immediately before travelling to Syria or Lebanon. The vaccination is practically without side effects and almost totally protective.

Vaccination against the following diseases are recommended:

Typhoid This is a disease spread by the insanitary preparation of food. A number of new vaccines against this condition are now available; the older TAB and monovalent typhoid vaccines are being phased out. The newer, eg Typhim Vi, cause fewer side effects, but are more expensive. For those who do not like injections, there are now oral vaccines.

Poliomyelitis Despite its decline in the world this remains a serious disease if caught and is easy to protect against. There are live oral vaccines and in some countries injected vaccines. Whichever one you choose, it is a good idea to have booster every 3-5 years if visiting developing countries regularly.

Tetanus One dose of the vaccine should be given with a booster at six weeks and another at six months and 10-yearly boosters thereafter are recommended. Children should already be properly protected against diphtheria, poliomyelitis and pertussis (whooping cough). Measles, mumps and rubella vaccine is also given to children throughout the world, but those teenage girls who have not had rubella (German measles) should be tested and vaccinated. Hepatitis B vaccination for babies is now routine in some countries.

Infectious Hepatitis This disease is less of a problem for travellers than it used to be because of the development of two extremely effective vaccines against the A and B form of the disease. It remains common however and protection is strongly recommended. A combined hepatitis A & B vaccine is now licensed and available; one jab covers both diseases. Use condoms against Hepatitis B.

Other vaccinations These might be considered in the case of epidemics: eg meningitis. There is an effective vaccination against rabies which should be considered by all travellers, especially those going through remote areas or if there is a particular occupational risk, eg for zoologists or veterinarians.

Staying healthy

Travellers' diarrhoea and vomiting is due, most of the time, to food poisoning, usually passed on by the unsanitary habits of food handlers. As a general rule the cleaner your surroundings and the smarter the restaurant, the less likely you are to suffer. **Intestinal upsets**

   Foods to avoid: uncooked, undercooked, partially cooked or reheated meat, fish, eggs, raw vegetables and salads, especially when they have been left out exposed to flies. Stick to fresh food that has been cooked from raw just before eating and make sure you peel fruit yourself. Wash and dry your hands before eating; disposable wet-wipe tissues are useful for this.

Tap water is generally safe to drink in larger towns and cities. If you want to be on the safe side however, bottled mineral water is readily available throughout Syria and Lebanon. Ice generally gets delivered in a pretty unhygenic fashion, so is best avoided.

Travellers' diarrhoea
Infection with various organisms can give rise to travellers' diarrhoea. They may be viruses, bacteria, eg Escherichia coli (probably the most common cause worldwide), protozoa (such as amoebas and giardia), salmonella and cholera. The diarrhoea may come on suddenly or rather slowly. It may or may not be accompanied by vomiting or by severe abdominal pain and the passage of blood or mucus – when it is called dysentery.

Types of diarrhoea & how to treat it
If you can time the onset of the diarrhoea to the minute ('acute') then it is probably due to a virus or a bacterium and/or the onset of dysentery. The treatment in addition to rehydration is Ciprofloxacin 500 mg every 12 hours; the drug is now widely available and there are many similar ones.

If the diarrhoea comes on slowly or intermittently ('sub-acute') then it is more likely to be protozoal, ie caused by an amoeba or giardia. Antibiotics such a Ciprofloxacin will have little effect. These cases are best treated by a doctor as is any outbreak of diarrhoea continuing for more than three days. Sometimes blood is passed in ameobic dysentery and for this you should certainly seek medical help. If this is not available then the best treatment is probably Tinidazole (Fasigyn) 1 tablet 4 times a day for 3 days. If there are severe stomach cramps, the following drugs may help but are not very useful in the management of acute diarrhoea: Loperamide (Imodium) and Diphenoxylate with Atropine (Lomotil) They should not be given to children.

Any kind of diarrhoea, whether or not accompanied by vomiting, responds well to the replacement of water and salts, taken as frequent sips, of some kind of rehydration solution. There are proprietary preparations consisting of sachets of powder which you dissolve in boiled water or you can make your own by adding half a teaspoonful of salt (3.5 gms) and 4 tablespoonsful of sugar (40 gms) to a litre of boiled water.

Thus the linch pins of treatment for diarrhoea are rest, fluid and salt replacement, antibiotics such as Ciprofloxacin for the bacterial types and special diagnostic tests and medical treatment for the amoeba and giardia infections. Salmonella infections and cholera, although rare, can be devastating diseases and it would be wise to get to a hospital as soon as possible if these were suspected.

Fasting, peculiar diets and the consumption of large quantities of yoghurt have not been found useful in calming travellers' diarrhoea or in rehabilitating inflamed bowels. Oral rehydration has on the other hand, especially in children, been a life saving technique and should always be practised, whatever other treatment you use. As there is some evidence that alcohol and milk might prolong diarrhoea they should be avoided during and immediately after an attack.

Diarrhoea occurring day after day for long periods of time (chronic diarrhoea) is notoriously resistent to amateur attempts at treatment and again warrants proper diagnostic tests (most towns with reasonable sized hospitals have laboratories for stool samples). There are ways of preventing travellers' diarrhoea for short periods of time by taking antibiotics, but this is not a foolproof technique and should not be used other than in exceptional circumstances. Doxycycline is possibly the best drug. Some preventatives such as Enterovioform can have serious side effects if taken for long periods.

Paradoxically **constipation** is also common, probably induced by dietary change, inadequate fluid intake in hot places and long bus journeys. Simple laxatives are useful in the short term and bulky foods and plenty of fruit are also useful.

Heat & cold
Full acclimatization to high temperatures takes about two weeks. During this period it is normal to feel a bit apathetic, especially if the relative humidity is high. Drink plenty of water, use salt on your food and avoid extreme exertion. Tepid showers are more

cooling than hot or cold ones. Large hats do not cool you down, but do prevent sunburn. Remember that, especially in the desert and mountains, there can be a large and sudden drop in temperature between night and day, so dress accordingly. Loose cotton is still the best material when the weather is hot.

Insects These are mostly more of a nuisance than a serious hazard. Mosquitos are the most troublesome. Malaria however is very rare in the region, although there have been cases reported in Syria. It is sensible to avoid being bitten as much as possible; cover bare skin and use an insect repellent. The most common and effective repellent is diethyl metatoluamide (DEET). DEET liquid is best for arms and face (care around eyes and with spectacles; DEET dissolves plastic). Aerosol spray is good for clothes and ankles and liquid DEET can be dissolved in water and used to impregnate cotton clothes and mosquito nets. Impregnated wrist and ankle bands can also be useful.

If you are bitten or stung, itching may be relieved by cool baths, antihistamine tablets (care with alcohol or driving) or mild corticosteroid creams, eg. hydrocortisone (great care: never use if any hint of infection). Careful scratching of all your bites once a day can be surprisingly effective. Calamine lotion and cream have limited effectiveness and antihistamine creams are not recommended – they can cause allergies themselves. Bites which become infected should be treated with a local antiseptic or antibiotic cream such as Cetrimide, as should any infected sores or scratches. When living rough, skin infestations with body lice (crabs) and scabies are easy to pick up. Use whatever local commercial preparation is recommended for lice and scabies. Crotamiton cream (Eurax) alleviates itching and also kills a number of skin parasites. Malathion lotion 5% (Prioderm) kills lice effectively, but avoid the use of the toxic agricultural preparation of Malathion.

Sunburn Most people fail to appreciate the burning power of the sun until it is too late. Always wear a wide brimmed hat and use some form of suncream lotion on untanned skin. Normal temperate zone suntan lotions (protection factor up to 7) are not much good; you need to use the types designed specifically for the tropics or for mountaineers or skiers with protection factors up to 15 or above. These are often not available in Syria. Glare from the sun can cause conjunctivitis, so wear sunglasses especially on beaches, where high protection factor sunscreen should also be used.

Other risks and more serious diseases

Rabies If you are bitten by a domestic or wild animal, do not leave things to chance: scrub the wound with soap and water and/or disinfectant, try to have the animal captured (within limits) or at least determine its ownership, where possible, and seek medical assistance at once. The course of treatment depends on whether you have already been satisfactorily vaccinated against rabies. If you have (this is worthwhile if you are spending lengths of time in developing countries or travelling far from the five-star circuit) then some further doses of vaccine are all that is required. Human diploid vaccine is the best, but expensive: other, older kinds of vaccine, such as that derived from duck embryos may be the only types available. These are effective, much cheaper and interchangeable generally with the human derived types. If not already vaccinated then anti rabies serum (immunoglobulin) may be required in addition. It is important to finish the course of treatment whether the animal survives or not.

AIDS AIDS is not a major problem in Syria and Lebanon, but care is obviously necessary. Heterosexual transmission is now the dominant mode and so the main risk to travellers is from casual sex. The same precautions should be taken as with any sexually transmitted disease. The AIDS virus (HIV) can be passed by unsterilized needles which have been previously used to inject an HIV positive patient. Check that needles have been properly sterilized or disposable needles have been used. The risk of receiving a blood transfusion with blood infected with the HIV virus is greater than from dirty needles because of the amount of fluid exchanged. Supplies of blood for transfusion should be screened for HIV in all reputable hospitals. Catching the AIDS virus does not always produce an illness in itself (although it may do). The only way to be sure if you feel you have been put at risk is to have a blood test for HIV antibodies on your return to a place where there are reliable laboratory facilities. The test does not become positive for some weeks.

Infectious hepatitis (Jaundice) The main symptoms are pains in the stomach, lack of appetite, lassitude and yellowness of the eyes and skin. Medically speaking there are two main types. The less serious, but more common is Hepatitis A for which the best protection is the careful preparation of food, the avoidance of contaminated drinking water and scrupulous attention to toilet hygiene. The other, more serious, version is Hepatitis B which is acquired usually as a sexually transmitted disease or by blood transfusions. It can less commonly be transmitted by injections with unclean needles and possibly by insect bites. The symptoms are the same as for Hepatitis A. The incubation period is much longer (up to six months compared with six weeks) and there are more likely to be complications.

Hepatitis A can be protected against with gamma globulin. It should be obtained from a reputable source and is certainly useful for travellers who intend to live rough. You should have a shot before leaving and have it repeated every six months. The dose of gamma globulin depends on the concentration of the particular preparation used, so the manufacturer's advice should be taken. The injection should be given as close as possible to your departure and as the dose depends on the likely time you are to spend in potentially affected areas, the manufacturer's instructions should be followed. Gamma globulin has really been superceded now by a proper vaccination against Hepatitis A (Havrix) which gives immunity lasting up to 10 years. After that boosters are required. Havrix monodose is now widely available as is Junior Havrix. The vaccination has negligible side effects and is extremely effective. Gamma globulin injections can be a bit painful, but it is much cheaper than Havrix and may be more available in some places.

Hepatitis B can be effectively prevented by a specific vaccine (Engerix) – three shots over six months before travelling. If you have had jaundice in the past it would be worthwhile having a blood test to see if you are immune to either of these two types, because this might avoid the necessity and costs of vaccination or gamma globulin. There are other kinds of viral hepatitis (C, E etc) which are fairly similar to A and B, but vaccines are not available as yet.

Typhus Typhus is carried by ticks. There is usually a reaction at the site of the bite and a fever. Seek medical advice.

Intestinal worms These are not very common in Syria and Lebanon. The more serious ones such as hookworm can be contracted from walking barefoot on infested earth or beaches.

Snake bite This is a very rare event indeed for travellers. If you are unlucky (or careless) enough to be bitten by a venomous snake, spider, scorpion or sea creature, try to identify the creature, but do not put yourself in further danger. Snake bites in particular are very frightening, but in fact rarely poisonous – even venomous snakes bite without injecting venom. What you might expect if bitten are: fright, swelling, pain and bruising around the bite and soreness of the regional lymph glands, perhaps nausea, vomiting and a fever. Signs of serious poisoning would be the following symptoms: numbness and tingling of the face, muscular spasms, convulsions, shortness of breath and bleeding. Victims should be got to a hospital or a doctor without delay. Commercial snake bite and scorpion kits are available, but usually only useful for the specific type of snake or scorpion for which they are designed. Most serum has to be given intravenously so it is not much good equipping yourself with it unless you are used to making injections into veins. It is best to rely on local practice in these cases, because the particular creatures will be known about locally and appropriate treatment can be given.

Reassure and comfort the victim frequently. Immobilize the limb by a bandage or a splint or by getting the person to lie still. Do not slash the bite area and try to suck out the poison because this sort of heroism does more harm than good. If you know how to use a tourniquet in these circumstances, you will not need this advice. If you are not experienced do not apply a tourniquet.

When you return home

If you have had attacks of diarrhoea it is worth having a stool specimen tested in case you have picked up amoebas. If you have been living rough, blood tests may be worthwhile to detect worms and other parasites. Report any untoward symptoms to your doctor and tell the doctor exactly where you have been and, if you know, what the likelihood of disease is to which you were exposed.

Further information

Further information on health risks abroad, vaccinations etc may be available from a local travel clinic. If you wish to take specific drugs with you such as antibiotics these are best prescribed by your own doctor. Beware, however, that not all doctors can be experts on the health problems of remote countries. More detailed or more up-to-date information than local doctors can provide are available from various sources. In the UK there are hospital departments specializing in tropical diseases in London, Liverpool, Birmingham and Glasgow and the Malaria Reference Laboratory at the London School of Hygiene and Tropical Medicine provides free advice about malaria, T0891-600350. In the USA the local Public Health Services can give such information and information is available centrally from the Centre for Disease Control (CDC) in Atlanta, T404-3324559.

There are other computerized databases which can be accessed for up-to-the-minute, destination-specific information. In the UK there is MASTA (Medical Advisory Service to Travellers Abroad), T0906-8224100 (calls charged at 60p per minute), or visit their website (www.masta.org), and Travax (Glasgow, T0141-9467120, ext 247). Other information on medical problems overseas can be obtained from the book by Richard Dawood (Editor) (1992) *Travellers' Health: How to Stay Healthy Abroad*, Oxford University Press 1992, £7.99. We strongly recommend this revised and updated edition, especially to the intrepid traveller heading for the more out of the way places. General advice is also available in the UK in *Health Information for Overseas Travel* published by the Department of Health and available from HMSO, and *International Travel and Health* published by WHO, Geneva.

Further reading

There is a wealth of books on all aspects of the Middle East, in fact probably enough to fill a few libraries and keep you going for a lifetime. The following is a small selection. Many contain more detailed bibliographies for those who wish to explore further.

History & politics

Aburish, Saïd K *A Brutal Friendship* (Victor Gollancz, 1997). A very readable and often highly controversial book which identifies the collusion between the Arab elite and the West as being at the heart of the Middle East's current problems. **Fisk, Robert** *Pity the Nation; Lebanon at War* (OUP, 1992). A moving account based on Fisk's thorough reporting of Lebanon's civil war, internationally acclaimed (and much disliked by the Israeli establishment), compelling reading. Highly recommended. **Freidman, Thomas** *From Beirut to Jerusalem* (Harper Collins, 1993). Though criticized by Edward Said as a classic example of 'Orientalism', this account of the Lebanese civil war is interesting for insights into both the Lebanese and Israeli experience. **Hourani, Albert** *A History of the Arab Peoples* (Faber and Faber, 1991). A comprehensive and highly regarded work which focuses as much on the social as the political history of the Arabs. **Hourani, A , Khoury, P, Wilson, M** (editors) *The Modern Middle East*. An authoritative survey of the Middle East. **Joffe, Lawrence** *Keesing's Guide to the Middle East Peace Process* (Cartermill, 1996). An excellent reference book on the Peace Process, including analysis of its relevance for Syria and Lebanon, and brief overviews of all the countries concerned. **Maalouf, Amin** *The Crusades Through Arab Eyes* (Al Saqi, 1984). An excellent, highly readable account of the Crusades, original and refreshing in its Arab perspective on this period of history. Highly recommended. **Mansfield, Peter** *The Arabs* (Penguin, 1992). A good, readable overview of the history of the region. Recommended. **Runciman, Steven** *A History of the Crusades* (1978). A detailed, traditional account in three volumes. **Salibi, Kamal** *A House of Many Mansions; the History of Lebanon Reconsidered* (IB Tauris, 1988). An excellent book in which Salibi examines what he describes as "the war over Lebanese history". **Seale, Patrick** *The Struggle for Syria* and *Asad: the struggle for the Middle East* (OUP and IB Tauris, 1965 and 1988). Scholarly but well written and compelling accounts. Recommended. The latter has recently been reprinted and is widely available in Lebanon. **Wilson** *Lawrence of Arabia, the Authorised Biography* (1989). Includes a discussion of Lawrence's disputed significance. Try also **Mack, JE** *The Secret Lives of Lawrence of Arabia* (1976).

Religion   **Brenton Betts, Robert** *The Druze*. Gives some fascinating insights into this secretive sect. **Dawood, NJ** (translator) *The Koran* (Penguin, 1993). A well regarded translation of the Qur'an. **Esposito, John L** *Islam; The Straight Path* (OUP). Excellent analysis of the origins and significance of Islam. **Halliday, Fred** *Islam and the Myth of Confrontation* (IB Tauris). Challenges the idea that a show-down between Islam and the rest of the world is imminent. **Lewis, Bernard** *The Assassins* (Al Saqi, 1985). A detailed and scholarly work, though still readable, examining the origins and history of the Assassins. **Netton, Ian R** *A Popular Dictionary of Islam* (Curzon Press, 1992). Useful reference book for those interested in learning more about Islam. **Said, Edward** *Covering Islam* (Vintage, 1997). Examines the basis of western stereotypes of Islam.

Travelogues   **Bell, Gertrude** *The Desert and the Sown* (various imprints). Gertrude Bell's classic account of her journey through the Middle East at the turn of the century. **Dalrymple, William** *From the Holy Mountain* (Flamingo, 1998). Highly readable account of a journey through the Christian world of the Middle East, starting at Mount Athos in Greece and travelling through Turkey, Syria, Lebanon, Israel and Egypt. His central thesis, that he is witnessing "the last ebbing twilight of Byzantium", is perhaps unnecessarily pessimistic. **Keenan, Brian** *An Evil Cradling* (Vintage, 1993). Won acclaim as one of the best accounts by the various Westerners held hostage in Lebanon in the 1980s. **Lawrence, TE** *Seven Pillars of Wisdom* (various editions). Lawrence's own account of the Arab Revolt and his part in it. Despite his somewhat impenetrable style, the book is a compelling one. **Makdisi, Said** *Beirut Fragments: A War Memoir* (Persea Books, 1990). A highly readable personal account of life in war-torn Beirut. **Thubron, Colin** *The Hills of Adonis, A Journey in Lebanon* (1987; first published in 1967) Penguin. Blends a travelogue of Thubron's walking trip through Lebanon with an engaging exploration of the country's ancient religions and mythologies.

Al Shaykh, Hanan *Beirut Blues* (Vintage, 1996). Other novels by the same author **Fiction** include *The Story of Zahra* and *Women of Sand and Myrrh* (Qartet Books). **Darwish, Mahmoud** *Memory of Forgetfulness; August, Beirut, 1982* (University of California Press). An account of the Israeli invasion of 1982, compellingly told through a series of prose poems by the acclaimed Arab poet Mahmoud Darwish. **Inea, Bushnaq** (editor) *Arab Folktales* (Pantheon). Includes a selection of Bedouin folktales under the heading 'Tales Told in Houses made of Hair'. **Maalouf, Amin** *The Rock of Tanios* (Abacus, 1995) . Winner of the 1993 Prix Goncourt, this wonderful piece of historical fiction brings alive the world feudal Mount Lebanon in the 19th century. **Nur and Abdelwahab Elmessiri** (editors) *A Land of Stone and Thyme* (Quartet). Excellent anthology of Palestinian short stories. **Salma Khadra Jayyusi** (editor) *Anthology of Modern Palestinian Literature* and *Modern Arabic Poetry; An Anthology* (Columbia UP).

Two map publishers stand out for their coverage of Syria and Lebanon: *GEO Projects* **Maps** and *Freytag & Berndt*. In the UK the best place for maps is Stanfords, 12-14 Long Acre, London WC2E 9LP, T020-78362121. The address for GEO Projects in the UK is 9-10 Southern Court, South St, Reading, Berkshire RG1 4QS, T01734-393567, F01734-598283. Probably the best map covering the whole region (including Jordan and Israel as well as Syria and Lebanon) is the *Hildebrand's* Travel Map of Jordan, Syria and Lebanon (1:1,250,000), 1996.

Websites

www.oranim.macam98.ac.il/geo/meast.htm ORANIM school of education (Dr A **General** Medzinin); geography of the Middle East. Vast number of excellent links.
www.columbia.edu/cu/libraries/indiv/area/MiddleEast/index.html Columbia University; Middle East Studies page. Excellent site, includes listings of internet resources on the Middle East by subject.
www.menewsline.com Middle East Newsline; a new regional internet service, now updated daily with the latest Middle East news, a diary of events, and special reports.
www.hrw.org/ Human Rights Watch; with an extensive Middle East section.
www.fco.gov.uk Homepage of the British Foreign and Commonwealth Office; gives current safety recommendations regarding travel in Syria and Lebanon.

www.syriatourism.org The official website of the Syrian Ministry of Tourism. **Syria**
www.arabia.com/syria Arabia On line; includes news, business, culture, etc.
www.syria-net.com Syria Net; useful general information on Syria.
www.arab.net./syria/syria_contents.html Arab Net; provides a basic outline of the country (history, geography, business, culture, government etc), plus links to a useful list of Syria-orientated sites.
www.odci.gov/cia/publications/factbook/geos/sy.html CIA Factbook; outline of Syria's geography, people, government, economy etc.
www.moi-syria.com/index.html Official website of the Ministry of Information.

http://almashriq.hiof.no/ Al Mashriq; a wide-ranging site focusing principally on **Lebanon** Lebanon, but with useful links to sites related to all the other countries in the region.
www.aub.edu.lb The official website of the American University of Beirut.
www.lebhost.com.lb Lebhost, a search engine dedicated exlusively to websites containing information on Lebanon.
www.odci.gov/cia/publications/factbook/geos/le.html CIA Factbook; outline of Lebanon's geography, people, government, economy etc.
www.lebanon-tourism.gov.lb The official website of the Ministry of Tourism.
www.arab.net./lebanon/lebanon_contents.html Arab Net; provides a basic

outline of the country (history, geography, business, culture, government etc), plus links to a useful list of Lebanon-orientated sites.

www.lebanonembassy.org Official website of the Lebanese embassy.

www.arabia.com/lebanon Arabia On line; includes news, business, culture, etc.

www.yalla.com.lb Extensive coverage of Lebanese current affairs, plus lots more.

www.cyberia.net.lb Extensive coverage of Lebanese current affairs, under 'News headlines', 'Art and entertainment' and 'Sports headlines', plus lots more.

www.solidere.com.lb Official website for the Solidere construction company.

www.baalbeck.org.lb Official website for the annual Baalbek Festival.

www.tradingplaces.com.lb Gives details of the programme for the Baalbek Festival, as well as ticket prices and how to book (much more useful than the official website).

www.beiteddine.org.lb Includes full details of the annual Beit ed-Dine Festival.

www.skileb.com Detailed information on skiing in Lebanon.

www.dailystar.com.lb Website of the *Daily Star*, Lebanon's English language daily.

Damascus دمشق and around

3

Damascus دمشق and around

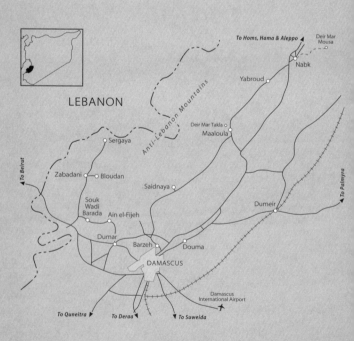

Although today a sprawling metropolis with all the trappings of a modern capital riven with traffic, pollution and high-rise development, Damascus is a place of great antiquity and beauty. The **Old City** with its mosques, souks, khans and narrow winding streets has an atmosphere of accumulated history, all still buzzing with life, much as it has done for centuries. Whether you are attracted by the beautiful and **delicate architecture**, or by the bewildering array of goods on sale in the **souks**, or whether you simply want an opportunity to watch the comings and goings of this fascinating quarter, you will come away enchanted.

In Straight Street, Ananias Chapel and St Paul's Chapel are names and places related directly to events described in the **New Testament**. For Muslims, meanwhile, this is one of the great holy cities of Islam, its importance embodied in the spectacular **Umayyad Mosque**, its huge dome and three minarets rising majestically above its surroundings. But if this is not impressive enough for you, the history of Damascus stretches far back beyond Islamic and biblical times. Alongside Aleppo (and dozens of other cities in the Levant region), it lays claim to that much disputed and problematic title of oldest continuously inhabited city in the world.

Once the heat of the city gets too much, why not try (along with half the population of Damascus if you do it at the weekend) the diesel-fired steam train which runs along the narrow-gauge line up to lively hill resorts of **Zabadani** and **Bloudan**; or ancient, originally sixth century BC, **Saidnaya**.

Ins and outs

See page 125 for detailed information on all international & long-distance transport to and from Damascus, and also local transport within the city, including to and from the airport

Getting there

Air Damascus International Airport is some 30 km to the southeast of the city centre and handles the vast majority of international flights arriving in Syria. There are also internal connections with **Aleppo**, **Lattakia** and **Qamishle**; flights to **Deir ez-Zor** had been suspended at the time of writing.

Rail Damascus has 2 railway stations. The attractive **Hejaz** station is right in the centre of the city, although you will only find yourself arriving here if you have come on the twice-weekly service from Amman (Jordan). This station also serves the hill stations to the northwest of the capital. **Kadam** station is around 4 km to the south of the centre and is the terminus for the daily service to Aleppo, the weekly service to Tartus and Lattakia, and the weekly service to Istanbul (Turkey).

Road Luxury coaches, buses, minibuses, microbuses and service taxis link Damascus with all main towns and cities in Syria, as well as several in Jordan, Lebanon and Turkey. The **Pullman/Harasta** bus station, inconveniently located 5 km to the northeast of the city centre, handles all the luxury coaches linking Damascus with the towns and cities to the north and northeast, as well Turkey. The centrally located **Baramkeh** bus station handles services linking Damascus with destinations in Jordan and Lebanon, as well as towns to the south of Damascus and local destinations around the capital. The remaining bus stations are only really relevant if you want to save a few Syrian pounds by going on a 'hob-hob' bus, the only exception to this being the **Maaloula microbus station**, the only place to catch microbuses to Saidnaya and Maaloula.

Damascus overview

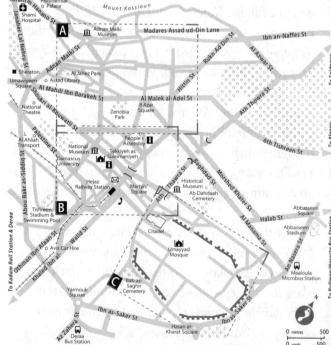

Related maps
A Salihiye, page 110
B Damascus centre, page 104
C Damascus old city, page 84

24 hours in the city

If that's all the time you've got, it's still possible to see a fair bit of Damascus, although such a brief taster is sure to leave you wanting more.

Once you have settled in, the first place to head for, without a doubt, is the **Old City**. You will probably want to spend most of the day here and possibly a good couple of hours in the Umayyad Mosque alone, people-watching and perhaps reading up on some of its history. Other places well worth dropping in on are the lavishly decorated **Azem Palace** (home to the Museum of Popular Traditions); the imposing **Khan Assad Pasha** and the **Maristan Nur ud-Din**. A visit to the **Hammam Nur ud-Din** also offers you the wonderful opportunity of worthily taking in yet more history whilst at the same time relaxing after a hard day's sightseeing and indulging in the more hedonistic delights of a Turkish bath.

If ablutions sound a bit low-key for you then you should use your precious time to explore the lively souks and narrow streets that offer endless opportunities for aimless exploration and unexpected discovery. (The **Hamidiyeh Souk** leading up to the Umayyad Mosque is a great introduction, while the souks to the south of the Umayyad Mosque and all along **Straight Street** are perhaps even more interesting. For **souvenir hunting**, this is a veritable treasure trove; numerous shops around here specialize in handicrafts, antiques or souvenirs.)

If you can drag yourself away from the Old City, you could head up to the summit of **Mount Kassioun** for sunset. There are great views out over Damascus from here. And dark comes quickly in this part of the world: before long the enchanting (some might say haunting) wails of numerous muezzins making the call to prayer will be replaced by a magical scene of twinkling lights against the night sky.

In terms of **nightlife**, Damascus isn't exactly Ibiza but there are plenty of cafés and restaurants to while away a pleasant evening in. Try either the **Naufarah** or **Al Shams** cafés situated opposite each other outside the east entrance to the Umayyad Mosque. Both are always busy with people exchanging news and gossip, smoking nargilehs, drinking tea and playing games of cards or backgammon.

There are some excellent **restaurants** to choose from in the Old City. Set in beautifully restored traditional Damascene houses and palaces, with their secluded, shady courtyards, they provide a welcome retreat from the bustle outside. The majority of these are open for both lunch and dinner. Try the **Jabri House** restaurant for some real atmosphere, or the **Elissar** for its sheer elegance.

The Christian quarter of the Old City also has a couple of trendy bars, the best of these being the recently opened **Café Mama**. Outside the Old City, the **Al Chamiat** is a popular and typically Syrian restaurant serving excellent Arabic food, while the **Damascus Workers' Club**, despite its traditional setting, serves both food and alcohol.

Damascus & around

Getting around

Damascus is a relatively compact city, and for the most part **walking** is the best way to get around (in the Old City it is really the only way). **Taxis** are plentiful and cheap (S£20-30 for shorter trips; S£30-50 for longer ones) and therefore a convenient way to get between districts, or to/from the more far-flung bus stations. These days, most have working meters; but if not, agree on a fare before setting off. The **microbuses** ('meecro' or 'servees') which zip all over the city are difficult to get to grips with unless you can read Arabic, though certain routes can be useful (see page 126). The **airport bus** which runs regularly between the airport and city centre provides a very cheap alternative to the taxis, which in this instance are relatively expensive.

Orientation

Although modern-day Damascus spreads over a large area, its core is surprisingly compact. The **Old City** comprises a distinct area, enclosed within city walls which for

☞ *Outside the Old City*

Although the Old City of Damascus is always going to be top of most people's sightseeing lists, there are several places outside its walls worth spending time on if you plan to spend more than a day here.

*In the modern part of the city, the **Tekkiyeh as-Suleimaniyeh complex** is not to be missed. As well as the beautiful 16th century Ottoman mosque, there is an excellent handicrafts/antiques/souvenirs market, part of which is housed in the courtyard of an attractive former madrassa (religious school). Next door to this complex is the **National Museum of Damascus**, which houses fine archaeological treasures from all over Syria and brings together more than 11 millenia of history. (Although the presentation isn't great, many of the exhibits are breathtakingly beautiful.)*

*Away from the main tourist trail, the **Sarouja/Bahsa** district is a small area outside the Old City walls which has survived the encroachment of the modern development which surrounds it. Its narrow alleys, lined by rickety old wooden houses draw you back through centuries' worth of living.*

the most part still survive. Immediately to the northwest of this is the **main centre** of the modern city. Here, Martyrs' Square (in Arabic 'al-Marjeh', but also known as Al Shouhada Square) is the focus for many of the cheap hotels and restaurants (unfortunately, this is also Damascus' 'red light' district).

Running **west from the citadel**, which is situated at the nothwest corner of the Old City, An Naser Street takes you past the Hejaz railway station, terminus for the famous Hejaz railway line, from where a major north-south axis runs along **Said al-Jabri**, **Port Said** and **29 May** streets, passing through the main commercial and business centre of the city. Intersecting this north-south axis is another major east-west axis, **Shoukri al-Kouwatli Street**. Heading west, this takes you past the Tekkiyeh as-Suleimaniyeh complex, the National Museum and International Fair grounds, separated from the main road by a branch of the Barada River, before reaching Umawiyeen 'Square' (in fact a huge roundabout).

Just west of the National Museum the large Assad Bridge crosses Shoukri al-Kouwatli Street. If you follow it south you come to the **Baramkeh district**, with Damascus University off to the right along Palestine Street, and the Baramkeh bus station to your left. Following it north and then northwest leads you up into the modern, fashionable **Abu Roumaneh district** where many of the foreign embassies are located. Further north still, the long ridge of Kassioun mountain dominates the skyline, with the ancient districts of **Salihiye/Al Charkasiye**, once separated from the old city by countryside, strung out along its lower slopes.

Extending southwest from Umawiyeen Square, meanwhile, is the modern district of **Al Mezzeh**, strung out along the busy thoroughfare of Fayez Mansour Street. This newly affluent area of Damascus also houses a number of foreign embassies.

Tourist information
Phone code: 011

There are 2 tourist offices in central Damascus. The main office is on 29 May St, on the left as you head north from Yousef al-Azmeh Square (also a roundabout), T2323953. Open daily, 0930-1400, 1600-2400 (approx). The second office is attached to the Ministry of Tourism building, just off Shoukri al-Kouwatli St, by the east entrance to the Handicrafts Market/Tekkiyeh as-Suleimaniyeh complex, internal phone only. Open 0900-2400 (approx). There is also a tourist information counter in the arrivals lounge of Damascus International Airport, T2248437. Open 24 hrs (in theory at least, though often unattended). The staff on duty at these offices can supply you with copies of the various maps/pamphlets published by the Ministry of Tourism, but otherwise they are of little help. They are even unable to agree on the opening times of their offices.

History

The setting of Damascus is the key to its historical importance, and that a permanent settlement should develop here is no surprise. The Barada River, flowing down from the Anti-Lebanon mountains to the northeast, waters the *Ghouta* plain below and has created a large, fertile oasis on the edge of an otherwise harsh and inhospitable desert stretching south and east. Over the centuries, Damascus has continually found itself at an important strategic and commercial crossroads.

See also History, page 607

It is precisely because Damascus has been inhabited continuously throughout its long history that there is very little physical evidence of the earliest stages of its settlement. Each successive civilization has built over the foundations of the one which preceeded it. Excavations in the Old City and at Tel as-Salihiye to the east have nevertheless revealed evidence of settlement during the fourth and third millenniums BC respectively. Our knowledge of the early history of the city, however, comes primarily from fragmentary literary sources.

Amongst the large numbers of tablets discovered at Mari (see page 388), some, which date back to 2500 BC, make reference to Damascus (then known as *Dimashqa*), while slightly later tablets from Ebla (see page 240) make reference to *Dimaski*, although its exact relationship with these important city-states is far from clear.

From around 2000 BC Damascus was settled by the **Amorites**, one of the many waves of Semitic peoples to migrate from the desert interior of the Arabian peninsular and settle in the fertile lands further north. Some 500 years later, the city came under **Egyptian** influence during the rule of Thutmosis III, as recorded in the Amarna tablets. In turn it then came under the control of the other great regional power of the time, the **Hittites**.

Some time after 1200 BC the **Aramaeans** established themselves in the city, and from the 10th to eighth centuries BC *Aram Damascus* was the seat of an important Aramaean kingdom. It was during this period that the Temple of Haddad was built on the site of what is now the Umayyad Mosque. The Aramaeans clashed repeatedly with the biblical kingdoms of Israel and Judah, limiting their northward expansion, as chronicled at length in the Old Testament. At the same time, the Aramaeans came under repeated attack from the growing **Assyrian** Empire in northern Mesopotamia, and finally in 732 BC the city was devastated by the Assyrian king, Tiglath Pileser III. The **Babylonians** followed in 572 BC, led by King Nebuchadnezzar, and the **Achaemenid Persians** in 539 BC, under King Cyrus.

Following the defeat of the Persians by the **Greeks** at the battle of Issus, one of Alexander the Great's generals, Parmenion, captured Damascus in 332 BC and it was under subsequent Greek rule that a planned grid pattern of development was first applied to the city.

With the death of Alexander the Great in 323 BC, Damascus then found itself caught for two centuries between the competing ambitions of the **Seleucid** and **Ptolemid** Empires. However, decline in the influence of both left the door open to the **Nabateans**, who under Aretas III (84-56 BC) extended their empire to include Damascus.

The first **Roman** conquest of Syria came as early as 64 BC, but Damascus at that point remained of peripheral importance, with Nabatean control over what was effectively a semi-independent city-state continuing until as late as 54 AD. Thus events such as the conversion of St Paul in the early years of Christianity took place before direct Roman control had been established. However, in the first century AD the Romans took direct control of Damascus and

Damascus & around

from that point onwards it grew in importance. In 117 AD the Emperor Hadrian declared it a metropolis, and in 222 AD Severus raised its status to that of a colony. Trade across what was now a relatively stable Roman Empire flourished, and Damascus reaped the rewards of being an important centre at the junction of major caravan routes.

There was a characteristically Roman flurry of building activity during this period. A *castrum* on the site of the citadel was established, the city walls strengthened and gates were installed, the Temple of Haddad was expanded and embellished to become the Temple of Jupiter, the Via Recta (Straight Street) was widened and colonnaded to create the *decumanus maximus* and aqueducts were built, adding to the system of irrigation first developed by the Aramaeans to harness the waters of the Barada.

During the **Byzantine** era (from the fourth century AD) Christianity became firmly established in the city. The Temple of Jupiter was converted into a church dedicated to St John the Baptist and Damascus became the seat of a bishopric, second only to the patriarchate in Antioch. However, the Byzantine Empire found itself under constant threat from the **Sassanid Persians** and eventually in 612 Damascus was briefly occupied by them, before being regained by Heraclius in 628.

This brief incursion by the Sassanids was the prelude to a far more permanent transition brought about by the expansion of the **Islamic** Empire of the nomadic tribes of the Arabian peninsular following the death of their Prophet Mohammad. Led by Khalid Ibn al-Walid, the Muslim army first took Damascus in 635, withdrawing to defeat Heraclius in the decisive battle of Yarmouk before occupying the city permanently in 636. Under this new regime, Damascus was at first a relatively unimportant outpost of an Islamic Empire whose political centre was Medina. However, in 661 the governor of Damascus, Mu'awiya, assumed the title of Caliph, initiating the **Umayyad** Dynasty and making Damascus the new capital of the Islamic Empire. For Syria, and particularly Damascus, this resulted in a great cultural flowering, most eloquently and enduringly expressed in the architecture of the Umayyad Mosque.

Umayyad rule lasted for nearly a hundred years until in 750 a new dynasty, that of the **Abbasids**, was established. Damascus was replaced by Baghdad as the capital of the Islamic Empire, and fell into decline. The unity of the now huge Islamic Empire began to give way to competing spheres of influence centred on Baghdad, Cairo, Mosul and Aleppo, with Damascus caught between them. From the ninth century it came under the control of the **Tulunids**, **Ikshidids** and **Fatimids** of Egypt, before passing in 1076 to the **Seljuk Turks** who had by then expanded from their capital at Isfahan to take control of both Aleppo and Mosul.

Seljuk rule was in an advanced state of decline by the time the **Crusaders** arrived in the 12th century. However, despite coming under attack three times in the first half of the century, Damascus was never taken by the Crusaders. Nur ud-Din, the **Zengid** ruler of Aleppo, assumed control of the city in 1154, and was followed by Salah ud-Din (Saladin) in 1174, who by that time had overthrown the Fatimids of Egypt to establish the **Ayyubid** Dynasty. Together, Nur ud-Din and Salah ud-Din led the Muslim resistance to the Crusaders and Damascus flourished once again as an important political centre.

The first **Mongol** invasion of 1260 brought devastation to Damascus and an abrupt end to Ayyubid rule. However the **Mameluke** Dynasty of Egypt quickly came to the rescue, defeating the Mongols and establishing their rule in Syria. Damascus flourished yet again, particularly under the rule of Baibars (1260-77) and later under the governorship of Tengiz (1312-39), becoming a second capital after Cairo and witnessing another burst of building activity. The Mongol threat continued, however, and after repelling an attack in 1299-1300, the city was largely destroyed by the Mongol leader Tamerlane in 1400. Although Mameluke rule was restored, the city never fully recovered under them.

In 1516 the **Ottoman Turks**, led by Selim I, took Damascus and incorporated Syria into their huge empire. The Ottoman's control and protection of the *Hajj* (pilgrimage to Mecca) helped reinforce their claim to the Caliphate, and throughout their 400 years of rule Damascus was of central importance as the last great staging post on the annual pilgrimage to Mecca. Inevitably for such a large empire, the city's governors enjoyed a large degree of independence. Indeed, the first Pasha of Damascus, **Al Ghazali**, declared himself independent of Ottoman rule and the city suffered considerable damage when it was retaken by the armies of Suleiman I in 1521. Later pashas exercised their independence more cautiously. Amongst the **Azem** family, who between themselves ruled for most of the 18th century, Darwish Pasha, Murad Pasha and most notably Assad Pasha were competent governors who did much to improve the city. However, corruption and stagnation began to set in and when Mohammad Ali, the Pasha of Cairo, rose against Ottoman rule in 1805, Damascus soon followed suit and control of the city passed to Mohammed Ali's son **Ibrahim** Pasha in 1832. His rule lasted until 1840 and saw a brief burst of civic improvements. But the return to direct Ottoman rule also saw a return to stagnation. In 1860, clashes between Christian and Druze minorities in Lebanon spread to Damascus and culminated in a massacre of Christians living in the city, the Christians having maintained a minimal presence here since the Byzantine era. **Midhat** Pasha brought further civic improvements towards the end of the 19th century, and at the same time Damascus, with its large concentration of intellectuals, became a centre of Arab nationalism.

When the Ottoman Turks allied with the Germans at the start of the First World War, Damascus became yet again an important strategic centre and its fall to the Allied forces in 1918 heralded the fall of the Ottoman Empire. The Arab nationalist dream of an independent Syria was briefly recognized under the leadership of **Feisal** (see page 623), who had been central to the Arab revolt upon which the Allies had relied so heavily. However, in the superpower carve-up which inevitably followed, this was replaced by French Mandate rule in 1920 and Damascus became for a while the capital of a mini-state. In 1925 an uprising against the French resulted in the bombing of Damascus which caused considerable damage, but it was not until 1945 that the city became the capital of an independent Syrian Arab Republic.

See page 624 for more on the French Mandate & Syria's independence

Sights

Old City

The Old City, retaining so much of its long and varied history, is certainly Damascus' greatest attraction. As soon as you step into it, you are drawn into a completely different world, barely touched by the 21st century. True, cars and minivans are becoming an increasingly common sight, nudging and beeping their way along the narrow lanes, but for the most part you are more likely to find yourself face to face with a donkey, or else swept along by the crowds of shoppers scouring the ancient souks for bargains. Around practically every corner, meanwhile, you will find another beautiful and atmospheric historic monument. Such immediate history might become overwhelming were it not for the fact that so many of these monuments are still in use, set firmly in the context of a living city.

Damascus & around

The various monuments are described here in as near as possible a logical order, although it is not really possible to conduct a detailed tour of the entire Old City without a considerable amount of doubling back on yourself. If you are here for a few days, you would do better to return more than once, concentrating on a different area each time. If your time is limited, however, you can still see the major monuments and get a good taste of the souks and different residential areas in a half or full-day (see '24 hours in the city' page 79).

Citadel The Citadel is an imposing structure standing at the northwest corner of the Old City, its massive western wall facing directly onto the modern thoroughfare of Ath Thawra Street. At the time of writing, it was undergoing extensive restoration – a painfully slow process which has been going on for more than five years – and closed to visitors. However you can view its walls from the outside and can get some insight into the different stages of its tumultuous history.

Damascus Old City

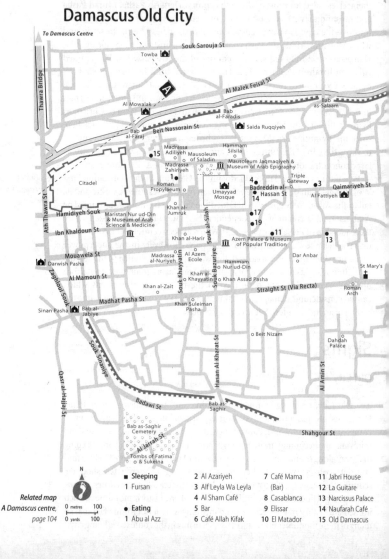

Related map
A Damascus centre,
page 104

0 metres   100
0 yards   100

■ **Sleeping**	2 Al Azariyeh	7 Café Mama	11 Jabri House
1 Fursan	3 Alf Leyla Wa Leyla	(Bar)	12 La Guitare
	4 Al Sham Café	8 Casablanca	13 Narcissus Palace
● **Eating**	5 Bar	9 Elissar	14 Naufarah Café
1 Abu al Azz	6 Café Allah Kifak	10 El Matador	15 Old Damascus

History The site appears to have been utilized as a *castrum* or military camp during Roman times (probably during the reign of Diocletian, 284-305 AD), the standard square walled compound with defensive towers at each corner and a gate in each wall standing in the eastern half of the present citadel. Then, during the Byzantine and early Islamic periods it was expanded to occupy roughly its present extent. After that there are no clear references to it until the Seljuk period (1058-1157) when a new fortress was constructed. After Salah ud-Din (Saladin) took control of Damascus in 1174 he strengthened it, adding a tower, and it became an important centre for his military operations. Most of what can be seen today, however, dates from the 13th century. Under threat from both the Crusader attack and local Syrian intrigues, Al Adil, brother of Saladin and successor to the Ayyubid leadership, set about building a new citadel in 1202. Work continued until well after his death, with new walls and towers being constructed along with a palace complex and mosque. In 1260 the great Mongol invasions from the east reached Damascus and the citadel was largely destroyed. It was subsequently rebuilt by the Mameluke Sultan Baibars, only to be attacked again by the Mongols in the 1300, and then destroyed by Tamerlane in 1400. During the Ottoman period the citadel was partially repaired but its importance declined and it gradually fell into disuse. Following Syrian independence, it was used once again as a barracks, and then later as a prison before work started on its restoration as a historic monument.

Tour of the citadel walls Facing the western wall of the citadel from Ath Thawra Street, the whole of the southwest tower along with the curtain wall up to the small central gate is an obviously modern reconstruction. The new stonework is rather too neat and crisp perhaps, but it gives a good idea of the full proportions of the massive, solid southwest tower. This tower has carried the full brunt of sieges, fires and earthquakes over the centuries; since Al Adil first built it in roughly its present form at the start of the 13th century, it has been destroyed and rebuilt no less than six times.

The remainder of the western wall has also been largely reconstructed, but this time using old stones from the Ayyubid and Mameluke periods. Various recycled architectural fragments bearing inscriptions and insignia can be seen in the upper parts of

The large metal statue of a mounted soldier in flowing gown which stands by the main gate is of Saladin

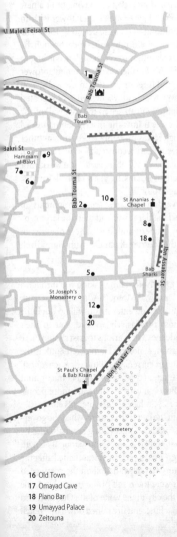

Damascus & around

these walls. At eye level, just to the right of the central gate, there is one interesting block carved with a dragon and rosette (though unfortunately placed upside-down, making it a little difficult to identify as such). Note also the recently discovered and only partially reconstructed tower to the right of the main gate, thought to be one of two flanking it which were built by Baibars but destroyed in an earthquake in 1759 and never rebuilt.

The northwest tower shows evidence of various different stages of construction and reconstruction in its stonework, from the Ayyubid through to the Ottoman periods. When Baibars restored the citadel, he had a belvedere built on top of this tower, from where he would review his troops and hold audiences.

From the corner of the northwest tower, you can follow the small cobbled street that runs between the Barada River and the northern wall (this also makes a pleasant alternative to Hamidiyeh souk as a way of reaching the Umayyad Mosque and surrounding areas). The stonework you see is entirely of Mameluke origin (with later reconstructions), Baibars having built a new wall some 10 m in front of Al Adil's. You first pass a small squat tower with an inscription on the north face commemorating its reconstruction in 1508. The street then passes under an arch with an inscription above it. Once through the arch you are in fact inside the remains of another tower, rebuilt according to the inscription by Nawruz al-Haifizi in 1407. Further on is a rectangular tower with just a very small central entrance and three arrow slits in the walls. You come next to the northeast corner tower which shows evidence of repeated repair and reconstruction. Turning right, you can see in the east wall of the tower an Arabic inscription in an elaborate frame; the inscription names Al Adil as the builder of the tower, although it was probably taken from another tower and re-used here during later repair and reconstruction work. (From here you can visit the nearby gate to the Old City, Bab al-Faraj, and work your way along the northern section of the city walls, taking in also Bab al-Faradis, Bab as-Salaam and Bab Touma (see page 100).

Following the eastern wall southwards there are various fragments of inscriptions in it, followed by a long rectangular tower and then the large central gateway, today largely obscured by modern buildings. The remainder of the east wall, along with the whole of the south wall parallel with Hamidiyeh Souk, are likewise obscured.

Hamidiyeh Souk

If you have lots of time on your hands and are interested in looking at antiques, souvenirs, handicrafts etc, talking to the people who will no doubt engage you in conversation can be a great way to spend an afternoon; and in traditional Syrian style you will be plied with endless cups of tea

This is the best way to enter the Old City for the first time, taking you through a colourful and lively souk directly to the Umayyad Mosque. Admittedly the souk has become rather tourist-orientated, and as you enter it you will no doubt be accosted by various people trying most persuasively to lead you to their 'cousin's' shop. Likewise (and often a sideline of the various tourist shops) there are lots of people on hand offering to change money (Hamidiyeh Souk is the main centre for the black market in foreign currency and travellers' cheques). But this is also a thoroughly Syrian market, and while westerners might hunt around for antique silver jewellery or Bedouin carpets, there are more people shopping for everyday items such as fabric, clothes, kitchen utensils etc.

In its present form the souk dates from the late 19th century, when the governor of Damascus, Rashid Nasha Pasha, modified the existing Souk al-Jadid by widening and straightening it, constructing two-storey shops along its length and erecting the corrugated iron roofing. On completion, it was named after the Ottoman Sultan, Abdel Hamid II. History has taken its toll on the corrugated iron roofing: the holes which pepper it were the result of the triumphant rifle shots of the Arab forces who rode into the city in the wake of the Ottoman and German retreat of 1917, and later, the machine-gun fire rained down by French planes during the Druze rebellion of 1925.

Paradise Lost?

"This is the Paradise which the righteous have been promised; it is watered by running streams; eternal are its fruits and eternal are its shades." (Koran, Sura 13; 35)

"...she is a city of hidden palaces, of copses, and gardens, and fountains, and bubbling streams... Close along the river's edge through seven sweet miles of rustling boughs, the deepest shade, the city spreads out her whole length..." (Alexander Kinglake, Eothen, 1844)

The close parallels between the traditional Islamic conception of Paradise and the descriptions given by travellers through the ages of Damascus as an idyllic garden have often been commented on. Looking down on the oasis from Mt Kassioun, the Prophet Mohammad is said to have turned away for fear that such an attractive earthly paradise would distract him from seeking heavenly paradise. Some traditions go further, arguing that this fertile oasis was in fact the Garden of Eden itself.

The images of bubbling streams and verdant, shady gardens are, however, a long way from the Damascus of today. The various branches of the Barada River as it passes through the city are channelled through concrete canals, meagre in size, polluted and uninspiring. The city, meanwhile, is a densely populated urban mass, beautiful and inspiring in places, but definitely not a garden. The only part of the city to retain some vestiges of this past is in the northeast, where a large area of nurseries and orchards survive, carefully fenced and not readily accessible to the casual visitor.

Damascus & around

As you approach the end of Hamadiyeh Souk, you get a glimpse of the towering, majestic southwest minaret of the Umayyad Mosque. At the same time, the remains of a **Roman Propylaeum** or monumental gateway (often mistakenly referred to as a triumphal arch) appear in front of you, marking the end of the souk. To the left are two huge free-standing columns and capitals, while to the right, three equally large columns and capitals support a segment of the original massive semi-circular arch, framed within a triangular pediment which would once have extended across six columns. The *propylaeum* marks the outer gateway at the western end of the Temple of Jupiter which once stood on the present site of the Umayyad Mosque (see below). The Temple would originally have been approached from the east side, so that this *propylaeum* was in fact primarily an exit and the decoration is therefore on the inside. Running at right angles to the *propylaeum* are the remains of an arcade, in fact a Byzantine shopping complex dating from around 330-40 AD. Today, various Koran sellers can be found plying their trade along its length.

The best way to view the Roman remains is from the mosque side; from here you can see the true scale of the arch as well as the intricate decoration which adorns it

Beyond this, you come out into an open square, cleared in recent years of the numerous shops and stalls which once filled the area. In front of you is the towering west wall of the Umayyad Mosque, 150 m in length and rising to over 100 m. Its stonework contains in it a record of the various historical phases, from the large-block lower courses of Roman origin, through the smaller stones of early Arab/Muslim times, to the occasional patches of modern restoration.

The large entrance in the western wall, the Bab al-Barid, is not officially for tourists, who are supposed to walk round to the entrance in the northern wall, the Bab al-Amara. Take the path through the area of garden alongside the northern wall; this takes you past the Mausoleum of Saladin (see below). The gardens are scattered with various re-erected columns and capitals, and other architectural fragments from the Roman temple which stood on the site of the mosque, while the approach to the Bab al-Amara is lined with a re-erected Byzantine colonnade.

Mausoleum of Saladin   For such a seminal figure in Arab history, the Mausoleum of Saladin is surprisingly small and unassuming. The dome-topped building which dates from 1196, three years after the death of Saladin, originally stood within a larger madrassa, but nothing remains of this other than a solitary arch nearby. The mausoleum itself was in such an advanced state of disrepair by the end of the 19th century that when Kaiser Wilhelm II of Germany visited Damascus in 1898, he financed its restoration and donated a new tomb of white marble. Inside, the chamber is decorated with blue and white glazed tiles and bands of black, white and yellow stone. Alongside the white marble tomb donated by Wilhelm II is the original, a wooden one richly carved in black and gold and encased in glass. ■ *Open daily 1000-1700. Tickets sold from small office around the side of the Mausoleum. Entry S£50 (no student discount), which also includes entry to the Umayyad Mosque. Cloaks for women (needed to enter the mosque) are available here.*

Umayyad Mosque - Great Mosque   However many times you visit the Umayyad Mosque, the impact of this architecturally unique and awe-inspiring building remains undiminished. If anything, it grows on you with every visit, and once you have paid due attention to the various architectural details, you are free to let the overall effect and atmosphere slowly soak in. And for all its grandeur and religious importance (it is one of the great holy sites of Islam after Mecca, Medina and the Dome of the Rock in Jerusalem), it is in no way a sombre place. Quite the contrary; gangs of young children run around the courtyard laughing and playing freely while families and groups of worshippers come and go, the scale and calm and beauty of the place easily absorbing and embracing the throng of human activity while never oppressing it. Here you can leave behind the crowds and congestion of Damascus and enter another world altogether, one which still manages to maintain a connection with the human and the ordinary, while at the same time somehow lifting it up into another level of significance.

History   The Umayyad Mosque stands on a site of religious importance dating back to the second millennium BC. At this time a temple to Hadad, the Aramaean god of rain and fertility, and his consort Atargatis, existed here, although little is known about its exact form or extent. These gods came in time to be identified with the Roman gods Jupiter and Venus, and under Roman patronage the temple was expanded in the first century AD and then further embellished under the reign of Septimus Severus (193-211 AD), becoming known in the process as the Temple of Jupiter. The inner enclosure or *temenos* of the temple corresponded approximately with the walls of the present mosque and within this would have been the *cella* or central shrine. Surrounding the *temenos* was a much larger outer courtyard marked by a portico pierced by four gateways, traces of which still survive in the western *propylaeum* (see above) and also in the eastern triple-arched *propylaeum* and the column bases to the north of it (see below).

With the adoption of Christianity as the official religion of the Roman Empire (the point which also marks the start of the Byzantine era), the Temple of Jupiter was converted into a Christian church and dedicated to St John the Baptist, most probably during the reign of Emperor Theodosius (379-395 AD), who is thought to have ordered the destruction of the pagan shrine in the first year of his rule. In 636 AD, following the defeat of the Byzantine forces of Heraclius at the Battle of Yarmouk, the Arab armies of Islam took Damascus. Initially, Christians continued to worship in the church, sharing the huge compound with Muslims who built a small *mihrab* in the south wall, which faced in the direction of Mecca.

However in 661 AD, under the Umayyad Dynasty, Damascus became the capital of the Islamic Empire and with this shift, pressure increased for a purely Muslim place of worship. It was under the Umayyad Caliph Khalid Ibn al-Walid that the huge compound was finally appropriated and work started on an Islamic mosque on a grand scale in 708 AD. The enterprise was an enormous one which suffered various setbacks and entailed massive expenditure, but the end result was the greatest monument to Islam of that period.

Over the centuries the mosque has survived invasions, sackings, earthquakes and fires, although with each calamity it has undergone a transformation of one sort or another. The most devastating and most recent came in 1893 when a fire largely destroyed the prayer hall. Restoration, involving the replacement of the interior columns and central dome, was undertaken by the Ottomans, although much of the original decoration and beauty were lost in the process. However for all that, and perhaps because of the amalgam of different influences and modifications over the centuries, today the Umayyad Mosque stands out as an unique and exceptionally beautiful monument.

Visiting the mosque The northern **Bab al-Amara** (2) brings you into the courtyard of the mosque, with the prayer hall and its striking mosaic-covered central transept in front of you. The **courtyard**, measuring over 50 m by 120 m, is a huge open space paved with white marble slabs. These date from the late-19th century restoration which followed the great fire of 1893. Their effect is quite striking, particularly in bright sunlight, although one can only imagine what it must have been like when the whole area was covered with mosaics.

The numbers in brackets refer to the plan below

Surrounding the courtyard on three sides is an **arcade**. Along the east and west sides of the courtyard the arcade retains its original pattern of two circular columns interspaced by a square pillar, the latter being newly clad in marble, while along the north side, except for a few columns at either end, all have been replaced over the centuries by square pillars and recently clad. The inside walls of the arcades have likewise been decorated with marble as part of ongoing

Damascus & around

Umayyad Mosque

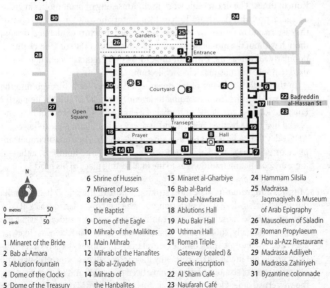

N

0 metres	50
0 yards	50

1 Minaret of the Bride
2 Bab al-Amara
3 Ablution fountain
4 Dome of the Clocks
5 Dome of the Treasury

6 Shrine of Hussein
7 Minaret of Jesus
8 Shrine of John the Baptist
9 Dome of the Eagle
10 Mihrab of the Malikites
11 Main Mihrab
12 Mihrab of the Hanafites
13 Bab al-Ziyadeh
14 Mihrab of the Hanbalites

15 Minaret al-Gharbiye
16 Bab al-Barid
17 Bab al-Nawfarah
18 Ablutions Hall
19 Abu Bakr Hall
20 Uthman Hall
21 Roman Triple Gateway (sealed) & Greek inscription
22 Al Sham Café
23 Naufarah Café

24 Hammam Silsila
25 Madrassa Jaqmaqiyeh & Museum of Arab Epigraphy
26 Mausoleum of Saladin
27 Roman Propylaeum
28 Abu al-Azz Restaurant
29 Madrassa Adiliyeh
30 Madrassa Zahiriyeh
31 Byzantine colonnade

Money no object: Khalid Ibn al-Walid and the Umayyad Mosque

The Umayyad period brought with it a great flowering of architectural expression in Syria, drawing inspiration from the rich Byzantine, Persian, Mesopotamian and local influences which existed at the time. Khalid Ibn al-Walid, the sixth Umayyad Caliph, was famous in particular for his architectural enterprises. He was responsible for the building of the Al Aqsa mosque in Jerusalem, and for the Great Mosque in Medina.

Al Walid ordered work to start on the building of the Umayyad Mosque in Damascus in 708 AD. The project lasted for seven years, reaching completion in 715, the same year as his death. Thousands of craftsmen were brought in from

Constantinople and Egypt to work alongside the Syrian craftsmen. Originally, practically every surface was covered with mosaics, including the whole of the floor of the courtyard. Inside the prayer hall, 600 gold lanterns hung from the ceilings, while all the column capitals were plated with gold.

According to one account, it cost the state's entire revenue thoughout this period. Another account relates how 400 chests each containing 14,000 dinars were needed to pay for the work, and that a total of 18 camels were needed to bring the receipts to Al Walid, who had them burnt without even looking at them, saying "We spent this for Allah and shall make no account of it."

restoration work. All three arcades are topped by a smaller upper-storey arcade of delicate columns and arches, with fragments of mosaic surviving in places.

In the centre of the courtyard there is an **ablution fountain** (3) of recent origin and on either side of it are small columns topped by newly added metal globes, meant to hold lanterns. Towards the west end of the courtyard, supported on eight columns topped by ornate Corinthian capitals, is a large, mosaic-covered octagonal structure with a domed top. This is known as the **Dome of the Treasury** (5) (*Khubbet al-Khazneh* or *Beit al-Hal*). The structure, as the name suggests, was the mosque's treasury. It is thought to have been built in 788 AD by the Abbasid governor of Damascus, Fadil Ibn Salih, although the columns and capitals on which it rests are clearly recycled from Roman times. The fine mosaic work itself, consisting of plant motifs in green and gold, probably date from 13th or 14th century restoration work. Towards the eastern end of the courtyard there is a smaller structure of identical design, though without the mosaic work and built much later (18th or 19th century), popularly known as the **Dome of the Clocks** (4). Predictably enough, it was used to house the mosque's clock collection.

In the northeast corner of the mosque, a doorway leads through into the **Shrine of Hussein** (6). According to legend, the head of the Shi'ite martyr Hussein, killed at the Battle of Karbala (see page 647) was brought here and placed in a niche by the Caliph Yazid as a way of humiliating the followers of Ali. Today the niche is fronted by a silver grille and has become an important place of pilgrimage for Shi'ites who come here in large numbers, although there are conflicting traditions as to the final resting place of his head.

A good time to view the mosaics of the western arcade is in the evening when they are floodlit

Mosaics and minarets The most striking feature of the prayer hall from the outside is the façade of the central transept, which is covered in mosaics. It is by looking at these mosaics that you can best conjure up an idea of what the mosque originally looked like when almost every surface was likewise adorned. The mosaic work on the central transept consists largely of restoration carried out in the 1960s, with only the darker patches being original. The other area where sections of mosaic have been preserved and restored is along the western arcade. On the inside wall, towards the northern end, is a section

The Dome of the Eagle

The Dome of the Eagle was perhaps the most ambitious aspect of the mosque. At the first attempt, the dome collapsed. According to one account, Al Walid was then approached by a craftsman who claimed he could build the dome, provided he was given total control over the construction work;

"The builder then dug until he reached water. Thereafter, he laid the foundation and covered it with mats. Then he disappeared. Al Walid's messengers searched for the man for one year, but they were unsuccessful in finding him. The man returned after an absence of twelve months and Al Walid enquired why he had deserted his job.

"The response was; 'come with me and I shall show you'. Al Walid joined him and they walked to the foundation where the builder removed the mats. Then they discovered that the base had dropped a small amount. The builder explained; 'This levelling process is why the failure occurred the first time. Now we shall build upon the settled foundation and it will never sink again, by the will of God.' " (Taken from The Mosque of Damascus by Afif Bahnassi).

The original Umayyad dome was made of wood. In 1069 it was destroyed by fire and subsequently replaced by a stone one. Ironically, the massive fire of 1893 which destroyed the prayer hall and resulted once again in the collapse of the Dome of the Eagle is said to have been caused by a nargileh (water pipe) of one of the workmen who was working at the time on its repair.

known as the **Barada Panel**. The theory is that this is a depiction of the Barada River, lined with lush vegetation and enticing villas, as it was in ancient times, although it could equally represent a scene from Paradise. In the entrance hall just inside **Bab al-Barid** (16) there are further elaborate mosaics which, like all the mosaics in the Umayyad Mosque, are notable for the complete absence of any human figures: such representations were considered blasphemous in Islamic tradition. The intricately painted wooden ceiling here (a restoration of the 15th century original) is also particularly beautiful. Note also the huge bronze panelled wooden doors of the Bab al-Barid, which date from 1416.

The mosque's three **minarets** can be viewed from different parts of the courtyard. Beside the Bab al-Amara in the centre of the northern wall is the **Minaret of the Bride** (1). The lower part dates from the ninth century, while the upper part was added in the late 12th century. According to a local story, its construction was originally financed by a merchant whose daughter was betrothed to the Caliph of the time, hence the name. In the southwest corner is the **Minaret al-Gharbiye** (15), also known as the Minaret Qait Bey after the Mameluke Sultan who built it in 1488. It is particularly graceful and shows the strong Egyptian influence typical of the Mameluke period. In the southeast corner is the **Minaret of Jesus** (7), the tallest of the three. The main body is Ayyubid, dating from 1247 and replacing an Umayyad minaret, while the tip is Ottoman. According to Islamic belief, Jesus will descend from heaven to do battle with the Antichrist before the Day of Judgement, and according to local Damascene tradition, he will descend via this minaret. Both the southeast and southwest minarets are believed to have been built on the foundations of Roman towers, although some scholars have questioned this, pointing out that no other examples of Roman temples have towers at the corners.

The **prayer hall** occupies the whole of the southern length of the mosque, and basically follows a basilica plan, although the long, narrow, triple-aisled hall is broken by a central transept topped by a massive dome which serves to orientate worshippers towards the mihrab in the centre of the south wall. Some scholars suggest that the Muslim architects followed the plan of the existing

Damascus & around

Byzantine church, modifying it by adding the central transept, thus shifting the focus of the building away from the east wall where the altar would have been, to the *mihrab* in the centre of the south wall. However, there is no firm evidence to indicate the exact form or extent of the Byzantine church, and others argue that Al Walid completely dismantled the church before starting work on the mosque. What you see today is largely the Ottoman reconstruction following the fire of 1893. Despite being in no way as elaborate as the original must have been, in its cavernous, cool, airy enormity it is still impressive. The floors are covered throughout with carpets, while numerous fans dangle from a huge height, wobbling as they spin. In the central transept, the towering **Dome of the Eagle** (9) resting on four colossal pillars is somewhat austere in its present form, though still awesome for its sheer size. Its name derives from the idea that the domed transept represents the head and body of an eagle, with the prayer hall extending to either side, representing the wings. As well as the main *mihrab* (11) and *minbar* beside it, there are three other smaller *mihrabs* or niches, dedicated to the Hanbalites (14), Hanafites (12) and Malikites (10), the three other schools of Sunni law besides the Shaffi school which was dominant in Damascus. To the east of the central transept, encompassing two columns of the line nearest the south wall, is the **Shrine of John the Baptist** (8), consisting of an elaborate, dome-topped mausoleum made of marble. This dates from the Ottoman period, replacing an earlier wooden shrine which was destroyed in the fire of 1893. According to legend, during the building of the mosque, Al Walid's workers discovered a casket buried underground containing the head of St John the Baptist, still with its hair and skin intact.

■ *The tourist entrance is via the north gate (Bab al-Amara). Open daily, but closed Fri 1230-1400 for main prayers. Entry S£50 (tickets from the small office around the side of the Mausoleum of Saladin, see above). Women are provided with a black hooded robe which must be worn inside the mosque. Men are required to dress modestly (shorts are not allowed; a long-sleeved shirt is preferable to a T-shirt).*

Madrassa Zahiriyeh (30) - School & Mausoleum of Baibars

A little to the northwest of the Umayyad Mosque, facing each other across a narrow street, are the Madrassa Zahiriyeh and Madrassa Adiliyeh. Originally the Madrassa Zahiriyeh was the private house of Ayub, the father of Saladin. Following the death of the Mameluke Sultan Baibars in 1277, his son converted it into a religious school, adding a mausoleum to house his father's body.

The recessed entrance which dates from the building's conversion is particularly imposing, consisting of contrasting black and yellow stonework, with three bands of marble above the level of the doorway carrying Arabic inscriptions and above these a finely executed semi-dome sculpted into intricate geometrical shapes. Today the building houses a library, but there is usually someone on hand to show you around and open up the mausoleum itself, which is kept locked.

Inside there is a small courtyard; the doorway immediately on the right leads into the mausoleum of Baibars, an ornately decorated, domed chamber which represents the main focus of interest. Opposite the entrance is a beautiful *mihrab* framed within strikingly patterned black and white marble. Each of the walls, themselves decorated with marble, contain two arched doorways, while running around the room is a wide band of lavish golden mosaic work in the same style as those of the Umayyad Mosque. ■ *There is no entrance fee as such but the caretaker expects a small tip for opening up Baibars' mausoleum.*

Construction work on this madrassa began towards the end of the 12th century, but it was left unfinished until the death of Sultan al-Adil Saif ud-Din (the brother of Saladin) in 1218, whereupon his son completed it to serve as the mausoleum of his father. The entrance, though impressive in its own right, is somewhat overshadowed by that of the Madrassa Zahiriyeh, while the mausoleum itself is a simple and unadorned domed chamber with broad arches in each wall. The remainder of the building, which consists of rooms arranged around a central courtyard, also houses a library.

Madrassa Adiliyeh (29)
The madrassa is currently undergoing major restoration work and is not open to the public

This madrassa is situated by the short colonnade leading to the northern Bab al-Amara gate of the Umayyad Mosque. The entrance is on the street, rather than from the adjacent gardens. Built by Jaqmaq al-Argunsawi, the Mameluke governor of Damascus from 1421-22 and later king of Egypt from 1438-52, this madrassa has an impressive entrance façade typical of the period, while the interior is also well preserved, housing a collection of Arab epigraphy, both in the form of carved inscriptions and some beautifully illuminated texts. ■ *Open 0900-1400, Fri 0900-1130, closed Tue. Entry S£150 (students S£10). Often seems to remain closed during its official opening hours.*

Madrassa Jaqmaqiyeh/ Museum of Arab Epigraphy (25)

Damascus & around

Continuing east from the entrance to the Madrassa Jaqmaqiyeh and then bearing right, you can weave your way through a series of narrow alleys to arrive on Badreddin al-Hassan Street, which runs east from the east gate of the Umayyad Mosque. But if instead you bear left and head north towards Bab al-Faradis, you pass on your right the Saida Ruqqiyeh Mosque. This Shi'ite mosque provides a complete contrast to anything else found in the Old City. For a start it was built in 1985. Its style, meanwhile, is entirely Iranian in inspiration (and indeed Iranian-built), as can be clearly seen from the distinctive onion-shaped dome. Inside, it is lavishly decorated with glazed tiles and copious amounts of marble, while the central dome is a dazzling mirror-mosaic. The overall effect is quite striking in its bright, fresh newness. It is also incredibly lively around evening prayers , thronging with families of Shi'ite pilgrims, mostly from Iran. The mosque stands on the site of a shrine to Lady Ruqqiyeh who died in 680 AD and was the daughter of Hussein, the great martyr of the Shi'ites. Hence its importance as a Shi'ite place of pilgrimage.

Saida Ruqqiyeh Mosque

You can also skirt around the outside of the Umayyad Mosque by following its southern wall. You first pass Bab al-Ziada (13), which leads directly into the prayer hall. Further along, partially obscured by an electrical installation, there are the remains of a Roman triple gateway in the wall of the mosque. Originally, this served as the southern entrance into the inner temenos of the Roman temple. The Greek inscription on the central lintel (*"Thy Kingdom, O Christ, is an everlasting Kingdom, and Thy dominion endureth throughout all generations"*) clearly demonstrates that it remained in use during the Byzantine period, perhaps serving also as an entrance for both Christians and Muslims when they shared the temple compound during the early years of Islamic rule. However, with the construction of Al Walid's mosque it was blocked up, since it interfered with the positioning of the central *mihrab* on the inside.

The South Wall of the Umayyad Mosque

The eastern gate of the mosque, Bab al-Nawfarah ('Gate of the Fountain') was originally part of the main *propylaeum* or monumental entrance to the inner temenos of the Roman temple, the climax of an approach which began from the agora further to the east and culminated in a huge portico (no longer surviving) and triple gateway (the present Bab al-Nawfarah). A broad flight of stairs descends from this impressive gateway, down into Bareddin al-Hassan

Bab al-Nawfarah (17) & Badreddin al-Hassan Street

Street. At the bottom of the steps, on the right, is the *Naufarah Café* and opposite it the *Al Sham*, both lively places to stop for refreshments and watch the comings and goings along this street (see 'Cafés', page 120).

Continuing east along this street, after a little over 100 m you reach the remains of the **Triple Gateway** which marked the eastern entrance to the outer compound of the Temple of Jupiter. The remains lie half buried in the ground, reducing their effect somewhat, though when you realize that the lintels which you can see just above ground level in fact crown the side portals, you get a sense of the original scale of the gateway. Like the monumental gateway at the end of Hamidiyeh Souk, the decoration is on the east-facing side.

If you follow the narrow street leading north immediately before the triple gateway (coming from the Umayyad Mosque), you can see on your left traces of the columns which formed the portico running around the outer courtyard of the Temple of Jupiter; in places just the column bases survive, elsewhere entire columns have been incorporated into the structures of buildings lining this street.

Continuing east from the triple gateway, the street becomes Qaimariyeh Street. Further along on the right is the **Al Fatiyyeh Mosque**, built in 1742 as a madrassa by Fat'hy Effendi, a poet and Ottoman treasury official. This beautifully proportioned mosque is interesting for its combination of a typically Syrian/Mameluke style in the bands of black and white stone and the elegant decorative tiling, with a typically Ottoman plan in features such as the triple-domed porch which precedes the prayer hall. The overall effect, with a two-storey arcade around the quiet, shady central courtyard, is very pleasing.

Further east, Qaimariyeh Street gives way to a maze of narrow alleys extending northeast and southeast; following these alleys northeast gives access (with a little careful navigation) to the Christian quarter of Bab Touma.

Directly to the south of the Umayyad Mosque is the **Azem Palace** which now also houses the Museum of Popular Tradition. To reach it, follow the narrow alley which runs south from the southwest corner of the mosque (this is **Souk al-Silah**, today largely given over to gold and jewellery, but previously the weapons market, or Souk Assagah), and turn left at what is effectively a T-junction.

Azem Palace & the Museum of Popular Tradition

Built in 1749-52 as a royal residence by the Ottoman governor of Damascus, Assad Pasha al-Azem, this palace is the largest, and amongst the most impressive, of the Ottoman period palaces to be found around Damascus. Entering it you are drawn immediately into another world of lavishly decorated rooms facing onto beautifully shady and tranquil courtyards with pools and fountains. The palace stands on the site of an earlier palace built by the Mameluke governor, Tengiz. It has been substantially restored, most notably after a fire in 1925, but the work was carried out carefully, preserving most of its original features. For a time it served to house the French Institute before being returned to the Azem family following independence. It was then sold to the Syrian government in 1951.

From the ticket booth, turn to the left and then right to enter the main

Old City street scene

haremlek or private family area. This, the largest courtyard, is particularly beautiful with its two pools and fountains, and its beds of tall, shady trees and shrubs. The rooms around the courtyard, luxuriously decorated with wood panelled walls and ceilings, each contain displays along a different theme: musical instruments; a reception room with elaborate inlaid furniture; a marriage room containing beautiful glassware; a pilgrimage room complete with a richly embroidered *mahmal* (the camel-mounted palaquin used to carry dignitories on the hajj to Mecca); an armoury (daggers, swords, pistols and rifles); a 'grand' reception room (very grand indeed); and the 'Salle de Djebel al-Arab' which houses various period costumes. There is also a private hammam complex and, in the south wall, a large, deep *iwan*. Given the grandeur of the rooms and exhibits, this part of the museum can hardly justify its title of 'popular tradition'!

A passage to the right of the ticket booth leads past carved wooden chests and panels and huge, richly decorated metal plates, through to the *salemlek* or visitors' area. There is another courtyard with a central pool which is surrounded by rooms, this time with displays more in line with a 'popular tradition' theme: domestic activities such as weaving and bread baking and handicrafts such as wood and metalwork, leatherwork, pottery, carpets and women's costumes and embroidered fabrics (some of them particularly delicate and beautiful). ■ *Open 0900-1730 in summer, 0900-1530 in winter. Closed Tue and 1200-1400 Fri. Entry S£300 (students S£15). There are postcards and various books/booklets on Damascus and Syria on sale at the entrance.*

The area which extends west from the Azem Palace, between Hamidiyeh Souk and Mahdat Pasha Street, is well worth exploring for its souks, khans and other historical monuments. Leaving the Azem Palace and turning left (south) into what is the main spice market, Souk Bazuriye, you pass on the left the Hammam Nur ud-Din, built by Nur ud-Din between 1154-72 in order to raise funds for the building of the Madrassa al-Nuriyeh (see below). It is one of the oldest in Damascus and despite undergoing several restorations, and housing a soap factory for a time, it is today the best example of a fully functional Turkish bath complex in Damascus (see page 108 for details of opening times etc). The large and elaborate domed reception chamber dates from the Ottoman period. A little further along on the same side is the entrance to Khan Assad Pasha.

Souk Bazuriye & Hammam Nur ud-Din

As well as building the Azem Palace, Assad Pasha al-Azem at the same time undertook the construction of this impressive khan between 1751-53. Extensively restored in recent years, the khan is currently used for exhibitions and occasional concerts, although there is talk of converting it into a tourist antiques/souvenir market or a museum.

Khan Assad Pasha

An imposing gateway of black and white stone leads through into what is easily the most ambitious and spectacular of Damascus's khans. It follows an essentially Persian design, with the main courtyard covered. There are a total of eight domes arranged around a large circular opening in the ceiling which allows light to pour down onto a circular pool below. Four huge pillars connected by elegant arches support the ceiling. Around the sides of the courtyard are two storeys of rooms (those below being the store rooms while those above were sleeping quarters). Above them there is a gallery running all the way round the walls, framed in arches which connect also with the arches of the four central columns to form part of the support for the eight domes. The alternating grey and white stonework, together with the ingenious and beautifully proportioned design of the building, combine to create something of an architectural masterpiece. Stepping into this khan from the crowded souk outside, you are certainly overwhelmed by the scale and sense of space. ■ *Open 0800-1700, closed Fri. Entry free.*

Damascus & around

Al Azem Ecole Following the street which runs due west from the entrance to the Azem Palace, you pass on the left the Al Azem Ecole. Originally this was the Madrassa Abdullah al-Azem Pasha, built in 1770 by the man of the same name who later went on to become the governor of Damascus and who represented the last of the Azem family, which governed Damascus between 1725 and 1809. Today the building houses an up-market tourist souvenir/antiques shop. Silk weaving is carried out on the premises, on what is claimed to be the last surviving loom working exclusively with natural silk to produce silk brocades. Even if you are not interested in buying anything, the interior of the building is well worth a look, with its small courtyard and delicate columns and arches supporting a two-storey arcade around the sides. If you can get someone to take you up onto the roof, there are good views from here of the Umayyad Mosque.
■ *Open 0930-1900 in summer, 0930-1800 in winter. Closed Fri. Entry free.*

Other madrassas & khans Just past the Al Azem Ecole there is a crossroads. Turning left into the narrow north-south souk (**Souk Khayyatin**, the tailors' souk), immediately on the right is the entrance to the **Madrassa al-Nuriyeh**. Today the Mausoleum of Nur ud-Din is the only surviving part of this madrassa, which was built between 1167 and 1172 to house the tomb of one of the great Arab leaders of this period; two more modern mosques now stand on either side of the main courtyard. The mausoleum (which has itself undergone a certain amount of modification) is reached through a doorway on the left in the initial entrance hall. The mausoleum is kept locked but the caretaker is usually on hand to open it up. If not, you can peer in through the iron-grille window in the street, to the left of the main entrance. The simple chamber is topped by a tall honeycombed dome, with a band of Arabic inscription running around the walls and the marble tomb in the centre of the floor.

Continuing south along this street, on the right is the **Khan al-Khayyatin**, with a particularly beautiful arched entrance of alternating black and yellow stone with intricately carved decoration and Arabic inscriptions (though unfortunately partially obscured by small stalls on either side). Inside, the central dome has long ago collapsed although the arches which supported it still survive. The khan is occupied today by cotton embroidery and fabric shops.

Returning to the crossroads by the Al Azem Ecole and Madrassa al-Nuriyeh, and heading north this time along the continuation of Souk Khayyatin, you pass first on the right the **Khan al-Harir**, the silk khan, the main entrance to which is via a narrow street on the right. The entrance doorway itself is the main feature of interest, being beautifully decorated. Continuing north, on the left is the entrance to the **Khan al-Jumruk** (the customs khan), a long L-shaped khan today occupied by brightly lit fabric shops, but still retaining its original domed roofing supported by arches.

If you head west from the crossroads by the Al Azem Ecole and Madrassa al-Nuriyeh, following the main street, the second turning on the right (after about 200 m) brings you to the entrance of the **Maristan Nur ud-Din**. This can also be reached by taking a short detour from Souk Hamidiyeh (to do this, take the right turn at the point where there is a break in the corrugated-iron roofing of the souk as you head east towards the Umayyad Mosque).

Maristan Nur ud-Din (or Bimaristan al-Nuri)
Undergoing restoration at the time of writing: some of the exhibitions may have been updated

Built by Nur ud-Din Zangai in 1154 as a hospital and medical school, this remarkable building was the most advanced medical institution of its time, and continued to function as a hospital until the 19th century. Restoration work was carried out on the building in the 13th and 18th centuries.

An archway with a honeycombed semi-dome frames the doorway, which utilizes a length of carved stone of clearly Roman/Classical origin as its lintel. The doors themselves, plated with metal and decorated with rivets arranged in patterns, are original. The entrance hall has an impressive central honey-combed dome and semi-domes to either side, decorated with a mixture of honeycombing and stalactites. A band of Arabic inscription runs around the room just below the level of the main dome.

Inside the main courtyard there is a large central pool and fountain. In each of the four walls there is a deep *iwan*, and on either side of each *iwan* is a door leading through to a room containing exhibits of the **Museum of Arab Science and Medicine** which is housed here. Note the beautiful arches of carved stone lattice work above each door. Displayed in the rooms is a varied collection of items from the world of Arab medicine; bottles of medicinal herbs, pharmacuetical accessories for measuring, grinding, distilling etc, surgical instruments for dentistry and operations, talismans and other 'spiritual medicine' accessories and also various astronomical instruments.

Arab medicine was far more advanced than anything practised in Europe during this period, and western medical knowledge only really began to progress with the translation of Arabic texts into Latin. The Arabs, for example, were the first to develop alcohol-based anaesthetics which could be inhaled. A sponge was soaked in a potent solution containing amongst other things hashish, opium and belladonna. It was then dried and stored, only needing to be soaked in alcohol prior to use.

From the entrance hall, a passageway to the right leads through to a hall containing a somewhat incongruous collection of stuffed animals and birds. From here there is access to a separate area of the maristan. ■ *Open 0800-1400, closed Fri. Entry S£300 (students S£15).*

Straight Street (Via Recta)

Known at its western end by its Arabic name, Madhat Pasha Street, the famous Via Recta or Straight Street runs through the entire Old City, terminating at its eastern end with Bab Sharki. Along its length, and as short diversions off it, there are several important historical monuments.

The Via Recta originates from Greek times when, following the conquests of Alexander the Great, a grid pattern was imposed on the Old City, which at that time was centred on a low mound just to the south of the street. During the first century AD, the Romans widened the street to make it into a major axis through the city (the *decumanus maximus*), a function which it continues to fulfil today.

In Roman times the street was around 26 m wide and lined with a colonnade, but over the centuries shops and buildings gradually encroached from either side, and today it is only a fraction of its former width. In fact at its western end, the tiny narrow souks which run parallel to it just to the south were originally part of the same street, only becoming separated from it when shops and stalls were erected in the middle of the wide thoroughfare. The gate at this important entrance to the Old City, the Arab period **Bab al-Jabiye** (Gate of the Water Trough) which stands on the site of the Roman Gate of Jupiter, is also in amongst these narrow souks, although you can't see much of it today.

The first section of Madhat Pasha Street is a lively, bustling souk boasting a wide variety of shops and traders. On the left after around 300 m (shortly before the turning left into Souk Khayyatin) are the entrances to three khans. The middle one, **Khan al-Zait** (the Olive Khan), is quiet and unassuming but its overall effect is very pretty with its pleasant, shaded courtyard and central pool surrounded by two galleries of arched arcading.

A little further along on the right, just past the turning for Souk Khayyatin, is **Khan Suleiman Pasha**, a rather vibrant but dilapidated place, full of the lively disorder of functioning workshops. It was built for the Ottoman governor of Damascus, Suleiman Pasha al-Azem in 1732. An unimposing entrance takes

Damascus & around

☞ *Bending words*

Straight Street in fact goes through two slight changes in direction along its course, the first at its junction with Souk Buzuriye and the second further east, at the point where the remains of a Roman arch still stand. Mark Twain comments on this fact in his book The Innocents Abroad, pointing out the rather laborious way in which the street is referred to in some bibles.

'St Luke is careful not to commit himself; he does not say it is the street which is straight, but the "street which is called Straight". It is a fine piece of irony; it is the only facetious remark in the Bible, I believe'.

you into a vaulted passage which leads through into a large rectangular courtyard. This was once covered by two large domes, now collapsed, although parts of the arches which originally supported them still survive. An upstairs gallery which can be reached via a staircase from the entrance passage runs around the whole courtyard.

Continuing east, after the next crossroads (left into Souk Buzuriye, right down towards Bab as-Saghir) the very much locals-orientated shops and stalls of Mahdat Pasha Street start to give way to more touristy shops selling brassware, swords and inlaid woodwork. If you take the second right turn after the crossroads, by a square black and white stone minaret (a small sign marks the turning), you reach (after around 100 m) the entrance of **Beit Nizam** on the left. This beautiful 18th century Ottoman house once served as the British consul's residence in Damascus. Today it is once again in the hands of the Nizam family, but it is open to the public. The decoration around the walls of the innermost courtyard is particularly beautiful. Although the rooms themselves are not usually opened up for tourists, their interior decoration is truly lavish and you can at least peer in through the windows. ■ *Open 0900-1400, closed Fri. Entry free.*

Returning to Straight Street, the first left turn after the turning for Beit Nizem brings you to the entrance of **Dar Anbar** on the right, another beautiful old house built for a wealthy Ottoman merchant in 1867. The building was used as a secondary school from 1920 and currently houses the offices of a team of architects charged with the restoration and preservation of Damascus' historical monuments. The inner courtyard (*haremlek*) has been completely restored, and the decoration around the walls of the courtyard is particularly beautiful and delicate. ■ *Open 0800-1400 in summer, 0800-1300 in winter, closed Fri. Entry free.*

Continuing east along Straight Street, the next feature of interest is the remains of a **Roman Arch**, today contained within a tiny fenced-off area of garden to the right of the modern road. The triple arch was discovered by builders during the period of French rule, buried underground by centuries' worth of debris, and re-erected on the surface. It is thought to have formed part of a tetrapylon which would have stood at what was once an intersection of the east-west *decumanus maximus* (Straight Street) with a major north-south street or *cardo maximus*.

If you take the right turn immediately before the arch, and then turn right again at the crossroads just after a small dog-leg in the street, you arrive at **Dahdah Palace** on the left. This little detour is fairly well signposted, which is a good thing because from the outside this beautiful 18th century house is entirely unremarkable. Inside, however, you have a typically Syrian/Ottoman layout of rooms arranged around a large, shady courtyard. The large, beautifully decorated *iwan* is particularly impressive. This area to the south of Straight Street is the traditional **Jewish quarter** (Haret al-Yehud) of the Old

City and there are still a few Jewish families living in the vicinity. ■ *Open 1000-1300, 1630-1800; ring the bell for entry and hope that the eccentric old owner, himself a member of the Dahdah family, is in a passably good mood.*

The Roman Arch also roughly marks the start of the **Christian quarter**, which extends to the northeast, reaching up to Bab Touma. Just beyond the arch, on the left, is the Greek Orthodox Patriarchate, **St Mary's Church** (Al Mariam). Looking somewhat modern, having just recently been clad in bright new stone, this church dates back to 1867. Its predecessor was burnt down during the great massacre of Christians and Druze in 1860. The site has been occupied by a church since Byzantine times.

Continuing east along Straight Street, you arrive eventually at **Bab Sharki** (literally 'Eastern Gate'). This is the only gate to preserve its original Roman plan (in Roman times it was the Gate of the Sun), but it has undergone extensive restoration, and only the left-hand arch of the triple arch (as viewed from the inside) contains any original stonework. Two columns stand just inside the gate, remainders of the colonnade which would have lined the street on either side during Roman times.

If you follow the narrow street to the left immediately before Bab Sharki, at the end of this street is St Ananias Chapel. A set of steps leads down to the cool, underground chapel reputedly standing on the site of the house of Ananias (see box 'Biblical Damascus'). The chapel appears to have existed since Byzantine times, when it was known as the Church of the Holy Cross ('Musallabah' in Arabic). Excavations first carried out on this spot in the 1920s revealed the apse of a small Byzantine chapel and, below it, the remains of a Roman temple. According to one line of reasoning, the house of Ananias was revered by early Christians. The Roman authorities, however, responded by building their own temple on the spot as a way of preventing Christians from coming here to worship. Only with the advent of the Byzantine era were the Christians able to build a church here. ■ *Open 0900-1300, 1600-1900 in summer, 0900-1300, 1500-1800 in winter, closed Tue. Entry free.*

St Ananias Chapel

This is popularly recognized as the site where Saul was lowered from the city walls to escape persecution by the Jews. It can be reached most easily by passing through Bab Sharki and following the line of the city walls on the outside. Going by this route, the entrance is via a driveway to the left of Bab Kisan as you face it, just before you reach a large roundabout. The main road which you must walk along is particularly busy and unpleasant, but you have the chance to get a good look at this section of the Old City walls; the first stretch as you walk from Bab Sharki consists mostly of recent restoration, but as you approach Bab Kisan you can see the huge old Roman-period stone blocks in the lower courses, along with smaller stones from the Arab period higher up.

St Paul's Chapel & Bab Kisan

An alternative route is to double back west along Straight Street and take a left turn (south) down a narrow street after approximately 500 m (the correct turning has the St Joseph's monastery a short way down on the right). Follow this street, going left and then right through a staggered crossroads to continue south, and at the end there is a gate which gives access via the modern St Paul's Monastery and Orphanage to the chapel. The disadvantage of this route is that the gate is generally kept locked and there is no real guarantee when you knock that there will be someone on hand to open it.

The chapel dedicated to St Paul is of 20th century origin and, like the rest of the complex, belongs to the Greek Orthodox church. At the rear of the chapel you can see massive stone blocks which are clearly of Roman origin. Originally the Roman gate of Saturn stood on this spot, but this was obliterated during

Damascus & around

☞ *Biblical Damascus*

There are three sites in the Christian quarter of Damascus which are mentioned in the Bible. The first, and the only one which definitely corresponds at least roughly with its modern counterpart, is Straight Street. The second is the House of Ananias. Both find mention in the story of the conversion of Saul (later to become St Paul) on the road to Damascus.

"As he neared Damascus on his journey, suddenly a light from heaven flashed around him. He fell to the ground and heard a voice say to him 'Saul, Saul, why do you persecute me?' 'Who are you, Lord?' Saul asked. 'I am Jesus, whom you are persecuting,' he replied. 'Now get up and go into the city, and you will be told what you must do.'

"The men travelling with Saul stood there speechless; they heard the sound but did not see anyone. Saul got up from the ground, but when he opened his eyes he could see nothing. So they led him by the hand into Damascus. For three days he was blind, and did not eat or drink anything.

"In Damascus there was a man named Ananias. The Lord called to him in a vision, 'Ananias!' 'Yes, Lord,' he answered. The Lord told him, 'Go to the house of Judas on Straight Street and ask for a man from Tarsus named Saul, for he is praying. In a vision he has seen a man named Ananias come and place his hands on him to restore his sight." (Acts 9: 3-12)

The third is the place where Saul was lowered from the walls in order to escape capture and murder by the Jews, traditionally (though without any real foundation) identified with Bab Kisan. This reference occurs shortly after (Acts 9:23-25).

"After many days had gone by, the Jews conspired to kill him, but Saul learned of their plan. Day and night they kept close watch on the city gates in order to kill him. But his followers took him by night and lowered him in a basket through an opening in a wall."

As for the place where St Paul received his divine vision while losing his physical sight, this was traditionally identified with the small village of Kokab, 15 km southwest of Damascus along the road to Quneitra, again without any firm evidence. However, in the 18th century tradition found itself shifting the site somewhat closer to Damascus, to a point in the vicinity of the large Christian cemetery to the south of Bab Kisan. More recently, a small chapel has been built there to mark the spot.

---

the time of Nur ud-Din and the present gate into which St Paul's Chapel is built is a 14th-century Mameluke construction. The gate itself is best viewed from outside the walls. An arch frames the central door and above it is a single machicolation. On either side are towers with a band of carved decoration and medallions bearing the *Chi-Rho* symbol (adopted by Constantine as the symbol of the new Christian empire).

Northern gates & walls of the Old City The city walls follow the same basic outline established in Hellenistic and Roman times, with a few minor variations. Various traces of the original Roman stonework can still be seen, although most of the surviving fabric of the walls is of Arab origin, dating from the 11th century onwards when extensive repairs were carried out in order to strengthen the city's defences against the threat of Crusader and later Mongol attack. The gates of the Old City also generally correspond with the original Roman gates, although most may have likewise been rebuilt in Arab times (Bab Sharki, dealt with above, is an exception).

Described below are Bab al-Faraj, Bab al-Faradis, Bab as-Salaam and Bab Touma which span the northern walls of the Old City. The remaining gates still in existence are dealt with separately (Bab al-Jabiye, Bab Sharki and Bab Kisan under 'Straight Street' and Bab as-Saghir under 'Around the Old City').

Bab al-Faraj (Gate of Deliverance), located in the northern city walls, close to the northeast corner of the Citadel, is one of the few gates which does not correspond with an earlier Roman gate. A gate was first built here by Nur ud-Din in the mid-12th century, although the existing double gateway is the result of later restoration. The inner doorway is a 13th century Ayyubid reconstruction while the outer doorway is a 15th century Mameluke reconstruction. In between the two, the covered passage between the two houses is a souk given over to blacksmiths and ironmongers.

Pass through the inner doorway and then, instead of turning left to go through the outer doorway, continue straight ahead (east) along Beit Nassorain Street, just inside the city walls. This picturesque, narrow lane is typical of the residential quarters of the Old City, with the ancient wood and plaster houses on either side leaning precariously and in one place actually touching, while elsewhere there are sections which are vaulted.

After around 250 m you reach a staggered crossroads. In front of you is the Saida Ruqqiyeh Mosque (see page 93), while turning left brings you to **Bab al-Faradis** (Gate of the Orchards, also known as Bab al-Amara and corresponding with the Roman Gate of Mercury). This gate is a 12th century Ayyubid construction, and like Bab al-Faraj originally consisted of two parts, although today only the outer doorway along with a solitary arch of the inner doorway survives.

Continuing east from here, you reach after another 250 m **Bab as-Salaam** (Gate of Peace, corresponding with the Roman Gate of the Moon). This is the best preserved and most impressive of the Old City's gates. In its present form, the gate is once again a largely Ayyubid restoration dating from 1243, although an earlier reconstruction of the Roman original was carried out in 1172. The central arch contains within it a rectangular doorway topped by a massive lintel bearing an Arabic inscription, dedicated to the Ayyubid ruler Sultan al-Salih Ismael. On either side of the arch are large machicolations.

Pass through the gate to continue east (Bab as-Salaam is unusual in this respect in that it has an east-west alignment). For the first stretch the **Old City walls** (now to your right) are obscured by houses. But after a while the street crosses a stream (a branch of the Barada River) and runs between it and the city walls, giving you the chance to inspect them close-up. The large Roman stone blocks in the lower courses are clearly distinguishable from the smaller stones of the Arab and Turkish periods. In one place there is a column section which has been placed horizontally in the walls so that just its end is visible. The use of a Classical column to reinforce the structure of a wall in this way was a technique typical of the Crusaders, and was perhaps borrowed by the Arabs during 11th-12th century repairs to the walls.

At the end of the street you come out at **Bab Touma** (St Thomas' Gate, corresponding with the Roman Gate of Venus). Today this gate looks somewhat forlorn and dislocated, standing at the centre of a large, busy roundabout, the walls to either side having been dismantled to make way for the flow of traffic. The original Roman gate was reconstructed in 1227 during the Ayyubid period, with the Mameluke ruler Tengiz adding the machicolation in 1334. The gate takes its name from the son-in-law of the Byzantine Emperor Heraclius, Thomas, who led the resistance to the first Muslim assault on Damascus in 635. The gate gives its name to the Christian area which surrounds it, both inside and outside the walls of the Old City. The main thoroughfare running south from Bab Touma through this Christian part of the Old City intersects with Straight Street.

Damascus & around

Around the Old City

There are a number of places of interest in the immediate vicinity of the Old City. People staying in the *Al Haramain* or *Al Rabie* hotels will be familiar with the picturesque old houses and narrow streets of Bahsa/Sarouja district. Less well known, however, is the extension of Souk Sarouja Street to the east of the modern Thawra Bridge.

Following this street east from Thawra Bridge, after about 500 m there is the **Towba Mosque** on the right (see Old City map). This large mosque was formerly a khan. According to local tradition, the khan gained a reputation as a brothel before being converted to a mosque – hence the name, which translates literally as Mosque of Repentance. The side entrance to the mosque (just off Souk Sarouja Street) is framed within a honeycombed arch, with a lintel bearing an Arabic inscription above the doorway. The courtyard with its black and white stone paving is reminiscent of that of the Umayyad Mosque, particularly in terms of the façade of the prayer hall. Inside the prayer hall, the *mihrab* is particularly beautifully decorated.

If you turn right at the junction by which this mosque is situated, and then right again immediately after, this narrow lane winds its way down to Al Malek Feisal Street (if you go straight across the junction here you arrive at Bab al-Faraj). A short distance east along Al Malek Feisal Street, on the right, is **Al Mowalak Mosque**, also often referred to as the Bardabak Mosque after the prince, Bardabak al-Jaqni, who was responsible for its construction. The mosque has a beautifully decorated minaret in marble, along with an impressive honeycombed arch to the right of the main entrance.

Heading back west to Ath Thawra Street and then following it south, past the entrance to Souk Hamidiyeh, on the right after around 250 m is the **Darwish Pasha Mosque**. Built in 1574 by a governor of Damascus of the same name, the long façade of this mosque with its alternating bands of black and cream stonework is quite impressive, despite the pollution from the heavy traffic running past which has left it in desperate need of cleaning. Inside, the pleasant courtyard with its central pool and fountain provides a peaceful respite from the frenetic activity outside. The panels of blue-glazed Damascene tiles on the façade of the prayer hall are particularly beautiful. Inside the prayer hall there is more tiling and an attractive *mihrab*, although a massive, intruding chandelier spoils the overall effect somewhat. The small octagonal building attached to the mosque by an arch contains the tomb of Darwish Pasha.

Continuing south, just past the entrance to Madhat Pasha/Straight Street, on the left this time, is the **Sinan Pasha Mosque**. The mosque dates from 1590, during the reign of an Ottoman governor of Damascus, Sinan Pasha (not to be confused with the great Ottoman architect of the same name who was responsible for the Tekkiyeh as-Suleimaniyeh mosque; see below). The façade is in the alternating black and cream bands of stone typical of Mameluke and Ottoman architecture, while the minaret is clad in distinctive green and turquoise glazed stone. Inside, there is once again a peaceful, shady courtyard and more panels of beautiful Damascene tiling in the arcades around the courtyard.

Just south of the Sinan Pasha Mosque, the road forks. Bearing right to head in a southerly direction, you are on Qasr al-Hajjaj Street, which becomes Midan Street a bit further south. Although now somewhat swamped by modern development, this axis represents the once distinct **Midan Quarter** which extended south for several kilometres. Its significance lay in the fact that this was the route taken by pilgrims as they set off from the Old City on the *Hajj*, or pilgrimage to Mecca. As such, it developed over the centuries into an important thoroughfare lined by numerous mosques, mausoleums, religious schools, baths and other amenities catering for the pilgrims. The monuments strung out along this route are today in a somewhat dilapidated condition, and only for the really dedicated sightseer.

Bearing left at the junction just south of the Sinan Pasha Mosque to follow the line of the Old City walls, you pass through **Souk Sinaniye** with its stores selling sheepskins. Bearing left at the next fork, you are in Badawi Street which heads east, passing on the left the **Bab as-Saghir** gate to the Old City (literally 'Little Gate', corresponding with the Roman Gate of Mars). The large stone blocks of the Roman foundations can still be seen, though the rest of the gate is a combination of Nur ud-Din's 12th century reconstruction and later Ayyubid work.

To the southeast is the Muslim **Bab as-Saghir Cemetery**, an important place of pilgrimage for Shi'ites who come to visit two of the tombs there. One is the **Tomb of Fatima**, daughter of the Prophet and wife of Ali. The other is the **Tomb of Sukeina**, the daughter of Hussein and great-grand-daughter of the Prophet. Most scholars agree that these are unlikely to be the genuine tombs of these two figures, but the tradition persists, attracting large numbers of Shi'ites from Iran. To enter, follow Al Jarrah Street, which branches southwest off Badawi Street and runs through the centre of the cemetery; a gate on the left gives access to the southern half of the cemetery containing the two tombs.

Modern Damascus

In many ways, modern Damascus is just like any other large capital city the world over, with it congestion, pollution and faceless concrete high-rise developments. At the same time, however, it does manage to retain a certain Syrian feel to it in places. This is particularly true of the area round Martyrs' Square, where the hawkers, market stalls and hole-in-the-wall restaurants selling roasted half-chickens and falafel or shawarma sandwiches leave you in no doubt that this is an Arab capital. Heading for the commercial districts around Yousef al-Azmeh Square, the bland uniformity of airline offices, expensive hotels and shops selling fancy designer goods starts to assert itself more strongly. By the time you get out to the districts such as Abou Roumaneh, where the foreign embassies have made their home amidst affluent, fashionable residential areas, there is little to remind you that this is not Europe or America.

There is no doubt that the Old City and its environs are the main focus of historical interest in Damascus, but the modern city has its important monuments and places of interest too. The most notable of these are the Tekkiyeh as-Suleimaniyeh complex and the National Museum, next to each other on the south bank of the Barada River, just to the south of the busy east-west thoroughfare of Shoukri al-Kouwatli Street.

Tekkiyeh as-Suleimaniyeh Complex

This large complex includes a mosque, the grounds of which now also house a military museum and a madrassa with a handicrafts market. The mosque was built by Sinan Pasha, the great Ottoman architect (most famous for the Suleimaniye Mosque in Istanbul), in honour of the Sultan Suleiman I (Suleiman the Magnificent, 1520-1566). Its purpose was to provide an alternative starting point for the annual pilgrimage to Mecca, the organization of which was traditionally the responsibility of the governor of Damascus.

From the arched entrance by the Tourist Information office a pedestrian street lined with jewellery and antique shops leads to the main mosque. Half way down on the left is the entrance to the old **Madrassa as-Selimiyeh**. This was actually a later addition, built during the reign of Suleiman's successor, Sultan Sleim II (1566-74) by another architect. The courtyard, with its subsided and uneven floor of black and white stone slabs and central fountain and pool, is rather atmospheric, with an slightly dilapidated charm about it. The surrounding arcade of arches and small domed rooms would once have housed religious students but is now given over to various handicrafts: inlaid woodwork, brass, copper and silverware, embroidered fabrics, paintings, carpets, musical instruments etc. In a small yard off the main courtyard traditional glassmaking is practised and you can watch the skilled craftsmen blowing glass in front of a blazing furnace even in the height of summer.

Damascus centre

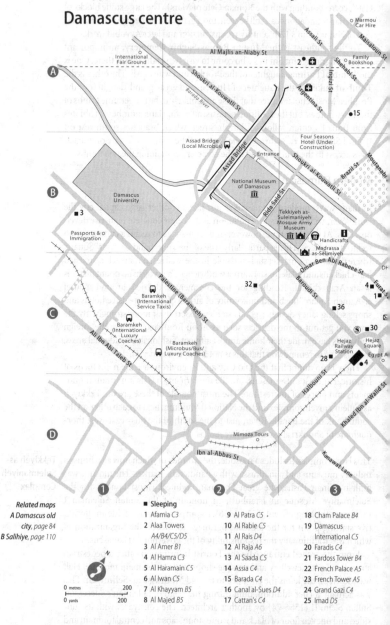

Related maps
A Damascus old
city, page 84
B Salihiye, page 110

0 metres — 200
0 yards — 200

■ Sleeping
1 Afamia C3
2 Alaa Towers A4/B4/C5/D5
3 Al Amer B1
4 Al Hamra C3
5 Al Haramain C5
6 Al Iwan C5
7 Al Khayyam B5
8 Al Majed B5

9 Al Patra C5
10 Al Rabie C5
11 Al Rais D4
12 Al Raja A6
13 Al Saada C5
14 Assia C4
15 Barada C4
16 Canal al-Sues D4
17 Cattan's C4

18 Cham Palace B4
19 Damascus International C5
20 Faradis C4
21 Fardoss Tower B4
22 French Palace A5
23 French Tower A5
24 Grand Gazi C4
25 Imad D5

The **Tekkiyeh as-Suleimaniyeh Mosque**, although not particularly grand in terms of its size, is a wonderful gem of Ottoman architecture. The mosque itself is clearly Turkish in inspiration, with its domed prayer hall and pointed, rocket-like minarets rising up on either side. The doorway of the prayer hall is decorated with honeycombing and delicately carved stalactites, while inside there is beautiful glazed blue and white tiling in the arches above the windows and doors. The courtyard in front of the mosque is more typically Syrian in

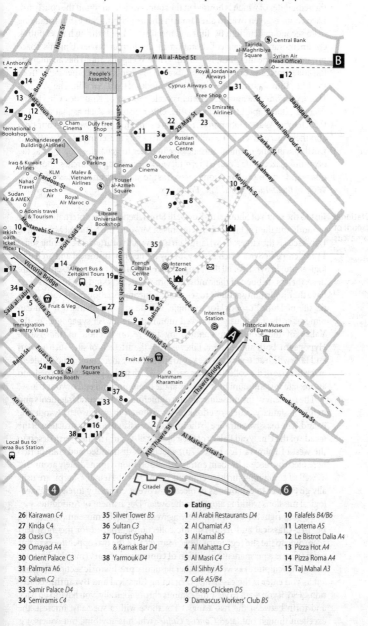

design, with its black and white stone slabs and large central pool and fountain. Surrounding it on three sides are rooms originally meant to house the pilgrims preparing for the *Hajj*. Unfortunately, the various MIG fighter jets, tanks and other items of military hardware dotted around the shady gardens of the compound clash incongruously with the spacious tranquility of this beautifully proportioned piece of architecture.

These odd intrusions represent part of the collection of the **Army Museum**, the remainder of which is housed in the rooms which surround the courtyard. Each room is given over to a separate theme or period, with exhibits ranging from second millennium BC flint and metal arrowheads through to a Sputnik commemorating Syrian collaboration in the former Soviet Union's space programme. The inexplicably named 'White Weapons' room has an interesting collection of swords, daggers, sabres, body armour and other items from the 12th-18th centuries, as well as a scale-model of Qalat Saladin. The 'Ancient History Room', meanwhile, contains scale-models of Krak des Chevaliers, Aleppo Citadel and Damascus Citadel. Other displays, such as that found in the 'October War of Liberation' room, are something of a waste of your time and their space. Even if the military theme of this museum puts you off, it is worth paying the nominal entrance fee in order to get a close-up look at the beautiful glazed blue floral pattern tilework decorating the arches above the doors and windows of the rooms, as well as the fine black and white stonework.

■ *Open 0800-1400, closed Tue. Entry S£5.*

National Museum of Damascus

If you are starting out on your travels from Damascus, it is worth thinking about the places you intend to visit and relating them to the things you can see here at the museum

Just to the south of Shoukri al-Kouwatli Street, between the International Fair grounds and the Tekkiyeh as-Suleimaniyeh Mosque, the National Museum of Damascus is the largest in Syria and boasts a wealth of artefacts covering some 11 millennia of Syria's rich history. Many of the great historical and archaeological sites in Syria, for all their importance and often spectacular settings, are nevertheless stripped of their most important artefacts, and it is here that you have the opportunity actually to see them. Your appreciation of the vast majestic site of Dura Europos, for example, will be greatly enhanced if you can remember the fabulously preserved murals of the Jewish synagogue, or the Valley of the Tombs in Palmyra by the reconstruction of the Yarhai Hypogeum, both housed here. Likewise, it is the artefacts of sites such as Mari and Ebla which actually hold the key to appreciating their significance. Indeed, given the size of the collection, it is perhaps worth making two visits in order to appreciate this museum fully, ideally at the beginning and end of your trip.

The gardens of the museum contain numerous architectural fragments and items of statuary, often overlooked by visitors but well worth wandering round. The massive entrance to the museum consists of a reconstruction of the façade of the Umayyad Palace of Qasr al-Heir al-Gharbi in the Syrian desert to the west of Palmyra (see page 170), which was dismantled and transported here piece by piece. The main entrance hall and rooms immediately around it, as well as containing further remnants from Qasr al-Heir al-Gharbi, are usually given over to exhibitions of recent discoveries made by foreign archaeological missions working alongside the Syrian Department of Antiquities.

To your right as you enter is the long west wing of the museum, containing the **pre-Classical** and **Arab-Islamic** collections, grouped for the most part according to the site (eg Ugarit, Ebla, Mari etc). In the two upper floors of this wing there is a permanent exhibition of **contemporary art** (mostly paintings and some sculpture) as well as a rather desultory **pre-historic** section. To your left as you enter is the east wing, containing **Classical** and **Byzantine** collections. (So, if you want to view the exhibits chronologically, you have to go back and forth between the two wings.) For those with a specialist interest, the excellent though outdated *Concise Guide* (which is anything but concise) is usually on sale at the ticket office (though it periodically sells out and the process of ordering another print run is painfully slow). Alternatively, if there is an organized group receiving a guided tour it is worth tagging along. Otherwise it is really a case of exploring and discovering as best you can for yourself.

Overall, the labelling is pretty appalling, given that this is Syria's most important museum. For the most part, the best you can expect is a couple of lines telling you which period each exhibit dates from and where it originates. Other than the display boards in the main entrance hall, there is nothing in the way of explanatory or interpretative texts. However, that said, some more detailed plaques have started to appear in the pre-Classical section giving decent explanations and interpretations of the exhibits, perhaps heralding a more comprehensive overhaul of the museum's presentation.

It is not possible to give a detailed commentary on so formidable a collection here, but there are certain collections/reconstructions which do deserve a special mention. Probably the most famous aspect of the museum is the reconstruction of the mid-third century AD **Dura Europos Synagogue** at the far end of the east wing, across a small courtyard. Discovered at the site of Dura Europos (see page 385) in the 1930s, the synagogue is unique in that its walls were decorated with frescos depicting scenes from the Old Testament, including human representations – something which goes against all Talmudic traditions. Equally remarkable is the fact that these frescos should be so well preserved (because they were buried under sand). The walls of the synagogue consist of the original frescos, much faded by time but still extremely impressive. The ceiling is a reconstruction of the original, with its painted wooden beams. The synagogue is sometimes kept locked (if so, ask an attendant to open it up). It is unlit and receives little natural light (in order to protect the frescos) so it takes a while for your eyes to adjust to the gloom.

Immediately before the courtyard leading to the synagogue, a flight of stairs leads down to the early second century **Hypogeum of Yarhai** from the Valley of the Tombs in Palmyra. The hypogeum (underground burial chamber) is reconstructed from the original, giving an excellent insight into what these underground tombs would have originally looked like, with the compartment-shelves for sarcophagi built into the walls and sealed by funerary busts, while at the end of the main chamber to the right is the *triclinium*, where a funeral banquet would have been held. The hypogeum is also sometimes locked.

Statue of Iku Shamagon, king of Mari

Returning to ground level, stairs also lead up from here to the first floor and the **Salle de Hommes**. This contains an impressive collection of jewellery and coins, including iron and gold funerary masks discovered near Homs and dating from the first century AD. ■ *Open 0900-1800 in summer (1/4-30/9), and 0900-1600 in winter (1/10-31/3), closed Tue. Entry S£300 (students S£15). There is a wide range of books, postcards and souvenirs on sale in the ticket office, and an excellent series of 10 small posters of some of the more important artefacts from different*

At the time of writing, this section was being refurbished. It is usually kept locked, but is well worth a visit

periods of Syria's history (very good value at S£50 each). Note that cameras cannot be taken into the museum. There is a pleasant, though expensive, open-air café in the grounds.

Hejaz railway station

Completed in 1917, the Hejaz railway station marks the terminus of the famous railway line that ran from Damascus to Medina. The brain-child of the Ottoman Sultan Abdul Hamid II (1876-1909), the main purpose of the railway was to facilitate the passage of pilgrims undertaking the *Hajj* to Mecca. However, with the outbreak of the First World War, it became a vital transport and communications link for the Ottoman and German forces, leading to concerted attempts by the Allies to blow it up.

The interior of the building is worth inspecting, with its beautifully decorated wooden ceiling and balcony running around the main hall, and its large silver chandelier. Outside there is a steam engine on display, dating from 1908. The station is only used today for services to the hill stations northwest of Damascus, as well as the twice-weekly service to Amman. On one of the platforms, the old wooden carriages of the private train of the last Ottoman Sultan, Abdul Hameed, have been converted into a restaurant and bar.

Historical Museum of Damascus

The display rooms are kept locked but will be opened for you by the caretaker, who expects a little baksheesh for his troubles

Little visited by tourists, this museum occupies the large **Beit Khalid al-Azem** (the palace of a former prime minister, Khalid al-Azem). The extensive complex is divided into a northern section which houses the museum, and a southern section which houses an important archive of historical documents not officially open to the public. From the entrance on the north side of the palace, a small initial courtyard leads through to the main courtyard, dotted with trees and shrubs, and with a fountain and pool on one side. This was the private family area of the palace (the *haramlek*). A large *iwan* occupies part of one wall, while the various rooms around the courtyard contain the museum's exhibits. The quality of the decoration in the rooms is superb, easily matching that of the more famous Azem Palace in the Old City. Lavishly carved marble-work and intricately decorated wood panelling adorn the walls and ceilings and there are numerous items of inlaid wood furniture. One room contains an intriguing fountain, fashioned from stone into something that resembles a water-maze and was used for games. Another room contains large scale models of the Old City, Salihiye district and various buildings and complexes around Damascus, as well as an interesting collection of old photographs.

A doorway at the end of the passage to the left of the *iwan* leads through to the southern half of the complex. This represents the public visitors' areas (the *salemlek*) and consists of a series of three courtyards. This is where the archive is housed and, although it is not officially open to the public, it is often possible to wander through and admire the impressive exterior decoration of the courtyards and rooms. If you do make it through to here, you can exit via the south door which leads out onto the eastern extension of Souk Sarouja Street.

■ *Open 0800-1400, closed Fri. Entry S£150 (students S£10). The entrance to the musuem is set back from Ath Thawra Street just to the north of Thawra Bridge, via an arched gateway in the parking area of a government building.*

Hammams

As well as being wonderful places to relax and unwind after a hard day's sightseeing, many of them are historically and architecturally fascinating buildings

Damascus has numerous hammams (Turkish Baths) dotted around the city (especially in the Old City). The most famous, and the most impressive, south of the Umayyad Mosque, in Souk Bazuriye, is the **Hammam Nur ud-Din** (see page 95), T2229513. Open 0800-2400 daily. Full package S£300 (including soap, sponge, abrasive cleaner, tea etc), steam bath S£125, massage S£70, sauna S£50. Men only. Less grand, though still very nice is **Hammam al-Bakri**, near Bab Touma, T5426606. Open 0900-2400 daily. Full package

S£190, steam bath S£100, massage S£50. Men only, but groups of women can book the whole baths for S£1,000 per hour, plus S£100 extra per massage. In a similar vein is **Hammam Silsila** (or 'Al Selselah Roman Baths'), T2220279. Open 0900-2300 daily. Full works S£200, steam bath S£100, massage S£50. Aside from booking the whole of the Hammam al-Bakri as part of a group, **women** can also try the **Hammam Zein**, near Bab al-Jabiye, which holds women-only sessions from 1200-1800 daily.

Just outside the Old City, in a beautiful old building on Souk Sarouja Street, to the east of Thawra Bridge, is the **Al Khanji Hammam**, T2314192. Open 0900-2300 daily. Full package S£200, steam bath S£100, massage S£50. By the vegetable market off Al Ittihad Street is the modern **Hammam Kharamain**, T2217483. Open 0800-2400 daily. Full package S£150, steam bath S£75, staff speak Arabic only.

Located in Abou Roumaneh district, on Adnan Malki Square, this tiny museum is rarely visited by tourists and, realistically, it is only worth doing so if you are in the area anyway (perhaps collecting a permit for Quneitra) and have time on your hands. It consists of just one room, dedicated to the 'martyr' Adnan Malki; his blood-stained shirt, the gun used to shoot him, a commentary written in English about him, photographs from this period and other bits of memorabilia.

Adnan Malki Museum

A lieutenant colonel, Malki was a leading Ba'athist and one of the most powerful figures in the Syrian army. He was assassinated in April 1955 by another member of the Syrian army as part of the Syrian Social Nationalist Party's (SSNPs) failed attempt to overthrow the Syrian government of the time. The Ba'ath and the SSNP were serious rivals for power during the 1950s, although after the failed coup attempt the SSNP were banned in Syria, while the Ba'ath took the opportunity to consolidate their position and thereafter rose to prominence. Ironically, following the failure of the United Arab Republic, the ideologies of the two, already in many respects closely parallel, converged even more. Although the SSNP remains banned in Syria to this day, it developed close links with Assad's Ba'athist regime from its base in Lebanon and became an important ally and instrument of Assad's regime during the Lebanese civil war. ■ *Open 0900-1400, closed Tue. Entry free.*

Salihiye/Al Charkasiye district

Most of the monuments in this district are concentrated along Madares Assad ud-Din Lane. Generally closed to the public, you can admire their façades from outside. The lane is lively and atmospheric; full of vegetable stalls by day and shops serving fuul and hummus at outside tables by night.The approach to this district, northwest of the city centre, is through areas dominated by modern development. However, as you reach the lower, more gentle slopes of Mount Kassioun, the streets begin to get narrower and the layout less regular.

This area was first settled during the mid-12th century when Hanbalite refugees, fleeing in the wake of the Crusader occupation of Jerusalem, were housed here by Nur ud-Din, who was keen to keep them separate from the rival Shaffi school which was predominant within the walled city. It then began to absorb the overspill from the walled city and with time became a well regarded district in its own right, inspiring many members of the ruling class to build mausoleums, mosques and *madrassas* in the area.

Damascus & around

Mohi ud-Din Mosque Roughly halfway along Mardares Assad ud-Din Lane, this mosque is open to the public and has a particularly beautiful Mameluke-style octagonal minaret. The mosque dates from the early 16th century and was built over the 13th-century burial chamber of the famous Sufi mystic, Mohi ud-Din Ibn al-Arabi. It remains an important pilgrimage site for Sufis. Inside, to your left as you face the prayer hall, a flight of steps leads down to a domed chamber decorated with glazed blue and white tiles which houses the tomb of Al Arabi. His tomb is the largest, contained within a silver grill surrounded by glass. The four other tombs in the chamber are of two of his sons (the double-tomb); Sheikh Mohammad Kharbutli, a devoted follower of Al Arabi; Mahmoud Pasha Sirri al-Khunaji, a son-in-law of an Egyptian Khedive; and Abd al-Kader al-Jazairi, a famous Algerian patriot who resisted the French occupation of his country before finally being exiled to Damascus.

Hanbala Mosque To the east of Mohi ud-Din Mosque, in a side street north off Madares Assad ud-Din Lane, this mosque dates from the early 13th century and was founded

Salihiye

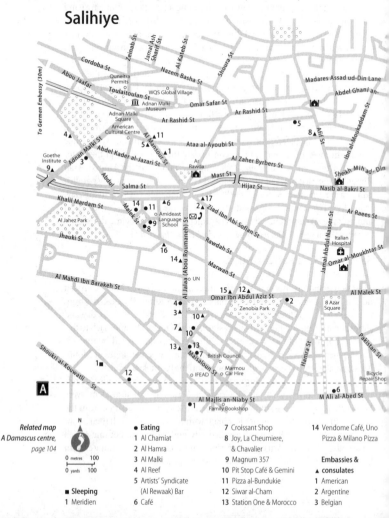

by Sheikh Omar Mohammad al-Maqdisi, the leader of the Hanbalite refugees from Jerusalem. Enclosed within unassuming (and easily missed) walls, the mosque interestingly has six classical columns in its courtyard.

Mount Kassioun

Rising steeply to the northwest of Damascus is Mount Kassioun (1200 m), a bare, dry ridge of mountain which dominates the city on this side and provides a useful point of orientation. The mountain has a number of legends attached to it. A mosque built over a cave on the eastern slopes of the mountain, near the town of Barzeh (on the road to Saidnaya) is believed to mark the birthplace of Abraham. Most famously, it was from the summit of Mount Kassioun that Mohammad is said to have looked down on Damascus, not daring to enter this oasis of gardens and streams lest its earthly delights distracted him from his quest for heavenly paradise.

At night, the densely populated lower slopes of the mountain make a beautiful twinkling backdrop to the city

There are several good vantage points on its lower slopes which can be

reached via the narrow lanes which lead off to the north from Madares Assad ud-Din Street in Salihiye district. But the best views out over Damascus are from the top, reached via a road which hairpins its way up the mountain. In summer there are various cafés and stalls close to the summit where tourists and Damascenes alike come to enjoy the cooler air and take in the panorama of the city spread out below: today a sprawling urban mass which is a far cry from the paradise of greenery said to have so impressed Mohammad, but nevertheless an impressive sight. The best times to come up here are late afternoon for sunset over the city, and at night when it is lit up in all its glory.

■ *There is no public transport to the summit; unless you have your own transport, you must take a taxi, in which case you are advised to negotiate a return trip since there is little traffic along this road.*

Saida Zeinab Mosque

This large mosque, 10 km to the south of central Damascus, like the Saida Ruqqiyeh Mosque in the Old City, is an important place of pilgrimage for Shi'ite Muslims. It is also similar to its counterpart in the Old City in that it is relatively modern, Iranian-built and equally bright and colourful in its decoration. The huge square courtyard features towering circular

If you are not a Muslim, you will generally not be allowed inside the prayer hall of the mosque, but you can get a good view from the courtyard outside

4	British
5	Chinese
6	Czech
7	Egyptian
8	French
9	Indian
10	Indonesian
11	Italian
12	Japanese
13	Jordanian
14	Netherlands
15	Portuguese
16	Saudi Arabian
17	Turkish

Damascus & around

minarets in two corners and a large gold-domed prayer hall in the centre. Practically every wall surface, including the entire height of the minarets, is decorated with boldly coloured glazed tiles bearing riotous floral patterns or elegant *Qur'anic* calligraphy. The overall effect is very striking indeed. Inside the prayer hall, the decoration is even more exuberant, with patterned mirror-work complementing the coloured glazed tile-work. In the centre of the prayer hall is the **tomb of Saida Zeinab**, the granddaughter of Mohammad and brother of the Shi'ite martyr Hussein (there is another mosque of the same name in Cairo which also lays claim to being the burial place of Saida Zeinab). The tomb is protected by a silver grille and is almost invariably surrounded by crowds of pilgrims seeking her blessings or intervention. ■ *A taxi to the mosque will cost around S£200-300 one way, depending on your bargaining powers. To get there by microbus ('servees'), take one from Fakhri al-Baroudi St to 'Garagat al-Sitt' (in the southern suburbs of Damascus), and change there for Saida Zeinab Mosque ('Jamiaat Saida Zeinab'). You can also catch the airport bus from outside the Kairawan hotel by Victoria Bridge; you need to get off where it turns off the ring road around Damascus, and pick up a microbus from there. Alternatively, the mosque is right on the road to Suweida (see the 'South of Damascus' chapter), so you could stop off on the way back from there.*

Essentials

Sleeping

■ *on maps, pages 84, 104 & 110*
Price codes: see inside front cover
Phone code: 011

NB Although on the whole hotel prices remain stable through the year, in some hotels, particularly around Martyrs' Sq, summer is the 'high' season, with lots of Saudi Arabian and Gulf state tourists arriving in Damascus and prices increasing accordingly. Likewise, during winter significant discounts can be found amongst some of the **C** category hotels. Where relevant, hotels have been categorized below according to their high season tariffs. Price categories also take account of the 10% tax usually added to the bill in **LL-C** category hotels; be sure to check whether the price you are quoted includes this tax. Bear in mind also that, as throughout Syria, in all but the cheapest hotels you will be expected to pay in US dollars; once you get down to **D** category and below, hotel managers can usually be persuaded to accept Syrian pounds, while in **F-G** categories this is the norm.

LL *Cham Palace*, Maisaloun St, PO Box 7570, T2232300, F2212398, www.chamhotels.com Comfortable, recently refurbished rooms with a/c, TV/dish, IDD, minibar and attached bath. 5 restaurants (see 'Eating') and also *Café Brésil*, 2 bars, and *Jet Set* disco. Full conference/banquet facilities and business centre. Swimming pool, squash, health centre, shopping arcade, travel agent (*Chamtour*), car hire (*Hertz/Chamcar*), 24 hr currency exchange. All very luxurious (a cut above the others in this price range), and centrally located. Recommended. **LL** *Meridien*, Shoukri al-Kouwatli St, PO Box 5531, T3738730, F3738661. Choice of 'superior' or 'non renovated' rooms, each with a/c, TV/dish, IDD, minibar, safe-deposit box, attached bath and balcony. 'Superior' rooms suitably luxurious; 'non renovated' rooms rather 1970s in style. Also 'VIP superior' and 'Royal Club' rooms. 5 restaurants and *Le Gourmet* café/patisserie, *Al Menchieh* café, *L'Oasis* bar and disco. Full conference/banquet facilities and business centre. Swimming pool, tennis, shopping arcade, travel agent (*Transtour*), car hire (*Europcar*), CBS bank for foreign exchange and *Air France* office. Lobby often exhibits paintings by local artists. **LL** *Sheraton*, Umawiyeen Sq, PO Box 4795, T2229300, F2243607, www.sheraton.com Comfortable rooms with a/c, TV/dish, IDD, minibar, attached bath. 5 restaurants and *Al Nairabein* café, *Salsabil* lobby bar and *The Pub*. Conference/banquet facilities, business centre, large outdoor swimming pool, tennis courts, shopping arcade, CBS bank for foreign exchange, travel agents, car hire (*Falcon* and *Europcar*). High standards of service, though not such a great location.

L *Semiramis*, Victoria Bridge, PO Box 30301, T2233555, F2216797, semirams@ net.sy Well appointed rooms with a/c, TV/dish, IDD, minibar, safe box, trouser press and attached bath. 4 restaurants and *Mandalon* bar and *Johno* 'super' nightclub (ie floor show). Conference/banquet facilities, business centre, small rooftop indoor swimming pool and health centre, shopping arcade, travel agent, car hire (*Europcar*). Centrally located, well run and comparatively good value for the level of facilities (small discounts outside Jun-Sep high season).

AL *Fardoss Tower*, off Maisaloun St, PO Box 30996, T2232100, F2235602, www.fardosstower.com A/c, TV/dish, IDD, minibar, attached bath. Restaurant (including open air terrace), bar and disco. Conference/banquet facilities, shopping, travel agent. Very posh lobby, but rooms themselves are rather functional and nondescript. **AL** *Omayad*, Brazil St, PO Box 7811, T2217700, F2213516, omayad_hotel@ net.sy Spacious rooms with a/c, TV/dish, IDD, fridge, trouser press, attached bath and small balcony. 3 restaurants, bar, roof terrace, nightclub planned, car hire (*Europcar*). Comfortable and tastefully furnished, centrally located, good value.

A *Damascus International*, off Yousef al-Azmeh St, PO Box 5068, T2311600, F2319966. Recently refurbished rooms with a/c, TV/dish, phone, fridge and attached bath. Restaurant, bar, disco, conference hall, shopping and travel agent. Discounts of around 10% readily available (bringing it into **B** category), but still overpriced, with the rooms only marginally better than those in some **C** category hotels. **A** *Faradis*, off Martyrs' Sq, T2246546, F2247009. Unremarkable rooms with a/c, TV/dish, phone, fridge and attached bath. Restaurant (11th floor), bar and roof terrace. Occupies the 8th-12th floors of a large tower block overlooking Martyr's Sq; the views are good but other than that it's pretty uninspiring and way overpriced.

B *Al Amer*, off Palestine (Baramkeh) St, T2116600, F2128889, alamerhotel@ net.sy Comfortable, spacious rooms with a/c, TV/dish, IDD, kitchenette area (sink, hob, fridge) and attached bath. Restaurant, café, business centre, shop, hairdresser. Not a prime location, but excellent value in terms of the quality of facilities (a much better deal than both the **A** category hotels above, and on a par with the **AL** category ones). Well run, helpful staff. Recommended.

B/C *Al Iwan*, Yousef al-Azmeh St, PO Box 6753, T2321476, F2315224. Small but comfortable rooms with a/c, TV/dish, phone, fridge and attached bath. Restaurant. Official prices make it an overpriced **B** category, but rooms generally available at slightly more reasonable **C** category rates. **B/C** *Al Majed*, off 29 May St, PO Box 13152, T2323300, F2323304. Comfortable rooms with a/c, fan, TV/dish, phone, fridge and attached bath. Attractive top floor restaurant. A striking hotel, lavishly decorated throughout with marble floors and traditional Arabic designs. Spotlessly clean, well run, friendly and good value, with reduced rates in low season (1/10- 31/6) making it one of the best deals in Damascus. Recommended. Opposite is the *Al Khayyam*, under the same management, which is identical in terms of the décor and facilities, except that the rooms are very small and consequently priced at **C/D** category rates in the high/low season.

C *Alaa Tower*, T/F2311221 (reservations and Branch 1). There are a total of 4 hotels in this chain – all with same name – dotted around the centre of Damascus (see map). All have a/c, TV/dish, phone, fridge and attached bath. Unremarkable but comfortable and reasonably good value. The better branches are No 1 (opposite the French Cultural Centre) and No 5 Brazil St (opposite the *Omayad* hotel). **C** *Al Boustan*, Basha Ibn Bourd St (opposite tourist information centre), T2224792, F2243468. A/c, TV/dish, phone, fridge, attached bath. Restaurant. Rather nondescript, but reasonable value. **C** *Al Patra*, Al Ittihad St, T2315914, F2315918. Reasonable rooms with a/c, TV/dish, phone, fridge and attached bath. Restaurant. Clean and fairly good value, though nothing to get too excited about. **C** *Assia*, Port Said St, T2314100, F2314101. Reasonable rooms with a/c, phone, fridge and attached bath. Restaurant. Fairly good value but often booked up by tour groups. **C** *Cattan's*, off Barada St, T2215785, F2212514. A/c, TV, phone, fridge, attached bath. Roof terrace area. Some rooms spacious with balcony, but building as a whole rather old and run-down. **C** *French Palace*, 29 May St, T2314015, F2314002. A/c, TV/dish, phone, soft minibar, attached bath. Newly opened place, spotlessly clean and furnished to a high standard, though the rooms are very small (and in some cases windowless). **C** *French Tower*, 29 May St, T2314000, F2314002. Clean, pleasant rooms with a/c, TV/dish, phone and attached bath. Some rooms with balcony. A little on the expensive side during the high season (Jul-Oct), but good value the rest of the year. **C** *Kairawan*, Victoria Bridge, T2313338, F2313343. A/c, TV/dish, fridge, phone, attached bath. Restaurant. Rooms rather run-down and in need of refurbishment. **C** *Kinda*, Al Ittihad St, T2319760, F2317438. A/c, TV/dish, phone, fridge, attached bath. Restaurant. Could do with some refurbishment but a reasonable deal. **C** *Orient Palace*, Hejaz Sq, T2231351, F2211512. Large, high ceiling rooms with a/c, TV, phone, fridge and attached bath. Some rooms have large balconies. Restaurant. Pleasant old building with grand reception and plenty of character, though a fraction on the expensive side for the quality of facilities. **C** *Samir Palace*, Martyrs' Sq, T2219502. Comfortable rooms with a/c, TV/dish, phone, fridge and attached bath. A recent refurbishment makes this hotel good value for the quality of facilities. Probably the best of the many in this category to be found around Martyr's Sq.

D *Afamia*, Furat St (behind Central Post Office), T2229152, F2214683. Choice of new rooms with a/c, TV/dish, phone, fridge and attached bath (very good value), or old rooms with fan, TV, phone, fridge and attached bath (rather more basic and not such great value). Unassuming but pleasant hotel in a relatively quiet location. **D** *Barada*, Said al-Jabri St, T2212546. Simple, clean rooms with fan, TV/dish, phone, fridge and attached bath. Pleasant, well kept old building. Good value off-season, when the absence of a/c is not a problem. **D** *Fursan*, Bab Touma St, PO Box 6400, T5421949. Clean, comfortable rooms with a/c, fan, phone, fridge and attached bath. Friendly, family-run place. Good value. Many of the foreigners studying Arabic at Damascus university live in this Christian area of the city. From a tourist's point of view, it is convenient for the Old City, but a long way from the commercial centre and attractions such as the National Museum. **D** *Imad*, Martyrs' Sq, T2314225. A/c, fan, TV/dish, phone, fridge, attached bath, balcony. Simple but reasonably clean. **D** *Silver Tower*, Souk Sarouja St, off Yousef al-Azmeh St, T2319518, F2315433. Clean, pleasant rooms with a/c, fan, TV, phone, fridge and attached bath. Restaurant. Quiet location, well run, good value. Recommended. **D** *Salam*, off Baroudi St, T2216674, F2215031. Comfortable, spotlessly clean rooms with a/c, TV/dish, phone, fridge and attached bath. Looks very unassuming from the outside, but this small hotel is actually excellent value. It may not boast a restaurant, bar or other such facilities, but the rooms themselves are on a par with (or even better than) many **C** category hotels. Recommended. **D** *Sultan*, Baroudi St, PO Box 221, T2225768, F2240372. Clean rooms with a/c, phone and attached bath (some slightly cheaper rooms with shared bath, and some rooms with fan only). Popular with foreign tourists, not so much for the facilities (it's actually relatively expensive for what you get), but for the quality of the service. A well run place with extremely helpful management (English, French, German spoken), able to arrange car hire, tours, etc. Advance booking essential in Mar/Apr, plus Jul-Oct, and advisable at other times. Recommended.

D/E *Tourist* (*Syaha*), Martyrs' Square, T2224890. A/c, fan, TV/dish, phone, attached bath, balcony. Rather shabby and run-down. **D/E** *Yarmouk*, off Martyrs' Sq, T2213283. Fan, TV, fridge, phone, attached bath, balcony. Rooms clean but small, and a little pricy, given the absence of a/c. **E** *Al Hamra*, Furat St (behind Central Post Office), T2210717. A/c, fan, TV, phone, fridge, attached bath. A little shabby and run-down. **E** *Palmyra*, 29 May St, T2318087. Fan, TV, phone, fridge, attached bath and balcony. Rather grotty, rooms at front very noisy. **F** *Canal al-Sues* (as in 'Suez'), off Martyrs' Square, T2222101. Simple but clean rooms with fan, TV, fridge, phone and attached bath. OK value at S£500 for a double, but in the high season you may have to bargain them down. **F** *Oasis*, 4th floor, Halbouni St, T2227724. Simple rooms with fan, phone and attached bath (double S£500). A little shabby and run-down, but passable.

Budget By far the best budget options in Damascus are the *Al Haramain* and *Al Rabie* hotels, close by to each other on a lovely vine-shaded pedestrian street down some steps off Ittihad St. Both are great places to meet other travellers, and have good travellers' information books. However, with the numbers of people visiting Syria steadily increasing, they are often full, so either book ahead or be prepared to make do with other cheapies. There are dozens of cheap hotels around Martyrs' Sq, particularly along and between the streets leading off towards the Citadel and Old City. However, this is the red light district of Damascus and many of these cheap hotels (and some of the more expensive ones in this area) are in fact brothels where they will either turn you away or try very hard to set you up with more than just a bed. The other budget options listed here are OK in this respect. **G** *Al Haramain*, Bahsa St, Souk Sarouja, T2319489, F2314299. A beautiful old Ottoman house, complete with (covered) courtyard and fountain, is the setting for this small but extremely popular backpackers' hostel. Dormitory beds (fan, share shower/toilet) cost S£185, and there are also some single and double rooms (S£235/395). Clean, well run, friendly and helpful. Cosy in winter. Booking essential in Mar/Apr, plus Jul-Oct, and advisable at other times. Recommended. **G** *Al Rabie*, Bahsa St, Souk Sarouja, T2318374, F2311875. Set in another beautiful old Ottoman house complete with courtyard and fountain. Dormitory beds (fan, share shower/toilet) cost S£175, or you can sleep on a mattress on a covered roof area for S£150 (an excellent option in summer). Single/double rooms cost S£250/375, and there are also a couple of doubles/trebles with attached bath (S£600/675). Well run, friendly and helpful. Distinctly shabbier than the *Al Haramain* , but with a great atmosphere of its own, and a larger and nicer courtyard which is blissfully cool and shady in summer. Booking essential in Mar/Apr, plus Jul-Oct, and advisable at other times. Recommended. **G** *Al Rais* (or *Al Raess*), off Martyrs' Sq, T2214252. Simple but clean rooms with fan, TV and fridge. Some rooms with attached bath. Double S£400. Friendly staff. One of the better budget options in the vicinity of Martyrs' Sq, and a reasonable option if the *Al Haramain* and *Al Rabie* hotels are full. **G** *Al Raja*, Baghdad St, T4440616. Simple but clean rooms with fan and sink, share shower/toilet (double S£350). Also some rooms with attached bath (double S£400). Hot shower extra (S£35). Clean, friendly, well run place. A good alternative option if the *Al Haramain* and *Al Rabie* hotels are full, though not as centrally located. **G** *Al Saada*, off Souk Sarouja St, T2311722, F2311875. Basic rooms with fan and shared shower/toilet. S£175 per bed. Also a couple of doubles with attached bath (S£325). A much smaller version of the *Al Rabie* hotel (and owned by the same family), with rooms around tiny courtyard shaded by creepers. Pleasant and quiet, but basic. **G** *Grand Gazi*, Furat St (just off Martyrs' Sq), T2214581. Simple rooms with fan, TV, phone and attached bath (double S£375). Basic and a bit dingy, but passable.

Eating

● on maps,
pages 84, 104 & 110

Damascus has a huge range of restaurants and eateries, offering perhaps the best choice in the country. Restaurants have been grouped below according location and price range. Prices per head are obviously only very approximate guides. Unless otherwise stated, they have been calculated to include any taxes, but not alcohol. If you stick to vegetarian dishes you can usually reduce the overall bill significantly.

Old City
In recent years a number
of restaurants have
opened in beautifully
restored tradtional
Damascene houses

There is an excellent selection of restaurants located within the Old City (convenient after a hard day's sightseeing, or for a well earned break at lunchtime), ranging from very expensive and luxurious establishments to more reasonable and, in some cases, very good value places.

Expensive *Casablanca*, Hanania St, Bab Sharki, T5417598. Open 1200-late, daily. A very upmarket, elegant restaurant in a beautifully restored old house. Primarily French cuisine, with a few Arabic touches. From around S£750 per head upwards. Live music in evenings. Full bar. Excellent service. *Elissar*, near Hammam al-Bakri, Bab Touma, T5424300. Open 1230-1700, 2000-late, daily. Set in the lovingly restored mid-19th century palace of Ibrahim Pasha, with seating in a beautiful central courtyard (covered in winter) or in the lavishly decorated 'banqueting' room (usually reserved for groups). The menu consists of a mixture of Arabic *mezze* appetizers and French/continental main dishes, around S£750-1000 per head. There is a bar in a separate room off the main courtyard, and a pleasant upstairs terrace in summer. One of Damascus' most elegant restaurants, booking usually necessary for evenings. *La Guitare*, off Straight St, near Bab Sharki, T5419823. Open 1200-late, daily. Very elegantly furnished dining rooms on 2 floors, plus an open terrace in summer. Mostly Italian/continental cuisine, with some Arabic dishes (*mezze* etc), from around S£500 per head. Alcohol served. *Narcissus Palace*, Al Amin St (north of Straight St, southeast of Umayyad Mosque), T5431205. Open 1000-late, daily. Set in a beautifully restored traditional Damascene house dating from 1735. Seating in the large central courtyard (covered in winter) or surrounding rooms. Choice of Arabic *mezze* appetizers and continental main dishes (escalope, steaks etc), though no written menu. From S£400-500 per head upwards. No alcohol. Live Arabic music and Whirling Dervishes in the evening. *Old Town*, just off Straight St, near the Roman arch, T5428088. Open 1300-1700, 1930-late. Lovely courtyard (covered in winter) and indoor seating. Italian/continental cuisine (including fresh pasta), as well as Arabic *mezze* etc. From around S£500 per head upwards. Pianist every evening from 2100. Alcohol served. Long-established place, friendly and well run. *Zeitouna*, off Straight St, near Bab Sharki, T5431324. Open 1800-late, daily. Yet another restaurant set in a beautifully restored old building with a courtyard and upstairs terrace. Arabic and continental cuisine from around S£400-500 per head upwards. Menu in English, with prices. Bar.

Moderate *Abu al Azz* (or just *Al Azz* or *Al Ezz*), just off Souk Hamadieh, near Umayyad Mosque, T2218174. Open 0900-late, daily. The narrow passageway-entrance, where delicious savoury pastries (*safiyah*) are served, conceals a spacious restaurant upstairs on 2 floors, elaborately decorated with marble mosaic walls and painted wood ceilings, also with 2 Bedouin-style 'tents'. Evening buffet (2100-late) of Arabic food (mezze, meat dishes, dessert, S£400 per person all inclusive) to the accompaniment of Arabic music and Whirling Dervish dancing, or choose from reasonably priced lunchtime menu (eat well for around S£200-300, but watch out for some of the waiters who have picked up the habit of overcharging foreign tourists). No alcohol. Along the same street there are a number of snack places for shawarmas, falafels, fresh juices etc. *Al Azariyeh*, off Bab Touma St, T5445173. Open 1200-late, daily. Small, cosy and intimate place decorated along the lines of a continental bistro with Oriental leanings.

Continental/international cuisine (eg pasta/lasagna, chicken Kiev, Mexican steaks etc) for around S£300 per head, or less for snacks. Alcohol served; also a wide range of *Lavazza* coffees. **Alf Leyla Wa Leyla** (*1001 Nights* or, as their own translation goes, *Thousand Night and Night*), on the street running east from the Umayyad Mosque, T5423021. Open 0900-late, daily. Set in a beautifully restored old building centred around an open courtyard with intricately decorated side-rooms. This was actually one of the first restaurants to open in a restored traditional house, though nowadays it seems to have become a bit of a tourist trap; it's suspiciously quiet, with never a local in sight, and the menu (Arabic cuisine) comes without any prices which is never a good sign. Alcohol served. **El Matador**, off Bab Touma St, T5443314. Open 1100-late, daily. Supposedly a Spanish restaurant/café/bar although, apart from the décor and the *paella* and *sangria* on the menu, its Spanish credentials seem a little tenuous. The other offerings are the usual Arabic dishes, pizzas, pasta etc. Full meals from around S£350 per head, less for snacks. Seating in the bar area downstairs, or in larger room upstairs, or in pleasant outdoor courtyard in summer. **Umayyad Palace**, situated in a small side-alley between the Umayyad Mosque and Azem Palace (a couple of doors down from the *Omayad Cave* restaurant), T2220826, F2248901. Beautifully restored Turkish building with all the traditional décor, geared very much towards attracting tourists and often host to large, organized groups. Lunch and dinner are both in the form of a good quality open buffet with a wide selection of Arabic dishes (*mezze*, grills, Damascene specials etc). Lunch is from 1200-1630 and costs S£350 per head. Dinner is from 2000-late, to the accompaniment of music and Whirling Dervish dancing, and costs S£600 per head. No alcohol.

Cheap **Jabri House** (or *Beit Jabri*), in narrow alley to southeast of Umayyad Mosque, T5416254. Open 0900-late, daily. Set in a beautiful traditional Damascene house dating to 1737 with seating in a large open courtyard with lemon trees, vine trellises, a fountain and pool, and a large *iwan* in one wall. Also seating indoors in the lavishly decorated grand reception room. Rather like eating in the Azem Palace, though at the same time the building has a slightly delapidated air to it, not having been meticulously restored, which somehow adds to the character. Traditional Arabic food at very reasonable prices (around S£200 per head upwards). Popular with locals and often busy. No alcohol. Recommended. **Old Damascus**, between the citadel and Umayyad Mosque, T2218810. Brightly lit, more modest place, aiming more perhaps at Syrian/Arab tourists. Usual range of Arabic food (menu in English posted on wall by cashier's desk. Eat well from around S£200 per head. Traditional Syrian music in evenings. No alcohol. **Omayad Cave**, in a small side-alley between the Umayyad Mosque and Azem Palace. Open 1000-late, daily. Cosy little place with seating downstairs in an underground vaulted room. As much a café as a restaurant during the day. Average Arabic food for around S£200 per head, plus pizzas (around S£100). Popular with young Syrians; with relatively modern décor, TV and pop music to offset any excessive 'Olde Worlde' pretensions.

Modern Damascus

Expensive **Laterna**, off 29 May St, T232 3185. Open 1300-1700, 2000-0100 (café section open 0900-0100). International cuisine with strong Italian leanings and various Asian and Far Eastern flourishes. Around S£500 per head upwards, excluding drinks. Originally established in 1918 as the *Al Kandil* (Arabic for lantern; the *Laterna* is a misspelling which stuck), this once slightly tawdry restaurant has recently undergone a radical refurbishment to make it certainly the most unusual, and possibly one of the trendiest, establishments in Damascus. You now enter across a glass-covered fish pond lit from below, past a relatively conventional café area, and into a large whimsical-modernistic space of bold colours, wavy contours and arty spotlights. Very recently opened at the time of writing, but already attracting chic Damascenes in their droves. Worth a visit as much for the atmosphere and social spectacle as the food. **Taj Mahal**, Ahmad Morewed St (off Argentina St), T223 7700. Open 1100-late,

This area of Damascus has the widest choice of restaurants. The expensive ones are generally in the luxury hotels. Moderate and cheap restaurants are dotted around all over the place, while the seriously cheap places are mostly around Martyrs' Sq

Damascus & around

daily. Pleasantly decorated a/c Indian restaurant. Set menu of starter, kebab, curry and ice cream for S£600 per head, or à la carte. Alcohol served (small can Heineken S£150).

Luxury hotel restaurants (expensive)   *Le Chinois*, *Cham Palace* hotel, Maisaloun St. Good quality and high prices. *Fuji Yama*, *Cham Palace* hotel. Japanese cuisine in luxurious surroundings with prices to match. *L'Étoile D'Or*, *Cham Palace* hotel. International cuisine. Very plush and expensive; aside from the food, the great attraction here is that this is a revolving restaurant situated up on the 15th floor, with superb panoramic views out over Damascus. *Le Panoramique*, *Cham Palace* hotel. French cuisine. Also with excellent views (up on the 11th floor), and live entertainment in the evenings. *Primavera*, *Cham Palace* hotel. Italian cuisine. Worth checking out for good-value seasonal 'specials'. *Luigi's*, *Sheraton* hotel. Italian cuisine. *Mihbaje*, *Sheraton* hotel. Arabic/international cuisine. Open all day, with set-price breakfast, lunch and dinner buffets (breakfast S£600 per person, lunch and dinner S£800). *Les Annees Folles*, *Meridien* hotel. International cuisine in a 1930s retro time-warp. Live entertainment. *Al Serane*, *Meridien* hotel. Arabic cuisine. Outdoor terrace in summer. *La Brasserie*, *Meridien* hotel. French cuisine. Set price open buffet for breakfast, lunch and dinner (breakfast S£660 per person, lunch and dinner S£825, including tax). *Golden Dragon*, *Semiramis* hotel. Chinese cuisine. *Villa Veduta*, *Semiramis* hotel. Italian cuisine. *Orzal*, *Semiramis* hotel. Arabic cuisine.

Moderate   *Al Arabi*, off Martyrs' Sq. This restaurant actually comes in 2 parts, either side of the *Canal al-Sues* hotel. Both branches are under the same management, though they seem to compete for passing trade. Pleasant for its quieter location on a pedestrian street just off Martyrs' Sq, though the Arabic fare on offer is distinctly mediocre. The absence of any prices on the menu, meanwhile, is a sure indication that as a foreign tourist you will be charged over the odds (S£300 per head upwards). *Le Bistrot Dalia*, Maisaloun St. Open 1200-2400, daily. Pleasant a/c restaurant-cum-café/bar (actually part of the *Omayad* hotel round the corner). Offers a range of burgers and snacks at around S£125-175, or main dishes (nominally French cuisine) for S£225-275 (set meals S£330). Attached is a second restaurant which at the time of writing was supposedly due to open soon as *Le Chalet*, serving Swiss-style fondues and raclettes. *Abou Kamal*, Yousef al-Azmeh Square (up on the 1st floor, next door to the CBS). Clean, brightly lit, long-established place with a good reputation. Wide range of Arabic dishes on offer (around S£350 per head upwards). The window tables overlooking Yousef al-Azmeh Sq are great for watching the comings and goings below. No alcohol. *Al Mahatta*, Hejaz Railway Station, T222 5876. Open daily, 24 hrs (or so they claim). If you fancy something a little different, this restaurant is housed in the restored wooden carriages of a steam train on one of the platforms of the Hejaz station in the centre of Damascus. Built more than 100 years ago, this was the private train of the Sultan Abdul Hameed (the last Ottoman Sultan and builder of the Hejaz railway line). Arabic cuisine (around S£300 per head upwards, excluding drinks). Seating inside the carriages or under an awning on the platform. Also functions as a café and bar, though as with the food, you are really paying for the location/novelty value (a very ordinary cup of tea here sets you back a rather unwarranted S£50, while a bottle of *Barada* beer goes for S£100). *Damascus Workers' Club*, off 29 May St, in Sarouja district (no sign in English, but the entrance is more or less directly opposite the impossible-to-miss *Majed* hotel). Open 1700-late, closed Fri. Housed in a well hidden traditional building featuring a beautiful courtyard and garden with fountains and seating dotted around outside under vine-shaded trellises. A delightful and atmospheric oasis of tranquility in the heart of modern Damascus. There is no menu as such, but they serve the usual range of Arabic food at slightly inflated prices (around S£300 per head upwards for a full meal). They also serve alcohol, and are quite happy for people to come here primarily (or indeed solely) for a drink, and/or to puff on a *nargileh*.

Cheap *Al Kamal*, 29 May St. Large, busy place offering a wide range of Arabic and continental dishes. Good value at around S£200 per head. No alcohol. *Al Sihhy* (or *Al Sehhy/Suhhy* or even *Al Sahiye*), off 29 May St. Spotlessly clean, brightly lit restaurant serving above-average Arabic food at very reasonable prices (around S£200-250 per head for a full meal). Menu in English, with prices. Family seating upstairs. Popular with locals, and often busy. Some of the waiters can be a little pushy for tips, but otherwise an excellent place. Recommended. *Pizza Hot*, Maisaloun St. Open 0800-late, daily. A popular and often busy meeting place amongst trendy upper-middle class Syrians. Incorporates the *Damascene Coffee Shop*, and is mostly a place for tea, coffee, cold drinks, cakes, ice creams etc, though, as the name suggests, it also serves pizzas (S£110/115). *Pizza Roma*, just off Maisaloun St. Open 0900-late, daily. A small, clean diner-style place offering pizzas (S£50-180), spaghetti and lasagne (S£40-70), or else burgers or *shish tawouk* (S£120/130 for 200 grammes). There are several ice cream parlours and falafel/shawarma places further along Maisaloun St, as well as a couple of great bakeries where you can get delicious chocolate-filled croissants.

Seriously cheap There are numerous cheap eateries dotted around Martyrs' Sq in the form of shawarma stalls (S£25 for a sandwich) and basic restaurants serving the usual range of Arabic food (roast chicken, meat grills, kebabs, *mezze* dishes etc). Watch out for some of the more brightly lit places which often tout rather pushily for passing tourists, and are quick to charge somewhat inflated prices; check how much your meal will cost before sitting down to eat.

For really good roast chicken at bargain prices, head east past the entrance to the *Karnak* bar and turn first left. In this narrow street there are a couple of places which serve nothing but roast chicken; the standard is a half-portion (S£75) which comes with a small dollop of creamy garlic sauce and some pickled veg, and which you eat shoulder to shoulder at a counter along the wall of the restaurant. The turnover is fast here and the chicken usually fresh and tasty (once you have been subjected to a few dried-out, chronically overcooked examples you'll appreciate how good these ones are). There are also a couple of more conventional sit-down restaurants here, which serve the usual range of *mezze* dishes as well as roast chicken etc.

The falafel restaurant marked on the Central Damascus map (on Korjiyeh St, to the east of 29 May St) serves, arguably, the freshest and tastiest falafels in Damascus.

Al Masri, Said al-Jabri St (next door to the *Barada* hotel; sign outside in Arabic only). More closely resembling a narrow corridor than a restaurant, this clean, simple and unpretentious place is popular with locals and often busy. Serves a wide selection of Arabic food at very reasonable prices (around S£150 per head for a substantial meal) and has a menu in English (complete with prices). The *fatteh* dishes are extremely generous and filling, costing S£60-70. Also a good place for *fuul* lovers to come for breakfast. Closes fairly early in the evening.

Expensive *Al Reef*, Al Jalaa (Abou Roumaneh) St. Arabic and continental cuisine. Supposedly a 4-star restaurant, but looking a bit run-down and neglected. Around S£500 per head and upwards. *Chevalier*, 'Restaurant Sq', off Abdul Malek St, T333574. Mostly French cuisine, also some Italian and Arabic. From around S£500 per head upwards. Pleasant traditional décor, alcohol served. *Joy*, 'Restaurant Sq', off Abdul Malek St, T3335697. Standard selection of Arabic cuisine with a few continental dishes, geared up for parties, occasional live music. From around S£500 per head upwards. Alcohol served. *La Chaumiere*, 'Restaurant Sq', off Abdul Malek St, T3338883. Mostly French cuisine, some Arabic. From around S£500 per head upwards. Pleasant traditional décor, no alcohol. *Pit Stop Café*, Al Amer Izz Eddin St, off Al Jalaa (Abou Roumaneh) St. Open 0800-late, daily. Modern, reaonably pleasant diner-style place offering sweet and savoury crêpes, sandwiches, omlettes and the like, as well as hot and cold drinks, milkshakes, ice creams etc. Upstairs is the extremely

Abou Roumaneh/ Salihiye *One of the more affluent districts, where lots of the trendier restaurants can be found, though there are also a couple of excellent cheaper places. In particular, check out Abou Roumaneh district's so-called 'Restaurant Square', off Abdul Malek St*

Damascus & around

trendy *Gemini*, a US-style restaurant and bar with a wide range of international cuisine meals and snacks. Everything is high quality (*Movënpick* ice cream, for example) and relatively expensive (from around S£500 upwards for a meal). Popular with the richer Syrian jet-set. *Vendome Café*, 'Restaurant Sq', off Abdul Malek St, T3338362. Super-trendy café/bar/restaurant imported wholesale from Lebanon. Housed in a swish glasshouse-type structure which manages to make all the others around the square look rather tacky. Fancy continental menu with Arabic touches. Snacks around S£150-300; meals from around S£500 per head and upwards.

Moderate *Morocco*, Maisaloun St (downstairs, next door to *Station One*). T3332410. Pleasant, if vaguely tacky, place offering an odd mix of Italian, French and some Moroccan dishes, as well as all kinds of burgers. All in all, the Moroccan connection seems pretty tenuous. Around S£300-400 per head. *Siwar al-Cham*, Moussa Bin Nusseir St (nearly opposite entrance to *Meridien* hotel), T3319568. Open 0800-late, daily. Simple but clean, pleasantly decorated and spacious restaurant serving the standard range of Arabic fare. Prices are higher than at the *Al Chamiat* for example, a meal here costs from around S£300 per head upwards. **Station One**, Maisaloun St. Trendy, modernistic place complete with occasional laser lightshow on the roof. Mixture of takeaway snacks (shawarma sandwiches etc) and sit-down meals. Rather expensive for what you get.

Cheap *Al Chamiat*, Al Majlis An Niaby St. Open 24 hrs, daily. A small, spotlessly clean, pleasantly decorated and typically Syrian restaurant. The Arabic food served here is excellent and the prices very reasonable (around S£200-250 per head for a full meal; menu in English). A gem of a place, reassuringly popular amongst Syrians (particularly for a family meal out). Traditional Syrian/Arabic food at its best. Recommended. *Al Hamra*, Omar Ibn Abdul Aziz St, by Zenobia Park. Large, fairly lively place with a good selection of Arabic food at reasonable prices (around S£150-250 per head) as well as various continental dishes and pizzas, hamburgers etc. *Al Malki*, Abdul Malek St, just short of junction with Adnan Malki St. Simple but attractively decorated and spotlessly clean restaurant serving traditional Arabic food; a good place to drop in for a bowl of *fatteh* or *fuul* and a cup of tea if you are in the area, though a long way from the centre. *Magnum 357*, 'Restaurant Sq', off Abdul Malek St. Modern, trendy ice cream, juice and milkshake parlour. *Milano Pizza*, 'Restaurant Sq', off Abdul Malek St, T3310875. Small, fairly traditional diner-style place. As well as pizzas (S£75-200), spaghetti and various sandwiches etc, they do a range of other main dishes (Arabic, continental, Tex-Mex, Chinese) for between S£130-200 a go. Also does take-away and home delivery. *New Pizza*, 'Restaurant Sq', off Abdul Malek St. Very much a fast-food style place, mostly takeaway/home delivery, but also with some seating. *Pizza al-Bundukie* (or *Venezia*), 'Restaurant Sq', off Abdul Malek St, T3310535. Fairly modern, trendy diner-style place. Good pizzas from S£110-150, sandwiches from S£40-60, or main meal dishes from S£120-200. Also does takeaway and home delivery. *Uno Pizza*, 'Restaurant Sq', off Abdul Malek St. Smaller version of *Pizza al-Bundukie*, with a similar menu and prices.

Cafés

Damascus' most famous café is the *Naufarah*, at the bottom of the steps leading down from the east entrance to the Umayyad Mosque in the Old City. This is a very popular place to come and hang out, for both Damascenes and visitors, and a great place to meet people, watch the general comings and goings or just rest after your sightseeing extravaganzas. Opposite it is the *Al Sham*, which is slightly more expensive. In the evenings; they generally put on a storytelling show (in Arabic, but theatrical and entertaining nevertheless) and there are often exhibitions of paintings by local artists. Also in the

Old City is the *Café Allah Kifak*, situated near Hammam al-Bakri, Bab Touma. Set in an old building with vaulted ceiling and bare stonework, and decorated with traditional handwoven Bedouin rugs, this is a fairly trendy place and considerably more expensive than your average café, but a great bolt-hole if you need to recuperate.

Rather less romantic perhaps, though still very typically Syrian, are the cafés to be found in the modern part of central Damascus. On An Naser St, between the main telephone office and the Hejaz railway station there is a large open-air café which is always lively and makes for a pleasant place to sit. On Moutanabi St there is a similar place with a pleasant outdoor patio which attracts a much older crowd and is quieter. The latter in particular is exclusively male, though foreign women will encounter nothing more than curious stares. If you feel like spoiling yourself, *Le Gourmet* café/patisserie in the *Meridien* hotel serves excellent bread, pastries, croissants, cakes and ice cream, as well as tea, coffee, fresh juice etc.

Bars

Many of the restaurants listed above also serve alcohol (for those Syrians who do drink, it is an activity usually associated with eating). Nevertheless, there are a few independent bars dotted around the city.

Old City

Although not exactly a powerhouse of nightlife, the Old City does have a few bars in the Christian areas (roughly speaking the eastern half), and it seems likely that more will open in the future. *Piano Bar*, near Bab Sharki (in the street leading up to Ananias Chapel). Open 1200-late, daily. A fashionable though rather expensive venue which aims to capture a certain 'hip' western atmosphere. Officially they operate a couples-only policy, though single punters are tolerated at the bar, with disdain. A bottle of *Barada* beer costs S£140 here. Food is also served, although it is overpriced (eg *Shish Tawouk* S£250, spaghetti S£200). *Café Mama*, near Hammam al-Bakri, Bab Touma. Open 1400-late, days. Set in a beautifully restored old building complete with the usual black and white stonework, ornate arches and heavy wood-beam ceilings, this place is very much a bar rather than a café, despite the name. They play a wide range of current pop music and there is a great atmosphere, making it popular with foreigners studying in Damascus and trendy Syrians. A bottle of *Barada* beer costs S£100 here, or S£150-200 for imported beers (including draught). Shots of whisky are S£150/200 for Red/Black Label, and cocktails S£210. There is also a limited food menu (salads, snacks, pasta dishes, chicken, steaks etc), though the main emphasis is on music and drinking. *Bar.* For a no-nonsense drink at a very basic hole-in-the-wall type of establishment, there is a tiny nameless bar on Straight St near to the turning leading down to *La Guitare* and *Zeitouna* restaurants. It's very much a locals' place, and definitely men-only, but a bottle of *Barada* costs just S£50.

Modern Damascus

All the luxury hotels in Damascus have their own bars, though they are rather expensive and a rather characterless. *L'Oasis*, in the *Meridien* hotel, features deep armchairs and a huge-screen TV. A bottle of *Barada* beer costs S£125, while a pint of draught *Lowenbrau* costs S£225. *The Pub*, in the *Sheraton* hotel is popular with expats. It comes complete with its own red telephone boxes for added British authenticity and has theme nights throughout the week.

Independent bars which are worth checking out include the following. *Artists' Syndicate* (*Al Rewaak*), off Afif St, in Salihiye district. An often lively place with outdoor seating in a pleasant courtyard/garden. Popular with the intelligentsia of Damascus. A great place to stop on your way back from exploring the monuments along Madares Assad ud-Din Lane in Salihiye district, but otherwise rather a long way from anywhere. *Bar Karnak*, Martyrs' Sq (entrance next door to the *Tourist (Syaha)* hotel, upstairs on the first floor). One of the cheapest bars in the centre of Damascus (a very reasonable

S£50 for a bottle of *Barada* beer complete with the obligatory dish of nuts and seeds to pick at). Also serves reasonable food (grills, *mezze* etc). Once a little seedy, but now redecorated and all clean and brightly lit, though still frequented mostly by solitary male drinkers. If you want some atmosphere, bring it yourself. **Damascus Workers Club**, off 29 May St, in Sarouja district. Also a restaurant (see above under 'Eating'), but at the same time a lovely place to come just for a drink.

Entertainment

Cinemas Other than the films and videos shown by the various cultural centres (see under 'Directory', below), the only 'serious' cinema is the **Cham Cinema**, attached to the *Cham Palace* hotel; films from Europe and North America appear here fairly regularly, several months after their release in the west. The cinema has 2 screens, at least 1 of which is usually showing a film in English. Tickets cost S£150. There are a number of other cinemas around Damascus where you can see the usual raunchy action pictures; the billboards outside give a good idea of what to expect.

Nightclubs The nightclub scene in Damascus is pretty dire. The independent nightclubs are best avoided, being seedy pick-up joints where you will find mostly East European/Russian prostitutes; the drinks are outrageously expensive and you are implicitly expected to sit with one of the many 'escorts' hanging around the bar and buy her a drink as well. The nightclubs attached to the luxury hotels do not have this seedy aspect to them, but are expensive and tend to lack atmosphere.

Theatre, music, exhibitions Most of the cultural events which take place in Damascus are arranged by the various cultural centres. The Centre Cuturel Français is the most active. See also 'Cultural centres', page 131.

Shopping

There are a couple of duty free shops (or 'Free Shops') in Damascus where you can buy imported brands of cigarettes, spirits, perfumes etc. One is around the corner from the Cham Palace hotel. The other is on 29 May St. All goods must be paid for in US$

Damascus has excellent opportunities for shopping, with the souks of the Old City being the obvious place to hunt for antiques, souvenirs and handicrafts. It is well worth shopping around to compare prices and quality. Although some operate a fixed-price policy, bargaining is the norm in most shops. Bear in mind that anyone who takes you along to a shop claiming that it is owned by his cousin, brother, friend etc, is guaranteed to be getting a commission on any sale that is made.

Following **Hamidiyeh Souk** into the Old City, there are numerous tourist-orientated shops. **Rugs** and **carpets** are concentrated close to the entrance and in the first couple of streets leading off to the right. All along this souk, around the south side of the Umayyad Mosque and outside its eastern gate, there are numerous shops selling **antique** coins and other **artefacts**, jewellery, silverware, brassware, inlaid wooden boxes and chess/backgammon boards, musical instruments, *nargilehs*, fabrics, rugs, carpets etc. Others specialize in **fabrics** and the silk brocades for which Damascus is famous. The eastern half of Straight St has many similar shops, including many specializing in **metal wares**, and in particular Damascene swords. To the south of Hamidiyeh Souk and the Umayyad Mosque are the **gold/jewellery** market (**Souk al-Silah**), fabrics market (**Souk al-Khayattin**), spices market (**Souk al-Bazuriye**) and many others. The **Al Azem Ecole** is entirely tourist-orientated, but they do have some beautiful things (see page 96 for details). Just inside **Bab Sharki** (at the eastern end of the Old City), the street leading north to Ananias Chapel has several very upmarket souvenir/handicraft/antique shops with a wide range of goods. The prices here are by no means the cheapest you will find, but the quality is high and it's a good place to get an idea of what's on offer.

In the **Tekkiyeh as-Suleimaniyeh Complex** beside the National Museum there is another tourist market with a good selection of **handicrafts/souvenirs/antiques** (see page 103). Again, although prices tend to be on the high side, this is the place to get an idea of what's available.

Although perhaps not of so much interest to tourists in terms of actually buying things, the pedestrianized section of **Salihiye St**, to the north of the People's Assembly, is a great place to wander around in the early evening, when it throngs with middle-class Syrians out shopping in the stylish **designer clothes** shops to be found along it. To the north, the lights of Charkasiye district on the lower slopes of Mt Kassioun can be seen twinkling almost magically up ahead. At various points along the street there are displays of paintings by local artists, and people posing for their portraits.

Bookshops

Avicenne Libraire Internationale, in a street running parallel to Maisaloun St near the *Cham Palace* hotel. Good selection of books on Syrian, Arab and Muslim history, art and architecture, as well as a range of western sci-fi, thrillers, mysteries etc. You can also buy a number of foreign papers here (usually not more than a couple of days out of date), and weeklies such as *Time*, *Newsweek* and the *Economist*. **Family Bookshop**, Al Majlis an-Niaby St. Mostly French books, but also a good range of fiction in English, and some books on Syrian art, history etc, as well as a selection of English language foreign newspapers. *Libraire Universalle*, in a small square just off Yousef al-Azmeh St stocks a smaller selection of books, but is still worth a look. All the luxury hotels also have bookshops attached to them and these can be good places to look. The bookshop in the *Meridien* hotel is one of the better ones.

Newspapers As well as the various bookshops, there are a number of ad-hoc news-stands where you can find foreign newspapers. The news-stand underneath Victoria Bridge (opposite the *Assia* hotel) has a good selection, though they may be several days out of date. Titles on offer include the *Herald Tribune*, the *Guardian*, the *Daily Telegraph* and the *Independent*, as well as *Le Orient le Jour* and the *Daily Star* (both Lebanese). Try also along Maisaloun St, to the west of *Cham Palace* hotel.

Photographic equipment

The shops attached to the luxury hotels are always well stocked with colour print and slide film, and many of the tourist shops in the Old City also sell film. Always check the expiry date before buying. There are several camera shops along Barada St and on Martyrs' Sq where you can get batteries etc as well as film. For processing and printing, try along Barada St, and on Mousalam Baroudy St (near the *Sultan* hotel), where there are shops with modern, fully automated processing and printing labs.

Sports

Swimming

The luxury hotels allow non-guests to use their swimming pools for a daily fee. The *Cham Palace* is the cheapest at S£400, though its pool is fairly small. The *Meridien* has a reasonably sized pool for which it charges S£500 per day. The *Sheraton* has the largest pool, with a baby pool alongside (S£550 per day). The *Tishreen Sports Stadium*, to the southeast of the town centre, has an Olympic-size swimming pool (open 0600-2000, S£40), though women may not feel entirely comfortable here.

Tennis

The *Sheraton* hotel has 3 tennis courts. They cost S£800 per hr to hire and should be booked 1 day in advance. You must become a member to use the tennis courts at the *Meridien* hotel (minimum period 3 months). There are also tennis courts at the *Tishreen and Al Jalaa Sports Stadiums*.

Squash

There are squash courts at the *Cham Palace* hotel. They cost S£250 for 30 mins, or you can get 1 month's membership for S£2500.

Damascus & around

Health centres   The *Cham Palace* is currently the only luxury hotel with a health centre. This includes a sauna, jacuzzi, gym, massage and sunbeds, as well as various beauty treatments.

Tours and tour operators

This is a small selection of the better tour operators based in Damascus

Adonis, 34-36 Moutanabi St, PO Box 4895, T5131643, F5116534, www.adonistravel. com Good professional service, dealing mostly with large organized tour groups but also able to cater for individuals and small ad-hoc groups. Organized tours (including city tours of Damascus), guides, car hire (with or without driver), international ticketing etc. Also have offices in Beirut and Amman, so well placed to provide tours taking in Lebanon and Jordan as well as Syria. **American Express**, Sudan Airways Bldg, Al Moutanabi Pl, PO Box 1373, T2217813, F2217938, amexrep@net.sy Tucked away on the 1st floor above the *Sudan Airways* office. Comprehensive service (whether you are an *AMEX* customer or not) includes international ticketing, guides, organized/tailor-made tours, car hire etc. Friendly and efficient. **Chamtour**, *Cham Palace* hotel, Maisaloun St, PO Box 7570, T2232300, F2226178. Part of the *Cham* group. Full range of services, aimed primarily at the luxury end of the market, and working mostly with large organized groups, but also able to offer tailor-made tours. **Mimoza**, Halbouni St (behind Hejaz railway station), PO Box 31162, T2235707, F2224627. Guaranteed daily tours of Damascus (full day/half day S£1500/1200), as well as organized tours to Saidnaya/Maloula (full day S£1750), Palmyra and other sites (cost and duration negotiable). Can also arrange car hire, international ticketing etc. **Nahas**, Fardous St, PO Box 3050, T2232000, F2232006, inbound@nahastt.com Large, well established company, acts as local agent for several foreign tour operators. Also acts as agent for *Thomas Cook* (see under 'Banks' in the Directory, below). Can arrange tailor-made tours for small groups and couples or individuals, as well as car hire, international ticketing etc. Also with offices in Beirut and Amman, so well placed to provide tours taking in Lebanon and

Damascus & around

Jordan as well as Syria. *WQS Global Village*, 19 Al Khansa St (behind Romanian Embassy), near Adnan Malki Square (see Salihiye map, page 110), PO Box 12104, www.wqs-globalvillage.com Small but friendly and well-run company offering tailor-made tours with English-speaking drivers (including also Jordan, Lebanon and Turkey). Can arrange car hire without driver (see under 'Car hire' in the Transport section, below), and/or hotel reservations.

Travel agents There are numerous travel agents in Damascus, the majority concentrated around Fardous St and along or just off Saad al-Jabri/Port Said/29 May St. Most of them only deal with international flights/reconfirmations etc, with some being General Service Agents (GSAs) for the international airlines listed under 'Airlines' in the Directory, below. It is worth shopping around for flights. For internal flights, most travel agents can make reservations, or you can go direct to the relevant *Syrian Air* office (see under 'Transport', below).

Transport

To/from the airport Damascus international airport is 25 km to the southeast of **Local** the city centre. There are several companies at the airport offering taxis into the centre of Damascus. During the daytime they charge around S£400-500/US$10, but late at night this rises to around S£1000/US$20. A taxi from the centre of town to the airport will cost in the region of S£300-500 depending on the time of day or night.

A bus service operates between the airport and the city centre. The journey takes 30-45 mins and costs S£10 (if you have a large amount of luggage you may have to pay an extra S£10 for it). The first bus leaves from the airport (from directly outside the arrivals/departures hall) at 0600, while the first bus from the centre of town (from outside the *Kairawan* hotel, beside Victoria Bridge) leaves at 0530. There are regular half-hourly departures in either direction up until 2400.

Car hire Damascus is the main centre of car hire in Syria, with an increasing number *See page 46 for* of small local firms now competing with the large international companies. Although *important information* the former are often significantly cheaper than the latter, be sure to check the rental *on car hire in Syria* conditions carefully, especially in relation to crash damage.

International companies *Avis*, Othman Ibn Afaan St, PO Box 12702, T2239664, F2239680. All cars are Mercedes. Cheapest car US$80 per day, limited mileage (up to 125 km), no insurance provided, minimum rental period 3 days, expensive. Much better value are the 10-24 seater minibuses/buses available for hire on a daily basis with driver for around US$65. *Budget*, Palestine (Baramkeh) St, T2122220, F2122210. Office closed at time of writing, but due to reopen shortly, along with several other offices around the city. Cheapest car US$60 per day including unlimited mileage and insurance (US$67 during peak season 1 Jul-15 Oct). Deposit/accident excess US$400, minimum rental period 3 days, expensive but good efficient service. *Europcar*, head office in Baramkeh district, T2120624, F2111304; hire desks at *Sheraton* hotel, T2229300; *Meridien* hotel, T2229200; *Semiramis* hotel, T2213813; *Omayad* hotel, T2217700; and at airport, T5431536. Choice of Hyundai, Peugeot or Volvo models. Cheapest car (Hyundai Atos) US$58 per day (open mileage, minimum rental 3 days). Includes full insurance; in case of an accident you will not be liable for any costs providing you obtain a police report. *Hertz/Chamcar*, Cham Palace hotel, Maisaloun St, PO Box 7570, T2232300, F2212398. Also with hire desk at the airport, and at all the other *Cham* hotels around Syria. Choice of Renault or Ford models. Cheapest car Renault Clio, US$66 per day (open mileage, minimum rental 3 days). Discounts for longer periods (eg 10% for 1 week, 20% for 1 month). Note that although PAI (Personal Accident Insurance) and CDW (Crash Damage Waiver) are compulsory, in case of an accident you may be liable for 50% of the repair cost and/or rental for the time the car is in the garage.

Local companies *Marmou*, Maisaloun St, PO Box 2810, T3335787, F2323084, www.marmou.com One of the longer established local companies with a good reputation. Cheapest cars (Opel Astra, Mazda 323, Suzuki Swift) US$60 per day (open mileage). Discounts for longer periods (eg 2 weeks or more; US$50 per day). Includes full insurance; in case of an accident you will not be liable for any costs providing you obtain a police report. *Rabwa*, off Palestine (Baramkeh) St (in side street on left, just before *Al Ahliah* ticket office as you head east along Palestine St), T2242804, F414023. Cheapest car Honda Civic S£1500/US$30 per day. Be sure to clarify rental conditions in event of an accident. *WQS Global Village*, (see under 'Tour operators', above, for details). This company arranges car hire through local companies, while at the same time guaranteeing the kind of rental conditions you would expect in Europe or North America. In case of an accident, providing you obtain a police report, you will only have to pay a US$200 excess (or less if the cost of repair is less). They will also automatically send you a replacement car in case of a breakdown or accident. The cheapest cars (all category B; eg Mazda 323, Mitsibushi Lancer, Hyundai Accent, Ford Escort) start from around US$55 per day (minimum 3 days, open milage, full insurance, a/c), with discounts for longer periods. They also offer minivans (with driver only) which seat 5-8 people and cost US$125 per day all in (including accommodation and food for the driver), with the added advantage that you can go into Lebanon and Jordan.

Some of the cheaper hotels can also arrange car hire. Although in effect they act as middlemen between yourself and the car hire company and therefore take a cut for themselves, they can still work out good value since they are generally able to obtain a better rate in the first place. They can also be useful in terms of firmly clarifying the rental agreement, especially in relation to crash damage. Try at the *Al Rabie* or *Haramain* hotels, or the *Sultan* hotel.

Taxi Taxis are readily available throughout Damascus. These days, most of them have working meters which makes life easier. If not, you should always agree a price before getting in. Shorter journeys within the city should not cost more than S£20-30. A taxi from the centre of town to the Pullman/Harasta bus station on the northeast outskirts of town (see below) should not cost more than S£30-50 on the meter. **NB** When arriving in Damascus by luxury coach, beware of taxi drivers eagerly waiting to meet you off the coach as they generally try to demand at least S£100; walk away from the station to find a more reasonable deal.

Bus/microbus Microbuses ('meecro' or 'servees') are an important part of the local transport network in Damascus, although they are not particularly easy to get to grips with since destinations are written in Arabic. The majority charge a flat fare of S£5. One of the main terminals for microbuses is under **Assad Bridge**. There are services from here to the **Abbasseen** and **Pullman/Harasta bus stations** (these do not pull into the parking bays and must be flagged down as they pass through; they also make a stop outside the fruit and vegetable market on **Al Ittihad St**, just east of Thawra Bridge, useful if you are staying at the *Al Haramain* or *Al Rabie* hotels). Bear in mind that they cannot really accommodate large items of luggage, although you can always try paying for 2 seats. Microbuses also run from under Assad Bridge to **Al Mezzeh** (useful for the Australian and Canadian embassies); ask for the 'Mezzeh Autostrade' service. There is a **bus** service from **Fakhri al-Baroudi St** to the **Deraa bus station** in the south of the city.

Long distance
Airport, T5430201. See above for information on transport to & from the airport

Air Domestic: *Syrian Air*; the office for domestic flights is on the roundabout at the north end of 29 May St, T2220700 (central switchboard), or T167, and ask for the 'Saba Bahrat' ('Seven Lakes') office. Open 0630-1930, daily. All domestic flights take around 1 hr and should be booked at least 1 day in advance. Exact timetables are subject to frequent changes. Fares given here are 1 way; return fares are double. **Aleppo,**

between 1 and 5 flights daily, S£602; **Lattakia**, 1 flight weekly, Fri, S£502; **Qamishle**, 3 flights weekly, Tue, Fri, Sun, S£902; **Deir ez-Zor**, 1 flight weekly, Sat, S£602 (NB flights to Deir ez-Zor suspended at time of writing, while airport under renovation).

International: there are a number of other *Syrian Air* offices dotted around the city which deal only with international flights. One of the more efficient offices is based in the *Semiramis* hotel, near Victoria Bridge. *Syrian Air* has services from Damascus to most major cities in Europe, the Middle East and Asia. Most other international airlines also have offices in Damascus (see under 'Airline offices' in the Directory, below) and between them offer services to all major destinations in the Middle East, Europe, USA and Australasia. **NB** Remember that an airport departure tax of S£200 is charged on all international flights.

Train There are 2 train stations for Damascus, the **Hejaz** station (T2217247 for info on services to the hill resorts to the northwest of Damascus, and to Jordan; T2212950 for info on services to Aleppo and Lattakia/Tartus) in the centre of the city and the **Kadam** station (T8888678 and see below) around 4 km to the south of the city centre. Unfortunately, the beautiful and centrally located Hejaz station is only for narrow-gauge services to the hill resorts of Ain Fijeh and Zabadani to the northwest of Damascus (see 'Around Damascus', below). Services are seasonal, operating between Jun and Oct only (you are advised to check timetables as they are subject to change). **Ain Fijeh**, daily, 0800 (0900 on Fri), S£20, 1½ hrs approx (return service departs at around 1730-1800). **Zabadani**, Tue, Thu, Fri, Sun, 0800, S£30, 3-4 hrs approx (Zabadani trains in fact carry on to **Serghaya**, just short of the Lebanese border, where they turn around; the return service departs Zabadani around 1730). Services to **Amman** in Jordan run twice weekly throughout the year. Mon, Thu, 0800 (get there at least 30 mins beforehand), S£160, 7 hrs minimum (more likely to be around 10 hrs). For those with lots of time and patience, the Amman train makes an interesting, although extremely slow, alternative way of crossing the border into Jordan.

All other services depart from the **Kadam** station (note that you can buy tickets at the Hejaz station for services to Aleppo and Lattakia, even through they depart from Kadam; tickets for the Turkey service must be bought from Kadam station). A taxi is the best way to get to Kadam (microbuses leave from along Ibn al-Abbass St to the south of Hejaz station, but this is quite a walk in itself). From Kadam station there are services to: **Aleppo** (via **Homs** and **Hama**), 1 train daily, 1600, 2nd class S£57, 1st class S£85, Sleeper S£325, 6 hrs approx; **Lattakia** (via **Tartus**, **Banias** and **Jableh**), 1 train weekly, Thu 1500, 2nd class S£60, 1st class S£90, 6 hrs approx; **Istanbul** (via **Aleppo**, **Adana** and **Ankara**), 1 train weekly, Tue 0530, 1st class S£1510, Sleeper S£3382 (tickets must be bought the day before, from Kadam station), 42 hrs approx.

Road The **Pullman/Harasta bus station** ('Garagat al-Pullman al-Jadide' or 'Garagat Harasta'/'Tariq Harasta') is the main station for luxury coaches to all towns and cities to the north and northeast of Damascus (ie **Homs**, **Hama**, **Aleppo**, **Tartus**, **Lattakia**, **Palmyra**, **Raqqa**, **Deir ez-Zor**, **Hassakeh** and **Qamishle**, as well as a few other smaller places). Coaches for **Turkey** also leave from here, but their main ticket offices are in the centre of town. The bus station is inconveniently located around 5 km to the northeast of the city centre, just off the Damascus-Aleppo motorway in a district known as Harasta. Over 30 different companies operate luxury coaches from here. Once inside the bus station, there are numerous touts shouting out the destinations of the different companies and eagerly trying to drag you off to their ticket offices (watch out for overcharging by the touts). Prices vary slightly for some destinations (see box for a guide to fares), but otherwise there is little to choose between the various companies and it is more a case of establishing which has the soonest departure to your destination. *Karnak*, the state-owned coach company, has its offices here for domestic services; it is slightly cheaper for some destinations, though the number

The 2 main bus stations in Damascus are the Pullman/Harasta & Baramkeh stations: between them they cover the vast majority of destinations

Damascus & around

of domestic routes they operate on is steadily dwindling. Given the number of competing companies and the frequency of departures, it is rarely necessary to book in advance. However, some companies have ticket offices in the centre of Damascus, so if you want to be absolutely sure, you can go to these offices the day before to buy your ticket. *Zeitouni* and *Kadmous* both have offices conveniently located in the same arcade as the *Kairawan* hotel, by Victoria Bridge. *Al Ahliah*, meanwhile, has a rather less convenient office towards the western end of Palestine (Baramkeh) St.

There are a number of **Turkish coach companies** offering direct services to Turkey from Damascus. All these coaches depart from the Pullman/Harasta bus station, but the main ticket offices for these companies are located in the centre of Damascus, in a small side-street just to the northwest of Victoria Bridge. You can buy tickets at the Pullman/Harasta bus station, but you are advised to book your seats at the main ticket offices in the city centre the day before. There are around half a dozen companies in all. Departures are at 2200 for all the companies, with the fare to **Antakya** varying from S£350-500. You can also buy tickets to anywhere else in Turkey, and to destinations such as **Sophia** or **Bucharest**, though in all cases you have to change first in Antakya; invariably it is quicker (and often cheaper) to buy a ticket only as far as Antakya and then pick up onward transport from there.

The **Baramkeh bus station** ('Garagat Baramkeh') is on Palestine (Baramkeh) St, close to the University and within walking distance of the city centre. The station is effectively divided into 3 parts (see Damascus Centre map). A mixture of luxury coaches, buses, minibuses and service taxis operate from here to international destinations (principally **Lebanon** and **Jordan**), towns to the south of Damascus and also to local destinations around Damascus. Services to **Amman** are shared between *JETT* (the Jordanian state-owned company) and *Karnak*, 2242169. Departures at 0700, 1500, S£300/US$6, approximately 4-5 hrs depending on border formalities. You are advised to book in advance. Note also that they are reluctant to sell you a ticket unless you already have a Jordanian visa, despite the fact that obtaining one on the border is relatively straightforward. With a little charm and persuasion you may be able to get a ticket without a visa. If not, you will have to take a service taxi from next door (see below). *Karnak* also operates services to **Beirut** 0730, 0830, 0930, 1200, 1430, 1530, 1630, S£175, approximately 3-4 hrs depending on border formalities. Note that a couple of these services may be cancelled if there is insufficient demand. There are various other companies (lined up on the right as you enter) with a mixture of small bus and luxury coach services to **Beirut** departing every hr or so, (S£200).

The **microbuses** (occupying the area to your left as you enter) run to local destinations around Damascus, departing when full. Destinations that are likely to be of use to tourists include **Zabadani**, S£20, 45 mins; and **Khan Arnabeh** (for **Quneitra**), S£20, 1 hr. Towards the far end of this section of the bus station, there are 2 luxury coach companies, *Al Muhib* and *Al Wasim*, which between them offer regular departures to **Bosra**, **Suweidha** and **Deraa**, all costing S£50 and taking around 2 hrs (services to Deraa are the most frequent, departing every 15-30 mins, while those to Suweidha depart every hr and those to Bosra at least every 2 hrs).

International service taxis These have the advantage of departing at almost any time of the day or night, although you have to wait around for the taxi to fill up (they take 5 passengers). They are also somewhat more expensive than the luxury coaches; **Amman** S£400 (you can also just get service taxis from here to **Irbid**, S£250); **Beirut** S£300; **Baalbek** S£300; **Chtaura** S£105; **Zahle** S£115. The drivers and touts waiting around the entrance to this part of Baramkeh station often try to charge more, particularly to tourists; go to the ticket office for the correct fare, though in practice you may find you have to pay whatever 'going rate' the drivers are asking.

The **Abbasseen bus station** ('Garagat Abbasseen' or 'Garagat Hob-Hob'), just to the east of Abbasseen Square, at the northeast edge of the city, is for cheaper, older and much slower buses (due to the frequent stops) serving the same destinations as the Pullman/Harasta bus station. The rickety old buses operating from here go to all the destinations covered by the luxury coach companies, as well as many other smaller places. They are significantly cheaper than the luxury coaches (for example **Hama** S£45, **Aleppo** S£60), and also significantly less comfortable and much slower, stopping en route wherever people wish to get on or off. Departures are frequent; they do not operate to a fixed timetable, with buses simply leaving when they are full.

Maaloula microbus station ('Garagat Maaloula'), is to the south of Abbasseen Sq. Regular microbuses operate from here to **Saidnaya**, S£15, 45 mins; and **Maaloula**, S£25, 1 hr, departing when full.

The **Deraa bus station** ('Garagat Deraa') south of the city centre, by the junction just south of Yarmouk Sq, is for buses and microbuses serving destinations to the south of Damascus (departing when full). Unless you really want to save a few S£, it is far more convenient to take a luxury coach from Baramkeh bus station to **Bosra**, **Suweidha** or **Deraa**, and change buses at any of these towns for other smaller places in the region.

Directory

The majority of the airline offices are located either inside the Mohandeseen Bldg on Maisaloun St (opposite the *Cham Palace* hotel), or along Fardous St, or along 29 May St. The remainder are all close by this central area. Many are represented by a General Service Agent (GSA). **Mohandeseen Bldg, Maisaloun St** *Austrian*, T2236001, F2236002. *Gulf Air*, PO Box 3050, T2221209, F2236002. *Iberia*, PO Box 2509, T2226085, F2212648. *Iran Air*, T2238660, F2217911. *Lufthansa*, PO Box 941, T2211165, F2242824. *Olympic* (Greece), PO Box 7584, T2217720, F2236660. *PIA* (Pakistan), PO Box 13463, T2211586, F2212648. *Saudi Arabian*, PO Box 386, T2214052. *Turkish*, PO Box 8176, T2239770. *Yemenai*, PO Box 535, T2220086, F2228855. **Fardous St** *Alitalia*, PO Box 49, T2222662. *Czech*, Rabat Bldg, T2225804. *Iraqi*, T2450301. *KLM*, PO Box 941, T2213395, F2245726. *Malev* (Hungarian), PO Box 5379, T2226188, F2216666. *Royal Air Maroc*, T2216265. *Sudan Airways*, Al Moutanabi Pl (off Fardous St), T2246800. *Tunis Air*, GSA *Nahas Travel & Tourism*, PO Box 3050, T2232000, F2236002. **29 May St** *Aeroflot*, T2317952. *Cyprus*, GSA *Al Patra Travel & Tourism*, Khalil Jadalla Alley (just off 29 May St), PO Box 12661, T2324513, F2324854. *Emirates*, PO Box 9633, T2313451, F2246640. *Royal Jordanian*, PO Box 2887, T2211267, F2231108. **Other** *Air France*, *Meridien* hotel, Shoukri al-Kouwatli St, PO Box 5531, T2218580, F2236860. *Air Malta*, Port Said St, PO Box 12734, T2311700, F2311704. *British Airways* (British Mediterranean), GSA *Sanadiki Travel and Tourism*, Argentine St (opposite Al Tawfiq hospital), PO Box 7784, T3310000, F3317880, also a travel desk at the British Council, off Maisaloun St, T3310631. *Egypt Air*, Hejaz Sq, PO Box 3175, T2240164, F2223992. *MEA* (Lebanese), Khouja Bldg, 88-90 Barada St, PO Box 10173, T2314998, F2314888. *Syrian Air* (head office), 5th floor, Social Secretariat Building, Port Said St, PO Box 417, T2220700 (central switchboard). They have several offices around the city; domestic flights are handled by the office on the roundabout at the north end of 29 May St (see under 'Transport' above).

Airline offices

There is a branch of the **Commercial Bank of Syria** (CBS) on Yousuf Azmeh Sq, where you can change cash (at the counter opening onto the street; open 0830-2000, Fri 0830-1400) and TCs (inside the building, up on the first floor; open 0830-1230, closed Fri). **NB** This is also the only branch of the *CBS* in Syria where you can change US$ TCs into 50% US$ cash and 50% S£ cash. There is another branch of the *CBS* occupying a small shop on Hejaz Sq opposite the Hejaz railway station which changes both cash and TCs. Open 0900-1900, Fri 0900-1400. If you need to change money while in the Old City (and wish to avoid the black market moneychangers), there is a *CBS* exchange booth on Straight St, just inside Bab Sharki, which changes cash and TCs. Open 0900-1900, Fri 0900-1400. Both the *Meridien* and *Sheraton* hotels have branches of the *CBS* in their lobbies which will exchange cash and TCs, open 0900-1430, 1515-2100, daily. The *Cham Palace* hotel is now authorized to change cash and TCs at the official bank rate, a service which they offer

Banks
You will not have to walk far in Hamidiyeh Souk before someone comes up and whispers "change money?" in your ear

24hrs a day. They will also give guests at the hotel small cash advances (up to around US$100) against credit cards. *Thomas Cook* are represented by *Nahas Travel and Tourism*, Fardous St, PO Box 3050, T2232000, F2232006, inbound@nahastt.com The representative here claims that he will provide a refund in US$ cash for lost/stolen TCs, and that he can also cash TCs (both *Thomas Cook* and *American Express*) into US$ and £Sterling, though there has to be a catch here (most probably in the size of the commission charged). In line with everyone else, cash advances cannot be given against credit cards. *American Express* is above the *Sudan Airways* office, Al Moutanabi Pl, PO Box 1373, T2217813, F2217938, amexrep@net.sy They cannot provide cash advances against credit cards (not even their own), but can help you find ways round this problem. Neither can they cash TCs, but they will arrange replacements for lost/stolen TCs (replacements must be sent by courier from the UK or Europe, so the process takes at least 3 or 4 days). They also operate a poste restante service and a full travel agency.

Communications

Internet There is a small but growing number of internet cafés in Damascus. As is the case throughout Syria, they are better described as internet offices – the 'café' aspect is more or less non-existant. *Alpha Centre*, 1st floor Abbedin Bldg, just off Souk Sarouja St, T231 2026. Open 0900-2100, closed Fri. S£5 per min, or buy time in advance at discounted rates (S£300 for 1½ hrs; S£500 for 3 hrs; S£750 for 5 hrs; S£1350 for 10 hrs). This place was initially opened as a computer training centre, but with the success of *Internet Zoni* upstairs (see below) has followed their lead. Friendly, helpful staff. *American Cultural Center*, 87 Ata al-Ayoubi St, PO Box 29, T3338413, F3321456 (see 'Cultural centres' below). *@ural*, 1st floor, Al Shark al-Awsat Café Bldg, Yousef al-Azmeh St (on south side of Al Ittihad St), T231 1253. Open 1000-2200, daily. S£5 per min, or buy 5 hrs in advance for S£750 (ie S£2.5 per min). Currently just 4 terminals, but more on the way, and the possibility of moving upstairs in the future, where there is room for a real internet café. *Internet Zoni*, 3rd floor Abbedin Bldg, just off Souk Sarouja St, T232 4670. Open 1000-2200, Fri 1300-2200. S£5 per min, or buy 5 hrs for S£750 (ie S£2.5 per min) to become a member, after which any additional time is charged at S£2.5 per min. This was the first private internet enterprise to open in Damascus, and now consists of 2 rooms full of computers. Staff are extremely helpful and knowledgeable, and can help you find your way around most obstacles. *Internet Station*, Souk Sarouja St, T231 3954. Open 0800-2000, closed Fri. Only just opened at the time of writing. 4 terminals. S£5 per min with reductions for extended use. *Muhajireen Centre*, at western end of Nezem Basha St, close to its junction with Jabal St. Inconveniently located way to the northwest of the city centre, at the foot of Mt Kassioun, and unfortunately just off our Damascus Overview map. From the junction by Shami Hospital (known as Ibrahim Hanano Sq), head due north up the hill, turn right at the junction 250 m further on and it is a short way along on the right, almost directly opposite Al Khair Mosque ('Jamaat al-Khair'). The sign just reads just 'Syriatel' and 'Investcom' in English. Open 0815-1815, closed Fri. S£2 per min. 9 terminals. This government-run place is often busy and, as it is not possible to book ahead, you just have to put your name on the list and wait your turn. *Telephone Office*, An Naser St, a block to the east of the Hejaz railway station. Open 0830-1330, closed Fri. S£2 per min. 9 terminals. This is the main government-run internet centre in Damascus. It is more conveniently located than the Muhajireen Centre and as such tends to be busier, so be prepared for a long wait.

Post The Central Post Office is a huge buiding on Said al-Jabri St, identified in English as the "Syrian Post Establishment". At the time of writing, the main entrance on Said al-Jabri St was closed; go instead to the smaller entrance around the right-hand side as you face the building. Open 0800-1900 (officially at least; in practice it often closes by 1800), Fri 0900-1200 for stamps only. There is a **poste restante** counter here (open 0800-1700, closed Fri). Bring your passport along as ID. There is a charge of S£10 per item of mail collected. **Courier** There is a *DHL* office just to the south of Shoukry al-Kouwatly St, near Victoria Bridge, PO Box 13293, T2227692, F2247486.

Telephone There are numerous cardphones dotted all over Damascus, with phonecards on sale from nearby shops, kiosks, juice bars and the like; just ask around. Finding a cardphone may be no problem, but the challenge is to find one which is not right next to a hopelessly busy/noisy junction or main road. One cardphone which is reasonably quiet is situated on Souk Sarouja St, just near *Zoni* internet café (very convenient if you are staying at the *Haramain* or *Al Rabie* hotels).

Bear in mind that, at the time of writing, phonecards bought in Damascus could be used in Damascus and Aleppo only, all other cities operate a different phonecard system. However, in the future (though exactly when is uncertain), the type of phonecard found in Damascus and Aleppo will replace the others.

Damascus & around

It is no longer possible to make international calls through the operator at the Central Telephone Office (which is situated on An Naser St, just to the east of the Hejaz railway station). There are several cardphones outside, and usually someone hanging around selling phonecards, but the office itself now only deals with bill payments for domestic/commercial phone lines and mobile phone accounts, as well as offering a **telegram** and **fax** service, and **internet** access. For sending/receiving faxes, hotels are more expensive, but infinitely less hassle. The mark-up at mid-range and budget hotels for telephoning or faxing is not excessive, but beware of the upper-range and luxury hotels, where telephone/fax charges amount to daylight robbery.

Cultural centres

American Cultural Center, 87 Ata al-Ayoubi St, PO Box 29, T3338413, F3321456. A programme is available from the centre listing occasional events organized by the centre, or telephone for details. There is also a library, open 1300-1700, closed Fri and Sat, which operates on a membership system, although tourists are generally allowed to come in and make use of the facilities. The resources here focus mainly on American culture and society, but you can read newspapers and magazines such as the *Herald Tribune* and *Time/Newsweek* here, and there is a TV showing CNN. Access to the **internet** is allowed "for research purposes only" (ie not for sending/receiving emails); the first 30 mins is free, after which there is a charge of S£1 per min. *British Council*, Shalaan, off Maisaloun St, PO Box 33105, T3310631, F3321467, www.britishcouncil.org/syria The BC in Syria is geared mostly to providing English language courses (though they also run Arabic language courses; see under 'Language schools' below) and information on studying in Britain. Library open 0900-2000, closed Fri. Limited collection of books, mostly focusing on Britain. Upstairs on the 3rd floor there is a cafeteria with a selection of British newspapers on offer. On Sat evenings 1700-1900 there is a video club, though this is meant primarily as a language teaching tool. Internet access is currently only for staff and students, though it may be opened up to the public in the future. There is a small *British Airways* office inside the building (see under 'Airlines', above). A bi-monthly newsletter gives details of occasional cultural events (theatre, music, exhibitions etc) arranged by the BC, or check their website. *Centre Culturel Français*, Bahsa, PO Box 3690, T2316181, F2316194. Open 0900-2100, closed Sun. Library open 0930-1330, 1600-1930, closed Sun and Fri morning. This is by far the most active of the cultural centres in Damascus, housed in a large modern building complete with its own theatre/cinema and exhibition hall. A programme of events, published every 3 months, is available from the centre listing the varied programme of films, theatre, music, exhibitions etc organized by the centre, or telephone for details. *Goethe Institute*, 8 Adnan Malki St, PO Box 6100, T3336673, F3320849. A programme of events, published bi-monthly (in German), lists films, lectures, music, exhibitions etc. *Institut Français d'Archéologie du Proche-Orient (IFAPO)*, Jisr al-Abiad, PO Box 3694, T3338727, F3325013. Open 0830-1300, 1600-2000, closed Sat and Sun. The nervecentre for French archaeological projects in Syria. *Institut Français d'Etudes Arabes de Damas (IFEAD)*, 22 Assali St, Abou Roumaneh, PO Box 344, T3330214, F3327887. Open 1000-1300, 1600-1900, closed Sun. The extensive specialist library housed here boasts more than 70,000 volumes and 1,100 periodicals dealing with the Arab world, while the institute acts as a focus for French research on the Arab world. *Russian Cultural Centre*, 29 May St, T2427155. *Spanish Cultural Centre*, Nazem Pasha St, T2714003.

Embassies & consulates

Australia, the embassy was closed at the time of writing; its business was being handled by the Canadian embassy. *Austria*, Sabri Malki Building, Chafik Mouayad St, Rawda, T6116730, F6116734. *Belgium*, Hashem Building, Ata al-Ayoubi St, T3332821. *Canada*, PO Box 3394, Autostrade, Al Mezzeh, T6116692. Open Sun-Wed 0830-1600, Thu 0830-1300, closed Fri and Sat. *China*, Al Mansour St (opposite US Embassy), Abu Roumaneh, T3339594. *Cyprus*, Al Salam St, Mezze, T6130812, F6130814. *Czech*, Maser St, Abu Roumaneh, T3331383. Open 0900-1100, closed Fri, Sat. *Denmark*, Chakib Arslan St, Abu Roumaneh, T3319304, F3337928. *Egypt*, Al Jalaa (Abu Roumaneh) St, T3333561. *Finland*, Yacoubian Bldg, West Malki Hawakir, T3338809, F3734740. *France*, Ata al-Ayoubi St, T3327992. Open 0900-1500, closed Sat, Sun. *Germany*, 53 Ibrahim Hanano St, T3323800. *India*, Adnan Malki St, PO Box 685, T3739081, F3316703. *Indonesia*, off Al Jalaa (Abu Roumaneh) St, T6119630. Consular section open 0830-1230, closed Fri, Sat. *Iran*, Autostrade, Al Mezzeh, T6120800. *Italy*, 82 Al Mansour St, T3332621. Open Mon-Thu 0930-1530, Fri 0930-1430, closed Sat, Sun. *Japan*, Omar Ibn Abdul Aziz St, T3338273. Open 0800-1500, closed Fri, Sat. Consulate open 0900-1200, closed Fri, Sat. *Jordan*, Al Jalaa (Abu Roumaneh) St, T3334642. Open 0830-1100, closed Fri, Sat. *Netherlands*, Al Jalaa (Abu Roumaneh) St, T3336871 (emergency number when closed, T6131102). Open 0900-1200, closed Fri, Sat. *Norway*, 1st floor, Shaheen Bldg, Ahmed Shawki St, Malki, T3310733. *Pakistan*, Sharah al-Farabi, East Mezzeh, T6132694, F6132662. *Saudi Arabia*, Abdul Malek Ibn Warden St, T3334914. *Spain*, behind *Hyatt* hotel, Al

Mezzeh, T6132900, F6132941. *Sweden*, Catholic Patriarchate Bldg, Chakib Arslan St, Abu Roumaneh, T3327261. *Switzerland*, Autostrade, Al Mezzeh, T6111972. *Turkey*, Hejaz St, Abu Roumaneh, T3331411, F3339243. *UK*, Kotob Bldg, 11 Mohammad Kurd Ali St, Malki, PO Box 37, T3739241, F3739236. Open Sun-Wed 0800-1515, Thu 0800-1400, closed Fri, Sat. Consular section open 0830-1030, closed Fri, Sat. *USA*, 2 Al Mansour St, Abu Roumaneh, T3718678, F2247938. Open 0800-1630, closed Fri, Sat (emergency number when closed, T3333232, or call in person; embassy marine guards on duty). Consular section open 0800-1200, closed Fri, Sat.

Language schools

AMIDEAST (*America-Mideast Educational & Training Services*), Wahab Bin Saad St, Abou Roumaneh, T/F3332804, www.amideast.org Open 0830-1430, closed Fri and Sat. Beginner, Intermediate and Advanced Conversation courses in Syrian Colloquial Arabic. All of these consist of 40 hrs spread over 8 wks, and cost S£6000. Courses usually start mid-Sep. *Arabic Teaching Institute For Foreigners*, 3 Jadet ash-Shafei, Mezzeh Villat Sharkiyeh, PO Box 9340, T2221538. Courses in Classical Arabic (with all the teaching given in Arabic) run from Jun-Sep and Oct-May. The fee is US$450 per term. Students enrolled on this course are entitled to apply for residence. *British Council* (see under 'Cultural centres', above, for details) offers Arabic courses. There is a 'Foundation' course, followed by a choice of 'Syrian Colloquial Arabic' or 'Modern Standard Arabic' courses. All of these consist of 32 hrs of teaching spread over 8 wks, and cost S£5000. Courses usually start in Sep and are repeated towards the end of Nov if there is sufficient demand. Private lessons can also be arranged, with discounts for university students. *Institut Français d'Etudes Arabes de Damas (IFEAD)*, (see under 'Cultural centres', above, for details) offers Arabic language courses aimed primarily at students and researchers working in Syria. The teaching is all in French, of course.

Laundry

Most hotels (including the better budget hotels) offer a laundry service and, on the whole, charge very reasonable rates.

Libraries

In addition to the libraries attached to the various cultural centres (see above), there is the *Assad National Library* by Umawiyeen Sq (entrance in Adnan Malki St).

Medical services

Chemists There are numerous chemists dotted around the centre of Damascus, particularly on the streets radiating off Yousef al-Azmeh Sq and in the vicinity of Martyrs' Sq. There is a rota for 24-hr opening, with details displayed in the windows of all chemists (though in Arabic only); ask your hotel for help if you need one outside normal opening hrs. In addition, the private hospitals all have their own pharmacies and may be better stocked. **Hospitals** Damascus has several good private hospitals with high standards of medical care. *Italian*, Omar al-Moukhtar St, T3326030. Recommended. *Shami*, Ibrahim Hanano St, by junction with Jawaher Lal Nahro St, T3734925. Also includes a dental clinic. Recommended. *Al Tawfik*, Argentina St, T2216364. *Muwasat*, Muwasat St, T2237800. *Razi*, Autostrade, Al Mezzeh, T2219445. *Damascus*, Al Moujtahed St, T2216000. Government-run. *Red Crescent*, T2421601.

Useful addresses

Ambulance T110. **Fire Headquarters** T113. **Traffic Police** T115. **Police** T112. **International Operator** T143/144. **National Operator** T141/142.

Visa extensions

These can be obtained from the **Passport and Immigration office** on Palestine St, opposite the University, open 0800-1400, closed Fri. You need 3 passport photos and must return to collect your passport the next day. This is one of the busiest places to extend your visa, and as well as having to come back the next day, expect to have to wait around quite a bit. Moreover, according to many travellers, the staff here are none too friendly or helpful. If you can time it right, it is far better to get this done elsewhere in Syria. The office at Aleppo is fairly efficient (same day service), or go for a smaller town such as Tartus or Homs.

Re-Entry Visa If you have only a single entry Syrian visa but wish to visit Lebanon and return to Syria, go to the Passport and Immigration office on Furat St, between Martyrs' Sq and Said al-Jabri St. They will not issue you with a re-entry permit as such, but will telex your details and permission to re-enter at the immigration office at the border (make sure you specify which border crossing you will enter and leave by). **NB** When you return to Syria you will still have to pay for a second Syrian visa, which will cost you just over US$50.

Quneitra Permits These are free, and can be obtained quickly and easily from the office just to the north of Adnan Malki Square/Museum (see Damascus: Salihiye map). The office is open 0800-1400, closed Fri. You should specify whether you want the permit to be valid for the same day or for the next day. Permits cannot be obtained more than 1 working day in advance.

Around Damascus

Damascus makes for a convenient base from which to explore the surrounding countryside. The places which are covered here are all easy day-trips (or less) from the capital. Bear in mind that the major sites to the south of Damascus (Bosra, Suweidha, Qanawat and Shahba), which are dealt with separately in the South of Damascus chapter (see page 143), can also be visited as longer day-trips. In addition Dumeir (on the route from Damascus to Palmyra, see page 170), and Deir Mar Mousa (a detour from the Damascus-Aleppo motorway, see page 202) are also feasible as day-trips, although if possible it is well worth staying overnight at the latter.

The Barada Gorge to Zabadani and Bloudan

From Damascus you can follow the narrow of the Barada River up through low hills which mark the southwest extremities of the Anti-Lebanon range, eventually arriving on the wide fertile plain of Zabadani. The town of Zabadani is the largest of several hill resorts in the area and popular amongst Syrians as a weekend retreat from the stifling summer heat of Damascus. Regular microbuses run from the Baramkeh bus station in Damascus, going via the modern Beirut motorway. However, by far the most picturesque route is by way of the 'old' Zabadani road, up through the green and well-wooded Barada gorge. This is also the route taken by the old narrow-gauge railway which runs as far as Sergaya, just short of the Lebanese border. Originally the line continued through to Beirut, with another branch following the Bekka valley northeast and continuing on to Homs.

Colour map 3, grid B1

At the time of writing, trains were still struggling up the narrow-gauge line from the Damascus Hejaz station via Ain Fijeh (in the Barada gorge) to Zabadani and on to Sergaya. These trains run only from June to October each year, when there is a daily service as far as Ain Fijeh, as well as a service on Tuesday, Thursday, Friday and Sunday to Zabadani and Sergaya (for more details, see page 127).

Train to Zabadani

An ancient Swiss-built diesel-fired steam train hauls equally antiquated wooden carriages on an excruciatingly slow trip taking 4 hrs to reach Zabadani. Perhaps the main reasons for taking this train are the novelty value, and the spectacle on weekends when it fills up with groups and families heading for the hills for a picnic, making for a lively occasion. The train stops briefly at a number of villages en route as it winds its way up the Barada gorge to Zabadani. From there it continues on to Sergaya, a small town just 5 km short of the Lebanese border with little of interest other than the backdrop of the Anti-Lebanon mountains. Here the train is turned around on a section of revolving track before starting on its return journey. If you are keen on taking the train but have limited time, take a microbus for the return journey (not more than 40 minutes). Services are most frequent from Zabadani; if you are only going as far as Ain el-Fijeh, bear in mind that microbus services from here are rather limited.

Damascus & around

The old road to Zabadani

There are various summer restaurants along the road as it winds its way through the Barada gorge. Although their setting amongst shady trees is pleasant enough, the river itself – generally little more than a stream – is unfortunately very polluted, particularly in summer when most people visit and flow is at its minimum.

From Umawiyeen Square head west along the continuation of Shoukri al-Kouwatli Street, keeping the *Sheraton* hotel on your left (signposted 'Dumar'). Continue straight through the busy town of Dumar (or 'Douma'). Around 10 km from Umawiyeen Square, shortly after passing the Barada Beer brewery on the left, there is a fork in the road with a petrol station in the wedge of the fork. Bear right here and just under 1 km further on you arrive at a T-junction with a large dual-carriageway. Go left here and right immediately after to rejoin the old Zabadani road.

The road first descends into a valley, the floor of which is surprisingly green and well-wooded, before starting to climb steadily, passing through several villages. At **Ain el-Fijeh** (just under 20 km from the Umawiyeen Square, off to the right below the main road) there are a few restaurants close to the railway station. In summer there is a daily train service as far as here. The village owes its name (and its existence) to the spring which emerges here and once used to add to the waters of the Barada River, though it is now piped directly to Damascus to supply the city's drinking water.

The small village of **Souk Wadi Barada** (28 km) stands on the site of the ancient Hellenistic town of **Abila**, which grew into an important centre on the route between Baalbek and Damascus. According to legend, it was on the mountain of Nebi Habil to the west of here that Cain buried Abel after killing him; hence the town's name. The only remains of the Hellenistic town, however, are in the occasional recycled architectural fragments to be found built into some of the houses.

Less than 2 km beyond the village, a series of rectangular doorways can be seen cut into the rockface on the opposite side of the now much narrowed gorge, marking a set of **Roman tombs**. The neatly hewn vaults each contain several compartments to house sarcophagi. To the left of the tombs (facing them from the road) a section of **irrigation channel** is visible, also of Roman origin or perhaps earlier, cut into the side of the rock face. Beyond this and above the level of the irrigation channel, there is a short stretch of **Roman road**, well preserved as it passes through a cutting. This is the road which connected Baalbek and Damascus. There are two inscriptions in the side of the cutting, both in Latin, which record how the road was restored following a landslide by the Legate Julius Verus, during the joint reign of Marcus Aurelius and Lucius Verus (161-180 AD).

Reaching the tombs, irrigation channel or Roman road is rather tricky, and only for the sure-footed

It is possible to **cross the gorge** from a point just past the Roman tombs, by walking across the rubbish-strewn bank from which the stream appears to emerge (if this is indeed one of the sources of the Barada, it can only be said that it starts as it means to go on), and then traversing a short though rather precarious section of concrete aquaduct to reach a path leading up to the tombs. Another option is to continue some 500 m along the modern road, around the corner to a point where a track leads off to the right. From here, double back along a track leading towards a small electricity pylon on a shoulder of the hillside. Just around the corner from this is the section of Roman road where it passes through a cutting. A little further on, it is possible to descend to the irrigation channel and follow it through a very deep and narrow cutting, followed by a short stretch of tunnel (not for the claustrophobic!), and then past a couple of tricky sections where the outside wall has fallen away, to arrive at the tombs.

Continuing along the main road, after just under 3 km you reach what is in effect a T-junction. Bear right here (left to reach the Damascus-Beirut motorway) and follow the road for a further 12 km to reach Zabadani. This last stretch is across a broad, fertile plain boasting **rich orchards** of apples, apricots, walnuts, plums and cherries.

Zabadani الزبداني

This popular hill resort has an affluent and, in summer at least, lively feel to it with plenty of well stocked shops along the main high street and a good selection of restaurants and cafés to choose from. Up on the hillside above the main town is a rapidly growing area of holiday homes owned by richer Syrians. The main high street, which crosses the railway line just by the station, is the focus for the modern town, with most of the shops, restaurants and cafés. Downhill from the station is 'old' Zabadani, quieter and more picturesque with an interesting old mosque in the centre and, close by, a Catholic church.

Phone code: 011

There is 1 hotel in Zabadani itself, the **D** *Al Siyaha (Tourist)*, on the main high street, about 100 m downhill from where the railway line crosses it, on the right by a small oval-shaped roundabout, T/F7116038. Fan, TV, phone, fridge, attached bath, reasonably clean and comfortable but nothing special. The various restaurants and snack places along the main high street all offer a fairly similar selection of traditional Arabic food. Prices are somewhat inflated, however, and it is worth checking them before ordering. Note that many of them remain closed during winter.

Sleeping & eating

Regular microbuses make the 45-min trip between **Damascus** and Zabadani (S£20), departing from the Baramkeh station in Damascus and touring Zabadani to pick up passengers for the return trip.

Transport

Bloudan بلودان

The town of Bloudan is situated 7 km to the east of Zabadani, at the slightly higher altitude of 1,400 m. It is a smaller and somewhat more exclusive version of Zabadani, consisting mostly of modern concrete construction which has largely swamped the original Greek Orthodox and Catholic village out of which it grew. Driving up from Zabadani, the road hairpins its way up the mountainside, offering great views out over the valley below, before arriving in the town's main square. This square is actually in the lower part of the town, and from here you can continue up the mountainside, passing ever more exclusive and fancy residences and restaurants along the way. Fridays are the best day to visit (this is true of Zabadani also), when the town is at its liveliest with day-trippers from Damascus, as well as visitors from Lebanon and Gulf-State holidaymakers.

Phone code: 011

AL *Regency Park*, on right as you head up to Bloudan, around half way up from Zabadani, T7115999, F7115990. Open all year. Suitably luxurious rooms with a/c, TV/dish, IDD, minibar, safe box, attached bath and balcony (good views). Choice of 3 restaurants; *Four Seasons* (international), *Sanawbara* (Arabic) and *Prego* (Italian), as well as a café, bar and nightclub. Other facilities include a conference hall, small indoor pool and a children's play area. All very modern and fancy. High season runs from Jun-Sep. **A/B** *Bloudan Grand*, in main sq. Closed at the time of writing, but due to open for the summer of 2001 according to locals. There are tennis courts and a swimming pool in the grounds. **C** *Akel*, in main square, opposite *Grand* hotel, T7128604, F7127959. Open from May-Dec. Simple but clean rooms with phone, TV, attached bath, balcony and great views. Restaurant. Room prices drop to a very reasonable **E** category outside of Jul/Aug high season. **C** *Alaa Tower*, on the left as you head up towards Bloudan, just before the arches over the road marking the start of the town, T/F7128997. Open May-Oct only. Part of the Damascus-based chain. Comfortable rooms with fan, TV/dish, phone, fridge, attached bath and balcony. Good views.

Sleeping & eating

Hotel categories given here are based on prices for the Jul and Aug high season; outside these months rates fall significantly. Except around the time of the Feast of Saidnaya (8 Sep). Many pilgrims stop here for lunch en route to Saidnaya

Damascus & around

If you want to dine out in style, try one of the restaurants in the *Regency Park* hotel, or else along the road heading up the mountainside above Bloudan (at the top of this road is the highly exclusive *Al Atlal*). For something a little less rarified, the *Akel* hotel features a large restaurant on the ground and first floors with open-air terraces. There is a menu in English displayed on the wall offering a wide range of Arabic dishes at very reasonable prices. The food is good quality and the service friendly and helpful. During the high season it gets very lively here (particularly on Fri).

Transport Being such an exclusive resort, there is no regular public transport up to Bloudan. If you do not have your own transport, you will have to hire a taxi from Zabadani, or else you could try hitching (there is plenty of traffic between the 2 towns on Fri).

Via Saidnaya and Maaloula to Yabroud

Colour map 3, grid B2

The two towns of Saidnaya and Maaloula were important centres of early Christianity and can both be visited as excursions from Damascus. If you continue on to Yabroud, this route also offers a more interesting alternative for part of the otherwise motorway-bound journey between Damascus and Homs.

From the Citadel, head north along Ath Thawra Street, over the flyover and under the underpass, following the signs for 'Barzeh'. Follow the road round to the right at Ibn Nafis Hospital (around 4 km from the centre of Damascus) and then go straight, ignoring the fork to the right soon after signposted for Aleppo and Lattakia. Just under 2 km beyond the Ibn Nafis Hospital, turn left at a crossroads. After this turning, there are frequent signs for Saidnaya and Maaloula. The road winds its way through rocky hills, passing first through the village of **Barzeh**, behind which, on the eastern slopes of Mount Kassioun, is a shrine said to mark the birthplace of Abraham. Around 4 km after the crossroads, bear right where the road forks (signposted), and then bear left soon after (not signposted). The road by now has emerged onto a wide flat plain. Around 27 km from Damascus you reach a large modern roundabout; go left here to ascend to the town of Saidnaya.

If you continue straight on past this roundabout, a little under 2 km further on there is second roundabout with a newly built hospital beside it and a left turn signposted for Saidnaya. Around 600 m beyond this there is another left turn for Saidnaya, followed immediately after by a left turn leading up to Cherubim Convent (see below). Continuing straight along the main road, after around 15 km you pass through the large village of **Al Tawani**, before arriving at a T-junction (just under 24 km from the turning for Cherubim Convent). Turn left here (you pass soon after through a pair of concrete arches, complete with towers and crenellations, which mark the start of **Maaloula** village), and it is another 4 km into the centre (turning right takes you down to the main Damascus-Homs motorway). Arriving in the village, bear right at a roundabout, follow the road round to the right and then sharply left through an S-bend to climb up to Deir Mar Takla. Note that if you are heading for Saidnaya from Maaloula, the small right turn after you pass through the concrete arches is signposted only as an alternative route back to Damascus.

Saidnaya صيدنايا

Phone code: 011
At the time of the Crusades, Saidnaya was second only to Jerusalem as a centre of pilgrimage in the region

Saidnaya is a rapidly growing town, with lots of new construction giving it a somewhat modern, nondescript air in places, despite an impressive array of convents, monasteries, churches, chapels and shrines. Its origins go back to ancient times, with evidence suggesting that it was inhabited at least from the sixth century BC, when it was known by the Aramaic name of 'Danaba'.

Evidence of occupation can be found right the way through Greek and Roman times, and it emerged as an important centre of Christianity well before this became the official religion of the Roman Empire.

In the centre, perched on a rocky hillock overlooking the town is the Greek Orthodox **Convent of Our Lady of Saidnaya**. From a distance it looks for all the world like a fortress and some people argue that this was the function it originally served. The convent is an important pilgrimage site for Christians and Muslims alike, the object of veneration being an icon of the Virgin Mary supposedly painted by St Luke. According to legend, the convent was founded by the Byzantine Emperor Justinian during the sixth century. Much damaged by earthquakes and the passage of time, today the convent is a jumbled mixture of old features and new restoration, much of the latter undertaken in recent years. Flights of stairs zigzag up from the parking area below the convent to the small low doorway leading inside. (Alternatively the tower to the left houses a lift!) The main chapel has numerous painted gold icons and a wooden *iconostasis* in front of the altar. The pilgrimage shrine, known as '*Shaghoura*' ('the famous') is a small dark room round the right-hand side of the chapel on the outside. The icon attributed to St Luke is kept hidden in an ornate silver-doored niche, while either side of this there are a number of later icons. Numerous beaten silver crosses and other religious symbols left by pilgrims are pinned to the walls. The large room off the courtyard to the right of the shrine houses a small museum, containing mostly painted gold icons. You will need to track down someone with the key if it is not open.

The hillock on which the convent is perched was certainly the site of earlier shrines, including possibly a sun temple dating from Greek and Roman times. As you ascend by the road up to the car park below the convent, a **cave tomb** is visible cut into the side of the rock, sealed by a metal door. Above it are three carved niches each containing a pair of figures (today very worn and headless) and a conch shell semi-dome in the arch of the niches. Greek inscriptions date these tombs to 178 AD, although in all probability they were first inhabited far earlier. Around Saidnaya there are a number of caves which have shown evidence of settlement since the early Stone Age, the most important of these being in the low rocky mound by the roundabout as you approach Saidnaya.

Amongst the houses which cluster around the convent there are numerous other small churches, monasteries and shrines dedicated to various saints. Some are very old, although the majority of these have undergone extensive restoration. The **Church of St Peter**, situated by the roundabout below the Convent of Our Lady of Saidnaya, on the southeast side, is a remarkably intact Roman building which has remained almost completely unmodified since its conversion to a church.

Just over 2 km to the northwest of Saidnaya, and accessible only by foot, is the **Monastery of Mar Thomas**, also originally a Roman Temple which was later converted into a monastery. The route is not obvious, so walk in the general direction and then ask – you should be pointed along the correct track with a bit of luck. The main building is a squat structure set in a courtyard. It has been partially restored, with a new cross of white stone now standing on the top. The building is locked and the keys kept at the main convent.

Around 8 km to the northeast of Saidnaya, strategically situated on the highest point of the local Qallamoun mountain range, is the **Cherubim Convent**. From the turning off the main Saidnaya-Maaloula road (see above), the narrow road winds its way steeply up to the convent, offering some excellent views along the way. The church itself is a small building, restored in 1982 when a new roof was added, but incorporating three classical columns and

The various caves dotted around the monastery, some of them with supporting pillars, doorways & windows, are thought to have been used as accommodation for the monks

Damascus & around

some huge stone blocks which attest to its origins sometime during the third century AD. Today the church is dwarfed by a large and somewhat ungainly new school/orphanage. The keys to the church are held by the resident caretaker. Dotted around the grounds are various architectural fragments from Greek and Roman times. Adjacent to the church is a rocky outcrop topped by two crosses, from where there are panoramic views out over the town of Saidnaya and the surrounding countryside.

Sleeping & eating There is only 1 hotel in Saidnaya, the **D** *Saidnaya*, on the western outskirts of town (heading up into town from the first roundabout as you arrive from Damascus, a sign on the right points the way down a steep narrow street to the hotel), T5953739. Simple but comfortable rooms with heater, phone and attached bath, some rooms with balcony. Restaurant and small swimming pool. Alternatively, it may be possible to stay at the convent.

On the main street just below the Convent of Our Lady of Saidnaya there are a couple of simple sandwich/snack places, as well as the *Al Massaya*, a small but clean and pleasant restaurant serving reasonable food. If you continue straight on at the first roundabout as you approach from Damascus, after just under 1 km there is a very large and fancy restaurant complex, the *Al Tilal* on the left, T5950001, F5950007. This actually consists of 5 different halls dedicated to French, Spanish, Italian, Chinese or Arabic cuisine respectively, although you have to book ahead for all except the Arabic hall. A meal here will cost from around S£500 per head upwards. At the time of writing, another restaurant was under construction by the first roundabout as you come from Damascus.

Festivals **The Feast of Our Lady of Saidnaya** (8th Sep). With its numerous churches and shrines, Saidnaya has a host of religious feast days. The most important of these is the Feast of Our Lady of Saidnaya. Vast numbers of pilgrims, both Christian and Muslim, flock here every year for this event from all over the Middle East. People start arriving a couple of days before, with the main celebrations taking place on the night of the 7th, and being repeated again on a smaller scale on the following night. Around this time practically every available inch of floorspace within the Convent of Our Lady of Saidnaya is taken up with pilgrims sleeping, praying, eating picnics etc. Rooms at the town's only hotel, meanwhile, double in price and are soon all full.

Transport Fairly frequent microbuses run from the Maaloula Station in **Damascus** directly to Saidnaya, departing when full (S£15). Public transport between Saidnaya and **Maaloula** is less frequent. Your best bet is to wait down on the main road and hitch; any traffic heading in that direction is sure to give you a lift.

Maaloula معلولا

Phone code: 011
Colour map 3, grid B2

Huddled strikingly against the sheer cliffs that mark the edges of the Qallamoun mountains, its blue-painted houses stacked tightly one above the other, Maaloula presents an angular and colourful picture. Also an important centre of Christianity, it is famous mostly as one of a few places in Syria where Aramaic, the language of Jesus, is still spoken.

Some of the caves around Maaloula suggest that it was a centre for pre-historic settlement, while others appear to have been dug during Greek and Roman times and subsequently used by the early Christians as refuges from persecution. (The occurrence of Aramaic in the region, together with the inscriptions found in some of the caves, confirm Maaloula as one of the earliest centres of Christianity.) Later, during the Byzantine period, Christianity flourished in the area.

Deir Mar Takla (Convent of St Takla) According to legend, this convent grew up around the shrine of St Takla (or St Thecla), daughter of one of the Selucid princes and a pupil of St Paul. The legend relates how Takla was being pursued by soldiers sent by her father to execute her for her Christian faith. Finding herself trapped against the sheer cliffs of Qallamoun, she prayed to God for help. Her prayer was answered when a narrow cleft was opened in the rock face, allowing her to escape to a small cave high up in the cliffs. Most of the buildings of the current convent are of recent origin, and none show any evidence of surviving Byzantine work. The main chapel has a number of icons inside, while the shrine of St Takla is above, in the side of the rock face.

The defile From the parking area below the convent, a path leads up through a narrow defile, the rock on either side pressing in, almost to form a tunnel in places. This is the cleft in the cliffs referred to in the legend of St Takla, and there are numerous shrines and caves which have been dug into the rock along its length. It is also to this defile that Maaloula owes its name, the word meaning literally 'entrance' in Aramaic. The defile brings you out eventually at the top of the cliffs. Close to where it emerges, there is the *St Takla* restaurant with a pleasant garden terrace set amongst poplar trees. Bear left and follow the road up past the *Safir Maaloula* hotel to reach the monastery of Mar Sarkis. If you do not wish to walk, you can get to the monastery by car – bear left at the roundabout in the village.

Deir Mar Sarkis The monastery of St Sarkis (or St Serge, from Sergius) is believed to have been founded in the early fourth century AD, on the site of an earlier Greek/Roman temple dedicated to Apollo. St Sarkis, along with St Bacchus, to whom the monastery is dedicated, were soldiers in the Roman army based at Rasafeh (see page 375). Having converted to Christianity, they refused to make sacrifices to the god Jupiter and were put to death. Their remains are believed to have been housed in the large basilica there, and during the Byzantine period Rasafeh was known as Sergiopolis in honour of St Sarkis.

The entrance to Deir Mar Sarkis is through a low, awkward doorway, presumably a defensive feature. This leads through to a small, recently restored courtyard. On your right is a room labelled 'Museum and Souvenirs'. There is an excellent series of postcards of the monastery's icons on sale here, along with various items of religious kitsch. The square pit hewn out of the stone floor in this room was for pressing grapes.

At the far end of the courtyard, on the right, a passage leads through to the monastery's church. The main altar of the church, in the central apse, is of particular interest, consisting of a semi-circular slab of marble with a 7cm rim around it. The fact that the altar is semi-circular is taken as evidence that it dates from before 325 AD, the date of the First Council of Nicea, when it was decreed that all altars had to be flat and rectangular. The rim around the edge of the altar is thought to be a feature which survived from pagan times, when altars were used for animal sacrifices in which the blood had to be collected. As the monks of the monastery are quick to point out, however, the rim appears to have been simply a stylistic feature, as in this case there is no drainage point from which to collect the blood, nor is the rim engraved with the animals which were suitable for sacrifice, as was the norm on pagan altars. Below the altar is a small crypt. In the side-apse to the left is another altar, this one also with a rim, though rectangular in shape. Note the fresco in the dome above the altar, depicting the heavens with the Virgin Mary and Jesus surrounded by the saints Mathew, Mark, Luke and John.

Damascus & around

Aramaic

Aramaic, much trumpeted as the language spoken by Jesus, first emerged in ancient Syria and Palestine far earlier, during the seventh to sixth centuries BC, when it began to replace Hebrew, with which it shares its roots as a Semitic language. It continued to be widely spoken throughout the region until the Arab conquest during the seventh century AD. Its importance to Christianity is undisputed and parts of the Bible, notably the Gospel of St Matthew, were originally written in Aramaic.

Sometimes referred to as West Syriac, Aramaic continues to be spoken in Maaloula, and in the nearby villages of Bakhaa and Jabadin, although in recent times it has been for the most part replaced by Arabic. This dialect also survives in the extreme northeast of Syria, amongst communities which have only recently returned to the area, preserving the language during centuries of exile in present-day northern Iraq and eastern Turkey.

Some of the icons in the church are thought to date back as far as the 13th century

The *iconostasis* of the church includes a number of particularly beautiful icons painted by St Michael of Crete in the early 19th century. The one above the entrance to the central apse is of St Sarkis and St Bacchus. On the pillar to the right of the entrance to the central apse is something you don't see often: Christ's crucifixion and the Last Supper portrayed in a single icon. It is also unusual in that Jesus is seated to the right of the table rather than in the centre. Also of interest is the icon of St John the Baptist, here smiling and relaxed, with his legs crossed (in contrast to the usual serious/formal depictions), having baptized Jesus and therefore completed his mission.

There is clear evidence in the church of its ancient origins. The lower part of the *iconostasis* consists of stone slabs taken from the earlier Greek/Roman temple, while some of the capitals appear to have originated from the same source. Above the arches separating the nave from the side-aisles, wooden beams can be seen incorporated into the stonework. These are thought to have served to reinforce the church against earthquakes. Samples taken from them have indicated that they are Lebanese cedar, and around 2,000 years old, suggesting that they too were recycled from the original temple. Outside the church, around the side, there is an even smaller arched entrance, now protected by a porch and sealed behind a metal door. In the immediate vicinity of the monastery there are several substantial rock-cut caves.

Sleeping & eating

There is only 1 hotel in Maaloula, the **AL** *Safir Maaloula*, up on the cliffs above the village, near Deir Mar Sarkis, T7770250, F7770255, safir@net.sy OK rooms with fan, heater, TV/dish, phone, minibar, attached bath. Restaurant, bar, coffee shop, playroom, swimming pool, sauna, tennis. Comfortable but not up to the same high standards as the *Safir* hotel in Homs, and a somewhat insensitive addition to the skyline. A new wing was under construction at the time of writing.

In addition to the hotel restaurant (expensive) and the nearby *St Takla* restaurant (pleasant and more reasonable), there is also a restaurant (in theory cheap, but check prices) and several simple snack places by the car park just below Deir Mar Takla.

Festivals

There are 3 feast days celebrated at Maaloula. The most important is the **Exhaltation of the Holy Cross**, on the 14th Sep, when fires are lit on top of the cliffs and there is dancing and celebrations and fireworks. The **Feast of St Takla** comes soon after, on the 24th Sep, while the **Feast of St Sergius** is celebrated on the 7th Oct.

Transport

Regular buses and microbuses run from the Maaloula bus station in Damascus. They usually take you right up to the parking area by the entrance to Deir Mar Takla. Be sure to check what time the last service is leaving for the return journey (usually a little before nightfall).

Maaloula to Yabroud يبرود

The road leading from the centre of Maaloula up to Deir Mar Sarkis is also the road to Yabroud. Four km from the roundabout in Maaloula, turn right at a T-junction and then keep going straight, passing through two villages before descending steadily to reach the town of Yabroud, 19 km from Maaloula. En route, the Qallamoun mountains present a very different aspect, sloping up gently to the west, and revealing themselves as part of the plain itself, tilted up and sheared off to create the sheer cliffs that characterize the setting of Maaloula as seen from the east. Shortly before arriving in Yabroud, you pass on the right more rock-cut tombs dating from Roman times. Bear left as you enter the town to reach the centre; right takes you directly on to the Damascus-Homs motorway.

Colour map 3, grid B2

There is evidence of settlement in the area of Yabroud going back at least to the Mesolithic period (10,000-7,500 BC), while in Roman times the town appears to have formed part of the territory placed under the control of Agrippa II. Its importance can be surmised from the discovery in Rome of an altar dedicated to *Malekiabrudis* or Jupiter Malek of Yabroud, the local form of Jupiter. Today Yabroud is a sizeable, prosperous and rapidly growing town, thriving on the narrow strip of fertile agricultural land in which it is set. In the centre there is the large Greek Catholic **Cathedral of Constantine and Helen**. This is thought to stand on the site of an earlier Temple of Jupiter, with stones from the temple having been incorporated into the fabric of the cathedral. Inside, the cathedral consists mostly of modern restoration, although there are some beautiful icons and traces of Roman architectural fragments in the apses. On the edges of the town the remains of another ancient church are being incorporated into a new church of modernistic design. Following the main road northeast out of Yabroud, after 8 km it joins the Damascus-Homs motorway just south of the town of Nabk.

Yabroud

Quneitra القنيطرة and the Golan Heights

Just 60 km to the southeast of Damascus are the Golan Heights, an area of high plateau between Mount Hermon and the northeastern shores of the Sea of Galilee, effectively marking the southern limits of the Anti-Lebanon mountains. Known in antiquity as the *Gaulanitis* and then later as *Jaulan*, historically this area forms part of the wider Hauran region. Today it has become emblazoned in most people's minds as a potent symbol of the Arab-Israeli conflict.

Colour map 3, grid B1

Originally part of Syria, the Golan Heights were lost to Israel during the 1967 war. In 1973 Egypt and Syria launched simultaneous attacks on the Israeli-occupied Sinai and Golan Heights. Despite initial gains by Egypt and Syria, they were both subsequently pushed back and it was only in the negotiations following a ceasefire that Syria was able to regain some 450 sq km lost in the fighting. A UN-supervised demilitarized zone was established to separate the two sides, with Syria now administering this area under continued UN supervision.

History

The town of Quneitra today stands at the very edge of this demilitarized zone, with Israeli-occupied territory immediately beyond the barbed wire fences on its western outskirts. When the Israelis withdrew in 1973, they completely demolished the town, leaving only the smashed, empty shells of buildings in their wake, and the Syrians have responded by leaving almost everything exactly as they found it, as a propaganda showcase against Israel.

Ins & outs **Permits** All visitors to Quneitra must obtain a permit in advance from Damascus. Although in the 1980s getting permission to visit Quneitra was rather difficult, the authorities now appear quite keen to encourage visitors. Permits are free and are generally issued within around half an hour (see page 133 for more details).

Getting there Microbuses run from the Baramkeh bus station in Damascus to Khan Arnabeh (S£20), from where a second bus will take you on to Quneitra itself. Set off early since this second bus runs less frequently as the day progresses. Returning, the guide who will have accompanied you around Quneitra will ensure that you get back to Khan Arnabeh, from where there are regular microbuses back to Damascus.

If you are **driving**, head out of Damascus on the Mezzeh road (from Umawiyeen Square head southwest, keeping the *Sheraton* hotel on your right). Keep going straight to pass under the Beirut motorway (Quneitra is prominently signposted straight ahead) and keep to this road all the way. After a while the looming outline of Mount Hermon comes clearly into view off to the right, often still streaked with snow as late as June. At the first checkpost you come to, around 30 km from Damascus by a right turn signposted for Beit Saber, your permit and passport details are recorded in a book. A little further on, there are the remains of a large fortress on the right as you enter the town of Sa'asaa. Beyond Sa'asaa the countryside gives way to the distinctive rocky black basalt terrain of the Hauran. At Khan Arnabeh, (61 km from Damascus) your permit and passport details will be recorded once again and a guide is assigned to show you around. It is a further 9 km on to Quneitra itself.

Quneitra

The sign outside the hospital proclaiming "Golan Hospital. Destructed by the Zionists and changed it to a firing target" clearly demonstrates (however ungrammatically) the jealousy with which the Syrians preserve this bitter legacy in crumbling concrete

How much time it is worth devoting to wandering around looking at the collapsed shells of buildings is debatable, but this battered ghost town does have an eerie atmosphere. Here, frozen in time, is an illustration of one of the great unresolved disputes of the Arab-Israeli conflict, a tangible episode of the modern history of the Middle East preserved in twisted metal and concrete. The UN military posts, the copious barbed wire and the Golan Heights themselves off to the west, all stand testimony to the continuing intractability of the dispute.

The **hospital** is a favourite showpiece. Inside you can inspect the heavily ruined shell of the building, while from the roof you can get good views over the town and the Golan Heights. Other prominent ruins include those of a **church** and a **mosque**. The **Liberated Quneitra Museum** is one of the few buildings to have been brought back into use. Housed in what was originally an Ottoman khan (of some interest in itself), the museum brings together a small collection of pre-historic, Roman and Byzantine artefacts; pottery, coins, architectural fragments etc.

Following the main street to the very western extemity of the town, barbed wire marks the start of a stretch of **no-man's land**, beyond which is effectively Israel. As if to make a point, the only other functioning building in the town is here, pressed right up against the barbed wire and used as a restaurant for the benefit of visiting tourists. Here you can sit up on the roof and sip on a coke while training a pair of binoculars onto Israeli occupied territory. Of the two mountains to the east beyond the wide strip of cultivated land, the one to the left, bristling with the paraphernalia of Israel's observation and early warning systems, is Abou Nader, while the one to the right is Araam. As for the restaurant itself, it caters mostly for organized groups, and overcharges heavily.

South of Damascus: the Hauran

4

South of Damascus: the Hauran

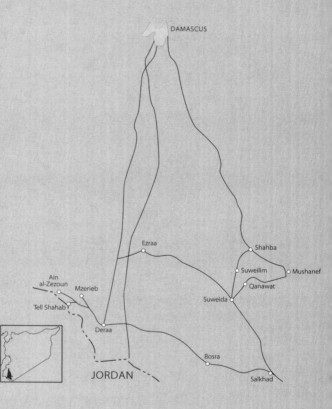

The Hauran is a plateau occupying the area to the south of Damascus as far as the Jordanian border and consisting of volcanic and basaltic rock interspersed by pockets of fertile soil. The black basalt rock which predominates gives the region a sombre air, extending also to its monuments, hewn out of the same dark and unyielding stone. Bathed in late afternoon sun, however, landscapes and monuments alike become almost luminous, revealing a beauty all their own.

In the southeast, the Hauran is defined by the mountains of the **Jebel al-Arab** (referred to as Mount Bashan in the Psalms and known until recently as the Jebel Druze). These rise to 1,800 m and act as a barrier against the desert to the east. Occupying the central region of the Hauran is an area known as the **Leja**, essentially an immense sheet of lava which has created a dramatic, if austere, landscape. The western limits of the Hauran are marked by the area known as the Golan (or Jaulan), rising in the southwest to the disputed Golan Heights. Between **Bosra** and **Deraa**, meanwhile, is the large and particularly fertile **Nuqra plain**, its fields golden with wheat and barley in spring.

A foot in the door

★ Far and away the most impressive sight in southern Syria is the immaculately preserved **Roman theatre at Bosra**. This is the largest theatre in the Middle East, and unique in that it is neatly enclosed within a medieval citadel. Every other year (usually at the beginning of September) it is the venue for a large **festival**; if your visit to Syria coincides with this event, it is well worth catching it.

★ The town of **Suweida** is not particularly inspiring, but the small museum here houses an extremely beautiful collection of mosaics, and is worth a visit in its own right.

★ Nearby, the small village of **Qanawat** boasts the ruins of a delicate and richly decorated Roman temple complex which was converted into churches during the Byzantine era.

★ Qanawat lies on the edge of the **Jebel al-Arab** area, and if you have your own transport you can take a detour through these picturesque, rolling hills to reach the town of Shahba, site of the Roman city of **Philippopolis** and also home to a small museum of beautiful mosaics.

Ins and outs

Getting around If you are travelling by **public transport**, some planning is required. Although there are regular direct services from Damascus to each of the major places of interest (most conveniently from the Baramkeh bus station, see page 128), connections between them are less reliable. The main problem is with the trip between Bosra and Suweida. For some reason there is no public transport along this route, making it very difficult to visit all the sites in one loop from Damascus. Instead it is more practical to make two separate trips (both can be day-trips, or longer): one to Bosra (and perhaps Ezraa and Deraa) and another to Shahba, Qanawat and Suweida. With your **own transport**, you are free to visit the sites in any order, although covering them all in one day would involve something of a hectic schedule.

Sleeping There is a luxury hotel in Bosra, as well as the opportunity to sleep inside the theatre in a basic hostel. There is basic and lower/medium range accommodation in Deraa and Suweida.

History

The Hauran was for a time colonized by the Greeks under Alexander the Great, before the conflicts of the rival Seleucid and Ptolomid Empires opened the region to competing Nabatean and Jewish claims. Thus in 23 BC Augustus, ruler of the newly expanding Roman Empire, granted control over it to Herod the Great, the king of Judaea. Then in 34 AD it was briefly made part of the Roman Empire before being handed over to Herod Agrippa I by Caligula. In 70 AD the Nabateans made Bosra the new capital of their empire, although they never succeeded in extending their control over the whole region.

In 106 AD the Romans, who until then had exercised for the most part only nominal control over much of Syria, established the province of *Arabia*, with Bosra as its capital. Subsequently the Hauran flourished under the new stability brought by the *Pax Romana*. Agriculture was developed, making this one of the great granaries of the empire, while the important trade routes which passed through Bosra brought further prosperity. The rise to power of Philip the Arab as emperor in the mid-third century AD ensured that the Hauran maintained its importance, with Shahba being developed into a prosperous imperial city alongside Bosra.

During the Byzantine period the Hauran continued to prosper as an important centre of Christianity. However, following the Muslim Arab invasions of the seventh century the region fell into relative decline, becoming an unstable zone of conflict, first between the rival Fatimid and Abbasid dynasties and later the Muslims and Crusaders.

In the 18th and 19th centuries large numbers of Druze migrated into the area, first from Mount Lebanon and later from Damascus and surrounding areas. Thus the mountainous massif in the southeast became known as the Jebel Druze, and today this region remains something of a Druze enclave.

Damascus to Deraa and Bosra

The easiest way to get to Deraa is via the motorway running due south from Damascus. To join the motorway (although this is by no means the most direct route, it is the best) is to head southwest from Umawiyeen Square along the Mezzeh Autostrade (keeping the *Sheraton* hotel on your right), and then, after just under 5 km, join the motorway ring-road around Damascus heading anticlockwise. The first exit you come to, after a further 5 km, is the motorway for Deraa, Bosra and the Jordanian border (clearly signposted). Around 77 km after joining the motorway, there is an exit clearly signposted for Ezraa, 3 km to the east (see below). From here it is just over 14 km to the exit for Deraa (clearly signposted). The exit for Bosra is just over 10 km further on, or you could continue on to cross into Jordan via the Nasib/Jabir border crossing. Taking the Deraa exit, after just over 9 km you arrive at a T-junction. Turn left here to join the old Deraa road. It is a further 6 km into the centre of Deraa, passing the huge new Assad's Athletic City sports complex on the way and entering the town along Damascus Street.

An alternative route is to take the **old Deraa road**, which runs roughly parallel to the motorway for the entire journey. From the Hejaz railway station, head south along Halbouni Street, eventually joining Khaled Ibn Walid Street and following it past Kadam railway station. Around 5 km south of Kadam station, continue straight past a right turn signposted for Deraa and Jordan (this turning takes you onto the motorway), and keep going straight. The old Deraa road is slightly more direct (105 km as opposed to 115 km), but also considerably slower and without any particular attractions along its route.

Ezraa إزرع

The town of Ezraa, identified with the ancient *Zorava*, was an important centre of Christianity during the Byzantine period, its bishop being invited to attend the Council of Chalcedon in 451 AD. It is famous for the ancient and well preserved Greek Orthodox St George's Church (Mar Georgis). *Colour map 3, grid B2*

Ins & outs The easiest way to reach Ezraa by public transport is from Deraa (main bus station). If there is no bus going direct, catch one to Ash Sheikh Miskeen, and change there for Ezraa. Services along this route are reasonably frequent. There are also less frequent buses from the Deraa bus station in Damascus.

From Ezraa, there is a good road running southeast which traverses the lava-strewn Leja region to arrive at Suweida, 37 km away. Ask directions in the centre of Ezraa to pick up the correct road.

Sights **St George's Church** is about 3 km to the north of the town centre. Arriving from the motorway, you pass the huge silos of a grain processing factory on the left; bear right here to arrive shortly after at a roundabout in the centre of town marked by a mosque with a distinctive black and white banded minaret. Bear left here (signposted 'Archeaological Area') and then straight across the next roundabout and keep following this road until you arrive at the church (or just ask for directions; locals are used to foreigners looking for the church).

An inscription on the lintel of the central portal of the west entrance (around to the left from the current entrance), reads *"What was once a lodging place for demons has become a house of God; where once idols were sacrificed, there are now choirs of angels; where God was provoked to wrath, now He is propitiated."* The inscription dates from 515, making this amongst the oldest functioning churches in Syria along with those of Saidnaya and Maaloula. As the inscription suggests, the church stands on the site of an earlier temple. Its design is of particular interest, representing one of the earliest examples of a basilica constructed on an octagonal plan and surmounted by a cupola. Inside, eight columns arranged in an octagon and connected by arches support the central cupola, a more recent metal and wood reconstruction of the original. This is enclosed within a basic square plan, with small chapels in each corner creating an octagonal effect. Note the corbelled ceiling of basalt slabs, one of which is carved with three medallions. On the east side, behind a simple wooded *iconostasis*, is an apse and two side-chambers which extend beyond the basic square plan to give a rectangular shape from the outside. In the central apse, behind the altar, is a tomb which according to local tradition is that of St George himself. ■ *If the church is locked, ask around and someone will send for the caretaker. There are no fixed opening times or entrance fee, though a donation towards the upkeep of the church, and perhaps a small tip for the caretaker, is expected.*

Just before you reach the church, on the right, are the **ruins of an Ayyubid mosque**; all that survives of it is the prayer hall, which is still largely intact, with two arcades of arches supported on a variety of pillars, columns and even a double column. The corbelled ceiling is still in place, as is the black and white banded *mihrab*.

Nearby, down a small side-street, is the Greek Catholic **Church of St Elias**. Although this is also very old, dating from 542, it has undergone extensive reconstruction and restoration in recent years. Architecturally it is also interesting, the east-west orientated cruciform plan being unusual for Syria. Inside, a central square of pillars and arches supports the cupola, which is a modern affair. The internal walls are now all plastered, but on the outside you can still see much of the original stonework, complete with various inscriptions and carvings.

Deraa درعا

Phone code: 015
Colour map 3, grid C1

Today, there is not a great deal of interest in Deraa, but the town has been identified with the ancient *Edrei*, mentioned in the Bible as one of the residences of Og, king of Bashan. During the Byzantine period it was known as *Adraa*. But it was during the early 20th century that the town grew in importance as a station on the Hejaz railway line between Damascus and Medina and the junction for the Haifa branch. Nowadays the town is useful mostly as a base for visiting Bosra, Tell Shahab and Ezraa. It is also the place to go from if you wish to cross the border into Jordan by local transport.

Ins & outs The main bus station is inconveniently located around 3 km to the east of the town centre, on the road to Bosra. There are regular luxury coach, bus and microbus services connecting Deraa with Damascus and Bosra, as well as less regular microbus services running between Deraa and Suweidha. You can also join the twice-weekly train service which runs between Damascus and Amman here. Deraa's hotels and restaurants are to be found along Ibrahim Hanano St, just to the south of the railway station, while the main sights are a couple of kilometres to the south, across the river in the older part of the town. There is a **tourist information** office on the old road to Damascus, just north of where it crosses the railway tracks (open 0800-1430, closed Fri, T232873). Further north, on the same side of the street, is the **post office**. The **telephone office** is on Ash Shouhada St, just east of the turning up to the railway station; the cardphones here are accessible only when the office is open.

In the southern part of the town is the **Omari Mosque**. Built in 1253 by the **Sights** Ayyubid Emir, Nasser ud-Din Osman Ibn Ali, it follows the same basic plan as the Umayyad Mosque in Damascus. In one corner is a distinctive square tower-minaret. Inside you find yourself in a large courtyard with the prayer hall to the right as you enter. Around the three remaining sides is an arcade supported by two parallel rows of columns and arches. The columns (almost certainly taken from the Roman theatre next door) are unusually short and topped by an odd assortment of capitals, with the stonework of the arches making up the remaining height. The prayer hall has three parallel rows of arches, also supported on squat columns, with a central transcept marking the *mihrab*.

Across the road from the mosque there is an area of excavations including, at the far end of the site, the scant remains of a **Roman theatre**, parts of which have been rather insensitively restored. In the excavated pits closer to the mosque you can see sections of columns and various capitals just like those found in the mosque.

For those with a fascination for the bygone days of steam, the **railway station**, in the centre of the modern (northern) half of the town, is perhaps worth a visit. Looking at the general state of dilapidation all around (various decaying steam engines can be seen standing in the sidings around the station), it is hard to believe that trains really do still run through here en route for Amman.

On Ibrahim Hanano Street there is the recently opened **Syndicate of Fine Arts**, which contains a small but interesting collection of paintings (and some sculpture) by artists from southern Syria. ■ *Open 0800-1400, closed Fri. Entry free.*

In the northeast of the town, near the junction of Bosra Street with Al Jumhouriyeh Street, there is a **museum** under construction, although work on this project seems to be progressing at a painfully slow rate and no one is sure when it will open.

Deraa

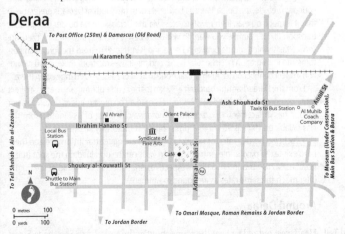

Sleeping & eating
■ *on map*
Price codes:
see inside front cover

D *Orient Palace (Al Chark)*, Ibrabim Hanano St, T/F238304. Clean, spacious rooms (technically 'suites', with a separate sitting area) with fan, TV, phone and attached bath. Large restaurant. The best available accommodation in Deraa, but a little pricey and nothing that special. **F** *Al Ahram*, Ibrahim Hanano St, T230809. Basic rooms with table fan and attached bath. Not very friendly, and way overpriced at around S£500 for a double; try bargaining. **F** *Al Hadood*, 3 km to the south of Deraa, just short of the Jordanian border, T237703. Basic but clean and friendly. Some rooms with attached shower/toilet (double room S£500). Convenient if you arrive too late to cross the border into Jordan.

As well as the restaurant in the *Orient Palace*, there are a number of simple restaurants along Ibrahim Hanano St where you can get the usual selection of falafels, shawarmas, kebabs, roast chicken etc. The open square to the south of Ibrahim Hanano St has a pleasant café for tea, coffee and nargilehs.

Transport

Train The twice-weekly trains bound for **Amman** stop in Deraa at around 1000 on Mon and Thu (S£150). Those bound for **Damascus** stop in Deraa at around 1200 on the same days (S£25), but are more likely to be delayed at the border.

Bus The *Al Muhib* coach company has regular services to Damascus (Baramkeh station) every 30 mins or so between 0530-2300, S£50. Their ticket office/bus stop is located at the east end of Ash Shouhada St, which saves you the trouble of going out to the main bus station.

A private taxi to the main bus station (3 km to the east of the town centre, on the road to Bosra) will cost around S£25. You can usually find taxis waiting around at the west end of Ibrahim Hanano St, by the local bus station, or at the east end of Ash Shouhada St, near the *Al Muhib* ticket office. Alternatively, you can catch a microbus ('servees') for S£5 from Shukri al-Kouwatli St, by the local bus station. There are regular luxury coach, bus and minibus services from the main bus station to **Damascus** (S£25-50) and **Bosra** (S£10-15), and most other towns and villages in the area. Service taxis run to **Ramtha** (the first town on the Jordanian side of the border) for S£150; it may also be worth trying to pick one of these up from the taxi stand at the west end of Ibrahim Hanano St.

Crossing the border into Jordan All the international coaches and the majority of the service taxis heading for Amman from Damascus now go via the Nasib/Jabir border crossing to the southeast of Deraa for the simple reason that it is on the motorway route between the two capitals, making it the quickest way to go. If you are travelling with your own vehicle, the Deraa/Ramtha border, 4 km to the south of Deraa, is preferable in that it is much quieter. If you wish to cross via the Deraa/Ramtha border using public transport (if, for example you want to visit Bosra before heading into Jordan), there are service taxis which shuttle between Deraa and Ramtha, 3 km from the Jordanian customs and immigration post. Regular buses and minibuses run from there; if you cannot find a direct connection for Amman, take one to Irbid or Zarqa and change again there.

From the Deraa/Ramtha border it is 92 km to the centre of Amman, the most direct route being via Jerash. Although this route is marked on most maps as simply a major road, it has in fact been upgraded to a motorway for most of its length. From the Nasib/Jabir border it is 96 km to Amman on a fast motorway all the way.

Whichever border you cross at, exit formalities are quite straightforward and there is no exit tax to pay. Single-entry Jordanian visas can be obtained on the spot (these now cost JD10 – around US$15 – irrespective of nationality). The banks at the border offer much the same rates as are found in Amman.

Around Deraa

Around Tell Shahab Head west out of Deraa at the roundabout at the end of Ash Shouhada Street and after 8 km take the road branching off to the left. Follow this road, passing a staggered crossroads before taking a small left turn after 8 km. Bear right after 1,500 m to arrive at Tell Shahab, where there are the ruins of a castle, at a point where the remains of the old branch line from Deraa to Haifa passes through a deep cutting. A short distance further on the road peters out in an open area of ground overlooking a **deep gorge** which drains into the Yarmouk River. On the opposite side a **waterfall** feeds two pools at different levels. The ruins of ancient irrigation channels and water-mills can be seen on either side. This picturesque spot is ideal for a picnic, and in summer there are usually a couple of snack stalls open. It is possible to scramble down to the foot of the valley, and then up to the pools if you fancy a swim.

Returning to the point where you took the small left turn (16 km from Deraa) and continuing along this road for a further 4 km, you arrive at the town of Ain al-Zezoun. Follow the road right through the town and bear off to the left at the roundabout at the far end of town. This brings you to a large, permanent spring feeding a waterfall, and a restaurant overlooking the deep valley of the Yarmouk River, which here forms the **border with Jordan**. The views out over the Yarmouk River Valley from the terrace of the restaurant are spectacular, although the food and drinks here are expensive. Traces of the old Deraa-Haifa railway line can be seen down in the valley. **Ain al-Zezoun**

If you continue straight on at the first junction 8 km west of Deraa, you arrive after 5 km at the town of Mzerieb. Taking a left turn in the centre brings you to a small lake, with a pleasant lake-side restaurant complete with pedalos and rowboats for hire. **Mzerieb**

From Deraa a good road heads east (ie out past the bus station), passing over the Damascus motorway (9 km) before arriving in Bosra (40 km). This road takes you through the fertile countryside of the **Nuqra plain**, which supports rich crops of wheat, barley, chickpeas, sesame and watermelons. During the Roman period this part of the Hauran region represented one of the major grain producing regions of the empire (the name Nuqra translates literally as 'granary'), although it is only in recent years that it has begun to recover from long centuries of decline and neglect. **Deraa to Bosra**
Colour map 3, grid C1/2

Bosra (Busra ash-Sham) بصرى الشام

The town of Bosra contains the most impressive and intact ruins of the Hauran region. Its most famous example is the huge theatre, but this is complemented by the extensive ruins of a Roman city along with some interesting later Byzantine and Islamic monuments. Although the modern town extends in a rather uninspiring sprawl to the northwest and east of the ruins, in places these contemporary houses are intermingled unexpectedly with Roman and Byzantine remains and there are constant reminders of the past in the present – the seventh- or eighth-century Umari Mosque is still in use today. The town can be visited as a day-trip from Damascus, but there are a couple of hotels here if you want to spend the night and explore at a more leisurely pace. *Phone code: 015*
Colour map 3, grid C2

Ins and outs

Regular luxury coaches run directly between Bosra and Damascus throughout the day, and there are regular buses and microbuses to Deraa, but no services to Suweida. The town itself is compact and easily explored on foot. There is a *CBS* exchange booth **Getting there & around**

South of Damascus

near the entrance to the theatre/citadel which changes cash and TCs. Open 0930-1400, 1600-1900, 7 days. Alternatively, the *Bosra Cham Palace* hotel can change cash and TCs at any time of the day or night. The small **tourist information** office is located just to the south of the theatre/citadel, though they can do little more than offer you the usual Ministry of Tourism free pamphlets/maps.

History

The earliest references to Bosra, then known as *Busrana*, can be found in the records of the Egyptian pharaoh Tuthmosis III (15th century BC). It was occupied by the Greeks following Alexander the Great's conquest of the region, and controlled by the Seleucids for a time after his death and the subsequent division of his empire. It was then in siezed by Judas Maccabeus in 163 BC after his campaign against the Ammonites, and during the first century BC came under the control of the Nabateans. Later, during the first century AD, they briefly made it the capital of their empire.

However, the most significant period in the city's history began with Trajan's conquest of the region and the imposition of direct Roman rule in 106 AD. The new Roman province of *Arabia* was established and Bosra chosen as its capital. A Roman Legion was stationed in the city, which was renamed *Nova Traiana Bostra* and major building works instigated, as befitted an important provincial capital. At the same time, the building of Trajan's road network linking Damascus, Bosra, Amman and Aqaba (the *Via Nova Traiana*) meant that Bosra found itself at the intersection of this north-south route and the east-west route between the Mediterranean and Mesopotamia, bringing great prosperity to the city. Alexander Severus (222-235 AD) raised its status to a colony, and under the rule of Philip the Arab (244-249) it was made a metropolis. Throughout this period the Romans also developed the agricultural potential of the surrounding Nuqra plain, building irrigation systems and introducing new crops.

During the Byzantine period Bosra continued to flourish as an important centre of Christianity, becoming the seat of a bishopric and later an archbishopric. During the sixth century one of the largest cathedrals in the region was built here, the remains of which can still be seen today. According to legend, Mohammad passed through the city around this time and was received by the monk Bahira (see box, page 156).

Bosra

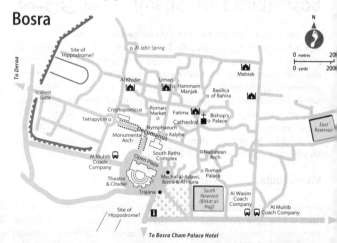

South of Damascus

Out on the edges of the desert, Bosra was amongst the first cities of Syria to fall to the Muslim invaders in 632. The Muslim era brought with it relative decline for Bosra, which soon found itself in a somewhat precarious position, caught in the ninth century between the competing ambitions of Fatimid Cairo and Abbasid Damascus. In the 12th century it was twice attacked by the Crusaders, though both times unsuccessfully. However, its location at the junction of important trade routes, as well as its new function as a halting place on the *Hajj*, or pilgrimage to Mecca, ensured it a continuing place in Muslim history, as demonstrated by the town's various Islamic monuments. The Ayyubids, responding to the threat posed by the Crusaders, completed the fortifications of the citadel which encloses the Roman theatre and these were substantially repaired by Baibars in 1261 following the first Mongol invasion.

Ultimately, however, the overall state of insecurity prompted the Mecca pilgrimage to shift westwards to the relatively safer route passing through Deraa, forcing Bosra into obscurity. By the 19th century the city was all but deserted, the citadel and theatre filled with sand and most of the other Roman, Byzantine and Muslim monuments either buried or abandoned. But the city had another renaissance after 1860 when significant numbers of Druze settled here and Bosra once again came to the attention of the outside world.

Sights

This is certainly the most remarkable of Bosra's monuments, and a good couple of hours are needed if you wish to explore it in detail. What you see from the outside is the **Arab citadel**, an imposing structure consisting of eight strongly fortified towers with connecting curtain walls built in a semi-circle to fit like a jacket around the theatre inside. These outer walls and towers of the citadel are of Ayyubid origin, built after 1200 by the Sultan of Damascus, Al Adil, and by his son As Salih, in response to the Crusader threat. Prior to this, the theatre had been less comprehensively guarded by two towers flanking the *scaenae frons*, built in 1088 by the recently installed Seljuk rulers of Damascus. A third tower was added in the southwest, backing onto the *cavea* of the theatre, in 1147-1148. Following Al Adil's construction of the Ayyubid outer fortifications, various other structures were built within the theatre itself, including a mosque and palace complex, although these were dismantled during the restoration work carried out from 1947-1970.

Entry to the citadel and theatre is from the east side, by a bridge across the moat. This brings you to a large entrance hall where the ticket office is located. Turning right, a vaulted passage slopes down, leading behind the *scaenae frons* of the theatre. Half way down, a stairway on the right (and a smaller one on the left) leads to the upper terrace of this part of the citadel, which serves as an **open-air museum** where various statues and architectural fragments collected from around Bosra are displayed. The central tower, halfway along the northern side of this terrace, houses a cafeteria in the first floor and a hostel (see 'Sleeping', below) on the top floor. The southwest tower of the outer fortifications houses a small **'Folk Traditions' museum**. Here you can view some eminently uninspiring depictions of everyday life, complete with tinny sound effects, as well as a rather sad collection of stuffed birds. It's worth a quick look, however, if only for a glimpse of the inside of the tower; if it is locked, ask at the ticket office to gain entry.

Bearing left from the entrance hall, after a short distance you come to a staircase which leads to an upper terrace which runs around the space between the citadel and the theatre, taking you past the 'Folk Traditions' museum and round to the open-air museum. Staying at ground level, you enter the system of vaulted

Theatre & citadel

See glossary page 661 for explanation of Latin terms

South of Damascus

tunnels running under the *cavea* of the theatre, and by ascending through any of the wonderfully named *vomitoria*, you can gain access to the **Roman theatre** itself. After the warren-like enclosure of the vaulted tunnels, the sheer scale of this is breathtaking. Built early in the second century AD, probably during the reign of Trajan, it was one of the many grand public buildings erected during this period, when Bosra flourished as the capital of the newly established *Provincia Arabia*. Although well preserved by the enclosing Ayyubid fortifications, and by the fact that it filled up with sand over the centuries, substantial restoration work was nevertheless necessary, both to the *cavea* and the *scaenae frons*. The *cavea* consists of a total of 37 tiers of seating which would have accommodated an audience of up to 9,000. Running around the top of the *cavea* are a series of columns which probably served to support a sunshade. The majority of the Corinthian columns behind the stage area are copies, but they give an idea of the decoration which once adorned the entire height of the *scenae frons*. Today the upper parts of this, stripped of their decoration, are somewhat severe. ■ *Open daily 0800-sunset. Entry S£400 (students S£15).*

Old City To the north of the theatre and citadel is the old Roman city of Bosra, its streets laid out in traditional grid pattern with an approximate north-south and east-west alignment. Until recently this was for the most part hidden under the buildings of the contemporary town, and it is only in recent years that these have started to be cleared away to reveal the full extent of the Roman settlement, although much undoubtedly still remains buried, particularly in the area further to the north.

From the northwest corner of the citadel an excavated street lined with column bases runs north to a **monumental arch** consisting of a central arch flanked by two smaller side-arches. An inscription dates it to the early third century AD and reveals that it was built in honour of the III Cyrenaica Legion. The monumental arch marks the intersection with the main east-west street, or *decumanus* of the old Roman town, which has been excavated along most of its length to show the column bases of the colonnade which once lined it. In places complete columns along with their Ionic capitals have been re-erected, although the majority of these appear to have been removed and reused in later buildings.

Turning to the right, on the right are the ruins of the extensive **south baths** complex. Dating from the late second to early third century AD, these baths (one of three in the town) were built on a grand scale, although they are now in an advanced state of ruin. The main entrance was from the *decumanus*, with an eight-columned portico (of which almost nothing remains) leading through to the *apodyterium* or changing room; a large octagonal hall, the domed ceiling of which has collapsed. Beyond this was the *frigidarium* (cold room), followed by the *tepidarium* (warm room), with a *calidarium* (hot room) on either side. The *calidarium* on the east side still has its ceiling largely intact (at the time of writing it was supported by a mass of wooden scaffolding to prevent its collapse), while the one on the west side is for the most part in ruins. Adjacent to the baths on the east side are the remains of what was perhaps an *agora* or public meeting place, a rectangular area lined with recently re-erected columns.

Almost opposite the baths, on the north side of the street, are four enormous Corinthian columns towering to a height of 13 m and placed at a 45° angle to the *decumanus*, spanning the corner with a major north-south street which leads off it at this point. These once formed part of what must have been a truly spectacular **nymphaeum**, or public water fountain. On the opposite corner there is a tall column and fragment of wall supporting a richly decorated section of entablature, along with a slender column to the north; this is the remains of a **kalybe**, a type of shrine used to display statuary.

The Bosra Festival

Heading north along the street leading off from the *decumanus*, on your left are the remains of a long rectangular **Roman market**. Part of the open plaza of this market has been repaved in recent years, while the long rectangular building with its arched doorways and niches (a later Muslim addition) has been consolidated.

Further north, also on the left, is the large **Umari Mosque**. This mosque is popularly attributed to the second Caliph, Umar Ibn al-Khattab (634-644), under whose leadership Syria was conquered in 636. If true, this would make it one of the earliest surviving mosques in Syria. Others argue that it was built during the reign of the Umayyad Caliph, Yazid II (720-724). However, in its present form, the mosque dates mostly from the 12th-13th centuries, when the Ayyubids extensively rebuilt and enlarged it. The distinctive square tower-minaret is most obviously Umayyad in style, although the upper parts of it show Ayyubid influences. The excavation of the main north-south street revealed a series of bricked-up Roman arches in the lower courses of this east wall (still visible today), thought to be the remains of a Roman temple on which the mosque was built. In the north wall of the mosque, meanwhile, sections of recycled basalt columns laid horizontally in the stonework as reinforcement can be seen, this pattern of construction dating from the 13th century enlargement of the mosque. If the main entrance from the north-south street is closed, try walking round to the west side where there is another entrance. Inside, the main courtyard (now covered by a tin roof) is surrounded on three sides by a double arcade, with a single arcade on the fourth side. Most of the columns of the arcades are clearly of classical origin, with a mixture of different capitals surmounting them. Having been abandoned and left derelict at some point, the mosque was restored in three phases from the 1930s onwards and today serves as Bosra's main mosque, as well as a *madrassa* (religious school) for children.

Opposite the Umari Mosque is the restored (though no longer functioning) **Hammam Manjak**, a Mameluke period bath house dating from 1372. These baths were built to service the pilgrims stopping in Bosra en route to Mecca. They represent the last phase of building work undertaken during the Muslim period before the Mecca pilgrimage route shifted to the west, precipitating the final decline in Bosra's importance. The entrance leads first into the main reception hall, a square room with a large pool in the centre and raised stone benches around the sides. Four arches forming a square once supported a central dome. A doorway in the north side of the room leads through to the bathing chambers, of which there are no less than eleven. If the baths are locked, ask at the Umari Mosque for the caretaker to open them up.

Retracing your steps to the main east-west *decumanus* and following it east, you pass on the right an area of excavations (ongoing at the time of writing) which has revealed part of a Nabatean building of uncertain function. The

👉 *A Prophet foretold*

According to Muslim tradition the future Prophet Mohammad, while still a young boy, used to pass through Bosra from time to time while accompanying the trading caravans of his uncle between Damascus and Mecca. There he met the highly respected Nestorian monk, Bahira, with whom he used to engage in theological discussions. Greatly impressed by his intelligence and perception, Bahira predicted that Mohammad would go on to be a great prophet. An almost identical tradition, even down to the name of the monk, is associated with the shrine of Nabi Haroun near Petra in Jordan. According to some, Bahira was also responsible for directly influencing Mohammad in the composition of the Qur'an, in so far as it incorporates aspects of the Law of Moses and Christianity. However, this particular interpretation finds no place in Muslim tradition, since according to Muslim belief the Qur'an is the direct word of God, and Mohammad was merely the medium through which that message was transmitted.

street ends with a **Nabatean arch** which was probably the entrance to a Nabatean temple compound or palace. The whole area to the east of the arch is thought to have been the site of the Nabatean settlement which grew up here when Bosra became the new capital of their empire, although nothing has been excavated. During the Roman period the arch appears to have been used to mark the eastern extremities of the planned Roman city.

To the south of the Nabatean arch are the ruins of a substantial **Roman palace** (perhaps the residence of the governor of *Provincia Arabia*), although little remains to be appreciated today. A little further to the south is the huge **south reservoir**. Of Roman construction and measuring over 120 m by 150 m in size, it represents one of the largest man-made water storages found in the region. One reason for Bosra's enduring importance was the existence of a reliable, year-round water supply, a resource which the Romans made full use of by building the reservoir, and something which was of equal importance during the Muslim period (the reservoir's Arabic name, *Birkat al-Hajj*, translates literally as 'pool of the pilgrimage').

Heading north from the Nabatean arch, you arrive first at the remains of a Byzantine **cathedral** on the right. Today the fenced-off site is in an advanced state of ruin, strewn with various architectural fragments and with only its basic outline and the semi-circular apse area clearly discernible, along with a couple of standing columns. The cathedral dates from 512 and was dedicated by Julianus, the archbishop of Bosra, to the Syrian saints Sergius, Bacchus and Leontius (Sergius and Bacchus were both from Rasafeh, see page 375). Although the size of the cathedral can only be appreciated today from the outline of the foundations, its present state of ruin is comparatively recent. Mid-19th century descriptions of the cathedral reveal that it was a complex and innovative structure for its period, consisting of a circle within a square, topped by a large central dome. On the east side is a choir surrounded by small side rooms extended beyond the basic plan. Just to the east of the cathedral are the indistinct remains of what was the **Bishop's palace**.

Just to the north of the cathedral, between two branches of the street, is the **Mosque of Fatima**. This small mosque consists of a simple square building with a distinctive square tower-minaret which actually stands separate from the main building. The mosque was built by the Fatimid rulers of Egypt during the 11th century and is named after the Prophet's daughter, Fatima, who was the husband of Ali, to whom the Shi'ite Fatimids traced their origins. The minaret, similar in style to that of the Umari Mosque, is an early 14th-century addition.

A little further to the north again, on the right, are the ruins of the **Basilica of Bahira**. Originally a civic building of some sort, probably dating from the third century, it was converted into a church some time during the Byzantine period. The basic structure of the building, rectangular in shape with a semicircular apse at the east end, survives up to the level of the roof. The church is associated with the legend of the monk Bahira (see box above).

Continuing north, you arrive after around 200 m at a newly cobbled street; turn right here to reach the **Mabrak Mosque** with its distinctive egg-shaped dome and half-ruined square minaret. According to legend, this mosque marks the spot where the camel carrying the first copy of the Qur'an to arrive in Syria knelt down to rest (the name translates literally as the 'kneeling mosque'). In another version of the legend, the mosque is said to mark the spot where Mohammad's own camel knelt when he stopped here to pray. Entry to the mosque is through a low doorway from the cobbled street which runs east-west along the northern edges of the town. Note also the small doorways on either side, still with their original solid stone doors (of Roman origin) in place. The room directly in front of the central entrance and courtyard currently serves as the prayer hall of the mosque. To the right is the oldest part of the mosque, dating in its present form to 1136. The *mihrab*, with its conch shell semi-dome (clearly of Roman origin) is slightly offset from the alignment of the wall in order to face exactly to Mecca. By the *mihrab* is a large stone slab with an indentation which is said to be the spot where the camel knelt. To the left of the central courtyard a set of steps and tiny doorway (actually originally a window) leads through to a large cruciform wing, built in the 12th-13th centuries as a *madrassa*, the earliest example of a religious school in Syria. The complex and somewhat awkward internal layout of the whole building is indicative of the numerous modifications made to it over time.

Returning to the main east-west *decumanus* of the Roman city and following it west, beyond the monumental arch on the left, you pass on the right a series of rectangular ventilation shafts at street level. These mark a long, narrow underground chamber probably dating from the first half of the second century AD and used for the storage of food and other products. Steps at its western end lead down, giving access to the vault, known technically as a **cryptoporticus**. Just to the west of this, past a turning leading to the north, the street can be seen to widen considerably to form an open circular area. Along with a large square platform on one side, this is all that remains of a **tetrapylon** which once marked the intersection with another north-south street. Continuing west, you arrive eventually at the **West gate** of the Roman city, known locally as the 'Bab al-Hawa' or 'Gate of the Wind'. Dating from the second century AD, it is a plain and imposing, if somewhat severe, structure consisting of a massive single arch topped by a barrel vault. To the north and south of the gate are the remains of the **Roman walls** of the old city, in places restored but for the most part in a poor state of repair, much of their stones having been removed during the building of the Arab citadel.

Essentials

There are just 2 options for accommodation in Bosra; a luxury 5-star hotel belonging to the Cham chain, and a budget 'hostel' inside the theatre/citadel. **AL** *Bosra Cham Palace*, T790881, F790996. Reasonably comfortable rooms with a/c, TV/dish, phone, minibar, attached bath and balcony. Restaurant, bar, swimming pool, shops, currency exchange. Eerily quiet, unless a tour group stops by. **G** *Hostel*, on the top floor of the central bastion of the citadel which encloses the theatre. Simple but clean dormitory, S£200 per person, share shower/toilet. Good value, and certainly the most unusual and atmospheric budget option in Syria. Recommended.

Sleeping

South of Damascus

Eating   *La Citadelle*, in *Bosra Cham Palace*. This is the most upmarket dining option in Bosra, with a set menu dinner costing S£660 per head. *Mechal al-Adawi* (or *Old City/Vieille Ville*), situated on the edge of the open square by the entrance to the theatre/citadel, T/F790966. Seating indoors in a lovely old building with basalt arches and corbelling, or outside in vine-shaded area. Interesting selection of local dishes from the Hauran region and Syrian specialities you don't usually find on the average menu. Around S£250 per head excluding alcohol. The owner (Mechal al-Adawi) speaks good English and Italian and works also as a guide, as well as selling traditional Syrian and Bedouin textiles. *Trajana*, situated across square from *Mechal al-Adawi*, and occupying a corner of the public gardens. Pleasant outdoor seating (and central covered area) with fountains etc. The standard range of Arabic food (*mezze* dishes, kebabs, grills, roast chicken etc). Usually around S£200 per head upwards, but it is worth checking prices before you order. There are a couple of other cafés/restaurants on the square by the entrance to the theatre/citadel, including the *Bosra* and *Al Huria*, which offer a fairly standard menu of Arabic dishes and snacks. For real cheapies (eg staples such as falafel sandwiches, shawarmas and roast chicken), try opposite the bus stands on the main road leading east towards Suweida, or else along the road which runs from the theatre along the outside of the city walls to the West Gate.

Transport   There are 2 luxury coach companies, *Al Wasim* and *Al Muhib*, offering direct services to **Damascus**. The ticket offices/bus stops for both are on the main road leading east towards Suweida (the latter also has a second office just to the west of the theatre/citadel; you can catch their coaches at either office). Departures every 2 hrs between 0800-2000, S£50. If you are visiting Bosra as a day-trip from Damascus, you are advised to buy your return ticket as soon as you arrive, and to check the departure time of the last bus as this may vary, particularly on Fri and outside the main tourist season when there is limited demand. Microbuses to **Deraa** leave from the bus stops on the Suweida road, departing when full (usually every 30 mins or so, though much less frequently on Fri), S£15. If you want to continue on to **Suweida** from Bosra, the easiest option is simply to charter a taxi or microbus (this will cost in the region of S£300-350). A much more roundabout option is to take a microbus back to Deraa, from where you can find buses and microbuses running to Suweida.

Bosra to   To continue on to Suweida from Bosra, with your own transport, head east out
Suweida   of the town past the bus stops. After 9 km, turn left at a crossroads and continue north for 24 km, passing through the villages of Qraya and Rassas, to arrive in Suweida. Going by this route, you also have the option of making a detour to Salkhad (see below).

Damascus to Suweida

Colour map 3, grid B/C2   To join the Suweida road from Damascus, the easiest (though by no means the most direct) route is to go via the motorway ring-road which encircles the southern half of the capital. Head southwest from Umawiyeen Square along the Mezzeh autostrade (keeping the *Sheraton* hotel on your right). After just under 5 km, join the motorway ringroad around Damascus heading anticlockwise. After another 9 km (having passed the exit for the motorway to Deraa, Bosra and the Jordanian border), the exit for the Suweida road is signposted, immediately before the airport road exit.

The Suweida road heads southeast from Damascus, taking you past the colourful Saida Zainab Mosque (see page 111). Once clear of the capital, the road first traverses a somewhat dreary plain before passing across the rather more atmospheric **Hauran plateau** with its landscape of dark, volcanic soils strewn with the ubiquitous black basalt rock typical of the region. Approaching the town of **Shahba**, the ridges of the **Jebel al-Arab** range come into view off to the left. The main road in fact bypasses Shahba; to reach the town, take the signposted fork off to the left, some 73 km after the Saida Zeinab Mosque (the fork is more or less opposite the distinctive cone of an extinct volcano to the right of the road). From the fork it is a further 2 km into the centre of town (see page 164).

Continuing along the main road past the fork for Shahba, you come next to the village of Suweilim (signposted 'Sleim' and marked 'Selim' or 'Salim' on most maps). Entering the village, the corner fragment of a **temple** is visible off to the right of the road in the northwest corner of the village. Clearly of Roman origin and thought to date from the late second-early third century AD, the decoration on this surviving fragment is impressive, although today nothing more remains of what would appear to have been a temple of considerable size. A little further along the main road, in the centre of the village, there is a left turn signposted to Qanawat (see below). **Suweilim**

Continuing south along the main road, 3 km beyond the left turn for Qanawat, there is another left turn leading into the centre of the village of Atil (marked 'Atheel' on some maps). Taking this turning, you can visit two small **Roman temples**. The first, down a side street on the left, is the best preserved, with the remains of a beautifully decorated door-frame and niches on either side. On the left, a stone bears a Greek inscription which dates the temple to 151 AD, during the reign of Antoninus Pius. Inside, there is a double arch structure which would have supported the roof. Continue along the same street and then turn right to reach the second temple. There is less to see here, the remains being partially obscured by surrounding buildings, though the roof is still largely intact. Note also the interesting course of carved stonework in one wall. **Atil**

Returning to the main road and continuing south, after 4 km you arrive in Suweida, passing first a roundabout boasting a huge portrait of Assad, followed by a second roundabout with an equally large bronze relief of his son Basel on horseback clutching a trophy, in an adaptation of the ubiquitous photograph of him.

Suweida السويداء

Today, Suweida serves as the capital of the Hauran region, a modern and rapidly expanding town with a mixed population of Druze and Greek Orthodox Christians, and a certain air of affluence about it; the northeastern area of the town in the vicinity of the new museum in particular boasts luxurious houses (and some extravagant architecture). Other than a few scant remains from the Nabatean and Roman periods dotted around the town, it is the museum which is the main attraction and reason for visiting Suweida, although if you wish to explore the Jebel al-Arab region in any detail, it is also the only place in the area with any accommodation, albeit somewhat basic and uninspiring. *Phone code: 016 Colour map 3, grid C2*

The main road from Damascus runs north-south through the centre of Suweida. The main bus station is beside this road (on the right as you head south), at the northern edge of town, by the roundabout with the bronze relief of Basel on horseback. The **tourist information** office is just to the north of this roundabout, on the same side, although it appears to be closed more often than not and is of little use in any case. **Ins & outs**

History During the first century BC Suweida was occupied by the Nabateans. Early in the second century AD it was conquered by the Romans and later named Dionysias. By the fifth century it had become an important centre of Christianity and the seat of a Bishopric, a position it still holds. Unfortunately, the town's most important ancient monuments were plundered prior to the First World War by Ottoman troops in search of building materials for their barracks. During the French Mandate period, the town was further remodelled. Those monuments which did survive suffered yet more damage with the building of the modern road which runs north-south through the town, although in recent years efforts have been made to salvage some of the town's heritage.

Sights **Suweida Museum** This small museum is a delight to visit. On the ground floor are various architectural fragments, statues and items of pottery, mostly from Shahba. The statues and architectural fragments dating from the Roman period are particularly delicately executed and all the more impressive for having been fashioned from the hard, unyielding basalt of the Hauran. The highlight of the museum, however, is the collection of mosaics, also from Shahba, displayed in the central domed hall. Going round the hall in an anticlockwise direction from the entrance, they depict Artemis surprised while bathing; Venus doing her makeup; Thetis (or Tethys) surrounded by sea monsters; four panels with scenes of lions chasing gazelle, and cocks and hens picking at flowers; Bacchus, Ariadne and Pluto, with personifications of the four seasons in each corner of the border; and Thetis and Peleus. The first three are the most impressive, and the expressiveness of the faces a testament to the remarkable skill of the craftsmen. The last two, however, are badly damaged. There are also a few interesting pieces of sculpture displayed in the central hall. Upstairs is a small 'popular tradition' display.

■ *Open 0900-1600 in winter, 0900-1800 in summer, closed Tue. Entry S£300 (students S£15). Situated 2 km to the northeast of the town centre, on the road to Qanawat. If you are arriving in Suweida with your own transport from the north, or if you find yourself deposited at the new bus station by the roundabout with the bronze relief of Basel on horseback, head east from this roundabout up the hill to reach the museum; turn left at the second crossroads and the museum is a few metres along on the right.*

Archaeological remnants Heading south through Suweida along the main road, in the southern part of the town you come to a roundabout with a large arch in the centre, while to the left of the road is a series of five columns. A little further on, to the left of the road below ground level is a rather intriguing section of richly decorated entablature supported on columns. Further on, on the same side, are the remains of a large church which has been modified and had contemporary houses built onto it. Another smaller church has also been identified nearby, believed to be one of the oldest churches in the world, though there is little for the casual observer to see and in any case it is hidden away

Suweida

To New Bus Station (600m), Tourist
Information (650m) & Damascus

To Suweida Museum (650m),
Shooting Club Hotel & Qanawat

Jamal Abdel Nasser St

To Ezraa & Arikah

Qanawat St

Microbuses to
Qanawat

16 Tishreen St

Assad
Square

CBS

Old
Governor's
Residence

Tourist
(Siyaha)

Asrar

Roddat
al-Jabal

Al Istiqlal St

Arch & Columns

Church Remains

N

Theatre
Remains

To Bosra

0 metres   100
0 yards   100

inside a walled compound. Back on the main road, a little further along on the right, are the remains of a small, partially restored theatre.

The government-run *Tourist (Siyaha)* was closed at the time of writing, and judging by the overall state of dilapidation is unlikely to open again. The only other non-budget option is the overpriced **D** *Shooting Club*, on the road to Qanawat, on the left, just over 1 km beyond the museum, T231929, F237548. Unfortunately it's nothing to write home about, being a big, decrepit, institutional type of building, featuring damp, blistering plasterwork on the walls and extremely dodgy plumbing in the rooms to go with the fan, heater and attached bath. There is also a restaurant. More realistically priced is the **G** *Roddat al-Jabal*, Sultan al-Atrush Sq (in the centre of town), T221374. Nice old building and friendly staff but very basic, S£150 per bed in shared rooms (4 beds), share toilet (recently painted but still pretty abysmal) and shower (cold water only).

There is no shortage of simple but reasonable snack places in the centre of Suweida. The *Asrar*, on the main road running north-south through town, does good shawarmas, sandwiches and pizzas. Alternatively, try exploring the maze of streets to the south and west of Sultan al-Atrush Sq, where there are numerous other snack places and simple restaurants.

Luxury coaches to **Damascus** depart from the main bus station (at the north end of town) every hour or so (S£50), or there is a choice of ordinary coaches, buses or microbuses costing anywhere between S£25-40, or 'hob-hob' buses for S£15. Note that only the *Al Muhib* and *Al Wasim* luxury coaches go to Baramkeh bus station, with the rest all going to the somewhat less conveniently located Deraa bus station. There are also regular microbuses to **Shahba**, **Deraa** and **Ezraa**. Taxis congregate on the main road by the roundabout, and there are local buses which shuttle between here and the centre of town. Microbuses to **Qanawat** are somewhat erratic; they leave from 16 Tishreen St, near the centre of town.

Qanawat قنوات

The village of Qanawat, 7 km to the northeast of Suweida on the slopes of the Jebel al-Arab massif, boasts some impressive ruins and definitely deserves a visit. In contrast to the other historical sites of the Hauran, Qanawat is set amongst a relatively verdant landscape of trees, vineyards and grassy terraces, providing a pleasant relief from the sombre and often arid black basalt landscape found elsewhere. The Wadi al-Ghar is the source of Qanawat's fertility, and the importance of harnessing its waters can be deduced from the village's name; it translates as 'canal'.

From Suweida, head northeast on Kanawat Street, past the museum on the right, and keep going straight. Entering Qanawat, you arrive at a roundabout with a statue of a lion in the centre (5 km from Suweida museum). If you turn right here, this road takes you directly up to the so-called Seraya, Qanawat's most impressive monument. If you continue straight on, it takes you past a number of minor remains before arriving at the Seraya (see below). The buses and minibuses which run from Suweida will drop you off in the square by the Seraya. Be sure to check when the last bus makes the return trip as transport to and from here is somewhat erratic, particularly off-season.

History

An edict discovered in the village relates how the Judaean ruler Herod Agrippa admonished the people of Qanawat for 'leading the life of wild beasts in their dens': probably a reference to the banditry prevalent in the region.

Although its origins certainly go back much further (there is a brief mention of *Kenath* being captured by Nobah, one of the leaders of the tribe of Manasseh, in Numbers 32: 42), the first detailed information about Qanawat dates from the time of Herod Agrippa I (37-44 AD). Herod Agrippa went on to suffer a major defeat at the hands of the various tribes of the region which the Nabatean and Jewish kingdoms struggled to control. During the Roman period it became one of the cities of the Decapolis, a loose confederation of cities in southern Syria and northern Jordan. Early in the second century AD it became part of the new Roman province of *Arabia*, and many of the major monuments which survive today date from the reign of Trajan (98-117 AD). By the end of the second century it had been renamed *Septimia Kanatha* by the emperor Septimius Severus. Christianity flourished here, as elsewhere in the Hauran during the fourth and fifth centuries, and it became the seat of a bishopric, with various Roman monuments being converted to churches. After the arrival of Islam, however, it appears to have fallen into decline, remaining all but abandoned until the Druze settlement in the region in the 19th century. If you wander through the village today, in addition to the surviving monuments, you can see evidence of Qanawat's ancient origins in the numerous architectural fragments taken from various ruins and reused in contemporary buildings.

Sights

Arriving from Suweida at the roundabout with the lion statue and going straight across, you pass after around 500 m the remains of the **Helios temple** off to the left, marked by seven standing columns, each still topped by delicately carved capitals. Along with the platform on which these stand, this is all that remains of the temple. There are excellent views from this vantage point out across the Hauran plateau. Further along, at the second small crossroads (just past a government building on the right which incorporates some columns of Roman origin), turn right to climb up the hillside, keeping the gorge of the Wadi al-Ghar to your left. Just on the opposite side of the stream, the ruins of a small **theatre** and **nymphaeum** can be made out from the road.

At the top of the hill, you arrive at an open square containing the ruins of the **Seraya**, now set within a fenced-off area. The Seraya, or Serai (from the Turkish for palace), consists of two adjoining Roman structures, which were later modified into Christian churches during the Byzantine period. The entrance is in the western side of the complex, through a small doorway just to the right of the central, elaborately decorated door. This western part of the complex is thought to have originally been a Roman praetorium or governor's palace, entered from the north via a columned portico. At the south end of the building are three semicircular niches probably originally used to display statuary, but used as a *martyrium* (a small shrine for holy relics) when the building was converted to a church. To judge from the candles which can be found placed in the niches, the shrine is still venerated by local Christians. In accordance with

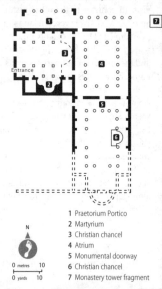

Qanawat Seraya

1 Praetorium Portico
2 Martyrium
3 Christian chancel
4 Atrium
5 Monumental doorway
6 Christian chancel
7 Monastery tower fragment

Christian tradition, the altar was built against the eastern wall, thus giving the building an east-west orientation, although nothing remains of this today. Passing through one of the openings in the eastern wall, you come to what appears to have been the Roman *atrium*, or courtyard, with two rows of columns still standing. The south wall of the atrium is pierced by a large monumental doorway which is particularly beautifully decorated. Passing through this, you come to the remains of a rectangular building, possibly a temple during the Roman period. Like the first building, its north-south orientation was rotated through 90 degrees during the Christian period by building an altar on the east side; the semicircular chancel on which the altar stood can still be seen. Today, a large circular stone basin occupies the chancel. According to one theory, the atrium and building to the south once formed a single rectangular courtyard surrounded by a colonnade, with the dividing wall and monumental entrance being added during the fourth or fifth centuries. ■ *Open daily 0800-sunset. Entry S£150 (students S£10). If the gate is closed, ask in the surrounding shops for the caretaker who will come and open it. One of the shops across the road from the entrance serves tea, coffee, soft drinks, and even beer and wine.*

Just to the northeast of the Seraya complex stands a precariously balanced **fragment of a tower**, thought to be part of a later monastery which was built here. Following the street which leads west from the open square in front of the entrance to the Seraya, and taking the first left turn, you come to an underground structure (originally a water cistern) consisting of a series of arches and columns, the tops of the arches corresponding with ground level. Beyond this, there are the scant remains of what has been identified as a temple dedicated to Zeus.

An alternative route from Qanawat to Shahba via Mushanef

Colour map 3, grid B/C2

If you have your own transport, you can drive from Qanawat to the village of Mushanef, with its interesting temple ruins, and on to Shahba. This pleasant, if somewhat roundabout, detour (43 km in all) takes you through the beautiful rolling hills of the **Jebel al-Arab**. From the Seraya in Qanawat, ask directions to pick up the road towards Mushanef. After passing through the village of Muf'Allah (3 km) the narrow road winds its way through fields and past apple orchards. In the village of **Taibeh** (13 km from Qanawat), bear right. The road descends into a valley and crosses a small bridge. Just after the bridge, bear right where the road forks and keep on following this road to arrive in Mushanef, 20 km from Qanawat.

Mushanef

In the centre of the small and otherwise uninteresting village of Mushanef are the remains of a **Roman temple**. The temple is set within a large open courtyard and stands on a podium, with steps leading up to it. On the basis of an inscription found here, it is thought to date to 171 AD, during the reign of Marcus Aurelius, though another inscription referring to Herod Agrippa I (37-44 AD) indicates that it already existed in some form at that time. A peculiar hotch-potch of architectural fragments have been incorporated into the fabric of the temple, reflecting reconstruction work at some point in its history. One of the walls is leaning at a precarious angle, while another part of the temple has been modified into a dwelling which is still lived in today. While not a particularly notable monument, the overall effect is somehow quite striking.

Ask directions again to pick up the main road to Shahba. Keep following this road, which passes through a number of villages along the way, to arrive eventually in Shahba, 23 km from Mushanef (arriving by this route you enter Shahba through the east gate of the old Roman city).

Shahba شهبا

Colour map 3, grid B2   Something of a white elephant of a monumental town to the Emperor Philip the Arab, it was only during the last century that Shahba (originally known as Philippopolis) became a centre of Druze settlement. Today the place is a small, bustling market town with an almost entirely Druze population.

Ins & outs   If you are visiting Shahba as part of a day-trip from Damascus, it probably makes more sense to catch a luxury coach from the Baramkeh bus station in **Damascus** direct to Suweida and then stop in Shahba on the way back, after making an excursion to **Qanawat**. Fairly regular buses and minibuses depart from the roundabout in the centre of town for Damascus and Suweida. Check what time the last bus leaves as this varies according to the season and demand.

History   Perhaps seeking to build a lasting monument to his own glory, and to re-create *The ancient city of* something of the imperial grandeur of Rome in the land of his birth, Philip the *Philippopolis was* Arab planned this new Roman city on a grand scale. At an altitude of 1,050 m *unique in that it was* on the outlying ridges of the Jebel al-Arab massif he built a city enclosed within *an entirely Roman* a rectangle of walls (of which only the outline now survives), with four gates *project, rather than* corresponding to the cardinal points of the compass. The town was laid out *a modification or* according to the traditional Roman grid pattern of streets and endowed with a *extension of a* number of large civic buildings meant to reflect its importance alongside *pre-existing city (as* Bosra, the existing provincial capital. Construction work started soon after *was the case with* Philip became Emperor in 244 AD, but the project appears to have been pre- *Bosra & most other* maturely abandoned following his sudden death five years later, with less than *cities developed by* half the town's area actually having been built upon. Although it continued to *the Romans in the* be inhabited well into the fourth century, Philippopolis failed to secure any *Middle East)* lasting role for itself in the region and was eventually abandoned altogether.

Sights   Entering the town from the north, you pass through the partially recon- structed remains of the northern gate of the Roman city, consisting of a large central arch flanked by two smaller ones. This main north-south street corre- sponds with the *cardo maximus* of the Roman city. The roundabout in the centre of the town likewise marks the junction with the east-west *decumanus*. The cobbled street run- ning west from this central round- about leads to the main cluster of Roman remains. A short distance up on the right there is a series of col- umns which mark the remains of a **portico** to a temple. Originally there would have been four columns, but the second from the right is missing and has been replaced by a stone block featuring a carved relief of a man with an inscription below. A lit- tle further on, to the left of the street, is a large open square, once the **forum** of the Roman town.

Dominating the far (western) end of the square is the imposing **palace façade**, consisting of a series of large

Shahba

To Damascus

Northern Gate

Portico Remains

Forum

Café & Snacks

Palace Facade

Temple

Baths Complex

Theatre

Mosaics Museum

To Mushanef

N

0 metres 100
0 yards 100

Southern Gate

To Suweida

Philip the Arab

Philip the Arab was unique amongst Rome's emperors in being the only Arab to rise to this position. Born in the Hauran region, possibly in a village standing on the same spot as Shahba, his father was a local chieftan of some importance. Philip himself joined the Roman army, soon rising to the position of Praetorian prefect. When the Emperor Gordian was killed during the course of a campaign against the Persians on the upper Euphrates, Philip was hailed as the new Emperor by his

legions, a position which the Senate in Rome opted to confirm in 244 AD. However, his rule was to last just five years, and in 249 he was murdered in a military mutiny. The year before that had marked the thousandth anniversary of the founding of Rome and he presided over fantastic celebrations in the Imperial capital. Nevertheless, his attachment to the land of his birth remained strong and it was at Shahba that he founded the new city of Philippopolis.

niches arranged in a semicircle. The broad flight of stairs leading up to the façade is a modern reconstruction. The purpose of the structure, though not entirely clear, is thought to have been to display statues of Philip the Arab and his family. The cobbled street continues via an arched tunnel under which are the further remains of the palace complex, although these are somewhat obscured by later buildings.

On the south side of the square, there are the remains of a small **temple**, thought to have been dedicated to Philip's father Julius Marinus. A Greek inscription can be seen over the doorway, while inside, the three remaining walls each contain a large arched niche flanked by smaller ones on each side. The stone benches arranged in a horseshoe shape around the inside suggest that the building perhaps also served as a meeting place of some sort. The small holes which can be seen in the stonework indicate that the interior was originally clad in marble. In the left-hand corner of the south wall, a set of stairs lead up to the roof, from where you can get a good overview the palace façade and the theatre.

Just to the south of the temple is the **theatre**. Although small in size and in no way comparable with the theatre at Bosra, this is the best preserved and perhaps most impressive remnant of Philippopolis. In recent years the *cavea* and *scenae frons* have been restored. At the time of writing, some restoration work was still being carried out on the outer walls.

Returning to the roundabout in the centre of town and following the main street south, the first turning on the left leads past the baths and museum. Although the **baths complex** is now for the most part in a fairly advanced state of ruin, the towering walls and arched doorways of the main reception hall are still standing, giving an idea of their monumental scale and elaborate layout. Again, the numerous small holes in the stonework indicate that the interior was marble-clad. At the east end of the complex, a walkway with a sign above it reading 'Especial Entrance' leads to a small Muslim shrine.

On the opposite side of the street, a little further on, is the **mosaics museum**. This small museum stands on the site of a private house dating from the second quarter of the fourth century and contains an impressive collection of beautifully preserved mosaics, all but one of which are displayed in situ. The mosaics depict a number of scenes from classical mythology: Bacchus, the god of wine; Tethys, goddess of the sea; the wedding feast of Dionysus and Ariadne; Orpheus, the Greek musician and poet; Aphrodite and Ares in a love scene (taken from Book Eight of *Odyssey*, lines 266-70); and the Three Graces.

■ *Open 0900-1800 in summer, 0900-1600 in winter. (NB If the museum is closed within these hours, ask at the 'Museum Shop' opposite and they will tele-phone for the caretaker.) Entry S£250 (students S£10).*

Leaving Shahba, if you head south along the main street, this road passes through the **southern gate** of the Roman city (identical in plan to the northern gate, though better preserved) and after 7 km rejoins the main Damas-cus-Suweida highway.

Eating There are various simple takeaway places along the main north-south street serving falafel sandwiches and the like, while by the roundabout in the centre of town you can get more substantial snacks of roast chicken etc.

Arikah
Colour map 3, grid B2

If you have your own transport, the village of Arikah, 27 km to the northwest of Suweida, is worth a visit for its interesting cave and adjacent restaurant; per-haps as a lunch-time stop en route back to Damascus.

Ins and outs From the centre of Suweida, pick up the road leading northwest towards Ezraa. After 12 km, entering the town of As Sijin, take the right turn clearly signposted for Arikah (amongst others). This road takes you through the village Najran, on the outskirts of which are a number of large, brightly painted villas, con-trasting rather incongruously with the somewhat desolate black basalt of the sur-rounding countryside. After 15 km you arrive at a roundabout in the centre of Arikah; turn left here, and the entrance to the restaurant and cave is on your right after less than 100 m.

The large, open-air restaurant in town is a typically Arab affair, with loud music and lively parties every Thursday evening. Stairs lead down below the platform on which the restaurant's tables are laid out, passing on the left a series of arches with a deep spring below. You pass through a low doorway, followed by a second one complete with a hefty single-slab basalt stone door. As with the arches above the spring, these doorways are of Roman origin. Once through the second door, you emerge into a huge cavern, spreading like a massive tunnel ahead of you. The cave (blissfully cool even in the height of summer) actually extends for some 1500 m, though after a couple of hundred metres it narrows in width and height until the roof is just a metre or so above the floor.

Salkhad
Colour map 3, grid C2

If you are en route between Suweida and Bosra with your own transport, you can make a short detour to the town of Salkhad, dominated by the ruins of a hilltop castle. It is easy to see why this hill would once have been of major stra-tegic significance, providing as it does such a commanding vantage point from which to control the surrounding countryside and, overall, it is these pan-oramic views which are the town's main attraction.

Salkhad has been identified with the biblical town of *Salecah*, which was within the territory captured by Moses from Og, the king of Bashan (Deuter-onomy 3:10; Joshua 12:5 and 13:11). Its importance continued into the Islamic period, with the present castle dating from the period of Ayyubid rule, when together with Bosra it served as a forward defence for the Damas-cus-based Caliphate against attacks from the south. You have to walk the last bit up to the castle, which is now in a fairly advanced state of ruin. Its continued strategic significance in the recent past can be seen from the various concrete structures of the Syrian army in amongst the older ruins, including a rather forlorn-looking hexagonal watchtower on the highest point of the castle. These days, however, the army appears to have all but abandoned it.

Palmyra تَدْمُر

5

Palmyra تدمر

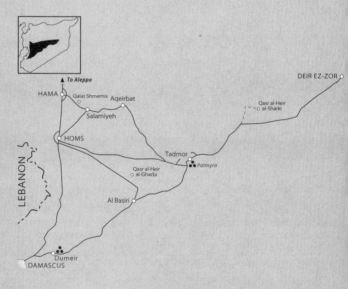

Beyond the fertile Ghouta oasis of Damascus, the Syrian desert stretches away to the east and northeast, a vast and inhospitable expanse of rocky limestone steppe interspersed by the parallel ridges of mountain ranges and giving way in the east to true sand desert. Despite the harshness of this environment, it is the home of numerous nomadic tribes, and although the ancient history of the Middle East region is closely tied to the productive agricultural areas around its fringes, this vast desert has also played a central role. Indeed, the earliest phases of civilization were characterized by a continual interplay between the nomadic peoples of the desert and the settled communities around its edges: successive waves of nomadic tribes left the desert to settle on the fertile agricultural land, displacing earlier societies and establishing new cultures.

The restless nomadism of the desert is reflected also in its historic role as a medium for the exchange of goods and ideas, the camel caravans of the Bedouin navigating this inhospitable vastness just as the ships of the Phoenicians had traversed the Mediterranean. It was this trade which allowed the oasis of Tadmor to flourish into the great caravan city of Palmyra, a vital link in the desert routes between Roman and Seleucid Syria to the west and Parthian Mesopotamia to the east. Today, the dramatic ruins of this once great city represent Syria's best known historic attraction. As for the Bedouins, while some have settled down, for many life continues much as it has done for centuries, except for the fact that you are more likely to see them at the wheel of a four-wheel drive than the reins of a camel.

A foot in the door

Having made the effort to get to Palmyra, it would be a pity not to explore the whole site in detail. Nevertheless, there are some things you must not miss.

★ The **Sanctuary of Bel** is in many ways the most impressive monument, and a logical place at which to start. From here you can follow the colonnaded street through the civic centre, passing important public buildings such as the carefully restored **theatre**.

★ Once you have reached Diocletian's Camp, you can climb up onto the low hillock behind for a good overview of the ruins.

★ The Arab castle known as **Qalat Ibn Maan** offers even more impressive views of the ruins and is a very popular spot from which to watch the sunset. It is here that you get a sense of Palmyra as an oasis, with its thick groves of date palms, and also of the seemingly limitless expanses of surrounding desert, austere and desolate yet strangely beautiful.

★ Another great way to enjoy the sunset is over a beer in the **gardens of the Zenobia hotel**; not only do you get a lovely view of the ruins from here, but the tables are actually ancient Corinthian columns taken from the ruins!

Damascus to Palmyra

Roman Dumeir
Colour map 3, grid B2

Ins and outs Leave Damascus on the Aleppo motorway, and after 24 km take the signposted exit for Palmyra. Having exited the motorway, turn left and then right soon after (it is well signposted). After a further 20 km, go straight ahead at a roundabout/fork as you enter the town of Dumeir (bear left to bypass the town). An old signpost by the roadside here indicates Baghdad, 800 km away.

There is an impressive **Roman temple** in the centre of the town, which is well worth a visit. The solid, imposing outline of the temple is visible at the end of the main street. Today it is set in a fenced-off enclosure, its foundations some 3 m below the level of the surrounding buildings. Although the existing structure, which has undergone extensive restoration, is of Roman origin, an altar to the Semitic god Baal Shamin dating from 94 AD found here suggests that it was originally a Nabatean temple. In 245 AD it was dedicated to the god Zeus Hypsistos, a local version of Zeus. At a crossroads on the east-west route between Homs and Palmyra and the north-south route between Damascus and Rasafeh, the building possibly started life as a staging post, which perhaps explains its square plan, unusual for a temple of this period. Some of the stone blocks in the walls bear Greek inscriptions. Inside, a small room to the right of the entrance contains a stone carved with figures on each face. During the Arab period the temple was used as a fortified tower which is why the large arched doorways at the front and rear have been bricked up, and the level of the walls raised above the pediments capping the arches.

■ *Both the enclosure and the temple are kept locked; ask around and the caretaker, who lives locally, will soon appear. From the roundabout/fork, follow the road towards the centre of town for just under 2 km, going straight over a second roundabout on the way, and then take the second right turn after a marked dip in the road as it crosses a wadi.*

Qasr al-Heir al-Gharbi
Colour map 1, grid C3

On your way east to Palmyra, it is possible to make a short diversion from the tiny settlement of **Al Basiri** to visit the ruins of Qasr al-Heir al-Gharbi (literally 'western walled palace'). Although this palace must once have been impressive, all the major architectural features have been removed, including the massive central gateway which now adorns the entrance to the National

Museum in Damascus. The remaining ruins are in a very advanced state of dilapidation and unless you have a special interest, the ruins of Qasr al-Heir al-Sharki ('eastern walled palace') to the northeast of Palmyra (see page 197) are far more rewarding to visit.

First occupied in the first century AD by settlers from Palmyra, and later the site of a Byzantine/Ghassanid monastery in the sixth century, the palace appears to have been built in the eighth century by the Umayyad Caliph Hisham Ibn Abd al-Malik, who is thought to have built Qasr al-Heir al-Sharki at around the same time. It is probable that the palace served primarily as a hunting lodge and desert retreat for the Umayyad rulers of Damascus, but, like its eastern neighbour, it perhaps also served as a means of maintaining close contacts with the desert tribes from which the Umayyads themselves had originated. It also appears to have supported gardens (watered by an aqueduct running from a dam built 15 km to the south by the Palmyrenes).

■ *To reach the ruins turn left towards Homs and follow the road for around 35 km, at which point the ruins can be made out 2 km off to the right.*

Hama to Palmyra via Qalat Shmemis

Palmyra

Covering the journey in 196 km, this route follows a recently built road (not marked on most maps) before joining the main Homs-Palmyra road. From Hama, take the road southeast towards Salamiyeh (the exit for Salamiyeh off the ringroad which passes to the east of Hama is clearly signposted). Around 18 km beyond the Hama ring road, at about the same time as you spot the huge concrete silos of a grain processing factory, **Qalat Shmemis** comes into view.

If you have your own transport, this is certainly the most beautiful route, combining both open desert & hilly steppes, as well as a chance to see some 'beehive' houses

This ruined castle is perched strikingly on the top of an extinct volcano whose perfect conical outline, completely bare of vegetation, contrasts sharply in spring with the green hills and fields surrounding it. The castle dates from the 13th century and was built by the Ayyubid Governor of Hama, Assad ud-Din Shirkoh. The climb up to the rim of the volcano on a path from the end of the metalled road is steep but fairly straightforward; getting into the castle, however, is more difficult. You must first descend into the crater and then scramble up. Note that the large slit in the rock wall of the castle, which looks like an entrance, is in fact a cave. You can gain entry from a point just to the right of the cave, which involves a tricky climb up through the last part (though there is a slightly easier access from the opposite side of the castle). Today little remains of the castle except for the walls themselves; there are panoramic views of the surrounding countryside, but the most striking thing about this site is the view of it from a distance. ■ *Depending on the season, there may be various tracks leading up to the volcano from the main road, or more conveniently there is a small surfaced road running from the town of Salamiyeh, a further 10 km away. Entering the town, turn left by the petrol station and then left again, and follow this road for a little over 3 km to the foot of the volcano.*

The town of Salamiyeh, 33 km from Hama, known in Hellenistic/Roman times as *Salamias*, was an important stopping place on the route to Rasafeh. It continued to flourish under the Byzantines, and during the Islamic era became an important Ismaili centre, being the birthplace of the first Fatimid Caliph Ubaydullah. Driven out by the Mongol invasion of 1401, many Ismailis left the refuge of the mountains during the 19th century and once again came to settle around Salamiyeh. Today, Salamiyeh is a small but lively market town used by farmers from the surrounding countryside. Recycled Byzantine architectural fragments can be seen in some of the older buildings, while in the centre is an Ismaili mosque, thought to date originally from the 11th century, and a beautiful

Salamiyeh
*Colour map 3, grid A3
There is a pleasant café on the main road on the left-hand side as you enter town*

old hammam. **NB** A road leads northeast from Salamiyeh to the Roman temple of Isriye, 90 km away (see page 237) and now extends all the way to Rasafeh.

Ask directions through the centre of town to pick up the road for Palmyra. Keep going straight through the villages of **Tal Atout** and **Bural Sharki** (the latter 16 km from Salamiyeh). The surrounding land becomes progressively less intensively cultivated, steadily giving way to scrubland and semi-desert. Around 26 km beyond Bural Sharki, bear right at the fork in the centre of the small town of **Aqeirbat** (80 km from Hama, petrol available), and then turn right at a crossroads just over 1 km further on. After heading across flat, stony scrubland, the road begins to climb, winding through low hills dotted with stunted pine trees, and then through dramatic desert scenery, desolate and bare. Around 75 km beyond Aqeirbat, you link up with the main Homs-Palmyra road. Turn left here and it is a further 45 km to Palmyra (see Homs to Palmyra, above).

Palmyra تدمر

Phone code: 031
Colour map 3, grid C4

Even as late as the 1920s the journey to Palmyra was a long (five days or so) and arduous one which required careful planning and usually an armed escort. Although the journey now involves no more than a comfortable cruise across the wide expanses of the Syrian desert in an air conditioned coach, it is still easy to understand why Palmyra, 'caravan city' and 'bride of the desert', with its almost improbable ruins spread majestically amidst bare desert, still fires our imaginations. As you approach from the west, the ruins come into view rather suddenly, scattered on either side of the road before you enter the modern town of Tadmor. But the ancient city's setting, bare desert contrasting sharply against the green oasis, makes the site all the more impressive.

Today, some of the magic and romanticism of the site has been tarnished by the throngs of tourist coaches which descend each day, and by the rapid, haphazard development of tourist facilities. Nevertheless, with such a vast site it is still possible to be the only person wandering around a particular area and with the ruins to yourself you can be transported back to the full glory of the city in its heyday.

Ins and outs

Getting there
See also Transport section page 196 for further details

Regular coaches run from Damascus, Homs and Deir ez-Zor to Palmyra, covering the journey in approximately 2-3 hrs (from Damascus it is 3 hrs, from Homs or Deir ez-Zor 2 hrs, though the slower local buses between Homs and Palmyra take around 2½ hrs). The route from Hama via Salamiyeh is only really viable if you have your own transport; there are regular buses/microbuses to Salamiyeh, and more erratic services to Aqeirbat, but along the final stretch there is no public transport, and not enough traffic to make hitching a reliable option.

Getting around

The main body of the ruins are within walking distance of Tadmor town, and the best option is simply to explore on foot. To reach the Valley of the Tombs, the Southwest Necropolis, Southeast Necropolis and Arab Castle you really need to organize transport (though if the weather is not too hot, the Valley of the Tombs, and perhaps even the Arab Castle, can be managed on foot). It is certainly worth spending a few nights in Palmyra in order to benefit from seeing the ruins at sunrise and sunset. Visiting Palmyra as a day-trip from Damascus or Homs is best avoided if at all possible; a minimum of one full day is recommended, and more if possible.

The tourist information office is on the roundabout near the museum, at the western end of Tadmor town, T910574. Open 0800-1400, 1800-2400 (in theory at least; in practice there is often no one in attendence after dark). The staff here are fairly helpful and well informed. Call here if you want an official tour guide to take you round the ruins. Alternatively, there are usually a few freelance guides hanging around outside the museum. In addition, many of the hotels offer a range of mini-tours (essentially transport only), most commonly to the Valley of the Tombs/southwest Necropolis, and/or to the Castle for sunset, or else to Qasr al-Heir al-Sharki. Another popular activity organized by many of the hotels is a visit to a 'Bedouin camp'. In many cases this simply amounts to a meal in a tent set up by the hotel outside of town, perhaps with 'traditional' music and dancing, though some hotels will arrange for an altogether more satisfying visit to an authentic Bedouin camp.

Tourist information, guides & tours

History

Evidence of the earliest periods of settlement in Palmyra is fragmented. Archaeological finds have confirmed that the oasis and surrounding area was a focus for settlement as far back as the Paleolithic and Neolithic eras, when the climate of the region would have been significantly wetter and milder.

The first written records concerning Palmyra date from the second millennium BC. **Cuneiform texts** found in the archives of Mari (see page 388) and Kultepe (in the Cappadocia region of present-day Turkey) dating from the beginning of the second millennium BC, as well as later **Assyrian texts** dating from the end of the second millennium BC, make reference to

Early accounts

Palmyra

Palmyra overview

To Deir ez-Zor

Kadmous Coaches

Al Wardeh Coaches

Damas Tour Coaches

Racecourse

TADMOR

B

Diocletian's Camp

Palmyra Museum

Colonnaded Street

Zenobia's Wall

Oasis

A

Ethnographic Museum

Sanctuary of Bel

Oasis

Southwest Necropolis

Oasis

To Damascus

Related maps
A Civic centre,
page 182
B Tadmor town,
page 193

N

0 metres   500
0 yards   500

■ **Sleeping**
1 Al Faris
2 Caracalla
3 Palmyra Cham Palace
4 Zenobia

● **Eating**
1 Garden

Archaeological sites
1 Funerary temple
2 Temple of Baal Shamin
3 Christian basilica
4 Peristyle house
5 Qalat Ibn Maan
6 Tower Tomb of Iamliku

7 Tower Tomb of Elabel
8 Tower Tomb of Atenatan
9 Tomb 36
10 Hypogeum of the Three Brothers
11 Afqa Spring

Tadmor: ancient and modern name

The origins of the name Tadmor, by which Palmyra was first known, and which is now applied to the modern town that has grown up beside the ruins, are unclear. The most popular explanation links it to the Semitic word 'tamr' meaning 'date', in the same way that 'Palmyra' is derived from the Greek and Latin 'Palma' meaning 'date-palm'. Another possible explanation is that the word is derived from the western Semitic root 'dh-m-r' meaning 'to protect' or 'guard-post'. Other possible derivations are from 'damar' meaning 'destruction', or 'tatmor' meaning to 'cover' or 'bury', although given that the town is known to have been called Tadmor during pre-Roman times, before there was any destruction or buried ruins, such a derivation seems unlikely.

Aramaic-speaking nomads from around Palmyra. The **Second Book of Chronicles**, meanwhile, relates the legendary tale of the founding of Tadmor by King Solomon during the first millennium BC. This reference is now recognized as being an error, the chronicler having confused Tadmor (Palmyra) with Tamar in the desert near the Dead Sea in present day Israel, but the mix-up in itself indicates that Palmyra was already a well known town.

Seleucid struggles Having been controlled for a time first by the Assyrians and then the Persians, Palmyra later became part of Alexander the Great's Macedonian Greek Empire. Following Alexander's death in 323 BC, the eastern part of the empire was divided between two of his generals, Ptolemy and Seleucus. Ptolemy controlled Egypt while Seleucus took control of Babylonia, soon extending his power to include Palmyra and most of Syria. Poor relations with Ptolemy's Empire, which likewise grew from its base in Egypt to encompass parts of southern Syria, including Damascus, meant that the Seleucids tended to favour the more northern (and therefore safer) trade route from their main capital Seleucia, along the Euphrates then across via Aleppo to Antioch. In time, however, the Seleucid Empire came under simultaneous pressure from the Parthians to the east and the emerging Roman Empire to the west. First the Parthians (successors to the Persians) took control of Babylonia, thus confining the Seleucids to Syria, and then in 64 BC the Romans annexed Antioch, establishing themselves along the Levantine coast and effectively bringing an end to the Seleucid Empire.

Profits from Parthians This new power balance left Palmyra in a no man's land between the Parthians and Romans. Threatened with the prospect of annihilation as the two powers locked into a continuing but inconclusive cycle of invasion and counter-invasion, the Palmyrans in fact managed to establish an unique, if precarious, niche for themselves. Despite the conflict between the two powers, there was also a common interest to be had in the continuation of trade between east and west. The collapse of the Seleucid Empire had resulted in the decline of the northern trade route along the Euphrates, which became an area of uncertainty and instability, and this provided the opportunity for Palmyra to establish itself as the principal trading post on a more direct desert route between Dura Europos and Emesa (Homs). Thus the Palmyran traders became middlemen in a mutually beneficial trade between two hostile powers. Pliny the Elder, writing in 77 AD, even went so far as to suggest that Palmyra played a mediating role between the two: "Enjoying certain privileges with the two Great Empires, that of the Romans and that of the Parthians, Palmyra is sought out whenever disputes occur."

Palmyrene art

The Palmyrene artistic style is highly distinctive and has been the source of much debate amongst scholars as to the different influences which have shaped it. The funerary sculptures which were such an important aspect of Palmyrene art are often referred to as Parthian in style due to the rigid representation of figures, always facing to the front with highly formalized facial features aimed at creating a timeless, other-worldly effect rather than depicting any realistic human expressions. Likewise, many of the statues are dressed in a distinctly Parthian style of clothing. Prior to the Roman presence in Palmyra, there was a strong Hellenistic influence in Palmyrene art and, with the growth of Roman influence, an increasing use of Graeco-Roman motifs. However, at the same time the eastern, 'Parthian' influence remained strong, allowing Palmyra to develop its own distinctive style. Thus for all their formulistic rigidity, elements of personal expression can be found in many of the sculptures, particularly those from later periods.

Roman renewal

The history of Palmyra up to this point provides the key to understanding its distinctive culture and style of art and architecture. First it came under Hellenistic influence, and then the competing influences of the Parthians and Romans, whilst all the time maintaining a certain degree of independence from all three. The exact balance of opposing influences and autonomy is difficult to determine, although it is clear that as time progressed, in practical terms it was the Roman influence that grew while Palmyra flourished as the most important caravan city of Syria. Thus when Mark Antony sent horsemen to loot Palmyra in 41 BC, the inhabitants fled with all their belongings to the safety of Parthian-controlled areas beyond the Euphrates. However, by 19 AD statues of Germanicus, Tiberius and Druses were erected in the Temple of Bel by Fretensis, the Roman legate of the 10th Legion, and by around 60 AD the Roman Senate was instituted as the sole governing body of Palmyra. Thus Palmyra in effect became a tributary buffer state of the Romans against the Parthians.

Even more important than the earlier collapse of the Seleucid Empire for Palmyra was the Roman annexation of the Nabatean Empire and its capital **Petra** in 106 AD. Previously Petra had rivalled and probably surpassed Palmyra as a trading city, but now a significant portion of that trade passed through Palmyra, with the rest going via Egypt. When **Hadrian** visited Palmyra in 128 AD, he awarded it the status of a 'free city', allowing it to set and collect its own taxes. This, now dominant, trading city flourished in the relative stability achieved under Hadrian and his successors, and it is this period, during the second and early third centuries AD, which is considered the height of Palmyra's wealth and success.

The Severans

The next series of events to influence Palmyra's fate came with the marriage of Septimus Severus to Julia Domna, the daughter of the high priest of Emesa (Homs), an event which ensured greater direct Syrian influence in the affairs of Imperial Rome. Severus divided the administration of Syria in two, with Palmyra becoming part of *Syria Phoenicia* with its capital at Emesa. Under his successor Caracalla, Palmyra was raised in status to a *colonia* and granted *ius italicum*, or freedom from the burden of paying taxes to Rome. At the same time, Rome's constant campaigns against the Parthians fully engaged its armies, forcing Palmyra to strengthen its own defensive capabilities.

Under Alexander Severus (222-235) Palmyra and the Syrian provinces successfully held out against the Sassanids, who rose to replace the Parthians as the great power in the east. But after his death, both internal Imperial power struggles and rebellions, together with invasions from outside, led to a period of decline in the empire which became a jungle of intrigue, blood and uncertainty. For Palmyra, this provided an opportunity to exercise greater independence. **Odainat** (Septimius Odaenathus), a local noble, assumed the title of king. His position was enormously strengthened when in 260 he defeated the Sassanid king Shapur, who in the same year had himself defeated the Roman emperor Valerian. Odainat's success in defeating this trouble-maker was a major relief for the struggling Roman Empire, and earned him the honorary title of *corrector totius orientis*. Ever ambitious, however, he went one step further in naming himself 'king of kings', a title borrowed from the Sassanids he had just defeated. In subsequent campaigns he succeeded in reaching their capital Ctesiphon (on the Tigris River in modern-day Iraq) thus effectively neutralizing the Sassanian threat. In 268 he was murdered during a campaign against the Goths in Cappadocia, according to some sources on the instructions of his wife Zenobia.

Zenobia Odainat had set the stage for the last great episode of Palmyra's history. Wahballat, his only surviving son was still a child, so his wife Zenobia took power as regent. A unique and almost legendary figure even in her own time, Zenobia was certainly the most colourful and unusual personality to emerge from Palmyra, even if her over-reaching ambition was ultimately to lead to the decline of what had become a rich and powerful city-state. Her assumption of power alarmed Rome and a force was sent to subdue her. But she easily defeated this force, and, perhaps seeking to outdo her husband's campaigning enthusiasm, she went on to seize control of the whole Province of Syria. Not content with this, she then besieged Bosra, the capital of the Province of Arabia, and shortly afterwards successfully invaded Egypt. **Aurelian**, the Roman emperor at the time, at first sought to appease her by 'granting' her son the various titles that Odainat had assumed, but when she declared Wahballat 'Augustus' (ie 'Emperor'), he was forced to confront this direct challenge to Rome's authority. After several clashes with the Palmyrene army, he took possession of Palmyra in 271. Zenobia was captured while trying to flee across the Euphrates and taken back to Rome as a captive of Aurelian.

Defeat & Early in 272, Palmyra revolted against Roman occupation, but was once again **decline** taken by Aurelian and his troops who this time sacked the city, though they did not completely destroy it. Palmyra never recovered from this defeat, and although it continued to function as a city for a couple of centuries, it never regained its former wealth and importance. Roman garrisons were stationed there, and **Diocletian** (284-305 AD) built a defensive wall around the main monuments, turning it into a fortified garrison town. This wall, along with other building projects such as the complex now known as Diocletian's Camp, fundamentally altered the appearance of the city from that of its original 'classical' period.

Christianity first became established around the late third to early fourth century and later, during the reign of the Emperor **Justinian** (527-65), the churches and fortifications of Palmyra were partially restored. Shortly after, however, the Eastern Roman (Byzantine) Empire collapsed. The next mention of Palmyra comes in 634 when the Arab Muslim general **Khalid Ibn al-Walid** captured the city after laying siege to it. From then on, it continued as a small and relatively insignificant settlement, fortified once more as a strategic desert outpost by the Arab general **Abdul Hassan Yussuf ibn Fairouz** in 1132-33.

Queen Zenobia

Little is known for certain about Queen Zenobia herself although, perhaps unsurprisingly, her ambitious exploits have inspired the imaginations of many a writer. The emperor Aurelian, who was at least qualified to comment on her from his own experience, wrote after capturing her: "Those who say I have only conquered a woman do not know what that woman was, nor how lightening were her decisions, how persevering she was in her plans, how resolute with her soldiers."

Edward Gibbon, in his Decline and Fall of the Roman Empire, *writes of her: "She equalled in beauty her ancestor Cleopatra and far surpassed that princess in chastity and valour. Zenobia was esteemed the most lovely as well as the most heroic of her sex. She was of dark complexion. Her teeth were of a pearly whiteness and her large black eyes sparkled with an uncommon fire, tempered by the most attractive sweetness. Her voice was strong and harmonious. Her manly understanding was strengthened and adorned by study." Certainly, the stories of her beauty were enduring, though quite how Gibbon, writing in the 18th century, was able to comment accurately on her chastity and the look in her eyes is quite another matter. Imbued with the aura of a legendary heroine, the details of her*

personality almost demand to be painted in the most noble and romantic colours.

What is clear about her is that she was a woman of exceptional ability. The 'manly understanding' to which Gibbon alludes probably refers to her fluency in Greek, Latin, Aramaic and Egyptian. Stories of her intelligence are reinforced by the fact that she was also able to attract to her court some of the best minds in the Hellenistic world, including the famous philosopher and rhetorician Cassius Longinus, who acted as her principal adviser. But most of all, her achievements in assuming power and challenging the might of the Roman Empire, all the more remarkable for a woman in the context of a rigidly male-dominated society, are a testimony to her capability and ambition.

Undoubtedly, however, that soaring ambition led ultimately to her downfall. Even when surrounded in Palmyra by Aurelian's troops and faced with hopeless odds, she still refused to accept the generous surrender terms offered to her and attempted instead to escape and seek the help of the Sassanians. After her capture, popular legend has it that Aurelian brought her to Rome and led her through the streets in gold chains as part of his triumphal parade through the city.

Palmyra

Notwithstanding the Arab's fortification of the temple of Bel in the 12th century, and possibly the building of the first castle on the hill overlooking the town at this time, Palmyra fell gradually from its former state of glory into disuse and then oblivion. Apart from the small village that established itself within the *temenos* of the temple of Bel, the monuments were left to the ravages of time and weather, becoming steadily more deeply buried in sand.

It was not until the second half of the 17th century that interest in the ruins began to be awakened amongst the European traders who had their headquarters in the khans of Aleppo's souks. Intrigued by tales of these fabulous ruins, an English expedition, led by Dr Huntington, a British trader based in Aleppo, set out to visit them in 1678. They fared badly, reaching the ruins only to be robbed, even of their clothes, before fleeing back to Aleppo. They returned again in 1691, this time led by a Dr Halifax, better prepared with a letter of introduction from a local tribal sheikh and a substantial armed escort. This second visit resulted in *Relation of a Voyage to Tadmor*, published in 1895, and the first descriptions and drawings of the ruins. Particularly interesting was the discovery of Greek inscriptions alongside the then unknown Palmyrene script, and through these, the identification of Odainat as king of Palmyra and husband of the, until then, purely legendary Queen Zenobia. Dr Halifax relates

'Rediscovery' of Palmyra: verification of myths & a tourist legend is born

how their interest in the inscriptions was interpreted: "for this notion stickes in ye heads of all these people, that the Frankes goe to see old Ruines only because there they meet with Inscriptions which direct them to some hid treasure ..."

In 1710 the Swede Cornelius Loos visited Palmyra on behalf of Charles XII of Sweden, making further drawings, but it was not until the detailed work of English architects Messrs Wood and Dawkins in 1751 that any systematic examination of the ruins was undertaken, and widespread interest began to be shown abroad. Subsequent visitors from the early 19th century onwards, amongst them in 1813 the eccentric Lady Hester Stanhope (see page 545), came more as tourists and did very little to further existing knowledge about the ruins.

Finally, before the **First World War** the Germans, who were by that time closely allied with the Ottoman Turks, carried out a detailed inventory of the city and its monuments, the first proper archaeological survey of the ruins. When it was finally published in 1932, it formed the basis of subsequent exploration which began in earnest after the War. In 1929 the French archaeologists H Seyrig and R Amy arrived at the site. They found the compound of the temple of Bel occupied by a small Arab village, which they set about removing, giving rise to the present town of Tadmor, before beginning excavations on the temple. In 1939-40 Seyrig excavated the Agora. Archaeological work intensified after the Second World War with a series of foreign archaeological expeditions, taken over after independence by the Syrian Directorate-General of Antiquities, and continuing to this day. Indeed, part of the magic of Palmyra lies not only in what there is to see, but in imagining what treasures remain hidden under the sands.

Sights

Remember to take adequate protection against the sun and a good supply of water

The main ruins, enclosed within what is commonly referred to as Zenobia's wall, are spread over a large area. While this makes it relatively easy to avoid the organized groups touring the site, it also means that during the summer, when it gets ferociously hot during the day, only the early morning and evening are really suitable for walking around the ruins. Likewise, you will get the best results in terms of photography during these times. The Sanctuary of Bel, Qalat Ibn Maan (Arab castle), the museums and the most important of the temple tombs observe fixed opening times and charge an entrance fee.

Sanctuary of Bel

A scale model in the Palmyra Museum gives a good idea of what the whole sanctuary would originally have looked like (see box, page 180)

At the eastern end of the ancient city centre, just by the main road, this is by far the largest and best preserved of the temple sanctuaries at Palmyra. The sanctuary consists of a central *cella*, or temple, contained within a large *temenos* (sacred enclosure) marked by huge walls, in places leaning precariously, shored up with concrete footings and buttresses, or else completely destroyed and replaced by low makeshift structures. These walls originally date from the second to third century AD, although they suffered severe damage from earthquakes and were subsequently reinforced and modified for defensive purposes during Arab times. A walk around the outside reveals examples of the original Palmyrene and later Arab building work. The northwest corner provides the best example of the original walls, with the sequence of pilasters and framed windows topped by triangular pediments well preserved. The later rebuilding work is clearly visible along the eastern (rear) wall, where various architectural fragments have been incorporated at random, and many of the recycled stone blocks have been placed on their sides, revealing the original locating grooves.

Palmyra

According to an inscription above the low doorway in the recessed arch of the main tower, the monumental entrance, or ***propylaeum***, to the enclosure was converted into a defensive citadel by the Arab general Abdul Hassan Yussuf Ibn Fairouz in 1132-33. Originally it would have consisted of a broad flight of stairs leading up to a massive portico supported by eight pillars and finally a triple gateway some 35 m wide. But it seems that the portico section had collapsed by the time Fairouz arrived, leaving him with three sides of a future 'keep' to complete along with the present fourth wall. Once inside the sanctuary, you can see the heavily weathered triple gateway consisting of an enormous central portal, its lintel now fallen, and two side portals. The space between the triple entrance and the outside Arab wall is strewn with massive tumbled blocks of stone.

Today you enter, rather boringly, through the ticket office to the left of the propylaeum

Today the courtyard of the *temenos* is striking for its size, a large open space littered with sections of fallen columns, in places neatly laid out in rows, with the *cella* in the centre. Originally, running around the inside perimeter there was a *peristyle*, or covered corridor, consisting of a double colonnade around the north, east and south sides and a single colonnade along the west side. The single line of columns along the west side are significantly taller, the *propylaeum* and outside wall forming the second line of support for the ceiling. To the left as you enter, seven of these columns are still standing, complete with their crowning *entablature*, although the decoration on this has been almost totally weathered away. A sunken passageway from outside leads under the columns by means of an arch. This passage was probably used to bring animals into the *temenos* to be sacrificed at the altar, the remains of which are in front and to the left of the central *cella*.

Approaching the *cella* from the monumental entrance, there is the sacrificial altar to the left, with only its base remaining. Its outline is partially obscured by the foundations of a later **banqueting house** (numerous clay tokens, distributed as invitations to the ritual banquets, were found here). On the right are the remains of a **sacred basin** where ritual ablutions presumably took place. Various **water channels** can still be seen leading to the basin.

The *cella* of the sanctuary of Bel is offset slightly to the east of the centre of the enclosure, creating a larger space between it and the monumental entrance. The present building can be firmly dated to 32 AD from a dedication inscribed on the pedestal of a statue found in the temple (now housed in the Palmyra Museum). However, this was also the site of an earlier temple of Bel, dating from the Hellenistic period and probably made from mud. The low mound, or *tell*, on which these temples were built has revealed evidence of worship dating back to between 1500-2200 BC. Surrounding the huge rectangular building was a broad *peristyle* supported by massive fluted columns; along the east (rear) side these columns, 18 m high, are still standing complete with their entablature and they provide a powerful sense of the colossal scale of the temple. The outer portal, which originally formed part of the peristyle, now stands alone, its

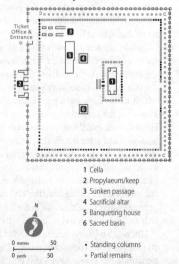

Sanctuary of Bel

1 Cella
2 Propylaeum/keep
3 Sunken passage
4 Sacrificial altar
5 Banqueting house
6 Sacred basin

N

0 metres 50
0 yards 50

• Standing columns
○ Partial remains

Palmyra

Palmyra

The Palmyrene pantheon

Unfortunately very little is known about the religion of Palmyra, except that like Palmyrene art, it was very much a synthesis of different influences. **Bel**, who was undoubtedly the most important of the Palmyrene gods given the dominant size of the Temple of Bel, was of Babylonian origin, and formed the apex of a trinity completed by **Yarhibol** and **Aglibol**, the sun and moon gods respectively, who were most probably of local origin. The second major trinity in Palmyra was that of **Baal Shamin**, Phoenician in origin, who was supported again by Aglibol and by another local god, **Malakbel**, also a sun god. To the Greeks, both Bel and Baal Shamin were equated with the god Zeus, although Baal Shamin was often depicted as an eagle with outstretched wings (there is a fine example of such a representation in the museum at Palmyra).

Two other gods are judged to have been of similar importance to Bel and Baal Shamin from the fact that they both had sanctuaries of their own and merited frequent mention in inscriptions. The first of these was the god **Allat**, of Arab origin and central to the Nabateans, who is often equated with Athena and was rare in being one of the few female gods (alongside the Babylonian **Ishtar**, herself identified with Allat) found in the Palmyrene pantheon. Indeed, Allat (or more accurately Ilah or al-Lat) is the female form of Allah, literally God in Arabic, and is interesting in that she represents the concept of monotheism amongst the Arabs long before the advent of Islam. The second was **Nebo**, of Babylonian origin, who is sometimes equated with Apollo, a pairing which was reinforced by the discovery of a statue of Apollo in the Nebo sanctuary.

massive lintel slightly slipped, but still in place following the restoration undertaken by the French in 1932. On the right as you pass through this portal there are two richly carved **stone beams** from the roof of the peristyle. The first depicts Aglibol, the moon god, hand in hand with Malakbel, here symbolizing fertility, while behind it the second depicts a camel carrying a tabernacle, attended by priests and worshippers. The swirling shapes of veiled women in the scene are well preserved and it is interesting to see that the use of the veil was a practice which long predated Islam. The **inner portal** has lost its lintel, but the walls either side are complete and the massive single-section stone slabs used to form the sides of the door frame are a good reminder of the awesome engineering feats involved.

The ceiling of the southern adyton was the inspiration for many decorated ceilings in country houses around Britain during the 18th century Neo-Classical period

Inside, the temple consists of a single chamber with an *adyton*, or large niche, at either end. Around the walls are various fragments of the original ceiling to the *cella*. At the southern end (to your right as you enter) is the smaller of the two *adytons*, possibly originally having contained a movable image of Bel which would have been paraded round the sanctuary on special occasions. However, the crowning glory is the **ceiling** inside: a massive single slab of richly carved, excellently preserved stone with a circular pattern of alternating acanthus and lotus leaves at its centre. This in turn is surrounded by a wide geometric border and enclosed within a square which is then surrounded by a broad border of octagonal shapes containing rosettes interspaced by a complex pattern of squares and triangles. A later addition to the south *adyton* was the small *mihrab* dating from the 12th century, when the temple was converted into a mosque. On either side of the *adyton*, at ground level, are entrance ways that give access to stairs leading up to the roof, although these are now locked.

The north *adyton* is larger and would have formed the main focus of worship. Its façade is more complex and imposing, while the absence of steps was meant perhaps to emphasize its elevated position above the mass of worshippers. The ceiling of the north *adyton* also consists of a single slab of carved stone; at the centre is a *cupola* with the busts of the seven planetary divinities (Jupiter at the centre, surrounded by Helios, Selene, Ares, Hermes, Aphrodite and Cronos) and surrounding this is a thin band containing the 12 signs of the zodiac. The underside of the lintel over the entrance to the *adyton* bears a carving of an eagle (representing Jupiter/Bel) with wings outstretched across a star-studded sky. Concealed by the façade are two side chambers to the left and right of the *adyton*, the one to the left containing stairs which give access to the roof of the *cella*.

■ *Open daily, 0800-1300, 1600-1800 in summer, and 0800-1600 in winter. Entry S£300 (students S£15). There are various postcards, booklets and souvenirs on sale at the ticket office, while just inside the compound there is a cardphone.*

Seen from the vantage point of the Arab castle, the colonnaded street clearly forms the backbone of the ancient city of Palmyra, its spidery line of columns stretching for over a kilometre. The street can be divided into three main sections, each with its own alignment. The first runs from the temple of Bel to the monumental arch, the second through the main civic centre from the monumental arch to the tetrapylon and the last from the tetrapylon to the partially restored funerary temple. The street was in fact built and developed from west to east, so in the following description, one should bear in mind the reverse chronology. The important temples and public buildings which are found along and off to either side of the street are described as they appear.

Civic centre & colonnaded street

Palmyra

Between the *propylaeum* of the temple of Bel and the monumental arch which today stands as the most prominent feature at the entrance to the civic centre of the ancient city, there was originally a section of colonnaded street, wider than the rest. From the temple of Bel a series of re-erected columns mark the left-hand side of this street, their line interrupted by some low buildings in front of the temple. Just across the modern road as you approach the monumental arch are four large re-erected columns, taller than the ones preceeding it. These formed the portico of an **exedra**, the paved area behind still visible. Further along the same side there are the foundations of what were probably shops and other buildings, including a small *nymphaeum* with a water tank at the rear.

The **Monumental Arch** towers impressively at the end of this section and combines great stylistic and decorative beauty with ingenious functional design. Essentially, due to the piecemeal development of Palmyra and resultant departures from what might otherwise have been a grand overall plan (see below), the monumental arch had to be carefully designed to link two sections of street which ran at a 30° angle to each other. In effect there are two monumental arches each aligned to their respective streets and joined together to form a V-shape. Approaching from the temple of Bel, the central arch of what was once a triple-arched arrangement is completely missing and only the side arches, themselves heavily weathered, remain. Seen from the opposite side, the triple arch is fully intact and the rich and varied decoration lavished on it has been well preserved, displaying a bewildering array of geometric and floral designs which are typically Syrian in their execution. Note also the decoration on the undersides (soffits) of the arches. Here the side arches would have been located under the covered *porticos* which lined the narrower street on either side.

Tellingly, this arch dates from the late 2nd to early 3rd century AD during the reign of Septimus Severus, when Palmyra was at the height of its prosperity

Passing through the arch, you enter the area of the **main civic centre**. To the left, immediately after the monumental arch, are the remains of the **Temple of Nebo** (or Nabu). The temple originally consisted of a trapezoid-shaped *temenos* with the main temple or *cella* at the centre. Today only the podium of the temple remains, together with the lower courses of the outer wall and the column bases of the *peristyle* (some now re-erected) which ran around three sides of the courtyard. The *propylaeum*, or monumental entrance to the temple, was on the south

The temple itself dates from the end of the 1st century AD, although work on the courtyard etc continued into the early 2nd century

side, so that what one sees from the colonnaded street is the rear of the temple compound, which also formed the back wall of the shops which lined the street. Between the *cella* and the *propylaeum* of the temple compound was an altar, today partially restored with concrete pillars. Nebo, identified with the Roman god Apollo, was particularly popular amongst the Palmyrenes. In the Babylonian pantheon he was the son of Mardok, Lord of Heaven. His role as scribe of the Table of Destinies gave him considerable influence over the fortunes of humans, a fact which the merchants of Palmyra, forever concerned with the uncertainties of trade in a continually changing world, must have kept at the front of their minds. Indeed, although the ruins are not much to look at today, this temple had a fundamental influence on the development of the layout of Palmyra. Were it not for the existence of the temple on this spot, it would have been possible for the colonnaded street to run in a straight line for its whole length from the funerary temple to the Temple of Bel. Rather than risk incurring his displeasure by relocating the temple, the Palmyrenes opted to alter the direction of the street at the Tetrapylon to avoid it, and again at the Monumental Arch to get back on course for the Sanctuary of Bel.

Returning to the colonnaded street, it is this next section between the monumental arch and the tetrapylon, dating from the mid to late second century AD (ie contemporary with the monumental arch), which is the best preserved. On one side, many of the columns which supported the covered *porticos* are still standing (or have been re-erected), complete with their characteristic protruding brackets which would have held statues of the civic notables who helped finance the building work, and crowning *entablature*. The porticos housed various shops, and many of the lintels from the doorways, now scattered on the ground, bear inscriptions identifying the trade and the proprietor.

On the right, a little further along from the temple of Nebo, is the entrance to the **Baths of Diocletian** (the sign reads 'Bathes of Zenobia'), marked by four monolithic columns standing forward from the main line of the portico and rising considerably higher. The columns are also distinctive for being of pink granite (brought from Egypt in the same way as the granite columns used at Baalbek, see page 589), in contrast to the locally quarried yellow limestone so

Civic centre

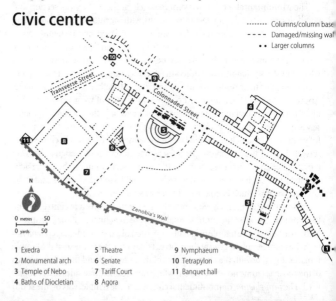

.... Columns/column base
– – – – Damaged/missing wall
• • Larger columns

1 Exedra
2 Monumental arch
3 Temple of Nebo
4 Baths of Diocletian
5 Theatre
6 Senate
7 Tariff Court
8 Agora
9 Nymphaeum
10 Tetrapylon
11 Banquet hall

characteristic of the rest of Palmyra. These columns once supported the portico to the entrance of the baths; they are also the only part of the complex actually dating from the time of Diocletian (284-305 AD), with the baths complex probably dating from around a century earlier, during the reign of Septimus Severus. The actual baths, which were excavated in 1959-1960, exist now for the most part only in outline. Most prominent is the large central basin, partially surrounded by a colonnade of Corinthian columns, which has been indentified as the *frigidarium*.

A little further along the colonnaded street, the columns of the portico on the left are interrupted by a wide, beautifully decorated arch marking the start of a transverse street which curves around the rear of the theatre in a semi-circle to rejoin the main street. A colonnade runs along the outside edge of this street and is joined half-way round by a colonnaded street coming from a large gate in Zenobia's wall to the south.

The **theatre** was until the 1950s for the most part buried under sand, giving no hint of its true scale. When it was first excavated, there were nine rows of seating rising up the *cavea*, divided into 11 sections. There are now 14 rows of seating, although it has been argued that in the original, above the twelfth row, only a wooden structure would have existed. The stage and elaborately decorated *scaenae frons* (stage façade) have been carefully restored.

Today the theatre serves as a venue for the shows put on during the Palmyra Festival

To the southwest of the theatre there are the remains of a number of other civic buildings. Three-quarters of the way round the transverse street, after the turning towards the gate in Zenobia's wall, there are the remains of a small building which is generally recognized as the **Senate**, although its small size has led some to dispute this. A row of eight truncated columns marks the portico to the entrance. Inside was a small peristyled courtyard, of which only the column bases remain, with an apse-shaped chamber at the far end. This apse, with its tiers of seats arranged in a semi-circle, is what led the archaeologist Seyrig to identify the building as the Senate.

Immediately to the southwest of the Senate is a large walled courtyard area, today known as the **Tariff Court**, primarily due to the fact that the Palmyra Tariff (see box) was discovered here. The main entrance to this courtyard was from the southwest side, although the elaborate portico was largely destroyed during the building of 'Zenobia's' wall (in fact the building work on this section was carried out by Diocletian during the third century) which lies just beyond it. The portico led to a grand triple entrance, of which two of the portals still remain. The southeast wall of the courtyard is no longer standing, but drawings made in the 1790s by LF Cassas indicate that it was identical to its northwest counterpart, with windows framed by strongly moulded architraves, interspaced with pilasters. In the northwest wall there are three doorways which lead into the adjacent Agora, the central one of which was known as the Senators' Gate.

The **agora** was the public meeting place of the city, a focal point where news and views were exchanged, and a great deal of the commerce on which Palmyra's wealth depended was carried out. The large, walled courtyard contained a colonnaded portico running around its edges, of which the majority of the columns, or at least their lower sections, still survive. The walls follow the same pattern as those of the Tariff Court, with windows interspaced by pilasters, and in addition a total of 11 doors. The columns would all have had the characteristic brackets bearing statues of civic notables (over 200 in all, including additional statues along the walls themselves). The accompanying inscriptions have provided a wealth of information on the public life of the city. Each colonnade was reserved for different social groups: senators along the east colonnade, Roman and Palmyrene officials along the north, soldiers along the

Judging by its size (48 m by 71 m), the Agora was clearly an extremely important civic institution

Palmyra

The Palmyrene Tariff

A huge inscribed stone slab (1.75 m by 4.8 m) found at Palmyra, known as the Palmyrene Tariff, dating from 137AD and now housed in the Hermitage Museum in St Petersburg gives an unique insight into the commerce of the city. Written both in the Palmyrene dialect and Greek, it meticulously details the taxes due on goods – from perfumes to bronze statues – sold in or passing through the city. The tariff also outlines charges for use of the all-important spring water and even mentions a tax on prostitutes working in

the city, as well as codifying various fiscal and other laws concerning the different traders based in the city. The merchants of Palmyra operated a far-flung network of trading caravans, both by land and sea, to reach out to the Arabian Gulf, India and China in the east, and across Syria to the Mediterranean coast and beyond in the west. In addition to those goods mentioned in the tariff, excavations have revealed the import of luxury items such as silk yarn, jade, muslin, spices, ebony, myrrh, ivory, pearls and precious stones.

west and caravan leaders to the south. On the lintel above the Senators' Gate in the east wall was an inscription (no longer in place) to the family of Septimus Severus, who through his marriage to Julia Domna, the daughter of the high priest of Emesa (Homs), came to have such a strong influence on Palmyrene politics. In the southwest corner of the courtyard steps lead up through a door-way into a small separate banqueting hall, complete with benches for guests, as well as an altar and niche which once would have housed the presiding deity. A bold, well preserved band of geometric decoration based around a swastika motif runs around the walls (the swastika is an ancient symbol, thought to have originated in India, and was associated with the sun, peace and good luck). Building work on both the Agora and the Tariff Court started around the mid-dle of the first century AD, with the earliest inscription in the Agora dating from 71 AD, at the beginning of Hadrian's reign.

Returning now along the last section of the semi-circular transverse street, you pass on the left a series of small cubicles, perhaps shops or ticket booths for the theatre. By the arch which leads back onto the main colonnaded street, there is a course of stone blocks with a hole bored through the centre which would once have carried a water pipe. This is part of an aqueduct dating from the Byzantine period, probably during the reign of Justinian (527-65 AD). Its presence suggests that the original Palmyrene water system must have failed by this time, while the fact that no attempt was made to conceal it below ground level is an indication of the relative decline in Palmyra's wealth by this time.

Opposite the archway leading back onto the main colonnaded street, there are the remains of a small **nymphaeum** or water fountain, marked by four col-umns (three still standing) set forward from the main colonnade to form a por-tico, and behind it a semi-circular *exedra* where the fountain would have been located. Just to the left of the columns are two large stepped platforms which once held honorific columns marking the start of a street leading towards the temple of Baal Shamin. A little further along is the imposing tetrapylon. Before reaching it, the last series of eight columns on the left (counting from the arch) are of particular interest for their inscriptions. Below the bracket of the sixth column is an inscription to "Septimius Odainat, King of Kings and Corrector of all the East". The bracket of the next column, however, is missing, the par-tially defaced inscription being dedicated to his wife, Queen Zenobia. Both inscriptions date from 271 AD, and it seems likely that after Aurelian's capture of the city in 272, the statue of Zenobia, who was considered a traitor by the Roman emperor, was destroyed and her inscription defaced. That of Odainat presumably survived, his loyalty to the Roman Empire being somewhat greater. (He had after all defeated the Sassanids and stopped short of his wife's Imperial ambitions.) Behind this series of columns there are the remains of a building with a peristyled courtyard of fluted columns.

The **tetrapylon** is an imposing structure which, like the monumental arch, conceals a change in the direction of the colonnaded street, as well as providing a suitably grand visual counterbalance to the Sanctuary of Bel. It consists of a large square platform set in an oval plaza with four huge pedestals standing at the corners of the platform, each originally bearing four massive granite columns (brought once again from Egypt) topped by an entablature. At the centre of each pedestal, amongst the columns, there would have been a statue. The monument was in ruins until the 1960s, with the columns all collapsed. When excavation work started, only the fragments of one of the granite columns were found. Much to the horror of purists, the monument was therefore reconstructed using coloured concrete for the other 15 columns. While the authenticity of the reconstruction can certainly be questioned, it undoubtedly enhances the overall effect of the ruins. Leading off at an angle to the left from the tetrapylon, a series of columns mark a second transverse street that runs down towards Zenobia's wall to the south.

In sharp contrast to the central section of the colonnaded street, the last section, from the tetrapylon to the funerary temple, has been subject to much less of the meticulous excavation and reconstruction lavished on the central stretch. The broken line of columns is matched by a confused jumble of fallen stonework scattered haphazardly along the street. Nevertheless, more than 60 columns have been re-erected along this stretch in recent years. The only clearly discernible feature is on the left, approximately 100 m from the tetrapylon, where there are the remains of an **exedra**, its semi-circular plan clearly visible, which was possibly another *nymphaeum*.

Approaching the end of the colonnaded street, there seems to be an even greater concentration of fallen masonry piled up in great heaps, while the bases of the last few columns on the right-hand side can be seen to rise in a stepped fashion. It has been suggested that there was a flight of steps here leading up to a large arch which would have framed the funerary temple beyond it in a dramatic fashion. The **funerary temple** itself is really more of an elaborate family tomb dating from the late second to early third century. The portico, with its six columns supporting the remains of a well proportioned pediment, stands today just as it was found, although the walls of the tomb itself have been reconstructed with the extensive use of concrete. A stairway behind the rear wall leads down into the crypt below, also extensively restored with concrete.

From in front of the funerary temple a wide transverse street dating from the second century leads southwest, its course marked by intermittent re-erected columns. This street led towards an oval piazza followed by a gate in the southern wall of the city, known as the Damascus Gate. Just a small part of the outline of the oval piazza is visible today, marked by a few standing columns, while the Damascus Gate is an indistinct pile of jumbled ruins. Before reaching this, an avenue, once framed by a huge portal, leads off to the right to the ruins of a complex known as **Diocletian's Camp**. The area is interesting in that although it represents one of the earliest settled areas of the city, it was subsequently extensively overlain by the later buildings of Diocletian's camp. This 'camp', dating from the late third to early fourth century AD, was built by Sosianus Hierocles, governor of Syria under the emperor Diocletian (284-305 AD) in the period following the defeat of Zenobia. Half way down the avenue, another one intersects it, running at right angles; this junction was once marked by a large tetrapylon, of which

Diocletian's Camp & Temple of Allat

The camp neatly reflects Palmyra's change in status from a powerful & largely independent trading city to a military outpost of the Roman Empire (see page 176)

only the pedestals and a couple of the columns remain. To the right of the tetrapylon is a series of distinctive fluted columns which, along with a heavily weathered doorway and the foundations of the inner *cella*, are all that remains of the **Temple of Allat**. These somewhat meagre remains date from the second century AD, although there was a temple compound on this site as early as the first century BC. At the end of the avenue are the foundations of a *propylaeum* which led through to what was once an enclosed square or miniature forum. In front of you, a broad flight of stairs, so heavily worn as to seem almost as if they have melted in the heat, leads up to what was the **Temple of the Standards**. At the top of the steps, four tall columns, one still standing, supported a portico which led directly through a triple doorway into the *cella* of the temple. This consisted of a large rectangular hall with an apse-shaped chamber opposite the entrance, parts of which

Diocletian's Camp

1 Temple of the Standards
2 Forum
3 Tetrapylon
4 Temple of Allat
5 Oval Piazza
6 Damascus Gate

0 metres 50
0 yards 50

still survive, where the various military insignia of the Roman army were housed. Strictly speaking, it is only this apsidal chamber which can be termed the Temple of the Standards; the exact function of the building as a whole is still unclear, and interpretation of the remains are further complicated by the fact that an earlier building was modified and extended in order to create it. It has been suggested that the whole area was previously Zenobia's Palace; the street plan and tetrapylon, which are known to predate Diocletian's occupation, certainly suggest a grand, monumental complex. Behind the Diocletian's camp is the low hill of Jebel Husseiniye, with a section of the northern fortifying wall running straight up its slope before swinging round and descending to run along the southern perimeter of the city. From the top of this hill there are good views out over the ruins.

Temple of Baal Shamin
The Temple of Baal Shamin is the most important of the ruins in the area to the northeast of the main colonnaded street. It can be reached either from the main tetrapylon on the colonnaded street, or from the main road via the Zenobia hotel. There are several stages of building work, the north courtyard being the oldest, followed by the *cella* and then the south courtyard. The main *cella*, restored in the 1950s by Swiss archaeologists, is today the only part of the temple compound still largely intact. Its construction in 131 AD was financed by Male Agrippa, a local merchant prince, who was so wealthy that when Hadrian came to visit the city in 129 AD, he paid for all the expenses associated with his visit. The *cella* has a large portico supported by six pillars, the front four originally supporting a triangular *pediment* rather like that of the funerary temple. On the projecting bracket of one of the front pillars is an inscription telling us of Male Agrippa's funding of the temple, and of Hadrian's visit to Palmyra. The inside of the *cella* consists of a central *adyton* fronted by a semicircular structure with fluted double columns on either side, and two side chambers. Although closed

off and partially obscured by a tree growing inside, you can still peer in. During the fifth century it was converted into a church. In front of the entrance is an altar dating from 113 AD. Parts of the north courtyard date from as early as 17 AD, while the smaller south courtyard dates from 149 AD. It is interesting to note the differing styles to be found in the capitals of the columns which formed the colonnaded peristyles of both courtyards; those of the north courtyard are mostly replacements dating from reconstruction work carried out by Odainat in 258 AD and show an apparently Egyptian influence, while those of the south courtyard are in the traditional Hellenistic Corinthian style.

Little else remains in this area to the northeast of the main colonnaded street, which once comprised Palmyra's more affluent residential area. There are the scant remains of a later Christian basilica about 150 m to the northwest, and another smaller one to the southwest of it. Elsewhere, only a couple of peristyles of Roman houses still survive.

Occupying a choice position on the high hilltop overlooking the ruins is the Arab castle of Qalat Ibn Maan. If for no other reason, the castle is worth a visit to see the panoramic views of Palmyra, as well as north along the ridges of Jebel al-Tadmoria. Sunset is the best time, with the ruins illuminated to a golden colour by the fading light. Sunrise is also very beautiful, although the ruins are then in silhouette against the rising sun. A metalled road winds its way up to the castle, or else there is a good, though steep, path which zig-zags up the side. A bridge, replacing the original drawbridge, gives access over the moat to the castle gate. Inside, there are several levels and numerous rooms to explore, with the best views being from the highest terrace to the south.

Qalat Ibn Maan

Palmyra

The castle is popularly attributed to Fakhr ud-Din, a Lebanese Maanite Emir who challenged the Ottomans in the early 17th century, extending his power base east from Mount Lebanon, deep into the Syrian desert, before being captured and finally executed by the Ottomans in 1635. However, it has also been suggested that Fakhr ud-Din only in fact occupied and extended an earlier castle which stood on the site, perhaps dating from the 12th century, around the same time as the temple of Bel was fortified by the Arab general Abdul Hassan Yussuf ibn Fairouz.

■ *Open daily 0900-dusk; in practice the opening times are a little erratic. Entry S£300 (students S£15).*

The Valley of the Tombs provides a fascinating insight into the burial practices of the Palmyrenes, and the great importance they clearly attached to honouring the dead. The oddly forlorn tower tombs found here are no match for the ruins of Palmyra itself, but their setting has an eerily unreal atmosphere (all the more so at twilight, or on a moonlit night). As well as the major tombs described below, the valley is scattered with numerous others in varying states of decay, the majority of which are open to the public. The Southwest Necropolis lacks the atmosphere of the Valley of the Tombs, but the Hypogeum of the Three Brothers is well worth a visit.

Valley of the Tombs & Southwest Necropolis
See map, page 173

Getting around and entry fees To gain access to Elabel, the largest and best preserved of the tower tombs in the Valley of the Tombs, and to the impressive Hypogeum of the Three Brothers at the Southwest Necropolis, both of which are kept locked, you must buy a ticket at the Palmyra Museum (S£150, students S£10). Visits are at 0830, 1000, 1130 and 1630. On Tue there are only 2 visits, at 0900 and 1100. On Fri there is no 1130 visit, while in winter the last visit is brought forward to 1430. In addition to these tombs, there are 2 interesting underground tombs at the Southeast Necropolis which have been recently restored (see below), although at the time of writing it was not clear whether these would be included in the official tour. Unless you have a specialist interest, or feel like wandering around the other tombs, these give the best insight into the burial practices of the Palmyrenes. During the peak season it can be somewhat chaotic, with several coach loads of people crowding into the tombs. Off-season it may be necessary to coax the caretaker to go out there. In theory you must organize your own transport, although as long as the caretaker is driven out with one of the groups, you can make your own way there on foot (an easy walk providing the weather is not too hot).

A newly surfaced road branches off from the main road around 100 m before the entrance gate of the *Palmyra Cham Palace* hotel and climbs up over a low saddle between the hills of Umm el Belquis to the right and Jebel Muntar to the left. At the point where the road bends to the left, one can follow a footpath leading off to the right to a series of tower tombs clustered in a row around the ridge of Umm el Belquis. The best preserved of these is the **Tower Tomb of Iamliku** which is unfortunately kept locked, although it is not included in the standard museum tour. Dating from 83 AD, this well preserved four-storey tower tomb has an impressive carved lintel above the door, and higher up an inscription identifying the family to which it belonged. Immediately above the inscription is a window decorated with a relief of two winged figures, their heads missing. The inside of the tomb consists of tiers of burial compartments, or *loculi*, built into the walls, stacked five high and interspaced by Corinthian pilasters; four sets on the right-hand wall and three on the left-hand wall with a stairway towards the rear where the fourth would otherwise be. The ceiling is elaborately decorated with a complex pattern of diamond and triangular designs. The other tower tombs in this group are less well preserved and have not been sealed. The next largest after that of Iamliku has a tunnel leading from the rear of the building directly into the hill behind, with burial compartments dug into the rock to either side. Stairs lead up as far as the third storey, although this has no floormaking access to the roof impossible.

Continuing along the main track, you arrive eventually at a small group of tower tombs set on level ground at a point where the valley has opened out. The excellently preserved **Tower Tomb of Elabel** dominates this group. This building dates from 103 AD and is named after one of the four founders, the other three being Shaqai, Moqimo and Maani. All were sons of the Wahaballat of Maani, who was closely involved in the building of the temple of Nebo. The doorway, with its impressive lintel, is in the south face of the tomb, while above it there is an inscription in Palmyrene and Greek and above that, an arched niche. Inside, the walls are arranged in the standard fashion, with tiers of compartments interspaced by Corinthian pilasters. Above the door there is a bust of the curator, Elabel's son and, as in the tomb of Iamliku, the ceiling is decorated with geometric designs and rosettes. Stairs lead up through three storeys, before arriving at the roof, from where there are excellent, if a little precarious, views out over the valley and across to the main ruins. At the rear of the tomb (outside) there are steps leading down to an underground burial chamber which is also kept locked. Although dank, smelly and strewn with rubbish, the presence of this underground chamber is interesting in that it shows the combination of a tower tomb with a *hypogeum* (underground tomb); generally tower tombs were of earlier origin and hypogea a later development, suggesting that this building represented a kind of transition stage. Amongst the same group is the **Tomb of Atenatan**, now kept locked and its tower disintegrated to a distinctive spire, and the minimal remains of the **Hypogeum of Yarhai** which has been dismantled and reconstructed in the Damascus museum.

From the tower tomb of Elabel it is possible to return to the main road via the course of the *wadi* (seasonal stream), which runs slightly to the north of the track you arrived by, keeping the ridge of Umm el Belquis and the Iamliku cluster of tower tombs to the right. This route takes you past numerous ruined tower tombs and temple tombs scattered across the floor of the wadi. Along this route there are the remains of what is simply labelled as '**Tomb 36**'. Only the base of the tower remains, with numerous fragments laid out within the foundation walls and in the immediate vicinity. Many of the fragments are beautifully decorated, with the added bonus that they can be inspected close-up, revealing the skill and precision with which the detailed carving work was executed.

To reach the **Hypogeum of the Three Brothers** at the Southwest Necropolis follow the main road south past the entrance to the *Cham Palace* hotel for around 300 m before branching off to the right along a rough track. This remarkably well preserved underground tomb (recently restored) dates from 160-191 AD and was still in use by 259 AD. Steps lead down to the entrance doorway, where the large lintel carries an inscription in Aramaic detailing how the hypogeum was founded by the three brothers Naamai, Male and Saadai, and how at a later stage certain areas of the tomb were sold off, perhaps suggesting that the family fell on hard times. Inside, the tomb follows a standard plan consisting of an inverted T-shape, with burial compartments built into the wall of each gallery. The main gallery, straight ahead of you as you enter, consists of plastered brickwork, the ceiling decorated with painted floral and geometric designs, the patterns still remarkably well preserved. A circular panel depicts the abduction of Ganymede, son of Troy, by Zeus (appearing as an eagle) who wanted him as his cup bearer. At the far end of the chamber is a scene from *Iliad* in which Achilles, disguised in women's clothes and concealed amongst the daughters of Lycomedes, king of Skyros, is discovered by Ulysses who has come to take him from the mortal world. Thus both frescos emphasize man's mortality, while at the same time offering the promise of a role in the afterlife. Another fresco depicts the three brothers, each framed in an oval medallion and held up by winged victories. In the right-hand side gallery there are three sarcophagi, with headless figures reclining on couches. In the left-hand side gallery there is a large sarcophagus of Male decorated with a frieze depicting him in Parthian dress reclining on a couch. Again, his head is missing but the detail of the decoration is impressive.

Palmyra

Southeast Necropolis

All the tombs of the Southest Necropolis are underground, so when you arrive here, there only appears to be desert. However, the lack of anything to see above ground is more than made up for by what is concealed below.

Getting around The Southeast Necropolis can be reached by continuing south along the main road from the *Cham Palace* hotel. Just over 2 km past the entrance to the *Cham Palace*, take the left turn immediately after the petrol station. Follow this road for a little over 3 km to arrive at the necropolis, just to the left of the road (at the time of writing it was not signposted and a small, squat building, partially built of ancient stones, was the only landmark). Returning, if you continue along the road, it will bring you out (after a few twists and turns) onto the eastward continuation of JA Al Naser St; turn left to head back into Tadmor's Main Bazaar.

The underground tombs here were accidentally uncovered in the 1950s when the *Iraq Petroleum Company* was laying an oil pipeline in the area. Running across the stairs leading down to the **Arteban Tomb** is a section of this pipeline. The doors of the tomb consist of two massive stone slabs, decorated with demon-like griffins and both still swinging on their hinges. Inside, the cradle-vaulted tomb follows much the same inverted T-shaped plan as the Hypogeum of the Three Brothers, except that there are two additional side galleries half-way down the main gallery. Many of the burial *loculi* still have their original funerary busts in place. Just inside the doorway, to your right, is one glass-covered *loculi* containing a skeleton. At the far end of the main gallery, framed within an arch, is a frieze depicting Arteban attended by various figures. The tomb dates from the second half of the first century AD.

This tomb takes its name from the fact that the restoration work was carried out by Japanese archaeologists (although the completely unpronounceable names of the tomb's two patrons, 'Bwlh' and 'Bwrp' might have something to do with it!

The nearby **Japanese Tomb** was officially opened in August 2000, having been first excavated in 1994. The immaculate crispness of the restoration work is not to everybody's taste, though it certainly gives you an excellent insight (perhaps even better than the reconstruction of the Hypogeum of Yarhai in the National Museum in Damascus) into what these tombs would have looked like originally. The entrance to the tomb consists of a massive single-slab stone door with carved panels and two small griffins. The lintel of the doorway is richly decorated, while above this is a carved satyr's head and an inscription dedicating the tomb, which dates from 128 AD, to the two brothers Bwlh and Bwrp. Leading off on either side of the main gallery as you enter are two arched side-chambers (note the medusa faces carved into the keystones of the arches, designed to ward off evil spirits). In each side-chamber is a sarcophogus topped by a sculpure depicting a family banqueting scene. Both these side-chambers are comparatively simple; according to the inscription above the door they were given away in 220 and 222 AD. Running around the main gallery is a particularly ornate frieze, while carved into the walls are the burial *loculi*, sealed by funerary busts. At the far end is a large frieze illustrating another family banqueting scene, presumably that of Bwlh and Bwrp.

Afqa Spring   The Afqa Spring, by the roadside in front of the *Palmyra Cham Palace*, was originally Palmyra's life source and raison d'être, providing the sole water supply to the oasis. The discovery of numerous incense altars in the vicinity, including two dedicated by the curator Bolanos in 162 AD to "Zeus the Most High", and others to Yarhibol, as well as the references in the Palmyrene Tariff, indicate the importance of the spring to the Romans. The name itself, which is Aramaic for 'source' or 'issue', confirms its existence since earliest times. Today, the spring has unfortunately dried up, probably because of the extensive digging of tube-wells. Water from the spring was sulphurous and warm, and used to emerge at a steady 33°C. Steps lead down to a bathing area, while a locked doorway leads to an underground cavern beneath the hill of Jebel Muntar, through which the water once flowed. Channels lead from the spring to the nearby groves of date palms, olives, pomegranates, figs and apricots, although today these are irrigated from tube-wells.

Palmyra Museum   The museum, by the entrance to Tadmor town, contains an interesting selection of artefacts, dominated by numerous Palmyrene religious artefacts and funerary art objects, along with a variety of other pieces.

The presentation here is nothing to get too excited about, but there are some beautiful pieces & on balance it is well worth a visit

The entrance hall contains an unconvincing reconstruction of a Stone Age cave and various stone implements. The original cave, situated 22 km west of Palmyra, was excavated in the 1950s by an American team. At the time of writing, the first floor of the museum was closed.

Going round in an anticlockwise direction, the first room contains a number of incense altars found around the Afqa Spring, and various large tablets and plinths for statues inscribed with dedications. These are written in the Palmyrene script, a dialect of Aramaic with a strong Arabic element, reflecting the large Arab population. Aramaic, and later Greek, were the *lingua*

*franca*s of the region before the
Roman era, and the continued use of
both in Palmyra emphasized its
independence from Rome.

In the centre of the second room is
an impressive scale-model of the
Sanctuary of Bel as it would have
looked in its heyday, and beside it a
smaller scale-model of Diocletian's
Camp. Around the edges of the room
are various elaborately decorated
architectural fragments, including a
particularly striking triangular pediment framing a carved bust.

Funerary bust,
150AD

The third room contains various
honorary statues and busts and a
bas-relief of a Palmyrene standing by his ship, an indication of the importance of
maritime trade for Palmyra, which through the ancient port of Spasinu Cherax
on the Euphrates-Tigris estuary, had access to the trade routes to India.

Along the length of the rear of the museum is a gallery displaying a variety of
artefacts: statues of various gods and goddesses, mosaics, glazed pottery, jewellery, coins, delicate Palmyrene and Byzantine glassware and carved reliefs. A
particularly fine piece is the lintel taken from the Temple of Baal Shamin with a
relief depicting the god Baal Shamin (fertility) as an eagle with outspread wings
sheltering Malakbel (a sun god) and Aglibol (the moon god). Two mosaics
taken from the Patrician Houses behind the Sanctuary of Bel, one depicting
scenes from the legend of Achilles and Odysseus, and the other of Centaur the
hunting god, are displayed. The collection of coins includes some with the heads
of Zenobia and her son Wahballat which were discovered in 1991, providing the
first evidence that Zenobia went so far as to mint her own currency. At the far
end of the hall is a partially restored statue of the goddess Allat-Athena with one
arm raised, found in the Temple of Allat by a Polish team in 1975.

The last three rooms contain a selection of excellently preserved funerary
busts, many of them with strikingly expressive features, as well as a number of
sarcophagi with elaborately carved reliefs and various fragments of textiles and
papyrus with Greek and Palmyrene lettering.

■ *Open daily; 0800-1300, 1600- 1800 in summer (1/4-30/9), and
0800-1300, 1400-1600 in winter (1/10-31/3). Entry S£300 (students S£15).*

Close to the Temple of Bel in a whitewashed building with an open courtyard,
is the Ethnographic Museum (or Museum of Popular Tradition). Originally
this served as the residence of the Ottoman governor of Palmyra, before being
converted to a prison during the French Mandate period. There are displays of
traditional spinning and weaving techniques, along with the colourful carpets
and rugs of the Bedouin, a collection of the distinctive chunky silver Bedouin
jewellery, and some beautifully embroidered traditional costumes, both Bedouin and urban, some of which can still be seen in everyday use. In the 'camel
room', perched on top of a model camel, is a towering *Hodaj* decorated with
cowrie shells, used to carry the bride at weddings. There are also reconstructions of the interiors of traditional Palmyrene houses and Bedouin tents and
displays of farming implements and village handicrafts such as baskets and
sandals. Unfortunately, the mannequins used to illustrate the scenes from
daily life are as lifeless and unconvincing as ever, and overall it is perhaps not
worth the full entrance fee. Explanations are in Arabic and French only.
■ *Open 0800-1430, 7 days. Entry S£150 (students S£20).*

**Ethnographic
Museum**

Palmyra

Palmyra Desert Festival

This annual festival is a popular event drawing people from all over Syria. Although it is advertised in English by the Ministry of Tourism, it is very much aimed at Syrians. If you are hoping for a quiet, crowd-free visit to the ruins, this is probably not the best time to go. During the day, horse and camel racing competitions are *held on the racecourse below the castle, while during the evening there are various performances of folk dancing and music, with the main ones being held inside the Roman theatre. In the past, the festival appeared to be something of a moveable feast, though for the last couple of years it has been held from the 2 to the 5 May.*

Essentials

Sleeping
■ *on map*
Price codes:
see inside front cover.
Categories below
are based on high
season prices

Palmyra experiences huge fluctuations in room prices between the high season, when hotels are often at capacity, and the low season, when the majority are empty. The official definition of 'high season' varies somewhat from hotel to hotel (and depends also very much on demand), but as a rough guide it generally runs from mid-Mar to the end of May, and from mid-Sep to mid-Nov, with some hotels counting an additional high season period over Christmas and New Year. Outside of these times it is often possible to negotiate significant discounts (up to 50% in some cases), although there are a few hotels which maintain fixed prices throughout the year. During the Palmyra Desert Festival, hotels are likely to be booked up well in advance and it can be difficult to find a room. Prices, meanwhile, go sky-high across the board, with many hotels charging as much as three times their normal high season rate. Many hotels include breakfast, though you should check this when enquiring after room prices. All the hotels listed here have heating, which is essential during winter; in the cheaper places you should check that it is actually working before taking a room.

LL *Palmyra Cham Palace*, 2 km from town, T912231, F912245. Comfortable rooms with a/c, TV/dish, IDD and attached bath. Also 2 restaurants, bar, swimming pool, shops, currency exchange, conference and banqueting facilities. Has benefited greatly from recent extensive refurbishment of rooms and lobby, though it is still hugely expensive for what you get, especially when compared with the best of Palmyra's **B** category hotels.

B *Heliopolis Palmyra*, T913921, F913923. Comfortably furnished (if slightly small) rooms with a/c, TV/dish, IDD, minibar and attached bath. Some rooms with excellent views across the oasis to the ruins. Restaurant on 5th floor with the best of these views. Small bar (beside reception). Good value for level of facilities. Prices drop by 25% in low season. **B** *Middle East*, T913844, F912401. Rather pokey and dark rooms with a/c, TV/dish, phone, minibar and attached bath. Restaurant on top floor. Palmyra's newest 'luxury' hotel doesn't really manage to live up to its price tag, though in the low season prices drop by nearly half. **B** *Villa Palmyra*, T913600, F912554. Comfortably furnished rooms with a/c, TV/dish, IDD, minibar and attached bath. Some rooms with views of ruins. Top floor restaurant with panoramic views. Basement 'pub' in a 'cave'. **B** *Zenobia*, T912907, F912407. French Mandate building, within perimeter of the ruins (and built with stones from the ruins!). Large, pleasantly furnished rooms (recently fully refitted) with a/c, TV/dish, phone, fridge and attached bath. Also camping (see below). Restaurant/bar with pleasant outdoor terrace and great views of the ruins. Certainly the best hotel in Palmyra in terms of location. Well run (new management). Recommended.

C *Caracalla*, T910879. Quiet, out-of-town location, near racecourse. Not your run-of-the-mill hotel. Consisting of just 4 comfortable and spacious suites, each with a large sitting/dining area (a/c, TV/dish, phone, fridge) and equally large bedroom (a/c, en-suite bath). Restaurant upstairs (all home cooking) and roof terrace. Use of kitchen facilities. Ideal for families. Owned by Jamal Fathalla who works at the *Palmyra Cham Palace* hotel as well as being a freelance guide. Excellent value (high season prices during Apr and Oct only; US$35 per suite for rest of year). Recommended. **C** *Ishtar*, T913073, F913260. Reasonably comfortable rooms with a/c, TV, phone and attached bath. Restaurant. Basement cave-type 'pub'. Mountain bikes for hire. Friendly owner, though a little pricy for what's on offer. **C** *Orient*, T910131, F910700. Reasonably comfortable rooms with a/c, fan, TV/dish, phone, minibar and attached bath. Best rooms on top floor. Restaurant. Acceptable but nothing special.

D *Oasis*, on Jamal Abd Al Naser St, east of Al Joumouriah Sq (just off our map, c100 m beyond *Al Bitar* restaurant), T911893. Recently opened. Clean, pleasant rooms with table fan (a/c promised by the time this book is published) and attached bath. Very ready to drop prices by half during low season. **D** *Odienat*, T/F911067. Mediocre rooms with a/c, TV/dish, phone, fridge, attached bath, balcony. Rather tacky décor and overall a slightly run-down feel to the place. Prices drop by more than half in low season. Breakfast served. **D** *Palace*, T/F911707. Clean but tiny rooms with fan and attached bath. Restaurant. Way overpriced. **D** *Tower*, T910116, F910273. Clean, though rather small, rooms with a/c, TV, phone and attached bath. Restaurant. **D/E** *Al Faris* (or *Knight*), T912514. Quiet, out-of-town location, near racecourse. Simple but clean rooms with fan, attached bath and balcony. Also 6 rooms on 2nd floor with a/c. Food served. Friendly, family-run place.

E *Al Nakheel*, T/F910744. Reasonable rooms with new a/c units, fridge and attached bath. Recently redecorated throughout. Nothing special, but friendly and honest. Breakfast served. **E** *Citadel*, T910537, F912970. Simple but clean rooms with fan and attached bath. Expanding each year; planning to install a/c in rooms. Restaurant/café downstairs. Prime location adjacent to the museum, which the owners exploit to the full; despite quoting a maximum of S£800 for a double during the high season, we have had reports of them charging as much as US$30! Take care.

Tadmor town تدمر

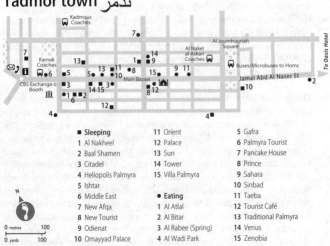

	Sleeping	11	Orient	5	Gafra
1	Al Nakheel	12	Palace	6	Palmyra Tourist
2	Baal Shamen	13	Sun	7	Pancake House
3	Citadel	14	Tower	8	Prince
4	Heliopolis Palmyra	15	Villa Palmyra	9	Sahara
5	Ishtar			10	Sinbad
6	Middle East		**Eating**	11	Taeba
7	New Afqa	1	Al Atlal	12	Tourist Café
8	New Tourist	2	Al Bitar	13	Traditional Palmyra
9	Odienat	3	Al Rabee (Spring)	14	Venus
10	Omayyad Palace	4	Al Wadi Park	15	Zenobia

F *New Afqa*, T/F910386. Clean, comfortable rooms with a/c or fan, phone and attached bath (S£500 with fan; S£700 with a/c). Plans to install a/c in all rooms, and also establish shaded roof area (sleep up here for S£100 per person including use of adjacent toilet and shower block). Restaurant. TV/dish in lobby. Friendly, helpful, family-run hotel. They have their eye fixed firmly on the backpacker market (though recent refurbishments make it look more like a mid-range place), and are consequently keen to keep their prices low. Good value. Recommended. **F/G** *Sun*, T911133. Clean rooms with fan and attached bath. Ground floor rooms rather dark; first floor rooms much better, and some with balcony.

G *Baal Shamen*, T910453. Basic but clean rooms with fan and attached bath. Doubles S£300, or a bed in a shared room for S£125, or sleep on the roof for S£75. Owned by same family as *Citadel* hotel, so prices perhaps vary with demand. **G** *New Tourist*, T910333. Dormitory rooms (3- or 4-bed) with fan and sink, share shower/toilet, S£125-150 per bed depending on the season. Doubles with attached toilet (share shower) S£325. Rather a decrepit old building, but clean bedding, friendly staff, unlimited free tea and a range of second-hand books for sale/swap, as well as the fact that it is one of the cheapest places in town, makes it ever popular with backpackers. **G** *Omayyad Palace*, T/F910755. Fairly clean rooms with table fan (some rooms with ceiling fan) and attached bath. Pleasant shaded internal courtyard. Very good value at S£300-350 for a double, or sleep on covered roof area for S£100 (including use of adjacent shower/toilet block). The owner swears blind that prices stay fixed throughout year (except during Palmyra Festival).

Camping The *Zenobia* hotel offers camping (S£200 per person, including use of toilet/shower facilities), though as this is in its gravel parking area it is really only suitable for camper-vans etc. For those who wish to pitch a tent, the *Garden* restaurant, across the road from the *Zenobia*, has a wonderful shady garden of date palms and olive trees where you can camp for S£100 per person (not including use of their small sulpherous swimming pool). The toilet/shower block is fairly basic but cleanish.

Eating

Most restaurants also offer a breakfast, usually consisting of Arabic or French bread, butter, jam or honey, cheese, olives and eggs in some form, which costs around S£50

Expensive/moderate For eating out in style, the hotel restaurants are your only option. The *Palmyra Cham Palace* is the most luxurious (although some visitors have complained of appalling service here). It has 2 restaurants, the *Zenobia* and *Al Nakhil*, though for most of the year only the former is open. When there are groups staying, they lay on a buffet dinner, which comes in at just over S£600 per head including tax, or else there is an à la carte menu (Arabic or Continental cuisine). The *Villa Palmyra* and *Heliopolis Palmyra* hotels both have restaurants on the top floor, with great views across the oasis to the ruins. Both do buffet dinners when there are groups staying (S£400 and S£250 per head respectively), or à la carte. The *Zenobia* hotel also does a buffet dinner when there are sufficient numbers staying (S£350 per head), or à la carte.

Cheap Most of the cheaper restaurants are concentrated along the Main Bazaar running east from the museum. Along the first stretch of this street are the more touristy restaurants, offering continental as well as Syrian cuisine, eg the *Gafra*, *Traditional Palmyra*, *Sinbad*, *Al Rabee* (*Spring*) and *Al Araby*. Despite the competition (someone is usually on hand to lure you into their establishment), prices are not exactly competitive and seem to fluctuate according to the season/demand; it is worth checking before you order. Further along there are some slightly less touristy places such as the *Zenobia* and *Sahara*, although what's on offer isn't desperately exciting. Continuing east there are some good cheap restaurants and falafal stalls, including the *Taeba*, a simple but clean place serving hummus and fuul only. Beyond Al Joumhouriah Sq, the *Al Bitar* is a small Lebanese-run restaurant which serves hummus, fuul and falafel only, as well as tea and cold drinks. Despite the limited menu, it is well furnished and even has a/c.

Al Wadi Park, is just to the south of the museum, at the end of the street with the *Citadel* hotel on it. Seating in a pleasant, shady garden. Standard range of Arabic food for around S£250 per head. *Garden*, on the edge of the oasis area, roughly opposite the *Zenobia* hotel, on the south side of the road, T911421. Set in a lovely shady garden of date palms and olive trees, and also boasting its own sulpherous swimming pool. Fairly standard range of Arabic fare for around S£200-250 per head. *Oasis*, T911439 and *Al Khayam*, T913056, next door to each other on the main road adjacent to the *Zenobia* hotel. Fairly standard Arabic fare for around S£250 per head. If there are groups booked in they lay on a lunch-time buffet (S£200 per head). *Palmyra Tourist*, opposite the museum. Pleasant, shaded outdoor seating. Standard range of Arabic food for around S£250 per head. Serves alcohol. *Pancake House*, 3 streets north of the Main Bazaar, T913733. Seating in pleasant central open-air courtyard shaded by a large date palm, or in surrounding rooms decorated with Bedouin rugs etc. Run by a local Palmyrene who lived in Romania for 8 years. As the name suggests, the speciality here is pancakes; whether sweet or savoury, they are thoroughly delicious and filling. A welcome change from the usual in Palmyra. Everything is freshly cooked (so be prepared for a wait, or order in advance). Also on offer is *mansaf* and various cous-cous dishes. Around S£200-250 per head. With any luck, a sufficient number of tourists will pluck up the courage to venture beyond the Main Bazaar, or this gem of a place will soon shut for lack of custom. Recommended. *Prince*, on street running parallel to the Main Bazaar on the north side, T911970. Seating in shaded outdoor terrace area, or Bedouin tent. Choice of standard Arabic fare or Continental dishes such as spaghetti. A little touristy but pleasant enough. Around S£200-250 per head. *Venus*, two streets north of the Main Bazaar, next door to *Odienat* hotel. Fairly varied menu of Arabic and Continental dishes. Around S£150-200 per head. Friendly staff and plenty of good write-ups in their visitors' book.

Cafés Adjacent to the museum, the *Citadel* hotel has a reasonable café, and next door is the pleasant *Al Atlal* café. Further east along the Main Bazaar, the *Tourist* café, next door to the mosque, is a more traditional Arabic coffee house where locals come for a *nargileh* and a game of backgammon or a chat. In a similar vein is the place a little further east again, on Al Joumhouriah Sq.

Bars There are no independent bars, though several of the hotels have bars, while one of the restaurants (*Palmyra Tourist*) also serves alcohol and will usually allow tourists to come just for a drink. The *Palmyra Cham Palace* hotel is predictably expensive, with a small bottle of imported beer (33cl) costing a whopping S£145 at their bar. The *Zenobia* hotel is certainly the most atmospheric place to come for a drink, with views out over the ruins and Corinthian capitals on the terrace acting as tables. A bottle of *Barada* beer costs a little under S£90 including tax. The *Heliopolis Palmyra* hotel has a small bar by reception, though it's not particularly atmospheric. A bottle of *Barada* costs S£115 here, while *Heineken* is S£150. The *Villa Palmyra* hotel has a basement 'pub' (*Barada* beer S£100, imported beers S£150). The *Ishtar* hotel has a slightly smaller, though otherwise identical, basement pub/cave arrangement (evidently furnished/decorated by the same company). (*Barada* beer S£75, imported beers S£100). The *Palmyra Tourist* restaurant is a nice place to sit around and drink. A bottle of Barada beer costs S£75 here.

Shopping Numerous antiques and handicrafts shops have sprung up along Tadmor's main bazaar, selling a wide range of Bedouin carpets, traditional costumes, jewellery, silverware etc. There are some beautiful items, particularly the carpets and rugs, although prices are often excessively high; don't be afraid to bargain hard. There is a good selection of books on Palmyra as well as postcards etc in the entry kiosk to the Temple of Bel, and also in the *Palmyra Cham Palace* hotel. Both colour slide and negative film

Palmyra

can be bought in the Main Bazaar; the *Al Zohbi Photoshop* generally has fresh stock, or try at the *Palmyra Cham Palace* hotel.

Sports **Swimming** The *Garden* restaurant has its own small swimming pool, filled from Palmyra's sulpherous spring water, and set in a lovely shady garden of date palms and olive trees. Use of the pool costs S£100 per person. Non-guests are allowed to use the more conventional pool at the *Cham Palace* hotel for S£300 per person.

Transport **Local** **Taxis** and **microbuses** can be hired readily, both for local sightseeing around Palmyra (around S£200-350 for the tombs and castle), and for longer trips such as to Qasr al-Heir al-Sharki (around S£1500-2000). Ask at your hotel, or outside the museum. There are no self-drive **car hire** companies in Palmyra. The *Ishtar* hotel has **mountain bikes** for hire (S£50 per hr or S£250 per day), which is a great idea providing it's not too hot. It's also a useful way of getting around the various tombs (provided of course that there are other groups or individuals also doing the tombs tour who will give the caretaker a ride out to the different sites). The ride up to the Arab castle is, however, extremely steep and only for the really fit (or dedicated).

Long distance **Bus**: There is no central bus station. Some of the private companies operate a mixture of luxury coaches, minibuses and microbuses. You are advised to check schedules for yourself as they are subject to frequent changes, particularly in the case of *Karnak*.

The state-owned *Karnak* coach company, T910288, has its ticket office and bus stop conveniently located opposite the museum. **Damascus**, 1015, 1230, 1345, S£100, 3 hrs. **Deir ez-Zor**, 1130, 1330, 1515, 1730, 2115, 2230, S£75, 2 hrs. The 1330 to Deir ez-Zor continues on to **Hassakeh** (S£135, 4½ hrs) and **Qamishle** (S£150, 5½ hrs). **Homs**, 1500, S£65, 2 hrs. With the exception of the Homs coach, all these services originate in Damascus or Deir ez-Zor. The staff in Palmyra phone their counterparts in these cities to check whether their are any seats available, with the result that tickets can only be bought a maximum of 1 hr before departure.

The private *Kadmous* coach company, T913077, has 1 ticket office/bus stop a little to the north of the museum (see Tadmor Town map), while its main ticket office/bus stop is way out on the edge of town in the *Sahara* restaurant, some 2 km to the north-east of the centre. You can catch services heading to Damascus, Homs, Tartus and Lattakia from the ticket office just to the north of the museum, but for services to Deir ez-Zor and other destinations to the northeast of Palmyra you must go to their ticket office/bus stop at the *Sahara* restaurant. **Damascus**, 0930, 1130, 1230, 1330, 1430, 1630, 1730, 1830, 1930, S£110, 3 hrs. **Deir ez-Zor**, hourly services (on the hour) between 1000-2200, S£85, 2 hrs. The 1200, 1500 and 1700 services to Deir ez-Zor continue on to **Hassakeh** (S£165), while the 1200, 1300, 1400, 1600, 1800 and 2300 services continue on to **Qamishle** (S£200). **Homs**, **Tartus** and **Lattakia**, 1630, 0230, S£65, S£105 and S£145 respectively. With the exception of the Homs/Tartus/Lattakia coaches, all these services originate in Damascus or Deir ez-Zor. In theory you should be able to get *Kadmous* to phone through to the departure office to check whether there is space on the coach, although in practice they often seem reluctant to do this; it may be worth asking your hotel manager to help you.

Two other private coach companies, *Al Wardeh* and *Damas Tour* operate limited services to **Damascus** and **Deir ez-Zor**; their offices are way to the northeast of the centre, near the *Kadmous* office. The *Al Nakel al-Askari* coach company, in a side street to the west of Al Joumhouriah Sq, has 1 bus daily (except Fri) to **Damascus**, 0600, S£75. As this bus starts from Palmyra, it is possible to book tickets the day before.

The most convenient place to catch buses and microbuses to **Homs** is from Al Joumhouriah Sq, towards the eastern end of the Main Bazaar. There are regular services throughout the day, departing when full (usually every 30 mins to 1 hr) and taking 2 hrs. The microbus fare is S£60 and the bus fare S£40, although foreign tourists tend to be charged an extra S£10-15 for luggage (officially there should be no extra charge, but this being Palmyra...).

Banks There is a *CBS* exchange booth right by the museum which changes cash and TCs. Open 0800-1300, 1800-2030, 7 days. The *Palmyra Cham Palace* hotel can change cash and TCs at any time of the day or night (at the official bank rate). **Communications** Post: the post office is by the roundabout at the western end of Tadmor, near the museum. Open 0800-1400, closed Fri. **Telephone** There are 2 cardphones for national and international calls just outside the post office (accessible 24 hrs), and another cardphone just inside the compound of the Sanctuary of Bel. You can buy phonecards inside the PO during opening hrs, but check first that one of the cardphones is actually working, as all 3 are sometimes out of order. **Useful addresses** If you run into any problems in Palmyra, ask your hotel manager for help, or go to the Tourist Information office. **NB** It is not possible to extend visas in Palmyra.

Directory

Around Palmyra

Qasr al-Heir al-Sharki قصر الحير الشرقي

Palmyra

Improbably set in the midst of the desert, without even an oasis in the immediate vicinity to justify its existence, is the desert palace known as Qasr al-Heir al-Sharki (literally 'eastern walled-palace'). Although it in no way matches the grandeur of Rasafeh to the north, it still makes an interesting day-trip from Palmyra, perhaps as much for the drive through the desert to get there and the opportunity to visit one of the many Bedouin camps in the vicinity, as for the site itself.

Colour map 1, grid B5

Qasr al-Heir al-Sharki is 110 km northeast of Palmyra on the road to Deir ez-Zor and then around 30 km north of the main road. The easiest way to get there is to hire a vehicle and driver in Palmyra which will cost around S£1500-2000 (good value if you get a microbus and go as a group). Make sure that your driver is familiar with the route and bear in mind that after rains a 4WD is essential. Visiting the site is perfectly possible with your own transport, providing the conditions are suitable, although the main difficulty is in finding it. The tracks left by Bedouin pick-ups are numerous and confusing. One option is to drive out to the 110 km point and then head roughly due north till you reach the site, but without knowing exactly where to turn off, the chances of getting lost are quite high. The easier route is to take the signposted turning left after around 70 km towards the village of Sukhneh. From Sukhneh there are reasonably obvious tracks leading towards the village of Taibeh 32 km away. This route leads you past a line of impressive fluted cliffs off to the left which fall away gradually before you reach Taibeh, a sizeable village complete with its own petrol pumps, although these look completely derelict and abandoned. From here you must bear off to the east (right), past a small oasis on the edge of the village to arrive at the ruins some 15 km away. This last stretch is the least obvious, with numerous tracks branching out into the desert, so it might be advisable to try to find a local to show you the way. From a distance, the ruins have an odd appearance, with the sections of newly cut limestone used in the restoration standing out sharply against the older, weathered stonework.

Ins & outs

While the Bedouins sometimes camped near the site are extremely friendly & hospitable, their dogs certainly are not; their impersonat- ions of rabid, demented, flesh-starved creatures intent on tearing you limb for limb are extremely convincing ... Beware

Very little is known about this site, both in terms of its inception and purpose. One theory, given some of its architectural features, is that it dates originally from the Byzantine period, while others argue that it was entirely an Arab project that borrowed materials from Roman and Byzantine sites around Palmyra. As to its purpose, theories range from it being an extravagant hunting lodge and pleasure gardens to an intensive market-garden/agricultural

History

community. The most generally accepted explanation is that the main complex was built by the Umayyad Caliph Hisham Ibn Abd al-Malik during 728-9 AD (he was also responsible for the Qasr al-Heir al-Gharbi to the west), perhaps on the site of an existing agricultural settlement and that it acted primarily as a khan, or caravanserai, on the route between Damascus and Mesopotamia, while also serving as a means of subduing the surrounding nomadic tribes.

Sights The site consists of two walled compounds adjacent to each other, a larger one to the west and a smaller one to the east. The larger compound to the west has an entrance gate in each of the four walls, which have been extensively restored with newly cut limestone to give such an odd appearance from a distance (and close up for that matter). Semi-circular towers are placed along the walls at regular intervals. Inside, there existed in effect a completely self-sufficient community. Although excavations carried out in the 1960s and early 1970s established the basic plan, today little can be distinguished with any certainty. The large brick-lined cistern, surrounded by a courtyard in the centre of the compound is still discernible, along with various fragments of the buildings which were ranged around the sides. In the southeast corner are the remains of what were a mosque, royal palace and olive press.

The second, smaller compound is kept locked (the key can be obtained from the nearby village of Karia). The main gateway in the west wall is well preserved, with the semi-circular towers either side of the gate decorated with distinctive bands of brickwork in a characteristically Mesopotamian style. Inside, it follows the same basic plan as the larger compound, with a cistern surrounded by a courtyard in the centre. Around this was a colonnaded porch (a few of the columns are still standing) with rooms ranged around the walls. This compound probably acted as a khan for passing caravans, and perhaps also as barracks for the army.

Between the two compounds is a small square minaret with steps climbing part of the way up inside. Surrounding the two compounds was a wall, traces of which are still visible. The whole complex was watered by means of an aqueduct that led from a dam by the village of Kom (or Qawm), 30 km to the north. To the east of the two compounds was a walled garden measuring 3 km by 6 km, and surrounding the whole settlement was a further mud-brick wall, over 22 km in circumference, sections of it still traceable as you approach from the south, some 5 km before reaching the main complex.

Palmyra to Deir ez-Zor

The route from Palmyra to Deir ez-Zor, 210 km away, is on a good road heading northeast across the desert. Four kilometres out of town there is a petrol station on the main road, which is the last one for just over 175 km, until 30 km short of Deir ez-Zor. This road takes you through a barren, inhospitable landscape of open desert and low steppes stretching into the distance in all directions. During spring there is a thin covering of grass and numerous Bedouin camps spring up, grazing their sheep and cattle on the short-lived pasture.

Orontes Valley

6

Orontes Valley

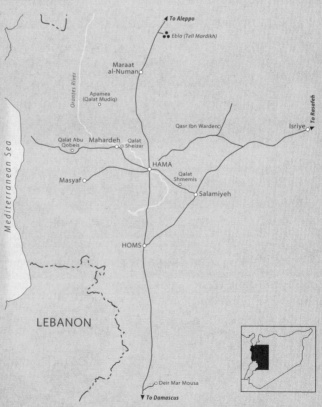

Together, the Orontes Valley and Central Plains form a long, narrow strip of land sandwiched between the coastal mountains to the west and the desert to the east. Isolated by mountains on one side and desert on the other, it was here that a string of powerful city-states – Homs, Hama, Damascus and Aleppo – grew up, and continue to flourish to this day. Others such as Kadesh (Tell Nebi Mend), Apamea and Ebla (Tell Mardikh) rose and fell with the fortunes of the civilizations which occupied them and now provide plenty of inspiration for archaeologists.

Today, a motorway runs between Damascus and Aleppo, forming the backbone of Syria's major north-south axis of communications. Heading north from Damascus, you first cross a rather barren and inhospitable plateau, skirting the northernmost reaches of the Anti-Lebanon mountain range. This drops down to an area of open plain known as the Homs Gap – historically a strategically crucial point of access to the coast. Between Homs and Hama you follow the course of the Orontes River, cutting a deep and dramatic gorge through the coutryside before continuing north across the fertile Central Plains to Aleppo. Here there is even enough rain to grow wheat, cotton and sugar beet without resorting to irrigation.

☞ *A foot in the door*

★ *The route from Damascus to Aleppo takes you right through the heart of Syria's most densely populated areas, and past a wealth of sites. Northeast of the small town of Nabk, the unique monastery of* **Deir Mar Musa** *has stunning views out over the desert and is possibly one of the most atmospheric places in the country.*

★ **Hama** *is a firm favourite amongst travellers, offering perhaps the best quality budget accommodation in Syria. As well as its famous waterwheels, or norias, there is now an excellent new archaeological museum.*

★ *Hama's other great attraction is as a base for visiting sites in the surrounding countryside. The most important of these is* **Apamea**, *with its impressive Roman colonnaded street, longer even than Palmyra's.*

★ *Also within easy reach of Hama is the imposing Ismaili castle at* **Masyaf**, *set against the backdrop of the Jebel Ansariye mountains. Being a former stronghold of the Assassins, the history of this castle is even more fascinating than that of the improbably well-preserved and much more famous Crusader castle of* **Krak des Chevaliers**, *which can also be reached from Hama (see page 258).*

★ *Some 60 km to the northeast of Hama, on the edges of the desert, the delicate ruins of the Byzantine complex of* **Qasr Ibn Warden** *are well worth the effort involved in getting there.*

★ *The town of* **Maarat al-Numan**, *en route between Hama and Aleppo, is worth visiting for its beautiful mosaics museum, housed within a huge 16th century khan.*

Orontes Valley

Damascus to Homs and Hama

The most direct route north from Damascus to Homs is on the Damascus-Aleppo highway, a fast though not altogether inspiring motorway. If you have your own transport, there is an interesting and scenic diversion for part of this journey, through the towns of Saidnaya, Maaloula & Yabroud. You rejoin the motorway close to Nabk. For details, see page 136.

Deir Mar Musa ديـر مـر مـوسـى

Colour map 1, grid C2　Perched in a ravine in the hills 14 km to the northeast of Nabk is the tiny monastery of Deir Mar Mousa. With stunning views out over the Syrian desert to the east, as well as some remarkable frescos in its church, it is a unique, almost magical place and well worth the effort involved in reaching it. The monastery can feasibly be visited as a day-trip from Damascus or as a detour en route to Homs, but staying overnight gives you the opportunity to really appreciate the sense of space, the tranquillity and the overwhelming beauty of sunset and sunrise.

Ins & outs　From the roundabout and large mosque at the centre of Nabk ask directions to pick up the rough track leading up to the monastery. The track winds its way up into the hills, terminating abruptly at the entrance to a ravine. Nearby, attempts are being made (as yet unsuccessfully) to drill a well to enable the monastery to irrigate some of the surrounding land. From here a footpath descends, gently at first but then more steeply with some scrambling involved, to reach the monastery (around 15-20 mins' walk).

History　An Ethiopian monk, Mar Mousa (St Moses), is believed to have retreated here some time in the sixth century, having founded several monasteries in the area. Already there was a Roman watchtower on the site, guarding the caravan route to Palmyra; the arched doorway to the kitchen of the present monastery is thought to represent part of the original tower. A parchment document now held in the British Museum confirms that a small community existed here by the end of the sixth century, though nothing else is known about this early phase of settlement. By the 11th century, the church had been built and for the next four centuries the monastery flourished, before falling into decline after the 15th century and eventually being abandoned in 1831. Then in 1984 restoration work began, initiated by an Italian former Jesuit, Paulo Dell' Oglio, with help from the Syrian Catholic community and donations from Italy. In 1991 the monastery and its community, an eclectic group of monks and nuns from Europe and the Middle East, was officially refounded under the aegis of the Syrian Catholic Church.

Aside from the stunning views out over the desert from the terrace of the monastery, the highlight is the **church** itself, in which a series of remarkable **frescos** have been preserved, some dating as far back as the 11th century, when the church was first built. Those on the rear wall have been cleaned and are particularly impressive. The overall effect inside the church, with the frescos gradually emerging as your eyes become accustomed to the gloom, is one of ancient, solemn religiosity, particularly if you stay for the evening service with its chanting and music. There is also a small museum housing a collection of pottery, coins and other archaeological finds from the area. Around the monastery there are numerous caves, some of which are used as sleeping quarters by the monks.

Sights

The monastery attracts plenty of pilgrims, as well as casual visitors, and all are welcome to stay overnight (or longer). There is accommodation for up to around 50 people. Meals are held communally. There are no fixed charges as such, although guests are expected to take part in the day to day life of the monastery, and perhaps make a donation towards its upkeep. Larger groups should make arrangements in advance (Deir Mar Mousa, PO Box 178, Nabk, Syria). Without your own transport, you will have to negotiate a ride from Nabk; be sure to make arrangements for the return trip in advance if you want to avoid a long, hot walk down. Around S£300 for a wait and return would be reasonable, or around S£200-250 one-way, although you may find you have to bargain hard.

Sleeping, eating & transport

Orontes Valley

North to Homs

Returning to the motorway and continuing north, the road begins to descend from the area of plateau around Nabk. Further north from here, the mountains of the Anti-Lebanon range to the west, which have until now run parallel to the motorway, begin to trail away, giving way to a corridor of flat plain which stretches to the sea, bounded by the Anti-Lebanon to the south and the Jebel Ansariye to the north. This corridor is known as the **Homs Gap**. Approaching Homs along the motorway, you can tell when you are parallel with the Homs Gap: the trees which line the road all lean precariously in the same direction, forced into this position by the winds which are funnelled through here between the mountains.

Immediately before a railway bridge crosses the road, 148 km from Damascus, there is a left turn signposted for Qusayr, amongst other places, 20 km to the southwest. Just under 3 km to the north of the village of Qusayr on the opposite bank of the Orontes River (here just a stream) is **Tell Nebi Mend**, site of the Bronze Age fortress-city of Kadesh, currently being excavated by a team of British archaeologists. This was also the scene of a great battle between the Egyptian king Ramses II and the Hittite king Muwatallis in the 13th century BC. However, despite the historical and archaeological importance of the site, there is little for the casual visitor to see.

The 'Homs Gap' represents the only unobstructed route from the sea inland into the heart of Syria, & as such has been a route of major strategic importance throughout history

Homs حمص

The city of Homs is at an important crossroads; here the Damascus-Aleppo high-way is intersected by the road east to Palmyra and west through the Homs Gap to the coast. Consistently maligned in guidebooks as a dull, industrial city with nothing of interest, Homs is certainly not one of the highlights of Syria, but on closer inspection its negative image is somewhat unjustified. As well as offering interesting contrasts between its Muslim and Christian areas, it also has a veritable maze of colourful, lively and seldom explored souks. Both the souks and the Christian quarter are dotted with numerous ancient buildings, many of them dilapidated but nevertheless providing intriguing glimpses of Mameluke architecture.

Ins and outs

Getting there
See also 'Transport',
page 211

Homs is a major road transport hub and has good luxury coach connections with the rest of the country, as well as numerous buses and microbuses serving surrounding areas. It is also on the railway line running between Damascus and Aleppo, though the station is a long way from the centre, and train times inconvenient. Homs is the most obvious (or at least closest) place from which to visit the Crusader castle of Krak des Chevaliers, and there are direct microbuses from here. However, given the better accommodation to be found in Hama, many people elect to stay there instead. For details of Krak des Chevaliers and the various routes by which it can be reached, see page 258.

Getting around

You really need a taxi (or a local microbus) to get to and from the main luxury coach station, the railway station and the Karnak/bus/minibus station (the latter is walkable if it is not too hot), but once you are in the centre, the city is best explored on foot. The **tourist information** office is in a small building in the centre of the strip of gardens on the south side of Shoukri al-Kouwatli St. Open 0830-1400, 1600-2100 (though the afternoon shift sees just a token presence here), closed Fri. The staff can supply you with the Ministry of Tourism pamphlet/map of Homs (in the morning at least).

History

Although there is evidence of settlement as early as the first millennium BC, Homs only rose to prominence during the Roman period under the Latin name *Emesa*, when it emerged as an important regional centre. It owed much of its wealth to its close trading ties with Palmyra to the east, a fact attested to by the numerous references to Emesa in Palmyrene documents.

More importantly, it also found itself close to the centre of Roman political life following the marriage of the future Emperor of Rome, Septimius Severus, to Julia Domna, a daughter of the High Priest of Emesa in 187 AD. In terms reminiscent of his musings on Queen Zenobia, Gibbon described her as possessing "the attractions of beauty ... united to a lively imagination, a firmness of mind and a strength of judgement seldom bestowed on her sex". Certainly, she played a central role during the reign of her husband (193-211) and following his death she managed to ensure that her sons, Caracalla and Geta, jointly inherited the position of Emperor. Continuing Syrian ascendency in Rome was ensured, but this period was marked also by a rapid decline into degeneracy. In 212 Caracalla murdered his brother Geta and took the title of Emperor for himself, embarking on a reign of terror which saw tens of thousands murdered. Following Geta's own murder in 217, Elagabalus, the grandson of Julia Domna's sister, Julia Maesa, rose to power. Although still only a boy of 14, Elagabalus was also the

High Priest of Emesa. He brought with him to Rome the sun god Baal, represented in Homs by a black stone, and raised the worship of the god to the status of an official religion. His reign was an orgy of debauchery bordering on madness and after four years he was murdered by members of the Praetorian Guard. The black stone was sent back to Homs, where it continued to be venerated locally. Fifty years later it once again rose to prominence throughout the empire when the Emperor Aurelian came to Homs to make offerings to Baal prior to his defeat of Queen Zenobia. Aurelian attributed his success to the sun god's intervention and went on to build a temple to *Sol Invictus* (the 'Invincible Sun') in Rome, raising Baal once again to the status of official religion. In the meantime, Elagabalus was succeeded by his cousin Alexander Severus who, although also only a young boy of 13, proved himself more worthy of the title of Emperor, bringing about a number of important reforms and checking the worst excesses of the imperial court. He was murdered in 235 following a revolt within the army, bringing to an end this unique Syrian Dynasty in Rome.

During the Byzantine period, Homs became an important centre of Christianity, and remains so today. There is a significant Christian population and various churches in the eastern part of the city. In 540 it suffered serious damage at the hands of the Persians, before falling in 635 to the Muslim invaders, led by the Arab general Khalid Ibn al-Walid, whose tomb is in the city's main mosque. The Islamic period saw it develop as a centre for the more puritanical elements of the Muslim faith, who opposed the relative liberalism of the Umayyad court in Damascus. Despite its proximity to the Crusader stronghold of Krak des Chevaliers, it resisted coming under their control, falling instead under the orbit of the new Zengid rulers of Aleppo in 1130. From this time onwards, although it continued to be an important commercial centre, in political terms it fell into relative obscurity, eclipsed by the larger and more influential city-states of Damascus and Aleppo. It was only during the 20th century that it developed as an important industrial centre, with oil and sugar refineries as well as phosphate treatment centres complementing and largely overshadowing the traditional spinning and weaving industries.

Orontes Valley

Sights

Although of recent construction (early 1900s), the Khalid Ibn al-Walid Mosque is an impressive example of Turkish architecture, with its large courtyard and walls strikingly decorated in alternating bands of black and white stone. Inside the large prayer hall, four massive columns support a central dome, while in one corner is a large, ornate domed mausoleum containing the tomb of the Arab General Khalid Ibn al-Walid. Walid is celebrated in Islamic history for leading the Muslim conquest of Syria, decisively beating the Byzantine army of Heraclius at the Battle of Yarmouk before taking Damascus. In addition to his military acumen, he showed great foresight in guaranteeing the security of the people, thus ensuring that the new invaders came to be accepted by the local population. However, once the Muslims had established themselves in Syria, the need for military expertise was replaced by a need for administrators, and Walid found himself excluded from the court of the Caliph Umar, living out the remainder of his life in obscurity in Homs. That this city was where he died is well documented, although whether the present mausoleum actually contains his remains is open to question.

Khalid Ibn al-Walid Mosque

The Great Mosque of Al Nuri is believed to stand on the site of a pagan sun temple (perhaps the temple of Baal), and was later the site of a Christian church dedicated to St John. As the name suggests, the mosque is attributed to

Great Mosque of Al Nuri

the 12th century Zengid ruler Nur ud-Din, although it has undergone extensive modifications over the centuries. The main arched entrance, with its black and white stone decoration and carved Arabic inscriptions on either side, is impressive. Inside, the large rectangular courtyard is unusual in that it includes a raised terrace area along one wall, perhaps representing a part of the podium on which the *cella* of the pagan temple would have stood. Note the ornate Corinthian capital decorating one side of the raised terrace area, opposite the main entrance (this terrace is used as an additional prayer area, so don't walk on it with your shoes). There are a couple of other architectural fragments dotted around the courtyard, including a rectangular basalt basin, perhaps a sarcophogus, with heavily worn decorations on it. The *mihrab* of the prayer hall has remnants of mosaics inside its arch, although this is spoilt somewhat by the amplifier bolted into it. A couple of the columns used in the mosque's construction are clearly of Roman origin.

Homs

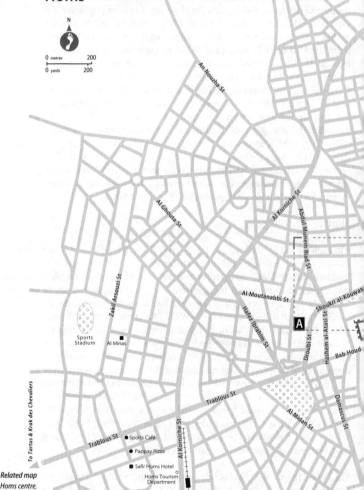

0 metres 200
0 yards 200

An Nouzha St

Al Ghouta St

Al Korniche St

Abdul Munem Riad St

Al Moutanabbi St

Shoukri al-Kouwat

Zakil Arsouzi St

Hafez Ibrahim St

Droubi St

Hashem al-Atasi St

Bab Houd

Sports
Stadium

Al Minas

Trablous St

Al Midan St

Damascus St

To Tartus & Krak des Chevaliers

Trablous St

Al Korniche St

Sports Café

Pappay Pizza

Safir Homs Hotel

Homs Tourism
Department

A

Related map
A Homs centre,
page 208

To Homs Grand Hotel (500m) & Damascus

A complex maze of narrow streets and covered souks extend south and east **The Souks**
from the Great Mosque of Al Nuri towards the ancient citadel. They are every
bit as lively and colourful as those of Aleppo or Damascus, and perhaps more
authentic, at least for the absence of antique/handicraft shops geared exclusively towards tourists. Mondays, when the fruit and vegetable markets are
freshly stocked, are particularly busy, and you can watch a huge variety of town
and country folk going about their business. There are also a number of good
clothes shops where you can pick up a lurid silk shirt (or perhaps even something a little more staid) for next to nothing. In any case, you can wander
around at will and absorb something of the atmosphere, safe in the knowledge
that you won't be dragged into someone's shop 'just for looking' ...

To the east of the main town centre is the Christian quarter, one of the few **The Christian**
remaining areas of the town alongside the souks which still retains many of its **Quarter**

old buildings and gives some idea of what the city must have been like before its recent industrial expansion. In contrast to the essentially very conservative Muslim areas of the town, the Christian quarter provides a strikingly different atmosphere, particularly early in the evening when groups of women stroll around sporting the latest fashions and hair-dos.

Al Zunnar Church In its present form, the Al Zunnar Church (Church of the Virgin's Girdle), dates from 1852, with further renovations carried out in 1966. However, it stands on the site of a much earlier church, probably dating back as far as the fourth century, and perhaps as early as 59 AD. In 1953 an old manuscript belonging to the church was found, detailing the existence of a sacred relic, the girdle of the Virgin Mary, which had been concealed in the altar of the church during its reconstruction a century earlier. The altar was subsequently dismantled and the relic duly revealed. Today the girdle, which consists of a small and not exactly awe-inspiring piece of decaying fabric, is rolled up inside a reliquary and displayed in a small shrine along with the original casket in which it was found. Beside the shrine is the hollowed-out stone block and cover from the altar in which it was hidden.

If the main gate of the church is locked, ring the bell of the small gate to the left and the caretaker will take you inside to view the relic.

Mar Elian Church This church looks every bit as unassuming from the outside as the Al Zunnar church. However, inside it contains **frescos** dating back at least to the 12th century. The church takes its name from St Elian, who according to legend was the son of an important Roman official from Homs. He refused to renounce his Christian beliefs and was put to death as a result towards the end of the third century. A church was built in his memory in the fourth century and his remains interred in the crypt. It was only in 1969 when renovations were being carried out on the church that the plaster which covered the walls was removed, revealing some beautiful frescos in the crypt area. Today these are complemented by bright new frescos painted in the main nave and side-aisles of the church by two Romanian iconographers, depicting various scenes from the life of St Elian. As well as being striking pieces of art in their own right, they provide an interesting reminder of how the older frescos would have appeared when first painted. The small chapel to the right of the main

Orontes Valley

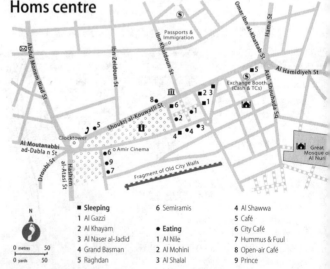

Homs centre

■ Sleeping	6 Semiramis	4 Al Shawwa
1 Al Gazzi		5 Café
2 Al Khayam	**● Eating**	6 City Café
3 Al Naser al-Jadid	1 Al Nile	7 Hummus & Fuul
4 Grand Basman	2 Al Mohini	8 Open-air Café
5 Raghdan	3 Al Shalal	9 Prince

crypt contains the tomb of St Elian, along with the oldest of the frescos, believed by some to date back as far as the sixth century. The beautiful wooden *iconostasis* which separates the crypt from the rest of the church has some interesting old icons in its upper register. The feast of St Elian is celebrated each year on 6 February, attracting large numbers of pilgrims. St Elian was a physician by trade and various miracles of healing are attributed to him.

Azze Hrawe This recently restored Mameluke residence was built by one Ali Ibn Abi al-Fadl al-Azzhari during the period of Baibars' rule (1260-77). There are plans to establish a National Folklore Museum here, but the building is already open to the public and well worth a look in its own right. Inside is a courtyard with a fountain in the centre. A large terraced *iwan* occupies one side of the courtyard, with an impressive conch shell semi-dome. In the wall opposite, note the two carved lions, popular symbols from the Mameluke era. You can explore the various rooms around the courtyard on the ground and first floors, and also get up onto the roof. ■ *Open 0800-1400, closed Fri. Once the museum is up and running there will be an entrance fee; in the meantime, the caretakers are happy to let you look around for free.*

Museum This small museum on Shoukri al-Kouwatli Street contains a selection of artefacts found in the region of Homs and covers the pre-historic through to the Islamic periods. There are some interesting pieces, but nothing is labelled in English. Upstairs there is a collection of paintings by the local artist J Traboulsi. At the time of writing the museum was undergoing extensive renovations, and with any luck this will culminate in an expanded and better presented collection; in the meantime the museum is only worth a look if you are paying the student price. ■ *Open 0800-1500/1600 in winter/summer, closed Fri. Entry S£300 (students S£15, though you may have to insist on your discount).*

Old City Walls To the south of Shoukri al-Kouwatli Street there is a short section of the Old City walls still standing (just). Most of what you can see here dates from the Ottoman period, though the tumbled remains of a much more ancient wall, built of huge stone blocks, is visible in places. At the western end of the wall there is a circular corner tower which has been converted into the minaret of a mosque, its lower courses built of large stone blocks and a couple of horizontally laid column drums. The remains are today somewhat dwarfed by a rather striking and impressive large new complex of government offices which is nearing completion. More fragments of the Old City walls can also be seen at the eastern edges of the Christian quarter, running south from Bab Tadmor. For the most part these walls have been lost to recent buildings, but in places you can still see traces of large, ancient stone blocks forming the foundations of contemporary buildings, or else later Mameluke/Ottoman stonework incorporated into walls, and at one point a semi-circular bastion tower.

Bust of Coré, Earth Goddess, daughter of Demeter, 1st century AD

Orontes Valley

Citadel The citadel, or at least the mound on which it stood, is at the southern edges of the Old City. Heading south along Damascus Street towards the *Homs Grand* hotel and Damascus, it can be seen to the left of the road. Traces of the original glacis along with fragments of the citadel walls still survive, although it is now topped by a communications tower and occupied by the Syrian army, making it off-limits to tourists.

Essentials

Sleeping
■ *on map*
Price codes:
see inside front cover

AL *Safir Homs*, Ragheb al-Jamali St (to the southwest of the town centre), PO Box 1746, T412400, F433420, safir@net.sy Suitably luxurious rooms with a/c, TV/dish, IDD, 'soft' minibar and attached bath. Choice of restaurants (see under 'Eating'), coffee shop, bar, nightclub, conference/banquet facilities, swimming pool, tennis courts, games room, shops. An excellently run hotel, far and away the best on offer in Homs. **A** *Homs Grand* (*Homs al-Kabir*), Damascus Rd (south of the town centre), PO Box 743, T412600, F423021. Comfortable, spacious rooms with a/c, TV/dish, IDD, minibar and attached bath. Restaurant, coffee shop, bar, conference/banquet facilities.

C *Al Minas*, off Corniche St (west of the town centre, near the sports stadium), PO Box 703, T/F220224, mh@mail.sy Simple but clean rooms with a/c, TV, phone, fridge and attached bath. Restaurant. Friendly, well run hotel in a quiet residential location, good value. **D** *Karnak*, located in the Karnak bus terminal (to the north of the town centre), T233099, F479572. OK rooms with a/c, TV, phone and attached bath. Overall a little shabby, though good value for having a/c, and surprisingly quiet given the location. Convenient if you only want to break your journey overnight, but otherwise a little far from the centre.

E The hotels in this category, although centrally located, are pretty abysmal for the price; if you are after some comfort, the next category up is much better value for money. **E** *Grand Basman*, Abu Alaa St, T225009. Fan, phone, attached bath, some rooms with balcony, reasonably clean but no a/c. **E** *Raghdan*, Kouwatli St, T225211. Some rooms a/c (others without even fan), attached bath, shabby and run-down. **E** *Semiramis*, Kouwatli St, T221837. No a/c or fan, phone, attached bath. Rather dingy and run-down.

G The 3 hotels given below in this category are all close to each other, along or just off Kouwatli St. The last is marginally the better of the 3. **G** *Al Gazzi*, T222160. Double room S£300, some rooms with fan, share shower (hot S£35) and toilet. Interesting building, and with a bit of work potentially a nice hotel. **G** *Al Khayam*, T223959. Double room S£275, some rooms with fan and sink, share shower (hot S£35) and toilet. Also dorm beds for S£125, making this the cheapest deal for solo travellers. Pretty basic. **G** *Al Naser al-Jadid*, T227423. Double room S£300, all rooms with fan and sink, share shower (hot S£50) and toilet. Reasonably clean all round, friendly management.

Eating **Expensive** *Mamma Mia*, *Safir Homs* hotel. Open 1800-late, daily. Good quality Italian cuisine for around S£500 per head upwards. During the summer the restaurant moves outdoors and there is usually a salad bar/set menu arrangement. *Mersia*, *Safir Homs* hotel. Open 24 hrs, daily. Arabic and Continental cuisine. Open buffet lunch and dinner (S£550 per head) every Fri and Sun, or à la carte.

Cheap *City Café*, off Shoukri al-Kouwatli St, near the clocktower. Open 24 hrs, daily. Modern, trendy and very popular café/diner-style restaurant, complete with shiny new décor, satellite TV and waitresses in berets. Mixture of Arabic and international cuisine, plus a huge range of fruit cocktails and milkshakes. Around S£250-300 per head for a full meal, or around S£100-150 for snacks. *Prince*, next door to *City Café*. Open 0900-0100, daily. Brand new, very shiny and modern, more of a take-away, but has some seating. Good shawarmas outside (small/large S£25/35), or there is a menu of pizzas, burgers, sandwiches, fresh fruit juices, fruit cocktails, ice creams etc. Around S£200-250 per head for a full meal, or less for snacks. *Sports Café*, near to the *Safir Homs* hotel. Open 1200-2400, daily. Trendy new place, very much in the same mould as the *City Café*, and equally popular amongst the young and monied Homsi set. Menu of pizzas, burgers, chicken dishes, steaks, salads etc. S£200-250 per head for a full meal, or less for snacks.

Seriously cheap *Al Mohini* (sign in Arabic only), off Shoukri al-Kouwatli St, facing the gardens. Simple place, often busy, which does a great fatteh for just S£20 (a really good filler), as well as falafel sandwiches, roast chicken, hummus etc. *Al Nile*, situated in the centre of the small pedestrian area just to the south of Shoukri al-Kouwatli St. Simple but clean and pleasant restaurant, decorated along an Egyptian theme, serving fuul, hummus and falafels only. Between the *Al Mohini* and *Al Nile* are a couple more simple restaurants serving mostly grilled meat, kebabs etc. *Al Shalal* and *Al Shawwa*, a few doors down from each other on Abu Alaa St, just to the east of the *Grand Basman* hotel. Both specialize in fresh fruit juices and shawarmas, as well serving burgers, shish tawouk etc. *Pappay Pizza*, located in the Christian quarter, just west of the Al Zunnar Church. Open 1200-2300. A small, modern-style pizza parlour offering pizzas for S£100-125 as well as sandwiches and soft drinks. On the corner next door to the *Prince* restaurant (on its south side), there is a small, simple, traditional restaurant which is good for hummus and fuul.

Chocolate If you are suffering from serious chocolate withdrawal, there is a great shop in the *Safir Homs* hotel which specializes in delicious, real chocolate which even the most discerning Belgian or Swiss would appreciate.

Cafés The *Safir Homs* hotel runs a poolside café during the summer months which is particularly popular on Thu through to Sun nights. On Shoukri al-Kouwatli St, near the museum, there is a large open-air café set in shady gardens which makes for a pleasant place to relax; it even has a separate seating area for women and families. A few doors down from this, near the telephone office, is another café with seating inside a large, smoky hall, or (more appealingly) out on the street.

Bars There are only 2 bars in Homs, in the town's two luxury hotels. The *Abo Nawas*, in the *Safir Homs* hotel, is the nicest. A bottle of *Barada* beer costs S£135 here, or there is draught *Heineken* and *Holsten* for S£185 per pint. The *Orontes*, in the *Homs Grand* hotel, charges S£115 for a bottle of *Barada* beer, or S£175 for a small can of *Heineken*, but it's somewhat lacking in atmosphere.

Sports There is a large outdoor swimming pool (open summer only) at the *Safir Homs* hotel, which non-guests can use for a daily fee of S£300 per person. There are also tennis courts here, which cost S£300 per hour for non-guests.

Transport **Local** The *Safir Homs* hotel can arrange a **car with driver** to take you to Krak des Chevaliers and back, for example, for around US$20, and they can also arrange self-drive **car hire**. There are always plenty of **taxis** waiting around at the luxury coach station. The fare into the centre of town shouldn't be more than S£30, though you may have to bargain hard (and perhaps insist that you do not want to be urgently whisked off to Krak des Chevaliers on the metre). Finding a taxi in the centre of the town is never a problem, and you are less likely to be overcharged (in any case, always agree a price in advance). If you stand outside the luxury coach station, the passing **microbuses** ('servees'; flat fare S£3) all turn around at the end of the street and head

Orontes Valley

The rebel river

The Orontes River is known in Arabic as the Nahr al-Assi, which translates literally as the 'Rebel River', a title it derives from the fact that, unlike other rivers in the region, it flows from south to north. Rising in the Bekaa valley in Lebanon, it meanders northwards through Syria, its deeply incised bed greatly reducing its usefulness as a source of irrigation for agriculture. Historically, however, the river *has always been of major significance as an obstacle to the movement of armies, with ancient towns and fortresses such as Jisr al-Shuhgur and Sheizar guarding the main crossing points. Having flowed through the Al Ghab region to the northwest of Hama, it enters Turkey, swings sharply west and passes through Antakya (Antioch) before draining finally into the Mediterranean.*

back along Al Korniche St, past the Karnak/bus/microbus station. Most continue along Al Korniche St, skirting to the west of the town centre. If you stand outside the entrance to the Karnak station (on that side of Al Korniche St), you can likewise catch a microbus towards the luxury coach station (ask for 'Garagat Pullman').

Road There are 2 bus stations in Homs. The Karnak/bus/microbus station is around 1.5 km to the north of the town centre along Hama St (see map). The luxury coach station ('Garagat Pullman') is further north, around 3 km from the centre, off Hama St. To reach it from the Karnak/bus/microbus station, continue north along Hama St (also the main road for Hama), past the large junction with Al Korniche St, and turn right at the next large roundabout you come to; it is around 500 m down on the right.

Karnak/bus/microbus This bus station is in 2 parts. The *Karnak* section of the bus station is accessible only from Al Korniche St. The ticket office (T225593) is open 0700-2100. You are advised to check these schedules for yourself, as they are subject to frequent change. **Damascus**, 0830, 0915, 1015, 1430, 1645, 1915, S£60, 2 hrs. **Aleppo**, 1400, 2000, S£75, 2-2½ hrs. **Palmyra/Deir ez-Zor** 0930, 1515, S£65/130, 2/4 hrs (note that this bus originates in Damascus, so bookings can only be made once it has started its journey, providing there are seats). **Tartus**, 1600, S£40, 1 hr. **Lattakia**, 1030, 1530, S£65, 2 hrs (direct service). **Tripoli/Beirut**, 1530, 0200, S£150/200. **Amman**, 2430, S£400.

The second section of the bus station, accessible from Hama St, or from the side street linking Hama St and Al Korniche St, is a bustling, chaotic place with microbuses, battered old 'hob-hob' buses and even some relatively comfortable coaches, which between them cover both local destinations and those further afield. Microbus services include **Qalat al-Husn (Krak des Chevaliers)** (this microbus will take you right the way to the village of Al Husn, just below the castle; be sure to specify that you want a 'servees', or someone may try to offer you a private booking), S£25, fairly regular departures until around 1600 (1400 on Fri); **Masyaf**, S£25; **Safita**, S£35; **Hama**, S£20, **Damascus** (Abasseen bus station), S£65; **Tartus**, S£35; **Tadmor (Palmyra)**, S£50. The 'hob-hob' buses covering many of these destinations are cheaper (eg Damascus S£35; Tartus S£25) but slower and less comfortable. There are also buses to Lebanon; **Baalbek**, S£150; **Beirut/Tripoli**, S£200.

Luxury Coach Between them, the various private luxury coach companies offer regular services to **Damascus**, S£70-75; **Aleppo**, S£80-85; **Tartus**, S£40; and **Lattakia**, S£80 *Kadmous* has 3 coaches daily to **Tadmor (Palmyra)/Deir ez-Zor**, 1400, 1500, 1700, S£75/200, and 1 coach daily to **Tripoli/Beirut**, 0400, S£150/225. **NB** There is talk of establishing regular bus services specifically for tourists directly from the luxury coach station to Krak des Chevaliers and Palmyra.

Train The train station is on Al Korniche St, to the southwest of the city centre. Heading south along Al Korniche St, just before you reach the large new 'Homs Tourism

Department' building, a subway gives access to the east side of the railway tracks, from where you can reach the station, a massive, Soviet-style edifice that is difficult to miss. Given that just 2 trains a day pass through here, it is improbably huge and predictably empty and echoing. **Damascus**, 0330, 1st class S£47, 2nd class S£32, 3 hrs. **Aleppo**, 1900, 1st class S£45, 2nd class S£31, 3 hrs.

Banks There is a *CBS* exchange counter for cash and TCs on the small street running parallel to Shoukri al-Kouwatli St on the south side. Open 0800-1900, daily. **Communications Post** The Post Office is located in a new building on Abdul Monem Riad St. Open 0600-1730, closed Fri. **Telephone** The Telephone Office is at the west end of Shoukri al-Kouwatli St, by the roundabout and clocktower. Open daily, 0800-2000. There are several international cardphones in the booths around the side and phonecards (the old STE variety) are also on sale here. Next door to the *City Café* restaurant, on the first floor of the *Amir* cinema, there is a private telephone office (open 1030-2300, daily) which is slightly cheaper. **Visa extensions** The Passport and Immigration office is on the 3rd floor of a building just off Ibn Khaldoun St; entry from the street is via a covered arcade. Open 0800-1400, closed Fri. Fairly chaotic and inefficient; not the best place to extend your visa. There are several photo studios on the ground floor if you need passport photos.

Directory

Homs to Hama

It is a further 47 km on to Hama from Homs. To pick up the motorway, head north out of town along Hama Street, passing the Karnak/bus/microbus station, and keep going straight. Once out of town, the road crosses a large open plain. After around 21 km a high bridge carries you over the Orontes River. To the west a dam has been built creating a large lake, while below the dam to the east the river is reduced to a small trickle. Most striking, however, is the sense you get here of the depth to which the Orontes River has cut into the surrounding countryside to create a deep gorge. The remainder of the route into Hama offers nothing of special interest.

Hama حماه

Hama is the fourth largest city in Syria after Damascus, Aleppo and Homs. Despite its recent history, it is today an attractive place, famous for its water-wheels or norias, and for its riverside parks and gardens. It has become something of a favourite stopping place for travellers, both for the excellent accommodation to be found here, and its pleasant atmosphere. It also makes a convenient base for visiting a number of interesting sites in the area. While the cooler months of April and September are the best times to visit in terms of the climate, it is during the summer months that you can see the otherwise idle norias in action.

Phone code: 033
Colour map 1, grid B2

Ins and outs

Hama is well connected with the rest of the country by luxury coach services, the majority of which stop in the centre of town. If coming from Damascus or Aleppo, it is worth choosing one of the companies which actually has a ticket office in Hama, as some of the other companies may simply drop you off on the outskirts of the town, rather than taking you right into the centre. Hama is also on the Damascus-Aleppo railway line, though once again the station is a long way from the centre, and train times far from user-friendly.

Getting there
See also 'Transport',
page 222

Microbuses (from the south microbus station) provide connections to places of interest in the surrounding countryside (or else you can opt for the organized tours laid on by the *Cairo* and *Riad* hotels; see 'Around Hama', page 224). For the most part Hama is

Getting around

Orontes Valley

small enough to explore on foot, or there are plenty of taxis and a couple useful local public transport routes which will get you to the south bus/microbus stations.

The **tourist information** office is on the north side of the river, in the garden area by the side of the main Aleppo road, T511033. Open 0830-1700, closed Fri (the afternoon shift, from 1400, sees only a token presence). They have the usual town/area map. In terms of advice and information, however, you are better off talking to the staff and guides at the *Cairo* and *Riad* hotels.

History

Although nothing remains to be seen of Hama's ancient history apart from artefacts preserved in the museum, evidence of settlement going back as far as the neolithic period has been uncovered in the course of extensive excavations of the large mound on which the town's citadel stood. This was also the site of a fortress during the late second to early first millennium BC when the town, then known as *Hamath*, was the capital of the Syro-Hittite kingdom of the Aramaeans. In 720 BC it was completely destroyed by the Assyrian armies of Sargon, and only regained some measure of prosperity under the Seleucids, when it became known as *Epiphania* after the Seleucid king Antiochus IV Epiphanes (175-164 BC).

Under the Romans and Byzantines it continued to prosper in relative obscurity until it fell in the Muslim conquest in the seventh century AD. It continued as a town of little importance during the Muslim period, caught between the competing city-states of Aleppo and Damascus. The Ayyubid period, however, brought with it relative prosperity. Given by Saladin to one of his nephews, the town subsequently managed to retain a certain degree of independence as a sovereign principality well into the Mameluke period. It was during this time that the first of the town's *norias* were constructed. During the Ottoman period Hama was incorporated into the *sanjak* of Tripoli, although within this it also enjoyed the position of chief town of a *pashalik*.

Perhaps due to its relative isolation, Hama developed as a fiercely conservative centre of Sunni orthodoxy, a fact which led to the tragic Hama Uprising of 1982, when the town was brutally wrenched from its relative isolation and obscurity (see box). Following the events of 1982, Assad ensured that a huge amount of investment was poured in, building new roads, public buildings and housing estates, in an attempt to create a 'new start' for the town. Today it is these modern aspects of Hama, with its wide streets and large new housing developments, which first make an impression.

Sights

The Norias

Even if you are simply en route to Damascus or Aleppo, many of the luxury coaches obligingly make a stop right in the centre of town, from where you can get a good view of a couple of the norias on the opposite bank of the river

Set in a natural depression surrounded by low hills, Hama faces a peculiar problem in that although the Orontes flows through it, all the surrounding land is at a higher level, making it difficult to irrigate. Previous attempts to tackle this problem were made as early as the Byzantine period, but the Ayyubids were the first to do so on a grand scale in the 13th century, and it is to them that Hama owes the earliest of its unique wooden waterwheels, or *norias*. These lifted the water from river level, depositing it in raised aqueducts which then carried it to nearby fields. Today there are a total of 17 of these enormous contraptions at various points along the river as it flows through the town. For much of the year they stand idle, the waters of the Orontes largely diverted to modern irrigation schemes, reducing the river to an insubstantial and heavily polluted trickle insufficient to power them. During the summer, however, the river is returned to its full flow and the restored *norias* turn as they did in the past.

The Hama uprising

In 1982 Hama was the scene of the bloodiest episode of Syria's modern history. The city had become the focus for opposition to Assad's regime, an opposition led by the extremist Islamic movement, the Muslim Brotherhood, which was intent on replacing the secular, modernist ideology of Assad's ruling Baathist regime with strict Islamic rule. The Brotherhood had been waging a bloody campaign of terrorism targeted at members of Assad's Alawi sect and at the foundations of the state for several years, carrying out numerous bombings and assassinations, including the murder of at least 32 Alawi officer cadets in a bomb attack on the Aleppo Artillery School in 1979. Assad responded to this threat to his authority with increasing brutality and to many it seemed that the country was on the brink of civil war.

The showdown finally came in February 1982, when an army unit was ambushed while patrolling the narrow souks of Hama's Old City. The Brotherhood quickly put out a call for a general uprising in the city. The government's response, led by Assad's brother Rifa'at, was swift, although the scale of that response shocked even those who understood the full implications of the showdown. As Patrick Seale comments in his book Asad; The Struggle for the Middle East: "Hama was a last-ditch battle which one side or the other had to win and which, one way or the other, would decide the fate of the country... Some such understanding that this was the final act of a long-drawn-out struggle may serve to explain the terrible savegery of the punishment inflicted on the city."

An all-out battle ensued which was to last for three weeks and devastate the city, leaving much of it flattened and thousands of its inhabitants dead (the site of the Apamee Cham Palace hotel, for example, was once a densely populated area of narrow streets and souks). The only westerner to offer an eye-witness account of the events in Hama was the reporter Robert Fisk, who arrived on the outskirts of the city in a taxi with a couple of soldiers who had asked for a lift back to their units: "It had been burning for a long time; a dense cloud of brown and grey smoke was steaming up from the walls and the narrow laneways beyond the Orontes....Parked on the banks of the Orontes was a line of Syrian T62 tanks, part of Rifaat's collection of armour from Damascus. Every minute or so, one of the barrels would shake, the tank would pitch backwards with the vibration and a shell would go hissing out over the river and explode amid the walls." (Robert Fisk, Pity the Nation). According to an Amnesty International report of November 1983, the estimates of the numbers killed ranged from 10,000-25,000.

Today it is hard to imagine that this peaceful, relaxing town with its waterwheels and riverside parks was the scene of such a devastating episode. As to people's attitudes towards what happened, there appears to be a certain ambivalence. On the one hand there is a deep sense of the terrible tragedy and brutality of those events, but on the other hand, the Muslim Brotherhood was also uncompromisingly brutal and had at its heart an extremist Islamic ideology completely at odds with the aspirations of Syria's younger generation at least. Certainly it is not something which people are keen to talk about, and you should not try to press them on the subject.

Orontes Valley

About 1 km upstream (east) of the town centre, there is a group of two pairs of *norias* known as the **Four Norias of Bechiriyat**, with the *4 Norias* and *Al Boustan* restaurants opposite. Heading west from the centre of town, the largest waterwheel, with a diameter of 20 m, is the **Al Muhammediyeh**, by a small stone footbridge to the west of the citadel mound. This was built by the Mamelukes in the 14th century (an inscription on the adjoining aquaduct gives the date as 1361) to supply the Great Mosque with water.

Old town The best preserved remnants of Hama as it was before 1982 are along the west bank of the Orontes River where it swings north in the centre of town. Just past the *Al Rowdah* restaurant and *Park* café, a small alleyway leads off to the right, immediately before one of the town's original aqueducts crosses the main road. If you follow this alleyway and bear right where it forks, you come first to the **Al Uthmaniyyeh Hammam** on the left (signposted simply as the 'Ottoman Public Bathing House'). ■ *In theory, this is open daily from 0800-1200 and 1900-2300 for men, and from 1200-1700 for women. In practice, however, it often remains shut. When it is open, a steam bath with all the extras costs S£150.*

Just past the hammam, on the same side, is the **Ateliers des Peintures**. This traditional building, its rooms arranged in typical Arabic style around a central courtyard, has been converted into artists' studios. The works on display here are also for sale, but even if you aren't interested in buying, it is well worth checking out the contemporary Syrian art scene. ■ *Open 0900-2200, daily. Entry free.*

Continuing north along the alleyway, past the Azem Palace, and bearing right where it forks (at this point you are confronted by a lengthy piece of wall graffiti outlining the Palestinian cause), you pass two large *norias* on the right and the *Sultan* restaurant opposite before going through a vaulted passage which meets the main road and bridge from where you get an excellent view of the **Al Nuri Mosque** to your left and the two *norias*.

Azem Palace (or Beit al-Azem) This 18th-century building was the palace of the governor of Hama, Assad Pasha al-Azem, who went on to become the governor of Damascus, where he built a larger version according to the same basic plan (see page 94). Extensively

Hama

To Aleppo
To Aleppo
Zigar St
Hama Archaeological Museum
Abi al-Fida
Omar Ibn al-Khattab
● 3
Citadel
● 4
■ 1
Roman Orthodox Cathedral
Al Nuri
Al Bahsa
Said al-Aas St
Grand Mosque
6 ●
Al Azem Palace
Ath Thawra St
Moutanabbi St
To Masyaf & Apamea
Ibrahim Hanano St
Kouwatli St
5 ●
Al Wahda al-Arabiye St
A
Khan Rustum Pasha
Jamal Abdul Naser St
Khan Assad Pasha
Al Murabet St
N
To South Microbus Station (300m)
To Homs & Damascus
Related map
A Hama centre,
page 219
0 metres 200
0 yards 200
■ **Sleeping**
● **Eating**
1 Apamee Cham Palace
1 4 Norias
3 Dream House
5 Railway Workers'
2 Al Boustan
4 Family Club
6 Sultan

Orontes Valley

damaged during the 1982 uprising, it has now been largely restored. Though not as grand as the Damascus Azem Palace, it nevertheless has a great deal of charm, evoking the atmosphere of such Ottoman buildings beautifully, with its shady courtyards, fountains and richly decorated rooms.

Various architectural fragments and pieces of sculpture are dotted around the main courtyard, which served as the *salemlek*, or visitors' area. Stairs lead up to the upper courtyard, where there is a particularly striking grand reception room; an arched portico protects the ornate façade, while inside every surface is lavishly decorated with painted woodwork, banded stonework and patterned marble. The central section of the room is topped by a large dome. The other rooms opening onto this upper courtyard contain 'popular traditions' displays, with costumed mannequins depicting scenes from everyday life, though it is the decoration in the rooms themselves which is most impressive. From the entrance area, you can also see the palace's private hammam, and from here you can go through to a smaller courtyard which served as the *haremlek*, or family and women's quarters. ■ *Open 0930-1430, closed Tue. Entry S£150 (students S£10).*

Al Nuri Mosque

Construction of the Al Nuri Mosque began in 1172 during the reign of Nur ud-Din, as detailed in the lengthy Arabic inscription on the outside wall, by the entrance opposite the prayer hall. The square tower-minaret of the mosque is original and features alternating bands of black and white stone, giving way in places to interwoven and chequered patterns. Inside, there is an arched and vaulted arcade around three sides of the courtyard, with the prayer hall occupying the fourth, and a pool for ablutions in the centre. Note the delicate classical column topped by a Corinthian capital incorporated into the arcade at one point. *The mosque is only open around prayer times. If the local imam shows you round, he will expect a small payment for his troubles.*

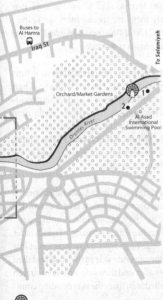

Buses to Al Hamra

Iraq St

To Salamiyeh

Orchard/Market Gardens

1

2

Al Asad International Swimming Pool

Orontes River

Noria (Water wheel)

Orontes Valley

Citadel

Practically nothing remains to be seen today on the archaeologically important citadel mound, which was subject to such extensive excavations by the Dutch. In the new archaeological museum (see below) you can see photos of these excavations. The summit of the mound is now occupied by a landscaped garden which is a popular picnic site amongst the residents of Hama, particularly on Fridays. This is also a good place to come for a bird's-eye view over Hama.

Roman Orthodox Cathedral

Following the main street which leads west from the roundabout to the south of the citadel mound, you pass first on your right the Roman Orthodox Cathedral, while further along on the left is the Grand Mosque. The huge modern Roman Orthodox Cathedral replaces an earlier one which was destroyed in 1982. Beside the cathedral there is a small chapel, also newly rebuilt. Known as the 'Church of the Entrance of Theotokus to the Temple', it is thought to originally date from the fourth century and to have stood on the site of an earlier pagan temple. In places the original, much larger, Roman-period stones have been used in the reconstruction. Beside the cathedral and chapel, overlooked by the large, modern residence of the Roman Orthodox Bishop, is an area of deep excavations. The foundations of another Byzantine church, complete with a fourth century mosaic (currently hidden under a layer of gravel for protection) have been discovered here.

Grand Mosque Almost completely destroyed in the 1982 Hama uprising, the Grand Mosque has now been fully restored. Although it has the feel of a modern replica, the reconstruction is faithful to the original in practically every detail and has been skilfully carried out. The original was built by the Umayyads, and like the Umayyad Mosque in Damascus, stood on the site of a Christian church which was itself built on top of the remains of an earlier pagan temple. The mosque has two minarets. One is a square tower adjacent to the prayer hall (visually the more striking of the two), which can be dated by an inscription to 1124, though some argue that its base in fact dates from the Umayyad period. The other is octagonal in shape, dating from 1427 and representing an excellent example of Mameluke architecture. In the courtyard there is a 'treasury' consisting of a domed structure supported on eight columns carved with Kufic inscriptions and topped by Corinthian capitals (clearly of Roman origin). It is identical to the treasury of the Umayyad Mosque in Damascus, except for the absence of mosaic decoration. The side entrance to the prayer hall, by the square tower-minaret, has a lintel of Roman or Byzantine origin which is richly decorated with floral designs; much of this wall of the prayer hall consists of large old stone blocks and contains several other architectural fragments from the Roman and Byzantine eras. A doorway in the side of the main courtyard (beside the treasury) leads through into a small square courtyard giving access to a domed mausoleum containing two tombs, said to be those of two 13th-century Ayyubid kings. ■ *Officially there are special times for tourists (0930-1230, 1600-1900 in summer; 0900-1130, 1400-1600 in winter), though in practice you can visit at any time. Be sure to dress modestly.*

Khans Two Ottoman period khans can be found along Al Murabet Street as it runs southwest towards the south microbus/bus stations. The first of these, **Khan Rustum Pasha**, dates from 1556. It is currently closed while undergoing restoration and will probably serve as a handicrafts market in the future. At the time of writing its impressive doorway of black and white stone was somewhat obscured by peeling posters of Assad. The second, **Khan Assad Pasha**, dating from 1738, has a larger and more impressive doorway, but is today used as the local Ba'ath party headquarters and is not open to visitors.

Souks Before reaching Khan Assad Pasha, extending north from Al Murabet Street is a maze of narrow streets housing the main concentration of Hama's crowded and colourful souks. On the north side of the river, meanwhile, running parallel to the main Hama road on the right, there are some remnants of much older souks which were largely destroyed in 1982. Turn right into a new street just before the tourist information office on the opposite side of the road and then immediately left to wander along a narrow alley and then into a covered stretch of these souks, which primarily serve the Bedouin from the surrounding countryside (mornings are the best time to come).

If you continue straight along the new street leading east, you will see after a short distance a small area of old buildings off to the right (practically all that remains of what was previously a dense area of souks; today this area is a rather bleak mixture of ruined buildings and half-completed modern housing blocks). At the end of a vaulted passage on the right is the 11th-century **Al Aubaysi Mosque**, still looked after by descendents of Sheikh Mohammad Aubaysi, who emigrated to Syria after the fall of Andalusia, and whose tomb is in the mosque. Attached to the mosque was a small palace and baths complex, though today this is completely in ruins. Approaching the mosque, on either side of the street are small, dark workshops where goat's hair is still spun into thread in the traditional way. The thread is then woven into bands of coarse goat-hair fabric which are sown together to make the panels for Bedouin tents. Along with the town of Jisr al-Shugur (between Aleppo and Lattakia), Hama is the only place where this traditional craft is still practised, an almost magical process to watch.

On the north side of the river, just past the huge new Omar Ibn al-Khattab Mosque, Hama's prestigious new purpose-built museum is excellently presented and well worth a visit. Dotted around the museum's gardens are numerous capitals, columns, carved basalt doors and various other architectural fragments. Of particular note are the artefacts housed under protective wooden structures: a series of mosaic floors, a couple of life-size statues, a set of huge amphorae and a richly carved sarcophogus. The museum itself is built around a central courtyard with a fountain and pool in the centre. You work your way around anti clockwise, with each hall being colour-coded according to the epoch it covers.

Hama Archaeological Museum

The first hall covers the **palaeolithic/neolithic** and **chalcolithic/Bronze Age**. It takes you from the earliest Stone Age, through the first settlements and beginnings of agriculture, to the development of urban centres with clear, well written interpretation boards and interesting displays.

The **Iron Age** hall includes some very beautiful artefacts, including an eighth-century BC human figurine made of bronze and covered in gold leaf, and

Orontes Valley

Hama centre

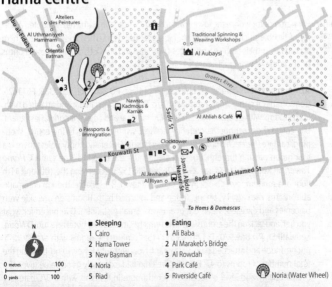

To Homs & Damascus

N
0 metres   100
0 yards   100

■ **Sleeping**
1 Cairo
2 Hama Tower
3 New Basman
4 Noria
5 Riad

● **Eating**
1 Ali Baba
2 Al Marakeb's Bridge
3 Al Rowdah
4 Park Café
5 Riverside Café

Noria (Water Wheel)

a ninth-century BC ivory cup with its handle carved into the shape of an ibex. Dominating the hall is a massive carved basalt lion (largely a reconstruction, but impressive nevertheless) found on Hama's citadel mound. This would have originally stood guard at the gates of the Royal Palace which occupied the citadel mound during the ninth century BC. Typically neo-Hittite in style, the similarity with the lions and figures at the entrance to Aleppo Museum, and the lion at Ain Dara, is quite striking. There is also a scale model of the Royal Palace and, on the wall behind, a series of photos of the excavations carried out on the citadel mound (all the work here was destroyed during the 1982 uprising).

Two halls are dedicated to the **Hellenistic/Roman/Byzantine** periods. The first contains various sarcophogi (including one of terracotta and lead, and a reconstruction of an unique wooden one), as well as gold burial ornaments, pottery, glassware, funerary stelae etc. Particularly striking is a statue of a female figure, possibly a deity, found in a Roman tomb dating from the second century AD, while the fresco on a fragment of stucco depicting Narcissus at a spring, found in a second to third century AD Roman tomb, is still remarkably clear. The highlight of the second hall is a really stunning Roman mosaic discovered at the village of Miriamin, to the southwest of Hama. This large, exceptionally well preserved third-century AD mosaic is made of unusually small *tesserae*, providing excellent detail. It depicts a group of women playing music and dancing, and provides an unique insight into the musical instruments of this period. Around the border is a broad band of lavish decoration with hunting scenes, cupids amidst swirling acanthus leaves and vine scrolls, and personifications of the four seasons.

The last hall, devoted to the **Islamic** period, contains some nice pottery and a very beautiful wooden *minbar* from the Al Nuri Mosque. Of great interest, though chronologically out of place, is a fragment of mosaic dating from 469 AD found at Apamea. This depicts part of a *noria*, confirming that this method of extracting water from the Orontes was already in use during the Byzantine era. ■ *Open 0900-1800 in summer, 0900-1600 in winter, closed Tue. Entry S£300 (students S£15).*

Essentials

Sleeping
■ *on maps*
Price codes:
see inside front cover

For better or for worse, the lower category (**D-G**) hotels in Hama have adopted a policy of flexible pricing according to the season/demand. They are categorized here according to their high season prices (Apr/May and Jul-Oct); outside these months prices come down significantly.

AL *Apamee Cham Palace*, on north bank of river, PO Box 111, T525335, F511626. Comfortable, if rather small, rooms with a/c, TV/dish, IDD, minibar and attached bath. Some rooms with good views of the Al Nuri Mosque and adjacent *norias*. Restaurant, bar, coffee shop, banquet/conference facilities, swimming pool, tennis courts, shopping, car hire (*Hertz/Chamcar*), currency exchange. Generally empty unless there is a tour group passing through, but staff are friendly and helpful all the same. **C** *Hama Tower*, off Kouwatli St, PO Box 297, T226864, F521523. Occupying the 10th and 11th floor of a modern tower block in the centre of town. Reasonable, though unremarkable, rooms with a/c, TV, phone, fridge and attached bath. Rooms on one side with balconies and excellent views out over Hama. Small restaurant. Overpriced for what you get, and lacking the enthusiasm with which Hama's other hotels are run. **D** *Noria*, Kouwatli St, PO Box 970, T512414, F511715. Comfortable rooms with a/c, TV/dish, phone, fridge and attached bath. Restaurant. Now with whole new wing, bringing the total number of rooms to 43. Friendly, well run and extremely good value given the overall quality and level of facilities offered (more in keeping with a B/C category hotel). Recommended. **D** *New Basman*, Kouwatli St, PO Box 754, T224838, F517776. Recently taken over by the family which runs the *Riad* hotel (see below). Clean, bright, fully refurbished rooms with a/c, fan, TV/dish, phone, fridge, attached bath and balcony. Restaurant in basement. Full range of tours and other services as offered by *Riad* hotel. Friendly, well run and excellent value. **F-G** There are 2 excellent value budget hotels in Hama, next door to each other on Kouwatli St, both very well run, friendly and highly recommended. Comfortable, spotlessly clean and with 24-hr hot water, they offer a standard of accommodation better than most D/E category hotels in Syria and are largely responsible for making a stay in Hama such a pleasant experience. *Cairo*, Kouwatli St, PO Box 970, T/F237206. Double room S£600 with a/c, fan, TV, phone, fridge and attached bath, or S£500 without the a/c. Dormitory beds cost S£150 each, or you can sleep on the roof for S£100. Small restaurant. *Riad*, Kouwatli St, PO Box 754, T239512, F517776. Double room S£600 with a/c, fan, TV, phone, fridge and attached bath, or S£400 without the a/c and with shared bath. Dormitory beds cost S£150 each, or you can sleep on the roof for S£100. Small restaurant.

Mid-range to cheap *Sultan*, located in the old town, by the river just to the south of the Al Nuri Mosque. Open 1200-late, daily. Lovely old building in pleasant surroundings with excellent views of the 2 *norias* on the river here. Good selection of Arabic cuisine for around S£250-300 per head. *Al Marakeb's Bridge*, occupying a prime location near the centre of town, on a small artificial island in the river, with good views of the nearby *norias*, T225169. Open 0700-late, daily. Large, bright restaurant/café with outdoor seating in summer. Usual range of Arabic cuisine for around S£250 per head upwards. Often with live music in the evenings. *Al Boustan* and *4 Norias*, 2 fairly up-market restaurants occupying prime locations next door to each other on the river at the eastern end of town. Both are somewhat cavernous places very much geared up to dealing with large parties and serve a rather uninspiring selection of Arabic food at slightly inflated prices (expect to pay from around S£300 per head). Of the 2, only the *4 Norias* serves alcohol. *Al Rowdah*, choice position overlooking the river near the centre of town. Unfortunately the Arabic food here is rather mediocre and the prices inflated (around S£300 per head upwards). *Castello*, located above the *Nawras/Kadmous/Karnak* luxury coach ticket offices to the west of the main bridge, overlooking the river and offering excellent views of the *norias*. Still under construction at the time of writing, but due to open as a comfortable a/c place lavishly decorated in the style of the Azem Palace (the restaurant is owned by a descendent of the Azem family).

There are 2 good restaurants in the Christian part of town near the Roman Orthodox church. *Dream House*, T411687. Open 1200-late, daily. Unassuming but pleasant, comfortable a/c restaurant. Choice of Arabic or Continental cuisine (wide range of *mezze* dishes, or steaks/grills/chicken dishes with chips and vegetables, as well as pizzas, burgers, soups, salads etc). Around S£200-300 per head. Alcohol served. Music and dancing on Thu and Sat nights. Friendly and well run. Recommended. *Family Club*. Open 1800-late, daily. Good selection of Arabic food for around S£250-300 per head, friendly relaxing atmosphere, outdoor terrace, alcohol served.

For something completely different, try the *Railway Workers' Restaurant* ('Al Mahatta al-Omali'), in the old railway station building in the southern part of town, T511498. Open 1600-2000, daily. Sign in Arabic only, but a distinctive French Mandate-period building with its wooden window shutters and tiled roof dotted with chimney stacks. Although better known for its somewhat tacky dancing/singing performances (see 'Entertainment'), it also has a reputation for serving good food.

Seriously cheap There are several cheap eateries along the western section of Kouwatli Ave and in the streets leading north from it towards the river. The usual selection of kebabs, half-chicken, hummus etc can be found, with a reasonable meal coming to around S£100-200 per head. For one of the best falafel, hummus and fuul places in Syria, try the *Ali Baba*, situated on Kouwatli St. The falafels here are particularly good.

Eating
● *on maps*
Price codes:
see inside front cover

Orontes Valley

Cafés　There are several pleasant riverside cafés in Hama. The *Park*, next door to the *Al Rowdah* restaurant, is offers good views and a garden with shady eucalyptus trees. A smaller and quieter place can be found to the east along the river, past the *Al Ahliah* bus stand, although it closes out of season.

Entertainment　As a small and still fairly conservative town, Hama does not exactly have a wild night-life scene. Alcohol can be bought from shops in the Christian part of town (there are a couple near the roundabout to the south of the citadel mound). Of the restaurants which serve alcohol, both the **Dream House** and the **Family Club** are good places for women on their own looking for a drink and a hassle-free evening. The former has a regular Thu and Sat night 'disco', while the latter tends to host wedding receptions etc for the Christian community. Definitely not a family affair, the **Railway Workers'** puts on a late afternoon show of female singers. As well as the stage performance, they also go round enticing the drunken all-male audience to shower them with money in return for a dance, while an assistant deftly collects the money from around their feet. It's tacky to an extreme, but quite a spectacle all the same. There is perhaps a vaguely seedy men-only atmosphere about the place, but at the same time it's friendly and foreign couples should be fine.

Shopping　Luxurious bath robes and towels made from mixed cotton and silk are a speciality of Hama, and this is one of the few places in Syria where they are still hand-woven on traditional looms. If you are interested, ask one of the guides at the *Cairo* or *Riad* hotels to take you to see the looms, where you can also buy their products at much cheaper prices than can be found in Damascus. At the southern end of the alleyway which follows the west bank of the river past the Al Azem Palace, there is the curiously named **Oriental Batman** shop, T224957. Open 0900-2100, Fri 1500-2100. Aimed very much at tourists, it offers an interesting range of jewellery, woven and painted fabrics, linen, traditional costumes and all kinds of antiques/bric-a-brac. The owner makes some of the jewellery himself.

　　If you are interested in contemporary Arab art, whether to buy or just to look, a visit to the *Ateliers des Peintures* is a must. The short stretch of souk on the north side of the river (see under Sights, above) is worth checking out for its brightly coloured Bedouin bags and rugs.

Sports　Non-guests can use the swimming pool at the *Apamee Cham Palace* hotel for a fee of S£200 per day. Alternatively there is an olympic-size swimming pool more or less opposite the *4 Norias* and *Al Boustan* restaurants, open 0800-1800 in summer, 0800-1500 in winter, closed Sat, entry S£25.

Transport　**Local** The *Apamee Cham Palace* hotel can arrange **car hire** through their *Hertz/Chamcar* desk. **Taxis** are readily available all around town; trips within Hama should cost no more than S£30. **Buses** and **microbuses** (S£2 and S£3 respectively) run from the centre of town (catch them from opposite the ticket offices/bus stops for *Nawras, Kadmous* and *Karnak*) to the south microbus/bus stations and the railway station, and vice-versa. For the south microbus/bus stations, just ask for 'Garagat'.

　　Road Conveniently (and rather unusually for Syria), all the luxury coach companies have ticket offices/bus stops in the centre of town (see 'Hama centre' map). For microbuses to destinations in the vicinity of Hama (Apamea, Masyaf, Salamiyeh, Homs), you need to go to the south microbus station, around 1 km to the south of the centre (see 'Hama' map). There is talk of all the luxury coach companies being made to relocate to a new terminal near the south bus station, though opinions are divided as to whether this will actually ever happen.

Luxury coach *Al Ahliah*, by the river to the east of the main bridge, T522551, is a locally owned private coach company with a good reputation. It has its own pleasant café/restaurant attached to the ticket office. **Damascus**, regular departures (19 daily), S£90, 3 hrs. **Homs**, regular departures (21 daily), S£20, 45 mins. **Aleppo**, regular departures (15 daily), S£65, 2 hrs. **Tartus/Lattakia**, 0600, 1215, 1700, 1815, S£70/100, 2/3 hrs. **Raqqa**, 0645, 1530, 1630, 1730, 1830, 2030, S£145, 5 hrs. **Idlib**, 1745, 1915, S£50, 1 hrs.

Nawras, by the river to the west of the main bridge, T510830, acts as agent for a number of private coach companies, including *Trans Orient, Express, Salama* and *Assia*. Between them, these companies offer regular departures to **Homs/Damascus** and **Aleppo**. Next door is *Kadmous*, T229219, which in addition to services to Damascus and Aleppo, runs a number of other useful services; **Lattakia** (small bus going via a direct but very scenic route across the mountains), regular departures (every 1-2 hrs) throughout the day, S£60, 2$\frac{1}{2}$ hrs; **Tartus/Banyas** (via **Homs** and the coastal motorway), 0530, 0730, 0930, 1245, 1615, 1715, S£65/75, 1$\frac{1}{2}$/2 hrs; **Palmyra** (via **Homs**, continuing on to **Deir ez-Zor**), 1345, S£105, 3 hrs; **Beirut/Tripoli** (small bus, goes via **Dabbousiyeh** border), 0930, 1100, S£250. Next door again is *Karnak*, the state-owned coach company, which despite having its own café/restaurant was at the time of writing only operating much reduced services, with just a few of its Damascus-Aleppo coaches stopping here (staff were unable to give times).

Al Riyan, on Badr ad-Din al-Hamed St (just off Jamal Abdul Nasser St, to the south of the clocktower), T227977, also has services to **Homs/Damascus** (7 daily) and **Aleppo** (6 daily). Just around the corner, on Jamal Abdul Nasser St itself, is *Al Jawharah*, T233904 (sign on shopfront just reads 'Nabulsi Insurance'), with one service daily to **Amman**, 2430, S£450, and **Antakya/Istanbul**, 2430, S£500/1500.

South microbus/bus stations The south microbus station is on Salah ud-Din St, to the southwest of the town centre (see 'Hama' map). Microbuses are frequent, departing when full, to (amongst others) **As Qeilebiyeh** (for **Apamea**), S£20; **Homs**, S£20; **Masyaf**, S£20 and **Salamiyeh**, S£15. Around 500 m further southwest, Salah ud-Din St ends in a T-junction; across the road to the left is the south bus station, where small buses and 'hob-hob' buses run to most the above destinations, as well as to places such as Damascus, Aleppo and Tartus, less frequently and more uncomfortably, but also more cheaply.

Al Hamra bus stand On the north side of the river, on Iraq St (see 'Hama' map), there is a bus stand for buses to **Al Hamra** (for **Qasr Ibn Warden**), S£15.

Train The railway station is way out on the eastern edge of town. Trains en route to **Damascus** stop here at 0230 (2nd class S£39, 1st class S£57, sleeper S£225), and those en route to **Aleppo** at 2000 (2nd class S£23, 1st class S£34, sleeper S£125), assuming they are not delayed.

Banks The main branch of the *CBS* is east of the roundabout and clocktower on Kouwatli Ave. **Directory** Open 0830-1230, closed Fri. Cash and TCs changed. The *Apamee Cham Palace* can change cash and TCs at any time, at the official bank rate. **Communications** Post and telephone Next door each other on Kouwatli Ave, by the roundabout and clocktower. The entrance to the post office (Open 0800-1400, closed Fri) faces the roundabout. The national/international cardphones are reached from a side street off Kouwatli St (open up to around 2200), while the phonecards are sold in a small booth round the side of the post office, just off Jamel Abdul Nasser St. **Medical services** There is a good private hospital, the *Markhaz al-Tobi ('Health Centre')*, T515801, in the eastern part of town. Ask first at your hotel for help if you need medical attention. The *Cairo* and *Noria* hotels have their own small supplies of medicines and can offer assistance for minor complaints. **Visa extensions** The Passport and Immigration office is located just south of the junction by the footbridge over the river in the centre of town; the building has a sign above the door reading 'Passports'. Open 0800-1400, closed Fri. Extensions of up to 1 month are generally issued on the spot. You need 4 passport photos.

Orontes Valley

Around Hama

Hama makes an ideal base from which to visit a number of sites in the surrounding countryside. Most obviously, these include Apamea (arguably the most impressive site in the area), Masyaf, Qalat Shmemis and Qasr Ibn Warden. Further afield, Krak des Chevaliers can reasonably be visited as a day-trip from Hama (see page 258), a popular alternative to using Homs as a base. The town of Maarat al-Numan (see page 238) with its beautiful mosaics museum and the nearby Dead City sites centred around Bara (see page 360) are also within reasonably easy reach, both in fact closer to Hama than to Aleppo.

Ins and outs

Guided tours Both the *Cairo* and *Riad* hotels run regular guided tours to the various places of interest around Hama. If you are pressed for time, these offer an excellent chance to see a great deal more than is possible by public transport. However, if you have plenty of time but a limited budget, they are relatively expensive and it is possible to get to the majority of the places by public transport (see under 'Transport' for each site). The most popular tours take in **Sheizaar**, **Apamea**, **Masyaf** and **Krak des Chevaliers** (or a selection of these for more detailed visits and a slightly less hectic schedule). They generally cost in the region of S£500 per person for a small group (excluding entry fees), though obviously this depends on the number of people in the group and how many sites are visited. Also popular (and not so easy by public transport) is a trip out to **Qasr Ibn Warden**, visiting some **beehive houses** on the way, and perhaps also taking in **Qalat Shmemis** and **Salamiyeh**. This usually costs in the region of S£250 per person for a group. Other tours venture further afield (eg to the **Dead Cities** and **Qalat Saladin**; to **Palmyra**; to **Rasafeh** and **Qalat Jaber/Ath Thawra dam**; or even to **Baalbek** in Lebanon), though these involve a lot of driving and are perhaps stretching the concept of Hama as a base for exploring a little too far.

Around Hama

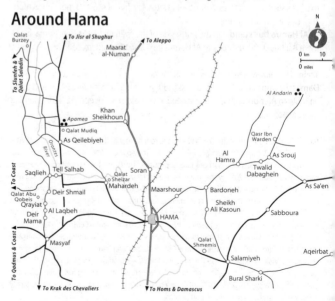

Hama to Apamea

The route from Hama to Apamea takes you past the castle of Qalat Sheizar, making for a convenient place to break the journey. If you are travelling by public transport, it makes more sense to leave this for the return journey, if you still have enough time.

At the time of writing there was a new motorway under construction between Hama & Mahardeh

From the centre of Hama, head west along Ibrabim Hanano Street, going straight across the double roundabouts near the railway station to continue northwest. Bear left at the next roundabout you come to (you have no option here) and then just after crossing the railway line (7 km from the centre of Hama), bear right (signposted for Mahardeh; left signposted for Masyaf). After a further 20 km, entering the Christian town of Mahardeh, turn left at a roundabout and then right at the next roundabout (both signposted for 'Afamia' and 'Sheizar'). Following this road, you soon pass on the right the ruins of Qalat Sheizar, strung out along a ridge above a village of the same name.

Continuing past the ruins and across the Orontes River, after around 15 km the road begins to climb up onto a low plateau giving good views of the surrounding countryside. Arriving in the centre of the town of As Qeilebiyeh (49 km from Hama), go straight across two roundabouts and follow the main road around to the right as it descends again from the plateau. Continue straight on this road to arrive in the modern village of Qalat Mudiq, 56 km from Hama.

Qalat Sheizar
Colour map 1, grid B2

According to legend this is the site of the Roman city of *Cesara*, thought to have first been settled by the forces of Alexander the Great. However, the most important period of its history dates from the 10th to the 12th centuries AD, when its great strategic value, guarding an important crossing point over the Orontes, ensured it a central role in the power struggles of the period. By the 10th century the Fatimids had built a castle and established themselves here, only to be driven out by Byzantine forces in 999. They in turn were eventually driven out by a local clan, the Banu Munqid, in 1081. In the following years Sheizar became a base for attacks against the Crusaders, who had established themselves in Apamea. Repeated attempts in the early part of the 12th century by the Crusaders to overrun it failed, resulting in an uneasy treaty between them and the Banu Munqid in 1110. The Byzantines similarly attempted unsuccessfully to take it on two occasions and it was only due to an earthquake in 1157 that the castle was eventually destroyed. The Zengid ruler Nur ud-Din subsequently repaired it and based a garrison here, but an earthquake again struck in 1170, and further repairs were not carried until 1233, under the Ayyubids. In 1260 it was overrun by the Mongol invaders, and following their defeat in 1281, Baibars restored it and established a Mameluke garrison here. However, it was abandoned as a military base soon after and quickly fell into ruin, becoming instead a source of building materials for the village below.

The ruins are best entered from the north end; head for the old, 11-arched bridge (known as *Jisr Ibn Munqid* after the Munqid family) off to the right of the modern road where it crosses the Orontes and climb up from there. This brings you to the northern gate complex, a largely Mameluke construction with evidence of recycled Greek/Roman columns. At the southern end of the ridge you can see the remains of an Ayyubid tower. Overall, the ruins are more impressive as seen looking up from the road, although there are good views from the top.

Orontes Valley

👉 *From swamp to farmland: Al Ghab*

To the northwest of Hama, the Orontes River flows into the Al Ghab, a long, narrow belt of low-lying land running parallel with the eastern edges of the Jebel Ansariye range. In the days of Alexander and the Seleucids, this area is known to have been intensively cultivated and highly productive, supporting large urban settlements such as at Apamea. Over subsequent centuries, however, it degenerated and until the 1950s this area, covering more than 800 sq km, was an unproductive, malaria-infested swamp. With World Bank funding an ambitious project was undertaken to drain the swamps and turn it once again into fertile, productive farmland. The result today is a complex grid of canals, dams and irrigation channels dissecting fruit orchards and fields of wheat, barley and sugar beet, making this one of the most agriculturally productive areas in Syria.

From the ruins of Qalat Sheizar or from the citadel of Qalat Mudiq you can look out over the fertile Al Ghab region, but for the best perspective you really need to get up onto the heights of the Jebel Ansariye. The road which descends from Slunfeh back down to the plains (see page 230) offers the best views, and those from Qalat Abu Qobais (see page 232) are also very impressive.

Apamea آفاميا

Colour map 1, grid B2 The Roman ruins at Apamea (Aphamia in Arabic, or Qalat Mudiq after the medieval hilltop citadel overlooking the ruins and the modern village on the main road) represent the most impressive site in the vicinity of Hama, reminiscent of Palmyra to the east, although in an entirely different setting to the latter's desert oasis. In spring in particular, the long line of columns marking the main colonnaded street is surrounded by a sea of wheat and bright flowers which come alive in the breeze.

Ins & outs If you are arriving in Qalat Mudiq by public transport, ask to be dropped off at the museum ('*mat-haf*' in Arabic), by the main road, on the right as you drive in from the south. Having visited the museum, you can then walk to the main ruins (a 15-20 min stroll). Turn right out of the museum entrance and left at the top of this short street, then bear off to the right to follow a rough track as it climbs up through the dusty village, with the citadel off to the left. Continue straight past the theatre ruins on your right, then bear off to the left slightly to join the modern road, which takes you directly to the ticket office and cafeteria at the southern end of the site. To drive right up to the site, continue straight on past the museum and take the sharp right turn at the northern edge of the village. This takes you past the old citadel of Qalat Mudiq, perched up on top of a steep hillock, and then down to the ruins.

Entry fees/opening times At the museum you have the option of buying a combined ticket for S£350 which covers you for both the museum and the main ruins. Individual tickets for each cost S£150 and S£300 respectively. Students must pay for the museum (S£10) and main ruins (S£15) separately. The musuem is open 0830-1430, closed Tue. There are no opening times as such for the main ruins since the site is not fenced in.

History Following the death of Alexander the Great and the subsequent break-up of his empire, Seleucus I Nicator rose to power in northern Syria, establishing the Seleucid Empire early in the third century BC. Previously known as *Pharnake* and renamed *Pella* by Alexander the Great, Apamea (named after Seleucus's Persian wife) was one of a number of settlements which he greatly expanded, making it into an important military base and provincial centre. Others in the area which received a similar treatment included Antioch (present day Antakya in Turkey), which became the capital, its seaport Seleucia, and Laodicea (present-day Lattakia), which served as Apamea's port.

During the Seleucid period, Apamea flourished in its new role. At its height it is estimated to have comprised a population of some 120,000. Strabo records that a stud was established here with no less than 30,000 mares and 3,000 stallions. Similarly, up to 500 elephants were kept here and trained for use in warfare.

The fortunes of the Seleucids fluctuated dramatically, their empire expanding and contracting repeatedly, but by the first century BC it was in terminal decline, and finally in 64 BC Apamea fell to the armies of Pompey. Under the Romans it continued to be an important military centre. A severe earthquake in 115 AD caused serious damage, but also resulted in a new burst of building activity, particularly during the reigns of Trajan (98-117) and Marcus Aurelius (161-180); thus almost all the archaeological remains to be seen at the site today date from the second century. By this time, Apamea was a flourishing city, with a population of perhaps half a million, and an important cultural centre. It was here for example that the philosophical school of thought known as Neo-Platonism was developed, combining Platonism with oriental elements, so continuing a process of synthesis between Hellenistic/Roman and oriental concepts which had begun under the Seleucids.

Its prosperity continued into the Byzantine period, when it became the seat of a bishopric and the capital of *Syria Secunda* province. However, in 540 the Persian armies of Chosroes I invaded Syria, sacking Aleppo and Antioch before descending on Apamea. Byzantine rule was restored for a while, albeit under tribute, but in 611 the Persians attacked Syria once again, taking Apamea in 612. Their occupation lasted until 628, when the Byzantines briefly regained it before finally losing it to the Muslim invaders in 636.

During the Islamic period Apamea declined in importance. In 1106 it was occupied by the Crusaders, led by the Norman, Tancred. They were eventually ousted by Nur ud-Din in 1149, but soon after, in 1157, it was all but destroyed in a severe earthquake. The Mamelukes still made use of the acropolis, building the present citadel there, while during the Ottoman period it retained a certain importance as a halting place on the pilgrimage to Mecca.

Sights

Museum This 16th-century Ottoman khan has been restored and converted into a simple but highly effective museum displaying some of the mosaics found at Apamea, along with numerous funerary *stelae* and various architectural fragments. In the centre of the large open courtyard are steps leading down to what was once a reservoir. Running around the courtyard are long vaulted chambers which once served as stables and now house a selection of the beautiful mosaics along with sarcophagi, inscribed stone tablets, statues etc. Spacious and deliciously cool in summer, the lighting inside is, however, a little dim.

Theatre In a depression to the right of the path coming from the museum, shortly before it joins the modern approach road to the main ruins, is the theatre. This was originally a massive structure, nearly 140 m in diameter, making it even larger than the theatre at Bosra. However, now in an advanced state of ruin, it is difficult to make out its plan from close up. A partially reconstructed doorway which would have led through to the *scenae frons* and stage area still stands, along with a stretch of passageway, but the *cavea* of the theatre has almost completely disappeared. A much better overview can be had by looking down onto it from the citadel.

Orontes Valley

Reconstruction archaeology

Wandering up and down Apamea's colonnaded street and admiring the variety and grace of its columns, capitals and entablature, you would do well to remember that this site was described as merely 'shapeless ruins' in the 1912 Baedeker guidebook. Since the 1930s the Belgians have more or less continuously been involved in archaeological work here, and in recent years the Syrian Department of Antiquities has undertaken further extensive work (still ongoing) to reconstruct the past glory of Apamea from the ample remains scattered around.

As such, the site provides a good example of the benefits of reconstruction archaeology. Purists complain about evidence of steel-reinforced concrete holding up the ruins, but the simple fact remains that practically nothing was standing in the early 1900s, whereas today, even the most casual of visitor cannot help but be inspired by what they see.

Citadel Perched on top of a steep hillock is the citadel and old village of Qalat Mudiq, quite an imposing sight from a distance. This strategic position has no doubt been utilized at least since Seleucid times, although all that remains today are sections of the 13th-century Mameluke walls, consisting of a mixture of recycled masonry from earlier fortifications. Inside, the village consists of a maze of narrow, cobbled streets and a jumble of new and old buildings. There are excellent views out over the Orontes Valley and Jebel Ansariye (as well as of the main ruins and theatre) from the main gate. If you are willing to let someone show you around, even better views can be had from various points along the walls and from the roofs of some houses. Be prepared, however, for very persistent attempts to sell you 'antique' artefacts, a thriving cottage industry in the village and something you are unlikely to escape in any case.

Main ruins The north-south **Colonnaded Street** or *cardo maximus*, forms the main backbone of the ruins and the prime attraction of the site. Stretching for nearly 2 km, it is longer even than Palmyra's. Little today remains of the porticoes which once lined the street on either side, but the original paving still survives in places, complete with the ruts worn in it by the passing of chariots. The re-erected columns are what really give it its grandeur, with their Corinthian capitals and connecting entablature which varies between Doric, Ionic and Corinthian in style. The modern approach road which intersects it near its southern end in fact follows the line of the ancient east-west *decumanus*. At the intersection is the *Apamee Cham Cafeteria* and a ticket booth.

Following the colonnaded street north, immediately on the right are the ruined remains of a **nymphaeum**. A little further up on the left you can see the outline of a small church, followed soon after by the **agora**. Consisting of a long rectangular area, little remains to be seen today other than two rows of column bases at its southern end (part of a short transverse street by which the agora was approached), and to the north a large pile of stones which once formed a second, monumental

Detail of Colonnaded Street

entrance. Further off to the west, hidden by a rise, a low mound is all that remains to be seen of the **Temple of Zeus**, the result of an order by the Bishop Marcellus in 384 AD that it be dismantled. Back on the main colonnaded street, opposite the pile of stones which mark the monumental entrance to the agora, the columns are deeply fluted in a corkscrew pattern with striking effect, a decorative device unique to Apamea. Continuing north, you pass along a section with rather obviously re-erected columns, their plainness emphasizing the elaborate floral decoration of the capitals. Immediately after these columns end there is the excavated base of a large, star-shaped votive column in the centre of the street. This marks an intersection (no longer visible), beyond which there is an open stretch with some more fluted columns on the right, followed by the foundations and low walls of buildings, also on the right. At the north end of these, three large stone slabs can be seen, two of which are carved with reliefs depicting scenes from the legends of Bacchus; one shows Lycurgus entangled by Bacchus in the branches of a vine, while the other shows Pan holding his pipes and tending to a flock of goats. A little further on, the remaining length of the colonnaded street has been the most extensively restored, and highly effectively, to give a good idea of its original glory. This last section is also the oldest, dating almost entirely from first phase of reconstruction carried out by Trajan following the earthquake of 115 AD. You come first to a recently restored and beautifully proportioned **portico** on the right, its taller columns set forward from the line of the colonnade and crowned by a triangular pediment. Further up there is a large re-erected votive column in the centre of the street (again marking an intersection), followed soon after on the right by the remains of a **baths complex**. This was built on a grand scale, although little remains to be seen of it now. Just beyond it the walls of buildings on either side of the street behind the colonnade have been reconstructed to show two storeys of windows. Finally, at the north end of the colonnaded street you reach the **Antioch gate**. Extending off to the left here is a well preserved section of the city walls. On a clear day there are good views from here across the Al Ghab, with the Jebel Ansariye beyond. The so-called Antioch gate appears to have been modified and extended at some stage to form a fortified keep. At the far end is a precarious looking arch surrounded by tumbled rubble. Parts of the keep have been excavated in recent years to reveal terracotta pipes which were laid at a later stage, above the level of the original paving.

Returning to the *Apamee Cham Cafetería* at the intersection of the *cardo maximus* and *decumanus*, and following the latter east, on the left after around 400 m there are the remains of a **Roman villa complex**. It has an impressive entrance complete with decorated lintel and porch on the west side, albeit extensively reinforced with concrete. Inside is a large

Orontes Valley

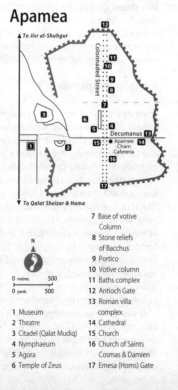

Apamea

↑ To Jisr al-Shuhgur

Colonnaded Street

12
11
10
9
8
7
6
5
4
3
2
1
15
13
14
16
17

Decumanus

● Apamee Cham Cafetería

▼ To Qalat Sheizar & Hama

N

0 metres 500
0 yards 500

1 Museum
2 Theatre
3 Citadel (Qalat Mudiq)
4 Nymphaeum
5 Agora
6 Temple of Zeus
7 Base of votive Column
8 Stone reliefs of Bacchus
9 Portico
10 Votive column
11 Baths complex
12 Antioch Gate
13 Roman villa complex
14 Cathedral
15 Church
16 Church of Saints Cosmas & Damien
17 Emesa (Homs) Gate

courtyard surrounded by 26 re-erected columns, and a smaller courtyard surrounded by rooms. On the opposite side of the road is an extensive area of ruins which has been identified as the **cathedral**. Now just a jumble of column bases, low walls and foundations, this was the most important of the Byzantine places of worship and underwent several stages of enlargement. Many of the mosaics displayed in Apamea's museum were uncovered here (the cathedral having been built over an earlier Roman structure), while according to legend the cathedral itself housed one of the relics of the True Cross, making it a major centre of pilgrimage.

Heading south from the cafetería and intersection, on the right are the remains of a **church**, dating from the sixth century during the reign of Justinian. Only the foundations remain, but these clearly indicate its basic circular plan, with a semicircular apse extending from the eastern side. Further south, on the left-hand side of the street, are the remains of the **Church of St Cosmas and St Damien**, again only consisting of the foundations and parts of the lower walls. This church, also of the sixth century, was an enlargement of an earlier fifth century church which in turn stood on the site of a fourth-century synagogue. The southern limit of the colonnaded street is marked by the **Emesa (Homs) gate**, of which little remains.

Eating Aside from the *Apamee Cham Cafetería* on the site itself, a rather expensive place selling tea/coffee, cold drinks and limited snacks (as well as a few souvenirs, books and film), there are only a couple of simple (and rather uninviting) places in the modern village on the main road where you can buy falafel sandwiches and the like. This is a good place to come armed with your own picnic.

Transport **Microbuses** run from the south microbus station in Hama via Mahardeh (for Qalat Sheizar) to the town of As Qeilebiyeh (S£20, 45 mins). Change here to pick up a second microbus to Qalat Mudiq (S£10, 10 mins). Departures are fairly frequent for both legs of the journey, although you should make sure that you set off for the return journey well before nightfall, and bear in mind that services are much less frequent on Fri.

North from Apamea

From Apamea you can continue due north through the Al Ghab to join after around 35 km the road between Aleppo and Lattakia, 7 km to the east of the town of **Jisr al-Shughur** (for details of this town and the route between Aleppo and Lattakia, see page 366). Following this route you also have the option of diverting off it to climb up into the Jebel Ansariye to the hill resort of **Slunfeh**.

To do the latter, take a small left turn 4 km to the north of Apamea and follow this road west. After a further 6 km, go straight over a crossroads at the village of Al Karim, to arrive at a T-junction 7 km further on (17 km from Apamea). Turn right here to head north. After just under 6 km you pass a right turn in the village of Mardash signposted for 'Afamea' and 'Al Rasief'. Just over 12 km further on, turn left (signposted in Arabic only). This road climbs steeply in a long series of switchbacks up into the mountains and then follows the line of a ridge, with various viewpoints providing spectacular views out over the Al Ghab and beyond (providing that it is not too hazy). You pass some radio transmitters on the left and soon after begin to descend to the town of Slunfeh (see page 305).

If you continue north past the left turn climbing up into the mountains, after approximately 4 km, a little way beyond a small artificial lake on the left, the ruins of **Qalat Burzey** come into view, up on the mountainside to your left. This 12th-century Crusader castle finally fell to Saladin during the remarkable campaign he conducted in the summer of 1188 in which the Crusader

Orontes Valley

presence in Syria was greatly weakened. The site appears to have been occupied more or less continuously since the Seleucid era, although today even the Crusader remains are fairly minimal. It is a steep scramble up to the ruins, and although they are not that impressive in themselves, there are excellent views out onto the Al Ghab. You can continue north on this road to join the Aleppo-Lattakia road just west of Jisr al-Shuhgur.

Masyaf مصياف

Masyaf is famous for its strikingly located and well preserved Ismaili castle. The old part of the town is also quite attractive, with its interesting medieval mosque, a lively market and a couple of khans, and is worth wandering round if you have the time. A major restoration and conservation project is planned for both the castle and the old town, to be funded in part by the Aga Khan Trust for Culture.

Phone code: 033
Colour map 1, grid B2

From Hama, follow directions as for Qalat Sheizar and Apamea, and then bear left instead of right at the signposted junction just after crossing the railway line (7 km from the centre of Hama). Continue straight on this road, heading west through fertile, open farmland to arrive in Masyaf, 42 km from Hama. Approaching Masyaf, the Ismaili castle looms up impressively above the plains, framed by the backdrop of the Jebel Ansariye. Both the castle and the old town are situated towards the northern edge of Masyaf.

Ins & outs

The origins of this castle are by no means clear. The Hellenistic, Roman and Byzantine architectural fragments which have been recycled in its existing fabric indicate that some sort of defensive structure existed here long before its rise to fame as an Ismaili stronghold in the 12th century. In 1103 it was captured by the Crusader Raymond St Gilles, and in 1127-28 it was purchased by the Banu Munqid clan who had by then entered into a loose treaty of non-aggression with the Crusaders. By 1140 it had been taken over by the Ismaili Assassins (see page 274), for whom it became an important strategic centre and one of a number of castles in the Jebel Ansariye in which they took refuge from Sunni persecution. In 1176 the newly established Ayyubid ruler Salah ud-Din (Saladin) laid siege to Masyaf, in an attempt to put an end to the wave of assassinations they were carrying out against Sunni leaders, including himself. However, he broke off the campaign rather suddenly, having apparently finally succumbed to the threats of the Assassins (see also page 274) and subsequently some sort of mutual agreement even appears to have been established between them. It was only a century later that the Assassins were finally ousted from their stronghold by the Mameluke Sultan, Baibars, in 1270.

The castle

In its present form the fabric of the castle is essentially Ismaili, as can be seen from the typically small, irregular stonework employed in its construction. Traces of earlier Crusader construction can also be seen in places, distinguished by more regular stonework employing larger blocks, as well as the occasional recycled classical column section laid horizontally to reinforce the walls. Entry to the castle is from the south side through a vaulted passage; note the large arch just inside the door, resting on Byzantine-period Corinthian capitals. The outer defensive walls and towers enclose a central keep. Although fairly ruined inside, there are still numerous passages and rooms to explore, and great views out across the plains from the central keep. In all, it is probably worth devoting at least an hour to visiting the castle. Of particular interest are the huge underground cisterns and chambers along the eastern side of the outer defensive walls. At the time of writing these still had to be fully excavated in order to determine exactly when they date from.

Orontes Valley

■ *Open 0800-1800 in summer, 0900-1500 in winter. Entry S£150 (students S£10). In practice this little visited castle is often kept locked; it may be necessary to ask around in order to find the caretaker.*

Sleeping   *Masyaf Tourist Hotel*, PO Box 3, just to the south of Masyaf, T713449, F711450. To get
& eating   there, head out of town as if for Krak des Chevaliers and after around 1 km take the
right turn signposted for Wadi al-Ayoun, Dreikish and Tartus; the turning for the hotel
is around 100 m up on the right. Formerly used by the military, this large old French
Mandate building has now been converted to a hotel by the municipality. Comfortable rooms with fan, heater, attached bath and balcony. A/c planned. Large shady
gardens with restaurant. Friendly, well run place.

On the Masyaf-Krak road, on the right just before the turning signposted for Wadi
al-Ayoun, Dreikish and Tartus, there is a pleasant restaurant set in large shady gardens
of eucalyptus and pine trees serving the usual range of Arabic food. There are a number of simple restaurants in the old part of Masyaf, close to the castle, where you can
get falafel sandwiches, kebabs etc, as well as a couple of cafés.

Transport   There are regular **microbuses** running between **Hama** and Masyaf (S£15), and less
frequently between Masyaf and **Apamea** (you may need to change in As Qeilebiyeh
for this journey). The microbus station has been relocated to a new site to the north of
the castle, though most microbuses also pick up passengers at the southern edge of
town, on the Masyaf-Krak road. Bear in mind that all services quickly dry up around
nightfall. Services are also much reduced on Fri.

Masyaf to Krak des Chevaliers

Colour map 1, grid B/C2   If you have your own transport, there is a particularly scenic route from
Masyaf to Krak des Chevaliers. Pick up the road heading south out of Masyaf.
After about 1 km you pass a right turn signposted for Wadi al-Ayoun, Dreikish
and Tartus (this road takes you across the Jebel Ansariye to Tartus on the Mediterranean coast; see page 266 for details of this route in reverse). Continuing
straight on along this road, you pass through several small villages, the road
climbing steadily up onto a plateau, until you reach a T-junction, 22 km from
Masyaf. Turn right here and then left soon after to continue south towards
Krak (turning right and then continuing straight on this road takes you up to
the hill resort of Mashta al-Helu; see page 270). Just under 6 km further on,
bear right at a fork and keep following this road. After a further 7 km you arrive
in the village of Nasra (signposted 'Nasira'). Shortly before, Krak begins to
come into view intermittently, in the distance off to the right. Leaving the village, bear left at a fork. Shortly after, you pass a very sharp right turn (the road
to St George's Monastery) followed a little over 1 km further on by the right
turn up to Krak des Chevaliers, 4 km away (see page 258).

Qalat Abu Qobeis   قلعة أبو قبيس

Colour map 1, grid B2   Although in a fairly advanced state of ruin, the beautiful setting for this small
castle on the eastern slopes of the Jebel Ansariye with its spectacular views
down onto the plains below, along with the particularly scenic drive to get
there, make it well worth visiting.

Ins & outs   Pick up the road heading north out of Masyaf and after 5 km take the right turn signposted for Deir Mama (going straight leads up over the Jebel Ansariye via Qadmus to
Banyas on the Mediterranean coast; see page 277). This small road skirts along the
edges of the mountains with views down onto the plains below. Note that the

Too hot to handle?

After the death of the great Zengid ruler Nur ud-Din in 1174, there followed a brief power struggle between his son, Al Salih and his nephew Salah ud-Din (Saladin). The latter quickly took possession of Damascus before marching on Aleppo where Al Salih had taken refuge. Al Salih meanwhile enlisted the help of the Assassins to try to kill Saladin. They were only too pleased to oblige, Saladin's championship of the orthodox Sunni Muslim cause against the various Shi'ite 'heresies' making him a natural enemy.

The first attempt on his life came early in 1175 when a team of Assassins penetrated Saladin's camp and attacked him, only narrowly failing to kill him. The next time, in 1176, it was only the fact that Saladin had taken to wearing extensive body armour that he again survived the attack. These two attacks prompted Saladin to lay siege to Masyaf in an attempt to stamp out the Ismaili threat once and for all.

In the event, however, Saladin soon abandoned the siege. Various explanations have been put forward as to why. According to one, the change in policy was the result of the mediation of the prince of Hama, who was an uncle of Saladin and on good terms with his Ismaili neighbours. According to another, Saladin's presence was urgently needed in the Bekaa valley following a Crusader attack there. The most colourful explanation, however, is one which neatly illustrates the deep fear bordering on superstition which the Assassins inspired at that time. Shaken by the two previous attempts on his life, Saladin had taken elaborate precautions to protect himself. Nevertheless, one night he awoke to catch sight of a figure leaving his tent, and found on his bed some hot cakes of a type commonly baked by the Assassins, a dagger and a piece of verse carrying the words 'You are in our power'. Believing that the leader of the Assassins, Rashid ud-Din Sinan (the 'Old Man of the Mountain'), had himself carried out this daring and seemingly impossible raid, Saladin lost his nerve and promptly lifted the siege. Whatever the reasons, it is a curious fact that Saladin never again launched a direct attack on the Assassins, despite the fact that in his eyes they represented a heretical branch of Islam.

In a similar vein, Bernard Lewis, in his book The Assassins, relates a story told by Kamal ud-Din, Sultan of Cairo from 1218-38: "My brother told me that Sinan sent a messenger to Saladin and ordered him to deliver the message only in private. Saladin had him searched, and when they found nothing dangerous on him he dismissed the assembly, leaving only a few people, and asked him to deliver his message. But he said; 'My master ordered me not to deliver the message unless in private.' Saladin then emptied the assembly of all save two Mamelukes, and then said; 'Give your message'. He replied; 'I have been ordered only to deliver the message in private.' Saladin said; 'These two do not leave me. If you wish, deliver your message, and if not, return.' He said; 'Why do you not send away these two as you sent away the others?' Saladin replied; 'I regard these two as my own sons, and they and I are as one.' Then the messenger turned to the two Mamelukes and said; 'If I ordered you in the name of my master to kill this Sultan, would you do so?' They answered yes, and drew their swords, saying; 'Command us as you wish.' Sultan Saladin was astounded, and the messenger left, taking them with him. And thereupon Saladin inclined to make peace with him and enter into friendly relations with him."

Orontes Valley

signposts for villages along this road appear several kilometres before the villages themselves; distances given here are to the approximate centre of each village. You pass first through the Alawi village of Deir Mama (5 km from the Masyaf-Qadmus-Banyas road) and then 3 km further on, entering the village of Al Laqbeh, turn right over a small bridge (going straight takes you into the centre of the village). Continue along this road, passing through the village of Qrayiat (2 km further on) and then after a further 4.5 km, fork left in the centre of Deir Shmail (signposted for Abu Qobeis). Soon after, the road descends almost to the level of the plain. Six kilometres beyond the fork in Deir Shmail, you arrive at a crossroads in the village of Saqliyeh. Turn left at the crossroads (signposted for 'Abo Kbais'). The road winds its way up through a beautiful wooded valley, passing several restaurants on the left, idyllically situated by the side of a stream (these are only open for the summer, closing down for the winter by around the end of Oct), before arriving in the village of Abu Qobeis, 5 km from the crossroads in Saqliyeh. A sharp left turn in the village leads up to the castle itself, 2 km away. From the road-head it is a short, steep climb up to the castle.

Along with Qadmus and Qalat al-Kahf high up in the Jebel Ansariye to the west, this castle was purchased by the Ismaili Assassins from a local emir, Ibn Amrun of the Banu Munqid clan, in the mid 12th century. Previously it had been occupied for a time by the Crusaders (who knew it as *Bokebeis*), and even when it came under the control of the Ismailis, they continued to pay an annual tribute of 800 gold pieces as well as a quantity of wheat and barley to the Hospitallers of Qalat Marqab. Most of what can be seen today dates from the period of Ismaili occupation, with the ruins bearing their distinctive hallmark of small, irregularly shaped stonework. Roughly circular in shape, the castle consists of an outer defensive wall with five towers and a central inner keep. A quick circuit of the area between the walls and keep reveals the existence of several large underground storage chambers. Some scrambling is involved to get in to the inner keep, which covers a tiny area and consists of a jumbled maze of half-ruined rooms, walls and vaulted chambers, as well as a crumbling tower. Most of all, however, it is the stunning views out over the plains to the east, along with the picturesque setting amidst olive groves, which make the visit worthwhile.

Abu Qobeis to the coast

Colour map 1, grid B1/2   The road from Saqlieh up to the village of Abu Qobeis continues west, following a very beautiful narrow, wooded valley to climb up into the mountains, leading eventually to the Mediterranean coast just north of Banyas. At the village of Ad Delieh, 21 km from Abu Qobeis, you can bear left (ask directions as the turning is not obvious) to make a detour to the ruins of Qalat Maniqa (or continue straight for the direct route to the coast). The ruins are above the village of Wadi al-Qalaa, 6 km beyond Ad Delieh. Just beyond the mosque in the village a set of concrete steps leads up the mountainside to the castle, a steep 15-minute climb.

Qalat Maniqa   Dating originally from the early 11th century, the construction of this castle is generally attributed to a local family. In the course of its history it appears to have been passed back and forth between the Ismailis and the Crusaders (who knew it as *Malaicas*), an example of the close but ambiguous ties which developed between the two. Thus, soon after being acquired by Rashid ud-Din Sinan, the leader of the Ismailis sometime between 1160-80, it came under the control of the prince of Antioch, Bohemond III, who subsequently entrusted it to the Hospitallers in 1186. However, before long it was back in Ismaili hands, and remained so until they were finally driven out by the Mameluke sultan, Baibars, in 1270-3.

The castle is strung out along a ridge running northeast-southwest, although today all that really remains are the outer defensive walls which can be best appreciated from outside; with a little bit of scrambling, you can also complete a circuit along the top of the walls. Inside, most of the area has now been cultivated. Towards the northeast end are the most substantial remains. Most of the fortifications were concentrated here, including the keep and a watchtower, as this was the weakest point in the castle's defences, being easily approached via a connecting spur. Nearby, there are several large, vaulted underground chambers, two of which appear to have served as stables.

Returning to the road and continuing west, just beyond the village of **Wadi al-Qalaa** you pass behind a waterfall gushing down from overhanging cliffs. The countryside around here is very beautiful, the steep, terraced valley given over to tobacco as well as olives and figs. Turn left at a T-junction 6 km further on to rejoin the main road between Abu Qobeis and the coast (this junction is 8 km from Ad Delieh by the main road, and the turning is signposted to Wadi al-Qala). Soon after, the road passes through the village of **Dweir Baabda**, which spreads over a considerable area. The final section of this route is rather confusing (or at least I seem to get lost every time). Basically, as long as you are going downhill, you cannot really fail to end up intersecting with the coastal motorway, or else with a smaller road which runs roughly parallel to it for a while; if in doubt, keep asking for directions to Banyas.

Qasr Ibn Warden قصر أبن وردان

Around 60 km to the northeast of Hama are the unique and remarkable Byzantine ruins of Qasr Ibn Warden. Out on the desert steppe at a point where ever less frequent patches of cultivation begin to give way to uninterrupted desert, this dramatic and austere setting provides a sharp contrast to the fertile irrigated Al Ghab region to the northwest of Hama.

Colour map 1, grid B3

Head north from the centre of Hama along the Aleppo road and turn right into Ziqar Street (at the crossroads just north of Omar Ibn al-Khattab mosque). After passing under the Hama motorway bypass you are in open countryside. You pass first through the village of Maarshour (15 km) and then Bardoneh (28 km), where there is a right turn signposted for Salamiyeh, 29 km to the south. Continuing straight, the surrounding countryside gradually begins to give way to semi-desert. In the village of Al Hamra (42 km), bear right where the road forks (signposted for Qasr Ibn Warden). The next two villages, Twalid Dabaghein (50 km) and As Srouj (53 km), are interesting for their distinctive 'beehive' houses (see box). Fork left in As Srouj (right takes you southeast to As Sa'en, en route between Salamiyeh and Asiriye; see below), and soon after the striking ruins of Qasr Ibn Warden loom up ahead.

Ins & outs
Distances in brackets are the cumulative distance from Hama

Along with sites such as Rasafeh and Halabiye/Zalabiye, Qasr Ibn Warden appears to have formed part of a network of fortified complexes built by the Byzantines in the sixth century to consolidate their control over Syria and to act as defensive positions against the Persians to the east. Inscriptions have dated the complex to the last years of St Justinian's rule (561-65). What is most remarkable about the buildings is that they display an architectural style which is not seen anywhere else in Syria, but appears instead to have been imported wholesale from the Byzantine capital, Constantinople. Even the building materials are not local, the basalt having been brought a considerable distance either from the north or south, while the marble columns and capitals are thought to have come from Apamea. It has been suggested that as it was set back considerably from the front line of Byzantine defences against the Persians (along the Euphrates), Qasr Ibn Warden was built primarily as a base from which to consolidate control over the Bedouin tribes of the area. The elegance and opulence of the buildings was perhaps intended to inspire a sense of awe and respect for the Byzantine rulers. Thus as well as fulfilling a practical function as the headquarters of an important military commander, Qasr Ibn Warden was perhaps as much a statement in itself, a piece of the grandeur of

History

Beehive houses

So called for their distinctive egg-domed shape, 'beehive' houses were once a feature typical across much of northern Syria and southern Turkey, though they are now becoming rarer with the inexorable spread of concrete construction (heading north from Hama along the motorway you see a few in the surrounding countryside, and also on the route along the Euphrates from Aleppo). The harsh extremes of heat and cold in the region gave rise to the unusual shape of these whitewashed, mud-built buildings, which are surprisingly cool inside during the searing heat of summer, and

equally well insulated against freezing winter nights. Today, most are used only for storage, but in the villages of Twalid Dabaghein and As Srouj they hold their own as traditional dwellings. If you are visiting Qasr Ibn Warden with a guide from Hama, they will undoubtedly arrange for a stop at one of the houses for tea. An electric fan and a TV may supplement the traditionally simple furnishings of rugs, cushions and the all-important family chest, but these villages still provide glimpses of a way of life that goes back centuries.

Orontes Valley

Constantinople recreated in the wilderness of the Syrian steppe, rather in the same way that the Umayyads attempted to make their own mark on the desert with the eastern and western Qasr al-Heirs.

Sights The complex consists of a palace, church and army barracks. Extensive restoration work has been carried out in recent years to both the church and the palace. Of the army barracks (to your left as you arrive at the site), only ruined fragments remain.

The **Palace** consists of a 50 sq m building with a large central courtyard. The south façade of the building, by which you enter, consists of wide bands of large, square black basalt blocks alternating with narrow bands of thin clay brickwork, creating a striking overall effect. The entrance has a frame of carved floral decorations along with Greek inscriptions and a Byzantine cross. Inside, you find yourself in a large entrance hall, with rooms off to either side, and the central courtyard ahead. Note the stone-carved symbols in each room, thought to indicate the function which it served. The first room on the right of the entrance hall for example has a symbol of a wine jar, perhaps indicating that it was a store room of some sort; the significance of the stone slab carved with an eagle in the adjoining room is open to speculation. A set of steps lead up from the right-hand wing to the first floor, probably used for accommodation. The restoration here is incomplete, but the basic plan, in the shape of a cross, is evident. Returning downstairs, in the room to the left of the entrance hall there is a symbol of a set of scales, perhaps indicating some sort of judicial function. This leads through to a set of rooms running down the west side of the courtyard, thought to have served as a school. In the first room there is a stone slab carved with images of a sheep and fish, both potent symbols in the early Christian church. To one side of this is a small room, perhaps the office or residence of the schoolmaster, while on the other side is the main school hall. By the door is a well and an underground passage leading to the northeast, presumably an emergency escape route, also said (more fancifully) to have once linked Qasr Ibn Warden to Anderin 25 km away. Note the central pillars in the shape of a cross. A set of stairs also leads up to the roof from here. The central courtyard is scattered with stone slabs, two of which can be identified as a sundial and calendar, while another was the door to a safe. The rooms along the north side of the courtyard (opposite the entrance hall and adjoining rooms) served as the stables, while along the east side was the baths complex, complete with a well, its 60 m depth protected by a metal cover.

The **Church**, though smaller, is architecturally more interesting. The huge lintel above the main entrance in the south side carries a Greek inscription, along with various symbols. Internally it follows a square plan with a central nave and two side aisles; on the north and west sides an upper-floor gallery of rooms overlooking the central nave still survives; these were reserved for women and reached by a set of stairs in the northwest corner. The north wall gives a good idea of the towering height of the building, although to this you must add the central dome (now collapsed), which would have brought the total height to 20 m. The dome was raised up on a drum, with *pendentives* (triangular segments of a sphere) used to make the architecturally difficult transition from a square plan to a circular dome, a challenge which the Byzantines were only just starting to get to grips with at this stage. ■ *Entry S£150 (students S£10). The caretaker, who lives right by the ruins, has the keys to the palace and church.*

Sleeping & eating The caretaker who lives beside the ruins is an extremely friendly Bedouin sheikh who is quick to extend his hospitality to visitors. You will almost certainly be offered tea, and perhaps a full meal at his house. It may also be possible to stay there overnight.

Transport Getting to Qasr Ibn Warden by public transport is something of a hit-and-miss affair. **Buses** run on an irregular basis from the fruit and vegetable market in Iraq St in Hama as far as the village of Al Hamra. From here you have to hitch or negotiate a ride (traffic is minimal along this last stretch, but anything which does come past will almost certainly stop for you if they have room). In the cooler months this offers lots of potential for a great day out, but in the full heat of summer you may be better off opting for an organized trip through the *Cairo/Riad* hotels, or hiring your own taxi.

Al Andarin
Colour map 1, grid B3

The ruins of Al Andarin, once a sizeable Byzantine settlement known in Latin as *Androna*, are 25 km beyond Qasr Ibn Warden. Thought to have been founded sometime in the second century AD, most of the ruins date from the mid-sixth century. The site is spread over an area of 3 sq km, and includes a large army barracks and a total of 10 churches. Very little remains to be seen today other than the jumbled ruins of the barracks and one church. Unless you have a special interest, it is perhaps not really worth the extra time involved in visiting. Traffic along this last stretch of road to Al Andarin is all but non-existent, making it essential to have your own transport.

Qalat Shmemis & Salamiyeh
Colour map 1, grid B2/3

From Hama a road heads southeast towards the town of Salamiyeh, passing close to the ruins of Qalat Shmemis en route. For details of this route and the castle ruins, as well as the possibility of continuing on to join the main Homs-Palmyra road, see page 171. There are regular bus and microbus services between Hama and Salamiyeh.

Isriye أصريا

Colour map 1, grid B3

From Salamiyeh a surfaced road heads northeast to the Roman temple of Isriye, 90 km away. This road has now been extended to continue all the way to Rasafeh (see page 375). Standing at the crossroads of the ancient caravan routes between Quinnesrin (ancient *Chalcis ad Belum*, to the southeast of Aleppo) and Palmyra, and between Homs and Resafeh, Isriye (ancient *Seriana*) was an important Roman staging post. Today all that remains to be seen is the small but impressive and well preserved *cella* of a third-century AD Roman temple. Built of limestone, it reflects very much the style of Baalbek, with which it is contemporary, particularly in the richly carved decorations around the main doorway and on the relieving arch above it. Inside, a set of stairs embedded in the wall to the right of the entrance gives access to the roof (now collapsed).

Orontes Valley

Much of the public transport running from Homs or Hama to Raqqa on the Euphrates River now uses this desert road, though you will probably be required to pay the full fare for Raqqa. Bear in mind also that the luxury coaches running along this route will not necessarily stop to pick up hitchers. On balance, this is a site for which you really need your own transport. Make sure that you have plenty of water and some food with you, just in case you are stranded with a puncture or breakdown.

Hama to Aleppo

Heading north from Hama, the motorway leaves the Orontes River to the west and begins its journey across the Central Plains, where an annual rainfall of more than 500 mm makes rain-fed agriculture possible, and you will see crops of wheat, cotton and sugar beet.

Maarat al-Numan معرة النعمان

Colour map 1, grid B2 Today the town of Maarat al-Numan is a small, dusty market town which at first sight offers nothing of obvious interest. It is well worth a visit, however, for its excellent mosaics museum, housed in an Ottoman khan. Known to the Greeks as *Arra* and to the Crusaders as *Marre*, the town takes its present name from a combination of these forms with the name of its first Muslim governor, Al Numan Ibn Bashir, a companion of the Prophet Mohammad who was appointed by the Umayyad Caliph Mu'awiya. As a small though relatively prosperous town it has been continually fought over throughout its history and controlled at different times by Damascus, Aleppo and Hama. The most famous (or infamous) episode in its history dates from the time of the First Crusade, when it was besieged by the forces of Raymond de Saint Gilles, Count of Toulouse and Bohemond, Prince of Antioch in 1099 (see box).

Maarat al-Numan also has a less gory claim to fame as the birthplace of the blind poet Abu al-Ala al-Maari (973-1057). Educated at Aleppo, Al Maari twice visited Baghdad where he came into contact with Hindus and adopted vegetarianism. He was recognized as a outspoken free-thinker for his time, even daring to write an artistic imitation of the Koran, an act considered sacriligious by Muslims (though unlike Salman Rushdie he appears to have avoided having a *fatwa* served on him). One of his most famous works provided the inspiration for Dante's *Divine Comedy*.

Sights The **museum** is just to the southeast of the main square (ask around for the 'mat-haf'; locals are used to pointing foreigners in the right direction). It is housed within a huge 16th century khan (the largest in Syria) built by the Ottoman governor Murad Pasha. The building is very impressive, and an ideal setting for the superb collection of mosaics which are displayed both in the central courtyard and also in the arcades and large vaulted halls surrounding it. The mosaics date from the Byzantine period (mostly fifth to sixth century) and come from various nearby 'Dead City' sites. Some of them have been restored, revealing their original, crisp colours. At the far end of the first hall to the right of the entrance is a particularly noteworthy mosaic depicting the legend of Romulus and Remus, the founders of Rome, being suckled by a wolf. At the far end of the next hall (going anticlockwise) is an equally impressive mosaic of a lion killing a bull. In addition, there are some beautiful statuettes, figurines, children's toys, pieces of pottery, coins and glassware dating from the Greek through to Ottoman periods. Unfortunately, the labelling of these artefacts is appalling; the

Orontes Valley

An unholy crusade of cannibals?

From the very beginning, the Crusaders gained themselves a reputation for their barbaric behaviour amongst the inhabitants of Syria, and much of that reputation would appear to have been founded on the horrific events which occured at Maarat al-Numan. Following the fall of Antioch, the Crusaders had been plagued by a shortage of food, their raids on the surrounding countryside in the lean winter months failing to bring in anything like sufficient supplies to feed their large numbers. By the time they laid siege to Maarat al-Numan, many were already dying from malnutrition and starvation. The walls of the town having been breached, as many as 20,000 of its inhabitants are reported to have been massacred, despite assurances from Bohemond that their lives would be spared.

But if such events were common during those times, what happened next was certainly not. In desperation, the starving Crusaders appear to have resorted to cannibalism. In a letter to the Pope one of the Crusader commanders wrote; "A terrible famine racked the army in Ma'arra, and placed it in the cruel neccessity of feeding itself upon the bodies of the Saracens." Another Crusader chronicler, Radulph of Caen, wrote even more explicitly how "In Ma'aarra our troops boiled pagan adults alive in cooking-pots; they impaled children on spits and devoured them grilled." For centuries after, the image of the Crusaders as fanatical cannibals lived on in Arabic literature. Some Arab commentators have even suggested that the behaviour of the Crusaders was born not of necessity, but rather out of fanaticism, their religious fervour leading them to view the Muslims as lower than animals. Thus Amin Maalouf, in his book The Crusades through Arab Eyes, points to the words of the Crusader chronicler, Albert of Aix, who wrote; "Not only did our troops not shrink from eating dead Turks and Saracens; they also ate dogs!".

Orontes Valley

Roman period is identified in some cases, but everything else is categorised as simply belonging to the 'idolotrous' or 'heathen' period. Attached to the khan (though accessible from outside only) is a hammam, still in use today and rather functional, with white ceramic tiles throughout. ■ *Open 0900-1800 in summer, 0900-1600 in winter, closed Tue. Entry S£300 (students S£15).*

Nearby, there is an interesting **mosque**, notable for its minaret, rebuilt after an earthquake in 1170 by the architect Hassan Ben Mukri al-Sarman in the style of the Great Mosque of Aleppo. To get there, turn right out of the museum and head down the main street. At the fourth side-street on your right you will be able to see the distinctive square tower-minaret; weave your way through the souk to reach it. In the courtyard of the mosque, the large pool for washing is particularly unusual. The water cistern itself is octagonal in shape, with 10 column sections topped by Corinthian capitals (clearly of Roman or Byzantine origin) supporting a dome on a 10 sided drum. Also in the courtyard is a smaller domed structure and a deep well. Close to the mosque is the **Madrassa Abu al-Farawis**, built by the same architect in 1199.

If you head northwest out of Maarat al-Numan on the road to Ariha, around 2 km from the centre you will pass on your left the remains of the original **citadel**. Consisting of a circular settlement surrounded by a dry moat, you can still see sections of the older, larger stonework dating from the Crusader period, interspersed with smaller, later stonework.

Transport

Regular **microbuses** and 'hob-hob' buses run to Maarat al-Numan from both Aleppo (from the Pullman/City Bus Station) and Hama (from the south bus/microbus stations) for S£15-20. It is a good couple of kilometres from the motorway exits into the centre of Maarat al-Numan, so try to avoid catching a Hama-bound service from Aleppo, or vice-versa, as these will drop you off by the side of the motorway

Around Maarat al-Numan If you have your own transport you can visit a number of Dead City sites to the northwest of Maarat al-Numan, including Bara and Serjilla. For details of these and the routes to reach them, see page 360.

Ebla (Tell Mardikh) تل مرديخ

Colour map 1, grid B2 Ebla is one of those sites, alongside Ugarit and Mari (Tell Hariri), which has provided a vital key to our understanding of Syria's ancient history, revealing the existence of a major Bronze Age civilization which was all but completely lost from the historical record. Excavations here in the 1960s and 1970s have placed Ebla firmly on the map. Yet the site itself is one which relies mostly on imagination if it is to inspire. For those not so inclined, and with no specialist interest, there is simply very little to see. A visit first to the museum at **Idlib** (see page 356), as well as those at Aleppo and Damascus, does, however, give an excellent insight into Ebla's significance.

History Excavations began at Tell Mardikh in 1964, carried out by an Italian team under the leadership of Paolo Matthiae from the University of Rome. By 1968 evidence of a substantial settlement had been uncovered, as well as a statue dating from around 2000 BC with an Akkadian inscription mentioning the name of a king, Igrish-Khep, of Ebla. Then in 1975 came the remarkable discovery of the Royal Palace and the virtually intact archives containing around 17,000 clay tablets inscribed in cuneiform script. These archives were invaluable. They provided unprecedented insights into a major civilization whose existence had only been guessed at until then, and they established beyond doubt that this was indeed Ebla, a once powerful and independent Bronze Age urban civilization.

The earliest stages of settlement at Ebla can only be guessed at, but it is now clear that the development of urban civilizations in southern Mesopotamia in the late part of the fourth millennium BC was mirrored also in Syria. By the mid-third millennium BC Ebla was flourishing as an important and distinctive urban civilization with a firm agricultural base supporting a population of up to 30,000. Its fame as a source of wood, textiles and metals was the basis for its wealth, fuelling lucrative trade which extended into Anatolia, Mesopotamia, southern Syria and beyond. Indeed, fragments of Egyptian alabaster vessels were found in the Royal Palace, along with quantities of lapis lazuli and tin (for smelting with copper) from Afghanistan, although it is likely that these were traded with Ebla through intermediaries. Politically, Ebla also wielded considerable influence, negotiating on equal terms complex treaties with neighbouring powers and even receiving a substantial tribute payments of gold and silver from Mari.

Some time around 2250 BC Ebla was attacked and largely destroyed by the first great Akkadian king, Sargon, or by his grandson, Naram-Sin. Nevertheless, it survived as an urban centre, now under Akkadian influence, and flourished once again on a more modest level from around 2150-2000 BC, later falling under the orbit of the local kingdom of Yamkhad, centred on Aleppo, before being finally destroyed in the wake of the Hittite invasions around 1600 BC.

By the time the Egyptian Pharaoh Thutmoses III marched through here around 1500 BC en route to the Euphrates, it was probably completely in ruins. During the ninth and eighth centuries BC there was a small fortified Aramaic settlement here, and the site was also occupied on an insignificant scale during the Persian through to Byzantine periods. The ancient city of Ebla,

The biblical controversy

The discovery of the Ebla archives brought with it a flurry of speculation as to their content and the light they might shed on our understanding of this period of history. Based on some early, tentative translations, the so-called 'biblical archaeologists' (those who seek to find archaeological evidence establishing the veracity and chronology of the Bible) leapt to a number of conclusions which have provoked severe controversy and animosity amongst experts. Essentially they argued that the tablets provided strong evidence to suggest that the people of Ebla were early ancestors of the Hebrews. Many of their claims were subsequently demonstrated to have been based both on erroneous readings of the texts and on somewhat creative historical distortions.

One of the most famous claims to emerge was that the names of the five Cities of the Plain mentioned in Genesis 14:2 (Sodom, Gomorrah, Admah, Zeboiim and Bela/Zoar) all appeared on one tablet, and in the same order. This claim was subsequently shown to be false, with the names of only two of the cities possibly appearing on a tablet (the others having been mis-readings). Similarly, the frequent occurence in the tablets of a word translated as 'Ya' was interpreted as meaning 'Yahweh', the Hebrew word for God, although closer examination suggested that the word was more likely to represent the pronoun 'he'.

It was also suggested that many of the names of the early patriarchs appeared in the tablets, and even that one of the kings of Ebla was a distant ancestor of the Jewish patriarch Abraham (thus leading to the assertion that the people of Ebla may have been the ancestors of the Hebrews). However, as J Pettinato points out: "Even if it were true that the study of proper names at Ebla left room for possible comparisons with the proper names in the Old Testament, at times subsequent to those of Ebla, there is no justification for regarding the Eblaites as ancestors of Israel. That the northwest Semitic proper names of Ebla should bear inherent characteristics which render them comparable with the proper names of all other northwest Semitic civilisations is too obvious to occasion any surprise or wonder."

Another claim was that the Ebla tablets recounted the biblical stories of the creation and the flood. The creation story turned out to centre on four lines of poetry which had not even been successfully translated, while the flood story had been built up around a single word which was translated as 'water'!

Leaving aside the early errors of translation, and the fact that any translation of the tablets relies to a certain extent on interpretation, the claims of the biblical archaeologists are more fundamentally flawed in terms of chronology. Thus the Ebla archives mostly date from around 2300 BC, while the age of the patriarchs is put at around 1000 BC. As Pettinato comments; "We cannot relate people historically who are at least 1000 years apart. It is impossible." P Matthiae made the point somewhat more graphically in a letter to the Telegraph, ridiculing the assertion that the tablets make references to biblical events or characters as being on a par with announcing the discovery of Roman documents referring to events and characters of the Renaisssance in Florence.

Nevertheless, the whole episode prompted accusations from the Syrian authorities of a Zionist plot to hijack the findings emerging from the translation of the Ebla archives, perhaps with the ultimate aim of making territorial claims on Syria. On the other hand the Syrians were accused of influencing decisions as to which tablets should be translated and published. The painfully slow pace at which translations are published has also been taken as evidence that the international team of experts, placed in an extremely delicate position, are effectively suppressing their contents.

Orontes Valley

meanwhile, was gradually completely buried under centuries of accumulated debris and the land eventually given over to agriculture, its existence only revealed once again to the world by the excavations carried out in the 1960s.

The Ebla Archives Despite having been stored on wooden shelves which were largely destroyed by fire during the Akkadian attack, the archives, although strewn across the floor in rooms below the Royal Palace, appear to have been in roughly the same order as they had been stacked before the burning shelving collapsed.

The majority of the Ebla tablets are written in the Sumerian cuneiform script. The term 'cuneiform' is taken from the Latin *cuneus*, meaning 'wedge', after the distinctive wedge-shaped impressions characteristic of this form of writing. However, the archaeologists' work was further complicated by the fact that while the Eblaites used written Sumerian, their spoken language (Eblaite) was fundamentally different; it was essentially Semitic in character, although its exact relationship to other Semitic languages such as Akkadian, Amorite and Hebrew is still a matter of conjecture. Around 80% of the words appearing on the tablets are straightforward Sumerian (although 'straightforward' is perhaps somewhat misleading, given that this language and script is still only partially understood by experts). Of the remainder, the scribes of Ebla appear to have adapted the Sumerian cuneiform script to express words in Eblaite. Given the intrinsic differences between the two languages, translating the tablets was an imperfect science to say the least (in much the same way as writing Arabic words in English is problematic), and it is in this respect that the tablets are particularly difficult to decipher. Moreover, the cuneiform script was progressively modified over time, with a set of conventions lasting for a certain period, though without ever becoming fully standardized or being clearly separated from those of another period. Add to this the fact that the scribes left no spaces or separating marks between the words and it starts to become clear just how problematic and open to interpretation the process of translating the texts really is. At least the Eblaites generally wrote the words in the order that they were meant to be read, something of an improvement on earlier Sumerian practice!

The vast majority of the texts are of an administrative nature: economic records of the production and trade in textiles, metals, agricultural goods etc. The remainder consists of lexical texts listing the Sumerian words for various objects, in some (though by no means all) cases with the Eblaite equivalent alongside, a few political and geographical texts and some literary texts. The political and geographical texts have been the main source of controversial claims regarding links with the Old Testament (see box), while the literary texts appear to consist of copies of older Sumerian texts as well as some purely Eblaite texts which have not as yet been translated.

Sights Extending over an area of 56 hectares, the site is dominated by a central mound or acropolis on which the Royal Palace stood, along with various religious and administrative buildings. Surrounding this was a large residential area, of which nothing survives, and surrounding the whole settlement was a stone perimeter wall with earth foundations 60 m thick. Parts of the lower acropolis, including stairs leading up past the famous archives to the Royal Palace have been reconstructed to give some idea of what the buildings would have looked like. Most impressive visually are the excavated foundations of a monumental gateway in the perimeter wall to the southwest of the acropolis.

■ *Open summer 0800-1900, winter 0800-1700, closed Tue. Entry S£300 (students S£15). A small booklet on the site is available. There is no shade, nor were there any refreshments facilities at the time of writing, so bring a good supply of water and adequate protection from the sun in summer.*

The Coast and the Jebel Ansariye

7

244

The Coast and the Jebel Ansariye

Syria's Mediterranean coastline extends north-south for over 180 km, marked by the Turkish border to the north and the Lebanese border to the south. Today the fertile coastal plain is intensively farmed, with large swathes given over to shimmering polythene-covered tunnels nurturing fruit and vegetables all year round. The two main coastal towns, **Tartus** and **Lattakia**, contrast sharply: Tartus still a small, relaxed provincial town, while Lattakia has become a thriving, vibrant city. Unfortunately, the beach resorts along the coast fall well short of most visitors' expectations: an unhappy combination of unplanned development and widespread pollution.

Running parallel to the coast is the **Jebel Ansariye** range. Isolated from the rest of the country, this is the least visited region of Syria and also the most beautiful; a detailed exploration is well worth the effort involved. A relatively narrow strip of mountains stretching for around 125 km from north to south but nowhere more than 30 km wide from east to west, the landscape varies from gently undulating terraced hills supporting olive groves, tobacco and rich fruit orchards, to rugged, steep and inaccessible mountains clad in thick forests with peaks of over 1,500 m. The tiny **villages** tucked away in hidden valleys and the ubiquitous olive groves give much of the area an almost Tuscan or perhaps Provençal feel, but it is the numerous Ismaili and Crusader **castles**, some in a near pristine state of preservation and others mere crumbling ruins, that bring you back from the western Mediterranean to the eastern magic of these mountains.

A foot in the door

★ Standing head and shoulders above all the other sites along the coast and in the mountains is the Crusader castle of **Krak des Chevaliers**. This is one of the great highlights of Syria, and easily the most formidable of the Crusader castles to be found anywhere in the Middle East.

★ The Jebel Ansariye mountains are home to numerous others, with **Qalat Marqab** and **Qalat Saladin** being the most famous and impressive after Krak.

★ Of the lesser known castles, **Qalat al-Kahf** is a great one for those who wish to get right off the beaten track; not much survives of the castle itself, but the setting (if you manage to find it) is truly magical. Indeed, in many ways it is the beauty of

these mountains as much as the sights themselves which make exploring this region so rewarding.

★ **Tartus** is a small, pleasant coastal town with an inviting, atmospheric old city area, and sea trips out to the tiny island of Arwad.

★ There is nothing of great note in the city of **Lattakia**, though its outward-looking, cosmopolitan ambience provides an interesting contrast with the rest of Syria.

★ The journey between **Lattakia and Aleppo** is perhaps the only instance in Syria where it is well worth going by **train**, as this line is efficiently run and offers excellent views of the mountains.

Ins and outs

Exploring the mountains

Even if you follow our route descriptions carefully, your chances of getting lost are quite high. On the other hand (as always in Syria), you can be sure of plenty of help if you need it

Travelling up and down the coast is easy and straightforward, but the mountains present more of a challenge. Tartus and Lattakia make good bases from which to explore the Jebel Ansariye; the major places of interest (Krak des Chevaliers, Safita, Qalat Marqab, Qalat Saladin) can all be reached fairly easily by public transport. Bus and minibus services also operate to more remote areas but tend to be pretty erratic, while finding out about them can be a challenge in itself. Having said that, if you have plenty of time and patience, it is certainly possible to get around the mountains using a combination of public transport, hitching and the odd bit of walking.

In order to explore this area in any detail, however, you really need your own transport. Even then, the greatest challenge is actually finding your way around. An intricate web of tiny roads criss-cross the region, and navigating them is made all the more difficult by the absence of any really accurate maps or consistent signposting. The best available map is in fact the Ministry of Tourism free hand-out entitled *The Coast*. This covers the whole coastal strip along with the Jebel Ansariye, extending as far east as the Al Ghab plains (thus including Masyaf, Apamea, Jisr al-Shuhgur etc). Unfortunately, however, in places the sheer density of tiny roads makes it very difficult (and in some cases, impossible) to read.

Over the last few years, the quality of the roads in the mountains has improved dramatically, with many of them having been widened and resurfaced. Nevertheless, there are still plenty of extremely narrow and heavily pot-holed roads (or worse still, sudden changes from one to the other). Together with the steep gradients and endless sharp twists and turns (not to mention the hazards of playing children or wandering animals), this makes for some extremely demanding driving conditions in places. Take care!

NB The route from Qalat Abu Qobeis west across the mountains via Qalat Maniqa to Banyas is dealt with in the Orontes Valley and Central Plains chapter (see page 234).

Best time to visit

With their higher elevation, the Jebel Ansariye provide a welcome escape from the intense heat and humidity which engulfs the coast during summer. However, spring and autumn are really the best times to see the mountains. During spring the countryside is resplendent with the colours of wild flowers, while in autumn the air hangs heavy with the fragrance of freshly pressed olives. Admittedly, more rain falls during these periods, but it tends to come in short, sharp bursts so that the gloom of low-hanging clouds quickly lifts, and the air turns crisp and clear. The heaviest rainfall occurs during winter, it can get bitterly cold (even down by the coast) and the highest peaks are snow-capped.

History

The Jebel Ansariye have historically acted as a barrier, with the Homs Gap, to the south of Tartus, providing the only easy access between the coast and the interior. As a result, the coast is culturally very distinct from inland Syria, its development linked to events in the Mediterranean basin rather than the Fertile Crescent or desert to the east. The success of the Phoenicians, who established a string of important city-states along the coast during the second to first millennium BC, was based firmly on maritime trade throughout the Mediterranean and indeed, all along the coast, wherever its natural features allowed for even the smallest of harbours, settlements have existed since ancient times. It was along this coast that the Crusaders established their foothold in the region during the medieval period, building castles up in the mountains to protect the corridor formed by the coastal plain and so allowing them to move between present-day Turkey in the north and Jerusalem, their ultimate goal and reason for coming to the region, in the south.

As well as presenting a natural barrier separating the coastal strip from the interior of Syria, the mountains have also served as a place of refuge for religious minorities facing persecution. Indeed, they take their name from one such group, the Alawis, also known as the 'Nusayriya' or 'Ansariya' (see box, page 304). Similarly, the Ismaili Assassins (see box, page 274) took refuge here during the 10th century, consolidating their military strength by building a series of castles in much the same ways as the Crusaders.

Tartus طرطوس

To visiting Syrians, Tartus is something of a beach resort, though this is a point on which few foreigners would agree. Yet despite rapid expansion in recent years, and the dominance of the large port facility to the north of the town, Tartus is not without its charm. It may not be the sleepy little fishing port it was a decade ago, but it is still a friendly, laid back place. The medieval old city area provides an interesting labyrinth of alleyways and passages to wander round and although parts of it have been restored, it still feels 'lived-in'. The imposing Crusader Church of Our Lady of Tortosa is essential viewing, and the small island of Arwad, a few kilometres off shore, provides an enjoyable half-day trip.

Phone code: 043
Colour map 1, grid C1

Ins and outs

There are 3 main luxury coach companies serving Tartus, all with ticket offices/bus stops in the centre of town, or within easy walking distance of the centre. *Kadmous* offers the most comprehensive and frequent services. For local destinations and places up in the surrounding mountains you must go to the bus/microbus station, a little under 2 km to the east of the sea front and town centre. Near to this is the rarely used train station.

Getting there
See also 'Transport'
section, page 255

For the most part Tartus is small enough to explore on foot. Taxis are readily available should you need them, or you could flag down a local 'servees' (microbus) if it is heading in your direction. The **tourist information** office is rather inconveniently located

Getting around

around 2 km to the south of the bus/microbus station and train station, on 6 Tishreen Ave (as in '6 October'; the date of the 1973 'October War of Liberation' better known as the Yom Kippur War), T223448. Open 0800-1800 (in practice there is only a token presence here after 1400), closed Fri. They can provide you with a free Ministry of Tourism map/pamphlet, but are otherwise of very little help.

History

In a classic example of the tail wagging the dog, Tartus really owes its existence to the small island of **Arwad** (ancient Greek: Aradous), some 3 km off shore from the modern city. In fact the town's name reflects this subservient status, being derived from anti-Aradous, or opposite Aradous. (For details of the history of Arwad island, see 'Sights', below.) The town was established by the **Phoenicians** (and called Antaradous) to act as a kind of service base for the more secure Arwad island. This situation continued following Alexander the Great's capture of both town and island for the Greeks in 330 BC, and the imposition of Roman rule in 64 BC. In fact, it was not until the **Byzantine** period (324-638 AD) that Tartus began to outstrip Arwad in importance. The deciding factor in the change is said to be the emperor Constantine's preference for the mainland Christian population over the pagan inhabitants of Arwad island. Tartus subsequently became known as Constantia, though the name does not appear to have stuck. The association of Tartus with the cult of the Virgin Mary, revived during the Crusader period, is attributed to the town's early Christian population, and there is reason to suppose that the chapel built here before the fourth century is one of the first in the region dedicated to the Virgin Mary.

The collapse of the Byzantine Empire in the seventh century saw the town fall into **Arab** hands, though the town was briefly recaptured in 968 AD when Nicephorus Phocas attempted to revive the moribund Byzantine Empire. However, by the time the **Crusaders** arrived from Europe in 1099, the town had been taken over first by the Fatimids (from Egypt), and then had fallen under the control of the Emir of Tripoli.

Excepting the town's recent development and transformation into Syria's second port, the most important era in Tartus' history was the medieval period. Tartus was of immense strategic value to the maritime Crusader forces, and though the port was lost to the Muslims almost as quickly as it had been gained in 1099, a concerted effort by Raymond, Count of Toulouse (at the head of the Genoese fleet) saw Tartus recaptured in 1102. He subsequently set about turning the town into a fortified stronghold, renamed **Tortosa**. In addition to the fortress, work also began on the construction of the Church of Our Lady of Tortosa.

However, divisions within the Crusader community allowed **Nur ud-Din**, the Muslim ruler of Aleppo, to capture the city briefly in 1152; an event which led Baldwin IV, king of Jerusalem, to hand over control of the city to the Knights Templar. Despite their formidable military reputation,

Crusader fortress

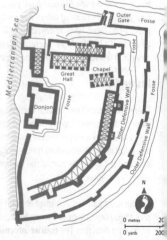

the Templars did not appear to have learnt the lessons of their Frankish predecessors, and in 1188 Nur ud-Din's nephew, Salah ud-Din (Saladin), was able to capture and sack most of the town. The Templar garrison survived by retreating into the *donjon* of the fortress, from where they managed to hold Salah ud-Din at bay. Following the withdrawal of the Arab army, the Templars set about refortifying not just Tortosa but the surrounding countryside as well, building a network of castles that guarded the approach to their coastal stronghold. Tortosa withstood several prolonged assaults by the Mameluke sultan, Baibars (1267, 1270), though the fall of the Templars' stronghold of Acre (in modern-day Israel) in 1291 meant that the writing was on the wall for the Crusader presence in the Holy Land. The Templars rapidly withdrew to Arwad island, and though they maintained a garrison there for the next 12 years, they were hardly able to influence events on the mainland; by 1303 the last of the knights had withdrawn to Cyprus.

Few details are known about the town's subsequent history, though it appears that most of the town may have been destroyed as early as the 14th century. Its revival began under the Ottomans (1516-1917), who used both Tartus and Arwad as a base, though the town's real expansion must be credited to period of post-Syrian independence. Tartus is now Syria's second port (after Lattakia), with a growing industrial sector.

Sights

Tartus' principal attraction is the remains of its the medieval city. Effectively, this actually means the Crusader fortress, an area covering little more than 500 m by 500 m. What makes it so interesting though is way in which the local population has blended the old with the new, adapting Crusader walls and vaults into integral parts of their homes. This is no carefully landscaped museum piece but a living community, warts (well, rubbish then) and all. Tracing the lines of the original Crusader buildings is rather problematic given the number of later additions, and you will probably be quite content wandering round the narrow alleyways, through the arches and vaults, and just seeing what turns up round the next bend. The open square in the centre is a great place to stop for a cup of tea, watch the comings and goings, and soak up the atmosphere. The most impressive remains identifiable today are those of the lower storey of the main **keep**, or *donjon*, facing the sea. This has now been restored and is used to host exhibitions and special events. When there is nothing on, you will just have to try your luck and see if you can find someone willing to show you round the huge vaulted halls inside. The former **chapel** is difficult to locate, it is hemmed in by contemporary dwellings, and in an advanced state of disrepair. When the fortress was constructed, the sea almost certainly extended right up to its walls. The *glacis* of the **southwest tower** of the outer city wall can be seen to the south of the fortresss, where Al Wahda Street meets the Corniche (it now has a model windmill on the top).

Old City

The fortress-like appearance of the church, with its heavily buttressed walls, is no accident: it was meant as much as a defensive structure as a place of worship. Originally there was a square tower at each corner, though today only those at the eastern (rear) end of the church remain, complete with their narrow arrow slits. The entrance façade to the west features a central arched doorway, with twin-arched windows above, topped in turn by a third smaller one. To either side, arched windows mark the north and south aisles. In the northwest corner is a small octagonal minaret, added in the late 19th century, although there is no eveidence that the church was ever actually converted into a mosque.

Church of Our Lady of Tortosa & museum
A thoroughly imposing piece of Crusader architecture. Though work began on it in 1123, much of what you see today actually dates to the 13th century

If possible, the interior is even more imposing than the exterior, austere yet beautiful with its massive pillars, soaring arches and barrel-vaulted ceiling towering above you. It follows the traditional triple-apsed basilica plan, with a central nave flanked by side-aisles. The symmetry of the church is broken only by the cube-shaped base of one of the pillars dividing the north aisle from the nave. It is thought that this was the result of an attempt to incorporate an earlier chapel dating from the Byzantine period into the plan of the Crusader church.

In turn the church has served as a mosque and a barracks, but is now used as a **museum**. Although poorly labelled (only in Arabic or English, if at all), there are some interesting exhibits. On the left as you enter is a series of striking marble coffins dating from the Phoenician period (fifth to fourth century BC), carved in the shape of human figures with carefully sculpted faces, each with different features and remarkably realistic expressions of serenity. The left-hand side-aisle contains fragments of sacrificial statues from Amrit (also

Tartus

To Port

Mediterranean Sea

To Arwad Island (3 km)

To Grand Hotel, Hawaii Restaurant & Al Manara Tourist Village

To Karnak Coach Office
To Cliapatra Hotel & Internet Centre (300m)

| 0 metres | 200 |
| 0 yards | 200 |

■ **Sleeping**
1 Al Baher
2 Ambassador
3 Antradous
4 Blue Beach

5 Daniel
6 Raffoul
7 Rawda
8 Republic
9 Shahin

10 Shahin Tower
11 Sihaya (Tourism)

● **Eating**
1 Al Nabil

fifth to fourth century BC), various pieces of pottery and a case of Stone Age tools. In the side-apse at the end is a large terracotta urn with various smaller jars arranged around it. Occupying the central apse is a massive marble sarcophagus dating from the Roman period (late second to early third century AD), its proportions every bit as imposing as the church itself. Tomb robbers made a hole in the rear, understandably enough electing not to try and lift the lid. Dotted around the central nave are various ornately carved capitals, a headless marble statuette of Bacchus with the obligatory grapes in hand, and a couple of other headless statues. The right-hand side-apse contains three mosaics from Jableh, all unfortunately with large sections missing; that of Psoiden, goddess of the sea, is most striking in that her face and most of her body still survive. The right-hand side-aisle contains a mixture of artefacts spanning 13th-14th century BC Ugarit through to the Islamic period. Dotted around the church grounds are numerous architectural fragments, as well as some statues and sarcophagi. ■ *Open 0900-1800 in summer, 0900-1600 in winter, closed Tue. Entry S£300 (students S£15).*

Jamal Abd al-Naser

To Coastal Motorway

To Tourist Information (2 km) & Amrit

2 Al Seraj
3 Al Yamak
4 Café
5 Cave
6 Cheap Restaurants
7 Sahara
8 Sary Express
9 Tee Tak
10 Venicya Pizza

Arwad Island

The tiny island of Arwad, measuring just 800 m by 500 m, has had a significant impact on this section of the Syrian coast. Indeed, Tartus owes its very presence to the existence of this island. The short boat trip out here is fun, while the island's narrow, twisting lanes which wind their way through densely packed houses make aimless wandering a delight. Unfortunately, however, the lack of any waste disposal facilities means that rubbish is just dumped on the beach, awaiting the high tides that take it ashore at Tartus; a most unappealing sight.

History The island appears to have been first settled in the third millennium BC by the Canaanites, though it subsequently became a pawn in the battle for hegemony between Pharaonic Egypt and the Hittite Empire. Arwad subsequently passed through the hands of the Assyrians, Chaldeans and Persians, when it formed part of the coastal Phoenicia province. Faced with the Greek invasion around 330 BC, the Arwadi fleet joined the Persian navy, though Alexander the Great's forces were too strong and the island fell. Nevertheless, Arwad enjoyed a degree of autonomy until the Romans annexed it in 64 BC.

The Coast & the Jebel Ansariye

The island declined in importance during the Byzantine period largely as a result of the development of Tartus, though the Muslim armies saw Arwad's strategic significance and constructed two small fortresses during the Crusader/Ayyubid period. The Knights Templar briefly occupied Arwad following their retreat from the mainland. Turkish troops refurbished the fortresses as barracks during the Ottoman period, with the French Mandate authorities later using them as prisons for those fighting against colonial rule.

Visiting the island You can quite happily spend a couple of hours randomly exploring the island's narrow lanes, perhaps having lunch at one of the many quayside restaurants, as well as checking out the two forts on the island. The first, generally referred to as the **Ayyubid fort**, is on the east side of the island (close to the harbour and clearly visible as you arrive). It is at present closed to visitors, and although officially undergoing renovation, the last three years or so have seen no progress on this front. On either side of the main gateway are carved reliefs of lions tethered to palm trees.

The **central fort**, reached by following the narrow lanes inland (west) from the harbour, is worth a visit. The original wooden doors, clad in steel bands, are still in place. As with the Ayyubid fort, the gateway is flanked by reliefs of lions tethered to palm trees, though these are more worn and faded. Inside, there is a green and shady courtyard and garden with large date palms growing in it. The fort doubles as a **museum**, with the displays housed in the rooms surrounding the courtyard. At the time of writing, these were being restored and refurbished. The fort also incorporates a small mosque, with its square tower-minaret and the two white domes of the prayer hall rising up from the roof, while another section is occupied by the local Ba'ath party. The battlements, with their distinctive crenellations topped by small pyramid-shaped decorations, together with the small overall size of the fort, give it the feeling almost of a model. ■ *Open 0900-1800 in summer, 1000-1600 in winter, closed Tue. Entry S£150 (students S£10); once the refurbishment is complete this may rise to S£300/15.*

At the northern edge of the island, huge weathered blocks of stone can be seen at the water's edge, remnants of a **Phoenician defensive wall**.

■ *Boats leave regularly for Arwad from the jetty of the small fishing harbour. The trip takes 20 minutes. You pay the fare of S£20 on your return from the island (last boat back is around sunset). Note that the island gets particularly busy on Fridays and public/religious holidays.*

Beaches

Syrian women bathe fully clothed, and any western women brave enough to run the gauntlet of the rubbish and raw sewage in the water will soon become the centre of attention (even in a one-piece bathing suit). Bikinis are a definite no-no. A swimming costume beneath a T-shirt is the absolute minimum you will get away with

The amount of rubbish strewn across the beaches, plus the clear evidence of raw sewage being pumped into the sea, deters most foreign visitors from viewing Tartus as a beach resort. In addition to this, at the time of writing the towering hulks of several grounded container ships washed up during storms the preceding winter could be seen at various points along the sea front. The prohibitive cost of refloating these ships, combined with the fact that they are now good for little more than scrap (if that), has left many local residents gloomy about the prospects of them being removed. Although they make for quite striking silhouettes, environmentally they are about as welcome as the raw sewage. None of this, however, deters Syrian holiday-makers, who come here in large numbers for their Mediterranean experience. Fridays are particularly popular, with numerous charabancs parked up along the sea front, with picnics and barbecues on the go, and families enjoying the surf. To the south of the town centre is the *Hawaii* restaurant, with two freshwater swimming pools and changing rooms (see 'Eating', below). To the south of this again is *Al Manara Tourist Village*, a complex of chalets with its own private stretch of supposedly cleaner beach. Further south, the coast is lined with private chalets.

Essentials

A *Shahin Tower*, Tarek Ibn Zaid St. New project by owners of *Shahin* hotel, still under construction at the time of writing, but scheduled to open by summer 2001. Once open, it will be the largest and most luxurious hotel in Tartus, with 156 rooms, 2 restaurants, coffee shop, bar, nightclub and conference/banquet facilities.

C *Grand*, Corniche, T315681, F315683. Reasonably comfortable rooms in odd colours with a/c, TV, phone, fridge and en suite bath. Rooms at front have balconies and sea views. Restaurant, coffee shop, bar. A little overpriced for what you get. Try bargaining. **C** *Al Manara Tourist Village*, Corniche (just over 1 km to south of centre), T323571, F327644. Family-orientated complex of chalets and apartments. Smaller units consist of bedroom, kitchen and bathroom; larger ones also have a sitting room, and some have an extra bedroom. All with a/c, TV, phone and balcony or terrace. Fairly comfortable and spacious (recently refurbished, but already showing signs of wear and tear). Gets very busy during high season (Jun-Oct), and especially on Thu and Fri (prices higher, booking necessary). Excellent value off-season (E/F category). Large restaurant hall, various children's facilities. Unfortunately, at the time of writing the beach here was rather spoiled by a couple of grounded container ships slowly rusting away. **C** *Antradous*, Ath Thawra St, T322488, F312712. Comfortable, clean and pleasantly furnished rooms with a/c, TV, phone, sink, hob, fridge and attached bath. Also 'suites', with separate sitting room/kitchenette area, and larger suites with 2 bedrooms, sitting room and kitchen. Well run and good value for level of facilities, especially with low season (Oct-May) discounts. Meals served. Restaurant planned for roof. **C** *Shahin*, Tarek Ibn Zaid St, T221703, F315002. Rooms with a/c, TV, phone, fridge, attached bath and small balconies. Much needed refurbishment planned once its sister hotel, the *Shahin Tower*, is open. Good restaurant on top floor. **D** *Al-Baher*, Corniche, T221687. Rather basic rooms with fan, TV, phone, attached bath and balcony. Rooms at front with pleasant sea views, but otherwise somewhat shabby, run down and overpriced. Restaurant.

E *Cliapatra* (sic), Ath Thawra St, T220915. Simple, reasonably clean rooms with fan, phone, rather decrepit attached bath and small balconies (but no views). Quick to offer discounts down to F category, but even then it's not very good value, and the location isn't up to much. **E/F** *Ambassador*, Tarek Ibn Zaid St, T220183. Simple but clean rooms with fan, attached bath (rather decrepit) and balconies overlooking the sea and fishing harbour. Overpriced for what you get, though prices fall considerably in low season. **E/F** *Blue Beach*, Tarek Ibn Zaid St, T220650. Essentially an identical set-up to the *Ambassador* next door, but a bit more run down. **F** *Daniel*, Al Wahda St, T312757, F316555. Simple but clean rooms with fan, heater and attached bath (single S£350, double S£600). Very friendly and welcoming family-run place, managed by Elie, whose enormous energy and enthusiasm for the job deserves a special mention. Excellent value breakfasts. Boat trips arranged to a small island to the south of Arwad (summer only). Recommended.

G *Raffoul*, Al Kowatli 1 St (up on 2nd floor, opposite Church of Our Lady of Tortosa), T220616. Small (10 rooms), friendly hotel. Simple but clean rooms with fan, phone and balcony. 4 rooms with attached bath, rest share bath. Single S£200, double S£400. The owner's main business is the small grocery store (T220097) on the corner below the hotel; enquire here if the hotel is locked. Good value. Recommended. **G** *Rawda*, Al Wahda St, T220639. Very basic rooms, some with fan, share shower/toilet. Dirt cheap at S£100 per bed, but equally grotty and dingy. **G** *Republic*, Al Wahda St, T223580. Very basic but cleanish rooms with sink and balcony. Share reasonably clean shower (hot S£35) and toilet. Single S£175, double S£275. An OK budget choice, but not a lot of English spoken. **G** *Siyaha (Tourism)*, entrance in 29 May St, just off Al Wahda St, T221763. Basic but cleanish and light, airy rooms with balcony. Share shower (hot S£25) and toilet. Double room S£250, or S£100 per bed in shared room. Friendly family-run place, probably the best of the rock-bottom cheapies.

Eating   Predictably enough, fish is popular here, though it is not cheap. If you wander past the fish market in front of the harbour, you can get an idea of what is available (and perhaps go for some self-catering). Prices vary significantly according to the type of fish, and the season. The cheapest period is from mid-Oct to mid-Nov, when it is excellent value.

Expensive/mid-range   *Al Yamak*, Corniche (on 4th floor of Chamber of Commerce, the large modern building adjacent to the southwest tower/windmill; the entrance is on the east side, not on the Corniche itself), T328755. Open 1200-late, 7 days. Smart, spacious place. Reputedly one of the best fish restaurants in Syria, and a favourite haunt amongst politicians, VIPs etc. Around S£500 per head and up for fish, depending on current market prices, or if you steer clear of the fish you can have an excellent value, high quality meal (Arabic cuisine) from around S£200 per head. Alcohol served. Live music in evenings and Fri afternoons. *The Cave*, Corniche, T221016. Open 1200-late, 7 days. One of the oldest restaurants in Tartus, set in a wonderfully atmospheric vaulted chamber which forms part of the 'Old City'. Seafood is the speciality here, though they also serve meat dishes (European cuisine). From around S£500 per head upwards. Alcohol served. *Sahara*, Corniche, opposite fishing harbour, T220220. Open 1200-late, daily. Recently opened fish restaurant. Seating indoors (slightly tacky décor), or outside on pleasant patio. *Shahin*, on top floor of *Shahin* hotel. Good quality Arabic cuisine from around S£300 per head. When the *Shahin Tower* hotel opens, it will include a couple of suitably up-market restaurants. There are a number of pleasant seafood restaurants on Arwad island.

Cheap   *Al-Nabil*, Al Wahda St, T222557. Rather basic place serving a standard range of Arabic food, plus fish. From around S£250 per head upwards. Have developed a habit of overcharging tourists, especially for fish, and the food is pretty mediocre, but the outdoor seating is pleasant in summer, and they serve beer. Agree a price before ordering. *Al Seraj*, tucked away on a side street off Ibrahim Hanano St. Open 1100-late, closed Fri. Small, friendly and spotlessly clean place serving the usual range of Arabic food (around S£200-250 per head for a full meal), as well as pizzas (S£125-150). Alcohol served. *Hawaii*, Corniche, to south of town centre (around 500 m south of *Grand* hotel), T318238. Open 1200-late, 7 days. Restaurant in large, simple hall with views overlooking sea. Standard range of Arabic cuisine for around S£150-200 per head, or more for fish. Also with a couple of rather dilapidated-looking concrete swimming pools (open in the summer only). Aimed very much at Syrian tourists. *Tec Tak*, Corniche, opposite fishing harbour. Open 1100-late, closed Fri. Simple but clean diner-style restaurant/snack place offering the usual mezzes, shish tawouk etc, as well as fish (to order), steaks and snacks such as pizzas, burgers etc. Around S£150-200 per head for a meal, or S£50-100 for snacks. Alcohol served (local beer S£40). *Venicya Pizza*, Tarek Ibn Zaid St, (next door to *Ambassador* hotel). Standard range of Arabic cuisine for around S£200 per head. Paradoxically, no pizzas. Alcohol served.

Seriously cheap   *La Younak*, Ahmad al-Azawi St, near *Shahin* hotel, T326086. Open 1100-late, daily. Snack bar downstairs, or sit-down restaurant upstairs. Clean, a/c place run by a Lebanese-Australian. Good value pizzas from S£115 upwards. *Sary Express*, Al Wahda St (below street level, diagonally opposite *Daniel* hotel). Unremarkable-looking diner/fast-food place, but clean, friendly and good value. Pizzas S£50-180, burgers, hot dogs, shish tawouk S£40-120. On **Ath Thawra St**, just to the south of the clocktower, there are several cheap take-away places for falafel, shwarma, half-chicken etc. On **Al Wahda St** there are a couple of good snack places where you can get mannoushi and other small savoury pastries, as well as the usual shawarmas. In the central square of the '**Old City**' there are a couple of simple snack places; the one next door to the mosque does particularly good fatteh, in addition to hummus, fuul and falafels.

Bars & cafés

Many of the restaurants in Tartus serve beer. *The Cave* restaurant has its own bar; they don't serve Syrian beer here, but a small bottle of *Lazizza* costs S£75, and there is a full range of spirits. The *Al Seraj* restaurant is another pleasant place to come for a drink. A bottle of Syrian beer costs S£40 here, or they also have *Heineken*, *Al Maaza* and *Lazziza* for S£50-65. The *Café Moulin A Vent*, on the Corniche (below the *Blue Beach* hotel), stands out as a nice place to sit with a tea, coffee or nargileh, read a book or watch the world go by. Other pleasant cafés can be found further north along the Corniche, and in the central square of the '**Old City**'.

Shopping

Anyone after truly awful kitsch souvenirs should try the stalls on Arwad island

Evening strolling and window shopping are popular in Tartus (mainly in streets branching off west and southwest of the clock tower), though the town is hardly a shopping paradise. There is a hard currency *Duty Free Shop* on al-Mina St near the port, selling alcohol, cigarettes, perfume etc. In a small kiosk on Khaled Ibn al-Walid St, you can buy beautiful model sailing ships, painstakingly built to scale with full working rigging and near perfect detail. Prices, however, are not cheap (US$500-1,000 depending on the size). Note that the afternoon siesta in Tartus is rigorously enforced and almost all shops close down for a couple of hrs, usually between 1400 and 1600.

Transport

Luxury coach *Kadmous* operate from a yard on Jamal Abd al-Naser St, T312829. Tickets can be booked up to 2 days in advance. **Damascus** (via Homs), hourly, S£110, 4 hrs (**Homs** S£40, 1 hr). **Aleppo**, 0630, 0900, 1130, 1330, 1630, 2100, 2330, S£115, 4 hrs (NB these coaches stop in either Homs or Hama en route; **Hama** S£65, 1½ hrs). **Lattakia**, every 10-15 mins (small bus), S£25, 1 hr. **Banyas**, every 10-15 mins (small bus), S£12, 30 mins. **Hassakeh** (via Homs, Palmyra and Deir ez-Zor), 1230, 2330, S£275 (**Palmyra** S£105, **Deir ez-Zor** S£190).

Al Ahliah has its ticket office/bus stop on Ath Thawra St, to the south of the centre, T222983. **Damascus**, 0600, 0730, 1215, 1430, 1715, S£100. **Lattakia** (small bus), 0815, 1100, 1330, 1430, 1600, 1730, 1930, S£30. **Homs/Hama**, 0815, 1530, 1815, S£40/70. **Aleppo**, 0645, S£120.

Damas Tour has its ticket office/bus stop on a small side street just to the west of Ath Thawra St, in the centre of town, T315100. **Damascus**, 0630, 0830, 1200, 1430, 1630, 1930 (Fri 0730, 1000, 1200, 1430, 1630, 1830, 2000, 2130), S£110. **Lattakia**, 0630, 0900, 1100, 1630, 2130, S£30.

Amal has its ticket office/bus stop on Al Mahatta St, from where it operates small buses to **Homs** (S£30) and **Banyas/Lattakia** (S£12/30), departing every 30 mins in both directions.

Karnak has its ticket office/bus stop at the southern end of Tarek Ibn Zaid St, around 1 km to the south of the *Shahin* hotel (the office is on the right, just after you cross a broad street with a strip of park running down the centre, and is marked by a sign reading 'Travel & Tourism'), T313210. Local microbuses run the length of Tarek Ibn Zaid St from the *Shahin* hotel southwards. Note that the *Karnak* office has moved several times over the last few years and may well move again (or close down altogether). **Damascus** (via **Homs**), 0700, S£100 (Homs S£40). **Tripoli/Beirut**, 0700, S£100/150.

Bus/microbus station On 6 Tishreen Ave. Transport from here operates on a 'depart when full' basis and consists of a mixture of microbuses and old 'hob-hob' buses. There are regular departures for **Safita** (S£12, 45 mins); **Dreikish** (S£12, 45 mins); **Sheikh Badr** (S£15, 45 mins); **Wadi al-Ayoun** (S£25, 1 hr); **Masyaf** (S£30, 1½ hrs); **Al Hamadiyyeh (for Amrit)** (S£5, 15 mins). You can also catch services to **Lattakia**

(direct or via Banyas and Jableh) and **Homs** from here. In addition, *Kadmous* operate buses to **Tripoli** (S£100) from here.

Service taxis These depart from the clock tower in the centre of town for **Damascus**, **Tripoli/Beirut** and **Lattakia**, though demand is fairly slack and it can take some time for them to fill up.

Train You would have to be a really dedicated rail buff to insist on taking the train to or from Tartus, with services now having dwindled to just one weekly in either direction. **Lattakia**, Thu, 1930. **Damascus**, Fri, 2445.

Directory **Airline offices** *Syrianair*, junction of Al Aruba 2 and Al Orouba, T326088. **Banks** The branch of *Commercial Bank of Syria* on Al Orouba St changes cash and TCs (open 0800-1200, closed Fri). There is another branch on Al Wahda St, open 1200-1400, 1600-1800 (in theory at least), closed Fri. **Communications** **Internet** At the time of writing there was one internet place in Tartus, the imaginatively named *Internet Centre*, Ath Thawra St (around 300 m off our map; on the right as you head south, just before you get to the *Cliapatra* hotel), T/F315906. Open 0900-2300 (this is perhaps a little optimistic?), closed Fri. Small, friendly place, 4 terminals, S£3 per minute. **Post** The post office is located on the corner of 6 Tishreen Ave and Jamal Abd al-Naser St (open 0800-2000, Fri 0800-1400). **Telephone** The telephone office is located on Ath Thawra St, just north of the *Kadmous* bus station. You can buy phonecards here and use the cardphones outside. There are also a couple of cardphones outside the post office. **Medical services** There is a good private hospital, the *New Medical Centre*, just off 6 Tishreen Ave, to the south of the railway station and bus/microbus station, T317319. There are several pharmacies around town, including the *Al Iman*, opposite *Daniel* hotel, and *Pharmacy Hajjar* on Al Orouba St. **Visa extensions** Ministry of Interior, Dept of Immigration and Passports, off Andalos St, to the east of the large park (see map). Open 0800-1400, closed Fri. You need to bring your passport, 2 photos, and then buy a form with an excise stamp on it (S£30) from the office on the 1st floor. Take the form to the 2nd floor, fill in a couple of forms and your extension will be issued on the spot. This is one of the more efficient places at which to get your visa extended.

Amrit عمرت

Colour map 1, grid C1 The site of Amrit, some 7 km to the south of Tartus, is a reminder of this stretch of coastline's early appeal to settlers. Several monuments remain from a number of different periods in the settlement's history, though it has to be said that unless you have a particular fascination with the archaeology and architecture of the periods concerned, Amrit is only of limited interest.

Ins & outs If you have your own transport, head south along Ath Thawra St, until you reach the right turn for Amrit, clearly signposted a little under 5 km from the centre of Tartus. Going by public transport, take an Al Hamadiyyeh bound microbus (S£5, 10 mins) from the bus/microbus station on 6 Tishreen Ave, and get off at the fork for Amrit. Follow this tree-lined road, passing the 'Biological Pest Control/Citrus Board' centre on the left after 400 m, and then the entrance to an army camp, also on the left, after a further 500 m. Having crossed a small bridge over a dried up stream (the Amrit/Maratos River), take the dirt track to the left where you see a sign on the right reading 'Rest Camp' (400 m beyond the army camp entrance). This track takes you to the caretaker's building, from where a path leads to the temple compound, stadium and tell.

It is not possible to walk directly across to the meghazils, situated to the south (the area is fenced off). Instead you must continue south on the paved road. After passing a sign announcing 'Amrit Touristic Project Phase I', the road bends round to the left and then you arrive at a gate on the left (just over 1 km from the 'Rest Camp' sign). Just inside are a couple of modern buildings and a path leading to the meghazils. The caretaker here will probably try to lend you his torch, for which he will expect some payment when you return (there is no official entrance fee for either part of the site). To return to Tartus, if you continue along the paved road you will rejoin the main road after a further 1 km, from where you can flag down any passing minibus.

The earliest remains here are located on the *tell* (mound) and date to the end of the third millennium BC. Some archaeologists suggest that the settlement here was founded by the Amorites as one of the many harbours that they established along the Syrian coast, whilst others contend that it was founded as a mainland religious centre by the Phoenicians of Arwad island.

Amrit reached its peak between the sixth and third centuries BC, with the religious buildings being heavily influenced in style by the Achaemenid Persians (who in turn borrowed freely from Egyptian and Mesopotamian architecture). Alexander the Great is believed to have rested here in 330 BC whilst his army marched on to Damascus, with the settlement taking the Greek name of Marathos. Amrit's subsequent history is not entirely clear. It has been suggested that it was wrestled from the control of the Arwadis in the second century BC, and that when they returned in 140 BC they destroyed it. Others suggest that Amrit gradually lost its importance with the expansion of Antaradous (Tartus) and was eventually abandoned.

The caretaker doesn't get many visitors, so he is keen to show guests around and share a cup of tea

The key attraction at the site is the **temple compound**, which dates from Amrit's era as a Phoenician religious centre. The temple compound comprises a 3 m deep sacred basin (38 m by 48 m) that was dug to form an artificial lake sometime in the late fifth or early sixth century BC. It was fed by a network of canals that delivered water from a spring that was believed to have healing properties. The floor and sides of the basin are made of natural rock and are unlined. At the centre of the basin stands a 5.5 m high platform hewn from the bedrock, upon which stood the central altar. It is topped by an Egyptian-style cornice. The basin is surrounded by a wide pavement which originally had colonnaded arcades on the south, west and east sides. Part of the colonnade, consisting of monolithic rectangular slabs, has been reconstructed. Whilst the general design on the temple compound strongly reflects Egyptian and Mesopotamian influences, the remains of a number of sixth to fourth century BC statues found in the basin have strong Greek and Persian characteristics. So possibly the temple had a number of dedications; the god Melqart (later assimilated in the Greek period with Hercules); the Egyptian god of healing, Echmoun; or indeed one of the many gods derived from the Baal root.

To the north of the temple compound the outline of a small **stadium** (230 m by 30 m) can be seen. Lines of seating are visible on the north and south sides, whilst two paths on the east side suggest an entrance and an exit. The west side was used as a quarry. Dating the stadium has been problematic. It is generally believed to be Hellenistic, dating to the fourth century BC, though some sources have suggested that it may have been the venue for a sporting event hosted by the ancient Syrians in the 16th century BC that the Greeks later adapted and called the Olympic Games!

Amrit

To Tartus

To Tartus
Army Camp
Communications Towers
Stadium
al-Amrit River (Maratas River)
Temple Compound
Tell (Mound)
Rock Cut House
Sign Saying 'Rest Camp'
Caretaker's Building
Sign Announcing 'Amrit Touristic Project'
Meghazils
Buildings
Al Qubil River
Mediterranean Sea
N
0 metres 300
0 yards 300
--- Fence
To Lebanese Border

The Coast & the Jebel Ansariye

The **tell** of the original settlement is located just to the east of the temple compound, though it is generally pretty unremarkable. The same can be said of the **rock-cut house** to the southeast of the tell. A number of artefacts found at the site can be seen in the modern building occupied by the caretaker.

Much of the area to the south of the temple compound is part of the Phoenician cemetery. Of particular note here are two giant funerary monuments, known locally as **meghazils** (spindles). The first is 7 m high, cylindrical, and features four lions carved in the Persian style around its base (unfinished). The second is a little smaller at 4 m high, and formerly featured a 5-sided pyramid at the top. Both have underground burial chambers below, with *loculi* cut into the walls. There is a third meghazil nearby (not within the bounds of our map), but it lies close to a military installation. The barrels of various heavy artillery pieces are visible sticking out from amongst the trees and undergrowth; be careful where you point your camera.

Krak des Chevaliers (Qalat al-Husn)

قلعة الحصن
Phone code: 031
Colour map 1, grid C2

Krak des Chevaliers (known as 'Qalat al-Husn' in Arabic, literally Castle of the Citadel) is certainly the best preserved and most impressive of the Crusader castles anywhere in the Middle East, and something of a must see for visitors to Syria. Although its setting is not quite as spectacular as some of the others in the area, the sheer scale and complexity of Krak's fortifications and its near perfect state of preservation will leave you breathless and speechless the first time you set eyes on it. And you will be in good company: TE Lawrence, who visited no fewer than 49 castles in a whirlwind tour of the region during a summer's vacation from Oxford, described it simply as "the finest castle in the world...quite marvellous".

Ins and outs

Getting there
There are a couple of more interesting and extremely scenic routes to Krak: one from Safita (see page 269) and the other from Masyaf (see page 232). Both are well worth trying if you have your own transport

Krak can be comfortably visited as a day-trip from Homs, Hama or Tartus, or there are a number of options for staying overnight in the vicinity of the castle, which allows you to enjoy it at sunrise and sunset, when the light is at its best. In any case, it is well worth making the effort to arrive early; by late morning coach loads of organized group tours will have arrived from Damascus and you will suddenly find yourself sharing Krak's splendours with hordes of other tourists.

By **public transport**, Homs is the easiest place from which to reach Krak, with direct microbuses (S£25) all the way to Al Qalaa village, just below the castle, making the journey in under one hour, although given the better accommodation situation in Hama, many travellers choose to stay there, which only adds another 30-45 mins for the trip to Homs. From Tartus there are no direct buses so you must catch a bus towards Homs, get off at the turning for Krak (ask for 'Qalat al-Husn'), and then hitch or wait for another bus from there; there is plenty of traffic, so you will not have to wait long. The last microbus back to Homs generally leaves at around 1500-1600 in summer, and around 1400 in winter, but check this and err on the side of caution as services vary greatly according to demand. A taxi back to Homs will cost in the region of S£300-350.

Driving, Krak des Chevaliers can be reached most easily by taking the exit off the Homs-Tartus motorway (clearly signposted on overhead signboards for 'Hosn Citadel' and 'Marmarita') and heading north. The exit is 40 km from Homs (or 32 km from the exit off the Homs bypass for the Tartus/Lattakia motorway) and 55 km from Tartus (coming from Tartus, there is another exit 9 km earlier which is signposted less clearly for 'Qalat Hosn' and 'Al Hosn'; ignore this). After leaving the motorway it is a further 15 km to the castle; follow the road for 11 km (ignore the left turn after 4 km signposted 'Al Hosn Castle' and 'Ammar Tourist Resort'), passing through two villages, before taking a rather poorly signposted left turn to climb for 4 km to the castle, passing through the village of Al Qalaa which nestles below it.

Open summer 0900-1800, winter 0900-1600, daily (NB the official government policy of Tuesday closing is waived in the case of Krak as it is such a popular attraction, but in the depths of winter it may be worth phoning the ticket office first just to check; T740002). Entry S£300 (students S£15). Official guides are on hand at the entrance (S£300 for a 1 hour tour). Postcards, booklets on Krak and various souvenirs are on sale at the ticket office (as well as outside, and in the various restaurants nearby). There are toilet facilities just inside the castle, a short way up from the entrance. A torch is very useful for exploring the darker corners of the castle.

History

The castle that you see today is primarily the work of the Hospitallers, who occupied it from 1144-1271. However, as with nearly all the Crusader castles in the Middle East, they occupied and expanded a pre-existing castle, in this case one originally built by the emir of Homs in 1031 and garrisoned by a colony of Kurds. The name 'Krak' is thought to have come from its original name *Husn al-Akrad*, 'the Castle of the Kurds'. Following the Hospitallers' occupation of the castle, it became known as Krak des Chevaliers, Krak of the Knights. Its strategic value lay in its location overlooking the all-important Homs Gap which gave access from the coast to the interior of Syria. Indeed, it has been suggested that the site may have been occupied by the Egyptians during their struggles against the Hittites, which culminated in the famous battle at Kadesh (Tell Nebi Mend) in the 13th century BC.

By the time the First Crusade entered Syria in 1097, the castle was largely deserted. However, with the Christians' imminent approach, preceded by horrific tales of the massacre at Maarat al-Numan (see page 238), the population in the immediate vicinity took refuge inside. Attracted by the provisions that had been stored there, the Crusaders, led by Raymond de St Gilles, laid siege. The inhabitants meanwhile, convinced that they would suffer the same fate as the people of Maarat al-Numan, soon abandoned it after a half-hearted attempt at resistance, slipping out under the cover of night. The Crusaders quickly moved on, however, and the emir of Homs reoccupied it.

In 1110 it was retaken by Tancred, the regent of Antioch, and placed under the control of the County of Tripoli, forming its easternmost outpost. But throughout their time in the Middle East, the Crusaders faced a continuing problem of insufficient manpower, constantly having to spread themselves thinly over a large area, and in 1144 Raymond II, Count of Tripoli, elected to hand over control of the castle to the independent military order of the **Hospitallers**. Nur ud-Din (then the emir of Aleppo and nominally aligned to the Fatimids of Egypt) besieged it in 1163 but was eventually driven back by the combined forces of Tripoli and Antioch. In 1170 the Hospitallers, by now a hugely wealthy and successful outfit, undertook a massive project to enlarge and strengthen it. Over the next hundred years, they transformed what had previously been a strategically located but somewhat insubstantial castle into an impregnable stronghold. So much so that in 1188, when Salah ud-Din (Saladin) was returning from his victory over the Kingdom of Jerusalem at Hattin, he abandoned his siege of it after just one day, concentrating instead on other easier targets in the area, including Tartus, Lattakia and Qalat Saladin.

It was not until 1271 that Krak des Chevaliers finally fell to the Mameluke sultan, **Baibars**, although his success appears to have stemmed as much from subterfuge as from military superiority. After a month of sustained assault, the

☞ ## The Rise of the Crusading Military Orders

"Cursed be he who keepeth his sword from blood," (Jeremiah, 48:10) was a quotation dear to the heart of Pope Gregory VII, under whose tender auspices the concept of Holy War was to become an integral part of Western European medieval life. Crusading clergy and holy men such as Peter the Hermit had acted as inspirational leaders and advisors during the First Crusade (1096-1100), but were hindered by a papal injunction that forbade the spilling of blood by men of the cloth. (In evasion of this unpalatable restraint, monks simply advocated the use of blunt or cudgelling weapons to crush rather than pierce the Unbelievers!) However, a more pragmatic fusion of military and monastic ideals emerged in the early 12th century. The order of the **Templars** was founded in around 1119 by Hugh de Payns, a knight from Champagne commissioned to protect the precarious pilgrim routes between the Mediterranean port of Jaffa and Jerusalem. They were granted a residence in Jerusalem by King Baldwin II, who was desperate to attract Frankish settlers. Situated within the Temple enclosure, the fledgling order became known as "The Poor Knights of Christ and the Temple of Solomon". Part of the popularity of this fresh knightly ideal stemmed from its supervision by the religious genius of the day, Bernard of Clairvaux, life-blood behind the Cistercian monk order. His eulogy of 1128 enthused: "The knights of Christ fight the battles of the Lord with untroubled minds, fearing neither sin from killing the enemy nor danger in their own death, since there is no guilt and much deserved glory in bearing death or inflicting it for Christ." (William Of Tyre, History). The **Hospitallers** (or Knights of St John), for example, who had their origins in a group dedicated to the care of the sick from the time of the First Crusade and hence were older than the Templars, were militarised during the course of the 12th century under Templar influence.

The Cistercian monks' ideal life of poverty, simplicity, purity, and self-denial could not win wars, but, artfully blended with an aggressive and arrogant military discipline it became a potent force. The military orders of the Templars and Hospitallers were to become the storm-troopers of the Church, infamous throughout the Muslim world.

The military orders in Syria Later, the Templars in particular were to add outstanding administrative ability and a legendary cupidity to their military discipline. The combination of the two social ideals had enormous recruiting appeal and as a result the orders accrued manpower, endowments and property in the West enabling the Templars to finance their Syrian adventures.

By 1200 the military orders had acquired territory throughout Syria. The local, often Syrian-born Frankish nobles had 'gone native' and were often keener to reside in luxury at villas on the coast, rather than in the isolated, oft-beleaguered strongholds of the desert. The financial clout and reserves of arrowfodder that characterized the military orders allowed them to assume the burden of defence. By 1140 many of the Crusader castles were in the custody of the orders. In Syria, the Templars held Tartus and the Hospitallers Qalat Marqab (Margat), Qalat Saladin (Saône) and the mighty Krak des Chevaliers.

By the 13th century they were operating in effect as sovereign powers, at times in conflict with each other and even with the Crusader states. The Templars at one point entered into a treaty with the Ayyubid prince of Damascus against Egypt at a time when both the Crusaders and the Hospitallers had entered into a directly opposing treaty with Egypt. Likewise, both were sufficiently powerful in the 13th century to demand tribute payments from the Assassins (see box page 274) as part of a loose treaty of non-aggression and when the Mongols invaded Syria in 1281, the Hospitallers fought alongside them against the Mamelukes. Although the Mameluke Sultan Qalaun soon had his revenge: soon afterwards defeating the Mongols and overthrowing the Hospitaller stronghold of Qalat Marqab in 1285.

Mamelukes had breached the outer walls, although the inner castle still remained intact. Daunted by the sheer strength of these inner defences, Baibars gave up hope of penetrating them by force and, according to some accounts, instead tricked the Hospitallers inside into a treaty of surrender, supposedly forging a letter from the Hospitallers' Grand Master in Tripoli ordering them to surrender. Whatever the exact circumstances, Baibars agreed to allow them safe passage to Tripoli, provided that they left the Middle East for good, and on the basis of this agreement the Hospitallers duly relinquished their castle. By this time they numbered just a few hundred, as opposed to the castle's full complement of 2,000 or so; and it is a tribute to Krak's formidable defences that despite such a paltry number of troops, they were still able to hold out for so long against Baibars, and in all probability could have continued to do so for much longer had they not agreed to surrender.

Under Mameluke control, further repairs and modifications were made to the castle, which they used as a military base. However soon afterwards, with the Crusader threat receding, the castle declined in military importance. Instead, it was occupied by local peasants, who lived within the castle walls until they were finally relocated in 1934 by the French authorities to the present village of Al Qalaa just below. Other than some fairly minor restoration work carried out by the French in the course of clearing the village from within the castle walls, and later by the Syrian authorities, the castle is essentially unchanged from the 12th-13th centuries, an impressive testament to its durability.

Sights

Outer defences Coming from the Homs-Tartus motorway (or else from Masyaf to the north), the final approach to Krak des Chevaliers is from the east, the road climbing up to it through the village of Al Qalaa. If you arrive via the route from Safita, however, the final approach is from the southwest. It is from here that you can get the best overview of Krak des Chevaliers (if you have arrived from the east, it is worth walking round to this point for an overall perspective on the castle before entering).

Built on a spur coming from a higher mountain to the southwest, the basic plan of the castle consists of two concentric defensive walls with bastions and towers encircling a central keep which is integrated with the inner walls. The ditch running between the outer and inner defensive walls could be filled with water, supplied by an **aqueduct** which flowed in from the south and in normal circumstances simply supplied the large reservoir between the walls at the southern end of the castle. The inner defensive walls were built raised up on a huge sloping base, or *glacis*, looming formidably above the outer walls, so that even if the outer walls were breached, the defenders would still occupy a commanding position above their attackers. Along the western side of the castle, the land falls away steeply into a 300 m deep valley, making an attack from this side all but impossible. The outer wall on this side is particularly well preserved (it was in fact never subject to attack), with five identical round towers evenly spaced along its length. The blunt southern end of the castle is its most vulnerable point, because it can be easily approached from the higher ground to the southwest and, consequently, there are more defensive towers on this side.

Inner defences The main entrance to the castle is from the east side, through a **square tower**. Today a modern bridge replaces the original drawbridge which most probably once existed here. Although built by the Crusaders, the lengthy inscription on the face of this tower commemorates the restoration work carried out on the castle by Baibars in 1271. The large **rectangular tower** to the left of it, and also the next one along, are of Mameluke construction. Once through the entrance doorway (note the huge metal-clad door, also Mameluke), a gently sloping **passage** climbs to the left, its low, wide steps designed to allow horses to negotiate it. The vaulted roof provided protection from above, while the opening in it served both to allow light in and to provide the defenders with a vantage point from which to pour boiling oil (or anything else unpleasant they could lay their hands on) onto any attackers who managed to penetrate this far. The first room on the left is part of the Mameluke tower to the left of the main entrance. Today this houses some toilets, while steps lead up to the room above. Continuing up the passage, the long vaulted chamber immediately after is thought to have served as **stables** (you can also get to these from the upper room of the Mameluke tower). Further along the passage there is access to the ramparts above the stables. Both these ramparts and the accompanying arrow slits have been restored. The passage next goes through a sharp U-bend. Instead of following it, bear off through an opening in the bastion in front.

This takes you through into the area between the inner and outer walls. In front of you is a large, stagnant **reservoir** running along the length of the southern wall of the castle, while rising up from it is a steeply sloping **glacis** (or *talus*) built up against the inner southern walls with their three massive towers. Usually such a glacis was meant to prevent attackers undermining the foundations of the walls and causing their collapse. However, since in the case of Krak these were built onto solid bedrock, it has been suggested that it was intended to reinforce the walls against the effects of earthquakes (one had caused extensive damage to the castle in 1170), or to prevent attackers from sheltering under the walls. With a thickness of some 25 m at its base, the glacis presents an imposing edifice; certainly its steep, precisely engineered stonework was enough to dissuade Baibar's troops (who dubbed it 'the mountain') from trying to scale it. The gateway from which you have emerged is set in an octagonal-shaped bastion. The two headless lions facing each other above the doorway (now partially obscured by grass and bushes growing from between the cracks in the stonework) appear at first glance to be Mameluke (the lion was Baibar's insignia). In fact they are Crusader in origin, this bastion having been built in the second half of the 13th century, towards the end of the Hospitallers' time here.

To your left is a complex which once served as **baths**. Dating from the Arab period of occupation, these are now in a fairly advanced state of ruin, the domed roofs of the various rooms all collapsed. Running along the inside of the southern outer wall is a long vaulted chamber which

Krak des Chevaliers

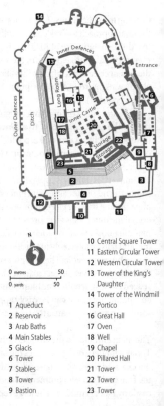

1 Aqueduct	**10** Central Square Tower
2 Reservoir	**11** Eastern Circular Tower
3 Arab Baths	**12** Western Circular Tower
4 Main Stables	**13** Tower of the King's Daughter
5 Glacis	**14** Tower of the Windmill
6 Tower	**15** Portico
7 Stables	**16** Great Hall
8 Tower	**17** Oven
9 Bastion	**18** Well
	19 Chapel
	20 Pillared Hall
	21 Tower
	22 Tower
	23 Tower

probably served as the castle's **main stables**, while above is a square central tower, flanked on either side by circular towers. Before entering the stables, take a look inside the **eastern circular tower**. A single arched window gives impressive views out over the village of Al Qalaa and the plain to the east. This tower, like its counterpart flanking the square central tower on the other side, dates from the time of Baibars. Entering the main stables and walking half way through them, a set of stairs lead down on the left to a secret door (now sealed) in the base of the central square tower. At the far end of the stables, you can gain access via a short passage to the **western circular tower**. The room inside, on the same level as the stables, contains a massive central octagonal pillar bearing an Arabic inscription. Stairs lead up, either from the passage linking the stables and circular tower or from outside, to give access to the ramparts of the outer defensive wall and also to the roof of the stables, from where you can gain access to the **central square tower**. According to an inscription, this was built by the Sultan Qalaun (the successor of Baibars) in 1285, though it probably stands on the base of an earlier Crusader tower. The main room is dominated by a massive central square pillar taking up much of the available space. A spiral staircase leads up onto the roof, from where you can get a good idea of the vulnerability of the southern end of the castle, as well as an impressive view of the glacis and towers of the southern inner wall behind.

Leaving the complex of towers and stables along the southern wall and following the ditch between the inner and outer walls around in a clockwise direction, the whole length of the western inner wall is also faced with a steep glacis. Meanwhile, to your left, you can see the arrangement along the inside of the outer western wall, with a protected gallery running below the upper ramparts. The square tower at the northern end of the inner western wall is known as the **tower of the king's daughter**. Three sets of relieving arches, one above the other, adorn the sheer face of this otherwise plain tower. The lowest of these was not entirely decorative, the arches concealing machicolations from which boiling oil or projectiles could be rained down on attackers. However, modifications carried out to this tower by the Crusaders resulted in it being raised to a higher level. The machicolations were filled in and two sets of blind arches built into the wall above, followed by new machicolations in a different style. Of the three towers in the northern end of the outer walls, the western-most known popularly as the **tower of the windmill** (Bourj al-Tauneh in Arabic), once housed a windmill. The remaining two form a barbican protecting a small postern gate in between, from which the Crusaders could mount surprise attacks against the enemy. Continue all the way round to enter the inner castle via a set of steps. This brings you to the top of the sloping passage by which you first entered, and which you branched off of at the point where it made a U-turn.

A set of steps leads up through a tall gateway into the courtyard of the inner **Inner castle** castle. In front of you is a portico which leads through into the great hall, to your left is a large vaulted area supported by square pillars (often dubbed the 'pillared hall'), and to your right is the chapel.

The **portico** (or *loggia*) is striking in that it is by far the most 'artistic' feature of the castle. Dating from the second half of the 13th century, towards the end of the Hospitallers' occupation, it shows a particularly delicate application of the Gothic style, which had begun to develop in France a century earlier. The façade consists of two arched doorways and five arched windows separated by pilasters. The windows in particular, each with a central dividing *colonnette* and circular *tympanum*, are typically Gothic. An inscription carved in Latin on the extreme right-hand window reads: "*Grace, wisdom and beauty you may*

The Coast & the Jebel Ansariye

enjoy but beware pride which alone can tarnish all the rest." Inside, the delicate ribbed vaulting of the ceiling, divided into seven bays, is also typically Gothic. In the rear wall of the portico are two doorways which lead through into the **great hall** beyond. Dating from the 12th century, this gloomy, austere space is much more in keeping with the typical Crusader style, although it is still essentially Gothic. It would have served as a banqueting and meeting hall. Behind this is a long vaulted chamber, stretching for 120 m along the whole length of the western inner wall, and arcing round at its northern end to terminate at the chapel. Dubbed the **'long room'**, this area served a number of functions, principally as the kitchens and main storage area, but also as accommodation. To the south (left as you enter) there is an old oven, and on the other side of a partition just beyond is a well. At the northern end (right as you enter from the great hall) are what appear to be 12 latrines.

The **chapel** dates from 1142-70, during the first phase of the Hospitallers' occupation. The interior is largely bare of decoration, except for the barrel vaulting, a plain cornice and shallow pilasters. Following the Mameluke occupation, the chapel was converted into a mosque, and you can see the *mihrab* which was built into the south wall. Originally the chapel was entered from the west, but this doorway was bricked up and an external staircase built against this wall, probably by the Hospitallers during their final years in the castle. Climbing this staircase takes you to the northern part of the upper courtyard. From here you can gain access to the **tower of the king's daughter** (which you can see during the tour of the inner defences from the outside). Today this houses an expensive restaurant/snack bar. A narrow spiral staircase leads up onto the roof of the tower, from where there are excellent views (on a clear day you can see Safita to the northwest).

Returning to the lower courtyard, the cavernous vaulted area supported by square pillars (the so-called **pillared hall**) probably served as a general area for cooking, eating, storage and accommodation. At the back (to the south) there are two **storage rooms** one behind the other, both containing huge olive oil storage jars with only their bases remaining, embedded in the ground rather like honeycombs or cocoons. The second room also contains a well. During the Crusader period, all the storage areas of the inner castle were said to contain sufficient provisions to last for five years.

A set of stairs climbing above the doorway by which you first entered the courtyard of the inner castle gives access to the roof of the pillared room. To your right parts of a circular stone structure, the purpose of which is unclear, still remain on the otherwise concreted-over terrace. In front of you is a slightly raised vaulted area, supported by square pillars. A set of stairs leads up to the roof of this, from where you can gain access to the three towers defending the inner southern wall of the castle. The central and left-hand (southeast) towers are the most imposing, their massive bulk designed to take the full brunt of any final assault on the castle. Basically rectangular in shape, the southern face of each is rounded in order to stand a better chance of deflecting missiles fired from the high ground to the south without sustaining serious damage. The right-hand (southwest) tower is circular in shape and much more delicately built. Although it also forms part of the inner southern defences, it is thought to have served primarily as the living quarters of the 'lord' of the castle. A spiral staircase gives access to a light and airy room with ribbed vaulting supported on *colonnettes* built into the walls and a frieze of rosettes running around the room. The roofs of the central and right-hand towers give the best views, both towards Safita to the northwest and the Homs Gap to the south.

Essentials

Of the hotels listed below, only *Le Table Ronde* and *Baibars* are really practical without your own transport. If you do have your own transport, it is also worth considering the various hotels along the road to St George's (see below).

AL/A *Francis*, close to *Amar Tourist Resort*. Still under construction at the time of writing. Similar to *Amar Tourist Resort*, but more luxurious. **B-D** *Amar Tourist Resort*, 4 km southwest of Krak (follow the road around to the west side of the castle and keep going; the resort is on your right, clearly signposted), T730512, F730558. Popular summer resort for Syrian families and visitors from the Gulf states. 14 family apartments each consisting of 2 double bedrooms, kitchen, living room, a/c, TV/dish, attached bath and balcony. Also 2 1-bedroom apartments. Restaurant, café, bar, swimming pool, games room. Gets very busy in peak Jul-Sep season (advance booking necessary); reduced rates off-season. Runs minibus excursions to Krak, St George's Monastery and other sites in the area. Clean, well run establishment. Friendly and helpful staff. **D** *Bebers* (as in 'Baibars'), across the valley to the west of the castle, a little over 1 km from the entrance (follow the road around to the west side of the castle, past the *Al Kalaa* restaurant, and take the right turn soon after), T/F741201. Owned and run by the same family that own/run the *Round Table*. Recently opened (further construction work still ongoing). Pleasant, comfortable rooms with attached bath; those at front with balconies and excellent views of Krak. Also 2 suites (2 double rooms, sitting room, attached bath). Breakfast included in room price. Can arrange car tours using Krak as a base. Friendly, helpful staff. **F/G** *Round Table*, situated around 200 m beyond (south of) the castle entrance, T740280. Primarily a restaurant catering for groups, but also with 4 rooms downstairs each containing 2-4 beds and attached bath. Rather basic and overpriced (S£500 for a double), although bargaining possible. **Camping** is also allowed in the grounds (suitable for tents and camper-vans) for S£125 per persons, which includes use of toilet/shower facilities, or you can sleep on the roof of the restaurant for the same price.

Opposite the entrance to the castle is the **Des Chevaliers**, T740411, with a pleasant shaded patio garden area or indoor seating. Buffet meals consisting of a selection of *mezze* dishes, chicken or meat, and fruit, cost S£250 per person, or S£150 for just the vegetarian *mezze* dishes. The food, however, is distinctly mediocre. Around 100 m beyond (south of) the castle entrance, the **Round Table**, T740280, F741400, offers better quality buffet meals for the same price in more comfortable indoor surroundings, and with a bar. Also just to the south of the castle, but reached by the road that runs around the western side, is the **Towers**, T740697, which again offers buffet meals for S£250 per head (this restaurant is owned by the same family that owns and runs the *Round Table* restaurant/hotel and *Bebers* hotel). Alcohol served. Good views from here of Krak's southern ramparts and defensive towers. Just under 1 km to the southwest of Krak (follow the road around to the west side of the castle and keep going past the *Towers* restaurant) is the *Al Kalaa*, T740493. A 2-storey affair offering good quality meals for around S£250 per head and the best views of Krak. Alcohol served. In the village of **Al Qalaa**, just below the castle, your options are limited to falafels and possibly the odd roast chicken if you are lucky, though a new restaurant, the *Al Nobalan*, was being fitted out at the time of writing.

Sleeping

While all the hotels in this area claim to stay open all year, during the winter months (late Nov to Mar), it is very cold up here &, except in the more expensive places, you may well find them closed, or perhaps with just a token caretaker in residence

Eating

The Coast & the Jebel Ansariye

St George's Monastery

In the valley to the northwest of Krak, visible from the castle's ramparts and towers, is the Greek Orthodox monastery of St George. Although now dominated by modern buildings, this monastery originally dates back to the sixth century, and the reign of Justinian. The modern church, to your right as you enter the main courtyard, dates from 1857. The entrance passage to the church features a delicate triple arch, with the two central supporting columns clearly of Byzantine origin. Inside the church is a beautiful carved wooden *iconostasis*, the gold painted icons depicting various scenes from the life of Christ. The old chapel, probably dating from 13th century, is located beneath the main courtyard, reached by a set of stairs opposite the modern church which leads down to a lower level courtyard. It contains a smaller *iconostasis*, also very beautiful, and icons depicting scenes from the life of St George. Also at this lower level, beyond an archway protected by a metal grille, is the entrance to what is believed to be the original sixth-century monastery, as well as various large earthenware *amphorae* which were used to store wine and olive oil. The monastery is a popular place of pilgrimage amongst Christians, particularly around the time of the feast of St George, held each year on 6 May, and the feast of the elevation of the Holy Cross, on 14 September.

The beautiful, wooded valley in which the monastery is located is known as *Wadi Nasara* or 'Valley of the Christians', having remained a centre of Greek Orthodox Christianity since the sixth century. Today 27 out of the 32 villages in the valley are Christian; of the remaining five, four are Alawi while just one, Al Qalaa (the village which nestles below Krak), is Sunni Muslim.

■ *To reach the monastery, return to the road leading north from the Homs-Tartus motorway, turning left to follow it north, and then bear left at a fork after just over 1 km. After a further 3 km you arrive at the monastery on the left.*

Sleeping There are 4 hotels along the road leading to St George's Monastery; after forking left to the north of the turning for Krak, you pass on the right around 200 m the *Al Riad* and, 300 m beyond it on the same side, the *Al Naeem*. On the left, around 600 m further on, is the *Al Wadi*, and just past it on the same side, the *Al Fahed*. **A/B** *Al Wadi*, T730456, F730399. Choice of 3-star rooms (fan, TV, phone, fridge, attached bath and balcony) or 4-star rooms (a/c, TV/dish, phone, minibar, attached bath and balcony). Restaurant, swimming pool, billiards/games room, children's play area. 4-star rooms very spacious and nicely furnished; 3-star rooms rather overpriced for the level of facilities. A rapidly growing establishment (now 6 storeys high, with 2 new wings going up). All 3-star rooms to be upgraded over the next couple of years. Well run, but pricey. **D** *Al Riad*, T735097, F730000. Simple but clean rooms with fan, attached bath and balcony (some with great views of Krak). Restaurant. **Camping** S£150 per person, including use of shower/toilet facilities. A little overpriced; try bargaining. **D/E** *Al Fahd*, T730822. Simple but pleasant rooms with fan, phone, attached bath and balcony. Tiny swimming pool. Good views. Friendly manager. **E/F** *Al Naeem* (to become *Layali al-Naeem*), T735044. 6 simple rooms with attached bath; some with balconies and good view of Krak. Restaurant (pleasant vine-shaded terrace with good views of Krak). Good value.

Tartus to Safita

The road from Tartus up to Safita is perhaps not the best introduction to the Jebel Ansariye region; having been widened to near motorway proportions along the first stretch, it is now seemingly always busy with traffic, and lined with haphazard, half-finished concrete buildings for most of the way. Nevertheless, as you get closer to Safita and the road begins to climb from the coastal plain, you begin to get glimpses of the olive groves, orchards and vegetable farming which make these fertile mountains so prosperous. Safita's tall square Crusader tower, meanwhile, comes in and out of view with the twists and turns of the road long before you reach the town itself.

Around 9 km after crossing over the motorway, a small unmarked right turn leads to the village and small fort of Qalat Yahmur, only really worth a detour if you have plenty of time. Taking this turning, bear left where the road forks and then continue straight through the village to arrive at the fort, 2 km from the main road. First fortified by the Byzantines under the Emperor Nicephorus in the 10th century, it was subsequently occupied by the Crusaders and came under the control of the Hospitallers in 1177. They carried out substantial modifications to the fort, which they knew as *Chastel Rouge*. Salah ud-Din (Saladin) briefly captured it during his campaign of 1188, but the Crusaders soon regained control and held it until 1289, when it finally fell to the Mameluke sultan, Qalaun. The fort consists of a solid, squat watchtower surrounded by defensive walls, all basically intact though in a poor state of repair.

Qalat Yahmur

Safita صافيتا

The town of Safita is spread across two hills, one dominated by the remains of the Crusader castle and the other boasting the somewhat less attractive *Safita Cham Palace* hotel. Although growing rapidly around its sprawling outskirts, the old part of town around the castle is still very picturesque, with lots of old buildings and narrow cobbled streets. The population is divided roughly equally between Alawi and Greek Orthodox, the latter having settled here early in the 18th century. Safita is popular as a summer resort, attracting lots of holidaymakers from the Gulf, and during the height of the season its small roads get heavily congested with traffic. However, the streets come alive with people in the early evening, as the younger generation of the Greek Orthodox population stroll around, women arm-in-arm and men watching, each side sizing up potential husbands and wives.

Phone code: 043
Colour map 1, grid C1

The name Safita (shortened from Bourj Safita) is the Arabic translation of the name by which the Crusaders knew it: *Chastel Blanc* or 'White Castle'. Thought to have originally been built by the Crusaders in the first years of the 12th century in the course of the First Crusade and designed to form a forward defence for the port of Tartus, it was subsequently largely dismantled by Nur ud-Din, to whom it fell in 1167. After reoccupying it, the Crusaders handed over control to the Templars. (The damage wrought by Nur ud-Din, along with a severe earthquake in 1202 necessitated major rebuilding work.) The Templars remained in possession of it until 1271, when it was taken by the Mameluke sultan, Baibars, who shortly after took Krak des Chevaliers.

History

Today, just about all that remains of *Chastel Blanc* is the central tower, or *donjon*, although originally this was surrounded by two lines of defensive walls, in typical Crusader style. The ground floor of the tower was the Crusader's chapel, and, never having been deconsecrated or turned into a mosque, it continues to serve as a Greek Orthodox church today, dedicated to St Michael. The entrance leads directly into the church from the west. The semi-domed apse at the far end together with the barrel-vaulted ceiling bear evidence in the marked fissures running through them of the damage caused by the earthquake of 1202. The stone and wood *iconostasis* in front of the apse is modern, although many of the icons in the church are clearly very old. The

The 'White Tower'

only source of light is from narrow arrow slits framed in arched bays. These arrow slits reveal the thickness of the walls and serve as a reminder of the building's primarily defensive function.

In the corner to your right as you enter is a long, steep flight of stairs leading up to the first floor, which was probably used as accommodation. This consists of a long vaulted chamber with three massive central pillars, cruciform in shape. The ceiling has been plastered at some stage, although much of this has fallen away to reveal the stonework underneath. Note the machicolation situated directly above the entrance to the church, allowing boiling oil to be poured on any would-be attackers. Note also the bell in the narrow arched window beside the machicolation. This arched window would appear to be a modified and widened arrow slit. A further flight of stairs takes you up onto the roof, from where there are superb views in all directions, with both Tartus and Krak des Chevaliers being visible on a clear day. On leaving, if you follow the cobbled street east, round past the rear of the tower, you pass through the remnants of the eastern outer gate and walls.

■ *There are no fixed opening hours or entry fees, though a donation towards the upkeep of the church is expected. If the tower is locked, ask at the* Al Bourj *restaurant by the entrance for the keys.*

Sleeping **B/C** *Safita Cham Palace*, PO Box 25, at the western end of the town, T531131, F525984. Rather more modest than the rest of the Cham's chain of hotels, and a little in need of refurbishment in places, but occupying a commanding position with great views out over the surrounding countryside. Comfortable rooms with a/c, TV, phone, attached bath and balcony (all with views). Restaurant, bar, swimming pool and sun terrace. The cost of a double room falls from US$75 to an excellent value US$40 during the low season (mid-Sep to mid-Jul). **C** *Al Nadeem Suites*, T/F534300. Consisting primarily of 3-bedroom suites (sleeping 6), with separate kitchen and sitting room areas, 2 bathrooms and balcony. All with a/c, TV/dish and phone. Also a small number of 2-bedroom and 1-bedroom suites. Small rooftop swimming pool. Restaurant and bar (also rooftop). Clean, pleasant and very good value. **D** *Safita Bourj* (from roundabout at eastern end of town, bear right – signposted Mashta and Kafroun – and hotel is on left after around 1 km), T521932. Reasonable rooms with fan, attached bath and balcony. A little run down and overpriced for what you get, but adequate. **G** *Syaha* (*Tourist*), on the roundabout at the eastern end of town. Very simple though reasonably clean rooms (S£100 per bed), cold shower, appalling toilets.

Eating Right by the entrance to the tower, the *Al Bourj* has excellent views out over the surrounding countryside. They serve a standard selection of Arabic meals and snacks at

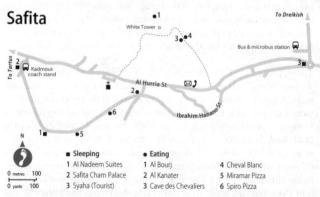

Safita

To Dreikish

White Tower

Bus & microbus station

To Tartus

Kadmous coach stand

Al Hurria St

Ibrahim Hanano St

To Safita Bourj Hotel (1 km), Krak

N

0 metres 100
0 yards 100

■ **Sleeping**
1 Al Nadeem Suites
2 Safita Cham Palace
3 Syaha (Tourist)

● **Eating**
1 Al Bourj
2 Al Kanater
3 Cave des Chevaliers
4 Cheval Blanc
5 Miramar Pizza
6 Spiro Pizza

slightly inflated tourist prices (around S£250-300 per head), or you can just have a cup of tea/coffee or a cold drink (alcohol also served). In a similar vein, with a pleasant garden as well as indoor seating, is the *Cheval Blanc*, just inside the remains of the castle's eastern outer gate, while opposite is the *Cave Des Cavaliers*, which appears as often as not to be closed. The overall best restaurant in Safita is the *Al Kanater*, on Ibrahim Hanano St, to the south of the tower, T524097. Occupying the first floor of what was formerly a *madrassa* (Islamic school) and later used by the French as a 'club', it has pleasant décor, friendly staff, good quality Arabic food at reasonable prices (from around S£250 per head). Alcohol served. Also on Ibrahim Hanano St, *Spiro Pizza* and *Miramar Pizza* both do reasonable pizzas as well as good value shish tawouk or burger snacks for around S£100. Alcohol served. On summer evenings they put tables out on the street. By the roundabout at the eastern end of town there are a number of cheap snack places for falafels, shawarmas etc.

The main bus station is near the roundabout at the east end of town. Most services are in the form of **microbuses**, which run to **Tartus** (S£5, frequent), **Homs** (S£35), **Dreikish** (S£10), **Mashta Helu** (S£10) and **Hosn Suleiman** (S£10, very limited services). If you are heading for Tartus, you could also follow the example of many locals and simply wait at the junction near the *Safita Cham Palace* hotel. | **Transport**

In addition, *Kadmous* operate **luxury coaches** from their ticket office opposite the entrance to the *Safita Cham Palace* hotel. In summer there are 2 services daily to **Damascus** at 0700 and 1500 (S£100). In winter this may be reduced to 1 service daily; in any case, timetables have a tendency to change, so check first. There is also a private **taxi** stand next door to the *Kadmous* ticket office.

The **post** and **telephone** offices share the same building (easily identified by the communications dishes on the roof), located on Al Hurria St, to the south of the tower. There is one cardphone inside, though finding someone to sell you a phonecard can be difficult. Alternatively, the *Al Nadeem Suites* hotel will let you make international calls at reasonable rates. | **Directory**

Safita to Krak des Chevaliers

This scenic route to Krak (around 34 km in all) is worth undertaking, providing you have the time and patience. In places the road is very narrow and heavily pot-holed, though sections of the route have been upgraded. | *See page 258 for Krak des Chevaliers*

Bear right at the roundabout at the eastern end of Safita (signposted for Mashta al-Helu and Kafroun) and then bear left at the next roundabout (1,500 m further on). Follow this road and take the second left turning you come to (a little over 6 km from the second roundabout). The first left turn, 1,500 m earlier and directly opposite a petrol station, is the turning for Mashta al-Helu (see below); there is a route to Krak via this road, but it is far more complicated.

Just over 1 km after taking the left turn, bear right where the road forks and then keep going straight. You pass through a small village, and then through the village of Burj al-Arab (6 km beyond the left turn), literally 'Arab Tower', so named after the small, solitary medieval watchtower of black and white stone which still stands in the village, clearly visible from the road. Continue straight, passing through the village of Tell al-Hawash (4 km beyond Bourj al-Arab), soon after which there are good views on your left, down towards a large lake formed by a recently built dam. A little over 2 km past Tell al-Hawash, turn left onto a good new road signposted for 'Amar Tourist Resort'.

After 3 km you come to a crossroads; at the time of writing the road straight ahead was still under construction. Turn left here, and then right 1 km further on. Bear right where the road forks soon after and then, in the village of Jereina, some 5 km after the last junction, turn left opposite an old church (signposted

'Amar Tourist Resort'). The road climbs very steeply from here, passing after a little over 1 km the *Amar Tourist Resort* on the left. A little further on there are wonderful views out over the valley to your left, with St George's Monastery visible on the far side. Continue straight, past the *Al Kalaa* restaurant, before arriving at Krak des Chevaliers, 4 km beyond the *Amar Tourist Resort*. Approaching from this direction, your first views of the castle are from above, providing an excellent overall perspective.

Bear right at the roundabout at the eastern end of Safita (signposted for Mashta al-Helu and Kafroun) and then bear left at the next roundabout (1,500 m further on). Follow this road and take the first left turning you come to (5 km from the second roundabout, situated directly opposite a petrol station). After just under 4 km, where there is a right turn signposted for St Georges, follow the road round to the left to keep going straight. Just under 3 km further on, after passing through a couple of small villages, there is another right turn signposted for St Georges. Both these turnings offer beautiful routes to Krak des Chevaliers, but you really need a local guide to get you through the maze of tiny roads and villages. Keep going straight, to arrive eventually in Kafroun (10 km further on), from where it is a further 3 km up to Mashta al-Helu.

Mashta al-Helu مشتى الحلو

Phone code: 043
Colour map 1, grid C2

The town of Mashta al-Helu is essentially a hill resort, popular amongst Syrians as a summer retreat from the heat of the plains. The surrounding countryside is beautiful and there are lots of pleasant walks in the area. Perched on a hilltop just before the town itself is the *Mashta al-Helu Resort*, a modern alpine-style complex of chalets which, if not actually dominating the skyline, stands out somewhat incongruously from its surroundings. In Kafroun, at the bottom of the valley, is the rather more modest *Al Widian* hotel.

Just under 2 km above Mashta are the **Al Douaiyat caves**, a network of caves leading a couple of hundred metres into the mountainside. To get there, turn right at the fountain and clocktower which mark the main square in the centre of Mashta al-Helu (coming from Kafroun and the *Mashta al-Helu Resort*). After 600 m follow the road around to the right (by a church), and then turn sharp left 200 m further on, immediately after a metal arch spanning the road. Follow this road up past a new housing development, and fork right after 500 m (signposted for the caves) to arrive at a café/restaurant and parking area 500 m further on. The entrance to the caves is just beyond this. At first they appear to be nothing special, but a narrow passage brings you to the most impressive part, thick with stalactites, stalagmites and pillars, all lit by strategically placed lights. ■ *Open summer only, 0900-1300, 1500-1900, daily. Entry S£25. The caretaker will show you around, armed with his torch. The café/restaurant here has fantastic views out over the valleys below from its shaded terraces.*

Mashta's other claim to fame is the nearby **Jebel Saidi**, an extinct volcano with a distinctive conical shape. To get there, take the turning on the right below the Mashta al-Helu Resort (heading down to Kafroun from the centre of Mashta), just after the twin metal arches over the road. Keep following this road (unsurfaced in places) as it winds its way to the top, just over 2 km from the main road. A Roman structure, either a fortress or a temple, is believed to have stood on the flat-topped summit. Today, the only structure is the outline of a small chapel, also believed to be very old, its walls standing to a height of just 1 m or so, with various contemporary statues of Mary adorning the semicircular apse. As the statues suggest, the chapel is dedicated to the Virgin

The Coast & the Jebel Ansariye

Mary. The mountain and chapel are a major focus for the Festival of the Virgin Mary, celebrated each year on 15 August. The festivities begin the evening before and carry on right through the night, with large crowds of pilgrims cramming onto the mountain top and celebrating to the accompaniment of fireworks and singing and dancing.

A *Mashta al-Helu Resort*, T584000, F584060. Choice of comfortable hotel rooms with TV/dish, phone, minibar, attached bath and balcony, or chalets set in mature gardens and sleeping up to 6 people, complete with kitchen and lounge. Restaurants, bars, swimming pool, tennis, sports hall. Good value for level of facilities offered. Gets very busy in the high season (mid-Jul to mid-Sep); during the low season double rooms come down to **B** category. **F** *Al Widian*, T581298. Simple but comfortable rooms with attached bath and balcony. Pleasant streamside location with gardens and outdoor restaurant, though the rooms on one side now look out onto a large new building.

As well as the restaurants attached to the hotels here, there are a couple of simple snack places grouped around the main square in town where you can get sandwiches and a cup of tea or coffee.

The microbus stand is in the main square. Services to and from **Safita** (S£10) are fairly frequent during the summer. You can also hire a microbus privately from here, to go to **Masyaf**, for example (around S£200), or to **Husn Suleiman** (around S£150), 20 km to the north of Mashta al-Helu. This route is rather complicated though and not really practical without a local driver who knows the area.

Sleeping, eating & transport

Mashta al-Helu to Masyaf

From Mashta al-Helu you can continue east to join up with the route running between Masyaf and Krak des Chevaliers. Coming from Kafroun and the *Mashta al-Helu Resort*, turn right in the main square and after 600 m bear right at the church. The road winds its way through the mountains, passing through the village of **Jweikhat** before starting to descend. After just over 7 km there is a right turn signposted for St Georges; this is the road to Krak. A little further on is a left turn which heads north towards Masyaf (see page 232 for details of the route between Masyaf and Krak des Chevaliers).

Colour map 1, grid B/C2

Tartus to Husn Suleiman

This route takes you through the village Dreikish (which can also be easily reached from Safita), and then through increasingly rugged and beautiful mountain scenery to the imposing ancient ruins of Husn Suleiman.

Colour map 1, grid C1/2

Head north along the sea front from the Crusader fortress/'old city' of Tartus, and then bear right at the roundabout. Keep going straight, along Khaled Ibn al-Walid St, then Jamal Abd al-Naser St, and across the railway line. Follow the road through a one-way system as you leave Tartus (there was some major road construction in progress here at the time of writing) and continue straight on over the coastal motorway (4 km from the centre of Tartus). Keep following this road, passing through the villages of **Bismaqa** and **Bamalkeh**, the latter with a couple of summer restaurants beside the road. Just under 29 km after crossing over the motorway, go straight across a large roundabout marking the start of Dreikish. Around 400 m further on, bear left at a mini-roundabout to head into the centre of Dreikish (bearing right at this mini-roundabout puts you on the road to Safita, around 14 km to the south).

Dreikish is a fairly large village famous mostly for its abundance of excellent spring water which is bottled and sold throughout Syria. The centre of the village

Dreikish

retains a certain charm, with several pleasant traditional cafés where locals while away the hours. Next door to one of these cafés there is a fountain where you can fill up with the famous Dreikish spring water for free. There is one small hotel here, the **G** *Dreikish*, behind the old mosque just before you emerge from the one-way system in the centre of town. It offers basic but clean rooms with shared shower/toilet (double S£200). The other hotel, the once grand *Dreikish Palace* (a large rather institutional-looking white building situated up on the hill behind the microbus stand) is now closed down and looking very dilapidated indeed. There are fairly regular microbus connections with Tartus and Safita.

Following the main road through Dreikish, around 12 km after leaving the vil-lage, bear right where the road forks in a small village (signposted 'Q. Hosson Suleiman'). The road climbs steeply from here and the scenery becomes increasingly picturesque. Just under 5 km further on, take a very sharp right turn (in effect a switchback), again signposted 'Q. Hosson Suleiman'. Around 500 m after taking this turning, bear left; the ruins of Husn Suleiman are visible from here less than 1 km down the narrow valley.

Husn Suleiman حصن سليمان

Colour map 1, grid C2   Seen from a distance, the ruins of Husn Suleiman look rather meagre, but close-up the sheer scale of the stone blocks used in the outer wall of the com-pound is truly awesome. It is reminiscent (although not in terms of its state of preservation) of the roughly contemporary Baalbek in Lebanon. That such a monument should have existed here is all the more remarkable when you con-sider its isolated location, high up in the mountains. It is as much this setting, as the site's ancient origins and monumental scale, that give it such a magical feel.

Ins & outs   There are very limited microbus services running between Safita and Hosn Suleiman. A more realistic option is to take a microbus from either Tartus or Safita to Dreikish and hire a taxi from there.

History   The name now given to the ruins (meaning literally Suleiman's Citadel) is entirely misleading: this was in fact a temple and it had nothing to do with Suleiman. Originally (during the late fourth to early third century BC) the site is thought to have been a Semitic/Canaanite centre of cult worship dedicated to the god Baal. Later, it probably came under the control of the Phoenicians, whose main base on the coast was the island city of Aradous (Arwad, just off the coast from Tartus). Baal subsequently became associated with the Greek god Zeus, and was worshipped here in his local form as Zeus Baetocecian, along with the god Astarte. Under the Romans, this tradition continued to flourish. The existing temple ruins date mostly from the second century AD, although construction probably first began a century earlier. Inscriptions found at the site confirm that it continued as an important centre for the wor-ship of Zeus well into the fourth century, long after Christianity had been adopted as the official religion.

Sights   The temple consists of a large open rectangular compound measuring 134 m by 85 m and pierced by gateways in each wall, in the centre of which is a small *cella*. The main entrance is on the north side; a triple doorway interspersed by two niches. This doorway was once enclosed both inside and out by a *propy-laeum*. However, all that remains today are the fragments of collapsed columns along with their bases which once formed the *portico* to the propylaeum. Carved lions, very weathered and faint, can be seen at either corner of the north wall. The undersides of the massive monolithic lintels which crown each entrance to the temple compound are carved with an eagle, its wings outstretched. Those in the east and west gates are the best preserved, while that of the central doorway on the north side is just discernible. On the east and west gates there are in addition winged victories on either side of the lintels, supporting it. The central *cella* is today a jumbled mass of stones; it stood on a platform and the stairs leading up to it can still be seen. Fragments of the walls of the *cella* also survive, on which can be seen semicircular engaged columns.

Across the road from the main temple there is a small building known locally as *Ed Deir* ('The Monastery'), suggesting that during the Christian era it served this purpose. Originally it almost certainly served as a secondary temple, perhaps dedicated to the god Astarte. The portico is well preserved, with a clearly visible winged eagle above the lintel. This temple once stood within a larger compound, and to the north of it traces can be seen of what appears to have been a Christian basilica.

Tartus to Masyaf

Follow directions out of Tartus as for Husn Suleiman, except instead of crossing over the coastal motorway, turn left onto it to head north towards Lattakia. Around 8 km after joining the motorway, take the exit signposted to Sheikh Badr and Hussein Bahr (ignore the exit signposted for Sheikh Badr and Tartus soon after joining the motorway: the exit you want is opposite a large mound topped by a towering statue of Assad). Having passed a huge cement factory, the road climbs up into the hills, passing through the village of Hussein al-Bahr before arriving at a crossroads in the village of **As Soda**, 6 km from the motorway. There is an interesting church here, as well as several Ottoman period buildings. Go straight over the crossroads and continue straight on to Sheikh Badr, 12 km further on, from where you can make the interesting detour to Qalat al-Kahf. Continuing straight along the main road, a road joins from the right at a mini-roundabout, follow the road round to the left in to Sheikh Badr. It is a further 4 km on to Sheikh Badr from here.

This route traverses the breadth of the Jebel Ansariye to arrive at the town of Masyaf with its Ismaili castle overlooking the plains to the east

This must surely be one of the most isolated and romantically located of all the castles to be found in the Jebel Ansariye. There may not be that much left to see of the castle itself, but its stunning location makes the considerable detour involved in reaching it well worth the extra effort.

Qalat al-Kahf
Colour map 1, grid B1

Ins and outs Though the castle is actually just 16 km from Sheikh Badr, the road is winding, narrow, steep and very rough in places, and you should allow at least 45 mins each way, plus time to explore once you get there. Approaching Sheikh Badr from the coast, a theatrical statue of an Arab fighter holding his rifle aloft marks the start of the village. Exactly 1 km beyond the statue, bear left at a mini-roundabout, and then left again at a second mini-roundabout 100 m further on. After 500 m, bear right at a third roundabout. Two km further on, entering a small village, bear left where the road forks. The road begins to climb; after around 700 m, follow the road sharply round to the left and then fork right immediately after in a second village. The road descends steeply through an increasingly rugged and beautiful landscape of steep, thickly wooded hills and rocky outcrops, crosses a small bridge and seasonal stream and then climbs again to another village just under 2 km further on. Fork left in this village to descend, before climbing again to arrive at a T-junction just under 1 km further on. Turn left here; the road descends steadily down the side of a valley, crosses a bridge and then climbs again up the other side in a long 'V' before arriving at a large concrete school building on the left, and a left turn signposted to 'Q. AlKahaf' (just

The Assassins

The Assassins were a radical branch of the Nizari Ismaili sect, founded by Hasan-i Sabbah. He was born some time in the middle of the 11th century in the town of Qom, to the south of Tehran in present-day Iran. From mainstream origins, he adopted the teachings of the Ismailis, later becoming an exponent of the Nizari Ismaili school after the schism which arose amongst Ismailis following the death of the eighth Fatimid caliph, Al Mustansir. In 1090 he acquired the castle of Alamut (meaning literally 'the nest of the eagle') in the Elburz mountains to the south of the Caspian Sea and from this stronghold he conducted his campaign of terror against the Sunni orthodoxy, persecutors of the Ismaili faith. He adopted the tactic of sending emissaries to kill his enemies, training them to become masters of disguise so that they could infiltrate the courts of foreign kings before carrying out their attacks, and instilling such a degree of discipline and obedience in them that they apparently went willingly to their deaths on what were in effect guaranteed suicide missions.

Such was the fame of the Assassins that the very word soon passed into common usage in the West, coming to mean someone who is hired, usually for political reasons, to carry out a killing. As to the origins of the word 'Assassin', this has been the subject of much debate. The most commonly accepted explanation is that it comes from the Arabic Hashishiyyin (literally hashish users). Numerous tales proliferated in the wake of this much feared and little understood sect. One suggestion was that the Assassins smoked cannabis prior to their suicide missions

and that this explained the fact that they were able to go to their deaths oblivious of their own safety and without even attempting to escape. Another suggestion was that the emissaries, drugged with cannabis, would be introduced into a secret 'garden of paradise' in the castle of Alamut where they experienced a foretaste of the heavenly joys that awaited them on their martyrdom. These tales of cannabis use amongst the Assassins were popularized in the West by Marco Polo, although most scholars agree today that the appellation Hashishiyyin was more likely an expression of the contempt and abuse with which orthodox Sunni Muslims regarded these fanatics. An alternative explanation of the origins of the word is that it is derived from the Arabic Assassiyun (literally followers of the Assass, or 'foundation' of the faith), and that foreign visitors confused the word with the similar sounding Hashishiyyin.

From the beginning of the 12th century the Assassins began to extend their influence into Syria, taking advantage of its fragmented state, nominally under the rule of the Fatimids, but also facing encroachment from the Seljuq Turks, the Byzantines and the Crusaders. At first they settled in Aleppo, where they received the support of its Seljuq ruler Ridwan, who appears to have enlisted their help in murdering his rival Janah al-Dawlah, ruler of Homs. Following Ridwan's death they were driven out, but later appeared to gain the support of Tughtigin, the Turkish ruler of Damascus, obtaining from him the fortress at Banyas and using it for a time

under 3 km from the last T-junction). Taking this left turn, the road climbs very steeply before arriving at another T-junction just over 1 km further on. Turn right here; after just under 1 km, follow the road sharply round to the right and keep going for another 3 km until you reach a sharp left turn signposted 'Qalat a Kahf 3 km'. One km down this track, fork left to arrive at the foot of the castle, 1,500 m further on.

History The strategic advantages of the site were first recognized by a local emir, Ibn Amrun of the Banu Munqid clan, who built a castle here some time during the 11th century. In 1134, Qalat al-Kahf was acquired by the Assassins, two years after their acquisition of Qadmus, as part of their policy of

as a base. On the whole, however, their presence in Syria was met with hostility, particularly in view of their willingness to form alliances with the Crusaders. But from the 1130s onwards they began to be successful in their attempts to establish secure fortress bases from which they could operate in relative safety, concentrating their efforts in the Jebel Ansariye. In 1132 they bought Qadmus, followed a couple of years later by Al Kahf, while in 1140 Masyaf was captured, with other castles in the region (including Qalat al-Khawabi, Qalat Maniqa and Qalat Abo Qobeis) coming under their control around this time.

In 1163 Rashid ud-Din Sinan, known to the Crusaders as the 'The Old Man of the Mountain', became head of the Assassins in Syria, and under his leadership they became a major player in the political intrigues of this period. Meanwhile, in 1164 the Assassins of Alamut underwent a remarkable transformation. The supreme leader there, Hasan (the great-grandson of Hasan-i Sabbah), declared that the 'Resurrection' had come and from that time onwards the Assassins no longer had to observe the Holy Law, since they had in effect attained paradise on earth. Thus the holy fast of Ramadan was broken, the drinking of alcohol allowed and, according to perhaps exaggerated later accounts, 'no man abstained from his sister or daughter'. Sinan appears at first to have accepted the proclamation of Hasan, but in later years put an end to the excesses that it encouraged. Indeed, he appears to have achieved independence from his superiors at Alamut, who tried to have him killed, fearing that he had become too powerful in his own right. According to some reports, his followers in Syria came to regard him as the supreme and divine leader of the Assassins. Certainly in Syria, his opponents regarded with a mixture of fear and respect. Most famously, after two unsuccessful assassination attempts, he is said to have personally threatened the life of Salah ud-Din (Saladin) (see page 233), prompting him to abandon his attempts to overthrow the Assassins. His relationship with the Crusaders was an ambiguous one: in competition and yet often loosely allied, and sometimes joined by formal treaties. In 1192 Sinan masterminded the murder of the king of Jerusalem, Marquis Conrad of Montferrat, according to some sources, at the request of Richard the Lionheart.

After his death one year later, the Assassins became less active in Syria. The fall of Alamut to the Mongols in 1260 greatly weakened their position. In 1270 the Mameluke sultan Baibars forced the Assassins of Syria to pay tribute to him instead of the Hospitallers, as had been the case previously. By 1273 he had subjugated them to the extent that they ceased to be a political force in Syria, though they continued to live in the Jebel Ansariye as an insignificant minority alongside the Christians and Alawis. In the 19th century many of them left the mountains to settle in Masyaf, and also in and around the town of Salamiyeh, to the southeast of Hama. Subsequently the sect died out, its members being reabsorbed into the Imaili sect.

establishing themselves in the Jebel Ansariye. It became one of the headquarters used by the Syrian leader of the Assassins, Rashid ud-Din Sinan (The Old Man of the Mountain) from 1164-1193. In 1197 Count Henry of Champagne, recently appointed by Richard the Lionheart as Regent of Jerusalem, visited the castle, seeking to secure an alliance with Sinan's successor against the Sunni Muslim threat to the Crusaders. According to legend, the new leader of the Assassins sought to prove to Henry the unswerving loyalty of his followers by ordering two of them to hurl themselves from the ramparts, which they promptly did. Ironically, Henry died shortly afterwards when he fell from a window of his palace at Acre.

During the next century it was the turn of St Louis of Acre (King Louis IX of France and leader of the ill-fated Sixth Crusade of 1249) to negotiate with the Assassins. The Assassins apparently sent emissaries to St Louis, demanding that he pay them an annual tribute. Louis responded by sending back the emissaries laden with gifts. Later he sent one of his friars, Yves le Breton, to Qalat al-Kahf and finally succeeded in securing an alliance.

That the castle only fell to the Mameluke sultan Baibars in 1273, two years after the fall of Krak des Chevaliers, is an indication of its near-impregnability. It continued to fulfil a military function well into the Ottoman era, but was finally destroyed in 1816. The English adventurer, Lady Hester Stanhope (see page 545), had taken up the cause of a French captain who was being held captive in the castle and managed to persuade the Ottoman governor of Tripoli, Mustapha Barbar, to lead an expedition against it to free the captain and also to destroy it once and for all.

Sights The ruins of the castle first come into view some way off, identifiable by the reinforcing stonework around the top of the high rocky outcrop on which it stands. From the end of the track, continue on foot along a narrow, overgrown path which leads around the right-hand side of the base of the outcrop. You pass first a gateway, its massive stone lintel now fallen, followed by a couple of vaulted underground chambers on the right. The path then passes through a small artificial cave cut into the rock, which formed the lower entrance to the castle (perhaps the source of its name, which translates literally as 'Castle of the Cave'). Note the Arabic inscription above the entrance to the cave. Further on, the path doubles back to climb up the side of the outcrop, giving access to the area inside the walls. Almost nothing remains here, the Ottoman governor of Tripoli apparently having carried out Lady Stanhope's wishes diligently. Here and there are the crumbling fragments of buildings half hidden amongst the undergrowth, some largely collapsed or earth-filled vaulted chambers and the circular openings of enormous water cisterns hewn into the rock. The views of the surrounding countryside, however, are stunning and this makes an excellent spot for a picnic.

Nearby is what is popularly believed to be the **tomb of Rashid ud-Din Sinan** himself. To reach it, take the right-hand fork as you make the final approach to the castle. This climbs to the summit of the ridge adjacent to the castle where, amongst the trees, there is a small whitewashed shrine said to contain his tomb. The views from here are also spectacular.

Wadi al-Ayoun
Phone code: 033

Returning to Sheikh Badr and continuing east along the main road, it is a further 12 km on to Wadi al-Ayoun (Valley of the Springs), a picturesque village famous for its plentiful spring water and its mulberry groves. The village is another popular summer retreat amongst Syrians and there are a number of houses where you can rent rooms or apartments. Ask around in the village if you are interested in doing this. There are several simple restaurants along the main road through the village. On the eastern outskirts of the village, to the right of the main road, there is a hotel and restaurant, the **F** *Sharfi* (sign in Arabic only), T720420, offering simple but clean rooms with kitchen, attached bath and great views (double S£500).

Leaving Wadi al-Ayoun, the road climbs through rugged limestone hills and pine forests before starting to descend. After around 10 km you come to what is in effect a T-junction. Turn left here (signposted 'Mosyaf'), and descend steadily with glimpses of Masyaf's castle and the plains beyond, before arriving after a further 10 km at another T-junction. This is the road running north-south between Masyaf and Krak des Chevaliers. Turn left here for the centre of Masyaf, around 1 km further on (for details of Masyaf, see page 231).

Tartus to Lattakia

The motorway from Homs to Tartus continues north along the coast all the way to Lattakia, passing en route the impressive Crusader castle of Qalat Marqab, the small town of Banyas (only really of interest as a base for visiting Qalat Marqab) and Jableh with its large, if ruinous, Roman theatre. It is a fast though often busy road, the journey direct from Tartus to Lattakia (around 90 km) taking no more than 1 hour.

Banyas بانياس

Despite its ancient history spanning the Phoenician, Greek, Roman, Byzantine and Crusader periods, there is nothing of particular interest in Banyas today. Ranged around its small fishing harbour, it is possible to imagine that the town was once quite picturesque, but today it is dominated by modern concrete construction and a large oil refinery to the north.

Phone code: 043
Colour map 1, grid B1

After they had established themselves here in 1098, it was known to the Crusaders as *Valenia* and formed the southernmost town of the principality of Antioch. The small river that flows into the sea here formed the boundary with the principality of Tripoli to the south. Owned by the Mansoer family, it was ceded along with Qalat Marqab to the Hospitallers in 1186. Both the town and the castle escaped capture by Salah ud-Din (Saladin) in 1188, eventually falling to the Mameluke forces of the sultan Qalaun in 1285. It subsequently fell into decline and was completely abandoned, only being resettled during the French Mandate period. Its principal use today (for tourists, at least) is as a base from which to visit Qalat Marqab.

There is a small hotel just off the main street running through the town, the **G** *Banyas*, T710173. Basic but reasonably clean rooms with fan, attached shower/toilet and heater. There are a few simple restaurants-cum-takeaways with the usual selection of falafel, shawarma, kebab, half-chicken etc nearby. Regular microbuses run from Banyas to **Tartus** and **Lattakia**, and less frequently up towards **Qalat Marqab** (see below), **Qadmus** and even **Masyaf**.

Sleeping, eating & transport

Banyas to Masyaf via Qadmus

This road has been upgraded to a broad highway for much of the way, making it a fast, easy (and at the same time very beautiful) route between the coast and the Al Ghab plains. From the centre of Banyas, head back up to the coastal motorway and cross directly over it (if coming from Tartus or Lattakia, the exit is signposted for Banyas and Qadmus). The road climbs steeply and follows the southern side of a wide, deep valley, with superb views across it. Around 22 km after crossing the motorway, a fork off to the right takes you into the centre of Qadmus, a distinctive village clustered around a pointed rocky outcrop.

Colour map 1, grid B1/2

Today an important centre of tobacco production, the town of Qadmus was once a major Ismaili stronghold. The rocky outcrop on which their castle stood is visible from a considerable distance, although all that remains today is the main gateway, and inside a few old buildings in amongst the more modern ones. Having been acquired by the Assassins from a local emir in 1132 (see Qalat al-Kahf above), control of the castle appears to have switched between the Crusaders and the Ismailis a number of times, although precise details of its history are surprisingly scarce. Finally, in the 19th century it was destroyed by

Qadmus

The Coast & the Jebel Ansariye

Ibrahim Pasha, during his brief challenge to the might of the Ottoman Empire. There may not be much left to see of the castle, but there are lots of beautiful old Ottoman-period houses dotted around the village, and an interesting mosque with an octagonal minaret. With the main highway now bypassing the village, it is also pleasantly relaxing and traffic-free, and worth stopping off at for a wander round. There are a couple of simple takeaway places, offering falafel sandwiches etc, along the main street.

Continuing east from Qadmus, the road climbs through rocky hills for a while, before beginning to descend. After a little under 18 km there is a left turn signposted to Deir Mama. This is the route to Qalat Abu Qobeis (see page 232). Continue straight to arrive at Masyaf, 5 km further on (see page 231).

Qalat Marqab (Margat) قلعة المرقب

Colour map 1, grid B1

Perched high up on a spur and dominating this stretch of the coastline where the coastal plain is reduced to a narrow corridor between sea and mountains, Qalat Marqab is striking even from a distance for its huge size and sombre, brooding appearance. Built from black basalt rock, it is one of the most impressive Crusader castles after Krak des Chevaliers and Qalat Saladin, and well worth a visit.

Ins & outs By public transport, take a **microbus** from either Tartus or Lattakia to Banyas. There are irregular microbuses running from Banyas to Zaoube (S£10) which pass right by the castle, though these only run until mid-afternoon so you may find yourself having to hitch back down. A microbus to Marqab village (S£5) will drop you around 2 km short of the castle. If you want to take a **taxi** from Banyas, you will have to negotiate a price according to how long you want to spend there. Around S£200-300 for the return trip with 1 or 2 hours for a visit would be reasonable.

If you are **driving**, probably the easiest way of getting to Qalat Marqab is to leave the motorway at the Banyas/Qadmus exit and head into Banyas. When you reach the sea front, turn left and follow the road south through the town for just under 2 km until you reach a left turn signposted (not very clearly) for Qalat Marqab. This road crosses over the motorway via a bridge and climbs up into the mountains. Four km after crossing the motorway, take a very sharp right turn to double back and climb up to the castle, 1 km further on, or else keep going straight to wind your way around the eastern side before arriving at the entrance.

Alternatively, coming from Tartus along the motorway, take the exit signposted for 'Marqab Citadel' and then 'Zobeh' and 'Al Baydar' (see above). Around 700 m after leaving the motorway, bear round to the left where the road forks to keep the castle directly in front of you. Around 1.5 km further on, take the small left turn signposted to 'Markab Castil' on a blue sign, and then after another 1 km turn right and then immediately left (both turnings are likewise indicated by blue 'Markab Castil' signs). The small road climbs very steeply, giving excellent views of the castle's hefty southern fortifications higher up. Finally, bear left to reach the entrance, just over 4 km from the motorway.

History Despite the obvious strategic significance of the site, commanding both the narrow coastal strip and the valley running east towards Qadmus and Masyaf (both of which were to become important Ismaili strongholds), a castle was only built here as late as 1062 by a local Muslim chieftain. Until then, it would appear that the far more ancient town of Banyas had fulfilled the function of controlling movement up and down the coast. When the Crusaders took Banyas in 1098 they made no attempt on the castle, and it was only in 1104 that it was occupied by the Byzantines. Sometime during the first half of that century it passed into Crusader hands, becoming part of the principality of Antioch. It was entrusted as a feudal endowment to the Mansoer family and then in 1186 sold to the Knights Hospitallers. It was known to the Crusaders as *Margat*, its Arabic name, Qalat Marqab, translating literally as 'Castle of the Watchtower'.

The Hospitallers immediately started major construction work to strengthen its fortifications, particularly at its more vulnerable southern tip. Just two years later it must already have been a formidable stronghold since Salah ud-Din (Saladin) opted to bypass it as he swept up the coast after his victory over the Crusaders at Hattin. It subsequently withstood attacks by the Emir of Aleppo Malik al-Daher in 1204 and the Turkoman emir Saif ud-Din Balban in 1280.

However, the fall of Krak des Chevaliers in 1271 greatly strengthened the hand of the Mameluke sultan Baibars, and he was able to enforce an agreement whereby the revenues from its dependent lands were divided between the Hospitallers and the Mamelukes. When Baibar's successor, Qalaun, besieged it in 1285, the dwindling manpower (and morale) of the Hospitallers made its capture relatively easy. Having successfully undermined the foundations of the huge south tower and so breached the castle's outer defences, the Mameluke forces began a sustained bombardment of the inner fortress. The Hospitallers soon decided that further resistance was futile and surrendered. Under the Mamelukes, the castle was repaired and continued to serve as an important military stronghold until the Ottoman period, although its primary function appears to have been as a prison.

Sights

The castle conforms to a basic triangular plan defined by the ridge on which it is situated. Like Krak des Chevaliers, it has an outer and an inner line of defensive walls. On the north, east and west sides the mountain falls away in an almost sheer drop, providing a formidable natural defence. Only at the southern end, the sharp point of the triangle, is the ridge connected to the main body of the mountain. It is here that all the castle's most formidable fortifications have been concentrated, including the main keep. As you approach, there are good views of the southern defences. The bands of white marble in the rounded tower of the outer walls here date from the Sultan Qalaun's repairs after he had caused its collapse.

Entry to the castle is through a **square tower** in the western walls. To the north can be seen a series of rounded towers in the outer walls. A set of stairs leads up to the tower, where there is a ticket office. Turn right to exit the tower and head south between the outer and inner walls. After a short distance, on the left, is a **barbican gate** giving access via a flight of stairs to the inner courtyard and main area of interest. In the centre of the courtyard is a **well** with a huge water cistern below.

Qalat Marqab (Margat)

To Banyas

Ruins of
Arab Village

11

Cemetery

1

2

10 3   6 7

Inner
Court-
yard

4

5

9

To Motorway

0 metres 40
0 yards 40

1 Entrance
2 Barbican Gate
3 Well
4 Chapel
5 Main Keep
6 Storage/kitchens
7 Great Hall
8 East Tower
9 South Tower
10 Offices
11 Ottoman Khan

'Stones which do the work of men, Qala'at Marqab (Castle Margat)

This imposing concentric fortress of black volcanic stone was built on a craggy southwesterly spur, looming above valleys to the east and south, and commanding views of the Mediterranean to the west. Originally the site of a Muslim-built fortification of 1062, it was taken by the Crusaders in the early 1100's. However, the commitments of the Count of Tripoli, to whom the castle was entrusted, were such that he 'realized that he could not hold the castle of Margat, as was necessary in the interests of Christianity, because of excessive expenses and the very close proximity of the infidel'. So in 1168 the castle was sold for a nominal fee to the Knights Hospitaller. Acknowledging the fortification's exceptional position, and following the dictum that a castle destroyed is a castle half-remade, they garrisoned and enlarged the site considerably until it become recognized as the most important Hospitaller castle of the Principality of Antioch. The military order's strongholds acted much as the aircraft carriers of today. They were manned to provide an impregnable base from which influence could be exerted over the surrounding area. The castellan of Margat was a senior commander who as well as launching knights on raiding sorties would have administrative powers over the local district. Caravans would stop at the castle to pay duty on their

goods and of course a Hospitaller castle would also be a centre of religious life. Although the knights lived in castle rooms decorated by paintings and mosaic floors they were essentially still monks following a religious rule and would eat in solemn silence while devotional readings provoked a contrast to their exceptional surroundings and silver plate!

Part of Margat's ability to withstand siege was its self-sufficiency. Castles of the period contained windmills to grind grain; wells; granaries; oil presses and dovecots (for both communication by carrier pigeon and food). Margat held ample provisions for a thousand inhabitants for five years: what it eventually lacked was a sufficient garrison. By 1285 the walls were always patrolled by four knights and 28 sergeants. It would have been one of these sentries, clad in his red surcoat emblazoned with a red cross, who raised the alarm when, on the 17th of April, without any warning, the immense hordes of Sultan Al Mansur Qalaun materialized before the walls.

Qalaun was Sultan Baibars' Mameluk successor and his Arab chroniclers have recorded the investment of Margat. The Sultan had honoured Baibars' treaty with the Christians but was enraged by the Hospitallers propensity to act as the auxiliaries of Mongol invaders from the North. So he prepared to treat 'al-osbitars' to a lesson. Pyrotechnicians and siege

At the southern end of the courtyard is the **chapel**, its simple, austere architecture reminiscent of the Church of Our Lady of Tortosa in Tartus. Built towards the end of the 12th century, around the time that the castle was acquired by the Hospitallers, it represents an early example of the Gothic style, with traces of Romanesque. The main entrance is on the west side, with a smaller one on the north. On either side of the main apse at the eastern end of the church are two small *sacristies*. On the ceiling of the northeast *sacristy* (ie the one to the left of the apse as you face it) you can see fragments of original frescos depicting the 12 apostles at the Last Supper.

To the south of the chapel are a number of rooms and vaulted halls forming a complex of buildings which probably served as the barracks and main reception area. These buildings surround the main **keep** or *donjon*, a massive 3-storey tower, rounded on its southern and eastern sides, with walls up to 5 m thick in places. You can climb via a series of stairs right up to the roof, from where there are excellent views, particularly west towards Banyas and the Mediterranean.

engineers were drafted into his forces to enable the assault on Margat. Dismantled mangonels were laboriously manhandled over the hills and reconstructed before the castle. The attackers also possessed the secret of projecting 'Greek fire', a form of napthma. This napalm substance was part of the exclusive preserve of the Sultan's arsenal, and was a notoriously feared weapon. Once surrounded, the castle was utterly isolated and could expect no quarter and no chance of relief from the pitifully inadequate forces of Frankish Tripoli. There were barely enough men to man the defences against the constant surprise assaults. Day and night the siege engines were hurling stone balls up to 270kg in weight at the walls. The constant pounding was accompanied by a battery of noise from horns and drums, the cacophony preventing anyone from snatching any sleep. Despite this, the several hundred defenders, stretched over parapets intended to be garrisoned by a thousand, responded to the bombardment by crippling the Mameluke's mangonels with their own engines, mounted on the wall-towers.

Meanwhile, Qalaun's miners had been tunnelling beneath the castle walls. These excavations were propped up by wooden beams that could be ignited, thus collapsing the tunnels and fatally damaging structures above. The world of the siege-miner was a perilous nightmare conducted in confined, claustrophobic conditions. Counter-mines would be sunk by defenders intent on breaking into the tunnels to fall upon the miners for deadly hand-to-hand scuffles, lit only by guttering torches that sucked the air from the combatant's lungs. Sometimes the tunnels were suddenly flooded from above or in a primitive form of biological warfare, 'stinkpots' were hurled down, releasing clouds of poisonous gases. It was these tunnel-rats who were to prove decisive in the siege of Margat. After a five week siege, the vital southwest tower was toppled and the Hospitallers fled into the circular tower-keep. By this time the foundations were riddled with holes and so a magnanimous Sultan Qalaun invited a delegation of defenders to examine the extent of the mines. The Knights realized the precarious nature of their position, and knowing that further resistance would entail the eventual taking of the inner defences and, according to the rules of medieval warfare, the subsequent massacre of the garrison, they accepted Qalaun's generous offer and evacuated the castle. The remaining 25 knights left under truce for Tortosa (Tartus). The castle was looted by Qalaun who removed the chapel's fine gothic columns to adorn the mosques of Cairo and the castle was never again held by the Christian crusaders.

Returning to the main courtyard, running along its eastern and northeastern side is a series of rooms which were most likely used as **storage chambers** and **kitchens**. The rooms on the eastern side lead through to a long hall facing onto the eastern outer defensive walls which perhaps served as the **great hall**. From here you can gain access to a large **eastern tower** built into the outer defensive wall.

On the western side of the courtyard (adjacent to the point at which you first entered the inner courtyard), steps lead up to a series of rooms. These give access to a room above the barbican entrance which has been restored and is now used as the office of the curator of the castle. Postcards are on sale here and the curator is generally on hand to offer visitors coffee or tea.

The large northern area of the castle is of lesser interest. Access to it can be gained most easily by heading north from the western tower by which you first entered the castle. In the centre are the remains of large Ottoman-period **khan**, with a later upper storey added and now topped by two communications masts. Scattered to the north of this are the ruins of an **Arab village** which grew

The Coast & the Jebel Ansariye

up here following the castle's fall to Qalaun, while the area to the southeast was used as a **cemetery**. Most of the inner wall, except on the western side, has been dismantled, its stones used in the construction of the village, but it is still possible to follow the line of the outer walls in places. However, the whole area is heavily overgrown, making it difficult to wander round.

■ *Open 0900-1800, 7 days, in summer (Apr-Sep); 0900-1600, closed Tue, in winter (Oct-Mar). Entry S£300 (students S£15). A torch is useful for exploring the castle. There are a couple of snack places outside.*

Jableh   جبلة

Phone code: 041
Colour map 1, grid B1

Like Banyas, the town of Jableh gained its importance from its small harbour, and has as a result been occupied since Phoenician times when it was known as *Gabala* and formed part of the kingdom of Arwad. After the Roman conquest led by Pompey in 64 BC it appears to have enjoyed considerable prosperity, to judge by the large theatre that was built during this period. It maintained its importance during the Byzantine era, when it became the seat of a bishopric under the patriarchs of Antioch. In 638 it fell to the Muslims, and then during the Ayyubid period was taken once again by the Byzantines in 969, only to fall once more to the Muslims in 1051. It was taken by the Crusaders, led by Raymond St Gilles, in 1098. Salah ud-Din (Saladin) captured it during his campaign of 1188, but after his death the Crusaders regained control, subsequently handing it over to the Hospitallers in 1207. Finally in 1285 it was taken by the Mameluke sultan Qalaun, shortly after he had captured Banyas and Qalat Marqab, and remained in Muslim hands thereafter.

Today it is a small but busy market town, famous mostly for the ruins of the enormous **Roman theatre** in the centre of the town, to the south of the main microbus station. Though nowhere near as well preserved as the theatre in Bosra, it is comparable in size, with an estimated capacity of around 7,000 people. Most impressive are the cavernous twin-vaults running underneath the semicircle of tiered seating, which together give some idea of its scale. Restoration work has been in progress here for the last few years, but the pace of work is so painfully slow that it is hard to see exactly what, if anything at all, has been achieved during this period. ■ *Open 0800-1700, Tue 0800-1400. Entry S£150 (students S£10).*

Nearby (between the microbus station and the theatre) is the **Mosque of Sidi Ibrahim Ben Adham**, named after a Muslim saint whose tomb it contains. Built following his death in 778, it stands on the site of an earlier church built by the Byzantine emperor Heraclius (610-41). In the souks and alleyways running between the town centre and the sea front there are various fragments of old buildings and tiny mosques in amongst the more modern buildings.

Sleeping, eating & transport

Opposite the microbus station is the **F** *Al Sham*, T824761. Simple but clean rooms with fan and shared shower/toilet. Almost opposite the theatre there is a much more basic hotel (**G** category, no sign in English), with beds in shared rooms (in the unlikely event that anyone else is staying) for S£150 per person.

There are a number of cheap restaurants offering the usual selection of Arabic food dotted around the centre of town. Down on the sea front, to the south of the two small fishing harbours, there is a pleasant café facing out to sea.

Frequent microbuses run from here to **Lattakia** and **Tartus**, departing when full.

Lattakia اللاذقية

Phone code: 01
Colour map 1, grid B1

Despite a long and eventful past, there are few physical reminders of Lattakia's historical importance. Instead, Lattakia remains today what it has always been throughout the centuries: a Syrian window opening onto the wider world. Lattakia's port is Syria's busiest and most important sea outlet, handling most of the country's import and export business, and this on-going process of contact with the outside world has surely been a factor in making Lattakia one of Syria's least conservative towns. It's not unusual to see confident young women striding out in outfits rarely seen in other parts of Syria.

There are precious few attractions in Lattakia that could be described as 'sights', though the town is not an unpleasant place in which to stroll or window-shop. Lattakia is a good base from which to visit a number of local attractions, notably Ugarit (Ras Shamra), Blue Beach (Shaati al-Azraq), Ras al-Bassit, Kassab, Qalat Saladin, Jableh and Qalat Marqab.

Ins and outs

There are dozens of luxury coach companies connecting Lattakia with major destinations throughout the country, as well as microbuses providing connections with smaller towns in the vicinity. However, most unusually for Syria, it is the railway which offers the most attractive option for the journey between Lattakia and Aleppo. This line is particularly beautiful, train times in both directions are convenient, and the train stations at either end are no more remote than the bus stations. Although the road through the mountains is slowly being upgraded to a motorway, for the time being it remains congested, slow and hazardous. Lattakia also has an airport (25 km southeast), though it is little used, with just 1 flight weekly to Damascus and Cairo.

Getting there
See also 'Transport', page 290

The train, luxury coach and bus stations are all around 1.5-2 km from the centre of town; manageable on foot if it is not too hot, or there are plenty of taxis and local microbuses. Otherwise, the town is for the most part best explored on foot.

Tourist information is on 14 Ramadan St, T416926. Open 0800-2000, daily. It offers the usual free maps/brochures, and if you come before 1400 you can usually find someone who speaks some English and is reasonably well informed.

Getting around

History

Lattakia was almost certainly founded as a small Phoenician fishing village around 1000 BC, though it was not until the fourth century BC that the emerging settlement developed into a town of any real significance. Having passed through the hands of the Assyrians, Persians and Alexander the Great's Greek army, it was the Seleucid ruler Seleucus I Nicator (311-281 BC) who established Lattakia as a major town within his empire (the town taking its name from the emperor's mother).

Lattakia continued to prosper after Pompey's Levantine adventure at the head of the Roman army in 63 BC, taking the Roman name of **Laodicea ad Mare**. Having been made a free town with tax raising rights, Laodicea's port developed further, with the town becoming renowned for its wine production and export. The Christian church appears to have gained an early toe-hold in Laodicea, and there are several mentions of the Christian community here in the New Testament (*Colossians 4: 13-16; Revelation 3: 14-22*). For a short period under the emperor Septimus Severus (r. 193-211 AD), Laodicea served as the capital of the Roman *Provincia Syria*, though this role later reverted back to the rival city of Antioch. The city was also one of those taken by the extraordinary Queen Zenobia (see box page 177) when she challenged the might of the Roman emperor Aurelian in the late third century AD.

During the Byzantine and early Arab periods, the town suffered badly at the hands of man and nature. It was devastated on several occasions not just by the battle for hegemony between the declining Byzantine Empire and the growing

Lattakia

To Iskandarun Square, Blue Beach & Ugarit

To Aden Square, Ugarit, Kassab & Ras al-Bassit/Al Badrusiyeh

Microbus Station

Al Jumhouria St

Hitteen Square

Al Maghreb al-Arabi St

Assad Sports Stadium

Visa Extensions

Al Montanabby St

Al Jumhouriah Square

Corniche/Jamal Abd al-Nasser St

8 Azar St

Service Taxis

Starco Car Hire

14 Ramadan St

Port

Assad Statue

Koumatli St

Saad Zaghloulo

Souria Av

Lattakia Museum

CBS

Al Quds St

Abdul Rahman al-Ghafiky St

Al Yaman Square

Hob-hob bus station

Abdul Kader al-Housseiny

Al Yarmouk St

Tetraporticus

Railway station

Luxury coach station

A

Baghdad Av

Boy Said St

Nadim Hassan St

Umar Ben al-Khattah St

Al Ourouba St

Beirut St

Al Ourouba St

South Corniche

Mediterranean Sea

Fishing Harbour

Persian and Arab powers, but also by a series of earthquakes. Hardly had the city recovered before it grabbed the attention of the Crusader forces. Between 1097 and 1287, control of it passed repeatedly between Crusader and Arab hands, before the Christians were finally expelled from the Holy Land. Even then, the successors to the Crusader legacy (the Cyprus-based Lusignans) returned to sack the city in 1367.

After much of the Levant fell under Ottoman Turk control, Lattakia went into decline as rival ports were preferred for development, and by the end of the 19th century Lattakia was once again little more than a fishing village. The town's revival began in the 1920s under the French Mandate authority, with Lattakia becoming the capital of the Alawi State administrative unit. The Alawi connection is also credited with Lattakia's recent rapid resurgence, the former Syrian President Hafez al-Assad's family links to the town being instrumental in the decision to redevelop the harbour into Syria's premier port.

Sights

Lattakia's small museum on Corniche/Jamal Abd al-Nasser Street is housed **Lattakia** in a former caravanserai dating from the Ottoman period. It features an **Museum** eclectic collection of artefacts excavated from sites in the surrounding area. The upper storey was added to the caravanserai during the French Mandate period, when the building served as the residence of the governor of the Alawi State. The imposing vaulted arcades of the caravanserai, partially clad in climbing plants and surrounding a small area of lawn and trees, provides a cool and peaceful respite from the throng and traffic of the city; likewise the museum's large gardens, which are dotted with an impressive array of columns, capitals, architectural fragments, sarcophagi and olive presses. Of particular note are the three beautifully carved marble statues in front of the caravanserai, one of them (the only one still with its head intact) sporting a thoughtful, melancholy expression.

Entering the museum, the first room on the right contains artefacts from Ugarit (mostly pottery items and clay tablets with cuneiform inscriptions) dating from the 16th to the 13th centuries BC. The second room features objects from a number of sites – stone tools and weapons, pottery jars, amulets, cylinder seals, human and animal figurines and jewellery – spanning the Stone Age through to the Roman and Byzantine periods. In the centre of the room is a large rectangular stone block with a depression chiselled into it in the shape of an animal skin. Unearthed at Ibn Hani (just to the north of Lattakia, near Ugarit) in 1982, it is believed to date to the Iron Age (14th-13th century BC) and to have been used as a mould for bronze and copper bullion. The third room features artefacts from the Greek, Roman and Byzantine periods found at various sites along the Syrian coast. These include coins, pottery figurines, glassware and a collection of oil lamps, some of which are beautifully decorated with delicate carved reliefs of animals, birds and mythical scenes. In the centre of the room is a pottery coffin with a distinctive cylindrical shape dating from the first century BC. The fourth room houses pottery, ceramics, coins, glassware, jewellery, armour and a Qur'an spanning the whole of the Islamic period, from the Umayyads through to the Ottomans. The fifth (and last) room is given over to a collection of contemporary paintings and sculptures. ■ *Open 0800-1800 in summer, 0800-1600 in winter, closed Tue. Entry S£300 (students S£15).*

There are several reminders of Lattakia's Roman past scattered across the **Roman remains** town, though none could be said to be particularly impressive. In fact, the two *Take care not to get run* main standing remains now serve as little more than centre-pieces to traffic *over when crossing to* islands. To the south of the city centre is the **tetraporticus**: a group of four *the traffic islands to view these remains!*

The Coast & the Jebel Ansariye

standing columns that with a vivid imagination could be envisaged as a four-sided gateway that once marked the east end of the *decumanus* (main east-west transverse street of the Roman town). It probably dates to the late second century AD.

At the point where Al Quds Street becomes Abd al-Rahman al-Ghafiky Street (opposite the *Ugarit* cinema), there are some standing granite **columns** that once formed part of a portico lining one of the Roman town's streets. The four columns on the traffic island in the centre of Al Jumhouriah Square, three of them topped by Corinthian capitals and two of them supporting a section of architrave, may be part of the Roman town's **Temple of Adonis**.

South Corniche

Occupying a small penninsula at the southernmost tip of Lattakia is a short stretch of coastline which is in many ways far more attractive than Blue Beach (see below). It may not offer the same opportunities in terms of swimming and watersports, but it is certainly more picturesque. The penninsula is marked by low cliffs leading down to a shoreline which is mostly rocky, but where there are a few patches of sand and shingle. The waters here are crystal clear, though the cliffs and shoreline are unfortunately predictably rubbish strewn. On the eastern side of the penninsula is a tiny fishing harbour. There are several restaurants along here (see 'Eating' below) and in summer numerous impromptu cafés with plastic tables and chairs occupying strategic postions along the cliffs. This penninsula appears to be Lattakia's new up-and-coming district, with numerous fancy-looking luxury appartment blocks springing up all over the place.

The South Corniche is quite a walk from the centre of town (around 2-3 km). Frequent microbuses shuttle back and forth from the centre, leaving from near the Assad Statue; ask for "Corniche Janoubi".

Essentials

Sleeping
■ *on maps*
Price codes:
see inside front cover

A *Riviera*, 14 Ramadan St, T421803, F418287. Small but reasonably comfortable rooms with a/c, TV/dish, phone, minibar, fridge and attached bath. Restaurant, bar, coffee shop. Friendly, helpful staff although a little pricey for what you get.

Lattakia's top-of-the-range hotels, namely the Cote d' Azur de Cham & Meridien, are located at Blue Beach, 6 km north of the town (see 'Around Lattakia', below, for details)

C *Casino*, Corniche/Jamal Abd al-Nasser St, T461140, F461142. Rather grand French Mandate-period building, though today that grandeur is very much faded, with peeling paint and a lingering smell of damp pervading the place. Large, echoing, high-ceilinged rooms with a/c, TV, phone, fridge and attached bath. Large restaurant and summer terrace. Quite an experience from a nostalgic (if not a comfort) point of view. **C** *Jamal*, Corniche/Jamal Abd al-Nasser St, T476156. Friendly, family-run hotel in a French Mandate-period building. Just 5 large rooms, share bathroom, a/c planned. Pleasant terrace garden overlooking the Corniche. Breakfast served. Potentially a nice place, but needs some refurbishment (and the promised a/c) in order to justify the price tag. **C** *Palace*, Ghassan St (continue north along Corniche, past Hitteen Sq), T469250, F470170. Comfortable rooms with a/c, TV/dish, IDD and attached bath. Restaurant and bar downstairs in basement. Slightly bland, with décor straight out of the 1970s, but excellent value in terms of level of facilities, and with friendly, helpful staff. **C/D** *Omar Khayyam*, Al Jalaa St, by Assad Stadium, T228219, F465698. A/c, TV, phone, fridge, attached bath and balcony. Hotel is a little dilapidated in places, but the rooms themselves are clean, comfortable and well maintained, with balconies overlooking the sports stadium or swimming pools. Pleasant rooftop terrace. Discounts available off-season. Good value for the level of facilities, but a long way from the centre of town (though ideal for the microbus station).

D *Al Gondole* (or 'Al Gandoul'), Corniche/Jamal Abd al-Nasser St, T477681. Simple but clean rooms with a/c, TV, phone, fridge attached bath and balcony. Overall looking a little faded and in need of refurbishment. Overpriced for what you get, though quick to offer discounts. Restaurant/café downstairs with large, elegant dining hall and pleasant outdoor terrace. D *Al Nour*, 14 Ramadan St, T423980, F468340. Simple but clean rooms with fan, phone and attached bath. Those at front have balconies, but are noisier. Friendly French-speaking manager. Well run hotel, but a little overpriced (single/double US$18/21). D *Al Riyad* (or *Al Riad*), 14 Ramadan St, opposite Assad statue, T479778. Simple but clean rooms with attached bath and balcony, most with a/c, others with fan only (same price; it may be worth trying to bargain fan-only rooms down to **E** category). Rather noisy location. D *Ambassadeurs* ('Al Soufaraa'), Corniche/Jamal Abd al-Nasser St, T477725. Simple but clean rooms with a/c, phone, attached bath and balcony. Claims to be the first hotel in Lattakia and has certainly seen better days (some much-needed refurbishment is promised). Rather overpriced as it stands. D *Haroun*, Al

Lattakia centre

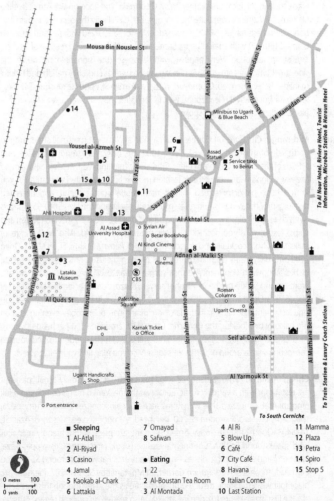

The Coast & the Jebel Ansariye

■ **Sleeping**	7 Omayad	4 Al Ri	11 Mamma
1 Al-Atlal	8 Safwan	5 Blow Up	12 Plaza
2 Al-Riyad		6 Café	13 Petra
3 Casino	● **Eating**	7 City Café	14 Spiro
4 Jamal	1 22	8 Havana	15 Stop 5
5 Kaokab al-Chark	2 Al-Boustan Tea Room	9 Italian Corner	
6 Lattakia	3 Al Montada	10 Last Station	

N

0 metres 100
0 yards 100

Jumhouriah Sq, T427140, F418285. Simple but clean rooms with fan, TV, phone, attached bath and balcony. Best rooms at rear, away from the noise of the main road. Friendly, helpful staff, but a long way from the centre and expensive for what you get.

F *Safwan*, off Corniche/Jamal Abd al-Nasser St, T478602. Clean, pleasant rooms with fan, attached bath and balcony (single/double/treble S£300/500/700). Also excellent value 'apartments' sleeping up to 5 people, with a/c, TV/dish, kitchen and bathroom (ideal for families or small groups). Quiet location. Friendly and helpful manager. Recommended. **F** *Al Atlal*, Yousef al-Azmeh St, T467121. Old building with high ceilings, large rooms with fan and sink, share shower and toilet. Quiet location, friendly manager, but overpriced for what you get (S£300 per bed, or S£500 for a double).

G *Kaokab al-Chark*, 14 Ramadan St, opposite Assad statue, T478452. Simple rooms with fan and attached bath (single/double S£200/325). Some rooms with balcony. Also some cheaper rooms with shared bath (single/double S£175/275). Despite the rather dingy, unappealing entrance, this is actually a fairly clean, well run and friendly budget place, though the location is rather noisy. **G** *Lattakia*, 2nd floor, on side-street leading off Yousef al-Azmeh St opposite the mosque, T479527. Easily the best deal in this category. Dorm beds for just S£100, singles/doubles for S£200/250 with fan and attached bath (S£150/200 with shared bath). Some rooms with balconies. Free use of kitchen, TV/dish in reception. Very popular with Japanese (the sign pointing down the side-street off Yousef al-Azmeh St is in Japanese as well as English). Friendly and helpful manager. Recommended. **G** *Omayad*, Yousef al-Azmeh St, opposite mosque, T479567. Very basic but relatively clean rooms with fan and sink, share shower/toilet. Cheap (double S£150), not much English spoken.

Eating   **Mid-range** *City Café*, off Corniche/ Jamal Abd al-Nasser St (on small street around north side of museum grounds). Open 1000-late, daily. Very trendy a/c place with photos of the likes of Claudia Schiffer, Cindy Crawford and Marilyn Monroe adorning the walls, along with more prosaic fashion models and a satellite TV beaming at you from a huge projector screen. Varied international cuisine menu; appetizers (eg nachos, spicy hot wings, squid rings, mozzerella sticks and the like) S£40-95; burgers (with chips and coleslaw) S£90-100; pasta and pizzas S£90-125; specials (eg fish and chips, fajitas, mushroom chicken, meat fondue) S£175-240. Also wide range of milkshakes, 'soft' cocktails and deserts. No alcohol. *Petra*, Al Akhtal St, T477207. Open 1200-late, daily. Fairly up-market a/c place offering the usual range of Arabic mezze dishes along with Continental dishes such as steak, escalope, pizza, spaghetti etc. From around S£300 per head. Alcohol served. *Plaza*, Corniche/Jamal Abd al-Nasser St, T461013. Open 2000-late, daily. Attractive, up-market Arabic and international cuisine restaurant. You can eat in the large a/c dining hall, or on cooler evenings out on the balcony overlooking the Corniche. Eat well for around S£300 per head upwards. Alcohol served. A good place, although if you are unlucky enough to find yourself competing with a group of Syrian VIPs for service you may find yourself ignored.

Cheap *Al Rif*, off Al Moutanabby St, T467198. Open 1300-late, daily. Small, pleasant a/c restaurant with a vaguely rustic/European theme. Varied menu combining a full range of Arabic mezze dishes with items such as steak, schnitzel, chicken curry, pizza, spaghetti, etc. From around S£200 per head. Alcohol served. *Cesar*, 8 Azar St, T475403. Open 1100-late, daily. Small, pleasant, a/c place with a friendly manager who speaks good English. Continental cuisine (steak, lamb chops, escalope, pizza, pasta etc) and a few Arabic dishes (shish tawouk etc). Eat well for around S£150-200 per head. Alcohol served. *Italian Corner*, Al Moutanabby St, T477207. Pleasant a/c place following the same rustic/European theme as the *Al Rif* (though this was actually the first in this genre to open in Lattakia). Also seating on covered terrace outside.

Continental cuisine (pizza, spaghetti, steak, escalope etc) and Arabic mezze dishes. Around S£250 per head for a full meal, less for snacks. Alcohol served. *Mamma*, 8 Azar St, T416929. Open 1100-late, daily. Small, popular place with just 6 tables. Continental cuisine along the same lines as the *Cesar*, and at similar prices, though with a rather more limited menu. Eat well for around S£150-200. Alcohol served. *Spiro*, Corniche/Jamal Abd al-Nasser St. Open 1200-late, daily. Traditional Syrian restaurant with a cavernous dining hall and a reputation for excellent Arabic food. From around S£200 per head. *Stop 5*, Al Moutanabby St. Open 1200-late, daily. Some good old (and somewhat tatty) 1970s décor here, with no trace of a rustic theme. Usual range of mezze dishes, plus steak escalope, pizza, spaghetti etc. Around S£200 per head upwards. Alcohol served. *"22"*, Faris al-Khury St (off Al Moutanabby St), T468042. Open 1200-late, daily. Small, pleasant, a/c bistro-style place (again furnished along a rustic/European theme). Usual range of steaks, pizzas, spaghetti etc. From around S£200 per head. Alcohol served.

Seriously cheap There are several places along 14 Ramadan St and Saad Zaghloul St (mostly in the vicinity of the Assad statue) offering half-chicken, kebabs, shawarma and falafels. A meal of half-chicken, hummus and salad shouldn't come to more than around S£100; check the chicken roaster first to see that its contents have completely dried and shrivelled. A few doors down from the *Lattakia* hotel is a small, recently opened and spotlessly clean place which serves excellent hummus, fuul and tea.

South Corniche The restaurants along Lattakia's South Corniche all offer a choice of indoor seating or open-air terraces with fantastic sea views. *Dolphin*, T473362. Open 0800-late, daily. Mixture of traditional Arabic fare (mezze dishes, shish tawouk etc) and pizzas, spaghetti, steaks etc. Around S£250 per head for a full meal, or you can just enjoy the views over a cup of tea or a beer. *Siwar* (sign in Arabic only), T220488. Open 1300-late, daily. Very much more up-market than the others along the South Corniche. Dishes from the seafood menu all at S£625, or standard range of Arabic cuisine (mezze, meat etc) for around S£300 upwards per head. Live music daily. Alcohol served. Popular with big-wigs from the Assad regime. *Somar* (sign in Arabic only), situated next door to *Siwar*, T232524. Open 0800-late, daily. Popular, bustling, family-orientated place with similar menu and prices to the *Dolphin*, but no alcohol.

Cafés *Al Boustan Tea Room*, 8 Azar St, has a pleasant sidewalk terrace and is a good place to take a tea or coffee (S£25) and watch the world go by. They also do fresh fruit juices and ice creams. *Al Montada Café*, off Corniche/Jamal Abd al-Nasser St, down a quiet side-street beside the museum. The usual tea, coffee, nargilehs, cards and backgammon is on offer here, but in significantly more classy surroundings than your run-of-the-mill café. Frequented by Lattakia's older, more traditional generation. As well as the formal restaurants along the South Corniche (all of which double up as cafés), during summer there are numerous ad-hoc open-air cafés at strategic points along the cliffs.

Bars Most of the restaurants mentioned above double as bars, serving Syrian beer for S£35-50 and imported beer for S£75-90 (though sometimes the imported beer has only come from not-very-exotic Lebanon). *Al Havana*, Ibrahim Hanano St (on corner with Andan al-Malki St). With its pleasant rooftop terrace, this is a good place to come for beer. A bottle of Al Chark costs S£50, or there are cans of imported beer for S£100. This is also a restaurant, serving the usual range of Arabic cuisine, though drinking seems to be the main pastime here. *Blow Up*, Al Moutanabby St. Despite being billed as a restaurant and bar, this place no longer does food. Popular with young Syrian couples looking for a bit of privacy, it has nothing in particular to recommend it, and charges an extortionate S£100 for a bottle of local beer.

The Coast & the Jebel Ansariye

Entertainment

Cinemas *Ugarit*, al-Quds St, shows usual diet of shoot-em-up Hong Kong flicks for S£35; *Al Kindi* on Adnan al-Malki St and the cinema on al-Moutanabby St offer pretty much the same.

Shopping

From a Syrian point of view, Lattakia has great appeal as a shopping destination. Evening strolls & window shopping are a favourite pastime

8 Azar St is probably the most up-market shopping street, featuring various designer-label stores. The heart of Lattakia's shopping area is the series of blocks enclosed by 8 Azar, Al Yarmouk, Maysaloun and Saad Zaghloul/14 Ramadan Streets. *Ugarit Handicrafts*, Al Yarmouk St, opposite port entrance, has some interesting craft items. Several shops along 8 Azar St sell the *Syrian Times*, though the only bookshop of note is *Betar Bookshop* on an alleyway called Jareer, just down from the Al-Kindi Cinema on Adnan al-Malki St. It has 2-week-old British newspapers (eg *Sunday Telegraph* S£350).

Sports

Key sporting events take place at the **Sports City Complex**, to the north of Lattakia before you reach Blue Beach. Other sporting events are held at the **Assad Stadium** on Al Jalaa St. This incorporates an outdoor Olympic-size swimming pool and diving pool (open daily 0700-1800 during summer only), though women may feel more comfortable paying to use the facilities at the luxury hotels at Blue Beach.

Transport

Local There are a couple of **car hire** companies in Lattakia. *Avis*, Saad Zaghloul St (by roundabout at northeast end, in same office as *TNT*), T/F478310. Cars from S£2,000 per day including insurance and open mileage (minimum 3 days), or S£1500 per day for 1 week or more. Deposit US$1,000, or credit card imprint. Also with hire desk at *Meridien* hotel, but only Mercedes available there (from S£4,000 per day, or S£3,700 for 1 week or more). *Starco*, 14 Ramadan St, T433103. Cheapest car S£1500 per day, but very little English spoken here; you may find yourself being directed to *Avis*.

As well as the microbuses to Blue Beach and Ugarit (see below, under Around Lattakia), and to South Corniche (see above, under Sights), there are local **microbuses** which run between Al Yaman Sq and the centre of town, and also between the microbus station on Al Jalaa St and the centre.

Shared or private-hire **taxis** prowl around town after customers, though most points are within walking distance. A private taxi from the train station or luxury coach station to the centre of town should not cost more than S£25-30.

Air Lattakia's **Al Basil International Airport** is 25 km to the southeast of town. Officially, a taxi should cost around S£200, though foreigners are likely to be charged more. There is 1 flight weekly (on Fri, 1020) direct to **Cairo** (hence the 'International') for US$164 one-way, and 1 flight weekly (on Fri, 1530) to **Damascus** for S£502 one-way.

Train Lattakia's train station is located on Al Yaman Sq, to the east of the town centre, T468131. It is one of the few in the country which actually has an air about it of being used. Check out the fine old German-built steam engine dating from 1891 on display to the right of the main hall. There are 2 trains daily to **Aleppo** at 0645, 1530. Tickets cost S£54 1st class and S£36 2nd class. There is 1 train weekly to **Damascus** via **Tartus**, on Fri at 2330. Tickets to Damascus cost S£90 1st class and S£60 2nd class; to Tartus they cost S£28/19 1st/2nd class. **NB** Before you board the train, your ticket must be stamped and your details entered in a register at the counter across the hall from the ticket windows.

Luxury coach station The luxury 'Garagat Pullman' coach station is on Abdul Kader al-Houseiny St, behind the railway station. There are at least a dozen private companies based here. Between them they offer regular departures to most destinations and it is rarely necessary to book in advance; ask around to find which company has the soonest departure to your destination. A selection of the more important companies covering the major routes is given here. *As Salaam* is one of many companies with departures to **Aleppo**, every 30 mins, S£100. *Kadmous* has departures to **Damascus** (along with lots of other companies), hourly or less, S£150; to **Tartus** (small buses), every 10-15 mins, S£25; to **Homs** (via Tartus, carrying on to **Palmyra** and **Deir ez-Zor**), 1230, 1430, 2300, S£80 (Palmyra S£150, Deir ez-Zor S£230); to **Hama** (small bus; direct route across the mountains), 0630, 0930, 1230, 1530, 1830, S£60; and to **Dreikish** (small bus), 0900, 1400, 1800, S£50. *Al Amir* has direct minibuses to **Safita**, 0815, 1215, 1415, 1830, S£50. *Al Ahliah* has departures to **Hama** (via Tartus and Homs), 0700, 1415, 1700, S£100. *Al Hassan* has departures to **Antakya** (in Turkey; crossing via the Kassab border), 0700, 0830, S£500. *Karnak* (also with a ticket office in the centre of town, see map, though all departures are from the luxury coach station) has departures to **Damascus**, 0700, 1430, S£110; to **Aleppo**, 1500, S£65; and to **Tripoli/Beirut**, 0600, S£125/175.

'Hob-hob' bus station The old (or 'hob-hob') bus station is located on Abdul Kader al-Houseiny St, between the railway station and the luxury coach station. Rickety old buses operate on a 'depart when full' basis to **Damascus** for S£55, and **Aleppo** for S£40, stopping on request en route. There are also microbuses to **Slunfeh** for S£20, and **Hama** (via the Al Ghab road) for S£40.

Microbus station The microbus station is located on either side of Al Jalaa St, just past the Assad Stadium. Microbuses depart when full to **Al Haffeh (for Qalat Saladin)**, S£10; **Slunfeh**, S£20; **Kassab**, S£25; **Ras al-Bassit/Badrussiyeh**, S£25; **Qardaha**, S£10; **Jableh**, S£10.

Service taxi There is a service taxi stand on 14 Ramadan St, opposite the *Al Nour* hotel. Service taxis depart when full to **Tripoli**, S£250-300; **Beirut**, S£500; **Damascus**, S£500; **Aleppo**, S£200.

Sea In the past there were irregular passenger services to Alexandria in Egypt and Izmir in Turkey, but for the last few years all of these have ceased to operate and it seems unlikely that they will resume in the forseeable future.

Directory

Airline offices *Syrian Air*, 8 Azar St, T476863/4. As well as buying tickets for flights from Lattakia (see under Transport above for details), you can book and reconfirm international flights with Syrian Air from Damascus here. **Banks** The main branch of *Commercial Bank of Syria* is on Baghdad Ave. Open 0830-1330. You can change cash and TCs here. Outside of these hours, you will have to go to Blue Beach, where the *Meridien* has a branch which is open 0800-2000, daily, while the *Côte d'Azur de Cham* can change money 24 hrs/daily. **Communications** Internet: at the time of writing there was just one computer terminal in the telephone office offering internet access (from 0800-2000 only, closed Fri, S£2/min). Already a couple of private computer shops in the centre of town have their own connections, and it is just a matter of time before private internet cafés start to open up. Post: the main post office is in a small cul-de-sac off Souria Av (around 200 m northeast of the roundabout known as Al Yaman Sq). Open 0800-1900, closed Fri. For stamps, poste restante etc go to the 1st floor. **Telephone**: the telephone office is on the corner of Al Moutanabby and Seif al-Dawlah St. Open 0800-2300, daily. There are 4 cardphones inside. When the desk selling phonecards is closed there is always at least one tout offering them for a small mark-up (eg S£500 card for S£550, or you can pay per unit used). **Couriers**: *DHL*, Seif al-Dawlah St, opposite telephone office, T479166. Open 0830-2030, Fri 0900-1400. To send a ½ kg packet of documents to Europe costs S£1,375, plus S£375 for each additional ½ kg. Better value is the package rate, which allows you to send a 'junior box' of 1-10 kg for S£5,000 or a 'jumbo box' of 1-25 kg for S£10,000. *TNT*, Saad Zaghloul St (on roundabout at northeast end, in same office as *Avis*), T/F478310. To send 1 kg of documents costs S£1,000, then S£500 for each additional kg. **Medical services** There are several chemists on Al Moutanabby St and 8 Azar St. Signs outside (in Arabic only) give information on late-night rotas. Lattakia's main (and best) **hospital** is the *Al-Assad University* in the centre of town on 8 Azar St, T478782/3. **Visa extensions** The Passport and Immigration Office is just to the northeast of Al Jumhouriah Sq (see map). The sign on the building reads 'Brancne Des Passeportes in Lattakia'. Open 0800-1400, closed Fri (though the 'big chief' doesn't get there until 0900 at the earliest). You need a grand total of 6 passport photos (!), and will be sent to-ing and fro-ing between the 2nd and 3rd floors in order to accumulate all the necessary paperwork. Otherwise, it's reasonably efficient and you should get your extension within an hour or so.

Around Lattakia

Blue Beach (Shaati al-Azraq) الشاطئ الأزرق

Phone code: 041 Around 8 km to the northwest of Lattakia is the resort known as Blue Beach (Shaati al-Azraq in Arabic), where the city's two premier hotels-cum-beach resorts are located, as well as a 'village' of private holiday apartments and a modest campsite nearby. The beaches here are relatively clean (by Syrian standards at least).

During the summer, the whole Blue Beach area throngs with Syrian families on holiday. The area around the *Côte d'Azur de Cham* hotel is alive with amusement arcades, stalls selling all kinds of souvenirs and seaside paraphernalia, snack bars and simple restaurants. Night-times are particularly lively, with all the stalls brightly lit and pumping out Arabic music, and couples and families out in their droves promenading. By contrast, in the low season everything closes down and the place is completely dead.

Ins & outs During the high season there are regular **microbuses** which run between the centre of Lattakia (from Antakiah St, behind the large white local government building just to the northeast of the Assad Statue) and Blue Beach (S£5).

To get there if you are **driving**, head north from the centre of Lattakia on 8 Azar Street and then follow signs for the Sports City Complex and *Meridien* hotel. A little over 4 km from the centre of town, go straight over a roundabout (the flyover which crosses this roundabout gives access to the Sports City, a huge complex built in the late 1980s when Syria hosted the Mediterranean Games). Another 3.5 km brings you to a second roundabout. Some 200 m in front of you is the *Côte d'Azur de Cham* hotel. Bearing left brings you after 600 m to the *Meridien* hotel. The spit of land beyond the *Meridien* hotel is given over to private holiday apartments. Bearing right at the roundabout, you pass a campsite on the left after a little over 1 km, and then after another 3 km, a small road on the left leading up to entrance to the site of Ugarit (signposted).

Activities Use of the private beaches and swimming pools at the *Côte d'Azur de Cham* and *Meridien* hotels costs S£250 per person for non-guests (though in practice foreigners shouldn't experience too many problems finding their way onto the beach for free). The *Meridien* is perhaps the better of the two in that all the facilities are integrated, while the *Côte d'Azur de Cham*'s swimming pool is situated in the 'Residence' wing across the road from the main resort. The latter also offers tennis (at the 'Residence' wing) for S£100 per hour for non-guests. In terms of watersports, the two hotels between them offer jet-skis, water-skiing, catamaran sailing, windsurfing and pedalos. As for nightlife, the *Meridien* tends to have more going on in the evenings (the *Côte d'Azur de Cham* is lively enough in summer, but the activity of choice here seems to be milling around the huge lobby area which gives it the atmosphere of an airport terminal).

One popular activity outside of the resorts (alongside just strolling around, visiting the amusement arcades and snacking) is bicycle hire with a difference. While you can find straightforward bicycles (a nice way to get to Ugarit from here if it is not too hot), someone has also been having fun with a welding machine. The result is a weird and wonderful range of tandems, 'quadems' (4-seaters), buggy-style 'pedalos', hi-rise bicycles, unicycles and anything else that the imagination (if not sound engineering practice) will allow!

There is a dramatic variation in prices between the high season (1/6-15/9), when both **Sleeping**
resorts are at their busiest, and the low season (the rest of the year), when they are
very quiet (or completely deserted in winter) and you can pick up rooms at bargain
prices. Sometimes there are also excellent deals on offer towards the end of the high
season. The price categories below reflect standard charges for the high season.

L *Le Meridien*, PO Box 473, T428736, F428732. Choice of sea-side or 'garden-side'
rooms (same price), all suitably luxurious with a/c, TV/dish, IDD, 'soft' minibar,
attached bath. Restaurants, bar, swimming pool, private beach, watersports, nightclub, shops, currency exchange (cash and TCs, open 0800-2000, 7 days), car hire (*Avis*).
Clearly the more luxurious of the two, both in terms of prices and facilities.

AL/A *Côte d'Azur de Cham*, PO Box 1097, T428700, F428285. Choice of sea-side or
considerably cheaper 'garden-side' rooms, all spacious and comfortable, with a/c,
TV/dish, phone, kitchenette, attached bath and balcony. Restaurants, bar, swimming
pool, private beach, watersports, tennis courts, mini golf, nightclub, shops, currency
exchange (cash and TCs, open 24 hrs, 7 days), car hire (*Hertz/Chamcar*). Fairly luxurious, but with more of a 'family resort' feel to it (tiled floors in the rooms for example,
rather than carpets). **G** *Camping*, T429319. Open during summer season only. Pleasantly located by a small bay and fishing harbour, and with its own small stretch of
beach. There are a couple of tents available for rent, or else pitch your own (or park up
your camper-van). The toilet/shower blocks are none too appealing, but otherwise
the site is well run. The beach and camping areas are kept tidy, and there is a reasonable amount of shade. Gets very busy at height of summer season. Small cafeteria.

The 2 luxury hotels between them offer a wide range of up-market eating options with **Eating**
prices to match. For budget eating, try the numerous snack stalls in the vicinity of the
Côte d'Azur de Cham hotel. As well as the usual shawarmas and falafels, mannoushi and
Syrian-style pizzas are particularly popular. There are also a few simple restaurants serving the usual range of Arabic cuisine, but watch out for overcharging.

Ugarit (Ras Shamra) رأس الشمرة

Known locally as Ras Shamra (literally 'Fennel Headland'), Ugarit is considered to   Phone code: 041
be one of the most important Bronze Age sites in the Middle East, providing as it   Colour map 1, grid B1
does one of the key 'touchstones' for archaeological and historical research into this
period. The Ministry of Tourism is keen to point out the importance of the site; what
a pity then that so little money and effort has been invested in presentation here.
The labelling and signposting is extremely rudimentary, and for much of the year
the site is completely overgrown (granted - the flowers look nice in spring!). And this
is despite the fact that excavations began here as long ago as 1929 and have contin-
ued, with few breaks, ever since. There are substantial remains on view at Ugarit,
particularly the royal palace complex, though unless you have a particular interest
in the Bronze Age period, prepare to be disappointed. Important artefacts discov-
ered at Ugarit can be seen in the National Museums in Damascus and Aleppo (and
to a lesser extent in the Lattakia Museum), though many of the more important
items are now in the Louvre Museum, Paris.

Ins and outs

Minibuses to Ugarit (S£5, 25 mins) depart from Antakiah St, behind the large white **Getting there**
local government building just to the northeast of the Assad Statue, passing via Blue
Beach and dropping passengers at the junction just 200 m from the site entrance. To
return, just flag down any passing minibus.

Driving, head north from the centre of Lattakia on 8 Azar St as if for Blue Beach. At Iskandarun Sq (signposted around 2.5 km from the centre), turn right, and then left at the junction 400 m further on to join Ugarit St heading north. Around 6 km from the centre of town, bear left at a large roundabout (signposted 'Meridien, Côte d'Azur, Ugarit'). Just over 2 km further on, fork left (signposted 'Raas Shamra'), and look out for the turning on the right just over 1 km further on, clearly signposted for Ugarit (the entrance is 200 m down this road). Alternatively, you can get there from Blue Beach (see above).

Entry & facilities   Open 0830-1830 in summer, 0830-1630 in winter. Entry S£300 (students S£15). Postcards, brochures, souvenirs etc are available both from stalls outside and from main ticket office. There are toilets and a simple café at the site entrance, but inside the site there is very little shade; bring plenty of water and adequate protection against the sun. In the full heat of summer, time your visit for the early morning or late afternoon, or else restrict yourself to the royal palace complex, which is in any case the most interesting area.

History

The town's growth & wealth were based on a combination of its location on a key commercial route between Mesopotamia & the Mediterranean, & the rich agricultural land that surrounded the city

Excavations on the tell (mound) at Ugarit have revealed evidence of occupation dating back to the seventh millennium BC. Nevertheless, it is the Bronze Age (3300-1200 BC) that most interests archaeologists and historians here. At some point in the late fourth or early third millennium BC, a population of Mesopotamian origin settled at the site, providing links to both Mesopotamia to the east and Cyprus to the west. The city's harbour (Minet al-Beida, some 1.5 km northwest, but now off-limits within a military area) became the point through which copper technology was largely introduced to the region.

For reasons that are as yet unclear, the city went into severe decline around 2000 BC, though layers of ash in the lower levels of stratum at the site suggest that the city may have been captured and burnt. Among subsequent migrants settling at the site were the **Canaanites**, who remained the dominant group here for the next eight centuries. The beginning of the second millennium BC represents the dawn of the city's first golden age, and by the 18th century BC we have textual proof that the name Ugarit was in common usage.

Ugarit's potential quickly drew the attention of the **Egyptians**, though Ugarit remained an independent kingdom (with a locally drawn royal dynasty) sandwiched between the far greater powers of Egypt and Mesopotamia. Ugarit's kings must have been statesmen of some ability to avoid having their kingdom subsumed into the mass of one of the neighbouring empires and there is even considerable evidence that Ugarit maintained close links with other empires, notably the **Minoan** civilization on Crete. The city also developed a reputation for excellence in bronze-working, adding another string to the bow of the city's economic base.

By the beginning of the Late Bronze Age (c.1550 BC), Ugarit was drawn closer and closer into Egypt's orbit, though the growing power of the **Mitannite** Dynasty in Mesopotamia meant that Ugarit still had to continue to walk the narrow tightrope of international diplomacy. It is even possible that Ugarit played an intermediary role between the Egyptians and Mitannites. They had much to gain from stability, the peace that emerged greatly enhancing Ugarit's wealth-generating capacity and resulting in the city's golden age of the 14th and 13th centuries BC. Under King **Niqmadou II** (r. 1360-1330), Ugarit traded with Egypt, Mesopotamia, Anatolia and the Aegean region, many of the transactions resulting from this great trade being recorded in the documents found at the site. Several of the buildings seen at the site today, including Niqmadou II's royal palace complex, date to this golden period.

The rise of the **Hittites** in the Anatolia region to the north posed a considerable threat to the independence of Ugarit, with the Ugarit kings going to great lengths to appease the Hittites (including requests to the Egyptian pharaohs to send gifts). However, correspondence discovered at the site here leaves no doubt that the Hittites considered Ugarit effectively part of their extended empire. Nevertheless, despite these pressures, the city continued to build links with the outside world, notably the Aegean region.

When Ugarit's end came it was remarkably swift, though not necessarily cataclysmic. The invasion of the region by the Sea Peoples (most famously the **Philistines**) around 1200 BC may have seen the city attacked, though there is reason to suggest that Ugarit's decline is equally attributable to the collapse of the palace-based economy brought about by changing technological needs that the subsequent Iron Age demanded. The site was later occupied during various periods, though Ugarit's golden past was never recreated, and the city lay largely forgotten until a chance find by a local farmer in 1928.

Sights

The tour of the site begins at the main entrance gate (**a**). Before ascending the steps to the ticket office (**b**), it is worth examining the remains of the **fortress walls and postern gate** (**c**) just to the right (south). The defensive wall was first built in the 15th century BC, though considerably strengthened during a later period. This involved levelling off the slope of the mound to an angle of 45° and covering it with stone, thus forming a difficult to climb *glacis*. The wall and *glacis* at this point was further fortified by a tower, probably built to defend the postern gate. It is generally believed that the gateway here was for royal usage, with the main gateway (along with most of the rest of the fortress walls) not having survived the ravages of time. Ascend the steps to the ticket office, then

The letters in brackets refer to 'Ugarit: Site Plan'. The numbers in brackets refer to 'royal palace complex'

The Coast & the Jebel Ansariye

Ugarit

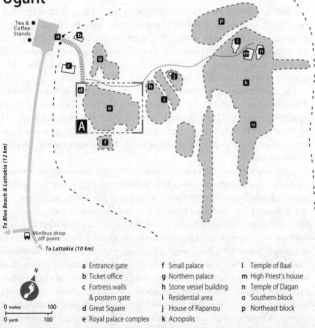

a Entrance gate	**f** Small palace	**l** Temple of Baal
b Ticket office	**g** Northern palace	**m** High Priest's house
c Fortress walls & postern gate	**h** Stone vessel building	**n** Temple of Dagan
d Great Square	**i** Residential area	**o** Southern block
e Royal palace complex	**j** House of Rapanou	**p** Northeast block
	k Acropolis	

Related map
A Royal palace complex, page 297

Tea & Coffee Stands

To Blue Beach & Lattakia (12 km)

Minibus drop off point

To Lattakia (10 km)

0 metres 100
0 yards 100

☞ *Ugarit alphabets*

Texts and tablets discovered at Ugarit reveal the use of eight languages. Much of the diplomatic correspondence is in Babylonian (or Akkadian), the lingua franca of the region. Other texts have been found in Hourrian, Cypro-Minoan, Hittite cuneiform, Sumerian, plus inscriptions in hieroglyphic Hittite and Egyptian. However, of greatest interest is the language now referred to as Ugaritic.

Prior to the 14th century BC, the two key regional forms of writing were hieroglyphic (evolving in Egypt) and cuneiform (from Mesopotamia). Both systems are complex, involving hundreds of signs and symbols representing either complete words or syllables. Excavations at Ugarit, however, revealed a greatly simplified form of writing, comprising just 30 signs based on a 'one sound, one sign' system. Tablets found at the site revealed a list of the 30 letters in the order in which they occur, thus allowing archaeologists

to decipher the texts discovered here. Dating to the 14th century BC, it is now claimed that Ugaritic is the most ancient alphabet in the world.

descend the other side towards the **great square (d)** at the entrance to the royal palace complex.

Royal palace complex (e) The palace complex dates to the city's golden age (14th-13th centuries BC), covering an impressive 10,000 sq m and featuring some 90 rooms, five large courtyards and an interior garden. It is worth bearing in mind that what you see today is merely the remains of the ground floor; the palace previously had an upper storey where most of the living quarters would have been (the remains of several staircases can still be seen).

The main entrance (1) to the complex was through a large wooden gateway, whose stone pillar bases can still be seen. Inside the entrance is a small paved square/reception area (2). A doorway on the east side of the square leads into a square room (3), which in turn leads north through a passage (4) into a secretary's office (5). The adjoining rooms (6, 7, 8, 9) are where the Western Archive was found.

Returning to the square room (3), head south into the palace's main courtyard (10). The courtyard's paved floor is well preserved, as are the conduits used to channel water throughout the complex. The well in the southwest corner of the courtyard provided much of the palace's supply of water. Pass from the main courtyard (10) into the porch (11), and then into what has been dubbed the 'throne room' (12). From here you can reach the banquet hall (13) to the east. From here, head south into another large, impressive courtyard (14), labelled the 'Reception Hall', at the centre of which stands a sunken pool with steps leading down into it from the east side. Remains of the channels that brought water from outside the palace walls can be clearly seen. Also of note here is the well on the west side of the courtyard and the cistern in the southeast corner. In the southwest corner a small oven (15) was found. The purpose of this oven was to bake the tablets upon which the letters, treaties, inventories and texts were written. The treasure of important finds gathered here is known as the Tablets of the Oven, whilst to the south of the courtyard lie the two rooms (**16,17**) in which the Southern Archive was found. The room to the west (**18**) revealed the Southwestern Archive.

Following the water channel east from the 'Reception Hall' (**14**), you come to the palace's large interior garden (**19**). The small structure on the north side (**20**) next to the well and bucket has been identified as the gardener's lodge. The three rooms to the north of here (**21, 22, 23**) are where the Eastern Archive was found. The two large structures on the south side of the garden (**24, 25**) are thought to have been shops or store rooms. The building in the northwest corner of the garden (**26**) appears to have been the workshop where the garden's ivory furniture was built (many fragments of ivory were excavated from the garden area). Just to the west of this you can walk through a large hall (**27**) and small room (**28**) to reach the north entrance (**29**) of the palace, where you can still see the notches in the wall on which the wooden gate used to hang. Retrace your steps through the large hall (**27**), and via another room to the west (**30**) to reach a large courtyard (**31**), signposted 'Courtyard II'. On the east side of this courtyard can be seen the bases of two stone pillars that once supported a porch, inside which is a well. In the main part of the courtyard, meanwhile, is a rectangular basin. Lying to the north of this large courtyard are a series of three sepulchral vaults dug beneath the rooms (**32, 33**) that served as the palace necropolis (signposted the 'Royal Tombs').

The so-called 'Small palace' is south of the royal palace complex; you enter it from the west side. It is fairly ruinous inside and nothing is labelled. The principal feature is the central room containing a large underground burial

Small palace (f)

Royal palace complex

1 Main entrance	**11** Porch	**19** Interior garden	**29** North entrance
2 Reception area	**12** Throne room	**20** Gardener's lodge	**30** Room
3 Square room	**13** Banquet hall	**21-23** Eastern Archive rooms	**31** Courtyard II
4 Passage	**14** Courtyard	**24-25** Shops/store rooms	**32-33** Necropolis
5 Secretary's office	**15** Oven	**26** Workshop	
6-9 Adjoining rooms	**16-17** Southern Archive room	**27** Large hall	
10 Main courtyard	**18** Southwestern Archive room	**28** Small room	

chamber with steps leading down to it from the west side and an arched roof which is still largely intact. The room immediately to the southeast contains another smaller but better preserved burial chamber.

Northern palace (g) & residential area (i) Following the path east from the entrance to the royal palace complex (**d**), along the outside of the north wall, you pass a fairly ruinous area on the left known as the **'Northern Palace'** (**g**). It is difficult to identify individual buildings here, though a section of the main sewer canal can be seen. Among the solid structures located in this area are the royal stables. Further on, you come to a sign for the **'Stone Vessel building'** (**h**), so-called because of the huge stone urn – completely intact – discovered inside. This marks the start of the **residential area** (**i**), comprising a fairly large concentration of spacious private houses, criss-crossed by a network of streets. Bearing off slightly to the left here, you come next to a sign for the **'House of Rapanou'** (**j**), a spacious 34-room villa, complete with its own excellently preserved underground mausoleum, belonging to a man named Rapanou. It was here that the so-called Library of Rapanou was discovered.

Acropolis (k) A little beyond the House of Rapanou, an arrow points you along a path towards the acropolis (**k**). Just before you get there you pass a deep trench. Dug by the archaeologists, this stratigraphic sounding covers the periods from the eighth to second millenium BC. A little further up, you come to the **Temple of Baal** (**l**), believed to have been the patron deity of Ugarit. Unfortunately, though it is signposted, it is now almost completely in ruins and there is little to see. Continuing along the path, you pass a deep water cistern, partially covered by a stone slab, and the indistinct ruins of the **High Priest's house** (**m**), where the Library of the High Priest was discovered. Further on is the **Temple of Dagan** (**n**), dedicated to the god of the underworld in the Ugarit pantheon. This temple, comprised of two rectangular courtyards surrounded by 4-5 m thick walls, is slightly better preserved though there is still not much to see.

To the south side of the acropolis is what is referred to as the **southern block** (**o**), though there is little to see here and it is badly overgrown. Many of the structures discovered here are thought to have been homes and artisans' workshops. Two separate dwellings in the southern block revealed the Southern Block Library and the Library of the Magician Priest.

Likewise, the **northeast block** (**p**) to the north of the acropolis is badly neglected, though the mound of accumulated debris from the various excavations does provide a good vantage point from which to view the site.

Kassab and Ras al-Bassit/ Al Badrusiyeh

To the north of Lattakia, right up against the de-facto border with Turkey, is the pleasant hill-resort town of Kassab, set amongst the foothills of the Al Aqra mountains. Immediately to the north and just inside Turkey is **Jebel al-Aqra** (1,728 m), the Mount Casius of antiquity, a mountain sacred to the Phoenicians and a focus for the worship of Zeus during Roman times. To the southwest, meanwhile, along the northernmost stretch of Syria's Mediterranean coast, are the beach resorts of Ras al-Bassit and Al Badrusiyeh, amongst the best in Syria (although that is not really saying very much). The scenery en route to Kassab is very picturesque (see below), and it is the drive perhaps more than the destinations which are the real pleasure.

Head north out of Lattakia as if for Ugarit and bear right at the large round-about around 6 km from the centre of town (signposted for 'Turkey, Kassab, Al Bassit'). Keep going straight along this road surrounded by fertile plains given over to highly productive agricultural land. Further north the road begins to climb into the foothills of the **Al Aqra** mountains, passing through olive groves and thick pine forests. A few kilometres after passing a turning right (25 km from the roundabout) signposted for the village of Balloram, you pass on your right a particularly beautiful lake set amongst pine forests. Towards the north end of the lake there are a couple of restaurants overlooking it. Just over 5 km beyond the right turn for Balloram, there is a left turn sign-posted to 'Al Bassit' and 'Badroussieh', the start of the road leading down to these resorts. Continuing straight, a little under 5 km further on you pass through the small village of Qastal Ma'af. After another 6 km you reach a right turn signposted to Aleppo (this road joins the highway between Lattakia and Aleppo). Continuing straight, after a further 7 km, fork left for Kassab. (If you carry on going straight on, you reach the Turkish border.) From the fork it is around 4 km on to Kassab.

Lattakia to Kassab

Kassab كسب

Sprawling out over the hillside, the town of Kassab, with its concrete high-rise apartment blocks springing up all over the place, is no oil painting. Its situation, on the other hand, is. The surrounding mountains are very beautiful and great for walkers. The predominantly Armenian population of the town is friendly and the place has a relaxed air about it. It is very popular as a summer retreat from the heat of the plains, particularly with Aleppines and visiting Gulf families, many of whom rent apartments for the whole of the summer. For around one week before and after the Feast of the Assumption on 15th August it gets particularly busy here and there is little chance of finding accommodation. In contrast, during low season (September-May) it gets very cold and wet, with heavy snow in the depths of winter, and the town more or less completely closes down.

Phone code: 041
Colour map 1, grid B1

D *Sevan (Razzouk)*, on the left as you drive into Kassab, before you reach the main square, T710267, F711485. Clean, comfortable rooms with TV/dish, phone, fridge, attached bath and balcony. A/c planned. Restaurant wth pleasant terrace area and great views. Friendly, well run place. Closed Nov-Mar. **E** *Al Rawda*, situated on left as you head up hill from main square, on back road to Ras al-Bassit, T711008, F711400. simple but clean rooms (double S£800) with attached bath. Closed Sep-May. **F** *Amira (Princess)*, on left as you head up hill from main square, on back road to Ras al-Bassit, T711007. Simple but clean rooms (double S£600) with shared bath (some with attached bath). Closed Sep-May. **G** *Motel Vahé*, beyond main square, T710224. Basic but clean rooms (S£200 per bed), some with attached bath. Pleasant courtyard. Closed Sep-May.

Sleeping, eating & transport

The restaurant in the *Sevan (Razzouk)* hotel serves good Arabic food for around S£250 per head upwards. Beyond the main square, the *Kilekia* is easily the nicest place to eat, with a lovely vine-shaded terrace and great views. They offer the usual range of Arabic fare, including fish, for around S£200 per head. There are several simple snack places along the main street.

During the summer season there are regular services from the **microbus** station in Lattakia (see above). Bear in mind that the last service back to **Lattakia** usually leaves well before nightfall. Out of season, services are much less frequent, drying up altogether in the dead of winter.

The Coast & the Jebel Ansariye

Ras al-Bassit رأس البسيط and Al Badrusiyeh بدروسية

From the turning for Ras al-Bassit and Badrusiyeh (see above), it is 12 km down to the coast, the road descending steeply through the mountains. Approaching the coast, there is a signposted right turn for Badrusiyeh, while keeping straight takes you into Ras al-Bassit. There is another route to Ras al-Bassit and Al Badrusiyeh directly from Kassab, along an extremely scenic and equally winding road. The turning is signposted from the main square in Kassab; keep following this road for around 16 km to arrive at the resorts.

The stretch of coastline here is unusual for its distinctive black sand beaches, relatively clean compared with elsewhere along the coast, but still beset by rubbish. However, the setting is quite beautiful, with mountains rising dramatically to the north and east. **Al Badrusiyeh** consists of a long stretch of sea front lined with a variety of stalls, snack bars, billiards tents and shops selling seaside paraphernalia; Syria's answer to Blackpool perhaps? **Ras al-Bassit** is much the same, although it is rather more developed. During the summer it gets extremely busy here. By around mid-September the crowds start to leave and it is much quieter, only picking up again towards the end of April/beginning of May.

Sleeping, eating & transport

Most of the accommodation here consists of chalets and apartments which are usually rented out for a period of weeks or months, although it may be possible to rent one on a nightly basis (around US$20-60 for 2 people depending on the facilities) subject to availability. There is one hotel in Ras al-Bassit, the **C** *Bassit Tourist*, some rooms with a/c, attached bath, restaurant. At the very northerly end of the beach in Al Badrusiyeh, meanwhile, there is a recently built eyesore, the **C** *Al Hammam Island*, offering a choice of small, medium or large suites, some with a/c.

There are numerous snack places and restaurants in both resorts. During the summer there are frequent services from the microbus station in Lattakia. The luxury coach company *Harsho* runs 4 coaches daily from Lattakia and Aleppo during the summer season only.

Qalat Saladin (Saône) قلعة صلاح الدّين

It is hard at first to understand why the Crusaders (or indeed the Byzantines and Phoenicians before them) should have chosen this wild and isolated location for a castle (its setting on a narrow ridge is far more dramatic than that of Krak des Chevaliers). Today the main route between Aleppo and Lattakia passes it by some distance to the north, but in ancient times an alternative route ran parallel to it, to the south, passing through the village of Al Haffeh. In fact the castle was sufficiently close to both routes to be able to control movement along them. It also had commanding views of the plains inland from Lattakia, an important consideration for the Crusaders, even though in the end they were powerless to stop Salah ud-Din (Saladin) taking it.

Ins and outs

Getting there

Regular **microbuses** run from Lattakia to Al Haffeh (S£10, 30-45 mins), from where you must walk (around 6 km, see route description below) or else negotiate a lift. The trip should not cost more than S£20-30 one way, although you may have to bargain hard since many of the vehicle owners in the village have cottoned on to the possibility of charging tourists exorbitant rates. Take care to return to the village well before nightfall in order to be sure of picking up transport returning to Lattakia. Microbuses also run from Al Haffeh on to the summer hill resort of Slunfeh.

Driving, from Jumhouriah Sq in Lattakia, head east along Aleppo Av, following signs for Damascus and Aleppo. Just after passing the Tishreen University grounds on the right, continue straight over a large roundabout (2 km from Jumhouriah Sq). Keep going straight (past an exit for the Aleppo road) following signs for Tartus and Damascus now, to join the coastal motorway heading south. Take the exit signposted 'Slunfeh, Al Haffeh, Saladin Citadel' (just over 14 km from Jumhouriah Sq), turning left at a T-junction after 700 m to go under the motorway. A little over 1 km further on, turn right at what is effectively a crossroads (signposted). Keep following this road for around 20 km to arrive in the centre of Al Haffeh. Drive through the village and take the clearly signposted right turn around 2 km further on. After 1,500 m fork left (also signposted, but not clearly). You pass on your left after 500 m a restaurant with excellent views across a deep ravine to the castle, before descending steeply and then climbing to reach the castle, just over 2 km beyond the restaurant.

Open 0900-1800 in summer, 0900-1600 in winter, closed Tue. Entry S£300 (students S£15). There are various postcards and souvenirs on sale at the ticket office. Toilets are at the bottom of the steps leading up to the entrance. There is no hotel at Qalat Saladin, or in the village of Al Haffeh. However, if you get stuck here it is worth asking at the **restaurant** on the way down to the castle from Al Haffeh. They may be willing to put you up for the night. Other than a couple of simple falafel/shawarma places in the village, and a tea house in the castle itself, this is the only place where you can get anything to eat.

Entry & facilities

History

Although known today as Qalat Saladin, this name was only given to the castle in 1957, in commemoration of Salah ud-Din's capture of it in 1188. To the Crusaders it was known as *Saône*, a name corrupted in Arabic to *Sayhun*. In its present form the castle dates mostly from the 12th century, although its origins go back much further. Early in the first millennium BC, the site was fortified by the Phoenicians and they were still in possession of it when Alexander the Great passed through Syria in 333 BC, en route for Egypt. In the second half of the 10th century the Byzantines, led by the Emperor John Zimisces, advanced into northern Syria, re-establishing the duchy of Antioch and seizing the site from the Hamdamid Dynasty of Aleppo. The remains of the fortifications they built can still be seen in the old citadel which stands on a small hillock in the centre of the eastern half of the castle, and also in the traces of defensive walls, all now enclosed within the later and more substantial work of the Crusaders.

The Crusaders first gained possession of the castle early in the 12th century. By 1119 it had been entrusted as a feudal endowment to Robert of Saône (from whom it took its name), by Roger, Prince of Antioch. It was to remain in Crusader hands until its capture by Salah ud-Din in 1188. During this period, the

Unlike other castles in the area, Qalat Saladin was never entrusted to either the Knights Templars or the Hospitallers

Qalat Saladin (Saône)

1 Rock needle	5 Stables	9 Mosque	12 Byzantine citadel
2 Entrance tower	6 Water cistern	10 Palace & baths complex	13 Tea house
3 Tower	7 Main keep	11 Water cistern	14 Byzantine chapel
4 Tower	8 Postern gate		15 Crusader church

Crusaders carried out major building works, largely rendering the Byzantine fortifications redundant and giving it the overall form you see today. As such, it represents a unique example of early Crusader castle architecture, unusual for this period in terms of its extravagant scale and execution.

Its fall to Salah ud-Din in 1188 is in many ways surprising. He had bypassed other major Crusader strongholds in the region (notably Krak des Chevaliers and Qalat Marqab), concentrating his attention on smaller, more easily taken castles. However, having conquered Lattakia, he moved on to Saône and laid siege to it. Two days later, the walls of the lower court on the north side were breached and the Crusader forces, insufficient in number to defend such a large castle, soon surrendered.

After its fall, the castle remained in Muslim hands. It was controlled first by the family of a local emir loyal to the Ayyubids, the Nasr ud-Din Manguwiris, before being handed over to the Mameluke sultan Baibars in 1272, during his campaign to drive the Crusaders from the region. In 1280 it briefly fell into the hands of Sonqor al-Ashtar, a governor of Damascus who rebelled against the Mamelukes, but was returned to Mameluke control under the sultan Qalaun (Baibar's successor) in 1287 after a brief siege. Subsequently its strategic importance appears to have declined and it fell into obscurity, housing a village for a time but later being abandoned.

Sights

The castle from outside   Approaching the castle from the village of Al Haffeh, it is worth stopping briefly before descending into the ravine for an overview of the castle. What you see from this side is the largely ruined western lower courtyard and the Byzantine citadel. Having dropped down to the bottom of the ravine, crossed a stream and then climbed again up the other side, you pass through a deep narrow **canyon** between two walls of sheer vertical rock. Incredible though it may seem, this is man-made, having been hewn out of the rock in order to separate the ridge on which the castle stands from the main body of the mountain to the east. Towards the northern end of the canyon is a free-standing needle of rock rising to a height of 28 m which was left when the surrounding rock was chiselled away in order to allow a drawbridge to be extended from the castle, providing an alternative entrance/exit. The eastern fortifications of the castle rise almost seamlessly from the natural rock, towering above you imposingly. The canyon is thought to have first been carved out by the Byzantines and then widened and deepened by the Crusaders.

Before entering the castle, follow the road as it climbs up the side of the ravine to the south. From this direction you get an even better view of the castle layout, in particular the concentration of Crusader fortifications along its more vulnerable eastern side, as well as the walls and towers along the southern side.

Eastern defences   Entry to the castle is through the last of three solid rectangular towers in the southern walls. A long flight of concrete steps climbs up to the tower. Leaving the entrance hall (where the ticket office is located), more or less directly in front of you is the mosque (see below). Turn right to follow the line of the southern walls towards the eastern fortifications. The three rectangular towers along the southern walls each have a staircase which gives access to the first floor and roof. These are typical of the early Crusader style, both in terms of their shape and the prominently bossed and neatly jointed large square blocks used in their construction.

A doorway immediately to the left of the easternmost rectangular tower gives access to the **stables** and **water cistern**. Going through the doorway, on your right are steps leading down into the huge barrel-vaulted water cistern. On the left, meanwhile, a second doorway leads through into the stables, a large vaulted area, its low roof supported by large, squat pillars. Tucked away in the far south-east corner of the stables is a doorway giving access to a small room in the central semicircular tower of the eastern defences. Along with the other semicircular towers along the eastern defences, this was originally built by the Byzantines and substantially modified and strengthened by the Crusaders. The northernmost of this set of three towers can likewise be accessed from the stables, and also has a stairway beside it leading up to the ramparts, from where there are truly vertiginous views down into the rock-cut canyon below.

Immediately to the north of the stables is the main **keep** (or *donjon*), a squat, solidly built two storey square tower which formed the final defensive position of the castle. With walls over 5 m thick it would certainly have presented a formidable challenge to any would-be attacker. A plain doorway in the west wall leads into a single large room, with a massive central pillar supporting the vaulted ceiling. The interior is very poorly lit, the only natural light coming through the doorway and the narrow arrow slits in the walls. A set of stairs on your left as you enter leads up to the first floor, the room here being identical except that the ceiling is lower and windows in three of the walls make it much lighter. The stairs continue up to the roof of the keep, from where there are good all-round views.

To the north again of the keep is a series of rooms, their ceilings collapsed, followed by a large hall with its arched ceiling still intact. The latter once formed the **postern gate**, giving access to the castle via a drawbridge supported on the needle of rock rising from the floor of the artificial canyon. This complex of buildings to the north of the main keep and extending around the northeast corner of the castle are all of Byzantine origin, with only the postern gate showing signs of later modification by the Crusaders. Note also the crumbling inner line of walls running parallel to the eastern fortifications; these are likewise of Byzantine origin.

Doubling back the way you came, you can visit next the mosque, which dates from the Mameluke occupation, probably during the reign of the Sultan Qalaun (1280-90). Steps lead up to an arched and vaulted porch which takes you in to the prayer hall. At the time of writing, the mosque was undergoing extensive restoration. On the higher ground just to the northwest of the mosque is the **palace and baths complex**, which has undergone some restoration in recent years. This dates from the Ayyubid period (late 12th to early 13th century). The main entrance, leading first into the palace, is from the eastern side, through a doorway elaborately decorated in typical Ayyubid style with stalactites and geometric patterns of interlocking stonework. Inside is a vaulted reception hall with an opening in the centre of the ceiling to let light in, and arched *iwans* to the left and right. Straight ahead is another doorway preceded by an arched semi-dome which leads into the baths complex. The main room here (its roof no longer intact) contains a shallow circular pool in the centre of the floor, with channels leading into it. On the north side of the room is an arched *iwan* flanked by two tall, arched passageways which lead through into the bathing rooms. To the west of the palace and baths complex, perched on top of a small hillock, is the original **Byzantine citadel**, now in an advanced state of ruin, its surviving stonework noticeably inferior to that of the Crusader fortifications.

A path leads north from the palace and baths complex taking you past the entrance to a huge **water cistern** set against the northern walls. The vast, echoing proportions of the interior, with its barrel-vaulted roof and steps leading

Mosque, palace & baths complex
Note the mosque's distinctive square minaret

Rest of the castle

The Coast & the Jebel Ansariye

The Alawis

Like the Ismailis, the Alawis are an offshoot of mainstream Shi'ite Islam, although very little is known about their origins, beliefs or practices. According to their own traditions they originated from the Arabian peninsula, moving to the Jebel Sinjar, a mountainous region between the Tigris and Euphrates, before arriving in Syria. The founder of their religion, Mohammad Ibn Nusayr, is thought to have developed its basic tenets in the ninth century, preaching that the One God was inexpressible and unknowable, but that a hierarchy of divine beings emanated from him, with Ali representing the highest of these. The term 'Alawi' (or 'Alawite') dates from the French Mandate period, meaning literally 'Followers of Ali'. Previously they were known as Ansaris or Nusayris after Mohammad Ibn Nusayr, and both names are used to describe Syria's coastal mountains (Jebel Ansariye or Jebel Nusayri), where they settled when they came to Syria.

Their doctrines are said to contain elements of Phoenician paganism, Manichaeism, Zoroastrianism and Christian Gnosticism. The Christian element, for example the belief in the symbolic significance of bread and wine and their observance of many Christian festivals, is strongly emphasized by many

commentators. Inevitably for such an esoteric religion, where even amongst themselves only a few are full initiates, the numerous stories surrounding their beliefs and practices all to a greater or lesser extent combine elements of truth and fabrication. Those emanating from their orthodox Sunni critics have tended to be the most fantastic and far-fetched, encompassing all manner of sexual perversions and secretive ritual practices.

The Islamic doctrine of Taqiya (concealing or disguising one's religion, especially in times of persecution or danger) provided the key to their survival and perhaps goes a long way to explaining the supposed syncretic nature of their beliefs. Thus the British traveller Maundrell, writing in 1697, described them as "of a strange and singular character. For 'tis their principle to adhere to no certain religion; but chameleon-like, they put on the colour of religion, whatever it may be, which is reflected upon them from the persons with whom they happen to converse... Nobody was ever able to discover what shape or standard their consciences are really of. All that is certain concerning them is that they make much good wine and are great drinkers."

down inside, is truly awesome. Next to it are two smaller and somewhat more ruinous cisterns. All of these were built by the Crusaders and, along with the first cistern in the southeast corner of the castle, provided a sufficient store of water to survive a lengthy siege.

From here you can follow a path westwards along the northern walls, passing the remains of the Byzantine citadel up on your left until you reach a Crusader-period building which today serves as a **tea house** selling refreshments and postcards. From here you can look down over the lower (western) courtyard of the castle, separated from the upper (eastern) courtyard by a ditch. This western half of the castle is almost entirely ruined and heavily overgrown. Only the line of the walls and towers are still discernible, along with a tiny **Byzantine chapel**. In the distance an artificial lake can be seen and, on a clear day, the plains around Lattakia and the Mediterranean Sea beyond. Unless you are really dedicated (and well protected against the thick brambles), it is not worth descending into this part of the castle.

Continue instead along the footpath, which completes a circuit around the hillock and Byzantine citadel to arrive back at the entrance tower, passing en route the ruins of a **Crusader church** on the left, on the far side of which are the ruins of a much smaller **Byzantine chapel**.

In the eyes of the Sunni orthodoxy of the Medieval period, they were nothing short of heretical, and as such their religion was widely condemned as an abomination to Islam. The Syrian theologan Ahmad Ibn Taymiya (1268-1328) described them as "more infidel than Jews or Christians" and argued that "war and punishment in accordance with Islamic Law against them are among the greatest of pious deeds and the most important obligations for a Muslim".

Certainly their history is one of constant persecution. From the time of the First Crusade (1098), their mountain strongholds were seized by the Crusaders, while early in the 12th century they faced similar encroachment from the Ismailis. Salah ud-Din (Saladin), when he swept through the mountains in his campaign of 1188 forced them to pay him a hefty annual tribute. The Mameluke sultans inflicted heavy losses on them, according to the Muslim chronicler Ibn Battuta, massacring 20,000, and tried forcibly to convert them to Sunni Islam, making them build mosques in their villages, to which they supposedly responded by using them as cattle sheds. The oppression continued, more or less unabated, throughout the Ottoman period, mostly through the imposition of punitive taxes.

Remarkably, however, from a position as late as the 1920s of almost total social exclusion, a poor, largely uneducated rural community discriminated against and isolated in a harsh mountainous environment, the Alawis underwent a dramatic transformation. The French courted them as potential allies, giving them a separate 'enclave' in the mountains around Lattakia where they were concentrated, just as they had done for the Maronites of Mount Lebanon. For the first time after centuries of relentless oppression they were presented with a unique opportunity, and it was one of which they made every use, totally reversing their situation and putting themselves at the heart of political and military power in the modern state of Syria. This is illustrated most clearly by the late president Hafez al-Assad, himself an Alawi, who held absolute power for three decades, and whose son, Bashar al-Assad, has succeeded him. Today the Alawi number around one million in Syria, representing nearly 12% of the total population. Over three-quarters of these live in the province of Lattakia where they form a two-thirds majority.

From the village of Al Haffeh, the main road continues east through the mountains to arrive in the centre of Slunfeh, 17 km away. Today a sprawling hill resort of considerable size, with plenty of new constructions going on around its edges, Slunfeh is a popular summer getaway for richer Syrians, many of whom have their own private villas here. There is a large hotel (closed during winter), situated by the roundabout in the centre of town: the catchily named **C/D** *Big Hotel and Restaurant of Slunfeh* T750606, F750035, a huge, grandiose, echoing building with reasonably comfortable rooms with attached bath, and a large restaurant. There are several restaurants and snack places around the main square. Definitely worth checking out are the excellent bakeries/takeaway places along the street to the east of the main square. They sell delicious savoury pastries and pizzas, as well as kebabs, burgers, chips etc.

Continuing east from Slunfeh, the main road continues to climb before bearing north along the easternmost ridges of the Jebel Ansariye. After passing some radio transmitters on the right there are various **viewpoints** by the roadside. Providing it is not too hazy, you can look out over the spectacular Al Ghab plains, spread out before you in a dramatic patchwork of fields, slashed through by the ultra-straight lines of irrigation canals. Just over 7 km from the centre of Slunfeh (soon after the viewpoints), a minor road forks off to the left;

Slunfeh

Phone code: 041
Colour map 1, grid B2

The Coast & the Jebel Ansariye

this road leads eventually to the main Lattakia-Aleppo highway. Keep going straight to start descending in a long series of switchbacks down to the plains. After 19 km you arrive at a T-junction in the tiny village of Jorin, the road here running north past the ruins of Qalat Burzey towards the town of Jisr al-Shughur, or south towards Apamea (see page 230).

Qardaha القرداحة

Phone code: 041
Colour map 1, grid B1

Qardaha's chief (and indeed only) claim to fame is that it is the birthplace of the late Hafez al-Assad, president of Syria for nearly 30 years. In the mountains some 30 km to the southeast of Lattakia, the exit for Qardaha is clearly sign-posted off the coastal motorway 17 km to the south of Lattakia. From here you follow a broad four-lane highway which is completely out of proportion to the volume of traffic travelling along it. This near-deserted highway is a suitable introduction to Qaradaha itself, which has something of a ghost town feel about it: all wide boulevards and fancy villas but not enough people. When Assad rose to power, Qardaha was a tiny, remote Alawi village hidden away in the mountains. The development which has been somewhat gratuitously lav-ished on it neatly reflects the remarkable reversal in fortunes which the Alawi community experienced during Assad's rule.

Other than the large, modern mosque in the centre of town, and the even more ubiquitous than usual portraits of Hafez-al-Assad and his two sons, Basel (deceased) and Bashar (the current president), there is nothing of particular interest here. However, in the unlikely event that you might wish to stay here, the authorities have thoughtfully built a huge, towering white elephant of a hotel, the 125-room **C/D** Qardaha International, T843231, F843234. The rooms here are actually quite good value for the level of facilities offered, with a/c, TV, phone and attached bath, but overall the hotel is rather run down, with peeling wallpa-per, stained carpets and a general air of having rarely seen any guests.

Aleppo حلب

8

Aleppo حلب

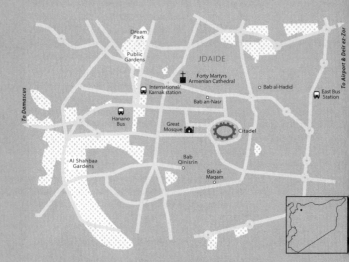

*Nestling in a depression on the stark, dry plateau which rises to the north of the Central Plains, Aleppo is Syria's second largest city, and vies with Damascus for the status of oldest continuously inhabited city in the world. Although its history is ancient, most of the city's surviving monuments date from the later Islamic era. It is famous for its formidable **Citadel**, and its labyrinth of covered **souks** and **khans** – it was through trade that Aleppo flourished, its fortunes rising and falling with those of the trade routes and traders it serviced. Wandering through the bustling souks and visiting the various khans, you quickly get a sense of the commercial life-blood of the city flowing to much the same rhythms as it did centuries ago: this is no historical theme park frozen in time, but a working city where past and present blend into one.*

Over the centuries Aleppo has enjoyed a number of periods of independence, as well as being subject to various outside influences, a fact that has given it a distinctive feel even in modern times: a Syrian city certainly, but one full of contrasts and with very much its own character. In terms of its majority Muslim population, it is much more conservative and insular than Damascus, without such an overtly modern and cosmopolitan atmosphere, although in earlier centuries all the major European trading powers set up shop here in the many khans which can still be seen today. Amongst its various Christian minorities (most notably Armenian, but also Maronite, Syrian Catholic, Greek Catholic and Greek Orthodox), meanwhile, can be found a completely different cultural dimension.

Ins and outs

Getting there
*See also the 'Transport'
section, page 339*

Air *Syrian Air* operates direct international connections between Aleppo and a number of European and Middle Eastern cities. For the most part, however, Aleppo's airport deals with the frequent domestic flights linking it with Damascus.

Rail Aleppo's railway station is relatively centrally located and getting here by train is an interesting option, particularly the services between Aleppo and Lattakia. This route is very beautiful and worth undertaking for the views alone, the railway snaking its way through the mountains with numerous bridges carrying it across narrow gorges and valleys. Train times in both directions are convenient, the journey time is only a little longer than by road and the train station in Lattakia is also relatively central. Train services to Aleppo from Damascus and Qamishle/Deir ez-Zor, however, both arrive at inconvenient times of the night, but trains from Aleppo to these destinations are overnight services and worth considering if you get yourself a sleeper.

Road Luxury coaches, buses, microbuses and service taxis connect Aleppo with the rest of Syria, and also with Turkey, Lebanon and Jordan. The relatively central **Hanano coach station** handles all the luxury coaches; there are regular services to most of the major towns and cities in Syria, as well as a limited number to Tripoli and Beirut in Lebanon. The **City/Pullman bus station**, also fairly central, handles a mixture of older

Aleppo

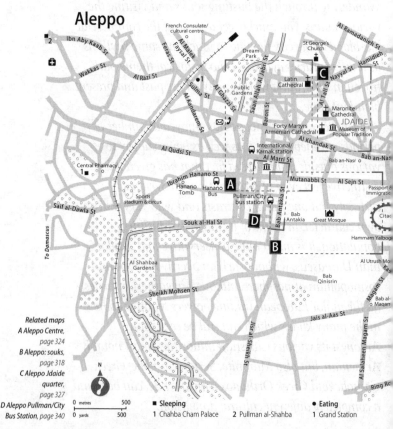

Related maps
A Aleppo Centre,
page 324
B Aleppo: souks,
page 318
C Aleppo Jdaide
quarter,
page 327
D Aleppo Pullman/City
Bus Station, *page 340*

0 metres 500
0 yards 500

■ **Sleeping**
1 Chahba Cham Palace
2 Pullman al-Shahba

● **Eating**
1 Grand Station

coaches, buses, microbuses and service taxis covering all the major destinations, as well as smaller places in the vicinity of Aleppo. The **International/Karnak station**, right by the central downtown area, handles all the coaches to and from Turkey, as well as Lebanon, Jordan and other more far-flung international destinations. Finally, there is the **East bus station**, way out to the east of the old city, though you need only deal with this one if you wish to get to Qalat Najm by public transport.

Getting around

Aleppo is reasonably compact and best explored on foot. Should you need them (to get to the coach, bus or train stations in the heat of summer with your luggage for example), taxis are plentiful and cheap: most journeys cost not more than S£25-30. The local bus system is pretty chaotic and best avoided. The one exception to this is the airport bus, which provides a cheaper alternative to catching a taxi.

Orientation

The Citadel and the Great Mosque, at the heart of the old city, are Aleppo's most important landmarks. Running east-west between the Citadel and Bab Antakya St are the main souks, with Bab Antakya St and its accompanying line of Mameluke city walls marking the western limits of the old city.

To the northwest of this is the main 'downtown' area of the modern city, where you will find the museum, the tourist office, the post and telephone office, many of the restaurants, and the majority of the hotels, the latter mostly clustered within a small area near the famous *Baron Hotel*. Taking its name from the hotel, Baron St, running north-south, is the main focus for travel agents and airline offices. To the west of the downtown area, beyond the railway line, is the modern university area, where there are also a couple of luxury hotels.

To the north of the Citadel the northern limits of the old city are marked by the modern Bab An-Nasr St (unlike Damascus, Aleppo's old city area is no longer clearly delineated; only along its western side do the city walls still survive). To the north of Bab An-Nasr St is the Jdaide quarter, where most of Aleppo's Christian population lives and works.

Tourist information

The tourist office is opposite the National Museum, T2221200. Open 0830-2400, daily (in theory at least; in practice there is only a token presence after 1400, and possibly none at all on Fri). Staff here are friendly and can supply you with the usual free maps/pamphlets, but have little else in the way of useful information. The Tourist Police are based in the same building. **NB** If you have your own vehicle, you can park it in the parking area in front of the tourist office. This is where camper-vans often seem to end up staying; for details of a good camping ground around 30 km to the west of Aleppo, on the road from the Bab al-Hawa border with Turkey, see page 358). Alternatively, there is an attended underground car park at the corner of Al Maari St and Bab al-Faraj St.

Aleppo

24 hours in the city

You can get to see quite a lot of Aleppo in a single day. The best place to start is probably the **Citadel**: don't forget to visit the sumptuous throne room in the upper storey of the formidable monumental gateway. The ramparts of the Citadel give excellent views out over the surrounding city, especially from the terrace of the café at the northern side.

An hour or so should be enough for the Citadel, after which you should head straight for the labyrinth of covered **souks** which are the heart of ancient Aleppo. From near the entrance of the Citadel you can follow Souk al-Atarin west, right the way through this fascinating world of commerce. The full length of the souk extends for less than 1 km, but what with the lively banter of traders and those inevitable offers of cups of tea (not to mention any of the possible detours and numerous monuments along the way), you can easily spend hours on end here without realizing it. Not to worry though: most visitors agree that this is Aleppo's greatest hightlight, so take your time!

When you have finally had enough, Aleppo's **National Museum** is worth a look for the insight it gives into the rich history of northern Syria. Like its counterpart in Damascus, the presentation isn't that great, but there are some stunning artefacts.

The **Jdaide quarter**, with its cathedrals and elegant 17th- and 18th-century houses of wealthy merchants, reflects the completely different world of Aleppo's Christian minorities. In this vibrant district you will find couples and families strolling around in determinedly western dress, seemingly at pains to assert their distinctiveness from the majority Muslim population.

Aleppo has even less than Damascus to offer in terms of nightlife, but there are some excellent **restaurants**. Perhaps the most attractive ones are in the Jdaide quarter, although there is stiff competition from those in the up-market district of Azizieh, and indeed from the more ordinary 'downtown' ones. Wherever you choose to eat, a drink or two at the archaic bar of the legendary **Baron hotel** (the favourite haunt of Lawrence of Arabia and a host of other celebrities over the last century) is a must.

History

Earliest stages Like Damascus, clues to the earliest stages of Aleppo's history come only from written records, the continuous layers of settlement since then having buried almost all archaeological evidence under a living city which still thrives and grows. The earliest references to the city (then known as *Halap*) come from Hittite archives of the second millennium BC found at Mari and at sites on the Anatolian plateau. At that time Aleppo was the centre of the powerful Amorite kingdom of **Yamkhad**, which counted Ugarit and Ebla (both of which were by that time in decline) amongst its vassal states, although its exact relationship with the Amorite (or Babylonian) Empire of Hammurabi remains uncertain.

Hittites Amorite rule in northern Syria gradually succumbed to pressure from the Hurrians and Mitannians from the northeast and east, and from the Hittites of the Anatolian plateau to the north. It was the **Hittites** who eventually held sway in northern Syria. Aleppo was probably made a vassal state during the 17th century BC under their ruler Hattusilis, and then in the early years of the 16th century BC his successor Mursilis I went on to overthrow Hammurabi's Empire. During the following centuries Aleppo was for a time controlled by the **Hurrians** and **Mitannians**, while also briefly coming under the control of the Egyptians following the campaigns of the Pharaoh Thutmosis III

(1490-36 BC). Around 1370 BC the Hittites, under the leadership of Suppiluliuma, once again took control of the city. The most significant power struggle of this period was between the Hittites to the north and the Egyptians to the south, culminating in the famous battle of Kadesh (Tell Nebi Mend) around 1275 BC which both sides claimed to have won but which effectively enabled the Hittites to maintain control over most of northern Syria.

However, soon afterwards, around 1200 BC, the Hittite Empire crumbled in the face of the invasion of the so-called **Sea Peoples**. In the aftermath of the destruction they wrought, small fragmented centres of **neo-Hittite** (or Syro-Hittite) power re-emerged, one of them centred on Aleppo. The absence of any centralized power in Syria created a vacuum which was eventually filled in the ninth century BC by the rising **Assyrian** Empire to the east. Aleppo was at first able to maintain partial independence as a vassal state, but was later totally subjugated by the Assyrian king Tiglath Pileser III (744-27 BC). The Assyrians were overthrown by the **neo-Babylonians** in 612 BC, and they in turn by the **Achaemenid Persians** following the capture of Babylon in 539 BC. The Persians ruled until the defeat of their king Darius at the hands of **Alexander the Great** in the battle of Issus in 333 BC. Following Alexander's death in 323 BC, Aleppo became part of the **Seleucid** Empire of Seleucus Nicator. A new city, named *Beroia*, was founded here and enjoyed a certain degree of prosperity thanks to its proximity to the Seleucid capital, Antioch.

Assyrians, Babylonians & Seleucids

Following the Roman conquest of Syria in 64 BC, Aleppo remained under **Roman** and **Byzantine** rule for the next six centuries. This period was one of relative stability, and although Aleppo was somewhat eclipsed by the rise of new trade routes through Palmyra to the south and Cyrrhus to the north, it nevertheless thrived, most notably as a centre for the export of olive oil, the Romans having established highly productive olive groves in the limestone hills to the north and west. It also served as an important military outpost guarding Rome's northern borders. Aleppo's earliest surviving monument dates from this period, in the form of the fourth-century **Cathedral of St Helena**, subsequently converted into a *madrassa* (the Madrassa Halawiye).

Romans & Byzantines

With the decline of Byzantine power in the late sixth to early seventh century AD, Aleppo suffered heavily at the hands of the **Sassanid Persians** who sacked the city, though it was subsequently retaken by the Byzantines for a brief period before falling in 637 AD to the **Muslim** Arab forces of Khaled Ibn al-Walid. Located on the peripheries of the Islamic Empire, it was eclipsed somewhat by Damascus, which soon became the seat of the Umayyad Dynasty, and later by Baghdad, seat of the Abbasid Dynasty. Instead, the city established a certain measure of independence under its own local dynasties, breaking away from the Abbasids in the 10th century to became the centre of the **Hamdanid** Dynasty, founded by a tribe of Arab refugees from Iraq. Under the leadership of Saif ud-Daula (944-67) the Hamdanids waged war energetically against the Byzantines, prompting them to retaliate and leading to the sacking of Aleppo in 962, and again in 969. In 1017 the **Fatimids** of Cairo briefly extended their influence north to include Aleppo, but by 1023 the city had once again achieved a certain degree of independence under the **Mirdasids**, a nomadic Arab tribe whose rule lasted until 1079 and depended on maintaining a delicate diplomatic balance between Fatimid and Byzantine interests.

Rise of Islam

In the meantime, the **Seljuk Turks**, who had already taken over effective control of the much weakened Abbasid Caliphate in Baghdad, began to make their

Seljuk Turks & Crusaders

Aleppo

presence felt in northern Syria. They took control of Aleppo in 1070, leaving it at first to be ruled as a vassal state by the Mirdasids but later installing their own Seljuk rulers. The rise to power of the Seljuks and the threat they posed to the Byzantine Empire prompted the First Crusade. Having taken Antioch in 1098, the **Crusaders** went on to surround Aleppo, cutting it off from its agricultural land and severing its trade links with the Mediterranean, although they failed to take the city itself. It again came under attack in 1124 from the Crusader forces of Jocelyn of Edessa and was only saved when the Seljuk ruler of Mosul, Bursuqi, sent a relieving force in response to the entreaties of Ibn al-Khashab, the *qadi* of Aleppo. Bursuqi incorporated Aleppo into his realm and his son, Zengi, established the **Zengid** Dynasty. Under his rule (1128-46) and that of his son Nur ud-Din (1146-74), Aleppo became a focus for resistance to the Crusaders. After years of neglect the city also experienced something of a renaissance, with lots of new construction being undertaken, most notably in the form of *madrassas* (religious schools) which were established in an attempt to restore Sunni orthodoxy in the face of the various heresies which prevailed at the time, particularly the Assassins (see page 274) who had been welcomed in Aleppo by its former ruler Ridwan.

Saladin's success Nur ud-Din's son Al Salih ruled the city until his death in 1183 and was succeeded by **Salah ud-Din** (Saladin), who had by that time overthrown the Fatimid Caliphate in Cairo and established the **Ayyubid** Dynasty which was at last able to fully unite the Muslim world against the Crusader threat. His son Al Zaher Ghazi ruled the city from 1193-1215. During his reign, most of the Citadel's existing fortifications were built, while the city flourished, establishing an international trading reputation through the signing of a number of treaties with Venice which allowed Europeans direct access to Muslim markets without having to go through the Crusader states along the coast.

Mongols & Mamelukes However, Aleppo was not able to withstand the new threat which came from the north in the form of the **Mongols**, who sacked the city in 1260. Although the **Mamelukes** quickly moved into Syria from their base at Cairo to drive back the Mongols, Aleppo remained largely forsaken at the northern extremities of their empire and it was not until the 14th century, when it became a base for Mameluke campaigns against the Armenians, that any attempts were made at repairing the destruction that the Mongols had caused. Even then, it was only in the 15th century, after the second Mongol invasion of 1400, that it began to regain its former wealth, with the trade routes which had been diverted to the north via the Black Sea and Cilicia once again being directed through Aleppo.

Ottoman rule In 1516 Aleppo became part of the **Ottoman** Empire and continued to flourish as a centre of trade. The souks and khans for which the city is famous nearly all date from the late Mameluke and early Ottoman period, with the British, French and Dutch setting up office in the city alongside the Venetians under a series of 'capitulation' treaties. The European presence in the city also ensured a special position for the various local Christian communities, who became important intermediaries for the merchants in carrying out their trade, and under the capitulations enjoyed a protected status. By the 18th century, however, Aleppo's fortunes were beginning to decline in the face of continuing competition from the new sea route to China and India, as well as routes through the Persian Gulf, Red Sea and across Russia. Apart from a brief spell from 1831-40 when it became part of Ibrahim Pasha's breakaway state, Aleppo remained under Ottoman rule until the collapse of their empire at the end of the First World War. Aleppo's Armenian community, which had been growing steadily in the last decade of the 19th century as a result of the brutal suppression of Armenian nationalism elsewhere in the Ottoman Empire, saw a massive influx when that repression degenerated into full-scale genocide during the First World War, and today the strong Armenian presence remains a distinctive feature of the city.

French Mandate rule

In the early years of French Mandate rule, Aleppo (like Damascus) was made the capital of an independent mini-state, although this arrangement only lasted for three years. By the time full independence came in 1945, the French had given much of the old Ottoman province of Aleppo to Turkey. This created great animosity between the two countries and resulted in a severing of the city's historically strong cultural and economic links with the Turks. As part of the Syrian Arab Republic it remained always of secondary importance to Damascus, but nevertheless grew steadily in size. Its historic function as a trading city continues today, although in somewhat truncated form with its traditional Mediterranean outlet, Antakya (ancient Antioch), now lying inside Turkey (though still disputed by Syria). The sanctions imposed on Iraq following the Gulf War of 1982 have likewise largely cut off its trade in that direction. However, in response to these changes it has developed strong links with the various states of the former Soviet Union to the north, and a prominent feature of the city are the groups of traders from these countries who come to buy up the textiles for which it is famous, frequently taking over whole hotels in the downtown area and stacking their lobbies full of huge packaged bales to be loaded onto buses and lorries for the journey home.

Sights

Citadel

Dominating the centre of Aleppo is the Citadel, its steep-sided, artificial-looking mound rising abruptly to a height of more than 50 m above the maze of surrounding souks and streets. Unusually for Syria, although the sides have been shaped over the centuries to give them their uniform slope, this is not an artificial mound (or *tell*) formed from the accumulated debris of successive settlements, but is a natural feature.

History

To date, the earliest evidence of settlement on the citadel mound comes in the form of two lions carved out of basalt rock dating from the neo-Hittite period (10th century BC), perhaps remnants of a temple. During the Seleucid period, the mound was used for defensive purposes and a citadel established here, along with the new town of *Beroia*. At the same time, a pre-existing temple to the local god Hadad was dedicated to the Greek equivalent, Zeus. Little is known about the site in subsequent centuries, although there is evidence of Byzantine occupation in the form of cisterns and a church, later incorporated into a mosque. It is also known that the Byzantine emperor Julian the Apostate came here to offer sacrifices to the god Zeus in the fourth century, suggesting that the temple still existed, despite the adoption of Christianity as the official religion. In the 10th century AD the Hamdanid ruler Saif ud-Daula built a royal palace on the mound and from then on it was occupied continuously. The most striking features of the Citadel today – the encircling moat, stone *glacis* and imposing entrance bridge and monumental gateway – all date from the Ayyubid period, during the reign of Saladin's son, Al Zaher Ghazi.

Following the Mongol invasions of 1260 and 1400, the Citadel underwent extensive repairs. During the Mameluke period it ceased to fulfil such an important defensive function, and was used instead as the governor's residence and barracks for troops.

Visiting the Citadel The Citadel is most imposing from the outside, although extensive restoration work, both to the ramparts and the buildings, is steadily transforming it. The stone cladding of the steep-sided (48 degree) *glacis* only survives in places, but coupled with the deep (22 m) encircling moat it gives a good idea of just how impregnable it would have appeared to any attacker. By far the most impressive feature overall is the sole entrance to the Citadel, consisting of an outer defensive tower followed by an entrance bridge leading up to a monumental gateway. The 20 m high **outer defensive tower** dates from 1211 but was restored by the Mamelukes early in the 16th century. Prior to the Mameluke restoration, it was approached via a drawbridge. (The ticket office is now inside.) After passing through this tower, the **entrance bridge** ascends up towards the monumental gateway, eight arches supporting it as it spans the moat.

The **monumental gateway** provides the crowning glory of this defensive ensemble, a solid and imposing rectangular tower of such massive proportions that it is practically a citadel in its own right. Either side of the tall and deeply recessed arched entrance is a series of box machicolations and above these an upper storey (representing the throne room, see below). The gateway which Al Zaher Ghazi built originally consisted of two towers which rose to the level of the machicolations. Following the first Mongol attack of 1260, the Mameluke sultan Al Ashraf Khalil carried out extensive repairs, commemorated in a long band of Arabic inscription just below the machicolations. The inscription praises the sultan in typically effusive terms as "lord of kings and sultans, champion of justice throughout the universe, the Alexander of his time, conqueror of capitals, he who put to flight the Frankish, Armenian and Mongol armies, and gave new strength to the glorious Abbasid Dynasty ..." In the early 16th century the gateway was further modified with the upper-storey throne room being added, so joining the two towers together. The gateway consists of a passage which passes through no less than five turnings and three doors before giving access to the inside of the Citadel. The first door is placed on the right inside the recessed arched entrance to prevent would-be attackers from using battering rams on it. Above it are two twin-headed serpents, their bodies intertwined in knotted coils. The doors themselves are of solid iron, reinforced with heavy studs and decorated with horseshoe and arrowhead motifs. The next two doors have carved lions, one pair facing each other on the lintel above, the next pair facing to the front and flanking the door on either side. These were believed to be imbued with magical powers aiding the defence of the citadel. The successive right-angled turnings were of more practical use in slowing the momentum of any attacker. After the last of the turnings, a rising passage takes you past various rooms, probably used as barracks and stables.

The palace & baths complex, & the whole surrounding area, were undergoing major restoration at the time of writing

From the monumental gateway, a street leads north across the top of the hill. On the right, immediately after you exit the monumental gateway, is a series of doors. The fourth doorway gives access to a chamber with a narrow passage at the end, and steps leading down to a large vaulted and pillared chamber, from where more steps (steep and uneven) lead down to another chamber. These chambers are thought to be of Byzantine origin, and to have been used as a prison and a storage room, and at a later date possibly also as a water cistern. Back on the street, a set of stairs on the right (immediately after the doorway leading to the underground chambers) doubles back and up towards the extensive remains of the **Ayyubid Palace**, built by the Ayyubid ruler Al Aziz in 1230, but destroyed by the Mongols 30 years later. The partially restored entrance to the palace consists of a striking doorway with beautiful honeycombing rising to a small conch shell semi-dome, and a surround of alternating bands of black and cream stone carved with geometric patterns. Built onto the palace (towards the rear) is a large Mameluke-period **baths complex** which has been extensively restored.

If you continue past the entrance to the Ayyubid Palace you can gain access, via a courtyard, to the Mameluke **throne room**, which occupies the upper floor of the monumental gateway by which you first entered the Citadel. The entrance to the throne room is particularly impressive, with a stalactited semi-dome and a surround of alternating bands of black and cream stone. This provides a suitably grand introduction to the throne room itself, a huge square room which has been immaculately restored to its former glory. The lavishly and intricately carved and painted wooden ceiling is particularly impressive. Four pillars support a central square, which in turn supports an octagonal drum with three panels of stained glass in each face of the octagon. Hanging from the centre is a large inlaid wood chandelier, and on the floor below a small fountain. The entire floor is paved with marble in intricate geometric patterns, while the lower parts of the walls are adorned with wooden panels similarly carved with geometric designs. In the right-hand corner, stairs lead down to a series of vaulted chambers with more holes in the floors for pouring oil onto attackers, and access to arrow slits overlooking the approach to the monumental gateway. (You can descend all the way down to the passageway leading through the monumental gateway if you wish.) Returning to the courtyard at the main entrance to the throne room, there is a set of stairs which lead to the **upper battlements**. From here you can get an excellent overview of the layout of the Citadel to the north. There is no railing on the inside edge, however, and it is a long drop down into the courtyard, making it a definite no-go for vertigo sufferers!

Note the 2 holes in the floor, 1 square & 1 circular, covered by grilles, which allowed oil to be poured on any would-be attacker as they passed through the twists & turns of the gateway below

Returning to the main street and following it north, on the left is another **baths complex** which has been fully restored, though at the time of writing it was not open to the public. Opposite the main entrance to these baths, a cobbled path with a channel running down the centre leads off to the right. This takes you to a large **amphitheatre**, an entirely modern concrete structure erected in the 1970s. Back on the main street, a little further up, on the left, is the small **Mosque of Abraham**, so called after the legend that this was the spot where Abraham used to milk his cow (this legend is also the source of Aleppo's Arabic name, *Halab*, derived from the Arabic for 'milk'). The mosque was built by Nur ud-Din in 1167 on the site of an earlier church, two columns of which are preserved inside the prayer hall, on the north wall. According to local legend, this church was also one of the many supposed resting places for John the Baptist's head (see also the Umayyad Mosque in Damascus, page 88).

A little further up past the Mosque of Abraham, to the right of the main street, is a deep area of ongoing **excavations** being carried out by a Syrian-German team. The excavations have uncovered the foundations of a temple dating back to the ninth century BC. There is not as yet that much to see of the temple itself, but the different types of stonework at various levels, from huge stone blocks towards the bottom to smaller ones higher up, are graphically displayed.

At the end of the main street, on the left, is the **Great Mosque of the Citadel**, built by the Ayyubid Sultan Al Zaher Ghazi in 1214. Much of what you see today is a reconstruction, though in places you can still see patches of the original stonework. The mosque is in fact quite small, but beautifully proportioned and has a quietly understated simplicity about it which somehow adds to the overall effect. Inside is a courtyard with a tiny central fountain and three fir trees, and surrounding the courtyard on three sides is an arcade. The prayer hall occupies the fourth side, and aside from the *mihrab* is adorned only with a dome in the ceiling, supported on an octagonal drum with a window in each face. In the northeast corner of the mosque is a square minaret.

To the east of the mosque (to the right of the path where it ends, as you face to the north) is a long rectangular building which served as a **barracks**. This dates from 1839 and was built by Ibrahim Pasha, son of Muhammed Ali, both Ottoman commanders who between them briefly challenged the might of the Ottoman Empire, ruling over Syria for a time. The building today houses a **café** and also a small **museum**, although without a student discount, the additional entrance fee of S£150 for the latter is somewhat expensive given the limited collection of artefacts. The terrace of the café, which occupies a section of the ramparts of the citadel, offers great views out over Aleppo.

■ *Open 0900-1800 in summer, 0900-1600 in winter, closed Tue. Entry S£300 (students S£15). There are usually guides on hand at the ticket office offering tours lasting 40 mins to 1 hr for around S£300-500 for individuals or small groups.*

Souks and khans

On Fridays the souks are closed and completely deserted, with metal roller-blinds pulled down over all the shops. An eerie silence replaces the usual bustle, broken only by occasional gangs of kids whizzing through on their bicycles

When you explore Aleppo's souks you are plunged into a world which lies at the heart of the city's very existence. The medieval maze of narrow alleyways, covered over not with corrugated iron as in Damascus, but with stone vaulting, are wonderfully atmospheric; the tiny shops trading in a bewildering array of traditional goods and wares, with only the occasional tourist-orientated handicrafts or antiques shop. Indeed, although the situation is rapidly changing, as a tourist you are still for the most part merely a little noticed observer of this bustling world, rather than the focus of commercial interest. With their stone vaulting, the souks are blissfully cool and shaded in the fierce heat of summer,

Aleppo souks

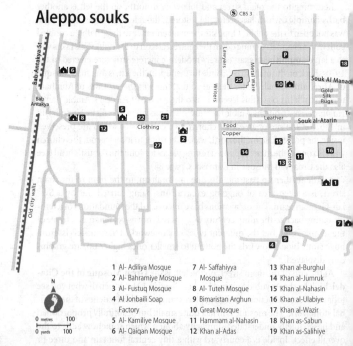

1 Al- Adiliya Mosque
2 Al- Bahramiye Mosque
3 Al- Fustuq Mosque
4 Al Jonbaili Soap Factory
5 Al- Kamiliye Mosque
6 Al- Qaiqan Mosque
7 Al- Saffahiyya Mosque
8 Al- Tuteh Mosque
9 Bimaristan Arghun
10 Great Mosque
11 Hammam al-Nahasin
12 Khan al-Adas
13 Khan al-Burghul
14 Khan al-Jumruk
15 Khan al-Nahasin
16 Khan al-Ulabiye
17 Khan al-Wazir
18 Khan as-Sabun
19 Khan as-Salihiye

and protected to some extent against the rain and cold in winter. The variety of sights, sounds and smells, meanwhile, is fascinating, as is the sheer diversity of peoples – Arab, Turkish, Armenian, Kurdish, Iranian – all drawn to what is one of the great commercial crossroads of the Middle East.

The main souk, known as **Souk al-Atarin** runs east-west between the Citadel and Bab Antakya, with smaller ones running parallel in places, and perpendicular branches to the north and south at regular intervals. This grid pattern of streets is believed to reflect the much earlier plan of the Hellenistic town established by the Seleucids in the fourth to third century BC, with Souk al-Atarin corresponding roughly with the later Roman *decumanus*. In their present form the earliest parts of the souks date from the 13th century, although for the most part they were built by the Ottomans from the 16th century onwards. The great khans (or *caravanserais*) which are to be found amongst the souks soon came to be occupied by the European traders who were drawn to the city. The Venetians were the first to arrive, in the 13th century, but within a few hundred years the English, French, Belgians and Dutch had all established themselves here.

The main 'heart' of the souks is to the south and east of the Great Mosque, and this is one place from where you can conveniently enter them, following the small alleys which lead south from Jamia al-Ayyoubi St on either side of the mosque. For the purposes of this description, however, the souks are followed from east to west, heading from the Citadel towards Bab Antakya, with detours off to the north and south to visit important places of interest en route.

Heading clockwise around the Citadel from its entrance (back towards Jamia al-Ayyoubi Street), a small arched entrance on the left, signposted 'Al Madina Souk' marks the point of entry into the souks. This first section (known in fact as Souk al-Zarb) sells mainly materials for Bedouin tents, before giving way to shops selling all manner of fabrics and clothing. Taking the first available right turn brings you to the entrance to the **Khan Khayr Bey**, on the right. This khan, with its entrance gateway of black and white stone, dates from 1514, shortly before the Mamelukes were swept from power by the Ottomans. It is now entirely given over to shops selling fabrics. The stretch of souk running past the entrance to the khan has been carefully restored to show off the domes in the roof to their full effect.

Returning to the main souk and continuing west, you soon arrive at a crossroads. Turning right here, you arrive at a dog-leg at a point where the covered vaulting of the souk ends. Here the elaborately decorated (though unfortunately largely obscured) entrance to the **Khan as-Sabun**, or 'soap factory' faces you. This building dates from the late 15th to early 16th century, and is an excellent example of Aleppo's Mameluke architecture. Inside, the khan today houses a variety different businesses,

no longer being given over entirely to soap production. Aside from the large rectangular building dominating the courtyard (a later addition), most of the architectural features of the khan are original, with some minor modifications here and there. The overall effect is actually quite picturesque, the courtyard still has its original cobblestones, and overhead vines provide some shade.

Back at the crossroads on the main souk, if you head south, just after the covered souk ends, on the right is the entrance to an attractively restored khan which today houses a couple of tourist-orientated antiques/handicrafts shops. This khan actually forms part of the Al Adiliye Mosque (see below), bordering the east side of its courtyard; it is possible to enter the mosque via a passageway just to the south of the khan (take the next doorway on the right after the khan). Further on, on the right, is the **Al Saffahiyya Mosque**. This mosque dates from 1425 and is decorated with alternating bands of black and white stone in typical Mameluke fashion, while the octagonal minaret is adorned with richly carved decoration.

Returning to the main souk and continuing west, the next right turn leads up to Jamia al-Ayyoubi Street along the east wall of the Great Mosque. This street is given over to **silks** and **fabrics**. Leading off it to the right at regular intervals is a series of tiny streets, the first couple selling **carpets** and **rugs**, while the next few form the heart of the brightly lit and affluent **gold souk**.

Back on the main souk (now **Souk al-Atarin**, the 'Spices Souk'), the next left turn takes you down to Bab Qinisrin, passing several interesting monuments en route. A short distance down on the left is the **Hammam al-Nahasin**, which dates originally from the 12th or 13th centuries. It has been restored in recent years and it now functions once again as a public bath house, although most of its original architectural features have been obscured as a result. Directly opposite is the entrance to the **Khan al-Nahasin** (literally 'Khan of the Coppersmiths'). This was the warehouse and consul of the Venetians from 1539. The building on the south side of the courtyard was lived in until recently by Adolphe Poche, who was born here in 1895 and who served as the consul of Austria-Hungary, Austria, the Netherlands and Belgium in turn. Adolphe Poche was a keen historian and archaeologist who amassed an impressive collection of antiques and archaeological artefacts which are still preserved within the building. To gain access to it you must apply to the present Belgium Consulate, now housed in the Khan al-Kattin, situated immediately to the south of the Khan al-Wazir (see above).

For my money, this is easily the most beautiful mosque in Aleppo, and it is also wonderfully tranquil, with its tree-lined courtyard far from the intruding noise of traffic

Continuing south, a small alleyway off to the left brings you to the **Al Adiliya Mosque**, built in the mid-16th century by the Ottoman governor of Aleppo, Mohammad Pasha, and stylistically similar to the slightly earlier Khusuwiye Mosque (see page 326). Two lines of columns and arches support a portico in front of the prayer hall, the inner arcade marked by a series of small domes. The main doorway to the mosque is particularly richly and finely executed, as are the blue and white glazed tiles in the arches above the windows, with their delicate foliate designs and Qur'anic calligraphy. Inside, a huge central dome dominates the prayer hall and the tilework is repeated, while above the *mihrab* is a panel of very beautiful stained glass.

Continuing south along the main street, go straight over a crossroads (left leads to the Al Saffahiyya Mosque, see above) and then, after following the street through a dogleg (here you pass the Ottoman-period **Khan as-Salihiye** on the left), you arrive at the **Bimaristan Arghun**. Originally a private house, this building was converted into a mental asylum in 1354 by the Mameluke governor Arghun al-Kamili. The impressive honeycombed entrance leads through to the main courtyard with a central pool and fountain, surrounded by tiny cells. A doorway opposite and to the right of the main

Project for the Rehabilitation of the old city of Aleppo

The old city of Aleppo, clustered around the Citadel, is characterized by densely packed neighbourhoods with narrow alleyways and souks, and inward-facing houses, khans and public buildings, typically arranged around a central courtyard. In sharp contrast to this pattern are the broad boulevards and high-rise developments laid out in the 1950s, many of which cut right through traditional neighbourhoods. While new road networks and modern housing developments continue to proliferate around the outskirts of Aleppo, since the 1980s a halt has been called to any further developments which involve the destruction of the old city. Indeed, the fabric of the old city has now been declared a national monument, and recognized as a World Heritage Site by UNESCO.

Initiated in 1993, the Project for the Rehabilitation of the Old City of Aleppo is actively supported by the Syrian authorities at both the local level (the project is partly funded by the municipality and headed by the mayor of Aleppo), and at the national level. The German government (through the German Agency for Technical

Cooperation, or GTZ) is also closely involved, providing expertise, training and additional funding.

The success of the project depends not just on restoring and preserving the historic monuments of the old city, but also on encouraging its social and economic regeneration. Thus there are initiatives to provide health services and kindergarten facilities, as well as basic public works projects to improve water supplies and sewage provisions. At the same time, interest-free loans have been extended for commercial ventures which involve preserving old buildings (this has been particularly successful in the Jdaide quarter, where several new restaurants and hotels have been opened in restored houses). It is only by involving local communities, and by making their neighbourhoods viable and attractive places to live and work, that Aleppo's cultural heritage can be preserved as a living entity rather than simply a museum piece. Thankfully for this unique city and its inhabitants, this project appears to be tackling the challenge with determination and imagination.

entrance leads through to three smaller courtyards, again each with its own pool and fountain surrounded by cells. The atmosphere is one of tranquillity, rather as if this were a *madrassa* of some sort, although the bars on some of the cells and the rings for chaining up the patients hint at a less serene past. The asylum was in fact still in use at the beginning of the 20th century. At the time of writing it was closed for restoration. Opposite is the **Al Joubaili Soap Factory**. Although recently fitted out with a new door, inside it remains distinctly unrenovated, being still used as a soap factory, with soap stacked up high in the gloomy vaulted chambers. Continuing along the street, now running southwest, you arrive after 200 m or so at **Bab Qinisrin**, the best preserved of Aleppo's old city gates. Variously dated to the 10th-13th century according to which source you consult, it is known for sure to have been restored in 1501 by the Mameluke governor Qansawh al-Ghawri. Outside the gate, around 200 m to the west, two towers of the old city's defensive walls can be seen; like the gate, in their present form they date to the Mameluke period.

Returning now to the main Souk al-Atarin and continuing west, you arrive next at the **Khan al-Jumruk** (literally 'Customs Khan', the place where customs duties were levied on goods arriving in Aleppo). This is the largest of Aleppo's khans. Completed in 1574, it accommodated the French, English and Dutch consuls, and also their financial offices. The impressive entrance gateway (on your left as you head west; the vaulting of the souk here is marked by a large dome) is decorated with alternating bands of black and white stone with a patterned surround and an inscription above. Inside, the khan, which covers an area of over 6,000 sq m, is still in use, accommodating for the most part fabric wholesalers. Stairs in the passageway leading through to the main courtyard, and in the corners of the courtyard, give access to the balcony running around the first floor; from here you can get a good overview of the khan and look down on the otherwise largely obscured mosque in the centre of the courtyard.

Continuing west, after about 150 m you come to the **Al Bahramiye Mosque** on the left. Built in 1583 by Ottoman governor of Aleppo Bahram Pasha, it is particularly notable for its beautifully decorated *mihrab*. The second lane leading off to the left after passing the mosque brings you to the entrance of the **Madrassa Muqaddamiye** on the left. Like the Madrassa Halawiye, this was originally a church before being seized and turned into an Islamic theological school in retaliation for the atrocities carried out by the Crusaders in 1124. The beautifully decorated entry porch is the most striking feature today. The inscription above it is dated to 1168.

Returning to the main souk, along this final stretch there are a few more khans to be seen, although they are not so interesting. Shortly before arriving at Bab Antakya, you pass the small **Al Tuteh Mosque** (literally 'Mosque of the Mulberry Tree'). Although rather dilapidated today and not particularly noteworthy, it is believed to stand on the site of the first mosque to be built in Aleppo, in the seventh century. In its present form it is largely an Ayyubid construction, the Kufic inscription and surrounding decoration dating to the late 12th century. Some of the large stone blocks used in its construction are clearly of Roman origin, probably recycled from the Roman triumphal arch which stood on the site of the present Bab Antakya.

A few twists in the lane bring you finally to **Bab Antakya**, in its present form a 13th-century Ayyubid construction, partly utilizing blocks from the original Roman triumphal arch which stood here, and further modified in the 15th century. Rather than exiting it onto the busy thoroughfare of Bab Antakya Street, you can bear off to the right just before, ascending along a beautiful cobbled street which runs along the **Mameluke ramparts** of the old city walls, from where you can look down onto the general chaos below. After around 50 m you pass the small **Al Qaiqan Mosque**, an early Ottoman period construction which incorporates two ancient basalt columns either side of the entrance. A stone block (now removed) bearing a Hittite inscription from the 14th century BC was found in the wall of this mosque. The higher ground off to the right as you follow the ramparts north is thought to represent the site of the ancient village which existed here and became incorporated into the new city of *Beroia* established by the Seleucids. At the north end of the ramparts you descend into a butchers' souk; turning left brings you out just south of the intersection of Bab Antakya Street with Mutannabi Street.

Great Mosque

The Great Mosque of Aleppo (also known as the Umayyad Mosque or the Jami Zakariye) illustrates very well the city's multi-layered history. Founded in the early eighth-century AD by the Umayyad caliph Al Walid, it was built on the grounds of the sixth-century Cathedral of St Helen, itself situated on the site of the Roman and Hellenistic market-place. Towards the end of the 11th century the first Seljuk sultan, Tutush, built the square minaret which still survives today. The rest of the mosque was destroyed by fire in 1169 and subsequently rebuilt by Nur ud-Din, with further extensive modifications carried out by the Mamelukes in the 15th century.

At the time of writing, the mosque was once again the focus of a massive repair project, this time involving the daunting task of underpinning the foundations of the pillars supporting the prayer hall and the arcades surrounding the courtyard; essential work in the face of serious subsidence. The courtyard was still open to the public, and it was even possible to weave your way between the underpinning work in the prayer hall, though obviously different parts of the mosque will be closed at different stages of the work. To judge by the scale of the project, work will last for a couple of years at least. Already the preparations for underpinning have unearthed a number of archaeological finds, slowing work and presenting the authorities with a serious dilemma. A huge earthenware *amphora* could be seen in a deep pit beside one pillar of the courtyard arcade, close to the west entrance to the mosque.

Overall, the mosque does not match the grandeur of the Umayyad mosque of Damascus. Nevertheless, the façade of the prayer hall is quite striking, with a series of large arches decorated with wooden lattice-work and an ornate central entrance. The patterning of the worn marble slabs of the courtyard is also quite effective, managing to achieve a certain understated elegance. Inside the prayer hall, the carved wooden *minbar*, dating from the Mameluke period, is particularly beautiful. Immediately to the left of the *mihrab*, in an arched recess protected by a metal grille, the head of Zachariah (the father of John the Baptist) is believed to be interned, hence one of the mosque's alternative names. Also desperately in need of restoration, the minaret rises to a height of 45 m. It represents the oldest part of the mosque and is considered to be amongst the earliest examples of the distinctive Syrian-Islamic architectural style which was later developed by the Ayyubids and Mamelukes.

■ *Before the repair project began, tourists were expected to enter the mosque by the west entrance and to pay an entrance fee of S£25, although this was very loosely enforced, particularly if you were not part of a group.*

Around the Great Mosque

Just to the west of the Great Mosque, and directly opposite its west entrance, is the entrance to the **Madrassa Halawiye**. This *madrassa* incorporates the remains of the Cathedral of St Helen. For a long time after the building of the Great Mosque in the grounds of the cathedral, the two institutions are believed to have co-existed harmoniously. However, some time after 1124 it was seized and converted into a *madrassa*, allegedly in retaliation for the atrocities committed by the Crusaders against the Muslims when they attacked the city.

Entering the *madrassa*, you find yourself in a rather unassuming courtyard surrounded on three sides by what were originally students' cells. The west wall (opposite you as you enter) has two large arches in it, the left one bricked up, while the right one has been glassed over. A doorway in the glassed-over arch leads into the *madrassa's* original prayer hall, notable for its beautifully carved wooden *mihrab*, dating from 1245, during the reign of Nur ud-Din. This hall is generally kept locked, but the caretaker is usually on hand to open it up. A wide range of postcards, as well as some books and pamphlets, are displayed for sale on a table inside. Returning to the courtyard, a doorway topped by a wooden porch in the left arch leads through into a large hall which was being used as an alternative prayer hall while the Great Mosque remained out of action. The ceiling is dominated by a central dome resting on an octagonal drum. The two arches which support the dome on the north and south sides rest on columns topped by ornately carved Corinthian capitals. On the west side, a semi-dome is supported on six columns arranged in a semicircle, the capitals of two of them even more exuberantly carved than the others, with their acanthus leaves curling in different directions as if caught by the wind. This is all that remains of the Cathedral of St Helen, but the beautiful columns and capitals, along with the traces of decoration on the walls, give an inkling of its former splendour.

Aleppo

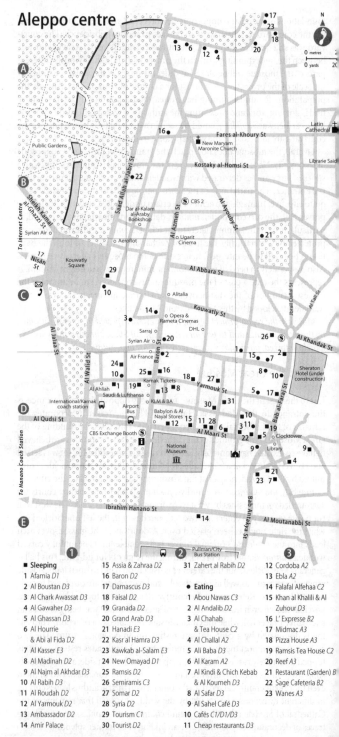

Aleppo centre

Latin Cathedral

Public Gardens

Fares al-Khoury St
New Maryam Maronite Church
Kostaky al-Homsi St
Librarie Said

Saad Allah al-Jabiri St

CBS 2

Dar al-Kalam al-Araby Bookshop

Al Azmeh St

Al Ayoubi St

Ugarit Cinema

Aeroflot

17 Nisán St

Syrian Air

Kouwatly Square

Al Abbara St

Alitalia

Kouwatly St

Opera & Rameta Cinemas

DHL

Sarraj

Baron St

Syrian Air

Air France

Al Walid St

Al Ahliah

Saudi & Lufthansa

Karnak Tickets

Yarmouk St

Al Khandak St

Sheraton Hotel (under construction)

Bab al-Faraj St

International/Karnak coach station

Airport Bus

Al Qudsi St

KLM & BA

Babylon & Al Nayal Stores

Al Maari St

Clocktower

Library

CBS Exchange Booth

National Museum 🏛

Jbrail Dallal St

Al Tari St

To Internet Centre
Sheikh Jamal al-Ghazzi St
Syrian Air

To Hanano Coach Station

Ibrahim Hanano St

Bab Antakya St

Al Moutanabbi St

Pullman/City Bus Station

Al Jalaa St

N

0 metres   2
0 yards   20

Aleppo

■ Sleeping		
1 Afamia *D1*	15 Assia & Zahraa *D2*	31 Zahert al Rabih *D2*
2 Al Boustan *D3*	16 Baron *D2*	
3 Al Chark Awassat *D3*	17 Damascus *D3*	● Eating
4 Al Gawaher *D3*	18 Faisal *D2*	1 Abou Nawas *C3*
5 Al Ghassan *D3*	19 Granada *D2*	2 Al Andalib *D2*
6 Al Hourrie	20 Grand Arab *D3*	3 Al Chahab
& Abi al Fida *D2*	21 Hanadi *E3*	& Tea House *C2*
7 Al Kasser *E3*	22 Kasr al Hamra *D3*	4 Al Challal *A2*
8 Al Madinah *D2*	23 Kawkab al-Salam *E3*	5 Ali Baba *D3*
9 Al Najm al Akhdar *D3*	24 New Omayad *D1*	6 Al Karam *A2*
10 Al Rabih *D3*	25 Ramsis *D2*	7 Al Kindi & Chich Kebab
11 Al Roudah *D2*	26 Semiramis *C3*	& Al Koumeh *D3*
12 Al Yarmouk *D2*	27 Somar *D2*	8 Al Safar *D3*
13 Ambassador *D2*	28 Syria *D2*	9 Al Sahel Café *D3*
14 Amir Palace	29 Tourism *C1*	10 Cafés *C1/D1/D3*
	30 Tourist *D2*	11 Cheap restaurants *D3*

12 Cordoba *A2*	
13 Ebla *A2*	
14 Falafal Alfehaa *C2*	
15 Khan al Khalili & Al Zuhour *D3*	
16 L' Expresse *B2*	
17 Midmac *A3*	
18 Pizza House *A3*	
19 Ramsis Tea House *C2*	
20 Reef *A3*	
21 Restaurant (Garden) *B*	
22 Sage Cafeteria *B2*	
23 Wanes *A3*	

Heading east (towards the Citadel) along Jamia al-Ayyoubi Street from the Great Mosque, after around 150 m you come to a small open square on the right, at the back of which is the **Al Fustuq Mosque** (literally 'Mosque of the Pistachios'). Built in 1349, this small mosque has been restored in recent years and is now once again fully functional. Across the road is the **Matbakh al-Ajami**, a 12th century Zengid palace with an imposing gateway of interlocking black and white stone in an arch, framed by geometric patterns. Restoration of this building was recently completed, and there is talk of opening it as a restaurant, though at the time of writing it remained closed to the public. On the east side of the small square in front of the Al Fustuq Mosque is the main entrance to the large **Khan al-Wazir**. This dates from the 17th century and is considered to be amongst the most impressive of Aleppo's khans. It is the entrance doorway which is the most striking feature, with its alternating bands of black and white stone and elaborately decorated arched window above the doorway. Note also the two medallions with reliefs of chained lions. Inside, the khan is imposing for its sheer size, with its original and heavily worn cobblestone paving still intact in places. Some carpet sellers have set up shop here, draping the walls and balconies with a colourful selection of old and new rugs from around the Middle East, and beyond.

South of the Citadel

There are a number of interesting monuments to the south of the Citadel which can be visited as a leisurely walking tour. None of them are dramatically spectacular, but they provide some interesting insights into Aleppo's medieval architecture, as well as offering the opportunity to get away from the main tourist trail.

Across the road from the entrance to the Citadel there are a couple of cafés. Although a bit touristy, they are nevertheless pleasant places to stop for refreshments & admire the Citadel's impressive fortifications

Immediately behind the cafés is the **Khan ash-Shouna** which has been restored as a handicrafts market, rather like the one in the Tekkiyeh as-Suleimaniyeh complex in Damascus. There is a wide selection of the usual handicrafts and antiques on sale here. Prices are on the high side, but the quality of the goods also tends to be better.

Following the road which encircles the Citadel anticlockwise (east) from the entrance, you pass on the right the Governorate building, a large, grand-looking complex dating from the 1930s, before arriving at the **Hammam Yalbogha al-Nasri**. These baths (also known as Hammam Lababidiyeh) are thought by some to date originally from the seventh century, although the present buildings are of 14th century Mameluke origin. Now restored to their former glory and in full working order, they are the largest and most lavish baths in Syria, and well worth a visit even if you don't plan on taking a bath. The entrance is typically striking, with its banded black and honey stone. A passage takes you past displays of decorated metalware and beautifully delicate glassware before you enter the large main hall with its domed ceiling and central pool. ■ *Open 1000-0200, daily. Women only Mon, Thu, Sat 1000-1700. T3623154. There is a sauna as well as the usual steam bath. For a complete service including massage, soap, towels, tea etc it costs S£415, or you can pay for each service individually. The basic steam bath costs S£200. Safe boxes are provided for valuables. There is a café outside during the summer; it can get busy at this time of year and booking may be necessary. If you are on a tight budget, Damascus has many smaller and considerably cheaper baths.*

Just to the south of the entrance to the citadel is the **Madrassa as-Sultaniye** (also known as the Madrassa Zahiriye), with a small green in front of it. Building work on this *madrassa* was started by Al Zaher Ghazi and completed around 1225 by his son Al Aziz. A squat octagonal minaret rises directly above the entrance, while inside, in the centre of the courtyard, are four tall palm trees. The *mihrab* in the prayer hall is particularly fine, decorated with beautifully delicate inlaid marble patterns. A small side room contains the tombs of Al Zaher Ghazi and other members of his family.

Behind (to the south of) the Khan ash-Shouna, meanwhile, is the **Khusuwiye Mosque**. Dating from 1537, this was the first Ottoman building to be erected in Aleppo, its distinctive rocket-shaped minaret typically Turkish in style. The man responsible for its construction was none other than Sinan Pasha, architect of the Tekkiyeh as-Suleimaniyeh Mosque in Damascus (see page 103) and, most famously, of the Suleimaniye Mosque in Istanbul.

The street leading east just to the south of the Madrassa as-Sultaniye brings you to the **Al Utrush Mosque**. This 15th-century mosque was started in 1403 by the emir Aq Bogha al-Utrushi who, in a typically Mameluke tradition, intended it to act also as his mausoleum. It was completed by his successor Emir Damir Dash. The main entrance façade of the mosque in particular is lavishly decorated.

Taking the main road heading southwest from the Al Utrush Mosque, go staight aross a mini-roundabout, then past the 14th-century Al Tawashi Mosque on the right, its windows flanked by slender colonettes, to arrive after around 500 m at the **Bab al-Maqam**. This southern gate of the Old City was first built by the Ayyubid governor Al Zaher Ghazi towards the end of the 12th century, and later rebuilt during the reign of the Mameluke sultan Qait Bey in 1493. Today this remnant of the old city stands rather isolated and forlorn-looking amidst the surrounding modern developments and roads.

Just under 1 km further to the southwest of Bab al-Maqam is the **Madrassa Faradis**, which manages to retain a wonderful overall atmosphere of antiquity and tranquillity, and is well worth the extra detour to reach it. Take the small road leading southwest from the square across the road from Bab al-Maqam (not the main road leading due south). Arriving at a fork, bear right along the road which passes through a cemetery on either side, then take the first left turn along a cobbled street and the *madrassa* is around 50 m down this street, on the right. The Madrassa Faradis (literally 'School of Paradise'), was built in 1234-47 by the widow of Al Zaher Ghazi, Daifa Khatun, who was also both the niece and daughter-in-law of Salah ud-Din (Saladin). The simple honey-combed entrance leads through to the main courtyard with a central pool surrounded on three sides by an arcade supported on slender columns of classical origin. The prayer hall, on the south side of the courtyard, has a triple-domed ceiling and boasts a particularly elegantly decorated *mihrab* with geometric designs of different coloured marble. At either end of the prayer hall are rooms containing the tombs of Muslim saints. On the opposite side of the courtyard to the prayer hall is a large arched *iwan*. Behind this is a vaulted hall (restored in recent years), which was the madrassa's original school room.

Jdaide quarter

The Jdaide Quarter (literally 'New quarter') was developed during the late Mameluke period to accommodate the growing numbers of Christians, mostly Armenian and Maronite, who were drawn to Aleppo by the commercial opportunities it offered for the astute entrepreneur. By the 17th and 18th centuries it had grown into a wealthy district with many elegant houses belonging to prosperous local Christian families. One of these now houses the Museum of Popular Tradition, although it is the architecture of the building itself which is the main attraction.

Today the district, with its narrow cobbled streets, retains much of its distinctive historic charm and the Maronite and Armenian cathedrals, although relatively recent constructions, are nevertheless fascinating to visit. (Sunday is probably the best day to visit, when there is a service in progress, or on one of the many religious festivals days.) At any time, but on Sundays in particular, the streets throng with Christian families, bringing with them an ambience worlds away from the atmosphere of Muslim Aleppo. True to the entrepreneurial spirit that spawned this district, it is also here that you can find several excellent restaurants and a couple of luxury hotels, set in elegant and stylishly restored houses and palaces dating from the 17th and 18th centuries. Most of these have complexes of underground caves and passages beneath them, dug to provide refuges during times of persecution. According to local tradition, some of these passages once led all the way into the Citadel.

From the large intersection at the north end of Bab al-Faraj Street, follow the small lane which runs east parallel to Al Khandak Street (the entrance to this lane is around 20 m to the east of the pedestrian street leading northeast from the main intersection). After 100 m or so, a small left turn brings you to the **Forty Martyrs Armenian Cathedral**. A small church dating from the 15th century originally stood on the site. This was replaced in 1639 by a larger complex, which was in turn partially rebuilt in 1869, then extensively restored in 1950. The interior is well worth a look for the beautiful paintings and icons which adorn the walls. There is also a bookshop and museum in the grounds of the cathedral.

Following the street due east from the cathedral, on the left just before you reach an intersection is the entrance to the **Beit Ajiqbash**, which now houses the **Museum of Popular Tradition**. Built in 1757 by the wealthy Christian Ajiqbash family, this is one of the best examples of such houses in Jdaide. In traditional Arab style the building is centred around a large courtyard with a fountain and trees for shade, and a large arched *iwan* in one wall with a richly decorated roof and porch. Combined with the Mameluke-style bands of black and white stone around the doorways in the courtyard, and the exuberant carved stone decoration above the windows, the overall effect is both striking and pleasing. The rooms themselves contain displays of old weaponry, inlaid wood furniture, intricately decorated copper pots and plates, jewellery, clothing and various depictions of 'traditional' life. The large room opposite the arched *iwan* is particularly lavishly decorated throughout. From the courtyard stairs lead up to the roof, from where there is access to one room containing an eclectic collection of old sewing machines, spinning wheels, a mangle, a press for shaping felt hats, wooden printing blocks and other assorted items. ■ *Open 0800-1430, closed Tue. Entry S£150 (students S£10).*

Aleppo

Jdaide Quarter

- Nayyal Hamidien St
- Al Malek Gori St
- Al Tall St
- Sissi St
- Al Raheb Buhayrah St
- Beit Balit 1
- Beit Basil
- Beit Dallal
- 4
- Al Hatab Square
- Maronite Cathedral 1
- Khan al-Arassa
- Al Jdaide St
- Beit Ghazale
- Al Kayyali St
- 2
- Beit Ajiqbash (Museum of Popular Tradition)
- 5
- 3
- Forty Martyrs Armenian Cathedral
- Al Khandak St

N

0 metres 200
0 yards 200

■ **Sleeping**
1 Beit Wakil
2 Martini/Dar Zamaria

● **Eating**
1 Al Mashrabia
2 Cantara
3 Kan Zaman
4 Sissi House
5 Yasmeen House

Turning left to head north at the intersection just to the east of the entrance to the Museum of Popular Tradition, after 40 m (soon after an alleyway leading to the *Yasmeen House* restaurant) you come to the **Beit Ghazale** on the left. Dating from the 17th century, it is similar in style to the Beit Ajiqbash, but sadly now very dilapidated, though this is one of the monuments which will be restored by the Project for the Rehabilitation of the Old City of Aleppo. In its heyday it must have been very grand, complete with its own *hammam*, while the main reception room still retains its original decorated woodwork. The carved decoration on the walls of the courtyard is much more delicate than in the Beit Ajiqbash, and the use of coloured stone to produce patterns around the doors and windows is particularly effective. Stairs give access to the roof, from where there are good views of the citadel. ■ *The family who live here and act as caretakers is usually on hand to let you in; they charge an unofficial entry fee of S£150 (students S£25). If the house is locked, ask at the Orient House antique shop on Al Hatab Square to the north of here.*

On the south side of Al Hatab Square is the **Khan al-Arassa**. Built in 1654, today the most interesting feature of this large khan or *caravanserai* is the entrance, with its heavy wooden doors and decorated band framing the main archway and the smaller inset arch. Inside, a barrel-vaulted passage leads through to the khan itself, which today houses a bakery. As part of the Project for the Rehabilitation of the Old City of Aleppo, there are plans to clear the modern structures from the centre of Al Hatab Square and to make this area a pedestrian zone.

Taking either of the left turns leading west from Al Hatab Square, you come to the large and comparatively recent **Maronite Cathedral**, dating from 1873-1923. The entrance façade is particularly imposing, consisting of a triple gateway flanked by square towers topped by pyramid-shaped roofs. This leads through to a courtyard with a statue of St Elie, to whom the cathedral is dedicated. The main doorway of the cathedral itself is framed by bands of black and honey stone, with interlocking patterns in the arch, and intricate geometric decorations above that.

In the series of narrow pedestrian streets leading north from the northernmost of the two streets running between the Maronite Cathedral and Al Hatab Square can be found a number of other elegant 17th-18th-century merchants' houses. Along Sissi Street, next door to *Sissi House* restaurant, there is **Beit Dallal**, while along Al Raheb Buhayrah Street are **Beit Balit** and **Beit Basil**. However, they have now been converted into schools or orphanages, or are privately owned and occupied, and gaining entry to them can be difficult.

National Museum

At the time of writing, some of the most important artefacts had been removed for restoration. The main focus is on archaeological finds from northern Syria covering the Iron Ages through to the classical period, but there is also a collection of artefacts from the Islamic era

Aleppo's National Museum is second only to the Damascus National Museum in terms of its remarkable collection of exhibits, and is well worth a visit. Unfortunately, the quality of the presentation does not always do justice to the subject matter, although efforts have been made to improve the labelling and interpretations.

Dotted around the gardens of the museum are some beautiful statues, *stelae* and architectural fragments. To the right of the museum entrance is a separate building housing mosaics, though this has remained closed for the last few years. The entrance to the museum is dominated by three huge basalt statues of gods standing atop equally massive animals. These were discovered at Tell Halaf (Guzana) in the Jezira region (in the far northeast of Syria) in 1912. They date from the ninth century BC and represent examples of the neo-Hittite (or Syro-Hittite) art which developed in Syria following the collapse of the Hittite Empire.

The modern building in which the museum is housed follows, in plan at least, traditional Arab design, with two storeys of rooms arranged around a central courtyard. For a chronological perspective you should work your way round in an anticlockwise direction. In the open area to your right as you enter are **pre-historic** artefacts covering the paleolithic, mesolithic and neolithic periods: flint tools, figurines, a burial urn and various pottery items, including some beautiful painted pottery from the Halaf and Ubaid cultures.

The **first hall** begins with artefacts from the Jezira region, including examples of the famous alabaster figurines from the so-called Eye Temple at Tell Brak (discovered by the archaeologist Mallowan, husband of Agatha Christie). This is followed by an extensive collection of Bronze Age finds from Mari (Tell Hariri), including distinctive statuettes of Mari priests, clay tablets inscribed with cuneiform text, cylinder seals, a larger statue of an Amorite spring goddess and a bronze lion from the Temple of Dagan. If you are planning on visiting Mari, it is here that you can get a real idea of the importance of the site in terms of the archaeological finds which were discovered there. Next there is a small section covering finds from Hama, including one of the huge basalt lions which guarded the Royal Palace on the citadel mound there. The rest of this hall is given over to finds from Ras Shamra (Ugarit), on the Mediterranean coast just to the north of Lattakia: bronze figurines, some inlaid with gold, dating from the second millenium BC, bronze tools and weapons, bronze and gold jewellery, ivory objects, stone friezes, painted pottery and alabaster figurines. Many of the pieces clearly show the strong Egyptian influence which resulted from the close trading contacts between Ugarit and the Pharaohs of Egypt during the 14th-13th centuries BC. Other pieces reflect Mycenaean and Lyprian styles, indicating the influence of trading links with the Aegean region.

The **second hall** is divided into three sections. The first is dominated by numerous massive basalt statues, sphinxes and friezes of gods and god-kings from Tell Halaf (Guzana). All are executed in the same style, and date from the same period as the statues at the entrance to the museum. The second section is devoted to items from Tell Arslan and Tell Hadjib (also in the Jezira region), and dominated by more massive basalt statues, friezes and a pair of carved lions. These all date from the Assyrian period (ninth-seventh centuries BC). In sharp contrast to the massive proportions of the basalt pieces is the collection of small, delicately carved ivory panels displayed in wall cases. These were discovered in the so-called Ivory House at Tell Arslan and date to the ninth century BC. Believed to have been used to decorate furnishings, the workmanship is generally recognized as Phoenician, with evidence of Egyptian, Aegean and Syrian influences. The last section contains artefacts from Tell Ahmar on the Euphrates (to the north of Lake Assad), where an Assyrian period royal palace was discovered within the walls of the citadel mound. There are several massive obelisks and friezes carved with figures in the Egyptian style from the palace on display here, but more interesting is the series of fragments of frescos (reproductions of the originals) which adorned the walls of the palace. They are strikingly life-like and beautifully executed, and all the more remarkable when you consider that they date from the eighth and seventh centuries BC.

The **third hall** is divided into two sections. The first contains a varied collection of artefacts from various different sites, including basalt friezes from Ain Dara (to the northwest of Aleppo) and alabaster figurines, pottery, jewellery, cylinder seals etc from Tell Chuera (in the desert region between the Balikh and Kabour rivers, to the north of the Euphrates). The second section is given over to artefacts from Tell Mardikh (Ebla), including a selection of clay tablets inscribed with cuneiform script, and various fragments of wooden furniture dating from the Early Bronze Age (2400-2250 BC) inlaid with shells and carved with delicate human and animal figures. The central courtyard of the museum contains various basalt pieces, a large rectangular mosaic floor, and a reconstruction of an underground tomb.

Upstairs, the first hall contains exhibits from various sites along the Euphrates, most of which were 'rescue' excavations carried out prior to their inundation by the river as a result of the construction of the huge dam at Ath Thawra. There are separate displays by the Syrian, German, Dutch, Belgian, Italian, French, British, American and Japanese missions which carried out the excavations. The second hall contains artefacts from the classical era, including pottery, coins, statues, glassware, mosaics and lots of funerary *stelae* from Palmyra. Although there are some beautiful pieces, unfortunately the labelling is very poor. The third hall (closed for renovation at the time of writing) is dedicated to the Islamic era and includes a scale-model of Aleppo's citadel and surrounding areas. Finally, the fourth hall houses **contemporary Syrian art**. For those interested it is well worth a look.

■ *Open 0900-1730 in summer, 0900-1530 in winter, closed Tue. Entry S£300 (students S£15). Postcards etc are on sale at the ticket office. The small 'Museum Guide' booklet on sale here is useful for a more detailed insight into the exhibits.*

Public gardens

On balmy summer evenings the gardens are busy with couples and families out strolling, chatting & enjoying the relative cool

As a rule, public gardens in Syria tend to be something of a let-down. However, the gardens which extend north from Kouwatly Square are an exception to this rule. Carefully tended and elegantly laid out, with extravagant fountains and a host of unusual contemporary sculptures along the main promenade, they are a feature of the city of which Aleppines are rightly proud. Occupying a small area on the northwest edge of the gardens (accessible only from Usman Basha Street) is **Dream Park**, with a modernistic internet café, a *Pizzaland* restaurant, a children's play area and ten-pin bowling alley.

Essentials

Sleeping

■ *on maps*
Price codes:
see inside front cover
Phone code: 021

There is something of a shortage of accommodation in Aleppo in the luxury through to medium range (**LL-C**) especially in peak spring and autumn periods. When demand is high, hotel owners (particularly in the **C**, **D** and **E** categories) are quick to mark up their prices. On the other hand, it is often possible to bargain in these places when it is quiet. There is no shortage of cheaper accommodation; but you are more likely to be driven away by the appalling conditions rather than an absence of rooms.

LL *Chahba Cham Palace*, PO Box 992, T2661600, F2270150. Suitably luxurious rooms with a/c, TV/dish, radio, IDD, mini-bar and attached bath. Those on upper floors (there are 22) have awesome views over the city. International cuisine restaurants, coffee shop, bar, disco. Conference/banqueting facilities, fitness centre, swimming pool, tennis, squash, shopping, currency exchange, travel agent (*Chamtour*), car hire (*Hertz/Chamcar*). Aleppo's premier hotel (with prices to match), but some way from the centre. **AL** *Amir Palace*, Al Raies Sq, Ibrahim Hanano St, PO Box 419, T2214800, F2215700, amir@net.sy A/c, TV/dish, radio, IDD, minibar and attached bath. 2 restaurants, bar, bookshop, car hire. Guests can send/receive emails from hotel's computer. Well run, comfortable 4-star hotel, with the advantage of being centrally located. **AL** *Beit Wakil*, Sissi St, Jdaide district, T2217169, F2247082. Set in a beautifully restored 18th-century palace. The reception area, with its lavish decoration, vaulting and high

Aleppo

The Baron hotel

When it was completed in 1911, the Baron hotel stood in an as yet largely undeveloped area to the west of Aleppo, surrounded by gardens and open countryside. Established by two Armenian brothers, it benefited from the custom brought by the Taurus Express (the eastward extension of the Orient Express; at that time the Taurus Express terminated in Aleppo, but eventually it extended all the way from Constantinople to Baghdad). The hotel was unique for its time in aiming specifically to cater for the needs of European visitors, providing such lavish creature comforts as central heating, attached bathrooms and, of course, a bar.

As such, over the years it attracted a veritable roll call of the rich and powerful, including such names as King Feisal (leader of the Arab Revolt), Kemal Ataturk, Theodore Roosevelt, the aviators Charles Lindbergh, Amy Johnston and Charles Kingsford-Smith, Freya Stark, Agatha Christie, the diplomat/spy Kim Philby and TE Lawrence (Lawrence of Arabia). The latter stayed there often, and earned a certain infamy for leaving without paying his bill on one occasion! The unpaid bill is displayed in a glass case in the lounge along with a few other pieces of memorabilia. The leather-bound visitors' book, however, is only brought out for inspection on special request.

Today you can still savour the romance and nostalgia of the hotel, which for the most part has changed little over the near-century of its existence. However, you do have a choice as to whether you wish that 'authentic' touch to extend to your room, or prefer to indulge in rather more up-to-date creature comforts, such as plumbing and a/c units which actually work!

---

dome-topped ceiling immediately gives you a sense of the historic atmosphere of this place, as well as the quality of the restoration. Apart from the suites, the hotel's 16 rooms are all arranged on 2 levels around a small, peaceful courtyard with a central fountain, and equipped with a/c, TV/dish, IDD, radio and attached bath. The hotel's restaurant (see 'Eating' below) occupies another courtyard, while the bar is in a small vaulted room below the restaurant (see 'Bars' below). Overall a very attractive place and well worth a visit even if you cannot afford to stay. Recommended. **AL** *Martini/Dar Zamaria*, Musa Bin Nusayr St, Jdaide district, T3636100, F3632333. Occupying another beautifully restored palace, this one dating from the 17th century. It is perhaps not quite as atmospheric as the *Beit Wakil*, but very tastefully done all the same. Suitably elegant rooms with a/c, TV/dish, radio, minibar and attached bath. Restaurant in beautiful covered courtyard (see 'Eating' below), and bar in underground chambers surrounding the restaurant. Recommended. **A** *Pullman al-Shahba*, PO Box 1350, T2667200, F2667213. Comfortable if unremarkable rooms with a/c, TV/dish, IDD, mini-bar and attached bath. Restaurants, coffee shop, *Fun Pub* (British-style 'pub' with pool table and BBC World on the TV; for that authentic British atmosphere, presumably), disco, shops, car hire (*Europcar*). Rather a long way from the centre of town.

B *Al Diwan*, off Nour al-Din al-Zanki St (behind the passport and immigration office, on the north side of the Citadel), T3322688. Still being fitted out at the time of writing, but scheduled to open by summer 2001. A restored old house along the same lines as the *Beit Wakil* and *Martini* hotels, views of the Citadel from the roof terrace. Promises to be a welcome addition to Aleppo's selection of upper range hotels.

C *Baron*, Baron St, PO Box 130, T2210880, F2218164. A/c, phone, fridge, attached bath. Aleppo's first and still most famous hotel (see box). You now have a choice between old rooms with rickety plumbing and battered a/c units, or much more comfortable and slightly more expensive ones with brand-new bathrooms and a/c units (good value). At the time of writing just 3 rooms had been refurbished in this way, with more to come. The reception, bar, restaurant and other common areas (and indeed the whole fabric of the hotel) remain unchanged, oozing with atmosphere from a bygone era. Parking available on hotel's grounds. **C** *Faisal*, Yarmouk St, T/F2213719. Clean, pleasant rooms with a/c, TV, phone, fridge and attached bath. Restaurant, roof terrace. Breakfast included in room price. Helpful management, but rather on the expensive side for the level of facilities. **C** *New Omayad*, off Baron St, T/F2214202. Simple but reasonable rooms with a/c (old units), TV, phone and attached bath. Some rooms with small balcony. Restaurant. **C** *Tourism*, Al Walid St, T2251602, F2251606. Comfortable rooms with a/c (rather old units), TV/dish, phone, fridge, attached bath and tiny balcony. 2 restaurants (including top floor with great views), bar, coffee shop. A little nondescript, but centrally located and reasonably good value for money. Popular with tour groups. **C** *Ramsis*, Baron St, PO Box 5097, T/F2216700. Large, high-ceilinged rooms with a/c (old units), TV, phone, fridge and attached bath. Restaurant. Big old building, and relatively basic given the price tag.

D *Al Boustan*, Bab al-Faraj St, T2217104, F2257629. Simple but clean rooms with fan, phone, attached bath and balcony. Rather noisy location, though rooms at the rear are quieter. Nothing special. Breakfast served. **D** *Ambassador*, Baron St, T2210231. Clean, reasonably comfortable rooms with a/c, TV, phone, fridge and attached bath. Fairly good deal. **D** *Granada*, off Baron St, T2224458. Large, high-ceilinged rooms with a/c, TV, phone, fridge, attached bath and small balcony. Grand breakfast/common room area with some great old paintings and elaborately upholstered furniture. Very good value for level of facilities (double US$25 including breakfast and tax), assuming prices hold steady in high season. **D** *Semiramis*, Kouwatly St, T2219991. Fan, TV, phone, fridge and attached bath. Also some rooms with a/c. The impression given by the newly decorated a/c lobby and new lift is undermined once you see the rooms themselves which are rather dingy and overpriced. **D** *Somar*, off Yarmouk St (off Baron St), T2212198, F2245925. Tucked away down a small alley just off Yarmouk St. Simple, spotlessly clean rooms with a/c, fan, TV and attached bath. Some rooms with fan only and shared bath. Lovely covered courtyard area with hanging plants draped down the walls. Fairly quiet, despite the central location. Good value (assuming quoted price of US$24 for a double holds good for the high season.

E *Hanadi*, off Bab al-Faraj St, T2238113, F2219657. Immaculately clean rooms, a/c, fan, TV, phone, fridge and attached bath. Lovely old building, carefully restored, with a pleasant 1st floor courtyard and a roof terrace. Free use of washing machine. Tours arranged to St Simeon/Dead Cities etc. Well run, with friendly and helpful staff. A wonderfully peaceful oasis in the centre of Aleppo. Recommended.

F *Afamia*, off Baron St, T2217078. Simple but reasonably clean rooms with fan and attached bath. Some rooms with balcony. Fairly good value at S£250/500 for a single/double. **F** *Al Chark al-Awssat*, Al Maari St, PO Box 232, T2211630, F2214115. Big, rambling old place. Reasonable rooms (though rather tacky décor) with a/c, fan, attached bath and balcony. Pleasant 1st floor terrace/courtyard. Fairly good value, and potentially an excellent hotel, but in need of a more thorough refurbishment and better management. **F** *Al Gawaher*, off Bab al Faraj St (behind the library), T/F2239554. Clean rooms with fan, phone and attached bath. Common area with TV/dish. St Simeon/Dead City tours arranged. Friendly staff. Good value (single/double S£300/600). **F** *Al Kasser*, Bab al-Faraj, T2239365. Clean rooms with fan, TV, phone, attached bath and balcony. Unremarkable, but reasonably good value at S£500 for a double. **F** *Syria*, Al Maari St, T2219760. Clean rooms with a/c, fan, phone, fridge, attached bath and small balcony. Good value for having a/c, though some of the rooms have excruciatingly tacky wallpaper. Tours to St Simeon and the Dead Cities etc

2

exodus
9 Weir Road
LONDON
SW12 0BR

BUSINESS REPLY SERVICE
Licence No SW4909

getaway tonight on
www.exodus.co.uk

exodus
The Different Holiday

arranged by the boss of the hotel who can be extremely pushy on this front. **F** *Tourist*, off Al Maari St, T2216583. Pleasant, clean rooms with fan, sink and attached bath (S£700 for a double, or S£350 per bed; some slightly cheaper rooms with shared shower/toilet). Spotlessly clean throughout and very popular, particularly amongst French, run by the venerable Madam Olga, helpful staff. Often full, booking advisable (especially in Apr, plus Jun-Aug). Recommended. **F** *Yarmouk*, Al Maari St, opposite museum, T2217510, Clean, comfortable rooms with a/c, phone, fridge and attached bath. All rooms to be fitted with TV/dish in near future. Rooms at front with balcony, but noisier. Very good value (from S£650 for a double; amongst the cheapest a/c rooms in Aleppo), but often booked up by Russian/East European groups.

G There are a great many budget hotels, nearly all concentrated in a small area bounded by Baron St, Al Maari St, Al Kouwatly St and Bab al-Faraj St. However, many are often booked out by groups of Russians who come to Aleppo on trading visits, while some are extremely basic and best avoided. Arrangements between hotel owners and Russian traders change frequently, making it difficult to recommend particular hotels since they may in future be booked up for weeks or months at a time.

Bear in mind that this is also Aleppo's red light district; some of the establishments in the area may try to offer you more than just a bed

G *Al Hourrie*, Al Maari St, T2215884. Situated above large tea house, bed in shared room with shared shower/toilet S£100. Very basic. The cheapest budget option in Aleppo, for those aiming to save every last penny. 1 floor up is the **G** *Abi al-Fida*, T2211725, with the same set-up and prices. **G** *Al Madinah*, Yarmouk St, off Al Maari St, T2210990. Basic but reasonably clean rooms with fan and attached bath (double S£400), or with shared bath (double S£350). Pleasant roof garden/patio area. **G** *Al Najm al-Akhdar (Green Star)*, Hammam al Tal (tucked away in the Armenian market to the southeast of the clock-tower at Bab al-Faraj), T2239157. Choice of singles/doubles with fan, sink and attached bath (S£300/450), or with fan, sink and shared bath (S£200/350). Also dormitory rooms with fan, sink and shared bath for S£175 per bed, or S£250 per bed with a/c and attached bath. Plans to install more a/c units in the future. Pleasant common balcony/terrace on 4th floor, and common sitting area with TV/dish at reception. Looking a little run-down and in need of refurbishment these days, but still a popular backpacker place. Friendly, helpful staff. **G** *Al Raoudah*, Al Maari St, T2233896. Small and basic but reasonably clean rooms with fan, phone, attached bath and balcony (double S£400). Unassuming but OK-ish. **G** *Assia*, 5th floor, Al Maari St, T2215214. Clean rooms with fan, phone and attached bath. Recently repainted. Reasonably good value at S£250/400 for a single/double. Friendly staff. Downstairs on the 3rd floor is the **G** *Zahra*, T2220184, which charges the same for rather grubbier rooms. **G** *Ghassan*, Al Maari St, T2210882. Basic rooms with fan, sink and shared bath (single/double S£200/300). **G** *Kasr al-Hamra* (or *Gaser al-Hamra*), Al Maari St, T2226934. Basic rooms with fan, phone and attached bath (single/double S£200/300). Pretty shabby and run-down. Ok-ish common area on 1st floor. **G** *Kawkab al-Salam*, Bab al-Faraj St, T2239121, F2249741. Basic but relatively clean rooms with fan, sink and attached bath (double S£375), or with shared bath (double S£325). Reductions in low season. Friendly staff. **G** *Zahert al-Rabih*, off Al Maari St, PO Box 10816, T2212790. Reasonable double rooms with fan and attached bath for S£350 (though some of these are small units built onto the roof, and so very hot in summer), or dorm beds (also with fan and attached bath) for S£125 per person. Popular backpacker option and good value, with plentiful hot water, free use of kitchen and a common sitting area with TV/dish. Also on offer are St Simeon/Dead City tours, email/internet access, and various other useful services.

Aleppo

Eating

Gourmet, *Amir Palace* hotel. Open 24 hrs, daily. International cuisine. Whenever there are more than 40 guests at the hotel, an open buffet dinner is served here each evening, as well as an open buffet lunch on Fri and Sun (S£600 per head). Every

● *on maps*

lunch-time (except Fri and Sun) there is also an open salad bar and plat du jour (S£358 per head). *Il Patio*, *Chahba Cham Palace* hotel. Open 24 hrs, daily, for breakfast, lunch and dinner. International cuisine (à la carte Italian for dinner). Fri and Sun lunch-time buffet (S£660 per person) when there are groups staying. *La Citadelle*, 22nd floor, *Chahba Cham Palace* hotel. Suitably elegant, with stunning views. French cuisine. From around S£750-1000 per head. *Panoramique*, top floor, *Amir Palace* hotel. Open 1230-2030, daily. Arabic, French and some Chinese cuisine, à la carte. From around S£500-750 per head. Live music and show each evening after 2030.

Jdaide quarter (expensive/ mid-range) This is where Aleppo's most interesting restaurants are to be found, many of them set in beautifully restored houses and palaces. *Al Mashrabia*, off Al Kayyali St, T2240249. Open 1000-late, daily. Pleasant, intimate restaurant, but without the atmospheric courtyards and sense of history of the other restored buildings in the area. Varied menu of Arabic and European cuisine for around S£300 per head upwards. Breakfasts served (choice of 'Oriental' – fuul, cheese, labneh, olives, tea/coffee – or Continental – jam, butter, croissant, juice, tea/coffee – for S£125/150 respectively). Also bills itself as a 'pub' and has a full menu of cocktails (S£150-175), as well as spirits, wines and beers. On Wed, Sat and Sun evenings there is live music (Arabic, Armenian or European) from 2200. *Beit Wakil*, Sissi St, T2217169, F2247082. Open 1300-1600, 1900-late, daily. Set in a beautiful shady courtyard of the *Beit Wakil* hotel, (see 'Sleeping' above). Arabic cuisine to a high standard from around S£350-400 per head upwards. Alcohol served. In the evenings, if there is a group staying, live music or perhaps even a Whirling Dervishes performance is usually laid on. *Cantara*, off Al Kayyali St, T2253355. Open 1200-1600, 1900-late, daily. Pleasant courtyard, as well as upstairs terrace and seating inside. Italian cuisine (pizza, pasta, lasagna, salad etc), as well as some Arabic food at lunch-times. Around S£300 per head upwards. Alcohol served. *Kan Zaman*, off Haret al-Yasmin St, T3630299. Set in another beautifully restored house. Very elegantly done, with 4 different dining areas comprising the main courtyard, 2 adjoining rooms and a covered roof terrace with views out over Jdaide. Varied menu of good quality Arabic cuisine from around S£300 per head upwards. Also with its own underground caves, which provide an alternative dining area, as well as serving as a bar/nightclub (see 'Bars' below). *Martini/Dar Zamaria*, Musa Bin Nusayr St, T3636100, F3632333. Open 0645-late, daily. Occupying a beautiful covered courtyard in the hotel of the same name, and also with a lovely roof terrace in summer with views of the Citadel. Arabic and European cuisine. Around S£350 per head upwards for Arabic food, and S£450-500 for European. *Sissi House*, Sissi St, T2219411, F2215700. Set in a beautifully restored 18th-century merchant's house, and offering a pleasant, atmospheric venue in which to dine out in style. Outdoor seating in summer in central courtyard, or indoors in lavishly ornate rooms. Downstairs is a bar in a hand-dug cave which, according to the owner, is believed to have once been connected by a network of tunnels to the Citadel. There is no menu as such, but the waiters will list the usual range of Arabic dishes (with the help of a local you could also sample aspects of Syrian cuisine not usually on offer at your run-of-the-mill restaurant). Alcohol served. From around S£400-500 per head upwards. *Yasmeen House*, off Al Kayyali St, T2224462, F2675366. Like *Sissi House*, this restaurant is set in a beautifully restored 18th-century merchant's house with its own courtyard, lavish rooms and hand-dug cave. You are presented with a simple menu (in English, with prices) of mezze, kibbeh, shish tawouk, kebabs etc, complete with photos of the dishes on offer. Despite the elegant surroundings, prices are very reasonable; there is a set menu for 1 or 2 people (S£200/380), though if you order for yourself and include a beer you are looking at more like S£300 per head.

Downtown area (mid-range/ cheap) *Al Andalib*, Baron St. Pleasant rooftop restaurant offering the usual selection of Arabic food. Popular with locals and often very lively in the evenings (once the arak starts to flow). Slightly inflated prices for tourists (S£250-300 per head), despite a sign announcing that an ordinary lunch costs around S£200 per head, but reasonable value all the same. *Al Chabab*, T2188041, off Baron St. Open 1300-late, daily. Friendly place claiming to be 'the first in Syria'. Outdoor seating in a large, pleasant patio garden with fountains and trees, as well as an indoor section. Standard range of Arabic dishes and a menu (of sorts) in English. From around S£200-250 per head. Alcohol served (this is a pleasant place to come just for a drink). *Abou Nawas*, off Zaki al-Arsuzi St, T2210388. Simple but clean and pleasant a/c restaurant serving the usual range of Arabic food. Around S£200-250 per head. No alcohol, so doesn't get as rowdy as places such as the *Al Andalib*. The *Restaurant* in the garden area between Al Ayouby St and Jbrail Dallal St has a cavernous dining hall and outdoor seating in the gardens, it serves good traditional Syrian food for around S£200-250 per head, alcohol served (in summer this is another pleasant place to come just for a drink). *Sage Cafeteria*, Saad Allah al-Jabri St. Large place offering a mixture of pizza, cakes, coffee etc, popular with families. Also a good place for Continental-style breakfasts.

If you head north from Kouwatly Sq along Saad Allah al-Jabri St, at the point where Al Ayoubi St converges with it, a right turn takes you into Mathilde Salam St (actually 2 parallel streets with a wide band of green running between them). Along this street, which forms the heart of the affluent Christian district of Azizieh, is a string of elegant restaurants, most of them in fact surprisingly affordable. As well as the restaurants listed below, there are 2 fast-food places to be found on Mathilde Salam St, and on a side-street leading off it; *Midmac*, complete with the trademark 'M', and *Pizza House*, which serves reasonable pizzas.

Azizieh district (mid-range/cheap)

   Al Challal, Mathilde Salam St, T2243344. Open daily 0800-late. Billed as a café and snack place as well as a restaurant, but the overall impression is very much of elegance. Seating in long glass-fronted section looking onto the street, or in large dining hall behind. Varied menu with the usual range of Arabic cuisine (including lots of mezze dishes), as well as Continental offerings such as steak, escalope, pizza, pasta, snacks (chips, chicken nuggets, spring rolls) etc. Around S£300 per head upwards for a full meal. Every Sunday, from 1200-1600, there is an open buffet (Arabic cuisine) costing S£350 per head. Alcohol served (some pretty serious drinking goes on here in the evenings alongside the eating). *Al Karam*, Mathilde Salam St, T2210110. Open 0900-late, daily. Fairly small, with décor bordering somewhere between stylish and slightly tacky. Combination of Arabic and European cuisine. Around S£250-350 per head upwards. Alcohol served. *Cordoba*, Mathilde Salam St, T2240868. Open 0900-late. Smart, pleasant restaurant offering a wide-ranging Arabic menu (including some local Aleppine recipies), as well as various Armenian and Turkish dishes. Some examples include; *Bastrama*, an Armenian dish of spiced potatoes; *Toshka*, an Armenian dish of spicy meat and cheese grilled between bread; *Yabrak*, a Turkish dish of vine leaves stuffed with rice and meat in a sour sauce; *Maajouka*, a typical Aleppine dish of kebab meat, cheese, pistachios, red peppers and pine nuts shaped into triangular segments and barbequed). Long-established, with a reputation for good quality food, and good value at around S£250-300 per head upwards for a full meal. Alcohol served. Friendly management and staff who will help you select from the less common dishes. *Ebla*, Mathilde Salam St, T2246103. Open 1000-late, daily. Comfortable-going-on-elegant place, decorated throughout to an 'Ebla' theme, with copies of statues and friezes from the site dotted around the place. Mixed menu of Arabic and European cuisine for around S£250-300 per head upwards. Alcohol served. *L'Expresse* (formerly *Chaumine*), Fares al-Khoury St, T2216241. Nicely furnished, intimate basement restaurant in the style of a French bistrot. Mixed Arabic and European cuisine. Menu in Arabic only (no prices), with the odd item translated. Potentially a lovely place, but suffering from poor service. Often empty and liable to close early as a result. *Reef*, Mathilde Salam St, T2235914. Open 0800-late, daily. Small, reasonably priced place serving the usual range of Arabic and European cuisine for around S£250 per head upwards. Alcohol served. *Wanes*, Mathilde Salam St, T2224353. Open 0900-late, daily. Large, elegant place, very much along the

Aleppo

same lines as *Al Challal*, with a wide-ranging Arabic and European cuisine menu. Around S£300 per head for Arabic meals, or rather more if you include European dishes such as steak, escalope etc. Alcohol served.

Others (mid-range) *Grand Station*, off Sheikh Kamal al-Ghazzi St (follow Sheikh Kamal al-Ghazzi St northwest from Kouwatly Sq and immediately before it passes under the railway line turn left into a side-road; it is a short way down on the left), T2215150. Open 0900-late, daily. Super-trendy and modern glass-fronted warehouse-style fast food place with seating on 2 floors. Fairly varied menu of pizzas, pasta, burgers, sandwiches, chicken meals, steaks, escalopes etc. Around S£300 per head for a full meal, or less for snacks. Very popular with Aleppo's young and hip middle/upper classes, and very busy most evenings. *Grand House*, University St, next door to the *Pullman al-Shahba* hotel. Open 0900-late, daily. Slightly less ostentatiously trendy than its sister restaurant, the *Grand Station*, but following the same modern theme and offering the same type of food. The upstairs part manages to combine the atmosphere of an American diner and a UK motorway service station. Downstairs there is a large cafeteria/restaurant, covered in winter, where families can eat or relax over a nargileh while their children amuse themselves in the adjacent adventure/play area. At the entrance to the whole complex is a short mall of shops selling designer clothes, computer games and other luxury goods. *Pasta Della Casa*, *Pullman al-Shahba* hotel. Open 1200-late, daily. Pleasant Italian restaurant. Reasonably priced dishes (with a little care it is possible to eat for around S£300-500 per head), though the drinks here are rather expensive. *Pizzaland*, inside 'Dream Park', a small section of the public gardens which extend north from Kouwatly Sq (access from Usman Basha St, on the northwest side of the gardens). Franchise outlet of the international chain offering the usual pizzas, pasta, lasagne etc. Like everything else in Dream Park it's fairly swish, though it doesn't appear to have caught on in the same way as places such as *Grand Station*. Around S£300 per head.

Seriously cheap There are several cheap restaurants towards the eastern end of Zaki al-Arsuzi St, including the *Al Safer*, *Khan al-Khalili*, *Al Zuhour*, *Al Koumeh*, *Al Kindi* and *Chich Kebab*. There is not much to choose between them, all offering the standard selection of kebabs, half-chicken, side dishes etc, as well as serving alcohol. With a little care it is possible to eat for under S£150 per head, although it is best to ask how much your meal will cost before ordering as foreign tourists are liable to be overcharged.

At the corner of Al Maari St and Bab al-Faraj St is a small pedestrian arcade/covered mall with underground parking below. There are several small, simple restaurants along here serving very cheap and filling meals (eg meat or vegetable stew and rice). Their breakfasts of fuul and tea for S£25 are also excellent value.

At the eastern end of Yarmouk St there are a few cheap places where a meal of 200g of kebab, plus hummus and salad, costs just S£100. The first restaurant on the right as you enter Yarmouk St from Bab al-Faraj St looks pretty dingy and grimy inside, but does the best kebabs in the street, complete with barbecued onions, and bread smeared in spicy paste and sprinkled with freshly chopped garlic and onion. They also do excellent grilled chicken (squashed flat Turkish-style between metal racks and smeared with spicy paste). Along this stretch of Yarmouk St there are also several good fresh juice stands on the opposite side.

Al Sham Pastries, off Baron St (next to the *Al Chabab* restaurant). Wide range of traditional Arabic savoury pastries for S£5-10 apiece, as well as mini-pizzas (Syrian style) for S£15. Takeaway, or eat in at a counter along the wall. Menu and prices displayed in English. Delicious and excellent value. *Falafel Alfehaa*, Baron St (on the corner of the side-road with the *Al Sham Pastries* and *Al Chabab* restaurant). This brightly lit takeaway does a roaring trade in fresh, tasty falafels (S£10 a go). Next door is another takeaway doing shawarmas, while next door to that is a simple sit-down place offering the usual half-chicken, salad and hummus etc.

On Musa Bin Nusayr St, in the Jdaide district (occupying a corner of the *Martini/Dar Zamaria* hotel), there is an excellent hummus and fuul restaurant; the fuul they serve here is very different from the standard Syrian style, with beans being mashed up and served with a generous amount of garlic juice and chilli sauce. You can also find good cheap snacks at various points along Souk al-Atarin in the Old City.

Cafés

There are several cafés in the downtown area. The one towards the north end of Bab al-Faraj St unfortunately often has its TV blaring at full volume. The one on Al Maari St (below the *Al Hourrie* and *Abi al-Fida* hotels) is more traditional; here you can get a very accurate picture of how most Syrian men, in particular the older generation, spend their seemingly endless hours of leisure. The **Al Saleh**, up on the 1st floor, with a large balcony area overlooking the clock-tower and the chaotic junction of Al Maari St/Bab al-Faraj St, is a pleasant place to watch the world go by. It has plenty of atmosphere and is relatively cool in summer. On Baron St, opposite the *Syrian Air* office, the **Ramsis Tea House** is a pleasant, more up-market café where you can get excellent real expressos (not the usual Turkish/Arabic coffee), as well as café au lait and tea etc. The café on Kouwatly Sq, on the corner opposite the *Tourism* hotel, features chess boards stuck to the tables; there are usually a dozen or so games on the go every evening, so if you fancy a game of chess, this is the place to come.

The 2 cafés opposite the entrance to the Citadel are comparatively expensive, although the outside seating is very pleasant and you have prime views of the Citadel from here. Most of the restaurants along Mathilde Salam St, in the Christian district of Azizieh, also double as rather up-market cafés, where Aleppo's well-to-do come to enjoy a drink and a nargileh.

Bars

The bar at the *Baron* hotel, steeped in atmosphere, is always popular with tourists, the décor and furniture largely unchanged since Lawrence's time, though its relatively expensive (S£100/150 for a local/imported beer). The *Al Chabab* restaurant has a pleasant outdoor patio/garden area and they don't seem to mind people coming just for a drink (local beer S£50; great with a plate of chips or a couple of mezze dishes.

Taverna, *Beit Wakil* hotel, Sissi St, Jdaide district. Set in a small underground vaulted room, this bar is about as intimate and atmospheric as you can get. Local beer is affordable at S£75 a bottle, while cans of imported beer cost the usual S£150. Stairs lead down from the bar into a miniature warren of caves and passages hewn into the solid bedrock. Watch out for one of the stairways; it is extremely steep and slippery, with the stairs only very roughly carved, and leads to a claustrophobically narrow dead end.

Entertainment

Nightclubs

There are quite a number of 'nightclubs' around Aleppo, most of them concentrated around the downtown area. However they tend to be seedy, to say the least, and probably best avoided. Perhaps a better bet are the nightclubs of the *Chabha Cham Palace* and *Pullman al-Shahba* hotels, although they are very expensive and frequently largely empty.

Cotton Club, in the *Panoramique* restaurant of the *Amir Palace* hotel, every Mon night from 1930-2200 (except end of Jun to end of Sep, and Christmas/New Year). An evening of jazz music organized by the French Cultural Centre. Entry S£100/200 per head including 1 soft/alcoholic drink. *Kan Zaman*, off Haret al-Yasmin St, Jdaide

Aleppo

district, T3630299. Although primarily a restaurant, this establishment also features its own underground caves. From 2230 on Thu, Fri, Sat and Sun nights these act as a bar/nightclub, with live music (Arabic and European). You can order mezze and other Arabic dishes along with your drinks.

Cinemas There are a number of cinemas along Baron St and Al Azmeh St to the north, as well as along Al Kouwatly St, including the *Ugarit*, *Opera* and *Rameta*. All provide a staple diet of crude violence and titillation, with garish posters outside to match. The *Al-Kindi* cinema occasionally shows more serious movies.

Shopping

Antiques, handicrafts & souvenirs
The souks of the Old City are an obvious place to look for things to buy. Although not specifically orientated towards tourists in the same way as the souks of Damascus increasingly are, there are still plenty of items which may be of interest. Aleppo is in particular famous for its silk and cotton textiles, and for its pistachio nuts. Items of traditional clothing, carpets, gold, copper and brass wares, spices etc can also be found. For a rough idea of where different goods are grouped together, see the Aleppo Souks map; bear in mind, however, that the grouping of specific trades is less pronounced than in the past, with a good deal of intermingling today.

In the downtown area there are several shops specializing in antique jewellery and carpets, as well as the usual range of handicrafts. The *Babylon* store on the corner of Baron St and Al Maari St has a good selection of the latter, while *Al Nayal*, next door in a basement (reached from Al Maari St), specializes in antique jewellery and carpets.

Opposite the entrance to the Citadel (behind the cafés which face it) is the *Souk ash-Shouna* which has been converted into a handicrafts market where you will find a wide range of handicrafts (see South of the Citadel in 'Sights' above). On Al Hatab Sq in the Jdaide quarter there are a couple of excellent antique shops with a wide selection of goods, including the *Orient House*.

Al Tilal St, which runs northeast from the large junction at the north end of Bab al-Faraj St, is a major hub of Armenian commercial activity. The first 100 m or so are pedestrianized and during the evenings this stretch (and indeed the rest of the street to the north) is brightly lit and very lively, thronging with people out strolling, chatting and window-shopping. Almost all the shops are Armenian-owned, with signs in Armenian as well as Arabic. Although unlikely to be of major interest to tourists in terms of shopping (it is mostly western clothing and household goods on sale here), this is a great place to wander round, soak up the atmosphere and generally just 'people-watch'.

Books The bookshops of the luxury hotels tend to have the widest selection of books, both in terms of the history etc of Syria, and western fiction. In the downtown area, the *Dar al-Kalam al-Araby* bookshop has a limited selection; it does however publish the best available map of Aleppo, in both Arabic and English. The *Librarie Said* has a good selection of Penguin Classics. Alternatively, try the bookshops at the *Chahba Cham Palace* and *Amir Palace* hotels.

Sports

Chahba Cham Palace hotel Non-guests can use the **swimming** pool for S£400 per day. Use of the **tennis** courts costs £300 per hr. In addition, there is a **fitness centre** here, with an indoor pool, gym, sauna, jacuzzi, massage, and squash (pay by the hr or become a member for 1 month minimum). *Fun Time*, Dream Park (access from Usman Basha St, on the northwest side of the public gardens which extend north from Kouwatly Sq). Open 1000-late, daily. Bright and colourful, with all the latest in

children's play; slides, tunnels, bouncy soft-ball areas etc. *Game Land*, Dream Park. Open 1000-late, daily. State-of-the-art computerized **ten-pin bowling** (S£550 per hr), plus **snooker** and **pool/billiards** (S£150 per hr). *Grand Fitness Centre*, University St (next door to *Pullman al-Shahba* hotel), T2688001. Open 0600-2300, daily. This large, modern sports complex is easily the best in Aleppo, boasting an Olympic-size indoor **swimming** pool complete with waterslide and café overlooking it (entry S£150; women-only sessions 1400-1800 Mon, Wed, Sat, and 1000-1400 Tue, Thu, Sun). It also has a fully equipped **gym** (membership S£1000 per month); a **health club** with sauna, jacuzzi and steam room (S£150); and **tennis** courts (S£150 per hr, or S£200 per hr when floodlit). **Turkish baths** There are 2 working hammams (Turkish baths) in Aleppo; Hammam Yalbogha al-Nasri (see page 325), and Hammam al-Nahasin (see page 320).

Tour operators and travel agents

Most of the luxury hotels, and some of the mid-range ones, have tour operators attached to them. In addition, most of the budget hotels which deal with backpackers offer tours to St Simeon and the 'Dead Cities'. If you can get a group together these can be reasonable value, and allow you to get round a greater number of sites more quickly than would be possible by public transport. For a vintage tour to St Simeon and sites around Aleppo, ask for Walid Mallahk or his son Mohammad, based at the *Baron* hotel. They can whisk you around in an immaculately restored 1955 Studebacker Commander (complete with a/c, and a Toyota engine, these days).

All the travel agents given here are situated on Baron St; *Atlantic*, PO Box 5698, T2222763, F2222763. *Baron*, T2242391, F2249054. *Ghazal*, PO Box 187, T2218775 (agents for PIA, Iberia, Air Algeria, Sudan Airways and Yemenia).

Transport

To/from the airport There are fairly regular buses which operate between the airport and the city centre. They depart from just outside the International/*Karnak* bus station (see Aleppo Centre map). **Local**

Car hire *Europcar* is based at the *Pullman al-Shahba* hotel, T2667200, F2667213. Cheapest car Hyundai Atos, US$58 per day for open mileage (minimum period 3 days), US$36 per day for limited mileage (up to 100 km per day, minimum period 2 days). Includes full insurance; providing you obtain a police report in case of an accident, you will not be liable for repair costs.

Taxis There is no shortage of taxis prowling the streets of Aleppo; indeed, they often seem to outnumber any other vehicles on the road. Many of them are huge, ancient American models from the 1940s and 1950s which are kept running by miracles of ingenuity, although modern imports are becoming more common. Fares should not exceed S£25-30 for journeys within the city.

Bus Aleppo has an extensive local bus system, although it is very difficult to make head or tail of it. The main terminal for local buses is just to the south of the *Amir Palace* hotel, part of the Pullman/City bus station (see below).

Air The airport is 10 km to the east of Aleppo, off the main highway to Raqqa and Deir ez-Zor. *Syrian Air* operate direct international flights from Aleppo to a number of European cities, including **Munich**, **Berlin**, **Frankfurt**, **Madrid**, **Paris**, **Rome** and **Athens**. Other destinations include **Istanbul**, **Cairo**, **Beirut**, **Dubai** and **Kuwait**. International flights with the majority of other airlines go from Damascus. Internally, *Syrian* **Long distance**

Aleppo

Air operate 2-5 flights daily to **Damascus** (S£602); timetables change frequently so check with their office on Baron St.

Train The train station is to the north of the main public gardens of the downtown area, a longish though manageable walk from the main hotel area, or a S£20-25 taxi ride. See under 'Ins and outs' at the start of this chapter for comments on rail travel to and from Aleppo. For the latest train information, T2213900, extension 296, or extension 205 for bookings. **Lattakia**, 2 trains daily, 0700, 1530, 1st class S£54, 2nd class S£36, 3½-4 hrs. **Damascus** (via Hama and Homs), 1 train daily, 2430, sleeper S£325, 1st class S£85, 2nd class S£57, 7 hrs approx. **Deir ez-Zor**, 1 train daily, 2330, sleeper S£225, 1st class S£87, 2nd class S£58, 5 hrs approx. **Qamishle**, 1 train daily, 2330 (same train as for Deir ez-Zor), sleeper S£350, 1st class S£132, 2nd class S£88, 10 hrs approx. **Istanbul** (Turkey): 1 train weekly, Tue 1100, sleeper S£1,950, 1st class S£1,050, 36 hrs approx.

Road Luxury coaches all depart from the **Hanano coach station**, to the west of the downtown area, on Ibrahim Hanano St (a good 15-20 min walk, or around S£20 by taxi). There are more than 50 companies located here, which between them offer regular departures to all the major cities in Syria, eg: **Hama**, S£65, 2hrs; **Homs**, S£80-85, 2½ hrs, **Damascus**, S£150, 5-6 hrs; **Lattakia**, S£100, 3-3½ hrs; **Tartus**, S£115-120, 4 hrs; **Raqqa**, S£85, 3 hrs; **Deir ez-Zor**, S£135, 5 hrs; **Qamishle**, S£175, 8½hrs. Note that for **Palmyra** you must go via Deir ez-Zor or Homs and change; going via Homs is considerably quicker. A couple of companies also offer services to Lebanon. With so many competing companies it is not necessary to book in advance; you will usually find a coach leaving for your destination within half an hour or so.

If you prefer, you can book your ticket in up to 1 week in advance with the better companies. A few of the coach companies also have ticket offices in the centre of town, including: *Al Ahliah*, off Baron St (a couple of doors down from the Afamia hotel), T2215286 (regular services to Damascus, Hama, Homs and Raqqa, and 1 service daily to Tartus at 0700); *Sarraj*, Baron St, T2246464 (regular services to Damascus, and 5 daily to Tripoli and Beirut); and *Zeitouni*, next to the International/Karnak station (hourly services to Damascus, from Hanano bus station).

South of the Amir Palace hotel, between Bab Antakya St & the southern continuation of Baron St, this is in fact a sprawling complex of several different bus stands (see map)

Pullman/City bus station Pullman station **(B1)** There are a number of competing companies offering 'Pullman' coach services from here to most major cities. On the whole these coaches are older and less comfortable than the private luxury coaches found at the Hanano bus station (though some are actually pretty good), and services tend to be less frequent. However, they are also slightly cheaper, eg **Damascus** S£90; **Deir ez-Zor** S£80. There are also hourly services to **Idlib** and **Maarat al-Numan** from here (both S£20).

Bus station (B2) The services operating from here are mostly the rickety old 'hob-hob' ('stop-stop') buses, together with various microbuses. They cover all the major cities in Syria. They are uncomfortable and slow (in particular the 'hob-hob' buses), stopping anywhere on demand. They do not operate to a fixed

Pullman/City bus station

timetable, departing when full. They are cheap; for example ('hob-hob'/microbus); Hama S£25/30; Homs S£30/40; Lattakia S£40/65. In addition, there are a few fairly respectable 'Pullman' coaches for Damascus, S£75. Tickets for all these services must be bought from the main hall at the north end of the station.

City station (B3) Local buses covering Aleppo itself run from here. The kiosk here sells tickets (S£10) which are valid for 4 separate journeys. However, the network of routes is difficult for the short-term visitor to get to grips with.

Microbus/service taxi station (B4) The microbuses operating from here cover all destinations to the northwest of Aleppo. You can get a microbus from here to **Daret Aazah**, S£25, from where it is a further 6 km or so of walking or hitching to **St Simeon (Qalat Samaan)**. There are also microbuses from here to **Azaz**, S£30 (28 km southeast of **Cyrrhus**); to **Afrine**, S£15 (10 km north of **Ain Dara**; to **Bab al-Hawa**, S£25; and to **Harim**. Service taxis operate to all major cities (including to international destinations such as **Tripoli**, **Beirut** and **Amman**), departing when full, though they are comparatively expensive and offer no real advantages over the luxury coach services.

International/Karnak station This coach station is conveniently located close to the downtown area, and just a few mins walk from the main concentration of cheap hotels. There are a number of different coach companies offering services to Turkey, Lebanon and Jordan, as well as further afield to Romania, Bulgaria, Saudi Arabia, Egypt, Libya and Iraq. You can buy tickets to anywhere in Turkey, but it is generally cheaper to buy one just as far as **Antakya** (S£200-250) and change there. Services to **Beirut** all seem to depart at 2400 and cost S£250. Services to **Amman** mostly seem to leave at 2300, with a couple going earlier at 1600, and cost S£450.

Karnak coaches also all depart from here, though their ticket office is on Baron St, T2210248. Note that their services have been greatly reduced in recent years. **Lattakia**, 0700, S£65, 3½ hrs. **Tripoli/Beirut**, 1300, 2400, S£200/250, 6/7 hrs. **Amman**, 2200, S£450, 9 hrs.

East bus station Inconveniently located way out to the east of the Old City (see main Aleppo map). A taxi to here will cost in the region of S£30. Buses and microbuses from here run (predictably enough) to destinations east of Aleppo. For the major cities such as Raqqa and Deir ez-Zor, unless you are really determined to go by the cheapest possible transport, it makes more sense to go by luxury coach. The East bus station is only of specific use if you wish to go to **Qalat Najm** by public transport; in which case buses and microbuses run from here to Ain al-Arab, passing en route the turning for Qalat Najm, from where you must hitch or negotiate a ride.

Directory

With the exception of *Aeroflot*, *British Airways* and *Egypt Air*, all the airlines given below, most of which are represented by General Service Agents (GSAs), are on Baron St. Other travel agents dealing with more than 1 airline are given under 'Tour operators and travel agents' above. *Aeroflot*, Saadalah al-Jabri Sq, T2247561, F2236652. *Air France*, PO Box 1482, T2232238, F2210530. *Alitalia*, T2222721. *British Airways*, GSA *Sanadiki Travel Services*, Kostaki al-Homsi St, T2274586, F2274588. *Egypt Air*, GSA *Byblos Travel & Tourism*, Kostaki al-Homsi St, PO Box 5956, T2247793, F2236601. *KLM*, PO Box 811, T2211074, F2246155. *Lufthansa*, T2223005, F2221503. *Saudi Arabian*, T2214114. *Syrian Air*, T2241232 (second office on Kouwatly Sq, T2236000).

Airline offices

Branch No. 2 of the *Commercial Bank of Syria (CBS)*, on Al Azmeh St (the northward continuation of Baron St) changes both cash and TCs. The bank is up on the 1st floor; entry is from the back of the shopping arcade here. Open daily 0800-1330, closed Fri. At the corner of Bab al-Faraj St and Kouwatly St, in the downtown area, there is a *CBS* exchange shop which changes cash only. Open 0800-2000, daily. The small *CBS* exchange booth next to the tourist information office also deals with cash only and is open 0800-2000, daily. The *Chahba Cham Palace* hotel is authorized to

Banks

change cash and TCs (at the standard bank rate), and offers this service 24hrs/daily. Nearly all black market financial transactions are made in the Souk al-Atarin; just wander up and down and you are sure to be asked before long.

Communications

Internet The number of places offering internet access in Aleppo is rather limited at present, although no doubt there will be rapid expansion in this area in the near future. *Compunet*, Ibn Aby Kaab St (near *Pullman al-Shahba* hotel), T2677532. Open 1600-2300, daily. Small outfit with 3 online computers, S£200 per hr. Phone first to check availability, as sometimes booked up for training courses. *Mac Café*, set in the so-called 'Dream Park', a small section of the public gardens which extend north from Kouwatly Sq (access from Usman Basha St, on the northwest side of the gardens). Open 0900/1000-late. Swish glass building housing a trendy café where you can indulge in croissants, ice creams, crêpes, cappuccinos and the like, and access the internet via an iMac machine for S£200 per hr. *Internet Centre*, 17 Nisan St (follow 17 Nisan St west from Kouwatly Sq for approximately 400 m and it is on the right, directly opposite the front entrance to the Abu Bakr Mosque; the sign outside just reads 'Internet'). Open 0700-2100 (best to come after 1100), daily. Simple outfit, currently with just 1 on-line computer, S£300 per hr.

Post The main post office is situated on the southwest corner of Kouwatly Sq in the downtown area and is open daily 0800-1700.

Telephone Aleppo operates the same *Easycomm/STE* cardphones (see page 130) found in Damascus. There are cardphones dotted around all over the city, with phonecards being sold from nearby shops, kiosks etc. You can also buy them from the central telephone office, which shares the same building as the main post office on the southwest corner of Kouwatly Sq. Some of the quietest cardphone locations (at night at least) are to be found along the narrow streets of Jdaide quarter. Alternatively, the *DHL* office just off Kouwatly St (open 0930-2300) will place international calls (and send faxes) with a minimum of fuss. Their rates work out slightly higher than if you use a cardphone, but there is no minimum charge.

Cultural centres

French Cultural Centre, 40 Rue Fayçal, PO Box 768, T2274460, F2216443. Open 1000-1300, 1700-1900, closed Sun. The cultural centre here is much smaller than the one in Damascus, but they still organize fairly regular cultural events. *British Council*, Al Sabeel, Franciscan, PO Box 5547, T2680502, F2680501. Geared primarily towards language teaching and promoting courses in the UK, but occasionally involved in organizing cultural events.

Embassies & consulates

All the foreign embassies are located in Damascus. There is a **French** consulate at the same address as the French Cultural Centre (see above), T2219823, F2219872. Open 0830-1230, closed Sat and Sun.

Medical services

The *Aleppo University Hospital*, T2236120, is in the modern western district of Aleppo, opposite the *Pullman al-Shahba* hotel. It offers a generally high standard of facilities and treatment. Opposite the *Chahba Cham Palace* hotel is the main lab of the *Syrian Clinical Laboratory Association*, T2231793, which conducts the full range of blood/urine/stool tests, though usually only through referral from a doctor (if you fall ill the best step initially is to seek help from your hotel which will call a local doctor for you). Upstairs from this is the *Central Pharmacy* which opens from 2300-0700 daily except Sun and public holidays. When it is shut there is a sign in the window (unfortunately in Arabic only) indicating which pharmacies will be open; there is always at least 1 which stays open when all the others are shut. There are plenty of pharmacies in the downtown area which are open during normal working hours.

Useful phone numbers

Ambulance T110. **Fire Headquarters** T113. **Traffic police** T115. **Police** T112. **International operator** T143/144. **National Operator** T141/142.

Visa extensions

These can be obtained from the Passport and Immigration office just north of the Citadel, open 0800-1330, closed Fri. You need 4 passport photos and must pay S£25. Get there early and you may be able to complete the process within less than an hr, but when it is busy it can take most of the morning. It is possible to get extensions of up to 1 month here (some travellers report getting 2 months, although there seem to be no fixed rules on this). If you want an extension of more than the standard 2 weeks, be sure to make this very clear at every stage of the process, otherwise 2 weeks are all that you will be given. There are several shops across the road from the office where you can get passport photos on the spot (S£125 for 4 mini-polaroid snaps).

Around Aleppo: Dead Cities

9

Around Aleppo: Dead Cities

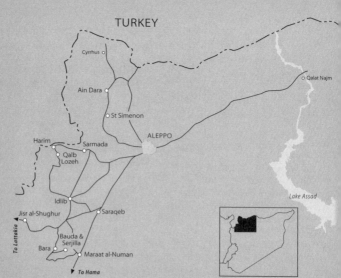

In spring, the rugged limestone hills surrounding Aleppo are illuminated by dramatic gold shafts of sunlight, the blues, pinks and yellows of **wild flowers** speckle the fields, and the **olive groves**, where they exist, are in full blossom. Showers are frequent but afterwards the air is fresh and the sun lights up the landscape. Such is the setting for the numerous ruins of Christian settlements dating from the Byzantine era (the so-called Dead Cities). The most famous, **St Simeon** (Qalat Samaan), is a remarkably well preserved fifth-century church embodying beautifully the early flowering of Byzantine architectural forms. Scattered through the limestone hills to the northwest, west and southwest of Aleppo there are literally hundreds more such sites. Even the most insubstantial assume an atmospheric, almost magical, beauty against this spring backdrop, but autumn can also be very beautiful.

In addition to the Dead Cities there are a number of sites dating from other periods which can also be visited as day-trips from Aleppo. These include the first millennium BC neo-Hittite temple of **Ain Dara** to the north of Qalat Samaan, the 12th-century AD Arab castle of **Qalat Najm** on the Euphrates River to the northeast of Aleppo (both covered in this section), the third millennium BC site of **Ebla** (covered as a diversion from the motorway between Hama and Aleppo, see page 240) and the town of **Maarat al-Numan** with its impressive mosaics museum (also en route between Hama and Aleppo, see page 238).

A foot in the door

★ Undoubtedly the crowning glory of the Dead Cities, you must not pass up the opportunity of seeing **St Simeon** under any circumstances. Once you are there, with your own transport it is easy to carry on north, perhaps making a quick stop at **Ain Dara** before continuing on to **Cyrrhus**, a journey which takes you through some of the best of the region's beautiful rolling limestone hills.

★ To the west of Aleppo, **Qalb Lozeh** is easily the most impressive site, though a detour through the ruins of **Baqerha** and

Khirbet Khateb is also well worth the extra effort.

★ To the southwest of Aleppo, **Bara** stands out as perhaps the largest of the Dead Cities, its ruins strewn in amongst the fields and olive groves of the modern village.

★ While in this area, it makes sense to visit the beautiful **mosaic musuem at Maarat al-Numan**. Wherever you choose to explore, you are sure to become enchanted both with the ruins themselves and the sheer beauty of the landscapes in which they are so atmospherically set.

Ins and outs

Getting around If you have your own transport and sufficient time, this is an area which amply repays detailed exploration. However, reaching even the major sites by public transport can be difficult and time-consuming, often involving some walking or hitching (or negotiating a ride) to get to the site itself. It makes a lot of sense, therefore, to hire a vehicle and driver to take you round. Divided among a few people, the cost of this is not prohibitive and it will greatly increase the number of sites you can visit within a given time. Some of the hotels in Aleppo organize trips to the main sites by microbus and most can help with hiring a vehicle and driver.

Background

To the west of the motorway en route between Hama and Aleppo there is an area of rugged limestone hills that starts a little to the north of Apamea and extends in a rough arc almost up to Cyrrhus, near the Turkish border northwest of Aleppo. Known in classical times as the *Belus Massif*, these hills consist of a broken series of ranges, averaging around 500 m in height but rising in places to over 800 m. Internally, they can be divided into three distinct areas: the northern **Jebel Samaan**; the central **Jebel al-Ala** and **Jebel Barisha**; and the southern **Jebel Riha** (also known as the Jebel Zawiye). Taken together, this arc of hills extends for around 140 km, though nowhere does it exceed 40 km in width.

On the face of it, this landscape appears harsh and inhospitable, dominated by jagged, broken limestone outcrops amongst which small, fragmented and barely productive pockets of land are painstakingly cleared and cultivated. And yet during the Byzantine era the *Belus Massif* flourished, supporting an unprecedented density of towns and villages. Its fascination today is that such a large number of these settlements should have survived (in all, more than 750 have been documented), and in such a remarkable state of preservation. Certainly, the ravages of time have reduced many to barely discernible scatterings of ruins, but others remain eerily well preserved – almost as if abandoned only in recent times – although their distinctive architecture hints at far more ancient origins.

Today they are known popularly, though somewhat misleadingly, as the 'Dead Cities' (none would appear to have ever grown to more than the size of a small town). The reasons as to why such a high density of settlements should have flourished in this region have been the subject of much speculation. The key, it would appear, lay in the relative political and economic stability which followed the Roman conquest of Syria. This allowed rich landowners from the plains to contemplate such long-term projects as planting olive groves in the hills of the *Belus Massif* (it takes at least 10 years before an olive tree actually starts to yield fruit). It also allowed trade to flourish unhindered so that the settlements which began to develop were able to sell their lucrative crop in regional centres – particularly Antioch with its access to more distant Mediterranean markets but also Aleppo and Apamea – and buy the items of everyday life which they were unable to produce in their otherwise marginal environment.

The economics of this trade obviously worked in the olive growers' favour, generating significant surpluses, so that by the Byzantine era these settlements were growing steadily in size and number. Fuelled by this newfound prosperity they flourished from the fourth to seventh centuries AD, and in the remains left behind can be seen examples of all the major trends in the early development of Byzantine architecture, most notably in terms of the churches, but also in the other public buildings, such as baths and markets as well as the 'vernacular' architecture of common houses.

However, the Persian invasions of the seventh century brought instability to the region, and soon after, following the Arab conquest, the region became a frontier zone between the Byzantine and Arab worlds. Trade was disrupted and as a result these settlements found themselves cut off from their all-important markets. No longer able to support themselves through the trade in olives, they were gradually forced to abandon their settlements and return to the plains where subsistence agriculture was possible; by the 10th century the region had been almost completely depopulated. It was not until this century that it began to be settled again (particularly the northern parts, where olives are once again being cultivated and you get a sense of how the region would once have appeared, at least agriculturally).

It is due to this abandonment of the region for 10 centuries or more (and to the use of durable limestone as the primary building material) that we owe the remarkable state of preservation of the Dead Cities; elsewhere around the Mediterranean basin, most early Byzantine architecture was adapted or built over, but in this region only time, the elements and the occasional earthquake have taken their toll, leaving largely intact these atmospheric relics of a bygone era.

Many of the ruins still stand in splendid isolation, hidden away amidst the limestone hills. Sometimes, however, you will find small, rather ramshackle contemporary farming settlements amidst the ancient remains, with former Byzantine buildings pressed into service as cattle shelters and sheep pens, or repaired and lived in once again. Elsewhere, stones from the ruins have been recycled and you may see a beautifully carved limestone lintel amongst the concrete and breeze-block of a modern house. Some might be taken aback at such seemingly flagrant disregard for these unique monuments, but the truth is that there are simply far too many sites for the Department of Antiquities to have any hope of preserving them all. And anyway, there is something quite refreshing about this blending of ancient and modern; as with the souks of Aleppo, what you see is living history, not some neatly packaged heritage theme park.

Northwest of Aleppo: Jebel Samaan

Colour map 1, grid A2

Not all these sites can feasibly be visited in a single day. If your time is limited, Mushabbak, St Simeon, Ain Dara & Cyrrhus can be combined in one long day. With a half-day or less to spare, stick to St Simeon

The Jebel Samaan is the setting for **St Simeon** *(Qalat Samaan), far and away the most spectacular of the Dead Cities, and also the easiest to visit as a day-trip from Aleppo. If you have your own transport, you can also combine it with a number of other sites in the area. The church of* **Mushabbak**, *directly en route to St Simeon is well worth visiting. The sites of* **Al Qatora** *and* **Rozzita** *are of lesser interest, but only a short detour from the main route.* **Basofan**, **Burj Haidar** *and* **Kharrab Shams**, *sites at intervals along the road heading east from St Simeon, have beautiful locations worth seeing quite apart from the ruins themselves. This road also joins up with the main road between Aleppo and Afrine, making for a convenient round-trip back to Aleppo. Alternatively, you can continue north from St Simeon to neo-Hittite* **Ain Dara**, *and from there continue on to Afrine. A detour to the north from the main Afrine-Aleppo road takes you to* **Cyrrhus**, *near the Turkish border.*

Aleppo to St Simeon (Qalat Samaan)

Head west out of Aleppo on Ibrahim Hanano Street, which subsequently becomes Saif al-Dawla Street. After passing under the railway line, turn right at a large junction consisting of a roundabout complete with flyover and underpass, and then first left around 150 m further on, at a junction with traffic lights. Go straight across one crossroads and then straight on again at a large roundabout with a statue of a soldier on horseback in the centre (this roundabout marks the junction with the main ring road around Aleppo). This road, which leads directly to Daret Aazah, is frequently signposted for 'Samaan Castle' or 'Qalat Samaan'. The road passes through Aleppo's rapidly expanding suburbs before reaching open countryside. After 25 km a turning (signposted 'Kasr al Mashabak') leads off to the left up a rough track to the ruins of Mushabbak Church, visible some 500 m away from the road on top of a small hill. Around 1 km before this turning there is a left turn signposted 'Camping Kaddour 10 km'; at the time of writing, however, this road was very poor, and the campsite in question is easier to reach via the Bab al-Hawa road (see page 358).

Mushabbak Church

This small but imposing monument is one of the best preserved Byzantine basilica churches in northern Syria, its basic structure still more or less completely intact. It probably dates from the late fifth century, around the same time that nearby St Simeon was developing into an important pilgrimage centre, and perhaps served as a stopping point on the pilgrimage route to St Simeon. It follows the standard *basilica* plan of a central nave and two side aisles, with two rows of five columns dividing the aisles from the nave. Note the variety of capitals atop the columns. The semi-domed apse at the eastern end is flanked by two side apses. The central nave has a *clerestory*, or upper stage, rising above the side aisles, with nine arched windows on either side. The clerestory and its windows would have added an overall sense of light and height to the church, probably an indication of the more advanced architectural influences coming from St Simeon. ■ *A caretaker is usually on duty here to collect an entrance fee of S£100 (students S£10).*

Outside the church, on its west side, is a **quarry** where the stone used in its construction was presumably cut. A little further away, to the northwest, is an **underground tomb** with three arched bays and nearby a small circular opening to a large water cistern as well as various other rock-cut features. Around 100 m to the east of the church are the ruins of what appears to have been a **monastery complex**, parts of which are today occupied by local shepherds.

From the turning for Mushabbak, it is a little over 4 km further to the centre of **Al Qatora** the village of **Daret Aazah**. Follow the signposts through the village to pick up **& Rozzita** the road for St Simeon. After 3 km there is a signposted turning left along a metalled road for Al Qatora (1 km) and Rozzita (4½ km). Taking this turning, in the village of Al Qatora there are various **fragmented ruins**, including one corner of a building – possibly a Roman villa. Continuing past the village, to the left of the road there are a number of **rock-cut tombs**, some with heavily weathered inscriptions and carvings of figures. These, like the ruins in the village itself, are of Roman origin, dating from the early second to mid-third century AD, when the settlements in the region were just beginning to achieve a certain level of prosperity. Further on, scattered amongst the village and surrounding fields of Rozzita (or Zarzita), are various fragments of what appears to have been a late fifth- to early sixth-century **monastic community**.

Returning to the main road, 2 km after the turning for Al Qatora and Rozzita, **Al Qatora to** bear right at a fork to reach St Simeon (straight on for Deir Samaan and Ain **St Simeon** Dara). A little further on, where the road again forks, bear left for St Simeon (right for Basofan, Burj Haidar and Kharrab Shams; see below).

St Simeon (Qalat Samaan) قلعة سمعان

The beautiful fifth-century church of St Simeon represents the largest and *Colour map 1, grid A2* most important surviving Christian monument of the early Byzantine period. It is surpassed only by the later (sixth-century) Hagia Sophia in Constantino- *If you see nothing* ple (Istanbul) and was not matched in Europe until the 11th and 12th centu- *else around Aleppo,* ries. On a steep-sided ridge with sweeping views out across the Afrine River *make sure that this* Valley to the northwest, and beyond to the Kurd Dag and Amanus mountains *is on your itinerary* across the Turkish border, the ruins of the church of St Simeon are remarkably well preserved, and really give a sense of the true splendour of this pilgrimage site in its heyday. It is worth timing your visit so you can see the ruins either in the early morning or the late afternoon, when the stones are illuminated to a golden glow. If you do this, you will also avoid the main rush of tour groups, which start to arrive from mid-morning and have usually all left by mid-afternoon. **NB** The site gets particularly busy on Fridays.

The construction of the church of St Simeon was an imperial project, under- **History** taken on a huge scale and employing architects and skilled artisans from Constantinople and Antioch. The cult status achieved by St Simeon during his life (see box 'Pillars of Wisdom') had considerable political significance. The eastern Church at that time was in a state of internal turmoil, brought about by obscure theological disputes as to the nature of Christ (most notably the Monophysite schism). This in effect pitted the church of Antioch against that of Constantinople, and to the imperial authorities in Constantinople the cult of St Simeon provided a welcome distraction from a dispute which was threatening their authority. After his death, by taking over responsibility for the construction of the church, they hoped to reinforce their power by associating themselves with this enormously popular saint.

In 526 and again in 528, only years after all the building work was completed, northern Syria was rocked by violent earthquakes, although the damage to the church appears to have been surprisingly minimal. In the seventh century the region fell to the **Muslim Arab** invaders. It was retaken by the **Byzantines** in the 10th century and subsequently the whole complex was fortified (it is probably from this time that its present name, Qalat Samaan, meaning 'fortress of St Simeon' originates). The **Hamdanids** of Aleppo, led by Said ud-Daula, recaptured it in 985, then in 1017 it was sacked by **Fatimid** forces from Egypt. Nevertheless, it continued to exist as a pilgrimage centre late into the 12th century, after which it was abandoned and, thanks to the depopulation of the area, left largely untouched until now.

Sights The site consists of a huge church, the most important feature of the pilgrimage site, and various accompanying buildings, all on a long, narrow ridge which was artificially levelled. The church is centred on St Simeon's pillar; a large octagonal courtyard surrounds the pillar, and radiating from this are four large basilicas arranged in the shape of a cross. Immediately to the southeast is an L-shaped monastery complex and chapel, while further to the south is a second group of buildings, including a small baptistry and basilica.

From the ticket office a path leads up onto the top of the ridge; to your left (south) is the baptistry, while to your right (north) is the main **Church of St Simeon**. Turning to the right, you are in fact approaching along the last stretch of the processional route, or *Via Sacra*, which originally led up from Deir Samaan on the plain below, past the baptistry and so to the church. In front of you is the main triple-arched entrance, leading via a *narthex* (entrance hall) into the southern basilica. In its architecture, the overall design of the entrance is typically Roman although the rich and **elaborate carved decoration** shows distinctive local influences. For example, the acanthus leaves on the capitals of the pillars curve delicately almost as if they were blowing in the wind. Decorative features such as this are believed to be innovations first employed at St Simeon which later became typical designs of Byzantine architecture.

It is the richness & variety of the carved decoration, & also the delicate yet monumental proportions of the design, which lend the building such beauty

Passing through the southern basilica you come to the octagonal courtyard, at the centre of which is all that remains of St Simeon's famous pillar, reduced to a worn and insubstantial lump of stone by the countless pilgrims who over the centuries have chipped away pieces to take home as holy relics. It has been suggested that the courtyard was originally covered by a wooden roof and that when this collapsed during one of the earthquakes of the early sixth century it was subsequently left open to the sky. Tall, wide arches link the columns which stand at the points of the octagonal courtyard, with four of these leading through to each of the basilicas.

The eastern basilica is longer than the others and ends in a large apse flanked by two smaller ones. This was the only section of the building where services were actually conducted; the other basilicas were in effect assembly halls in which pilgrims could gather. The eastern basilica is also slightly out of line with the symmetry of the overall cross-shaped design of the complex. The reasons for this are not entirely clear. It has been suggested that the builders wished to orientate it towards true east. However, while the other three basilicas do not quite line up exactly with the cardinal points of the

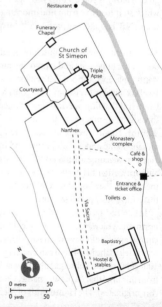

St Simeon (Qalat Samaan)

Restaurant ●

Funerary Chapel

Church of St Simeon

Triple Apse

Courtyard

Narthex

Monastery complex

Café & shop ○

Entrance & ticket office

Toilets ○

Via Sacra

Baptistry

Hostel & stables

N

0 metres 50
0 yards 50

Pillars of wisdom

St Simeon Stylites (literally 'St Simeon of the Pillar') was born in 386 AD, the son of a Cilician farmer. At the age of 16 he joined the monastery of Teleda on the slopes of Mount Hermon, and stayed there for 16 years. In 412 he joined the recently established monastic community of Deir Samaan (then known as Telanissos or Tell Nisheh, literally the 'mountain of the women' in Greek and Aramaic respectively).

Increasingly drawn to a life of asceticism, he gained permission to withdraw from the main community and lead a life of solitude and meditation on the hill where the Church of St Simeon now stands. He soon gained a reputation for his extreme piety and asceticism and began to attract large numbers of pilgrims from far and wide. Wishing to maintain his detachment in the face of so much attention, he had a 3 m tall pillar constructed with a platform on top.

From then onwards, until his death in 459, 42 years later, he lived his life on top of a pillar, or in fact a series of pillars, each taller than the one before, culminating in one between 17-20 m high. And as if living on top of a pillar, utterly exposed to the elements for years on end was not a sufficiently extreme act of asceticism in itself, he spent most of his time standing, with his arms raised to heaven in prayer, or else bowing repeatedly. Once a week his disciples brought him food by means of a ladder (quite what arrangement he had for relieving himself is unclear).

Perhaps in keeping with the times, his attitudes towards the opposite sex were severe; no women were allowed to come anywhere near him, he even refused to see his own mother. From his vantage point he preached to the pilgrims who continued to arrive in ever increasing numbers, gave advice on their problems and mediated disputes. According to one of his contemporaries, Bishop Theodoret of Cyrrhus, his fame was such that pilgrims came from as far away as France, England, Spain and Italy, while in Rome representations of him stood in every workshop. Such was his influence meanwhile that the Byzantine emperor himself was said to have sought his advice several times on doctrinal matters.

After his death, despite fierce local opposition, his body was taken by imperial troops of the Byzantine court to the cathedral at Antioch where he was buried. At a later stage his body appears to have been moved to Constantinople. Work began almost immediately on the church of St Simeon, which was built around his famous pillar. Meanwhile his unusual form of asceticism, though not original, popularized the cult of stylites, with numerous others following his bizarre example both during his life and after.

compass, neither does the eastern one, even with its adjusted alignment. Certainly, the architects were constrained to some extent by the local topography, and the need to centre the whole structure on the position of St Simeon's pillar. This can be seen at the far end of the western basilica, where an artificial terrace had to be built out from the steep slope of the ridge in order to support it. There are particularly good views from here out over the Afrine Valley to the mountains beyond.

Outside the northern basilica is an area of higher ground from where you can get a good overall perspective of the layout of the church. Just inside the outer enclosure wall (this was part of the fortification work carried out following the Byzantine reoccupation of the site in the 10th century) is a small funerary chapel. From here you can also work your way round to the outside of the triple apse at the end of the eastern basilica. Interestingly, the curve of the apses extends beyond the basic rectangular shape of the basilica, a design for which the only precedent was at Qalb Lozeh (see page 359) but which was later to become typical of Syrian Christian architecture.

In the area between the south and east basilicas, there are the ruins of a **chapel** and **monastery** complex, much of it now reduced to a tumbled mass of stones but with the odd section still standing. This would have housed the resident monks and more important visitors (most people would have stayed at Deir Samaan down below).

The **baptistry** stands 150 m or so to the south of the main church. Here, those who had made the pilgrimage to the church of St Simeon but were not Christian would be baptized before being allowed into the church itself. The neatly proportioned building is topped by an octagonal drum which would once have supported a domed or conical wooden roof. Inside, there is an octagonal room, on the east side of which is a semi-circular apse with a half-dome roof and steps leading down to what was in effect a walk-through baptismal font. In the bottom of the baptismal font a fragment of patterned mosaic floor still survives. Immediately to the south, attached to the baptistry, are the remains of a small **basilica**, now largely in ruins. To the right of the baptistry as you approach from the main church, there are the scant remains of what appear to have been a hostel and stables. Below this (to the southwest of the baptistry), two arches still survive of a triple-arched **monumental gateway**, with two imposing square towers immediately to the south. The gateway stood at the top of the *Via Sacra* from Deir Samaan, marking the main entrance to the complex. The towers, meanwhile, are part of the 10th-century fortifications added by the Byzantines. If you clamber up onto one of these towers, you can get a good overview of the ruins of Deir Samaan below. You can descend on foot by this route to the ruins of Deir Samaan, scattered amongst the field below. Alternatively, if you are heading north to Ain Dara by car, the main road passes through them. ■ *Open daily, 0900-1800 in summer, 0900-1600 in winter. Entry S£300 (students S£15). There are lots of postcards, as well as various booklets and souvenirs, on sale at the ticket office. The toilets are in the block to your left after you enter the site.*

Deir Samaan This complex started life as a small agricultural community. Early in the fifth century a monastery was founded here, where for a short time St Simeon lived as part of the monastic community (hence Deir Samaan: 'Monastery of Simeon'). Following his death and the construction of the church of St Simeon, Deir Samaan flourished as the last stopping point for pilgrims before they made the final ascent up to the church. **Hostelries**, **bazaar stalls**, **monasteries** and a **church** were established here in the fifth and sixth centuries, in what must have been a thriving centre accommodating thousands of pilgrims at a time. A little way up the hill is a partly reconstructed **monumental arch** which marks the start of the *Via Sacra* leading up to the church of St Simeon. Most of the other surviving remains of Deir Samaan are in a fairly advanced state of ruin, although the basic outlines of the buildings and in places sections of walls etc can be clearly discerned. The ruins are interesting to wander round, although they in no way match the splendour of the church of St Simeon itself.

Sleeping There is a small café/shop just inside the main entrance to St Simeon. If you continue
& eating past the entrance, where the road ends there is a small restaurant serving the usual kebabs, roast chicken hummus etc. However, the food is expensive and mediocre. Most Syrians, for whom St Simeon is a popular outing, bring their own picnic. Alternatively, there is a good restaurant some 15 km to the north of St Simeon, on the road to Ain Dara (see below). There is no accommodation at the site, although **camping** is a viable option, providing you have your own equipment. Ask the staff from the café/shop or restaurant for permission.

Fairly regular microbuses run from the Pullman/City bus station just south of the *Amir* **Transport**
Palace hotel in Aleppo as far as the village of Daret Aazeh, from where it is a further
6 km or so to the site. If you do not want to walk or hitch, it is usually possible to negotiate a ride for the last stretch privately, perhaps with the microbus you came on from
Aleppo, although you may be charged as much as S£200 to go and come back.

East to Basofan, Burj Haidar and Kharrab Shams

The turning heading east from the road leading up to St Simeon traverses a rug-   **Basofan**
ged upland section of the Jebel Samaan, arriving after 23 km at the main road
which runs between Aleppo and Afrine. After 5 km you reach the village of
Basofan. To the right of the road, largely concealed amongst the fields and
houses of the village, are various scattered ruins, including a column and arch
attached to a contemporary house. A large church once existed here dedicated,
according to an inscription, to St Phocas and dating from 491-92 AD. However,
little of it remains to be seen. Most of the ruins here are half-buried, the ground
level having risen over the centuries, and other are now used as cattle shelters.

A further 3 km along the road, you come to the village of Burj Haidar, where   **Burj Haidar**
there are more substantial ruins amongst the houses. Many of the modern
buildings feature stones recycled from antiquity. The ancient settlement here
dates back at least to the end of the third century AD. By the sixth century it had
grown to become a thriving Christian community with several churches and a
monastery. The ruins of a mid-fourth-century church lie in the centre of the
village, inside a farmyard. Originally a three-aisled structure, only two rows of
columns and arches which separated the aisles survive. To the north of it is a
large tower built of huge roughly cut slabs of stone. On the west edge of the village are the ruins of a sixth-century monastery. To the left of the road as you
head east out of the village there is a small well preserved chapel with a rectangular building attached to it.

Continuing east, after 5 km you arrive at the village of **Kharrab Shams**. Just
before you reach the village, clearly visible off to the left of the road are the
remains of a well preserved fourth-century church. The side aisles of the
church have completely collapsed but the central arcaded nave with its five
arches on either side is almost perfectly preserved, giving the building a striking, if slightly odd, appearance. The church bears a strong stylistic resem-
blance to the church at Mushabbak, which dates from the late fifth century,
leading to suggestions that it was rebuilt around this time. Certainly, there is
evidence of different phases of construction. Note, for example, how on the
south side there are 10 windows in the upper *clerestory*, while on the north
(older) side there are only five. There are numerous other ruins scattered
around the church, including door frames, parts of walls, dwellings which
have been built onto natural caves and rock-cut tombs. The first settlement
here in fact goes back to the pre-Roman era. On top of the hill behind the
church there are the ruins of a small chapel and, on the way up to it, what
appears to have been a Roman villa, its well preserved walls built of massive
slabs of stone. From the top of the hill, away to the northwest a cluster of ruins
– the Dead City site of Barad – are clearly visible.

Returning to the road and continuing east, 10 km or so beyond Kharrab
Shams you arrive at a T-junction. Going right (south) takes you back to Aleppo, 15 km away. Going left (north) you are on the main road to Afrine; a detour
from this road takes you to the ruins of Cyrrhus near the Turkish border (the
route described below heads north from St Simeon, passing Ain Dara, to join
the Aleppo-Afrine road at Afrine).

Around Aleppo: Dead Cities

North to Ain Dara and Cyrrhus

From the fork for St Simeon, the main road passes through the ruins of Deir Samaan, heading north across a fertile plain. It then follows the **Afrine River** as it winds its way through fields, orchards and gently rolling hills. Towards the northern end of the village of Basoutah, 15 km from the St Simeon turning, there is a petrol station and, soon after, the *Al Basota* **restaurant** on the left, with a pleasant covered terrace and fountains. The food here is good quality and reasonably priced (around S£200-250 per head). It is just under 4 km further on to the village of Ain Dara, where there is a clearly signposted left turn for the ancient mound and archaeological site of Ain Dara, 2 km away along a newly surfaced access road.

Ain Dara The large mound, or *tell*, at Ain Dara shows evidence of settlement from the first millennium BC through to the 16th century AD. The feature of greatest interest, however, is the **neo-Hittite temple** dating from the 10th-ninth century BC. In 1980 of a relief depicting a figure identified as Ishtar was discovered which suggests that the temple was dedicated to this Semitic fertility goddess. Of Babylonian/Assyrian origin, Ishtar was equated with Astarte, the Phoenician goddess of fertility and love, who was in turn identified with the Egyptian goddess Isis and later with the Greek and Roman goddesses Aphrodite and Venus. Despite the archaeological importance of the site, some may find it somewhat disappointing to visit. The main temple is encircled by a band of concrete supported on pillars, the beginnings of a seemingly abandoned plan to erect a protective structure over the ruins.

The main temple occupies the northwest area of the mound. The steps leading up to the south entrance of the temple are flanked by two carved lions, and running around the outer walls are more friezes of lions and sphinxes. However, the elements have caused extensive damage to the carvings, the black basalt stone cracking and flaking so that many of the reliefs are barely discernible. Carved into the stone paving leading from the entrance to the inner temple are huge footprints, perhaps meant to convey the presence of the goddess Ishtar at the temple. To the southwest of the main temple there is a huge statue of a lion carved from basalt, its crude, massive proportions typical of the neo-Hittite style (as seen at the Aleppo Museum). ■ *Open daily during daylight hours. Entry S£150 (students S£15). The caretaker lives in the archaeologists' buildings at the foot of the tell, from where it is a short walk up to the top.*

Transport You can either continue hitching north from St Simeon (although there is little traffic on this road), or else get a microbus direct from the Pullman/City bus station in Aleppo to Afrine. From Afrine you again have to hitch (or walk) the 7 km to Ain Dara, or negotiate a return ride with a taxi.

Ain Dara **to Cyrrhus** Continuing north from the turning for Ain Dara, after a further 6 km you arrive at a T-junction with the main Aleppo-Afrine road. Turning left here takes you into the small, predominantly Kurdish town and district centre of **Afrine**, where there are a few simple restaurants, but no hotel. Turning right, the road leads first northwest, before bearing south towards Aleppo. After 11 km you arrive at a crossroads; the left turn here is clearly signposted for 'Nebi Huri' (the Arabic name for Cyrrhus). However, a recent dam building project, and the associated creation of a large lake, has rendered this a rather complicated route by which to approach the site, involving a lengthy and confusing detour.

The more straightforward option is to go via the town of **Azaz**. Around 5 km further along the main road, take the clearly signposted left turn for Azaz. Go straight across the first roundabout you come to (just under 4 km from the main road; the microbus station is located here), and then go left 400 m further on at a second roundabout in the centre of the town (signposted 'Turkia as-Salama'). After a further 600 m, turn left again (at the time of writing this turning was not signposted, nor was it particularly obvious; ask directions for Nebi Huri).

After around 17 km you pass through the small village of Deir Sowan, and then some 2½ km further on you come to the first of two steeply hump backed **Roman bridges**. This first one consists of three arches spanning the upper reaches of the Afrine River, while the next one (1½ km further on) consists of six arches spanning the Sabun Sayu River. Both date from the late second century AD. They show signs of having been repaired and strengthened in the Byzantine and Islamic periods, but, even so, the fact that they are still serviceable is no small tribute to the original engineering skills of the Romans, and clearly illustrates the importance they attached to road building. A little under 2 km further on, you come to a sharp right turn signposted to 'Al Nabi Houry' (just under 1 km away along a rough track), while a little further on, on the left, is a distinctive hexagonal Roman tower tomb.

This road is very scenic, taking you through the rolling limestone hills & olive groves

Cyrrhus نبي حوري

Cyrrhus (known in Arabic as 'Nebi Huri') was originally founded soon after 300 BC by Seleucus I Nicator, and named after a town of the same name in Macedonia. Despite developing as an important regional centre, its location on the northern borders of the Seleucid Empire meant that its position was always precarious. And sure enough, early on in the first century BC it was absorbed into the Armenian Empire to the north. Following the conquest of Syria by Pompey in 64 BC, it became part of the Roman Empire. In the mid-first century AD it was made into an administrative centre and headquarters of a legion. Its interest to the Romans was both as a military base from which they could conduct their campaigns against the Armenians to the north, and as a commercial centre on the trade route between Antioch and the Euphrates River crossing at Zeugma (in Turkey, near Birecik). During the third century it suffered invasion and occupation at the hands of the Persians on a number of occasions, but began to recover as an important centre of Christianity in the fourth century. It was here that the remains of St Cosmas and St Damien were buried, making it a popular place of pilgrimage, known at that time as **Hagiopolis**. Theodoret, to whom we owe much of our knowledge of St Simeon, was bishop here from around 423-450. During the mid-sixth century the town was refortified and its garrison strengthened by the emperor Justinian in an attempt to make it into a bulwark against the Persian threat. Even after the Muslim conquest of 637 it continued as an important Christian centre. During the early 11th century it was taken by the Crusaders and placed under the control of the Count of Edessa. In 1150 it was recaptured by Nur ud-Din but subsequently appears to have lost its strategic significance, and was abandoned soon afterwards.

Colour map 1, grid A2

Although the ruins here are not particularly substantial, the site is worth a visit as much for its setting & for the dramatic & beautiful scenery en route

Beside the road is a **Roman tower tomb** dating from the late second to early third century AD. The squat, solid hexagonal tower has a pyramid-shaped roof with a bulb of carved acanthus leaves at its apex. The lower floor now houses the tomb of a 14th-century Muslim saint and has been extended to accommodate a small mosque as well. Steps lead up inside the tower to the upper floor, where arched windows in each face look out onto the surrounding countryside.

The track leading from the road to the main ruins of Cyrrhus passes first through the heavily ruined remains of the **South Gate** of the city. From here it follows what was the north-south oriented *cardo maximus*, to arrive at the

Sights

Around Aleppo: Dead Cities

e **theatre**, which dates from around the mid-second century AD, making it roughly contemporary with the theatre at Bosra. Measuring 115 m in diameter originally, it would have been even larger than the theatre at Bosra, though today, in its half-ruined state, this is difficult to imagine. The theatre formed the main focus of excavation and reconstruction work carried out here by French teams from the 1950s onwards. Its basic outline is still clearly discernible, while scattered all around are column sections, carved capitals and huge slabs of masonry. Around 500 m to the north of the theatre, further along the line of the *cardo maximus*, the outline of a very large rectangular building or compound can be seen. In the southwest corner of this you can see the remains of what appears to have been a tower with an arched gateway. Directly to the east of (and downhill from) the theatre, the apse and basic outline of a basilica **church** can be discerned, while further east and downhill again are traces of further buildings.

Sitting on top of the steep hill, directly behind the theatre is the city's **citadel**, now largely ruined but with parts of it surviving, including a bastion and arch. As you would expect from a fort, it has impressive panoramic views. Also up on the hill, traces of the **defensive walls** can still be seen following the contour of the hill, particularly to the northeast of the citadel. Both the citadel and defensive walls date from the refortifications carried out by Justinian, although they stand on the foundations of the Hellenistic/Roman defences, reusing much of the original stonework.

Transport There are direct microbuses from the Pullman/City bus station in Aleppo to the town of Azaz, 23 km to the southeast of Cyrrhus. From there the only viable option is to negotiate a return ride with a taxi, since traffic is very limited on the road to the site.

West and southwest of Aleppo

*There are two main groupings of ruins to the west and southwest of Aleppo. To the west, near the Syrian/Turkish border crossing of Bab al-Hawa, the hills of the **Jebel al-Ala** are the setting for the beautifully preserved church of **Qalb Lozeh**, as well as a number of other sites. To the southwest, meanwhile, in the area between the towns of Ariha and Maarat al-Numan, the hills of the **Jebel Riha** (or Jebel Zawiye) boast a wealth of sites, all concentrated within a small area.*

*Although all these sites generally tend to be visited as excursions from Aleppo, the second grouping of sites in particular can equally be visited as a diversion en route between Hama and Aleppo, or even as a day-trip from Hama. Alternatively, the town of **Idlib**, where there are a couple of hotels, can be used as a base for visiting all the sites.*

Idlib إدلب

Phone code: 023
Colour map 1, grid B2

Idlib is the chief town of the Mouhafazat (Governorate) of the same name. A series of roads radiate from the town, connecting it with the road leading to the Syrian/Turkish border crossing of Bab al-Hawa (see below, West to Qalb Lozeh), the main Aleppo-Damascus motorway and the road to Lattakia. Other than as a possible base for visiting surrounding Dead City sites, the town's main attraction is its museum, where there is an impressive collection from the excavations at Ebla (Tell Mardikh). As well as the large new luxury hotel recently opened in Idlib, there is a brand new **tourist information** office nearby, though at the time of writing it was not as yet open.

The **museum** is on the east side of town, beside Ath Thawra Square (actually a large roundabout on the ring road). There are various pieces of mosaics, carved friezes, capitals and other architectural fragments in the gardens of the museum which are worth a look. Inside, on the ground floor, there are more mosaics (some of them very impressive), terracotta figurines, various items of pottery and ceramics, and an extensive collection of coins spanning the Roman through to the Ottoman periods. There are also some displays of costumes and fabrics (very much in the usual 'popular traditions' mould), and some contemporary paintings. The main focus of interest, however, is the 'Ebla Pavilion' on the first floor. The displays here are well presented and there is an impressive collection of the famous clay tablets inscribed in the Sumerian cuneiform script. Other artefacts include fragments of furniture covered in gold leaf, incredibly intricate terracotta figurines, gold and lapis lazuli jewellery, fragments of inlaid friezes and a relief of the Semitic fertility goddess Ishtar. All these artefacts, together with the various photos of the site at the time of the excavations, go a long way towards bringing Ebla to life. Also upstairs, at the opposite end to the 'Ebla Pavilion' are cases displaying a rich and impressive collection of artefacts from various other sites in the vicinity of Idlib. ■ *Open 0900-1800 in summer, 0900-1600 in winter, closed Tue. Entry S£300 (students S£15).*

AL *Carlton*, on the Ariha road on the southern outskirts of the town, T240780, F241624/223592. Brand new luxury hotel intended primarily to cater for tour groups. Comfortable though somewhat bland rooms with a/c, TV/dish, phone and attached bath. Also some bungalows arranged around a courtyard, with 'beehive'-style domed ceilings and traditional hammam-style bathrooms. Restaurant, coffee shop, bar. Small outdoor swimming pool, as well as a large and very ornate hammam (Turkish baths) downstairs in the basement. **C** *Grand*, on south side of town by Hanano Sq, T221137. Reasonable rooms with fan, TV, phone, fridge, attached bath and balcony. Little visited and rather run-down overall, and unfortunately way overpriced (single/double US$20/40); try bargaining. Heading west out of town along Al Ba'ath St (the road for Harim), in a side road beside the sports stadium, there is a **F/G** *Hostel* where you may be able to get a room; the accommodation is fairly basic, but hot showers are available. There are also a couple of tiny and very basic hotels in the centre of town. As well as the restaurants in the *Carlton* and *Grand* hotels, there are several simple restaurants in the centre of town where you can get the usual kebabs, roast chicken, hummus etc.

Sleeping & eating

The main bus/microbus station is on the east side of town, south of the museum and set back slightly to the east of the ring road, here known as Palestine St. There are fairly regular services to **Aleppo**, **Lattakia**, **Ariha**, **Maarat al-Numan** and other local towns.

Transport

Jebel al-Ala

Extending north-south in a narrow ridge of hills, the Jebel al-Ala is perhaps the most rugged and isolated stretch of the Belus Massif, and yet somehow strangely beautiful. Scattered amongst the hills are a number of small Druze communities which have been here since the 10th century, long before the waves of Druze who came to settle the Jebel al-Arab region of the Hauran to the south of Damascus in the 19th century.

Aleppo to Qalb Lozeh

Head west out of Aleppo on Ibrahim Hanano Street to join the Damascus motorway. After around 6 km, take the exit signposted for Bab al-Hawa. The

Around Aleppo: Dead Cities

exit appears rather suddenly, but don't worry if you miss it as there is a second exit 800 m further on which joins up with the first. To begin with the road is a busy four-lane highway which passes through an area of fairly built-up linear settlement. Around 18 km after leaving the motorway, where the main road swings round to the right, there is a left turn signposted for Idlib (and also, slightly confusingly, to Jisr al-Shughur and Lattakia).

Camping Kaddour Following the main road round to the right (signposted for Turkey, amongst others), 3 km further on there is a right turn signposted 'Camping 2 km' which takes you to *Camping Kaddour*; taking it, turn right again after 1½ km and follow the road through a small village for 400 m until you arrive at the large walled compound which encloses the campsite. Inside, the olive and fig trees dotted around provide a limited amount of shade. There is a simple but clean toilet/shower block and a 'Bedouin tent'-style café. Camping here costs S£150 per person, plus S£100 for vehicles (motorbikes free). This is a friendly, well run place, and something of a haven for overlanders who have just crossed into Syria via the Bab al-Hawa border. With your own transport, it also makes for a great base from which to explore the Dead City sites in the surrounding areas.

Through Tal al-Karamah & Sarmada Back on the main road, just under 4 km further on there is a second left turn signposted to Idlib. Carrying straight on, after a little under 9 km, just as you enter the village of **Tal al-Karamah** and the main road bends round to the right, it crosses a particularly well preserved section of **Roman road**. The most impressive section branches off straight ahead from the righthand bend. It is raised above the level of the surrounding countryside and built of large, carefully hewn stone blocks, heavily worn but surprisingly intact.

Just over 1 km further on there is a right turn signposted to St Simeon and Daret Aazah, and then after a little under 4 km you come to a large (and rather confusing) roundabout/junction. Go straight across, and then bear right immediately after, following signs for 'Harem' (Harim). The road passes through the small town of **Sarmada** before heading across open countryside characterized by dramatic and desolate hills of bare rock. Around 6 km from the roundabout/junction, the ruins of a couple of buildings (the remains of a sixth-century **Byzantine monastery complex**) are clearly visible off to the right, halfway up a rocky ridge. Soon after, you come to a crossroads; a path from here leads between drystone walls towards the ridge, from where you can reach the ruins. Of far greater interest, however, are the ruins of Baqerha and Khirbet Khateb.

Baqerha & Khirbet Khateb To reach this impressive 'Dead City' site, turn right at the crossroads and follow the narrow winding road as it climbs steeply up onto the ridge and then through a small village, to arrive after 3 km at an extensive cluster of ruins on the right. Dating from the late fifth to early sixth century AD, this was clearly a substantial settlement. Amongst the ruins you can identify at least three **churches** and numerous **private houses**, as well as **civic buildings**, **towers** and deep **wells**. Continuing another 800 m or so up the road, you come to a small solitary **chapel** on the left, with the remains of what appears to be a **tower** next to it. The roof of the chapel is missing, but otherwise it is remarkably well preserved, and adorned with a distinctive style of wave-pattern decoration running around the ground floor and upper storey windows (a feature common to many of the ruins at this site). Higher up the hillside there are more ruins. Though it doesn't look like it, you can actually reach these ruins by following the road; turn left at a T-junction after 500 m and they are to the left of the road after a further 500 m. There is plenty to explore here, but the hightlight is the remains of a large triple-aisled basilica **church**. The most impressive feature is the elaborately decorated front façade, leaning precariously but still standing in all its glory right the way to the tip of its third-storey gable end. Another 200 m further up the road, marked by a gateway of heavy stone slabs beside the road on the left, are the remains of a second century AD **Roman temple** dedicated to Zeus Bombos (literally Zeus of the Altar). The gateway is just about all that remains of the temple's *temenos*, but the *cella* is quite well preserved, with the rear wall and parts of the side walls still standing. On a clear day there are excellent views from here out across the plains below.

Another 1 km brings you back to the main road, a little over 3 km beyond the crossroads; turn right to continue west towards Harim. Very soon after, you pass through a small village. A little under 5 km further on there is a left turn signposted for 'Qalb Lawza' and 'Hattan', but the more interesting route is to go via the town of Harim. After just over 11 km you arrive at a roundabout in the centre of Harim. On a steep hillock near the centre of the town are the crumbling ruins of a **fortress**. Although a stronghold was first established here by the Byzantine emperor Nicephorus Phocas in 959, the existing ruins date largely from the construction work carried out by the Ayyubid ruler of Aleppo, Al Zaher Ghazi, in 1199. From 1097 when it was captured by the Crusaders prior to their siege of Antioch until the late 13th century when it was largely destroyed during the Mongol invasions, control of Harim passed back and forth repeatedly between the Crusaders and Muslims. Today little remains of the fortifications, although there are good views from the top, and a couple of pleasant **restaurants** down below.

Harim

From the roundabout in Harim, take the signposted turning for Qalb Lozeh. After just under 2 km, fork right onto a rough old road (clearly signposted for 'Kalb Lawza', 'Bnabel' and 'Kafer Keela'). The road, narrow and poorly surfaced in places, climbs steeply up into the hills of the Jebel al-Ala, with excellent views back down onto the plains below. At the village of **Bnabel**, 4½ km beyond the fork, the well preserved remains of a Roman villa are visible to the right of the road. After another 4 km, having passed various scattered ruins, you arrive at what is effectively a crossroads. Immediately before, a small road leads off to the left to the site of **Kirk Bizeh** (clearly visible from the road), where there are the ruins of a fourth-century church and assorted other buildings. Turn sharp right at the crossroads and it is less than 1 km to the village of Qalb Lozeh. The church of Qalb Lozeh is towards the far end of the village, close to the road.

Harim to Qalb Lozeh

Around Aleppo: Dead Cities

Qalb Lozeh قلب لوزة

The small village of Qalb Lozeh (literally 'Heart of the Almond'), predominantly Druze like most of the villages in this part of the Jebel al-Ala, is an unlikely setting for this unique church. Thought to have been built as early as 450 AD, it was (like the church at Mushabbak) perhaps conceived as a stopping place for pilgrims en route to visit Deir Samaan – already an important pilgrimage centre even before St Simeon's death. Thus it pre-dates the church of St Simeon, and in its layout represents the earliest example of a broad-aisled basilica church. Both its design and decoration provide an excellent early example of the Syrian style of Byzantine ecclesiastical architecture.

Colour map 1, grid A2

Initially it is worth making a tour of the outside of the church. The *narthex* or entrance hall at the west end of the church is flanked by two towers which were originally joined by a broad arch (now collapsed). Beyond this, the lintel of the central doorway is topped by its own, much smaller arch. At the opposite end of the church, the apse, decorated with engaged colonnettes between the windows, extends beyond the basic rectangular plan. Known as a *chevet*, this extension of the apse represents a departure from earlier church designs where the apse was contained within the exterior rectangular plan. It is a feature repeated in the eastern basilica at St Simeon. The south side of the church has three richly decorated doorways, once protected by wooden porches, and a line of arched windows. The north side has two doorways, one of which you enter through. Inside, two rows of three broad arches supported on piers divide the central nave from the side aisles. The southern side aisle still retains parts of its roofing, consisting of long slabs of limestone laid horizontally. The central nave would originally have been covered with a wooden roof, the windows of the *clerestory* providing light to the interior, unobstructed by the flat-roofed side aisles. At the east end of the church, the half-domed semicircular apse, framed with elaborate decoration, is beautifully preserved. ■ *Open daily during daylight hours. Entry S£150 (students S£10). The church is kept locked and the current caretaker lives in the village of Bnabel, 5 km away, so if you arrive late in the day you may find that he has already gone home.*

Transport Microbuses run from the Pullman/City bus station in Aleppo as far as Harim, although services are erratic. It may be easier to go first to Idlib and then to get a microbus from there to Harim. From Harim hitching is not really practical given the extremely limited amounts of traffic on the road to Qalb Lozeh, so you will have to negotiate a return ride with a taxi (or anyone you can find who is willing to take you).

South from Qalb Lozeh

Rather than returning the way you came, you can continue south from Qalb Lozeh, following the line of a high exposed ridge of the Jebel al-Ala, before descending to join the main road between Harim and Idlib. Around 2½ km to the south of Qalb Lozeh a rough track on the left leads in 500 m or so to the site of Behyo.

Behyo The settlement here is thought only to have been established in the fifth century (quite late compared with other Dead City sites). Despite the particularly harsh and rugged environment in which it is set, it quickly grew to a substantial size and what remains to be seen today, although heavily ruined, extends over a wide area. Bathed in sunlight the ruins are very atmospheric, and the views from here quite spectacular. The partially standing remains of a sizeable church are clearly discernible, while all around amongst the scattered ruins are large masonry blocks bearing fragments of carved decoration and Byzantine crosses, as well as a number of olive presses.

Returning to the road and continuing south, you pass some insubstantial ruins and then through a couple of villages, before descending steeply down to a T-junction in the town of Kafr Takhariem (17 km from Qalb Lozeh). Turning left here leads south and then southwest to Idlib (35 km), while right leads back to Harim, 10 km to the north.

Jebel Riha (Jebel Zawiye)

The Jebel Riha, with its gently rolling landscape and pockets of rich, fertile agricultural land is less isolated than the Jebel al-Ala. You can reach the concentration of Dead City sites in the Jebel Riha either from the Lattakia highway or from Maarat al-Numan on the Damascus-Aleppo motorway. From Maarat al-Numan (see page 238), pick up the road heading due west towards Kafr Nubbul, passing through a more or less continuous string of villages along the way. Turn right at the mini-roundabout in the centre of Kafr Nubbul (12 km), and then after 1 km take the small right turn signposted for Bara, 7 km to the north, passing a number of other sites en route. From the Lattakia highway, take the turning leading south 6 km to the west of Ariha (see below, Aleppo to Lattakia). Follow this road, bearing left wherever it forks ambiguously, passing through the village of Ehesem before arriving at the village of Bara, 14 km away.

Bara بارة

The modern village of Bara, strung out along the main road, is growing rapidly and close on becoming a small town in size. The ruins are scattered over a large area, in amongst the drystone walls of fields, olive groves and orchards to the west of the modern village, with a number of narrow roads and tracks linking the most important ruins. Without your own transport, getting around the ruins involves quite a bit of walking; in hot weather be sure to bring plenty of water and adequate protection against the sun.

Phone code: 023
Colour map 1, grid B2

History

The settlement of Bara developed from around the fourth century. By the fifth and sixth centuries it was a flourishing town (it is certainly the largest of the Dead City sites), with at least five churches, three monasteries and numerous large villas. The fact that its inhabitants even began to build themselves elaborate burial tombs is an indication of its wealth. It owed this wealth both to its position on an important north-south corridor of communication, and to the richness of the agricultural land here which allowed for the cultivation of grape vines as well as olives. Thus the settlement developed into a major centre, producing wine and olive oil on a large scale, and probably acting as a processing centre for surrounding villages. Interestingly, it continued to be inhabited even after the disruption of the trade routes which led to the gradual abandonment of other settlements from the seventh century onwards. This was probably thanks to the relative diversity and inherent wealth of its economy. In 1098, shortly before the infamous massacre at Maarat al-Numan, Bara was occupied by the Crusader forces of Raymond St Gilles. It remained under Crusader control until 1123 when it was retaken by the Muslims, who built a small fortress there.

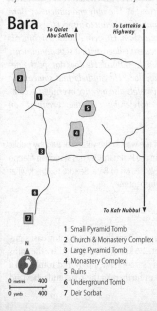

Bara
To Qalat Abu Safian
To Lattakia Highway
To Kafr Nubbul

N

0 metres 400
0 yards 400

1 Small Pyramid Tomb
2 Church & Monastery Complex
3 Large Pyramid Tomb
4 Monastery Complex
5 Ruins
6 Underground Tomb
7 Deir Sorbat

Sights

As you enter Bara from the north, there is a sharp right turn at the start of the village signposted for the 'Ruins of Bara'. Taking this turning, fork left after 500 m and follow the narrow road past various fragments of ruins to arrive in a further 600 m at a **pyramid tomb** on the left. This is the smaller and plainer of two such tombs to be found at Bara. Its pyramid-shaped roof is almost completely intact, while inside there are the broken remains of three sarcophagi. Next to the tomb are the remains

Around Aleppo: Dead Cities

of a large rectangular building, with one arch inside still standing. A little way away, across the road from the pyramid tomb and up on higher ground, the remains of a large church and monastery complex are clearly visible. Back on the road, turn left immediately beyond the pyramid tomb and keep going for around 500 m, past various other fragments of ruins, to arrive at the **large pyramid tomb** on the right. Only about half of its pyramid roof survives, but, as if to make up for this, it is much more ornate. The lintel above the door is richly decorated, while running around the top of the square base on the outside of the building are two bands of carved decoration. In each corner is a carved pilaster, and in each face two small, arched windows. The entrance to the tomb is protected by a locked iron grille, but you can peer inside, where there are five sarcophagi, all still with their lids intact and with carved medallions containing Byzantine crosses. A short walk across the fields more or less directly opposite the pyramid tomb brings you to the ruins of a large monastery complex, distinctive as you approach it from this side for the large rectangular window flanked by two smaller square ones, each with Byzantine crosses on the lintels. A little further on is a large complex of several buildings, though to the untrained eye it presents little more than a confusing jumble of walls, arches and tumbled-down ruins. Back on the road, just past the large pyramid tomb, a left turn leads back towards the modern village. Going straight on, you pass on the right an **underground tomb** with a triple-arched porch protecting a square portal which leads into the burial chamber, where arched bays have been carved into the walls to hold sarcophagi. Further on you come to the monastery of **Deir Sorbat**, Bara's best preserved monument after the pyramid tombs. At the centre is a church with its walls still standing to a height of two storeys, pierced by windows and doorways decorated with Byzantine crosses. Various rooms have been built onto the church, while dotted around are the ruins of several other buildings. The remains of the various other **churches** are scattered around the area between the modern village and the road linking the two pyramid tombs; a path leads past one of them, but the others can only be reached by scrambling over a number of drystone walls. To the northeast of the main concentration of ruins are the remains of the Arab fort of **Qalat Abu Safian**, today in an advanced state of ruin. ■ *The only monument at Bara which is kept locked is the large pyramid tomb. If you want to inspect the sarcophagi inside in more detail, contact the site guardian, Hussein Aboud. His office is on the main street running through the modern village, with a sign announcing 'Directeur General D'Antiquities, Guardien de Al Bara'. He does not speak English, but the local teacher, Hassan Al Shaf, does. He can help find someone to guide you around the site if you wish, and possibly also arrange overnight accommodation; contact him in advance (preferably in the evening) on T450134/450901.*

Transport For a change, it is actually possible to get all the way to the village of Bara by public transport. Microbuses run fairly regularly from the Pullman/City bus station in Aleppo to Ariha, where there are less frequent microbuses on to Bara. Be sure to check what time the last microbus leaves Bara for the return journey.

Bauda سيرجيلة and Serjilla بودة

Colour map 1, grid B2 Just 300 m or so south of the modern village of Bara there is a turning east signposted for Bauda and Serjilla. On the right, 2½ km down this road are the ruins of Bauda, consisting of several large stone sarcophagi, a pyramid tomb and a very dilapidated church. A little over 1 km further on the road ends; beyond are the ruins of Serjilla.

Serjilla, like Bara, was an extensive settlement that prospered from the cultivation of grapes as well as olives. The ruins here are scattered across a depression in the hills. From the road-head, a path leads down past the well preserved remains of a **baths complex** on the left, and next to it an **andron**, or meeting hall. The baths, which have been dated to 473, are an indication of the wealth of this community and are unusual in that they date from the Christian rather than the Roman period. The American team from Princeton University which carried out excavations here in 1899 discovered a large mosaic covering the floor of the main hall of the baths, but when they returned six years later it had been removed. Traces of murals (now destroyed) were also found on the walls. Continuing along the path, also on the left, are the ruins of a **church**, of which little remains, with an underground burial chamber below it. On the hillside to the left above the church is a particularly large and well preserved **villa** with its two storeys still standing. Note how two of the rooms inside each contain an arch which would have supported the ceiling. This is a feature which can be seen amongst the ruins of many of the Dead Cities; here the good state of preservation makes its structural significance much clearer. Behind the house is a sunken building containing an olive press. Scattered across the hillside to the southeast are the ruins of numerous other houses.

There are a number of other ruins of lesser interest which can be visited as short diversions off the road heading south from Bara. Three kilometres to the south of Bara there is a turning west signposted for the ruins of **Bshala**, 1½ km away. Six kilometres to the south of Bara a turning east is signposted for the ruins of **Rabia** and **Shinshrah**, 3 km and 5 km away respectively. While these sites do not have anything particularly notable to offer amongst the scattered ruins, the isolated setting of the latter two, with their panoramic views of the the surrounding rolling hills and olive groves, is gently impressive.

South of Bara

Ruweiha and Jerada جيرادة

The two Dead City sites of Ruweiha and Jerada are east of Bara. The best way to get to them is by turning south off the Lattakia highway into the the town of **Ariha** (see below, Aleppo to Lattakia). After turning off the highway, go straight on past a fork with a petrol station in the crook of the fork and then bear left at the roundabout soon after. The road climbs steeply into the Jebel Riha, passing a couple of summer restaurants with excellent views down onto Ariha and out over the plains around Idlib. Some 14 km after the Lattakia highway exit, where the road bends round to the right, there is a fork off to the left signposted for the 'Ruins of Roweiha and Gerada' (straight on leads to Maarat al-Numan).

Colour map 1, grid B2

You come first to the ruins of **Ruweiha**, to the left of the road after 4 km, set in a dramatic landscape of rolling hills on an open plateau. There are a couple of modern buildings, but elsewhere surviving buildings of the ancient settlement have simply been reoccupied. Some scrambling is necessary as many of the ruins are now enclosed within drystone walls. Close to the road there are the ruins of a **church**, with a series of columns and arches which once separated the nave from a side-aisle still standing. Many of the buildings here are of almost palatial proportions, an indication of the high degree of prosperity which the town must have achieved. Their excellent state of preservation, meanwhile, gives an idea of the quality of workmanship involved. Further away from the road to the northeast, after passing through the main body of the ruins, there is a second larger church, now used as a farm. This has been identified from an inscription as the **Church of Bissos**, dating from the sixth century. The domed structure on the

The ruins are scattered over a considerable area & now accommodate a small farming settlement (beware of the dogs!)

south side of the church housed the tomb of Bissos, who was perhaps the local priest or bishop. At the eastern end of the vilage there is a small, perfectly intact **funerary monument** with even its roof still in place. It looks distinctly Roman in style, with two hefty columns supporting the triangular *pediment* of the porch. A little further to the east is what was clearly the burial area of the settlement. Close to the road there are a couple of **underground tombs** with decorated entrances. Various other underground burial chambers are dotted around, their entrances sealed by massive stone lids, though some of these have been jacked up on stones, allowing you to peer inside. There are also a couple of more elaborate above-ground mausoleums, one topped by a massive sarcophagus which, along with its lid, is still intact.

The most impressive remains are at the east end of the village, just to the left of the road

The ruins of **Jerada** are 3 km further on, interspersed with the buildings of a contemporary village. They include a couple of **watchtowers** dating from the fifth or sixth century, one of them still standing to its full height, along with the ruins of several buildings and a church. The presence of watchtowers perhaps indicates the greater vulnerability of settlements such as this, which were closer to the desert and so liable to attack from nomadic tribes.

Continuing east from Jerada, you arrive after a further 3 km at the sliproad leading from the Damascus-Aleppo motorway to the village of Babila. **NB** If you wish to reach Jerada and Ruweiha from the motorway, the turning is signposted for 'Babila, Grada', 70 km to the south of Aleppo and 14 km to the south of the turning for Ebla, or 6 km to the north of the turning for Maarat al-Numan.

Northeast of Aleppo

Heading northeast from Aleppo, the landscape is flat and featureless, with vast expanses of rain-fed arable land gradually giving way to arid semi-desert. By the time you reach Qalat Najm, on the banks of the Euphrates, the land is parched and barren, despite the presence of this mighty river. Although certainly an impressive site (and all the more so for its setting), it is a long way to come, particularly as a round trip from Aleppo. If you have your own transport and are planning to visit the Jezira region, you could use this as an alternative route into the Jezira.

To join the road leading northeast towards Qalat Najm, follow directions as for the Euphrates highway (see page 370). After leaving the Euphrates highway, the first 31 km or so, up until you arrive at a roundabout and exits for Tadef and Al Bab, is along a broad four-lane highway. A further 45 km along a normal two-lane road brings you to a second roundabout, the left turning here signposted to 'Monbej', 2 km away.

Membij

The town of Membij was a centre for the cult worship of the Mesopotamian goddess Atargatis and her consort Hadad during the Persian period. The town was Hellenized and renamed Hierapolis by Seleucus I Nicator in the third century BC. The worship of Atargatis, which involved various bloody ritualistic practices including the sacrifice of children, continued during Roman times and Membij became perhaps the most important religious centre in Syria, its fame spreading throughout the Roman Empire. Today, however, Membij is a dusty, uninspiring place with nothing to see and little to recommend it.

Some 17 km further on from the roundabout/exit for Membij there is a small left turn signposted to 'Qalaat Najem', 14 km away. Taking this turning, after passing through a couple of small villages, the Euphrates River appears, almost like a mirage, up ahead. Soon after, you arrive at the castle itself.

Qalat Najm قلعة نجم

Colour map 1, grid A4

Known as *Caeciliana* to the Romans, this site was an important crossing point on the Euphrates, from where Roman forces were able to launch offensives against the Parthians of Mesopotamia. The present castle was first built by Nur ud-Din in the 12th century but subsequently largely reconstructed by the Ayyubid ruler of Aleppo, Al Zaher Ghazi (the son of Saladin), in the early 13th century. Al Zaher Ghazi was also responsible for much of the fortification work carried out on Aleppo's citadel and the parallels between the two are obvious, particularly in terms of the stone *glacis* surrounding the castle. The Mongol invasions of the late 13th and early 14th century took their toll on the castle, however, and soon afterwards it was abandoned.

The castle stands on a natural high point by the banks of the Euphrates, with inspiring views out over the river, which flows past here in a broad and majestic sweep, and the mud-brick village of Qalat Najm nestled below. In recent years a joint Syrian-Spanish team has carried out extensive restoration work on the castle, to impressive effect. The stairway and neatly arched bridge leading up to the entrance is a modern reconstruction. The inscription above the tall arched entrance gate details the work carried out by Al Zaher Ghazi in the 13th century. This leads through into a large vaulted entrance hall. Bearing off to the left from here and ascending, you arrive at the castle's **palace**, built around a central courtyard with a basin and fountain in the centre and arched *iwans* around the sides. Steps lead down from here to the **dungeons**, where traces of a church dating from the early Byzantine period have been identified. A passage leads from the courtyard through to the palace's **hammam**, where traces of ceramic waterpipes can be seen. A number of large, cool rooms served as storage, with deep grain pits and water cisterns. Two flights of stairs take you up to the roof of the palace, from where there are excellent views. Returning to the entrance hall, if you go right and then left through a dogleg, you find yourself in a long, vaulted passage which has been identified as the **souk** or market; note the remains of rings cut into the walls for tethering animals. From here you can gain access to the upper **ramparts** of the castle (once again with excellent views), and the **mosque**. ■ *Open daily during daylight hours. At the time of writing there was no official entrance fee, though it seems likely that the standard S£300/students S£15 will be applied in the near future. For the time being, the caretaker (or his son) is usually on duty to show you around, and afterwards offer you tea or soft drinks, though he expects a payment for his troubles.*

Transport Buses from Aleppo's East bus station run to Ain al-Arab via Membij and the turning for Qalat Najm; make sure that someone understands where you are going so that you can be dropped off at the right place. From the turning it is still a further 14 km, however, and there is little traffic along this road. You may be better off negotiating a ride with a taxi driver in Membij.

Aleppo to Lattakia

The route to Lattakia is varied and picturesque. Having crossed the plateau to the southwest of Aleppo, it traverses the northern reaches of the Jebel Riha, before descending to the fertile plains of the Orontes River (and crossing it at Jisr al-Shughur). Having crossed the Orontes, it climbs steeply, winding its way through the Jebel Ansariye mountains before descending to the broad coastal plain surrounding Lattakia.

Unfortunately, the road is also extremely busy with heavily laden lorries crawling along what is the only route connecting Lattakia with the main transport corridor between Aleppo and Damascus. A motorway is planned which will eventually connect Lattakia with Aleppo. The first stretch after leaving the Damascus-Aleppo motorway has already been upgraded to motorway dimensions, while west of Ariha a certain amount of widening work is in progress. For the most part, however, the road is narrow and, particularly through the Jebel Ansariye mountains, quite treacherous in places. You are strongly advised to avoid driving this route at night. If you are travelling between Aleppo and Lattakia by public transport, the train journey along this route is easily the most scenic in Syria and well worth considering as an alternative to going by road.

From the centre of Aleppo, head west along Ibrahim Hanano Streeet to join the Aleppo-Damascus motorway. Continue past the exit for the Syrian/Turkish border post at Bab al-Hawa (6 km; also signposted for Idlib and, slightly confusingly, Ariha, Jisr al-Shughur and Lattakia). Take the next major exit, just over 40 km further on, signposted for Ariha, Jisr al-Shughur and Lattakia (and also Saraqeb and Idlib). Following this road (effectively a motorway for this first stretch), you arrive after 22 km at an interchange (left for the town of Ariha and the road to the Dead City sites of Ruweiha and Jerada; right for the town of Idlib, see above). Continue straight, passing after another 6 km the left turn for Bara. Further on the road begins to descend from the hills of the Jebel Riha with views down onto a fertile, patchwork quilt landscape of fields extending over the Al Ghab plains of the Orontes River. In the small village of Frikeh (or Ferayka), a little over 28 km from the Ariha/Idlib junction, there is a left turn signposted for amongst others 'Madiq Citadel'. This road runs due south along the Al Ghab plain to Apamea (Qalat Mudiq), 34 km away (see page 230). After a further 7 km, you arrive in the centre of Jisr al-Shughur.

Jisr al-Shughur
Colour map 1, grid B2

Note the V-shape of the bridge pointing upstream, so designed to strengthen it against the force of the current

The town of Jisr al-Shughur has since ancient times been an important crossing point over the Orontes River. In the Seleucid period it was known as *Seleucia ad Bellum* and in Roman times as *Niaccuba*. The bridge across the Orontes here in fact dates back originally to Roman times, although it has been repaired and strengthened numerous times over the centuries (note the variety of stones from which the piers and arches are built). In its present form it is essentially a Mameluke construction of the 15th century. The town itself is busy with traffic passing through, but quite attractive in its way, with a number of old buildings from the Ottoman period still surviving. There are a number of cafés and simple restaurants along the main road.

Just over 1 km after leaving the town, where the road swings round sharply to the right, a road branches off to the left (ie straight ahead). This road runs south along the edges of the Al Ghab plain, with the mountains of the Jebel Ansariye rising immediately to the west, taking you past the ruins of Qalat Burzey and the turning for Slunfeh (and also past Apamea, off to the east, and eventually all the way to Masyaf). Following the main road round to the right, you soon begin to climb steeply into the Jebel Ansariye. The road winds its way through picturesque hills dotted with cherry orchards, fields and small villages, with the Aleppo-Lattakia railway repeatedly crossing and recrossing it on high viaducts. There are numerous turnings off the main road, including (distances from Jisr al-Shughur); 32 km turn left for Salma and Slunfeh; 36 km turn right for Rabia and Kassab (see page 299); 41 km turn left for Salma and Slunfeh (alternative route); 46 km turn left for Haffe (or Al Haffeh, from where you can visit Qalat Saladin; see page 300). Having descended from the Jebel Ansariye, the road runs across the coastal plain to arrive in Lattakia (see page 283), 75 km from Jisr al-Shughur and 180 km from Aleppo.

Euphrates River الفرات and the Jezira الجزيرة

10

Euphrates River and the Jezira

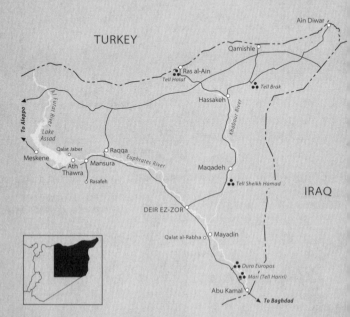

The Euphrates is one of the great rivers of the Middle East, historically both a major cultural and geographical boundary, and an important medium for trade and communications. Rising in Turkey's eastern Anatolian plateau, it flows southeast through Syria, dividing the Syrian desert from the rain-fed plains of the Jezira. Rather like the Orontes, the Euphrates does not offer its waters easily to the surrounding countryside, cutting its way instead through low hills or irrigating narrow strips of land along its banks, while beyond the land rises to desert-steppe stretching away into the horizon. Despite the irrigation from the Euphrates Dam at Ath Thawra, it is still the desert which makes its presence most strongly felt.

The northeastern region of Syria is known as the Jezira (literally 'island' in Arabic), a large expanse of land bounded by the Euphrates and Tigris rivers which also extends into Iraq and Turkey. In effect, the Syrian Jezira corresponds roughly with the northern part of ancient Mesopotamia ('the land between two rivers' – again the Tigris and Euphrates), most of which lies now within present-day Iraq. Physically, the Jezira is often beautiful: rolling hills and rippling fields of wheat extend as far as the eye can see. Culturally, the region is also interesting, two of its major towns, Hassakeh and Qamishle, are home to sizeable Christian communities and most of the one million Kurds in Syria are concentrated in the Jezira. Enormously friendly and consistently cheerful in outlook, it is sometimes hard to believe that this ethnic group has experienced so much persecution and hardship in their search for a homeland.

☛ *A foot in the door*

★ *Of all the historic sites along the Euphrates, **Rasafeh** is perhaps the most spectacular in terms of its standing remains.*

★ *Also impressive, **Qalat Jaber**, **Halabiye** and **Dura Europos** are actually memorable as much for their dramatic settings on the Euphrates as for the ruins themselves.*

★ ***Mari**, for all its archaeological significance, has been stripped of its treasures, which all now reside in museums.*

★ *Given the huge distances involved, you can't really help but stop overnight in **Deir ez-Zor**, which gives you the opportunity*

*to visit its excellent **museum**, and to appreciate the broad sweep of the **Euphrates** from the comfort of a restaurant or café.*

★ *The Jezira region has just one small historic monument, a **ruined Roman bridge at Ain Diwar** in the extreme northeast; even if you don't make it down to the bridge, the views looking out over the **Tigris** at Ain Diwar, which here forms the border between Syria and Turkey, are particularly dramatic.*

★ *Alongside the beautiful scenery of the Jezira, it is its people, and in particular the **Kurds**, which make it such a rewarding area to visit.*

Ins and outs

Getting around Of the major sites along the Euphrates river, Dura Europos and Mari are within walking distance of the main road, but the others are not, making reaching them by public transport more difficult. There are only 2 towns of any size along the Euphrates. Raqqa, the smaller, has just 3 hotels (none of them very appealing) and for all its recent rapid growth still has a very provincial feel to it. It is useful primarily as a base for visiting Rasafeh, the Euphrates dam and Qalat Jaber. If you have your own transport, it is possible (in a long day) to visit these sites en route to Deir ez-Zor, which has better hotels and is generally more appealing. Deir ez-Zor, at an important transport cross-roads, has flourished in recent years on oil-generated wealth. It serves as a useful base for visiting Halabiye, Dura Europos and Mari, as well as the Jezira and Palmyra.

Aleppo to Raqqa

For the first 80 km or so out of Aleppo, the road passes through a rather monotonous landscape, cultivated in places but often barren, the Euphrates being a long way to the northeast. Even after the town of Meskene, when you are running parallel to this great river, irrigated farmland comes in small patches, with the desert never far away.

Euphrates Highway To join the Euphrates Highway you have to head east out of Aleppo in the direction of the airport. However, Aleppo's often confusing one-way systems and chaotic traffic make this no mean feat. This is one route out of the city. From the junction at the north end of Bab al-Faraj Street in the centre of Aleppo, head east along Al Khandak St. After a short distance, the one-way system forces you to turn right; go left at the next roundabout you come to (into Al Sejn Street), then left again at the T-junction at the end of this street, and then right at the next T-Junction. You are now on Bab an-Nasr Street, the continuation of Al Khandak Street. At the Bab an-Nasr roundabout on the northeast corner of the old city, turn left and follow Al Abbassin Street north up to the next major junction. Turn right here and follow signs for Aleppo Airport. Just over 9 km from the centre of Aleppo by this route, take the exit sign-posted for Raqqa and Membij to join the Euphrates Highway (at this stage a motorway) heading east. The exit immediately before (signposted for Hama and Damascus) puts you on the motorway in the opposite direction to bypass Aleppo and join the Aleppo-Damascus Highway.

There is an exit clearly signposted for **Membij** 6 km after joining the Euphrates Highway. This is the start of the route to Qalat Najm. At this point, the Euphrates Highway turns from a motorway into a normal two-lane highway. After a further 39 km, you pass through **Deir Haffer**, a half-built, rather miserable looking place, and then, in another 40 km, arrive at **Meskene**, also somewhat uninspiring, although there is an interesting monument nearby.

Around 5 km to the northeast of Meskene (as the crow flies), on the edges of Lake Assad, there is a solitary 13th-century Ayyubid brick-built octagonal minaret with stairs inside leading up to the top, from where there are panoramic views out onto the lake. A little beyond the minaret there are a few insubstantial ruins dating from the Byzantine period on the shores of the lake. This is all that remains of an ancient transit point on the Euphrates where caravans on the trade route between the Mediterranean and Mesopotamia switched between land and river transport.

Meskene minaret
For Ath Thawra & Qalat Jaber, see page 378

Ins and outs The area of land between the modern town and the minaret is criss-crossed by irrigation channels, making it difficult to reach it directly. One route is as follows: 2 km beyond Meskene's police post (by the road on the right at the east edge of the town), turn left along a small road running along the east side of a large irrigation channel. After just over 4 km, turn left to cross over the channel on a bridge and follow a smaller irrigation channel running off the main one at right angles. After just under 2 km, turn right cross over this channel on another bridge. The surfaced road now turns to a rough track running through a village. Around 500 m further on you come to a kind of T-junction, from where the tower is visible up ahead.

Raqqa الرقة

The small, rather sleepy, provincial town of Raqqa stands on a section of the Middle Euphrates, at its junction with the Balikh River (the classical *Balissus*). There is not a great deal to see and do in the town, despite efforts to restore its historical remains. Anyway, it is the town's function as a market centre for the surrounding countryside which gives Raqqa its greatest appeal, attracting Bedouin from far and wide and creating a colourful spectacle on market days. Notwithstanding the extremely limited and uniformly appalling accommodation on offer here, Raqqa is also the ideal base from which to visit Rasafeh, Qalat Jaber and the Euphrates Dam.

Phone code: 022
Colour map 1, grid B5

Raqqa is well connected by road with Aleppo to the west and Deir ez-Zor to the southeast. There are also services connecting it with Damascus, either via Aleppo, or else the desert road via Salamiyeh. The main luxury coach/minibus station, a little to the south of the town centre, handles all these services. Raqqa's train station is inconveniently located way to the north of the centre. Services in both directions pass through during the early hours of the morning, making them of little practical use. Raqqa is easily managed on foot, though there are taxis available should you want one. There is a new **tourist information** office on the road into town (coming from the Euphrates), though at the time of writing it was not yet open.

Ins & outs

The great historian-geographer Pliny suggests that the town here was first established by Alexander the Great, though the credit probably lies with his general Seleucus Nicator, who went on to establish the **Seleucid** Empire. In

History

fact, the settlement's development is really due to one of his successors, Seleucus II Callinicus (246-225 BC), who gave his name to the early town. The strategic importance of a town controlling much of the Middle Euphrates basin was further emphasized when the battle lines became drawn between the Byzantine Empire and the rising power of the Sassanid Persians. The town was close to this zone of contact and was the scene of a major battle in 531 AD in which the Christian army was resoundingly beaten.

The rise of **Arab** power across the region produced the town's golden period (the settlement becoming known as 'Raqqa', or 'flat land' in Arabic). The Umayyad caliph Hisham (724-743 AD) is said to have built two palaces here, though it was the succeeding (and rival) **Abbasid** Dynasty who enhanced Raqqa's status as a major Euphrates town. The caliph Al Mansur (754-775 AD) made the town the administrative capital of the province of Jezira, and laid the foundations of the stout defensive walls that can still be seen today. The later Abbasid caliph Harun al-Rashid (786-809 AD) substantially remodelled the town, and added a neighbouring twin settlement to serve as his summer capital.

Raqqa's subsequent history is not so glamourous. It may have enjoyed a brief period of fame as the centre of a noted glazed ceramicware industry, possibly introduced by Salah ud-Din (Saladin), though following its sacking by the Mongols in 1258 the town went into terminal decline. In fact, Raqqa's recent revival is very recent indeed, dating just to the last four decades. It is once again the administrative capital of the province in which it stands, and is the main commercial market for the region.

Sights

Because Raqqa has so few reminders of its historical past, great efforts are being made to make the best of what is left

Old city walls and gates The rebuilding and refurbishment of the Abbasid city walls and gates proceeds at a startling pace, with much of the southeast and east sides now returning to something approaching their former glory.

The **city walls** are credited to the Abbasid caliph Al Mansur, who fortified Raqqa as his advance headquarters against the Byzantine threat. The distinctive horseshoe shape is said to be based on the original circular plan for the

Raqqa

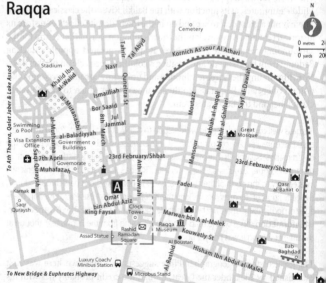

*Related map
A Raqqa centre,
page 374*

defence of Baghdad, though adapted here to take account of the Euphrates to the south (the walls on this south side, parallel to the river, have largely disappeared). The bases of many of the 100 or so round towers that punctuated the city walls at every 35 m or so can still be seen, though only one gate has survived to any great height. In fact, there is now reason to suppose that the substantial **Bab Baghdad** (Baghdad Gate) in the southeast corner is actually mid-12th century AD and not Abbasid.

Qasr al-Banat Around 400 m north of Bab Baghdad are the remains of the ninth-century AD Qasr al-Banat, or 'Palace of the Maidens'. The palace features a fountain set in a courtyard at its centre, with a high-arched hall (or *iwan*) on each side, though for whom the palace was built is still not entirely clear. The palace has been partially restored, though it is now fenced off and the gate on the west side is usually locked.

Great Mosque The great Friday mosque complex occupies a whole city block more or less at the centre of the old walled city. Like the city walls it was originally built by the Abbasid caliph Al Mansur (around 772 AD), though much of what you see today dates to the restoration programme undertaken by Nur ud-Din (1165-6). In its prime the complex would have been an impressive sight, surrounded by a 100 m by 100 m wall (up to 5 m high) complete with 11 towers, though the remains to be seen today can only hint at this former splendour. In the northeast corner stands a 25 m high tower, probably part of Nur ud-Din's efforts, whilst along the south side stand 11 remaining arches of his impressive colonnade (that bears the inscription detailing his restoration work). At the centre of the complex is a small green-domed shrine.

Raqqa Museum Raqqa's recently refurbished (or at least redecorated) museum features a small collection of artefacts excavated from the numerous sites of different periods in this region. Some of the figurines and items of pottery dating back as far as the fourth millennium BC are quite impressive, but most of the more important finds are now housed in the National Museums in Aleppo and Damascus, or else have gone abroad. All in all, its certainly not worth the full price entrance fee. ■ *Open 0900-1800 in summer, 0900-1600 in winter, closed Tue. Entry S£300 (students S£15).*

■ *on map*

Sleeping

Unfortunately, Raqqa's 3 hotels have precious little to recommend them

C/D *Karnak*, Saqr Quraysh St, T232265. Large, echoing and generally empty hotel, owned by the government-run *Karnak* transport company. Ageing, decrepit rooms with a/c, TV, phone, attached bath, small balcony and that musty smell which comes from lack of use. Restaurant, duty-free shop, children's play area. Friendly, helpful staff, but desperately in need of refurbishment. **G** *Ammar*, Quneitra St, near clock tower, T222612. Basic but cleanish rooms with sink, balcony and shared shower/toilet. 2 5-bed rooms with fans (more promised for next year). Overpriced for what you get at S£400 a double. Close to noisy mosque and even noisier clock tower. **G** *Tourism*, Kouwatly St, east of clock-tower, T220725. Basic but cleanish rooms with fan, fridge and balcony. Some rooms with attached bath, and a/c of sorts. Also overpriced at S£400 for a double.

Eating

Options for eating in Raqqa are marginally less limited than they are for sleeping. Though these places deserve a mention

Al Bustan, Hisham Ibn Abdul al-Male St. Pleasant open-air rooftop restaurant offering the usual range of Arabic dishes for around S£250 per head, as well as unlimited supplies of arak. *Al Rashid*, King Faysal St, to west of clock tower (enter through arch, sign above just says 'restaurant'). Looks distinctly decrepit from the outside, but is not so bad once you're in, with seating in large open garden. Usual range of Arabic food, including fish from the Euphrates. Around S£250 per head. Alcohol served. Beware of the cats who will try to join you for your meal. *Corner of Hamburger*, just off Ath

Euphrates River & the Jezira

Thawra St, offers excellent value burger and coke for S£50. There are several places selling traditional Arabic sweet dishes (eg *al-Waleed*) on Ath Thawra St, just off the clock tower square. There are several cheap places around the clock tower square offering the usual staples of shwarma, kebabs, falafels etc. The *Al Nawair*, opposite the *Al Waha* café, is good for kebabs, while a few doors down, the *Al Jamal* specializes in roast chicken. Heading down from the museum towards Hisham Ibn Abdul al-Male St, there are several simple restaurants specializing in particular in kebab meals. The *Al Waha* restaurant is actually exclusively a café; it's friendly and spotlessly clean inside, or you can sit out on the street.

Sports

Bear in mind that swimming in Raqqa must be an exclusively male experience

There is a huge public **swimming** pool just off Saqr Quraysh St, about 300 m north of the *Karnak* hotel. On my last visit it was half empty, with the remaining water looking pretty green and filthy, but if it's cleaned up during the summer it would be worth a go (entry S£15).

Transport

The **luxury coach/minibus station** is to the south of the large statue of Assad on Rashid Ramadan Sq, close to the centre of town. There are regular minibuses for **Deir ez-Zor**, departing every 45 mins, S£60. Several private companies operate from here. *Kadmous* runs the most frequent luxury coach services. **Aleppo**, 0715, 1115, 1415, 1915, S£85, 2½ hrs. **Damascus** (via Salamiyeh and Homs), 1430, 2400, 0115, S£190, 5½ hrs (Homs S£125, 3½ hrs). **Deir ez-Zor**, 0930, 1145, 1400, 0100, S£60, 2 hrs. *Al Ahliah* runs 2 coaches daily to Damascus, the first departing at 1200 and going via Aleppo, Hama and Homs, the second departing at 1330 and going via Salamiyeh and Homs. *Nahhas* operates cheaper, older coaches to Damascus (S£150) via Salamiyeh and Homs (S£125).

Across the road is the **microbus stand**. Regular services depart when full to **Mansura (for Rasafeh)** (S£15), **Ath Thawra** (S£25), **Aleppo** (S£75) and **Deir ez-Zor** (S£60).

The **train** station is inconveniently located around 2 km to the north of town; keep following Quneitra St northwards to reach it. There is a daily service to **Aleppo** at 0400, and to **Deir ez-Zor/Hassakeh/Qamishle** at 0200.

Directory

The **post office** is on the southeast corner of the clock tower square. The **telephone office** shares the same building. Phonecards (the old STE variety) are on sale here, and there are several cardphones just down the hill. The town's **hospital** is on Saqr Quraysh St, just to the north of the *Karnak* hotel. For an ambulance, T110. **Visa extensions** can be obtained from the Department of Immigration and Passports, in the police station on Al Baladiyyah St (enter through alleyway around the back, where you pay for the stamp in the kiosk).

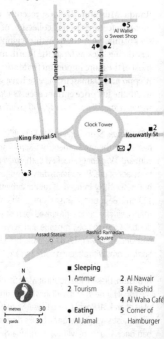

Raqqa centre

Al Walid o Sweet Shop

Quneitra St

Ath Thawra St

King Faysal St

Clock Tower

Kouwatly St

Assad Statue

Rashid Ramadan Square

N

0 metres 30
0 yards 30

■ **Sleeping**
1 Ammar
2 Tourism

● **Eating**
1 Al Jamal

2 Al Nawair
3 Al Rashid
4 Al Waha Café
5 Corner of Hamburger

Euphrates River & the Jezira

Rasafeh الرصافة

Rasafeh, the dramatic ruins of a huge walled city on the fringes of the desert, is perhaps the most impressive sight you will see along the Euphrates. The road south from Mansura to Rasafeh (25 km) passes through land which is now cultivated in patches with the help of irrigation water from Lake Assad. However, as you approach Rasafeh the desert begins to make its presence felt more forcefully and by the time the imposing walls of the city come into view you are left wondering why such a large settlement should have developed in so remote and inhospitable an area.

Colour map 1, grid B5

Ins & outs

Microbuses run regularly between Raqqa and Mansura, but traffic from here along the road to Rasafeh is limited, making hitching difficult. Unless you are lucky, you really have no choice but to try to negotiate a ride, but be warned that the locals here have cottoned on to the possibilities of charging rather exorbitant rates for the return trip.

There is a makeshift tea shop on the road by the site, but it is not always open. You need at least 2-3 hrs to explore the site in any detail. Try to time your visit for the early morning or late afternoon when the light is at its best.

History

Rasafeh is thought to be the *Rezeph* of the Bible (2 Kings 19: 12 and Isaiah 37: 12) and it is also possible that it was referred to in certain Assyrian texts, although no firm archaeological evidence has as yet been discovered to confirm this. During the third century AD the Roman Emperor **Diocletian** established a fortified caravan town here, on what was an ancient trade route between Damascus and the Euphrates (via Dumeir and Palmyra; later named the *Via Diocletiana* in his honour). Following the fall of Dura Europos to the Sassanid Persians in 256, Rasafeh also marked the new boundary between Roman west and Sassanid east.

It rose to fame after the martyrdom in 305 of **Sergius**, a Roman soldier who converted to Christianity and was executed for refusing to perform sacrifices to Jupiter. With the official recognition of Christianity following the Edict of Milan in 313, Sergius soon came to be revered as a saint and his burial place here began to attract large numbers of pilgrims. By the late fourth to early fifth century his fame was such that the settlement was renamed *Sergiopolis* in his honour. New ramparts were constructed, along with a basilica and water cisterns to supply its growing population. During the reign of **Justinian** (527-565), it reached the height of its prosperity. As part of a chain of frontier defences against the continuing Sassanid threat (including also Halabiye and Zalabiye on the Euphrates, see page 379), Justinian stationed a large garrison here and completely rebuilt the defensive walls surrounding Rasafeh on a far grander scale, constructing them out of stone instead of mud-brick. At the same time he undertook an extensive programme of building works within the city (although Procopius ascribes the water cisterns mentioned in the box below to Justinian, they appear to have been started earlier, and perhaps only enlarged during his reign).

Ultimately, however, Rasafeh was unable to withstand the repeated attacks of the **Sassanid Persians** and in 616 it was finally sacked by Chosroes II. Following the Arab Muslim conquest of Syria, the **Umayyad Caliph Hisham** restored much of the city and built a palace for himself here in the eighth century. However, Abu al-Abbas, the founder of the **Abbasid Dynasty** in 750, largely destroyed his palace, and is even said to have had Hisham's bones dug up and flogged, such was his hatred for this Umayyad caliph. Despite a severe earthquake towards the end of the eighth century the city continued to be occupied, although in a much impoverished state. A small Christian community appears to have coexisted alongside the Muslim one until the 13th century, by which time its population had greatly dwindled. Following the **Mongol** invasions it was abandoned altogether. In the ensuing centuries the encroaching sands of the desert did much to protect what remained of the city from the ravages of time.

Sights

Bring plenty of water & adequate protection against the sun; even in winter it can get extremely hot during the day, while in summer the heat is ferocious

Rasafeh's walls form a rough rectangle averaging 500 m by 400 m, with a variety of differently shaped towers at regular intervals and circular bastions on each corner. The main entrance is through the **North Gate**, off to the left of the approach road. Dating from Justinian's reconstruction of the city walls, its triple gateway is remarkably well preserved and represents a beautiful example of Byzantine architecture. Originally there was a single outer entrance (now missing) leading through to a courtyard and so to the inner triple gateway, consisting of a large central portal flanked by two smaller side ones. The capitals of the six columns framing the portals, and the five arched friezes spanning them, are a riot of exuberant decoration, and a suitably grandiose introduction to this great caravan city.

Once through the gateway, you get a sense of Rasafeh's size (over 20 ha); a strange, almost lunar landscape spread out before you, the result of years of digging by the Bedouin in search of treasure. The north wall of the city in particular deserves closer inspection from the inside. You can see clearly the semi-circular vaulting of the arcades which allowed troops to move under protection between the towers. With a little care it is possible to climb up to the upper galleries for good views out over the city. The building material used here is a coarse crystalline stone known as gypsum, which would have been a brilliant white when first cut but has been dulled over the centuries by the elements.

From the North Gate a path (excavated along the first stretch to reveal one of the city's main thoroughfares) is clearly discernible running south, though at a slightly southwesterly angle. Following it, on the left after around 100 m are the remains of what was probably Rasafeh's **metropolitan church**. Today the best preserved feature is the main apse, with part of its semi-dome surviving and a band of decoration above the three windows which pierce it. On either side is a square chapel, in typical Byzantine style. More unusual is the fact that the basic rectangular basilica plan was modified so that the walls curved outwards to give a circular effect, perhaps in order to accommodate a central domed roof. Dated to around 520, similar examples of this 'circle within a square' plan (at Bosra and Ezraa) also date from the first half of the sixth century.

Continuing southwards along the path, after around 100 m, the somewhat insubstantial remains of a **khan** can be seen on the left. After another 100 m or so, shortly before the south walls of the city, you come to a set of underground **water cisterns** on the right; two huge ones which are interconnected, with a set of very rough and uneven steps leading steeply down to them (to the left of the path), and two smaller ones. The sheer size

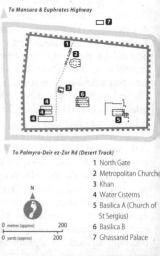

Rasafeh

To Mansura & Euphrates Highway

To Palmyra-Deir ez-Zor Rd (Desert Track)

N

0 metres (approx) 200
0 yards (approx) 200

1 North Gate
2 Metropolitan Church
3 Khan
4 Water Cisterns
5 Basilica A (Church of St Sergius)
6 Basilica B
7 Ghassanid Palace

of the two larger ones in particular is breathtaking; 13 m deep, 58 m long and with a combined capacity of over 15,000 m³. Their near-perfect state of preservation after nearly 15 centuries is equally remarkable.

Heading roughly east from the cisterns brings you to Rasafeh's two main basilica churches, imaginatively dubbed 'basilica A' and 'basilica B' by the German archaeologist Johannes Kollwitz who was responsible for their excavation. The first one you come to, **basilica B**, is poorly preserved, except for a completely intact semi-domed side apse, and tall tower built onto the central apse with a staircase leading up inside (do not climb up, as the upper part of the tower is very unstable). Its ground plan reveals it to have been almost as large as the second, much better preserved church. The second church, **basilica A** (often referred to as the Church of St Sergius, but in fact revealed by an inscription discovered in 1977 to have been dedicated as the Church of the Holy Cross), is the best preserved and most impressive of the ruins at Rasafeh, after the walls themselves. Completed in 559, this church is thought to have replaced the earlier basilica B as the main focal point for the ever-increasing numbers of pilgrims. Some restoration work has been carried out on it in recent years, giving a better idea of how it would have looked. Most striking are the two rows of three enormous arches which separate the central nave from the side aisles, in much the same style as the earlier church at Qalb Lozeh (see page 359). However, in this case the architects appear to have been somewhat over-ambitious and soon afterwards (perhaps due to an earthquake) it was necessary to insert an arrangement of two smaller arches and three columns within each of the main arches for additional support. The apse of the church is also well preserved, with two rectangular chapels flanking it.

Outside the city walls, to the northeast of the North Gate, are the ruins of a building closely resembling a church (and mistakenly identified as the burial spot of St Sergius until recently) which has now been identified as a **Ghassanid palace** or audience chamber. The Ghassanids were an Arab tribe who entered into an alliance with the Byzantines, patrolling the desert on their behalf and helping to control the other tribes of the region. ■ *Open daily during daylight hrs. Entry S£300 (students S£15). The site is not kept locked and there is no ticket office as such; the caretaker will track you down and sell you a ticket.*

Southwest to Homs

As you approach the site there is a turning off to the left along a newly built road. This runs southwest across the desert, passing Isriye (see page 237) and Salamiyeh (on the route between Hama and Palmyra, see also page 237) before arriving in Homs. Although this is a good quality road, used by some of the luxury coaches running between Raqqa and Homs, Hama or Damascus, it is still an isolated desert route. If you intend to drive this way, make sure you have plenty of water and some food, just in case of a breakdown or puncture.

South to Palmyra

It probably will not be long before a surfaced road runs for the whole distance across the desert between Rasafeh and the town of Sukhneh, just off the highway running between Deir ez-Zor and Palmyra. Currently, surfaced roads extend south from Rasafeh and north from Sukhneh, with just some 50 km or so of open desert in-between. Where the surfaced road ends, there is no fixed trail as such, the desert being criss-crossed by numerous tracks left by the pick-ups of the Bedouin. Therefore, a local guide is strongly recommended, as is a four-wheel drive vehicle or off-road motorbike. You do need to be properly prepared for such a trip, with adequate supplies of food, water and spares for your vehicle (and the ability to fix it if necessary).

This being limestone steppe as opposed to true sand desert, the ground is generally firm, although you should not attempt the journey after rain

Euphrates River & the Jezira

The Euphrates dam and Lake Assad

Work began on the construction of a dam across the Euphrates River in 1963 and 10 years later it became operational. It represents the most ambitious construction project ever undertaken in Syria and is, at least officially, a great source of national pride. To quote the project's own publicity material: "Since 5th July 1973 when [the] old course of the river closed and the water was diverted to pass through the hydro-electric station, the farmer in the Wadi al-Furat slept comfortably (sic), not worried about his land being flooded. This brutal feudalism fell for ever and the glorious rovolution (sic), March Revolution, and the arms of the workers, the builders of the great dam, are belessed (sic) for good."

The dam itself is certainly a remarkable piece of engineering. Measuring no less than 4,500 m in length and 500 m wide at its base, it is filled with some 41 million m^3 of sand and gravel. Lake Assad, created by the dam, measures around 80 km in length, with an average width of 8 km and an estimated volume of 11.9 billion cu m of water.

The main objectives of the project were to meet Syria's growing demand for electricity through hydroelectric generation, to provide irrigation water with which to reclaim vast areas of the desert for cultivation and to regulate the flow of the Euphrates and so control flooding. It was also seen as a way of developing a large pool of skilled engineers and technicians within the country for future projects. The hydroelectric installation, consisting of eight massive turbines and spillways, was projected to be able to generate a total of 1.1 million kilowatts of electricity at full capacity. The irrigation waters from the lake, meanwhile, aimed ultimately to bring a total of 640,000 ha of desert into cultivation in six areas (Balikh basin, Euphrates valley, Lower Khabur, Rasafeh, West Meskene plain and Mayadin plain).

However, obtaining accurate information as to the extent to which the project has met its objectives is more difficult. Certainly, its successes have been considerable, and unlike other major dam projects, its negative environmental impacts have been relatively limited. The main setback has been the building of the Ataturk dam in Turkey, which has significantly reduced the flow of the Euphrates through Syria, diminishing both the hydroelectric power generating capacity and the irrigation potential of Syria's Euphrates dam. A second major dam was completed at Birecik in 2000 as part of an overall programme of dam building in Turkey which Syria fears will ultimately halve the flow of the Euphrates through Syria and render its dam all but redundant. The fate of a third dam at Ilisa, representing the next stage of Turkey's programme, currently hangs in the balance after Britain made its promised £200 of financial support conditional on Turkey first reaching an agreement with Syria and Iraq on the issue. Syria claims that Turkey has failed to honour water sharing agreements reached between the two countries and has broken international laws relating to 'international rivers' such as the Euphrates. As relations between the two countries have become increasingly strained, Syria has started to accuse Turkey of manipulating the Euphrates waters issue in order to apply political and economic pressure on Syria.

Ath Thawra Dam, Lake Assad and Qalat Jaber

Colour map 1, grid B4 From the turning off the Euphrates Highway it is 10 km to the start of the dam, passing through **Ath Thawra** en route, a rather anodine town of wide streets, gardens and modern apartment blocks. Ask directions through the town to reach the dam as it is somewhat confusing. There is a covered viewing area from which you can look out over the dam itself, which is a truly awesome construction (see box), with a road running across the top of it.

Once you have crossed to the north side of the dam, follow the road for just **Qalat Jaber**
under 3 km and take the left turn signposted for Qalat Jaber. The castle is a further 14 km from the turning. Standing on a promontory now lapped by the
waters of Lake Assad and reached by a narrow causeway, the first views of Qalat
Jaber as one approaches are extremely impressive. Indeed, you could argue that
it is the vast expanse of Lake Assad rather than the castle that is the real attraction.
Some local fishermen supplement their income by taking tourists out on the
lake, and there are numerous excellent picnic spots along its shores.

Before the creation of the lake, the castle guarded an important crossing
point on the Euphrates. During the 11th century it was controlled by the local
Beni Numeir tribe before falling to the Seljuq sultan, Malik Shah in 1087. Early
in the 12th century it fell to the Crusaders and came under the control of the
Count of Edessa. Zengi, the ruler of Aleppo, having occupied Edessa in 1144,
was assassinated while laying siege to the castle in 1146. Three years later, however, it fell to his son Nur ud-Din, who later carried out extensive rebuilding
work. It remained in Ayyubid hands until the Mongol invasions of the 13th
century, after which it was abandoned, except for a brief period of occupation
by the Mamelukes. The walls are perhaps the most impressive feature of the
castle. They have been extensively restored, in places quite subtly, but elsewhere with somewhat incongruous modern bricks. Enough of the original
brickwork (consisting of small red bricks, typically Mesopotamian in style)
survives to give a good idea of how it would have looked originally. Entered via
a long sloping ramp and monumental gateway, the inside of the castle is largely
in ruins and little has been excavated. In the centre there is a large brick minaret (all that survives of the mosque) and the foundations of various buildings.
The main attraction, though, is undoubtedly the spectacular views out over
Lake Assad. ■ *Open 0900-1800 in summer, 0900-1600 in winter, closed Tue.
Entry S£300 (students S£15).*

There are regular microbus services between Raqqa and Ath Thawra (45 mins-1 hr), **Transport**
and less regular services to and from Aleppo. However, there are no services to Qalat
Jaber itself; either negotiate a ride with a taxi driver in Ath Thawra, or try hitching
(there is much more traffic on Fri, when many families head out there for a picnic).
Bear in mind that services between Ath Thawra and Raqqa tail off towards nightfall.

Raqqa to Deir ez-Zor

Halabiye occupies a strategic position on the Euphrates where it narrows as it **Halabiye**
passes through a gorge, allowing for the more effective control of the commercial **& Zalabiye**
river traffic plying it. The site was fortified by Queen Zenobia when Palmyra was *Colour map 1, grid B6*
at the height of its power and challenging even the might of the Roman Empire,
and later refortified by Diocletian after he had occupied Palmyra in 273 AD. The
remains you can see today date from the sixth century AD, when the emperor
Justinian greatly expanded and again refortified the site as one of the frontier
posts forming a line of defences against the Sassanid Persian threat. Like all the
Byzantine positions along the eastern frontier, it did eventually fall to the
Sassanids, and after the Arab conquest was largely abandoned.

Ins and outs The turning left (north) off the highway to reach these sites is clearly signposted (for 'Halapiye' and 'Zalapiye') in the tiny village of Shiha, 84 km from the Raqqa
exit (if you arrive in Tibni you have gone too far). If you are coming from Deir ez-Zor, it is
44 km to Tibni and then a further 4 km to the village of Shiha and the turning. Once you
have turned off the main highway, the narrow road joins the river and follows it, passing
through a small village before arriving at the ruins of Halabiye on the left after 9 km.

Euphrates River & the Jezira

To reach the site of Zalabiye, cross the river on the rickety wooden bridge to the north of Halabiye and follow the road which doubles back southwards and climbs up past Zalabiye railway station. Approximately 1 km beyond the station, branch right on a rough track and cross over the railway line to arrive at the ruins (in all just under 6 km from Halabiye).

Any public transport running along the Euphrates Highway between Deir ez-Zor and Raqqa/Aleppo can drop you off at the turning in the tiny village of Shiha, but from there you have to be prepared to walk or hitch the remaining 9 km. There is a shop by the turning selling cold drinks; a sign on the wall reads 'Welcome You'. The trains passing through Zalabiye station all do so at inconvenient hours of the night, and anyway you are still a 6-km walk from Halabiye, the more interesting of the two sites.

Sights The most impressive feature of **Halabiye** is the **walls**. Those facing the river have for the most part been eroded away, but to the north and south, rising up the hillside, are two lines of well preserved walls that meet in an apex at the top of the hill, where the main citadel is located. Built of the same crystalline gypsum as found at Rasafeh, the walls are marked by large bastions placed at regular intervals. Three-quarters of the way up the north wall, one of the bastions has been extended to accommodate a large building, the **praetorium** or imperial barracks. It is a steep climb up to the **citadel** at the top of the hill, but the views out over the Euphrates once you get there are well worth the effort. Of the town which existed within the walls, only the outlines of some of the buildings can be made out, including two churches and a forum occupying the central area.

On the opposite bank of the river, **Zalabiye** was the twin fortification of Halabiye. Very little remains to be seen here, due in part to its position on the outside edge of a bend in the river, which has over the centuries undercut the riverside walls and swept them away. The views out over the river as it sweeps past in a wide curve are nevertheless impressive.

Deir ez-Zor دير الزور

Phone code: 051
Colour map 2, grid B1

Spread along the southern banks of the Euphrates, Deir ez-Zor stands at an important crossroads. Two major routes intersect here: the Euphrates Highway running between Aleppo and the Iraqi border at Abu Kamal, and the desert route from Damascus through Palmyra and on to Hassakeh and Qamishle in the northeast of the country. Its importance as a transport hub has more recently been complemented by the discovery of extensive oilfields nearby. As a result, Deir ez-Zor has rapidly increased in size, and today is a thriving, prosperous town. Although there is little to see (with the exception of the new museum), it is a pleasant and convenient place to break one's journey if coming from or heading to Palmyra, and the most practical base for visits to the various sites along the banks of the Euphrates to the north-west and southeast.

Ins & outs
See also page 383 for more details

Getting there There are good transport links by road with the rest of the country. The new luxury coach station ('Garagat al-Jdaide') is situated a little over 1 km to the south of the centre (a longish walk or short taxi ride). If you want to walk into town, turn right onto the main road and then first left after around 100 m. Keep following this road (8th Azar St) into the centre of town. On the way, you pass the bus/microbus station, which covers local destinations, and some further afield. Deir ez-Zor's airport was closed at the time of writing. The train station is inconveniently located, and train times of little use in any case.

Euphrates River & the Jezira

Getting around Aside from the luxury coach station and train station, everything in Deir ez-Zor is within easy reach on foot. Taxis are readily available should you want one. The **tourist information** office is down a small side street off Khalid Bin Walid St (heading east, take the first right turn after the turning with the entrance to the *Al Jamia al-Arabia* hotel and it is less than 100 m down on the right). They have a photostat map of the town in English and a few of the usual handouts. There is also an office at the luxury coach station, though it is seemingly permanently closed.

Sights

Museum Opened in 1996 this excellent museum is the result of extensive collaboration with, and funding from, Germany. For those who were disappointed by the quality of the presentation (if not the subject matter) at Damascus and Aleppo museums, this museum will come as a welcome surprise, and is definitely worth a visit. Adopting a modern format that incorporates reconstructions and clear, informative explanations, the fascinating and often strikingly beautiful exhibits are truly brought to life.

There are four main sections to the museum, covering prehistory, ancient Syria, the classical periods and Arab-Islamic/popular traditions. It is the first two, and to a lesser extent the third sections, which are the most impressive. The Jezira has proved to be a treasure trove for archaeologists; and the region, which is littered with *tells* marking prehistoric and ancient settlements, is still very much a focus for archaeological research. The museum brings together some of the most fascinating (and most recent) finds from the region, and is successful in drawing together in a dynamic, coherent manner the historical phases and cultural developments at the various sites, as well as the way in which they relate to each other, and to the wider history of the region. ■ *Open 0900-1800 in summer, 0900-1600 in winter, closed Tue. Entry S£300 (students S£15).*

Deir ez-Zor

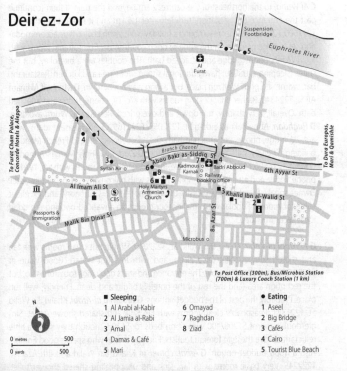

Euphrates River & the Jezira

■ Sleeping		● Eating
1 Al Arabi al-Kabir	6 Omayad	1 Aseel
2 Al Jamia al-Rabi	7 Raghdan	2 Big Bridge
3 Amal	8 Ziad	3 Cafés
4 Damas & Café		4 Cairo
5 Mari		5 Tourist Blue Beach

Holy Martyrs Armenian Church Built in 1990, this church has a quiet, understated beauty about it. Steps lead up from the street into a peaceful courtyard. Inside the main chapel, a central cross-topped pillar rises up from a lower ground level where the bones of those who died in the Armenian genocide are preserved around the base. Windows in the dome of the chapel allow the sunlight to play on the cross, contrasting with the semi-darkness below. ■ *If the church is closed, ring on the bell and someone will open it up for you.*

Euphrates River On arriving in Deir ez-Zor, you may be forgiven for mistaking the small, disappointing branch channel which runs through the town for the Euphrates itself. A walk across the bridge from the central square brings you to the suspension footbridge which spans the actual river. More than 1 km wide at this point, it is altogether a far more impressive sight! In the late afternoon and early evening the bridge throngs with people out strolling and enjoying the views; at sunset the river is at its most beautiful. While the restaurants on the south bank of the river are perhaps best avoided (see below), the gardens and café on the far side make for a nice spot from which to enjoy the river.

Sleeping
■ *on map*
Price codes:
see inside front cover

L *Furat Cham Palace*, to northwest of centre, on main road into town, PO Box 219, T225418, F222672. Suitably comfortable rooms with a/c, TV/dish, IDD, mini-bar and attached bath. Restaurants, café, bar, banquet/conference facilities. Swimming pool, fitness centre (gym, sauna, massage), tennis, squash. Shops, currency exchange, car hire (*Hertz/Chamcar*). Used mostly by staff from nearby oilfields and organized tour groups. Beautiful location on the banks of the Euphrates, but a long way from the museum (3 km) and centre of town (4½ km).

C *Al Waha*, to the northeast of the centre, 2 km beyond the train station (continue past the entrance to the station, turn left after 1½ km and it is 400 m further on), T221500, F221001. Rather resembling a holiday camp, with chalet-type accommodation set in large gardens on the edge of open countryside. Comfortable rooms with a/c, TV/dish, phone, fridge and attached bath. The doubles are a bit pokey, but the suites (sleeping 4; US$80) have additional sitting room area and kitchen. Restaurant, bar, swimming pool. Well run place, but a long way out of town. **D** *Mari*, off Al Imam Ali St, T224340. Rather unappealing rooms with a/c, TV, phone, fridge and attached bath. Overall, very shabby, run-down and overpriced. Restaurant. Worth avoiding. **D** *Raghdan*, Abou Bakr as-Siddiq St, T222053, F221169. Clean, pleasant rooms with a/c, TV, fridge, phone and attached bath. Breakfast served. Big old French Mandate building. Friendly staff and fairly good value. **D** *Ziad*, near Holy Martyrs Armenian Church, T214596, F211923. Comfortable, immaculately clean rooms with a/c, TV/dish, phone, fridge and attached bath. Some rooms with balcony. Well run, friendly hotel. Owner speaks fluent German. Easily the best hotel in this category, and excellent value for money. Popular with smaller tour groups so advanced booking is a good idea. Recommended.

G *Al Arabi al-Kabir*, Khalid Bin Walid St, T222070. Simple but clean rooms with fan and shared shower/toilet (also clean, and with free hot water). Good value at S£200/300 for a single/double. The entrance and stairs don't look too promising, but the reception area (and the rest of the hotel) is bright and clean. Friendly, well run place. Probably the best of the budget options. **G** *Al Jamia al-Arabi*, Khalid Bin Walid St, T221371. Reasonably clean rooms with fan, sink and shared shower/toilet. Single/double rooms S£200/400, also dorm beds for S£100, though they seem a little reluctant to give these to foreign tourists. Friendly owner who speaks good English. Also a good budget option. **G** *Amal*, corner of Khalid Bin Walid and 8th Azar St, T222245. Very basic rooms with fan, sink and unappealing shared shower/toilet.

Cheap (double S£250, dorm beds S£100), but all in all very grotty and noisy. **G** *Damas*, corner of Abou Bakr as-Siddiq and 8th Azar St, T221481. Very basic rooms with fan and shared shower/toilet. Dirt cheap at S£100-125 for a dorm bed, or S£250 for a double, but very unappealing, and all the more so for the persistent reports from women of harassment by owner. Women in particular are advised to give this place a miss. **G** *Omayad* (sign outside just says 'hotel' in English), off Al Imam Ali St, T221220. Nice old building, but rather shabby rooms with fan, sink and unappealing shared shower/toilet. Not particularly good value at S£250/400 for a single/double.

The *Furat Cham Palace* hotel has 2 upmarket restaurants, *La Louisiana Steak House*, offering supposedly American fare, and the **Four Seasons**, offering an à la carte menu of Arabic and European cuisine. With the hotel often completely empty, however, these can be somewhat cheerless places to eat.

To the left and right of the suspension footbridge on the south side of the Euphrates are the *Bridge* and **Tourist Blue Beach** restaurants respectively. Although pleasantly located overlooking the river, they both charge inflated tourist prices for distinctly mediocre Arabic food (around S£300 per head upwards), particularly the latter. Likewise for the *Aseel* and *Cairo* restaurants, both on Abou Bakr as-Siddiq St, overlooking the branch channel of the Euphrates. Better quality is the **Nadi Mohandiseen**, on the north side of the Euphrates, more or less directly opposite the *Tourist Blue Beach* (cross by the suspension footbridge and turn right just past the sports stadium and mini-funfair), T220469. There is seating in the large hall or out on a pleasant garden terrace overlooking the river. A good meal of Arabic food will come to around S£300 per head here. All of these places serve alcohol.

Along Khalid Bin Walid St, to the east of the main square, there are several cheap eateries serving the usual roast chicken, kebabs, hummus, falafel etc. The *Ugarit*, just past the *Al Jamia al-Arabia* hotel is one of the better ones. Heading north towards the bridge along 8th Azar St, there are couple of good falafel, hummus and fuul places.

A nice place to enjoy a cup of tea or cold drink is in the large café/garden on the north bank of the Euphrates (cross the suspension footbridge and turn left). The cavernous tea house beneath the *Damas* hotel is a popular place with locals; there are usually tables out on the street where you can watch the world go by. There are a number of similar places to the west, along Abou Bakr as-Siddiq St, and along Khalid Bin Walid/Ali Imam streets.

The **swimming** pool at the *Furat Cham Palace* hotel is open to non-guests for a daily fee of S£200 (children S£100). There are also **squash** and **tennis** courts (both S£200 per game) here, while use of the **gym** and **sauna** costs S£250 per person, and a **massage** costs S£300.

Air The *Syrian Air* ticket office (T221801, open 0830-1230, closed Fri) is on a small side street to the north of the bank (see map). The airport is 7 km to the southeast of the town centre, on the road to the Iraqi border. At the time of writing, the airport was closed for repairs, and no one seemed very sure as to when it would reopen.

Road Although all the luxury coaches go from the new **luxury coach station** to the south of the town centre, *Kadmous* and *Karnak* have additional ticket offices in the centre of town, next door to each other on one side of the same covered complex which houses the railway booking office. *Kadmous*, T212921, offers the most frequent services. **Damascus (via Palmyra)**, 0700, 0900, 1000, 1100, 1200, 1415, 1500, 1700, S£175, 5 hrs (Palmyra S£85, 2 hrs). **Qamishle (via Hassakeh)**, 1445, 1630, 1730, 1830, 1845, 2015, 2430, S£110, 3½ hrs (Hassakeh S£75, 2¼ hrs; if you want to go in the morning, go by microbus). **Aleppo (via Raqqqa)**, 0500, 0630, 0800, 0900, 1030, 1200, 1530, 1700, 1800, 1900, S£135, 5 hrs (Raqqa S£60, 2 hrs). *Karnak*, T218200, has a more limited timetable but is slightly cheaper. **Damascus (via Palmyra)**, 0800, 1000, 1500, S£150 (Palmrya S£75). **Qamishle (via Hassakeh)**, 1600, S£100 (Hassakeh S£65). There are a few other companies offering services to these destinations.

The **bus/microbus station** on 8th Azar St is mostly for microbuses, though there are still a few old 'hob-hob' buses operating from here. There are no fixed timetables, with services simply departing when full. **Mayadin**, S£25. **Abou Kamal**, S£50. **Raqqa**, S£60. **Aleppo**, S£135. **Palmyra**, S£75. **Hassakeh**, S£75.

Train The railway booking office (T222406) is in the centre of town, in the covered complex just west of the main square. The station itself is a little under 3 km to the northeast of the town and best reached by taxi. To walk there, cross the suspension footbridge, and then turn right when you reach a T-junction. The daily train to **Aleppo** passes through at 0130 (2nd class S£60, 1st class S£90, sleeper S£225). The daily train to **Qamishle (via Hassakeh)** passes through at 0400, in theory at least, though delays are common (1st/2nd class S£60/40; Hassakeh S£40/30).

Directory **Banks** The *Commercial Bank of Syria* is on Al Imam Ali St. Open 0800-1400, closed Fri. Cash and TCs can be changed here. The *Furat Cham Palace* can change cash and TCs at any time of the day or night (at the official bank rate). **Communications** The **post office** is on 8th Azar St, near the bus/microbus station. Open 0800-2000, closed Fri. The **telephone office** is on Al Imam Ali St, west of the main square. Open 0800-2200, daily. Phonecards (the old STE variety) are sold here, while the cardphones are around the side from the main entrance. This used to be where the post office was located and a counter for stamps is open 0800-1400, closed Fri. **Medical services** The best hospital in Deir ez-Zor is the private *Badri Abboud*, on Abou Bakr as-Siddiq St (next door to the *Raghdan* hotel, T221341, F228407. The Shell and Elf oil companies have a special contract with the hospital for their expatriate workers and so there are a couple of doctors here who speak good English. In an emergency they will also admit patients to their intensive care unit, which includes an operating theatre etc. **Visa extensions** The passport and immigration office is on Malik Bin Dinar St. Open 0800-1400, closed Fri.

Southeast to the Iraqi Border

Mayadin &
Qalat al-Rabha
Colour map 2, grid C1

From Deir ez-Zor, the Euphrates Highway continues southeast down to the Iraqi border at Abu Kamal. After 44 km you come to a big roundabout and fork leading off to the left to the small town of Mayadin on the banks of the Euphrates, 2 km from the main road. There are two pleasant tea shops here, on the banks of the river which flows past, broad and powerful at this point.

Near the town, and clearly visible from the Euphrates Highway, are the ruins of Qalat al-Rabha. From the fork for Mayadin, continue southeast along the main road for 1½ km to a crossroads and turn right (signposted) towards the castle (left to Mayadin). After 1½ km, turn left and follow this road for a further 1½ km to reach the castle. The ruins stand on the edge of the desert plateau which stretches away to the southwest. What remains to be seen today dates largely from the reign of Nur ud-Din (1146-1174), who built a castle here on the foundations of an earlier Abbasid fortification as part of his attempts to unite Syria into a single cohesive Arab Muslim Empire. The castle is in an advanced state of dilapidation, although impressive from a distance and with plenty of underground chambers and passages to explore inside (for which a torch is essential).

Mayadin to
Dura Europos

The next stretch of the Euphrates Highway passes through farmland and an almost continual string of villages and settlements. The largest of these is **Al Ashara** (23 km from the turning for Qalat ar-Rabha), where there are shops and a couple of simple restaurants. After passing through the village of Tishreen (14 km further on), the road climbs up onto a desolate and forbidding plateau, from where there are occasional glimpses of the Euphrates. Off to the left of the road, the western walls of Dura Europos gradually come into view, and soon you come to a metalled access road leading to the site just over 1 km from the main road. The turning is 46 km from the Mayadin junction and 90 km from Deir ez-Zor.

Dura Europos الصالحية

The ancient city of Dura Europos occupies a section of plateau directly over-looking the Euphrates River to the east and bounded to the north and south by deep ravines. Only on its western flank is it exposed to the desert, and it is along this side that the city's most substantial defensive walls were built. Most remarkable from an archaeological point of view are the frescos discovered here, and the unique insight these have provided into Judaic and early Christian art. Today the site is a dramatic one to visit for its setting overlooking the Euphrates, but all the most important treasures are now housed in museums around the world (most notably the frescos from the synagogue, now in the National Museum at Damascus).

Colour map 2, grid C2

Although its history appears to go back even further (*Dura* is an Aramaic word meaning 'fortress'), the city as we know it is of Hellenistic origin, founded during the reign of **Seleucus I Nicator** by one of his generals named Nicanor around 300 BC (the *Europos* was added at this time, after the name of the birth-place of Seleucus in Macedonia). Once again, its role was to protect and control trade along the Euphrates, as well as forming part of a defensive chain of military/caravan towns strung out along the northern and eastern borders of the Seleucid Empire, including also Edessa (present-day Urfa in Turkey), Nisibin (present-day Nusaybin, just across the border from Qamishle) and Seleucea-on-the-Tigris (southern Iraq). Planned on an ambitious scale and containing within it a fully fledged city laid out in traditional Hellenistic grid pattern, its position soon became precarious with the steady westward advance of the Parthians.

History

Eventually, as the Seleucid Empire declined, whether by assault or accommodation, Dura Europos became in effect a **Parthian** city sometime around the first century BC and thus began to absorb many eastern influences. With the Roman conquest of Syria in 64 BC, the city found itself in a delicate position at the contact point between the Parthian and Roman empires. Given the importance of the Euphrates River as a trade route to both powers, an uneasy truce was maintained for the best part of two centuries and Dura Europos was able to flourish alongside Palmyra (though always to a certain extent eclipsed by it) as a trading city. In 115 AD the Roman emperor **Trajan** occupied Dura Europos in his attempts to extend the Roman Empire beyond the Euphrates. Despite his initial successes, he was soon forced into retreat and died in Turkey on his way back to Europe. His successor, **Hadrian**, allowed Dura to return to Parthian control and reverted to a policy of non-interference.

In 164 AD Lucius Verus, the co-emperor alongside Marcus Aurelius, again occupied the city and by 211 it had been formally declared a Roman colony by **Septimius Severus** who established a permanent garrison there. The Romans built temples, baths and other public buildings while steadily increasing the size of the garrison in response to the growing threat from the newly emergent **Sassanid Persians** who were replacing the Parthians as the major power in the east. Despite its military importance to the Romans, and its continuing close ties with Palmyra, its importance as a commercial city was by this time steadily declining because of the Sassanid threat. Finally, in 256 it fell to the Sassanid

Euphrates River & the Jezira

king **Shapur I**, who sacked the city. It was subsequently briefly occupied by the **Palmyrenes**, but during the Byzantine period was left abandoned in favour of other sites such as Rasafeh and Halabiye/Zalabiye.

The site was first **'rediscovered'** in 1920, when a British expeditionary force took refuge there and uncovered a fresco in one of the ruined buildings. Systematic excavations were then carried out by the Americans and French in the 1920s and 1930s. Ironically, the final frantic attempts of the Roman garrison to defend Dura Europos against the Sassanids were directly responsible for preserving the frescos for which it is so famous. In order to reinforce the western wall the Romans built a makeshift embankment against it from the inside, burying many of the buildings along its line in the process, including the synagogue, and so protecting its frescos from the elements. A joint Syrian-French team has been carrying out restoration work on the site in recent years.

Sights

There are no refreshments or toilet facilities here. Take adequate protection against the sun and a plentiful supply of water

The approach road brings you to the main **Palmyra Gate**. Set between two solid bastions linked by a passageway over the inner arch, the gateway is functional and imposing. It is thought to date from around 17 BC, when the Parthians began strengthening the original Seleucid walls. The **walls** represent a combination of the original Seleucid work consisting of stone surmounted by mud-brick, and the later Parthian work which is entirely in stone. In places they stand up to 9 m high, with the regularly spaced towers for the most part still surviving. At the time of writing, the entrance to the site was through the small subsidiary gate to the right (south) of the Palmyra Gate (now restored but still closed). Entering by this subsidiary gate, the **Christian chapel** is just to your right, one of its walls recently reconstructed in stone after collapsing. Converted from a private house around 240 AD, it represents the earliest known example of a Christian place of worship in Syria. Murals depicting scenes of Adam and Eve, a shepherd tending his flock and various miracles were uncovered here and are now displayed in the Yale University Art Gallery. Further to the south was the **temple of Zeus Kyrios**. To the north of the Palmyra Gate, amongst a cluster of ruins close to the walls that included also the **temple of Adonis**, is the site of the **synagogue**.

The main path running eastwards from the Palmyra Gate follows the line of the **decumanus**, or main east-west thoroughfare of the Seleucid city. You pass first a heavily ruined **baths complex** on the right. After about 300 m, on the left are the jumbled and indistinct remains of the Seleucid **agora**, covered in Parthian times with a more chaotic bazaar. A little further on, just to the right of the path, are the remains of the **temple of the Gaddé**. One block further to the south is the site of the **temple of Atargatis**, and next to it the **temple of Artemis**. Just to the southeast of this is a restored **theatron** (minature theatre), with nine tiers of seating arranged in an oval. Continuing along the main path, just after the temple of Gaddé, you pass through the remains of a **monumental gateway** before descending into a wadi. Across the wadi, on the hillside to the right, are the remains of what is generally

Dura Europos

Euphrates River

Palace of the Dux Ripae

Temple of Bel
Temple of Azzanathkona
Praetorium
Mithraeum

Main Citadel & Palace

Strategion Palace

Agora
Synagogue
Temple of Adonis

Temple of the Gaddé

Temple of Atargatis
Temple of Artemis

Palmyra Gate

Baths Complex
Christian Chapel

Temporary Entrance

Theatron

Temple of Zeus Kyrios

To Highway

N

0 metres (approx) 20
0 yards (approx) 200

The cultural and religious development of Dura Europos

The Seleucids founded Dura Europos as a Hellenistic city, settling it with Macedonian soldiers from Alexander the Great's campaigns and giving them land to farm in surrounding areas. They formed the ruling class and brought with them their own institutions, including Greek as the official language. However, it also incorporated a significant indigenous Aramaean population, and with it the influences of the numerous different cultures – Iranian, Indian, Babylonian, Mesopotamian, western Semitic, Arabic, Anatolian – which had previously existed within the vast and loosely defined realms of the Persian empire.

Following its absorption into the Parthian empire, it retained a substantial degree of autonomy. Greek continued to be used as the official language, while the descendants of the original Macedonian settlers remained in place as the local ruling class, maintaining Seleucid forms of civic administration and law. However, under this Hellenistic veneer, oriental Parthian influences increasingly made themselves felt. The local Aramaean population grew in size, the Macedonians intermarried, and all the time the city was open to Parthian influence from the outside. The overall result was a startlingly diverse society where different traditions and influences co-existed and merged.

The complex religious life of the city demonstrates this best. The earliest temple at Dura Europos was dedicated to the Greek goddess Artemis, who continued to be worshipped in her Greek form throughout the city's history, although the layout of the temple itself underwent several transformations. In 31 AD a temple dedicated to the Mesopotamian goddess Atargatis was established alongside the Artemis temple, reflecting the growing Parthian influence (the Parthians had shortly before reclaimed the city from the Romans following Trajan's brief occupation). Possibly around the same time a third temple, dedicated to a local goddess, Azzanathkona, was established (found only at Dura Europos, Azzanathkona was clearly in the Syrian mother-goddess tradition and appears to have become identified with Artemis). These three goddesses, one Greek, one Mesopotamian and one purely local, dominated the city's religious life and neatly characterized the major influences at work at the time. In addition, the Palmyrene influence was strong, with the Palmyrene trinity of Bel, Yarhibol and Aglibol all represented in Dura Europos, along with a temple dedicated to the Gaddé, or Fortunes.

When the city came under lasting Roman control during the 2nd century AD, the Roman garrison occupied the northern part of the city, keeping itself largely separate from the main focus of settlement around the central agora. While the soldiers were required to worship the official Roman pantheon (which was soon represented through a number of temples), the local population were allowed to continue in their own varied forms of worship. Interestingly, well before Christianity became officially recognized, small Christian communities were allowed to develop, establishing their own places of worship in converted houses. The Jewish community, meanwhile, developed its own unique art forms, depicting human figures in direct contravention of Talmudic injunctions.

referred to as the **strategion palace**. Dating from the original Seleucid founding of the city, this is thought to have acted either as the residence of the *strategos* or chief magistrate, or else to have been the city's original citadel. Its façade has been rebuilt by French and Syrian architects using local stone and traditional stonecutting techniques. Beside the strategion palace is a reconstruction showing what a typical house at Dura Europos is thought to have looked like. From the wadi you can ascend to the **main citadel and palace**, which occupies a long ridge of high ground directly overlooking the

Euphrates. Dating from the later Seleucid period (early second century BC), only the western face still survives, the rest of it having been undercut and swept away by the Euphrates over the centuries. Although little remains, it is worth climbing up to for the views it gives out over the Euphrates.

In the northern section of the city there are further remains, mostly relating to the Roman military camp which was established in this area in the second century AD. All the ruins are discernible in outline only. To the northwest of the main citadel and palace, also overlooking the Euphrates, is the **palace of the Dux Ripae** (literally the 'palace of the commander of the river bank') which housed the Roman garrison commander and dates from the final period of Roman occupation in the third century. Against the north wall of the city is the **praetorium** or main barracks, also occupying the site of the **temple of Azzanathkona**. In the far northwest corner where the north and west walls meet is the **temple of Bel** (or temple of the Palmyrene Gods). This was the building first uncovered by the British expeditionary force, revealing the wall paintings which inspired further excavation work at Dura Europos. To the south of it, against the west wall, is a temple, or **mithraeum**, dedicated to the worship of *Mithras*, a cult of Persian origin which became popular amongst the Roman military. Other remains in the area include assorted barracks, baths and a small amphitheatre. ■ *Open daily 0900-1800 in summer, 0900-1600 in winter. Entry S£150 (students S£15).*

Transport Frequent **microbuses** run from Deir ez-Zor down to Abu Kamal on the Iraqi border; just ask to be dropped off at the Dura Europos turning (Tell Salihiye in Arabic). The site is just over 1 km from the main road, a manageable walk, though hot in summer. It is usually fairly easy to pick up transport on to Mari or back to Deir ez-Zor from the turning, although Fridays are not a good day.

Mari (Tell Hariri) تل الحريري

Colour map 2, grid C2 The low mound rising from the plain between the main road and the Euphrates looks unassuming enough as you approach it. Yet it was here in 1933 that the chance discovery by a Bedouin nomad of a fragment of statue led to the subsequent excavation of an archaeological site which, like Ebla and Ugarit, has proved to be of crucial importance to our understanding of the ancient history of Syria. However, despite its enormous archaeological significance, very little remains to be seen at Mari, and for most visitors it is not a place that fires the imagination. The Aleppo and Damascus museums (and also the Louvre in Paris) are where the most significant finds are now displayed. In addition, the excellent museum at Deir ez-Zor contains many beautiful artefacts from Mari as well as a reconstruction of part of the famous Zimri-Lim Palace.

Ins & outs **Getting there** From the turning for Dura Europos, the Euphrates Highway continues southeast, descending from the plateau and passing through two small villages, before arriving at the turning left for Mari (signposted) 400 m from the main road. The turning is 28 km from the Dura turn-off and 118 km from Deir ez-Zor.

History The earliest evidence of settlement so far discovered at Mari dates back as far as 4000 BC. However, it was during the **Early Syrian II** (or Early Dynastic) period (c 2900-2300 BC) that Mari rose to become a powerful independent city-state on the Euphrates. Its wealth depended both on the intensive cultivation of the surrounding land using irrigation water from the Euphrates, and widespread trading links. Excavations from this period have revealed large temples dedicated to the goddesses Ishtar, Ninni-Zaza, Ishtarat, Ninhursag and Dagan which were lavishly decorated and filled with statues, as well as a successively rebuilt palace/temple complex. Close relations existed with the city of Ebla, with which it was contemporary, their often conflicting interests being resolved through payments of gold and silver.

Following the rise to power of the **Akkadian** Empire founded by Sargon of Akkad around 2350 BC, Mari came for a while under its control and was somewhat eclipsed by it. With the break-up of the Akkadian Empire around 2200 BC, a period of unrest followed about which little is known. One local dynasty, that of the city of Ur in southern Mesopotamia, is known to have extended its control as far as Mari at one point. Sometime around 2000 BC, however, the arrival of the **Amorites** (a Semitic people who migrated from the south) saw a renewed period of prosperity and independence for Mari. An Amorite, Yaggid-Lim, founded the Lim Dynasty there and began work on the famous Zimri-Lim palace.

Undoubtedly the most significant find from the palace was an archive containing around 15,000 clay tablets inscribed in Akkadian (or Old Babylonian) cuneiform script. These have given us an unprecedented insight into the Lim Dynasty and the political, economic and social life of Mari under their reign. Agriculture was highly developed with complex irrigation systems which, as well as allowing intensive cultivation, appear also to have served as transport canals. The city raised revenues by taxing the long distance trade which passed through it between southern Mesopotamia, Anatolia and southern and western Syria. It also engaged in its own trade, most importantly in the raw materials for the production of bronze (tin from northwestern Iran and copper from Cyprus), but also wood, oils, wines and semi-precious stones. An inscription found on the foundation stone of the Shamash temple which was built by Yakhdun-Lim (the son of Yaggid-Lim) details his exploits in this respect: "...no other king residing in Mari had ever – since, in ancient days the gods built the city of Mari – reached the (Mediterranean) Sea, nor reached and felled timber in the great mountains, the Cedar Mountain and the Boxwood Mountain, he, Yakhdun-Lim, son of Yaggid-Lim, the powerful king, the wild bull among kings, did march to the shore of the sea, an unrivalled feat, and offered sacrifices to the Ocean as (befitting) his royal rank while his troops washed themselves in the Ocean..." (translation by AL Oppenheim).

The period of Amorite rule was also one of complex political relations. We know from the Mari archives that around 1800 BC Zimri-Lim (the grandson of Yaggid-Lim) was driven from Mari by Shamshi-Adad, another Amorite who was in effect the founder of the Assyrian Empire. Interestingly, Zimri-Lim took refuge in the kingdom of Yamkhad with its capital at Aleppo, indicating the importance of this power centre at the time. Following the death of Shamshi-Adad, Zimri-Lim was able to regain control of Mari around 1775 BC, allowing himself a brief but highly successful period of rule (it was during this period that he greatly extended the palace begun by his grandfather and richly decorated it, leading archaeologists to attribute it entirely to him initially). By around 1758 BC he was overthrown by Hammurabi, the ruler of Babylon, who was steadily expanding his empire across southern Mesopotamia and even into Assyria. Hammurabi largely destroyed Mari and afterwards it was abandoned, with the exception of brief periods of limited occupation centuries later in the Seleucid, Parthian and Sassanid periods.

Sights

From the tea shop and archaeologists' base, head northeast onto the *tell*, to arrive at the main covered area of excavations, representing the **Palace of Zimri-Lim**. Inside, you can wander around the complex (and confusing) network or rooms, corridors and courtyards which formed this huge palace (in all it consisted of 275 rooms spread across 2.5 ha). What you see is only the basic plan of the building (more like a reconstruction of First World War trench conditions according to one couple!), with all the murals which adorned it having been removed not to mention the numerous statues and treasures and the huge archive of clay tablets.

Outside, the other excavated remains of the city of Mari, covering an area of 60 ha, have largely been eroded away by the elements. To the east of the southeast corner of the covered excavations of the Palace of Zimri-Lim a high terrace marks the site of what has been identified by some as a **ziggurat**, which would make it a forerunner of the later Mesopotamian ziggurat (stepped tower) tradition. Clustered around it are the temple of Dagan, the temple of Shamash and the temple of Ninni-Zaza, all of them only barely discernible. This was also the site of a palace dating from the mid-3rd millennium BC (partly built over by the later Zimri-Lim palace). To the west of the southwest corner of the covered excavations is the **temple of Ishtar**, dating from around 2500 BC. ■ *Open daily, 0900-1800 in summer, 0900-1600 in winter. Entry S£150 (students S£10). There is a small, friendly tea shop by the archaeologists' base at the entrance to the site, with postcards etc on sale.*

Transport As for Dura Europos, microbuses running between Deir ez-Zor and Abu Kamal can drop you off at the turning for the site.

Abu Kamal It is a further 10 km to the small town of Abu Kamal (or Al Bukamal). There are a few cafés and simple restaurants in the centre of town, and even a small, very basic hotel. However, other than engaging in predictable conversations as to the rights and wrongs of the Gulf War with Iraqis living in the town, the only conceivable reason for coming here is to be able to boast that you have been to within 10 km or so of the Iraqi border.

The Jezira الجزيرة

Background

The climate of the Jezira is semi-arid, with long, dry and hot summers and cool, wet winters. Rainfall decreases to the southeast (where irrigation-based agriculture becomes the norm), but over the northern parts of the region it is sufficient to support rain-fed farming. The Khabur River, a tributary of the Euphrates, is formed by a number of streams that rise in the Taurus mountains of Turkey and join just north of Hassakeh before flowing south and draining into the Euphrates near Mayadin to the southeast of Deir ez-Zor. The various tributary streams of the Khabur to the north of Hassakeh form an area known as the 'Khabur triangle', the most fertile part of the Jezira.

The Jezira region is of enormous importance in archaeological terms, forming part of the 'Fertile Crescent', and ongoing archaeological research is beginning to reveal its central role in the early origins of settled agriculture. Sites such as Tell Brak and Tell Halaf (ancient Guzana) have already been extensively excavated, yet in all there are more than 250 such tells or artificial mounds. While increasing numbers are being excavated, the majority have yet to be explored. Many are partially built over with settlements, or have been used as graveyards, creating yet another layer of history to be excavated by some future generation.

Deir ez-Zor to Hassakeh

From the centre of Deir ez-Zor, head east along 6th Ayyar Street (following the branch channel of the Euphrates), and then turn left to cross over the Euphrates itself and join the main road to Hassakeh and Qamishle. After leaving behind the irrigated farmland of the Euphrates basin, the road heads northeast through desert before turning more northwards at the village of **Suar** (52 km from Deir ez-Zor, village centre off to the right from the main road, signposted for 'Tal Sheikh Hamad', amongst others).

Taking this turning, you can make a diversion to visit the archaeological site of Tell Sheikh Hamad, on the east bank of the Khabur River. After crossing the river, follow the road north for around 20 km to reach the site. The excavations carried out here have revealed it to be the ancient *Dur-Katlimmu*, a provincial capital of the **Middle Assyrian** Empire that emerged in the second half of the 14th century BC following the collapse of the Mittanian Empire. Administrative archives discovered here demonstrate that it exerted control over a sizeable area. A so-called 'Dark Age' followed the arrival of the '**Sea Peoples**' around 1200 BC, but during the ninth century BC the **Assyrian** Empire (in this period usually termed neo-Assyrian) rose to prominence once again. By the late eighth century BC Dur-Katlimmu had tripled in size, with 4 km of walls enclosing a town of around 100 ha. The citadel stood at the southeast corner overlooking the river (corresponding with the existing tell), while the town extended north along the banks of the river (parts of it are revealed in a series of excavated plots complete with mud-brick walls, paved floors, sections of a drainage system, a well and bread-baking oven).

Tell Sheikh Hamad

Continuing north from Suar along the main road, it follows the west bank of the Khabur River, passing through fertile agricultural land. At the village of **Al Husein**, 22 km from the turning for Suar, you can see Tell Sheikh Hamad across the river, along with another smaller *tell* nearby. Entering the village of **Marqadeh** (88 km from Deir ez-Zor and 13 km from Al Husein), there is a small Armenian chapel up on the hillside to the left of the road, dedicated to those massacred here during the genocide. Completed in 1996, it houses some of the bones of the dead. After another 43 km you pass a right turn for **Shahddadi**, and soon after the road swings north again (having curved northwest to follow the Khabur River), running parallel to the railway line between Deir ez-Zor and Hassakeh. Numerous tells can be seen dotted around the countryside. Finally you arrive in Hassakeh, 188 km from Deir ez-Zor and 100 km from Marqadeh.

Marqadeh

Euphrates River & the Jezira

Hassakeh الحسكة

Hassakeh is the largest town in the Jezira region and the capital of the Mouhafazat (Governorate) of the same name. Its main importance derives from its role as a market centre for agricultural produce from the surrounding countryside. There is nothing of special interest in the town, although it is a pleasant enough place to wander round and makes a convenient point at which to break the journey up to Qamishle to the north. At the time of writing, work was due to start shortly on a new museum in the southwest corner of town which will display the many artefacts uncovered at archaeological sites in the surrounding countryside. Work is also in progress on a new 5-star luxury hotel nearby, the *Al Jazira*, scheduled to open in 2002.

Phone code: 052
Colour map 2, grid A2

Ins & outs
See also 'Transport'
page 393

The main bus station ('Garagat Intilaqkh') is in the northwest corner of town, around 2 km from the centre (there are shuttle buses, or catch a taxi). It handles all the luxury coaches, buses and microbuses, except for some of the microbuses coming from Deir ez-Zor which stop at the south microbus station ('Garagat al-Janubi'), around 2 km to the south of the centre (again, there is a shuttle service into the centre. The train station is around 1 km to the northwest of the centre, at the east end of Al Mahatta St. Other than for getting to and from the bus stations, and perhaps the trains station, Hassakeh is small enough to wander around on foot.

The **tourist information** office (T313960) is hidden away up on the first floor of a complex on Fares al-Khoury St, near the roundabout and Assad statue. Open 0900-1400, closed Fri. A new office is planned for the near future, to be situated near the bridge and clock tower at the southern end of town. The manager speaks good English and is helpful.

Sleeping
D *Al Bustan*, T221721. Clean, comfortable rooms with a/c, fan, TV, phone, fridge, attached bath and balcony. Large restaurant downstairs. Quiet location in the grounds of the sports stadium. Currently the best hotel in Hassakeh, and good value.
D *Sanabel*, T314019. Clean but slightly tatty rooms with a/c, TV, phone, fridge and attached bath. Restaurant and bar upstairs. Doesn't quite live up to the standards

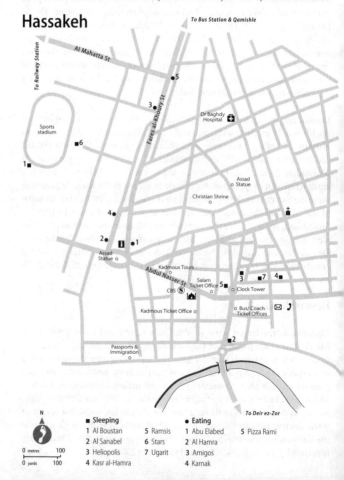

Hassakeh

Euphrates River & the Jezira

■ Sleeping
1 Al Boustan
2 Al Sanabel
3 Heliopolis
4 Kasr al-Hamra
5 Ramsis
6 Stars
7 Ugarit

● Eating
1 Abu Elabed
2 Al Hamra
3 Amigos
4 Karnak
5 Pizza Rami

0 metres 100
0 yards 100

suggested by the reception area, and rather expensive for what you get. **E** *Kasr al-Hamra* (only the word 'Hotel' appears in English on the sign), T316301. Clean rooms with fan, phone, sink and shared shower/toilet. OK, but way overpriced for what you get. **F/G** *Stars* ('Njoum'), T/F319299. Simple but reasonably clean rooms with fan and shared shower/toilet (double S£500). Better rooms downstairs with attached bath (double S£750). The main advantage of this hotel is its quiet, shady location in the grounds of the sports stadium. **F/G** *Ugarit*, T227000. Simple but clean rooms with fan, a/c, TV and fridge. Some rooms with attached bath (double S£550), others shared (double S£450). Very good value given that there is a/c, and way ahead of the **G** category hotels in terms of cleanliness. Recommended. **G** *Heliopolis* (sign outside reads 'Al Frsan Hotel', though now known as the *Heliopolis*), T220272. Very basic rooms (no fan) with shared shower/toilet. Single/double S£150/300. **G** *Ramsis*, T221026. Very basic and grotty rooms with fan, sink and shared toilet (no sign of showers). Single/double S£175/275.

Right by the Assad statue and roundabout, the *Al Hamra* (sign in Arabic only; also known as the Abu Ziad after the name of the owner) is the best restaurant in Hassakeh. It is clean and well run, with menus in English listing a range of mezze dishes and the usual kebabs etc. Highly recommended is the roast chicken, which is juicy and tasty, and comes with a delicious garlic and lemon sauce. They also serve fuul etc in the morning, and falafel and shawarma sandwiches during the evening. A few doors along is the *Karnak*, which has outdoor seating in a small garden and serves the usual kebabs, chicken, hummus etc, as well as alcohol. Across the road, the *Abou Elabed* (sign in Arabic only) is similar, and doubles as an ice cream parlour during the day. Further north along Fares al-Khoury St, on the left, *Amigos* is a modern, diner-style snack bar with neon lighting and satellite TV, offering burgers, pizzas, milkshakes etc (also serves alcohol). Further up, on the right, *Pizza Rami* is a tiny place which does good pizzas. At the southern end of Fares al-Khoury St, on the paved area in the middle, there are small kiosks and seats where you can enjoy a cold drink.

Eating
Most of the restaurants are concentrated along Fares al-Khoury St

The grounds of the sports stadium, where the *Stars* and *Al Bustan* hotels are located, also include the *Tishrin Swimming Pool*, complete with its own restaurant and bar (open during the summer only).

Sports

Road To get to the **main bus station** from the centre of town, walk north along Fares al-Khoury St from the Assad statue and turn left at the large roundabout; it is by the next roundabout you come to (around 2 km). Although all the **luxury coaches** depart from here, most of the companies have additional ticket offices in the centre of town. The *Kadmous* ticket office is off Abdul Nasser St (down the side street by the large mosque), T313698. It has the most frequent services to Aleppo and Damascus. *Salam* has its ticket office on Abdul Nasser St. Inside a covered arcade between the clock tower and the bridge there are ticket offices for *Zeitouni*, *Salam* and *Dijleh*. Between them, all these companies offer regular services to **Aleppo**, S£150, 5 hrs (some of these coaches go on to Hama, Homs and Damascus or Tartus); and **Damascus (via Deir ez-Zor and Palmyra)**, S£250, 8 hrs (Deir ez-Zor S£75, 1¼ hrs; Palmyra S£150-165, 4½ hrs). **NB** For Damascus, check that the coach is going via Deir ez-Zor and Palmyra, rather than via Aleppo, Hama and Homs, as this latter route is both more expensive (S£300) and considerably longer (10-11 hrs). There are also regular **microbus** services from here to all the surrounding towns and villages, including to **Qamishle** (S£35) and **Deir ez-Zor** (S£75); for Deir ez-Zor it is more convenient to go from here than from the south microbus station). The 'hob-hob' buses cover all the same destinations; they are even cheaper, but very slow as compared with the microbuses. Both the microbuses and 'hob-hob' buses operate on a 'depart when full' basis.

Transport

Euphrates River & the Jezira

Train To get to the train station from the centre of town, walk north along Fares al-Khoury St and turn left into Al Mahatta St; the station is at the end of this street. Booking office/info: T 221996. Services bound for **Aleppo** pass through at 2345 (2nd class S£100, 1st class S£130, Sleeper S£350). Services for **Qamishle** pass through at 0600 (2nd class S£15, 1st class S£21).

Directory **Banks** The main branch of the *Commercial Bank of Syria* is on Abdul Nasser St, west of the clock tower. It is open 0800-1230, closed Fri, and changes cash and TCs with a minimum of fuss. **Communications** The **post and telephone office** is on Abdul Nasser St, east of the clock tower. Open 0800-1400, closed Fri. STE phonecards can be purchased here and there are cardphones outside. **Medical services** There is a small, modern private hospital, the *Dr Baghdy*, on Al Khabour St, T320940. **Visa extensions** The passport and immigration office is on the street running west just north of the bridge over the Khabur River. Open 0800-1430, closed Fri.

Hassakeh to Qamishle

Colour map 2, grid A2 The route used by luxury coaches travelling between Hassakeh and Qamishle goes via Tell Mansour to join the highway linking Aleppo with the Jezira region. A quieter and somewhat more scenic route, however (and the one still used by buses and microbuses), goes via Tell Brak on the old Qamishle road. Head north out of Hassakeh and then fork right after 13 km (signposted for Tell Brak; straight on signposted for Amuda). It is a further 27 km to the village of Tell Brak; turn right at the roundabout in the village for 2 km to reach the tell itself, which is clearly visible from a distance.

Tell Brak This large tell was first excavated in 1937-39 by the British archaeologist Max Mallowan (Mallowan was married to Agatha Christie. She accompanied her husband on his research in the Jezira and wrote an entertaining account of their experiences together: *Come, Tell Us How You Live*). The site proved to be of pivotal importance in terms of the insight it gave into Bronze Age settlement in the area. Amongst the best known finds was the **Eye Temple**, dating from between 3100-2900 BC (Late Ubaid/Uruk to Early Syrian I Period), so called due to the discovery of large numbers of small, highly distinctive idols with oblong flat bodies and `heads' consisting of a large pair of eyes and eyebrows. Some of these are displayed in the new museum at Deir ez-Zor, or you can see them in Aleppo's museum. More recently, a later **Akkadian** palace and fortress was also discovered, dating from 2400-2300 BC, and also a 15th-16th-century BC **Mitannian** palace. A British team is currently carrying out further excavations. Aside from the numerous pottery shards scattered all over the site, there is little for the casual visitor to see. However, it does make a lovely picnic spot, with good views in all directions over the surrounding plains.

Tell Brak to Qamishle Returning to the main road and continuing north, after 36 km you arrive at a roundabout. Go straight over this (right for Yarobia on the Iraqi border, left for Aleppo 412 km) to arrive in the centre of Qamishle, 10 km further on.

Qamishle القامشلي

Phone code: 052 *Colour map 2, grid A2* Pressed right up against the Turkish border, Qamishle is a thriving town with an interesting mix of Kurds as well as various Christian denominations (Armenian, Syrian Orthodox, Syrian Catholic, Roman Catholic and Roman Orthodox) who together make up around half of the total population. There is nothing of special interest in the town, but it is a friendly place and makes a good base from which to visit Ain Diwar and Ras al-Ain. It also provides an alternative crossing point into Turkey, although the ongoing conflict between the PKK and Turkish government troops has made this part of Turkey a very sensitive area. You are advised to check the situation before attempting to cross the border here.

Ins & outs

The main bus station, around 2 km to the southeast of the town centre, handles all the luxury coaches, and the majority of buses and microbuses. The train station is a further 1 km or so to the southeast. Small yellow buses shuttle between the centre of town and the main bus station and the train station, or else a taxi for either of these journeys should not cost more than S£20-25. The airport is 3 km south of the town on the main road to Hassakeh.

Sleeping

E/F *Semiramis*, T421185. Large, reasonably pleasant old building. Clean rooms with fan, TV, phone, fridge and attached bath. Also some cheaper rooms with shared bath. **F** *Mamar*, T420428. Clean rooms with fan, fridge, attached shower (share toilet) and small balcony (single/double S£450/650). Also some rooms with a/c. Well run place, spotlessly clean throughout. Friendly manager (fluent Swedish, good English). Good value. Recommended. **G** *Chahba* (sign outside just says 'hotel'), T420874. Relatively clean but rather small and cell-like rooms with fan and shared shower/toilet (double S£200). Also some rooms with cooler units (double S£250). **G** *Omayad*, T420444. Basic rooms with fan, sink and shared shower/toilet (double S£270). Quieter rooms at rear.

Eating

Probably the most upmarket establishment is the cavernous *Gabrielle*, to the south-west of the town centre, opposite the microbus station. Despite billing itself as a 'res-taurant-pizzeria', the menu here appears to be exclusively Arabic, with the usual range of dishes on offer. Around S£250 per head upwards. Alcohol served. Next door is *Simoneeds*, a fast food place which does do pizzas, as well as burgers, shawarmas, chips etc. On Al Kouwatly St there is the simpler *Al-Batric Cafeteria*, which serves piz-zas, hamburgers, falafels etc.

There are several simple kebab/chicken restaurants on Al Wada al-Arabia St, all with names in Arabic only; the one on the right one block south of the junction with

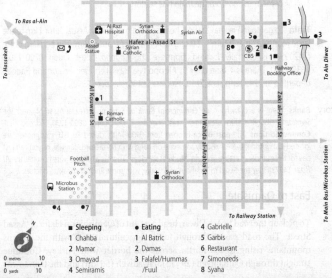

Qamishle

To Turkish Border
To Ras al-Ain
To Hassakeh
To Ain Diwar
To Main Bus/Microbus Station
To Railway Station

Al Razi Hospital
Syrian Orthodox
Syrian Air
Assad Statue
Hafez al-Assad St
Syrian Catholic
CBS
Railway Booking Office
Al Kouwatli St
Roman Catholic
Al Wahda al-Arabia St
Zaki al-Arsuzi St
Football Pitch
Microbus Station
Syrian Orthodox

0 metres   10
0 yards   10

■ **Sleeping**
1 Chahba
2 Mamar
3 Omayad
4 Semiramis

● **Eating**
1 Al Batric
2 Damas
3 Falafel/Hummus /Fuul
4 Gabrielle
5 Garbis
6 Restaurant
7 Simoneeds
8 Syaha

Euphrates River & the Jezira

Hafez al-Assad St stands out as being clean, and also has a menu in English. There are several similar places on Hafez al-Assad St, including the *Damas* and *Syaha*, as well as various falafel places (the small restaurant east of the bridge is very good for falafels hummus and fuul).

There are quite a few tea shops and cafés along Hafez al-Assad St and in the side streets off it, but note that the more upmarket ones such as *Garbis* charge up to 3 times the usual rate for tea and coffee.

Transport

Air The *Syrian Arab* airlines office (T420713, open daily 0800-1400) is in the centre of town, near the junction of Al Wahda St and Hafez al-Assad St.There are 3 flights weekly to **Damascus**, Tue, Fri, Sat, departing 0930 (S£902, 1 hr).

Road To get to the **main bus station** from the centre of town, head south along Zaki al-Arsuzi St, take the second available left turn and keep straight along this road for around 1½ km. The bus station is on the right, shortly after a crossroads. **Luxury coach** companies operating from here include Kadmous, Zeitouni, Damas Tour, Izla Tour, Harsho and Karnak. There are several departures for **Damascus (via Hassakeh, Deir ez-Zor and Palmyra)**, between around 0800-1200, and then more from around 2000, but nothing in-between. The fare is S£300 (Hassakeh S£35, Deir ez-Zor S£110, Palmyra S£200). The pattern of departures for **Aleppo** is similar (note that Aleppo-bound coaches take the direct desert road via Tell Amr and Membij, not via the Deir ez-Zor and the Euphrates Highway). The fare is S£175. Some of the Aleppo coaches continue on to Hama, Homs and Damascus, though for the latter, the coaches going via Palmyra are quicker and cheaper. In addition, there are lots of **microbuses** operating from here on a 'depart when full' basis to towns and villages in the area; eg **Hassakeh**, S£30; **Malkiyeh** (for Ain Diwar), S£35; **Derbassiyeh** (en route to Ras al-Ain), S£10; **Amuda**, S£10; **Tell Maruf**, S£15; **Tell Hamis**, S£15; **Tell Brak**, S£15.

There is also a **microbus station** to the southwest of the town centre (opposite the *Gabrielle* restaurant), with frequent departures to most of the destinations covered by the microbuses operating from the main bus station. There are also direct services to **Ras al-Ain** from here, though they are somewhat erratic; it may be easier to get a microbus as far as Derbassiyeh and then change there. Note that for microbuses to Malkiyeh you must go from the main bus station.

Train To get to the railway station, head south along Zaki al-Arsuzi St for 1 km to the large roundabout and turn left there; it is on the right after 2 km. The booking office (T420950) is centrally located, opposite the *Chabha* hotel. Open 0700-1300, 1630-1800. There is 1 train daily to **Aleppo** (via Hassakeh, Deir ez-Zor and Raqqa), departing at 2245 (2nd class S£90, 1st class S£135, sleeper S£350).

Directory

Banks There is a branch of the *Commercial Bank of Syria* on Hafez al-Assad St, near the *Semiramis* hotel which changes cash and TCs. Open 0800-1230, closed Fri. **Communications** The *post office* is open from 0900-1400, closed Fri. STE cardphones are located just outside; there is usually someone on hand with phonecards for sale, or you can just pay for the number of credits you use. **Medical services** There is a good private hospital, the *Al Razi*, T427303, by the Assad roundabout and statue, with some English-speaking doctors.

East of Qamishle

To pick up the road to Ain Diwar, head east out of Qamishle on Hafez al-Assad Street. The road passes through fertile agricultural land, with the Taurus mountains rising to the north, across the border with Turkey. Continue straight through Qahtaniyeh (29 km), Jawadiyeh (56 km) and the twin towns of Roumelian and Mabada (67 km). Several old-style 'nodding donkey' oil wells can be seen in the area, still functioning though their significance is now completely eclipsed by the vast new oilfields which have been opened up near Deir ez-Zor. After 82 km, where the road forks, keep straight (left), to arrive at Malkiyeh, 95 km from Qamishle. Turn left in the centre of town to pick up the road to Ain Diwar, 17 km further on.

The village of Ain Diwar is perched on the edge of a plateau overlooking the **Ain Diwar** Tigris River (the *Dijlah* in Arabic). The river here winds lazily through its wide valley in a broad sweep, while across the border to the northeast, the mountains of southeast Turkey rise up majestically, capped with snow for most of the year. Beyond the village, down on the banks of the Tigris, are the ruins of a **Roman bridge** which once spanned the river (over time the course of the river has changed so that the ruins now stand on dry land). The bridge dates originally from the second century AD, although it was subsequently modified by the Seljuks and Arabs in the 11th-12th centuries, and partially reconstructed by the Turks more recently. A rough track winds its way down from the plateau and then snakes round a low ridge to reach the bridge (approximately 7 km). After rain this track can be impassable except by four-wheel drives as it fords a substantial stream and is often churned up into deep mud.

The Tigris at this point marks the border with Turkey, and unfortunately the bridge is officially off-limits to tourists (although unofficially the local Kurds are more than ready to take you down there). Relations between Turkey and Syria are strained over the Kurdish question, with Turkey accusing Syria of harbouring PKK activists amongst its Kurdish population. Officials talk of regular incidents of Turkish soldiers firing across the border; around 10 people are said to die each year in this way. Although the bridge itself is officially off-limits (and is likely to remain so), a visit to Ain Diwar is still worthwhile for the superb views out over the Tigris River and the Taurus mountains beyond. Just beyond the village, right on the edge of the plateau, there is a new restaurant with a shaded terrace where you can enjoy the views.

Microbuses run regularly from Qamishle to Malkiyeh, but not to Ain Diwar. To hire a **Transport &** taxi for the last stretch (17 km) is relatively expensive, costing S£200-300; it is also pos- **registration** sible to negotiate a ride there by motorcycle for around S£100. If you want to hitch, Fri is a good day to try as lots of families go there for picnics; otherwise there is usually next to no traffic on the road between Malkiyeh and Ain Diwar. **NB** Due to the sensitive situation, tourists are officially required to register with the police in Malkiyeh before visiting Ain Diwar.

West of Qamishle

To pick up the road heading west out of Qamishle to Ras al-Ain, head west along *Colour map 2, grid A1* Hafez al-Assad Street. Go straight across the Assad roundabout and then bear right at the next roundabout. After 27 km you pass through the village of Amuda, the road from then on running closely parallel with the Turkish border.

Around 8 km beyond Amuda you pass on the right a large tell. This is Tell **Tell Mozan** Mozan, excavated by Giorgio Buccellati and Marilyn Kelly-Buccellati, and identified in 1995 as the ancient *Urkesh*, capital of the late third millennium BC Hurrian Empire which arose in the wake of the collapse of the Akkadian Empire. In Hurrian mythology Urkesh was also a holy city, the seat of the 'father of the gods', *Kumarbi*. Hundreds of seals were found at the site, some of them inscribed with cuneiform script. These were used to label jars, baskets and other

Euphrates River & the Jezira

containers that were kept in the royal storehouse. Their style is highly distinctive and gives unique insights into the little understood Hurrian civilization.

Around 28 km from Amuda you pass through the small town of Derbassiyeh, from where it is a further 60 km on to Ras al-Ain.

Ras al-Ain This town and Turkish border crossing point is famous mostly for the nearby archaeological site of Tell Halaf. There is very little for the casual visitor to see at the tell, but nearby there are various **sulphur springs** where you can swim. To reach the tell, take the road leading west from the telegraph office (distinguished by its tall communications mast) in the centre of town. After 4 km, just after crossing a small bridge, the tell is on your right.

The **Tell Halaf (Guzana)** site was first discovered in 1899 by Baron Max von Oppenheim, an engineer attached to the German diplomatic mission in Cairo who was sent to survey the route of the Berlin to Baghdad railway. He left the diplomatic service in 1911 in order to excavate the site, returning after the First World War to complete his work from 1927-29. The earliest evidence of settlement here (known as the 'Halaf culture' after the site) goes back to the first half of the fifth millennium BC and is noted for its distinctive style of painted pottery consisting of very fine, thin wares made by hand or turned on a slow wheel and decorated with rich polychrome designs in a luminous glaze-like paint. This style was common to a vast area extending over much of eastern Turkey and northern Iraq during this period. The site then appears to have been abandoned until the beginning of the first millennium BC, when it became the seat of one of the easternmost Aramaic (or neo-Hittite) states that had established themselves across northern Syria following the collapse of the Hittite Empire. Referred to in Assyrian records as *Guzana*, it was the capital of a region called *Bit Bahiani*. In the ninth century BC it began to pay tribute to Assyria, becoming an Assyrian province during the eighth century BC. The most substantial finds date from the period when it was the capital of an independent Aramaean state ruled by the *Kapara* Dynasty (probably ninth-eighth century BC, but possibly earlier). A sizeable walled citadel and palace/temple complex occupied the main mound at this time, and it was from the palace/temple that the huge, imposing statues which form the entrance façade to the Aleppo Museum were found.

Just past the tell there is a turning left off the main road which leads to the **Kapreet sulphur spring**. Follow the side road for 1½ km and then turn left again to arrive at the springs after 2½ km. There is a deep pool fed by the spring which makes for a pleasant and popular (though exclusively male) place to swim.

Eating Along the ring road around the south side of the town the *Sirob* and *Riad* restaurants both have pleasant outdoor seating with tables set in shallow pools of flowing sulphur spring water, allowing you to cool your feet while eating during the summer! There are a few cafés and simple restaurants in the centre of town.

Transport From Qamishle the easiest option is to get a bus or microbus to Derbassiyeh and then another one from there onto Ras al-Ain. Alternatively, there are direct buses and microbuses from Hassakeh. In either case, check what time the last services leave in the afternoon for the return trip.

Beirut بيروت

11

Beirut

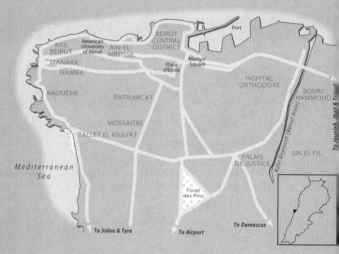

RAS BEIRUT
American University of Beirut
AIN-EL-MREISSE
BEIRUT CENTRAL DISTRICT
Port
MANARA
HAMRA
Place d'Etoile
Martyrs' Square
HOPITAL ORTHODOXE
BOURJ HAMMOUD
To Jounieh, Jbail & Tripoli
RAOUCHE
PATRIARCAT
Nahr Beyrouth (Beirut River)
MOSSAÏTBE
SIN EL FIL
TALLET EL KHAYAT
PALAIS DE JUSTICE
Mediterranean Sea
Foret des Pins
To Sidon & Tyre
To Airport
To Damascus

You'll either love Beirut or hate it. This city embodies so many of the hopes and aspirations as well as the frustrations and fears of modern Lebanon. Before the civil war, the Lebanese proudly referred to Beirut as the 'Paris of the East', and it is this reputation which they are striving so hard to recapture. But for most foreigners the very name Beirut is synonymous with seemingly endless civil war and destruction. There is still plenty of evidence of the devastation wrought by the fighting, for example in the towering, derelict shell of the Holiday Inn skyscraper, or the crumbling, bullet-riddled buildings along the old Green Line. Essentially, however, the image of Beirut as a war-torn city is long past its sell-by date. This is perhaps best demonstrated by the downtown area, which was almost completely flattened during the war, but has now been largely redeveloped and is well on its way to becoming the political, cultural and commercial centre of the city once again. Today's Beirut is a thriving, cosmopolitan capital of stylish shops, gourmet restaurants and trendy nightclubs, where the Mediterranean influences typical of the country are most in evidence. Apart from the various excavations in the downtown area and the truly magnificent National Museum, there's not much in the way of historical sites or places of interest in the traditional sense, but what it lacks in this respect it more than makes up for in its irrepressible vibrancy and chic, modern ambience.

Ins and outs

Getting there

Air Beirut International Airport, 10 km to the south of the city centre, is the only airport in Lebanon and handles all the international flights into and out of the country. It has recently been expanded and completely refurbished throughout to present arriving travellers with a gleaming, state-of-the-art first impression of the country.

Road Public transport connections with the rest of the country and the surrounding region are improving steadily. If you are arriving in Beirut from Syria, whether coming from Damascus or from the north via Tripoli, you will find yourself at the recently reopened Charles Helou bus station by the port area in the eastern half of the city. Beirut's other major transport hub, Cola bus stand, is primarily for services to destinations in the south of the country, as well as to the Bekaa valley. The third transport hub, Dora bus

Beirut: Overview

Related maps
A West Beirut, page 410
B Beirut central district
(Downtown), page 415
C East Beirut, page 419

0 metres 100
0 yards 100

N

■ **Sleeping**
1 Holiday Inn Dunes
2 Marriot
3 Mövenpick Resort (Under construction)
4 Sheraton Coral Beach (Under construction)

stand, mostly handles local buses serving greater Beirut as well as service taxis running to the north of the country.

Getting around

Service taxis (shared taxis, known as 'serveece') are the most common form of local transport within Beirut, costing LL1,000, or LL1,500 for longer journeys. These days there are an increasing number of bus services, most notably the small LCC buses (usually red and white but sometimes emblazoned with advertising logos) which cost just LL500. There are also plenty of private taxis, though these are considerably more expensive. Exploring on foot is fine within specific districts, but Beirut is a sprawling city and for getting between districts you really need to take a taxi or bus.

Beirut forms a headland bounded to the north and west by the Mediterranean and to the east by the southernmost reaches of Mount Lebanon. Today the Green Line that divided Beirut (marked by Rue de Damas) is still distinguishable by the concentration

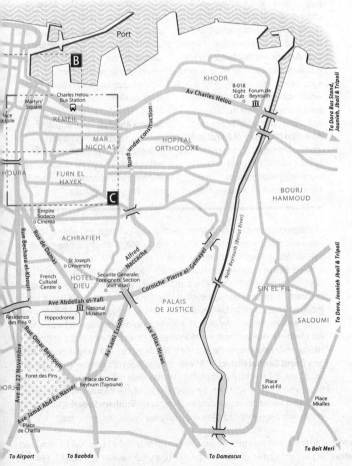

5 Summerland

24 hours in Beirut

An early morning stroll along the **Corniche** is a great introduction to Beirut in all its cosmopolitan diversity. Wandering along this broad pedestrian strip by the seafront, you'll mingle with a typical cross-section of Beiruti society out exercising, fishing, chatting or just enjoying the Mediterranean views over a strong black coffee. Heading east from Ain el-Mreisse, it's just under 2 km to Ras Beirut, from where you can continue south through Manara to Raouche, though you're probably better off seeing this stretch at sunset or at night.

Hamra will give you a taste of Beirut's lively, bustling commercial side, which is about as westernized as you can get. Rue Hamra is the main thoroughfare, and there are a couple of great cafés – the **Cafe du Paris** and the **Modca** – where you can sit and watch the world go by (or, if you prefer to remain firmly in the grip of western commercial imperialism, there is a recently opened branch of Starbucks). Just nearby, but a world away, is the **American University of Beirut** (AUB for short), with its tranquil, shady, beautifully laid-out gardens and views out over the shimmering Mediterranean. There is a small, well-presented museum

on the AUB grounds, but if you've only got one day, be sure not to miss out on the recently restored **National Museum**. It boasts some stunningly beautiful artefacts, all excellently presented, and is not so big that you feel overwhelmed.

The old '**Downtown**' district (also known now as Beirut Central District, or BCD) was devastated during the war, but has been the focus of one of the biggest redevelopment projects in the world. Place d'Etoile and the streets which radiate from it form the heart of this area, and many of the beautiful Ottoman and French Mandate-period buildings here have been meticulously restored to their former glory. In amongst all this period elegance there are also plenty of modernistic office blocks of glass and steel, though the blending of old and new has been done with care and sensitivity to impressive effect.

Depending on how you are doing for time, you may want to visit the Christian areas of East Beirut, and in particular the **Sursock Museum**. This is actually a contemporary art gallery set in a beautiful, elegant private house which miraculously survived the ravages of the civil war, along with several other similarly elegant houses in this area.

---

of bullet-pocked and bombed-out buildings which lie along it, and while it no longer exists as a physical barrier to movement, the division of the city between Christian east and Muslim west is as marked as ever.

West Beirut is focused on Hamra, which following the destruction of the old downtown area became the business and commercial centre of the city with most of the hotels, restaurants, banks, shops and other services. To the north of Hamra are the grounds of the American University of Beirut (AUB) overlooking the Mediterranean. To the west are the exclusive districts of Ras Beirut and Manara overlooking the western Mediterranean seaboard. Ain el-Mreisse forms a small area to the northeast of Hamra, while extending to the east of it is what was once downtown Beirut, now the new **Beirut Central District**. At its eastern edge is Beirut's port complex. Extending south from the port up the hill are the Christian areas of **East Beirut**, a series of districts climbing up to Achrafieh, the most elegant of them. Sprawling south towards the airport are the poverty-stricken and ramshackle **Southern Suburbs**, home to the city's Shi'ite population and a few remaining Palestinian refugee camps.

Tourist information The tourist information office is on the ground floor of the Ministry of Tourism building on the corner of Rue Banque du Liban/Rue de Rome, T343073, F340945, www.lebanon-tourism.gov.lb Open 0800-1600 (0800-1800 Aug-Oct), closed Sun. They have a good selection of pamphlets on all the main tourist attractions in

Whether from the downtown area or East Beirut, it's quite a haul through the traffic back to Raouche in West Beirut, but this is the place to be when the sun sets over **Pigeon Rocks** and the Mediterranean. The outdoor terrace of the **Bay Rock** café/restaurant is probably the best place from which to enjoy the sunset, over a tea/coffee, juice or a beer, and perhaps indulge in the delights of a nargileh. Once night falls, the red glow of the sun is quickly replaced by the multicoloured glow of neon signs and the headlight beams of cars out cruising up and down the Corniche.

As for the question of **where to eat**, the overwhelming range of choices could easily render you helpless with indecision. My first choice would be the **Abou Hassan** restaurant, a little way inland from Raouche/Manara. This no-nonsense, traditional Lebanese restaurant serves excellent Arabic food at very reasonable prices. If you fancy something a bit more elaborate, East Beirut is the place to go. Either the **Al Mijana** (Arabic cuisine) or the **Al Dente** (Italian), both set in beautiful Ottoman-period houses on Rue Abdel Wahab El Inglizi, are excellent top-of-the-range establishments. Nearby,

along Rue Monot, there are literally dozens of restaurants ranging from Japanese sushi bars and Thai takeaways to the best of French haute cuisine.

Although there are some good bars in West Beirut, East Beirut is arguably the best place to come for **nightlife**. The oddly named B-O18 ('Bee Oh Eighteen') is a highly unusual and hugely popular venue, though difficult to get to. There are also plenty of nightspots on Rue Monot; clustered together on a small side street are *Rai* (low lighting, Moroccan décor and food), the **Hole in the Wall** (a small, unpretentious English-run pub) and **Pacificos** (big, loud Latino-style bar). Further up Rue Monot is the laid-back, arty **Bongos Pub** and **Circus**, a very trendy bar/restaurant with occasional live music. Others in the area worth investigating include **Zinc**, another extremely trendy bar/restaurant with good music and food, and **Sports Café**, a large American-style (though English-run) sports-theme bar. On a Thursday, Friday or Saturday night you could easily see the night out at many of these places and make the best of every one of your precious 24 hours, though you might need as long to recover!

Lebanon, as well as booklets covering each of the regions in more detail. The staff are generally friendly and helpful although their usefulness in terms of practical information and advice is somewhat limited.

History

Various stone implements discovered in the vicinity of Beirut reveal evidence of human activity dating back as far as the **Palaeolithic** era, although exactly when a permanent settlement was first established here is not known. Recent excavations in the redevelopment area of central Beirut have revealed traces of a **Canaanite** settlement, the earliest phases of which appear to go back to the 19th-18th century BC. The earliest known references to Beirut (known then as Birûta, probably derived from the Semitic word for 'well' or 'spring') come from cuneiform tablets discovered at Tell Amarna in Egypt in 1887. These date from the early 14th century BC and consist of letters sent by Ammunira, a Canaanite king of Beirut, to the Pharaoh Amenhotep IV pleading for help in repelling the invading Hittites. The tablets also indicate that Beirut enjoyed close links with Byblos. In the so-called **Phoenician** period after around 1200 BC, despite its favourable location close to reliable water sources and with a sheltered natural

Pre- & early history

harbour, Beirut was largely eclipsed by the more important Phoenician cities of Sidon, Tyre and Byblos. Certainly, the historical record is all but silent as to its fate, while the other coastal cities find frequent mention in Assyrian, Babylonian and Persian records. Although not mentioned in accounts of Alexander the Great's conquest of the coastal cities, Beirut does reappear in later **Hellenistic** records, named *Laodicea in Canaan*, possibly by the Seleucid emperor Antiochus IV in the second century BC (a total of five cities were named *Laodicea* by the Seleucids in honour of a Seleucid queen, *Laodice*). Excavations carried out in 1994 have confirmed that the later Roman city closely followed a typical grid pattern of streets that was essentially of Hellenistic origin.

Roman reaction

The city only really began to flourish during the **Roman** period, becoming an important commercial port and military base. It was first conquered by the emperor Pompey in 64 BC. Later, the emperor Augustus (r 27 BC to 14 AD, formerly Octavian) placed Beirut under the governorship of Vespasianus Agrippa, the husband of his daughter Julia, raising it to the status of a colony and renaming it *Colonia Julia Augusta Felix Berytus* in her honour. An extensive city was laid out over the earlier Hellenistic foundations, and baths, markets, a theatre and other public buildings erected. The Herodian kings of Judaea (which was at that time in effect a Roman client-state) financed many of these building works in order to gain favour with the Romans. Veterans from the *V Macedonica* and *VIII Gallica* legions were given land and settled there, while the local inhabitants received Roman citizenship and were exempted from taxes. Between 190-200 AD the Roman emperor Septimus Severus established a School of Law at Beirut, and from the early third century the city flourished as one of the great centres of Roman jurisprudence. It was here that the substance of the famous Code of Justinian, to which the Western legal system owes its origins, was developed by Papiniam and Ulpian. Beirut was unique in that culturally it was distinctively Roman, with its Law School and community of veterans, in contrast to other cities where Hellenistic cultural influences remained strongest.

Byzantines, catastrophe & Crusader control

Beirut continued to flourish during the **Byzantine** period, not least because of the fame of its Law School, becoming the seat of a bishopric by the end of the fourth century. Its reputation as a commercial centre was enhanced meanwhile by the manufacture and trade in silk. However, in 551 the city was all but destroyed by earthquakes and associated tidal waves which caused devastation all along the coast. The Law School was moved to Sidon and although Beirut was subsequently rebuilt, it never regained its former glory. When it fell to the Muslim Arab conquest in 635, it was still a relatively insignificant port, and remained so for nearly four centuries of Arab rule.

In 1110 it was captured by Baldwin I after a lengthy siege, and remained in **Crusader** hands until 1187 when it was retaken by Salah ud-Din (Saladin). Just six years later, however, it was occupied by Amoury, king of Cyprus, so passing back into Crusader hands. In 1291 it was captured by the Mamelukes and the Crusaders were driven out for the last time. There were a number of attempts to recapture it during the 14th century, but ultimately when Europeans started to settle there during the 15th century, they came as traders rather than conquerors.

Ottomans & oligarchs

In 1516 the Mamelukes were defeated by Sultan Selim I and Beirut subsequently became part of the Ottoman Empire. However, Ottoman rule was never directly applied, local rulers being appointed instead and given a large degree of autonomy provided they faithfully collected and passed on the taxes that were due. Two local rulers were particularly notable for their role in reviving Beirut's commercial reputation. **Emir Fakhr ud-Din II Maan** (1590-1635) was perhaps the most powerful and famous of Lebanon's local rulers during the Ottoman period. After a brief period in exile in the Italian duchy of Tuscany from 1613-18, he returned, bringing with him many modernizing influences. Although originally from the Chouf Mountains, he made Beirut his main residence, building an elaborate palace and gardens there and energetically encouraging trading links with the Venetians and other European states, so reviving something of Beirut's prosperity. Once again silk, manufactured in the Chouf Mountains and traded through Beirut (and also Sidon), formed the basis of this prosperity.

During the 18th century Beirut's fortunes fluctuated, favoured for a while by one Emir, only to be neglected by the next. It began to flourish more consistently under **Emir Bashir Shihab II** (1788-1840). However, he also laid the seeds of his own downfall in 1832 by entering into an alliance with **Ibrahim Pasha**, the son of the viceroy of Egypt Mohammad Ali, who had risen against the Ottoman Empire and was threatening to overthrow it. Britain was alarmed at this upset to the balance of power in the region and the threat it posed to her interests. In 1840 a combined Anglo-Austro-Turkish fleet bombarded Beirut. Emir Bashir was captured and sent into exile and direct Ottoman rule was re-established. The opening up of Damascus to European trade from this time fuelled ever greater commercial activity in Beirut, along with an increasing **European presence**. In 1860, the massacre of Maronites at the hands of the Druze, first in Lebanon and then in Damascus, prompted direct European military intervention. French troops landed in Beirut and thousands of Maronites fled to the city for protection. These events led to the establishment of 'Mount Lebanon' as a semi-autonomous province, although Beirut itself remained under direct Ottoman control. With its population vastly expanded by the influx of Maronites, and with an ever growing European presence, Beirut's position as the commercial capital of the eastern Mediterranean was further enhanced.

During the First World War the British, French and Russian navies blockaded Beirut's port in an attempt to dislodge the Ottoman military forces from Lebanon. This, combined with a series of natural disasters, brought famine to the country on a massive scale. In 1916 the leaders of a local revolt against the Ottomans were executed in Beirut, in what afterwards became known as Martyrs' Square. On the 8 October 1918, eight days after the fall of Damascus, the British army entered Beirut with a detachment of French troops. Under the provisions of the secretly negotiated Sykes-Picot treaty of 1916, Lebanon (as part of Syria) was placed under French Mandate rule in April 1920. Under pressure from the Maronites, the French promptly created the new, enlarged state of 'Grand Liban' (Greater Lebanon), separate from Syria and with Beirut as its capital. The inter-war years were peaceful ones in which Beirut was able to consolidate its position as capital of the new state.

First World War

See also page 634 for more on the French Mandate period, Independence & the Civil War

The Second World War saw the return of Allied troops to Beirut, with full independence only being established for the country in 1946. Since independence, the fate of Beirut has always been closely linked to and shaped by the country's (and indeed the wider region's) complex and tumultuous history. The Arab-Israeli war of 1947-49 resulted in a massive influx of Palestinian refugees, many of whom settled in the southern part of the city. When tensions over support for Nasser's pan-Arab vision degenerated into civil war in 1958, some 15,000 US Marines landed in Beirut to restore order. In 1970 the PLO, having been driven out of Jordan, set up their headquarters in Beirut, launching

Independence & war

Beirut

frequent attacks on Israel and establishing themselves as a virtual 'state within a state'. When all-out civil war finally erupted in 1975, Beirut was the main focus. The city became divided by the infamous Green Line between Muslim West Beirut and Christian East Beirut. The devastation and suffering was on an unprecedented scale and continued more or less unabated through Syrian occupation, Israeli invasion and the presence of various United Nations and multinational peace-keeping forces. Fighting eventually subsided in 1989 and by 1991 the Green Line had been dismantled, finally heralding a lasting peace.

Sights

South of the centre

National Museum

This is a sight which deserves at least 1 or 2 hours in order to do it justice, perhaps even more if you find yourself mesmerized by the beauty of the artefacts

Opened once again to the public in 1999, the National Museum is the jewel in the crown of Beirut's cultural heritage, and a powerful symbol of the city's regeneration. It boasts a superb collection of excellently presented artefacts, with everything labelled in English, French and Arabic, while information boards provide brief outlines of each period.

Situated right on the so-called 'Green Line' separating East and West Beirut, the museum took a veritable pounding during the civil war. Some of the artefacts were removed for safe-keeping when hostilities broke out, while the larger ones, such as the stone sarcophagi and mosaics which could not easily be removed, were sealed within thick concrete shells in order to protect them from damage. For nearly a decade, the museum has been the focus of a massive restoration project. Not only did the building itself have to be extensively repaired, but the museum's collection had also suffered severe damage, not least because the basement, where many items were stored, became flooded. At the time of writing, work was still ongoing behind the scenes to restore the basement.

As you enter the museum, you are first confronted by a large mosaic depicting Calliope, the muse of philosophy, surrounded by Socrates and the seven wise men all framed within ornate roundels. Dating from the third century AD, this beautiful mosaic was discovered at Baalbek, in the dining room of a Roman villa. In the central area of the hall, arranged around the mosaic, are four large marble sarcophagi discovered at Tyre and dating from the second century AD. The delicately carved reliefs adorning their sides depict scenes of drunken banquets and epic battles from the legend of Achilles, and show a quite remarkable degree of artistry in their execution.

In the hall to your right are various artefacts from the Sanctuary of Eshmoun near Sidon, the most striking of which are the statuettes of young children and babies, offered by parents in thanks for the healing of their children. Dating from the fifth century BC, they already show clear Greek influences, even though Alexander the Great did not arrive in the region until a century later.

In the hall opposite are various artefacts from the first and second millenniums BC, including the sarcophagus of Ahiram, king of Byblos (10th century BC). Though rather clumsily carved in comparison with the Roman sarcophagi from Tyre, its significance is enormous in that it is inscribed with the earliest known example of the Phoenician alphabet, upon which our own Latin one is based. Many of the artefacts here are of Egyptian origin, or else Egyptian-inspired, notably the stela of the Pharaoh Ramses II, complete with a hieroglyphic inscription, found at Tyre. Dominating the small room at the far end of this hall is a carved Colossus from Byblos, also Egyptian in style. Equally striking is the reconstruction of a marble column base in the shape of a pumpkin, and a capital decorated with carved bulls' heads, both from the fifth century BC Sidon.

Tucked away in the corner to the left of the stairs leading up to the first floor is a beautiful fragment of Roman mural from Tyre depicting a figure carrying a load on his shoulder, the colours still surprisingly vivid. In the corner to the right of the stairs is a Roman carved limestone altar from Nihan in the Bekaa valley, with two lions flanking a central god. Flanking the stairs themselves are two graceful and beautifully preserved marble statues, the one on the right being Hygeia, goddess of health, while the one on the left is an unidentified Roman woman, clearly of noble blood.

The first floor houses all the smaller pieces. Going round in a clockwise direction, you work your way through the prehistoric eras, Bronze Age, Iron Age, Greek, Roman and Byzantine periods to the Arab Muslim era. The quality and beauty of the artefacts from all these periods is really stunning, but perhaps most breathtaking of all is the vast wealth of Bronze Age pieces from Byblos. Particularly striking are the hundreds of gilded bronze sticklike figurines with their distinctive Egyptian style peaked hats found in the Temple of the Obelisks. Note also the beautifully fashioned solid gold axes. It is thought these were presented as to Reshef, the Amoritic god of war and destruction and his consort, the goddess Anat in order to secure their blessings for the continued cutting of the cedar forests. The fact that they are solid gold is an indication of how important these trees were to the wealth of Byblos. Similarly, the jewellery and weapons from the tombs of two Amoritic (early second millenium BC) princes of Byblos, Abi Shemou and Ip Shemou Abi show the extremely high levels of skill and craftsmanship which were applied to making such ceremonial offerings.

Returning to the entrance lobby, in the wing opposite the ticket office and museum shop, there is an audio-visual hall where a 15-minute video about the museum is shown every hour between 0900-1600 (if it is quiet, ask at the ticket office and the staff will probably run it for you whatever the time). The video gives a short history of the founding of the museum, as well as fascinating footage of the building at the end of the war, revealing the full extent of the devastation. The footage of the concrete encased sarcophagi being broken open is particularly dramatic, although the subsequent tour of the opened museum, zooming in on all the artefacts you've already seen is perhaps unnecessary. ■ *0900-1700, closed Mon. LL5,000 (students and under 18s LL1,000). The museum shop sells postcards and souvenirs, but is extremely pricey. Official guided tours cost US$15.*

At the turn of the century the Ottoman rulers of Lebanon granted a concession for the building of a race track, casino/private club and public gardens in a section of the large pine forest which then still existed to the south of Beirut. However, it was not until after the fall of the Ottomans in the First World War that a member of the prestigious Sursock family established a race track here. Today the Beirut Hippodrome is once again up and running and regaining its former popularity after falling into disuse during the civil war. ■ *Racing takes place every Sun, starting at 1300 in summer and 1100 in winter with 8 races through the day. There are also plans to hold races on Sat and in the evenings in the future. Entry is LL5,000-15,000 depending on where you sit. There is a cafeteria and 2 restaurants in the main stadium. Although somewhat run-down after years of neglect, the facilities are steadily being upgraded. For more information, T632515.*

Beirut Hippodrome & Residence des Pins

The Residence des Pins, the impressive Ottoman period building just to the west of the race track, was originally intended as the casino/private club, but it was leased instead to the French and used as the ambassador's residence. When the lease ran out, the French obtained ownership of it in exchange for other buildings belonging to them. During the civil war it was badly damaged by tank fire, but it has now been fully restored and serves once again as the

Beirut

ambassador's residence. ■ *Unfortunately, visits to the Residence des Pins can be made by special invitation only.*

West Beirut

Hamra Hamra district emerged as the new financial and commercial centre of Beirut during the civil war. Here you will find most of the banks, hotels, restaurants, and shops. It is not exactly picturesque and there is nothing really to 'see' as such, but it is buzzing with life. Rue Hamra, running east-west, forms the main

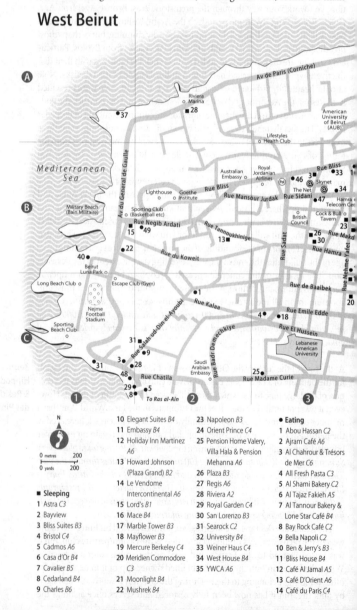

West Beirut

	10 Elegant Suites *B4*	**23** Napoleon *B3*	**● Eating**
	11 Embassy *B4*	**24** Orient Prince *C4*	**1** Abou Hassan *C2*
	12 Holiday Inn Martinez *A6*	**25** Pension Home Valery,	**2** Ajram Café *A6*
	13 Howard Johnson	Villa Hala & Pension	**3** Al Chahrour & Trésors
	(Plaza Grand) *B2*	Mehanna *A6*	de Mer *C6*
	14 Le Vendome	**26** Plaza *B3*	**4** All Fresh Pasta *C3*
	Intercontinental *A6*	**27** Regis *A6*	**5** Al Shami Bakery *C2*
■ Sleeping	**15** Lord's *B1*	**28** Riviera *A2*	**6** Al Tajaz Fakieh *A5*
1 Astra *C3*	**16** Mace *B4*	**29** Royal Garden *C4*	**7** Al Tannour Bakery &
2 Bayview	**17** Marble Tower *B3*	**30** San Lorenzo *B3*	Lone Star Café *B4*
3 Bliss Suites *B3*	**18** Mayflower *B3*	**31** Searock *C2*	**8** Bay Rock Café *C2*
4 Bristol *C4*	**19** Mercure Berkeley *C4*	**32** University *B4*	**9** Bella Napoli *C2*
5 Cadmos *A6*	**20** Meridien Commodore	**33** Weiner Haus *C4*	**10** Ben & Jerry's *C4*
6 Casa d'Or *B4*	*C3*	**34** West House *C4*	**11** Bliss House *B4*
7 Cavalier *B5*	**21** Moonlight *B4*	**35** YWCA *A6*	**12** Café Al Jamal *A5*
8 Cedarland *B4*	**22** Mushrek *B4*		**13** Café D'Orient *A6*
9 Charles *B6*			**14** Café du Paris *C4*

N

0 metres   200
0 yards   200

thoroughfare. Apart from exploring the rough grid pattern of streets surrounding it and shopping, dining and snacking to your heart's content, the two cafés to be found on Rue Hamra (the *Café du Paris* and the *Modca*) make for very pleasant places from which to watch all the comings and goings. Although practically all the buildings in Hamra are modern and rather ugly, here and there you can see the odd few dating from the French Mandate period; isolated reminders of a more elegant past. Heading down towards Ain el-Mreisse (see below) and Rue Minet el-Hosn along Rue John Kennedy and Rue Omar ed-Daouk you pass a number of these, including the old French embassy building.

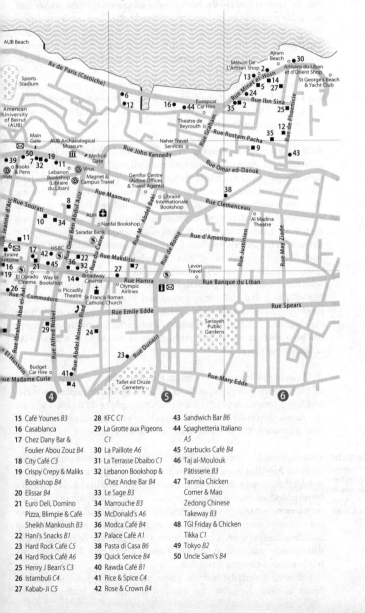

Beirut

American University of Beirut

Extensive grounds, spreading down the hillside towards the Mediterranean, provide a wonderful oasis of leafy green tranquillity - a world away from the congestion & noise outside

The American University of Beirut, or AUB for short, was first established in 1866 and named at that time the Syrian Protestant College. Founded by the American Protestant missionary Daniel Bliss, it was one of several foreign educational establishments which were opened following the advent of direct European involvement in the affairs of Lebanon in 1860. Others included the Beirut Women's College, likewise founded in 1860 and also in West Beirut (it became Beirut University College and is now the Lebanese American University), and the University of St Joseph, founded in 1874 and located in East Beirut (still functioning under the same name). The AUB gained a reputation over the years as perhaps the most prestigious university in the Middle East and today it remains an exclusive, much sought-after (and extremely expensive) place to study. It continued to function throughout the civil war, remaining largely unscathed notwithstanding the kidnap and murder of various of its staff and a car bomb in 1991 which destroyed College Hall, the original building of the college founded by Bliss.

■ *The main entrance is on Rue Bliss, just to the east of the intersection with Rue Jeanne d'Arc. There is a post office on the grounds, and a small archaeological museum. The university newsletter* Campus *gives details of university concerts, theatre productions, films etc.*

AUB Archaeological Museum This small museum houses an interesting collection of artefacts which have been gathered from around the wider Middle East region as well as from Lebanon itself. The emphasis is very much on the prehistoric and ancient periods up until Roman and early Byzantine times; stone implements of the Palaeolithic, mesolithic and neolithic periods; varied examples of the pottery styles/techniques of Mesopotamia and Egypt during the fifth and fourth millenniums BC; Sumerian administrative tablets from the kingdom of Ur; pottery, jewellery, figurines and fertility goddesses of the second and third millenniums BC from the Euphrates region of North Syria and from Phoenician coastal sites such as Byblos; the strikingly more sophisticated later Phoenician fertility goddesses and figurines of the Middle Iron Age (900-600 BC); and Hellenistic, Roman and Byzantine artefacts, including coins reaching up to the Umayyad period. Although many of the artefacts are very impressive, the labelling is unfortunately rather patchy and no attempt has been made at interpretive explanations of the displays. ■ *0900-1600, closed Sat and Sun. Free.*

AUB Geological Museum Upstairs in the same building as the Archaeological Museum, the scale model of Beirut and the surrounding mountains on display here gives a useful perspective on the topography of the region. There are also various displays of fossils and rocks here, as well as a good geological relief map of Lebanon. ■ *0900-1700, closed Sat and Sun. Free.*

Corniche

This is where Beirutis come to exercise, socialize, enjoy the sunset & generally 'see & be seen'

Running the full length of West Beirut's northern and western sea front is the corniche. As well as being a prime stretch of road along which Beirutis love to indulge their deep passion for aimlessly cruising around in cars, there is also a broad pedestrian thoroughfare on the seaward side. Wandering along it in the early evening you mingle with a broad cross-section of Lebanese, from families out enjoying a stroll to walkman-toting joggers and roller-bladers gliding up and down clad in the latest lycra fashions. This is post-war Beirut eagerly and determinedly reclaiming its freedom, a people getting back down to the serious business of enjoying themselves.

Following it west, the corniche proper starts from its junction with Rue Minet el-Hosn (opposite the *Hard Rock Café* and recently opened

*View of Corniche
from Ain el-Mriesse*

McDonalds). The first stretch passes through an area known as **Ain el-Mreisse** after the spring and tiny fishing bay located there (the entrance to the bay passes under the road, so you must cross over to see inside). Beirut's coastline is for the most part rocky, with concrete breakwaters piled up in places. Fishing is another popular activity along the Corniche, anglers cast their lines from the railings or perch down on the rocks, in either case seemingly more for the pleasure of it than in hope of catching much. Further on is the **AUB 'beach'** (see under 'Beaches and beach clubs') and the university grounds stretching up the hill on the opposite side of the road, followed by the flashy *Riveria* hotel complete with its own private beach club/marina. A little further on the road swings south following the coastline. The small headland here is a particularly popular fishing spot. To the south, the military-only Bain Militaire is followed by a cluster of restaurants, cafés and private beach clubs, a couple of the latter behind the **Luna Park** fairground, dominated by a large ferris wheel, and the football stadium. The road then climbs steeply up to the cliffs that mark this stretch of the coast, known as Raouche, now an area of exclusive new residential apartments, cafés, restaurants and brightly lit fast food outlets. Just beyond the cliffs, the famous **Pigeon Rocks** rise from the sea, two tall pillars of rock with arches hollowed through them at their bases by the action of the sea. Continuing south, the road descends, past the new *Mövenpick* resort (under construction at the time of writing) and down to a long stretch of sand beach, known as **Rafiq Hariri beach**.

The term 'Beach Club' is something of a misnomer, since there are only a couple of real sand beaches in Beirut. For most Lebanese, however, the absence of any beach at their favourite beach club is neither here nor there. What is important is that it is a club, a private place for relaxing, socializing and enjoying a sense of exclusivity (though these days the majority are open to the public for a straightforward entrance fee, without the need to be a member). Starting at St George's and following the coast round west and then south, the main clubs are as follows.

St George's Yacht Club, Minet el-Hosn, T365065. Formerly this was a luxury hotel with its own private beach club and marina, but like most of the hotels and restaurants in this area, St George's was devastated during the civil war. The large hotel building still stands in a state of ruin (there is a long-standing legal battle between the owners and Solidere, with the latter claiming ownership of the land/sea frontage as part of the redevelopment area), but the beach club and marina is up and running, and popular as ever amongst wealthy Beirutis. Facilities include a swimming pool, waterslide,

**Beaches &
Beach Clubs**
*Turning up at these
clubs without a gently
tanned & perfectly toned
body, & of course a
mobile phone, is verging
on the subversive*

Beirut

children's play area, restaurant, three bars, a small marina for motor yachts, jet skis for hire and a privately run diving club. During the summer, evening entertainments are often laid on (singers, bands, dancing etc). ■ *The entry fee is LL20,000 (LL15,000 on Mon), or LL12,000/10,000 for children.*

Ajram Beach, Minet el-Hosn. Shower/changing room facilities and cafeteria. The only women-only beach club in Beirut, but rather basic. Closes down for the winter. ■ *Entry LL10,000.*

La Plage, Ain el-Mreisse (part of the *Café d'Orient* complex). Very smart terrace restaurant and bar, together with its own swimming pool. Jet skis and powerboats for hire. ■ *Entry LL20,000.*

AUB Beach, Ras Beirut. Only open to AUB students and reached via a tunnel from the university grounds. If you have friends studying at the university they may be able to get you in. Along the sea front either side of AUB beach there are a number of places where you can climb over the railings and down onto stretches of rocks. These areas are popular with children, although not exactly clean.

Yacht Club, *Riviera* hotel, Ras Beirut. This highly prestigious private club features its own small marina, outdoor swimming pool, health centre (with jacuzzi, sauna, massage and gym), as well as a restaurant and bar. There is a fully equipped diving centre here, and the usual watersports on offer (jet skis etc). ■ *Officially it is only open to hotel guests and members (full membership costs US$400 per year, or you can pay US$85 per year, plus an entry fee of US$13/10 on weekends/weekdays). In practice, providing it is not too busy, non-guests may be able to pay an entrance fee without having to go for full membership.*

Long Beach Club, Manara. Two large swimming pools and a children's pool with full shower/changing room facilities. Restaurant and bar/snack bar. Large concrete sunbathing area and steps down to the sea. Jet skis for hire. ■ *Entry LL10,000.*

Sporting Beach Club, Manara, T742481. Strong family emphasis. Two large swimming pools and a children's pool with full shower/changing room facilities. *Maharaja* (Indian) and *Feluka* (Arabic/seafood) restaurants, two bars, cafeteria, basketball and volleyball. Large concrete sunbathing area and steps down to the sea. ■ *Membership based, though foreign tourists are allowed in for an entry fee of LL17,000 in the summer and LL15,000 in the winter.*

Rafiq Hariri Beach, to the south of Raouche heading down towards the *Summerland* and *Coral Beach* hotels (see 'Beirut: Overview' map). As well as having a decent stretch of good sand which is kept relatively clean, a sectioned-off swimming area, snack bar and basic shower and changing facilities, this beach has the advantage of being open to the general public, with no membership or entrance fees.

Club 500, *Summerland* hotel, Jnah district, South Beirut. This is the only hotel with its own private *sand* beach. There is also an Olympic-size outdoor swimming pool (and another 'waterfall' pool). A wide range of watersports is on offer, including diving, sailing, windsurfing, water skiing, jet skiing, parasailing, boat tours etc. ■ *Non-guests must pay an entrance fee of LL20,000 to use the beach and pools.*

Beirut Central District (Downtown Beirut)

Known now as Beirut Central District (BCD), the downtown and heart of old Beirut was largely devastated during the civil war. The classic early 1970s photo of Martyrs' Square that you see so often in Beirut gives a glimpse of what it once was: a thriving financial and commercial centre of offices, hotels, cafés and markets. In recent years it has been the scene of one of the largest urban redevelopment projects in the world (see box) and already this district has been completely transformed.

Place d'Etoile and the streets radiating from it are now all but completely restored. Thought to stand on the site of the forum of the Roman city, this area was laid out in its present form by the French, with the north-south Rue Maarad being modelled on the Rue de Rivoli in Paris. Today, the architecture is striking, combining the quiet grace and elegance of restored Ottoman and French Mandate period buildings with the loud modernity of glass and steel office blocks. At the time of writing, cafés, fancy Italian restaurants and expensive boutiques were slowly starting to open up, though the majority of the outlets were still empty. The overall effect can be distinctly odd at times, without any of the bustle or lived-in feel that you would expect from a city centre, almost as if you are walking around an enormous semi-deserted film set. Time, no doubt, will change all that.

On an area of higher ground to the west of Place d'Etoile, overlooking the old centre of Beirut is the **Grand Serail**. This was built in 1890 and acted both as a barracks and the seat of the Ottoman government. Following independence it served as the Ministry of Interior. Now fully restored, the building houses the Council of Ministers and the prime minister's offices. The smaller building immediately to the north of it was the Ottoman military hospital and now houses the Council for Development and Reconstruction (CDR), responsible for coordinating these activities at a national level.

Between the Grand Serail and Rue Riad es-Solh there is a long, narrow area of excavations where the remains of a Roman baths complex have been uncovered, preserved today as an archaeological 'garden'. The three rooms identified as the *caldarium*, *tepidarium* and *frigidarium* can be clearly discerned,

Place d'Etoile

Grand Serail & Roman baths

Beirut central district (Downtown)

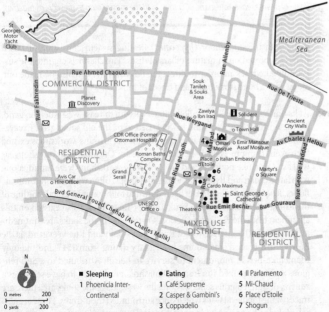

■ Sleeping	● Eating	4 Il Parlamento
1 Phoenicia Inter-	1 Café Supreme	5 Mi-Chaud
Continental	2 Casper & Gambini's	6 Place d'Etoile
	3 Coppadelio	7 Shogun

☞ *Walking on Solidere*

In 1994 the Société Libanaise pour le Développement et la Reconstruction du Centre-Ville de Beyrouth, known as **Solidere** *for short, was formed. The brain-child of the then Lebanese prime minister, Rafiq Hariri, the primary objective of this private real estate company is to reconstruct the old downtown area of central Beirut in accordance with a government-approved master plan. The scheme is highly ambitious, involving the redevelopment of 180 ha of land including over 60 ha of landfill reclaimed from the sea.*

The single greatest obstacle to initiating a redevelopment project on such a large scale was the complex web of local land/property ownership and tenancy rights that existed within the area. In all, more than 40,000 active property owners were involved, while in one celebrated case it was revealed that 4,750 people held ownership or tenancy rights to a single plot of land in the souks. To get round this problem, all those with property rights of one sort or another were given shares in Solidere amounting to a total value of US$1.17bn, this being the estimated total value of private real estate in the BCD. In

addition, outside investors were allowed to buy shares in the company to a value of US$650m.

Solidere has been responsible for carrying out all infrastructure works (roads, tunnels, bridges, public squares, gardens etc), and also for treating the landfill on the reclaimed land and developing the sea defences and two associated marinas. In the historic core of the district (centred on Place d'Etoile), it has been responsible for the restoration of more than 250 Ottoman and French Mandate period buildings. While as much as possible of the historic core of the city is being restored in its original form and layout, the 60 ha of reclaimed land are going to be developed to include a financial district along with entertainment, recreational, cultural and shopping facilities (scheduled for completion in 2003).

The redevelopment of the whole of the centre of the city presented archaeologists with an unique excavation opportunity. Remains from every period of occupation from the Canaanite period onwards were uncovered, and provisions were included in the master plan to preserve as much as

---

along with the underfloor (*hypocaust*) heating system consisting of raised floors supported on miniature pillars of discs. The channels cut into the surrounding bedrock in order to direct the flow of water can also be made out, along with a huge stone basin and traces of mosaics.

Old souks area   At its north end, Rue Riad es-Solh intersects with the east-west Rue Weygand. To the north of Rue Weygand is what used to be the old souks area. Excavations have revealed that a market and complex of artisans' workshops existed here even from pre-Hellenistic times. Traces of Ottoman silk workshops, as well as Mameluke potteries and glass-blowing workshops were found, along with late Roman and Byzantine houses and shops, often with elaborate mosaic floors. Rue Weygand has in fact been shown to follow almost exactly the line of the Roman *decumanus*, while Souk Tawile ('Long Souk') also existed on this alignment from the Hellenistic period. On the edge of the souks area, immediately opposite the intersection of Rue Riad es-Solh and Rue Weygand, is the **Zawiye Ibn Iraq**, a small domed sanctuary dating from 1517 and the only Mameluke-period monument to survive in Beirut. Attributed to a Sufi religious authority named Ibn Iraq al-Dimashqi, it is thought to have served as a *zawiye*, or Sufi religious school. Along the west side of the souks area there are traces of the medieval walls which once surrounded the old city. These are also scheduled to be preserved in an archaeological 'garden'.

possible of these remains in the form of archaeological gardens and mini-museums in the basements of new buildings.

Solidere sees the project as being about much more than just rebuilding the physical fabric of the city and sets itself some lofty aims: "At stake is the rebirth of the centre of a capital city after its destruction by war. The pattern of development it engenders must inform the future and cherish the past. In the renewal of the great city squares and the making of new public spaces, it must provide a social arena and a means to reconnect a once-divided city. In the quality and example that it sets, and in the value placed on the city's heritage and its archaeological treasures, it must also instill a renewed sense of national pride and identity. Finally, under the pressure of private sector reconstruction of the city centre, the plan must be sufficiently all-embracing to protect the public interest." (Beirut Reborn, Solidere 1996).

However, perhaps inevitably for an undertaking of this size, the project has drawn a great deal of criticism. Former property owners in the project area have

claimed that the real value of land and property has been massively underestimated, describing Solidere as having pulled off the "biggest land-grab in history". Others claim that many of the old buildings which could have been restored have been demolished, the bulldozers coming "like thieves in the night" to clear away what would have been costly restoration projects offering limited returns compared with the new office developments that will replace them. At the same time, the differing priorities of archaeologists keen to uncover and preserve as much as possible, and developers impatient to get on with the job of rebuilding the city centre have led at times to tensions and even hostilities.

Whatever the rights and wrongs of the various issues associated with the project, it at least represents a carefully planned and coordinated attempt to rebuild the city centre; elsewhere in Lebanon the total absence of any planning structure whatsoever is all too evident. Time will tell whether the new city centre will "reconnect a once-divided city" and "instill a renewed sense of national pride and identity".

Further east along Rue Weygand, on the south side of the road, is the Omari **Omari Mosque** Mosque (or Grand Mosque), originally built in the mid-12th century by the Crusaders as the Church of St John the Baptist (on the site of an earlier Byzantine church which was itself built on the foundations of the Roman temple of Jupiter). In 1291, after the Mamelukes had finally driven the Crusaders from Beirut for the last time, it was converted into a mosque.

The Solidere information centre, in the grid of pedestrian streets to the north **Solidere** of Rue Weygand, boasts a huge and elaborate scale model of the BCD which **information** gives an excellent overview of the area, as well as more detailed scale models of **centre** different areas, and even individual buildings. Information boards provide insights into various aspects of the downtown area, including the excavations. ■ *0900-1500, 1600-1800, closed Sat and Sun. Free.*

To the southeast of Place d'Etoile, on Rue Emir Bechir before you reach Mar- **St George's** tyr's Square is the Maronite Cathedral of St George. Heavily damaged during **Cathedral** the war, it has now been completely restored to its former glory. In its present form it dates from 1890, though it stands on the site of an older Maronite church built during the early 18th century. The towering façade, which is modelled on the Santa Maria Maggoria in Rome, is extremely imposing. The interior, with its richly decorated ceiling and vast expanses of marble, is both lavish and yet at the same time somehow austere. Particularly striking is the wooden dome-topped structure which stands over the altar, supported on four massive wooden columns carved into twisting muscle-like corkscrews and topped by ornate Corinthian capitals. Behind it, on the wall of the apse, is a large painting of St George slaying the dragon. The cathedral has a basement of cavernous Ottoman barrel vaults which served as a storage and inventory centre for the archaeologists who worked so hard to rescue what they could of Beirut's past before it headed briskly into the future.

Immediately to the left of the cathedral as you face it, a number of re-erected columns mark the **Cardo Maximus** of the Roman city. The whole area surrounding the cathedral to the north was the focus of intensive excavations which have uncovered a large portion of the Roman market area and the remains of a number of important buildings. It is not clear exactly which of the excavations in this area will be preserved in the final plan.

Martyrs' Square Still just a bare area of gravel at the time of writing, Martyrs' Square is eventually to be restored. Popularly known in Arabic as 'Al Bourj' (literally 'tower'), after a medieval watchtower which once stood at its southern end, it was later known as the 'Place des Cannons', when a huge cannon was set up here in 1772 during a brief occupation of the city by the Russian fleet of Catherine the Great. The name, Martyrs' Square, dates from the execution here of the leaders of the rebellion against Ottoman rule in 1840. Until recently, a statue commemorating the martyrs stood in the square. During the civil war the square lay right on the Green Line; the statue was riddled with bullet holes but remained standing, becoming a poignant symbol of the city's suffering. It is currently being restored and will eventually be returned to its original place. Martyrs' Square was always a social focal point of old Beirut and in 1994 the famous Lebanese singer Fayrouz performed there to a mixed Christian and Muslim audience, her first live performance since the start of the war, in a concert which embodied the re-emerging peace and unity of the city.

Heading east from Martyrs' Square along Avenue Charles Helou, if you look over the north side of the avenue, you can see below you traces of the ancient **Canaanite and Phoenician city walls**. In the corner, by the point where the avenue crosses over Rue George Haddad, are the foundations of a later circular tower. At the time of writing it was not clear whether these archaeological features would be preserved or built over.

East Beirut

Rue de Damas marks the boundary between East and West Beirut, the various districts of East Beirut extending south up the hillside from the main port area. Although generally ignored in favour of West Beirut, there are an increasing number of restaurants as well as bars and nightclubs in this area (see under the respective headings in Essentials). Unlike West Beirut, it has also managed to retain far more of its Ottoman and French Mandate architecture, giving a taste of what the city was like before it was overtaken by developers. The most striking example of the opulent architecture of the late Ottoman period can be seen in the Sursock Museum building and in a number of the other houses along Rue Sursock.

Sursock Museum The strikingly elegant building in which this privately run museum is housed is one of several to be found around this affluent quarter of Christian East Beirut, but is of special interest in that it is open to the public. Built in 1902, it was dedicated as a museum on the death of its owner Nicolas Ibrahim Sursock in 1952 and since then has been maintained by the Sursock family as a museum (or, more accurately, a gallery of contemporary art). There is a small permanent exhibition which is supplemented by annual retrospective, foreign and other exhibitions. As well as being worth a visit simply to see the building, the exhibitions give an interesting insight into contemporary Lebanese art, much of it of a very high standard. ■ *1000-1300, closed Sun (except if there are special exhibitions, in which case it stays open on Sun and also opens in the afternoon from 1600-1900). Free. For details of current exhibitions, T334133.*

Around Beirut

Given Lebanon's small size, Beirut can effectively be used as a base for visiting the entire country, with just about all the places of interest reachable as day-trips from the capital. However this involves the tiresome process of repeatedly having to negotiate the city's sprawling and congested suburbs. The

East Beirut

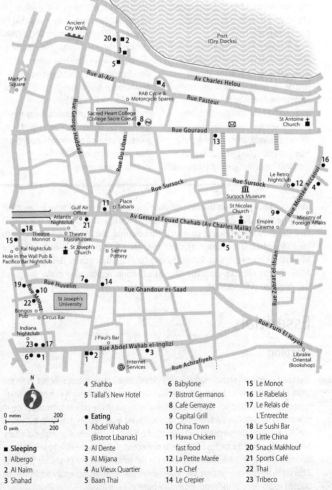

Beirut

	4 Shahba	6 Babylone	15 Le Monot
	5 Tallal's New Hotel	7 Bistrot Germanos	16 Le Rabelais
		8 Cafe Gemayze	17 Le Relais de
	● **Eating**	9 Capital Grill	L'Entrecôte
	1 Abdel Wahab	10 China Town	18 Le Sushi Bar
	(Bistrot Libanais)	11 Hawa Chicken	19 Little China
■ **Sleeping**	2 Al Dente	fast food	20 Snack Makhlouf
1 Albergo	3 Al Mijana	12 La Petite Marée	21 Sports Café
2 Al Naim	4 Au Vieux Quartier	13 Le Chef	22 Thai
3 Shahad	5 Baan Thai	14 Le Crepier	23 Tribeco

War and extravagance: the Summerland Hotel

The Summerland Hotel epitomizes some of the more surreal aspects of Lebanon's civil war. Opened in 1979, it was, as Thomas Friedman put it, "the first resort hotel designed for people who wanted to vacation inside a civil war zone – in style." The idea of a luxury hotel resort being built in the midst of a brutal civil war may sound somewhat incongruous, not to mention precarious. However, the demand was certainly there amongst wealthy Lebanese for a fantasy world where one could escape from the grim realities of death and destruction, for a place where, according to the hotel's publicity literature, "life is always shiny and warm...". And the Summerland offered the shiniest and warmest fantasy that money could buy.

But in order to immerse themselves in this fantasy, people needed to feel that they really had escaped from the war just outside. They needed a sense of security. The Summerland provided this on a grand scale, establishing itself as a completely self-sufficient enclave-going-on-fortress. The hotel's specifications certainly must have been reassuring; two 12,000 gallon fuel tanks capable of keeping its generators running for a month; a 3,400 gallon reserve of petrol for its private fleet of taxis and cars; 18 industrial freezers which could hold enough food to last for the whole summer season; its own artesian well and water purification system; an underground bomb shelter; and most importantly, its own fully armed private militia.

The rich and the famous flocked to the hotel, and within its well guarded walls flourished an elegant and extravagant life of champagne and cocktail parties round the pool. In 1980, in what must have been a sublimely ironic event, the hotel even managed to fly Gloria Gaynor in to sing I Will Survive to the guests, half of whom would have been arms dealers and drug barons. In 1990, however, the politics of the war, if not the actual fighting, found their way inside the Summerland when President Hrawi and his cabinet set up headquarters here in opposition to General Michel Aoun who ruled from the Presidential Palace at Baabda. Today the hotel has lost none of its glamour and reputation, though now there are plenty of new competitors in the luxury extravagance industry.

most obvious places in the immediate vicinity of the capital which can most easily be visited as day-trips include Nahr el-Kalb, Jounieh and Byblos (Jbail) (see Coast North of Beirut chapter); Broumanna, Beit Meri and Jeita Grotto (see Mount Lebanon chapter); Deir el-Qamar and Beit ed-Dine (see Chouf Mountains chapter); and Sidon (Saida) (see Coast South of Beirut chapter). Many of the trips up into the Mount Lebanon region also make for good day-trips from the capital.

Essentials

Sleeping

Sleeping
■ on maps pages
402, 410, 415, & 419
Price codes:
see inside front cover

The luxury end of the hotel market is ridiculously over-represented in Beirut. With the tourist/business visitor boom yet to arrive, this means that there is still competition between hotels. The price categories below are based on the official full room price; in practice, however, discounts of as much as 50% are often readily available. It is worth checking around the websites, or emailing the hotels for details of any special offers. Similarly, if you go through a Lebanese travel agent, they may be able to secure huge discounts from the advertised rack rates. On the other hand, watch out for the hefty 21% (16% service charge plus 5% government tax) which is generally added to the quoted room price in the more expensive hotels.

Beirut

LL *Bristol*, Rue Madame Curie, T351400, F351409, bristol@dm.net.lb Luxurious rooms with a/c, TV/dish, IDD, minibar, safe box and attached bath. Restaurants, bars. Conference and banqueting facilities. Free access for guests to swimming pool, gym, sauna and squash at the *Heliopolis* health centre. Full shopping facilities etc. All very elegant (classic 1920s style) with lots of attention to detail. Worth checking for special offers, which can be excellent value (eg, at the time of writing, US$100 for a single/double with lots of extra perks). **LL** *Holiday Inn Martinez*, Phoenicia St, Ain el-Mreisse, T368111, F370333, www.holidayinn-martinez.com Suitably luxurious rooms with a/c, TV/dish, IDD, minibar, safe box and attached bath. Asian/international cuisine restaurant, coffee shop, bar and nightclub. Full conference and banqueting facilities. *Inn Shape* fitness club, complete with indoor pool etc. Shops, *Payless* car hire, *Khayat* travel agent. Recently opened and all very swish, though the dodgy nightclubs across the road lend a distinctly seedy atmosphere to the area. There is also a second branch, the *Holiday Inn Dunes*, in the upmarket Verdun district of Beirut (see 'Beirut: Overview' map), which incorporates a huge shopping complex (see under shopping), though it is a long way from the centre of town. **LL** *Le Vendome Inter-Continental*, Ain el-Mreisse, T369280, F360169. The *Phoenicia's* smaller sister, described as a 'boutique hotel'. Luxurious rooms with a/c, TV/dish, IDD, minibar, safe box and attached bath. Most rooms with balcony and sea views. Restaurants, bar, coffee shop. Conference and banqueting facilities. Free access to *St George's Yacht Club*, *La Plage* and the *Riviera* hotel's marina/beach club. *Hala* car hire. All very nice, but equally expensive. **LL** *Meridien Commodore*, Rue Commodore, Hamra, T350400, F345806, www.commodore.com.lb Luxurious rooms with a/c, TV/dish, IDD, minibar, safe box and attached bath. Restaurants, bar, coffee shop. Full conference and banqueting facilities. Outdoor swimming pool, plus free access to *Lifestyles* health club (see under Sports). Shops, *Avis* car hire, *Air France* office, travel agents. Favoured haunt of foreign reporters during the war, this hotel acquired a legendary reputation for managing to stay open in the midst of total bedlam. Now part of the Meridien chain, but still popularly known as just the 'Commodore'. **LL** *Phoenicia Inter-Continental*, Minet el-Hosn, T369100, F369101, www.interconti.com A huge complex comprising three towers and an extensive commercial centre. Super-luxurious rooms with a/c, TV/dish/video (plus interactive email, internet, movies etc), IDD, minibar, safe box and attached bath. Numerous restaurants, coffee shop, bars etc. Full conference and banqueting facilities (the biggest in Beirut). Indoor and outdoor pools, health spa (still under construction at the time of writing), shopping arcades, *Avis* car hire, *Kurban* travel agent/tour operator, *MEA* airline office. This was Beirut's most prestigious hotel before the war, and no expense has been spared this time round in recreating an atmosphere of lavish 1920s opulence. The broad sweep of the red-carpeted main stairway (with escalators to one side for those not inclined to strain their legs), the huge hanging chandelier and the endless expanses of marble set the tone for the rest of the hotel. Dripping with money, and worth a gawp, if nothing else. **LL** *Riviera*, Av de Paris (Corniche), Ras Beirut, T373210, F365239, www.riviera_hotel.com.lb Luxurious rooms with a/c, TV/dish, IDD, minibar, attached bath and balcony (great views over Corniche, marina and sea). Also cheaper rooms (**L** category) without sea views. Restaurants, bar and coffee shop. Full conference and banqueting facilities. Private *Yacht Club* across the road (linked to the hotel by a tunnel), complete with marina, watersports, diving centre, health centre etc. Prime location on the Corniche. **LL** *Summerland*, Al Akhtal as-Saghir St, Jnah district, South Beirut, T858000, F856666, www.summerland.com.lb Reasonably luxurious rooms with a/c, TV/dish/video, IDD/fax, minibar, attached bath and balcony with sea view. Restaurants, coffee shop, bar and nightclub. Own private sand beach, Olympic-size swimming pool plus 'waterfall' pool, tennis, volleyball, basket ball. *Club 500* for wide range of watersports, plus full health club and beauty parlour. Conference and banqueting facilities. Shopping centre, car hire and travel agents. Beirut's most famous luxury hotel complex during the civil war (see box). Today somewhat eclipsed in terms of luxury by the likes of the *Phoenicia Inter-Continental*, but still the best in terms of its private sand beach, swimming pools and wide range of watersports.

Beirut

L *Albergo*, 137 Rue Abdel Wahab el-Inglizi, Achrafieh, T339797, F339999, albergo@ relaischateaux.fr Lavish rooms with a/c, TV/dish, Hi-Fi, IDD/fax, minibar and attached bath. In a welcome departure from the usual massive proportions of Beirut's 5-star chains, this intimate hotel is full of atmosphere and character. Set in a beautiful Otto-man-period mansion, each room is individually furnished in opulent style. As well as the *Al Dente* restaurant downstairs (see 'Eating'), there is a dining hall upstairs and a lovely rooftop terrace/bar complete with its own small swimming pool. **L** *Marriot*, Rue Adnan Hakim, Jnah district, South Beirut, T840540, F840345, www.marriott. com Luxurious rooms with a/c, TV/dish, IDD, minibar, safe box and attached bath. Restaurants, bar, coffee shop. Rooftop swimming pool and health club. Conference facilities. Modernistic complex, built around a central glass-covered courtyard with its own shopping mall etc occupying part of ground floor. Very swish, but no sea views and somewhat remote. **L** *Plaza*, off Rue Hamra, T755777, F751241. Luxurious though somewhat characterless rooms with a/c, TV/dish, IDD, minibar, safe box and attached bath. Notable mostly for its franchise outlets, namely *Ciros Pizza Pomodoro* and *Churrascos* (an Argentinian steak house), as well as its own *Café Plaza 1954*. Quick to offer discounts which bring the rooms down to **A** category.

AL *Bayview*, Rue Minet el-Hosn, Ain el-Mreisse (entrance next door to *Hard Rock Café*; rooms above it), T/F373090. Luxurious rooms with a/c, TV/dish, IDD, minibar, safe box and attached bath. Choice of sea view rooms (with balcony), or slightly cheaper 'busi-ness' rooms. Restaurants/bars (rooftop, with great views). Conference and banquet-ing facilities. Now part of the *Golden Tulip* chain. Great location. Reasonably good value. **AL** *Cadmos*, Rue Minet el-Hosn, Ain el-Mreisse, T374892, F374898. Small but reasonably comfortable rooms with a/c, TV/dish, IDD, minibar, attached bath and small balconies with sea view. Restaurant, café, bar. Lacking that touch of luxury dis-played by its neighbours, but quick to offer discounts. **AL** *Cavalier*, Rue Makdissi, Hamra, T353001, F347681, cavatel@dm.net.lb Comfortable, fairly spacious rooms with a/c, TV/dish, IDD, minibar, attached bath and balcony. Restaurant and bar. Recently refurbished. **AL** *Royal Garden*, Rue Emile Edde, Hamra, T350010, F353241, rogarden@dm.net.lb Comfortable rooms with a/c, TV/dish, IDD, attached bath and 'garden' balcony. Restaurant, coffee shop, pub, small rooftop swimming pool. Rather expensive for what you get, try bargaining. **AL** *Searock*, Rue Salah ud-Din el-Ayoubi, Raouche, T788488, F787741, searock@cyberia.com.lb A/c, TV/dish, IDD, minibar, safe box, attached bath and balcony (rooms at rear with excellent sea views). Restau-rants, café, bar, business centre. Now run by *Signature Series*. Nice location. **AL** *Weiner Haus*, Rue Lyon, Hamra, T350050, F351322, weinerH@cyberia.net.lb Comfortable rooms with a/c, TV/dish, phone, attached bath, and balcony. Restaurant, coffee shop, 'super nightclub', conference room, health club. Overpriced, but quick to offer dis-counts of up to 50%, bringing it down to **B** category and making it much better value.

A *Bliss Suites*, Rue Bliss, Hamra, T367531, F367164, blisshotel@terra.net.lb Spacious rooms with a/c, TV/dish, IDD, fridge and attached bath. Restaurant and bar. Brand new hotel, and all very luxurious. **A** *Casa d'Or*, Rue Jeanne d'Arc, Hamra, T347850, F347840, casador@cyberia.net.lb A/c, TV/dish, IDD, kitchenette (fridge, cooker, sink) and attached bath. Restaurant and bar. Comfortable but a little overpriced. **A** *Elegant Suites*, Rue Sourati, Hamra, T/F755600, www.elegantsuites.com.lb Studios with a/c, TV/dish, IDD, kitchenette area, sitting area and attached bath. Also suites (**AL** category) with sep-arate kitchenettes, sitting room and bedroom. All very comfortable, with significant dis-counts for longer stays. **A** *Howard Johnson (Plaza) Grand*, Rue Tannoukhiniye, Ras Beirut, T739860, F739866, www.hojo.com A/c, TV/dish, IDD, minibar and attached bath. Restaurant, bar, 'super nightclub' and *Versaille* theatre downstairs. Full conference and banqueting facilities. Small rooftop swimming pool and health centre. Recently fully refurbished throughout. Good value. **A** *Mercure Berkeley*, Rue Jeanne d'Arc,

Hamra, T340600, F602250, mercurbk@cyberia.net.lb A/c, TV/dish, IDD, minibar and attached bath. Restaurant and bar. Small, friendly well run place, now part of the *Accor* group's *Mercure* chain. **A** *Napoleon*, Rue Nehme Yafet, Hamra, T340013, F354658. A/c, TV/dish, IDD, attached bath and balcony. Restaurant and bar. Conference and banqueting facilities. Small swimming pool on 6th floor. Comfortable and characterless.

B *Charles*, Rue Rustam Pacha, Ain el-Mreisse, T362268, F363244, charle@cyberia. net.lb A/c, TV/dish, IDD, attached bath and balcony. Recently opened. Smart but rather characterless. Fairly good value. **B** *Lord's*, Manara, T740382, F740385. A/c, TV/dish, phone, minibar and attached bath. Recently refurbished. Best rooms at front with balconies and sea views. Also some cheaper non-refurbished rooms (**C** category). **B** *Marble Tower*, Rue Makdissi, Hamra, T354586, F346262, www.marbletower. com.lb A/c, TV/dish, IDD, minibar, attached bath and balcony. Restaurant and *Pickwick* pub. Reasonably comfortable but a little expensive; try bargaining down to **C** category. **B** *Mayflower*, Rue Nehme Yafet, Hamra, T340680, F342038. www.mayflower. com.lb A/c, TV/dish, IDD, fridge, attached bath and balcony. Also cheaper **C** category rooms with same facilities but in old wing of hotel. Restaurant, pleasant *Duke of Wellington* pub. Small rooftop swimming pool. Friendly, well run hotel. Good value. Recommended.

C *Astra*, Rue Nehme Yafet, Hamra, T346600, F347733. A/c, TV, phone, fridge and attached bath. Looking a bit run down, with peeling paint. Worth it only if you can bargain them down to **D** category. **C** *Cedarland*, Rue Omar Ben Abdul Aziz, Hamra, T340233, F853579. A/c, TV, phone, attached bath and balcony. Simple and reasonably clean, though some rooms are in a better state of repair than others. **C** *Embassy*, Rue Makdissi, Hamra, T/F340814. A/c, TV, phone, fridge and attached bath. Quieter rooms at rear, with balconies overlooking small, pleasant patio garden. Fairly simple, but OK. **C** *Mace*, Rue Jeanne d'Arc, Hamra, T/F344626, macehot@cyberia.net.lb A/c, TV/dish, phone, fridge, attached bath. Restaurant and bar. Simple, clean and unassuming place. Fairly good value (particularly the trebles for US$50). **C** *Orient Prince*, off Rue Emile Edde, Hamra, T340030, F343012. A/c, TV, phone, fridge, attached bath and balcony. Restaurant, pool table in lobby. Rather shabby 1970s décor but reasonably clean and comparatively good value. **C** *West House Residence*, Rue Sourati, T350450, F352450. Primarily long-let apartments, but also rooms on daily basis with a/c, TV, kitchenette and attached bath. Unassuming but fairly good value, especially for longer stays (eg 1 week **D** category, 1 month **E** category).

D The limited number of hotels in this category, though good value by Beirut standards, are overpriced for what you get, offering only a marginal improvement (if any at all) over cheapies such as the *Pension Home Valery*. **D** *Moonlight*, off Rue Hamra, T352308. Shabby rooms with fan, attached bath and balcony. Relatively cheap (single/double US$20/25), but rather run-down, with a slightly seedy atmosphere. Not recommended for women travellers. **D** *Mushrek*, Rue Makdissi, Hamra, T345773. Simple, reasonably clean rooms with fan, sink, balcony and shared bath. OKish. **D** *San Lorenzo*, Rue Hamra, T348604. Simple/basic but reasonably clean rooms with fan, attached bath and balcony. Also slightly cheaper rooms (single/double US$15/20) with shared bath. *Taverne Suisse* restaurant and bar attached to hotel. OK value but nothing to get too excited about. **D** *University*, Rue Bliss, T365391. A/c, phone and attached bath. Some rooms with balcony. Common area with TV/dish. Use of kitchen on 5th floor. Simple going on rather shabby and run-down but friendly and safe. Generally fully booked up by AUB students during term time; more likely to have vacancies during holidays. **D/E** *Regis*, off Rue Ibn Sina, Ain el-Mreisse, T361845. Simple, reasonably clean rooms with a/c, TV, fridge, attached bath and balcony (double US$30), or much more basic ones with just fan and attached bath. Pretty run-down overall, but friendly and reasonably good value for Beirut.

Beirut

E/F Women travellers, who might not feel comfortable in the budget places mentioned below, particularly if travelling alone, might consider trying the *YWCA*, Rue Rustom Pacha, Ain el-Mreisse, T368019, F371519. Shared double rooms here cost US$15 per night/US$175 per month, or a bed in the dormitories (sleeping 6-8 people) costs US$10 per night/US$150 per month (both with shared shower/toilet facilities). There are also a small number of private rooms with attached bath for US$25 per night/US$300 per month. People staying here can use the kitchen facilities. It is all very clean, well maintained and safe/hassle free, as well as being a great place to meet young Lebanese women. However, doors close each night at 2300. **NB** The hostel is generally fully booked up during term-time; the only time rooms are likely to be available is during the summer vacation period (July-Sep), but even then it is essential to book ahead as they are not used to taking in people without a prior arrangement.

Budget hotels are very thin on the ground in Beirut, and pretty basic. In West Beirut there is the *Pension Home Valery* and its various offshoots (all in the same building). In East Beirut, by the port area, there are several slightly cheaper places which cater primarily for Syrian workers in Beirut, though they are getting used to backpackers turning up. **F/G *Pension Home Valery***, 2nd Floor Saab Building, Rue de Phoenicie (no sign outside, but entrance is next door to the *Wash Me* car wash which features a Mini suspended from the wall of the building; go to the very back and take the lift, or use the stairs), T362169. Dormitory beds US$6. Fan, share shower/toilet. Single/double rooms (same facilities) US$8/12. Rooms all simple but clean, with clean bedding. A/c lobby area, with TV/dish. Free use of kitchen. Very popular with backpackers and probably the best of the budget options in Beirut (some room for bargaining). Friendly, helpful staff. Recommended. Down on the first floor is the *Villa Hala* (same phone number, plus under the same management), which is slightly cheaper (dorm beds US$5) but deals primarily with Syrian workers. On the 3rd floor there is another *Pension Home Valery* (T364906), run by a member of the same family, though now completely separate. Prices are identical to its counterpart on the 2nd floor, though the facilities are not quite as good. On the 4th floor is the *Pension Mehanna*, T365216. Dorm beds here cost LL7,000, with fan and shared shower/toilet. A hot shower here costs an extra LL2,000. Clean and OK, though there have been reports of thefts from the rooms in the past. **G *Al Naim***, off Av Charles Helou (by the port area), T447297, F387375. Dormitory beds LL5,000, or rent a treble for LL15,000 (also one double room, LL10,000). Fan, shared shower/toilet. Free use of kitchen. Basic but fairly clean, and friendly. The quietest of the cheapies in this area. **G *Shahad*** (sign outside just says 'hotel'), off Av Charles Helou (by the port area), T564154. All rooms are trebles; LL5,000 per bed, or rent the whole room for LL15,000. Fan, shared shower/toilet. Free use of kitchen. **G *Shahba***, off Rue al-Arz/Rue Pasteur (by the port area), T564287. Dormitory beds LL5,000, or rent whole room for LL15,000. Fan and shared shower/toilet. Free use of kitchen. Basic but fairly clean, and friendly. **G *Tallal's New Hotel***, off Av Charles Helou (by the port area), T/F562567. Dormitory beds with fan and shared shower/toilet LL5,000. Doubles LL15,000 with fan and TV/dish, or LL12,000 with just fan; share shower/toilet in either case. Free use of kitchen. Overall the cleanest of the cheapies in this area, with reliable hot water, but rather noisy now that Av Charles Helou is open to traffic.

Eating

● *on maps pages 410, 415 & 419*

Beirut is bursting at the seams with restaurants and places to eat, so the following is of necessity just a small selection of what's on offer. New places open on an almost daily basis and, with such fierce competition, existing ones frequently close down or change hands, so be prepared for significant differences between what's listed here and what you find on the ground. The Ministry of Tourism's annual *Restaurant, Nightclub and Café Guide* is fairly comprehensive. There are also various privately published booklets giving restaurant listings, though they are not that accurate or informative. The excellent *Beyrouth à Table* (unfortunately in French only) has not been updated since 1996 (the publishers/editors apparently felt that it was no longer possible to keep pace with the changes in the restaurant sector!). Note that many of Beirut's bars and nightclubs also double as excellent restaurants in their own right (see also 'Entertainment', below).

Aux Quatre Saisons, *Summerland* hotel. Open for breakfast, lunch and dinner. French cuisine. *Benihana*, *Meridien Commodore* hotel. Japanese cuisine. Open sushi bar on Tue and Wed lunchtimes (US$25 per head; eat as much as you want). *Blue Elephant*, *Searock* hotel, Rue Salah ud-Din el-Ayoubi, Raouche, T788588. Extremely upmarket Thai restaurant. Around US$40-50 per head. *Eau De Vie*, *Phoenicia Inter-Continental* hotel. Open 1230-1530, 2000-2300, closed Sat lunchtime and all day Sun. Up on the 11th floor. Described as offering 'progressive French' cuisine. Very elegant and nouveau, and seriously pricey. *Indochine*, *Phoenicia Inter-Continental* hotel. Open 1230-1530, 2000-2330, closed Sat lunchtime and all day Sun. Vietnamese cuisine in a French colonial setting. Set lunch US$25, including a glass of wine and service, but with 5% tax extra. *Kona Kai*, *Marriott* hotel. Open 1900-late, closed Sun. Chinese cuisine. Fixed menu during the week, around LL30,000 per head, plus 5% tax. *La Casbah*, *Meridien Commodore* hotel. Open 2030-late, closed Sun. Lebanese cuisine to the accompaniment of live singers and belly dancing shows. *Le Jardin*, *Summerland* hotel. Open for lunch and dinner. Lebanese cuisine. *Mosaic*, *Phoenicia Inter-Continental* hotel. Open daily 0700-2330. A la carte or buffet breakfasts (US$18) and lunch/dinner (US$30). Choice of Lebanese or international cuisine. *Palms*, *Marriott* hotel. Open daily 0630-1130. International cuisine. Buffet lunch LL39,000 per head, plus 5% tax. Sunday brunch LL45,000 per head, plus 5% tax.

Luxury hotel restaurants: Expensive

As well as being the focus for much evening cruising and posing, the Corniche around Raouche/Manara is an area where expensive, upmarket establishments compete with increasingly popular western fast-food chains and restaurants such as *KFCs* and *Pizza Hut*. (We have not bothered to list such places; if you are interested in eating at them, you know what to expect, but bear in mind that they are not as cheap as in Europe or North America).

West Beirut: Raouche & Manara

Expensive *Al Chahrour*, Av du General de Gaulle, Manara, T869300. Upmarket restaurant combining Arabic and European cuisine (seafood, grills and fondues a speciality). Around US$20-30 per head. *Tokyo*, Rue Negib Ardati, T740602. Open 1200-1430, 1900-2400, closed Sun. Japanese restaurant and bar specializing in sushi (sushi sets US$25-35), or from around US$20-25 per head upwards. *Tresors de Mer*, Av du General de Gaulle, Rauche, T789789. Open daily 1200-late. Smart, upmarket seafood restaurant. From around US$30 per head upwards.

Mid-range *Abou Hassan*, Rue Salah ud-Din el-Ayoubi, Manara, T741725. Open daily 1200-late. Hidden away on a small street leading inland back towards Hamra and Ras Beirut, this small, traditional Lebanese restaurant has a well deserved reputation for serving excellent Arabic food at very reasonable prices (from around US$10 per head for a full-blown meal). Pleasant atmosphere and friendly staff. Recommended. Conveniently, there is even a 24-hr taxi company next door (*Caracas Taxi*, T741959). *Bay Rock*, Av du General de Gaulle, Raouche. Open daily 0500-0300 (22 hrs!). A pleasant, unpretentious café/restaurant with seating out on a long, narrow terrace or indoors. Excellent views out over Pigeon Rocks, and a lovely place from which to watch the sun go down over them. Reasonably priced for tea/coffee (LL2,500) and fresh fruit juices (LL3,000-3,500). Breakfasts (omlettes LL5,000-7,000, fuul LL4,000, fatteh LL5,000), as well as a full lunch and dinner menu (Arabic/international; around US$10-15 per head). *Bella Napoli*, Rue Salah ud-Din el-Ayoubi (off Av du General de Gaulle), Raouche, T863332. Pleasant, intimate Italian restaurant. From around US$10-15 per head. *La Grotte aux Pigeons Petit Café*, Av du General de Gaulle, Raouche, T03-886633. Open daily 0900-late. Now part of the *Petit Café* chain. Arabic cuisine for around US$10-15 per head, or more for fish. Live music in the evenings. Large dining hall (great views overlooking Pigeon Rocks) and outdoor terrace in summer. *La Terrasse Dbaibo*, Av du General de Gaulle, Raouche T812893. Prime location on the cliffs looking out to sea. Pleasant outdoor terrace in summer. Arabic and European food (US$10-15 per head, or more for seafood), or just go to enjoy a nargileh and drinks, also with *Bouzouki* restaurant/dancing club. *Rawda Café*, off Av du General de Gaulle, Manara (set back from the road, around the side of the *Luna Park* fairground and overlooking Bain Militaire). Pleasant café/restaurant with terraces overlooking the sea and a shaded garden area. Popular with families. Arabic food from around US$10 per head, or you can just come for tea/coffee, cold drinks, snacks etc. *TGI Fridays*, Av du General de Gaulle, Raouche, T802587. Part of the international chain of bar/restaurants. American/international cuisine, from around US$15-20 per head upwards. Regular live music. Often booked out for private parties. Upstairs is the *Chicken Tikka* (Arabic cuisine), with great views, but otherwise just a large, rather characterless hall geared very much towards Gulf state tourists.

Seriously cheap This part of West Beirut is really the last place to come for seriously cheap eats, but if after walking the length of the Corniche you find yourself staggering around Raouche, weak with hunger and drooling at all the fancy restaurants, one possible option is *Al Shami Bakery*, Av du General de Gaulle. As its name suggests, it is essentially a bakery and sells mostly biscuits, sweets etc, but out on the terrace there is usually a bread oven on the go, baking up delicious *mannoushi*, which makes for an excellent cheap snack. Just off the Corniche in Manara, meanwhile, is *Hani's Snacks*, Rue de Bahrain (off Av du General de Gaulle). Although perhaps nudging at the 'cheap' category, this fast food place serves reasonably priced burgers and chips etc (around US$5 per head for a meal, or less for snacks).

West Beirut: Ain el-Mreisse & Minet el-Hosn

As well as the inevitable arrival of *McDonalds*, across the road from the *Hard Rock Café* (see 'Entertainment', below), there are several good restaurants around this area.

Expensive *Café d'Orient*, Rue Minet el-Hosn, T366222. Newly opened, very plush and upmarket place incorporating 3 restaurants, all overlooking the sea. The first serves international cuisine (pizzas, steaks etc), the second is a fish restaurant (à la carte, or set menus of US$28 or US$38 per head, minimum 4 people), while the third is downstairs in *La Plage* beach club (see 'Beach Clubs', above), and also offers international cuisine, though in slightly more informal surroundings. *Casablanca*, Rue Dar el-Mreisse, T369334. Open 1200-1600, 2000-late, closed Mon. Set in a beautiful old Ottoman building with stylish modern internal décor. International cuisine. From around US$20-25 per head upwards (lunchtime fixed menu LL27,000 per head), or around US$10-15 for Sunday 'brunch'. Also a popular drinking place later on in the evening. *La Paillote*, Rue Minet el-Hosn, T369113. Open daily 1200-2400. Pleasant, recently opened seafood restaurant. Great sea views from the window tables. More reasonably priced than most other seafood restaurants in Beirut (set menus from US$23 per head for fish and mezze). *Spaghetteria Italiano*, Rue Dar el-Mreisse, T363487. Open daily 1200-1700, 1800-2400. Large, modern a/c restaurant with views over the Corniche. Around US$20-25 per head (more for fish), or slightly less with some careful selection.

Mid-range *Café Ajram*, Rue Minet el-Hosn. Simple, unassuming terrace café/restaurant overlooking the sea. You can come here just for a tea, coffee or juice (LL2,000), a *nargileh* (LL7,0000), or a beer (LL3,000). If you fancy something to eat, the usual range of Arabic food is on offer (mezze dishes and chicken or meat grills etc) for around US$10 per head, or you could go for fish (from US$25 per kilo). A pleasant place to come and enjoy the sunset. *Pasta Di Casa*, just off Rue Clemenceau (nearly into Hamra district), T366909. Open daily 1200-late. Small, pleasant, unpretentious Italian restaurant specializing in fresh pasta made on the premises. Around US$10-15 per head.

Cheap *Al Tajaz Fakieh*, Av de Paris (Corniche). Open daily 1200-late. Fast food-style place (barbecue chicken LL5,750, or barbecue chicken meal LL10,000). Also with café section on terrace outside. *Café Al Jamal*, off Av de Paris (Corniche). Open daily 0530-1300, 1700-late. Pleasant wooden shack-style restaurant/café serving simple Arabic food at reasonable prices, eg fuul or hummus LL3,000, fatteh LL4,000, mezze dishes LL3,000 (all plus 12% service), as well as tea, coffee etc.

Seriously cheap *Mardo's Gourmet Snack*, Rue Graham, Ain el-Mreisse (next door to *Theatre de Beyrouth*). On the borderline between cheap and seriously cheap in terms of what you actually get for your money, but a friendly, well run and spotlessly clean sandwich bar serving freshly made sandwiches for LL2,000-3,000, as well as salads (LL4,000) and soft drinks. Also a fairly good deal is the sandwich bar towards the top (south) end of Rue de Phoenicie. There are a couple other simple sandwich bars along Rue Ibn Sina.

Mid-range *All Fresh Pasta*, Kalaa St, Ras Beirut (near Lebanese American University), T785556. Specializes in fresh pasta made on the premises. From around US$10 per head for a full meal (less for snacks). Eat-in or take away (also free delivery). *Elissar*, Bliss St, T365285. Open 0900-late, closed Sun. Smart, modern café-style restaurant/bar. Some Lebanese food, but mostly international cuisine. Around US$15-20 per head upwards. *Istambuli*, Rue Commodore (near *Commodore* hotel; officially Rue de Baalbek), T352049. Open daily 1130-2400. Traditional Lebanese restaurant with an extensive menu of good quality Arabic food. Popular at lunchtime with businessmen. From around US$15-20 per head upwards. *Marrouche*, Rue Sidani, T803600. Divided into 2 parts, with a 24-hr snack bar serving good shawarmas and other sandwiches and a restaurant downstairs (also open 24 hrs) where you can eat hummus, fuul, fatteh etc as well as sandwiches and admire the unusual décor. Good value (from around US$10 per head for a full meal). *Panda Shohai*, Rue Sadat (between *The Net* internet café and *Bliss Suites* hotel), T738609. Open daily 1100-2400. Chinese restaurant and takeaway. Around US$10 per head. Good value set meals (LL10,000-15,000). *Rice & Spice*, Rue Madame Curie (opposite the *Bristol* hotel), T340973. Open daily 1100-1700, 1900-2300. Small, smart, pleasantly furnished restaurant serving good Chinese food. From around US$10 per head upwards (or more like US$20 plus if you go for duck or seafood). Takeaway service (free delivery on orders over US$10). *Uncle Sam's*, Bliss St, T353500. Trendy/stylish sit-down restaurant. International and Arabic cuisine. Around US$10-20 per head for a full meal. Lunchtime specials (salad, hummus, main dish, soft drink and ice cream) LL10,000. Also sandwiches/subs LL6,000.

Cheap *Kabab-Ji*, Rue Hamra. Part of a national chain. Brightly lit, spotlessly clean and efficiently run, this place is primarily a takeaway offering a range of sandwiches for LL3,000-3,500. There is also a sit-down area where you can tuck into any of the sandwich items served as a platter for LL7,000. A bowl of fuul, complete with a spread of olives, chillis, tomatoes, mint and radishes, costs LL5,0000, though if you eat in there is an additional 14% service charge. *Mao Zedong Chinese Takeaway*, Rue Sidani (next door to *Tanmia Chicken Corner*), T750528. Open daily 1130-2330. Free delivery on orders over LL15,000. Good value 'specials' consisting of a main dish, rice and a soft

> **West Beirut: Hamra**
> *The main emphasis in Hamra is on fast food/snack bars (particularly along Rue Bliss, see below), although there are also some good restaurants*

Beirut

drink for LL6,000. Simple place, also with a couple of tables for eating in. *Tanmia Chicken Corner*, Rue Sidani, T749822. Open daily 1100-2400. New chicken place claiming to offer 'the first natural chicken in Lebanon' (no antibiotics, no chemicals, no animal fats, no animal proteins). A whole range of chicken meals and snacks is on offer here, from whole chickens (roasted LL10,000 or firewood grilled LL7,000), to platters (LL4,500-7,000) or sandwiches (LL2,000-4,000). Primarily a takeaway, but you can also eat-in. Fresh, uncooked chicken also for sale here. Free delivery service.

Rue Bliss is home to the greatest concentration on **fast food** places and **snack bars**, catering for the throngs of university students who gather here. The places listed here are in the order they appear as you walk west along Rue Bliss from its junction of Rue Omar Ben Abdul Aziz. *Bliss House*, divided into 2 parts, the first serving juice and ice cream, while the second does a roaring trade in subs (French bread sticks with a rich filling of your choice), burgers, etc. Whether the large crowds seemingly always gathered here are a reflection of the good quality and value of the food, or AUB students' sheeplike mentality is open to debate. *Crispy Crepy*, subs, crêpes, hot dogs, sandwiches, donuts, ice cream, coffee etc. *Al Tannour Bakery*, specializing in *saj* (a thin flat bread topped with *zaatar* (a seasoning of thyme and sumak) much the same as *mannoushi*, but here the dough is cooked on what looks like an upturned wok instead of a bread oven). *Dip'n'Crunch*, trendy takeaway place basically serving chips (French fries) and a choice of all sorts of different flavoured dips, as well as hot dogs etc. *Sub Station*, *Bakkur* and *Universal Snack* (all on Rue Jeanne d'Arc, just off Bliss St) between them offer a range of reasonably priced sandwiches, subs and burgers etc. *Quick Service* (no proper sign outside; look out for the stained glass effect on the windows), a simple, somewhat quirky café-style sit-down place, rather down-at-heel compared with all the other flashy places in this area, but unpretentious and friendly. Reasonably priced Lebanese/Western snacks/meals for LL3,500-8,000. *euro deli*, very trendy café/snack place (branches in Montreal and Tokyo according to the sign) serving soups, pasta, lasagna, sandwiches, salads as well as tea, coffee, juices etc. *Domino Pizza* and *Blimpie* (subs/sandwiches), both on lower ground level, together with *Café Sheikh Mankoush* (see 'Bars and nightclubs', below). *Ben & Jerry's*, large new outlet of the American chain. As well as the usual range of ice creams, frozen yoghurts, sorbets, shakes etc, they also offer an extensive breakfast menu (croissants, pancakes, bagel, waffles, crêpes etc). *Le Sage*, tiny hole-in-the-wall takeaway serving saj. *Taj al-Mouklouk*, traditional Lebanese pâtisserie, plus ice cream parlour.

Seriously cheap Many of the numerous snack bars along Rue Bliss could technically be described as seriously cheap, though when you take into account the size of the portions they don't turn out to be such good value. The same goes for the various shawarma/burger takeaways to be found along Rue Hamra. One exception, however, is the *Foulier Abou Zouz*, Rue Ibrahim Abd el-Aal (just off Rue Hamra, next door to the *Chez Dany* bar). Right in the heart of Hamra, but nevertheless a simple, unassuming and genuinely cheap place serving good hummus, fuul, falafels and various other simple snacks. A filling bowl of fuul here costs LL2,500.

Beirut Central District (Downtown) Restaurants and cafés were only just starting to open up around the newly redeveloped Downtown area at the time of writing, with most of them concentrated around Place d'Etoile and the streets radiating from it. No doubt plenty more will open in this area in the coming years. It would appear that those already open are holding down their prices to attract custom while the area re-establishes itself in people's minds as something more than just a bombed-out wasteland or massive building site. Once it begins to gain in popularity, prices will no doubt rise to reflect the high cost of real estate here.

Beirut

Mid-range *Coppadelio*, Rue Emir Bechir (opposite St George's Cathedral), T988444. Open daily 0800-late. Italian pizzeria and café. Large, recently opened and stylish (mostly modern décor, with traditional touches). Also seating out on the street in summer. Wide range of pizzas, pasta etc, as well as fish, meat and chicken dishes. Daily specials at LL22,000, or from around LL30,000 per head upwards for a full à la carte meal. *Il Parlamento*, Rue Omari, T985296. Open daily 1200-1600, 1900-late. Cosy, nicely furnished Italian restaurant. Around US$15-20 per head upwards. *Place d'Etoile*. Open daily 0800-late. Very smart and trendy café, restaurant and bar right on Place d'Etoile. Already starting to reap the benefits of its prime location and set to become an extremely popular hang out. European cuisine. Around US$15-20 per head for a full meal. Also some good value snacks on the menu. *Shogun*, Rue Maarad. Open 1200-1600, 2000-2400, Sun 2000-2400. Teppen Yaki and Sushi bar.

Cheap *Café Supreme*, Rue Maarad. Small sandwich bar/café selling a range of sandwiches, salads, juices and tea and coffee. *Casper & Gambini's*, corner of Rue Emir Bechir and Rue Maarad. Open daily 0730-late. Smart, ultra-modern and trendy snack bar/café with a pleasant outdoor terrace overlooking the Roman cardo and excavations next door to St George's Cathedral. Wide range of hot and cold sandwiches, panini, wraps (tortilla bread), baked potatoes and 'specials' (most items between LL5,000-12,000). Also an excellent range of real fresh coffees, including lots of speciality coffees (LL3,000-7,000). The full-on English breakfast of bacon, sausage, mushrooms, baked beans, eggs, toast, orange juice and tea/coffee (LL12,500) looks very promising (if a little extravagant!), or there are more restrained continental and Lebanese breakfasts for LL3,500-7,000. *Mi-Chaud*, Rue Maarad. Small snack bar serving shawarmas, burgers, sandwiches, juices, tea and coffee etc.

Seriously cheap *Snack al-Mathaf*, Rue de Damas. Open daily, 24 hrs. This snack bar is actually nowhere near Downtown Beirut, being opposite the National Museum. Unless you're visiting the museum it's a long way from anywhere, but all the same it stands out for its excellent value sandwiches. Their shish tawouk sandwich, for example (LL3,500), is at least twice the size of most others and pretty much a meal in its own right. There is a whole range of other options on offer, including shawarmas. A great place to fill an empty stomach on the cheap.

Some of Beirut's most elegant (and expensive) restaurants are in the eastern half of the city: places which offer sumptuous and atmospheric surroundings as well as the finest Middle Eastern and European cuisine. There are also plenty of more reasonably priced places and, these days, a choice of cuisines from all over the world.

East Beirut

In recent years, there has been an explosion of new restaurants of all kinds along Rue Monot

Expensive *Al Dente*, 137 Rue Abdel Wahab el-Inglizi, T202440. Open daily 1200-late. Upmarket Italian restaurant set in a beautiful old Ottoman-period house, lavishly furnished throughout. Set menu evening meal US$29 (or US$36 for fish), plus 19% tax and service, or order à la carte. *Al Mijana*, Rue Abdel Wahab el-Inglizi, T328082. Open 1230-1530, 2030-2330, closed Sat lunchtime. Upmarket Arabic cuisine restaurant set in another beautiful Ottoman period house a few doors down from the *Al Dente*, and very much in the same style. Lavish set menu lunch and dinner for US$37 per head (plus 5% tax), including open bar, or simpler version for US$25 per head (plus 5% tax) including 2 drinks. *Au Vieux Quartier*, Rue Michel Bustros, T200870. Open 1230-1500, 2030-2330, closed Sun. An extremely elegant going on opulent French restaurant with quite a strong emphasis on fish/seafood. Excellent, long-standing reputation, though also very expensive (around US$40 per head upwards). *Babylone*, 33 Rue Abdel Wahab el-Inglizi, T219539. Open 1200-1600, 2000-late, closed Sun. Intimate, elegant restaurant, set in a beautiful Ottoman-period house. International/fusion nouveau cuisine. From around US$20 per head upwards. Livens up after 2400 on Thu, Fri and Sat nights. *Capital Grill*,

Beirut

off Rue Montée Accaoui (around the back of the *Empire* cinema complex), T215500. Open 1200-1500, 1930-2300, closed Sun (except in winter). Mostly European cuisine (some Arabic), specializing in grills, roasts and seafood. Extensive wine list. From around US$40-50 per head upwards (excluding alcohol). Large, very grand and elegant dining hall. Officially there is no dress code here, but in practice it's a pretty exclusive suit and tie kind of place. Advance booking essential. *La Petite Marée*, Rue Sursock, T204111. Open 1230-1530, 2030-2300, Sat 2030-2300, closed Sun. Upmarket fish restaurant. From around US$30 per head upwards. *Le Rabelais*, Rue Montée Accaoui, T204433. Open 1200-1515, 2100-2400, closed Sun. Very smart and swish French restaurant. Lunch menu around US$20 per head upwards. Set menu evening meal US$35, or order à la carte. *Le Sushi Bar*, Rue Monot, T338555. Very smart, upmarket sushi bar and Japanese restaurant. Around US$30 per head upwards.

Mid-range *Abdel Wahab (Bistrot Libanais)*, Rue Abdel Wahab el-Inglizi, T200552. Open daily 1200-2300. Large, elegant restaurant serving excellent Arabic cuisine. Rooftop terrace in summer. Around US$15-20 per head. Also with a good value takeaway menu. *Baan Thai*, Rue Selim Bustros, T321710. Open 0930-2400, closed Sun. Good Thai food for around US$10 per head upwards. Takeaway section downstairs (free delivery), sit-down restaurant upstairs. *China Town*, Rue Monot, T325069. Open daily 1130-late. Fairly average-looking Chinese restaurant. From around US$10-15 per head upwards. *Le Chef*, Rue Gouraud, T445373. Open 0600-1800 only, closed Sun. Simple but friendly place serving good value European and Lebanese food for around US$10 per head upwards, or around US$3-5 for snacks (menu in Arabic only). Popular with expats. Recommended. *Le Monot*, 83 Rue Monot, T326956. Open daily 1200-2400. Mostly French and some Middle Eastern cuisine in pleasant, comfortable surroundings. Set menus for US$15-20 per head (one main dish, plus open salad bar), or à la carte. Also cheaper snacks for around US$5-10 per head. *Little China*, Rue Monot. Closed for refurbishment at the time of writing. *Le Relais de l'Entrecôte*, Rue Abdel Wahab el-Inglizi. Open daily 1230-1530, 1930-2330. Popular institution with branches in Paris and Geneva. Fixed menu of entrecôte (steak), chips and salad for LL25,500 plus 5% tax (service included). Drinks and deserts extra. No reservations; just turn up and wait for a free table. *Thai*, Rue Monot, T329313. Open 1200-2300, closed Sun. Primarily a takeaway (free delivery), but also with a small space (just 5 tables) for eating-in. 'Modern Thai cuisine' (ie variations on traditional Thai). Around US$10-15 per head. Well run place with a good reputation.

Cheap *Bistrot Germanos*, Rue Huvelin. Small, low-key restaurant/pub with a nice atmosphere where you can get snacks/meals for US$5-10 or just have a drink. *Le Crepier*, Rue Ghandour es-Saad. Small, friendly snack bar serving sweet and savoury crêpes, as well as sandwiches, subs, burgers, pizzas etc. Most items are around US$2-3. Beer also served (small Al Maaza LL1,500). *Tribeco*, Rue Abdel Wahab el-Inglizi, T332666. Open daily 0800-late. Smart and trendy American-style coffee and bagels café (all bagels freshly baked on the premises). Straightforward bagels from LL1,500, through to full-on bagel sandwiches and specials for LL5,000 and up. Also with an interesting range of other breakfast items, salads, desserts and all kinds of excellent fresh coffees (LL2,000-4,500).

Seriously cheap There are several good cheap restaurants and snack bars around the entrance to the port, just on the edge of the redevelopment area. Opposite the *Al Naim* hotel there is a branch of **Snack Makhlouf**, which does good sandwiches, while at the bottom of the same street, on the corner on the right, there is a small **snack bar/restaurant** which does good fuul, hummus etc in the mornings and filling lunchtime 'specials', in addition to the usual sandwiches etc.

Cafés

There are lots of excellent cafés dotted around Beirut. The following is just a small selection. *Café du Paris*, Rue Hamra. Long established French-style café, looking a bit run-down these days, though expensive as ever (LL3,250 for a coffee). All the same, still a pleasant place to read the papers, write postcards or watch the world go by. Also serves beers and snacks. *Café Younes*, Rue Nehme Yafet (opposite the *Astra* hotel). Tiny café serving a wide variety of teas and coffees at reasonable prices (you'll probably get a waft of freshly ground coffee before you reach the place). Snacks of croissants, biscuits, chocolate bars etc also served. *Caffe Mondo*, *Phoenicia Inter-Continental* hotel. Open daily 24 hrs. The really 'in' place to seen these days, attracting much of Beirut's high society, as well as crowds of wannabes. Also offers a full Italian menu of pizzas, pasta etc. *City Café*, at the southern end of Rue Sadat. A trendy venue for students from the Lebanese American University. Gets particularly busy on summer evenings. *Palace Café*, Av de Paris (Corniche), Ras Beirut. Occupying a prime position right on the water's edge at the very tip of Ras Beirut, this is a wonderful spot from which to enjoy the sunset or watch the fishermen perched up on oil drums amongst the rocks. You can just come for a cup of tea or coffee, and perhaps a *nargileh*, or they also serve food. *Starbucks*, Rue Hamra. It was kind of inevitable that this chain would find its way into Lebanon sooner rather than later. It's certainly popular, and providing stiff competition to *Café du Paris* amongst others. The coffee is great, but the prices are on the steep side. *Theatre Café*, Rue Maarad (next door to *Casper & Gambini's*). Much smaller and simpler than its neighbour. Takes its name from the old theatre (as yet still just a bombed out shell, but awaiting restoration) over on the south side of Rue Emir Bechir.

Entertainment

Beirut's nightlife all but died during the civil war, with most of it shifting up the coast to Jounieh. These days it's alive and kicking once again, with a good selection of bars and nightclubs around the city and new ones opening on a regular basis. Jounieh may still have the greatest concentration of venues, but they tend either to be rather ostentatiously extravagant and exclusive (ie ridiculously expensive), or else somewhat tacky (floorshows etc) going on downright dodgy. By contrast, Beirut has the best in stylish, trendy and innovative clubs. Most places only really get going on Thu, Fri and Sat nights, and even then only after around 2300. All are very expensive, with drinks generally around the US$5 mark, even for a humble bottle of beer. But then the Lebanese like to do things in style which in Lebanon inevitably means money. A selection is given here, but there are many more and inevitably this is a rapidly changing scene; ask around for the latest hotspots.

Bars & clubs

East Beirut appears to have taken the lead in re-establishing the city's nightlife with many of the newest and most imaginative venues opening up here. *Atlantis* (incorporating *Jules Verne Brasserie*), off Av General Fouad Chehab. Nightclub housed in a cavernous vaulted and pillared hall, while built onto this is a large conservatory housing the brasserie (all very stylish and modern, serving nouvelle cuisine). Barely open at the time of writing, but promising to be another very trendy nightspot. *B-018* (pronounced 'Bee Oh Eighteen'), off Av Charles Helou (adjacent to the landmark Forum de Beyrouth), T580018. Open daily 1900-late (may close on Mon during winter; phone to check). This is one of the largest and most spectacular nightclubs in Beirut. Set in a huge underground bunker, it features a hydraulically operated roof which can be opened up to let in fresh air, and some truly zany musically themed furniture and décor. Extremely popular, though difficult to get to and pretty expensive (drinks from LL10,000). *Bongos Pub*, Rue Monot. Open daily 2000-late (may close on Mon during winter). Newly opened and

Beirut

already extremely popular, this is just a big, straightforward bar, but the arty décor and mix of jazz, Latin, Cuban and funk have succeeded in striking a chord. Usually packed solid by 2200 on Fri and Sat nights, but more laid-back during the week. A pint of draught *Lazizza* costs LL5,000, bottles of *Al Maaza* are LL3,500, or there is a large range of cocktails for LL8,500-9,500. *Circus*, Rue Monot, T332523, www.circus.com.lb Open daily 2030-late. Large, modernistic building with a spacious, open plan tentlike effect inside. Though it bills itself as a restaurant/bar (and the food is certainly a major element) this place is definitely much more than just a place to eat. Extremely trendy and hugely popular, with live music on Tue, Thu and some Sat nights (check their website for a monthly programme of events). The food is described as 'fusion cuisine', bringing together Arabic, Asian and European influences (around US$20-25 per head upwards, advance booking essential on Thu, Fri and Sat nights), or you can just come for a drink at the large downstairs bar (bottled beer US$4, cocktails from US$9). Well worth a look. *Hole in the Wall*, just off Rue Monot (squeezed between *Rai* and *Pacifico*). Small, friendly unpretentious pub offering a welcome respite from all the hype of surrounding nightspots, though it still gets packed to overflowing on Thu, Fri and Sat nights. English-run and popular with Expats. *Indiana* (formerly the *Monkey Rose*). Open 2130-late, closed Mon. The graceful exterior of this beautiful Ottoman period house, complete with its lovely courtyard garden, conceals a modern, trendy interior. Plays a lively mix of dance music, attracting a younger crowd. All drinks LL10,000 (including soft drinks!), except cocktails at LL12,000. *J Pauls*, Rue Abdel Wahab el-Inglisi, T204779. Open daily 1200-late. Upmarket American-style 'dining saloon', as much a place to come and eat (salads, T-bone steaks etc) but with regular live music and a general ambience geared towards making it an all-in-one evening's entertainment. *Le Retro*, Rue Sursock (next door to *Le Petit Marée* restaurant, and sharing its kitchens with it), T202118. Open Thu, Fri and Sat nights only. Extremely trendy, exclusive and expensive nightclub. No entrance fee, but very careful vetting at the door (money and looks appear to be the main criteria). Booking essential on Sat nights. Drinks start at US$10 (even for a bottled beer!), though they'll be quite happy to accept US$100 bills if you don't have any small change. *Pacifico*, just off Rue Monot (next door to the *Hole in the Wall*), T204446. Large, very trendy Latino-style bar. Food served (Mexican/Cuban and North American). Fairly relaxed and laid-back during the week, but hopelessly busy and loud on the weekends. *Rai*, Rue Monot. Open from 2100, closed Mon. Occupying a large basement, this bar/club is furnished in Moroccan style, with low couches and cushions strewn all over the place, and also serves Moroccan food (snacks for US$5-10, more substantial dishes such as tajine or couscous for US$12-15. Very trendy and totally packed out on Fri and Sat nights. *Sports Café*, Av General Fouad Chehab. Open daily 1200-late (opens earlier if there are any important sporting events worth screening). Huge, American-style sports theme bar and restaurant. Lots of sporting memorabilia, and TV screens around the place showing sporting events. Some tables equipped with monitors and computer games. Children's play area downstairs. Pint of draught Heineken LL6,000 (happy hour 1700-2000, LL5,000). Cocktails LL5,000. Mix of American/Mexican/Italian food on offer, from around US$10-15 (weekends minimum charge US$15 per head for food). Sat nights are dance night, with Arabic and Western dance music.

West Beirut also has its fair share of venues, though the emphasis is more on bars, sometimes with live entertainment, rather than nightclubs. *Blue Note*, Rue Makhoul, T743857. Jazz café, often with live music. Pleasant atmosphere. European and Arabic food served. *Café Sheikh Mankoush*, Rue Bliss. Fancy upmarket basement bar. Spacious, with nice décor and a good atmosphere. Occasional live music. Beers LL4,000-5,000. Various Lebanese snacks also served (*Manakeesh* a speciality). *Chez Andre*, set back from Rue Hamra inside a small arcade (same entrance as Lebanon Bookshop). This tiny bar is one of the few left over from before the war; walking in is rather like stepping back in time from all the glitz and modernity outside. It's a friendly, cosy place, oozing with atmosphere (almost sleazy, in fact, but in an unthreatening sort of way). Draught *Heineken* costs LL6,000 for 500 ml (just under a pint). *Chez Dany*, Rue Ibrahim Abd el-Aal (just off Rue Hamra). This tiny, very simple bar is friendly and unassuming, more in the mould of *Chez Andre* rather than the fancy, upmarket places which dominate Beirut. A small bottle of Amstel beer costs LL2,500. *Cock and Bull Tavern*, Rue Nehme Yafet (next door to the *Napolean* hotel). Now under new ownership/management, and recently refurbished. Small, friendly place with a pleasant atmosphere. Working hard to attract the student crowd from AUB. Quizz night every Wed. Gets lively on Thu, Fri and Sat nights. Pint of draught Lazizza LL6,000. *Hard Rock Café*, Rue Minet el-Hosn, Ain el-Mreisse. Open daily 1200-late. Part of the international Rock'n'Roll-theme chain, decked out with the usual music industry memorabilia. Live bands on Wed and Fri nights from around 2130 (free entry). Drinks are predictably expensive (eg a small bottle of *Al Maaza* for LL4,000), though they sometimes put on 'buy one get one free' promotions. Also serves various US-themed snacks and meals (burgers, grills, fries, etc). There is also another branch on Concorde Square, Verdun, though it lacks the atmosphere of the Ain el-Mreisse branch. *Henry J Beans* (or *'Harry JBs'*, or just *'Hanks'*), Rue Madame Curie, T809199. Large American-style pub/bar (part of an international chain). A lot of effort has gone into conjuring up the spirit of America in terms of décor and atmosphere, making it hugely popular amongst young Lebanese. Food (burgers, steaks, salads etc) also served. *Lone Star* Café, Rue Bliss, T341605. Mexican style bar/restaurant, a popular venue with students from the AUB across the road. Friendly and relaxed, local beer reasonably priced (US$3 for a bottle), likewise the Mexican-food (most dishes around US$5). *Rose and Crown*, Rue Makdissi, T349930. Traditional English-style pub with a restaurant thrown in for good measure. Pleasant, intimate atmosphere. Draught beer US$5, varied menu around US$15-20 per head, lunch-time specials US$10.

Cinemas

The *Circuit Empire* group have a chain of comfortable, modern cinemas around Beirut (and beyond) showing all the latest American and European releases. The following are to be found inside the capital. *Empire Dunes*, Dunes centre, Verdun St, Verdun (in the same complex as the *Holiday Inn Dunes* hotel). 4 screens. *Elite*, Marriott hotel, Jnah district. 4 screens. *Empire* Sofil, Sofil Centre, Av General Fouad Chehab, Achrafieh. 2 screens. *Empire Sodeco*, Sodeco Centre, Sodeco. 6 screens. There are 3 performances each day at 1600 or 1630, 1900 or 1930, and 2200 or 2215. Tickets at all these cinemas cost LL10,000 (half price all day Mon, and for the 1600/1630 performance throughout the week). There are numerous other cinemas dotted around Hamra showing mostly Arabic (ie Egyptian) or else generic Kung Fu-type movies. The various Cultural Centres are also worth checking out for their video clubs (see 'Directory', below).

Circuit Empire publish their own monthly movie guide (available free from any of their cinemas) or The Daily Star newspaper has full listings of what's on throughout the country

Children

Planet Discovery, Rue Omar ed-Daouk, Beirut Central District, T980650, info@solidere.com.lb Described as a 'children's science museum', there are lots of different activities and interactive games for children here, from age 3 through to 15. There are puppet shows every Sat, while during the week there are special organized programmes. The organized programmes last around 3½ hrs and cost LL15,000. Alternatively, a 1½ hr visit (without the organized programme, but including supervised activities) costs LL5,000.

Galleries

The *Sursock Museum* (see 'Sights', above) is the best place to check out Beirut's art scene, but there are also a couple of private galleries which put on regular exhibitions open to the public. *Agial*, 63 Rue Omar Ben Abdul Aziz, Hamra, T345213. *Chahine*, 103 Rue Madame Curie (near the Concorde cinema), Hamra, T/F346522, www.chahinegallery.com.lb

Theatres

Theatre de Beyrouth, Rue Graham, Ain el-Mreisse, T363466. Established in the 1970s, this theatre has an enduring reputation as the focus of innovative new works and also runs a regular programme of dance, music, films, exhibitions and talks, mostly in Arabic but with some in French or English. *Theatre Ivoire*, Sin el-Fil, T490380. Occasionally hosts *Caracalla*, the Lebanese dance company of worldwide renown. *Theatre Al Madinah* (*City Theatre*), Rue Justinian (just off Rue Clemenceau), T371962. Regular programme of high quality modern Arabic productions. *Theatre Masrah.com*, opposite St Joseph's Church, Achrafieh, T329171. Small, recently established place specializing in political satires and sketches, mostly in Arabic, but with some performances in French and English. *Theatre Monnot*, adjacent to St Joseph's Church, Achrafieh, T202422. Part of the University of St Joseph. Regular programme of plays and performances (often in association with the Centre Culturel Français), mostly in French and Arabic. Also runs a video club every Mon night at 1900 (LL5,000). Check the University of St Joseph website (www.usj.edu.lb) for programme details. Both the AUB and Lebanese American University often put on student productions (usually in English) which are open to the public. The Centre Culturel Français also has a regular programme of plays (see 'Cultural Centres', in the directory below).

Shopping

Handicrafts, antiques & souvenirs

Maison De L'Artisan, Rue Minet el-Hosn, Ain el-Mreisse. Open 0930-2000, closed Sun. Large, newly opened government-sponsored place with a wide range of souvenirs and traditional handicrafts from all over Lebanon: ceramics, tapestries, woven rugs, silver jewellery, nargilehs, pottery, metalware, cutlery, glassware, inlaid wood items, fabrics etc. A few doors down is the privately run *Artisans du Liban et d'Orient*, open 100-1800, Sat 1000-1330, closed Sun, with an interesting selection of handicrafts and local produce including handwoven rugs, fabrics, glassware, soaps, spices and some books. There are numerous souvenir/antique shops in Hamra district, particularly along Rue Hamra. In East Beirut, particularly around Achrafieh, there are numerous antique shops, most of them specializing in elegant furniture and furnishings along the lines of reproduction Louis XIV items, but there are also lots of places selling smaller items such as jewellery etc. *Sienna Pottery*, Rue des Saints Coeurs, Achrafieh, T204529, has very delicate and beautiful handmade pottery items fashioned on the premises, although it is very expensive.

General

For an insight into the preferred shopping experience of wealthy Beirutis, try visiting the *Dunes* shopping centre. This huge multilevel steel and glass complex features all the most expensive designer shops, as well as the *Holiday Inn Dunes* hotel, the 4-screen *Empire* cinema, a 'food court' with a *McDonalds* and various other outlets, an amusement arcade and state of the art bowling alley, and an internet café.

Books

Beirut has some excellent bookshops stocking a wide and varied selection of books; if you are coming from Syria, the sudden explosion of choice is quite overwhelming, though by no means unwelcome. Amongst the better ones in West Beirut are: *Lebanon Bookshop* (*Libraire du Liban*), main branch in Rue Hamra, another on Rue Bliss; *Libraire Antoine*, Rue Hamra (between junctions with Rue Jeanne d'Arc and Rue Ibrahim Abd el-Aal); *Way In Bookshop*, Rue Hamra; *Libraire Internationale*, Rue M Abdel Baki (opposite the Gefinor Centre), with a second branch on Rue Phoenicie; *Books and Pens*, Rue Jeanne d'Arc, near junction with Rue Bliss; *Naufal Booksellers*, Rue Sourati. In East Beirut, *Libraire Oriental*, at the junction of Rue Achrafiyeh and Rue Furn el-Hayek, has a good selection of books.

Sport

For details of Beirut's beach clubs, most of which are equipped with **swimming pools**, as well as offering a range of **watersports**, see page 413. Note that all the health centres listed below also feature swimming pools. For details of **horse racing** at the Beirut Hippodrome, see page 409.

Big Blue Dive Centre, St George's Yacht Club, T365065 (or mobile T03-747789), www.bigbluelebanon.com Fully equipped five star IDC centre. Everything from 'Discover Scuba' introductory dives and PADI Open Water courses through to all kinds of technical and specialist diving. For more details check their website. *National Institute for Scuba Diving*, Yacht Club, Riviera hotel, T373210 (or mobile T03-204422, F739206, www.nisd-online.com Fully equipped dive centre. For details of prices etc check their website. *Lebanon Divers*, T03-602614, www.lebanondivers.com For some general information about diving in Lebanon, see page 64.

Diving

Escape Sports Club, Manara (opposite the Luna Park fairground), T740995. Offers a wide range of fitness classes, as well as having its own tennis courts, squash courts, gym and swimming pool (summer only). *Health Club*, *Summerland* hotel. Gym, sauna, steam room, jacuzzi, indoor pool. Entry LL30,000 (LL20,000 in winter), includes use of the hotel's beach and swimming pools, as well as the tennis courts etc. *Inn Shape Fitness Club*, *Holiday Inn Martinez* hotel, Phoenicia St, Ain el-Mreisse. Very elegant place with Roman-style décor throughout. Indoor swimming pool, jacuzzi, sauna, steam room, massage and full gym. Free for guests at the hotel (except the massage service, US$30); non-guests pay US$10 per day, or US$99 per month. *Lifestyles*, Al Mada Building, off Rue Bliss, Ras Beirut, T366555. Open 0630-2300, Sat and Sun 0900-2100. Very fancy, state-of-the-art health centre in the basement of a huge, equally swish apartment tower. Facilities include an indoor swimming pool (plus a teaching pool and hydro pool), sauna, jacuzzi, 2 squash courts, fully equipped gym, café, club room, internet/games room and even a snooker room. One year's membership costs US$1,600, or you can take a one month trial for US$189. Alternatively, overseas visitors can buy special tickets entitling them to 10, 20 or 30 visits for US$160, US$300 or US$425 respectively. Guests at the *Meridien Commodore* hotel are entitled to free entry. In the same building, and with the same phone number (though a separate enterprise), is *The Spa*, offering a bewildering range of beauty treatments.

Health/ fitness clubs

Tour operators and travel agents

If you have limited time, there are several local **tour operators** which offer guided tours of the major sights in Lebanon. These range from half-day tours (eg of Beirut, or to Byblos, costing US$20-25 per person), through to full-day tours venturing further afield (eg to Baalbek, Aanjar and the Ksara vineyards and caves, costing US$55). *Kurban Tours*, Amine Gemayel St, Achrafieh, T614914, F611125. Second office Rue de l'Armee, Kantari, T371013, F370129. Also with offices at the *Phoenicia Inter-Continental* hotel and *Meridien Commodore* hotel. Now the largest tour operator in Lebanon. Regular tours to all the major sites in Lebanon, as well as trips to Syria, Jordan and Cyprus. *Nakhal & Cie*, Ghorayeb Building, Sami el-Solh Av, T389389, F389282, www.nakhal.com.lb Regular tours to all the major sites in Lebanon, as well as trips to Syria and Jordan. Long established company with good reputation. *Tania Travel*, Rue Sidani, opposite Jeanne d'Arc Cinema, Hamra, T739679, F340473, taniatvl@cyberia.net.lb Regular tours to major sites in Lebanon and trips into Syria.

There are plenty of travel agents in Beirut for **international airline tickets** (many of them in Hamra), or you can go directly to the airlines (see 'Airline offices', below). *Campus Travel*, Rue Makhoul (just off Rue Omar Ben Abdul Aziz), Hamra, T744588, F744583, www.campus-travel.net Stands out as the only travel agent in Lebanon able to offer heavily discounted student fares on international flights (to qualify you must either have an ISIC card and be under 31, or have a Go 25 card and be under 25). The staff here are very helpful, and can provide lots of useful information and leads on

Beirut

NAKHAL &cie

The best way to discover Lebanon

GUARANTEED TOURS ALL YEAR ROUND
English & French speaking guides

HALF & FULL DAY TOURS WITH LUNCH

DAYS	TOURS	EXCURSIONS
Sunday	1	Baalbeck, Anjar & Ksara
	4	Jeita, Harissa & Nahr El-Kelb (1/2 day a.m.)
	5	Byblos, Tripoli & Rachana
	6	Cedars, Becharreh & Kozhaya
	BYB	Byblos (1/2 day a.m.)
Monday	1	Baalbeck, Anjar & Ksara
	3	Sidon, Tyre & Echmoun
	8	Damascus Cultural Tour
	BYB	Byblos (1/2 day p.m.)
	BAT	Batroun (May till October).
Tuesday	1	Baalbeck, Anjar & Ksara
	2	Beirut, Beiteddin & Deir El-Kamar
	BDE	Beiteddin & Deir El-Kamar (1/2 day with lunch)
	BH	Beirut Historical Tour (1/2 day a.m.)
	4	Jeita, Harissa & Nahr El-Kelb (1/2 day a.m. & p.m.)
	7	Baalbeck, Cedars & Kozhaya (July/August/September)
Wednesday	1	Baalbeck, Anjar & Ksara
	3	Sidon, Tyre & Echmoun
	4	Jeita, Harissa & Nahr El-Kelb (1/2 day a.m. & p.m.)
	5	Byblos, Tripoli & Rachana
	6	Cedars, Becharreh & Kozhaya
	BYB	Byblos (1/2 day a.m.)
Thursday	1	Baalbeck, Anjar & Ksara
	2	Beirut, Beiteddin & Deir El-Kamar
	BDE	Beiteddin & Deir El-Kamar (1/2 day with lunch)
	BH	Beirut Historical Tour (1/2 day a.m.)
	BYB	Byblos (1/2 day p.m.)
	4	Jeita, Harissa & Nahr El-Kelb (1/2 day a.m. & p.m.)
	8	Damascus Cultural Tour
Friday	1	Baalbeck, Anjar & Ksara
	3	Sidon, Tyre & Echmoun
	4	Jeita, Harissa & Nahr El-Kelb (1/2 day a.m. & p.m.)
	5	Byblos, Tripoli & Rachana
Saturday	1	Baalbeck, Anjar & Ksara
	2	Beirut, Beiteddin & Deir El-Kamar
	BDE	Beiteddin & Deir El-Kamar (1/2 day with lunch)
	BH	Beirut Historical Tour (1/2 day a.m.)
	4	Jeita, Harissa & Nahr El-Kelb (1/2 day a.m. & p.m.)

PRIVATE TOURS ON REQUEST WITH LANGUAGE OF YOUR CHOICE

- Circuit tours in Syria & Jordan
- Incentive programs
- Assistance in congresses & fairs
- Hotel bookings
- Transfers with meet & assist
- Car rental
- Cultural & pilgrim tours
- Trekking
- Shore excursions
- Night programs

Sami el Solh avenue - Ghorayeb bldg - Tel: (01) 389389 - Fax: (961 - 1) 389282
E-mail: tours@nakhal.com.lb - Internet: www.nakhal.com.lb

Beirut

tours within Lebanon. **Nahas Travel Services**, Tina Centre, Rue John Kennedy, Ain el-Mreisse, T376600, F374135, nta2-lbn@nahastt **Sogetour** (*American Express Travel Related Services Representative*), Gefinor Centre, Bloc 'A', PO Box 11-5865, T/F739793, gefinor@sogetour.com.lb offers a comprehensive service for international ticketing and can also arrange tours in Lebanon.

Transport

Car hire Beirut is the main centre for car hire. There are literally hundreds of companies, of which only a small selection is listed here. It is worth booking well in advance, particularly during the summer season when demand is high. See page 49 for important information on car hire in Lebanon. **Avis**, main office Sioufi Garden, Amine Gemayel St, Achrafieh, T611000, F611125, www.avis.com.lb Desks at the airport (T629890, F629891), *Phoenicia Inter-Continental* hotel (T363848, F363851) and *Meridien Commodore* hotel (T749997, F749998). Rates from US$30-40 per day (Kia Pop, Ford Fiesta). Unlimited mileage on rentals of 3 days or more. **Budget**, Minkara Centre, Rue Alfred Nobel (near the *Bristol* hotel), T740741, F740999, www.lebanon.com/budget Rates from US$35 per day (Citroen Saxo, Peugeot 106, Fiat Punto, Kia Young). Unlimited mileage on rentals of 3 days or more. **Europcar**, main office Saarti Building, Hayek Av, Sin el-Fil, T480480, F500788. Branch at Ain el-Mreisse, T363636 (see 'West Beirut' map). Rates from US$35 per day (Citroen Saxo, Renault Clio, Nissan Micra). Unlimited mileage on rentals of 1 week or more. **First**, Saloumeh roundabout, Sin el-Fil, T/F488884, www.firstrentacar.com.lb Office at *Royal Garden* hotel, T618181. Rates from US$30 per day (Nissan Micra), including unlimited mileage. **Hala**, main office Av Sami el-Solh, Badaro, T393904, F384121, www.halacar. com Branches at the *Vendome Inter-Continental* hotel, Ain el-Mreisse, T369280, F360169 (see 'West Beirut' map), and at *Holiday Inn Dunes* hotel, Verdun, T793333. Rates from US$20 per day (Kia Pop). Good value. Recommended.

Local
See page 36 for details of getting to & from the airport

Service taxi Service (shared) taxis are the most popular form of local transport in Beirut. They are numerous and highly persistent, beeping and kerb crawling anyone who looks like a potential customer (which in effect means anyone on foot; trying to cross the road can sometimes be very frustrating with service taxis constantly slowing down in front of you just when there would otherwise be a gap in the traffic). They either run on fairly loosely defined set routes, or else simply head for the destination of their first passenger and then look for more customers along the way. The average fare for journeys within Beirut is LL1,000 per person (LL1,500 for longer trips), with 5 passengers constituting a full taxi. Always confirm that the taxi is operating as a service taxi ('servees') before getting in or you are likely, particularly as a foreigner, to be charged an inflated private taxi fare. Alternatively, if

you are in a hurry, you can simply offer to pay the equivalent of a full taxi load (ie LL5,000 in most cases).

Getting to grips with the system takes some time. When using service taxis to get around, it is useful to think in terms of travelling between Beirut's major transport hubs in order to get as close as possible to your destination. These include Cola and Dora bus/service taxi stands, the junction by the National Museum ('Mathaf') and the Balbirs junction (to the west of the National Museum). The National Museum and Balbirs junctions are useful staging points for getting between East and West Beirut, with lots of service taxis passing through, as well as LCC buses (see below). It also helps to position yourself along a major road heading in the overall direction that you wish to go, bearing in mind the one-way system. Thus to head east from Hamra you need to be on Rue Emile Edde/Rue Spears which is one-way eastwards; service taxis running along Hamra St will all take you out towards Manara and Raouche.

Private taxis are also numerous in Beirut, particularly in more affluent areas such as Hamra. Local journeys should cost roughly 5 times the equivalent service taxi fare, although at night when service taxis are very rare you can expect to pay a lot more. In any case, always agree a price before setting off; once you have made a journey it is much more difficult to dispute an unreasonable fare. Most hotels can book a taxi to pick you up, or try calling one of the following. *Allo Taxi*, T366661. *Caracas Taxi*, Rue Caracas (next door to *Abou Hassan* restaurant), Manara, T741959. Open 24 hrs. *Lebanon Taxi*, Rue Banque du Liban, opposite Ministry of Tourism, T353153. Open 24 hrs. Also with minibuses (11 seat) and buses (24 seat) for hire with driver.

Bus Beirut's bus system has been much improved by the setting up of the privately owned Lebanese Commuting Company (LCC), which operates small and medium-sized red and white buses along fixed routes. The buses are numbered, in English, and run relatively frequently. There is a flat fare of LL500 within Beirut, rising to LL750 for journeys beyond the capital. The company is steadily expanding their services, taking over existing government-run bus routes, though the large government buses can still be found on certain routes in Beirut. They are cheaper (LL250 flat fare) but also slower and less comfortable.

Long distance **Air** **Beirut International Airport** is around 10 km to the south of the city centre (see page 36 for full details of the airport, and how to get to and from it). The number of international airlines once again operating services to Beirut is increasing steadily; see under 'Airline offices' below for the current list. Between them, these airlines provide regular connections with most European cities as well as major destinations in the Middle East.

Road There are 3 bus stands in Beirut. **Charles Helou Bus Station**, underneath an elevated section of Av Charles Helou, just to the east of the port area (see 'Beirut: overview' map), is the most important. It is divided into 3 sections. Arriving from the port and working your way from west to east, the first section (Zone C) is for buses to **Tripoli**. There are 3 companies here which between them offer regular departures (every 15-30 mins) between around 0600-2000. *Adhab* and *Tripoli Express* have the better coaches and buses, with tickets costing LL2,000. *Al Kutb* has somewhat older and more decrepit coaches, but is slightly cheaper at LL1,500 for a ticket. International service taxis to Damascus and Amman also depart from this section, though they are more expensive than the luxury coaches and often driven by suicidal maniacs. The next section (Zone B) handles local buses, with the LCC No 13 running between here and Cola bus stand being the most useful. The last section (Zone A) is for services to Syria. As well as *Karnak* (the Syrian government-owned coach company), there are around a dozen private luxury coach companies. The most regular departures are to **Damascus** (every 30 mins-1 hr, LL7,000, around 3½ hrs) and **Aleppo** (every 30 mins-1 hr, LL11,000, around 6½ hrs). There are also 3 departures daily to **Lattakia** via Tartus

(LL9,500, around 4 hrs). In addition to the luxury coaches, there are dozens of microbuses and old buses serving a whole range of destinations in Syria. Prices are the same as for the luxury coaches. Note that you can pay for tickets to destinations in Syria in Syrian Pounds as well as Lebanese Lira (and of course US Dollars). There is an exchange booth in this section which is open daily/24 hrs. If you are heading for Syria, note that the rates on offer for changing foreign currency into Syrian Pounds are usually roughly equivalent to the black market rate in Syria.

Cola bus stand is spread around a large, chaotic roundabout underneath a flyover to the southwest of the centre (see 'Beirut: overview' map). A mixture of luxury coaches, buses, minibuses, microbuses and service taxis operate from here, primarily to destinations to the south of Beirut, but also to the Bekaa Valley, and to Tripoli. From the west side of the roundabout there are regular services to **Sidon (Saida)** (luxury coach LL1,500, minibus LL1,000 LTC bus LL750). For **Tyre (Sour)**, go to Sidon and change there. For **Chtaura/Zahle** and **Baalbek** there are regular microbuses (generally referred to as 'vans') costing LL2,000 and 3,000. All these destinations are also covered by service taxis, though they charge far more than anybody else. For other destinations in the south you have no choice but to go by service taxi. A service taxi to **Deir el-Qamar/Beit ed-Dine** will cost in the region of LL4,000. From the east side of the roundabout you can catch occasional microbuses to **Tripoli** (LL2,000), though the departures from Charles Helou Bus Station are more frequent and more convenient. It is also from this side that you can catch the LCC bus number 6 to Jounieh and Byblos (Jbail), going via Balbirs, the National Museum and Dora.

Dora bus stand (pronounced 'Dauwra') is to the east of Beirut, underneath a flyover section of the motorway to Jounieh and the north. Service taxis operate from here to all destinations along the coast to the north of Beirut: **Jounieh** LL2,000; **Byblos (Jbail)** LL3,000; **Batroun/Chekka** LL4,000; **Tripoli** LL4,000. You can also catch the LCC bus number 6 for Jounieh and Byblos (LL750) from here (between Jounieh and Byblos it follows the much more scenic old coast road, but it is also much slower). Finding service taxis to places up in the mountains to the north of Beirut is more difficult. You can sometimes find ones going up to **Bikfaya** or **Aajaltoun** (both LL2,000), but for destinations such as Qartaba, Laqlouq etc you are better off going from Byblos, while for destinations in the Qadisha valley you are better off going from Tripoli. Alternatively, you could arrange to be dropped off at the appropriate turning off the motorway, and then pick up another service taxi, or hitch, from there.

Directory

The following airlines have offices within the **Gefinor Centre** on Rue Clemenceau in Hamra district (see 'West Beirut' map; the tall, prominent building is a useful landmark). *Aeroflot*, T/F739596. *Air Malta*, T751100, F751200. *American*, T353637, F346807. *British Airways (British Mediterranean)*, T747777, F739552. *Cathay Pacific*, T747748 ext 120, F341596. *Egypt Air*, T741402, F341656. *KLM*, T746599. *MEA*, T737000, F738825 (central reservations T629999, head office, Airport Blvd, T629125, F629260, airport office T629125 ext 2929, F838086). *Turkish*, T741391, F341956. *Yemenair*, T747748 ext 124.

Most of the remaining airlines can be found around **Hamra/Ras Beirut**, including: *Air France*, *Meridien Commodore* hotel, T740300, F740305 (central reservations T204506, head office in Achrafieh, T200700, F200710, plus an office at the airport, T628000 ext 1688). *Alitalia*, T340280, F343011. *Emirates*, Hamra, T739042, F739888. *Lufthansa*, Rue Hamra, T349001, F346595. *LOT* (Polish), Rue Makdissi, T342415, F739727. *Malev* (Hungarian), Hamra, T366107, F368102. *Olympic*, Rue Hamra, T340285, F340287. *Royal Jordanian*, Rue Bliss, T/F379990. *Tarom* (Romanian), Rue Jeanne d'Arc (between *Mercure Berkeley* and *Mace* hotels), T/F742966.

Airlines with branches **elsewhere in the city** include: *Austrian*, Ain el-Mreisse, T/F343620. *Cyprus*, Rue Sursock, Achrafieh, T200886, F444382. *Gulf Air*, Bourj el-Ghazal building, Av General Fouad Chehab, Achrafieh, T323332, F323364. *Syrian Arab*, El Nisrine Building, Mar Elias St, T375632, F375363.

Airline offices

Beirut

Banks Beirut is awash with banks, most of which are now equipped with ATMs (cash machines), making a credit (or debit) card the easiest and most convenient way to obtain cash. All the major cards (Visa, Mastercard, Cirrus, +Plus, Global Access etc) are accepted, and you can draw your money either in US Dollars or Lebanese Lira.

For changing **cash**, there are dozens of money changers with small offices along Hamra St who will change practically every imaginable currency. All of them stay open until early evening, and some of them are also open throughout the day on Sat. Rates vary slightly between them, so if you are changing a large amount it is worth shopping around. Most of the banks will also change cash for you, though their rates are no better than that offered by the money changers.

For some reason, changing **travellers' cheques (TCs)** is more problematic. *Sogetour* (the American Express Travel Related Services Representative), Block A, Gefinor Centre, Hamra, PO Box 11-5865, T/F739793, can change American Express TCs, but only if they are in US$. They charge a 1% commission (minimum fee US$5) for this service. Most banks will also only deal with US$ TCs and though their commission rates vary they all seem to apply the same minimum fee of US$5. To change TCs which are in any other currency than US$, you must go to the *Saradar Bank*, tucked away on Rue du Caire (just south of its junction with Rue Sourati). They charge a 1% commission, with a minimum charge of US$5, plus a US$2 'handling fee' (thus for any amount up to the value of US$500, you must pay a total of US$7). The numerous money changers along Rue Hamra are extremely reluctant to deal with anything other than US$ TCs, for which they charge commissions of between 4-5%. *Jalloul Exchange* was one of the few which offered to change UK£ TCs, though they were asking for US$5 commission on *each* TC.

Credit cards *American Express*, Bloc C, Gefinor Centre, Hamra, PO Box 113-5953, T749574, F749577. Open 0900-1600, Sat 0830-1330, closed Sun. Although previously a fully operational bank, this office now just deals with credit card enquiries etc (this is the place to come if your credit card is lost or stolen).

In an emergency, you can have money sent to you quickly through *Western Union Money Transfer*, although this can work out quite expensive. The main agents in Beirut include *Byblos Bank*, *Khalaf Trading* and the *Lebanese-Canadian Bank*, which between them have branches all over the city. The head office contact number is T601315.

Communications **Internet** There are now dozens of internet cafés in Beirut, with most of them being concentrated in the Hamra district of West Beirut, particularly in the vicinity of AUB. *Internet Services*, off Rue Abdel Wahab El Inglizi, Achrafieh. Open daily 1030-2400. Internet access LL3,000 per hr. Recently opened, very functional place (more internet office rather than internet café) with 9 terminals. *Magnet*, off Rue Omar Ben Abdul Aziz, Hamra, T03-988102. Open 0900-2400. Sun 1000-2400. Internet access LL5,000 per hr. Café area downstairs (sandwiches, burgers, crêpes, tea, coffee, soft drinks, beer etc), and around 25 terminals upstairs. *The Net*, Rue Mahatma Gandhi (just off Rue Bliss), Hamra, T740157. Open 0900-0400, Sun 1600-0400. Internet access LL3,000 per hr. Pleasant, airy, open-plan arrangement. Hot and cold drinks, crisps etc served. Plans to introduce more substantial snacks in the future. *Planet Discovery* (downstairs from the children's science museum), Rue Omar ed-Daouk, Beirut Central District. Open 1000-1700, Sat and Sun 1030-1900. Sponsored by *Microsoft*, there are 20 terminals here. At the time of writing a free promotion was just finishing, after which internet access was to be charged at somewhere between LL3,000-5,000. *Sky Net*, Rue Sidani, Hamra, T751897. Open daily 0930-0130. Internet access LL3,000 per hour. Only 7 terminals in a cramped room upstairs given over to internet use, with the whole of the downstairs dedicated to computer games (LL2,500 per hour). Free coffee. *Virus*, Rue Omar Ben Abdul Aziz (just off Rue Bliss), Hamra, T374794. Open 0900-0200, Sun 1000-2400. Internet access LL3,000 per hour. Large, trendy place, popular with AUB students. Lots of terminals (including plenty given over to computer games). Separate non-smoking area. Tea, coffee, soft drinks and sandwiches served. *Web Café*, Rue Khalidy (just off Rue Jeanne d'Arc), T348880. The first internet café to be established in Beirut. Internet access LL5,000 per hour. Fast machines, no games, and a strong emphasis on the café as well as the internet side of things (breakfasts from 0800-1200, as well as burgers, sandwiches, main meals and tea, coffee, soft drinks etc). Pleasant atmosphere, and spacious (each monitor on a separate table). Worth paying that bit extra for if you prefer to surf in more comfortable surroundings. Internet phoning possible from here. Scanning and printing service also available.

Post The Central Post Office is located in Beirut Central District (BCD) on Rue Riad es-Solh. At the time of writing, however, this building was undergoing restoration, and another branch, on Rue Fakhreddine (on the edge of the BCD, up the hill from the *Phoenicia Inter-Continental* hotel) was the 'acting' Central Post Office. Open 0800-1700, Sat 0800-1200, closed Sun (these opening times apply to all the other branches in Beirut, except the AUB branch). Nobody seems very sure as to when, or indeed if, it will re-locate back to the main building on Rue Riad es-Solh. There are several other branches dotted around Beirut, including one in East Beirut, on Rue Gouraud near *Le Chef* restaurant, and another in Hamra, on Rue Makdissi across the road and a few doors down from the *Embassy* hotel (upstairs on the first floor, now with a signboard outside bearing the distinctive blue and yellow *Liban Post* logo). Perhaps the best option, however, is the small post office within the American University of Beirut grounds in Hamra, open 0800-1600, closed Sat, Sun. Entering by the main gate, turn left and it is a short distance along on your left. This is also the best place to have mail sent to you **poste restante**; have people address your mail to you (surname underlined and in capitals), c/o AUB, PO Box 11-0236/Poste Restante, Riad el-Solh, Beirut 1107 2020, Lebanon. (This way, mail will come to the AUB post office via its PO Box at the Central Post Office, which may seem rather roundabout, but saves you the hassle of dealing with the Central Post Office directly). Alternatively, *Sogetour*, the American Express Travel Related Services Representative, will hold mail for AMEX members, or for those with AMEX TCs (have mail sent to; c/o AMEX Clients' Mail, Sogetour, Gefinor Centre, Bloc 'A', PO Box 11-5865, Beirut). **Parcels** (up to a maximum weight of 10 kg) must be sent from the Central Post Office. See page 54 for details of rates.

Telephone The main telephone office ('Centrale') is by the Tourist Information office on the ground floor of the Ministry of Tourism building, on the corner of Rue Banque du Liban/Rue de Rome. Open daily 0730-2300. There is a 3-min minimum for international calls; Europe/USA LL2,100 per min; Australia LL2,400 per min; New Zealand LL3,600 per min; Syria LL500 per min. Between 2200-0700, reduced rates apply (with the exception of Syria); Europe/USA LL1,800 per min; Australia LL2,100 per min; New Zealand LL3,300 per min. You can also make local and national calls from practically any shop. In addition, there are numerous private telephone exchanges dotted around Beirut which offer significantly lower rates. *New Links*, at the southern end of Rue du Caire, where it intersects with Rue Emile Edde (see West Beirut map) is amongst the cheapest. Open daily 0800-2400. International calls to anywhere in the world cost LL1,500 per min, with a 2-min minimum. You can also send and receive faxes from here. Most hotels in Beirut also have their own fax machines which is convenient for receiving faxes, though they generally work out very expensive for sending faxes (or making international calls). *Hamra Telecom Centre*, on the corner of Rue Sourati and Rue Nehme Yafet, keeps the same opening times and charges the same flat rate of LL1,500 per min. Another possibility worth considering is internet-based telephone calls, a service which is offered by a few of the internet cafés in Beirut (the *Web Café* seems to be the best bet). The great advantage is that you just pay for the cost of the internet access. The disadvantage is that at present the quality of the connections are extremely variable (calls to the USA and Canada seem to work best), though no doubt this will improve over time.

British Council, Rue Yamout (off Rue Sadat), T740123, F750105, www.britishcouncil.org/ lebanon Open 1000-1300, 1500-1700, Fri 1000-1300, 1400-1600, closed Sat and Sun. Mostly geared towards disseminating information on study opportunities in the UK. However, the library does have a good selection of British newspapers and international news magazines which you can browse, as well as a TV tuned into BBC World. There is also internet access here, but it is meant for 'educational purposes' only (ie not for sending or checking your emails). You can borrow videos by joining the video club (membership LL160,000, plus LL65,000 deposit). Check the notice boards, or the website, for details of any cultural events (though the British Council is nowhere near as active as the *Centre Culturel Français* in this respect). There are no Arabic language courses on offer here. *Centre Culturel Français*, Espace de Lettres, Rue de Damas (near National Museum), T615859, F615863, www.lireenfrancais.org Open 0800-1900, closed Sun. This large complex is host to a lively programme of events and includes a library, cinema, theatre, exhibition hall, teaching facilities and café/restaurant (the *Café des Lettres*), as well as the French consulate (a full embassy is under construction next door). The library is open Tue-Fri 1000-1300, 1400-1730, Sat 1000-1500, closed Sun and Mon. There is a good range of books, videos and CD-roms, as well as French language newspapers and magazines; visitors are welcome to browse, but to borrow you must become a member (LL40,000 per year, plus an additional LL20,000 if you want to borrow videos). The cine club shows films every Wed at 1915, with tickets costing LL2,000. Details of films, as well as any exhibitions, plays, music or other performances are listed in a monthly programme leaflet available from the centre. *Geothe Institute*, Rue Bliss, T740524, F743524, www.goethe.de/beirut With its own library, as well as an exhibition hall and cinema. Ask for a programme from reception for details of films and other events, or check their website. *Italian Cultural Centre*, Rue de Rome, T749801. *Cervantes Institute*, Rue Commodore (or Rue de Baalbek), T347755.

Cultural centres

Beirut

Embassies

You are advised to phone before visiting since many embassies are still at temporary addresses & may move during the lifetime of this book

Australia, Fara Building, Rue Bliss, Ras Beirut, T374701, F374709. **Austria**, Rue Sadat, T354238. **Belgium**, Baabda (near Municipality), T05-468487. **Canada**, Coolrite Building, Autostrade, Jal el-Dib, T04-521163 (same building as UK embassy, see below). **Egypt**, Rue Thomas Edison, Ramlet el Baida, T867917. **France** (NB a new embassy was under construction next door to the *Centre Culturel Français*/consulate compound at the time of writing, due to open late 2001), Mar Takla, Hazmieh (on road heading out of Beirut towards Damascus), T429629, www.ambafrance-liban.org.lb Consulate; Espace des Lettres, Rue de Damas (in the same compound as the *Centre Culturel Français*), T616578, F616585. **Germany**, Mtayleb, T04-914444. **Greece**, Naccache, T04-521700. **Italy**, Place d'Etoile, Beirut Central District, T985200, F985308. **Japan**, Baabda, near municipality, T05-922001. **Jordan**, Baabda, near municipality, T05-922500. **Spain**, Chahab Palace, Hadath, T05-464120. **Turkey**, Tobi Building, St 3, Zone II, Rabieh, T04-412080. **UK**, Coolrite Building, Autostrade, Jal el-Dib, T04-715900, F04-715904. Inconveniently located on motorway to Jounieh. Heading out from Beirut, it is on the left just before the Jal el-Dib flyover. A pedestrian bridge gives access to the building if you are dropped off on the northbound carriageway. In case of a real emergency, you can contact the chancellery outside office hours; 8th St, Rabieh, T417007, F402032. **USA**, Aoucar, opposite municipality (PO Box 70-840, Antelias, Beirut), T04-417774, F04-407112.

Medical services

There are numerous private hospitals dotted around Beirut. The *American University Hospital (AUH)*, T340460, at the north end of Rue du Caire in Hamra is centrally located and has excellent facilities, as well as a well stocked pharmacy.

Language schools

The *Centre Culturel Français* (see above under 'Cultural Centres' for details) runs lessons in spoken and Classical Arabic. Each course consists of 60 hrs of teaching spread over 10 weeks, and costs US$200. It may also be worth enquiring at the AUB for details of any Arabic language courses they are running.

Laundry

All the hotels in Beirut offer a laundry service. In the budget places this can be very good value (you may even simply be allowed to use the washing machine for a small fee, or for free). In the more expensive hotels everything will be painstakingly dry-cleaned, ironed and folded (and probably individually wrapped in plastic), but you will pay through the nose for the service.

Useful addresses

Police: T160, or T350901. **Fire**: T175, or T310105. **Ambulance**: T865561. **Red Cross**: T140, or T863295. **Directory inquiries**: T120, or T200100. **International operator**: T100 or T885801.

Visa extensions

The main office for tourist visa extensions is the Securite Generale, Rue Habib Abi Chahla, near Cola bus stand. The building is on the corner with Rue Baghdad which joins Rue Habib Abi Chahla from the north. There is no sign in English. The relevant office is on the 1st floor. Open 0800-1300, Fri 0800-1000, Sat 0800-1200, closed Sun. You must leave your passport with them (you will be issued with an official receipt) and collect it after approximately 10 days. The new visa will generally be for the same period as the old one and you will be charged the appropriate fee. If the prospect of giving up your passport for up to 10 days does not appeal, or if you are only intending to overstay your visa by a week or 2, there is a much more straightforward option. Simply allow your visa to expire and then 1 or 2 days before you plan to leave the country, go to another branch of the Securite Generale (Service des Etrangeurs), this one near the National Museum. To get there follow Av Abdallah el-Yafi east from the large junction by the National Museum, and take the second left turn just before a church; the turning is signposted for the Securite Generale. The building is on the left after about 100 m. The office, situated on the first floor, is open 0800-1330, closed Sun. They will issue you with an exit stamp on the spot and free of charge. You must then leave the country within 72 hrs. **NB** This information was correct at the time of writing and the procedure worked fine for this editor. However regulations change frequently in Lebanon and you are strongly advised to check for yourself before allowing your visa to expire.

Motorcycle spares *RAB (Rizkallah A Boustany)*, behind Sacré Coeur College, Gemmayzeh, East Beirut, T448173, F446165. Wholesaler for Honda, Suzuki, Kawazaki and Yamaha spares. Can put you in touch with dealers specializing in European and US (ie Harley Davidson) bikes (note that there are no dealers for BMW motorcycles in Lebanon). If the shop is closed, check round the side alley where there is an entrance to the main basement storeroom/parts section.

Coast North of Beirut

12

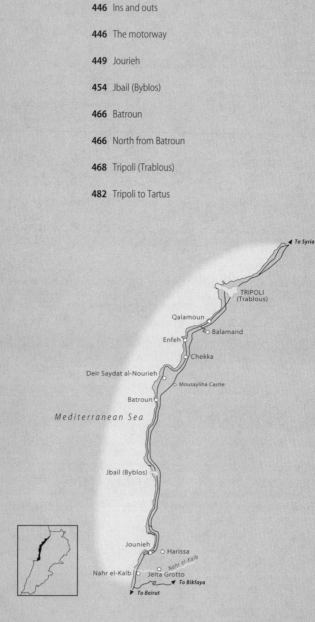

Coast North of Beirut

*The development of this stretch of coastline, particularly
between Beirut and Jbail, but also to a lesser extent
further north, has been a relentless process, with only the
occasional vestiges from the past still peeping through
here and there. Today many of the villages and coastal
resorts between the major towns merge into one another,
at times a continuous linear sprawl of unplanned and
often ill-conceived development. In short, although there
are some interesting places to visit, with a few rather
spectacular exceptions, Lebanon's Mediterranean
coastline is not outstandingly beautiful.*

*The main centres along the coast north of Beirut are
Jounieh, Jbail (Byblos), Batroun and Tripoli. Of these,
Jbail stands out for its beautifully preserved medieval
town and fascinating ancient excavations. Likewise, the
old part of **Tripoli**, the second largest city after Beirut, still
retains the atmosphere of a traditional Islamic city, with its
numerous Mameluke monuments and chaotic maze of
narrow, bustling souks. Elsewhere, you are faced with the
stark contrast of the glitzy (or some might say tacky) face
of **modern Lebanon**, embodied most dramatically in the
neon and high-rise of **Jounieh**, slashed through by the
never-ending roar and buzz of traffic making its way up
and down the coastal motorway.*

A foot in the door

★ Jounieh's congestion, and its endless beach resorts, hotels, restaurants, and garish 'super nightclubs' may not be to everybody's taste, but the **telepherique** (cable car) is definitely not to be missed. Starting down by the coast, it climbs steeply up the towering slopes of Mount Lebanon to Harissa, where a massive statue of the Virgin Mary looks down on the sprawling scenes of relentless materialism below. Whatever you make of it all, the views are truly spectacular.

★ If the dazzle of so much ostentatious wealth whets your appetite for the high life, you could always pay a visit to the **Casino du Liban**, in Maameltein overlooking the bay of Jounieh. Famous the world over during the 1960s, this huge complex with its numerous gaming tables and vast halls of fruit machines has now been fully restored and is open for business once again.

★ In complete contrast, **Jbail (Byblos)** offers another world of ancient Phoenician remains, carefully restored medieval souks, and a thoroughly picturesque and quintessentially Mediterranean fishing harbour. Once you have had your fill of sightseeing or browsing for souvenirs in the souks, the legendary **Byblos Fishing Club** restaurant, overlooking the harbour, is the place to relax and enjoy the sunset over a delicious meal of fish and mezze.

★ **Tripoli's medieval souks** are fascinating to explore, being every bit as colourful and lively as those of Aleppo and Damascus in Syria, and boasting a wealth of impressive Mameluke monuments. There is also some great **shopping** to be had here, whether in the form of lavish jewellery from the gold souk, ornate copperware, or the traditional, all-natural soaps made in the ancient Khan al-Saboun (soap factory). With excellent views overlooking the city, the Crusader castle of **St Gilles** is easily the best preserved castle in Lebanon.

Ins and outs

Two routes lead up the coast from Beirut. The main route is the motorway (or to the Lebanese the 'autostrade'), which now extends all the way to Tripoli and provides a rapid, if less interesting, means of travelling up and down the coast. As far as Kaslik this is in fact the only option, but at Kaslik you can join the slower and more scenic old coast road which runs parallel to the motorway, passing directly through all the towns along the coast en route. As well as linking places along the coast, both the motorway and the old coast road also provide access to the various routes leading inland up into the mountains. (These routes are dealt with separately in the Mount Lebanon chapter.)

The motorway

To join the motorway heading north from Beirut, follow signs through Beirut Central District first for the Port and then for Dora. The first 20 km or so consist of an unbroken urban sprawl of high-rise office buildings, shops, hotels, restaurants etc. This stretch also seems to be permanently congested: a nightmarish free-for-all as traffic jostles for space, with cars, trucks and lorries overtaking, undertaking, cutting each other up and somehow managing to squeeze themselves into more lanes than actually exist.

The unbroken nature of this urban sprawl makes it difficult to distinguish the various districts along this stretch. However, there are a number of important junctions, marked by flyovers, which correspond with each district and make for useful landmarks. Immediately to the east of the port, you pass the new **Charles Helou Bus Station**, and then the **Beirut Forum** (a large exhibition/concert hall) on the left, after which a flyover takes you over the **Dora** junction. Dora is an important transport hub for service taxis and local buses, as well as being one turning for Sin el-Fil. You then pass the **Jdaide/Sin el-Fil** exit, going under a flyover this time. After this you pass over the **Jal el-Dib** flyover (immediately before this is the Coolrite Building housing the British and Canadian embassies). Next is the **Antelias** flyover (the junction under this flyover is the turning for Bikfaya which provides an alternative route across to Zahle, see page 491). A little further on, an exit signposted for 'Dbayeh' also gives access to a large new marina and seaside development.

Around 16 km out of Beirut (counting from Ain el-Mreisse) and a little under 5 km after the Antelias junction, the motorway passes through twin tunnels cut into a shoulder of mountain which reaches right down to the sea. A new section of motorway has now been completed which carries southbound traffic around the promontory, although this has done little to ease the congestion around here. Immediately after the tunnel is the **Nahr el-Kalb** (Dog River). Emerging from the tunnel, turn right (signposted 'Vallée Archeologique de Nahr el-Kalb' on a Ministry of Tourism sign) to visit the monuments of Nahr el-Kalb.

While today it is the tunnel which is the source of so much modern-day congestion, in ancient times it was the Nahr el-Kalb which presented a major obstacle. Before the building of the motorway and tunnel, the Nahr el-Kalb was faced on either side by steep cliffs which invading armies were forced to negotiate in single file, leaving themselves highly exposed to attack. As a result it became something of a tradition to leave *stelae* (commemorative inscriptions) in the rock here, celebrating successful crossings of the river. The earliest of these inscriptions, left by Ramsis II of Egypt, dates from the 13th century BC, while the most recent, left by Christian Phalange militias, dates from the 1975-90 civil war in Lebanon. All the pre-1920 inscriptions have been numbered with Roman numerals, which are given below where appropriate.

Nahr el-Kalb (Dog River)

The first inscription (No I) is on the north side of the river. It records in neo-Babylonian script the campaigns of Nebuchadnezzar II (605-565 BC) in Mesopotamia and Lebanon, although it is heavily eroded and is not really worth the extra detour to reach it.

The first of those on the south side of the river (No II) is a little way up the valley, opposite an elegant triple-arched bridge spanning the river and the entrance to the Happy Valley/McMagic complex. It consists of a lengthy inscription in Arabic, weathered but still clearly discernible, which attributes the construction of the bridge to a Mameluke sultan.

Heading back towards the motorway, you then come to a set of steps which lead up to a large obelisk erected by French and Allied troops in 1942, commemorating the construction of the old coastal narrow-gauge railway. Back at the road level, just beyond the steps, is a Latin inscription (No III) left by the Roman emperor Caracalla (211-217 AD); the words 'Antonius' and 'Maximus' are discernible.

This is followed soon after by an inscription commemorating the 'liberation' of Syria and Lebanon from the Vichy French; "June-July 1941; First Australian Corps captured Damour while British, Indian, Australian and Free French Troops captured Damascus bringing freedom to the Syria and the Lebanon". The next inscription (No IV) is written in French and records the taking of Damascus on 25 July 1920 by General Gouraud, thus heralding the start of French Mandate rule.

Shortly after is a plaque which has been cemented into the rock depicting a small coat of arms, and an Arabic inscription with the date 25/3/1979. Next is a second large plaque cemented into the rock, depicting the national symbol of

The Legends of Nahr el-Kalb

No one knows really where the name Nahr el-Kalb, or Dog River, originated from. The Egyptians are believed to have associated the river with the jackal-headed god Anubis who controlled the entrance of the underworld which makes sense given that the river's main source is the Jeita Grotto (see page 494). The Greeks referred to it as the Lycus, meaning 'wolf'. According to one legend a demon chained an enormous wolf to the mouth of the river whose howls could be heard as far away as Cyprus. Others suggest that it was simply the howling of the wind and sea at the mouth of the river on stormy days which gave rise to the name. One American-Lebanese student visiting the site offered an alternative explanation, "It was a son-of-a-bitch to cross in those days, so they called it Dog River…"

the Lebanese Cedar, and with an Arabic inscription commemorating the final evacuation of French troops from Lebanon in 1946.

This is followed by an inscription (No V) left by the army of Emperor Napoleon III commemorating an expedition to Lebanon in 1860-1861. After this are two inscriptions adjacent to each other (Nos VI and VII), both depicting Assyrian kings, the first worn but clearly discernible, while the second is almost completely eroded.

Above these is an inscription (No IX) which records the capture of Damascus, Homs and Aleppo in Oct 1918: "The Desert Mounted Corps composed of British, Australian, New Zealand and Indian cavalry with a French regiment of Spahis and Chasseurs D'Afrique and the Arab forces of King Hussein captured Damascus, Homs and Aleppo, Oct 1918".

Further along is a heavily worn Assyrian stelae (No VIII) which is easily missed. Then, right by the motorway, is an inscription (No X) which records the occupation of Beirut and Tripoli by the "XXI British Army Corps with Le Detachment Français de Palestine et Syrie", also in Oct 1918. Right by the latter inscription, steps climb up the mountainside, leading over the motorway and entrance to the tunnel.

Having crossed over the motorway by means of the steps and a path, you come to a Greek inscription (No XI), very weathered and with the lower part defaced. After passing a cross symbol carved into the rock you come to an inscription (No XII) which is extremely weathered. It has also been identified as Greek, although nothing is really discernible today.

You then pass a Phalange version of the Lebanese Cedars symbol carved into the rock before zigzagging up the hillside to a pair of stelae (Nos XIII and XIV), the one on the left depicting an Assyrian king, the one on the right depicting a Pharaoh, identified as Ramses II (1298-1235 BC) by the accompanying inscription, carrying out a ritual sacrifice to the god Harmarkhis.

Along a dead-end side path off to the right is another stela (No XV) depicting an Assyrian king. The main path doubles back on itself and descends, leading to the final pair of stelae (Nos XVI and XVII), the first depicting once again the Egyptian Pharaoh Ramses II, this time making a sacrifice to the god Ammon, and the second with a cuneiform inscription relating the campaigns of the Assyrian king Esarhaddon against Egypt in 671 BC.

Eating Returning to the road leading up the Nahr el-Kalb valley, the triple-arched bridge spanning the river gives access to the *Tazka* restaurant on the north side, with a pleasant, shaded outside patio area. Alternatively, cheaper refreshments can be found within the *Happy Valley/McMagic* complex.

On the opposite side of the river is an old irrigation channel built against the cliff face, much of it still surviving. High up on the hillside meanwhile is a huge cathedral topped by a towering statue of Jesus with arms outstretched, part of the **Christ the King** Jesuit monastery and school. It is possible to continue up the Nahr el-Kalb valley, following a narrow, steep and scenic road as it climbs up into the mountains. Shortly before the modern village of **Diyarna**, there is a beautiful old chapel by the roadside. Continuing along this road and passing through the village of **Beit Chebab**, it is possible to join the alternative route across to Zahle via Bikfaya (see page 491).

Continuing north along the motorway, the next section is somewhat chaotic in that there are several small, unmarked exits off the motorway, as well as numerous shops, restaurants and snack bars lining the route. Take particular care of vehicles pulling out or stopping abruptly. Some 4 km after the Batroun exit, just before the start of a crawler lane for lorries, there is a small exit (signposted 'Museilha Castle') for the castle of **Mousayliha** (the castle is only accessible from the motorway).

North from Dog river

Mousayliha is 'fairytale' in the sense of its precarious position perched on top of a rocky outcrop, and its peculiarly small and compact proportions. Almost nothing is known about its origins: some have speculated that it was an Ayyubid construction, others that it was built by the Crusaders to guard this narrow section of valley where the old coast road was forced to swing inland by the promontory of Ras ech-Chekka. However, there is no mention of it in the records from Arab/Crusader times, and the construction appears to be more in line with techniques used during the 16th century. A steep stone staircase leads up to the castle, and once inside you can appreciate just how tiny it really is, its proportions restricted by the narrowness of the outcrop on which it is perched.

Mousayliha Castle
With your back to the motorway (& earplugs to block out the roar of traffic), Mousayliha has all the elements of a fairytale castle

The motorway continues its steep descent to the coastal plain north of Ras ech-Chekka. Five km beyond the tunnel (66 km from Beirut) there is a checkpost and, immediately after, an exit clearly signposted for **Ehden**, **The Cedars** and **Chekka**. As well as giving access to the coastal town of Chekka, this is the main route heading east via **Amioun** to **Bcharre** and the **Qadisha valley** (see page 510). From here the motorway continues for a further 18 km to arrive in **Tripoli** (see page 468), 84 km from Beirut (or more exactly, at the junction by the telegraph tower between Tripoli proper and the port area of El Mina).

Jounieh جونية

The civil war had a dramatic if somewhat unusual effect on Jounieh. Most of East Beirut's nightlife relocated here to create a world of hedonistic escapism for the privileged amongst Lebanon's Christian community (of which the war ironically created many). What was just a sleepy Christian port in the shadow of Beirut suddenly became the focus of a mad frenzy of development, free from any of the constraints, dare one mention the words, of urban planning. Today, the result is a chaotic stretch of neon and high-rise squeezed between the broad sweep of the bay and the mountains: Lebanon at its brightest and brashest.

Phone code: 09
Colour map 4, grid A2

Coast North of Beirut

Bus is the easiest way to get to and from Jounieh, though there are also plenty of service taxis (see 'Transport', below). The old coast road through Kaslik, just to the south of Jounieh, is lined with restaurants, bars and cafés, as well as numerous fancy shops and the huge *Espace 2000* cinema complex. On summer evenings this stretch of road performs the same function as the Corniche in West Beirut, playing host to a nose-to-tail parade of flash sports cars plying back and forth on see-and-be-seen

Ins & outs

missions. The road descends to a roundabout at the southern end of Jounieh: left takes you towards Jounieh's port; straight ahead (one way in the opposite direction for the first stretch) is the road running along the sea front through the centre of old Jounieh; right takes you back up to the motorway, or bearing off to the left, through the one-way system and past the municipality building ('Baladiyé') to rejoin the coast road north of old Jounieh.

Sights Jounieh is really a place to hang out and spend money in the restaurants, beach clubs and nightclubs, rather than a sightseeing destination. However, a trip up to Harissa by the telepherique (cable car) provides some spectacularly dramatic views, while nearby, **Jeita Grotto** (see page 494) is not to be missed. The inscriptions at **Nahr el-Kalb** (see above) are also worth visiting. Despite the new development all around, the old centre of Jounieh still retains a certain charm with several old Ottoman-period houses surviving.

Were it not for the devout praying at the shrines, & the modern octagonal chapel beside the pond, it would be easy to mistake this place simply as some sort of recreational park (indeed there are slides & swings in one corner for children)

St George's Grotto Beside the road leading towards the port, St George's grotto provides a reminder of a bygone era. Enclosed within a neatly landscaped area of park is a pond at the foot of an overhanging cliff face with several small shrines dedicated to St George and the Virgin Mary cut into the rocks. This was almost certainly a shrine to Adonis before the Christian period, and the grotto is said to have once been connected via a tunnel with the Greek Catholic monastery of Sarba further up the mountain side, itself built on the site of an ancient acropolis. People still come here to seek cures for their sick children. The landscaped park, the fountains bubbling away in the pond, and the filtered lighting at night are all recent additions, and very typically Lebanese.

Head north towards Maameltein for more space, less pollution & in some cases better sand

Beach clubs and watersports Practically the whole of the bay of Jounieh has been turned into a continuous line of fenced off private beach clubs. All charge an entrance fee, ranging from anywhere between US$1-10, while the most exclusive operate on a membership basis. Many have chalet apartments which are rented out on a monthly or seasonal basis, although these get booked up a long way in advance for the peak summer season. Most have a variety of watersports on offer (jet skis, water-skiing, etc) and a restaurant and bar. Some also have a swimming pool. Particularly at the southern end of the bay, however, the feeling is distinctly claustrophobic, with each beach club jostling for space with the next. One good place is the rather unfortunately named **Slimy Beach** in Maameltein, which is in fact quite clean. It is mostly a pebble beach, but there is a narrow band of sand by the water's edge, and comparatively spacious, stretching for a good 200 m. Entry is free and there is a café.

Gazing down on the scenes of mammon spread out below her, the Virgin has an expression that could be interpreted as compassion, & arms spread out in a gesture that could be interpreted as despair

Harissa and the telepherique Perched high up on the mountains overlooking Jounieh is a huge statue of the Virgin Mary. Inaugurated in 1908, the huge 15 tonne bronze statue (now painted white) is known locally as Notre Dame du Liban or Notre Dame du Harissa (Our Lady of Lebanon/Harissa). Beside it is a towering, modernistic cathedral of concrete and glass.

Although there is a road leading up to Harissa from Jounieh, the most exciting way to get there is by the **telepherique**, a cable car which climbs steeply from the coast up to the summit, passing indecently close to some of the high-rise apartments en route and providing spectacular views out over the bay of Jounieh from higher up. The cable car starts from the coast road a little to the north of the one-way stretch running through old Jounieh.

Once up there, you can join the numerous pilgrims in climbing the spiral staircase around the base of the statue, although you soon realize that for the pilgrims this is a serious religious experience rather than mere sightseeing.

There is also a small chapel inside the base of the statue and nearby a souvenir shop doing brisk business in religious souvenirs. A short distance to the south of the statue and modernistic cathedral, is the Byzantine-style **St Paul's Basilica**, built between 1947-62 by a Greek Catholic society of preaching fathers, the Missionaries of St Paul.

■ *The cable car operates Tue 1300-2000, Wed and Thu 1000-2000, Fri-Sun 1000-2300, closed Mon (except holidays). Return tickets cost LL7,500 and LL3,500 for children under 10. One-way tickets cost LL4,000 (children LL2,000). Officially, student discounts are only given to groups of 20 or more who have a letter from the Ministry of Tourism. However, if you show an ISIC card and ask nicely, you may get a slight reduction.*

Casino du Liban If ever there was a national symbol of Lebanon's reputation as the 'playground of the Middle East', this is it. The brain-child of Camille Chamoun, president of Lebanon from 1952-58, and first opened in 1959, the Casino du Liban was an extravagant multimillion dollar project. According to Victor Moussa, the first general manager of the casino, it was conceived as a means of containing the burgeoning gambling industry by bringing it all together in one establishment, while banning gaming activity in the rest of the country. Other commentators have criticized it as a symbol of the grossly iniquitous development policies which Chamoun presided over, favouring the Maronite community at a time when the country was in desperate need of a more balanced approach which would help unite the Christian and Muslim communities and create a sense of common national identity. Be that as it may, the Casino du Liban was built, and soon gained a reputation as one of the most prestigious casinos in the world, attracting the rich and famous from both East and West, and boasting lavish cabarets and musical extravaganzas, a huge theatre and numerous bars and restaurants in addition to the gaming rooms.

The Casino's minimum age of entry is 21 & a strict dress code is enforced, but aside from this all you need is lots of disposable income, & the inclination to dispose of it, fast

Badly damaged and subsequently closed down during the civil war, the casino underwent a massive US$50 million reconstruction and refurbishment programme in the 1990s, and was finally opened to the public once again in 1996. Facilities include 60 gaming tables, a slot machine area with over 300 machines, 6 restaurants, various bars, a nightclub, a 1,200-seat theatre and 750-seat 'Salles des Ambassadeurs' (for cabarets etc). A luxury hotel complex is also planned.

■ *The casino is in Maameltein, overlooking the bay of Jounieh from the north. The main entrance is via the motorway (heading south the turning is clearly signposted just over 1 km south of the Tabarja exit; heading north, take the Tabarja exit and double back). It is open all year round (the gaming rooms from 2000-0400, the slot machine area from 1200-0400). For more information T 932932, F 932779, www.cdl.com.lb*

Coast North of Beirut

There are numerous hotels in Jounieh, of which we have only included a small selection. However, bear in mind that in high season there is nothing below **B** category, other than the one **E/F** category hotel listed here. **L** *Emilton*, Maameltein (on coast road), T/F853344, www.emiltonhotel.com Luxurious rooms with a/c, TV/dish, IDD, minibar, safe box and attached bath. Restaurant, and bar. Very elegant and stylish place on the seaward side of the coast road, complete with its own small marina and swimming pool. Can arrange watersports and diving. A cut above the usual, sometimes rather tacky, resorts, and more spacious. **AL** *Aquarium*, Jounieh (on coast road, just south of telepherique), T936858, F935098. Reasonable rooms with a/c, TV/dish, IDD, minibar, attached bath and balcony (good sea views). Restaurant, bar, small swimming pool across the road (still under construction at the time of writing). OK, but rather overpriced (discounted low season rates better value). **A** *Bel Azur*, Jounieh

Sleeping
Prices quoted are for the high season (mid-May to mid-Sep); at other times there are usually substantial discounts on offer (anywhere between 15%-50%)

(south end of town, on coast road near roundabout), T/F930612, www.belazur.com Comfortable rooms with a/c, TV/dish, phone and attached bath (only the suites have balconies). Restaurant, large swimming pool, private beach, marina and a wide range of watersports on offer (jet skis, water-skis, scuba diving, paragliding, etc). **A** *Holiday Suites*, Jounieh (on coast road in old Jounieh, more or less opposite municipality), T933907, F639038, www.holidaysuites.com Comfortable rooms with a/c, TV/dish, phone, sink/fridge and attached bath. Best rooms with sea views and balcony; also cheaper rooms without either. Restaurant, bar, small swimming pool and access to the sea. **B** *Montemar*, Maameltein (set back slightly from coast road), T/F851624. A/c, TV, phone, fridge, attached bath and balcony. Rooms a little run-down and rather in need of refurbishment, though those at the front have great sea views. Restaurant, bar, swimming pool. **E/F** *St Joseph*, Jounieh (on coast road in centre of old Jounieh, just north of municipality), T931189. Beautiful Ottoman period building offering simple, spacious, high-ceilinged rooms with attached bath (double US$20). Also a couple of more basic singles for US$15. Lovely upstairs shaded terrace area. Very friendly and welcoming. Book ahead in summer. The only budget option amidst all the overpriced glitz of Jounieh (apart from a couple of dodgy sleaze-pits). Recommended.

Eating

There are numerous restaurants & snack places lining the road through Kaslik, the coast road through Jounieh as far as Maameltein, & also the motorway. Again, only a small selection are given here

Expensive *The Beach House*, Jounieh (on coast road to south of telepherique), T642888. Open 1200-late, closed Mon. Very stylish Lebanese cuisine/fish restaurant set in a stylishly restored red-roofed Otttoman building. Modern interior décor, light and airy, plus outdoor seating on sea front 'deck'. 'Oriental' restaurant planned for upstairs. From around US$30-40 per head. *Chez Sami*, Jounieh (on coast road to south of telepherique), T646064. Open daily 1200-late. Very stylish Lebanese cuisine/fish restaurant set in a carefully restored red-roofed Ottoman building complete with its own outdoor sea front 'deck'. From around US$30-40 per head. *Don Carlos*, Jounieh (on coast road to south of telepherique, T03-3388622. Open daily 1200-late. Spanish restaurant (plus some Eastern European and Russian cuisine). Pleasant interior, though looking a bit down-at-heel from the outside. From around US$20-25 per head. *St Pierre*, Maameltein (on coast road), T930141. Open daily 1200-late. High class French and international cuisine restaurant set in a carefully restored Ottoman building. Light and airy inside, while outside there is a pleasant terrace, as well as a large swimming pool and private (shingle) beach. Set menus of US$25 and US$30 per head, or order à la carte. Also just does poolside snacks in summer, as well as offering jet skis etc. *Les Tziganes*, Maameltein (on coast road), T915780. Open daily 1200-late. Big, upmarket place offering Lebanese, French and Russian cuisine (lots of steaks etc), as well as live entertainment in the evenings. Around US$25-30 per head.

Moderate *Abou Samir*, Jounieh (on coast road, a little to the north of the telepherique), T910209 and T936531. Open daily 1100-late. Two separate restaurants next door to each other, both Lebanese cuisine, with the same name and owned by the same company but run separately. The right-hand one is for fish/seafood only, while the left-hand one also does meat and chicken grills etc. Reasonably priced at around US$15-20 per head, though if you opt for more expensive types of fish/seafood this will push up the price to more like US$25-30 per head. *L'Entrecôte de Paris*. Maameltein, (on coast road), T917736. Open 1200-late, Mon 1800-late. Pleasant French restaurant with large bar in centre. Set meals of salad, entrecôte, chips and dessert for LL18,000 per head (or with fresh salmon fillet instead of entrecôte for LL23,000 per head). No advance booking. *La Crêperie*, Kaslik (on the right as you begin to descend into Jounieh), T933594. Open 1200-late, closed Mon. Set in a beautiful Ottoman period building with wonderful views out over the bay of Jounieh. As the name would suggest, crêpes (sweet or savoury) are the house speciality here, though they also serve raclette (actually jacket potatoes with melted cheese), steaks and various other dishes. With a little careful choosing you can eat for around

US$10-15 per head, though if you want to splash out you're looking at more like $20-25 per head. *Momentos*, Maameltein (on coast road), T03-822903. Open daily 1900-late. Specializes in fondues, with a set-menu for 2 of salad, soup, meat or cheese fondue and a bottle of wine for LL25,000 per head. *Pizza Hut*, Jounieh (a little to north of telepherique). Part of the international chain. Usual range of pizzas, pasta, salads etc for around US$15 per head. *Taj Mughal Mahal*, Maameltein (on coast road, opposite Slimy Beach), T851590. Open daily 1230-late. Comfortable, spacious Indian restaurant. Extensive menu, including lots of vegetarian options. Around US$15-20 per head. Also offers a free delivery service.

Cheap *Le Cuistot*, Jounieh (old coast road, just to north of roundabout at southern end of old Jounieh), T936745. Simple, pleasant Lebanese restaurant where you can have a meal of mezze, chicken or meat grills etc for under US$10 per head (though fish will set you back considerably more). Also sandwiches and snacks for under US$5. *KFC*, Jounieh (by mini-roundabout at northern end of one-way system through old Jounieh). Part of the international chain. No surprises, just your bog standard chicken meals etc for under US$10 per head.

Seriously cheap On the coast road near the mini-roundabout by the northern end of the one-way system through old Jounieh, both *Makhlouf* and *Snack al-Karkour* offer the usual selection of shawarmas, kebabs, pastries, sandwiches etc. The former is a big, brightly lit place, part of a chain and somewhat overpriced for what you get. The latter looks slightly less overpriced, but is basically very similar.

You'll be hard-pressed to find any genuinely budget dining options in Jounieh

Not the easiest of places to get to, but much better value and well worth a mention is *Abou André*, Jounieh (beside northbound carriageway of motorway; sign in Arabic only; just after passing the *West House* hotel off to the left and then going under the telepherique, look out for a large sign on the right for *Galerie Decorel* – the restaurant is next door). Open daily/24 hrs. No-nonsense traditional Lebanese diner offering delicious fatteh, fuul, hummus, falafels etc, eat in or takeaway. A filling bowl of fuul, complete with a full spread of crudité (raw onion, olives, mint, tomatoes, pickled gerkins etc), is great value at LL5,000.

Back in Jounieh itself, *Café Toni*, on the one-way section of the coast road as it runs through old Jounieh, is a juice bar which serves excellent, wonderfully refreshing freshly squeezed juices.

The choice in terms of nightlife is huge, although Jounieh's numerous 'super night-clubs' are rather tacky and outrageously expensive affairs involving glitzy floor-shows and lots of female 'escorts' hanging around waiting to be bought a drink. Even the regular nightclubs, without the floor shows, are extremely expensive. Note that most venues also include restaurants or bar food. If you want to splash out, here is a small selection of what's on offer. *Options*, *Century Park* Hotel, Kaslik, T212727. Huge venue on 3 levels (claims to be the biggest in Lebanon), popular on Sat nights but otherwise often half-empty, entry US$25, drinks from US$10. *Opera*, Debs Centre (next door to *Century Park* hotel), Kaslik, T900296. Dinner and dance, Lebanese music, older, more 'traditional' crowd. *Alecco's*, Val de Zouk Building, Kaslik, T918898. Similar to *Opera*, reputation as a classic Lebanese venue. *Piper's*, Kaslik, T931961. Traditional English-style pub complete with darts board, beers from US$5. *Old Wheel Pub*, Jounieh (part of Lagon beach club, opposite Le Cuistot restaurant), T916342. Nice décor but rather pricy. *Oliver's*, Maameltein (on coast road), T934616. Friendly, unpretentious restaurant/bar in a cosily furnished cellar with very reasonably priced snacks and meals (pizza, chilli con carne, pasta etc, US$5-15 per head) and a great atmosphere, attracts a young crowd, gets very lively on weekends, with more dancing and drinking than eating going on.

Bars & nightclubs

Coast North of Beirut

Shopping Jounieh itself is not particularly noted as a shopping destination, though there are some sylish shops along the coast road running through the old part of town. **Zouk Mikael**, to the north of Kaslik, is more likely to be of interest to tourists. Here, an area of old souks has been immaculately restored in much the same style as the Ottoman souks of Jbail (Byblos). There are numerous shops selling all the usual souvenirs, hand-icrafts etc, as well as a couple of restaurants and cafés.

Transport **Bus** The LCC bus No 6 (flat fare LL750) from Cola bus stand in Beirut goes via Dora, along the motorway and then down into Jounieh just to the north of the old part of town before continuing along the old coast road to Jbail (Byblos). Some of the other private buses on this route also go through Jounieh, but you may find yourself being dropped off on the motorway and having to walk into town. Buses back to Beirut can be caught from the roundabout at the southern end of town, but for Jbail (Byblos), you need to be on the coast road to the north of the one-way system through the old part of town. To pick up transport heading north to Tripoli you are best off walking up to the motorway and flagging down a bus or service taxi there. A **service taxi** from Dora to Jounieh will cost LL2,000, though unless all the passengers are heading for Jounieh, you may be dropped off on the motorway. It is usually possible to find taxis in Jounieh itself, although these tend to be private ones.

Directory **Banks** There are several banks and money-changers along the coast road in old Jounieh. *HSBC*, more or less opposite the municipality ('Baladiye') has an ATM which accepts Visa, Mastercard, Cirrus, Global Access, +Plus and Bankernet. **Communications** The **post** and **telephone** office are in the same building, opposite the municipality. **Medical services** 2 private hospitals with good facilities are the *Notre Dame du Liban*, in a side street off the coast road just north of the roundabout at the southern end of town, T644644, F831630, and *St Louis*, opposite the telepherique station, T912970. There are a couple of chemists in the centre near the municipality.

Jbail (Byblos) جبيل

Phone code: 09
Colour map 4, grid A2

As you entering Jbail, at first there seems little hint at the beauty of the place. But as soon as you wander down into the medieval part of town or towards the tiny fishing harbour, you are drawn into another world of tranquil, unhurried Mediterranean charm. The atmosphere is perhaps a little artificial in places, with touristy souvenir shops at every turn of the immaculately restored souks, but it provides a welcome relief from frenetic chaos beyond. Indeed, others would argue that Jbail's relaxed ambience and rich historical heritage makes it one of the most evocative and enchanting places in Lebanon.

Steeped in history, Jbail shows traces of settlement stretching back through seven millennia. This was one of the great city-ports of the ancient Canaanite-Phoenician period, and revered by the Egyptians as the 'land of the gods'. It was the Greeks who dubbed it Byblos (from the Greek for papyrus, bublos), because of it's control of the trade in papyrus between Egypt and Greece, and it was from this word that 'Bible' was derived.

Ins and outs

Getting there
The guide to Byblos by Maurice Dunand, first published in 1973, is still the most detailed guide to the ruins & can be found in most of the town's shops

The town is easy to reach by bus or service taxi (see 'Transport', below), whether you are coming from Beirut/Jounieh or from Tripoli. Arriving by bus or service taxi, you will be dropped off in the centre of town, by the sharp bend in the old coast road, from where you can explore on foot. From here, the heart of old Byblos extends south through the souks towards the Crusader castle and archaeological site, and west down towards the tiny fishing harbour. If you have your own transport, there is a large new parking area a little to the north of the fishing harbour.

There is a small tourist information office in the square at the entrance to the Crusader castle and archaeological site. Open daily 0830-1700 (in theory at least). Here you can pick up a selection of Ministry of Tourism brochures, but other than a friendly welcome, the staff have little else to offer in practical terms.

Tourist information

History

The earliest evidence of settlement dates back to around 5000 BC, when a small **neolithic** community lived here in round mud huts and engaged in simple agriculture, animal husbandry and fishing, using implements of stone, wood, bone, and pottery. Obsidian blades found here indicate that some form of trade existed with Anatolia.

During the **Chalcolithic** period (3800-3200 BC), ceramics and copper weapons began to make their appearance, the copper imported from Cyprus and the Caucasus, along with ebony from the Sudan and lapis lazuli from Central Asia. After around 3200 BC, the dwellings show a marked change, the round mud huts being replaced by more sophisticated rectangular buildings, with roofs supported by timber posts and beams. The settlement steadily grew, the houses becoming more densely packed inside an area now enclosed within ramparts.

According to Philo of Byblos, Canaanite-Phoenician religious tradition held that Byblos was founded by the god El, who built a wall around it and later bestowed it to the goddess Baaltis (Baalat-Gebal)

By the early to mid-third millennium BC, Byblos began to flourish in its role as a great commercial and religious centre. The source of its wealth was timber from the vast cedar forests of Mount Lebanon, which was traded with the Old Kingdom pharaohs of Egypt. To the Egyptians, who lacked any such forests, cedar was of enormous practical importance, used to build ships, palaces and temples, and even in the construction of the pyramids. In turn, the pharaohs made generous endowments to the temple of Baalat-Gebal (Baalat was the female form of Baal, known locally as Baalat-Gebal), whom the Egyptians identified with Hathor. By the end of the third millennium BC, trade had reached new heights, with timber, pitch, resin, wool and olive oil being shipped down the coast to Egypt in return for gold, alabaster, papyrus, flax, rope, cereals and pulses. Byblos also traded with Anatolia to the north and Mesopotamia to the east and in effect became a conduit for the passage of goods and ideas between Egypt and these two centres of civilization.

From around 2100 BC Byblos was overrun by waves of **Amorites**, a nomadic Semitic people from the deserts of Arabia. The Amorites settled in Byblos, bringing with them their own influences. Soon, however, trading relations were re-established with the Egyptian pharaohs of the Middle Kingdom and Egyptian influence began to reassert itself, fusing with that of the Amorites and indigenous Giblites (people of Jbail). What emerged is seen by many as the first truly Canaanite culture. Thus the so-called obelisk temple dating from this period was dedicated to *Reshef*, the Semitic god of war and destruction, while the obelisks themselves were clearly an idea borrowed from Egypt. The temple of Baalat-Gebal, having been partially destroyed by fire, was restored in modified form and worship of Baal-Gebal continued, though with new Semitic influences. The early kings of this period had names belonging to the same family as those of the first Babylonian Dynasty (also of Amorite origin), but adopted Egyptian titles. Burials were in the Egyptian style, in lavishly furnished royal tombs at the bottom of deep shafts.

Towards the end of the 18th century BC, the first of several waves of invaders, the **Hyskos** arrived (the so-called 'Shepherd Kings', although the name more accurately translates from Egyptian as 'rulers of foreign lands'), bringing with them new military techniques in the form of horse-drawn chariots, squadron formations, javelins and lances. They settled in Byblos and overthrew the Middle Kingdom Egyptians, remaining in power for over a century and a half.

Osiris and Isis at Byblos

The strong links between Egypt and Byblos led the closely parallel myths of Adonis and Astarte and Osiris and Isis to become entwined and confused. According to Giblite-Egyptian versions of the legend, Osiris was murdered by his brother Seth and floated out to sea in a wooden coffin. The coffin was washed up at Byblos, where it became encased in a splendidly tall and straight erica tree which the king of Byblos cut down and used as a pillar to support the roof of his palace. Eventually the goddess Isis, the lover and sister of Osiris, was guided to the palace at Byblos by a divine wind. She settled herself by the palace's well and wept for Osiris. In time she gained the favour of the queen and, having revealed her identity and the fate of her brother, the coffin was removed from the column and restored to her. The column itself became an object of worship in the temple, while Isis brought Osiris back to life and returned with him to Egypt.

However, in 1580 BC the Egyptian pharaohs of the New Kingdom retaliated, driving the Hyskos from Byblos and this time establishing more direct control, with Byblos becoming in effect a vassal state. Often referred to as the period of **Egyptian** domination, it was during this period that the cult of Isis and Osiris was at its strongest in Byblos. By the end of the 13th century BC what is considered to be the forerunner of our own alphabet emerged (the first evidence of it to be found on the sarcophagus of King Ahiram). Although the Ugaritic alphabet came earlier, it still relied on cuneiform imprints on clay tablets, while the script at Byblos was more cursive, making it better suited to writing on papyrus, and so spread more easily through Europe and the West. While Byblos (along with Beirut, Sidon and Tyre) remained faithful allies of the Egyptian pharaohs, other local rulers gave their allegiance instead to the newly emergent **Hittites** and the famous Tell Amarna tablets of Egypt record the desperate and futile pleas of the kings of Byblos for assistance from the declining pharaohs against the Hittite threat.

Ultimately, however, the period of Egyptian domination at Byblos was brought to an end not by the Hittites, but by the arrival of the so-called **Sea Peoples** around 1200 BC. Although the heyday of Phoenician culture is generally identified as coming after this invasion, Byblos itself (perhaps mirroring the fate of Egypt) appears to have fallen into decline, with Tyre to the south and Arwad to the north (ancient *Aradus*, the island that gave rise to present-day Tartus) taking the ascendency. The archaeological record shows little in the way of building activity, although Byblos continued as a small centre of trade, most importantly in papyrus between Egypt and Greece, coming first under **Assyrian** and later **neo-Babylonian** (Chaldean) control. Following the conquest of Babylon by Cyrus the Great in 539 BC, the **Persian** period saw a new flourishing of trading activity and wealth at Byblos. Submitting peacefully to Alexander the Great in 332 BC, it continued to prosper during the **Hellenistic** period, still ruled by its own semi-independent kings.

From the time of Pompey's conquest of the region in 64 BC, the **Roman** period saw Byblos fall into economic decline again, its main source of wealth, the cedar forests of Mount Lebanon having been all but completely exhausted. Nevertheless, it remained an important religious centre based on the cult of Adonis, which survived well into the second century AD, and the Romans undertook an extensive building programme there. During the **Byzantine** period, paganism was gradually replaced by Christianity and Byblos became the seat of a bishopric.

Coast North of Beirut

The Cult of Adonis and Aphrodite

Throughout the Greek and Roman periods, Byblos was a major centre of the cult of Adonis (see page 501) and the starting point for the annual pilgrimage to the source of the Adonis river at Afqa. It also had a special significance in terms of the myths surrounding Astarte, the 'Lady of Jbail', known to the Greeks as Aphrodite and identified with Venus by the Romans. Writing in the second century AD, Lucian gives some insight into the cult at that time: "I saw too at Byblos a large temple, sacred to the Byblian Aphrodite.... this is the scene of the secret rites of Adonis; I mastered these. They assert that the legend about Adonis and the wild boar is true, and that the facts occurred in their country, and in memory of this calamity they beat their

breasts and wail every year, and perform their secret ritual amid signs of mourning through the entire countryside. When they have finished their mourning and wailing, they sacrifice in the first place to Adonis, as to one who has departed this life; after this they allege that he is alive again, and exhibit his effigy to the sky. They proceed to shave their heads too, like the Egyptians on the loss of their Apis. The women who refuse to be shaved have to submit to the following penalty, viz., to stand for the space of an entire day in readiness to expose their persons for hire. The place of hire is open to none but foreigners, and out of the proceeds of the traffic of these women a sacrifice to Aphrodite is paid." (Lucian, The Syrian Goddess)

Following the **Arab Muslim** conquest of the seventh century AD, Byblos fell into obscurity and only regained a certain measure of importance during the **Crusader** period. When Byblos was captured by Raymond St Gilles in 1104, a castle was immediately built overlooking the small harbour which gave the town a major strategic significance to the Crusaders. After the death of Raymond in 1105, the town was controlled by the Genoese and benefited from trade with Europe. In 1187 it was captured by Salah ud-Din (Saladin) and colonized with Kurds before being retaken by the Crusaders in 1199 and remaining in their hands until they were finally driven out by Baibars in 1266.

Under **Mameluke** and **Ottoman** rule, although the fortifications left by the Crusaders were repaired in anticipation of their possible return, Byblos returned to relative obscurity, no longer an important centre of trade. The significance of the site was first highlighted by Ernest Renan, who carried out a survey in 1860. Detailed excavations were carried out by Pierre Mentet from 1921-24 and continued by Maurice Dunand until 1975 when work was interrupted by the civil war.

Sights

Built largely from recycled Roman stones and columns and standing on the site of an earlier Fatimid fortification, the castle consists of a solid central keep or *donjon* enclosed within defensive walls with towers at each corner and an extra tower in the north wall defending the original entrance. Restoration work is in progress to the outer fortifications of the castle. From the roof of the northwest and southwest towers you can get an excellent overview of the layout of the archaeological site.

Crusader castle & archaeological site

With so many layers of settlement enclosed within such a small area, excavation of the most ancient monuments involved removing later monuments which had been built on top of earlier ones and relocating them. Thus the small Roman theatre was originally between the northeast entrance of the city and the temple of Reshef/Obelisk temple, but was obstructing excavation of the latter and so was dismantled and moved piece by piece to its present location.

What you see is a somewhat rearranged version of what previously existed

Coast North of Beirut

You exit the Crusader castle through a small doorway in the base of the northwest tower (follow the steps leading down just beside the main doorway by which you first entered). Turn left to follow the west wall of the castle southwards (note the column drums used to reinforce the lower parts of the castle walls). On your right are the remains of successive stages of the city's ancient **ramparts**. The three most northerly *glacis* date from late second to early first millennium BC. Immediately south of these is a *glacis* of large stone blocks erected during the Hyskos period (1725–1580 BC). The southernmost rampart, clearly identifiable by its regularly spaced square buttresses, dates from the second half of the third millennium BC. To the south of it are indistinct traces of an even earlier rampart dating from the early third millennium BC.

Bear left once you are clear of the southwest tower to follow a clockwise circuit around the site

The ancient ramparts to the east of the Crusader castle (early to mid-third millennium BC) are pierced by a **gateway** which was the main entrance to the city. Steps lead up to a narrow passageway between the ramparts and down the other side, though, depending on the season, you may find this route to the Archaemenid Persian fortress very overgrown and impassable.

To the south of the gateway are the remains of a **third millennium BC temple** (labelled 'Temple En L, c 2300 BC'), dedicated to an unknown deity. Towards the end of the third millennium it was burnt down, probably during the Amorite invasions. The large depression to the west, now with pine trees growing in part of it, is thought to have been a **sacred pool**, associated with this

Crusader castle & archaeological site

1 Ticket office	8 3rd millennium BC temple	16 Amorite quarry
2 Crusader Castle	9 Obelisk temple/	17 Roman theatre
3 Glacis (late 2nd to	Temple of Reshef	18 Royal tombs
early 1st millennium BC)	10 King's well	19 Roman colonnade
4 Hyskos Glacis	11 Pre-urban settlement	20 Temple of Baalat-Ge
(1725–1580 BC)	12 Great residence	21 Roman Nymphaeun
5 Buttressed rampart	13 Ottoman building	22 Byzantine oil press
(3rd millennium BC)	14 Neolithic and	23 Achaemenid Persian
6 Ramparts	Calcolithic dwellings	fortress
(3rd millennium BC)	15 Early Bronze Age	24 Monumental podium
7 Gateway	settlement	

temple and the contemporary temple of Balaat-Gebal on the opposite side (see below). To the southeast of the third millennium BC temple is the more interesting **obelisk temple**, now surrounded by a wrought-iron fence and generally kept locked. This temple was built on the ruins of the third millenium BC temple by the Amorites in the early second millennium BC. Standing in the centre of the raised inner sanctuary of the temple is the cube-shaped base of a large obelisk, thought to have been a symbolic representation of Reshef, the god of war and destruction. Dotted around the surrounding courtyard are numerous smaller obelisks, probably erected by the devout as a means of soliciting the god's favour. Referred to as the *masseboth* in the scriptures and cursed and doomed to destruction by the prophets, the majority of these obelisks were nevertheless found still in their upright position when the temple was excavated. Numerous votive offerings were also uncovered, consisting of small bronze figurines covered with gold leaf (a collection of these is on display in the National Museum in Beirut).

From the obelisk temple a path runs west to the so-called **king's well**. This consists of a deep crater-like depression at the bottom of which is the base of a well. The sides of the depression are lined with stone and steps lead down to the well itself. Originally this was in fact a spring, which provided the whole of the town's water supply. During the Roman period, a system of earthenware pipes brought water to the town from the surrounding mountains and the spring water was only used for religious purification rituals. However, the rising earth level over the centuries threatened to choke the spring, so a well was constructed which was still in use as late as 1936. What you see today is the base of the well, the depression having been excavated to the level of the spring to reveal the steps by which it was reached in earlier times. According to legend, this was the well where Isis sat weeping when she came to Byblos in search of Osiris.

To the south of the king's well are traces of a late fourth millennium BC **pre-urban settlement**, while to the west of this are the remains of a large third millennium BC Early Bronze Age settlement generally referred to as the **great residence**. This is the best preserved of the settlement compounds dating from this period, consisting of a long central hall with three sets of rooms on either side. The roof of the central hall and those of the side rooms were held up by thick wooden columns, the stone locating bases of which can still be seen (120 of them in all). Some have sought to identify this complex as the palace in which stood the column containing the coffin of Osiris. A little to the west again, on the edge of the cliffs overlooking the sea, there is a large red-roofed Ottoman period house, the only part of the 19th-20th century village which once covered the whole of the excavation area not to have been cleared away. Dotted around it are the indistinct remains of various **neolithic** and **chalcolithic** dwellings (fifth and fourth millenniums BC). In the latter, numerous earthenware burial jars were discovered, complete with skeletons inside curled up in foetal positions.

A rough path leads north from the Ottoman house, passing between an area of Early Bronze Age settlement on the left and a large Amorite quarry on the right, to arrive at the **Roman theatre**. Built around 218 AD, the theatre is surprisingly small, even taking into account the fact that the four tiers of seating represent only a third of the original number. Note the holes in the first tier, which served to locate poles supporting an awning as protection against the sun. The miniature porticoes decorating the low wall of the stage are unique to this theatre. The square of black basalt pebbles in the centre of the semi-circular pit of the theatre mark the spot where a mosaic of Bacchus, now in the National Museum, once lay.

To the east and north of the theatre are the **royal tombs**, nine of them in all, dating from the second millennium and consisting of deep shafts dug into the bedrock. Although all but three of them had already been looted by the time they were excavated, many of the sarcophagi remained. The most important, that of king Ahiram, with the earliest known example of alphabetic writing engraved on it (a curse against would be tomb robbers), is now in the National Museum. Steps lead down into one of the shafts, with a tunnel at the bottom giving access to another, where there is a massive stone sarcophagus still in place, that of Yp-shemu-Abi, son of Abi-shemu, a 19th-century BC prince of Byblos.

Up on the hill to the east of the main cluster of royal tombs are the remains of a **Roman colonnaded street**, with six re-erected columns. These stand on the level of the original mound, giving some idea of the depth to which the surrounding excavations have been carried out. At their south end is the **temple of Baalat-Gebal**. This was the largest and most important of the temples at Byblos. First founded around 3000 BC, it continued to be used right through to the Roman era when it was dedicated to Astarte/Aphrodite (the colonnaded street was built by the Romans as an approach to it), undergoing numerous rebuildings and transformations over the intervening millennia. The excavated remains you can see today date from the third millennium BC when the temple was a focal point for the close relations which developed between Byblos and Egypt. Numerous fragments of alabaster vases given by the pharaohs as offerings were uncovered here, dating from this period. Some of these fragments, inscribed with the names of the Old Kingdom pharaohs of Egypt, including Cheops, the builder of the pyramids (26th century BC), can be seen at the National Museum, and the AUB archaeological museum.

Returning to the Crusader castle, a path leads under the bridge by which you entered and along the north wall of the castle. By the northeast tower are the remains of a **Roman nymphaeum**, only its base still standing, but with the remainder laid out on the ground beside it. Beyond this, following the old rail tracks used by the excavators to shift earth and stones, you come to the remains of a **Byzantine oil press**, followed by an **Achaemenid Persian fortress** (late fifth century BC) built against a **monumental podium** (early fifth century BC) which covered part of the ancient ramparts and which was topped by a building.

■ *Open daily 0800-sunset. Entry LL6,000 (students LL1,500). Multi-lingual guides are usually on hand (ask at the ticket office, or else at the tourist information office if you are interested). A guided tour (around 1 hr) for up to 12 people costs US$10.*

Medieval town The medieval town was surrounded by **ramparts**, of which the north section is best preserved, along with parts of the east section. These were first built by the Crusaders in the early 12th century at the same time as the castle, although they were subsequently repaired during the Mameluke and Ottoman periods and have been further restored in recent years. The cobbled **souks**, running north-south just outside the east ramparts, and leading north, east and west from the square by the Crusader castle and entrance to the archaeological site, have likewise been carefully restored in recent years and now boast a growing number of touristy souvenir/antique shops and small cafés. The overall effect is perhaps a bit too neat and contrived, though the beautiful Mameluke and Ottoman period buildings do still have a certain charm.

Fossils museum In the restored souks just near the small square by the entrance to the Crusader castle and archaeological site, this musuem is well worth a visit. There are impressive displays of the fossil fish and other organisms found in this region (see also under 'Shopping', below), and interesting explanations of their role in helping us understand the evolutionary process. For Jurassic Park fans there are also a couple of models of dinosaur heads. ■ *Open 0900-1300, 1500-1800, closed Mon. Entry free.*

Built in 1115 by the Crusaders in the Romanesque style, this church underwent several modifications and additions over the subsequent centuries. Perhaps the most striking feature from the outside is the open-sided **baptistry** built onto the side of the church, with its domed top and gracefully decorated arches. Added around 1200, the diverse decoration on the arches of the baptistry, incorporating rosettes, ribbing and zigzags, is clearly Italian in style, reflecting the influence of Genoese who occupied Byblos at this time. The adjacent entrance is of 18th-century origin, but around the opposite side of the church the entrance is purely Romanesque. Note the heavy buttressing along this side, thought to have been added following a severe earthquake in 1170. Inside, the barrel vaulting above the central nave is on an impressive scale. The church suffered serious damage during the British bombardment of 1840 and was only fully restored in 1947, at which point the bell tower was added.

Church of St John the Baptist (Mar Yuhanna)

Set within a rectangular garden adjacent to the paved courtyard in which the church stands (on the west side), traces of **mosaic paving**, foundations and a single standing column are all that remain of an earlier Byzantine church. There is grass growing amidst the mosaic, but in places its geometric patterns are discernible.

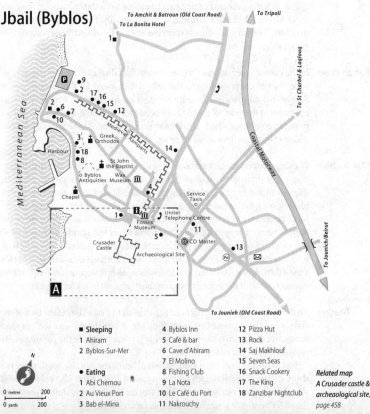

Jbail (Byblos)

Coast North of Beirut

■ Sleeping	4 Byblos Inn	12 Pizza Hut
1 Ahiram	5 Café & bar	13 Rock
2 Byblos-Sur-Mer	6 Cave d'Ahiram	14 Saj Makhlouf
	7 El Molino	15 Seven Seas
● Eating	8 Fishing Club	16 Snack Cookery
1 Abi Chemou	9 La Nota	17 The King
2 Au Vieux Port	10 Le Café du Port	18 Zanzibar Nightclub
3 Bab el-Mina	11 Nakrouchy	

Related map A Crusader castle & archaeological site, page 458

Pepe Abed and the Byblos Fishing Club

Pepe Abed and his restaurant, the Byblos Fishing Club, have become something of a legend. Born of mixed Lebanese and Mexican parentage, Pepe grew up in Mexico and travelled extensively before coming to Lebanon and establishing his restaurant in Byblos. A keen diver and collector of archaeological artefacts, Pepe also picked up a taste for the high life during his years of travelling, and his charm and charisma soon drew the rich and famous to his restaurant. A collage of fading photographs on the walls (together with more recent ones) bear witness to the numerous politicians, film stars and celebrities who have come to wine and dine here over the years; Marlon Brando, Sophia Loren, Brigitte Bardot, David Niven, David Rockefeller, Mick Jagger, Carlos Menim, Vaklav Havel and countless others.

Now in his eighties, Pepe leaves the running of the restaurant to his son, but is still to be found here, entertaining friends, taking it easy and generally enjoying the quiet, slow pace of life in Byblos. In a vaulted hall adjacent to the restaurant is a small musuem (dedicated under the auspices of UNESCO) displaying Pepe's small but remarkable collection of artefacts spanning the Phoenician, Persian, Greek and Roman periods. Here you can see statues, jewellery, amphorae, anchors, friezes, capitals and other archaeological fragments retrieved by Pepe from the sea around Byblos over the years. Also Included are various Mayan artefacts brought back from Mexico.

A little further down the same street, heading towards the harbour, there is a small **Greek Orthodox church**, a squat, heavily buttressed, fortress-like structure. The various remains scattered around the church's garden point to its Byzantine origins.

Roman street In the central reservation of the short stretch of dual carriageway which runs from the old coast road up to the coastal motorway are the remains of the Roman-period main north-south street, or *cardo maximus*. Around half way up, traces of the original paving have been excavated, and a series of columns from the colonnade which lined the street re-erected. At the top is a tumbled pile of column sections awaiting re-erection.

The harbour Walking down to the tiny harbour, which today shelters just a few small fishing boats, it is difficult to imagine that this was the port from which cedar was shipped to the Egyptian pharaohs for the building of the pyramids and that Phoenician merchants carried out extensive trade from here throughout the Mediterranean and beyond. The Crusaders built towers on either side of the narrow harbour mouth, of which the north tower still stands, and controlled entry and exit to and from the port by means of a chain strung between the two. A visit to Pepe's *Byblos Fishing Club* overlooking the harbour is a must, if not for a meal then at least for a drink and to see his small private museum (see box). In summer, some of the fishing boats run short trips out to sea for tourists.

Beaches To the south of the fishing harbour a path leads to a small bay at the foot of the cliffs below the excavated archaeological site, where there is an excellent sand beach, free and open to the public, and as yet without any of the paraphernalia typical of Lebanese beach resorts.

Just to the north of the fishing harbour (below the *Ahiram* hotel) there is a short stretch of public beach with a couple of snack bars. The beach here is shingle, but it is reasonably clean. Note that the beach shelves quite steeply into the water here, so it is not really suitable for children.

Heading south out of Byblos towards Jounieh, and reached by turnings off the old coast road, there is a series of more conventional beach resorts; *Byblos Riviera Beach*, *Tam Tam Beach* and *Paradise Beach*. Each charges a parking and/or entrance fee of between LL2,000-3,000. *Tam Tam* is the most developed in terms of facilities (showers, changing rooms, snack bar/restaurant, bar, watersports etc), but there is not that much to choose between them.

Essentials

AL *Byblos-Sur-Mer*, Byblos Port, T548000, F944859, www.byblossurmer.com.lb Fairly luxurious rooms with a/c, TV/dish, IDD and attached bath. Best rooms with balconies overlooking sea. Restaurant (also floating restaurant and swimming pool down by the sea in summer) and bar, watersports (jet-skis etc), sauna, conference facilities. The top hotel in Byblos, ideally located overlooking the sea right by the old port.

B *Ahiram*, overlooking the sea a little way to the north of the port and old town. T540440, F944726. Comfortable, recently refurbished rooms with a/c, TV/dish, phone, attached bath and balconies (all facing out to sea). 2 restaurants (Italian pizzeria and Lebanese/fish) both with good sea views, bar and 'disco'. Access to pleasant public beach below, and use of salt water swimming pool (US$5 per person) in private appartment complex next door. Quiet residential location, homely atmosphere, friendly staff. **B/C** *Abi Chemou*, in the small square opposite the entrance to the Crusader castle and arachaeological site, T540484. Above the café and restaurant of the same name the owner has converted 4 rooms of his home for rent. Fan, 1 room with attached bath, others shared, use of common sitting room area. Comfortable, homely and very central, but a little overpriced for what you get. **B/C** *Byblos Fishing Club*, T/F540213. Although famous for his restaurant, Pepe also has 12 delightfully secluded bungalows on the hillside overlooking the port. Some have their own private garden at the front, and all offer a pleasant change from the usual run of modern hotel blocks. At the time of writing these were closed for refurbishment (a/c etc being fitted), but due to open again in the near future.

D *La Bonita*, to north of port and old town (follow road past *Ahiram* hotel and *Byblos Marina*, then turn right soon after and it is the new appartment block on the right), T342076. Primarily long let, but will also rent to foreign tourists on a daily basis if there is room. Simple but clean studios with sink units, attached bath and balcony. Good value (**F** category for 1 month lets), though could do with a/c or fans for the summer.

D-G *Camping Amchit Les Colombres*, on the coast 2 km to the north of Byblos, in the village of Amchit (the left turn is around 500 m north of the bridge over the deep Nahr el-Joura, by a big blue and white sign for 'Housing Gallery; by the time this book is published the campsite should have its own sign in place), T540322. Lebanon's first campsite, and the only budget place on the coast between Beirut and Tripoli. Within easy walking/hitching distance of Byblos, and also useful as a base for trips up the Adonis valley and to surrounding areas. There is a range of accommodation here; comfortable, recently refurbished chalets with a/c, phone, fridge/sink units, attached bath and balcony (double US$30; also larger ones sleeping 4-6); 'tungalows' (tent-like bungalows, double US$20) with attached shower/toilet, though very cramped (going on claustrophobic) and hot in summer; and camping (plenty of shade; US$3 per person with your own tent; also a few tents for rent). Campervans etc also welcome. Small café/snack bar, access to the sea (rocks only). The owner, Françoise Matta, is also establishing a 'country club' up in the mountains, with bungalows, camping, restaurant, activities etc.

Sleeping
Price categories are based on high season rates. During the low season (mid-Nov to end Feb, excluding Christmas/ New Year), discounts are often available, bringing hotels down 1 category

Coast North of Beirut

Eating **Expensive/moderate** *Byblos Fishing Club*, beside harbour, T/F540213. Open daily 1200-late. Oozing with character and idyllically situated with a covered terrace overlooking the old port of Byblos, this is *the* place to go in Byblos (and indeed Lebanon for many afficianos). As you would expect, seafood is the speciality here. A full-scale à la carte meal will cost from around US$30 per head, but there are also a couple of cheaper options. A set menu meal of starters (8 mezze dishes), a fish main course, fruit and coffee costs a very reasonable US$20 per head, or else there is a mixed grill variation (chicken/meat) for US$17 per head (both set menus are plus 5% tax, but without any service or cover charge). Recommended. *Au Vieux Port*, overlooking the sea-front parking area to the north of the old harbour, T541893. Lebanese cuisine (seafood a speciality). Around US$25-30 per head. *Bab el-Mina*, next door to *Byblos Fishing Club* restaurant, T540475. Open daily 1100-late. Similar set-up to its more famous neighbour, with a pleasant terrace overlooking the harbour, though without the atmosphere. Set meal for 2 of grilled fish, chips, salad and beer US$15 per head, or order à la carte (from around US$20 per head). *Le Café du Port*, opposite *Byblos-Sur-Mer* hotel, T547447. Open daily 1100-late. Recently opened café/restaurant with a pleasant open-air terrace overlooking the harbour. From around US$20 per head for a full meal with fish, or less for snacks. *Cave d'Ahiram*, next door to *Byblos Sur Mer* hotel, T540206. Lebanese cuisine (seafood a speciality) in pleasant, intimate surroundings. Around US$25-30 per head.

Moderate *Abi Chemou*, in the small square opposite the entrance to the Crusader castle and archaeological site, T540484. Downstairs is a pleasant café for tea/coffee, beers (small Amstel LL1,500), snacks (sandwiches LL2,000-3,500) etc, while upstairs is a restaurant with a pleasant balcony, European/Lebanese cuisine, around US$15-20 per head à la carte. Also 2 set menus; US$10/15 per head for meat/fish respectively. *Byblos Inn*, just inside the eastern medieval ramparts, T547884. Open daily from 1100 (book for evening dining). Small, friendly European/Lebanese cuisine restaurant set in a restored barrel-vaulted hall which formed part of the Ottoman souk. Set lunch menu US$15 per head, or simpler option US$10. *El Molino*, T541555. Open 1200-late, closed Mon. Pleasant, intimate restaurant and bar serving good Mexican cuisine, around US$15-20 per head. Fixed menu lunch (1200-1500) US$10 per head.

Cheap/seriously cheap Following the road that runs west from the coast road, along the outside of the northern medieval ramparts and down to the port, you pass a new *Pizza Hut* restaurant on the right. Just past this are three pleasant snack places, grouped together in a row with terraces facing out onto the street; *Seven Seas*, *Snack Cookery* and *The King*, all offering a range of sandwiches (from LL3,000), pizzas, burgers, crêpes etc, as well as some more substantial dishes (mostly under US$10) and serving draught Amstel (LL5,000 for a pint).

Just inside the old souks, *Nakrouchy* is a pleasant snack bar/diner offering a wide range of sandwiches from LL2,500-3,000 upwards, as well as crêpes, pizzas and grilled meat/chicken platters etc (most dishes under US$10). The menu is entirely in Arabic, though the staff are generally helpful.

There are several cheap snack bars and takeaways along the old coast road as it passes through town, mostly rather anodine western-style fast-food places. For the best falafel and shawarma sandwiches, try the *Rock*, a brightly lit and spotlessly clean place which also does all manner of kebabs etc, either as a sandwich (from LL3,000) or as a platter (around LL7,000). Again, the menu is all in Arabic, but the cashier will help you out (you pay for your order first, then give your ticket to the people serving). Another good place is *Saj Makhlouf*, specializing in *saj* (a thin, flat round bread cooked on what looks like an upturned wok and served rolled into a sandwich). Fillings range from traditional *zaarta* – a seasoning of thyme and sumak – to ham, vegetables, cheese etc. A basic *zaarta saj* costs just LL1,000 (though you'd need quite a few to fill you up), while the more substantial ones are LL3,500.

All the expensive/moderate restaurants listed have their own bars, with those overlooking the harbour being the obvious places to go for a sundowner. *La Nota*, next door to *Au Vieux Port* restaurant, is primarily a 'pub'/café, though it also serves sandwiches, burgers etc, as well as some main dishes.

Bars & nightclubs

There is one dedicated nightclub, by the old harbour; *Zanzibar*, below *Byblos Fishing Club* restaurant, T541516. Open from 1900, closed Mon. Owned by same management as *El Molino* restaurant. Entry LL10,000 (including 1 drink). Rather a small place. Only really gets going on Fri and Sat nights, though Thu nights (Latin/Salsa) also popular. If you are looking for a wild night out you really need to head back down to Jounieh or Beirut.

There are plenty of tourist shops selling **souvenirs**, **jewellery** and **handicrafts** in the restored Ottoman souks of the old town, and around the small square by the entrance to the Crusader castle and archaeological site. *Byblos Antiquities*, just up from the Byblos Fishing Club has one of the better selections of jewellery, antiques and archaeological artefacts, though it is worth shopping around. Bear in mind that the majority of the 'antique' and 'archaeological' artefacts you see are probably reproductions, however convincing the shop owner may seem. For a more unusual gift, most of the souvenir shops sell rocks bearing imprints of **fossil** fish like those to be seen in the Fossils Museum; if you are interested in these you might also want to consider visiting the small village of Haqel (see page 509), 17 km away in the mountains to the east of Byblos, where most of these fossils are found and where there are several more shops selling them. Colour slide and print **film** is readily available in most of the tourist shops. The *Mayadoun Bookshop*, just inside the eastern medieval ramparts, has a good selection of books and maps.

Shopping

Service taxis congregate in the centre of town, on the old coast road close to the main entrance to the Ottoman souks. The service taxi fare from Beirut (Dora bus stand) is LL3,000. Most of those which you see waiting around in the centre of town are looking to fill up with people heading for Jounieh/Beirut. For Tripoli you should go up to the northbound side of the motorway where you can flag down either a service taxi (LL3,000) or one of the regular Beirut-Tripoli buses which pass this way.

Transport

Buses coming from Beirut/Jounieh also turn around in the centre of town on the old coast road close to the main entrance to the Ottoman souks. As well as the LCC bus service (No 6), which runs from Cola bus stand in Beirut going via Dora and Jounieh, there are several other private bus companies which make the same trip, though these have to be caught at the Dora bus stand. The LCC bus No 6 goes through Jounieh itself and then follows the old coast road to Jbail (Byblos); some of the other private companies do the same, while others simply stick to the motorway. The bus fare is LL750-1,000 depending on the company.

Banks One of the souvenir shops in the small square by the entrance to the Crusader castle and archaeological site offers exchange (look for the sign in the window). There are several banks along the old coast road as it passes through town (most of them with cash machines), as well as a couple of official money changers. **Communications** Internet There is currently only one internet 'café' in Byblos, *CD Master*, tucked away in a narrow lane to the south of the old coast road. Mostly given over to computer games, though always with a few terminals dedicated for internet access (LL4,000 per hr). Claims to be open 24 hrs/7 days. Post The *Liban Post* office is on the first floor of an anonymous-looking building to the southeast of the town centre, between the old coast road and the motorway. **Telephone** The government telephone office ('Centrale') is on the main road to the north of the town centre. Open daily 0700-2300. Same rates as per Beirut. Cheaper and more convenient is the private *Unitel* office down inside the old souks. Open daily 0800-2400. LL1,500 per min flat rate for all international calls.

Directory

Coast North of Beirut

Batroun البترون

Phone code: 06
Colour map 5, grid B1

The town of Batroun, modern and not particularly inspiring, along the main road, preserves something of its traditional past in the old part of town around its small fishing harbour. During Phoenician times it was a centre of some significance, finding mention in the 14th-century BC Tell Amarna tablets of Egypt as a dependency of Jbail. During the Hellenistic and Roman periods it was known as *Botrys*, whilst in the medieval period it was known as *Butron* and came under the control of the County of Tripoli.

Ins & outs   Batroun is some 16 km to the north of Jbail (Byblos). Following the old coast road north, after crossing the deep Nahr el-Joura, you pass through **Amchit** (2 km), where Ernest Renan lived for a time and where his sister died and was buried. For the remaining 14 km on to Batroun the coastline is on the whole relatively unspoilt. Service taxis run fairly frequently from the centre of town to Tripoli and Beirut, or if coming from either of these, buses and service taxis doing the motorway route will drop you off by the Batroun exit, from where it is a short walk into town. From Jbail there are less frequent service taxis along the coast road to Batroun.

Sights   In the centre of town a signpost points you in the direction of the small **Roman amphitheatre** (to the east of the main road). Set in the garden of a private house (visitors are welcome), all that remains of it is a small section of the tiered seating, cut into the natural rock. More interesting is the old part of town to the west of the main road, leading down towards the fishing harbour. Many of the old Ottoman-period buildings remain, and there are two interesting churches. The main one is the Maronite **church of St Stephan**, with square towers in each corner and crenellations around the top. Covered until recently with render, this has now been removed to reveal the original stonework, both inside and out. The second one is the Greek Orthodox **church of St George**, topped by a dome and with an interesting arrangement of arched machicolations around the main door. Close to the tiny fishing harbour there is a section of sea wall cut from the natural rock, thought to date originally from Phoenician times and used as a quarry in the Hellenistic and Roman periods.

Sleeping & eating   Although there are no hotels in Batroun itself, around 1 km to the south of town on the old coast road there are a couple of luxury hotel/beach resort complexes: **A** *Sarawy*, T620100. Apartments rented on a seasonal basis or privately owned, but some available for rent on a daily basis (usually out of season). A/c, TV/dish, phone and attached bath. Restaurant, bar, swimming pool, health centre, small private harbour and beach. **A** *San Stephano*, T643041, F741540. Choice of apartments or rooms with a/c, TV/dish, phone and attached bath. Restaurant, bar, swimming pool.

Just south of these is the *Taj al Mansour* restaurant, serving Lebanese cuisine for around US$20-25 per head, or more for seafood. In the centre of Batroun there are several small restaurants and snack places along the main road, and a couple more in the old part of town. Opposite the Roman theatre, *Chez Merchak* is both a restaurant and pub/bar, serving mostly European cuisine, around US$10-15 per head.

North from Batroun

Heading north, shortly after leaving Batroun, a small chapel is visible perched on a hillock to the right of the road. This is the **church of the Holy Saviour**, a beautiful, recently restored 12th-century Crusader construction which overlooks the Nahr el-Jaouz. To reach it, take the small turning by some houses just beyond it (the turning just before it does not give access). Continuing along the coast road, it begins to climb as you approach **Ras ech-Chekka**, a shoulder of mountain reaching right down to the sea. Known in classical times by its Greek name *Theouprosopon* (literally 'the Face of God'), successive invaders had the choice of following the exposed path around this precipitous headland, or else heading inland to follow a narrow valley to the east (later guarded by Mousayliha castle, see page 449).

As the coast road climbs approaching Ras ech-Chekka, you come to a Syrian army checkpost and a small turning off to the right, signposted to Hamat. Taking this turning, the road climbs up to the village of Hamat (3 km). Turn sharp left in the village to reach Deir Saydat al-Nourieh, a large Greek Orthodox church and monastery dating from the 17th-19th centuries, parts of which are being restored. Steps lead down from the monastery to a small chapel cut into the cliffs of Ras ech-Chekka, from where there are wonderful views out over the Mediterranean. From the village of Hamat, you can also descend to the motorway, joining it just beyond Mousayliha castle. Nearby there is a bizarre remnant of Lebanon's civil war; the **Pierre Gemayel International Airport**, a huge airport complex including runways large enough to take Boeing 747s. The brain-child of Bashir Gemayel, the project was undertaken at a time when the Christians of Lebanon saw the partition of Lebanon into Christian and Muslim statelets as a very real possibility.

Deir Saydat al-Nourieh
Colour map 5, grid B1

Continuing along the coast road from the turning for Hamat, there is an excellent viewpoint offering wonderful view out to sea, followed by a tunnel which cuts through a section of the Ras ech-Chekka promontory. The road then begins to descend, passing the **C** *Beaulieu Sur Mer* hotel/beach resort and a series of four somewhat tacky beach resort complexes lower down, followed by the unfortunate juxtaposition of a cement works. Chekka, 15 km from Batroun, is a small village with a couple of restaurants and snack places along the main road. Just before the centre of the village, you pass an unmarked right turn which is the start of the road leading via Amioun to the Qadisha valley (see page 510). Continuing north, you pass a second huge cement works before getting to Enfeh.

Chekka
Phone code: 06
Colour map 5, grid B1

The town's name translates literally as 'nose', in reference to the shape of the coastline here. It consists of a largish village with several small restaurants, cafés and shops along the main road. Mentioned in the 14th-century BC Tell Amarna tablets as *Ampi* and known to the Crusaders as *Nephin*, Enfeh was, like Batroun, a dependency of the County of Tripoli and once boasted its own castle. However, little of the Crusader castle, which occupied the narrow peninsula jutting out from the coast, remains today. There are several churches in the village, including the ruins of two Byzantine and Crusader churches by the sea. Around Enfeh there are various **salt pans** consisting of shallow rectangular pools where sea water is left to evaporate.

Enfeh
Phone code: 06
Colour map 5, grid A1

Sleeping Around 2 km to the north of Enfeh there are two luxury beach resort complexes, each with their own private marina, swimming pool, tennis, health centre, restaurant, bar, etc; the **A** *Las Salinas*, T540970, F611647 and **B** *Marina del Sol*, T645216. Accommodation in the latter is only available on a daily basis from Oct-May, with the chalets being rented on a monthly or seasonal basis during the summer.

Around 4 km north of *Marina del Sol* there is a right turn signposted for Balamand University (5 km), which incorporates the monastery of Deir Balamand (or Belmont Abbey), high up on the mountainside overlooking the sea. Also referred to in some Crusader chronicles as *Valmont*, the monastery

Deir Balamand (Belmont Abbey)
Colour map 5, grid A1

Coast North of Beirut

was first founded (possibly on the site of an earlier Byzantine monastery) by Cistercians in 1157, and remained in their hands until the fall of Tripoli to the Mameluke Sultan Qalaun in 1289. The monastery is known to have come under the authority of the Greek Orthodox Church in the early 17th century, although according to some sources it has been occupied by Greek Orthodox monks since the Cistercians were driven out in 1289. The main church, dating from the original founding of the monastery, is noted for its austere simplicity (typical of Cistercian architecture). Its bell-tower (probably early 13th century) is one of the few to have survived from the Crusader period, although the bell itself was removed at some point and relocated above the west wall of the courtyard (visible from the outside only). The overall atmosphere of the monastery, with its ancient church, cobbled courtyard and arched cloisters, as well as its setting amidst olive groves with stunning views out over the Mediterranean and across to Tripoli, is one of great tranquillity and beauty. The monastery runs a seminary and is famous for its library. Most of the buildings have been carefully restored and you can usually find someone to show you around.

Qalamoun
Colour map 5, grid A1

Continuing north from the turning for Balamand, after 2 km you come to the centre of Qalamoun, a town famous for its **brassware**, which is sold in various shops along the main road. From Qalamoun it is a further 8 km into the centre of Tripoli, with several hotel/beach resort complexes lining the road en route.

Tripoli (Trablous) طرابلس

Phone code: 06
Colour map 5, grid A1

Tripoli was at one time earmarked to become the capital of the country. In the event, that honour went to Beirut, and Tripoli, Lebanon's second largest city, was left something of its old character and quiet, friendly ambience. The medieval core of the city in particular, with its wealth of Mameluke and Ottoman period monuments and its narrow, chaotic souks, give it a distinctly Arab feel and make it a fascinating area to explore. The population is predominantly Sunni Muslim and, without the same degree of cosmopolitan or westernizing influences, more conservative than Beirut's. Tea shops and cafés, where men often seem to while away whole days, are still very much the way, and despite the inevitable congestion and press associated with a large Lebanese city, things somehow seem to move at a slower pace.

By contrast, the wide boulevards leading from the medieval city to the port area of El Mina are lined with modern apartment blocks and fashionable shops and restaurants, giving a taste of Tripoli's 21st-century face. El Mina itself, although the site of the ancient city, is also largely modern, and its main attractions are walks along the sea front, fishing boat excursions and dining out.

Ins and outs

Getting there
Regular buses, coaches and service taxis shuttle back and forth between Beirut and Tripoli. There are also plenty of Syrian-operated luxury coaches connecting the city with various destinations in Syria (the most frequent services are between Aleppo and Tripoli, going via Hama and Homs, and crossing the border at Dabbousiyeh or Arida).

Getting around
The only way to explore Tripoli's medieval souks is on foot, though for the 3 km trip between the medieval city/'downtown' area and El Mina you are best off taking a service taxi or private taxi.

Tripoli consists of 2 distinct areas. Occupying the narrow coastal headland is the port area of **El Mina**, while around 3 km inland from this is the main centre and **medieval**

city, overlooked by the Crusader castle of St Gilles. Entering Tripoli along the old coast road from the south, you come in along Rue Sheikh Bechara el-Khoury. A distinctive clock-tower off to the right (east), on Rue Tall, stands more or less opposite Sahet et-Tall (Tall Sq) and together they form the focus of the main 'downtown' area, with the bus/service taxi stands and most of the banks, hotels etc. Beyond this, to the southeast, extending to the Abu Ali River and Crusader castle, is the heart of the medieval city. To the west of Rue Sheikh Bechara el-Khoury, meanwhile, are the modern boulevards extending northwest to El Mina. Entering Tripoli from the south along the coastal motorway, you come out on Rue Riad Solh (Mina Av), roughly half way between El Mina and the medieval city/downtown area.

The tourist information office is on the large roundabout heading south out of Tripoli on Rue Sheikh Bechara el-Khoury, T433590. Open 0800-1700, closed Sun and holidays. The staff here are helpful and well informed. As well as offering the usual array of Ministry of Tourism pamphlets, they can help you out with hotel bookings and organize fully trained French/English speaking guides for tours of the city (around US$30 for a 3 hr tour, or more for large groups). **Tourist information**

History

The earliest evidence of settlement here dates back to the **Late Bronze Age** (14th century BC), although it seems likely that a settlement of some sort existed here even earlier. By the 9th-8th centuries BC a small **Phoenician** trading station had been established, with traders from Sidon, Tyre and Arwad (ancient *Aradus*, the island that gave rise to Tartus) each forming their own separate communities on the headland around the port. During the 4th century BC, the three Phoenician city-states represented here formed a federation based at Tripoli (then known as *Athar* or *Kadytis*) and declared independence from their **Persian** overlords. The focus of this revolt soon shifted to Sidon, still the most important of the Phoenician city-states, and the Persians crushed the uprising just as their empire fell to the armies of Alexander the Great.

During the **Hellenistic** period the town became known as *Tripolis*, literally 'three cities', in reference to the separate Sidonian, Tyrian and Aradian communities there, and began to prosper as a centre of trade, thanks to its coastal position and its easy access to the interior. Under the **Seleucids**, like most of the cities along the coast, it gained almost complete autonomy. During the **Roman** period, it maintained this position and continued to flourish. In 551 AD, however, towards the end of the **Byzantine** period, Tripoli was almost completely destroyed by an earthquake.

It soon recovered, and by the time it was besieged in 635 by the **Muslim** armies of Mu'awiya, the future founder of the Umayyad Dynasty, it was once again a walled city of some importance. The inhabitants fled the city by sea with the help of the Byzantine fleet, and Mu'awiya subsequently resettled it with a Jewish colony. From 685-705 it fell into the hands of the Byzantines again, before being recaptured and incorporated into the **Umayyad** Empire. Towards the end of the 10th century, in the anarchy which followed the steady decline of the **Abbasid** Dynasty, Tripoli came under the rule of the Egyptian **Fatimids** who stayed in control until 1069, when the Shi'ite *qadi* (religious judge) of the city, Amin al-Dawlah ibn Ammar, declared its independence. Under the rule of the Banu Ammar family, Tripoli, already a flourishing industrial city surrounded by rich fruit orchards, olive groves, date palms and fields of sugar cane, became renowned as a centre of learning, famous for its school, the *Dar al-Ilm* (literally 'House of Culture') with a library said to contain 100,000 books.

Coast North of Beirut

Its very prosperity made it highly attractive to the **Crusaders**. Raymond St Gilles did not attack it the first time he passed by in 1099, frustrated by his unsuccessful siege of nearby Arqa (see page 528), anxious to press on to Jerusalem and persuaded perhaps by the generous gifts of gold, horses and supplies which Jalal al-Mulk ibn Ammar, the ruler of Tripoli at that time, had showered on him. However, he was later impressed by the wealth of its hinterland and in 1102 he returned with just 300 men. Believing that he could be easily beaten, Fakhr al-Mulk ibn Ammar, Jalal al-Mulk's successor, convinced the rulers of Damascus and Homs to join him in an offensive against Raymond's derisory force. But Raymond routed all three armies, inflicting heavy losses on Fakhr al-Mulk's forces. The following year, he set about building a formidable castle, Chateau Pelerin, on a hill a few miles inland from the fortified city of Tripoli, which at that time occupied only the headland around the port of El Mina. Later named St Gilles citadel in his honour, it was around this castle that the Mameluke and Ottoman period city subsequently developed.

Raymond's castle provided him with a means of controlling all the land trade entering and leaving the coastal city. Fakhr al-Mulk responded by launching repeated raids against the castle, the most daring in 1104 resulting in Raymond receiving burns which were to eventually prove fatal. On his deathbed, he negotiated a deal whereby the Tripolitians would cease these attacks in return for free passage in and out of their city. This uneasy truce lasted for a while until his cousin, Guillaume Jourdain, count of Cerdagne, who took over on Raymond's death in 1105, once again tightened the blockade on the city, aided this time from the sea by the Genoese fleet. The situation inside grew ever more desperate, with the price of a pound of dates reputedly reaching one gold piece, enough to feed an entire family for several weeks under normal circumstances. As a last resort, in 1108 Fakhr al-Mulk slipped out of the city and went in person to Baghdad to plead with the all-powerful Seljuk sultan and the largely nominal Abbasid caliph for help. Although he was royally received, no help was forthcoming and in the meantime his cousin, who had been left in charge of Tripoli, handed it over to the Fatimids. They merely looted Fakhr al-Mulk's family treasure, while the Crusader's grip tightened. Finally, on 26 June 1109, it fell to the Crusaders, who ransacked the city, burning down the *Dar al-Ilm* and destroying its famous library in the process. Thus the County of Tripoli was formed with Tripoli as its capital, its territory extending from Jbail (Byblos) to Qalat Marqab (in present-day Syria).

The city was quickly rebuilt and soon began to flourish once again. Glass making and silk weaving were its major industries, but it also regained its former reputation as a centre of learning, with the Nestorians and Jacobites establishing famous schools of philosophy and medicine. Numerous hospitals, monasteries and churches were established and the city became the seat of a Latin bishopric. Tripoli remained in Crusader hands for 180 years until they were finally driven out by the **Mameluke** Sultan Qalaun in 1289 after more than a month's siege. Most of the population was massacred or captured and Qalaun ordered that the city be razed to the ground. Abandoning the old site, he instead built a new city around St Gilles' castle. Under Mameluke and then Ottoman rule, this new city flourished once again as a commercial and cultural centre, with thriving souks and khans and numerous mosques and madrassas. After the creation of the *Mutasarrifiyah* of Mount Lebanon in 1860, Tripoli (along with Beirut and Sidon) remained under direct Ottoman rule, but was incorporated into the new French Mandate territory of Greater Lebanon in 1920.

As a predominantly Sunni Muslim city, Tripoli remained after independence a focus for the dissatisfaction felt by many at being included in a new country dominated by the Maronite Christian community. When the country

War and peace amongst the Crusaders and Muslims

Although a Crusader state, the County of Tripoli was largely independent and often found itself more in conflict with the other Crusader states along the coast than with the Muslims who were their supposed enemies. In 1185 Raymond of Tripoli (a descendant of Raymond St Gilles), secured a truce with Salah ud-Din (Saladin) which extended an earlier agreement between Damascus and Jerusalem guaranteeing the free movement of goods and people in the region. Visiting Damascus in 1184, the Andalusian traveller Ibn Jubair was surprised to find caravans moving freely between Damascus and Cairo, writing; "The Christians make the Muslims pay a tax, which is applied without abuses. The Christian merchants in turn pay duty on their merchandise when they pass through the territory of the Muslims. There is complete understanding between the two sides, and equity is respected. The men of war pursue their war, but the people remain at peace."

However, in 1186 Raymond's chief rival, Reynald of Chatillon, broke the truce by attacking a caravan of pilgrims en route to Mecca. This, together with previous attacks including one on Mecca itself, provoked Saladin to declare jihad, rallying Muslim forces for an attack on Jerusalem. In the meantime King Guy of Jerusalem, seen by some as a mere puppet of Reynald of Chatillon, launched an attack on Tiberias, which belonged to the wife of Raymond of Tripoli. Raymond sought the help of Saladin, who sent a detachment of troops to reinforce Tiberias, and King Guy was forced to withdraw. In return, Raymond

allowed Saladin's troops free passage through the territory of Tiberias as they carried out a reconnaissance of the coast of Lake Galilee. On their return, they were ambushed by a troops of the Knights Templars and Hospitallers, who were not bound by any truce with the Muslims. In the event Saladin's troops massacred their attackers and only the leader of the Templars survived.

Subsequently, Raymond was threatened with excommunication for his alliance with Saladin and persuaded to join the other Crusader states in their defence of Jerusalem. The Crusaders were nevertheless resoundingly defeated at the battle of Hattin (4 July 1187) and Jerusalem taken. Raymond escaped back to Tripoli while Reynald of Chatillon was captured and executed. King Guy, who was also captured, was spared his life.

Until Saladin succeeded in uniting the Muslims under his leadership, they were even more notorious for their internecine struggles and treacheries. In 1100, the Seljuk Sultan of Damascus, Duqaq, prepared an ambush at Nahr el-Kalb for Baldwin of Edessa, who was marching on Jerusalem in the hope of installing himself as king there following the death of its former ruler. Fakhr ul-Mulk ibn Ammar, fearing Duqaq's designs on Tripoli more than he feared the prospect of Baldwin, a man renowned for both his brutality and military genius, installing himself as king of Jerusalem, gave the Crusader detailed information of Duqaq's planned ambush, allowing him to avoid it and continue on to the Holy City.

briefly descended into civil war in 1958 over the issue of Nasser's pan-Arab vision, Tripoli soon became a focus of fighting, with the Sunni leader Rashid Karami fronting an insurgency which prevented government troops from entering the city for several weeks. Although Tripoli on the whole escaped the terrible devastation which was wreaked on Beirut during the 1975-90 civil war, it did suffer several months of tragically ironic bombardment in 1983. Having returned to Lebanon after being driven out following the 1982 Israeli invasion, Yasir Arafat joined his remaining loyal supporters in the city but soon found himself under siege from rival splinter factions of the PLO, aided by Lebanese Ba'athists and Syrian forces: Palestinians fighting Palestinians while the civilian Muslim inhabitants of Tripoli suffered heavy casualties. By the end of the year he finally left by ship (for the second time), this time bound for Tunis.

During and after the civil war, Tripoli experienced a population explosion – both from refugees (many of them Palestinian), and natural increase. Today the city is thriving, building its reputation as a commercial and tourist centre.

Sights

The main focus of historic interest is the numerous Mameluke and Ottoman monuments in the old part of Tripoli around the Crusader castle. The port area of El Mina is of course much older, although almost nothing of its ancient past remains today. Joining the port area of El Mina with the city centre is a burgeoning area of modern high-rise development, with fancy shops and restaurants lining the grid of parallel streets.

St Gilles Citadel

The entry fee entitles you to a copy of the excellent Tripoli Municipality map of the souks; it is worth coming here first so that you can explore the souks armed with this map

Perched on a hilltop dominating the medieval city is the huge Crusader castle known as St Gilles Citadel (or in Arabic *Qalat Sanjil*), after its founder Raymond St Gilles (see above). The external fabric of the castle is remarkably well preserved, presenting a formidable edifice, particularly when viewed from the east bank of the Abu Ali River, from where its sheer walls tower above you forbiddingly. In fact, much of what remains today represents later rebuilding work carried out by the Mamelukes and Ottomans.

The entrance to the castle is on the north side. A small arched gateway of Ottoman origin is followed by a bridge across the moat. After crossing the bridge, you must turn to the left and then right to pass through the outer Mameluke period tower and gateway (the turns were designed to prevent any would be attacker using a battering ram). The portal is decorated with alternating black and white bands of stone, while the massive wooden doors, heavily reinforced with bands of iron covering their entire surface on the outside, are still in place. A little further along is the inner tower and gateway, this time in plain stone, and even more massive iron-clad doors still in place. From here a gently sloping passage leads through a vaulted hall, past three hefty basalt sarcophagi and into the inner castle.

Once inside, you are confronted by a fascinating though confusing jumble of courtyards, staircases, passageways, vaulted chambers and buildings, reflecting the different stages of occupation and construction work, the most recent dating from the 19th century. Extensive restoration work has been carried out to the interior in recent years, and many of the buildings refurbished.

Tripoli

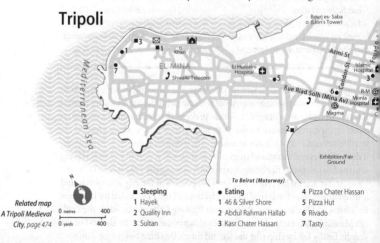

Related map
A Tripoli Medieval City, page 474

0 metres 400
0 yards 400

To Beirut (Motorway)

■ Sleeping	● Eating	
1 Hayek	1 46 & Silver Shore	4 Pizza Chater Hassan
2 Quality Inn	2 Abdul Rahman Hallab	5 Pizza Hut
3 Sultan	3 Kasr Chater Hassan	6 Rivado
		7 Tasty

Unfortunately nothing is labelled, so if you want to identify the different functions and stages of construction you really need to take a guide, though it is really more fun simply to explore at will. Most rewarding are the excellent views from the terraces and upper ramparts of the castle; northwest, out over the medieval town, with El Mina and the Mediterranean beyond; and east, across the Abou Ali River to the densely packed buildings of Qubbeh district rising steeply up the hillside.

■ *Open daily, summer 0800-1800, winter 0800-1600. Entry LL7,500 (students LL3,750). Guided tours cost LL20,000 (or LL30,000 if there are more than 7 people).*

Medieval city

NB At both the Great Mosque and Taynal Mosque, signs outside request women to don gowns before entering, and not to visit during prayer times, though this is only loosly enforced. Most of the smaller mosques are only open at prayer times, so unless you are really dedicated, you will not get to see the interiors of all of them. Women should wear clothing which covers their arms and legs, and preferably also a scarf over their heads. Even then, whether you are allowed in or not will depend on the caretaker or *imam*.

The medieval city is surprisingly compact, with a wealth of ancient monuments tucked away amongst the narrow, bustling *souks*, making it a fascinating and rewarding area to explore on foot. Indeed, most of the souks are pedestrian only, being too narrow for vehicles, and little changed from medieval times in most other respects too. Many of the old buildings are in a poor state of repair, although there is also a great deal of restoration work being carried out.

The **Great Mosque** lies at the heart of the medieval city. During the 12th century the Crusader cathedral of St Mary of the Tower stood on this site. Destroyed by an earthquake in 1170, it was restored in the early 13th century only to be largely destroyed again by the Mamelukes, who built instead the Great Mosque, or *Jami al-Kabir*, using parts of the earlier cathedral in their construction. Started by Khalil, the son of Qalaun, in 1294, it was not completed until 1315. The courtyard is surrounded by arched porticos on three sides, with the prayer hall occupying the fourth side and a large dome-topped structure in the centre containing a fountain for ablutions. The mosque's large square minaret was probably originally the cathedral's bell-tower, reminiscent of the style of Lombardy.

To Syria (Tartus)
Sports Stadium
Azmi St
Jarrous Bookshop oli Net
City complex
Car Hire
Budget Car Hire
Dar el-Chimal Bookshop
Nini Hospital
Mazloum Hospital
Rue Sheikh Bechara el-Khoury
St Gilles Citadel
Cemetery
A
To Chateau des Oliviers & Beirut (Old Coast Road)

The beautiful north entrance to the mosque also appears to be a remnant of the original cathedral. Flanking it are two 14th-century madrassas, the **Al Machhad** and **Al Shamsiyat**. Of the two madrassas on the opposite side of the street, the **Al Khairiah Hassan** and **Al Nouriyat** (also both 14th century), the former is now an undertaker's office, while the latter is still in use as a madrassa, with impressive black and white banded stonework around the doorways and windows, and inside carefully restored rough stonework and an intricately patterned and inlaid mihrab. The large **Hammam al-Nouri** on the corner adjacent to the north entrance to the mosque is contemporary with the madrassas, although it is now derelict inside.

Attached to Great Mosque on its east side, and reached via the narrow alley between the mosque and the Hammam al-Nouri, is the **Madrassa al-Qartawiya**. This was built by the Mameluke governor Qartawiya (1316-25), probably on the site of the baptistry of the cathedral. The front entrance is particularly impressive, consisting of a beautifully decorated arched doorway framed by black and white bands of stone, with patterned geometric designs above, and topped by a honeycombed and stalactited semi-dome. The rear wall is of the same black and white banded stone, with several beautiful inscriptions in Arabic. Inside there is a large marble water tank for ablutions. The mihrab and the wall either side of it are intricately decorated, but it is the view of the entrance from the outside, as well as the rear wall, which are most striking.

The passageway which takes you past the Madrassa al-Qartawiya emerges on a long straight souk running northeast-southwest. Following it southwest, you come to the mid-14th-century **Al Muallaq Mosque** on the left. Its name (literally 'the hanging mosque') is a reference to its location on an upper storey above the street. Almost opposite it is the **Hammam al-Jadide**. These baths were built

Medieval City

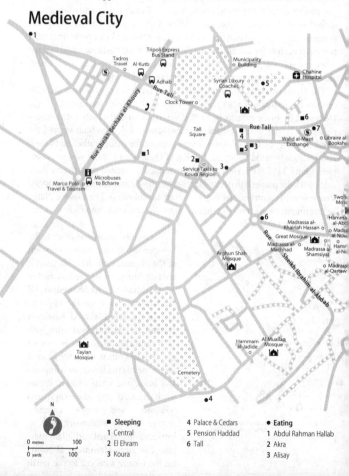

■ Sleeping
1 Central
2 El Ehram
3 Koura

4 Palace & Cedars
5 Pension Haddad
6 Tall

● Eating
1 Abdul Rahman Hallab
2 Akra
3 Alisay

around 1740 by Assad Pasha al-Azem, who was governor of Damascus from 1743-52 and was famous for building the Azem Palace and Khan Assad Pasha there (see page 94). Still in use during the 1970s, this is the largest of the public baths in Tripoli, and also the best preserved (with the exception of Hammam al-Abd which is still in use today, see below). It is kept locked, but ask around and you will be taken to a nearby shopkeeper who has the key. In the main room, a large dome pierced by numerous glass-filled apertures illuminates a large shallow pool and fountain below. The pool and surrounding floors are paved with multicoloured marble slabs arranged in geometric patterns.

Taking the street running northwest just before the Al Muallaq Mosque, you come to the **Arghun Shah Mosque**, dating from the late 14th to early 15th century and notable mostly for its distinctive circular tower-minaret, expanding higher up in a series of patterned bands to a 12-sided top.

A longish walk to the southwest from here (but well worth the detour), brings you to the beautiful **Taylan Mosque**, on the far side of the large walled cemetery. According to a lengthy inscription, this mosque was built between 1326-33 by the Saif ud-Din Taylan, the Mameluke governor of Tripoli at that time. However, like the Great Mosque, it stands on the site of an earlier church, possibly built by the Carmelites, elements of which can be found in the mosque. The large twin-domed prayer hall appears to correspond with the nave of the church and the columns of Egyptian granite topped by Corinthian capitals, were probably also taken from the church and perhaps in turn recycled from an earlier Roman monument. The bare simplicity of the stonework of this prayer hall contrasts dramatically with the huge inner portal, a wholly Mameluke construction strikingly decorated with alternating bands of black and white stone, finely executed Arabic inscriptions, panels of geometric designs and a honeycombed and stalactited semi-dome. This leads through into an inner prayer hall, again of simple undressed stone with an unadorned *mihrab*, although the wooden *minbar*, dating from 1336, is intricately carved.

Returning to the north entrance to the Great Mosque and following the narrow street east, you soon enter the **gold souk**. You pass on your left the **Madrassa al-Tuwashiyat**, c.1471, with an elaborate façade and towering portal. The small alleyway on the left immediately after leads to the **Hammam al-Abd**. Dating originally from the late 17th century, these are Tripoli's only working baths (see under 'Sports' in the Essentials section, below).

4 Cafés
5 Garden Café
6 Rush Rush
7 Tres Bien

Coast North of Beirut

Back on the gold souk, you come next to the large **Khan al-Saboun** on the left. Meaning 'soap khan', this is exactly what it was; a soap factory and warehouse. Thanks to the efforts of the Hassoun family, soap is made here once again (see box), and forms an enticing display at the entrance to the khan, with brightly coloured balls of soap, and pieces carved into all manner of shapes, from pine cones to cedar trees. Inside, the khan itself is rather dilapidated, with many of the shops and workshops which once occupied it now closed down, though there are plans to restore it to its former glory as a handicrafts market, and perhaps establish a luxury hotel on the upper floor.

A little careful navigating through the narrow souks will bring you to the **Abdul Wahed Mosque**. Dating from 1305-06, this is one of the oldest mosques in Tripoli and has been carefully restored in recent years. Built by a Moorish holy man, it features an unusual octagonal minaret, probably added at a later date. Inside, original features such as the typically Moorish vaulted arcades combine with more recent modifications. Nearby, the 15th-century **Al Uwaysiat Mosque** has also recently undergone restoration, with the plaster which once covered its walls now removed to reveal the original stonework beneath. The mosque has a beautifully proportioned central dome and circular minaret. Inside, there are two smaller prayer halls alongside the main one.

Continuing to work your way eastwards through the souks, on this side of the main street which intersects them is the **Madrassa al-Qadriyat**, dating from the second half of the 15th century and notable for its tall and graceful arched entrance of black and yellow banded stonework. Across the street, the **Hammam Izz ed-Din** is today largely derelict having suffered heavy damage during the civil war, although there are plans to restore it. Built by the Mameluke governor Izz ed-Din Aybak towards the end of the 13th century, it incorporates fragments of earlier Crusader structures.

Entering the next section of souks by the passage to the left of Hammam Izz ed-Din as you face it, off to the left is the somewhat delapidated **Khan al-Misriyin**, or Egyptian khan, while off to the right is the **Khan al-Khayattin**, or tailors' souk, a stretch of souk spanned by graceful arches at regular intervals along its length, and lined with small tailors' workshops. Built during the first half of the 14th century, this souk has been carefully restored and is architecturally the most impressive, if not the most authentic. Emerging from its eastern end, you come out on the main street running alongside the Abu Ali River. Across the street, in a small compound by the river, is the **Madrassa al-Burtasiyat**. Built in 1315 as a madrassa and later converted to a mosque, it is notable for its beautiful square tower-minaret and its typically Mameluke-style entrance portal decorated with alternating bands of black and white stone, and featuring a honeycombed and stalactited semi-dome.

Returning to the souk running northeast between the Khan al-Misriyin and Khan al-Khayattin and following it northeast, a short way along, off to the left, is the easily missed 14th-century **Mosque al- Attar**, or Perfumers' Mosque, with its Mameluke portal and striking patterned marble designs. Further on, turn right then first left at a junction with a small fountain in the centre to arrive at the **Souk al-Haraj**, possibly the site of an earlier Crusader church, its high vaulted ceiling supported by two massive granite columns in the centre, with further columns around the sides. A little further on, where you emerge from the souks, in front of you to your right is the **Al Tawbat Mosque**, dating originally from the 14th century, but restored in the 17th century. Opposite it is the large **Khan al-Aksar**, or Soldiers' Khan, originally a 13th-14th century Mameluke construction, but later restored and modified by the Ottomans in the 18th century and today occupied by a number of families.

Emir Bachir Street, also known as the 'Street of Churches' makes for an

The art of soap

The famous Greek physician Galen mentioned soap in his writings as early as the second century AD, though it was not until the 14th century that it found its way to Europe, probably via the traders of Castile and Venice. Long before this, however, it was being manufactured in the Middle East, with Tripoli being one of the oldest known centres for the craft, alongside Nablus (in the present-day Palestinian Authority-controlled West Bank).

Until recently, traditional soap making had died out in Tripoli, but the efforts of Badr Hassoun and his family have seen the craft revived. Unlike the chemical cocktails which form the basis of soap manufacture in the west, Tripolean soap is made using only natural ingredients, with olive oil forming the base. As well as the standard blocks of plain olive oil soap, the Hassoun family make colourful balls streaked with natural dyes. Building on a local tradition of infusing soap with herbal remedies, they have also developed a range of so-called 'aromatherapy' soaps. Along with the olive oil base, these are made from as much as 20-30% pure honey combined with various essential oils. The result is a sticky, black, almost tar-like concoction with deliciously rich fragrances. Whether or not the aphrodisiac version has the desired effect is open to debate, but it certainly makes for a wonderful bathing experience and will leave you smelling thoroughly delicious!

interesting alternative route back into the centre of town. There are no less than six churches on or near this street, the largest of which is the imposing, almost fortress-like Greek Orthodox **St Georges church**, with a tall pillared arcade surrounding it. Opposite is the Syrian Catholic **St Elie church**.

As recently as 1966, the Hatchette guide to the Middle East was able to describe how "in the triangular plain separating Tripoli from El Mina, lie a multitude of gardens with rich vegetation". Today the picture couldn't be more different, giving some idea of the city's explosive growth in recent decades.

El Mina

Although a far more ancient site than the medieval city, the port area of El Mina has very little in the way of historic monuments. One exception is the **Bourj es-Saba** (Lion's Tower), on the north side of the headland by the now derelict railway station, close to the modern port. A square tower of massive yet squat proportions, it has sections of recycled Roman columns laid horizontally in the walls to reinforce them. Built by the Mamelukes during the 15th century, it served as part of a series of defences along the coast against Ottoman attack. The typically Mameluke entrance with its bands of black and white stone lead into a single chamber occupying the whole of the ground floor. Steps lead up to the first floor and then onto the roof, from where there are views over the port on one side and the apartment blocks lining the route towards Tripoli proper on the other.

Also on the north side of the headland, set back from the Corniche to the west of a large mosque, the remains of a rather delapidated **khan** can be seen. A little further on, a restored vaulted and pillared building now houses a *Sleep Comfort* showroom, and beyond the *Sultan* hotel is a small area of gardens containing some re-erected **Roman columns** and other architectural fragments.

That's about it though, and for most Tripolitians, El Mina's main attraction is as a place to come for a walk along the **Corniche** on summer evenings. Like a smaller (and somewhat more conservative) version of Beirut's Corniche, it throngs with families and children out strolling and enjoying the cool sea air. The small fishing **harbour**, meanwhile, busy with brightly painted boats, adds a colourful dimension not found in Beirut.

Palm Island There are several small islands a few kilometres off the coast of El Mina. The largest, known as *Jezira al-Nakhil* in Arabic (literally 'palm' or 'sandy' island), is some 20 acres of beautiful beaches, plentiful stands of palm trees and fresh water springs. It is also known as *Jezira al-Aranab* or 'rabbit island', from the French Mandate period when rabbits were introduced to provide hunting for the French administrators. During the Mameluke period, some of Tripoli's Christian population took refuge here, and you can still see the ruins of a church. The islands provide nesting place for a variety of rare birds, and green turtles also come here to lay their eggs. In an attempt to protect the green turtles and other fauna and flora, the islands are officially closed to the public during the winter (from October-May). Indeed, the islands were actually declared a nature reserve in 1992, though a proper management and conservation plan has yet to be implemented. In the meantime, during the summer local fishermen do a brisk trade taking tourist out to the islands, charging LL2,000 for the privilege.

Essentials

Sleeping
■ *on maps,*
pages 472 & 474
Price codes:
see inside front cover

AL *Chateau des Oliviers (Villa Nadia)*, Heykalie (4 km outside Tripoli). From the centre of town, head south on Rue Sheikh Bechara el-Khoury and turn left after 2 km (shortly after a right turn signposted for the motorway to Beirut; if you pass under the motorway you have gone too far). Bear right soon after and take the left turn, continue past the Haykel hospital and the left turning for the hotel is a little further on. T411170, F440981, www.villanadia.com Much more than just a hotel, this unique place really has to be seen to be believed. Set amongst olive groves on a hillside overlooking Tripoli and the sea, and with its own pleasant gardens and swimming pool, the 'chateau' is an enormous private house converted into a hotel. Inside, the common areas have been sumptuously furnished with a veritable museum of antiques and objets d'art collected over the years by the voluptuous owner, Nadia. All the rooms are individually and elegantly furnished, with private balconies and panoramic views (as well as all the usual mod-cons. 3-course meals for guests cost around US$25 per head, bar, 'nightclub' downstairs. A welcome if idiosyncratic contrast to the usual blandness of luxury international-style establishments. **AL** *Quality Inn*, by the exhibition/fair ground between El Mina and Downtown Tripoli, T211255, F211277, qualityinn1@inco.com.lb Luxurious (if a little anodine) rooms with a/c, TV/dish, IDD, minibar, safe box and attached bath. Restaurants, bar, conference and banqueting facilities, health club (see 'Sports' below), *First* car hire. Tripoli's only full size luxury hotel, converted from an existing office block in record time for the 2000 Asian Cup.

El Mina There are 2 hotels in El Mina, both overlooking the Corniche and sea. **C** *Sultan*, T292493. Somewhat shabby rooms with a/c and attached bath. Some rooms with balconies overlooking sea. The rather dilapidated attempted grandeur of the lobby, with its ornate wood panelling and mirrors, gives way to more straightforward dilapidation in the rooms themselves. Prices come down to **D** category outside the summer season, which is not too bad value given the sea views, but otherwise overpriced for what you get. **E** *Hayek*, set back slightly from the Corniche (ask for the post office; the hotel is more or less directly opposite) T601311. Simple but friendly family-run place. Double rooms US$20, or US$10 per bed, share shower/toilet (no fan).

Downtown Tripoli There are several hotels, all close to the main square (Sahet et-Tall). **D/E** *Palace*, Rue Tall, T432257. Basic rooms with sink (no fan) and shared shower/toilet (single/double US$10/20). Also a couple of doubles with attached bath (US$30). Beautiful old building but noisy location, rather run down and in need of refurbishment. Friendly management. **D/E** *Tall*, Rue Tall, T628407. Simple but clean rooms with fan and choice of shared bath (double US$20) or attached bath (double

US$23). Quieter rooms at rear, some rooms with balcony. Friendly place. Reasonably good value. **E** *Central*, T441544. Simple but clean rooms with attached bath and large common balcony area (single/double US$10/20). The hotel is up on 6th floor – a long climb if the distinctly rickety lift isn't working. **F** *Pension Haddad*, 2nd floor, off Rue Tall, near Tall Sq, T624392. Very friendly place, run by the ever-welcoming Haddad family. Clean, comfortable dormitory rooms with fan and shared shower/toilet (US$6 per bed). Also a couple of double rooms (US$12). You really are staying in the family home here, with the common area (complete with TV/dish) being their front room. This sort of arrangement may not be to everybody's taste, but you can't fault it for its homely atmosphere and friendliness. Safe for women travellers. Quiet location. Recommended. **G** *Cedars*, Rue Tall (next door to *Palace* hotel), T503335. Very basic rooms (no fan), share grotty shower/toilet. Doubles US$10, or US$5 per bed. Noisy location and not very appealing. **G** *El Ehram*, Tall Sq, no phone. Very basic rooms with fan and choice of shared bath (double US$10) or attached bath (double US$8). In either case, the showers and toilets are really grotty. Also dorm beds for US$5. Noisy location and not very appealing. **G** *Koura*, Rue Ezz al-Din, T03-306803. Friendly family-run place. Simple but clean rooms with shared shower/toilet (double US$10, or US$5 per bed). Also 2 much more comfortable (and excellent value) **D** category rooms; 1 double and 1 triple, both with a/c and attached bath (US$25 and US$30 respectively). Safe for women travellers. Quiet location. Recommended.

Expensive *Kasr Chater Hassan* (sign in Arabic only, but difficult to miss), Monla St (between El Mina and downtown), T600286. Open daily 1100-2400. A large, very elaborately furnished place serving Lebanese cuisine for around US$20-25 per head. *Silver Shore*, Corniche, El Mina, T601384 (entry is from around the back, not from the Corniche itself). Open daily 1200-2030. An upmarket establishment specializing in fish and seafood. Meals cost in the region of US$30 per head. Elegant décor and great views; the place to come if you fancy splashing out.

Moderate *'46* (as in 1946, the date it was first established), Corniche (next door to *Silver Shore*, and under the same management), El Mina, T212223. Open 1200-2400, closed Mon. Comfortable, pleasantly decorated and airy restaurant/coffee shop overlooking the Corniche. Reasonably priced food (pasta, chicken, steaks etc) for around US$10-15 per head for a full meal, or less for snacks. Live music (one man show) on Fri and Sat nights, and Sun lunchtime. *The Canyon*, City Complex (lower ground floor), Mina Av. American-style steak house/fast food place offering steaks, chicken meals, burgers, snacks etc. Around US$10-20 for a meal, or less for snacks. *Pizza Hut*, Mina Av, T211600. Open daily 1200-2400. To actually fill yourself up you need to spend more than US$10 per head. *Rivado*, Mina Av (between El Mina and Downtown). Open daily 1100-late. Downstairs is a small bar decorated to a slightly tacky wood and hessian theme, while upstairs is the restaurant part. Rather generic international cuisine of steaks, hamburgers etc. Around US$10 per head for a meal, or less for snacks.

Cheap *Pizza Chater Hassan* (aka *Chater Hasan Café*), off Monla St (between El Mina and downtown). Open daily 0600-0200 (20 hrs). Diner-style place offering pizzas, burgers, sandwiches etc, plus a wide range of traditional Arabic pastries, mannoushi etc. Eat well for around US$5-7 per head, or less for snacks. Clean, pleasant and good value. *Tasty*, Corniche. Simple diner-style place with outdoor seating on pleasant terrace. Pizzas, meat/chicken platters, burgers, sandwiches etc. Eat well for around US$5-7, or less for snacks. Draught *Heineken* good value at LL3,500 per pint, or small bottles of *Al Maaza* LL1,250. Friendly owner, speaks English and an avid collector of British football memorabilia. Recommended.

Eating

Most of the expensive & moderate restaurants are in El Mina, or else in the streets running between 'downtown' and El Mina. Cheap and seriously cheap restaurants are generally found around downtown Tripoli

Coast North of Beirut

There are also plenty of small, traditional snack places hidden away in the souks; try around Hammam al-Jadide

Seriously cheap On Rue Tall, to the west of the clocktower, is a cluster of fast food places serving burgers, subs, shawarmas, falafel sandwiches, roasted half-chickens etc. One place has seating, allowing you to sit down to a meal (half chicken LL4,000) but the majority are takeaway, and have names with 'Quick' in them. At the east end of Rue Tall, on the corner, the small *Tres Bien* serves excellent fuul, hummus and hummus, though it closes for the evening. On a small side street to the south of Rue Tall *Alisay* (sign in Arabic only) is a simple unassuming place. It's not overly clean, but does good food (the usual range of Arabic cuisine) at reasonable prices. On the round-about at the northeastern end of Rue Sheikh Ibrahim, **Rush Rush** (sign in Arabic only) is a simple bakery (takeaway only) offering excellent mannoushi, Arabic-style pizzas and other savoury pastries; very tasty and excellent value (items from LL1,000). In a tiny alleyway near Khan al-Saboun, the *Akra* serves excellent fuul, hummus etc.

Around El Mina, there are a number of cheap snack bars along the sea front in the vicinity of the *Qasr e-Sultan* hotel, though the seriously cheap eats in this area are tucked away in the small streets inland from the sea front.

Cafés There is a great café by Tall Sq where you can sit out on the street and watch the comings and goings. The cluster of cafés by the small square and park to the southeast of the Taylan Mosque are also lovely, while up on the hillock opposite the municipality building there is a café in shaded gardens which sometimes also serves food.

Tripoli is famous for its sweets and cakes and there are a number of pâtisseries along Rue Tall. Established in 1881, the most famous is **Abdul Rahman Hallab**, towards the downtown end of Mina Av. There is seating inside, and as well as a mouthwatering selection of Arabic sweets, you can enjoy a cup of coffee here.

Bars Nightlife is pretty limited in Tripoli, with most places closing well before midnight. *Tasty* restaurant, in El Mina (see above), is a good place to come for a drink; if there is any football on the TV, it will be showing here.

Cinemas *Planete*, inside City Complex, Mina Av, T442471, www.circuiteplanete.com 4 screens showing American and European films (and the occasional Lebanese one), usually in English or French. Tickets for afternoon screenings (1445 and 1715) and all day Mon and Wed cost LL5,000. Evening screenings (1945 and 2215) LL10,000. Phone/check the website, or see the inside back page of the *Daily Star*, for details of what's showing.

Shopping

Tripoli's souks are an obvious place to look for interesting items. They are closed on Fri

If you are interested in **jewellery**, the gold souk (to the east of the Great Mosque) is good value, with prices reported to be much lower than in Damascus or Aleppo. The different types of **soap** on sale at the Khan al-Saboun are very attractive and make ideal gifts. Along the street which runs northwest past Hammam Izz ed-Din there are several shops selling a wide range of **copperware**. The first couple of shops on the left belong to genuine craftsmen and have their own workshops attached, where beautifully decorated copper plates are fashioned, along with massive *arak* distillers. Even if you are not interested in buying, they are fascinating places just to look inside. Further along, the shops are more touristy, with lots of nargilehs, inlaid wood items, samovars, trinkets etc. On the east side of the Abu Ali River, just off the main road, the tiny *Al Kahf* is a veritable treasure trove of unusual bric-a-brac and antiques.

Books Tripoli has nothing like the same range of bookshops (or books) as Beirut. *Jarrous*, Rue Nadim el-Jisr, has a limited selection of books (mostly in Arabic and French), but a vast array of magazines. *Dar el-Chimal*, Rue Rachide Karamé has a limited selection of English classics, as well as books on Lebanese history, art, architecture etc.

Sports The *Leisure Club* at the *Quality Inn* hotel offers sauna, Turkish bath, massage, a fully equipped gym and and 2 swimming pools (the latter were still under construction at the time of writing). Use of the facilities here costs US$10 per person (massage extra).

The *Hammam al-Abd*, in the souks of Tripoli (see 'Sights'), offers a traditional Turkish bath complete with massage and all the extras (soap, scrubbers, towels etc) for US$10. Open daily 0700-2200. Men only.

Fernand Rachid Chaptini, Rue Ezz al-Din (below *El Koura* hotel), T431715. Agent for *Air France*. *Marco Polo*, next to Tourist Office, T433304. Agent for international flights and reconfirmations. *Tadros*, Rue Tall, T628504, F624190. Agent for British Airways. | **Tour companies & travel agents**

Car hire *Budget* shares an office with a Fiat garage on Rue Rachide Karamé, opposite the *Dar el-Chimal* bookshop, T431654. See Beirut for details of rates etc. A little further down on the right, set back from the main road, *VIP*, T03-531588, is a very small outfit with cars from US$35 per day. *First*, *Quality Inn* hotel, T221255 or T03-898964. **Local taxis** Service taxis shuttle back and forth between Downtown Tripoli and El Mina for a flat rate of LL1,000 (catch them from anywhere along Mina Av). Private taxis are more expensive; agree a price before getting in. | **Transport**

Syrian luxury coaches There is an office off Rue Tall, near the clock-tower, which acts as an agent for all the Syrian luxury coach companies (only *Transtour* have their logo on the door, but *Kadmous*, *Zeitouni*, *Nahas*, *Amir*, *Karnak* and a couple of others are all represented). You can pay for tickets in LL, US$ or S£; due to rounding up, it works out fractionally more expensive to pay in LL for some destinations. The various companies between them offer regular departures to **Aleppo (via Homs and Hama)**, hourly from 0900, LL8,000/US$5/S£250 (Homs/Hama LL5,000/US$3/S£150). *Transtour* have 2 departures daily to **Damascus** (direct), 0500, 1500, LL6,000, US$4, S£200. *Karnak* have 1 departure daily to **Tartus/Lattakia**, 1500, Tartus LL5,000/US$3/S£150, Lattakia LL6,000/US$4/S£200.

Beirut coaches/buses There are 3 different companies offering regular coach/bus services to **Beirut** throughout the day, a journey which takes around 1 hr 15 mins, depending on the traffic. On Rue Tall, to the west of the clock-tower, is the large ticket office for *Adhab*, with departures every 15 mins or so, LL2,000. Around the corner, on Rue Sheikh Bechara el-Khoury, *Tripoli Express* also has departures roughly every 15 mins, LL2,000. On the west side of the junction of Rue Tall with Rue Sheikh Bechara el-Khoury, *Al Kutb* (or *Kotob*) has regular departures every 30 mins or so, and is slightly cheaper at LL1,500, though its coaches are older and more decrepit than the others.

Microbus There are 4 microbuses daily to **Bcharre** (LL2,500), from the large roundabout as you head south out of Tripoli on Rue Sheikh Bechara el-Khoury (they leave from outside *Marco Polo* travel agents, next door to the Tourist Information office). Exact timings vary, but you can count on 2 in the morning and 2 in the afternoon. From the corner of Rue Tall and Rue Sheikh Bechara el-Khoury (by the *Adhab* ticket office), you can catch microbuses to **Halba** (LL1,000), from where you can pick up onward transport to **Qoubaiyat**.

Service taxis Service taxis depart when full from beneath the clock-tower on Rue Tall for **Beirut** LL4,000 (there is an office for service taxis within the clock-tower itself). Syrian-operated service taxis depart when full from the vicinity of the clock-tower to various destinations in **Syria**, though they are around twice as expensive as the luxury coaches and offer no real advantages. Drivers stand around beside their vehicles touting persistently for passengers.

At the back of Tall Sq (on the southeast side, beside the *El Ehram* hotel) there is a smaller triangular square known as Sahet el-Koura. The service taxis which congregate here serve most destinations in the Koura region to the south and southwest of Tripoli (eg Kousba, Amioun etc). Of more interest to tourists are the services to

Bcharre from here (going via Kousba, Hadath el-Jobbe, Hasroun and Bazroun). The fare is LL3,000, though departures are not that frequent; make it clear that you want a service taxi, or you will be offered a much more expensive private booking. There are also services to **Sir ed-Danniye** from here, LL2,000.

Directory **Banks** There are several banks along Rue Sheikh Bechara el-Khoury, most of them with cash machines. In addition, there are literally dozens of money-changers along Rue Tall which can change just about every major currency, as well as Syrian Pounds. *Walid al-Masri Exchange*, opposite the *Tall Hotel* is one of the major money-changers and usually offers good rates, but it is worth shopping around. **NB** At the time of writing, changing TCs in Tripoli was problematic (even US$ ones); banks were refusing outright, and most money changers were extremely reluctant to do so.

Communications Internet With 3 internet cafés inside the City Complex on Mina Av, this is the obvious place to go, though there is another good place further northeast along Mina Av, and a couple of others just off it. There is a considerable amount of competition between internet cafés, so prices for internet access are likely to fall over time. Look out for any special deals (eg 6 mins free access for checking emails, or reduced rates at certain times). *Compu Games*, City Complex, Mina Av (1st floor). Open daily 1000-2400. Internet access LL4,000 per hr. 6 terminals; a bit cramped and office-like. *In-Side*, City Complex, Mina Av (ground floor), T432738. Open daily 1000-2400. Internet access LL4,000 per hr. Clean, smoke-free place with good music. Currently only 4 terminals linked to internet (rest for games), but very fast machines. Internet phone calls possible from here. Plans to expand into larger upstairs premises. *Magma*, Mina Av. Open 1000-2400, Sun 1500-2400. Internet access LL3,000 per hr. Fairly trendy place with 12 terminals. Tea/coffee and snacks available. *R-M* (name may change), tucked away in a side street off Mina Av. Open daily 1030-2300. Internet access LL2,000 per hr. Simple, rather office-like but clean place with 13 terminals. *Tripoli Net*, tucked away in a side street running parallel to Mina Av. Open daily 0930-2300. Internet access LL3,000 per hr. Simple place with 10 terminals. Tea/coffee and snacks available. *W lan*, City Complex, Mina Av (1st floor). Open daily 1000-2400. Internet access LL4,000 per hr. 17 terminals on 2 floors. Rather smoky and office-like, but OK. **Post** The central post office is just off Rue Sheikh Bechara el-Khoury. Open 0800-1700, Sat 0800-1200, closed Sun. **Telephone** The main telephone office ('Centrale') is on Rue Riad Solh near the start of the coastal motorway, easily identified by its large circular tower. Open daily/24 hrs. Rates for international calls are the same as per Beirut. There is a smaller branch in the centre of Tripoli, near Tall Sq. *Shwaiki Telecom*, on Mina Av in El Mina, is a small private shop which also offers international calls (and fax) and was quoting a flat rate of LL750 per min at the time of writing which is excellent value.

Medical services Private hospitals include the *Haykel* (near *Chateau des Oliviers* hotel), T430600, the best (and most expensive) in Tripoli. *Mazloum*, off Rue Sheikh Bechara el-Khoury (heading south, take the right turn for the main post office and then the first left), T430325, F628305. *Monla*, corner of Monla St/Rue Riad Solh, T600112. *Nini*, near exhibition/fair ground, T431400, F448442. Also has women's clinic. The main government hospital is the *Al Hakoumi* near University, to the east of the city centre, T441769. There is also a charitable hospital, the *Islamic*, Rue Azmi, T210179. Free treatment, also with private ward. All these hospitals have dispensaries, or there are a number of good pharmacies on Rue Tall and in El Mina district. **Useful phone numbers Fire**: T175. **Police**: T112. **Ambulance (Red Cross)**: T140. **Directory enquiries**: T120.

Tripoli to Tartus

Heading northeast out of Tripoli on Rue Sheikh Bechara el-Khoury, keep going straight to join the coast road heading up towards Syria. After about 5 km you pass through El Baddoui, where there is a large oil refinery on the coast. At Aabdé, 17 km from Tripoli, instead of bearing right towards Halba (see page 526), bear left to keep to the coast. It is a further 15 km to the Lebanese/Syrian border post of El Aarida, passing en route a string of rather depressing Palestinian refugee camps. Once across the border and inside Syria, it is a further 37 km on to Tartus.

Mount Lebanon جبل لبنان

13

Mount Lebanon
لبنان جبل

*The term 'Mount Lebanon' (in Arabic 'Jebel Lubnan') refers as much to an idea as a geographical entity. We have taken 'Mount Lebanon', somewhat arbitrarily, to mean the mountainous areas to the north of the Beirut-Damascus highway; that is the **Metn**, **Kesrouan**, **Mount Lebanon** proper and **Jebel Akkar** (the administrative district of Mount Lebanon which exists today differs considerably from this definition). These mountains, rising abruptly from the coast and running in a spine parallel to it, reach a height of 3,083 m in the peak of **Qornet es-Saouda**, average around 2,000 m and provide some of the most spectacular and varied scenery in Lebanon. Most striking is their proximity to the coastal plain: in just 20 minutes or so you can drive from the busy and congested sprawl of coastal towns and resorts, swelteringly hot and humid in summer, up into a deliciously **cool alpine climate**. Though the spread of new development has reached far into the mountains, there are still plenty of unspoilt areas where narrow mountain roads wind their way tortuously through picturesque villages set amidst stunningly beautiful valleys and soaring peaks.*

☞ *A foot in the door*

In many ways it is the very act of exploring Lebanon's mountains and taking in the stunning scenery which is the greatest high, rather than what is to be found at specific sights and destinations.

★ *One exception to this rule is the spectacular **Jeita Grotto**, deep inside the bowels of the mountains. Easily accessible as an excursion from Beirut or Jounieh, this vast network of caverns is brimming with some of the largest stalactites and stalagmites in the world.*

★ *If you don't have time for lengthy trips up into the mountains, but want to get a taste of the views, head up to **Beit Meri** and **Broummana**. These two summer resorts are only half an hour's drive from Beirut and have amazing views back down onto the capital and the shimmering Mediterranean. To the east of Jounieh, **Faraya Mazaar** and **Faqra** offer the best **skiing** in Lebanon, and certainly the most luxurious ski resort accommodation. Faqra is also the setting for the ruins of a Roman temple.*

★ *Rising to the east of Jbail (Byblos), the stunningly beautiful **Adonis Valley** (Nahr Ibrahim) climbs steeply up to the dramatic Afqa spring, where in legend Adonis and Aphrodite first kissed.*

★ *To the southeast of Tripoli, the **Qadisha Valley** is also dramatically beautiful. Something of a heartland of the Maronite faith, it is easy to see why the early Maronites should have chosen it as a refuge from the outside world. Today it is dotted with numerous monasteries, churches and shrines, many of them built into the sheer sides of this deep gorge.*

★ *At the head of the Qadisha valley, **Qornet es-Saouda** towers above an area known as **The Cedars** (Al Arz), where you will find the most famous of Lebanon's remaining stands of cedars. Nearby, in the **Horsh Ehden Nature Reserve**, and on the road leading into the Qadisha valley from Tannourine el-Faouqa via Arz Tannourine, are larger and more impressive though less well known stands.*

★ *The Cedars (Al Arz) is also a popular **ski** and **paragliding** resort. But if you prefer to keep your feet firmly on the ground, there are plenty of opportunities for **hiking** and **mountain biking**, both up here and down in the Qadisha valley.*

History

It is important to distinguish Mount Lebanon from the Lebanon mountain range, the latter consisting of the entire coastal range running the whole length of Lebanon. Arab geographers used the term, Mount Lebanon, rather loosely to refer to the higher northern parts of the Lebanon mountains, between Tripoli and Byblos, and this appears to be the perception of Crusader chroniclers. During the 17th century the Druze emir Fakhr ud-Din II Maan, who had his base in the Chouf mountains, was appointed by the Ottomans to administer what were then the Sanjaks of Beirut and Sidon (essentially the Chouf and Kesrouan). He briefly managed to extend his control northwards also to include Mount Lebanon, before being deposed by the Ottomans who feared that he had become too powerful. By the early 19th century the emir Bashir Shihab II had once again succeeded in uniting all the mountain districts from Mount Lebanon in the north to the Chouf mountains in the south under his control, this time more permanently and the whole of this mountainous area became known as 'Mount Lebanon'. After 1860, when the Ottomans were forced under pressure from the European powers to create the special semi-autonomous *Mutasarrifiya* of Mount Lebanon, it was defined as including all of this area and for the first time, officially at least, Mount Lebanon became a political entity.

The motivation behind the creation of this entity was to protect the Maronite Christians, who formed a majority within it but who had suffered terrible massacres at the hands of the Druze in 1860. The presence of significant numbers of Maronites in the Chouf mountains dates back to the 17th century when Emir Fakhr ud-Din II Maan began encouraging them to come and settle in these areas to help with the labour-intensive production of silk, which soon became a flourishing and highly lucrative industry. Earlier, in the 16th century, the Maronites had begun the process of southward migration, settling in the Kesrouan at the invitation of the Assaf clan (see page 494). This process continued through the 18th and early 19th centuries under the Shihab emirs, to the extent that Maronites came to be responsible for most of the silk production, although the land they worked was mostly rented from Druze landowners. When the Ottomans imposed their direct rule over the former territories of Emir Bashir Shihab II in 1840, they divided that territory into two administrative regions, and began playing off the Maronites and Druze against each other in an attempt to subdue them both. It was to a large extent this policy of divide and rule which led to the massacres of 1860. The civil war of 1975-90 saw what was in many ways a repeat of these events in the coastal mountains, with the Druze establishing their supremacy in the Chouf mountains, while the Maronites became concentrated once again in Kesrouan and traditional Mount Lebanon areas. The Metn, meanwhile, and the Beirut-Damascus highway in particular, became the front line between the Maronites and Druze.

The Metn المتن

For details of the Beirut-Damascus highway (which passes through the Metn), see page 579.

Directly east of Beirut the mountains of the Metn rise steeply from the coastal plain. A number of summer resorts have grown up in these mountains – places where Beirutis can come to escape the heat and humidity of the city. The most popular are Beit Meri and Broummana, which can both be visited as a short round trip from Beirut, returning via the town of Bikfaya on the alternative route between Beirut and Zahle. While the views may be impressive and the summer climate appealing, the popularity of this region and its proximity to Beirut have also in a sense been its undoing, with an often ugly sprawl of development spreading up the mountainsides along the roads leading out of Beirut.

Beirut to Beit Meri & Broummana

Navigating your way out of Beirut and picking up the road to Beit Meri is a little tricky. Head southeast from Downtown on Rue de Damas. Turn left at the National Museum junction, and then after around 500m turn right at the large intersection and flyover to join the broad dual carriageway of Ave Elias Hrawi (signposted for Chtaura). Towards the end of Ave Elias Hrawi, major construction work was in progress at the time of writing, with a mass of new flyovers, underpasses and feeder roads springing up. Follow signs for Sin el-Fil (this involves looping underneath Ave Elias Hrawi by the glass *Cellis* building), and then for Mkalles. Arriving at a large roundabout ('Place Sin el-Fil'), turn right. At the next roundabout ('Place Mkalles'), go straight across, this being the start of the road up to Beit Meri and Broummana (signposted 'Route de Baabdat').

The road climbs steeply into the mountains through a more or less continuous sprawl of suburbs. Two km from the Mkalles roundabout the road forks; left is signposted for Beit Meri, though in fact both branches join up again before Beit Meri. Going by either route, a little over 9 km from the Mkalles roundabout, soon after a sign announcing the start of Beit Meri, you can either follow the road sharply round to the left to continue on to Broummana, or bear off to the right to visit Deir el-Qalaa (see below; signposted 'Ruines de Beit-Mery' on a Ministry of Tourism signboard). Following the road sharply round to the left, after just over 1 km bear left at a roundabout with a column in

Mount Lebanon

the centre. A little under 2 km further on, you have the option of forking left (signposted 'Centre Ville') by the massive new *Grand Hills* resort development, or else carrying straight on. Both roads take you through Broummana before joining up again at the western end of town; the left fork is the more interesting route through town and gives the best views.

Beit Meri بيت مري and Broummana برمّانة

Phone code: 04
Colour map 4, grid A2

At an altitude of between 770-800 m above sea level, both Beit Meri and Broummana are refreshingly cool in summer and offer spectacular views out over Beirut and the Mediterranean. Beit Meri, where the historic/archaeological site of Deira el-Qalaa is located, has grown to a considerable size in recent years, with numerous private villas and apartments belonging to rich Beirutis spread across the hillside. There are a couple of hotels here, and on the road between Beit Meri and Broummana, but it is Broummana itself which is the prime summer resort. The town is spread out for several kilometres along the main road, with another road running parallel to the southeast (the fork off to the left at *Grand Hills*). There is nothing of special interest as such in Broummana, this being more a place to come and enjoy the views and lively atmosphere in summer, dine out in style and indulge in a bit of nightlife. In terms of accommodation, there are some excellent off-season deals to be had and Broummana is worth considering as an alternative base to Beirut (there are even regular bus services from near the National Museum). On the other hand, the Mad Max-style rat race of bumper-to-bumper traffic careering up and down the mountainside each day may leave your nerves a little frayed.

Deir el-Qalaa

Part of the site is currently occupied by the Syrian army; they don't seem to object to tourists wandering around, but be careful where you point your camera

Deir el-Qalaa consists of a 17th-century Maronite monastery standing on the ruins of a Roman temple, with further Roman and Byzantine ruins nearby. To reach the site, bear right at the junction soon after the start of Beit Meri (coming from Beirut; see route description, above), and then bear right again at a mini-roundabout 400 m further on. After a further 400 m or so, a track off to the left (with a large Ministry of Tourism sign beside it) leads up to the site.

Inscriptions discovered here by Julius Löytved (the vice-consul of Denmark during the late 19th century and a keen amateur archaeologist) have identified the Roman temple as being dedicated to *Baal Marcod* (the 'Lord of Dances'), and there is evidence to suggest that this was built on the site of an earlier Phoenician temple. The Maronite monastery, built of stones from the Roman temple, was heavily damaged during the civil war and still stands empty today, although parts of it have been restored. A number of hefty columns can be seen, including one built into the wall of the monastery, and also a large square platform built of massive stone blocks, possibly the base of the *cella* of the Roman temple. Nearby there are the remains of other smaller temples, including one dedicated to the goddess Juno, dating from the reign of Trajan (98-117 AD). Heading back down the track to the road, off to the right there is an extensive area of Roman and Byzantine ruins. A Syrian army unit is camped here, with their tents pitched amongst the fallen columns and capitals; (you are advised to make your presence known before wandering around). Beyond the main area of the Syrian army camp are the remains of a baths complex and an area of mosaic flooring which was part of a sixth-century Byzantine church. Following the track down the hill, the baths complex and mosaic floor are on the right, behind the first first house you come to.

On the main road a short way past the track up to the ruins, the Tigre restaurant/café has fantastic views & makes an ideal stop for a rest after your visit (see 'Eating', below)

Sleeping

Price categories are for the high season, when advance booking is recommended. During the low season, all the hotels offer substantial discounts (as much as 50% in some

Mount Lebanon

cases). Traditionally the high season lasts from the beginning of May or Jun through to the end of Nov or Dec, though in practice it is much shorter these days, really only lasting from mid-Jul through to mid-Sep. All the hotels listed below stay open all year round. **LL** *Al Boustan*, Beit Meri (occupying the highest point of the village and signposted from all directions), T870400, F972439, albustan@inco.com.lb The most luxurious hotel in the area (with prices to match – doubles from US$215 plus 16% service). Suitably lavish rooms with a/c, TV/dish, IDD, minibar, safe box and attached bath. Restaurants (see 'Eating', below), bar, swimming pool, business centre (complete with Reuters, internet access etc) and large banqueting/conference facilities. Under the same management is the *Merybel*, closed for renovations at the time of writing.

L *Beit Mery*, on the main road between Beit Meri and Broummana, T873111, F972512, www.beitmeryhotel.com A/c, TV/dish, phone, minibar, attached bath and balcony. The open fireplace in each room is a nice feature, but otherwise the décor is a bit odd. Restaurant, bar/nightclub and conference/banqueting facilities.

Broummana centre L *Printania Palace*, Broummana centre, T/F862000, www.printania.com Tastefully furnished and suitably luxurious rooms with a/c, TV/dish, IDD, minibar, attached bath and balcony. Restaurant, bar, swimming pool, pleasant gardens. Conference/banqueting facilities. **A** *Garden*, Broummana centre, T960579, F960259, www.gardenhotellb.com Friendly family-run hotel. Reasonably comfortable rooms with a/c, TV/dish, phone, attached bath and balcony. Restaurant, swimming pool. Very good value **C** category rates in low season (1/10-31/5). **A** *Pax*, Broummana centre, T960027, F862303. Recently fully refurbished throughout. Comfortable rooms with a/c, TV/dish, phone, fridge, attached bath and balcony. Restaurant and bar. Large sun terrace. High season rates a little on the steep side, but also good value **C** category rates in low season (1/10-31/6). **B** *Le Crillon*, Broummana centre, T/F960221, www.lecrillon.com Friendly family-run hotel. Comfortable rooms with a/c, TV/dish, phone, minibar, attached bath and balcony. Restaurant, bar, swimming pool, gym/health club. Conference/banqueting facilities. Good value for level of facilities. High season rates in Aug only; excellent value **C** category rates for rest of year.

Expensive The *Al Boustan* hotel in Beit Meri has 2 restaurants: *Il Giardino*, which offers excellent Italian cuisine from around US$30 per head; and *Les Glycines*, with even more refined French cuisine from around US$40-50 per head (buffet lunch, Sun 1200-1500, US$40 per head all inclusive). *Burj al-Hamam*, around 1 km out of Broummana heading towards Baabdat and Bikfaya (signposted off to the right of the road), T960058. Open daily 1200-late. Huge, very upmarket Lebanese cuisine restaurant, seating 500 indoors plus a further 1,000 in summer on a shaded terrace with expansive views. From around US$35 per head à la carte, or fixed menu meal of mezze, meat grill etc for US$25 per head. Provides something of a spectacle in summer, when the seriously rich come in their droves. Dress smart and arrive in a flash car or you may not be made to feel overly welcome. Inside the same complex is *Boccalino* (closed Mon), a fancy Italian restaurant costing around US$30 per head. *Le Gargotier*, Broummana centre, T960562. Open 1200-1500, 1900-2400, closed Mon. Pleasant, cosy, traditional French restaurant. Long established (1971) and with an excellent reputation. From around US$20 per head. *La Gargotte*, Broummana centre, T960096. Open daily 1200-1500, 1900-2400. Under the same ownership as *Le Gargotier*, with the same menu and prices etc. Even longer established (1966), though perhaps not as stylish and intimate as its counterpart. *Janna*, Beit Meri, T03-367777. Open daily 1200-late. Pleasant, popular restaurant with large gardens and terrace area. Steaks, burgers, grills, mezze dishes etc. From around US$25 per head. *Jdoudna*, Beit Meri (on main road to Broummana, just above junction for Deir el-Qalaa), T873888. Open daily 1200-late. Pleasant, traditional Lebanese restaurant. Large

Eating

There are numerous restaurants & cafés, most of them in Broummana, but also several between Broummana and Beit Meri, & a few in Beit Meri itself

Mount Lebanon

dining hall complete with a huge woodburner in one section, plus an outdoor terrace. Live music (one-man show) on Tue, Fri and Sat nights. Set menu meals from US$21 per head, or more for à la carte. *Mounir*, off main road between Beit Meri and Broummana (coming from Broummana, just after you pass the *Bellevue Palace* hotel, a signposted fork off to the right leads down steeply to the restaurant), T873900. Open daily 1200-late. Large, very classy, upmarket Lebanese restaurant with extensive gardens and terrace, as well as a children's play area. Long established, with an excellent reputation. From around US$30 per head. *Pasta Commedia*, on main road between Beit Meri and Broummana (opposite *Bellevue Palace* hotel), T864777. Open 1200-late, closed Mon. Large, upmarket Italian restaurant and bar. From around US$30 per head.

Moderate *Crepaway*, Broummana centre. Large, trendy American-themed (or mostly; the Moto Guzzi on the wall is presumably a cheaper alternative to a Harley Davidson) fast food/diner style place. As well as crêpes, they offer burgers, pizzas etc. *The Hunters Meet*, Beit Meri. See 'Bars and nightclubs', below. *Manhattan*, Broummana centre, T961967. Fairly upmarket diner-style restaurant. European/ American cuisine (steaks, escalope, pizzas, burgers etc), as well as mezze. From US$15 per head. *Rincon Espaniol Chayenne*, Broummana centre, T961378. Open 1200-late, closed Mon. Pleasant, if a little dimly lit, Spanish restaurant. Around US$15-20 per head. *Tigre*, Beit Meri (just past the track leading up to the ruins of Deir el-Qalaa). Simple, unpretentious place with a pleasantly shady and breezy outdoor terrace and stunning views out over Beirut, and north along the Mediterranean coast. Traditional Lebanese cuisine for around US$10-15 per head during summer, or a great place to come just for a coffee after visiting Deir el-Qalaa. *Via Venetto*, Broummana centre, T961342. Large French and Italian cuisine restaurant. Live music every night during the summer months (Fri/Sat nights only for rest of year). Around US$15-20 per head.

Cheap/seriously cheap *Greedies*, Broummana centre. Small fast food place offering a full range of sandwiches, including shawarma and falafel, as well as pizzas, burgers etc. Fill up on snacks for less than US$5. *Tonino's Crepes*, Broummana centre. Simple, pleasant place with seating under roadside awning and kitchen in converted cargo container. Reasonable crepes, mannoushi etc. The cheapest place in Broummana from which to enjoy the 5-star views. *Wakim's Golden Bakery*, Broummana centre, T961450. Small, clean, friendly place specializing in mannoushi, but also doing pizzas and planning to expand into sandwiches etc. Their mannoushi are very good value, starting from just LL1,500. Free delivery.

Broummana

■ **Sleeping**
1 Garden
2 Le Crillon
3 Pax
4 Printania Palace

● **Eating**
1 Cheers Club & Pinnochio Bar
2 Crepaway & 401 Bar
3 Greedies

4 Kanaan/High School Ba
5 La Cantina Bar
6 La Gargotte
7 Le Gargotier
8 Manhattan
9 Pizza Hut
10 Rincon Espaniol Chaye
11 Tonini's Crepes
12 Via Venetta
13 Wakim's Golden Bakery

0 metres (approx) 200
0 yards (approx) 200

401, Broummana centre. Small, trendy pub/bar above *Crepaway*. Open during the summer months only. *La Cantina*, Broummana centre. Mexican-style bar. Also serves food. *Cheers Club*, Broummana centre, T03-819243. Friendly, popular, no-nonsense bar. Live music (covers C&W, Blues, Jazz, Golden Oldies etc) by the guitar-happy owner/manager. Attracts a young crowd, and gets really packed out on Fri and Sat nights. Upstairs is the outdoor *Pinnochio bar*, also very friendly and a pleasant, easy-going place to come on summer evenings. *The Hunters Meet*, Beit Meri (on the main road to Broummana, just above the junction for Deir el-Qalaa, opposite the *Jdoudna* restaurant). T871601. Open 1100-late, closed Mon. Traditional British-style pub. Live band on Fri nights. Draught *Murphy's* and *Guinness* LL7,000 per pint. Wide range of bar snacks (LL3,000-8,000), plus fish and chips (LL15,000) and Sun lunch (roast etc, LL15,000). Friendly atmosphere, popular with expats and a good place to meet people. *Kanaan/High School*, Broummana centre. Taking its names from its owner and the nearby Broummana High School, this place hovers undecidedly somewhere between a bar and a café. Very smart and trendy. Gets busy on Fri and Sat nights.

Bars & nightclubs
Most of the restaurants listed above have their own bars, while some also have live music & get pretty hectic later on

Bus The easiest way of getting here is by LCC bus No 7 or OCFTC bus No 17, both of which leave from near the National Museum in Beirut (just to the southeast of it). These pass the junction for Deir el-Qalaa and through the centre of Broummana. They then continue on through Baabdat before turning round and doubling back a couple of km short of Bikfaya. The fare is LL750 (flat rate). **Service taxis** are pretty thin on the ground; you might find one going from Cola bus stand in Beirut, though you are more likely to find one going from the Mkalles roundabout.

Transport

Banks There is a branch of *Credit Libanais* in the centre of Broummana with a cash machine which accepts Visa, Mastercard, Cirrus and +Plus. There are also a couple of money-changers with offices nearby. **Communications** Internet: *Challenge Net*, in the centre of Broummana, offers internet access for LL4,000/hr. The **post and telephone** offices are in the same building. Post office open 0800-1700, Sat 0800-1200, closed Sun. Telephone office open daily 0700-2400. Rates as per Beirut. There is a small private telephone office, next door to the *Aswad* minimarket in Broummana, offering international calls at LL1,500/min.

Directory

With your own transport you can continue northeast from Broummana along a picturesque road leading to Bikfaya. After passing through the village of Baabdat, there is a viewpoint offering excellent views of Jebel Knisseh to the right (east). Soon after, go straight across a roundabout (right for Douar) and then through a couple more villages to arrive at a roundabout at the eastern end of Bikfaya, 11 km from Broummana. Turn sharp left here to head back down to Beirut, joining the coastal motorway at Antelias (see below).

Broummana to Bikfaya

Beirut to Zahle via Bikfaya

As well as offering a much quieter and more scenic alternative route to Zahle compared with the main Beirut-Damascus highway, this road gives you excellent views of Jebel Sannine. **NB** Beyond Mrouj, the road is blocked by snow during the winter; if you wish to attempt it in early spring or late autumn, check first that it is open. At the time of writing, the road was being widened and upgraded; it may remain open all year round once this work is complete. A lengthy diversion off this route brings you to the small ski resort of Qanat Bakich, from where you can also continue on to Faqra. En route to Qanat Bakich you pass through the village of Baskinta, from where a narrow mountain road loops around the lower slopes of Jebel Sannine to rejoin the Bikfaya-Zahle road between Majdel Tarchich and Zahle.

Mount Lebanon

Beirut to Bikfaya   From Beirut, join the coastal motorway heading north and take the Antelias exit (see page 447). The road climbs steadily through a more or less continuous built-up sprawl to arrive at Bikfaya (14 km from the motorway exit), the start of which is marked by a roundabout with a large modernistic monument in the centre. Bearing sharp right here (signposted to Baabdat and Broummana, amongst others) puts you on the road to Broummana and Beit Meri (see above). Continuing straight on into the centre of town, bear right after 600m to pick up the road for Dhour ech-Choueir (signposted) and Zahle (going straight leads you into a confusing though very scenic maze of tiny mountain roads).

Bikfaya
Colour map 4, grid A3   Bikfaya has a certain air of prosperity about it. This is the home town of the Gemayel family; Pierre Gemayel, founder of the Phalange party in 1936; Bashir Gemayel, the leader of the Phalange militia and Lebanese president-elect for less than a month before his murder in 1982; and Amin Gemayel, Lebanese president from 1982-88. Their presence is strongly stamped on the town, most notably in the family's 'Presidence', a beautiful Ottoman period mansion signposted off to the left (north) of the main road (though strictly off-limits unless you have some pretty good connections). Bikfaya suffered heavily during 1987 when fighting broke out between the Phalange and various other Christian militias for control of the area. However, the wealth and influence of the Gemayel family ensured that it was rapidly rebuilt. During August of each year a **flower festival** is held in the town. There are several restaurants and a number of hotels, but otherwise the town has little to offer of special interest.

Transport   During summer, service taxis run from Dora in Beirut to Bikfaya (LL2,000) and there are buses from here as well. Services are much less frequent in winter.

Bikfaya to Zahle   Heading out of Bikfaya on the road towards Dhour ech-Choueir, you pass first through the village of **Douar**, where the damage caused by the internecine fighting between Christian militias in 1987 can still be seen.

Continue straight through the village, passing a right turn leading towards Broummana and Beit Meri, to arrive in **Dhour ech-Choueir**, 5 km from Bikfaya. Travelling in this direction, the main road bypasses the centre of the village; turn left to reach the centre, where there is the imposing Maronite St Mary's church, and also a brand new hotel; the **B** *Dhour Choueir*, T04-391270, F391269. Comfortable rooms with fan, TV/dish, IDD, minibar, attached bath and balcony. Restaurant, bar, café. Good value.

Continuing along the main road, you pass through a beautiful area of pine forest known as **Bois de Boulogne** (marked on most maps as **Bolonia**), arriving after 7 km at a crossroads and checkpost. On the right immediately before the checkpost and crossroads there is a large, old hotel, the **B** *Grand Hotel Bois de Boulogne*, T04-295100, F295143. Pleasant rooms (some a/c) with TV/dish, phone, attached bath and balcony. Restaurant and bar. Friendly and family run. Turning left at the crossroads leads via Baskinta to the small ski resort of Qanat Bakich, around 20 km to the northeast (see below).

Continuing straight at the crossroads and checkpost, 1 km further on you arrive at a roundabout and church in the centre of **Mrouj**. Turn right here for Zahle (or straight on – keeping the church to your left – to reach the private, members only skiing club of **Zaarour**, 7 km away). Taking the Zahle road, after 5 km you pass through **Ain Toura**, a small, rather ugly village consisting mostly of new concrete buildings. The road then begins to climb steeply into the beautiful and rugged limestone mountains of Jebel ech-Chaoukat/Jebel Knisseh. At **Majdel Tarchich** (9 km from Mrouj) there are a couple of snack places. The road continues to climb through an ever more outlandish scenery of weathered limestone rock before reaching the crest of the mountains, from where there are stunning views down into the Bekaa valley, with the Anti-Lebanon mountains beyond. From here the road descends steadily down to Zahle, 31 km from Mrouj (see page 583).

Qanat Bakich via Baskinta

If you turn left at the crossroads and checkpost by the *Grand Hotel Bois de Boulogne* (coming from Bikfaya), the road descends to the village of **Bteghrine** (follow signs for Baskinta and Qanat Bakich). You may have to ask directions through the village as the route through it is rather confusing. From here the road winds its way steeply down into the deep Wadi el-Jamajin and up the other side to arrive in **Baskinta** (15 km from the crossroads/checkpost), a picturesque mountain village with many of its traditional red-roofed houses still surviving. Turn sharp left in the village (signposted in Arabic only, so ask directions), and then bear right at a checkpost/fork 1 km further on (signposted to Qanat Bakich, and also to Faqra and Faraya). The road, narrow and poorly surfaced in places, climbs steadily for a further 7 km to arrive in Qanat Bakich.

Colour map 4, grid A3

This ski resort, on the slopes of Jebel Sannine, is the smallest in Lebanon. It was established in 1967 by the Karam family which owns the land and built the first ski lift here. The one existing ski lift is operational during the winter season, and there are plans to build a new complex of hotels, restaurants and shops, as well as further ski-lifts.

Popular in the early 1970s for its good snow & interesting slopes, the resort suffered considerable damage during the civil war & is only now being redeveloped

Sleeping There is currently just 1 hotel here, the **C** *Snow Land*, T03-345300 (or in Beirut T01-870077, F01-870518). Simple but comfortable rooms with heater, TV, phone and attached bath (some with balcony). Restaurant. There is ski equipment available for hire here (and down in Baskinta), and there are instructors and rescue/first aid teams based at the hotel on weekends. The hotel also has its own 'baby' lift and teaching slope. Contact the owner of the hotel, Joseph Karam, in advance in Beirut if you are interested in skiing here.

Continuing past the *Snowland* hotel and bearing left after 500m (right for the ski lift), it is a further 4 km on to the private **Faqra Ski Club** (see page 499). On a clear day, you can see spectacular views down the Wadi Daraiya and Nahr el-Kalb valley to the Mediterranean. Arriving in Faqra Ski Club, there is a barrier across the road here, though the attendent seems happy to let people through. You can then continue on to Faraya/Faraya Mazaar and/or head back down to the coast via Aajaltoun.

If you continue straight on through the village of Baskinta instead of turning sharp left to head up to Qanat Bakich, you can rejoin the Bikfaya-Zahle road roughly half way between Majdel Tarchich and Zahle. This narrow and extremely beautiful mountain road works its way around the head of the green and wooded Jamajin valley, with the bare, imposing southwest slopes of Jebel Sannine rising majestically above. After around 8 km you pass through the village of **Sannine**, where there are several restaurants all with stunning views down the valley. From here, the road climbs up over the lower slopes of Jebel Sannine, passing a couple of small, high altitude lakes before descending and arriving at the Bikfaya-Zahle road (19 km from Baskinta). Turning left, it is around 11 km down to Zahle, or turning right, around 20 km to Mrouj.

The mountain road from Baskinta

Mount Lebanon

Kesrouan كِسرَان

The Kesrouan mountain region rises to the east of Jounieh, dominated by the northwest flanks of Jebel Sannine (2,628 m). The ski resorts of Faraya and Faqra, on these northwestern slopes of Jebel Sannine, are the largest and best developed in Lebanon. The road leading up to them is a fast, busy one and, for the first stretch at least, not the most scenic of routes through the mountains. Higher up, however, the clutter of new development gives way to striking mountain scenery dominated by the dramatic eroded limestone formations typical of the area. While the excellent winter skiing facilities are the main attraction, there are also some interesting ruins at Faqra. This is also the way to get to the spectacular Jeita Grotto, and higher up you can divert off the main road to approach Afqa spring and the Adonis valley (Nahr Ibrahim) from the southwest. Above Faraya, the road crosses the ridges of Jebel Sannine to the north of the main summit and descends into the Bekaa valley, although this road is blocked by snow during winter.

History Although today predominantly Maronite, Kesrouan was originally inhabited by Shi'ite Muslims. In the late 13th and early 14th century the Sunni Muslim Mamelukes subdued the area, settling it with Turkoman families whom they charged with maintaining control on their behalf. In the late 14th century these Turkoman clans fell out of favour with the Mamelukes and were forced into obscurity. However, under Ottoman rule they regained their influence, headed by the Assaf clan. Although themselves Sunni Muslim, the Assafs forged close links with the Maronites, encouraging the latter to come and settle in the Kesrouan region and act as their political agents. One such family in particular, the Khazins, rose to prominence and by the end of the 18th century had gained possession of almost the entire Kesrouan region, driving out nearly all the original Shi'ite inhabitants in the process. During the 20th century, the Kesrouan region provided the main heartland of support for the Phalange militia of the Gemayel family. The Gemayels, like the Khazins, had themselves migrated from the north at the invitation of the Assafs during the 16th century, settling in Bikfaya, slightly further south in the Metn district.

Beirut to Faraya and Faqra

Head north from Beirut on the coastal motorway and 1 km after passing through the tunnel at Nahr el-Kalb, take the exit signposted clearly for Ajaaltoun, and less clearly for Jeita Grotto. If you are coming from Jounieh (ie heading south along the motorway) there is an exit and bridge across the motorway. The road climbs steeply from the motorway. After a little over 3 km there is a right turn signposted for Jeita Grotto. This side-road winds its way down into the picturesque Nahr el-Kalb valley to arrive at the entrance to Jeita, 2½ km away.

Jeita Grotto The enormous Jeita Grotto contains one of the largest collections of stalactites
Colour map 4, grid A2 and stalagmites in the world. The formations are a breathtakingly beautiful example of the forces of nature and time at work. The grotto in fact consists of an
For details of any upper and lower network of caverns which together extend for more than 6 km
concerts or special into the mountainside. It was first discovered in 1836 by an American, the Rev-
events, T09-220840, erend Thompson, who was living in Beirut. Sheltering in a cave while out on a
F220844, or check the hunting trip, he heard the sound of running water coming from inside. Firing his
website: gun into the cave he realized its size and reported his find to the authorities in
www.jeitagrotto.com

Beirut. It was not until 1873 that a team from the Beirut Water Supply Company explored further and established that this was one of the major sources of the Nahr el-Kalb. With its substantial output, the spring was subsequently used as a source for Beirut's water supply. Further explorations carried out in the early part of this century culminated in the discovery of the upper network of caverns in 1958. In 1969 Jeita was opened to the public as a tourist attraction and the German composer Karlheinz Stockhausen held a series of concerts in the upper caverns, which were shown to have excellent acoustics.

A somewhat unnecessary cable car (altogether very tame compared with Jounieh's telepherique) takes you the short distance from the main ticket office to the entrance to the upper grotto. By the entrance there is a "Sound and Images Theatre", the 20 minute film here giving good explanations of how the caverns and rock formations evolved (English language versions at 0930, 1330 and 1730; French at 1130 and 1530). A long tunnel complete with sound effects leads into the upper grotto. A concrete pathway then runs for around 800 m through an awesome network of huge caverns, atmospherically lit and brimming with the most spectacular stalactites and stalagmites imaginable, including one stalactite which at 7 m is said to be the longest in the world. In places the stalactites hanging down from the roof have joined with the stalagmites rising from the floor to form solid columns, while elsewhere the steady seepage of calcium carbonate-rich water through the limestone rock over millions of years has created all manner of other weird and wonderful formations. The temperature here remains a steady 22°C throughout the year.

During the civil war, Jeita was used as a weapons & ammunition store by Christian militias, & it was only in 1995 that it was once again opened to the public

If the cable car taking you to the entrance to the upper grotto seemed a little pointless, the miniature 'train' which takes you to the entrance to the lower grotto is downright silly. Once inside, a motorized boat, expertly manoeuvred by its skipper, takes you through the water-filled caverns (here the temperature is 16°C all year round). In comparison with the upper grotto, the lower one is perhaps not as spectacular, though still extremely impressive in its own right.

■ *Summer (1/7-15/9) 0900-1900, closed Mon (open daily Jul/Aug). Spring/autumn (16/9-31/10 and 1/4-30/6) 0900-1800, closed Mon. Winter (1/11-30/3) 0900-1700, closed Mon.* **NB** *Jeita closes completely for 4 weeks from 7 Jan each year, while around the end of Mar, when the water level rises, the lower grotto closes for about 2 weeks. Entry LL16,500. Children (4-12 years) LL9,250. No student discounts except for organized groups by prior arrangement. When the lower grotto is closed, entry LL10,500 (children LL6,250). Parking LL2,000. Allow 1½ hrs for a full visit. There is a restaurant and cafeteria, gift shop and toilet facilities at the entrance. Photography strictly prohibited; cameras must be deposited outside. There is no public transport to Jeita. The easiest option is to hire a taxi to take you privately (from Jounieh this shouldn't cost more than US$10-15 for the return trip). Alternatively, get a service taxi or bus to drop you by the turning off the motorway and walk, hitch or negotiate a taxi from there.*

Jeita to Faraya

Continuing along the main road from the Jeita turning, after 9 km there is a right turn signposted for 'centre ville' just after you pass under a bridge; this takes you into the centre of the sprawling summer resort of **Aajaltoun**. There are a couple of hotels here, though other than the views out over the bay of Jounieh and the cooler climate in summer, there is little reason to stay. On the right, around 400 m past the turning for the town centre, is the *Club Thermique Parapente* shop (see 'Sports and special interest travel' in the Essentials chapter, page 62). A litte under 3 km from the turning for the centre of Aajaltoun, you come to a large roundabout. Bear right here to continue straight on (signposted 'Centres de Ski' on a Ministry of Tourism sign). A little under 4 km after the roundabout, there is a large fork off to the right (signposted to Kafr Debian

Mount Lebanon

and Faqra); this is the start of the alternative route via Kfar Debian to Faraya Mazaar and Faqra (see below). Continuing straight on, after just under 3 km (immediately after *La Rocha* restaurant), there is a small left turn with a sign by it for 'La Reserve'. This turning joins the road leading up to Afqa Spring (see page 503); taking it, turn right at the top of the road (which forks just short of what is in effect a T-junction), bear left soon after (signposted to 'Qehmez') and keep going straight for 19 km.

Carrying along the main road to Faraya, you pass through the village of Mairouba and, 4½ km after the Afqa turning, a right turn leading to the *Guest Palace* hotel. From this turning, it is a little under 8 km to the roundabout in the centre of Faraya, passing the *St Georgio* and *Coin Vert* hotels along the way.

Via Kfar Debian to Faraya Mazaar & Faqra

Taking the large fork off to the right as you come from Aajaltoun (signposted to Kafr Debian and Faqra), this road winds its way through dramatic mountain scenery before passing through the sprawling village of Kfar Debian. Just under 9 km from the fork (still in Kfar Debian), take the left turn signposted for 'Faqra Club' and then bear left wherever the road forks ambiguously. Just over 3 km further on you pass a major left turn; this is a brand new road, still under construction at the time of writing, which will lead directly to Faraya and form the main route up to Faraya Mazaar and Faqra when it is completed.

Continuing straight on, after 1 km you pass though a checkpost, and then 500 m further on you arrive at a crossroads and sign for 'Archeologic sites of Faqra' (see below, under 'Faqra'). Continuing straight on again, after 1½ km you pass the right turn up to Faqra Ski Club itself, followed 500 m further on by a natural rock bridge off to the left of the road. Another 1½ km brings you to the junction/checkpost on the road between Faraya and Faraya Mazaar; left leads around to Faraya, while right leads up to Faraya Mazaar.

Faraya فاريّا and Faraya Mazaar (Ouyoun es-Simaan) مزار فاريّا

*Phone code: 09
Colour map 4, grid A3
NB During winter
telephone lines are
invariably broken by
storms, so all the hotels
make use of mobile
phone numbers (code
03) as well as landlines*

During the winter the whole area around Faraya and Faraya Mazaar comes to life, with many people renting chalets and apartments for the whole skiing season, while many more make the trip up from Beirut and Jounieh on weekends and holidays. Without the snow, however, there is not really very much to do around here, other than visit the dramatic ruins at Faqra. There are several hotels in and around Faraya, with a couple more located closer to the slopes. In Faraya Mazaar itself there is a new luxury hotel complex run by the *Inter-Continental* chain, as well as a couple of mid-range hotels.

Ins & outs

For information on cost of ski passes, snow conditions etc, contact Faraya Mazaar Co, T341034, T03-771211, or check the website: www.skileb.com

The village of Faraya lies around 6 km below the actual ski resort, which is known as Faraya Mazaar or Ouyoun es-Simaan. Turning left at the roundabout in the centre of Faraya, the road climbs steadily, passing the *Chateau d'Eau* hotel, before arriving at a checkpost and junction after a little under 5 km (just past the junction is the *Dallas* hotel). Turning right at this junction takes you past the rock bridge, the turning for Faqra Ski Club, and the temple ruins of Faqra (see 'Faqra', below), while continuing straight on, you arrive soon after in Faraya Mazaar.

The ski resort

The resort gets extremely crowded on weekends, but is much quieter during the week, so plan accordingly (ski passes are also much cheaper on weekdays)

There are now a total of 12 lifts (2 baby-lifts, 5 ski-lifts and 5 chair-lifts) providing access to slopes suitable for all levels of abilities, including the recently opened 'Piste Rouge' chair-lift for advanced skiers. The 'Mzaar' chair-lift reaches the highest point of the resort (2,463 m) from where there are stunning views out over the Bekaa valley to the east, Mount Hermon to the south, Laqlouq and the Cedars to the north and the Mediterranean to the west. The resort has two snow machines which can be used on even the steepest slopes. Snowploughs are on hand to keep the main road up to the resort open throughout the season. Various skiing competitions are held from February to March and there is occasionally floodlit night skiing on the 'Refuge' slopes. Medical services throughout the season include an ambulance and qualified mountain rescue team, with an additional doctor and Red Cross team on weekends and holidays. When buying ski passes, check whether insurance is included or needs to be arranged separately. Skiing lessons can be arranged and ski equipment is available for hire at the foot of the slopes. There are also a number of ski hire shops in Faraya and on the main road between Aajaltoun and Faraya.

Most of the accommodation is in the form of chalets and apartments which are **Sleeping** rented out for the whole of the skiing season and often booked up as much as 1 year in advance. The hotel accommodation which exists fills up quickly during the season, particularly on weekends, so make sure you book in advance. Price categories below are for the high season. Substantial discounts (often as much as 50%) are available in the low season (with the exception of the *Inter-Continental*, this is basically when there is no snow; ie from around late Apr/early May until Nov/Dec).

LL *Mazaar Inter-Continental*, Faraya Mazaar (in centre of village), T340100 or T03-777991, F03-777933, mzaar@interconti.com A brand-new super-luxurious complex which even boasts its own ski slope ('Refuge'), with access to this ski lift being directly from the hotel. Suitably luxurious rooms arranged around a central atrium, with a/c, heater, TV/dish, IDD, minibar, safe box, attached bath and balcony. Note that slightly cheaper standard rooms have an additional kitchenette; otherwise they are identical to deluxe rooms except that they are a little further from the core of the hotel. Restaurants (see 'Eating'), bar, nightclub, conference and banqueting facilities. Swimming pool (complete with a retracting glass roof for the summer months), health club/spa, gym, bowling alley, squash, basketball, volleyball, games room, mountain bike hire, children's playground and computer games arcade, mini-cinema and shops. Discounts during low season (1/4-15/6 and 16/9-15/12) bring rooms down to **AL** category. It is also worth asking about any special packages on offer. **AL** *San Giorgio*, on main Aajaltoun-Faraya road just over 2 km before the centre of Faraya, T/F720720 or T03-720750, s.giorgio@cyberia.net.lb Comfortable rooms with heater, TV/dish, phone, attached bath and balcony. Restaurant, bar, swimming pool. Pleasant, well run hotel, though rather expensive. **A** *Merab*, Faraya Mazaar (in centre of village), T/F341000 or T03-345679. Small but comfortable rooms with heater, TV/dish, phone, minibar, attached bath and balcony. Brand new hotel, though rather on the expensive side (25% discount in low season).

B *Auberge Suisse*, Faraya Mazaar (above main village) T953841 or T03-210101. Comfortable rooms with heater and attached bath. Dorm beds (minimum 10 people) for US$32 per person full board. Restaurant and bar. Simple but cosy and friendly family-run place. 50% discount in low season brings rooms down to **C** category. **B** *Chateau D'eau*, 3 km above Faraya, en route to Faraya Mazaar, T341424, or T03-605790. Reasonable rooms (great views) with heater, phone and attached bath. Some rooms with balcony. Cosy restaurant and bar with a huge open fireplace. **B** *Dallas*, by junction/checkpost en route between Faraya and Faraya Mazaar, T341048, or T03-341048. OK(ish) rooms with heater, TV/dish and attached bath, or considerably more comfortable suites with open fireplace. Restaurant and bar. **B** *Guest Palace*, off main Aajaltoun-Faraya road, just under 8 km before Faraya, T720420, or T03-639000. Comfortable suites with bedroom, sitting room/kitchenette (heater, TV/dish and phone), bathroom and balcony. Restaurant and nightclub. Recently fully refurbished throughout. Good value.

C *Coin Vert*, Faraya (on main road, just before roundabout in centre), T/F720812, or T03-724611. Comfortable rooms with heater, phone and attached bath. Restaurant and bar. Friendly and family-run. Ski equipment available for hire. **C** *Tamerland*, Faraya (just up from roundabout in centre, off to left of road), T/F321268 or T03-818981. Big old building. Reasonably comfortable rooms with heater, phone, attached bath and balcony. Also apartments (2 double rooms) with kitchen, fireplace and attached bath. Restaurant, bar. Pleasant location surrounded by trees and set back from road. **D** *Grand Hotel Faraya*, Faraya (by roundabout in centre of village), T321534. Simple, clean rooms with heater and attached bath. Restaurant. Friendly, and the nearest you will find to a budget hotel (double rooms US$25).

Eating All of the hotels listed above have restaurants; most of them offer inclusive full or half-board deals, so there is not that much in the way of independent restaurants. If you want to dine out in style, the *Mazaar Inter-Continental* hotel has 3 excellent restaurants; *Les Airelles* (international); *Al Kantara* (Lebanese); and *Le Refuge* ('mountain').

Down in Faraya, on the main road, the *Pancho Vino*, T321309 or T03-517070, is a fairly upmarket place serving steaks, pizzas and various Mexican dishes from around US$25 per head. Nearby, the *Jisr al-Qamar*, T03-877993, and the *Al Aarab*, T720496, both serve good Lebanese food for around US$15-20 per head. Upstairs from the latter is the *Café Paradiso*, a café/bar which also serves snacks. Others here include the *Country House* and *Soleil d'Or*. The *Snow Man* and *Quick Food*, both on the main road, are both good snack places. By the roundabout in Faraya there are a couple of much simpler snack places offering good value saj (a thin, flat, round bread) with fillings of zaarta (thyme and sumak) and/or cheese and ham.

Transport Most people coming up here have their own transport, but during the skiing season there are also service taxis which run from Beirut (Dora bus stand) to Faraya, and between Faraya and Faraya Mazaar. You may find, however, that it is easier to hitch.

Faraya Mazaar to the Bekaa Valley The road which climbs from Faraya Mazaar up over the northern slopes of Jebel Sannine has now been widened and resurfaced. Having climbed steeply, it winds its way through a desolate, hilly upland plateau before starting to descend. Around 15 km from Faraya Mazaar (soon after you begin to descend), you pass through a Syrian army checkpoint. The road then descends steeply, and stunning views of the Bekaa valley spread out before you. A little under 8 km further on you come to a roundabout/junction with a restaurant beside it. Bearing left here, the road climbs again, crossing the mountains to arrive near Afqa, at the head of the Adonis valley (Nahr Ibrahim); see page 505. Bearing right, the road continues to descend, passing through the village of **Hadet** and then through a second Syrian army checkpost, before arriving at a crossroads (just over 8 km from the junction/roundabout and restaurant) with yet another Syrian army checkpost. Turn right here to head towards Zahle, or left to intersect with the road between Baalbek and Bcharre. (Going straight on, you should in theory be abe to intersect with the main road between Rayak and Baalbek, though the soldiers on duty here seem reluctant to let you do this for some reason). Turning right, you pass through the village of **Nabi Rchade** and then after 5 km, in the village of **Chimstar**, turn left to pick up the main road, from where it is a further 21 km on to Zahle (see page 583).

Faqra فقرا

Colour map 5, grid B1 There is no village of Faqra as such (except for the artificial 'village' of the Faqra Ski Club). Other than the ski club, the scenery, historical monuments and rock bridge are all worth checking out. En route between Faraya and Faraya

Mazaar, if you turn right at the checkpost and junction (5 km from Faraya), after 1½ km you come to a signpost for 'Pont Naturel Kfardebian', off to the right of the road. A short track takes you down to a **rock bridge** over a stream, looking for all the world as if it has been carved by hand, although in fact it is a natural feature, eroded by the forces of nature out of the limestone rock. Around 500 m further on there is a left turn signposted for the **Faqra Ski Club**.

Continuing straight on, you arrive after 1½ km at a crossroads and sign for 'Archeologic sites of Faqra'. Visible off to your right, up a short track, are the remains of a curious cube-shaped structure, heavily ruined though solidly built of huge stone blocks. This is known as the **Claudius tower** – a Greek inscription above the entrance stating that it was rebuilt by the Emperor Claudius in 43-44 AD and dedicated to the 'very great god' (almost certainly Adonis). The cube base was once topped by a stepped pyramid which has now all but completely collapsed. Inside, steps lead up onto the roof. Given its unusual design and the style of the stone blocks used in its construction, it seems likely that the building is actually much older than its inscription suggests. To the right of the track leading up to the Claudius tower is the base of an altar, while to the left of the track is another smaller altar which has been restored, with 12 miniature columns arranged like a mini *portico* supporting the altar-top.

Temple ruins

Turning left at the crossroads, 500 m away at the bottom of this road, are the more substantial remains of two **temples**, both within fenced-off enclosures. The larger temple (to your right as you enter) was probably also dedicated to Adonis. It is set amidst limestone rocks which have been eroded into bizarre fluted shapes and look almost as if they have themselves been carved by hand. In front of the temple is a squat structure of huge stone blocks which probably served as an altar. The walls of the temple enclosure or *temenos* are still largely intact, while inside extensive restoration work has been carried out, including the use of dubious amounts of concrete in the reconstruction of the six columns which formed the *portico* of the *cella*.

The smaller temple (to your left as you enter) was originally dedicated to the Syrian goddess Atargatis and later became identified with Astarte, before being partially dismantled in the Byzantine era to build a church. The basic outline of the temple still stands, consisting of a rectangular building divided into a large antechamber followed by a smaller inner sanctum. Low niches line the walls of the latter, while on the ground there is a large circular stone basin with carved decorations on it. Adjacent to the temple, the ten standing columns which can still be seen formed the nave of the church; carved on one of the fallen stones in the compound is a Byzantine cross.

■ *Open 0900-sunset, closed Tue. Entry free (with the site now fully fenced in and supervised, it seems likely that an entry fee will be applied in the near future). There are a couple of simple snack places down by the entrance to the ruins, and another one on the main road, by the crossroads.*

This is a private ski club complete with its own mini-village of privately owned chalets and a luxury hotel. The resort has one chair-lift, two ski-lifts and a baby ski-lift, giving access to some 200 ha of slopes suitable for all levels of ability. All the land on which the ski-lifts and slopes are located is also privately owned, so to ski here you must be staying at the hotel (or else be invited as the guest of a member), although it may be possible to arrange to ski as a visitor here during the week when it is much quieter (enquire at the hotel in advance). Various skiing competitions are held during the season. Skiing lessons can be arranged and ski equipment is available for hire. There are good medical and rescue arrangements during the season. The club is also popular as a summer retreat, with another 'high season' from June-September.

Faqra Ski Club
Colour map 5, grid B1

Sleeping L/AL *L'Auberge de Faqra*, T300600, F300610, or T03-211127, aubergef@dm.net.lb Comfortable rooms with heater, TV/dish, phone and attached bath. Some rooms with balcony. Restaurant, bar, nightclub. Heated outdoor swimming pool, tennis, squash, sauna/health club, horse riding, shops. Cheaper room rates apply during the week (Sun-Thu) and during the low season. A large new hotel and restaurant, *Le Chateau Fort de Faqra*, is under construction next to the temple ruins at Faqra.

Eating As well as the various restaurants in *L'Auberge de Faqra* and around the Faqra Ski Club, there is the excellent *Chez Michel*, off the main road just below the turning for Faqra Ski Club, T341021 or T03-694462. This is a very smart, stylish restaurant/bar which attracts a pretty exclusive crowd. It is open throughout the year, serving high quality Lebanese cuisine for around US$25-35 per head. During the winter ski season and the summer months it also features live music or DJs on Sat nights, and cheese and wine soirées.

Adonis Valley (Nahr Ibrahim) وادي نهر إبراهيم

The Adonis valley (Nahr Ibrahim) climbs steeply into the mountains to the east of Jbail (Byblos). As well as being the source of numerous extraordinary legends surrounding the cult of Adonis, and the setting for some interesting ancient ruins, this valley and the surrounding mountains are also stunningly beautiful. The main point of interest is the Afqa spring, which is the source of the Nahr Ibrahim. You can only get here with your own transport, by private taxi, or by hitching (best done on the weekend when many Lebanese head up here for a picnic), but it is well worth making the effort to get there.

A round-trip via Qartaba and Aajaltoun

Heading north on the coastal motorway from Beirut/Jounieh, take the Qartaba exit (see page 449) to join the road heading up to Qartaba. To join the Qartaba road from the old coast road, head south out of Byblos and through the villages of Fidar and Halat. Around 700 m after passing the *4 Seasons* hotel on the right, turn left to cross over the motorway and head up towards Qartaba (if you cross a stream – the Nahr Ibrahim – you have gone too far). Heading

Adonis Valley & Jebel Tannourine

To Qadish Valley

To Tripoli

Naht Madtoun

Bcheale Douma Tannourine el-Tahta Arz Tannouri

Hadtoun

Tartij Chatine

Maifouk

Haqel Jaj Tannourine el-Faouqa

Amchit Nahr el-Joura Mechmech Troglodyte dwellings Jebel Tannourine

Annaya (St Charbel's Monastery) Ehmej Laqlouq Aaqoura

Jbail (Byblos) Kfar Baal Jebel Laqlouq Majdel Jebel Mnaitra

Fidar Nahr el-Fidar Checkpost Machnaqa Qartaba Mugheir

Halat Adonis El Mnaitre

Nahr Ibrahim Nahr Ibrahim (Adonis River) Lassa Ghabat Afqa Spring

Aqaibé

To Hadet & Faraya Mazaar

Bouar N

To Jounieh & Beirut To Aajaltoun & Faraya 0 km 2 / 0 miles

The cult of Adonis

The cult of Adonis flourished in Byblos and the Adonis Valley from Phoenician times. Adonis is said by some to be derived from the earlier Mesopotamian deity Tammuz, who was the lover of Ishtar, the great fertility goddess. According to this interpretation, to the Semitic peoples of ancient Syria, Ishtar became known as Astarte, and her lover as the graceful shepherd Adonis (from the Semitic 'Adon' or 'Lord'). Astarte in turn became identified with the Greek goddess Aphrodite and later, in Roman mythology, with Venus. As Colin Thubron comments, "The permutations in the legends and history of Astarte are of such tortuous richness that it has been impossible to assign her any permanent rites or character." Throughout these transformations, the legend of Adonis and Astarte-Aphrodite-Venus lived on, with each civilization adding its own embellishments and variations.

According to one Greek version of the legend, Adonis was the offspring of an incestuous relationship between Cinyrias, the king of Cyprus, and his daughter Myrrha. Famed for his good looks, Aphrodite, the goddess of love, soon fell in love with him and at Afqa they exchanged their first kiss. Her husband Ares (to the Romans, Mars), jealous of their love, caused a wild boar to attack Adonis while he was out hunting in the mountains of Lebanon. Mortally wounded, Adonis died in his lover's arms. Where his blood fell, crimson anemones sprung up (anemones are still known in Arabic as 'the wounds of Naaman', Naaman meaning 'darling' and being an epithet of Adonis). Aphrodite, inconsolable at her loss, petitioned the god Zeus (Roman Jupiter) to allow her to be reunited with Adonis, either through her own death or else by his resurrection. Eventually a compromise was reached whereby Adonis was allowed to leave the underworld for half of each year, providing he returned for the remainder.

Thus every spring, Adonis was born again into the world and reunited with Aphrodite, only to die again in autumn.

In another version Myrrha, out of shame for her incestuously conceived child, is turned into a tree (the myrrrh tree), while the infant Adonis is taken by Aphrodite and placed in the care of Persephone, the queen of the underworld. Seeing the great beauty of the child, Persephone refuses to return Adonis to Aphrodite. Eventually Zeus intervenes and decrees that Adonis may spend half the year with Aphrodite but must return to the underworld for the other half. The two become lovers and Aphrodite's jealous husband Ares turns himself into a boar and kills Adonis in revenge. But the judgement of Zeus still stands and Adonis is freed each year from the underworld to return to his lover.

Although on the surface a love story, the legend also clearly has its roots in those primordial themes of fertility, death and rebirth. Adonis is closely identified by some with vegetation, visibly prosperous during the six favourable months of the year, and lurking hidden under the cold ground during the remainder. Others see evidence of a sun myth in which Adonis, the short-lived sun, is slain by the boar, the demon of darkness, and passionately mourned by the dawn or twilight (Venus), who utterly refuses to live without him. With the advent of Christianity, the cult of Adonis was banned, but found new life in the form of St George, ever popular in Lebanon. Astarte-Aphrodite-Venus, meanwhile, became identified with the Virgin Mary. It has also been suggested that the Christian festival of Easter, celebrating the resurrection of Christ, may have replaced the pagan celebration of the resurrection of Adonis. Certainly, the Adonis Valley is today fervently Christian, and many of the numerous shrines and chapels along its length were clearly converted from earlier shrines to Adonis.

north from Jounieh on the old coast road, having passed through the villages of Tabarja, Safra, Bouar and Aqaibé, take the right turn around 100 m after the bridge across the Nahr Ibrahim (a sign by the bridge announces the start of Nahr Ibrahim village).

The Qartaba road, rather busy and built up to begin with, climbs steeply into the mountains, with superb views west out over the Mediterranean coast. To the south, meanwhile, there are spectacular views down into the deep, sheer-sided gorge of the Nahr Ibrahim, and to the north occasional glimpses, equally spectacular, down into the Nahr el-Fidar. After 12 km you come to a checkpost and right turn leading down to the village of Adonis. Continuing straight on, the road narrows considerably and after a further 10 km brings you to the tiny village of Machnaqa.

Machnaqa
Colour map 5, grid B1

The literal translation of this village name is 'place of the hanging'

Just before entering the village, you can see some **temple ruins** off to the right of the road, on a level-topped hill. A rough track leads past a tiny chapel (built partly of stones from the temple) up to the ruins. Alternatively, a little further along the road, a set of steps right by the signpost announcing the start of Machnaqa village leads up to the ruins, passing through a narrow cleft cut into the rocks with heavily weathered reliefs on either side (said to depict Adonis and Astarte but no longer clearly discernible). Dotted around are a number of trenchlike tombs cut into the rocks. The main temple (almost certainly dedicated to Adonis) consists of a large rectangular *temenos* entered through a monumental gateway. The gateway and the lower courses of the walls, built from massive stone blocks, are fairly well preserved, although on one side a more modern house encroaches on the compound. At the far end, opposite the entrance, are the remains of the *cella*, with four columns in one corner still standing, topped by sections of *entablature*, and with more sections propped up on the ground beside it. Scattered around are the remains of further columns, capitals and various architectural fragments.

Qartaba
Phone code: 09
Colour map 5, grid B1

From Machnaqa it is a further 11 km on to Qartaba, the road en route giving ever more dramatic, and at times extremely vertiginous, views down into the Nahr Ibrahim valley. The small town of Qartaba is beautifully located, overlooking the valley, and is itself rather picturesque, with its large church and square, and substantial, well built houses giving it a certain air of affluence. Surrounding the town are fertile olive groves, mulberry orchards and vineyards. There are a couple of seasonal hotels/restaurants in the town, making it a pleasant place to stay during the summer. The main road passes along the top of the town, which spreads down the hillside below. Entering the village, bear left where the road forks to keep to the upper road, and then bear right at the next junction (with an *United/Esso* garage beside it; left leads across to Laqlouq on a road which was being upgraded at the time of writing). Immediately after is the *Palma* restaurant. Around 300 m further on, bearing right leads down to the *Rivola* hotel, or bear left for the road to Afqa.

Sleeping and eating D/E *Rivola*, T405002. Friendly family-run hotel in a big old house. Simple but comfortable rooms with attached bath and balconies offering lovely views out over the valley. Restaurant. Open May to Oct approximately (depending on the weather; phone to check). The *Palma* restaurant, T405011, or T03-385011, is no longer a hotel, despite the sign, and opens from around early Jun to late Aug only. Below it is the *Octane* bar/'nightclub'.

Mugheir
Colour map 5, grid B2

A little under 6 km beyond Qartaba, you come to a set of **temple ruins** right by the road. The rectangular building, dating from Greek or Roman times and again most probably dedicated to Adonis, has three fairly well preserved walls, with traces of its original decoration still visible. During the Byzantine period, the temple was converted into a church, with the missing fourth side of the building (originally the entrance) forming the apse. The site is known locally as *Mar Jurios Azraq* (literally 'St George the Blue', the epithet 'the Blue' perhaps being derived from the greyish-blue granite from which the church was built). Surrounding the temple/church are the remains of a larger compound, built from huge blocks of reddish stone. Although the stones from which this compound has been constructed are certainly much older, in their present form they are thought to have been arranged as fortifications by the Crusaders during the 12th century.

Continuing on from Mugheir, after 1½ km you cross a stream on a small bridge (this is a tributary valley of the Nahr Ibrahim). To the right of the road, down by the stream just before you cross the bridge, is the **D** *Al Rabih Motel*, T439625, or T03-249051. This is a very friendly place and beautifully located. Simple but clean and pleasant rooms with attached bath and balcony, and lovely views out over the stream and down the valley. The restaurant here serves fresh trout from its own trout pools, as well as the usual range of grills, mezze etc. Open Apr/May to Sep/Oct (depending on the weather; phone to check). From the bridge, the road climbs steeply through the village of **Majdel**. A further 1½ km after crossing the stream, there is a sharp right turn signposted 'La Reserve Afqa' (straight on is signposted 'Laklouk', this road passing first through Aaqoura to reach Laqlouq, see below).

Majdel & Mnaitre
Phone code: 09

Taking the sharp right turn, after a little under 3 km you come to a left turn signposted once again for 'La Reserve'. As well as taking you past *La Reserve* camping/activity centre, this is the start of a new road which crosses the high ridges of Mount Lebanon and descends into the Bekaa valley (see below). Continuing straight on, it is a further 2½ km to Afqa spring. Shortly before you reach the spring, you pass through the tiny village of **Mnaitre**. This is where a Maronite missionary by the name of Abraham is said to have first settled when he came to Lebanon during the fifth century, and it was in his honour that the Adonis Valley was later named the Nahr Ibrahim. There are hot springs in the village, while up on a hilltop above the village there are traces of ruins, said by some to be the Crusader castle known as Le Moinestre, which was destroyed by Salah ud-Din (Saladin) in 1110.

Afqa أفقا

The scenery approaching Afqa is beautiful and dramatic. Arriving at the spring, you are confronted by enormous cliffs towering nearly 200 m above you, their sheer face broken by a huge cavern from which the Afqa spring, the source of the Nahr Ibrahim, gushes out in a forceful torrent. A rough path leads steeply up to the gaping opening; depending on the season (and therefore the level of the waters), if you negotiate the unseemly tangle of pipes which emerge from it, you can scramble right up inside the cavern. The roof, noticeably uniform, shows signs of having been chiselled, and according to some sources there was originally a temple dedicated to Adonis inside the cavern itself.

A little further along the road, to the right, a fenced-off area contains the tumbled ruins of a **temple**, its form no longer distinguishable, though the mass of scattered stones indicate that it must have been of substantial proportions. Exactly when it was first constructed is uncertain, though in legend it was Cinyras, the king of Cyprus and father of Adonis, who built it. Whoever was responsible obviously went to great lengths, as the granite column discovered

Colour map 5, grid B2

In Arabic the name Afqa translates as 'source', but in Greek Aphaca means literally 'the kiss' – this allegedly being the place where Adonis and Aphrodite first met and fell in love

Mount Lebanon

here which must have been transported from Egypt shows. Originally dedicated to Astarte, during Roman times its importance continued as a temple of Venus. Wishing to eradicate the licentious pagan cults which held such sway in this region, the Byzantine emperor Constantine ordered that it be destroyed. However, it was not until the end of the fourth century, during the reign of Arcadius, that it was finally reduced to ruins under the directions of St John Chrysostom. At the base of the ruins there is an arched opening from which a small spring emanates, and which still serves as a shrine, with candles inside and bits of cloth tied to an overhanging fig tree. So Afqa remains a sacred site in the minds of local people. Christians identify it with the Virgin Mary and Shi'ite Muslims with a woman named *Zahra*, of uncertain origin, and both groups make pilgrimages to the site in search of fertility or cures for illnesses.

Heading down the hillside from the temple ruins, you get the best views back up to the cavern and spring, and also a good view of the old stone arched **bridge**, now contained within the larger arch of a later bridge.

Sleeping If you wish to spend longer exploring this area, *La Reserve*, 3 km away, offers a spec-
& eating tacular camping spot (see below). There are also plenty of idyllic places to camp around Afqa itself, and an abundant supply of fresh spring water! Alternatively, there is the *Al Rabih Motel*, 7 km away, just past the village of Majdel (see above).

Just below the road, by the bridge and stream, there is a small restaurant, open only in the spring and summer months, where you can get tea, coffee etc and a limited range of snacks/meals for around US$5-10 per head, although it is more fun to follow the Lebanese example and bring your own picnic with you. Bear in mind that Afqa is a popular destination on summer weekends and can get quite busy.

Aaqoura and the road to Laqlouq

Coming from Qartaba, if you continue straight on past the turning for Afqa, the road runs along the east side of the picturesque tributary valley of the Nahr Ibrahim, arriving after just over 3 km at Aaqoura. Nestling beneath towering cliffs of sheer rock, the village of Aaqoura is an important Maronite centre, with numerous churches and shrines, including one dedicated to Mar Butros (St Peter) which is perched in a natural grotto in the cliff face and reached by a steep stairway cut into the rock. The grotto, with its hollowed-out tombs cut into the rock, appears to have originally been a Roman necropolis before being converted into a Christian shrine. (Aaqoura is said to be one of the first to have undergone conversion to Christianity by the Maronite missionary Abraham, see under 'Majdel and Mnaitre, above). At the back of the grotto, faint traces of the rare *Estrangelo* script can be seen, painted in red on the rock. This vertical Syriac script is thought to have been developed by Nestorean Christian missionaries who visited China in the seventh century and adopted elements of the Chinese script. (Although Estrangelo soon died out, modern Mongol and Manchu still contain elements of ancient Syriac.) There is also a well preserved section of Roman road in the village, part of a route which once led over the mountains and down to Yammouné in the Bekaa Valley (see page 598). In pre-Christian times, after visiting Afqa, Adonis pilgrims would come to Aaqoura and cross the Lebanon mountains by this route, carrying out the final purification rituals of their pilgrimage in the lake there. **NB** Although a tempting hiking option, the mountains here were extensively mined during the civil war and remain dangerous.

Continuing on from Aaqoura, the road climbs steadily and the mountains begin to open out. After just over 5 km you come to a very sharp right turn, followed 300 m further on by a very sharp left turn. Another 1 km brings you to a second sharp right turn; this is the start of the road to Tannourine el-Faouqa. The rather vaguely and confusingly aligned signpost by the junction reads 'St Charbel-Annanaya 14 km'. Continuing straight on, just past the junction there is a signpost announcing, equally confusingly, the start of Ehmej; in fact you are approaching the ski resort of Laqlouq (see page 507), Ehmej is some distance further down the valley.

La Reserve and the road across to the Bekaa Valley

Taking the signposted turning for 'La Reserve' 2½ km to the north of Afqa spring, *La Reserve* itself is off to the right of the road 400 m further on. The awesome mountain scenery and stunning views make this a truly dramatic wilderness camping location. Tents (sleeping up to 4 people), complete with mattresses and all bedding, are available (US$10 per person), including use of good, clean shower/toilet facilities (and hot water), or you can pitch your own tent. There is also a café/restaurant here. Activities on offer include archery, horse riding, mountain biking, abseiling, potholing, canoeing and rafting. ■ *The place is generally open from around early May to late Sep, depending on the weather. For more information, contact La Reserve directly on T03-727484, or in Beirut T01-498774, F01-492660, www.lareserve.com.lb*

Returning to the main road (a brand-new well built affair), and continuing east, you climb steeply up, with ever more vertiginous views back down the valley, before winding your way through an upland plateau of rolling hills. After 14 km you pass through a Syrian army checkpost, and then around 1 km further on begin to descend, with panoramic views of the Bekaa valley spread out below. Some 5 km after the checkpost (and 1 km after passinng a sharp right turn), you arrive at a roundabout/junction with a restaurant beside it. Bearing right here takes you back up over the mountains to Faraya Mazaar, while bearing left takes you down into the Bekaa Valley (see page 579 for details of the remainder of this route to Zahle).

Jebel Tannourine جبل تنّورين

There are several interesting and extremely scenic trips which can be made from Jbail (Byblos) into the mountains. The most obvious route is the one leading due east up to the monastery and shrine of St Charbel at Annaya, and then via the village of Ehmej to the ski resort of Laqlouq. From Laqlouq there are several options. One road leads via the village of Aaqoura down to Qartaba, with the possibility of diverting to Afqa, while another continues north to Tannourine el-Faouqa, from where you can either head across to the Qadisha valley, or else round to the pretty town of Douma and then return via a winding mountain road to the coast at Amchit (just north of Jbail).

Jbail (Byblos) to Laqlouq

Heading in either direction along the coastal motorway, take the Jbail (Byblos) exit (see page 449). Coming from the old coast road in the centre of Jbail, follow the dual carriageway with the remains of the Roman street running along the centre and cross over the coastal motorway. From here a broad highway climbs up through Jbail's suburbs and into the mountains. Higher up, there are lots of snack bars and small restaurants strategically placed to make the most of the panoramic views out over the Mediterranean. Some 14½ km after crossing over the motorway, you arrive at a checkpost and junction, preceded

Mount Lebanon

by several more restaurants as well as a number of shops lining the road; fork left here to make a short detour up to the monastery and shrine of St Charbel at Annaya (a little over 2 km further on, see below), or right to head towards Laqlouq. Bearing right, the broad highway gives way to a narrow mountain road. You pass first through the village of Kfar Baal, and then the *Hafroun* hotel on the right, before getting to **Ehmej**, which spreads out for a couple of kilometres along the road. From the church which marks the approximate centre of the village (6 km from the checkpost and junction), it is a further 6 km up to the lower section of Laqlouq, the valley gradually narrowing as you ascend.

St Charbel Monastery دير القديس شربل

Phone code: 09
Colour map 5, grid B1

Although first established in the early part of the 19th century, there have been substantial later additions to the monastery. Today, a visit is interesting more for the somewhat bizarre experience of seeing a flourishing modern-day Maronite pilgrimage centre in action, rather than for the building itself. Inside the monastery there is a small museum where various items from St Charbel's life are displayed, including piles of crutches belonging to those cured by his miracles, the papal letter of canonization, pieces of his blood-stained clothing and a mega-tacky display of mannequins depicting his family praying before a meal. There are no less than three tombs for the Saint, his remains having been transferred to a new one each time they were disinterred. The devout can also obtain pieces of cloth stained with the blood which is said to still issue from his body. A souvenir shop sells all sorts of St Charbel-related souvenirs, while opposite the monastery there is another shop selling locally produced wine. Unfortunately, the rapid development of the area and the rather crude commercialization of the monastery as a pilgrimage site have robbed it of the sense of solitude and isolation which must have existed in St Charbel's lifetime.

You can get to the nearby hilltop **hermitage** to which he retreated by following the signs from the monastery, rather than the fork soon after the checkpost and junction. Though it still has something of a pilgrimage theme park atmosphere about it, it does retain something of its original tranquillity along with spectacular views out over the Mediterranean.

Sleeping & eating
As well as the hotel restaurants, there are dozens of restaurants down by the checkpost and junction, & along the road leading to the monastery

There are several hotels near St Charbel Monastery. **C** *Al Mayadine* (sign in Arabic only), on the left, 500 m from the checkpost and junction, on the road leading towards Ehmej, T760333. Large, comfortable rooms (some with separate lounge area) with heater, TV, phone and attached bath. Huge restaurant. **C** *Hafroun*, on the right, at the start of Ehmej village, T504620. Heater, phone, attached bath. Some rooms with balcony. Restaurant, bar and 'Tit Hits' nightclub! **C** *Mawal*, just past the checkpost and junction, on the road leading towards the monastery, T760077. Large, comfortably furnished rooms with heater, TV/dish, phone, attached bath and balcony. Restaurant, and bar/'nightclub'. **D** *Oasis St Charbel*, right next door to the monastery itself, T760130. Simple (going on spartan) but spotlessly clean rooms with heater, phone and attached bath. Restaurant/snack bar. Run by the monastery and really only meant for bona fide pilgrims (unmarried couples must take separate rooms).

Transport

A private taxi from Jbail should not cost more than US$10-15 for the round trip up to St Charbel's monastery and back, although this depends on the length of time you expect them to wait. On Sun there is a good chance of finding a service taxi heading up there from Jbail, or you could try hitching.

St Charbel

Born in 1828 in the tiny village of Bqaa Kafra in the Qadisha valley (see page 518, St Charbel (christened Joseph) first studied as a novice at the Monastery of Our Lady of Maifouk (see below), before being transferred to what was then the Monastery of St Maroun at Annaya. After completing his studies at the Monastery of Kfifane (to the east of Batroun), he returned to Annaya, where was ordained as a monk in 1859 and where he remained for the rest of his life, first in the monastery itself for 16 years and then in a nearby hilltop hermitage for 23 years. During his lifetime he gained a reputation for his piety, and various minor miracles were attributed to him. Several months after his death in 1898, his body was disinterred and found to be undecomposed, with blood still issuing from it. Three further disinterrments in 1950, 1952 and 1955 all revealed the same state

of affairs, and to this day blood is still said to seep from his undecomposed body. In the meantime, numerous miracles involving the curing of the terminally ill or disabled have been attributed to him, including three formally recognized as such by the papal authorities in Rome. In 1965 he was beatified and in 1977 canonized, thus becoming the first (and to date only) officially recognized Maronite saint. Today he is one of the best loved and most popular figures of the Maronite church, with statues and pictures of him to be found all over Lebanon. As well as attracting large numbers of pilgrims each Sunday, even larger crowds flock to the monastery on the 22nd of each month to witness the latest miracle in the form of a local woman who since 1992 has displayed the bleeding wounds of the stigmata every month on this date.

Laqlouq لقلوق

The ski resort of Laqlouq doesn't really have a centre as such; the first part you come to consists of the *Lavalade* hotel and several chalet developments. Some 2 km further on, the *Shangri La* hotel is signposted off to the right of the road. This hotel complex is close to the foot of the slopes, and there are a number of private chalet complexes nearby.

Phone code: 09
Colour map 5, grid B1

Originally Laqlouq was one of the smallest ski resorts in Lebanon alongside Qanat Bakich, but following development of the resort in 1996/7 there are now three chair-lifts, three ski-lifts and three baby-lifts. Most of the slopes are quite gentle (suitable for beginners to medium ability), although one technical Alpine slope has recently been approved by the International Ski Federation as suitable for Giant Slalom events at international competition level. There are also excellent opportunities for cross-country skiing. As always, weekends are the busiest (and most expensive times) to ski. The ski school includes French instructors and has a good reputation. Skiing equipment is available for hire and there are rescue and medical facilities on hand. The direct route up from Jbail (described above) is kept open throughout the season by snowploughs. The area around Laqlouq is very beautiful, with Jebel Tannourine rising to the east, while to the west there are still stands of Lebanese cedars down in the valley. Although essentially a winter ski resort, the *Shangri La* hotel stays open all year round and offers various activities during the summer.

The ski resort

B *Shangri La*, T621436 or T03-448825, F01-336007. Comfortable rooms with heater, phone and large attached bath. Some rooms with balcony. Restaurant and bar. Pleasant, old-style hotel with friendly management. Geared very much towards families/children. Lots of common areas for socializing. Full range of ski equipment available for hire, as well as mountain bikes and ATVs/quad bikes in summer. Slightly cheaper rates

Sleeping & eating

during week (Mon-Thu) and off season. Also various chalets, though these are generally rented out for the whole season. **B/C** *Nirvana*, next door to *Shangri La*, and sharing the same phone numbers. Rather 1970s in style. Simple but clean rooms with heater, phone and attached bath. Restaurant and bar. Large outdoor swimming pool. Previously run as part of the *Shangri La*, but due to open under separate management. **C** *Lavalade*, T904100 or T03-885810. Sign outside announces it as just a hotel, but also with rooms for rent. Open weekends only during winter, daily during summer. Large rooms with sofa-beds (sleeping max 6 people, price according to number of people), heater, kitchenette and attached bath. Large restaurant.

There are a couple of snack places at the foot of the slopes (open during the winter only), but otherwise the only restaurants are those attached to the hotels.

Transport　On weekends during the winter skiing season, it may be possible to find service taxis running to Laqlouq from Jbail (Byblos) or from Dora bus stand in Beirut, but otherwise the only way to get here is by your own transport or a private taxi.

Routes from Laqlouq

There are plans to build 2 new roads leading up from the coast, one from Batroun and the other from Amchit, which will join up shortly before Tannourine el-Tahta

If you continue up past the turning for the *Shangri La* hotel, after just under 1 km you come to a junction; bear left for Tannourine el-Faouqa (signposted for 'Tannourine', amongst others) or continue straight on (signposted rather confusingly 'Laklouk') to head down to Aaqoura and then Qartaba, passing en route the turning for Afqa (see above). Bearing left, after 600 m you come to a striking cluster of protruding limestone rocks eroded into weird shapes beside the road. Cut into these rocks are tiny **troglodyte dwellings** of uncertain origin. They were once used as an army barracks but are now deserted. Continuing on, you pass the village of Chatine, clinging prettily to a steep-sided rocky outcrop off to the left of the road, before arriving in a fork in the centre of the village of **Tannourine el-Faouqa**, 9 km from the junction above Laqlouq. The fork off to the left (signposted to Batroun and Tannourine el-Tahta, amongst others) leads to Douma. The fork off to the right leads across to the Qadisha valley; around 100 m further on, bear round to the right in front of a large, very grand looking church, then go left immediately afterwards. Start asking directions through the village from here – picking up the correct road is rather tricky.

The road across to the Qadisha valley is spectacularly beautiful. It climbs steeply from Tannourine el-Faouqa and then follows a wide arc around the head of a valley with sizeable stands of Lebanese cedars – the **Arz Tannourine** – below you off to the left of the road, before descending to Hadath el-Jobbe (18 km, see page 519). This road has recently been resurfaced, making it an extremely pleasant alternative approach to Bcharre and the Qadisha valley, and well worth doing if you have your own transport.

The road to Douma takes you through dramatic scenery of towering rock mountains and deep, sheer-sided gorges, before descending steeply to **Tannourine el-Tahta**, just over 5 km from Tannourine el-Faouqa. Go straight on at the junction in Tannourine el-Tahta, and then, after a further 1½ km fork left at the 'Speed' petrol station. Around 2½ km further is the *Douma* hotel on the left, and beyond it the town of Douma.

Douma دوما

Phone code: 06
Colour map 5, grid B1

Douma is unique in that it has largely escaped the modern concrete construction you find practically everywhere else in Lebanon. Instead, the town has managed to preserve its beautiful Ottoman period houses with their distinctive red-tiled roofs. With strictly enforced town planning regulations, it has also managed for the most part to preserve a distinctive scorpion-shape layout, clearly discernible when viewed from above.

During the Ottoman period the town flourished as a centre for the production of swords and guns, with the inhabitants using the wealth they accumulated to build the grand red-roofed houses that can be seen today. Although there is nothing of special interest in Douma, it is a picturesque town with several pleasant cafés in the centre where the local men come to pass the time drinking tea and coffee, smoking nargilehs and playing *towleh* (the Arab version of backgammon). There are also plenty of opportunities for hiking in the surrounding hills (the *Douma* hotel organizes hiking trips).

The town's name is said to be derived from Julia Domna, the wife of the Roman Emperor Septimus Severus (193-211 AD), who supposedly used it as a summer retreat

The only hotel is the **C** *Douma*, T520202 or T03-611406, F520106. Reasonably comfortable rooms with heater, TV/dish, phone, attached bath and balcony (good views). Restaurant and bar. Friendly, well run hotel, though a little on the expensive side, and rather an ugly circular building, somewhat out of keeping with the spirit of Douma. Other than the hotel's restaurant (Lebanese, French, Italian food, around US$15-20 per head), there are a couple of snack places in town where you can get sandwiches etc.

Sleeping & eating

Douma back to the coast

Coming from the *Douma* hotel, turn left in the centre of Douma. The road climbs steeply from here, with various vantage points giving excellent views of the town and its distinctive scorpion shape spread out below. After crossing a watershed, the road descends through strikingly eroded limestone rock formations, passing through the village of **Bcheale** (a little over 3 km from Douma), also notable for its red-roofed houses, before arriving in **Tartij**, 5 km further on. Turn right in the centre of Tartij (marked by a statue of St George slaying the dragon, and signposted for Hadtoun, Maifrouk and Aale) to pick up the road leading down to the coast at Amchit.

The road leading down into **Maifouk** takes you past numerous tombs and the chapel of St Elije. The centre of the village is marked by a mini-roundabout with a hand-like sculpture in the centre. Bearing right here brings you to the entrance to a large monastery and school, also dedicated to St Elije (the 'Monastery of Our Lady of Maifouk'). In its present form this dates from 1904. Opposite is a tiny chapel which was part of the original monastery.

Bear left at the mini-roundabout in Maifouk to continue on towards Haqel. Around 3 km beyond Maifouk, you pass a fork off to the left signposted to Jaj and St Charbel's Monastery (Annaya). Keep going straight and then 2 km further on follow the road round sharply to the left (ignoring a right turn on the bend signposted in Arabic only) to descend into a narrow valley. The road crosses the valley's stream near its head (look out for the remains of an old dry-stone bridge by the stream) then loops round to the right to double back along the opposite (south) side before arriving in Haqel, 7 km from Maifouk and 22 km from Douma.

Haqel The valley here is famous for its marine fossils and there are a couple of shops in the village selling stones with the fossilized skeletons of fish imprinted on them, ranging in size from a few centimetres up to a metre and more. The presence of such fossils at this altitude (600 m) is evidence of the fact that during the cretacian and cenomanian eras (90-110 million years ago) most of Lebanon was immersed under the sea.

The road continues along the south side of the valley, which develops steadily into a deep gorge, passing through a number of small villages. Keep going straight, descending through the old part of Amchit. Around 16 km from Haqel you cross over the coastal motorway, before joining the old coast road 2 km to the north of Jbail.

Mount Lebanon

Qadisha Valley and Cedars of Lebanon

The Qadisha valley, the heartland of the Maronite Christian community, is arguably one of the most beautiful of north Lebanon's mountain areas. From the fertile Khoura plains which spread inland around Batroun, the valley climbs steeply in a deep gorge up to the amphitheatre of mountains that surround the Cedars, dominated by Qornet es-Saouda, at 3,083 m the highest peak in the Lebanon mountain range.

From Chekka via Amioun

Heading north on the coastal motorway, the exit for Chekka and Amioun (clearly signposted for Ehden, the Cedars and Chekka) is just after a checkpost, 6 km beyond the tunnel through the promontory of Ras ech-Chekka (see page 449). Heading south on the coastal motorway, the Chekka/Amioun exit is 18 km from the start of the motorway in Tripoli, just before you reach the checkpost. Heading south on the old coast road, the turning for Amioun (not signposted) is the first left turn you come to immediately after leaving Chekka (just after the signposted right turn for the *St Francoise* hotel). Heading north on the old coast road, after the tunnel through the promontory of Ras ech-Chekka, the road descends past various small beach resorts; the right turn for Amioun is just under 1 km beyond the left turn signposted for the *Palmara* resort.

After leaving/crossing over the motorway, a good road climbs gently up through the fertile Khoura plain, passing through rich olive groves and orchards. A little over 5 km from the motorway, go straight at a crossroads and Syrian army checkpost. From here it is 4 km into the centre of Amioun.

Amioun
Colour map 5, grid B1

Amioun, at an altitude of 400 m, is the principal town of the Koura region, and has a predominantly Greek Orthodox population. As you approach the centre, above the road to the left you can see a chapel on top of a rocky outcrop, with lots of small, square chambers cut into the rock below. This is **St John's chapel** ('Mar Youhanna') a relatively recent construction, while the rock-cut chambers below it are **burial vaults** dating from the Roman period, or perhaps even earlier. Spread out over this long, narrow outcrop of rock is the old village of Amioun, which is well worth exploring.

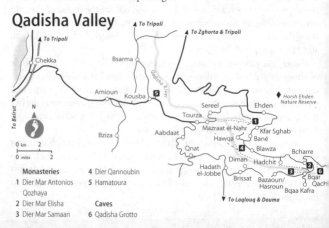

Qadisha Valley

Monasteries
1 Dier Mar Antonios Qozhaya
2 Dier Mar Elisha
3 Dier Mar Samaan
4 Dier Qannoubin
5 Hamatoura

Caves
6 Qadisha Grotto

To get up to it, turn left at the traffic lights around 200 m beyond St John's chapel and the burial vaults and take the small left turn around 200 m further on. Although the first part is accessible by car, the road is extremely steep and it is best to go on foot. Wandering around the narrow streets, you can forget for a moment all the glitzy new development which lines the modern road (itself only constructed in 1986) and get a glimpse of the quiet, parochial atmosphere which once would have reigned in this small village overlooking the Khoura plain. There is a fascinating blend of old Ottoman architecture mixed in with more modern construction, the latter often built straight onto the former. The size of many of the old houses gives an indication of the wealth generated by the olive-based economy of the village during the Ottoman period. At the far end of the ridge is the large **Church of St George** ('Mar Gorjius'). This appears to have been built from an earlier Roman temple, as can be seen from the large stone blocks used in the lower courses of the walls, as well as the sections of columns laid horizontally as reinforcement. Higher up, the walls are of smaller, more recent stones while the belltower is clearly a recent addition. The interior is plain vaulted with a stone *iconostasis* decorated with numerous painted icons in front of the apse. Flanking the apse there are two Roman columns, the capital of the left-hand one with a carved face still discernible on it. In the centre of the village there are a couple more churches of recent origin, and the austere looking **Church of St Phocas** ('Mar Fauqa') probably built in the 12th century by the Crusaders. Inside, the walls are decorated with Byzantine-style frescos dating from the 12th and 13th century.

Around 500 m past the traffic lights and crossroads in the centre of Amioun, there is a right turn signposted for the village of Bziza (amongst others), 5 km away; ask directions along the way as the route is not very clear. Nearby there are the remains of a **Roman temple**, dedicated originally to the Semitic god *Azizos*. The four limestone columns which formed the *portico* of the temple are still standing, three of them still topped by Ionic capitals and supporting the original *architrave*. Beyond the *portico*, the doorway of the temple is also well preserved, complete with its entire crowning *entablature*. During the Byzantine period, a church was erected within the temple.

Bziza

Returning to the main road and continuing east, turn left around 3 km after the crossroads and traffic lights in the centre of Amioun (signposted for Ehden). Go straight across the crossroads 1 km further on, in Kousba, another predominantly Greek Orthodox village and important market centre. Around 700 m after the crossroads, there is a small left turn, signposted (none too clearly) for the **Chateau du Liban**. Built during the civil war as the fulfilment of a local man's dream (ask for a leaflet explaining the building's symbolic significance), this is a bizarre-looking, wedding cake-like construction of black basalt rock. The 'chateau' houses a restaurant on the ground floor (open daily 1100-2200), serving Lebanese food for around US$10-15 per head (excluding alcohol), while behind it there is an open air theatre. The upper storeys of the chateau are eventually to house a 'museum' featuring all manner of faces, animals and weird and wonderful creatures fashioned from wood and stone.

Kousba
Phone code: 06
Colour map 5, grid B1

In many ways, the best thing about the Chateau du Liban is the spectacular views it offers across the deep, narrow Qadisha valley (known here as the Nahr Abu Ali) to the Greek Orthodox Hamatoura monastery. Built precariously into the almost sheer cliff face, the monastery is accessible only on foot by means of a zig-zagging trail and steps leading up from the valley floor. The rock strata in the cliffs angle sharply upwards from the valley floor and then bend

Hamatoura monastery

Mount Lebanon

round in a broad arc, graphically revealing the geological processes of uplift and folding which formed these mountains. To reach the start of the trail up to the monastery, continue past the Chateau du Liban, and follow this narrow road as it winds its way down to the bottom of the valley (around 2½ km). The road ends at a hydro-electric station and a bridge across the river giving access to the trail and steps leading up to the monastery (a steep 30-45 minute climb).

When you get there, you pass through a short section of tunnel running under a newly constructed wing. The monastery's tiny chapel is partly built into the cliff face. Carved into the stonework above the entrance to the chapel is a Crusader-style cross (with twin horizontal members), while carved above the entrance to a cave behind the chapel is a Byzantine cross. Inside the chapel, there are a few small fragments of frescos, revealed after a fire in 1993 caused the plaster covering the walls to peel and flake. The frescos are all 10th century in style, except for one, which is thought to date from the sixth century. According to some estimates, the monastery may have been established as early as the fourth century. At its height, during the 14th century, there were some 200 monks in residence here, though following a massacre at the hands of the Mamelukes, it went into decline. In 1850 the Ottomans bombed the monastery, causing serious damage and killing 50 monks, while in 1917 it suffered further damage due to an earthquake. Since 1994, the Abbot, Father Pandelemion, has overseen its gradual restoration.

Two routes on to Bcharre Continuing east along the main road, 4 km beyond the turning for the Chateau du Liban and Hamatoura monastery you come to a checkpost and fork in the road. If you fork right, the road climbs up over a shoulder of mountain, passing through the villages of **Aabdaat** (or Aabdine) and **Qnat**, off to the right of the road, before descending to **Hadath el-Jobbe** and continuing on to **Bcharre**.

Forking left, the road descends through the red-roofed villages of **Tourza** and **Mazraat el-Nahr**, before crossing the stream of the Qadisha valley (3 km from the checkpost). From here on, the valley is spectacularly beautiful. The road climbs, gently at first and then more steeply, to arrive at a mini-roundabout in **Sereel**, 2½ km further on. Turn right here, and after a further 4 km you pass a right turn signposted to the 'Couvent St Antoine Kosbaiya' (this is the road leading down to Deir Mar Antonios Qozhaya, see page 522).

From Tripoli

Via Kousba From the centre of Tripoli, head south on Rue Bechara El Khoury and turn left after 2 km (shortly after a right turn signposted for the motorway to Beirut; if you pass under the motorway you have gone too far). Bear left shortly after taking the left turn (right for *Haykel* hospital and the *Chateau des Oliviers* hotel). After 9 km, turn left again (straight on leads back down to the coast at Chekka) and then keep going straight. In the village of **Bsarma** (2 km further on), follow the road round to the left where it forks and keep going straight until you reach a left turn (4 km from Bsarma) signposted for Ehden in the village of **Kousba**. Turning left here, this is the road which leads past the Chateau du Liban (see above).

Via Zghorta & Ehden In the centre of Tripoli, cross over to the east side of the river by the citadel and turn right to pick up the dual carriageway leading southeast towards Zghorta. The highway passes first through Majedlaya before arriving in the centre of **Zghorta** (8 km), a not particularly inspiring town whose main claim to fame is as the home town of the Franjieh family. Straight ahead of you, you can see the peak of Qornet es-Saouda towering impressively in the distance. Continue straight across the roundabout at the far end of the town and keep going straight, climbing steadily on a wide, good quality road (complete with road markings for most of way) passing through a number of villages before arriving at a right turn with a statue of St Charbel in the centre of the junction (around 24 km from Zghorta). This turning is the start of the road leading down to the coastal highway at Chekka, via Kousba and Amioun, while straight on the road leads through Ehden and on to Bcharre.

Bcharre بشرّي

The staunchly Maronite village of Bcharre is dramatically located near the head of the Qadisha Valley, on the edge of sheer cliffs which plunge down to the valley floor. The town is famous as the birthplace of Gibran Khalil Gibran, one of Lebanon's most famous poet-artists. Largely dormant during the winter months (along with all the other villages in the vicinity), Bcharre gets busy in the summer when people come to escape the heat and humidity of the coast. As well as the various sights around the town, Bcharre is the obvious base from which to explore the stunningly beautiful Qadisha valley, while the Cedars (Al Arz) is also within easy reach from here.

Phone code: 06
Colour map 5, grid B2

Ins & outs

Bcharre is best reached by microbus or service taxi from Tripoli. The village itself is easily manageable on foot. To the east of the village, just past the waterfall, a turning up the hillside is clearly signposted to the Gibran Museum, Notre Dame de Lourdes Grotto and Phoenician Tomb, all within walking distance. It is possible to walk down into the Qadisha valley directly from Bcharre, or there is a road leading down to the valley floor from the south rim. To reach the Qadisha Grotto and Cedars (Al Arz), you really need transport; private taxis are available in the village, or else you can hitch.

Sights

Churches Two large churches stand out clearly from a distance: **Mar Saba church** in the centre by the main square is the largest, while a short way up from it is the **Virgin Mary church**. A third church to the west of St Saba along the main street is now a school.

In a small garden at the top of the main square opposite Mar Saba church is **Khalil Gibran's house**, the exterior of which has recently been restored, although at the time of writing it was empty inside.

The **Gibran Museum**, with its excellent views out over the Qadisha valley, has the most beautiful setting and brings together an extensive collection of Khalil Gibran's (1883-1931) paintings and drawings, some 440 in all, of which 170 are displayed. Known primarily in the West for his poetry, in particular the book *The Prophet*, his paintings and drawings are in themselves remarkable and certainly merit greater recognition, although some critics point to their uncanny similarity with the works of William Blake. There is also some of his furniture and personal effects on display, while down a flight of stairs leading to one of the caves is his tomb, furnished with some more of his personal effects, including his

The museum has recently been renovated and the collection is well presented, although one could do without the accompanying ephemeral flute music presumably intended to enhance the spiritual atmosphere

Mount Lebanon

Bcharre

▼ To The Cedars & Qadisha Grotto

Virgin Mary

Open Square

Kahlil Gibran's House

School

Mar Saba

To Ehden

To Hasroun, Hadath el-Jobbe, Gibran Museum, Notre Dame de Lourdes Grotto & Phoenician Tomb

N
Not to scale

■ Sleeping	● Eating		
1 Chbat	1 Cafeteria Aryda	3 Makhlouf Elie	5 Shallal
2 Palace	2 Les Copains	4 RTC	6 Snack Mado

bed (!) and a large painted fabric alter-piece of the crucifixion which he was particularly fond of because it depicted Jesus smiling.

The history of the building is varied and interesting. From around the seventh century, followers of Mar Sarkis (St Sergius) lived in the caves here and in time also built a hermitage. In the 15th century a small residence was erected for the Papal Nuncio (representative), which later expanded, along with the caves and hermitage, to become a monastery. In the 16th century it became the summer residence of the French Consul, and then in the 17th century it was donated to the Carmelite monks of the area. The present buildings date from this time and the monastery was then bought by Gibran who intended to use it as a retirement retreat. However, he died shortly afterwards and so it became instead a museum for his works, as well as his tomb. ■ *Open daily 0900-1800 in summer, 0900-1600, closed Mon in winter (mid-Oct to end Apr). Entry LL3,000 (students LL2,000). Postcards, posters and framed prints of Gibran's paintings are on sale, along with a brochure about the museum. Photography prohibited. T/F671137.*

Just behind the museum a footpath leads up a short distance to a small cave and spring dedicated to the Virgin Mary known as **Notre Dame de Lourdes Grotto**. According to legend, the location of the spring was revealed to one of the Carmelite monks in a vision by Mary, who took pity on the monk having to carry water all the way up to the monastery each day in order to irrigate his small vegetable garden.

Further up along the same path is a **Phoenician tomb**, consisting of a large conical obelisk of rock rising up out of the hillside (presumably carved into its present shape), with a chamber cut into its base and compartments inside for four coffins. The structure is thought to date from 750 BC.

Around 2 km out of Bcharre on the road to the Cedars, a signposted turning right leads up to the **Qadisha Grotto**. Follow the road as far as the *l'Aiglion Hotel* (3 km further on), and take the footpath opposite. The narrow path traverses the mountainside for around 1½ km with views down into the Qadisha valley, the last sections passing through tunnels cut into the rock face, before reaching the entrance to the grotto, where there is a simple restaurant/cafetería.

The grotto is the source of the Qadisha River which gushes out of the rock face in a powerful torrent. A natural tunnel carved out by the water extends for around 500 m into the side of the mountain, at the end of which there is a large cave with some stalagmites and stalactites. The grotto itself is not that impressive, and certainly no match for Jeita Grotto, but the walk to reach it is pleasant, and the views from the restaurant area are superb. ■ *Open daily 0800-1700. Closes with the first snows and remains closed until spring (usually Dec-May). Entry LL4,000.*

Sleeping

■ *on maps*
Price codes:
see inside front cover

Price categories are for the peak summer season; when it is quieter it may be possible to negotiate a discount

There are just 2 hotels in Bcharre itself but a number of other places in nearby villages along the north and south sides of the Qadisha valley (see below), and several more at the Cedars. **A** *Chbat*, T671270 or T03-292494, F671237, schbat@cyberia.net.lb Comfortable rooms with heater, phone, attached bath and balconies offering stunning views out over the Qadisha valley. Also some **D** category dorm rooms sleeping 4-6 people (US$20-25 per person; minimum 4 people). Restaurant, bar, swimming pool, sauna/gym and 'nightclub'. Large screen TV/dish in lobby area. Pleasant, well run hotel. The owner, Mr Wadih Chbat, can help organize hiking trips all over the Qadisha valley, and also around the Cedars. **C** *Palace*, T/F671460. Pleasant, spacious rooms with heater and attached bath. 2 rooms with balconies. Common area with open fire and TV/dish. Breakfast served (and other meals if busy). Most of the rooms have now been refurbished, making them good value, although the hotel does not have the same stunning views as the *Chbat*, or the range of facilities.

Moderate As well as the restaurant in the *Chbat* hotel, there are a number of restaurants along the road leading from Bcharre towards Bazaoun/Hasroun and Hadath
el-Jobbe, along the south rim of the Qadisha valley. *Mississippi*, around 1 km beyond
the waterfall, on the right, T671074. Cavernous place with seating on three levels, and
an arrangement of trout pools and mini-waterfalls cascading down beside it. Geared
very much towards dealing with large groups and special occasions (bills itself as a
'casino restaurant'). Lebanese cuisine for around US$10-20 per head. *River Roc*, next
door to the *Mississippi*, T671169 or T03-576996. Open all year round. Pleasant, well run
place with seating indoors or out on terrace with great views. Lebanese cuisine for
around US$10-20 per head. *Al Sabbagh*, on left around 200 m past *River Roc*, T671217
or T03-341754. Modern, comfortably furnished place. Seating indoors only, but with
large windows along whole length of restaurant offering great views. Lebanese cuisine for around US$10-20 per head. *Shallal*, on the main road at the west end of town,
right beside the waterfall. Open air café and restaurant serving standard Lebanese
cuisine (grills, mezze etc) during summer. *Zahret al-Dawalib*, on the left just before
the *Mississippi*, T671265 or T03-927052. Open May-Oct. Friendly place with a pleasant
shaded terrace area. Lebanese cuisine for around US$15-20 per head.

Cheap/seriously cheap *Les Copains*, occupying part of the forecourt of the *Coral*
petrol station, on the main road close to the waterfall at the west end of town. Mostly
pizzas (LL6,000-12,000), as well as burgers, sandwiches etc. Seating out on a small
covered terrace, or takeaway. *Makhlouf Elie*, on the main road, towards the east end
of Bcharre. Small, friendly place with a covered upstairs terrace. Filling meals (shish
tawouk platters, chips, hummus, salads etc) for under US$10. They also serve a full
range of sandwiches etc, and do a great bowl of fuul for under US$5. Tiny kitchen, so
be prepared to wait for your order. *Snack Mado*, on main road, towards west end of
Bcharre. Simple takeaway place, with a couple of tables out on the street. This is the
only place which does that perennial budget staple, falafel sandwiches, as well as the
usual range of other sandwiches and roast chicken.

On the main road at the east end of Bcharre, opposite Snack Mado, is the *Cafeteria*
church. By the junction beyond the Chbat hotel heading up towards the Cedars there is
the *RTC*, a small, fairly trendy café/bar which also serves some food. The *River Roc
Nightclub*, opposite the restaurant of the same name, is open during the summer only,
on Fri and Sat nights only. Entry US$5. There is also a 'nightclub' in the *Chbat* hotel.

There is a **private taxi** company, *Transport Al Arz*, tucked away beside the Mar Saba
church, to the left as you face it, T672166. A taxi up to The Cedars or to Ehden will cost
LL10,000. To Tripoli they quote a fare of LL30,000. **Service taxis** congregate in the
square in front of Mar Saba church. They are most frequent during the peak summer
season, and during the winter skiing season when many people head up to the ski
resort at the Cedars. The fare to Tripoli is LL3,000, and to Beirut LL5,000. **Microbuses**
also go to Tripoli (usually 4 daily) via the south rim of the Qadisha valley, for LL2,500.

Banks There is a bank (as yet without a cash machine) and a money-changer's office on the main
road, towards the east end of Bcharre. **Communications** Internet: there are 2 internet cafés on
the main road in the centre of Bcharre. The first, more or less directly opposite the turning leading
down to the *Palace* hotel, is a slightly run down place given over to video games, billiards and
table football downstairs, with computer games and internet access (LL4,000 per hr, or LL3,000
after 2100) upstairs. The 2nd, a few doors down to the east, is a clean, pleasant café and bar (tea,
coffee, soft drinks, cakes, snacks, beers etc available), charging LL4,000 per hr for internet access.
Post and telephone: the post office and telephone office ('Centrale') share the same building, on
a side street above the main road through Bcharre. National and international calls can be made
from the office of the *Transport Al Arz* taxi company. International calls are made via the internet,
so sometimes the line is very poor, but rates are also very cheap (LL500-1,000 per min).

Exploring the Qadisha valley from Bcharre

Ins & outs   The deep gorge of the Qadisha valley is an excellent place for walking, combining spectacularly beautiful natural scenery with some of the most important religious centres of the Maronite faith. There are numerous paths (some rather precarious) leading down into the valley at various points, and numerous isolated grottoes, hermitages, chapels and monasteries, but you really need a local **guide** to find many of these. If you are interested in spending some time hiking around here, contact Wadih Chbat, the owner of the *Chbat* hotel in Bcharre (see above). He is a mine of useful information about the area, and can put you in touch with local guides. Another person worth contacting is Joe Rahmé (T03-832060, ialine@ifrance.com); as well as being an experienced guide himself, at the time of writing he was hoping to set up an ecotourism project in the Qadisha valley, organizing camping trips and training local youngsters to act as guides. One easily accessible route along the valley floor which takes in two important Maronite monasteries is described here, followed by the main villages and sites along the south and north rim of the Qadisha valley.

Deir Mar Elisha   Heading east out of Bcharre and following the road as it loops round to head
(St Elisée or   west along the south rim of the Qadisha valley, after a little under 3 km there is a
St Eliseus)   right turn which leads steeply down to the floor of the Qadisha valley (a small sign by the turning reads 'Visiter Monastere St Elisée'). Immediately below the road on the way down is the modern monastery of Mar Elisha, which has replaced the much older monastery of the same name near the valley bottom, built into the rock face on the far (north) side of the valley. On the valley floor, by the stream, there are several seasonal cafés and restaurants. Just across the stream, a narrow surfaced road climbs steeply up to the original monastery. It is also possible to reach Deir Mar Elisha directly on foot by heading down the steep valleyside from Bcharre. The path is a little tricky in places, and unfortunately also takes you through some rather unsightly ad hoc rubbish tips.

The history of this monastery has been that of a gradual evolution from an extremely basic of hermits' retreat which originally occupied the caves in the rock face. Written evidence of Deir Mar Elisha as a functioning monastery, and indeed as the seat of a Maronite bishop, goes back to 1315, while artefacts discovered during restoration work in 1991 suggest that it may already have been in existence by the late 11th or early 12th century. Various phases of enlargement, modification and restoration have been identified during the 16th, 17th and early 20th centuries. Of great significance to Maronites is the fact that the Lebanese Maronite Order, the first formal Maronite religious order (initially known as the Aleppines, after its founders, who came from Aleppo), was founded here in 1695 and officially sanctioned by the Patriarch Stephen Douweihy in 1700.

The monastery's current chapel, to the right of the main entrance, was completed in 1835. Just inside the entrance to the monastery, steps lead up to a small grotto which formed part of a much earlier chapel and today houses the tomb of François de Chasteuil, a respected Capuchin, or Franciscan friar, who died here in 1644. The main body of the monastery stretches off to the left of the entrance and consists of a series of monks' cells on two levels. Today the monastery is in effect a museum, with information boards in Arabic, French and English detailing its various special features, and aspects of its history and that of the Maronite church in general. On the lower level you can see a small basin cut into the rock to collect water dripping from the rock face above, a much older entrance to the hermitage, a monk's hiding hole and a water cistern dug into the rock. On the upper level, check out the black stone slab bearing an inscription in Estrangelo, or East Syriac (see page 504), brought by the founders of the Lebanese Maronite Order when they arrived from Aleppo.

Returning to the valley floor, you can follow a good track along the north bank of the Qadisha river to Deir Qannoubin. Although it is possible to drive along it for all but the final couple of kilometres, it is much more rewarding to walk. The valley here is wooded and green, and carpeted with flowers during the spring, with terracing and cultivation wherever possible on the steep slopes, and waterfalls cascading down from the sheer cliffs above. After around 1 km steps on the left lead down to the stream, with a bridge across to a particularly beautiful and secluded restaurant with a terrace area shaded by vines (open only during the summer months). Around 2 km further on, the track forks; bear right here to keep to the upper level. A couple of km further on, the track gives way to a concrete-covered irrigation channel (not wide enough for cars). Follow this, passing a simple café/restaurant, until you reach a clearly sign-posted path off to the left, leading steeply up to Deir Qannoubin. Allow at least 1 hour to walk here from Deir Mar Elisha, or more like 1½-2 hours if you want to take it slowly or stop along the way.

Along the valley floor

This is perhaps one of the oldest monasteries in the Qadisha valley, founded according to some sources by Theodosius the Great in the late fourth century AD. According to Maronite legend, the Mameluke Sultan Barquq (1382-99), having escaped from Kerak castle (in present-day Jordan) where he was imprisoned after being briefly deposed in 1389, came to the Qadisha valley and stayed at Qannoubin, before going on to regain his Sultancy. Impressed by the hospitality he received and the way of life of the people there, he subsequently made substantial endowments, allowing the monastery to be restored after centuries of decay. From 1440 until 1790, Qannoubin was the permanent resi-dence of the Maronite Patriarchs.

Deir Qannoubin
The name Qannoubin is taken from the Greek Koinobion, meaning literally 'community' ('koinos' = common 'bios' = life)

Today it is in fact a working convent run by Antonine sisters, and in its sim-plicity and isolated tranquillity (except perhaps on Sundays during the sum-mer months when it is generally busy with pilgrims) gives a genuine sense of the Maronite monastic/hermitic tradition, without any of the commercializa-tion or crisp restoration to be found elsewhere. The monastery's church, with its barrel-vaulted ceiling, is partly built into the cliff face. On one of the side walls there is a large fresco depicting 'Le Gloire de Marie' (the coronation of the Virgin Mary by the Trinity, witnessed by an assembly of Maronite Patriarchs). The lower parts of the fresco are peeling badly due to dampness, but the upper part is still clearly discernible. Below the fresco there is a small baptismal font set inside a recess. In the semi-domed apse behind the altar there is a fresco depicting Jesus flanked by the Virgin Mary and St Stephen (this being a varia-tion on the traditional formulation of Jesus flanked by Mary and St John the Baptist, known as a *Deisis*), while two niches on either side depict St Joseph holding the baby Jesus and Daniel in the lion's den.

Just to the west of the monastery is the **Chapel of Mar Marina**, containing the tombs of the Maronite Patriarchs of Qannoubin. Born at Qalamoun on the coast just south of Tripoli, St Marina is said to have disguised herself as a monk and lived her life as a hermit at Deir Qannoubin. Finding an abandoned baby, she saved it by breast-feeding it herself (much to the surprise of her fellow monks), and today mothers unable to produce breast milk make pilgrimages to Deir Qannoubin seeking her intervention. It is possible to continue up the side of the valley from here, along a very steep (and in places tricky) path, to arrive eventu-ally in Blawza, but you are advised to take a local guide for this hike.

The south rim of the Qadisha valley

Heading west on the main road running along the south rim of the Qadisha valley, around 1½ km beyond the turning down to Deir Mar Elisha you come to the village of **Bqar Qacha**. Here a left turn is signposted on a large motorway-style overhead signboard to the village of Bqaa Kafra, a steep 2 km climb up a narrow road which zig-zags its way up the mountainside. Unusually, street lights line this road all the way up; at night they are clearly visible across the valley from Bcharre, and look for all the world like a Christmas tree!

Bqaa Kafra
Colour map 5, grid B2

At an altitude of 1,750 m, this tiny village is the highest in Lebanon. Its main claim to fame, however, is as the birthplace of St Charbel (see page 507). The simple wood-beamed house where he was born has been converted into a small chapel, and around this has grown a small monastery which includes a museum with contemporary paintings depicting scenes from his life, as well as statues and busts of the man. The annual feast of St Charbel is celebrated here on the third Sunday in July.

Deir Mar Samaan (St Simon's hermitage)

Back on the main road, some 400 m past the turning for Bqaa Kafra (still in Bqar Qacha village), there is a small blue sign with white writing in Arabic indicating the start of a footpath leading off to the right, down to Deir Mar Samaan. This hermitage is believed to have been originally founded in 1112 by Takla, the daughter of a local priest and later inhabited by St Simon. A concrete path and steps lead steeply down to the cave where St Simon lived as a hermit. The views down into the Qadisha valley are truly spectacular. When you reach a concrete bell-tower you can either continue down to a small shrine below the cave, or follow a narrow ledge and then climb via a metal ladder up into the cave itself. This involves crouching and squeezing through two tiny doorways cut into the rock and is only for the agile or determined. There are candles and offerings in the tiny and surprisingly exposed cave, as well as a book in which the faithful have written prayers. One can only wonder what it must have been like to live in such conditions through winters at this altitude.

Continuing along the main road, a short distance further on there is a cemetery off to the right of the road. A track leads round the side of the cemetery and down past a quarry to a rocky outcrop (in fact the top of the cliff in which St Simon's hermitage is located), from where there are even more spectacular views down into the Qadisha valley.

Bazaoun & Hasroun
Phone code: 06

Around 1 km further along the main road you come to the twin villages of Bazaoun and Hasroun, some 5-6 km from the centre of Bcharre. Both villages, and Hasroun in particular, are very picturesque, much more so than Bcharre in fact. Here the old Ottoman period buildings with their distinctive old stonework, arched windows and pyramid-shaped red-tiled roofs still outnumber the modern concrete buildings. Away from the sometimes frenetic traffic along the main road, there is a relaxed, unhurried atmosphere about the place. Bearing off to the right in the centre of Hasroun to head downhill, you come to the **church of the Virgin Mary** (Eglise Notre Dame). The church features a large clock-tower with a dial giving the date in Arabic below the standard clock face, and a pretty bell tower to the right. In front of it is a fountain and statue of Josephus Simon Assemani, a 17th-century doctor from the village. Further down you come to the tiny **church of St Jude** (Knisset Mar Leba), with steps leading down into the plain, barrel-vaulted interior of undressed stone. A little further on, past a couple of modern buildings, there are further marvellous views into the Qadisha valley, which drops away in a sheer cliff face from here.

Sleeping and eating There are 3 hotels here. In **Bazaoun** (just on the border with Hasroun; **C** *Karam*, on the left (coming from Bcharre), shortly before a signpost reading 'Bienvenue a Hasroun', T/F591189. Open all year. Friendly hotel in a lovely old building. Simple but clean and pleasant rooms with heater, phone, brand new attached bath and balcony. Restaurant downstairs with pleasant terrace (Lebanese food, around US$15 per head). In **Hasroun**; **C** *Green*, above the main village, turn left at crossroads in centre (signposted to 'Gendamerie and Eglise St Anne'), follow road around to right and keep climbing for around 1 km, T/F590180. Open all year. A modern, rather nondescript building. OK rooms with heater, phone and attached bath. Those at rear have balconies offering fantastic views. Restaurant (closed in winter). **D/E** *Palace* (no sign, on left heading west along main road, towards the outskirts of the village), T590115. Open early May to mid/late Nov only. Family-run hotel occupying a beautiful old building with a large garden at the rear and terrace out front. Simple but clean rooms with attached bath and balcony. Excellent value (the cheapest accommodation in the Qadisha valley). Meals served. As well as the hotel restaurants, there are several traditional cafés and simple snack places along or just off the main road through Bazaoun and Hasroun.

Diman

Around 4 km beyond Bazaoun and Hasroun is the village of Diman. There is a large, imposing monastery and church here which today serves as the summer residence of the Maronite Patriarch (in winter he retreats to his main residence at Bkerke, above Jounieh). Dating from 1939 the monastery and church are not particularly beautiful and without a formal introduction you are unlikely to be allowed inside anyway. Just beyond Diman is the tiny village of **Brissat**, with a couple of snack and pizza places, as well as a small new church.

Hadath el-Jobbe

A couple of kilometres beyond Brissat on you come to the village of Hadath el-Jobbe, 13 km from Bcharre. In the centre of the village there is a left turn opposite the police station ('gendarmerie') which is the start of the road leading via the cedars of Arz Tannourine to Tannourine el-Faouqa, from where you can continue on to the ski resort of Laqlouq in Kesrouan region or to the town of Douma (see page 508). Continuing straight along the main road, around 1 km beyond Hadath el-Jobbe, just after a checkpost, there is a hotel on the right, the *Barakat* (closed down at the time of writing). Continuing along this road, if you bear right where it forks near the village of Qnat, this route takes you back towards the coast via Amioun (see above).

The north rim of the Qadisha valley

Hadchit

Heading west out of Bcharre to follow the north rim of the Qadisha valley, you come first to the village of Hadchit (3 km). Although signposted on the main road, the heart of the old village is off to the left (south) of the road. On the way down to the village square you pass the **church of St Sarkis**, with part of a Roman column still standing outside. In the square itself is the **church of St Raymond**, with a Roman statue outside, minus its head and arms. Previously this stood inside the church, until it was condemned as a pagan idol and its head and arms smashed off before being removed. The feast of St Raymond is celebrated each year in the village from the last Sunday in August to the first Sunday in September. Nearby is the smaller **church of the Virgin Mary**. A difficult path (you really need a local guide for this) descends steeply from Hadchit down to the grotto of **Deir es-Salib** (monastery of the cross), a tiny monastery built into caves in the side of the cliff face, although today in an advanced state of ruin. Deir es-Salib can also be reached by a path leading up from the track along the floor of the valley (see above), but again you really

Mount Lebanon

need a local guide to find it. There are the remains of numerous other hermitages, chapels and tiny monasteries in the immediate vicinity.

Blawza &
Hawqa
Phone code: 06

Returning to the main road and continuing west, 2 km further on you pass through the village of Blawza, where there is *La Luna* restaurant (T617440) offering Lebanese, Italian and Chinese cuisine for around US$15-20 per head. A path descends from Blawza to Dier Qannoubin, down in the Qadisha valley (see above). A little over 1 km further on there is a left turn signposted for 'Hawka'. This road leads through the village of Hawqa, from where you can carry on down to the monastery Deir Mar Antonios Qozhaya (5 km) on a winding, at times almost precarious, road with dramatic views down into the Qadisha valley. The more commonly used approach to the monastery is via a turning off the main road beyond Ehden leading down towards Amioun (see below). Note that it is not possible to do a loop, descending by one road and leaving by the other, as the monastery itself blocks access between the two roads. A steep footpath leads down from Hawqa to **Saydet Hawqa** (Our Lady of Hawqa), consisting of a small chapel and monks' cells built into a shallow cave. On 14 August each year a high mass is celebrated in the chapel, during the feast of the Assumption of the Virgin.

Bané &
Kfar Sghab

Beyond the turning for Hawqa, the main road veers northeast, following a side valley which drains into the Qadisha valley and passing through the villages of Bané and Kfar Sghab. Many of the inhabitants of these villages (along with those of Blawza and Hadchit) emigrated to Australia during the civil war, the majority of them settling in Sydney. During the summer many of them return home to visit relatives, and you can hear many a thick Australian accent twanging around.

Ehden إهدن

Phone code: 06
Colour map 5, grid B2

The large village of Ehden is popular as a summer resort and famous for its springside restaurants up on the hillside to the northeast of the main town (see below). The old village (at the east end of town) is quite picturesque, while extending to the west along the main road (which widens out to a two-lane affair) is some modern development. To the right of the main road as you enter the old village coming from Bcharre is a pleasant square with a fountain in the centre and a number of cafés and small restaurants, all thronging with people on summer evenings.

Ehden's other claim to fame is as the summer residence of the Franjieh family. The summer 'palace' of Suleiman Franjieh, president of Lebanon from 1970 to 1976, is near the roundabout at the far western end of town. Today it is occupied by his grandson, Robert Franjieh, his son Tony having been murdered in 1978 by gunmen of Gemayal's rival Phalange militia, along with his wife and daughter and 32 of his supporters. The Mouawad family also have a summer residence in Ehden; René Mouawad was elected president in 1989 but survived just 16 days before being blown up by a car bomb in West Beirut.

Statue of
Youssuf Bey
Karam and St
George's church

Opposite the square in the centre of the old part of Ehden, a signpost points up to the statue of Youssuf (Joseph) Bey Karam (1823-89), a Maronite hero of the struggle against Ottoman rule in Lebanon who drew wide support for his cause from the Greek Orthodox, Sunni and Shi'ite communities as well as fellow Maronites. Born in Ehden, he was finally defeated and driven into exile after leading rebellions against the Ottomans in 1864 and 1867. The statue, depicting him riding proudly into battle on horseback, stands in front of **St George's**

church, in which there is a glass-topped mausoleum containing Karam's mummified body. Many of the families in this area bear the surname Karam, a clan which rose to importance in the region long before Joseph Bey Karam's time.

High up on the hillside to the northwest of Ehden, dominating the skyline, is the large, modernistic church of Saydet el-Hosn (Our Lady of the Castle). Next to it, and completely dwarfed by it, is a much smaller and older church of the same name, which was probably originally built on the site of a Roman fortress (hence the name). Note the small face (said to be that of Jesus) carefully carved into a stone in one corner of the church exterior. On the way up to Saydet el-Hosn, you pass a **statue of Stephen Douweihy**, Maronite Patriarch from 1670-1704, who was responsible for many of the important reforms of the Maronite church during this period and who acquired a reputation for his piety and dedication. Another interesting church is that of St Mema, on the main road as you head out of Ehden towards Bcharre, which dates back to 749 AD.

Saydet el-Hosn & St Mema

Covering approximately 1,000 ha of mountain terrain above Ehden, the Horsh Ehden Nature Reserve was established in 1991 by the Friends of Horsh Ehden in an attempt to preserve the area's unique natural forest habitat. Nearly half the reserve is forest-clad, with large stands of Lebanese cedars (accounting for 20% of Lebanon's remaining cedar forests), as well as some 39 other species of trees. Horsh Ehden is also home to a wide variety of mammals, including wolves, wildcats and striped hyenas, as well as weasels, badgers, hares, hedgehogs and porcupine. Birds to be seen here include the Imperial eagle, Bonnelli's eagle and the globally threatened cornrake.

Horsh Ehden Nature Reserve
Colour map 5, grid B2

In all, more than 1,000 species of plants have been identified here, of which more than 100 are endemic to Lebanon, while 10 are endemic to the reserve

Marked hiking and 4WD trails have been established through the reserve's often dramatically beautiful scenery (there are entrances to the reserve above the *Masters* hotel and beyond Ehden's springside restaurants). As well as working to raise public awareness on conservation issues and overseeing research and monitoring projects, the Friends of Horsh Ehden can also organize guided tours with local rangers. ■ *There is an office for the reserve on the road above the* Masters *hotel (this road also takes you up to Saydet el-Hosn by an alternative route), or you can contact the reserve manager, Sarkis Kawajah, by email; fohe@cyberia.net.lb*

A *Ehden Country Club* (signposted off main road heading west out of Ehden), T/F560561, or T03-252700 ehdencc@sodetel.net.lb Open all year (room rates **B** category during winter). Membership-based luxurious modern complex geared primarily towards families, many of whom buy or rent apartments on a long term basis, but also catering for foreign tourists on a short stay basis. Comfortable rooms with heater, phone, kitchenette and attached bath. Restaurant, bar and conference facilities. Leisure facilities include a large outdoor swimming pool, tennis, squash, sauna, and health centre. **B** *Masters*, on mountainside around 2 km above Ehden (clearly signposted from the roundabout at the west end of town), T561052 or T03-727711, F561054. Open all year. Comfortable, pleasantly furnished rooms with heater, TV/dish, phone, attached bath and balcony (stunning views all the way down to Tripoli and the Mediterranean, and north into Syria). Restaurant, bar, tennis, horse riding and baby-ski-lift/beginners slope. Recently opened, well run hotel. Fantastic location. Good value. **C** *Belmont* (near roundabout at west end of town), T560102. Open all year. Modern hotel offering comfortable rooms with heater, phone and attached bath. Some rooms with balcony. **C** *Grand Hotel Abchi* (above main road towards west end of town; impossible to miss), T561101 or T03-300948, F561103, www.abchihotel.cm Open all year (restaurant closed in winter). Large imposing building in traditional style with futuristic UFO-shaped restaurant/nightclub.

Sleeping
Price categories are for the peak summer season (approximately early Jul-end Sep, when advanced booking is usually necessary). Discounts can generally be negotiated out of season

Mount Lebanon

Comfortable recently refurbished rooms with heater, TV/dish, phone, attached bath and balcony (wonderful views). Swimming pool. **C/D** *Provençal*, in old village square. Open summer (Jun-Oct) only. Simple but pleasant rooms with heater and attached bath. Geared mainly towards families.

Eating & nightlife

To reach Ehden's famous springside restaurants (open in the summer only), take the turning opposite the small church of St Mema and bear right around 200 m further on, at a mini-roundabout with a church beside it. Follow this road for around 1½ km to the point where the Nebaa Mar Sarkis spring emerges from the hillside. Here there are 3 large restaurants, the *Firdous*, *Shafak* and *Asmer*, and a little further on the *Al Arz*, each with shaded terraces and channels carrying water from the springs. All specialize in Lebanese cuisine, in particular lavish mezze spreads (from around US$15-20 per head), and there is often live entertainment on summer evenings.

In the centre of the modern part of Ehden, above the main road, is *El Hatillo*, (coming from Bcharre, go sharp right at the mini-roundabout at the western end of town and it is on the left after 400 m), T560401. This is a very smart, recently opened place serving mostly Italian food, but also with some Asian (Chinese, Thai, Japanese and Korean), as well as Venezuelan, dishes. From around US$15-20 per head.

In the old village square, below the *Provençal* hotel, is the *Zaghloul*. This restaurant has a large indoor section, as well as a few tables out on the square. Lebanese cuisine, plus pizzas, steaks etc. From around US$10 per head. There are several other cafés/restaurants in the square, including *Best Corner*, *Drop In* and *Gypsy*, as well as a couple of patisseries serving Arabic sweets.

The *Grand Hotel Abchi* has its own nightclub, the *Midnight*. Heading east out of Ehden on the road to Bcharre, *Magnum* nightclub has the best reputation in the area, attracting large crowds in the summer. It is in *La Marie* hotel (which has gone rather downhill in recent years and is in need of refurbishment). Open Fri and Sat nights only. Entry US$10 (includes 1 drink). T560108 or T03-239333 for further info. Further along the road towards Bcharre is the *Au Pere Loup* (a restaurant and nightclub) and the *Titanic* (just a nightclub).

Transport

During the summer there are **service taxis** which operate between Tripoli and Ehden, and between Ehden and Bcharre. However, most people coming up here have their own transport; if you don't, hitching is probably your best option.

Ehden to Deir Mar Antonios Qozhaya

Continuing west out of Ehden along the main road, 2 km beyond the roundabout at the west end of town, you come to a left turn (marked by a statue of St Charbel in the centre of the junction), the start of the road leading down towards the coast via Amioun. Taking this left turn, after just under 4 km you come to a left turn signposted for 'Couvent St Antoine Kosbaiya'; take this turn to get to Deir Mar Antonios Qozhaya (Monastery of St Anthony Qozhaya).

Deir Mar Antonios Qozhaya ديـر مـارا نطنيوس قزحيّا

Built into the side of a cliff face in the same way as Deir Mar Elisha, this is one of the largest monasteries in the Qadisha valley. First founded as a monastery in the 10th or 11th century, it is famous for having established the first known printing press in the Middle East, during the late 16th century. Today the monastery is a popular pilgrimage site, though somewhat commercialized and lacking entirely the sense of isolation found at Qannoubin. Built up against the cliff face along one side of a large courtyard is the façade of the **church**. Its doorway is beautifully decorated with alternating bands of stone and intricate carved patterns. Above is a long row of small arched windows, again intricately decorated, and a triple bell tower. Inside, the vaulted stonework of the church blends in with the natural rock of the cave behind. By the entrance to the main courtyard and church there is a large cave, the **grotto of St Anthony**, where you can see the chains and shackles used to restrain the insane, who were brought here in the belief that they would be cured by the saint.

Below the courtyard and church there is a large souvenir shop selling all sorts of tacky religious souvenirs. This leads through to a **museum** displaying a number of old manuscripts (including a Syriac-Arabic dictionary dating from 1702 and a Latin-Arabic dictionary dating from 1639), various sacred relics and items of religious paraphernalia, and a printing press imported from Edinburgh (although itself dating from 1609, this press was only purchased during the 19th century, replacing earlier ones). ■ *Open daily 0930-1930 in summer, 0930-1730 in winter. Entry free. If you find the museum closed during these times, ask at the monastery and someone will open it up for you.*

The Cedars (Al Arz) الأرز

From Bcharre, a road snakes its way up the mountainside to a plateau surrounded by an amphitheatre of mountains, known as the Cedars, or *al-Arz* in Arabic. On the way up, you can either turn sharp right to go via the *l'Aiglion* hotel, or else keep going straight; both roads join up at top. You come first to the ski resort (8 km from Bcharre), with various hotels, restaurants and chalet complexes dotted around. Further up, beyond the ski resort, is the stand of cedars itself. If you are lucky, you may find a service taxi heading up here from Bcharre (particularly during the skiing season), but don't count on it. A private taxi from Bcharre to the Cedars costs around LL10,000. Without your own transport, the only other option is to hitch (anyone with room will usually stop).

Ins & outs
Phone code: 06
Colour map 5, grid B2

When the French established an army skiing school here in the 1930s, the Cedars became the first of Lebanon's ski resorts. Today it is the second most popular ski resort after Faraya Mazaar. Although not as developed, its higher altitude (maximum 2,800 m) means that the season generally runs for slightly longer (mid-November to late April). Being a considerable distance from Beirut, it also has the largest selection of accommodation of all the resorts. As well as the main **Pic de Dames** chairlift which reaches 2,800 m, there are now 6 ski-lifts and 4 baby-lifts. Ski equipment is available for hire from a number of the hotels, while the *Tony Arida Centre* has its own skiing school with professional instructors. There is a duty doctor at the resort during the season and Red Cross teams in attendance on weekends. The main road up to the resort (via Amioun, Hadath el-Jobbe and Bcharre) is kept open throughout the season. The Cedars is also trying to market itself as a summer resort, with many of the hotels offering mountain bikes for hire. In addition, this is one of the main locations where you can learn to paraglide during the summer (see page 63).

The ski resort
The excellent slopes and high quality of the snow have given the Cedars something of a reputation as a resort for 'serious' skiers

The resort tends to get extremely busy on weekends, and this is also when ski passes are most expensive

Today all that remains of the once extensive forests which gave the area its name is a small, somewhat forlorn stand of around 300 cedars in a landscape otherwise practically bereft of any trees. Although at first sight something of a disappointment, this stand nevertheless contains some of the oldest and largest cedar trees in Lebanon, rising to a height of 35 m and estimated to be between 1,000-1,500 (or by some accounts up to 2000) years old. The steady depletion of Mount Lebanon's cedar forests has taken place over literally thousands of years, but it was only by the mid-19th century it began to dawn on the local people that they would soon disappear altogether. The Maronite Patriarchs of Bcharre placed them under their personal protection, building a small chapel in the midst of the stand in 1843 and forbidding any further felling of

The cedar trees

Mount Lebanon

The Cedars of the Lord

The Lebanese Cedar (Cedrus libani) is the country's national symbol, and a source of great pride amongst the Lebanese. Once, much of the Lebanon mountain range was clad in rich cedar forests (conservative estimates suggest that these would have covered as much as 80,000 ha) but heir exploitation goes back just about as far as recorded history.

According to legend, Gilgamesh, the third millenium BC king of Uruk in southern Mesopotamia, came to Lebanon to cut down cedars for his city. Inscriptions discovered at Mari in Syria relate how the Amorite king Yakhdun Lim did likewise in the second millenium BC, while the campaign history of Tiglath Pilser I, the late second millenium BC Assyrian king, tell a similar story. Similarly there are numerous references in the Bible to the exploitation of Lebanon's cedar forests by the Phoenicians of Tyre, Sidon and Byblos, both for the building of ships and for export to Egypt and Israel. Most famously, the Bible recounts how King Solomon's temple in Jerusalem was built of cedarwood beams, and panelled throughout with cedar, "So give orders that cedars of Lebanon be cut for me... So Solomon built the temple and completed it... The inside of the temple was cedar, carved with gourds and open flowers. Everything was cedar; no stone was to be seen." (1 Kings 5; 6, 9, 1 Kings 6; 14, 18)

The exploitation continued more or less unabated through the Roman, Byzantine and Islamic periods, right up until the trees most recently felled by the Ottomans for use as sleepers in the building of the Hejaz railway, and during the First World War as fuel on the trains. Today, despite attempts to regenerate the remaining stands of

cedars through planting schemes, there is evidence to suggest that they are under serious stress from pollution, soil erosion and infection, and that their ability to survive naturally in such small numbers is debatable.

Locally the cedars are known as Al Arz al-Rab (The Cedars of the Lord), and numerous biblical references, in places all too poignantly relevant to Lebanon's present environmental predicament, make it clear that the tree had enormous symbolic significance. In Ezekiel 31, God warns the Egyptians against their arrogance, reminding them of the fate of Assyria and comparing its grandeur to that of the cedar, "Son of man, say to the Pharaoh king of Egypt and to his hordes; 'Who can be compared with you in majesty? Consider Assyria, once a cedar in Lebanon, with beautiful branches overshadowing the forest; it towered on high, its top above the thick foliage... All the birds in the air nested in its boughs, all the beasts of the field gave birth under its branches; all the great nations lived in its shade... I made it beautiful with abundant branches, the envy of the trees of Eden in the garden of God... Because it towered on high, lifting its top above the thick foliage, and because it was proud of its height, I handed it over to the ruler of the nations, for him to deal with according to its wickedness. I cast it aside, and the most ruthless of foreign nations cut it down and left it. Its boughs fell on the mountains and in all the valleys; its branches lay broken in all the ravines of the land... Because of it I clothed Lebanon in gloom, and all the trees of the field withered away." (Ezekiel 31: 2-3, 6, 9, 10-12, 15)

the trees. In 1876 Queen Victoria financed the building of a protective wall around the cedars, important for keeping out grazing goats. Today, the **Friends of the Cedars' Committee at Bcharre** has taken over responsibility for protecting them, repairing the enclosure wall and marking out a path through the trees. In addition there are various projects to carry out further research into the trees and to plant new stands in the surrounding areas. There are numerous souvenir shops around the entrance to the enclosure selling all kinds of cedar wood trinkets (carved from naturally fallen timber only), as well as a number of cafés and snack places.

Note that many of the hotels offer a choice of full/half board, B&B or room only, while some also include the cost of ski equipment etc; check in advance what is included. **A** *L'Auberge des Cedres*, T03-633503. Reasonably comfortable (though a little gloomy) suites (1-3 bedrooms, sleeping 2-6 people) with common siting area, heater, phone and attached bath. Restaurant and bar. All very nice and cosy downstairs, but rooms are little pricy for what you get. **A/B** *Alpine*, T671057 or T03-213102. Pleasant, cosy hotel with a friendly atmosphere. Comfortable rooms with heater, TV/dish and attached bath. Restaurant (Lebanese and Italian cuisine). Ski hire, as well as various activities during the summer (early May to end Oct), including horse riding, ATVs, mountain biking and paragliding (this hotel is one base for the *Thermique School of Paragliding*; see 'Sports and special interest travel' in Essentials, page 62). **A/B** *St Bernard*, T03-289600. A very comfortable and plush hotel above the main village and cedars. Rooms with heater, TV/dish, phone, attached bath and balconies offering lovely views (suites also have open fireplace). Restaurant and bar. Ski hire and mountain bikes. **A/B** *Tony Arida Centre*, T/F678198, aridac@hotmail.com   Selection of cosy chalets sleeping up to 8 people. All with common siting area (TV/dish, phone and open fire), kitchenette (gas hob, sink, fridge/freezer), bedrooms (most with 2 doubles plus 1 with bunkbeds for 4 people), bathroom (most with 2) and balcony. Across the road is simpler place where groups of 6 or more can sleep for US$10 per head (minimum charge US$100 on weekends). Restaurant (Lebanese and European cuisine), nightclub, ski shop and rental, own baby-lift/beginners slope and ski instructors. Owned by Tony Arida, Lebanon's first qualified ski instructor and a real character, with a great repetoire of conjuring tricks.

B *Mon Refuge*, T03-734312. Choice of standard double rooms with heater, phone and attached bath, or chalets sleeping up to 6 people (common sitting area with open fire etc). Large restaurant (French and Lebanese cuisine) and bar. Pleasantly furnished common areas (wood panelling, log fires). Friendly, homely hotel run by Sabah Succar, ex-Lebanese skiing champion. **C** *L'Aiglion*, around 2 km before you reach the Cedars, opposite the track leading to the Qadish Grotto (see under Bcharre Sights, above), T671529 or T03-684998. OK rooms with heater and attached bath. Some rooms with TV and 2 rooms with really stunning views. Restaurant. Overall, a little run down and in need of refurbishment. **C** *Cortina*, T678061. Simple rooms with heater, attached bath and balcony. Restaurant. Nice open fire in lobby, but overall a little run down and overpriced. **D** *Rancho Grande*, T671501. Small, simple rooms with heater and attached bath. Restaurant and bar (open fire in centre). The cheapest hotel here, but looking distinctly run down and desperately in need of refurbishment.

As well as the hotel restaurants, there are several snack bars and restaurants around the main village and near the foot of the slopes, although most of them are only open during the winter skiing season. One good independent restaurant/bar which stays open all year is *Le Pichet*. Open daily 0800-late. Breakfast options range from bacon and eggs (LL6000) to fuul (LL4,000), while for lunch and dinner there is a varied menu of mostly European dishes (around US$10-20 per head; plat de jour on weekends good value at around LL12,000), or cheaper snacks (sandwiches, burgers etc). In the *Tony Arida Centre*, *La Casa* is a large nightclub which is popular during the summer (Sat nights only; entry US$10; drinks US$7).

The Cedars to Baalbek

From the Cedars a road continues up the mountainside, crosses the high ridges of the Lebanon mountain range and descends into the Bekaa valley beyond before arriving in Baalbek. Check that it is open before you attempt it, from around late October to late May it is usually blocked by snow. Once open, the road is reasonably good, though pot-holed in places, particularly on the far side.

Sleeping
Price categories are for the winter skiing season; outside this period there are substantial discounts

Eating & nightlife

Mount Lebanon

Qornet
es-Saouda
Colour map 5, grid B2

It is perhaps typical of
the car-obsessed
Lebanese that they
should have built a
motorable track to the
summit of their highest
mountain. For walkers
there are a number of
other routes to the
summit, ask in Bcharre
or the Cedars for a guide

On the way up, around 7 km from the stand of cedar trees, a narrow side road (marked by a large overhead sign with Arabic writing and Coca Cola logos) branches off to the left at a point where the main road hairpins sharply round to the right. Taking this side road, after 2½ km a rough jeep track branches off to the left. This jeep track climbs up to the summit of Qornet es-Saouda (3,083 m). In summer it is passable in a four-wheel drive almost all the way.

Continuing along the metalled road, it climbs up to a ridge before descending to **Ouyoun Orogosh**, a series of small lakes fed by a spring and set in a wide depression. A popular spot for outings and picnics, there are now several restaurants dotted around the edges of the lakes. From here, the metalled road climbs up past a church with a small chapel beside it and over the lip of the depression, winding its way through bare hills before descending through scattered orchards to a small, newly built church dedicated to St Charbel.

Down into the
Bekaa valley

Continuing along the main road from the turning for Qornet es-Saouda and Ouyoun Orogosh, after another couple of kilometres of climbing you reach the watershed of the Lebanon mountain range. Here, once again, there are spectacular views down into the Bekaa valley, its patchwork landscape of orchards and farmland spread out before you, with the bare mountains of the Anti-Lebanon range beyond. From here it is a long, sweeping descent through numerous hairpins, down to **Ainata** (15 km from the summit), a small village with a couple of simple restaurants offering snacks and tea/coffee etc. Leaving Ainata, you pass through a Syrian army checkpoint, and then 3 km beyond this there is a sharp right turn for Yammouné (see page 598). Continuing straight, you pass through a couple of tiny villages, and then through the sprawling village of **Deir al-Ahmar** overlooking the flat plain of the Bekaa. Just beyond the village you pass through a second Syrian army checkpoint and then after a further 5 km, at yet another checkpoint, fork left for Baalbek (signposted). Follow this road across the flat plain, going straight over a crossroads (15 km from Deir el-Ahmar; right for Zahle), to arrive in the centre of Baalbek (see page 589).

Sir ed-Danniyé and Sfiré

Phone code: 06
Colour map 5, grid A2

Up in the mountains due east of Tripoli is the town of Sir ed-Danniyé, a popular summer resort amongst Tripolitians. Beyond it are the isolated ruins of a Roman temple at Sfiré. Both the summer resort and the Roman temple ruins command spectacular views across the valleys to the north, while their relative proximity to Tripoli makes them an attractive option as a day-trip (or possibly half-day excursion) from the city.

Getting there
from Tripoli

Head north out of the centre of Tripoli along Rue Sheikh Bechara el-Khoury (as if to join the coast road heading northeast to the Syrian border). Go straight across the first large roundabout you come to and then, 3 km from the centre, bear sharp right at a junction (at the time of writing a new section of flyover was under construction here; the road layout around here may be rather different when it is completed). The road climbs through Tripoli's poor, ramshackle eastern suburbs. A little further on, turn left where the road goes sharply round to the right, and then soon after, turn right and then left at a T-junction to join the road heading up towards Sir ed-Danniyé (ask directions through this section as it is very confusing). The road climbs through several small villages which all more or less merge into each other, before passing through **Kfar Habou** (13 km from Tripoli; follow the main road round to the left here). Bear right in **Bakhoun** (7 km further on), a sizeable village with lots of high-rise construction, continuing through **Haqel Azzine** and **Aassoun**. Again, these villages all merge with each other, but now it is the dramatic scenery of precipitous gorges, forest-clad mountainsides and terraced valleys which begins to dominate. Soon after you arrive in the centre of Sir ed-Danniyé (27 km from Tripoli).

The main attraction of this resort is its pleasant climate in summer, although at just 900 m in altitude, at least two of the hotels stay open throughout the year, and it is equally beautiful in spring and autumn. There are plenty of possibilities for walking in the area, while in the village itself there are several pleasant cafés and restaurants, some of them built around the spring-fed streams which cascade down from the mountains. Despite all the ugly new concrete construction springing up all over the place, the village is still a very pleasant place to stay and the views out across the valley are really stunning.

Sir ed-Danniyé (Sir)
سير الضّنّية

B/C *Syr Palace*, on the main street, T490202, F490065. This is the best hotel in Sir, occupying a beautiful, grand old building dating from 1934. Simple but clean rooms with attached bath (those at the back have balconies and the full benefit of the views). Restaurant (and large open terrace, again with great views, in summer). Room prices appear to be flexible, try bargaining. **C** *Peace*, on main street opposite the *Syr Palace*, T490360. A modern, rather characterless building without the views. Small, simple rooms, some with attached bath and balcony. Restaurant. Friendly, but no English spoken here. The other 2 hotels here, the *Fathat* and the *Grand*, were both closed when this researcher visited. The former occupies a nice old building but looked rather run down and basic, while the latter is more modern and appeared in better condition.

Sleeping

Service taxis run frequently from Tripoli in the summer, but less so in spring and autumn, and rarely in winter. The one-way fare should be around LL4,000. To continue on to Sfiré you will need to hire the taxi on a private basis.

Transport

Take the left turn immediately beyond the *Syr Palace* hotel to head downhill, keeping the *Grand* hotel on your right. Continue to descend through the village of **Qattine**, and after just under 5 km (at a sign indicating the start of **Hazmiye** village) bear right at a junction. The narrow road winds its way through **Ain et-Tine** and **Beit el-Faqs**, before arriving in Sfiré (8 km from Sir ed-Danniyé).

Sfiré
صفير

Continue climbing up through the village, and after a couple more kilometres, take a small left turn to reach the remains of a **Roman temple**, up above the road (the turning is not at all obvious, so ask around). Known locally as *Qalat al-Hosn* (literally 'Castle of the Citadel'), what survives of this temple is the *cella*, a simple, largely unadorned structure built of hefty limestone blocks, with no evidence of a surrounding colonnade. In the corners either side of the main portal, steps lead up within the walls to what would have been a roof terrace. Inside, a set of steps at the rear lead up to a raised platform with a barrel-vaulted chamber below. Much of the courtyard in which the *cella* stands is still paved, and the whole site is strewn with rubble and architectural fragments. In front of the *cella* are the remains of a subsidiary building, and to the right another one with four columns still standing. Note the Greek inscription on the outside wall of the *cella*. High up on the adjacent hillside are the ruins of another smaller temple. A good path continues on to the top, from where there are really spectacular panoramic views on a clear day.

NB Although most maps suggest that you can continue northeast from Sfiré to join the road between Hermel and Qoubaiyat, or else branch off to the northwest to rejoin the coast road at Aabdé, in the former case the road deteriorates to

Mount Lebanon

an extremely rough jeep track for which a 4WD and considerable off-road experience is necessary, while in the latter case the road disappears altogether.

The Akkar عكّار

In the extreme north of Lebanon, the Akkar region consists both of the northernmost reaches of the Lebanon mountains (the Jebel Akkar), which stretch in an arc to the northeast of Tripoli, and the coastal plain, which broadens out to the north of Tripoli to form a triangle between the coast and the line of the Jebel Akkar, extending also north into Syria. In all its isolated and largely untouched beauty, the Jebel Akkar, like the extreme south, is today one of the least developed areas of Lebanon. The region as a whole is home to a mix of Sunnis, Maronites and Greek Orthodox, and in the extreme northwest, to small communities of Turkomans. The Akkar Turkomans, who are unique in having retained their original language in some villages such as Kouachra to the northeast of Qoubaiyat, are thought to have arrived in Lebanon later than their counterparts in the Kesrouan, being settled there by the early Ottomans, possibly during the rule of Sultan Selim I (1512-20).

Northeast from Tripoli Head north out of the centre of Tripoli on Rue Sheikh Bechara el-Khoury to join the coast road leading northeast towards Syria. After around 7 km, a smaller road forks off to the left from the main dual carriageway; this road follows the coastline more closely before rejoining the main road at Aabdé. Keeping straight along the dual carriageway, it is 17 km from the centre of Tripoli to Aabdé. Bear right at the junction here and follow this road for a further 10 km to arrive in **Halba**, a sizeable town with a few simple restaurants and a service taxi stand. Rather bizarrely, the crossroads in the centre of the town is marked by a statue of Hafez al-Assad, the former president of Syria.

Tell Arqa
Colour map 5, grid A2 Shortly before arriving in Halba, the road passes close to Tell Arqa, the site of the Roman city of *Arca Caesarea* ('Caesarea in Lebanon') and birthplace of Septimus Severus, emperor from 222-35 AD. Excavations here have revealed evidence of settlement dating back as far as the Neolithic period (7500 BC-4500 BC), and references to Arqa appear in the Tell Amarna tablets of Egypt and Assyrian texts, as well as in the Bible. During the 11th century Arqa boasted a prosperous fortified town which held out against the Crusaders in 1099, though it later fell to them in 1109 and was subsequently controlled by the Templars before being recaptured by Baibars in 1266. The scattered architectural fragments from the various periods of occupation can be seen all around the tell, including sections of pink granite columns, similar to those found at Baalbek. From the top of the tell there are panoramic views of the plains to the north, while to the south the low hills climb steadily up towards the high peaks of Mount Lebanon.

Halba to Akkar el-Atiqa From Halba you can continue along the main road, which runs in an arc along the northernmost edges of the Jebel Akkar to reach Qoubaiyat (to do this, turn left at the crossroads in the centre of town marked by the statue of Assad). The more interesting route, however, is to turn right at the crossroads to follow a road which winds its way through the Jebel Akkar to Qoubaiyat, passing en route Akkar el-Atiqa.

Taking this turning, the road climbs up into the mountains, through the small village of Aadbel and past a major fork off to the left (7 km from Halba; go straight on here), to arrive in the village of Gebrayel (around 11 km from

Halba). Leaving the village, follow the road round to the left where there is a fork to the right signposted 'Welcome to Rahbe', to arrive in Tekrit village, 2 km beyond the fork. Around 1 km further on, entering the village of Beit Mellat, bear right where the road forks. In Aayoun village, 1 km further on again, bear right at a fork to keep to the main road (left signposted to 'Chataha' and 'Baino'). Five hundred metres beyond this fork, just after a sign announcing the start of Bezbina village, turn left at a crossroads. Go straight over a small crossroads and sign announcing Al Borj village, and around 200 m beyond this, follow the road round to the right in the centre of the village. Over the next couple of kilometres, bear right wherever the road forks ambiguously. The road climbs steeply, passing through the sprawling village of Dawra, and then descends to the floor of a picturesque sidevalley and a bridge across a stream (around 7 km from Al Borj village). Where the road crosses the stream, if you look up the sidevalley, you can glimpse the ruins of Akkar castle on a rocky spur. From the stream and bridge it is a couple of kilometres up into the centre of Akkar el-Atiqa.

Akkar el-Atiqa ('Old Akkar') عكار العتيقة

The main point of interest here is not Akkar el-Atiqa itself (a sizeable though essentially unremarkable village), but the strikingly situated ruins of **Akkar castle** nearby. Said to have been built in the late 10th century by Mouhriz Ibn Akkar, a local chieftain, the castle was subsequently controlled first by the Fatimids of Egypt, and then by the Seljuk Turks, before being handed over to the Crusaders as part of a treaty agreement following their capture of Tripoli in 1109. Briefly taken by Nur ud-Din, it was recaptured by the Crusaders in 1170 and used as a base from which to make raids on the main route between Homs and Baalbek. The Crusaders were finally driven out by Baibars, who laid siege to it in 1271, immediately after taking Krak des Chevaliers. It was not until the 17th century that the Druze emir, Fakhr ud-Din II Maan, reduced it to something approaching its present state of ruin. According to some sources he used its stones in the building of his own palace at Beit ed-Dine.

Heading up the hill from the bridge and stream at the bottom of the side valley below Akkar el-Atiqa, after 500 m you pass a small fork off to the left (this is the road to Qoubaiyat, see below). Just under 1 km further on, at a point where the road swings round sharply to the left (by a small sign for 'Agfa Studio Hady'), a concrete driveway leads down steeply to the right past a number of houses before turning into a footpath. Follow this path, which descends to the level of the stream, where you can cross easily (providing it is not swollen with rains) and then follow shepherds' paths steeply up to the castle ruins. The castle occupies a strategic spur between twin sidevalleys which drain down from the mountains to the south before joining just below it. Although now in an advanced state of ruin, its basic outline, defined by the topography of the spur, is still clearly discernible, with sections of the defensive walls still standing, along with traces of towers and vaulted rooms. At its southernmost end, where it was most vunerable to attack from the main shoulder of the mountain above, is the castle's main keep and best preserved feature.

Taking the fork for Qoubaiyat, this road was being widened and resurfaced at the time of writing. It winds its way through the mountains before descending to Qoubaiyat, 10 km further on. Around 3 km before reaching Qoubaiyat, you pass a brand-new hospital complex on the left, the Hopital Notre Dame De La Paix Des Soeurs Antonines. Bear left at a fork 2 km further on to reach the centre of Qoubaiyat.

Akkar el-Atiqa to Qoubaiyat

Qoubaiyat قبيّات

Colour map 5, grid A3 Qoubaiyat is the largest town and administrative centre of the Akkar region. Standing at the foot of the northernmost reaches of the Lebanon mountain range, this predominantly Maronite town flourished during the Ottoman period as a centre of silk manufacture. Today the town still has a quietly affluent air about it, with several pizza restaurants, smart cafés and pattisseries along the main road, although there is no hotel here.

St Charlita Just over 3 km out of Qoubaiyat there is an interesting chapel dedicated to St Charlita. Head south out of town along the main road and fork right by the post and telephone office with its distinctive communications mast (signposted 'Couvent St Charlita). Turn right immediately after, past a Carmelite monastery and school, and then take a small left turn (around 600 m from the post and telephone office; signposted in Arabic only). This narrow road runs along a valley of fir trees and orchards, with the chapel coming into view off to the left after a couple of kilometres. Continue past it and then take the small turning which doubles back to reach it.

The chapel has been restored from a state of near complete ruin (the photos inside give an idea of the work that has been done). It consists of a small square building with a bell-tower in one corner and a vaulted interior. Most striking, however, are some of the huge stone blocks from which it is built, clearly of Roman or Greek (or perhaps even Phoenician) origin. The chapel is set in a garden shaded by a large old tree and surrounded by stone walls (recently restored), with small shrines to various saints dotted around. For its tranquillity and natural beauty, the setting really couldn't be finer.

Transport The easiest way to reach Qoubaiyat from Tripoli is to take a **microbus** first to Halba, and then change there, or else you may be able to find microbuses runnning directly between the two. **Service taxis** also operate between Tripoli and Qoubaiyat, though they are steadily being replaced by microbuses. Without your own vehilcle, to reach Akkar el-Atiqa or St Charlita you will need to negotiate a private taxi from Qoubaiyat.

Routes from Qoubaiyat From Qoubaiyat, instead of going back the way you came, you can return to Tripoli on the faster main road via El Biré and Halba. This road climbs up through low hills and then runs along the edge of a plateau, with views north across the plains to the Jebel Ansariye range in Syria, before descending to the Akkar plain and swinging gradually south to Halba. From Qoubaiyat to Halba by this route is 26 km. Alternatively, a road leads south through the mountains to Hermel in the northern Bekaa valley (see page 600).

South Lebanon

14

South Lebanon

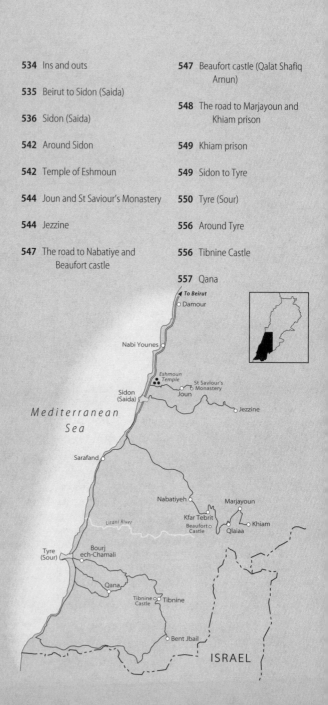

Until recently, visitors to the south of Lebanon were essentially restricted to the two cities of Tyre and Sidon and a few places inland. Much of the rest of southern Lebanon was either directly occupied by Israel as part of its so called 'Security Zone', or else controlled by Israel's proxy army, the South Lebanon Army (SLA). However, since the Israeli withdrawal of May 2000, these areas have been opened up once again. It is still rather early to talk of a return to complete normality, but already Lebanese and foreign tourists alike have begun visiting, intrigued to see this previously forbidden area. Sidon and Tyre, though often overlooked, have a great deal to offer. Both have to a large extent escaped a frenzy of unplanned development, their small fishing communities and still functioning Ottoman period souks offering glimpses of a way of life which has all but disappeared elsewhere. Towards Tyre, the landscape becomes increasingly 'tropical' and rich orange, banana, date and sugar cane plantations line the road.

The hill country inland from the coast has nothing of the dramatic, soaring peaks of the higher reaches of Mount Lebanon, and consequently has seen nothing like the same amount of development. Instead, what you find here are low, rolling hills, in places stony and arid, supporting little more than gnarled olive groves, elsewhere green and fertile and dotted with springs feeding rich orchards of apples, almonds, apricots and mulberry trees, fields of corn, or else forests of oak, poplar, willow and pine. One might even be tempted, not inappropriately, to call the scenery biblical: this is land after all, through which Jesus and the apostles travelled and preached.

South Lebanon

☞ A foot in the door

★ **Sidon** is best known for its picture book **Sea Castle**, but its **atmospheric souks** and small **fishing harbour** are also very attractive, and nearby are the intriguing ruins of the **Temple of Eshmoun**, dating back to the seventh century BC. After you've had your fill of sightseeing and exploring, the **Rest House** restaurant, overlooking the Sea Castle, provides the ideal setting for a meal. Alternatively, if you have a sweet tooth, go to the **Pâtisserie Kanaan**, and choose from a vast array of Arabic sweets accompanied by a cup of strong black Arabic coffee on the verandah.

★ Up in the hills to the east of Sidon, **Jezzine** is a pretty summer resort, famous for its distinctive **hand made cutlery**,

40 m high **waterfalls** and locally brewed **arak**. From here you can head north along a stunningly beautiful valley to Beit ed-Dine, in the Chouf mountains.

★ To the southeast of Sidon, the towering ruins of the **Crusader castle of Beaufort** occupy a dramatic position overlooking the deep gorge of the Litani river. Its recent history has seen it occupied by both Palestinian guerrillas and Israeli forces, its rather battered silhouette against the skyline a poignant testimony to the long and bloody conflict in southern Lebanon.

★ **Tyre** has substantial ruins from the Roman period, including a huge **Hippodrome** and its tiny **fishing harbour** has a number of excellent fish restaurants.

Ins and outs

Accommodation & transport

Accommodation in the south is extremely limited. There are now 4 reasonable hotels in Tyre, and a couple more on the road between Sidon and Tyre. In Sidon itself there is just one extremely basic hotel. However, you can easily see both Sidon and Tyre as day trips from Beirut.

There are regular coaches, buses, microbuses and service taxis linking both Sidon and Tyre with Beirut. Fairly regular microbuses and service taxis operate between Sidon and Nabatiye, but to get to most other places inland you need to hire a taxi privately or else have your own transport. The coastal motorway now extends all the way to Sidon. To the south of Sidon there is another short stretch of motorway as far as the highway leading inland to Nabatiye, though it is steadily being extended and will one day reach all the way to Tyre (and link with the motorway north of Sidon via a bypass).

Safety

The coastal cities of Sidon and Tyre are perfectly safe to visit. The situation in the rest of southern Lebanon is much more stable now that the Israelis have withdrawn from their so called 'Security Zone'. Nevertheless, Hezbollah are still active here, and the continued UN presence is an indication that the potential remains for conflict to flare up again. It is a good idea to keep abreast of events in the local news (the *Daily Star* generally reports even the smallest incidents) and, in the case of trips inland from Tyre, enquire at the UNIFIL base in Tyre before setting off. The soldiers at the numerous Lebanese army and UN checkpoints throughout southern Lebanon will also advise you of any trouble in their areas. The Lebanese authorities are very keen to avoid foreign tourists being involved in any 'incidents', and the soldiers on duty at Lebanese army checkpoints will stop you going into a particular area if they feel that there is any chance of trouble.

In the areas formerly occupied by Israel or controlled by the South Lebanon Army (SLA), landmines are a major problem. There are known to be at least 130,000 still in place, and in all likelihood many more. That said, as long as you stick to the roads and do not wander off cross-country, you will be safe. All the roads in the area have been checked, and it is only away from the roads (often, tragically, in fields that farmers are trying to work) that they are found.

Beirut to Sidon (Saida)

Following Av Du General Fouad Chehab around Beirut Central District (Downtown), the exit for the new airport highway is signposted 'City sportif, Aeroport, Saida'. There are signposts all along this highway for Saida, though at the time of writing it did not connect with the coastal motorway. Instead, you had to take the exit signposted for Ouzai and turn left at the end of this road to join the road running through Beirut's southern suburb of Bourj el-Barajneh.

Another way to join the coastal motorway heading south is to follow the Corniche around past Raouche and Pigeon Rocks, then bear right at the large intersection to continue along the sea front down past Rafiq Hariri beach. Bear right again at the next junction to continue south, passing the *Summerland* hotel and the new *Sheraton Coral Beach* complex on the right. The next stretch, practically always heavily congested and chaotic, takes you through Beirut's crowded and sprawling southern suburb of Bourj el-Barajneh. You then join a brand new section of motorway which takes you past Beirut International Airport and passes underneath the airport's recently extended main runway. Soon after you arrive at a large intersection where you join the motorway proper heading south. (Returning along the motorway from Sidon towards Beirut, remember to take the exit here signposted for Beirut centre, rather than going straight on, which takes you into Beirut via a long and confusing route from the southeast).

The motorway passes to the west of **Damour**, a Christian town which was the scene of a bloody massacre in 1976, carried out by Palestinian troops in retaliation for an earlier massacre by Phalange militias of Palestinian refugees in the Beirut suburb of Karantina. Soon afterwards, there is an exit signposted for Damour and Beit ed-Dine. This is the start of the road up into the Chouf mountains, to Deir el-Qamar and Beit ed-Dine (see page 562). If you continue south along the motorway, it ends 17 km further on, around 3½ km to the north of Sidon (Saida).

Around 1 km after the exit signposted for Damour and Beit ed-Dine, there is an exit to the old coast road. The coastline here is fairly built up, one village more or less merging into the next, interspersed by various beaches and beach resorts. After rounding the rocky promontory of **Ras es-Saadiyat**, popular with fishermen, you come to **Nebi Younes**. There is a small shrine here by the sea, which is said to contain the tomb of Jonah, of Old Testament whale fame. According to local Muslim tradition, it was here that Jonah was disgorged from the whale's stomach. Nebi Younes is situated on **Jiyyeh bay**, which has been identified by some with ancient *Porphyreon*, an important centre of the murex (see page 537) industry during Phoenician times. A fifth-sixth century Byzantine church containing numerous mosaics was uncovered here, suggesting that it continued to flourish right through to the Byzantine era. The mosaics are now displayed in the museum at Beit ed-Dine. Jiyyeh bay has good sand **beaches** and there are a couple of beach resorts with restaurants, (although just to the south is a large oil refinery and storage facility complete with its own mini-port). South of the oil refinery you pass more sand beaches, before the motorway joins with the old coast road (around 42 km from Beirut). A kilometre further on, after crossing over the Awali river and going through a checkpost, you pass the large, new **Saida Sports Stadium** on the right (built for the Asian Cup 2000 games) and more or less directly opposite the right turn for Eshmoun (see below). A new flyover is being built here, perhaps to allow southbound traffic to access the Eshmoun road, or else as part of a bypass around Sidon. A little under 2 km further on, fork right for the Sea Castle and the old part of Sidon. If you go straight on, you arrive at the town centre.

Sidon (Saida) صيدا

Phone code: 07
Colour map 4, grid B1

Sidon is today a thriving and rapidly growing town, the administrative and commercial 'capital' of the south. Although one of the great Phoenician city-states of the second-first millennium BC, almost nothing from this period survives. Instead it is the Crusader Sea Castle and the medieval town arranged around the small harbour which give it its charm. There is little of the carefully spruced up atmosphere of Byblos here; the souks are very much as they have always been, authentically ramshackle, chaotic and dirty, and away from the modern part of town you have the sense of an essentially provincial community still founded on fishing and agriculture, where tourism remains a largely insignificant sideline.

Ins and outs

All public transport services from Beirut to Sidon depart from the Cola bus stand. Arriving in Sidon, whether by luxury coach, bus, microbus or by service taxi, you will be dropped off by the large Sahet al-Najmeh (Place d'Etoile) roundabout. This is within easy walking distance of the Sea Castle and the old part of town, both to the west of here. Indeed, all the main sights are grouped together within a relatively small area around the harbour, and can easily be visited on foot in the space of a few hours. Rue Riad Solh, which runs to the north and south of Sahet al-Najmeh roundabout, is a major thoroughfare through the modern part of the town, with sprawling modern suburbs extending east from this line up into the hills.

History

According to the Bible, Sidon was the first-born son of Canaan (Genesis 10: 15), and in Isaiah the city of Tyre to the south is referred to as the "Virgin daughter of Sidon" (Isaiah 23: 12)

The earliest archaeological evidence of settlement at Sidon dates back to the late **neolithic** or early **chalcolithic** period (around 4000 BC). Although politically it remained subservient to Byblos, during the second millennium BC it developed in importance as a commercial centre, establishing close trading links with the pharaohs of New Kingdom **Egypt**. Like many of the Canaanite/Phoenician settlements along the coast, it made use of a promontory and facing island which together provided a sheltered harbour for ships and a refuge against attacks from the hinterland. But Sidon only really began to come into its own towards the end of the second millennium BC, when both Egyptian and Hittite influence declined and Phoenicia began to enjoy a period of relative peace and independence. It extended its trading links throughout the Mediterranean and beyond, and gained hegemony over southern Lebanon. Much of its wealth was founded on the murex industry which produced the purple dye for which the Phoenicians were famous.

Around 1200 BC the **Philistines** (the only clearly identifiable group amongst the so called 'Sea Peoples') destroyed the city along with its fleet of trading ships, and it was Tyre which later emerged as the most important of the Phoenician city-states. Nevertheless, Sidon soon recovered its importance as a centre of commerce, at times semi-independent, but more often ruled by Tyre. The **Assyrians** periodically extracted tribute from the city from the 11th century BC, although along with Tyre it repeatedly rebelled against their somewhat tenuous control, until in 675 BC it was comprehensively destroyed by Esarhaddon. Control of the Mediterranean coast subsequently passed to the neo-**Babylonians** (Chaldeans), who under Nebuchadnezzar eventually put down a new revolt, though only after a 13-year siege of Tyre.

After the capture of Babylon in 539 BC by Cyrus the Great, the **Persian** Empire soon extended its control over Phoenicia, which peacefully succumbed

The colour of money

The Phoenicians are credited with discovering the distinctive purple dye that in time became a colour closely associated with royalty, no doubt because of the huge expense involved in producing the it. This was the colour favoured by Cleopatra and donned by Roman emperors. During the reign of Diocletian (284-305 AD) purple-dyed silk was worth three times its weight in gold.

According to legend, it was first discovered by the god Melkart and his lover Tyrus, a nymph. Walking on the beach one day, Tyrus noticed how their dog had bitten a murex shell, causing its mouth to be stained purple. She demanded that Melkart make her a dress of the same colour, and so Melkart set about collecting the shellfish to fulfil her wish. According to a Greek version of the legend, it was Helen of Troy who noticed the purple colour around her dog's mouth after it had chewed on the shellfish. She subsequently demanded that any suitor for her hand in marriage produce a dress dyed in the same colour.

Although the origins of the discovery are lost in legend, what is certain is that the murex industry was of enormous importance both to Sidon and Tyre, where superior varieties of the Murex trunculus mollusc was found in great quantities. And great quantities were what was needed. An estimated 10,000 murex molluscs produced just one gramme of purple dye. The process was also extremely laborious. According to Pliny it involved extracting fluid from a vein of the mollusc while still alive, mixing it with salt and allowing it to stand for three days, and then boiling it gently for a further 10 days before it was ready to be used. Except for the tiny amounts of fluid which formed the basis of the dye, the rest of the mollusc was discarded, leaving large mounds of murex shells as evidence of the industry. By all accounts the distillation process also produced an unbearable stench, and it was due to this that even in its early history Sidon developed as two cities; the coastal one around the harbour and an inland suburb reaching up the hillsides, at a safe distance from the dye-works.

to its new rulers. Sidon was made the capital of the fifth satrapy (province), which included both Syria-Palestine and Cyprus, and began to experience its greatest period of prosperity and power. It was during this period that the temple of Eshmoun was built, along with lavish Persian gardens and palaces. The king of Sidon acted in effect as the admiral of the Phoenician fleet, which was put at the disposal of the Persians and used first to defeat the Egyptians in 525, and later in the wars against the Greeks, for example at Miletus in 494 BC and Salamis in 480 BC. Indeed, such was the importance of the Phoenician fleet that these wars were often characterized as being between the Greeks and Phoenicians, and made the Phoenicians almost allies rather than vassals of the Persians. They even refused to take part in the conquest of Carthage planned by Cambyses (530-21), Carthage having been originally founded as a colony of Tyre.

Early in the fourth century BC the Phoenician city-states further asserted their independence by forming a federation based at Tripoli. In 360 Straton, the king of Sidon, established friendly trading relations with the Athenians, and when the Phoenician city-states collectively rose against their Persian overlords, it was Sidon which soon became the focus of the rebellion. The Persian king, Artaxerxes III Ochus, led a huge army against the city in 350. The Greek historian Diodorus relates how the people of Sidon, seeing the Persian army massacre a delegation of notables which had attempted to surrender, destroyed their own fleet and then set fire to the city with themselves inside, more than 40,000 people dying in the process.

According to legend, Alexander installed a gardener as king, at Sidon, this being the only man of royal lineage to have survived

After the defeat of Darius at Issus in 333 BC, Alexander the Great proceeded unchallenged down the Mediterranean coast, with only Tyre bravely attempting to resist the new **Greek** domination (see page 552). Control of the city later alternated between the **Seleucids** and **Ptolemids**, although in both cases it was able to maintain a large degree of autonomy. In 64 BC it was incorporated into the **Roman** Empire and for a time continued to enjoy some independence. During the **Byzantine** era, although declining in importance, it was still made the seat of a bishopric. Following the great earthquake of 551 AD, its fortunes were revived somewhat when Beirut's famous Law School was transferred there.

After 667 it was incorporated into the **Umayyad** Empire of the Muslims, becoming known by its present Arabic name, Saida. Although historically of no major significance, it remained a wealthy city. The Persian Ismaili missionary Nasir-i-Khosrau, who visited in the mid-11th century, was certainly impressed, writing, "The well built stone wall of Sidon has four gates. The bazaars are so splendidly decorated that the stranger might imagine that the sultan was expected to visit them. The orchards are such that one might say each was planned to meet the caprice of some king." In 1110 it was captured by Baldwin I and remained in **Crusader** hands until 1187, when it surrendered without a fight to Salah ud-Din (Saladin) as he marched up the coast triumphant from his capture of Jerusalem. Saladin dismantled the city's walls, hoping to render it useless to the Crusaders. But their interest in it continued and it passed back and forth between the Muslims and Christians no less than five times, suffering destruction and restoration on each occasion, until finally it was taken from the Crusaders by the **Mamelukes** in 1291, its defences dismantled for the last time.

It was not until the 17th century, under the patronage of **Fakhr ud-Din II Maan** (1590-1635), that Sidon regained something of its former importance. The Druze emir developed trading relations with Europe, building the Khan of the Franks to accommodate French merchants and a French consulate. At its height, some 20 ships arrived from Marsailles each year. But this period of pre-eminence was short-lived: in 1634 the North Harbour was allowed to silt up for fear of the hostile Turkish fleet landing there. In 1791 **Ahmad Jazzar**, the Ottoman pasha of Acre, drove the French merchants from the town, and subsequently Beirut evolved as the main port for commerce with Europe. In 1837 Sidon was rocked by an earthquake and then three years later bombarded by the combined Anglo-Austro-Turkish fleet sent to drive out Ibrahim Pasha and his local ally Bashir Shihab II. After 1860 the town came under direct **Ottoman** rule and it was only in 1920 that it was incorporated into the enlarged **French Mandate** territory of 'Greater Lebanon'.

During the 1950s Sidon flourished as the terminus for the Trans Arabian Pipe Line (Tapline), and in 1955 a new oil refinery was established to the south of the town, bringing further industrial activity. All that came to an end with the outbreak of the civil war

Sidon (Saida)

Sea Castle

North Harbour

Khan o al-Franj

Khattakdar Mosque

Great Mosque

Castle of St Louis

Murex Hill

Sahet al-Najmeh Roundabout

Service Taxi/ Bus Stand

Natout Telephone Office

Rue Riad Solh

To Tyre

N

0 metres 200
0 yards 200

■ **Sleeping**
1 Orient

● **Eating**
1 Abou Ramy Falafels
2 Kanaan Pâtisserie
3 Rest House

in 1975, during which the town suffered greatly, control of it passing between the Palestinians, Syrians, Israelis and Hezbollah/ Amal. Since 1991, recovery has been swift, its fortunes closely linked to the fact that this is the birthplace of the prime minister, Rafiq Hariri, who has ensured generous contributions towards reconstruction and redevelopment through the charitable Hariri Foundation.

Sights

Standing on a tiny island just off the coast and reached by a narrow man-made causeway, the so called 'Sea Castle' is the most prominent of Sidon's historic monuments. This island appears to have been the site of an earlier temple, probably built originally by the Phoenicians and dedicated to Melkart, and adapted by the Greeks and Romans who identified Melkart with Herakles and Hercules respectively. The present castle was built by the Crusaders to defend the town's main harbour soon after they had recaptured Sidon from the Ayyubids in 1228. It was largely dismantled by the Mamelukes when they expelled the Crusaders for the last time in 1291 and later rebuilt, successive local rulers adding further embellishments. Its present much reduced state is largely a result of the damage it received during the bombardment of 1840.

    Approaching the castle along the narrow causeway, note the extensive use of Roman columns (taken from the earlier temple) laid horizontally in the walls for reinforcement. This is a feature you can also see at Jbail (Byblos) and is typical of Crusader architecture wherever such materials were available. In the stonework above the entrance to the castle are carved reliefs of lions and human figures. The main tower of the castle, to your left as you approach, is the best preserved, with a large vaulted room at ground floor level and steps leading up to the roof, from where there are good views out over the harbour and back across the town. The smaller tower is topped by a small domed building, a later addition which served as a mosque and perhaps replaced an earlier church.

    The harbour which the castle overlooks was in fact one of four which together allowed ships to shelter and sail from here whatever the prevailing winds. Known as the **North Harbour**, it is the only one still in use. A system of sluice gates created a through current which prevented it from silting up. The bay to the south of the North Harbour was known as the Egyptian Harbour and was the second most important. The Foreigners' Harbour and the Pomegranate Harbour to the north and south respectively were of lesser importance. ■ *Open daily 0900-1800 in summer, 0900-1600 in winter. Entry LL3,000.*

Sea Castle (Qalat al-Bahr)

Extending south from the North Harbour are Sidon's souks, where you will find Sidon's other historic monuments. The souks are something of an attraction in their own right, particularly the core area between the Khan al-Franj and Great Mosque. Still very much alive and little changed over the centuries, they are wonderfully atmospheric and well worth exploring. The cafés in the square opposite the Great Mosque attract an elderly clientele of nargileh smoking, card playing gentlemen.

Souks

Donated to the French by Fakhr ud-Din II Maan in 1610 as part of his drive to encourage trading relations with Europe, the Khan al-Franj (literally 'Foreigners' Khan', also referred to as the 'Khan al-Faransawi' or 'French Khan'), was the largest and most elegant of Sidon's khans. In typical Ottoman style it consists of a large rectangular courtyard with a central fountain surrounded by two storeys of rooms fronted by arched arcades. The ground floor would have been used as workshops, storehouses and stables, while the upper floor served as living quarters. As well as housing merchants and their wares, it also served

Khan al-Franj

as the residence of the French consul and later the Franciscan Fathers. After independence it housed an orphanage run by the Sisters of St Joseph of the Apparition. In recent years the khan has been carefully restored to its former glory. Some of the rooms on the ground floor now serve as handicraft and souvenir shops, while a large vaulted and pillared hall is used for occasional exhibitions. There are plans to establish a cultural centre, complete with a library, museum and tourist information office in the upper floor rooms. ■ *Open 0700-1500, Fri 0700-1100, closed Sun.*

Great Mosque
Non-Muslims are not always allowed inside the mosque itself, though this appears to depend on who is on duty at the time. To improve your chances, avoid prayer times and dress modestly (long trousers/sleeves, and a head-scarf for women)

Dating from the 15th century, the Great Mosque was converted from an earlier fortified structure built by the Knights Hospitaller in the 13th century. The prayer hall of the mosque corresponds with the Church of St John which stood within the fortified complex. Viewed from the road running along the harbour front, what you see is the original Crusader stonework, which presents an imposing and impregnable façade. Approaching through the souks, you come first to a monumental gateway flanked by two large lanterns, followed by a passage which leads to the entrance of the mosque itself. Inside there is a courtyard surrounded by arched porticos on four sides, with the prayer hall to your left as you enter. The entire structure has been carefully restored in recent years.

Castle of St Louis

This castle was built on the foundations of an earlier Fatimid fortress during the Crusaders' first occupation of Sidon from 1110-1187. However, the existing ruins largely reflect later Mameluke and Ottoman period reconstruction work. It takes its name from the fact that King Louis IX of France, leader of the Seventh and Eighth Crusades (and later canonized as St Louis), made it his headquarters when he retook the town from the Ayyubids in 1253. Now in an advanced state of ruin, the castle stands on an acropolis which has revealed evidence of occupation from at least the 17th century BC.

Murex hill

The hill to the south of the castle of St Louis is formed largely from the crushed remains of murex shells accumulated over centuries of purple dye production during Sidon's Phoenician period. Today the hill has been built over and is also occupied by a cemetery. However, if you walk down towards the sea along the street just south of the castle of St Louis, you can still see traces of the debris.

Essentials

Sleeping

The only hotel in Sidon itself, on the street leading south from the sea castle, is the rather shabby **E-G** *Orient*, T720364. A bed in a very basic shared room here (share basic shower/toilet) costs LL8,000, which is fine, though the rooms are far from appealing. The quoted price for an equally basic double room (share shower/toilet) is an something of a rip-off at US$20 or more, try bargaining. Alternatively, on the old coast road in the village of Khaizarane, a little over 18 km south of Sidon, there is the **C** *Mounes*, T/F07-390677. A/c, TV/dish, phone, attached bath and balcony. Restaurant. The rooms are a little basic for the price but the setting is lovely, on a spit of land surrounded by sea with fishing boats moored around it.

Eating

Mid-range *Rest House*, adjacent to the Sea Castle, T722469. Open daily 1100-late. Set in a beautifully restored 17th-century khan, the interior is lavishly decorated in traditional Ottoman style, and during summer you can sit outside in the lovely garden area overlooking the sea and the castle. Good quality Lebanese cuisine. The set menu (minimum 6 people), consisting of a mezze spread, mixed grill, sweet, coffee and 1 alcoholic or soft drink, is good value at LL18,000 per head (plus 5% tax). If you order à la carte (perhaps including some fish), you are looking at more like US$15-20 per head (note the LL1,500 cover charge and additional 20% tax and service). *Palamera*, Rue Riad Solh (on the main road to the north of Sahet al-Najmeh), T729543. Open 1200-late. Pleasant, comfortable restaurant offering an eclectic mix of European, Mexican and Chinese cuisine. From around U$15 per head, or less for a light meal.

Cheap *Pizza Hut*, Rue Riad Solh (on the main road to the north of Sahet al-Najmeh, next door to *Palemera* restaurant), T751132. Open daily 0830-late. Part of the international chain. The usual range of pizza, pasta etc for around US$5-10 per head.

Seriously cheap Along Rue Riad Solh, to the south of the Sahet al-Najmeh roundabout, there are several snack places where you can get the usual sandwiches, roast chicken etc. *Abou Ramy*, set back just to the south of the entrance to the Sea Castle, serves the best falafel sandwiches in town. This is all they do, serving a steady stream of hot, light and fluffy falafels in fresh bread with salad and tahini/yoghurt sauce to eagerly waiting customers. Excellent value at LL1,000 each. Although basically just a takeaway place, there are a couple of tables at the front where you can sit and eat.

Pâtisserie Kanaan, on the sea front, around 500 m north of the new Saida Sports Stadium (ie around 3 km to the north of the centre of town). This is Sidon's best known pâtisserie, with a bewildering variety of Arabic sweets. Out at the back they have a covered terrace overlooking the sea where you can sit down with a coffee and a selection of sweets, the waves drowning out the noise of the highway. This is a great way to fortify yourself for the drive back into Beirut, though it is a nightmare crossing the highway here if you park on the northbound carriageway. Also have a branch on Rue Riad Solh, just to the south of Sahet al-Najmeh roundabout.

Coffee & sweets

Sidon is famous for its Arabic sweets, the local speciality being a kind of biscuit known as 'senioura'

Transport

Luxury coaches, buses, microbuses and service taxis congregate at the Sahet al-Najmeh roundabout. There is a bus stand in a parking lot by the roundabout where you can catch microbuses to Beirut (Cola bus stand) or Tyre (Sour) for LL1,000. Alternatively, you can just wait by the main road, on the appropriate side of the roundabout. The fare to Beirut by luxury coach is LL1,500. Service taxis charge LL3,000 to both Beirut and Tyre. There are fairly frequent microbuses and service taxis to Nabatiye (LL1,00 and LL1,500 respectively). Service taxis to Jezzine are less frequent, though this may change as the town begins to regain its status as a summer resort. To visit Eshmoun, Joun and St Saviour's monastery you will have to negotiate a private taxi.

Directory

Banks There are several banks along Rue Riad Solh and on the road leading east from Sahet al-Najmeh roundabout towards Jezzine, the majority with cash machines accepting most major cards. In addition, there are several moneychangers along Rue Riad Solh, south of Sahet al-Najmeh roundabout. **Communications** Internet: there is an internet café on Rue Raid Solh, south of Sahet al-Najmeh roundabout. **Post** The main post office is on Rue Riad Solh, north of Sahet al-Najmeh roundabout (on the left just past a large mosque). **Telephone**: the government telephone office ('Centrale') is around 300 m to the east of Sahet al-Najmeh roundabout, on the right just past the *Coral* petrol station (rates as per Beirut). There is also a private telephone office, *Natout*, on Rue Riad Solh to the south of Sahet al-Najmeh roundabout. Although you are less likely to have to queue here, it is more expensive than the Centrale (eg UK LL3,000 per min).

Around Sidon

Temple of Eshmoun مبعد أشمون

Colour map 4, grid B2 Set amidst rich orange groves close to the Awali River in an area known as *Bustan esh-Sheikh* or Sheikh's Garden, is the Phoenician temple of Eshmoun. The site is unique in that more than just the foundations of the temple have survived. Although of great archaeological significance because of this, to the non-specialist the site is rather confusing, spanning as it does nearly eight centuries of occupation. In addition, all the important archaeological finds have been removed, while much of the stonework of the various temples has been taken by local villagers over the centuries. Nevertheless, the remaining ruins give some idea of the scale of the original complex, and the rather sombre jumble of ancient stones is somehow rather atmospheric.

Ins & outs The turning for Eshmoun is a little under 3 km north of Sahet al-Najmeh roundabout (see Beirut to Sidon, page 535). Coming from Sidon, take either of the right turns immediately before or after the fairground on the right (signposted; if you go through the checkpost you have gone too far). Follow this road past some riverside snack places, a bridge over the Awali River, and then the fancy new *Wadi Eshmoun* restaurant. The site entrance is on the left soon after (around 1½ km from the Sidon-Beirut highway).

History The earliest parts of the temple complex appear to date back to the late seventh century BC, although most of it dates from the sixth-fourth centuries BC during the period of **Persian** suzerainty over Sidon. This is reflected in the distinctly Persian style terraced podiums built against the hillside. After the fourth century BC, further subsidiary temples were erected during the **Hellenistic** era, while the **Romans** built a colonnaded street lined with shops and processional stairway leading to the temple, along with their own nymphaeum. The presence of a church suggests that even during the **Byzantine** era, long after Eshmoun or his Greek and Roman equivalents had ceased to be worshipped here, the site retained its importance, probably still as a place of pilgrimage and healing. At its height the temple appears to have attracted great numbers of pilgrims and numerous statuettes inscribed with the names of those who came to be healed were unearthed during excavations.

Sights Entering the site, bear right past a newly excavated area on your left, followed by the remains of a **Byzantine church**, its floor plan still discernible along with its patterned mosaics. Beyond this, also on the left, is a large **courtyard**, probably part of a Roman house, with a mosaic floor depicting the four seasons. At the time of writing this was in a very poor condition, with the detail shown on the Ministry of Tourism brochure all but completely defaced, although restoration work was being carried out on it. To your right, opposite the courtyard is an enclosure which has been identified as a **Roman nymphaeum**, with badly damaged mosaics and niches in the fountain, in which statues would once have stood. The path you are following is the route of the later **Roman colonnaded street** and along it are the bases and fragments of large columns.

The main area of interest, however, is the large **Phoenician temple complex** built up against the hillside in the southeast corner of the site, the most striking feature of which is the towering **main podium**, probably erected by the Sidonian king Eshmounazzar I (literally 'Eshmoun helps me') in the fifth century BC. The podium appears to have been enlarged at a later stage, and excavations carried out around the base of the thick retaining wall at the front (which as a result is

The Legends of Eshmoun

The Phoenician god Eshmoun appears to have been none other than Adonis (see page 501) in a different guise. Born as a mortal in the city of Beirut, Eshmoun was a keen hunter who soon attracted the attention of the goddess Astarte. She fell in love with him but he spurned her advances and finally took his own life in order to escape her. However, Astarte was not to be so easily thwarted and promptly brought him back to life, giving him immortality so that she could enjoy his company for eternity. Thus, like Adonis, Eshmoun was to the Phoenicians a symbol of fertility and the cycle of death and rebirth represented by the cycle of the seasons.

He also appears to have had associations with healing, the Greeks and Romans identifying him with Asklepios/ Aesculapius, their god of healing. According to Roman legend, Aesculapius was the son of Apollo and Coronis. Having wooed Coronis as his lover, Apollo shot her with an arrow in a fit of rage after discovering that she had taken a second lover. Immediately he regretted his hasty action and employed all his skills as a physician in a desperate attempt to revive her. However, he was too late and she died, leaving him with their son Aesculapius, to whom Apollo imparted all his medical skills. Once grown up, Aesculapius outstripped his father in the practice of medicine and even managed to bring the dead back to life, prompting Jupiter to kill him with a thunderbolt out of jealousy.

now largely free standing) revealed lengthy inscriptions left by the king Bodashtart. To the right of the main podium as you face it is an even older **pyramid-shaped podium** dating from the sixth century BC when Sidon was still under neo-Babylonian cultural and political influence. Two faces of it survive pressed up against the main podium, along with a section of wall to its right. Between the nymphaeum and the temple compound a flight of **Roman stairs**, complete with traces of mosaics still surviving, climbs up and joins a path which leads to the top of the main podium. From here you can get a good overview of the layout of the site. Ascending the stairs, note on your left the square shaped **altar** on which is placed a capital carved with four bulls' heads. The area of courtyard around the main podium contains a complex jumble of structures spanning several different eras. Immediately to the left of the Roman stairs (as you face them from the colonnaded street) are the remains of **ablution basins**, while to the left of these is a broad flight of stairs leading up to an ablution basin, followed by a narrow flight of stairs leading up to a lower level of the main podium. To the left of this again is the **sanctuary of Astarte**, within which there is a stone throne flanked by two sphinxes (the 'Throne of Astarte'). Finally, to the left of this are the remains of a third-century BC **temple** with badly weathered but still discernible friezes in the corner section of the walls depicting hunting and banqueting scenes, while behind it, in the extreme southeast corner of the site, there are more ablution basins and traces of a water channel which runs all the way around the front of the main podium. The system of water channels and ablution basins reflects the importance of water (in this case taken from the Awali River, known then as the *Bostrenus* and considered sacred to Eshmoun) in the healing rituals of the temple. ■ *Open daily 0730-sunset. At the time of writing no entrance fee was charged.*

Joun جون and St Saviour's Monastery دير المخلص

Colour map 4, grid B2 A short detour into the hills to the northeast of Sidon takes you to the village of Joun, just beyond which is the ruined house of Lady Hester Stanhope and St Saviour's monastery. To get there, head north out of Sidon and around 1½ km after the bridge over the Awali River (instead of going up onto the motorway, bear off to the right), take the right turn signposted for 'Convent St Saviour'. This road winds its way up into the mountains to the sizeable and prosperous village of Joun. Continuing straight through the village, after around 2 km you come to a left turn signposted 'Stanhope' (the sign is actually for the Stanhope tyre factory!). Taking this turning, follow the road down to the bottom of the hill and bear right and then right again. The road climbs steadily before ending at the ruins of **Lady Hester Stanhope's house**. Although once a substantial building (according to one account it had 35 rooms), the house is now in ruins. In the olive grove beyond the house is the grave where she was buried. By all accounts this was also once an impressive monument, but it was looted and completely destroyed during the civil war and today all that remains is a forlorn, rubble-strewn hole in the ground. All in all there is not a lot to see here now, but the setting is very beautiful and the site makes an ideal, although somewhat macabre, picnic spot.

Returning to the main road from Joun and continuing east along it for another 3 km or so, you arrive at the Greek Catholic **St Saviour's Monastery (Deir Moukhalles)**. Founded in 1711, the monastery was damaged by an earthquake in 1956 and then abandoned during the recent civil war, but has now been carefully restored and contains some beautiful icons. According to legend, the monastery was founded as a result of a miracle. The bishop of Tyre and Sidon was passing through the area when one of the priests in his entourage was accidentally shot in the stomach. The bishop cried out "Holy Saviour", whereupon the priest got up and was found to be unharmed, the bullet having melted into a flat disc instead of piercing his body. Duly impressed by this divine intervention, the bishop ordered that a monastery be built on the site.

Jezzine جزين

Phone code: 07
Colour map 4, grid B2 The town of Jezzine, around 32 km to the east of Sidon, was until recently under the control of the SLA, and therefore completely off-limits. Before the war and the Israeli invasion, it was a popular summer resort, famous for its beautiful setting and 40 m high waterfalls, and also for its distinctive, ornately decorated cutlery. Readily accessible once again from Sidon or from Beit ed-Dine, Jezzine has something of an affluent air about it, having seemingly come out of the war and SLA occupation in good shape. There are two hotels here, and a couple of pleasant restaurants beside the waterfalls.

Ins & outs To get to Jezzine from Sidon, follow the road leading east from Sahet al-Najmeh roundabout, and go straight across the next 2 roundabouts you come to. The road climbs up through a string of villages, and then passes through a couple of checkposts. At the village of **Anane** (a little under 22 km from Sidon), there is a large artificial lake to the right of the road, followed soon after by dramatic views down into the Nahr Awali to the left. In the village of **Roum**, just over 3 km further on, there is a hotel, the *New Granada* (see 'Sleeping' below). From here, it is a little over 7 km to Jezzine, the road winding its way through picturesque pine woods. Entering the town, you pass a large, striking statue of Our Lady of Maabour on the right. For details of the route to Jezzine from Beit ed-Dine, see page 570. **NB** Although there is a road which heads south from Jezzine before looping north again towards Mashghara in

Lady Hester Stanhope: the "Princess of Europe"

Born in 1777, Lady Hester Stanhope's life was colourful to say the least. She was the granddaughter of Lord Chatham (William Pitt the Elder) and niece of William Pitt the Younger. Her upbringing was highly unconventional for the time, and whatever its merits or otherwise, she proved to be an extremely intelligent and able woman. She developed a close friendship with her uncle, and when he became prime minister worked closely with him as his adviser and confidant during the crucial early years of the Napoleonic wars. However, after William Pitt's death in 1806, she found it difficult to make the transition to a more mundane everyday life. To make things worse, three years later her fiancé, Sir John Moore, was killed at Corunna in Spain, along with her brother Charles. Heartbroken and disenchanted with her life in England, she set off for the Middle East in 1810.

In the course of her travels she earned herself a formidable reputation. At Constantinople she was royally received by Ottoman Sultan Mahmoud, while in Syria she made a deep impression on the bedouins of Palmyra, who hailed her as a latter-day Queen Zenobia when she became the first European woman to visit the ruins.

However, the reverence with which she was received wherever she travelled started to go to her head and soon she was involving herself in the politics of the region. In 1816 she persuaded the Ottoman pasha of Tripoli to lead an expedition against the remote castle of Qalat al-Kahf in the Jebel Ansariye mountains, where a French captain had been imprisoned (see page 276). In 1818 she settled down near the village of Joun in the Chouf mountains of Lebanon, arrogantly requisitioning the house of a local farmer. When the farmer objected to the local emir, Lady Hester Stanhope wrote directly to the Ottoman sultan in Constantinople, who reputedly responded with the injunction that the emir was to "Obey the Princess of Europe in everything!" She also managed to make a lifelong enemy of the emir Bashir Shihab II of nearby Beit ed-Dine who, angered as he was by her continual meddling in his affairs, nevertheless couldn't help but respect her audacity. She likewise succeeded in antagonizing Mohammad Ali, the viceroy of Egypt, who reputedly complained that she caused him more trouble than all the peoples of Palestine, Syria and Lebanon. In 1838 she was even credited with inciting the local Druze rebellion.

Amongst ordinary people she was greatly respected and admired, at least from a safe distance, for her seemingly limitless generosity, which was steadily ruining her financially. In her later years she appears to have become increasingly eccentric, leading a reclusive life and receiving only reluctantly European visitors, among them Lamartine and Alexander Kinglake, the author of Eothen. Lamartine praised her great beauty, writing, "She has those features which years cannot alter", while Kinglake wrote of her that, "She never, she said, looked upon a book, nor a newspaper, but trusted alone to the stars for her sublime knowledge; she usually passed her nights communing with these heavenly teachers." By the time she died she was bankrupt and heavily in debt. All her servants promptly fled with whatever remained of value in the house. When the British consul arrived from Beirut, he ordered a hurried burial that very night in the tomb which contained the remains of a young captain in Napolean's Imperial Guard who had been her lover. As the 1966 Hatchette Guide to the Middle East put it, "Ruined by her prodigality, forsaken by everybody, she gave herself up to sorcery and astrology and died miserably in Joun in 1839."

the southern Bekaa Valley, at the time of writing traffic was not being allowed through at an army checkpost around 7 km to the south of Jezzine.

Sights Jezzine's main attractions are its setting and the 40 m high **waterfalls** which cascade down into the valley below. The old part of the town is also worth exploring, with plenty of beautiful old Ottoman buildings still surviving (two of these once housed hotels, the *Palestine* and the *Ahiram*, though they have now closed). Being predominantly Christian (including a sizeable population of Maronites), there are several **churches** and **monasteries** dotted around the town and its environs. Across the valley to the northeast of Jezzine are the so called **caves of Fakhr ed-Dine**, where the famous emir is said to have been finally captured, having fled his previous refuge at nearby Qalat Niha (see page 571).

A somewhat bizarre sight is the **Farhid Serhal Palace** to the south of Jezzine. Take the road heading south out of town, fork off to the left after around 3 km by a sign for 'Ain Majdalain', and then turn left less than 100 m further on. What you find here is a huge, lavishly decorated palace, reminiscent in style of Beit ed-Dine, with intricately carved stonework of geometric and floral designs, inlaid tilework, richly decorated doorways, delicately arched windows, *ablaq* patterning, and just about every other traditional Arabic architectural feature imaginable. However, the whole structure is entirely modern, and indeed as yet incomplete, with bits of steel-reinforced concrete showing through in places, and the occasional pile of building materials dotted around. It was begun in 1967 by a Dr Farhid Suleiman Serhal who, in a now somewhat forlorn testament to one man's delusions of grandeur, sank most of his considerable personal fortune into the project for nearly three decades before his death in 1996. Since then it has stood abandoned, its future uncertain, his children perhaps understandably wary of investing their own time or money in such a huge white elephant.

Sleeping **C** *Al Wehbe*, above main street in centre of town, T780723, F781011. A rather grand building with an equally grand reception area consisting of a pillared and vaulted hall sporting leopard skins, stags' heads and wild boar tusks on the walls. The rooms themselves are simpler, but clean and very comfortable nonetheless, with heater, phone and attached bath. Restaurant and swimming pool. Good value. **D** *Rizk Plaza Motel*, tucked away in the upper, old part of town (ask directions), T781066. Simple but clean and comfortable rooms with TV/dish, kitchenette and attached bath. Some rooms with balcony. (Many of the rooms are really suites, with a separate sitting room). Restaurant. Also good value, especially for groups of 3 or more, with beds then working out at around US$10 per person. **D** *New Granada*, Roum (7 km to the west of Jezzine, on the road to Sidon), T710080. Simple but reasonably clean rooms with heater, attached bath and balcony. Restaurant. Great views of the coast from here.

Eating & drinking

Jezzine is well known for its arak, which is brewed locally, & for most Lebanese diners this is a major component of a meal here

Moderate There are 2 good restaurants in the centre of town, by Jezzine's famous waterfalls; the *Rock Fall*, T03-505016, and the *Al Shallal*, T780067. Both have pleasant shaded terraces as well as seating indoors. You have to crane your neck somewhat to see the waterfalls, but the views out over the valley are very impressive. Both serve Lebanese cuisine, with a standard spread of mezze dishes, mixed grill etc costing around US$15-20 per head.

Cheap/seriously cheap On the main road in the centre of town, *Joe's Cascata Snacks* is a simple but clean and pleasant diner-style place offering pizzas, burgers, sandwiches, subs etc. A filling meal will come to less than US$10, and a substantial snack to less than US$5. Eat in or takeaway.

Transport You may be able to find a service taxi heading up to Jezzine from Sidon, depending on demand. If not, your only option is to hire a taxi privately from Sidon or Beit ed-Dine, or come with your own transport.

South Lebanon

The road to Nabatiye and Beaufort castle

Around 9 km to the south of Sidon (counting from the Sahet al-Najmeh roundabout; see Sidon to Tyre, below) a broad, fast dual carriageway climbs southeast into the mountains, to the town of **Nabatiye**, around 23 km from the coastal road/motorway. Approaching Nabatiye, bear right at a roundabout and then fork left after 1 km, heading downhill along the main road to arrive in the centre of town, 1 km further on. Prior to the Israeli withdrawal, Nabatiye stood on the very edge of the occupied zone, with Israeli positions overlooking it from the hills to the southeast. There are several good snack places along the main street where you can get shawarma and other sandwiches, as well as good fuul, hummus etc. Otherwise, there is nothing of special interest in this large, bustling town.

Colour map 4, grid C2
With its predominantly Shi'ite population, Nabatiye was a major centre of resistance to the occupation, and suffered frequent reprisals from Israeli forces in response to Hezbollah attacks

Heading down the hill along the main road into the centre of town, follow the road round to the left at the bottom and keep going straight to pick up the road to Beaufort castle. After a little under 4 km you arrive at a mini-roundabout and junction; go straight across here (signposted to Arnoun and Yohmor; bearing left takes you along the main road towards Marjayoun). After around 500 m, Beaufort castle comes clearly into view, perched on a hill-top up ahead. Keep going straight on, past a right turn leading to the village of Yohmor and then past Arnoun village, before climbing steeply up to the castle, 5 km from the mini-roundabout and junction.

Beaufort castle (Qalat Shafiq Arnun) قلعة الشقيف

This is the only castle in the Middle East with the dubious distinction of having remained, until very recently, in active service: right up until it was evacuated by the Israelis in May 2000 in fact. It is the castle's setting, with dramatic views down into the deep gorge of the Nahr Litani, and the rather poignant sense of it having been witness to the latest twists in Lebanon's tortuous history, rather than the remains of the castle itself, which are its main attraction.

Colour map 4, grid C2

The exact origins of the castle are unclear. According to some accounts, it stands on the site of a Roman fortification which was later developed by the Arabs before being taken over by the Crusaders. According to William of Tyre, however, it was the Crusaders who first built it. Whatever the truth, by the early 12th century it formed part of the Crusader principality of Sayette, falling for a short time into the hands of a local Arab emir before being recaptured in 1139. It was here that many Crusader knights took refuge following Salah ud-Din's (Saladin) devastating campaigns against them in the late 1180s, and in 1192 Salah ud-Din laid siege to it. He is said to have enticed Renaud, the prince of Sayette, out of the castle for negotiations by sending his ring as a token of trust, and then had him clapped in irons and tortured in view of the defenders. However, it was only after Salah ud-Din's death, following a blockade of two years, that hunger finally forced them to surrender. In 1240 it was returned to the Crusaders under a treaty with the sultan of Damascus, though the Muslim garrison resisted their orders and were only forced to leave after a lengthy siege. In 1260 it was sold to the Knights Templar and remained in their possession until the Mameluke sultan Baibars captured it in 1268. Subsequently it fell into disrepair, and it was not until the 17th century that Fakhr ud-Din II Maan set about restoring its defences with a view to resisting the forces sent by the Ottoman authorities to overthrow him. In the event, however, when the governor of Damascus pounded it with his artillery, Fakhr ud-Din's troops soon surrendered. In the 1970s, the Lebanese Department of Antiquities began to restore

History

South Lebanon

the castle, but soon had to abandon its work when the PLO occupied it, remaining entrenched there through the Israeli invasion of 1978. It was only following heavy bombardment by F-16 fighters during the 1982 invasion that they were finally driven out and the castle occupied by the Israelis.

Sights Scattered all around the castle are piles of shattered concrete and twisted metal. Just to the south of the castle (to your right as you arrive), steps lead up to a bunker built by the Israelis as a lookout post. The easiest point of access to the castle itself is from the east side (walk around the outside of the castle anti-clockwise to reach it), or there is a metal stairway and ladder arrangement leading up the outside of the walls from the north side. Inside, the castle is heavily ruined, though hastily installed metal railings and walkways link the surviving sections. At the southern end of the castle a lookout post, topped by a Hezbollah flag, sits perched on the remains of a medieval tower. Half-way along the west side of the castle are the partial remains of another tower, this one topped by an Amal flag and reached by a ladder. The views in all directions are really spectacular, especially to the east, where sheer cliffs drop away vertiginously to the deep gorge of the Litani River.

Transport There are fairly frequent microbuses and service taxis running between Sidon (Saida) and Nabatiye (LL1,000 and LL1,500 respectively), and less frequent microbuses between Beirut and Nabatiye (LL2,000). For the trip to Beaufort, you may be lucky and find a service taxi going to Arnoun village (LL1,000), but it is far more likely that you will have to hire a taxi privately (around LL15,000 for the return trip with a bit of bargaining; be sure to agree on how long you wish to spend there). Some of the taxi drivers already seem used to dealing with tourists wishing to visit the castle, and may offer to take you on to Khiam prison (see below) afterwards. The microbus stand in Nabatiye is on the right, on the main road as you head down into town, just past the *Liban Post* office. Service/private taxis congregate at various different points around town; there are usually several on the main road close to the microbus stand.

The road to Marjayoun and Khiam prison

The road to Marjayoun follows the course of the Litani River for a while, with sheer cliffs to the west rising precipitously up to the ruins of Beaufort castle, silhouetted imposingly against the skyline. Indeed, the views of the castle from this side are altogether more imposing than approaching from Nabatiye via Arnoun village. At the time of writing, in order to continue on to Marjayoun, you had to go back to the mini-roundabout and junction on the main road 4 km out of Nabatiye (though it looks like a road is under construction cutting across from Arnoun village to the Marjayoun road). Following the main road from here towards Marjayoun, you pass through the village of Kfar Tebnit, and then through a checkpost (just over 2 km from the mini-roundabout and junction). A little over 7 km further on there are a couple of riverside restaurants on the banks of the Litani. Continuing on, keep to the main road as it winds its way southwards before swinging northeast to arrive at a mini-roundabout in the village of Qlaiaa (a little under 9 km from the riverside restaurants). From here it is a further 4 km into Marjayoun.

A predominantly Christian town, Marjayoun was the headquarters of Major Saad Haddad, the much feared commnader of the SLA

Entering **Marjayoun**, you pass first through the modern part of the town. There is a group of three restaurants/cafés – the *Al Rasheed*, *Boulevard* and *Chedid* – in a parade of shops on the left as you drive in, where you can get tea, coffee, snacks etc, and more substantial meals. Around 1½ km further on, you pass through the old part of the town; rather dilapidated but boasting some graceful Ottoman period buildings.

Following the main road through town and continuing eastwards, after around 2 km you come to a sharp right turn beside a blue and white petrol station which leads towards Khiam. Taking this turning, bear right where the road forks after just under 1 km, and then 2 km further on, turn left opposite a reservoir to climb up into the village of Khiam, some 4 km up the hillside.

Khiam prison الخيام

The village of Khiam, though reasonably large and prosperous, would be of no greater note than dozens of others like it in the area, were it not the setting for the infamous Khiam prison. During the Israeli occupation, hundreds of people – both men and women – were held here. Over the years, both the Red Cross and Amnesty International repeatedly expressed grave concerns about the use of torture, with numerous first-hand statements from former inmates suggesting that this was a routine occurrence. The Israelis never allowed either organization, or the UN, access, claiming that it was run by Haddad's SLA, and therefore nothing to do with them. Although termed a prison, and its inmates prisoners, none were ever formally charged. Instead, they were simply held under suspicion of being involved in, or supporting, the resistance to Israeli occupation, and in some cases, purely on the basis of being related to suspected resistance fighters. Indeed, as Robert Fisk points out in *Pity the Nation* (and the militias who controlled Khiam openly admitted), they were held not as prisoners, but "as hostages for the good conduct of their fellow villagers in southern Lebanon".

Colour map 4, grid C2

It may sound a little macabre and in bad taste for Khiam prison to have become a tourist attraction, though others argue that it helps educate an often ignorant public as to what went on in the occupied south. Certainly, Hezbollah have lost no time in exploiting its propaganda potential. Posters of the 'martyrs' who died in Khiam, or fighting the Israelis, are displayed on lamp posts all through the village. The prison itself is perched on a ridge, towards the top end of the village at its southwest end (ask directions to reach it). Its a rather squalid, poignant and depressing place, much what you might expect from a military prison. Those so inclined can wander around the various buildings where inmates were held and tortured.

There is no regular public transport around this area as yet, so your only option is to hire a taxi privately or bring your own transport. There is 1 hotel on the road between Marjayoun and Hasbaya. Returning to the turning by the blue and white petrol station (2 km out of Marjayoun) and continuing eastwards, go straight on past a fork off to the left after 600 m, and then a little over 2 km further on you arrive at a large UN checkpost by the right turn to the village of Ebel es-Saqi. Around 300 m down this turning is the **B** *Dana*, T03-421233. This large, cheerful place bills itself as a hotel and recreation centre, and boasts a large outdoor swimming pool set in pleasant gardens, as well as offering basketball. Comfortable rooms with a/c, TV/dish, phone, attached bath and balcony. Restaurant. 24 hr electricity (seemingly something of a special feature here).

Sleeping & transport

Sidon to Tyre

Heading south from Sidon, you have the option of following the new motorway or the old coast road for the first stretch. Heading south along Rue Riad Solh from Sahet al-Najmeh roundabout, you must fork off to the left towards the southern end of town (signposted to Nabatiye) if you wish to join the motorway, or continue straight on for the old coast road. Currently the motorway extends around 5 km beyond the junction for the highway up to Nabatiye, though eventually it will run all the way to Tyre. By either road, it is around 9 km to the junction for Nabatiye. Following the old coast road from here, after another 6 km you come to the town of Sarafand, which extends along the main road for a couple of kilometres, merging with Khaizarane to the south.

Sarafand
Colour map 4, grid B1

Although today a modern and rather nondescript place, Sarafand has been identified as the ancient *Sarepta* or *Zarephaph*, famous in biblical accounts as the place where the prophet Elijah raised the son of a widow from the dead (1 Kings 17: 7-24). An important Phoenician trading town with a large harbour consisting of three separate bays, Sarepta was famous for its glassware (the name is derived from the Hebrew *seraph*, meaning 'to melt'). At the time of the Crusades it was still a large town enclosed within defensive walls and had its own castle. Although some excavations were carried out here in the late 1960s-early 1970s, revealing traces of a Bronze Age settlement, these were abandoned during the civil war and today there is nothing of particular note to be seen.

Continuing south, around 3 km from the start of Sarafand (9 km from the junction for the highway up to Nabatiye), you come to the *Mounes* hotel on the right (see under 'Sleeping, in Sidon, above'). Around 9 km further on you pass through a checkpost by a left turn. Continuing straight on, a further 3 km brings you to a fork off to the left signposted to the *Abou Deeb* hotel (see Tyre 'Sleeping' below).

Continuing along the coast road, just under 1 km beyond the fork for the *Abou Deeb* hotel, you come to another checkpost where the road crosses the **Litani River**, which has its source in the Bekaa Valley near Baalbek. This is the *Shihor Libnat* of the Old Testament and the *Leontes* of antiquity. To Zionists the river represents the northernmost limit of the Promised Land, and it was to this point that the Israelis advanced the first time they invaded Lebanon in 1978. A little over 6 km further south, entering Tyre, fork right to reach the harbour and the old part of town, 3 km away. Going straight on takes you through the modern part of town and past the El Bass area of excavations.

Tyre (Sour) صور

Phone code: 07
Colour map 4, grid C1

Like Sidon, little remains of Tyre's once proud Phoenician past, although the excavations carried out here prior to the civil war uncovered impressive Greek and Roman period remains, while further excavations in 1991 resulted in the dis-covery of a first millennium BC Phoenician graveyard. Today Tyre is a fairly large town with plenty of new development in evidence, although economically it remains handicapped by the closed Israeli border to the south. The population is predominantly Shi'ite Muslim, though there are some Sunni Muslims, and a sig-nificant Maronite and Greek Catholic Christian community, as well as large numbers of Palestinians housed in three refugee camps surrounding the town. The archaeological excavations are well worth visiting, the ruins giving some idea of the city's former grandeur. The small picturesque fishing harbour is full of atmosphere, and to the west and south of it is the Christian quarter and the Otto-man period souks.

Ins and outs

Getting there & around

There are frequent buses, microbuses and service taxis running between Sidon and Tyre, and less frequently directly between Beirut and Tyre. Arriving in Tyre by public transport, you will be dropped off beside the large parking area near the fishing har-bour, a little to the west of the UNIFIL base. From here you are within easy walking distance of all the sights on the 'island' part of Tyre. To reach the inland sights, it is worth taking a taxi (particularly in summer) if you do not have your own transport.

Tyre occupies a large promontory formed by the accumulation over centuries of sand and silt against the causeway which Alexander the Great rebuilt (see below). This promontory joins what were once two separate islands with the mainland. The island part includes the small **fishing harbour** on the north side, surrounded by the **Christian quarter** and the **Ottoman souks**, as well as the **El Mina** excavations on the south side. Around 2 km inland, on the original mainland part of Tyre, are the **El Bass** excavations, which include a large necropolis, a colonnaded street which passes through a large triumphal arch and the massive hippodrome.

History

Known in Arabic by its ancient Semitic name, Sour (literally 'rampart' in Arabic, or 'rock' in Hebrew), the earliest stages of settlement at Tyre have yet to be uncovered. According to Herodotus, it was founded around 2750 BC. Like Sidon and Byblos, Tyre came under the influence of **Egypt** during the second millennium BC and, although it was of far lesser importance than either during this period, it also benefited from the trade with Egypt.

The city's golden age came later, from the early 10th century BC onwards, when it emerged as a powerful independent state after the destruction of Sidon at the hands of the Philistines. Both Sidon and Byblos appear to have paid tribute to Tyre during this period. The most famous of the Tyrian kings, Hiram I (or Ahiram, ruled 969-936 BC), cultivated close ties with the Israelite kings David and Solomon, and it was Hiram who supplied Solomon with the cedar and pine for the building of the Temple of Solomon (1 Kings: 5, 6), receiving an annual payment in wheat and olive oil in return, as well as a gift of 20 towns in Galilee (1 Kings 9: 11-13). At this time Tyre consisted of a mainland city with two small islands just offshore which provided sheltered anchorages for ships. Under Hiram's rule the main island grew into an important city in its own right and eventually Hiram linked both islands and the mainland to create a large promontory reaching out to sea, with sizeable harbours on the north and south sides, known as the Sidonian and Egyptian harbours respectively. The Bible also records how Hiram joined with Solomon in mounting trading expeditions along the coasts of north and east Africa and Arabia, returning from Ophir with 420 talents, or around 14 tonnes, of gold (1 Kings 9: 27-28). Under Hiram and his successors, Tyre flourished to become the most important trading centre of all Phoenicia.

In the 9th century BC Tyre came under **Assyrian** domination after its conquest by Shalmaneser III in 842. It paid tribute to its new masters but at the same time retained a large degree of autonomy. Close relations with the Israelite kings continued, and Jezebel, of biblical infamy, the daughter of the king and high priest Ithobaal, was forced to marry King Ahab of Israel against her will. Tyre continued to flourish commercially, extending its trading links through the Straits of Gibraltar and down the west coast of Africa as well as north to Britain. During the eighth century Tyre repeatedly rebelled against Assyrian domination, at times finding itself isolated by alliances between its rival Phoenician city states and the Assyrians. When Hiram II rebelled against Assyrian rule in 727 BC, Sidon, mainland Tyre and Acre allied themselves with Assyria and provided 60 ships and 800 oarsmen for an attack on Hiram's island stronghold. In the event, the island held out for five years until a treaty was signed following the death of the Assyrian king Shalmaneser V in 722. In 701 a rebellion by the pro-Egyptian king Elu-eli (or Elouli) was put down more rapidly by Sennacherib. In 672, three years after the destruction of Sidon, Tyre again rebelled under the leadership of King Baal and this time it was not until 664 that Ashurbanipal comprehensively subjugated the city state.

With the fall of Nineveh in 612, control of Tyre passed relatively peacefully over to the **neo-Babylonians** (Chaldeans), until in 586 it once again rebelled. The neo-Babylonian king Nebuchadnezzar laid siege to the town for 13 years from 585 to 572, but its king, Ittobaal II, held out tenaciously, withdrawing to the island city and destroying the causeway that linked it to the mainland. Although the siege was eventually lifted and a treaty signed, the mainland city had been destroyed and Tyre's period of ascendancy was over. During the **Persian** era (538-332 BC) it was Sidon which flourished as the most important of the Phoenician city-states. Nevertheless, Tyre was able to recover something of its former significance under Persian rule, and when the **Greeks** led by Alexander the Great marched down the Phoenician coast in 332 exacting tribute from each of the city-states, it was only Tyre that chose to resist. The city held out for seven months, far longer than any other had previously resisted for. Alexander painstakingly rebuilt the causeway linking the island to the mainland and finally stormed the walls. Angered at its stubborn resistance he destroyed much of the city and either massacred or sold into slavery the majority of its inhabitants. Even so it recovered with time and began to hold Greek-style festivals, one of which was attended by the **Seleucid** emperor Antiochus IV Epiphanes on coming to power in 175 BC. Fifty years later Tyre had achieved complete autonomy within the Seleucid Empire.

After passing into **Roman** hands in 64 BC, Tyre continued to enjoy a certain degree of autonomy and, to judge from the massive hippodrome and the monumental arch which survive from this period, considerable prosperity. The city flourished also as a centre of intellectual activity, producing men such as Marinus, who founded the principals of mathematical geography and provided the basis of much of Ptolomy's subsequent work. As one of the first Lebanese towns to embrace Christianity, Tyre occupied a position of considerable importance during the **Byzantine** era, becoming the seat of a bishopric and then of an archbishopric.

Tyre (Sour)

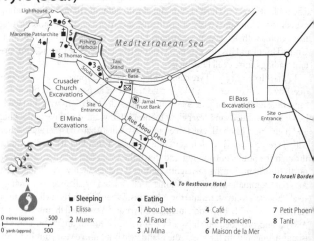

Conquered by the Muslim **Arabs** in 636 AD, Tyre continued to flourish as a commercial centre, becoming also a naval base under the Umayyad caliph Hisham (724-43 AD) and later falling under the control of the Fatimids. When the Persian Ismaili missionary Nasir-i-Khosrau visited in 1047, he talked of "The bazaars of opulent and flourishing Tyre". In 1099 Tyre escaped attack by the **Crusaders** as they marched on Jerusalem by paying a substantial tribute. In 1011 Baldwin laid siege to the city but was eventually forced to give up after the Tyrians succeeded in setting their siege tower on fire. Finally in 1124, with the help of a sea blockade mounted by the Venetian fleet, the Crusaders succeeded in taking the city after a five-month siege. In 1187 it repelled an attack by Salah ud-Din (Saladin) after his capture of Jerusalem, and it was not until 1291 that the Crusaders finally abandoned it along with Sidon and Beirut following the fall of Acre to the Mamelukes, thus relinquishing their last remaining enclaves in the Holy Land, with the exception only of the tiny island of Arwad which held out until 1302.

The **Mamelukes** dismantled much of the city, using the ruins as a quarry for building materials and thereafter it never really recovered its former importance. The causeway which Saladin had rebuilt and the two associated harbours were left to silt up. **Fakhr ud-Din II Maan** attempted to rebuild it in the 17th century, but ultimately it was Beirut and to a lesser extent Sidon which flourished. Under **Ottoman** rule it prospered moderately on the basis of its surrounding agricultural land, noted in particular for its sugar cane crop. Incorporated into **French Mandate** Greater Lebanon in 1920, it suffered greatly after 1948 from the closure of the Israeli-Lebanese border, which doomed it to a peripheral position at the end of a road leading nowhere. It was heavily damaged during the 1975-90 war, and though now slowly recovering, remains something of a backwater.

Sights

The **fishing harbour** (the original Sidonian harbour of the Phoenicians) is certainly the most picturesque aspect of modern-day Tyre. Here you can see small, brightly painted fishing boats, workshops where traditional wooden boat building techniques are still practised, and fishermen mending their nets just as they have done for centuries. There are also several pleasant restaurants and cafés in the vicinity (see below). The **souks**, which run east-west between the main square to the southeast of the harbour and the westernmost tip of the promontory, are no comparison with those of Tripoli, but they are lively and interesting all the same. Following the road that runs around the edge of the harbour and then winds its way through the Christian quarter, you pass on your left the **Maronite Patriarchite**. If you continue round in a loop to head south along the westernmost tip of the promontory, on a side street off to your left is the Greek Catholic **St Thomas church**. Dating originally to 1750, restoration work was carried out to the apse following bomb damage during the civil war, though miraculously the church was otherwise unharmed. The exterior is marked by a pretty arched and vaulted portico at the front. Inside, the original stonework has been left bare, giving the church a simple, unassuming feel. The nave is barrel vaulted, with tall columns separating it from the side-aisles.

The El Mina excavations are divided into two parts, the most interesting being the southernmost part. To your right as you enter is a double line of columns, thought to represent one side of the Roman **agora**. Going straight, you soon join the main **colonnaded street**, still paved in places with mosaics and marble and lined with re-erected columns of distinctive variegated marble brought

Fishing harbour, souks & churches

El Mina excavations

South Lebanon

from Greece. On your right as you follow the colonnaded street down towards the sea is a large **rectangular arena** or theatre with terraced seating. Its rectangular shape is unique, and it is thought that it used to be filled with water to allow nautical games of some kind to be held. Between the arena and the colonnaded street is a double row of small cells each connected by a doorway, which perhaps served as shops. To the left of the colonnaded street meanwhile is an extensive **baths complex**, identifiable by the profusion of distinctive stone discs which would have supported a raised floor heated by hot water flowing underneath. Just beyond the baths complex a single row of columns leads off from the colonnaded street at right-angles. This is believed to be part of a **palaestra**, or training area for athletes. It is as much the setting of the site, overlooking the ancient Egyptian harbour (now silted up) and the Mediterranean, as the ruins themselves that impresses, especially when seen in the late afternoon with the setting sun illuminating the sea and the stone of the ruins.

■ *Open daily 0800-1930 in summer, 0800-1800 in winter. Entry LL6,000 (students LL3,500; officially this is for Lebanese students only, though with a little gentle persuasion they will usually relent for foreign students).*

To the north of the main El Mina excavations and separated from them by a road is a smaller, fenced off area. Although there is no access to this site, from the road you can get a good view of the excavations which have revealed the basic outline of an early 12th-century **Crusader cathedral**, complete with a few huge re-erected granite columns. The line of smaller columns running across the site of the cathedral represents part of an earlier Roman road. It is thought that the cathedral was built on the site of the original temple of Melkhart, the god of ancient Tyre. Towards the seaward side of this site are further somewhat jumbled excavations dating from the Roman and Byzantine periods, including what is believed to be a much earlier Byzantine church dating from the early fourth century.

El Bass excavations
The entrance to the El Bass excavations is from the main road leading south through town towards the Israeli border. A track leads to a parking area from where you can join the **colonnaded street**, which would originally have joined up with the section of colonnaded street seen in the El Mina excavations. The first stretch of the street passes through what was a huge **necropolis** and is lined with a veritable forest of sarcophagi and funerary monuments. The majority of these date from the second century AD, although the earliest dates from the second century BC and the latest from the fourth century AD. Also lining the street is a portico, best preserved on the left-hand side. About two-thirds of the way along the street you come to a huge **triumphal arch**, marking the Roman entrance to the city. Approaching the arch, look out for traces of the underground water channels which formed part of the system of aqueducts supplying water to the island city from the spring of Ras al-Ain to the south of Tyre. Beyond the arch, the street drops to a lower level and is paved with larger, heavily worn stone slabs, in contrast to the neatly patterned stone paving which came before. To the left of the colonnaded street after the triumphal arch is the second century AD **hippodrome**, awesome for its sheer size. Measuring 480 m in length and with a total capacity estimated at 20,000 spectators, this is believed to be the largest ever built during the Roman period. Three sections of the tiered seating surrounding the track still survive in a relatively complete state, while in the centre is a narrow strip or *spina*, marked at either end by the bases of stone turning posts (*metae*), around which charioteers would have had to turn sharply as they circuited the track. Traces of mosaics can be seen covering the central *spina*, although these are very badly worn, while at the centre point there is an obelisk of Egyptian pink granite. The base of a structure towards the south end of the *spina* was perhaps a later Arab tower.

Essentials

A *Murex*, a brand new hotel on the sea front in the centre of Tyre, T347111, F347222, www.murexhotel.com All very smart: comfortable rooms with a/c, TV/dish, IDD, safe box, attached bath and balcony (all rooms with sea views). Restaurant on top floor, also with sea views. **A** *Rest House*, on the sea front to the south of the centre of Tyre, T740677, F345163, www.resthouse-tyre.com.lb This large, well run complex boasts a large outdoor swimming pool, a health club and its own private stretch of beach, with all the usual watersports on offer in summer. Comfortable rooms with a/c, TV/dish, phone, fridge and attached bath. Restaurant, bar, conference facilities. Room rates drop to just inside **B** category in winter. **B** *Abou Deeb*, around 10 km to the north of Tyre, T07-360250, F07-360251. Coming from Tyre, fork off to the right around 100 m past the *Mobil* petrol station (don't take the right turn by the petrol station itself). After around 400 m, go through a checkpost and cross over the Litani River, then turn left just after and the entrance to the hotel is on the left around 500 m further on. Pleasant, well run hotel with a lovely tranquil setting amidst lush vegetation overlooking the Litani River. Comfortable rooms with a/c, TV/dish, phone, attached bath and balcony. Restaurant, swimming pool, garden and children's play area. Good value. **B** *Elissa*, on the sea front in the centre of Tyre, T347551. Recently refurbished rooms with a/c, TV/dish, phone, attached bath and balcony. Also some slightly cheaper non-refurbished rooms though these are rather shabby and smell strongly of damp. Restaurant. Overall somewhat overpriced, try bargaining. **C** *Al Fanar*, on the sea front in the centre of Tyre, T741111, F740111, salwalid@inco.com.lb Although primarily a restaurant, this place has 4 simple but comfortable rooms with a/c and attached bath (some with sea views), with further rooms being prepared at the time of writing. There is also a 'studio' sleeping up to 5 people (4 in bunk beds) for US$80. Pleasant common balcony, and sitting room with TV/dish.

Sleeping
There are now 4 hotels in Tyre itself, as well as one on the banks of the Litani to the north of Tyre (see 'Sidon to Tyre', above)

Moderate *Al Fanar*, on the northern tip of the promontory, behind the lighthouse, T741111. Open daily 1000-late. Shaded, airy seating downstairs under a large awning, or upstairs on a covered terrace. Lebanese cuisine from around US$10-15 per head. The owners are also restoring 2 ancient barrel-vaulted basement rooms and fitting them out as a bar. *Maison de la Mer*, next door to *Al Fanar*, T03-648429. Open daily 1000-late. Seating indoors, or out on a large, very pleasant terrace area overlooking the sea. Lebanese cuisine from around US10-15 per head. *Al Mina,* by the fishing harbour, T347190. Open daily 0900-late. Slightly more upmarket a/c restaurant in a tastefully restored old building. Lebanese cuisine from around US$15-20 per head. *Le Petit Phoenician*, by the fishing harbour, T741562. Open daily 1200-late. Simpler version of *Le Phoenicien*, though very much in the same vein. Fish meals around US$15 per head, or around US$10 for meat. *Le Phoenicien*, by the fishing harbour, T740564. Open daily 1000-late. Prime location with seating inside or out on a covered terrace right on the edge of the fishing harbour. Lebanese cuisine. Around US$17-20 per head for mezze and fish. *Tanit*, T740987. Open 0930-1530, 1830-late. Attractive restaurant and bar set in a beautifully restored barrel-vaulted hall. Lebanese and European cuisine from around US$10-15 per head. Draught *Al Maaza* and *Heineken* LL4,000 per pint. Good atmoshere, popular with UNIFIL personel. The owner, a one-time resident of Northampton, UK, is very friendly.

Eating
As you might expect, seafood figures prominently on the menus here, typically accompanied by a spread of mezze dishes. Prices for fish are not as exhorbitant as they are in Beirut

Cheap/seriously cheap Along and just off Rue Abou Deeb, and around the bus/service taxi stand, there are several fast-food and snack places serving both falafels, shawarmas etc and pizzas, burgers etc. The *Abou Deeb*, owned by the same family as runs the *Abou Deeb* hotel, is clean and friendly and serves reasonably priced Lebanese food.

South Lebanon

Transport Buses, microbuses and service taxis all depart from beside the large parking area near the fishing harbour. By bus or microbus the fare to Sidon (Saida) is LL1,000, and to Beirut LL2,000. The fare by service taxi to Sidon is LL3,000, and to Beirut LL6,000. You may find the occasional microbus or service taxi heading to Tibnine, but you are far more likely to have to negotiate a taxi privately. For other destinations inland of Tyre, a private taxi is the only option.

Directory **Banks** There is a branch of the *Jamal Trust* bank near the post and telephone office with a cash machine which accepts Visa, Mastercard, Cirrus, +Plus and Visa-electron. There is also a small *Bureau de Change* near the main square/parking area to the southeast of the old fishing harbour, on the road which leads between the 2 parts of the El Mina excavations. **Communications** The **post** and **telephone office** is above the main square/parking area as you approach the harbour, opposite the UNIFIL base. Open 0800-1400, closed Fri. **Useful addresses** If you want up-to-date information on the **security** situation for places inland and south of Tyre such as Tibnine castle and Qana, ask at the UNIFIL base. They have a press office there and will be glad to give you advice.

Around Tyre

Tibnine Castle قلعة تبنين

Colour map 4, grid C2

Around 30 km to the southeast of Tyre, the Crusader castle of Tibnine stands out from miles around, perched on a steep hilltop with the Shi'ite town of Tibnine spread out across the slopes below

Heading south through Tyre along the main road, take the left turn signposted clearly for Bent Jbail. The road passes first through the densely populated Palestinian refugee camp of **Bourj ech-Chamali**. After just over 10 km you come to a small crossroads (signposted to 'Aitit' and 'Kana' to the right, this being the road to Qana, see below) with a UN observation post beside it.

Continuing straight on, after a little over 3 km, bear left where the road forks (at the time of writing, the road was being widened, so its configuration may change when completed). You pass next through the villages of Jouaiya, Mjadel and Chhabiye, the latter two, which blend into one another, with a UN checkpost between them (unmanned at the time of writing). After passing through another unmanned UN checkpost, bear right where the road forks in the village of Bir es-Salassel (14 km from the turning for Qana; a sign by the road reads ' Khirbet Selem', which is off to the left).

A little further on, after passing through the village of Sultaniyeh, Tibnine castle comes into view on a hilltop across the valley. The road descends to the bottom of the valley (bear right here; signposted to Tibnine), then climbs up the other side. Immediately after passing through a UN checkpost (this one still manned by an Irish regiment at the time of writing), you come to a junction. Straight on is signposted to Bent Jbail, while the fork off to the right up a steep hill is signposted for Tibnine castle. This route to the castle will get you lost or gridlocked in Tibnine's narrow network of streets. Better to *turn* right (signposted to the 'Serail'), this route taking you up to the castle on a good road. The 'Serail' which you pass on the way up is a large, modern government building established by Nabih Berri, who was born here and is the current Parliamentary Speaker, and leader of the Shi'ite party, Amal, since the disappearance of Moussa Sadr in 1979).

The castle The castle was built in 1104 by Hughes de Saint-Omer, lord of Tiberias, and named *Le Toron* by him, an old French word meaning 'high place' or 'isolated hill'. It was captured by Salah ud-Din (Saladin) in 1187 and remained in Arab hands until 1229 when it reverted to Crusader control. In 1266 it was captured by the Mameluke sultan Baibars and subsequently fell into disrepair, although it was rebuilt in the 17th century by the governor of Acre, Daher el-Omar.

Today, most of what remains dates from the 17th century, with only a few traces of the larger, older Crusader stonework. The outer defensive walls and towers are well preserved, although inside the castle is mostly in ruins. Extensive restoration work has been carried out on the main entrance gate and tower and on the cluster of buildings in the northwest corner of the castle. The massive bronze doors at the entrance to the castle are replicas, commissioned by the Norwegian contingent of UN soldiers stationed for a time here. (The originals on which they are based were found in Jerusalem, having been removed to there following the castle's capture by Salah ud-Din). At night the whole castle is floodlit and there is lighting inside each of the restored rooms, but taking things a little far are the 'exit' signs in each room, even when the only exit is the one you entered by. Perhaps the most impressive features are the views of the castle as you approach and the panoramic views of the surrounding countryside from the castle itself.

Continuing south from Tibnine, it is a further 12 km or so to the village of Bent Jbail. At the bottom of the hill a little under 2 km out of Tibnine, follow the road round to the left. A few kilometres further on, the road, previously narrow and rather pot-holed, suddenly turns into a wide and perfectly surfaced affair, this change marking the start of the former Israeli-occupied zone. A couple of kilometres before the town, where you arrive at what is in effect a T-junction, there is a sprawling military base, the former HQ of the Israeli Western Brigade. A large Hezbollah signboard by the entrance gives details about the base; when it was constructed, its function, capacity etc, and the "date of the ignominious departure" of the Israelis. Also detailed are the various military operations carried out against the base, complete with the numbers of Israelis killed and wounded. Particulary chilling is the series of photos showing a suicide bomber being blessed by a bearded imam, sitting in his vehicle, his vehicle seen exploding from afar, and then the wreckage being towed away.

Bent Jbail
Colour map 4, grid C2

Turning left at the T-junction takes you into the centre of Bent Jbail, a rather nondescript town with nothing of special note. Turning right, you can follow a road which winds its way first southwest and then west, passing through several small villages, and running close to the Israeli border (for one stretch you come quite literally to within a stone's throw of it). The scenery, of low, rolling hills, olive groves and orchards, is very picturesque, though obviously you should check that all is quiet along the border before driving along this route. The road descends into the coastal village of Naqoura around 38 km from the T-junction just outside Bent Jbail. From here it is a further 21 km back to Tyre.

Qana قانا

The village of Qana (or 'Cana') can be reached via a turning off the main road to Tibnine (see above). Taking this turning, bear right as you enter the village of Aitit, 3 km further on, and then right again in the centre of the village (signposted for 'Kana'). Around 2 km further on, turn right by the large Qana UN base (see box), to arrive after just over 2 km in Qana. Go straight across the mini-roundabout in the centre of the village (going left here brings you to a large memorial commemorating those killed in the massacre), follow the road round to the right immediately after, and then keep going straight on to arrive at the entrance to the site, on the right, a little over 1 km further on.

An alternative route from Tyre is to head south along the coast road and fork right a little over 2 km beyond the turning for Tibnine (clearly signposted for Qana). Just over 6 km further on you come to the **Tomb of Hiram**, by the roadside on the right. Although clearly of Phoenician origin, its popular

Colour map 4, grid C1

In the village of Qana itself several olive presses, grape presses and stone urns have been excavated, the latter said to have contained the water which Jesus turned into wine. Ask directions to find these – they are tucked away in an obscure corner of the village and rather difficult to find

South Lebanon

Operation Grapes of Wrath and The Qana Massacre

In April 1996 Israel initiated 'Operation Grapes of Wrath', the stated aim of which was to retaliate against Hezbollah 'nerve centres' responsible for coordinating attacks on northern Israel from within Lebanon. This was probably the most intensive shelling of Lebanese territory by Israel since the end of the civil war. It was also a dramatic departure from the usual pattern of low-level fighting in that Israeli artillery fire was directed at targets in and around Beirut as well as the more familiar targets in South Lebanon and the Bekaa Valley. The most infamous incident to occur during the operation was the shelling of the UN base at Qana, which resulted in the death of more than 100 civilians. It soon emerged that some Hezbollah guerrillas had entered the base shortly before the attack took place and the subsequent investigation carried out by the UN suggested that the base was deliberately targeted, although the Israelis denied this saying that the tragedy was an accident resulting from inaccurate maps of the area and an error in the coordinates given to the artillery unit. However, an amateur video showed an Israeli drone (pilotless reconnaissance aircraft) in the area in the time, suggesting that the Israelis would have known exactly what they were aiming at, and that there were civilians sheltering in the base at the time.

identification as the tomb of the 10th century BC king of Tyre is based more on local legend than any firm historical evidence. Built of huge stone blocks, the tomb once rose to a height of nearly 4 m. Today, however, it is rather forlorn and battered, covered by grafitti and with rubbish strewn around it. Its somewhat stunted size is partly due to the accumulation of earth around it over the centuries, and also the raised level of the modern road. The archaeologist Ernest Renan uncovered steps at the rear leading down to an underground chamber beneath the tomb, now blocked by an old car tyre. Continuing along the road, the entrance to the ancient site of Qana is on the left after a little over 2 km, in the outskirts of Qana village.

At the time of writing the site was being developed in a concerted effort to attract pilgrims and tourists, with a large new parking area under construction, complete with souvenir shops, vine-shaded seating areas, toilet facilities and a restaurant. The hillside below has been neatly landscaped, with carefully tended beds of shrubs, pathways and stone stairways leading past the various **rock carvings** of human figures and down to a **cave**, said to be where Jesus' followers sought refuge from persecution. Originally the carvings were thought to be of Egyptian origin, but more recently it has been suggested that Qana is the same Qana of Galilee where Jesus performed his first miracle, turning water into wine at a wedding (John 2: 1-11). Traditionally Qana of Galilee has been identified with Kafr Kanna in Israel, but there is considerable evidence to suggest that the Lebanese Qana is the true site, most notably the writings of Eusebius in the third century AD and those of St Jerome in the fourth century AD, both of whom refer to Qana as being close to Sidon. The carvings themselves are rather heavily worn, but the setting is pretty. ■ *At the time of writing there were no fixed opening hours or entrance fee, but this may well change once all the facilities here are up and running.*

Chouf Mountains تلال الشوف

15

Chouf Mountains الشوف

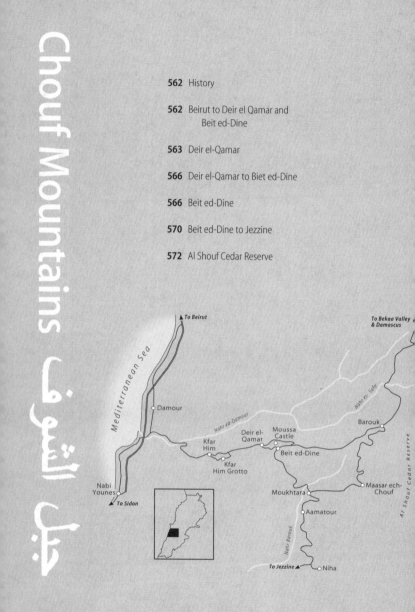

*Running parallel to the coast south of Beirut, the Chouf mountains are effectively a continuation of the Lebanon mountain range. They are considerably lower and less rugged than the Lebanon mountains further north and therefore more intensively cultivated. At the same time, the Chouf mountains have retained far more of their forest cover, a result of the ecologically minded outlook of the predominantly **Druze** population. Even in the thick of the civil war, the Druze leader Walid Jumblatt managed to enforce strict planning regulations and initiate tree planting projects. Today, the region has the largest nature reserve in the country, the **Al Shouf Cedar Reserve**, and the most extensive surviving stands of Lebanese cedars.*

*Traditionally the Chouf mountains were the centre of the **silk industry** which brought such wealth to its leading families. It was here that the house of Maan, the Ottoman appointed governors of the region, established their seat of government in the late 16th century, at **Deir el-Qamar**. In the early 19th century Emir Bashir Shihab II, a member of the Shihab family which took over from the Maans in the late 17th century, moved across the valley to **Beit ed-Dine**. Today Deir el-Qamar and Beit ed-Dine, with their variety of well preserved monuments and palaces remain the greatest historic attractions in the Chouf. Beit ed-Dine's beautifully restored palace built by Emir Bashir Shihab II is without a doubt Lebanon's most spectacular surviving monument from this period.*

Chouf Mountains

☞ *A foot in the door*

The Chouf mountains have plenty to offer besides the palace of Beit ed-Dine and the village of Deir el-Qamar, though these two sights should certainly be top of your list.

★ *If you really want to indulge yourself, the beautiful* **Mir Amin Palace** *hotel, a smaller version of the nearby Beit ed-Dine palace, has been lovingly restored, combining all the elegance of a 19th-century palace with the creature comforts of a five-star hotel. If such luxuries are beyond your budget you could always just come for a meal.*

★ *For those interested in nature and wildlife, the* **Al Shouf Cedar Reserve** *provides an enchantingly beautiful wilderness escape from all the congestion and sprawling development of Beirut.*

There are lots of walks and hikes you can do through the reserve, with trained rangers on hand to guide you.

★ *The* **road across into the Bekaa Valley** *from Maaser ech-Chouf offers a dramatically beautiful alternative route to the hectic Beirut-Damascus highway, and takes you right past some of the oldest cedars in the reserve.*

★ *Also extremely beautiful is the road leading south from Beit ed-Dine, following first the Nahr Barouk and then the deep gorge of the Nahr Aaray to arrive at the town of Jezzine. On the way, those with a head for heights can make a detour to* **Qalat Niha**, *a rock-cut network of caves reached by a narrow ledge running along an otherwise sheer cliff-face.*

History

From the 11th century onwards the Chouf mountains were the stronghold of the Druze. However, during the 17th century increasing numbers of Maronite Christians came to settle here at the invitation of the Druze emir, Fakhr ud-Din II Maan, to the extent that by the mid-19th century Christians actually formed the majority. The massacres of Maronites which occurred in the Chouf in 1860 resulted in a large-scale exodus of Maronites, a process which was repeated during the civil war of 1975-90. Today, considerable numbers of Christians are returning to their former villages and there have been concerted attempts to restore the largely harmonious relations which existed between the Christians and Druze prior to the communal conflicts of the 19th and 20th centuries.

Beirut to Deir el Qamar and Beit ed-Dine

Head south out of Beirut to join the coastal motorway for Sidon and then after 25 km take the exit clearly signposted on an overhead sign for Damour and Beit ed-Dine (see page 535 for details of this first section of the route). Having left the motorway, the road first follows the Nahr ed-Damour, with several pleasant restaurants and snack bars along the road, before starting to climb steeply into the Chouf mountains. After a little under 12 km you come to a mini-roundabout in the village of **Kfar Him**. A short diversion off the main road here takes you to the Kfar Him grotto. Turn right at the mini-roundabout and follow this road for 1½ km to reach the grotto, on the right, now topped by a large building incorporating a souvenir shop, restaurant and hotel.

Kfar Him grotto
Colour map 4, grid B2

Although no match for Jeita Grotto and really rather expensive given the small size of the caves, a lot of effort has gone into making the best of the rock formations here through the careful use of lighting (and a fair bit of judicious sculpting). The exit has been arranged so that you pass through the large shop above, where a vast array of polished stones, crystals and all kinds of other souvenirs and handicrafts are on sale. The restaurant is open during the summer only, while on the top floor is the **B/C** hotel, T05-720500. Reasonably comfortable rooms with a/c, TV/dish and attached bath. ■ *Open daily, 0800-1900 in summer, 0800-1700 in winter. Entry LL6,000.*

Deir el-Qamar دير القمر

Arriving at Deir el-Qamar's main square you find yourself confronted by a small pocket of carefully preserved 17th-18th century Lebanon. Late in the 16th century Emir Fakhr ud-Din II Maan made Deir el-Qamar his capital, abandoning his former capital at Baakline due to water shortages there, and it remained the capital of the local rulers of Mount Lebanon until the late 18th century. Concerted efforts on the part of the Department of Antiquities in the 1950s helped ensure that the various buildings from this period were carefully preserved and new ones prevented from spoiling the overall effect. The village is a pleasant place to wander round and its buildings a worthy primer for the splendours of Beit ed-Dine palace across the valley.

The majority of the interesting buildings are grouped around the main square. **Fakhr ud-Din's mosque** was first built in 1493 and later restored by Fakhr ud-Din II Maan. Small and simply designed, its octagonal minaret nevertheless adds a graceful touch to the square. Immediately behind the mosque on a higher level is the **old souk**, which still houses some small shops, as well as a snack bar selling sandwiches, soft drinks etc.

Behind this again, on the other side of the road which climbs up around the back of the square, is **Younes Maan's palace**, boasting a particularly elegant entrance doorway. Housed in the ground floor of the palace is a new **Holograms museum**. It may sound a little gimmicky but actually the displays, consisting of a fascinating range of different types of holograms (even stereograms, or 'moving' holograms), all of very high quality, are thoroughly absorbing and well worth the entrance fee. The hall in which they are displayed is a large, vaulted and pillared affair which remains wonderfully cool and airy even in the height of summer. ■ *Open daily 0900-1900 in summer, 0900-1600 in winter. Entry LL6,000 (children LL4,000).*

The **silk khan and warehouse** of Fakhr ud-Din II Maan occupies much of the northeast side of the square. Dating from 1595, the scale of these buildings reflects the great wealth generated through the silk industry. At the level of the square are the halls which were used as servants quarters and stables. Upstairs, meanwhile, was the main part of the silk khan and warehouse, now housing the **Centre Culturel et Linguistique Français**. You are free to wander around the cultural centre, which

Phone code: 05
Colour map 4, grid B2

Deir el-Qamar was one of the first places in the Chouf mountains to succeed in restoring a harmonious balance between its traditionally mixed Druze and Christian population

Sights

Younes Maan was the brother of Fakhr ud-Din II Maan, and ruled from 1613 to 1618 while his brother was in exile in Italy

Chouf Mountains

Deir el-Qamar

To Moussa Castle & Beit ed-Dine

To Beit ed-Dine (Direct route)

N

metres   100
yards   100

6 Palace of the poet Nicolas el-Turq
7 Fakhr ud-Din's palace (Marie Baz museum)
8 Ahmed Chehab's Palace
9 Church of Saidet et-Tallé (Notre Dame de la Colline)
10 Salle de Colline
11 Plaque de Martyrs
12 Fountain
13 Youssef Chehab's serail (Palace de Justice)
14 Fakhr ud-Din Mosque
15 Old Souk

Younes Maan's Palace (Holograms museum)
Silk Khan & warehouse
Jesuit School
Terrace (Pedestrian only)
Synagogue

Emir Fakhr ud-Din II Maan

In 1590 the Druze leader Fakhr ud-Din II Maan was appointed local governor of the Chouf mountains by the Ottomans, following more than six decades in which the Ottomans had struggled to subdue repeated rebellions amongst the Druze, many of them instigated by the chieftains of the House of Maan. Although the Ottomans chose Fakhr ud-Din in the hope that he would prove to be loyal and subservient, he soon rose to be one of the most powerful local rulers in Lebanon's history. Indeed, many Lebanese history books characterize him as the historical founder of the Lebanese state, since he succeeded in uniting most of present day Lebanon under his rule, the first local ruler to achieve this. Initially he only controlled the Ottoman Sanjak (administrative district) of Sidon. Soon after, however, Beirut was added to this, and by 1621 he had extended his control to include the Maronite heartland of the Qadisha valley, and the Sanjak of Tripoli. Indeed, his power stretched far beyond the boundaries of present day Lebanon, to include the Sanjaks of Safad (in present day Israel) and Ajloun (in present day Jordan). At one stage he is even believed to have reached as far as Palmyra in Syria, and to have built the castle which overlooks the Palmyrene and Roman ruins.

But Fakhr ud-Din II Maan did more than just amass territory. According to the historian PK Hitti, his aims from the beginning included "building up a greater Lebanon, severing the last ties between it and Turkey and setting it well on the path of 'modernism' and progress". Hitti goes on to observe, "By intermarriage, bribery, intrigue, treaties and battles - the recognized media of the day - he came very near achieving full success. The man was incontestably the ablest and most fascinating figure in the history of Ottoman Lebanon, and indeed one of the most colourful of the entire empire."

In terms of developing and modernizing his kingdom, Fakhr ud-Din drew much of his inspiration from Europe. From 1613-18 he was forced into exile in the Italian duchy of Tuscany after entering into a treaty with Ferdinand I, the Medici grand duke of Tuscany, which included a secret military article against the Ottomans. During his stay in Florence he picked up many ideas, and on his return set about expanding, strengthening and modernizing his kingdom with great zeal. New agricultural techniques were applied throughout the kingdom, with the development of the silk industry forming one of the mainstays of the economy (and also providing the impetus for the migration of Maronite Christian families into the Chouf mountains, see page 486). Fakhr ud-Din was also responsible for carefully nurturing trading relations with Europe and it was under his auspices that European trading missions in Lebanon, notably French and Tuscan, first became firmly established.

Ultimately, however, the Ottomans became uneasy at his growing power and independence. In 1633 they ordered the pashas of Syria and Egypt to march against him, sending also a fleet of ships to attack the coastal towns. His son Ali led a brave resistance but was eventually captured and beheaded, while Fakhr ud-Din was forced to flee from his capital at Deir el-Qamar, taking refuge first at Qalat Niha and then in a small cave nearby, before being captured and taken to Constantinople. Two years later, on 13 April 1635, he was put to death, the Ottoman authorities fearing his influence even in exile.

incorporates a school and library, although large groups should get prior consent to visit. Note the beautiful open-arched window overlooking the main square. The library occupies what was originally the warehouse, built in 1616 to store merchandise etc. From the road which climbs up around the back of the square, a terrace on the right allows you to view two interesting buildings from the outside. The first was the **Jesuit school** while the second was the **synagogue**, dating from the 17th century.

Returning to the main square, adjacent to the silk khan and warehouse is **Fakhr ud-Din's palace**. Fakhr ud-Din built this palace in 1620: his earlier palace had been burned down by the pasha of Tripoli while he was in exile in Italy and according to legend, after defeating his adversary Fakhr ud-Din built his new palace with stones from the pasha's fortress at Akkar (see page 529). The palace, owned by the Baz family who acquired it in 1925, now houses the **Marie Baz museum**. This consists of an impressive collection of waxworks of Lebanon's major historical and political figures (worthy of Madame Tussaud's in terms of the quality of the modelling) displayed in what was the harem of the palace. There is a small cafeteria in the courtyard, with another rooftop café/restaurant due to open soon, as well as plans for a bar. ■ *Open daily, 0800-2200 in summer 0900-1700 in winter. Entry LL6,000 (children LL4,000).*

Next door to the Marie Baz museum is **Ahmad Chehab's palace**, also owned by the Baz family, though this building is closed to the public (Ahmad Chehab was of the same Shihab family as Emir Bashir Shihab II, the names Chehab and Shihab being interchangeable). This palace was built in 1755 at the request of Ahmed Chehab's wife, who refused to live in her first house where two of her sons had died. In 1784 Ibrahim Pasha lived here while coordinating resistance to Ottoman rule.

To the south of the main square, on the opposite side of the road, is **Youssef Chehab's Serail**, or Palais de Justice. Today this serves as the local town hall, but parts of it are open to the public. Note the two carved lions in circles above the doorway, representing symbols of justice. The entrance leads through into a large courtyard, decorated with beautifully carved stonework and a variety of different keystone arrangements in the arches above the windows and doors. The royal apartment occupies one side of the courtyard: there is a central dome in the ceiling and in one wall a large square bay window, complete with its beautiful original wood panelling, looking out across the valley towards Beit ed-Dine. One doorway from the courtyard gives onto a steep flight of stairs leading up to the roof. ■ *Open weekdays 0900-1400 only. Entry free.*

Reached via the small road which winds its way steeply down into the valley and then up again to provide a direct route across to Beit ed-Dine is the **Church of Saidet et-Tallé** (literally 'Our Lady of the Hill' or 'Notre Dame de la Colline'), and beside it a **Maronite monastery**. Though in its present form the church dates mostly from the 16th century onwards, it is believed to have been built orginally in 451, on the site of a temple dedicated to the goddess Astarte. The church is the focus of a major feast dedicated to the Virgin Mary which is held each year on the first Sunday in August, attracting pilgrims from far and wide. In the large courtyard of the church is the **Plaque de Martyrs**, commemorating those who died in the massacres of 1860.

On the south side of the church, carved above the original doorway, is a rosette containing a cross and an inverted crescent. It is from this symbol that the village takes its name (Deir el-Qamar translates literally as 'Monastery of the Moon')

Off to the right of the road leading past the Church of Saidet el-Tallé there are a couple more churches down narrow cobbled streets, the 17th-century **Our Lady of the Rosary** and the 18th-century **church of St Elie**.

Sleeping

C *La Bastide*, on the left, just over 1 km out of Dier el-Qamar, on the main road to Beit ed-Dine, T505320, F505849, bastideir@hotmail.com Friendly, family-run place offering spotlessly clean, pleasantly furnished rooms with hob and sink unit, fridge, heater and attached bath. Rooms at the front have balconies and impressive views across to Beit ed-Dine. Good value. Recommended.

Eating

On the right as you enter the village (coming from the coast) is the *Gardenia*, with a pleasant shaded terrace, offering Lebanese cuisine for around US$10-15 per head. Just past Moussa castle, on the way to Beit ed-Dine (see below) is the *Farah*, T503233, offering excellent views down into the valley and serving good Lebanese cuisine for around US$15-20 per head. When it opens, the rooftop café/restaurant in the Marie Baaz museum looks like it will be a very pleasant place to eat.

For **cheap eats**, there are several simple snack places along the main road through the village, and around the main square, where you can get the usual sandwiches etc.

Transport   **Service taxis** stop in the main square in Deir el-Qamar en route between Beirut and Beit ed-Dine. The fare from Beirut (Cola bus stand) is LL4,000. They are fairly regular, though less frequent out of season. After nightfall they are very scarce. During the summer season you may be able to find **microbuses** running to here from Cola bus stand for less (around LL2,000).

Deir el-Qamar to Beit ed-Dine

The main road through Deir el-Qamar continues east, past Moussa castle (2 km) before rounding the head of the valley, just after which a very sharp left turn (4 km) leads back towards the Beirut-Damascus highway via Barouk and Ain Zhalta (see below). The main road, meanwhile, continues on to Beit ed-Dine (6 km from Deir el-Qamar). Alternatively, if you bear right at Youssef Chehab's Serail in Deir el-Qamar (coming from the coastal highway), a minor road descends steeply to the bottom of the valley and then climbs directly up to Beit ed-Dine, 3 km away by this route. If it is not too hot, this makes for a very pleasant walk.

Moussa castle   Mr Moussa, the man responsible for this rather bizarre Disney-style castle, is
Colour map 4, grid B2   sometimes on hand to tell the story of how, as a child, he was beaten by his schoolmaster for dreaming of living in a castle and as a result vowed one day to make his dream come true. Having achieved success as a businessman, he poured much of his wealth into building the edifice you see today which for all its tackiness is every bit as popular amongst Lebanese tourists as the monuments of Deir el-Qamar and the palace of Beit ed-Dine. Each of the castle's large embossed stones is carved with scenes and symbols from Lebanon's history, while inside is a museum with mannequins in costume portraying scenes from traditional Lebanese mountain life. The added touch here is that each of the mannequins is mechanized, so that they actually grind corn, spin wool, smoke nargilehs etc ... Downstairs a whole room is given over to depicting Moussa as a young child being beaten by his schoolmaster for dreaming of his castle. It's all a bit silly, but if you have the time worth a visit for its kitsch value if nothing else. ■ *Open daily 0800-1800. Entry LL6,000 (children LL3,000). For more info, try the website; www.moussacastle.com.lb*

Beit ed-Dine بيت الدين

Phone code: 05   The village of Beit ed-Dine is the setting for the beautifully restored palace built
Colour map 4, grid B2   by the emir Bashir Shihab II in the early 19th century. This is amongst the most impressive sights in Lebanon dating from this period. Its grand scale, elegant architecture and sumptuous interiors give some idea of the power and independence which Bashir achieved as the Ottoman appointed governor of what was to become Mount Lebanon.

Bashir also built three further palaces nearby for his sons, one of which still survives and has now been converted into the luxury *Mir Amin Palace* hotel (see 'Sleeping' below).

History   Beit ed-Dine translates literally as 'House of Faith' and the palace was in fact built around a former Druze hermitage. Bashir employed the very best artisans

Emir Bashir Shihab II

Emir Bashir Shihab II ranks alongside Fakhr ud-Din II Maan as one of the most important figures of pre-independence Lebanon. He came to power in 1788, having outmanoeuvred other members of his family to secure the position of Ottoman appointed governor of the Chouf region with the help of the Jumblatts, a powerful local Druze family. He proceeded to consolidate his position ruthlessly, killing, blinding, imprisoning and exiling rival members of his own family and later turning against other influential families. In 1825 he persuaded the Ottoman pasha of Acre to have the leader of the Jumblatts, Bashir Jumblatt, hanged. During the course of his earlier intrigues he triggered riots in Deir el-Qamar after executing a popular Maronite prince and as a result decided to move his government to Beit ed-Dine.

The Shihab family first came to power in 1697, after the death of Ahmad Maan, the last of the Maanid dynasty. The Shihabs were descended from the Maans through the female line, but unlike the Maans who were Druze, they were Sunni Muslims. As such they had little support amongst the Druze of the region (not withstanding the initial support of the Jumblatts) and turned for support to the Maronite Christians. Towards the end of the 18th century, they converted to Maronite Christianity, although Bashir Shihab II took great care not to emphasize his own faith, striving instead to achieve unity amongst his subjects through even-handed and just rule. His palace at Beit ed-Dine had no chapel, and engraved on the wood panelling of the hall in which he held court was his motto, "The homage of a governor towards God is to observe justice, for an hour of justice is better than a thousand months of prayer." Indeed, despite his ruthlessness, Bashir was noted for his

enlightened rule, building roads and bridges and initiating irrigation schemes, as well as promoting health and education. By 1821 he had extended his rule to the Maronite heartlands of Mount Lebanon proper (centred on the Qadisha valley) and thus, like Fakhr ud-Din II Maan, succeeded in uniting under his rule the whole of what became the political entity of Mount Lebanon.

Although known both locally and abroad as 'Emir', a title befitting a local ruler of considerable power and independence, to the Ottomans, Bashir was officially nothing more than a local tax collector answerable to the pashas of Tripoli and Sidon. It was only the weakness of the Ottoman empire at this time which allowed Bashir to consolidate his position of power. Ever eager to secure greater autonomy from his Ottoman overlords, Bashir was quick to offer his support to Mohammad Ali Pasha, the viceroy of Egypt, when he rose against Ottoman rule. In 1832 he allied himself with Ibrahim Pasha, the son of Mohammad Ali, who occupied Syria on his father's behalf. However, this state of affairs alarmed the European powers and in particular Britain, who feared that this upset to the balance of power in the region threatened her commercial interests. In 1840 Britain and Austria helped the Ottomans drive Ibrahim Pasha from Syria. Emir Bashir Shihab II was captured and sent into exile. Just one year later Shihab rule collapsed and direct Ottoman rule was established, to be replaced soon after by a new arrangement which divided Mount Lebanon into two separately governed Maronite and Druze enclaves. The Shihabs are still one of the leading families in Lebanon, though the name is today generally spelt 'Chehab'.

and craftsmen from Damascus and Aleppo for its construction, as well as architects from Italy. According to some sources the palace took 30 years to complete. After Bashir was sent into exile in 1840, it was used by the Ottomans as a government building. During the French Mandate period it served as a local administrative office before being declared a historic monument with restoration work starting in 1934. After independence the palace was used as the summer residence of the president. During the recent civil war it suffered heavy damage, but after 1984, when the fighting in the Chouf had receded, the Druze leader Walid Jumblatt (currently an MP and leader of the Progressive Socialist Party) ordered restoration work to be carried out once again. Today the palace serves once again as the president's summer residence, so sections of it are closed to the public.

Sights Approaching the main entrance, note the lions above the entrance doorway, as on Youssef Chehab's Serail in Deir el-Qamar. At the end of the entrance hall is a room which now contains the small **museum** chronicling the life of Kamal Jumblatt. Born in 1917, Kamal Jumblatt studied sociology, psychology and law at the Sorbonne in France and St Joseph's University in Beirut before rising to become probably the most important and enigmatic leaders of the Druze. In 1949 he founded the Progressive Socialist Party, establishing close links with the Soviet Union and China. As well as being a committed politician, he was deeply interested in philosphy and eastern mysticism, visiting India in 1953 and returning with a Hindu guru. In 1977 he was assassinated, probably by the Syrians, and assumed an almost cult status amongst the Druze.

Leaving the entrance hall you find yourself in a huge courtyard, open on one side to give views out over the valley. This first outer section of the palace is known as the **Dar el-Baraniyyeh**. Along the entire length of the right-hand side of the courtyard is a long vaulted hallway supported by a double line of columns. Half-way along this stairs give access to the upper floor, consisting of an open terrace with a series of interconnected rooms behind. These two floors provided accommodation for guests, with sleeping quarters above and stables below. Offering hospitality to passers-by was a matter of honour, particularly amongst people of social standing. According to tradition, visitors could stay for up to three days without having to reveal their identity or their business. Today the upper floor houses the **Rashid Karami Archaeological and Ethnographic museum** (Rashid Karami was prime minister of Lebanon six times between 1955-70). You start at the eastern end, where there is a scale model of the entire palace, and then work your way through the rooms. A variety of artefacts is displayed: Canaanite/Phoenician pottery; Roman glassware; jewellery, figurines and statuary; Islamic period glazed pottery; weapons ranging from swords and armour through to rifles and semi-automatic machine-guns; traditional costumes; and old photographs.

Beit ed-Dine Palace

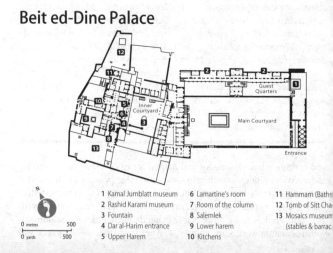

1 Kamal Jumblatt museum	6 Lamartine's room	11 Hammam (Baths)
2 Rashid Karami museum	7 Room of the column	12 Tomb of Sitt Cha
3 Fountain	8 Salemlek	13 Mosaics museum
4 Dar al-Harim entrance	9 Lower harem	(stables & barrac
5 Upper Harem	10 Kitchens	

0 metres 500
0 yards 500

Returning to the main courtyard, at the western end a double staircase leads up to an elaborately decorated doorway leading through to the middle section of the palace, known as the **Dar el-Wousta**. The vaulted entrance hallway leads through to a beautiful **courtyard** with a central fountain and graceful arcades around the sides. The arcades on the north and west sides are on the upper floor and reached by double stairs. The southern side of the courtyard consists of an open raised terrace once again providing views out over the valley. The rooms around this courtyard were used as reception rooms, conference rooms and offices and are all very beautifully decorated with wood panelling, gold and silver leaf, marble etc. One of the conference rooms is equipped with a small separate conferring room; inside, an arrangement of water flowing over marble served both as a cooling device and as a means of drowning out voices to allow privacy during delicate negotiations. The upper floor arcade on the west side of the courtyard (opposite you as you enter) boasts particularly beautifully decorated stonework. This is the **upper harem** of the Dar al-Harim; the room to the left is known as **Lamartine's room**, it was here that the poet stayed when he visited in 1833.

To the left of the double staircase leading to the upper harem is a monumental archway and behind it a richly decorated doorway providing access to the inner section of the palace, or **Dar al-Harim**. The doorway leads first into a waiting room, known as the **room of the column** due to the single column in the centre supporting the vaulted ceiling. To the south of this is the reception hall or **salemlek**, built on two levels with a beautiful mosaic floor and richly decorated marble walls. It was here that Bashir would hold court; on one of the walls is inscribed the motto which underpinned Bashir's philosophy of government (see box). To the west of the waiting room is the **lower harem** or private living quarters of Bashir and his family, consisting of a small courtyard with two *iwans* and rooms arranged around it. To the north of this are the kitchens, which in their heyday served up enough food to feed more than 500 people each day. To the north of the kitchens are the palace's **hammam** or baths (accessible also via a doorway from the courtyard of the Dar el-Wousta), consisting of a series elaborately decorated rooms; the *frigidarium* (cold room), *tepidarium* (warm room) and *caldarium* (hot room). To the north of the baths is a shaded garden, in one corner of which is the **tomb of Sitt Chams**, the first wife of Bashir. The ashes of Bashir, brought back from Turkey in 1947, are also contained in the tomb.

Much of this area, together with the Dar al-Harim beyond it, is closed to the public, though exactly which rooms are closed depends on whether the president is in residence &/or holding audiences when you visit

Chouf Mountains

Detail of fountain, Beit ed-Dine Palace

Returning to the Dar el-Baraniyyeh (the outer section of the palace), to the left of the double staircase giving access to the Dar el-Wousta or middle section, steps lead down to a series of large vaulted halls which served as stables and barracks. These were large enough to accommodate 600 horses and their riders, as well as 500 foot-soldiers. Today the stables and barracks house a **mosaics museum** containing an impressive collection of mosaics gathered from various sites around Lebanon. The majority come from a fifth/ sixth-century Byzantine church uncovered during the course of excavations at Jiyyeh (ancient *Porphyrion*), on the coast 30 km to the south of Beirut (see page 535). Some of the mosaics have been incorporated into an area of garden adjacent to the stables/barracks. ■ *Open 0900-1800 in summer, 0900-1600 in winter, closed Mon. Entry LL7,500 for foreigners, LL5,000 for Lebanese, LL2,000 for students and free for children. Official guides are on hand for detailed tours of the palace; if you take a guide you may be able to gain access to parts of the inner palace which are otherwise out of bounds. There is a souvenir shop and café (tea, coffee, snacks etc) in the main outer courtyard of the palace.*

Sleeping **L** *Mir Amin Palace*, PO Box 113-5881, T/F501315 miramin@cyberia.net.lb This smaller but equally lavish version of the Beit ed-Dine palace, built by Emir Bashir Shihab II for his third son, Emir Amin, offers panoramic views from its hilltop location and has been beautifully restored to serve as a luxurious hotel. To get there, head south out of Beit ed-Dine in the direction of Jezzine, and then take the signposted left turn to climb up to the hotel, just over 1 km from the centre of Beit ed-Dine. Large, comfortable, elegantly furnished rooms with a/c, TV/dish, IDD, minibar and attached bath. Restaurants, bar, conference and banqueting facilities, large outdoor swimming pool, tennis courts and children's playground. 40% discount in low season (1/10-31/5) brings rates down to **A** category. An excellently run place with real character and class. Recommended.

In terms of mid-range accommodation, there is *La Bastide* hotel just outside Deir el-Qamar (see above), and the *Barouk Palace* hotel 12 km from Beit ed-Dine in the village of Barouk (see below). There is also a hotel in **Samqaniyeh**, a little over 2 km from Beit ed-Dine, on the road to Jezzine (see 'Beit ed-Dine to Jezzine', below). **C** *SJS Motel*, on the right as you head down into Samqaniyeh, T05-501567. Most the rooms here are actually suites with separate sitting room (TV/dish), kitchen (hob, sink, fridge) and bathroom. Clean and comfortable but right on the main road and so a little noisy.

Eating There are 2 excellent restaurants in the *Mir Amin Palace* palace hotel. The **Al Diwan** serves Lebanese cuisine and offers a Sun lunchtime buffet (1200-1700) costing LL25,000 per head, children LL5,000 (+5% tax). You can eat in a large vaulted hall, or on the terrace, with stunning views out over the valley. The **Arcadia** serves Italian/European cuisine for around US$20-30 per head.

Heading up the hill out of Beit ed-Dine towards the *Mir Amin Palace* hotel, on the left is the **Amirah** (sign in Arabic only; next door to the clearly signed *Moulin*, which was closed at the time of writing), T503003. Small, slightly dingy but friendly, family-run place offering Lebanese cuisine for around US$10-15 per head, or good value snacks (eg mannoushi or sandwiches) for LL2,000-3,500.

Continuing up the hill, a fork off to the right 800 m from the main square in Beit ed-Dine brings you after a further 1 km to the **New Garbatella**, T301411. Cosy, pleasantly furnished restaurant and bar with seating indoors or out on a lovely shaded patio terrace offering great views. Serves a mixture of European (particularly Italian; pizza, pasta etc) and Lebanese cuisine for around US$10-20 per head.

At the top of the hill (1½ km from the main square in Beit ed-Dine and around 400 m past the turning leading up to the *Mir Amin Palace* hotel), by the roundabout and war memorial, is the **Al Dawar**, T501309, a large, traditional Arabic-style restaurant serving Lebanese cuisine for around US$10-15 per head.

Beit ed-Dine to Jezzine

The road south from Beit ed-Dine to Jezzine is particularly beautiful, especially to the south of Moukhtara. From here the road first follows the Nahr Barouk, and then the deep gorge of the Nahr Aaray which plunges away to the right, while to the left is a steep mountainside rising up to sheer cliffs (these being the setting for Qalat Niha, which can be clearly seen from the road, to the south of the turning up to Niha).

Heading south out of Beit ed-Dine (ie up the hill from the main square), you pass the left turn for the *Mir Amin Palace* hotel to arrive after 1½ km at a large roundabout and war memorial. Bear left here (signposted to 'Moukhtara 6 km' and 'Cedres du Chouf 22 km'). A little over 1 km further on you enter **Samqaniyeh**. Though marked on most maps as a small village, nowadays it is more like a medium-sized town, spreading for a couple of kilometres along the main road and boasting lots of shops, a couple of banks, restaurants and one hotel. Keep going straight through the town and then, soon after leaving it, bear left where the road forks (a little over 4 km from the roundabout and war memorial).

From here it is a little over 3 km into the centre of the picturesque village of **Moukhtara**. This is the home of the Jumblatt family and boasts an impressive 'palace', occupied today by Walid Jumblatt, the current leader of the Druze. On weekend mornings he opens his doors to his followers, listening to their problems and grievances and dispensing advice. A sharp left turn in the village leads up towards Maaser ech-Chouf, providing an alternative route up to the Al Shouf Cedar Reserve (see below). Continuing straight on (south) along the main road, you pass through the small villages of Ain Quern and Aamatour, and then through the sprawling village of Baytar, to arrive after a little under 15 km at a left turn and checkpost. This checkpost marks the former 'border' with what was until May 2000 territory controlled by Israel's proxy army, the South Lebanon Army (SLA). The left turn leads up to the village of Niha, and also to the shrine of Nabi Yacoub and and the mountain eyrie of Qalat Niha. Continuing straight on, fork right after just over 6 km to arrive in the centre of Jezzine, 1 km further on (see page 544).

Shrine of Nabi Yacoub

Taking the left turn for Niha by the checkpost, the road climbs steeply to arrive after 4 km at what is in effect a fork (in fact you intersect with another road at the point where it goes through a hairpin bend). Bear right here (left for Niha village) to continue climbing, arriving a little under 3 km further on at the Shrine of Nabi Yacoub (or Nabi Ayoub), revered in Druze tradition as the tomb of the prophet Jacob. The complex is a simple, modern affair, with the main focus being the dome-topped building housing the tomb. For Druze especially, but also for Christians and Muslims, this is an important place of pilgrimage. For the less devout, it is the panoramic views of the surrounding mountains which are the main attraction (including a particularly imposing ridge with exposed seams of rock strata running in dead-staight parallel lines like some massive giant's highway).

Qalat Niha

Heading up from the checkpost on the main road, around 100 m before you arrive at the fork, an unmarked turning on the right doubles back sharply up the hillside. Taking this turning, at the first hairpin you come to (around 300-400 m further on, marked by a couple of concrete bunkers), go staight on along a rough track and then turn right after 200 m (signposted 'Qalat Fakhr ed-Dine' on a Ministry of Tourism sign). From here it is possible to continue on for some of the way by car, but much nicer to walk. After around 1 km the track turns gradually to a path, following a ledge along the otherwise sheer cliff-face, with dizzying views down into the Nahr Aaray.

In terms of its isolation and stunning natural setting this place is hard to match, though it's definitely not recommended for vertigo sufferers!

The so called 'castle' (known locally as 'Qalat Niha' or 'Shafiq Tiron') consists of a series of natural and man-made caves in the cliff face, many of which are no longer accessible except with climbing equipment, being on a higher level than the main ledge. In places you can see traces of rock-cut stairs, but most striking are the numerous huge water cisterns hewn into the solid rock and lined with plaster; evidence that this mountain eyrie was designed to withstand a lengthy siege. The complex is thought to date back to at least the 12th century, built either by the Crusaders or a local Arab ruler. According to legend, this was where Fakhr ed-Din II Maan took refuge from the Ottomans in 1633, holding out for several months. Eventually, however, his besiegers succeeded in poisoning his water supplies, forcing him to flee to another set of caves near Jezzine, where he was finally captured.

Al Shouf Cedar Reserve أرز الشوف

Colour map 4, grid B2

The reserve is home to 26 species of wild mammals, including mountain gazelles, wolves, hyenas, caracal lynx, wild cats, porcupines, badgers and squirrels, as well as more than 200 species of birds

Officially established in 1996 and opened to the public in 1997, the Al Shouf Cedar Reserve covers an area 550 sq km (some 5% of Lebanon's total area), making it the largest nature reserve in the country. It stretches north-south along the Jebel Barouk and Jebel Niha ranges, which form the watershed between the Chouf region to the west and the Bekaa Valley to the east. Within the reserve, around 550 ha are forested, primarily with cedars (representing 25% of Lebanon's remaining cedars), but also with some 16 other species, including oak, juniper and pine. In all, some 524 species of plants have been identified so far. There are three main areas of forest; the Barouk forest, which is the largest, covering over 400 ha; the Ain Zhalta forest covering over 100 ha; and the Masaar al-Chouf forest, which is the smallest, at just 6 ha, but boasts the oldest trees.

As well as protecting the flora and fauna and encouraging the regeneration of the cedar forests, the reserve aims to provide real economic benefits to the local community. It is already achieving this by providing local people with employment as rangers, and by providing an outlet for the sale of local nature-based products. There are also plans to initiate scientific research projects within the reserve.

Ins and outs
The *Al Shouf Cedars Society*, which is responsible for administering the reserve, has its office next door to the *Barouk Palace* hotel in the village of Barouk, en route between Beit ed-Dine and the Beirut-Damascus highway. The office is open daily 0900-1900 all year round. To organize a visit, contact the Tourism Coordinator, Jean Daou, T/F05-240166 or T03-885751, arzshouf@cyberia.net.lb, www.shoufcedar.org

To get there from Beit ed-Dine, head back towards Deir el-Qamar along the road which runs via Moussa castle, but fork off to the right (ie straight ahead) before rounding the head of the valley. Just over 10 km from this junction you arrive at the hotel and reserve office, on your right in the centre of the village. If you continue north along the main road from here, you pass through the villages of Ain Zhalta and Ain Dara before intersecting with the Beirut-Damascus highway at Dahr al-Baidar (see page 579).

Visiting the reserve
The main starting point for visits to the reserve is the *Al Shouf Cedars Society* office in El Barouk village, next door to the *Barouk Palace* hotel. The staff here can arrange for a qualified ranger to take you on hikes of anywhere between 1-4 hours (or more) through different parts of the reserve. There is currently an entry fee of LL5,000 for the reserve. Payments to the rangers for their services are at your own discretion, though they are relying on people giving reasonable sums if this arrangement is to be sustainable in the long term. If you have limited time, you can also go for a tour of the Barouk cedars from here by jeep (including a short walk through the forest if you wish). The tours cost LL10,000 per person and last around 1-2 hours. The advantage of doing it this way is that you get driven right into the reserve to the more impressive areas of forest, whereas private vehicles are not allowed further than the entrance gate (around 4 km from Barouk village).

You can also just drop in at the Maasar ech-Chouf ranger station, beside the road between Maasar ech-Chouf village and the Bekaa Valley (see below). There is a shop here selling locally made natural products (honey, jams, olive oil, pickles, preserves and herbal essences etc). The station closes during the winter months, from around late November or early December through to late March or early April (exact dates depend on the weather). There is a very pleasant short circular walk you can do from here (around 30-45 minutes), or longer hikes to the Barouk or Ain Zhalta forest areas. If you want to do the longer hikes (for which a ranger/guide is required) you ideally need to arrange this at the office in Barouk village first.

B *Barouk Palace*, El Barouk village, T05-240251 or T03-630055, F05-240253 or **Sleeping**
F03-649734, www.baroukpalace.com Comfortable, nicely furnished rooms with a/c, TV/dish, phone, attached bath and balcony. Large restaurant (including seating outdoors down by the river in summer), bar. Discounts during winter (1/11-30/5) bring room rates down to **C** category. Well run. Good value. **Camping** There is a campsite inside the reserve, in the Dalboun oak forest to the south of Barouk village. There are tents available for hire, or bring your own. If you are interested in camping you should arrange this in advance with the Al Shouf Cedars Society office in Barouk village.

A road leads east from the village of Maaser ech-Chouf, crossing the high **Maasar**
ridges of the Jebel Barouk before descending down into the Bekaa Valley at **ech-Chouf to**
Kefraya. This route takes you right past the Maasar ech-Chouf ranger station, **the Bekaa**
where you can see some of the oldest and most impressive cedars in the area. **Valley**
The road is closed by snow from around late November or early December through to late March or early April.

There are two routes up to the village of Maaser ech-Chouf. One runs from Barouk village (take the turning right by the *Barouk Palace* hotel; the first section through the village after you leave the main road is a rather confusing, so ask directions). The road was quite rough and narrow in places at the time of writing, though widening and resurfacing work was in progress. It is 11 km to Maaser ech-Chouf by this route. The other route runs from the village of Moukhtara (see 'Beit ed-Dine to Jezzine', above). Taking the turning in Moukhtara, the road climbs steeply, passing through a small village before arriving at Masaar ech-Chouf after just over 7 km. By the junction where these two routes meet up, at the entrance to the village, there is a clean, friendly snack place, *Fast Food La Gare*, which does excellent mannoushi, as well as sandwiches etc.

The picturesque village of **Maasar ech-Chouf** stands at an altitude of 1,250 m. As well as enjoying a beautiful and tranquil setting, with the high peaks of the Jebel Barouk rising to the east, it still has many of its traditional red-roofed houses surviving. In the centre of the village is the church and monastery of St Michel.

From here the road climbs steeply up the flanks of the Jebel Barouk, hairpinning sharply, and narrow in places, to arrive after 7 km at the Maaser ech-Chouf cedars and ranger station. It is a further 1 km or so to the watershed of the range, marked by an army checkpost. On a clear day, the views from here out over the Bekaa Valley are truly awesome. Heading down into the Bekaa Valley, the road is equally steep and winding, but wider and newly resurfaced all the way. Towards the bottom you pass a sharp right turn leading into the village of Kefraya before arriving at a crossroads and checkpost, just under 13 km from the top. Turning left here takes you northeast to the Beirut-Damascus highway near Chtaura, while turning right takes you southwest to Lake Qaraoun. Straight ahead is the Chateau Kefraya vineyard (see page 601).

Bekaa Valley

16

Bekaa Valley

To Qoubaiyat
Hermel
Deir Mar Maroun
Ain Zarqa (Springs)
Hermel Tower
Mahattet Ras Baalbek
Ras Baalbek
Yammouné
Baalbek
Temnin el-Fawqa
Niha
Furzol
Zahle
Dahr el-Baidar Pass
To Beirut
Chtaura
Rayak
Quabb Elias
Aanjar
Masnaa
Jdaide
SYRIA
Khirbet Qamafar
Jobb Janine
Qalaoun Lake
To Marajayoun
Ain Ata
Hasabaya

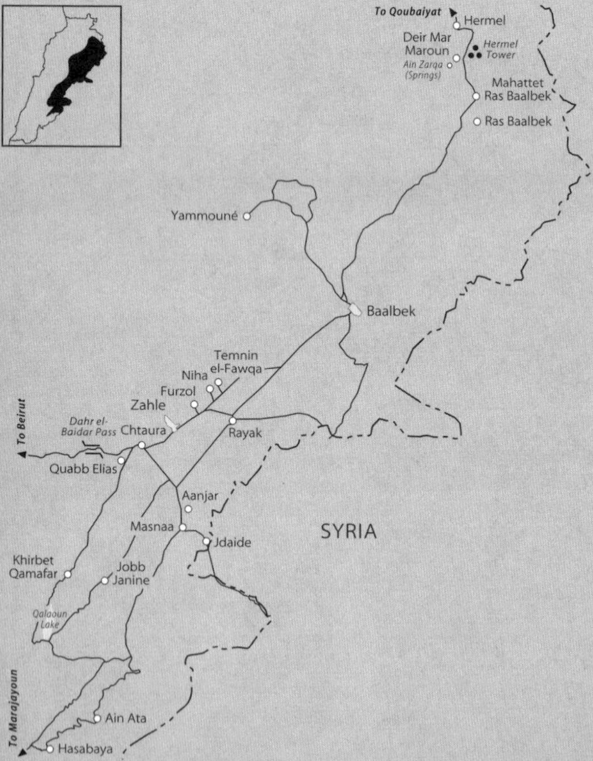

The Bekaa Valley, sandwiched between the Lebanon and Anti-Lebanon mountains, is more accurately a plateau, its altitude ranging from 750-1150 m. Geologically, it forms part of the Great Rift Valley, a massive fault line extending south through the Jordan Valley, the Dead Sea, the Gulf of Aqaba and on into Africa. The Greeks and the Romans referred to the area as Ceole Syria, literally 'Hollow Syria' and for millenia it has formed a natural corridor of communication – a continual traffic in ideas, commerce and invading armies passing through it. The legacy of its historical importance can be seen most spectacularly in the world famous Roman temples at **Baalbek**, but dotted all over the Bekaa there are literally dozens of other ancient sites.

One of the 'bread baskets' of the Roman Empire, the Bekaa Valley is also arrestingly beautiful, both in the broad expanse of its rich, fertile patchwork of agricultural land and in the crisp light and clarity of colours, the product of higher altitude and clearer air. Today the area is more famous for its **wines**, but is also still a producer of grains, cereals, fruits and vegetables. The best time to come here is in spring, when the countryside is at its most beautiful. Despite the higher altitude, it can get very hot during the daytime in the summer months. The autumn is also very beautiful but during the winter it gets very cold, particularly at night.

👉 *A foot in the door*

★ The **temples of Baalbek** are undoubtedly the main attraction of the Bekaa Valley (and arguably the whole of Lebanon). You really need a good half-day at the very least to do the site justice, but if at all possible it is well worth spending a night here so that you can appreciate the ruins at sunrise and sunset.

★ The remains of the **Ummayad Palace at Aanjar** is also very beautiful indeed, its graceful columns and arches still standing after nearly 13 centuries of wars and earthquakes.

The town of **Zahle** is a pleasant, relaxing place, famous in summer for its riverside restaurants. It also makes a good base from which to explore the numerous remains of Roman temples to the northeast.

★ **Wine lovers** can visit two vineyards in the Bekaa Valley and sample some of the excellent wines for which Lebanon is becoming increasingly well known. **Ksara**, just outside of Zahle, one of the oldest in the country and **Château Kefraya**, to the southwest of Chtaura, which, although it only began making its own wine in the 1970s, is already drawing international acclaim.

★ The road from **Baalbek to Bcharre** (in the Qadisha Valley) crosses the high ridges of Mount Lebanon, passing close to Qornet Souada, the highest peak in the range, and has spectacular views looking back down onto the Bekaa Valley. Equally spectacular are the various other **routes across the mountains**, to Afqa, Faraya Maazar, Bikfaya and, further south, to Maaser

Ins and outs

Sleeping & transport

There is good accommodation in Zahle, and also a couple of hotels in Baalbek and Chtaura. In the southern Bekaa, there are 2 good hotels near Qaraoun lake, and (heading into South Lebanon) 1 near Marjayoun. Public transport connections to and from the major centres – Chtaura, Masnaa, Zahle, Baalbek and to a lesser extent Rachaya – are generally good. However, for more out of the way places, unless you are ready to hitch, you really need to organize your own transport.

Safety

There is still a strong military presence in the Bekaa Valley, with numerous Syrian army checkposts complementing those of the Lebanese army in northern Bekaa. The travel advice issued by the British embassy still suggests that tourists should only visit the Bekaa (or anywhere else outside Beirut for that matter) as part of an organized tour. As always with official embassy advice, this errs heavily on the side of caution. In practice, Baalbek and all the other towns and historic sites covered here are perfectly safe to visit.

However, in the southern part of the Bekaa in particular tourists are a still very rare sight and you may find that military personnel at checkposts are more than a little suspicious of your reasons for wishing to explore the area. The Ministry of Tourism's excellent pamphlet on the Bekaa Valley can be very useful in this respect since it contains colour photos of almost all the sights in the area, allowing you to point out what it is you wish to visit.

Note that to the south of Machghara and Rachaya you are entering territory that was occupied by Israel until May 2000. You are advised to stick to the roads in these areas since there is still a very real danger from **landmines** in remoter countryside areas. All the routes described in the section on the southern Bekaa have been cleared and are in regular use by Lebanese. At the time of writing, the **continuing escalation in the Israeli-Palestinian conflict** was adding considerably to tensions in Lebanon, with the Bekaa Valley – a stronghold of Hezbollah – being a potential flashpoint. As long as tensions remain high over the Israeli-Palestinian problem, it is a good idea to keep abreast of events in the local news and follow any advice given by locals. If you are turned back at a checkpost, don't argue – it is probably for a good reason.

The Beirut-Damascus Highway

The Beirut-Damascus highway winds its way up through the mountains of the Metn to the east of Beirut, crosses the Dahr el-Baidar pass, and then descends into the Bekaa Valley. Being the major transport artery connecting not just Beirut and Damascus, but the whole of the Mediterranean coast with the Bekaa Valley and the interior in general, it is always heavily congested, and perhaps one of the most hair-raising routes in Lebanon. Along the steep mountain sections, impatient drivers at the wheels of their flash BMWs and Mercedes find themselves stuck behind heavy lorries crawling along at agonizingly slow speeds. Or at least they would be stuck, but this being Lebanon, it is not unusual to witness two cars double-overtaking a lorry on a blind corner, only to be met by a similarly suicidal overtaking manoeuvre taking place in the oncoming lane; the only surprise is that multiple head-on collisions are not a more frequent occurrence.

Beirut to Chtaura

Head southeast from Downtown on Rue de Damas. Turn left at the National Museum junction, and then after around 500 m turn right at the large intersection and flyover to join the broad dual-carriageway of Av Elias Hrawi (signposted for Chtaura). Towards the end of Av Elias Hrawi, major construction work was in progress at the time of writing, with a mass of new flyovers, underpasses and feeder roads springing up. Keep following signs for Chtaura and Hazmieh in order to rejoin Rue de Damas. Bear left at the rather chaotic junction by the large Baabda Plaza buiding and then go straight on past the fork off to the right signposted to 'La Presidence'.

The road climbs steadily up into the mountains overlooking Beirut, passing on the right the Ministry of Defence headquarters, where you can see a surreal **war memorial**. Created by the French artist Armand Fernandez and unveiled in 1996, it consists of a 10-storey high monument made from tanks, armoured cars, anti-aircraft guns and other items of military hardware embedded in solid concrete.

After passing a right turn for **Aley**, the road forks (both branches join up again further on). Soon after is the town of **Bhamdoun**. There are several luxury hotels and numerous expensive restaurants to be found in both towns, although the steady sprawl of new development spilling out of Beirut and up the mountainside means that the area is heavily built-up. Nevertheless, the views back down onto Beirut and the Mediterranean beyond are very impressive.

Both Aley & Bhamdoun are popular summer resorts where wealthy Beirutis come to escape the heat – the name Bhamdoun is shortened from Biet Hamdoun, literally 'House of Pleasure'

The road passes next through **Sofar** (around 29 km from Beirut). Despite the evidence of war damage, the village has many beautiful old Ottoman houses and impressive views looking north out over the valley of the Nahr el-Metn. Beyond Sofar the sprawl of new development begins to peter out, giving way to open scenery and beautiful views of the surrounding countryside. After 3 km you arrive at a checkpost and crossroads. Turning right here takes you through Ain Zahlta and Barouk to Beit ed-Dine (see page 572).

Continuing straight on, the road winds its way up to the **Dahr el-Baidar pass** (37 km from Beirut), where there is another checkpost, and then descends, with spectacular views down into the Bekaa Valley. On the way down, keep an eye out for sections of the old narrow-gauge railway line which once wound its way through the mountains, linking Beirut and Damascus. Towards the bottom you pass a right turn signposted 'Bekaa - Oest -Sites Archéologique et Touristique' on a large Ministry of Tourism sign. This is the start of the road leading sothwest, past Château Kefraya, to Qaraoun Lake, see page 600). Continuing straight on, you arrive after a few hundred metres in the town of Chtaura (47 km). Towards the eastern end of Chtaura, a road forks off to the left for Zahle and Baalbek (clearly signposted on Ministry of Tourism signs) while the Beirut-Damascus highway continues straight on.

Chtaura
Phone code: 08
Colour map 4, grid B3

Situated on an important transport hub where the main north-south route between Baalbek and the southern Bekaa intersects with the Beirut-Damascus highway, the town of Chtaura has grown to become the commercial and banking centre of the Bekaa Valley. Originally it gained its importance as a spa town, with sulphur springs said to be beneficial to rheumatism and arthritis sufferers. While there are still some pleasant stream-side gardens here, the weight of traffic passing through makes it rather less inviting than it once would have been. However, with its numerous restaurants and snack bars, it makes for a convenient place to stop for refreshments en route between Beirut and Damascus. There are also a few hotels should you need to stop overnight, as well as lots of shops and supermarkets where you can stock up on provisions. If you are coming from Syria, this is a good place to change money (though, as with most places in the Bekaa Valley, Syrian pounds are widely accepted alongside US$ and LL). There are numerous banks along the main road, all with cash machines accepting all the major cards, and equally numerous moneychangers.

Sleeping **L** *Chtaura Park*, set back from the main road, behind the impossible to miss *McDonald's* restaurant, T540011, F542686, www.chtauraparkhotel.com Comfortable rooms with a/c, TV/dish, IDD, minibar and attached bath. Restaurant, bar, nightclub, conference facilities, health centre, swimming pool, tennis, shopping. This is where Elias Hrawi was elected President on 24 November 1989, following the assassination of René Mouawad after just 17 days in office. The hotel has become a venue for high level meetings, particularly between Lebanese and Syrian officials. Quick to offer substantial discounts when it is quiet, bringing rates down to **A** category. **A** *Massabki*, on main road, T03-709710. Hotel nearing completion at the time of writing. **C** *Al Khater*, on a side road around 300 m to the north of the main road, technically in Jdita village, T540659. Simple but clean and reasonably comfortable rooms with heater, attached bath and balcony, some rooms with TV, phone and fridge. Restaurant. Large, old building in a relatively peaceful location away from the main Beirut-Damascus highway. Lovely garden. Good value. **D** *Khater*, on the main road, T540133. Simple rooms with attached bath. Quieter rooms with balconies at rear. Perhaps worth trying to bargain the price of double rooms down, singles good value at US$15.

Locally produced cheeses and yoghurt are a speciality, as are fresh fruit & nut syrups

Eating *Akl*, T540699. Open daily 1200-late. Large, long established Lebanese restaurant with a good reputation. Seating indoors or on large, shaded terrace area. Geared mostly towards catering for special occasions or large groups, but also with a good value set menu of mezze dishes, 1 main meat course, fruit, coffee and 1 alcoholic drink for just over US$10 per head. *Green's Café*, T542223. Open daily 0800-late. Very smart and modern café/restaurant. Breakfast menu of croissants, omlettes and Lebanese dishes. Large selection of coffees, juices etc, salads, sandwiches, burgers, pizzas and main dishes (European cuisine). Snacks around US$5, main dishes from around US$10. Dozens of cheap restaurants/snack bars line the main road through town, some stay open 24 hrs.

Transport **Microbuses** and **service taxis** congregate on the main road, by the fork for Zahle and Baalbek. The microbuses are on the whole cheaper, and offer regular departures to **Zahle** (LL500), **Baalbek** (LL1,000), **Beirut**, (LL2,000), **Masnaa** (LL500) and **Damascus** (LL5,000), and less frequent departures to **Rachaya** (LL1,500) and **El Qaraoun** (LL2,000). If you can't find a microbus to where you want to go, try the service taxis.

Continuing straight along the Beirut-Damascus highway, you pass a more or less continual sprawl of factories etc, before arriving next in **Bar Elias**, which spreads along the road for several kilometres. Just under 6 km from Chtaura (counting from the fork for Zahle and Baalbek), in the centre of Bar Elias, there is a left turn followed immediately after by a right turn and then a Syrian army checkpost. The right turn (marked by a sign reading 'Bienvenu à Marj') leads southwest towards Jobb Jannine and El Qaraoun (on the east side of Qaraoun lake). A little under 3 km further on there is another Syrian army checkpost by a left turn, this road leading towards Rayak (just to the south of the main Zahle-Baalbek highway). A further 3 km brings you to a fork off to the left by a *Caltex* petrol station and sign announcing 'Welcome to Aanjar'. This fork takes you to the Umayyad ruins at **Aanjar**. Continuing straight on, you enter the town of **Masnaa**. Off to the right of the road, up on a small hill above the village of **Majdel Aanjar**, there are the ruins of a Roman temple, reached by any of several small turnings off the main road. Soon after you arrive at a fork off to the right (3½ km from the fork for Aanjar) which leads southwest towards Rachaya (see page 602). Going straight on, you arrive after a few hundred metres at the Lebanese border post of Masnaa. Once through the Lebanese customs and immigration, it is a further 8 km on to the Syrian border post, known as **Jdaide**, from where it is a further 45 km on to Damascus.

Aanjar عنجر

The Umayyad ruins at Aanjar represent perhaps the most impressive site in the Bekaa Valley after Baalbek, the graceful columns and arches of the palace standing majestically against the backdrop of the Lebanon and Anti-Lebanon mountains, their summits capped with snow for much of the year. The modern village of Aanjar, known in Arabic as *Haouch Moussa* (literally 'Farm of Moses'), was founded by Armenian refugees fleeing the genocide in Turkey.

Colour map 5, grid C2

There is no regular public transport to Aanjar, so just ask to be dropped off at the fork by the *Caltex* petrol station and 'Welcome to Aanjar' sign, and then walk or hitch from there. Taking this fork, you arrive after just over 1 km at *Le Soleil* and *Shams* restaurants on the right. Turn left at the crossroads here to arrive at the entrance to the site 1 km further on (when the walls of the site come into view, keep them to your right, following them round to reach the entrance, on the north side).

Ins & outs

Excavations carried out here in the late 1940s were aimed initially at uncovering the ancient city of Chalcis, founded during the second-first millennium BC and later the capital of the Ituraeans, to whom it was known as Gherra. Although Aramaic speaking, the Ituraeans were of Arabian origin. They established themselves here in the first century BC when Seleucid power was on the wane, carrying out raids on the coastal cities of Lebanon and earning themselves a reputation as professional robbers. They retained a semi-autonomous status under Roman rule until around the end of the first century AD. The name Aanjar is thought to be derived from *Ain Gherra*, literally 'the spring of Gherra' – 3 km to the northeast of Aanjar there is a substantial spring which forms one of the sources of the Litani River. Until it was drained in the 14th century this spring fed a large lake where, according to local tradition, Noah's ark came to rest. Traces of ancient stonework discovered by the spring are perhaps part of a place of worship associated with Chalcis.

Instead, what the archaeologists uncovered at Aanjar was an Umayyad settlement, founded probably by the sixth Umayyad Caliph Walid I (705-715 AD). Although the settlement is an entirely Islamic construction, there is

History

plentiful evidence of recycled Hellenistic, Roman and Byzantine materials having been used, particularly in the columns and capitals of the colonnades lining the main streets. Indeed, the layout of the town, enclosed within a rectangle of defensive walls and divided into four quarters by a north-south *Cardo Maximus* and an east-west *Decumanus*, is typically Hellenistic/Roman. The stonework, meanwhile, is typically Byzantine in style, consisting of alternating courses of large stone blocks and narrow bricks (reminiscent of Qasr Ibn Warden in Syria, see page 235). The purpose of the settlement appears to have been primarily commercial. However, the two palaces and the public baths suggest that it was more than this, perhaps serving also as an imperial residence and strategic outpost. Whatever its purpose, the settlement only lasted for 50 years or so before being largely destroyed and abandoned when the Umayyad Dynasty was overthrown by the Abbasids.

Sights   Entering through the north gate (the main entrance), the **Cardo Maximus** runs south through the centre of the settlement. To your left, beside the northern walls, are the remains of a **baths complex**, laid out according to the Roman style. To your right is another smaller baths complex. The Cardo Maximus itself was lined with shops and an arched colonnade, both of which have been partially reconstructed. Note the holes and stone covers in the street, which were access points to an underground sewerage/drainage network. At the intersection of the Cardo Maximus with the east-west Decumanus is a **tetrapylon**, with one of its sets of four columns now re-erected. Continuing straight on, off to your left, in the southeast quadrant of the settlement, is the **great palace**, the most impressive feature of the site. The partially reconstructed sections of walls and the two storeys of slender columns and arches have about them an air of delicate beauty which is altogether enchanting. Just to the north of this are the remains of a **mosque**, while to the north again, across the Decumanus, is what has been termed the **little palace**, more ruined than the great palace, but still interesting to explore. The partially excavated southwest quadrant of the settlement appears to have been given over to **residential quarters**, while in the northwest quadrant there are two large enclosures which perhaps served as animal pens. ■ *Open daily, 0800-1900 in summer, 0800-1700 in winter. Entry LL6,000. There are usually a couple of registered guides at the entrance. Toilet facilities just inside, right of the entrance.*

Majdel Aanjar   Perched on the hill above the village of Majdel Aanjar are the heavily weathered ruins of a **Roman temple**. Take any one of the several turnings right off the main road as you approach the Syrian border and head through the village of Majdel Aanjar in the direction of the ruins, which are clearly visible from a distance (around 2-3 km from the main road). Only the *cella* of the temple remains standing, though scattered around it are numerous sections of massive columns and fragments of capitals and entablature. The temple is thought to date from the first century AD, and was perhaps built by Herod Agrippa II during the reign of the Emperor Claudius (41-54 AD). During the seventh-eighth centuries AD the Abbasids converted it into a fortress guarding the all-important pass and caravan route through the Anti-Lebanon mountains, dismantling the outer courtyard (*temenos*) of the temple to build defensive walls.

Eating   *Le Soleil* is a large, spotlessly clean Armenian-run restaurant. It specializes in freshwater trout which are farmed here and kept in large tanks to be selected live and cooked to order. You can also get the usual selection of grilled chicken, meat, sandwiches and snacks. A meal of half-chicken, chips etc costs US$5-10; fish meals are more expensive. You can pay in US$, LL or S£. Next door is the *Shams*, offering a very similar deal.

Zahle زحلة

Because of its altitude (945 m), the town of Zahle enjoys a pleasantly cool and dry climate during the summer, making it a popular summer resort. Built along the banks of the Bardouni River, which flows down from the heights of Jebel Sannine to the northwest, Zahle is famous for its shaded outdoor restaurants which line the banks of the river, and for the wine and *arak* which is produced in the area, particularly at the nearby Ksara vineyards. Today Zahle is Lebanon's third largest urban centre, and the town serves as the administrative centre of the Bekaa Valley. Its population of around 150,000 includes a significant number of Greek Catholics, the largest concentration of this denomination in Lebanon. As well as its wonderful restaurants, the town still has many of its beautiful Ottoman period houses still surviving (two of them now hotels), making it a picturesque and relaxing place to visit and also a good base from which to explore the Bekaa Valley.

Phone code: 08
Colour map 5, grid C2

The birthplace of the actor Omar Sharif, Zahle has something of a reputation as a centre of cultural and intellectual activity. Some 50 poets and writers have been born here in the last 100 years

Ins & outs

If you take the fork off to the left in the centre of Chtaura (coming from Beirut), this road brings you after just over 6 km to a large roundabout surrounded by modern buildings at the bottom of Zahle. Turn left here to climb up into the older and more picturesque part of town. Most **service taxis** will drop you off by the parking area in the centre, though **microbuses** tend to deposit people by the roundabout at the bottom of town. With either type of transport, if they are just passing through en route to Chtaura or Baalbek, you may find yourself left by roundabout on the bypass (another 1 km or so to the south).

En route between Chtaura & Zahle, after 4 km, a road branches off to the right, the start of a bypass around Zahle: take this if you wish to head directly to Baalbek

There is a **tourist information** office on the 3rd floor of the Chamber of Commerce, Industry and Agriculture (clearly signposted off to the left, above Rue de Brazil, as you head up through the town, see map), T802566. Open 0800-1400, closed Sun. They have the usual selection of Ministry of Tourism brochures and are keen to help.

History

Being predominantly Greek Catholic, Zahle suffered heavily in the communal fighting which erupted between the Druze and Christians in 1860. Large numbers of its inhabitants were massacred and much of the town was razed to the ground. However, the opening in 1885 of the railway line connecting Beirut and Damascus (the same one that still runs between Damascus and Zabadani in Syria), brought with it economic prosperity. In 1885 the town's only stone building was the church: 25 years later, Zahle had grown into a sizeable town, boasting many grand stone-built, red-roofed houses. During the recent civil war Zahle again suffered heavily, coming under bombardment in 1981 from Syrian artillery after Bashir Gemayel's Phalangists (see page 637) started building a road linking it with the ski resort of Faraya, in the heart of Phalange territory. Although the Syrians had worked closely with the Phalangists when they first entered Lebanon in 1976, the fact that the Phalangists also had close links with the Israelis meant that the building of such a road was a serious threat to Syria, which had most of its troops stationed in the Bekaa Valley. Although the bombardment caused considerable damage, the post-war recovery has been swift and enough of the town's 19th-century heritage escaped destruction to allow it to retain something of its former atmosphere.

Sights

There are numerous monasteries and churches dotted around Zahle, including the Maronite, Greek Catholic and Greek Orthodox **Bishoprics**. Perhaps the most rewarding thing to do is simply to wander around, taking in the various examples of Ottoman architecture, enjoying the relaxed atmosphere of the town, and sampling the food in the famous riverside restaurants. Above the town on the west side of the valley, on the road that leads across to Beirut via

Bekaa Valley

Bikfaya, is **Our Lady of Zahle and the Bekaa**, with a huge 54 m concrete tower topped by a bronze statue of the Virgin Mary. A lift takes you up to the top of the tower, from where there are spectacular views out over the Bekaa Valley.

Caves de Ksara Heading back towards Chtaura from the large roundabout at the southeast end of town, the Caves de Ksara are on the right after just over 2 km (just before the bypass around Zahle joins from the left). Originally the site of a fortified palace during the medieval period (hence the name Ksara, derived from *Ksar*, Arabic for palace), the land here was planted with vineyards during the late 17th or early 18th century. In 1857 it was acquired and developed by the Jesuit Fathers before being sold in 1972 to a private company which now runs the estate. The chalky soils of the Bekaa Valley together with its excellent climate of bright sunshine and minimal amounts of rainfall during the growing season combine to give an environment particularly well suited to grape vines. Many of the **wines** produced here have won international acclaim. Dug into the mountainside is an extensive network of underground tunnels (extending for nearly 2 km in all) where the wine is matured. Visitors are shown a short video outlining the history of Ksara and giving details of the wine-making process. You then have the opportunity to taste some of the wines before going on a short tour of the tunnels. ■ *Open daily 0900-1600 (closed Sun in winter). T813496. The tours (lasting around 30-45 mins in all) are free.*

Zahle

0 metres   200
0 yards   200

Sleeping

During summer it can get very busy here and advanced booking is advisable. Out of season, however, it is much quieter and it is often possible to negotiate some very good value deals

L *Grand Hotel Kadri*, T813920, F803314, kadrotel@dm.net.lb Built in 1908, this elegant building served as a headquarters and hospital for the Ottomans during the First World War. During the French Mandate period it housed the chief of the French army in Lebanon, and it was from here that the creation of 'Greater Lebanon' was announced in 1920. It was subsequently converted into a luxury hotel, but was badly damaged during the 1981 bombardment. In recent years it has been fully restored and refurbished, and opened to the public once again. The rooms are luxurious and tastefully furnished and have been restored so that some of the building's original stonework is left exposed. A/c, TV/dish, IDD, minibar and attached bath. Restaurant, bar, conference and banqueting facilities, outdoor swimming pool, health club, tennis courts, *Avis* car hire. Special discounts often available, bringing rates down to **AL** category. Friendly and well run. **B** *Casino Arabi*, T821214, F812443. Lovely, tranquil setting, at the start of the green and leafy stretch of riverside restaurants at the top end of the town. Comfortable rooms with a/c, TV/dish, phone, attached bath and balcony. Restaurant (see 'Eating' below). Good value for the quality of facilities.**B** *Monte Alberto*, up on the hillside above the riverside restaurants and town centre, on the east side of the valley, T810912, F801451, www.montealberto.com Comfortable rooms with a/c, TV/dish, phone, fridge, attached bath and balconies offering excellent views out over the valley. Revolving restaurant and large banqueting hall. **B** *Monte Alberto 2*, higher up the hillside above its sister hotel (immediately below *Sunny Land*), T810812, fax and website as above. Slightly simpler (and cheaper) rooms with fan, TV, phone, fridge, attached bath and balcony (also with great views). Restaurant, bar and basement theatre. **B** *Sunny Land*, up on hillside overlooking town, on east side of valley, T804940, F806770. Primarily a resort complex with privately owned or seasonally rented chalets, but also has a hotel section. Rooms with heater, TV/dish, phone, fridge and attached bath. Restaurant, bar, dance hall, swimming pool, tennis courts and health club. **C/D** *Akl*, Rue de Brazil, T820701. Set in a beautiful old Ottoman period house. Choice of rooms with attached or shared bath, all with balconies. Friendly place, rather like stepping back into a bygone era. **D** *Traboulsi*, Rue de Brazil, T812661. Simple, clean rooms with attached bath and balcony. Set in another beautiful and wonderfully atmospheric old Ottoman period house, but a little more run down than the *Akl*.

Moderate/Cheap The largest, and one of the longest established *casinos* (founded in 1922) is the *Casino Arabi*, belonging to the hotel of the same name, but there are plenty more further along, including (in order of appearance) the *Casino Kraitem* (sign in Arabic only), *Casino Mhanna*, *Casino Nmeir* and *Casino Wadi*. All the restaurants specialize in Lebanese mezze dishes, with a full-blown spread consisting of up to 50 different salads, dips and side dishes. These are traditionally washed down with liberal quantities of arak, followed by a relaxing nargileh. Expect to pay in the region of US$15-20 per head for a meal (excluding alcohol), depending on how many dishes you go for. **NB** These restaurants are only open from around mid-May to mid-Oct (daily from around 1100-late), closing down during the winter months, although the *Casino Arabi* also has an indoor section which stays open all year.

Up on the hillside above the riverside restaurants, on the east side of the valley, there are some more good restaurants. Pleasantly set amidst the vineyards which surround Zahle, and offering great views, these are also well worth trying. They include the *Casino Ain el-Daouk*, and the *Casino Green House*.

Le B.K., *Grand Hotel Kadri*. An international cuisine restaurant. Sunday lunchtime buffet for US$18 per head. *The Bridge Pub*, Rue de Brazil. Smart, pleasant, rather trendy restaurant/bar. Open daily, in the mornings for croissants and coffee, then from around 1400-late. Seating indoors or out on terrace beside the river. Wide range of snacks (Mozerella sticks, buffalo wings, tacos, spring rolls etc), sandwiches, pizzas etc (most items under US$5), as well as main dishes for around US$7-10 each. A small bottle of Al Maaza beer here costs LL3,500. A popular evening venue for drinking and socializing. *Chez Charles*, Rue de Brazil, T823564. Open daily 1030-late. Pleasant, cosy restaurant and bar, though rather 1970s in décor (this being when it was first established). Friendly owner. Varied menu; mostly European cuisine, with a few Arabic dishes. Around US$15-20 per head for a full meal. Daily specials good value at around US$7 per head. *Nuggy's*, Rue de Brazil. Open daily 1100-late. Rather cavernous place, and an odd cross between a fast food diner and a bar. Sandwiches, pizzas, burgers etc.

Eating

The riverside restaurants (known locally as 'casinos') for which Zahle is so famous are at the northwest end of the town, with dozens of them clustered along a green & shady tree-lined pedestrian street running beside the river

Snacks for under US$5; meals for around US$10-15. *Old Arabesque*, New Boulevard, T821216. Open daily 1000-late. Small, pleasant pub/restaurant in a carefully restored old building. The usual selection of sandwiches, pizzas, burgers etc for under US$5, or around US$10-15 for a full meal.

Cheap/seriously cheap In the centre of town, particularly along Rue Brazil, there are several cheaper Lebanese restaurants/snack bars and western-style fast-food places where you can get the usual range of roast chicken, kebabs, fuul, falafels, shawarmas, sandwiches etc, or pizzas, burgers etc. *Adonis Snacks*, Rue de Brazil. Open daily 0900-late. Fast food/diner-style place doing good sandwiches and fresh fruit juices and milkshakes. *Chinese House*, Rue de Brazil. A simple diner-style place with not a whiff of Chinese about it: just fresh fruit juices, ice creams, coffee, tea etc. *Tanmia Chicken Corner*, Rue de Brazil, T818088. Large, modern, spotlessly clean takeaway outlet specializing in naturally reared chicken from their own poultry farms. Wide range of chicken dishes, either as 'platters' (LL4,500-8,000), or as sandwiches (LL2,500-4,000). Free delivery. Restaurant section due to open upstairs in 2001.

Transport **Service taxis** congregate on the square/parking area half way along Rue Brazil (see map). They run regularly to **Chtaura** (LL1000), **Beirut** (LL4,000), and **Baalbek** LL2,500. **Microbuses** are best caught from the large roundabout at the southeast end of town. As usual they are slightly cheaper; eg Chtaura LL500; Baalbek LL1,000; Beirut LL2,500.

Directory **Banks** There are dozens of banks in Zahle. *Credit Libanais*, down by the large roundabout at the southeast end of town, has a cashpoint machine which accepts Visa, Mastercard, Cirrus, +Plus, Amex and Diners Club International cards. *Byblos Bank* and *Bank Audi*, further up into the centre of town, on New Boulevard (running parallel to Rue de Brazil) also have cash machines accepting most of these cards. There is also a currency exchange shop a few doors down from the *Chinese House* snack place on Rue Brazil. **Communications** **Internet** There is an internet café, *Dataland*, on Rue de Brazil. Open daily 0800-2400. Internet access LL4,000 per hour. Slightly cheaper is *Compunet*, on the same side-street as *Naim Maalouf Calling Centre* (see below). Open daily 0900-2400. Internet access LL3,000 per hour. The **post** and **telephone** office is on Rue Brazil. Post office open 0800-1700, Sat 0800-1200, closed Sun. Telephone office open daily 24 hrs (rates as per Beirut). There is also a private telephone office, *Naim Maalouf Calling Centre*, tucked away on a side street above Rue de Brazil, to the south of the post and telephone office. Open 0900-1400, 1600-2400 (if it is closed, ask at the grocery store next door). International calls from here cost between LL500-1,000 per minute (via the internet, so lines are not always very good). **Cultural centres** There is a branch of the *Centre Culturel Francais* on Rue de Brazil, T821293. It contains a small library and organizes occasional cultural events. **Medical services** There are several **hospitals** in Zahle. One of the best (and most conveniently located) is the private *Khoury*, opposite the *Akl* hotel, T800911. There are several good chemists along Rue de Brazil.

Around Zahle

Heading northeast from Zahle, there are a number of interesting places off the main road. Using a combination of service taxis and hitching/walking it would conceivably be possible to get to all these in one day and then back to Zahle or on to Baalbek, but realistically you need your own transport or a private taxi.

Karak
Colour map 5, grid C2

Coming from the centre of Zahle, turn left at the large roundabout at the southeast end of town. After 1½ km, in the suburb of Karak, there is a left turn signposted 'Karak Nouh/Karak Noah' on a Ministry of Tourism sign. Head for the minaret of a mosque, clearly visible from the main road. According to local tradition, the 40 m long stone structure inside the mosque is the **Tomb of Noah**, although a more convincing explanation is that this is a section of an aqueduct dating from the Roman period.

Returning to the main road and continuing northeast, after just under 1 km the Zahle bypass joins from the right. Just over 2 km further on, in the centre of the modern part of the village of Furzol, which is spread out along the main road, there is a left turn opposite a tiny Christian roadside shrine. The turning is signposted 'Habiss el Furzol' on a Ministry of Tourism sign, but only coming from the opposite direction. Taking this turning, the road climbs up to the old village of Furzol. As you enter the village, bear right where the road forks (just past a traffic island with a small, rather forlorn tree growing in it). In the centre of the village, where the road descends steeply to cross a wadi, bear off to the left to follow the road running along the left bank of the wadi.

Furzol
Colour map 5, grid C2

The road comes to an end at an area of **rock-cut tombs** peppering the limestone cliffs near the head of the valley (3 km from the main road). There is a pleasant *restaurant* here with good views down the valley. You can climb up behind the restaurant to get to the tombs, some of which are easily accessible, though others can only be reached by a combination of precarious ladders and some fairly tricky scrambling. Some of the caves appear to have been dwellings, while others were clearly tombs, with compartments cut into the rock to accommodate bodies. The tombs are thought to date from the Roman period, while the dwellings were probably early Christian hermitages. Traces of a **Roman temple** can be found in the old village of Furzol, which is known to have later developed into an important centre of Christianity, becoming the seat of a bishopric after the fifth century. Around 100 m before arriving at the restaurant, a rough track leads off to the left and climbs up the hillside. To the right of the track, higher up the hillside, there are two areas of cut rock (possibly ancient quarries). The second of these has a **relief carving** of a man on horseback and a woman holding a large bunch of grapes. Beside it is a huge rectangular stone slab which looks as if it was in the process of being quarried. From the metalled road it is a 15-20 minute walk up to the relief carving.

Returning to the main road and continuing northeast, after around 600 m the main road bears off to the right, passing through a checkpost to head towards Rayak and Baalbek. Fork left here to keep going straight along a minor road and 2½ km further on there is a left turn by a petrol station signposted for 'Niha Temple' on a Ministry of Tourism sign. Taking this turning, continue straight, following signs for 'Le Temple'.

Niha
Colour map 5, grid C2

The impressive **Roman temple complex** is set amidst a small stand of pine trees at the top end of the village. Entering the site, the **main temple** is off to the left. An inscription found during the course of excavations identifies this temple as having been dedicated to the Syro-Phoenician god *Hadaranus*. Built of massive stone blocks, the *cella* of the temple has been extensively reconstructed using concrete in places and many of the features are not in their original positions. Nevertheless, the overall effect of this edifice, towering above you, is very imposing. A large stone slab to the left of the monumental stairs leading up to the *cella* bears a relief carving of a figure making an offering, possibly a priest/guardian of the temple, or a Roman dignitary. Inside the temple, a broad central stairway flanked by narrower stairs to either side leads up to where the altar would have been. Some of the columns which lined the central stairway have been re-erected, one is topped by a Corinthian capital. The side-stairs on the right lead to a small door and steps down into a barrel-vaulted chamber with an underground passage at the rear running along the length of the rear wall of the temple. In front of you as you enter the site are the remains of a **small temple**, its structure much less complete: only the foundations and the first few courses of stonework, together with various fragments of columns still remain. ■ *Open daily 0800-sunset. Entry LL2,000.*

Despite its ruinous state, if you have the time Hosn Niha is well worth visiting for its dramatic setting amidst rugged hills & newly planted vineyards – it makes an ideal spot for a picnic

A rough track to the right of the temple complex climbs up the right side of the valley: following it, bear right wherever it forks to keep to the upper route. The track is very steep in places and only really suitable for a four wheel drive vehicle. After around 3 km you arrive at the remains of another Roman temple known locally as **Hosn Niha**. Parts of the lower walls and entrance portal of the *cella* are still intact, but for the most part the site consists only of massive tumbled stone blocks, even larger than those used at Niha itself. In places there is evidence of smaller, rougher stonework dating from the Arab period when the temple was fortified and used as a castle (the name Hosn Niha means literally 'Niha Fortress').

Temnin el-Fawqa
Colour map 5, grid C2

Returning to the main road and continuing northeast, after 1½ km you come to a right turn signposted for Temnin el-Tahta, followed 100 m further on by a left turn signposted for Temnin el-Fawqa. Taking the left turn, after just under 2 km you need to cross over the stream in the village and continue up the left bank of the wadi. After a further 600 m you arrive at a small **Roman shrine**, on the right below the road in a dense stand of fir trees. Large amounts of concrete have been used in the reconstruction of the doorway. The inside of the shrine is barrel vaulted with a niche in either side-wall and what looks like a *mihrab* at the far end, perhaps indicating that the shrine was converted into a mosque during the Arab period. A shaft in the floor leads down to what was a well: the shrine is believed to have been built originally in honour of a local god of flowing water. Although the detour involved in getting here is pleasant enough and the upper reaches of this small side-valley very picturesque, the shrine itself is not that impressive and perhaps best left off your list if you have limited time.

Qsarnaba
Colour map 5, grid B2

Returning to the main road and continuing northeast, after 1½ km you come to a left turn signposted for 'Roman Temple - Qsarnaba' on a Ministry of Tourism sign. Taking this turning the road climbs steeply up through the village. Head for the mosque, the brightly coloured minaret of which is visible from some distance. Once you reach the mosque (towards the top of the village, just over 2 km from the main road), there are signs for the temple ruins, 100 m further on.

Within a fenced-in area are the remains of a **Roman temple**. Ask around and someone will fetch the key to the site for you. Only the lower part of the main temple remains: the foundations, the podium (of huge stone slabs), the steps leading up to the *cella* and the first few courses of the walls, on top of which on one side have been placed sections of the cornice, decorated with carved lions' heads as at Niha. Beside the temple the *pediment* which would have surmounted the entrance portal has been reconstructed on the ground. In the apex of the triangle is a carving of the head and shoulders of a figure with a Latin inscription above it. In front of the stairs leading up to the *cella* of the temple is a small altar, while dotted around the site are various stone-cut tombs. There are excellent views out over the Bekaa Valley from here.

North from Qsarnaba

Returning to the main road at the turning for Qsarnaba and continuing northeast, go straight across a crossroads after just over 1 km. Around 2 km further a road forks off to the right to join the main highway to Baalbek. Carrying straight on, after passing through the village of Chmistar, you will eventually reach a checkpost and junction, where turning left will take you up over Jebel Sannine to the ski resort of Faraya Mazaar (see page 496).

Baalbek بعلبك

What Palmyra is to Syria, so Baalbek is to Lebanon – simply the most outstanding example of Roman ruins to be found in the country, and arguably in the whole region. Certainly Baalbek's temple complex is the best preserved of any in the Middle East, its buildings still largely intact having survived the ravages of time, earthquakes, wars and plunderers. Awesome in their sheer scale and mesmerising in their richness of decoration and enduring atmosphere of ancient splendour, Baalbek's temples cannot fail to leave a deep impression. This is undoubtedly one of the great highlights of a visit to Lebanon and if possible an experience to be savoured in the golden light of the rising or setting sun, when the deep, rich colours of the ruins are illuminated in their full glory. After all, Baalbek was known to the Greeks and the Romans as Heliopolis, 'City of the Sun'.

Colour map 5, grid B3

Bekaa Valley

Ins and outs

Coming from Zahle, the main route to Baalbek bears off to the right after 5 km (600m beyond the turning for Furzol, see above), bypassing the centre of Rayak, and then continuing northeast along a fast, straight road (now upgraded to a dual carriageway for much of the way) to arrive in Baalbek, 36 km from Zahle. If you are coming directly from Chtaura and the Beirut-Damascus highway, you can take the bypass round Zahle. **Microbuses** are the main form of public transport these days, with regular services from Beirut, Chtaura and Zahle. There are still **service taxis** operating on these routes, but they are less frequent and more expensive.

Getting there

Arriving in Baalbek, the main temple complex is right in the centre of town, close to where the microbuses and service taxis terminate. All the other sights are within walking distance, though the taxi drivers hanging around outside the main temple complex will happily drive you out to Ras al-Ain or the Quarry if you prefer. There is no tourist information office in Baalbek, try asking at the ticket office of the main temple complex, or at the *Palmyra* hotel, if you need any help.

Getting around

Bear in mind that this is a conservative Shi'ite town: modest dress is the order of the day. Out of respect for local values and to avoid causing offence, revealing items of clothing (shorts, singlets etc) are best avoided, both on men and women.

History

Baalbek's origins go back to the **Phoenician** period. The earliest evidence of settlement dates back at least to the end of the third millennium BC, while during the first millennium BC a temple compound was established here, which became a centre for the worship of Baal. Of the history of Baalbek during the Phoenician period very little is known, but situated on the important north-south caravan route through the Bekaa Valley and surrounded by fertile agricultural land on the watershed between the Litani and Orontes rivers and fed by water from its own spring, it clearly occupied a position of importance.

The name Baalbek has variously been translated as 'Lord of the Land' ('Baal' translating as 'Lord' & 'Bek' as 'Land') or 'Lord of the Bekaa'

Incorporated in the fourth century BC into the empire of Alexander the Great, it later became part of the **Seleucid** Empire. Equating Baal with their sun god Helios, the Greeks renamed the town *Heliopolis*. However, it was during the **Roman** era that Baalbek really came into its own. Having been made part of the Roman Empire by Pompey in 64 BC, the Emperor Augustus Caesar made it into a Roman colony, naming it Colonia Julia Augusta Heliopolis and settling a garrison of troops here. Work on the temple of Jupiter itself started around 60 BC and was nearing completion towards the end of Nero's reign

(37-68 AD). Under **Antoninus Pius** (138-161 AD), a grandiose series of enlargements were initiated, with work starting on the Great Court complex adjoining the temple of Jupiter to the east, and on the so called temple of Bacchus and temple of Venus. Finally, under **Septimus Severus** (193-211 AD) and **Caracalla** (211-217 AD), work on the Hexagonal Court and the Propylaea began, although some scholars attribute the Hexagonal Court to **Philip the Arab** (244-249). Such was the scale of the undertaking that even with the advent of the Byzantine era, parts of the complex were still uncompleted. It has been estimated that the project employed the labour (and cost the lives) of more than 100,000 slaves over 10 generations. Artists and craftsmen from throughout the empire came to Baalbek to carry out the elaborate carved decorations and to produce the numerous statues which adorned the temples. Around 90% of the complex was built from locally quarried limestone, but the granite columns were imported from Egypt. They were shipped to Tripoli and then rolled along stone tracks around into the Bekaa Valley via the Homs Gap.

Exactly what inspired successive Roman emperors to build such a massive temple complex here is not entirely clear. Admittedly, Jupiter Heliopolis grew to become one of the most popular cults in the Roman Empire, and altars dedicated to him have been found right across Europe. But the temple of Jupiter at Baalbek surpassed in size and grandeur anything else ever built in the Roman Empire, even in the imperial capital itself. To a certain extent the motivation was perhaps political: by erecting such awesome monuments the Romans were asserting their superiority over their subjects, proclaiming to the barbarian hordes of the East their supremacy and invincibility. It may also have been religious: an attempt in a period when Christianity was steadily gaining ground to reassert the influence of the pagan gods. Whatever the reasons, during its heyday Baalbek was undoubtedly one of the most important religious centres of the Roman Empire.

Ultimately, however, Christianity did triumph over the pagan gods of the Romans. Under **Constantine the Great** (324-337) pagan worship was suppressed, briefly reasserting itself during the reign of Julian the Apostate (361-363), before being finally crushed by Theodosius I (379-95), who ordered the destruction of the altars of the Great Court and had a basilica built there, using stones from the earlier Roman temples. Under **Justinian** (527-65) a number of the massive granite columns from the temple of Jupiter were transported to Constantinople and used in the construction of the Hagia Sophia. In 634 AD it fell to the Muslim **Arabs** and subsequently became known once again by its ancient Semitic name. The main temple complex at Baalbek was later converted into a fortress, and although many of the stones from the temples were used in the defensive walls, these ultimately also helped preserve what was left. Although it remained in Muslim hands, it was repeatedly attacked: in 1139 by Zengi, the Seljuk ruler of Aleppo; in 1176 by Raymond of Tripoli; in 1260 by the Mongol hordes of Hulagu; and again by Tamerlane in 1400.

Under Ottoman rule Baalbek fell into obscurity and although visited in the 16th century, it was not until the visit of the English architects **Robert Wood** and **James Dawkins** in 1751 that the ruins were 'rediscovered'. Already battered by earthquakes in 1664 and 1750, the remaining monuments suffered from another massive earthquake in 1759, and while Wood and Dawkins were able to report that nine of the columns of the temple of Jupiter were still standing, when Volney visited in 1784 there were only six. After the visit of Kaiser Wilhelm II in 1898, German archaeologists began clearing the clutter of houses from the ruins and excavating them. French archaeologists continued the work during the **French Mandate** period and since **Independence** the

Lebanese Department of Antiquities has been responsible for excavating and preserving the ruins.

During the early 1980s several hundred **Iranian Revolutionary Guards** stationed themselves here and began preaching their radical brand of Islam, exhorting the Shi'ite population to embrace martyrdom as a means of overthrowing American and Israeli imperialism. Later it became the base for Islamic Jihad, Islamic Amal, Hezbollah and other radical Shi'ite groups, and in all likelihood it was here that the suicide bombers who wrought such terrible destruction on the American embassy in Beirut and later on the US and French military headquarters were trained. This is also where John McCarthy, Terry Waite, Terry Anderson and others were held for much of their time as hostages of Hezbollah. Predominantly Shi'ite and still a Hezbollah stronghold, until very recently Baalbek remained a no-go area for foreigners. Alongside the roads into and out of the town you can still see larger-than-life billboard cut-outs of the Ayatollah Khomeini, even in death (perhaps more so) the supreme figurehead of the Iranian-backed Hezbollah, and also those messages of brotherly love and friendship addressed to Israel ... In recent years, however, the prevailing atmosphere has changed markedly and even Hezbollah have adopted a stated policy of welcoming tourists to Baalbek.

Sights

Propylaea From the ticket office, walk round to the propylaea or monumental entrance. The stairs leading up to the propylaea were built during the course of German restoration work carried out in 1900-1904. The original staircase, which was more than 50m wide, was used in the Arab fortifications. The *portico* of the propylaea was supported by 12 granite columns, some of which have been re-erected by the Department of Antiquities in recent years. On the bases of some of the columns are Latin inscriptions. The most clearly discernible one, on the third column base from the left, reads, 'For the safety and victories of our lord Caracalla'. The *portico* was flanked by two towers which would have housed the imperial guards of the temple. Modified during the Arab period to serve as bastions, the right-hand one was restored by the French in 1933, but the left-hand one was in an advanced state of ruin and so dismantled. The *portico* would have originally been covered by a roof of cedarwood and paved with mosaics.

Hexagonal court From the propylaea a doorway with a raised threshold leads through into the hexagonal court, the raised threshold serving to delineate the propylaea from the sacred enclosure beyond where sacrifices and religious

Main temple complex
Consisting of the temples of Jupiter and Bacchus, this is overwhelmingly the main focus of interest for a visit to Baalbek, although there are a number of other sites which are worth visiting if you have the time

Main temple complex

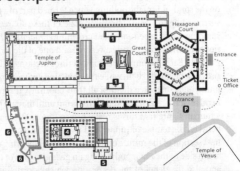

1 Stone basins
2 Observation tower
3 Raised altar
4 Temple of Bacchus
5 Mameluke tower
6 Arab fortifications

dances, perhaps to the goddess Venus, were performed. The six-sided layout of this court is a reflection of the Eastern influences which guided the Roman architects. Thirty granite columns originally supported a covered arcade around the central hexagon, which was paved with mosaics and left open to the sky. The central hexagon is believed to have been covered over with a dome during the Byzantine era and converted into a church. The upper parts of the walls of the hexagonal court were added during the Arab period while the four rectangular *exedrae* around the court had arrow slits added.

Great court   From the hexagonal court you pass through to the huge great court (or sacrificial court), where you begin to get a sense of the enormous scale of the temple complex. Around the north, east and south sides of this court were 12 semi-circular and rectangular *exedrae*, with numerous niches on two levels for statuary, and a covered arcade supported by 84 granite columns. Some of the columns of the arcade have now been re-erected, while scattered all around on the ground are numerous architectural fragments (some bearing inscriptions), allowing you to examine their richly carved decoration close up. In the centre of the court are two large structures. The larger one to the east (of which only the lower parts are still standing) is believed to have been an observation tower, while the taller one immediately to the west of it appears to have been a raised altar where sacrifices were made. Immediately to the east of the observation tower is a deep trench where archaeologists have excavated down to the original Phoenician foundations over which the great court was built. Also in the central area of the court, to the north and south of the altar and observation tower, are two large stone basins which most probably served as ablution pools where animals were ritually cleansed before being sacrificed. The basin on the north side is the more richly decorated of the two, with intricate relief carvings of cupids riding on sea creatures, medusae, tritons and nereids. Note how some of the carvings are unfinished. During the fourth century AD Theodosius I built a large basilica in the great court. Much of this basilica was still standing when excavations were carried out this century, but French archaeologists cleared it away. In doing so they discovered the bases of the altar and observation tower, which had been dismantled and used in the fabric of the church, and after careful analysis of the stones, partially reconstructed them. Today all that remains as evidence of the former basilica is the semicircular apse cut out of the broad stairs at the west end of the great court leading up to the temple of Jupiter itself.

Temple of Jupiter   Ascending these stairs you arrive at the top of the huge raised podium on which the temple of Jupiter originally stood. Completely dismantled to provide stone for the Byzantine basilica and later Arab fortifications, today all that remains of the *cella* are the six massive Corinthian columns on the south side of the podium which formed part of a *peristyle* of 54 columns surrounding the *cella*. The sheer scale of these six remaining columns, still standing undisturbed with their crowning *entablature*, having survived centuries of earthquakes, is truly awesome and one of the most enduring images of Baalbek. Each column, consisting of three sections, is 2.5 m in diameter and rises to a height of 20 m, while the crowning *entablature* is nearly 5 m tall. Yet until you actually see them in all their enormity, it is impossible to comprehend their true size, and even then it is not until they are put into perspective by a human figure that this is really driven home. Descending to the open area between the temple of Jupiter and temple of Bacchus, you can examine close up a section of the *cornice* of the *entablature*, now lying on the ledge below the south side of the main podium, again giving an idea of the scale of the temple, and also the detail of the decoration which adorned it. The massive carved

The many faces of Baal

The god Baal was of Semitic origin, a sky god associated with the elements thunder, lightning, rain and the sun, and so essentially a fertility god, closely linked to the natural seasonal cycle. To the peoples of the richly productive Bekaa Valley, the importance of the cycle of the seasons for the success of their crops is easily appreciated. Baal was synonymous with the Aramaean/Mesopotamian god **Hadad**, also a fertility god closely associated with lightning and thunder. References to Baal-Hadad have been found in Egyptian and Assyrian inscriptions, and also in the epic poems discovered at Ugarit (Ras Shamra) in Syria, where mention is made of the rituals associated with Baal. According to the Ugaritic texts and later Roman writings, at Baalbek these involved licentious festivals where animal and perhaps even human sacrifices were made and sacred prostitution was practiced in a kind of human re-enactment of the cult of nature's fertility. Baal-Hadad's consort was **Atargatis**, goddess of the earth, in whom the fertility bestowed by Baal-Hadad found expression, while completing the trinity was a third god whose Phoenician identity remains uncertain.

Baal-Hadad was worshipped throughout ancient Syria, in numerous different guises and with as many local interpretations of his attributes. The Greeks associated Baal-Hadad specifically with the sun and identified him with the sun god **Helios**, and with

Zeus. The Romans, meanwhile, identified Baal-Hadad with **Jupiter** and his consort Atargatis with Venus, adding Mercury to complete the trinity.

Baal also represented the main challenge to the supremacy of the Hebrew god Yahweh. The historian PK Hitti observes, "The acknowledgement of Yahweh as the supreme deity did not preclude considering the local deities as controllers of land productivity. At times the Hebrew deity acquired many attributes of Baal which made him lord of heaven, sender of rain, controller of storms. Hebrew parents often named their first-born after Yahweh, but the younger after Baal... In the Ugaritic literature 'rider of the clouds' is an epithet of Baal as it is of Jehovah in Hebrew (Psalms 68; 4)... Psalm 29 in its entirety is of clear Canaanite origin, a modified hymn to Baal." Hitti also notes, "It should, however, be added that later on the Hebrew prophets rose... to think of God in terms of oneness and of social righteousness and to emphasise conduct rather than cult... Abraham's substitution of the ram for his eldest son Isaac marks the beginning of a cultural stage in Semitic development in which human sacrifice was considered no more acceptable." While the Phoenicians appear to have practiced human sacrifice, Hitti also notes that, "In the sixth century before Christ the practice was entirely abandoned by them. In Western Europe offering human sacrifice to appease the gods lingered for centuries after Christ."

lion's head conceals a spout in its mouth through which rainwater would have been drained from the roof of the temple. From here you can also get some sense of the sheer enormity of the stone blocks used to build the podium on which the temple of Jupiter stood. While still on the podium of the temple of Jupiter, if you look over the north edge you can see more of these massive stone blocks, which appear to have been intended to form a terrace surrounding the main podium. At the west end of the podium, three of the largest of these stone blocks were completed and put in place: known as the 'trilithon' each of these measures more than 19 m by 4 m by 3 m and weighs more than 1,000 tonnes.

Temple of Bacchus Although dwarfed by the temple of Jupiter and as a result often referred to as the 'small temple', the separate temple of Bacchus is itself an enormous structure. More importantly, it is perhaps the most complete temple in the Middle East ever to survive from the Roman period, and apparently one of the most lavishly decorated. Monumental stairs ascend from the east to the massive entrance portal to the *cella* of the temple. The frame of the entrance portal is richly decorated with grapes, vines and other Bacchian motifs. The keystone, shown hanging down precariously in the drawings of David Roberts in the 1830s, has now been more securely pushed back in place and reinforced. On the underside of the keystone is a carving of a winged eagle carrying in its claws a *caduceus*, the snake entwined rod which was the symbol of the god Mercury, and in its beak a garland held up by two winged genii. Inside the *cella*, the walls are decorated with engaged fluted columns and niches for statuary. At the far (west) end of the *cella*, stairs lead up to *adyton* (now vanished) where the image of the deity of the temple would have been housed. The peristyle surrounding the *cella* is still largely intact, its columns in places still supporting the massive stone slabs that covered the it. Elsewhere, these slabs lie propped up on the ground, the carved images of various gods today heavily weathered but still discernible. One of the columns of the peristyle leans precariously against the wall of the *cella*.

The structure to the left of the stairs leading up to the entrance portal of the temple is a **Mameluke tower** which today houses a small **museum**. In the upstairs chamber of the tower are artefacts dating mostly from the Ayyubid and Mameluke periods, including funerary stelae, pottery pieces and a carved stone lion from Hadeth. The information boards here give details of Baalbek's Islamic history, and there are interesting photos of the temple complex at the beginning of the 20th century. The ground floor chamber contains mostly Roman period artefacts from Baalbek's various necropoli. Of particular interest is a small room containing the 'Dourris' sarcophagus. This still contains the skeleton of the deceased, together with the thin gold sheets, some decorated, which were laid over the eyes, nose, mouth, forehead and torso of the corpse.

Returning to the open area between the temple of Bacchus and temple of Jupiter, in the southwest corner are the remains of further **Arab fortifications**, along with a number of pillars which probably formed part of a **mosque**. A path running beside the south side of the foundations of the Great Court of the temple of Jupiter brings you back to the parking area at the entrance to the site.

Main musueum Baalbek's main musuem occupies a vaulted tunnel which runs underneath the whole length of the eastern side of the Great Court. The museum contains some very beautiful pieces of Roman statuary and architectural fragments, as well as numerous information boards detailing Baalbek's history, geography, strategic significance, method of construction etc. If anything, there is too much information to absorb in one go, and unfortunately as yet no museum brochure which you can take away and read. A side-room on the right towards the end of the tunnel contains a collection of photographs by the German photographer Hermann Burchardt illustrating everyday life of the Bekaa Valley at the end of the 19th century.

■ *Open daily from 0830 to around 30 mins before sunset. Entry LL12,000. Guides are available for detailed tours of the site. The official, government-set rates are LL20,000 for 1-6 people, LL25,000 for 7-14 people, and LL30,000 for groups of 15 or more, though the guides tend to expect a hefty additional tip.*

Temple of Venus Opposite the entrance to the main temple complex, on the other side of the road, a fenced in area encloses the remains of the temple of Venus (or round temple). At the time of writing the temple could only be observed from outside the enclosure, though in the future it may be opened to the public. Its tiny, delicate proportions are somewhat out of keeping with the massive scale of the temples of Jupiter and Bacchus. The *cella* forms three-quarters of a circle, rather like a horseshoe, surrounded by a *peristyle* with five concave bays, each with a niche built into the outside walls of the *cella*. Originally a staircase led up to the podium on which the *cella* stands, its entrance preceded by a large rectangular *pronaos* topped by a triangular *pediment*. During the Byzantine era the temple was converted into a church and dedicated to St Barbara, the daughter of a local dignitary of Baalbek. According to legend, when her father learnt that she had embraced Christianity, he took her up onto the slopes of Mount Lebanon and slaughtered her. He was in turn immediately struck down by lightning and reduced to ashes: as a result prayers to St Barbara are offered in the hope of protection against lightning.

Also opposite the main temple complex, to the northeast of the temple of **Umayyad** Venus, is the Umayyad Mosque (or Great Mosque). Built by the Umayyads in **Mosque** the seventh-eighth century AD, the large square courtyard of the mosque has a pool and fountain in the centre, surrounded by four columns. To your right as you enter is a series of parallel rows of arched colonnades, the columns and capitals of which are clearly Roman in origin, taken from the nearby temple complex. In the northwest corner of the courtyard is the partially ruined minaret, its square tower terminating in an octagonal top.

Opposite the *Palmyra* hotel is an area of excavations carried out in the 1960s. A **Roman civic** stretch of colonnaded street lined with re-erected columns can be seen here, **monuments** with a particularly striking column at one end topped by a fragment of richly decorated arch, appearing, with the help of a little reinforcement, to defy gravity. Across the road to the northeast of this is another area of semi-excavated ruins. None of these have been conclusively identified, but it seems likely that together they represent some of the civic monuments of the Roman town which existed alongside the temples: perhaps the public baths, agora (market place/meeting area), Hall of Justice etc, or possibly the theatre.

To the southwest of the main temple complex, at the end of Ras al-Ain Boulevard, is the spring of Ras al-Ain. The waters from the spring, which provided **Ras al-Ain** the town and the temple complex with their principal water source, flow out into a large shallow pool before being channelled alongside the road towards the main temples. The spring and its stream are surrounded by parks with various restaurants and cafés around. Beside the spring are the ruins of a mosque dating from the Mameluke era with only its walls, gateway, a couple of the arches of the prayer hall and a few columns still surviving.

On the way into Baalbek (coming from Chtaura/Zahle), you pass the Quarry, **The Quarry** signposted 'The Roman Quarry' off to the right. To get there from the centre of town, head southwest along Rue Abdel Halim Hajjar past the *Palmyra* hotel: it is signposted on the left immediately after the Coral petrol station.

Here you can see a massive slab of stone, known locally as Hajar el-Qublah (literally 'Stone of the South') or Hajar el-Hubla ('Stone of the Pregnant Woman' or 'Stone of the Mother Stone'). Although still attached at one end to the bed-rock, the greater part of the slab has been perfectly hewn into a rectangular block. Its dimensions are enormous (bigger even than the three 'trilithon' blocks in the west end of the podium of the temple of Jupiter), measuring 21.5 m by 4.8 m by 4.2 m and weighing well over 1,000 tonnes. Presumably intended to form part of the terrace of this podium, according to one calculation it would have required 40,000 men to move it, although the builders evidently gave up and abandoned their over-ambitious undertaking. According to local superstition, when touched the stone has the power to make women fertile. There are several rock-cut tombs in the walls of the quarry. There is a souvenir stall beside the quarry, and a tea tent down in it. Considerable effort has gone into sprucing up the site in recent years: rubbish has been cleared, trees planted and the area attractively landscaped.

Essentials

Sleeping The best hotel in Baalbek is the perversely named **B** *Palmyra*, T370230, F370305. Built in 1874 and boasting names such as Kaiser Wilhelm II, General Allenby and Charles de Gaulle in its visitors' book, this is very much a hotel in the same mould as Aleppo's *Baron* hotel – steeped in atmosphere and faded grandeur (though without any signs of modern refurbishment in this case). The rooms (doubles US$53 including tax and service) are large, cool and pleasantly furnished, with fan, heater and attached bath (rather decrepit, hot water in mornings and evenings only). The best rooms have balconies with views of the temples. There is a restaurant serving meals for around US$10-15 per head, a bar serving alcohol and a shaded garden area. **D** *Jupiter*, T376715. Small hotel with just 6 rather simple, reasonably clean rooms with fan and attached bath arranged around a courtyard. Overpriced for what you get. Try bargaining. **F-G** *Al Shams*, on the 1st floor above a tailors, T373284. Small, rather basic hotel, but OK. US$6 for a bed in a shared room, or US$14 for a double. In either case, share shower/toilet. **F-G** *Al Shoman*, no phone, offers a similar deal but is even smaller with just 3 rooms and the toilets here are very basic indeed.

Eating The restaurant in the *Palmyra* hotel scores better for its atmosphere than for its food. As an alternative, there are several restaurants and cafés towards the southeast end of Ras al-Ain Boulevard, and around Ras al-Ain spring. These are built over the stream which issues from the spring, with shaded outdoor terraces providing a pleasant setting for meals in the summer. The *Riviera* is one of the larger ones, serving traditional Lebanese mezze dishes for around US$10-15 per head for a full meal, while further along is the *King* offering a similar deal.

Related map
A Main temple
complex, page 591

For cheaper meals and snacks explore along Rue Abdel Halim Hajjar, Ras al-Ain Boulevard and around the souks off Ras

Baalbek

■ Sleeping
1 Al Shams
2 Jupiter
3 Palmyra
4 Pension Shuman

● Eating
1 Assyla Café
2 Café
3 Cafés & Restaurants
4 Khaillame
5 King
6 Restaurants
7 Riviera
8 Sndibad

The Baalbek Festival

During the 1960s and early 1970s the temples of Jupiter and Bacchus were the venue for what was undoubtedly the most prestigious annual festival in Lebanon and indeed the whole of the region, combining music, dance, theatre and sound and light shows. The festival attracted performers of international renown, including Duke Ellington, Ella Fitzgerald, The Who, Rudolf Nureyev, and the Bolshoi ballet. In July 1997 the Baalbek Festival was reinstated on a modest scale for the first time since 1974, with the Lebanese Caracalla dance troupe inaugurating the four nights of performances culminating in an appearance by the cellist Mstislav Rostropovitch. Since then it has grown in

size and popularity each year, and is fast regaining its former reputation. The summer 2000 festival included a performance of Puccini's Tosca and an appearance by Compay Segundo of Buena Vista Social Club fame, as well as a host of big names from the Arab world. At the time of writing, Sting was signed up to play in 2001. The festival is held from early July through to mid-August each year. Tickets at the 2000 festival are priced at anywhere from LL20,000 to LL250,000 depending on the perfomance and where you sit.

For precise dates and details of current line-ups, go to www.tradingplaces.com.lb (bookings can be made on T01-611600). The website of the festival organizing committee is www.baalbeck.org.lb

al-Ain Boulevard. Towards the northwest end of Ras al-Ain Boulevard, there are several reasonable snack places and juice bars where you can get the usual falafels, shawarmas etc and excellent fresh fruit juices and milkshakes. Opposite each other on Rue Abdel Halim Hajjar there is the *Sndibad* (sic) and *Khaillame* both simple restaurants serving reasonably priced Arabic food, while to the southwest of the entrance to the temples there are 2 restaurants/cafés in a similar vein. The *Exotica* café/restaurant, just down from the *Palmyra* hotel does good sandwiches, and the Assyla café/restaurant, more or less opposite the *Palmyra* hotel is also good. One of the best cafés is opposite the *Al Shams* hotel. It has a quiet, shaded garden area where local men gather to drink tea and coffee, smoke their nargilehs, exchange gossip and play cards or backgammon.

Microbuses congregate in the square just to the north of the *Palmyra* hotel. They run regularly via **Zahle** (LL1,000) and **Chtaura** (LL1,000) to **Beirut** (LL3,000). Microbuses to **Hermel** (LL2,000) depart from the stretch of road between the *Al Shoman* hotel and the Umayyad Mosque. **Service taxis** also congregate in the square just to the north of the *Palmyra* hotel, and in the square to the north of Ras al-Ain Boulevard. They are slightly more expensive than the microbuses, and seem to be a lot less numerous these days.

Transport

Banks The *Jamal Trust* bank, near the temple complex, has a cash machine which accepts Visa, Mastercard, Cirrus, +Plus and Visa Electron. You can also change cash at the *Palmyra* hotel, or at various moneychangers in the narrow souks near the square and fruit/vegetable market to the north of Ras al-Ain Boulevard. Syrian pounds are widely accepted in Baalbek alongside US$ and LL. **Communications** Internet There is a small internet café, *Network*, just up the side street next door to the *Palmyra* hotel. Open daily 0900-2400. Internet access LL4,000 per hr. They have 6 terminals, often taken up by young kids playing computer games. The **post** and **telephone** office is just off Ras al-Ain Boulevard, on the left as you head down towards Ras al-Ain (see map). **Medical services** The *Imam Khomeini* hospital near Ras al-Ain spring, T870880, is a Hezbollah funded institution but the staff are friendly and, in the true Islamic tradition, they will be more than happy to see to the needs of any sick unbelievers.

Directory

North of Baalbek

Baalbek to the Cedars and Bcharre

Distances in brackets are the cumulative distance from Baalbek

Following the road leading northwest from Baalbek, go straight across the first major crossroads you come to (left for Zahle, Chtaura and the Beirut-Damascus highway, right for Homs and Hermel). Beyond the village of **Iaat** (5 km), look out for a solitary 18 m tall **column** topped by a heavily worn Corinthian capital standing in the fields off to the right of the road. Local tradition attributes the column to St Helena, although it is more probably a Roman funerary monument. Arriving at a checkpost and junction (12 km), bear right (going left takes you through the village of Chlifa, past the turning up to Faraya Mazaar and back eventually to Zahle). The road continues across the flat fertile plain of the Bekaa Valley before climbing up to the large sprawling village of **Deir al-Ahmar** overlooking the plain (17 km, Syrian army checkpost entering the village). Continuing straight on, you pass through a couple of tiny villages before coming to a left turn (24 km) signposted for 'Yammouneh Public School Construction Project' on an USAID signboard. This road takes you to the village of Yammouné.

Yammouné
Colour map 5, grid B2

Yammouné boasts many very luxurious looking houses, a legacy of the days when this was a major hashish producing area. Today the main crops are potatoes and apples

Taking the turning for Yammouné, the road descends into a wide fertile basin surrounded on all sides by mountains (almost like a separate Bekaa Valley in miniature). In the centre of the village there are several shallow pools with pleasant shaded cafés beside them and the ruins of a **Roman temple** consisting only of the first couple of courses of the enclosure wall, built of massive stone blocks, within which is a still unexcavated tell. The temple probably dates back to the Phoenician period, when it was dedicated to the goddess Astarte (Greek Aphrodite and Roman Venus). This was the final destination for pilgrims after visiting Afqa (see page 503), where they would undergo a ritual purification having climbed up from the village of Aaqoura and over the high ridges of Mount Lebanon. According to legend it was here that Astarte turned herself into a fish to escape the wrath of the monster Typhon. On the slopes of Mount Lebanon to the northwest of the village is the **spring of the Forty Martyrs** (Ain Arbaeen), the waters of which only flow from March to August each year. Locals will tell you that it begins to flow each year on exactly the same date, the 8 March, which is also the Feast of the Forty Martyrs. Until it was drained by French engineers earlier this century, much of the basin in which Yammouné stands was covered by a large lake fed by this and other springs in the area. A legend which goes back at least to Roman times suggests that the waters of the Ain Arbaeen spring are connected directly with those of the Adonis River. Below the spring local people have carried out excavations in recent years, uncovering traces of a building dating from the Roman period and various Roman architectural fragments.

Baalbek to Qoubaiyat

Distances in brackets are the cumulative distance from Baalbek

Joining the road leading northeast from Baalbek you pass through the villages of Labwé (or Laboué, 29 km) and then through Nabi Osmane, Al Ain and Jdaide, all of them more or less merging with each other, before arriving at a right turn (40 km) signposted for Ras Baalbek.

Ras Baalbek
Colour map 5, grid B3

The village of Ras Baalbek, you will find the Greek Catholic **Monastery of Notre Dame de Baalbek** standing on the site of what was probably a Roman temple. A church existed here during the Byzantine period and the smaller side entrance to the monastery includes one stone carved with a Byzantine cross surrounded by laurels. The monastery's smaller chapel dates from the 16th century, although the main church was built in 1925 when the whole monastery was restored. There is a small museum containing Roman artefacts uncovered here in the course of restoration work, as well as fossils and various religious items. The monastery still owns substantial pistachio orchards in the area – in the museum there is a sand timer which was used to allocate irrigation water. In the courtyard of the monastery there are a few Roman columns and capitals, as well as doors to ancient Christian tombs. The monks here are very friendly and will happily show you round. They also have some rooms available for visitors and may be willing to put you up.

Returning to the main road and continuing northeast, after a further 5 km you arrive at a Syrian army checkpost and junction known as **Mahattet Ras Baalbek** (literally 'Ras Baalbek Railway Station'), there having been a railway station here on the old line which used to run from Homs and connect with the Damascus-Beirut line. Taking the left fork (towards Hermel), continue past two small left turnings and shortly after the road bends round to the right there is a third left turn (6 km beyond the Mahattet Ras Baalbek) which leads to the spring of Ain Zarqa and rock-cut monastery remains of Deir Mar Maroun.

North from Ras Baalbek

After a couple of kilometres you arrive at the spring of Ain Zarqa (literally 'Blue Spring'), down a short track off to the left of the road. This is one of the main sources of the Orontes River or Al Assi ('Rebel River'). The spring emerges from the rocks into a large pool, its waters deliciously cool and refreshing in the heat of summer, while a large overhanging tree provides an idyllic shaded picnic spot. During the spring and summer a small restaurant operates here. Just beyond the track leading down to the spring the road comes to an end: on the right, cut into the rocks above you is what is known as Deir Mar Maroun. The name derives from the Maronite belief that St Marun, effectively the founder and first saint of the Maronite church, lived here as a hermit for a time. During the Arab period the caves appear to have been fortified, with walls pierced by arrow slits built across the entrances to the caves. You can scramble up from the road and explore the various caves.

Ain Zarqa & Deir Mar Maroun
Colour map 5, grid A3

Returning to the main road and continuing north, a little under 2 km further on there is a right turn, leading to the Hermel tower. Standing on the top of a low hill which rises above the surrounding plain, the Hermel tower can be seen from miles around (it first comes into view shortly after forking left at the Mahattet Ras Baalbek checkpost and junction). The structure consists of a pedestal of black basalt stone on which stands a large square base in two tiers surmounted by a pyramid-shaped top. Large sections of it have been restored, with the new, cleanly cut stone contrasting sharply with the rougher, darker original blocks. On each face of the lower tier of the square base, where the original stone survives, there are worn friezes depicting what appear to be hunting scenes. As to the origins or purpose of the monument, no-one is entirely sure. Its unique style is clearly not Greek or Roman and most scholars believe it to be a second-first century BC tomb of a local Syrian king. There is, however, some similarity between it and the pyramid-topped tombs of Bara in Syria (see page 361) and a medieval Arabic manuscript now housed in Cairo's National Library relates the story of Hermelos, a local Christian king of the northern Bekaa, whose sudden death while out on a hunting expedition was commemorated by a pyramid-topped tomb.

Hermel tower

North to Qoubaiyat

Returning to the road and continuing north, the road descends steadily and then crosses the Orontes River. There are several pleasant, shaded riverside restaurants here specializing in trout, and also a couple of hotels, the **D** *Asamaka* and the **D** *Al Fardos*, both offering clean reasonable rooms with attached shower/toilet. Note that the hotels and restaurants close for the coldest winter months. Shortly after the river crossing the road bends round to the east before arriving in the town of Hermel, 60 km from Baalbek.

Hermel is the northernmost town of the Bekaa Valley and predominantly Shi'ite. Although it is fairly large, it has no real centre, or anything of particular interest to the visitor. There are a few simple restaurants along the main road, and occasional microbuses and service taxis running to and from Baalbek.

Following the main road through the town, ask directions to pick up the road for Qoubaiyat as it is a small, easily missed left turn off the main road. Once on this road, it climbs up into the hills, arriving after 9 km in the village of **Charbine**. Entering the village, fork right and then after a further 3 km turn left at a T-junction near the tiny village of **Fissane**. The road continues to climb through rugged limestone hills of shrub interspersed with occasional orchards before starting to descend through pine forests and eventually arriving in the town of Qoubaiyat, 48 km from Hermel (see page 530). NB this road is generally blocked by snow during the winter months.

Southern Bekaa Valley

The southern Bekaa Valley is in places very beautiful and well worth exploring. Rather confusingly, this area is often referred to as the 'West Bekaa' (presumably because it is further to the west than the northern half of the Bekaa Valley).

Chtaura to Qaraoun Lake

Public transport along this route is very erratic, so unless you resort to hitching, you really need to organize your own transport. Taking the turning leading southwest from the Beirut-Damascus highway just to the west of Chtaura (see page 579), after 2½ km (soon after a sign reading 'Bienvenue a Kabb Elias') there is a fork off to the right leading into the centre of Qabb Elias.

Qabb Elias
Colour map 5, grid C1

This small town is spread across the steep slopes of the hillside to the right of the main road. The population here is a mixture of Shi'ite Muslim and Christian, and there are a number of interesting old buildings, including mosques, churches and a large monastery. At the top of the hill there is a fragment of ancient wall supporting a tangle of electric and telephone wires – all that remains of a 12th century **fortress**. It is possible to drive up, but more interesting to walk via the steep winding stairways which climb up through the town. On a rocky outcrop on the south edge of the town there is a large rock-cut **altar** carved into the sheer rock face and framed within a carved rectangular border. This is thought to date from late Greek or early Roman times.

Southwest from Qabb Elias

Returning to the main road and continuing southwest, the next stretch is particularly beautiful. The road closely follows the Jebel Barouk and Jebel Niha ridges of the Lebanon mountain range to the west, while to the east the flat plain of the Bekaa with its rich, fertile soils, stretches into the distance. At one point you pass a sign for the '**Ammiq Wildlife Reserve**', off to the left of the road. This 100 hectare wetland area is rich in birds and fish, and also home to fresh-water turtles. Soon after (around 11 km from the Qabb Elias turning), off to the right of the road at the foot of the mountains, is the village of **Ammiq**, dominated by a distinctive, brand-new church. Just under 18 km beyond the turning for Qabb Elias you arrive at a crossroads and checkpost. Turning right here takes you past the village of Kefraya and up over the ridges of the Jebel Barouk mountains on a good road, then down past the Maaser ech-Chouf ranger station of the Al Shouf Cedar Reserve (see page 572). Turning left takes you to the Château Kefraya vineyards, the entrance to which is on the right after around 700 m.

The setting for Château Kefraya is very beautiful indeed. The estate's vineyards stretch away into the distance against the backdrop of the Lebanon mountains, while nearby is the private Moroccan-style château of the owner, standing on a small cypress-covered hillock.

Château Kefraya
Colour map 5, grid C1

> First established in the 1950s, the Kefraya estate initially supplied all its grapes to other wine producers in the area. In the late 1970s, however, the owner Michel de Bustros decided to go into production himself, and by 1979 had his own winery up and running, despite the outbreak of the Lebanese civil war. The estate now has some 300 hectares of vines, with more planned. Its wines, meanwhile, have gained a reputation internationally for their quality, winning many prestigious awards.

> Although Kefraya does not have the attraction of the rock-cut tunnels dug into the mountainside at Ksara, the guided tour takes you through the entire wine-making process (seen only on video at Ksara). Here you shown all the different stages, with someone to explain in detail the pressing of the grapes, the fermentation process in massive steel tanks or concrete underground tanks lined with epoxy, and the bottling process. Last, but not least, you come to the cellars where the wine is aged before being released onto the market. The *Compte de M*, Kefraya's premier red, is aged in oak barrels made from Spanish and French oak, though all the other varieties are aged in their bottles. The tour culminates in a wine-tasting session in the *L'Accueil Dionysos*, the estate's showroom/shop/restaurnat.

> ■ *Each year, during October, a* **wine festival** *is held to celebrate the first tasting of the Kefraya Nouveau before its release onto the general market the following month. The festival is by invitation only, but if you are interested you should contact the estate in advance and they will send you an invitation; T08-645333 or T03-322005, F08-645151, chateau-kefraya@lebanon.com, www.lebanon.com Tours of the winery (free; lasting around 30 mins) are available Mon-Fri 100-1600. The showroom/shop, for wine tasting and sales, is open daily from 0900-1700. The restaurant is open daily 1000-2200.*

Continuing southwest along the main road, after 3½ km there is a right turn signposted to 'Khirbet Qanafar - Centenarian Oak Tree' on a Ministry of Tourism sign. Taking this turning, fork left after around 400 m and head for a small building topped by a white dome. This simple shrine is said to be the mausoleum of **Sheikh Adi ibn Mousafir**, a 12th century Sufi saint. Mousafir (literally 'the traveller') was the founder of the **Yezidi** sect, which incorporates aspects of Judaism and Christianity, as well as various folk traditions, with traditional Islamic teachings.

Khirbet Qanafar

Returning to the main road, a little over 1 km further on you pass the *Al Khraizat* hotel on the left (see below). Soon after you get your first views of the **Litani River** flowing through a green and wooded valley into the Qaraoun lake, its waters shimmering enticingly in the distance. Keep going straight, passing after around 3½ km the *Abou Antoun* restaurant on the right. Around

Southwest from Kefraya

700 m further on, just after a fork off to the right leading up to the village of **Saghbine** you pass a steep driveway on the left leading down to the *Macharaf Saghbine* hotel (sign in Arabic only). A little further on you pass the *Blue Lake* and *Chalet du Lac* restaurants before coming to a left turn which leads down to the lake itself, just under 3 km from the main road.

Qaraoun Lake & Litani Dam
Phone code: 08
Swimming in the lake is not recommended due to the high levels of bacteria, particularly when the water level is at its lowest in late summer and early autumn

Created by the building of the Litani Dam in 1959, the building of the dam was undertaken both with a view to generating electricity and providing irrigation water for large areas of the southern Lebanon. For years, the civil war and Israeli occupation of the so called 'Security Zone' in southern Lebanon prevented many of the dam's objectives being fulfilled. One of the more ambitious aspects of the project, which may now be taken up once again, envisaged building four further dams and boring a tunnel through the Jebel Niha mountains to supply irrigation water to the land around Nabatiye. The views of the lake from a distance are altogether more impressive than from the shores itself, which are muddy and not particularly inviting.

Sleeping & eating C *Khraizat*, T/F645188. Comfortable rooms with a/c, TV/dish, phone, attached bath and balcony. Restaurant, bar and small rooftop pool. **C/D** *Macharef Saghbine*, T671200, F670362. Comfortable rooms with a/c, TV/dish, phone, attached bath and balcony. Restaurant, bar, large swimming pool. Recently built, well run hotel offering stunning views of lake. Excellent value low season discounts (from 1/11-31/5; double room US$25). Recommended. The 2 restaurants along the main road, the *Blue Lake*, T860146, and the *Chalet du Lac*, T860022, both offer Lebanese cuisine (fresh trout a speciality) in pleasant surroundings with terraces overlooking the lake. A meal at either will cost in the region of US$20 per head.

Routes from Qaraoun
At the time of writing, traffic was being prevented from passing through an army checkpost around 7 km to the south of Jezzine

Continuing south along the main road from the turning down to the lake, you pass through a couple of small villages to arrive after 6 km at a checkpost and junction. Going straight on here takes you after a further 2 km into **Machghara**, a small town with nothing of particular note scattered across the side of the deep valley of the Nahr Litani. A rather poor road continues south from Machghara (into what was Israeli-occupied territory until May 2000), eventually looping north to **Jezzine**.

Forking left at the checkpost and junction takes you across the **Litani Dam**. The dam itself is 60 m high and 1,350 m long. On the other side you come to another junction and checkpost. Going left here takes you back up the other side of the lake to the village of **El Qaraoun**, and then northeast, passing through **Jobb Jannine** en route, to join with the Beirut-Damascus highway at **Bar Elias**. Going straight, you can reach the town of **Rachaya** (see below); after a couple of km you come to another checkpost and a right turn. Continue straight on here. The road winds its way through low hills and vineyards, passing a couple of turnings to small villages before arriving at another checkpost. Bear left here and then after just under 5 km take the turning to the right to head up to Rachaya.

Masnaa to Rachaya

Taking the fork off to the right in the border town of Masnaa (see page 581), after 6½ km you come to a left turn signposted to 'Roman Temple - Manara' on a Ministry of Tourism signboard. The temple referred to is 5½ km from the main road, and accessible only by foot or by four wheel drive. Continuing straight on, after a further 3 km you come to a checkpost and left turn signposted to 'Aita el Foukhar'.

There is a whole cluster of Ministry of Tourism signboards by this turning – to 'Yanta Ruins', Aita el Fakhar Ruins', 'Roman Temple Deir el Ashayer', 'Roman Temples Khirbet el Kneiseh' and 'Bakka Ruins'. Finding these sights is quite difficult and really best undertaken with a local guide. The sights themselves, meanwhile, are all very minor Roman temple ruins and not particularly impressive, though the scenery en route is very beautiful. In the case of Deir el-Ashayer, this village is right up against the Syrian border, with a large Syrian army base nearby; a local guide who can explain the reason for your presence here is definitely a good idea.

Continuing southwest along the main road, after a little over 3 km you pass a checkpost and right turn, this road leading to Jobb Jannine. Keeping straight on, after a further 11½ km, in the centre of Dahr el-Ahmar, take the left turn signposted for 'Rachaya Ruins' on a Ministry of Tourism sign. From the turning it is a little under 6 km to the castle. The road climbs steeply up through Rachaya; keep following the signs through the town to arrive at the castle.

The town of Rachaya is famous for its hilltop **castle**. It was here in November 1943 that the French Mandate authorities arrested the President, Beshara al-Khoury, the Prime Minister, Riad al-Solh, and most of the Lebanese Cabinet in response to their demands that Lebanon be given full independence. They were imprisoned in the fortress, but widespread protests both within Lebanon and abroad led the French to capitulate, and on 22 November the President and Prime Minister formally declared Lebanon an independent state. It was not, however, until 1946 that the last French troops finally left. You can see the rooms where the Lebanese politicians were held by the French, the castle's vaulted stables and various French artillery pieces dating from the French Mandate period. From the upper parts of the castle there are excellent views of **Mount Hermon** to the south, although sadly the mountain remains strictly off-limits. There is talk of the army vacating the castle and handing it over to the Ministry of Tourism in the future. ■ *Open daily 0700-1900. Entry free.*

Rachaya was also the scene of an earlier revolt in 1925 when its predominantly Druze population rose against French Mandate rule, though on that occasion the uprising was brutally suppressed and parts of the town destroyed. Nevertheless, enough of it evidently survived since today it retains much of its Ottoman character, with many old red-roofed houses still standing and attractive, cobbled souks, which have been carefully restored in recent years.

Rachaya
Colour map 4, grid B3

Built during the 18th century, the castle is now occupied by the Lebanese army, but if you ask at the gate you will be allowed in and shown around

Eating and transport There are a couple of simple snack places/restaurants down in the old part of town, at one end of the restored souk, where you can get falafel sandwiches and other snacks. There are fairly frequent microbuses to Rachaya from Chtaura (LL1,500). You may also be able to find a microbus or service taxi running from Masnaa; wait by the fork on the Beirut-Damascus highway.

From Rachaya you can follow the mountain road southwest to the town of Hasbaya. Ask directions to pick up the road going via Ain Harsha and Ain Aata (there is another road to Hasbaya, along the valley floor, but it is less scenic). This road first descends into a side-valley and then climbs steeply up the right-hand side of the valley. After around 11 km you come to a left turn leading to **Ain Harsha**, across the valley.

On the mountainside high above the village is a small, well preserved **Roman temple**. Dated according to an inscription in Greek, to 114-115 AD, the temple is only accessible on foot, a walk of 30-40 minutes from the top of the village.

Continuing straight on, the road climbs steeply up to the village of **Ain Ata**, 5 km further on. The road through the village is very narrow and rather

Rachaya to Hasbaya

Bekaa Valley

confusing in places. Once out the other side, there are dramatic views down into the Wadi el-Fater. The road then descends steeply to the village of El Kfair (7 km from Ain Ata), crosses the stream of a side-valley, and climbs again before descending once more to the village of Mimes, some 4 km further on. The scenery en route, boasting pine forests, olive groves, vineyards and brightly coloured wild flowers in spring, is particularly beautiful. From Mimes it is a further 6 km or so to Hasbaya.

Hasbaya
Colour map 4, grid C3

The town of Hasbaya is spread across a steep hillside, with views down towards the Nahr Hasbani to the west. According to some sources, Hasbaya corresponds with the biblical town of *Baal Gad* (Joshua 11: 17). The principal attraction today is the so called **Shihabi Citadel** (or Chehabi Citadel), an unusual complex dating back at least as far as the Crusader period. It was taken over by the Shihab (or Chehab) family after they helped drive the Crusaders out in the 12th century. It remained their main ancestral home until the late 17th century, when they took over from Maanid dynasty as rulers of Mount Lebanon, moving to the Maanid palace at Deir el-Qamar in the Chouf mountains (see box, page 567). However, a branch of the family remained at Hasbaya, and even today ownership of the complex is shared between some 50 descendents of the Shihabs.

Over the centuries the complex has been repeatedly added to, damaged, repaired and modified. The octagonal tower which you see from the outside when you arrive dates back to the Crusader period, as do elements of the main entrance, on the south side of the complex. The main entrance consists of an arched gateway flanked by carved reliefs of lions, the symbol of the Shihab family. In this case the lions are tethered by chains and faced by small rabbits, though the significance of this is anybody's guess. These reliefs are repeated on the inner part of the arch, though without the rabbits, while in the centre is an Arabic inscription detailing building works carried out in the early 17th century. The massive wooden door is still in place, while above the gateway is a large machicolation which has been converted into a balcony with three tall, graceful arches. Once inside, you find yourself in a large courtyard. To your right is an arched recess leading to a vaulted area supported by massive pillars. Part of the complex (in the far left-hand corner of the courtyard) is still lived in, while adjacent to this some rooms were being renovated at the time of writing. Apart from this, however, the complex is in a rather sorry state of dilapidation. Upstairs, you can wander through the various rooms, some piled high with discarded antique furniture. A long passageway leads to a particularly beautiful small courtyard with a fountain in the centre. On two sides of the courtyard are delicate arched porticos supported on slender columns, while the doorways to the courtyard are all richly decorated with intricate geometric designs.

If you follow the road down through Hasbaya, you can descend to the bottom of the valley along a tree-lined avenue. A sharp right turn by a petrol station is the start of the road leading back northeast along the valley floor (going via Dahr el-Ahmar and bypassing Rachaya). Continuing straight on, you pass through a UN checkpost, over a staggered crossroads and then through another UN checkpost (10 km from Hasbaya). Just to the south of this checkpost is the *Dana* hotel, while just under 3 km further on (2 km before Marjayoun) is the turning for Khiam village (see page 548).

Background

17

Background

Regional history

Though Syria and Lebanon only came into existence as nation-states during the 20th century, the region they occupy has a history dating right back to the dawn of civilization, and indeed beyond. Traces of human activity stretching back as far as the Old Stone Age or Paleolithic era (as much as 1 million years ago). Moreover, this region has witnessed the evolution of the three great monotheistic religions – Judaism, Christianity and Islam – as well as playing a central role in the development of civilization in terms of the development of settled agriculture, cities and indeed writing.

The prehistoric era

Around 700,000 years ago, during the **Paleolithic** period, *Neanderthal* man in the Middle East was engaged in primitive forms of hunting and gathering, utilizing simple stone tools to hunt large mammals such as elephants and hippopotami. This is the earliest evidence of 'human' activity to be recorded in the area.

Hunter-gatherers

During the **Epipaleolithic** or **Mesolithic** period (17,000-8500 BC), following the end to the last Ice Age some 15,000 years ago, *Homo sapiens sapiens* first made their appearance. The predominance of smaller, faster animals such as gazelles and wild goats necessitated the development of more sophisticated hunting skills, and correspondingly more specialized tools such as flint arrow-heads, spear-heads and knives have been uncovered from this period. Simultaneously, the gathering of wild plants began to take on a greater importance.

All around the peripheries of the Middle East, the so called Fertile Crescent provided the ideal conditions for the development of settled agriculture. This occurred towards the end of the Epipaleolithic (Mesolithic) period and during the early stages of the **Pre-Pottery Neolithic** period (8500-6000 BC). Wheat and barley appear to have been first cultivated around 10,000 years ago, while 8,000 to 9,000 years ago sheep and goats began to be fully domesticated. Hunting and gathering still played an important role, while the domestication of sheep and goats still required a semi-nomadic lifestyle in order to find suitable grazing. Gradually, however, small permanent settlements became more widely established.

Early settlement

During the **Pottery Neolithic** period (6000-4500 BC), baked clay (ceramic) wares made their first appearance. This period witnessed a marked reduction in levels of rainfall, and settlement tended to shift to riverside and coastal sites. In northern Mesopotamia and Syria, centred around the Kabur Triangle, the so called Halaf Culture developed (named after pottery finds dating from this period at Tell Halaf), overlapping with the Samarra culture of southern Mesopotamia. At sites such as Jbail (Byblos) and Ras Shamra (Ugarit) on the Mediterranean coast, small settlements were being established.

The **Chalcolithic** period (4500-3300 BC) heralded the appearance of copper (first used in eastern Anatolia and central Iran). Village settlements based on agriculture spread throughout the whole of the region. Agriculture and animal husbandry both became more sophisticated. Wheat and barley began to be complemented by pulses, olives and flax, while further south, dates and grapes were being cultivated. As well as sheep and goats, cattle and pigs were kept, and the remains of dogs, donkeys, gazelle and foxes have also been found. Styles of pottery became more varied, while basalt was also being used for many utensils. By now there was a thriving trade in obsidian with Anatolia.

Background

Chronology of archaeological and historic periods

Lower Paleolithic	1,500,000 - 100,000 BC
Middle Paleolithic	100,000 - 40,000 BC
Upper Paleolithic	40,000 - 17,000 BC
Epipaleolithic (Mesolithic)	17,000 - 8500 BC
Pre Pottery Neolithic	8500 - 6000 BC
Pottery Neolithic	6000 - 4500 BC
Chalcolithic	4500-3300 BC
Early Bronze Age	3300 - 2250 BC
Middle Bronze Age	2250 - 1550 BC
Late Bronze Age	1550 - 1200 BC
Iron Age	1200 - 539 BC
Persian Period	539 - 333 BC
Hellenistic Period	333 - 64 BC
Roman/Nabatean Period	64 BC - 395 AD
Byzantine Period	395 - 636 AD
Early Islamic Period	
Arab Conquest	632 - 661 AD
Umayyad Period	661 - 750 AD
Abbasid Period	750 - 969 AD
Fatimid Period	969 - 1171 AD
Crusader Period	1097 - 1291 AD
Late Islamic Period	
Zengid and Ayyubid Periods	1128 - 1260 AD
Mameluke Period	1260 - 1516 AD
Ottoman Period	1516 - 1918 AD
Modern Period	1918 AD - Present

The ancient era

The first cities & empires Out of these early settlements the first cities and city-states developed during the **Early Bronze Age** (3300-2250 BC). Initially, this took place in southern Mesopotamia, where the **Sumerian** civilization began to evolve from the fifth millennium BC. Here, an economy based on animal husbandry and large-scale irrigation of the river valleys between the Tigris and Euphrates rivers produced substantial surpluses. This in turn allowed powerful city-states to emerge with their specialized divisions of labour and complex social hierarchies and administrations. The most important was **Uruk** in southern Mesopotamia, from which the term 'Late Uruk culture' is derived. The most significant feature of the Sumerian civilization was the development of a form of writing based on the cuneiform script.

At the same time, from around 2900-2300 BC (a period in Syria generally referred to as the Early Syrian II period and in Egypt as the Early Dynastic period), the settlements at **Mari** (Tell Hariri) on the Euphrates and **Ebla** (Tell Mardikh) on the Central Plains to the south of Aleppo were also evolving into powerful city-states in their own right. Both developed their own systems of writing based on the cuneiform script of the Sumerians. The comparative developmental histories of southern Mesopotamia, Mari, Ebla and the Khabur plains have been described by one historian as a "research frontier looming on the horizon". Certainly the relationships between the various city-states and their embryonic empires were complex. Indeed, the discovery (made only in the 1960s) of a thriving Bronze Age city-state of the mid-third millennium BC at Ebla has forced historians to revise the emphasis previously given to the city-states of southern Mesopotamia in the early

Geographical/Historical Syria

Historically, the whole of the area covered by present day Syria and Lebanon (and Jordan and Israel) was referred to as 'Syria', though the actual definition of this term has shifted over the ages. The word itself was originally Greek, derived from the Semitic Suriyon, or perhaps the Babylonian Suri. Amongst the earliest examples of its usage comes from the fifth century BC when Herodotus, writing in Histories, used the term to refer to Cappadocia in present day Turkey. Herodotus himself believed the term 'Syria' to be a corruption of 'Assyria', denoting the western parts of the loosely defined Assyrian Empire. By the Roman era, 'Syria' had come to mean 'those regions of the Near East between Asia Minor and Egypt which belonged to the Roman Empire' (indeed, the Roman conquest of 64 BC saw the creation of the Roman Provincia Syria, with Antioch as its capital). The Roman definition endured through the Byzantine era and, with the coming of the Muslim Arabs, though the terminology changed, the broad definition remained the same.

In Arabic, the region was referred to as Ash Sham or Bilad ash-Sham (literally 'The North' or 'The Country of the North', although somewhat confusingly Damascus is also referred to as Ash Sham in Arabic). From the point of view of the nomadic Arab tribes who conquered this region, it was indeed to the north of their heartlands in the depths of the Arabian desert; by the same token, they used the

term al-Yaman (literally 'The South') to refer to southern Arabia, this term gaining currency in English as Yemen and becoming the name of the modern day country occupying the southern tip of the Arabian peninsula. In Europe, the term 'Syria' (or in French 'Syrie') continued to be used, and with the growing European influence in the region, became Arabized during the 19th century as 'Suriya'.

Thus a distinction needs to be made between 'geographical/historical Syria', which PK Hitti describes as, "the lands between the Taurus and Sinai, the Mediterranean and the desert", and the modern nation state of Syria (or more properly the Syrian Arab Republic).

Within geographical/historical Syria there were many other regional definitions. Modern day Israel was, roughly speaking, Palestine, while in Europe the term 'Southern Syria' was largely interchangeable with 'Palestine', though it tended to include parts of what was otherwise referred to as 'Transjordan', the land across (to the east of) the Jordan river. Likewise, 'Lebanon' and 'Mount Lebanon' are broad geographical terms, the latter in existence since earliest history, though they only emerged as political entities in the 19th and 20th centuries. The paradox of this region as a whole is that while it represents a geographically cohesive unit, broadly but clearly definable, historically and politically it has rarely been similarly united.

development of empires. It would appear that while the growth of the southern Mesopotamian cities was fuelled by intensive irrigation based agriculture, the extensive rain-fed plains of the Jezira and northwest Syria were also fuelling a similar growth in powerful city-states. Moreover, there appears to have been a steady shift in the centre of power, first from the southernmost portion of the Tigris-Euphrates alluvium to the dry farming plains of the Jezira, and then to the plains of northwest Syria around Aleppo. It has been suggested that the decline of the southern Mesopotamian centres of power was due to water-logging and salinization brought about by the intensive irrigation on which these city-states depended, a problem not encountered in the extensive rain-fed, grain producing regions of the Jezira and northwest Syria.

The development of these city-states was interrupted (or at least modified) in around 2350 BC by the invasion of the **Akkadians**, the first territorial empire to emerge in the ancient Middle East. This empire was founded by Sargon (2334-2271

☛ *The desert and the sown*

Identifying a series of distinct geographical zones running north-south in parallel (see 'Land and environment', below) provides a useful means of visualizing the physical geography of the region. However, there is another perspective which is equally valuable, and perhaps more so in historical terms. Viewing the Middle East as a whole, its single largest feature is the vast Arabian desert. This forms the core of the region, around which is a periphery of fertile land: the **Fertile Crescent**. *This stretches in a broad arc from southern Jordan up through Lebanon and Syria following the eastern plateau of the Great Rift Valley, the Jordan River, Bekaa Valley, the Lebanese and Syrian coastal plains and mountains and the Orontes river, right up to the Taurus mountains marking the border between Turkey and Syria, following them east and then bending southwards to follow the Euphrates and Tigris rivers right the way down though Iraq to the Arabian Gulf.*

In many ways, the ancient history of this region has been to a large extent shaped by the relationship between the central core of desert and the Fertile Crescent surrounding it. While the Fertile Crescent provided the best environment for the emergence of agriculture and permanent settlements, the desert itself was the source of successive waves of migrations. Nomadic tribes of the deserts gradually (and in some cases more abruptly and violently) moved into the fertile peripheries, displacing those that were already there and bringing with them their own new cultures and languages. In ancient times, the most important of these included the **Amorites**, **Aramaeans** *and indeed the* **Hebrews**. *All shared a common mother tongue which developed into different languages, but still had a common Semitic root. More recently, the arrival of the* **Muslim Arabs** *and their conquest of the Middle East during the seventh century AD represents another wave of migration from the desert interior into the fertile settled lands of the periphery.*

BC), who initiated its expansion from its base in Mesopotamia, while his grandson Naram-Sin continued the process, extending the empire eastwards towards the Persian Gulf and westwards towards the Mediterranean.

Meanwhile, on the Mediterranean coast, **Byblos** was evolving into an important commercial and religious centre, establishing close relations with the Old Kingdom pharaohs of Egypt and trading timber from the vast cedar forests of Mount Lebanon with them. The Egyptians, having no forests of their own, needed timber to build ships, palaces and temples. In return they brought goods such as gold, alabaster, papyrus, flax, rope, cereals and pulses, as well as making generous endowments to the temple of Baalat-Gebal in Byblos.

The **Middle Bronze Age** (2250-1550 BC) brought with it major upheavals. Towards the end of the third millennium BC, the region was overrun by the **Amorites**, a Semitic people who emerged from the deserts to the south and east. After an initial period of disruption, city-states such as Byblos and Mari absorbed these new peoples and began to flourish once again. Ebla, meanwhile, became part of the newly emergent Amorite kingdom of Yamkhad, based in present day Aleppo. By the 18th century BC, Mari had been destroyed by the **Babylonian** king Hammurabi, also of Amorite origin, who was extending his own empire from its base in southern Mesopotamia. Byblos at this time was settled by the **Hyksos**, who overthrew the Middle Kingdom Egyptians. **Ugarit**, however, now entering its first golden age as a great trading city, continued to flourish by maintaining a delicate balancing act with the more powerful civilizations of Mesopotamia and Egypt.

Ancient 'super-power' rivalries
The **Late Bronze Age** (1550-1200 BC) saw further upheavals in the region. The expulsion of the Hyksos from Egypt by the pharaohs of New Kingdom Egypt in around 1550 BC was soon followed by a far greater **Egyptian** involvement in the region,

particularly along the Mediterranean coast in centres such as Byblos and Ugarit. Around the same time, a new peoples of Indo-European origin, the **Hittites**, were advancing into the region from the northwest. These were complemented by the **Hurrians** and later the **Mittanites** who arrived from the northeast. The latter two blended into a federation known as the **Mittani** kingdom. For a time, the Egyptian, Hittite and Mittani Empires formed a triangle of 'super-powers' fighting for control of the region. Eventually the Mittani kingdom was absorbed into that of the Hittites, the struggle for supremacy becoming a straight battle between the Egyptians and Hittites. Byblos, along with Sidon and Tyre, allied themselves with Egypt, though their pleas for assistance in the face of the Hittite threat, as recorded in the famous Tell Amarna tablets discovered in Egypt, were largely ignored by the Egyptian pharaoh of the time. The armies of the two powers finally met head on at Kadesh, though the outcome of the battle was inconclusive, with both sides claiming victory.

Despite these upheavals, it was during the Late Bronze Age that the first **alphabets** were developed, offering a massive improvement on the hugely complex cuneiform system first developed by the Sumerians, and the equally complex hieroglyphic system of the Egyptians. This momentous development occurred initially at Ugarit during the 14th century BC, and later at Byblos towards the end of the 13th century BC, the latter being considered by many experts to represent the forerunner of our own alphabet. It was also probably towards the very end of the Late Bronze Age that the famous **Exodus** took place, when Moses led the **Israelites** out of slavery in Egypt and back to the 'Promised Land', his successor Joshua leading the 12 tribes across the Jordan River into Palestine.

The start of the Iron Age saw two major migrations which brought with them fundamental changes to the region. The first was the violent invasion of the so called **'Sea Peoples'**, about which remarkably little is known. As JD Muhly points out: "While the Egyptian texts refer to massed invasions by land and by sea of various groups collectively known as the 'Peoples of the Sea', it has been notoriously difficult to find any trace of such people in the archaeological record. Only the **Phillistines**, who gave their name to what was thereafter known as Palestine, subsequent to their settlement in the area as Egyptian garrison troops, can be identified in the archaeological context by their distinctive painted pottery" (JD Muhly in *Ebla to Damascus*). What is known, however, is that these 'Sea Peoples' overthrew the Hittite Empire and largely destroyed Ugarit.

In the wake of the 'Sea Peoples' came the **Aramaeans**, a semi-nomadic Semitic people who arrived from the deserts of Arabia and settled in central and northern Syria, blending with the small **neo-Hittite** kingdoms which had arisen in the wake of the destruction of the Hittite Empire. The Aramaeans also established themselves in Damascus, where they checked the expansion of the kingdoms of Judah and Israel to the south.

Along the Mediterranean coast, meanwhile, although Byblos appears to have fallen into relative decline, the other **Phoenician** city-states (most notably Tyre) which evolved from the former Canaanite communities flourished. This was the golden age of Phoenicia, when the king of Tyre supplied Solomon with cedar for the building of the Temple of Solomon, and Phoenician ships voyaged throughout the Mediterranean and beyond, carrying out lucrative trade and establishing numerous colonies, most famously that of Carthage in North Africa.

From the ninth century BC a new empire, that of the **Assyrians**, arose in northern Mesopotamia and gradually extended its control over most of the region. The Assyrians were in turn overthrown by the **neo-Babylonians** or **Chaldeans**, who captured their capital, Nineveh, in 612 BC.

Iron Age (1200-539 BC)

Background

The Canaanites and Phoenicians

During the late fourth or early third millenium BC a people, possibly of Semitic origin, who became known as the Canaanites, established themselves along the Mediterranean coast of present day Israel, Lebanon and Syria. However, the origins of the Canaanites and the exact moment when they first appeared, remains shrouded in uncertainty. Some historians consider Canaanite culture to have only truly emerged as a result of a fusion of local and Amoritic influences which followed the Amorite invasions of the late third millenium BC.

The term 'Canaan', known to us from the Bible, is thought by some to have originated during the Late Bronze Age and to have referred to the Egyptian province of Canaan (Palestine west of the Jordan river). According to one interpretation, the word is of Semitic origin, meaning literally 'lowland'. An alternative interpretation suggests that it derives from the non-Semitic Hurrian word kinahhu or knaggi, literally 'belonging to (the land of) purple'. The Greek term 'Phoenician' is likewise thought by some to come from a

Canaanite word for the all important purple dye for which the Canaanites and Phoenicians were famous (see page 537). Tyrian purple, as the colour was known to the Greeks and Romans, was made from the crushed shells of the sea snail Murex trunculus, and heaps of crushed Murex shells are a common feature at most Phoenician sites.

While the origins of the Canaanites remains a mystery, most scholars agree that the Phoenicians evolved from the Canaanites. To quote FM Cross on the subject: "Arbitrarily we use the term Canaanite to refer to a people of a homogeneous culture who lived in Syria-Palestine before 1200 BC and spoke a related group of dialects ... After the series of destructive attacks which engulfed the Levant about 1200 BC [the invasions of the so called 'Sea Peoples'], the remnants of the Canaanites, whose centres were now restricted to the Lebanese coast and northern Palestine, were called Phoenicians, their Greek name. Thus the Phoenicians' ancestors were the Canaanites."
(FM Cross in Ebla to Damascus).

Persian period (539-333 BC)   Neo-Babylonian dominance of the region was short lived, with the **Achaemenid Persians**, led by Cyrus, capturing their capital Babylon in 539 BC, taking over control of their empire and extending it to include all of the Middle East, Egypt and Asia Minor. Persian rule was on the whole very well organized, with an excellent network of roads encouraging trade and communications within the empire. The coastal cities of the Phoenicians in particular flourished. Sidon, which was made the capital of the fifth satrapy, encompassing both Syria-Palestine and Cyprus, benefited greatly, and it was during this period that the nearby temple of Eshmoun was built. The Sidonian fleet aided the Persians in their defeat of the Egyptians in 525 BC, and played a crucial role in their wars with the Greeks. Ultimately, however, the Sidonians overstepped the mark by establishing close trading relations with the Athenians and leading a coalition of Phoenician city-states in a rebellion against Persian rule, prompting the Persian king Ataxerxes III Ochus to lead a massive army against them in 350 BC.

The Classical Era

Hellenistic period (333-64 BC)   Although the Persians were at first successful in their battles with the **Greeks**, ultimately it was the latter who triumphed, Alexander the Great of Macedon defeating the forces of Darius III at the battle of Issus in 333 BC. When he died at Babylon in 323 BC, Alexander was only 33 years old, but in the space of just 10 years he had succeeded in creating an empire larger even than that of the Persians.

After his death, Alexander's Empire was partitioned between his generals. Ptolemy I Soter gained control of Egypt, southern Lebanon and southern Syria (including Damascus), founding what became known as the **Ptolemid** Empire. Seleucus I Nicator, meanwhile, gained control of Mesopotamia, Asia Minor and northern Syria, establishing what became known as the **Seleucid** Empire. Over the next century, the Seleucids extended their control southwards, driving the Ptolemids back into Egypt, though at the same time they lost Asia Minor to the **Romans** and Mesopotamia to the **Parthians** (who arose from the ashes of the Persian Empire). Thus much of present day Syria and Lebanon came to be controlled by the Seleucids.

The Seleucids continued the process, begun under Alexander, of Hellenization, 'founding' new cities such as Antioch (which they made their capital), Apamea and Dura Europos. Most of these had already existed as small settlements, and in addition the Seleucids made their mark on the great cities of the region, including Aleppo, Damascus, Beirut and many others. They laid out a distinctive grid pattern of streets and erected civic buildings and monuments, bringing with them Greek political and legal institutions, and indeed the Greek language. All the same, many of these cities were able to establish a high degree of autonomy within the empire, often amounting to near independence. The Seleucids, being relatively few in number, had no choice but to let them run their own affairs, albeit in a Hellenistic way. In the countryside, they made little or no impression.

By the second century BC, the Seleucid Empire was beginning to crumble. The sacking of Jerusalem and desecration of the Temple there prompted the Maccabean revolt of 173 BC, which in turn led to the creation of the independent Jewish **Hasmonean** Dynasty within Palestine. The Hasmoneans subsequently extended their power to the east of the Jordan River, capturing Jerash in 84 BC. At the same time, the **Nabateans**, who had already established themselves as a powerful, semi-independent trading state in Petra, began to push northwards. Under King Aretas III (84-56 BC), they briefly succeed in extending their empire to include Bosra and Damascus. Similarly, the **Itureans**, a local tribal dynasty from the Bekaa Valley, began making raids on the coastal cities and inland centres. In the northern part of the empire, the Seleucids faced more serious threats from the Romans to the west, the **Armenians** to the north and the **Parthians** to the east.

Roman period (64 BC-395 AD)

The final fall of the Seleucid Empire came with the conquest of Antioch by the Roman general Pompey in 64 BC. The Romans created the province of Syria in their newly acquired territory and adopted Antioch as its capital. Initially, the Romans were much more concerned with their own internal power struggles, and at one stage the Parthians even succeeded in occupying much of Syria. Rome's bloody intrigues finally drew to an end with the abolition of the Roman Republic and the appointment of Octavian (Augustus Caesar) as the first Roman emperor in 29 BC.

Thus at first the Romans were only able to exercise loose political control, declaring the former city-states of the Seleucid Empire 'free cities'. In the south, the Nabatean kingdom continued to exist as an independent entity, keeping Damascus until as late as 54 AD. After that it was pushed back into its former confines of Petra, though in 70 AD it pushed northwards again and briefly made Bosra the capital of its empire. Although Pompey had taken Jerusalem when he first conquered the region, a reduced Hasmonean kingdom was allowed to maintain its independence, a state of affairs which continued under the rule of the Herod the Great (37-4 BC) and his successors. By 44 AD, however (following the death of Herod Agrippa I), it had been brought under direct Roman rule.

Octavian's rise to the position of emperor in 29 BC heralded a gradual improvement in the overall state of affairs in the province of Syria. Though there were many areas over which they still had only nominal control, Roman rule brought with it peace and an orderly, efficient administration – the so called *Pax Romana* – which allowed the region to flourish economically. The loose federation known as the **Decapolis**, or 'Ten Cities', emerged, straddling the borders of present day southern Syria and northern Jordan, with cities such as Bosra and Jerash benefiting from the north-south trade between Damascus and the Red Sea. In Damascus, the former temple of Haddad was gradually expanded and converted into a temple dedicated to the Roman god Jupiter, and the principal *Via Recta* (the Straight Street of the Bible) was widened and colonnaded. Likewise, Baalbek began to rise to prominence as a major centre for the cult worship of Jupiter, work on its main temple nearing completion towards the end of Nero's reign (37-68 AD). In the Syrian desert Palmyra began to emerge as a major trading post on the direct route between Dura Europos and Emesa (Homs). Ironically, in the case of Palmyra, it was actually its position in the no-man's-land between Parthian and Roman power which helped it to flourish. Palestine, however, continued to cause problems, the Jews rising against Roman rule in 66 AD (the First Jewish Revolt). But by 70 AD, the revolt had been crushed, the Romans taking Jerusalem and destroying the Temple.

The Romans also developed their new province agriculturally. The Bekaa Valley and the area around Bosra became major grain producing regions, the so called 'bread baskets' of the Roman Empire, while in the rocky limestone hills around Aleppo, richer landowners were able to embark on the long term project of developing olive groves. Throughout Syria and Lebanon, it is the monuments of the Roman era which have survived, the ubiquitous building projects of the Romans having overlain those of the Greeks whom they replaced. Socially and culturally, however, the region's Hellenistic influences continued to be felt long afterwards. Greek remained the official language, and the Romans relied heavily on pre-existing Hellenistic administrative structures.

In 106 AD, during the reign of Trajan, the empire was substantially reorganized. The Nabatean kingdom of Petra was incorporated into the empire and a new province of Arabia created alongside that of Syria, with Bosra as its capital. As a result of this, Palmyra entered its golden age, surpassing Petra in significance as a centre of trade. Soon after, the Second Jewish Revolt (or Bar Kokhba Revolt) of 132-135 was even more brutally suppressed than the first.

The marriage in 187 AD of Septimus Severus to the daughter of the High Priest of Homs, Julia Domna, heralded a 'Syrian' line of Roman emperors, ensuring a greater direct Syrian influence in the affairs of Imperial Rome. It was during the rule of Septimus Severus (193-211) that Beirut's famous Law School was established and the city subsequently flourished.

However, during the rule of Caracalla (211-217) and his successor Elagabalus (217-222), the empire began to descend into degeneracy. The reigns of Alexander Severus (222-235) and Philip the Arab (244-49) provided brief respites, but by that time Rome's Empire in the Middle East was under serious threat. Since the late second century, the advances of the Parthians from the east had become a major preoccupation. In the early part of the third century the Parthians were replaced by the **Sassanid Persians**, who posed an even more pressing threat. In 256 Dura Europos fell to the Sassanids. Four years later, the emperor Valerian was captured by the Sassanids and disaster was only averted when the king of Palmyra, Odainat, defeated them the same year. This set the stage for the legendary Queen Zenobia to establish Palmyra as an independent kingdom until the emperor Aurelian captured it in 271.

Diocletian's rule (284-305) saw relative stability, but his death brought with it 20 years of civil war between the newly created eastern and western administrations of the Roman Empire. These only came to an end when Constantine managed to establish himself as sole emperor in 324, founding Constantinople as a second imperial capital in 330.

In 312 Constantine had converted to Christianity, which was already spreading throughout the empire, despite the attempts of Diocletian to suppress it. A year later, the Edict of Milan officially gave Christians the right to practice their religion and by 380, Christianity had been adopted as the official religion of the Roman Empire. Although the Byzantine period can be said to have effectively started earlier (according to some interpretations with the rise of Constantine to the position of sole emperor in 324), most historians date the Byzantine period from the official division of the Roman Empire into East and West in 395, with the Eastern Roman Empire becoming known as the Byzantine Empire.

Byzantine period (395-636 AD)

Many of the former pagan temples of the Romans were converted into great churches during this era, for example at Baalbek and Damascus. In addition, numerous Christian communities flourished, particularly in the so called 'Dead City' region around Aleppo (and most famously at the pilgrimage site of St Simeon), but also throughout the rest of the empire. The Byzantine period in the Middle East spawned many fundamentally important innovations in religious architecture, the influence of which can still be seen today.

Under the reign of Theodosius II (408-50), the '100 Year Peace' was established with the Sassanids, and the region was able to prosper as it had done under the Romans. During the reign of Justinian (527-65), the Byzantine Empire again came under repeated attacks from the Sassanids, who on several occasions made deep incursions into Byzantine territory. Nevertheless, Justinian's rule was also marked by a flowering of Byzantine culture and architecture.

In 602, under the leadership of Chosroes II, the Sassanids launched a massive invasion. By 614 they had reached right down into the southern part of the empire and captured Jerusalem. In addition, Antioch, Aleppo, Damascus and Jerash were all occupied. In 616 they simultaneously conquered most of Egypt and Asia Minor, laying siege even to Constantinople. In 622 the Byzantine emperor Heraclius led a counter attack. His six-year campaign against the Sassanids drove them from most of the empire, but his success was short lived. The Byzantine Empire was on its knees, and in no position to resist the onslaught of the new power emerging from the deserts of Arabia, that of the Muslim Arabs.

The Islamic Era

After the death in 632 of the founder of Islam, the Prophet Mohammad, the Arab tribes which he had welded together into such a formidable force set about conquering the fertile lands to the north and west. Led by the military commander Khalid Ibn al-Walid, the Muslim Arab army captured Damascus in 635 and then withdrew to defeat the forces of Byzantium at the Battle of Yarmouk in 636, effectively marking the end of Byzantine rule in the region. They again occupied Damascus the same year, and then proceeded to sweep through the lands of present day Syria and Lebanon, meeting little resistance from the local peoples. By 656 the whole of Persia had also been conquered.

Arab conquest (632-661 AD)

These conquests took place under the rule of Mohammad's first three successors, the caliphs Abu Bakr (632-34), Omar (634-44), and Uthman (644-56), who all maintained Medina as their capital. The fourth caliph, Ali (656-61), whose assumption of the title of caliph was opposed both by the kin of Uthman (who had been assassinated) and by others in Medina, moved the Arab Muslim capital to Kufa in southern Iraq. However, the governor of Syria, Mu'awiya, was a close kinsman of Uthman, and he rose up in revolt. After Ali was murdered by disaffected members of his own camp (see 'Religion': Sunnis and Shi'ites, below), Mu'awiya assumed the title of caliph, thus founding the Umayyad Dynasty.

**The Umayyads
(661-750 AD)**

Mu'awiya promptly made Damascus the seat of the caliphate and capital of the empire, heralding the start of one of the most glorious periods in the city's history, and that of the region as a whole. Under the Umayyads, the empire grew to its greatest extent and by the end of the seventh century it stretched from Spain in the west to the Indus River in the east.

Though their origins were nomadic, the Umayyads were quick to adopt many aspects of the civilizations which had previously existed in the lands they now ruled. As Albert Hourani comments: "Gradually, from being Arab chieftains, they formed a way of life patterned on that traditional among rulers of the Near East, receiving their guests or subjects in accordance with the ceremonial usages of Byzantine emperor or Iranian King." (Albert Hourani, *A History of the Arab Peoples*.) The synthesis of different influences – Graeco-Roman, Byzantine, Persian, Mesopotamian and indigenous – which occurred under the Umayyads is most graphically displayed in their architecture, and in particular their religious architecture. The famous Umayyad Mosque in Damascus, built during the reign of the sixth Umayyad caliph Khalid ibn al-Walid (705-15), is the most spectacular example of this. But the Umayyads were also responsible for many other monuments, including the delicate palace at Aanjar in the Bekaa Valley and the desert complex of Qasr al-Heir al-Sharki near Palmyra.

In retrospect, the Umayyads were seen as lax and corrupt by future Islamic Dynasties. Certainly, they did not place a major emphasis on religion, concentrating instead on developing their empire economically and politically. But eventually they did indeed fall into degeneracy. The last truly great Umayyad caliph, Hisham (724-43) was followed in quick succession by a series of incompetent and debauched caliphs. The last of these, Marwan II, was overthrown following an uprising led by Abu al-Abbas, who went on to found the Abbasid Dynasty. One grandson of Hisham did manage to flee to Spain, maintaining the Umayyad lineage there for another 500 years.

**The Abbasids
(750-1258 AD)**

The Abbasids sought to bring Islamic rule back to the more rigorous and theocratic interpretations they felt it deserved. They transferred the seat of the caliphate to Iraq, first to Kufa and then Baghdad. In doing so, they abandoned the blending of eastern and western influences which characterized Umayyad rule and brought to the empire a distinctively Mesopotamian and Persian emphasis. Syria and Lebanon, previously at the political heart of the empire, became relatively insignificant backwaters.

Initially, the Abbasids managed successfully to administer an empire which included the whole of the former Umayyad Empire except Spain and Morocco. By the mid-ninth century, however, their power was beginning to fragment, with numerous local dynasties appearing in Syria and Lebanon. The **Tulunid** and **Ikhshidid** Dynasties of Egypt in turn controlled parts of southern Syria from 868 to 969. The latter were ousted by the **Fatimids**, who went on to make Cairo their capital in 973 and later extended their power into Syria. The Fatimids represented the Ismaili branch of Shi'ite Islam, and as such were a direct threat to the power of the Sunni Abbasids, having set up their own rival caliphate. In the north, meanwhile, the **Hamdanid** and **Mirdasid** Dynasties ruled in turn in Aleppo from 944-1070. Both, however, were only nominal rulers, being at one time or another subject to either the Fatimids to the south or the Byzantines to the north (the Byzantines were making the most of the chaos and trying to regain territory in their former empire).

While all this was happening, the **Seljuk Turks**, originally chiefs of the Oghuz tribes of Transoxania, had conquered Persia and established a kingdom there with Isphahan as their capital. Being Sunni Muslims, they came to the aid of the Abbasids, who were experiencing their own domestic problems in Baghdad. In return the Seljuk ruler forced the Abbasid caliph to recognize him as 'Sultan' (literally 'Sovereign') of the Universal State of Islam. Thus the Abbasids became in effect helpless puppets of the Seljuks. The Seljuks occupied Aleppo in 1070 and defeated the Byzantines at Manzikert in eastern Anatolia in 1071. By 1076 they had extended their control over most of Syria, including Damascus, and largely ousted the Fatimids, though they were never strong enough to completely expel them from the region. After 1095 two Seljuk rulers emerged in Syria with Aleppo and Damascus as their capitals. These rulers set up what were in effect their own rival dynasties, both only nominally subservient to the Seljuk sultan in Isphahan.

Though the Abbasid caliphate continued to exist, nominally at least, until it was conclusively destroyed by the Mongols in 1258, in practice it faded into total insignificance.

During the first part of the 11th century, the Fatimid caliph Al Hakim had ordered the destruction of 30,000 churches in Egypt, Palestine and Syria (including the Church of the Holy Sepulchre in Jerusalem). This, along with the pleas of the Byzantine emperor, who was becoming increasingly alarmed at the Seljuk threat, prompted Pope Urban II to call for a crusade to restore the Holy Lands to Christian control.

The First Crusade

Thus the **First Crusade** set off from Europe, arriving in Syria in 1097. To their surprise, instead of a formidable enemy in the form of the Seljuk Turks, what they found was a region deeply divided and fragmented into numerous petty principalities. While the Crusaders were united by their religious mission of a 'Holy War', the Muslim peoples against whom they were marching were thoroughly embroiled in their own domestic conflicts. After a nine-month siege they took Antioch, massacring many of its inhabitants, including it's Greek Orthodox community. They then continued southwards along the Orontes River. Despite meeting little resistance, they were by this time in a sorry state, riven by disease and famine. The shortage of food in particular was reaching crisis point, prompting the infamous massacre at Maarat al-Numan. Continuing south, they swung inland through the Homs Gap, briefly occupying the castle which was later to become Krak des Chevaliers. After unsuccessfully besieging Aqra (near Tripoli), they headed straight down the Mediterranean coast, turning inland again near Jaffa to arrive at Jerusalem. After just over a month, on 15 July 1099, the Holy City fell to the Crusaders, its inhabitants, like those of Antioch, being subjected to an indiscriminate massacre.

By this time, three Crusader states had been established under the rule of the principal leaders of the Crusade: the **Kingdom of Jerusalem**, which went to Godfrey of Bouillon; the **Principality of Antioch**, which had been left in the possession of Bohemond; and the **County of Edessa** (present day Urfa in Turkey), which Baldwin, Godfrey's brother, had carved out for himself. After the fall of Jerusalem, Raymond St Gilles headed back north along the coast and laid siege to Tripoli. The siege cost him his life, but eventually Tripoli fell in 1109 and a fourth state, the **County of Tripoli**, was created. Meanwhile, other cities along the coast fell to the Crusaders and were incorporated into the Kingdom of Jerusalem or County of Tripoli. By the early 12th century the Crusaders controlled a narrow strip of land stretching along the whole of the eastern Mediterranean (and various inland sites in the coastal mountains), as well as the area around Edessa.

After capturing Jerusalem, the great majority of the soldiers of the First Crusade returned home. Though the Crusaders were to remain in the region for another 200 years or so, their numbers were always dangerously few. In the absence of manpower they resorted instead to building formidable castles which could be easily defended with the minimum of soldiers. Today, numerous examples of these remarkable pieces of military architecture can be seen throughout Syria and Lebanon. Many of them (most famously Krak des Chevaliers, but also others such as Qalat Marqab, Qalat Saladin and St Gilles) are still in an excellent state of preservation.

Background

Frankish and Arabic cultural exchange (East meets, and gets to know, West)

When the European Crusaders swooped upon Syria in 1097 the local population assumed that this infidel warband were in transit through their lands, like the more local Muslim warlords with whom they were so familiar. Yet these interlopers decided to lay roots. They constructed vast fortresses and it was to be 200 years before the Muslims saw the last of the people they referred to generically as 'Franks'. People who came from chilly but fertile lands and were distinguished by their fanatical bravery and poor personal hygiene.

Initially the Crusades were marked by the kind of ferocity that occurs whenever an army encounters a foreign and threatening culture. Christian propaganda had painted the Arab rulers of the Holy Land with all the lurid traits of atrocity: holy places defiled; beasts butchered in Christian shrines; and pilgrims plundered, massacred and otherwise harassed. Most of the Crusaders would never before have travelled more than a few miles from their home villages and their perception of this alien people, inflamed by the rhetoric of hysterical priests and the berserk intoxication of battle led to predictable and bloody slaughter. The followers of Peter the Hermit began the First Crusade (1096-1102) by obliterating the peaceful Jews of the Rhine who populated their overland route. As the Frankish warriors fought their way through Syria they made imaginative use of the Arabic innovations they stumbled across. Upon being informed by captives that the pigeons carried by the Arab armies were used to communicate with their towns, they released the birds bearing word of the Christian owner's victories – written in the blood of their erstwhile owners.

It was perhaps the brutal slaying of every inhabitant, Muslim, Jewish or otherwise, after the capture of Jerusalem (the ostensible object of the First Crusade) that brought a slowing of savagery. Having flushed their quarry, the Westerners found themselves alone, outnumbered and unloved, hundreds of miles from home and surrounded by a hostile population. Maintaining their tenuous toehold in the East required the conquerors to become colonists. Imperceptibly, they began to blend in with the locals, Syrian-born Franks (or poulains) merged with Arabs or Jews who had aligned themselves with this new power: the Crusaders were 'going native'.

Popular history of the Crusades indicates that the pilgrimages and crusades to the Holy Land spawned generations of sophisticates who, weary of battle, returned to Europe to initiate their barbaric western brethren into the wonders of the East. Coming during a particularly productive phase in Islamic scholarship, science and poetry, the epoch of Nizam-al-Mulk and Omar Khayyam, the First Crusade brought many thousands of western Europeans into

The Zengids and Ayyubids (1128-1260 AD)

A concerted response to the Crusaders came from the **Zengids**, nominally subservient to the Seljuks. The Zengid Dynasty was founded by Zengi, who in 1124 had helped lead a Seljuk force in the relief of Aleppo from a Crusader siege. In 1128 he became the ruler of Aleppo. Under his rule, and that of his son Nur ud-Din (1146-74), Aleppo became a centre of resistance against the Crusaders.

In 1144 the County of Edessa fell to Nur ud-Din, prompting the **Second Crusade**. Their attempts to besiege Damascus failed and the whole expedition ended in something of a fiasco. By 1154 the Zengids had themselves gained control of Damascus, uniting the Muslim opposition to the Crusaders in Syria. In 1169 Nur ud-Din sent a huge force against the Fatimids in Egypt. Led by **Salah ud-Din** (better known to us as Saladin), the Zengid forces over threw the Fatimids in 1171, restoring Sunni orthodoxy there and, nominally at least, the authority of the Abbasid caliph. After Nur ud-Din's death, Salah ud-Din returned to Syria and by 1186 had succeeded in uniting

contact with an alien, but highly developed civilization. Direct trade routes to Asia Minor were opened and Mediterranean trade became dominated by the West, who freely traded with the Arab states even when at war with them. Eventually popes had to impose trade restrictions and arms embargos to prevent Christians from running arms to the east. Plus ça change!

Paradoxically, as the Arab's political power in the east declined, their cultural influence increased, and eastern textiles, glassware, cutlery, mirrors; as well as banking and agricultural methods; mathematical and medical knowledge; hindu numerals (now known as Arabic); armorial and heraldic devices; all made their way westwards. The accuracy and geometrical ingenuity of Islamic building was an inspiration to the architects of the west. Exported craftsmen and masons transmitted architectural knowledge of cross-vaulting and barrel-vaults; pointed and semi-circular arches and their use in colonnades; as well as the distinctive oriental dome that first appears in Islamic architecture at the Dome of the Rock in Jerusalem (688).

The returning Franks also brought an eastern flavour to cookery, by cutting out the Arabic middleman from the lucrative spice-trade they popularized the usage among the rich of eastern spices, sugar, rice, lemons and melons. Spice of a different kind was represented by the European's introduction to Islamic polygamy. The Crusaders were familiar with eunuchs, the pope kept them for his choir, but shadowy impressions of the seraglio of the Sultan hinted at a more intriguing role for the castrated hulks.

So the nobles of Frankish Syria wallowed in luxury on the coast. Abandoning the wool and furs of their homelands they swathed their Turkish wives in damask and muslin fabrics and cosmetics. Secure in their villas, they guzzled peacocks and swilled Lebanese wine while the frugal warrior-monks of the military orders garrisoned the harsh rebellious interior. They hunted lion with the Arab aristocrats and visited bath-houses and bazaars almost identical to those of today.

The tragedy of the Crusades is that the cultural benefits of contact with the East were already being transmitted through trade. Christians wishing to visit the Holy Land on pilgrimage did make the journey, arduous though it could be, and Muslim Spain was a conduit for cultural exchange. The lasting legacy of Outremer is the memory of militant Christianity. The common theological roots and beliefs of 'the peoples of the book' were obscured by conflict as armies of Islam and Christendom vied for prestige, power and land. Muslims today still evoke the Crusades as a harbinger of the later colonialism and Imperialist attitudes of the Christian West.

---

all the Muslim lands from Cairo to Baghdad under the **Ayyubid Dynasty** (named after his father Ayyub). In 1187, having defeated the Crusaders at the Battle of Hattin, he recaptured Jerusalem and also regained Acre, Sidon, Beirut and Byblos. The following year he conducted a whirlwind campaign which saw no less than 50 Crusader positions fall, although he avoided their most important and impregnable strongholds: Krak des Chevaliers, Qalat Marqab and Antioch.

The fall of Jerusalem prompted the **Third Crusade**, which by 1191 had recaptured Acre. The King of England, Richard I (Richard the Lionheart) is perhaps the best known figure of this Crusade, but despite twice coming to within sight of Jerusalem, he failed to take it. Instead, he signed a peace treaty in 1192 which guaranteed pilgrims free right of passage. After Salah ud-Din's death the following year, his successors failed to capitalize on the gains he had made and the Crusaders were able to recapture much of their former territory along the coast. The Ayyubid

Sultan Baibars (1223-1277)

Baibars, a former slave and renowned Muslim captain known as 'the crossbowman', had been instrumental in the military coup that saw the Ayyuyid dynasty of Saldin replaced by the Mamulukes in 1250. By 1260 his primacy as a general enabled him to seize power in Cairo. The reign of the Mameluke sultans had evinced a hardening of Muslim attitudes towards the Franks and Baibars was to invoke the most brutal expression of this attitude. His reduction of Antioch (now Antaka in Turkey), a Frankish city for 170 years, took only four days, and culminated in a massacre that he boasted of to Prince Bohemond VI, "Be glad that you have not seen your knights lying prostate under the hooves of horses, your palaces plundered, your ladies sold in the quarters of the city, fetching a mere dinar apiece – a dinar taken, moreover, from your own hoard!" (From his official chronicler, Ibn Abd-al-Zahir in A history of the crusades through Arab Eyes.)

Baibars consolidated Muslim Syria,

reducing Crusader possessions to a strip of coastal lands and cities. He simultaneously broke the power of Mongol invaders from the East and ejected the Ismailis from their 'Assassin' fortresses in the north. One of his most impressive feats was the capture of the legendary Krak des Chevaliers from the Knights Hospitallers in 1271.

The Mamuluke forces had already taken Chastel Blanc at Safita from the Templars when they besieged this supreme achievement of medieval military architecture that even Saladin had failed to reduce. It took under a month for the severely undermanned castle to fall. The Hospitallers or al-osbitar as the Arabs called them, were driven into a tower in the inner ward, and when mangonel siege engines were introduced into the courtyard they capitulated.

By the time he was poisoned in 1277, Sultan Baibars had sealed the fate of the Frankish barons, their inevitable departure was now just a matter of time.

line continued until 1260, ruling from the twin capitals of Cairo and Damascus. It came to rely increasingly on Turkish slaves to man its armies and administer its empire. These slaves grew in power, giving rise to what became known as the Mameluke Dynasty (from *mamluk*, meaning 'owned').

The Mamelukes (1260-1516) The Ayyubid line in Damascus was brought to an abrupt end in 1260 by the invasion of the **Mongols**, who swept across Syria leaving a trail of destruction in their wake. Already in Cairo the **Mamelukes** had risen to power in a coup in 1250, and they were able to defeat decisively the Mongols at the Battle of Ain Jalud in Palestine. One of the Mameluke generals at this battle was a man named Baibars, who subsequently made himself sultan and took over from the vanquished Ayyubids. Baibars (1260-77) proved himself to be a formidable adversary, unleashing the full force of his military genius on the Crusaders. By the end of his rule he had driven them from Antioch, Krak des Chevaliers and Safita. The offensive was continued by Qalaun (1280-90) who dislodged the Crusaders from Qalat Marqab, Lattakia and Tripoli, and by his successor Khalil who took Acre and Tartus in 1291. The Crusaders continued to cling to a tiny foothold on the coast, occupying the island of Arwad until 1302, but already they had been reduced to little more than an anachronism.

The Mameluke genius was not purely military. During the 14th century they also presided over a remarkable programme of building works, the legacy of which is still very much in evidence in Damascus (their second capital after Cairo), Aleppo and Tripoli. However, towards the end of the 14th century they were riven by internal power struggles which left their empire in Syria increasingly vulnerable to renewed attacks by the Mongols. The most devastating of these, led by Tamerlane, came in 1400, bringing devastation to much of their empire. Under the sultan Qait

Bey (1468-95), the Mamelukes recovered somewhat, but they never achieved their former greatness, and in the first quarter of the 16th century they were overthrown by the Ottomans.

The Ottoman Turks, who had already established themselves in Asia Minor during the middle of the 15th century and made Constantinople their capital, met little resistance when they swept into Syria in 1516, led by the sultan Selim I (1512-20). Under his rule, the Ottomans extended their empire into Egypt, capturing the last Mameluke sultan, and even into Arabia, taking the Islamic holy cities of Mecca and Medina. His successor, Suleiman the Magnificent (1520-66), further extended the empire to include Serbia, Hungary, Mesopotamia and all of North Africa except Morocco. Thus present day Syria and Lebanon formed just a small part of a vast empire.

The Ottomans (1516-1918)

Nevertheless, the region benefited considerably from its incorporation into this new empire. An efficient administrative system was put in place, new trading links were established and ambitious building projects undertaken. It was during Suleiman's reign that the great Tekkiyeh as-Suleimaniyeh complex in Damascus was built. One of the first things Selim I had done on capturing Cairo was to proclaim himself caliph (since the final collapse of the Abbasid caliphate in 1258, the title had been held by a puppet of the Mamelukes). The Ottomans took great care also to ensure that the great pilgrimage route to Mecca, which they now controlled almost in its entirety, was managed properly. As a result, they soon succeeded in legitimizing their assumption of the caliphate and establishing themselves as Protectors of the Faith. Damascus flourished in its role as the last great staging post on the *hajj* to Mecca. Aleppo, meanwhile, was opened up to European traders by 'capitulation' treaties with the European powers and prospered even more vigorously, its souks and khans thronging with commercial activity.

Inevitably for such a vast empire, Ottoman rule was rarely directly applied, with *pashas* or local governors holding office in the major cities and exercising control over large administrative districts. As long as taxes were collected and paid on time, and peace maintained, the sultans in Constantinople were happy not to interfere. At times, the local governors, or even their subordinate tax collectors, were able to carve out what amounted in effect to more or less fully independent kingdoms for themselves. The first Pasha of Damascus, Al Ghazali, declared his independence, though he was quickly ousted. In the mountains of Lebanon, the **Emir Fakhr ud-Din II Maan** (see page 564) ruled over a largely independent principality from 1590 to 1635, and the **Emir Bashir Shihab II** (see page 567) achieved a similar state of affairs in Lebanon from 1788 to 1840. Both these periods are considered crucially important to the history of pre-independence Lebanon, representing the first examples of political autonomy for what was otherwise just a geographical entity.

The 18th century saw a period of stagnation in the Ottoman Empire, which was followed in the 19th century by a more serious revolt. The viceroy of Egypt, Mohammad Ali (1805-49) succeeded in establishing his own independent power base there, shaking off the authority of the Ottomans. His son, **Ibrahim Pasha**, carried the uprising into Syria and Lebanon in 1831, ousting the Ottoman forces from the region and carrying out wide ranging modernizing reforms. At one stage it seemed that the Ottoman Empire would collapse, but in 1840 the European powers chose to intervene on the side of the Ottomans, alarmed at this upset to the balance of power in the region and the threat that it posed to their interests. In Lebanon, where Emir Bashir Shihab II had collaborated with Ibrahim Pasha, direct Ottoman rule was imposed. Ottoman 'divide and rule' policy was at least in part responsible for the terrible massacres of Maronite Christians in the Lebanon mountains at the hands of the Druze in 1860. As a direct result of these massacres, the Ottomans were forced under pressure from the European powers to create the semi-autonomous *Mutasarrifa* (province) of Mount Lebanon (see page 486). This special new province

Background

was ruled by a non-Lebanese Ottoman Christian appointed by the Ottomans and approved by the European powers. This arrangement continued up until the First World War and the collapse of the Ottoman Empire, and formed the basis for the creation of French Mandate 'Grand Liban' from which the modern state of Lebanon emerged.

The immediate result of greater European involvement was to open Syria and Lebanon up to greater European influence. Protestant educational/missionary schools were established in Damascus and Beirut, and the latter began to flourish as the point of commercial and cultural contact with Europe. At the heart of Ottoman political power in Constantinople, meanwhile, the Ottoman sultan was deposed in 1909 by the revolutionary movement known as the 'Young Turks', who established the *Committee of Union and Progress (CUP)*. This brought with it an upsurge of Turkish nationalism which served to awaken amongst the Arab peoples a sense of their own Arab identity. Turkish nationalism was also behind the brutal genocide carried out against the Armenians during the First World War.

First World War & the Arab revolt

The modern political geography of the Middle East was largely shaped during the decade from 1914 to 1924. The onset of the First World War was of enormous significance to the region, which suddenly became a focus of international concern. The decision of the Ottoman Turks to ally themselves with the Central Powers (Germany and Austria-Hungary) placed them in direct opposition to the Allies. The harsh indifference of the Turks to local Arab peoples, along with a breakdown of civic administration as the Turks focused their attentions on the war, brought widespread famine and epidemics. Arab feelings against the Turks increased, culminating in the Arab Revolt, with the Sharif of Mecca, Hussein Ibn Ali, as the figurehead.

By the beginning of the 20th century, the emirate of Mecca (in the Hejaz peninsula of Arabia) was rather different to other political and administrative units found within the Ottoman Empire. As Salibi observes, "it was neither a principality nor a province, but merely an office to which members of a particular line of Hijazi sharifs were regularly appointed." More importantly, however, "it represented a Muslim office of considerable antiquity, based in Islam's most holy city, and commanding general deference." Crucially to the Arab world, "it was the only Muslim institution which continued to be the preserve of an Arab Dynasty long after political sovereignty in the world of Islam had passed into non-Arab hands." (Kamal Salibi, *The Modern History of Jordan*, 1993.) As the concept of Arab nationalism began to develop at the turn of the century, notably amongst the urban middle classes of Syria, it soon became clear that the only source of leadership to which they could turn was provided by the emirate of Mecca – an Arab Dynasty of great Islamic standing that was directly descended from the Prophet. Among those who had recognized this were the British, who in 1882 had established themselves across the Red Sea in Egypt. The contacts that the British had established early on with the various sharifian factions paid dividends when the Ottomans entered World War I on the side of the Central Powers.

When the CUP's puppet caliph Mohammad V declared the expected *jihad* against the Allies on behalf of the Islamic world, the impact on the Muslim populations in the Arab world and India was in fact negligible. The Ottoman-German advance into Aden did, however, mean that the Central Powers could threaten Allied shipping in the Red Sea and Suez Canal area (particularly now that the Germans had U-boats). Furthermore, their armies could be resupplied and reinforced by way of the Hejaz railway. Thus, for the Allies (and British in particular) a revolt in the Hejaz and Syria against the Ottomans would not only disrupt the Central Powers resupply lines to Aden, it might actually cut off the whole of the Ottoman-German forces in southern Arabia. Henceforth efforts were made by the British staff at the Arab Bureau in Cairo to increase contacts with Sharif Hussein and his sons.

The subsequent call to armed revolt against the Ottoman Empire that Sharif Hussein made in 1916 – the **Arab Revolt** – has been the subject of much reinterpretation over the years. How much the revolt was British inspired and how much it was the result of an indigenous bid for Arab independence is a moot point. The fact that many of the desert tribesmen appeared only to have joined for pay and the booty of conquest, and that many villages and towns remained at best neutral, at worst loyal to the Ottomans until their fate was decided, has left many questions surrounding the 'popular' nature of the revolt. Likewise, the revolt's actual military contribution to the war effort is often queried.

Much of the controversy over the interpretation of the Arab Revolt centres on the role of TE Lawrence and the degree to which his account of it, most famously told in his book, *Seven Pillars of Wisdom*, is accurate or realistic. Sceptics argue that Lawrence vastly over inflated and romanticized the significance of the revolt, and indeed his own role in it. Certainly, the Arab Revolt was of minor significance in the wider scheme of things. However, it was important in that by harassing vital Turkish lines of communications, most notably the Hejaz railway line which Lawrence and his band spent so much time blowing up, it forced the Turks to tie up large bodies of troops defending strategically unimportant corners of the Arabian peninsula (Medina included), allowing the British to consolidate their military position in Palestine, Egypt and the Red Sea. It should also be made clear what Lawrence does and doesn't say in *Seven Pillars of Wisdom*. Though there are instances in the book where Lawrence appears to lie about his exploits (the 49-hour march across Sinai from Aqaba to Suez being one), he himself plays down both his own role and that of the Arab Revolt in the First World War. Indeed, Lawrence describes the Arab Revolt as "a side show of a side show".

End of First World War & broken promises

The triumphant entry of the Allies and the Arab nationalist forces into Damascus on 1 October 1918 signalled the final collapse of the Ottoman Empire and defeat of the Central Powers. The end of the First World War saw Sharif Hussein's third son, **Feisal**, established in Damascus as the head of an Arab government that recognized the suzerainty of his father, the ruler of the Hejaz. Feisal, however, only controlled one of three Occupied Enemy Territory Administrations (this consisted of present day Jordan, Syria and the inland areas of Lebanon, while the British controlled Palestine and the French the coastal areas as far north as present day Turkey). Each of these OETAs was under the overall control of the British commander General Allenby who, while recognizing Feisal's government, described it as 'purely provisional'.

Feisal attended the Paris Peace Conference of 1919 and secured the promise of an International Commission of Inquiry to look into the question of Syrian unity. The **King-Crane Commission**, as it became known, recommended that, "the unity of Syria be preserved, in accordance with the earnest petition of the great majority of the Syrian people". However, in response to increasing French pressure, Britain agreed in September 1919 to withdraw its troops from Syria and Lebanon. In January 1920 Feisal managed to negotiate an agreement with the French Premier, Georges Clemenceau, which allowed a temporary French military presence along the coast in return for French acknowledgement of Syrian unity and Feisal's rule over the interior. The end of Clemenceau's term in office saw the agreement repudiated and in response the General Syrian Congress proclaimed Feisal king of all Syria. A month later, however, at the **San Remo Conference** in April 1920, Britain and France formally divided historic Syria between them, the French Mandate covering present day Syria and Lebanon, while the British Mandate covered Palestine, Transjordan and Iraq. On 24 July 1920 Feisal was forced out of Damascus by the French, and later installed instead as the king of Iraq by the British.

The San Remo Conference had put into effect the **Sykes-Picot Agreement** of 1916. Despite this secret wartime agreement to carve the region up between the

Background

British and French, the British had also entered into the so called '**Hussein-McMahon Correspondence**' that had appeared (albeit vaguely) to commit Britain to assist the Arabs in attaining independence. In addition, in 1917, in a letter addressed to Lord Rothschild (and subsequently known as the **Balfour Declaration**), the British government appeared to commit herself to the establishment of a 'nation home for the Jewish people in Palestine'. Thus the Arabs were denied their own government, the region was divided along artificial lines, and the seeds of the bitter dispute over 'Palestine', still so fundamental to Middle Eastern politics today, were sown. It is interesting to note now how Israeli sources refer to the moral obligation of the Balfour Declaration whilst dismissing the other agreements as wartime expediency. Most Arab sources, meanwhile, focus on the perceived treachery of the British.

Post-independence history of Syria

French Mandate & Independence (1920-46)

The French Mandate was for Syria a period of traumatic dismemberment. First the French carved out *Grand Liban* in August 1920, adding Tyre, Sidon, Beirut, Tripoli, the Akkar region, the Bekaa Valley and the south to the protected Maronite enclave of Mount Lebanon to create the basis for the modern state of Lebanon. Then parts of the old Ottoman province of Aleppo were given to Turkey. Internally, meanwhile, the French dissected the country, creating two mini-states centred on Aleppo and Damascus while establishing separate Alawi and Druze 'enclaves' (in the mountains around Lattakia and the Hauran region to the south of Damascus respectively) and maintaining direct French rule in the northeast. By the time of the French withdrawal in 1946, Syria comprised an area of a little over 185,000 sq km, compared with the former Ottoman province of Syria which ran to around 300,000 sq km.

Within Syria, the desire for an united 'Greater Syria' was matched by the strength of feeling against the French administration and their policy of 'divide and rule'. In 1925 a revolt broke out amongst the Druze of the Hauran region, initially over local disagreements with the French, though it soon spread to Damascus and other parts of the country. The French response, which included the bombing of Damascus, was uncompromising and by 1927 the revolt had been suppressed.

In an effort to appease opposition to their rule, they allowed elections to take place in 1928 to a Constituent Assembly which was charged with drafting a constitution. The draft constitution declared that, "the Syrian territories detached from the Ottoman Empire constitute an indivisible political unity. The divisions that have emerged between the end of the war and the present day do not diminish this unity." This was unacceptable to the French and, after attempts to negotiate a compromise failed, they dissolved the Assembly in 1930 and unilaterally issued a new constitution less hostile to their rule.

New elections were held in 1932 and negotiations started on a Franco-Syrian treaty, but these also broke down and the Assembly was again dissolved in 1934. By 1936 growing opposition and disturbances which threatened to escalate into a full scale revolt prompted the French to send a Syrian delegation to Paris to discuss their demands.

The new French Popular Front government was more sympathetic and in September 1936 a Franco-Syrian Treaty was signed recognizing the principal of Syrian independence after a three-year 'hand over' period. In 1938, however, with tensions growing in the wider region, the French announced that the treaty would not be ratified. The following year, in an effort to ensure Turkish neutrality in the Second World War, the enclaves of Antioch (Antakya) and Alexandretta (Iskanderun) were formally ceded to the Turkish (the source of a continuing territorial dispute between Syria and Turkey).

Background

After the surrender of France to Germany in 1940, Syria came under the control of the Vichy government. In 1941, against a background of rioting in Syria, Free French and British troops soon succeeded in overthrowing the Vichy government and in September 1941 Syrian independence was formally recognized, in theory at least. In practice, however, the French held on to power, refusing to restore constitutional rule while the war still raged. In 1943 elections were finally held and a nationalist government formed with Shukri al-Kuwatli becoming the President of the Syrian Republic in August of that year. The hand over of power was gradual and acrimonious. The Syrians refused to give in to French demands for a new Franco-Syrian Treaty as a condition for the final transfer of administrative and military services, leading to fresh disturbances in 1945 (and again the French bombing of Damascus). These were only quelled following British military intervention and the final departure of all French troops and administrative personnel. The departure of British troops in April 1946 at last heralded full independence for Syria.

The early years of the Syrian Republic were marked by chronic instability and bitter disappointment. Having already been in existence as a separate entity for a generation, the appeal of restoring 'Greater Syria' (expressed in various proposals of union with Iraq) was tempered by a new sense of Syrian nationalism and a fear of being absorbed within such a union. Indeed, the parallel ambitions of Jordan's King Abdullah to lead a united 'Greater Syria' were viewed with outright hostility and politically Syria was more closely aligned with Egypt and Saudi Arabia than with either Iraq or Jordan.

Early years of instability (1946-58)

The defeat of the Arab countries by the newly formed State of Israel in the **1947-49 war** shook Syrian confidence and created much resentment within the country. In 1949 there were no less than three military coups. In 1950 a new constitution was put in place and Hashim al-Atasi, a widely respected politician, installed as president. In 1951 there was another coup, engineered by Adib al-Shishakli (the leader of the final coup of 1949), who by 1953 had installed himself as president. The following year he in turn was ousted after popular demonstrations in Aleppo and Damascus. The 1950 constitution was restored, Atasi reinstated as president and new elections held.

On the international scene, Syria's position was full of paradox. The reappointment of Shukri al-Kuwatli as president in 1955 signalled increasingly close relations with Egypt. Syria was at the same time becoming much more anti-Western and pro-Soviet, protesting strongly against the formation of the Baghdad Pact (a defensive alliance aimed at curbing Soviet communist designs in the Middle East, which included Turkey, Iraq, Iran, Pakistan and Britain). The **Suez Crisis** and subsequent invasion of Sinai by Israel in 1956 with help from Britain and France only served to bolster anti-Western sentiments. Syria blew up the oil pipelines from Saudi Arabia and Iraq which passed through her territory en route to the Mediterranean and refused to repair them until Sinai was fully restored to Egypt. When America's **Eisenhower Doctrine** of 1957 was warmly received by King Hussein of Jordan and the Christian president of Lebanon Camille Chamoun, Syria found herself at loggerheads, politically at least, with every one of her immediate neighbours. Only Egypt appeared to share a similar outlook.

The pan-Arab nationalism being espoused by Gamal Abdul Nasser of Egypt had massive popular support throughout the region. Swept along in the tide of popular sentiment, in February 1958 Syria formally united with Egypt to form the United Arab Republic (UAR), with Nasser as its president. Though popular in the beginning, the relationship soon soured, with the inevitable Egyptian political domination of Syria, as well as the economic cost, causing resentment. Despite the formation of a

The UAR (1958-61)

single UAR cabinet in August 1961, by September a military coup had put an end to what most now regarded as Egyptian imperialism and Syria announced her withdrawal from the UAR, leaving it defunct.

The Ba'ath rise to power

The Ba'ath ('Renaissance') party was founded by a Christian Arab academic, Michel Aflaq in 1947. It espoused a combination of socialism, secularism and pan-Arabism and grew steadily in influence in Syria, spreading also to Lebanon, Jordan, Iraq and Egypt. It was the Ba'ath party which was one of the driving forces behind Syria's short lived union with Egypt, though within Ba'ath there were divisions between the pro-Egyptian, pro-Iraqi and nationalist camps. Following the collapse of the UAR, Syria experienced a couple more years of uncertain rule which saw the president ousted and then reinstated. In March 1963 a coup was staged by a Ba'athist military junta calling itself the National Council of the Revolutionary Command. The Ba'athist regime which followed purged the remaining pro-Nasserists from power, foiling a coup instigated by them, and set about implementing its socialist agenda, nationalizing banks, initiating land reform etc. This disaffected the influential land-owning and merchant sections of society. In addition, by relying heavily on the military, which was dominated by religious minority groups and in particular the Alawis, the Ba'ath failed to win the support of the Sunni Muslim *ulema*. Politically the country was becoming polarized between conservative/traditional elements and modernizing socialist elements. In April 1964 these tensions erupted into civil disturbances in Hama which were swiftly suppressed.

At the same time, there were growing tensions within the Ba'ath party itself, between the more moderate and long standing civilian politicians, and the more extreme left-wing elements (including many radical young officers from the military). These tensions finally came to a head in February 1966, with the radical elements seizing power. Many of the moderate Ba'ath politicians, including the founder of the Ba'ath Michel Aflaq and the head of state General Amin Hafiz, were placed under arrest.

It was against this background of radicalism that the build up to the **Six Day War** of 1967 with Israel took place. In November 1966 Syria entered into a defence pact with Egypt, soon to be followed by Jordan. Throughout 1966 and early 1967 Syria increasingly became the focus for cross border attacks on Israel, while Egypt's actions in Sinai and the Gulf of Aqaba finally resulted in the outbreak of war on 5 June 1967. The war proved to be a disaster for Syria, with Israeli troops gaining control over the strategically vital Golan Heights and pushing forwards as far as the town of Quneitra (just 67 km from Damascus) before a UN-brokered ceasefire was implemented on 10 June.

Assad assumes power

The Six Day War of 1967 was another bitter disappointment for Syria and once again a serious blow to her self-confidence. The credibility of the 'progressive' Ba'athist regime which had come to power in 1966 was seriously undermined. In particular it began to be criticized for its heavy reliance on the USSR, and for its overriding emphasis on the importance of developing a neo-Marxist economy. The level of Soviet involvement in Syria was seen by many as bordering on imperialism, while the debacle of the Six Day War was seen as evidence that the regime was more interested in neo-Marxist ideology than the struggle against Israel.

A 'nationalist' camp within Ba'ath began to gain ground, one which recognized the need for a pragmatic approach to the economy and emphasized the importance of developing stronger ties with Syria's Arab neighbours and overthrowing Israel. The 'nationalist' camp was led by Hafez al-Assad, who gained control of the all-important Ministry of Defence. Initially Assad was constrained by Soviet threats to withdraw all aid, which would have left Syria greatly weakened militarily and economically. However, improved relations with China strengthened his hand. The power struggle came to a head over the question of Syria's support for the Palestinian guerrilla groups in Jordan, whose might was being challenged by King Hussein in a showdown which became known as Black September. Assad disapproved of direct Syrian military intervention on the side of the Palestinians, fearing that it would damage pan-Arab unity, and that the Palestinian guerrilla groups were about to trigger another confrontation with Israel at a time when Syria's military forces were too weak to have any chance of success.

In November 1970 Hafez al-Assad seized power, assuming the position of prime minister. By March 1971 he had made himself president, with a referendum confirming his position for a seven-year term. A legislative body, the People's Assembly, was formed, with the Ba'ath party being guaranteed 87 of its 173 seats to give it an overall majority (the Assembly was later enlarged to 200 seats). In order to broaden his power base, Assad went on to form the National Progressive Front, a coalition of parties headed by the Ba'ath. In March 1973 a new constitution was put into effect.

On 6 October 1973 Syria and Egypt launched simultaneous attacks on Israel in an attempt to regain territory lost during the 1967 war. The attacks were timed to coincide with the Jewish Day of Atonement, Yom Kippur, the holiest day in the Jewish calendar, hence the popular name the **Yom Kippur War**, although in Syria the encounter is known officially as the **October War of Liberation**. Having taken Israeli forces by surprise, Syria and Egypt were able to make dramatic advances, Syria reclaiming a substantial portion of the Golan Heights. The subsequent Israeli counter-offensive saw both the Egyptians and the Syrians pushed back, in the case of the Syrians to within 32 km of Damascus. Egypt signed a disengagement agreement on 18 January 1974, but on the Golan fighting dragged on, with an agreement not being signed until 30 May of that year. The outcome of this conflict was at best inconclusive, but it did at least allow Syria to claim some degree of victory and went a long way to restoring Syrian self-confidence, as well as strengthening Assad's position.

Assad's close co-operation with Egypt during the October War reflected the improved relations he had effected in that direction. Ties with the Soviet Union were likewise restored, and Syria began to receive substantial amounts of military and economic aid once again. In June 1974 diplomatic relations with America were also restored. The **Rabat Conference** of October 1974 resulted in a declaration which recognized the PLO as the "sole legitimate representative of the Palestinian people". From Assad's point of view this was highly significant in that it meant that Jordan had implicitly relinquished its claim to the West Bank and signalled that the Arab world was at last united in its approach to the Palestinian question.

The new found stability of Assad's regime, along with its relatively enlightened approach to economic development brought with it a veritable flow of foreign aid into Syria from Arab oil producing countries, the UN, World Bank, Europe and even the US. Before the October War foreign aid had averaged just US$50 million annually; after 1974 it jumped to US$600 million. At the same time, the sharp rise in world oil prices saw Syria's oil exports rocket in value from US$70 million in 1973 to US$700 million in 1974. Remittances from Syrians working in the Arab oil producing countries likewise shot up. In short, after faltering along without any real direction from one unstable regime to another, Syria suddenly started to experience a sustained period of solid economic development which brought with it tangible benefits to ordinary people.

The Alawis in particular benefited from the economic boom, but also other minority groups and previously neglected sections of society. Perhaps inevitably, however, the socialism of the Ba'ath regime gradually started to give way to more selfish opportunism. By 1976 there were around 3,500 millionaires (in S£s), as compared with just 55 in 1963, the majority beneficiaries of the commissions,

Background

October War of Liberation (Yom Kippur War) 1973

Economic boom

kickbacks and outright corruption which accompanied the government's close involvement in economic affairs. Mohammad Haydar, the vice-premier of Economic Affairs, was notorious for the personal wealth he amassed and became known as "Mister Five Percent". Assad's youngest brother Rif'at, unassailable in his position as commander of the elite Defence Companies which acted as a kind of praetorian guard for Assad's regime, indulged himself in a luxurious international jet-set lifestyle and enjoyed access to unlimited government funds.

Such gross iniquities began to breed resentment towards the Alawis. At the same time, the *nouveau-riche* started to outstrip traditional merchants and landowners, whose political influence had already been weakened by the Ba'ath rise to power. Venerable religious families and the Sunni Muslim *ulema*, meanwhile, found themselves undermined by the rising tide of secularism. The seeds of a backlash against Assad, the Ba'ath and the ruling Alawi elite were being sown.

War in Lebanon When Lebanon erupted into civil war in April 1975, Syria, understandably enough, took a keen interest and followed events closely. A destabilized Lebanon might open the door to an Israeli occupation of all or part of the country (or at least result in the emergence of pro-Israeli government in Lebanon). It also threatened the stability of Syria itself. Direct Syrian military intervention was therefore perhaps inevitable, and indeed came the following year. By the end of May 1976 there were an estimated 40,000 Syrian-controlled troops in Lebanon, and the following month Syria launched a full scale invasion. Initially Syria's stated aim had been to protect the Palestinians, and subsequently to control their activities in Beirut. However, it soon became clear to Assad that his best hope lay in restoring stability to Lebanon by crushing the PLO and ensuring that a pro-Syrian government held power. Following the appeal of the Maronite president Suleiman Franjieh for help, Syria switched sides.

Thus Assad found himself attacking the PLO and their allies and defending the Maronite Christians, much to the dismay of the rest of the Arab world. (During the 15 years of civil war, Syria found itself aligned with practically every Lebanese faction at one time or another). By October the Arab League had 'regularized' the Syrian presence in Lebanon by giving authority to an Arab Deterrent Force (ADF) to maintain peace. The ADF was, however, dominated by Syrian troops and the Arab League in no position to dictate policy to Assad in what he regarded as his own backyard.

Syria's military involvement in Lebanon's civil war was a bitter, costly and long, drawn-out affair. On two occasions, following the 1978 and 1982 Israeli invasions of Lebanon, it very nearly resulted in another full scale war between Syria and Israel, and in the latter case did result in military humiliation for Syria. Ultimately, however, Syria has been able to maintain its military presence in Lebanon and continues to exercise a strong influence over most aspects of Lebanese politics.

Insurrection at home, disunity & war abroad Syria's intervention in Lebanon in 1976 coincided with an upsurge in discontent at home. The economic boom was running out of steam, with many Gulf states withdrawing their aid in protest at Assad's assault on the Palestinians in Beirut. Social inequality was growing, and opposition to the regime was finding a further focus in the form of extremist Sunni Muslim groups which resented minority Alawi rule and the Ba'ath promotion of secularism. The most prominent of these groups was the **Muslim Brotherhood**, which originated in Egypt during the 1920s. Its original aim had been to bring about an end to British rule in Egypt and to establish an Islamic state in its place. In the context of Ba'athist Syria, its Islamist ideology quickly became a banner behind which all the disaffected sections of Syrian society could unite. Acts of terrorism against prominent Alawi figures became ever more frequent, the most prominent being the massacre of at least 32 Alawi officer cadets at Aleppo Artillery School in June 1979. Almost exactly a year later, an assassination attempt was made on Assad himself.

Hafez al-Assad: the Lion of Syria

Hafez al-Assad was certainly one of the most enigmatic and controversial political figures in the Middle East. Born into a poor peasant family of the Alawi community, he changed his family name from Wahsh meaning 'wild beast' in Arabic, to Asad meaning 'lion' (Hafez al-Asad; 'lion's guard'), and went on to achieve the ultimate position of President of the Syrian Arab Republic in 1971, a position he held on to until his death nearly 30 years later in 2000. If his rise to power from an obscure background amongst a minority religious group was remarkable, the tenacity and skill with which he hung onto that power was all the more extraordinary.

As an Alawi (see 'Religion', below), Assad was a member of a small religious minority sect comprising just 12% of the total population and regarded at best as parochial, backward and misguided, and at worst as heretical, by mainstream Sunni Muslims who make up some 74% of the population. In the circumstances, the odds would seem to have been stacked heavily against him. Yet not only did Assad succeed personally in his quest for power, he also radically changed the composition of the political and military élite of the country, replacing the Sunni Muslim urban upper classes with lower class young people from the villages and small towns.

Whatever their personal opinions of him, most ordinary Syrians agree that Assad brought political stability and continuity to the country, and that as a direct result Syria was able to develop economically and achieve a level of regional influence which it never before possessed. That there was continuity under Assad is self evident (in stark contrast to the country's notoriously divided and vulnerable position during the first couple of decades following independence). That the economy benefited as a result, although a complex question, is essentially undeniable. That Syria managed to carve for itself a pivotal role in the wider region's affairs is likewise undeniable and perhaps best demonstrates the full scope of Assad's shrewdness and pragmatism. His banner was a simple one: Arab unity in the face of Zionism. Ultimately, however, he was unable to prevent the signing of bilateral agreements between Israel on the one hand, and Egypt, Jordan and the PLO on the other. In his final years he came close to securing the return of the Golan Heights, one of his most cherished goals (he had been defence minister during the 1967 war in which they were lost to Israel). On this count too, in the end he ultimately failed, having played a waiting game for too long.

To his supporters, he was an exceptionally gifted man who demonstrated great talent and selfless dedication in leading his country. In short, for many he was precisely the strong hero-figure and leader that the Arab world so desperately needed, a kind of modern day Saladin restoring pride and uniting the Arab world against a hostile and aggressive Jewish state. To others, however, he was a brutal and devious man who ruthlessly crushed all opposition in order to create a highly dictatorial regime, and whose only real aim was to perpetuate his own power.

This growing internal threat to the stability of the country was occurring in the context of serious setbacks for Assad abroad. The **Camp David** accords of 1978 led the following year to a full peace treaty between Egypt and Israel, seriously weakening the pan-Arab unity against Israel which Assad so cherished. On the Lebanese front, by 1981 the stand-off between Syria and Israel over the positioning of SAM missiles in the Bekaa Valley was threatening to escalate into a full scale confrontation, while at the same time Syrian troops found themselves fighting the Christian Phalangists they had previously been sent to protect. Israel, meanwhile, formally annexed the Golan Heights. To the east, the outbreak of the **Iran-Iraq War** in 1980 further added to the regional tension. Syria gave its support to Iran, reflecting the long standing hostility which existed between the Syrian and Iraqi branches of the Ba'ath party. With Jordan offering its support to Iraq, Syria and Jordan found themselves once again at loggerheads and tensions between the two countries nearly escalated into open hostilities on several occasions.

At home things finally came to a head in February 1982 with a full scale uprising against Assad's regime in the conservative town of Hama. It took three weeks before the uprising was finally quelled, and in the process much of Hama was devastated (see page 215). Though Assad survived this challenge to his authority, the Israeli invasion of Lebanon in June of that year presented him with an even more serious problem. Many of Syria's fighter aircraft in the Bekaa Valley were destroyed, along with most of its SAM missiles. The Syrian presence in Lebanon was rendered all but impotent in the face of the sheer might of the Israeli military. By 1983 Syrian forces in Lebanon were under attack not only from the Israelis but also from Sunni Muslims in Tripoli, Maronite Christians in the centre of the country, and guerrillas loyal to Yasir Arafat in the Bekaa Valley (Assad had backed extremist elements within the PLO which were attempting to overthrow Arafat).

In November 1983 Assad suffered what was widely believed to be a heart attack and for several weeks disappeared completely from the public eye while convalescing. A power struggle ensued, with Assad's younger brother Rifa'at spearheading the challenge to Assad's supremacy. By March 1984 a showdown seemed certain. Eventually, following a dramatic face to face meeting between the two brothers, Rifa'at lost his nerve and Assad was able to reassert his authority. That year Rifa'at went into effective exile, along with others who had played a part in the confrontation.

In 1985 Assad was elected to a third seven-year term as president and his position at home appeared once more secure. On the international scene, however, Assad was isolated from the rest of the Arab world, both due to his support for Iran in the Iran-Iraq war, and his attempts to oust Arafat from the PLO. Suspicion in the West that Syria was involved in international terrorist attacks led to the US and most members of the EU imposing sanctions in 1986. Britain broke off diplomatic relations entirely. The Soviet Union, Syria's chief sponsor since 1980, became Assad's only firm ally, with economic and military aid from this quarter growing massively throughout the 1980s.

Gulf War The Iraqi invasion of Kuwait in August 1990 gave Assad a chance to mend his bridges with the West. Having restored diplomatic relations with Egypt (severed since 1977 in protest at Sadat's peace overtures towards Israel), Syria agreed to send troops to Saudi Arabia as part of a pan-Arab deterrent force. Despite strong support for Saddam Hussein amongst Syria's Palestinians, Assad supported calls for an unconditional Iraqi withdrawal from Kuwait. By December it was estimated that Syria had more than 20,000 troops in Saudi Arabia. Officially, Assad maintained that they were only there to help defend Saudi Arabia from a possible Iraqi invasion, and they did not directly participate in the massive Desert Storm offensive against Iraq in early 1991. However, the very fact that Assad had aligned himself with the US-led anti-Iraq coalition represented a major turning point in Syria's international standing, both in the Arab world and in the West.

Assad's efforts to secure the release of Western hostages held in Lebanon helped to further improve relations with the US and Europe. Britain restored diplomatic relations and, at a time when the break up of the Soviet Union heralded the end of its economic and military support, Syria began to receive substantial amounts of aid from Europe, Japan and the Gulf states. In Lebanon, Syria gained almost complete freedom to pursue its own ends. In October 1990 Syria suppressed the revolt led by General Michel Aoun and set about implementing the 1989 Taif Accord (see below). By May 1991 Syria had signed a formal Treaty of Brotherhood, Cooperation and

Coordination with Lebanon, followed later that year by a Pact of Defence and Security. Although Syria was implicitly obliged as a result to recognize Lebanon as a sovereign state, it at the same time gave Syria complete control over Lebanon's economy and foreign policy.

Perhaps the most important consequence of Syria's stance in the Gulf War was that America began to acknowledge Syria's key role in any future Arab-Israeli peace deal. Following the end of the Gulf War, America intensified diplomatic efforts to initiate negotiations between Israel, the Arab states and Palestinian representatives. In July 1991 Assad agreed to participate in direct negotiations with Israel at a regional peace conference. Although the historic **Madrid conference** of October 1991 was largely symbolic, a series of bilateral negotiations between Syria and Israel followed. From the Syrian point of view, the primary aim of these talks was to secure an unconditional Israeli withdrawal from the Golan Heights (occupied since the 1967 Six Day War) in return for peace. At the same time, however, Assad made it clear that any agreement with Israel would have to form part of a comprehensive settlement in the Middle East. Assad was well aware that Israel hoped to reach separate agreements with each of its neighbours, as it had already done with Egypt, so weakening the collective bargaining power of the Arab world, something which he wished to avoid at all costs.

Assad's decision in 1992 to allow Syrian Jews to leave the country if they wished was seen as a conciliatory signal towards Israel. Though a breakthrough on the issue of the Golan Heights at times seemed imminent, the various rounds of bilateral talks dragged on without any real progress. The signing of the Declaration of Principals (DOP, better known as the **Oslo Accords**) between Israel and the PLO in September 1993 represented a serious setback to Assad's attempts to maintain an united Arab front. Nevertheless, after a meeting between President Clinton and Assad in Geneva on 20 January 1994, Syria indicated its willingness to establish, "normal, peaceful relations" with Israel. Progress continued until late 1994, when Assad suspended negotiations, ostensibly in protest at Israeli demands for a mutual reduction in the military presence around the Golan, but no doubt also in protest at the signing of a formal peace treaty between Israel and Jordan in October 1994.

Talks resumed in March 1995 and by May a "framework of understanding on security arrangements" was announced. Syria maintained that any agreement on the Golan Heights would have to be linked to an Israeli withdrawal from southern Lebanon. Eventually the US-brokered plan collapsed after Syria objected to Israeli demands for early warning stations on the Golan. The assassination of Yitzhak Rabin in November 1995 threw the Peace Process into renewed uncertainty. Negotiations resumed with the new Israeli prime minister Shimon Peres. Initially there were promising signs of progress, with Peres advancing a new 10-point plan. However, Hezbollah attacks on Israel from southern Lebanon continued, prompting Peres to retaliate with 'Operation Grapes of Wrath' in April 1996. Apart from the renewed carnage and bloodshed, this resulted in the negotiations stalling once again. In May 1996 the right-wing Likud leader Benjamin Netanyahu was elected prime minister. Netinyahu's uncompromising stance, refusing to cede an inch of the Golan to Syria (not to mention his policy of promoting Jewish settlements in the West Bank and East Jerusalem, and insisting on an extremely narrow interpretation of the Oslo II accords), effectively brought the Peace Process to a complete halt.

The May 1999, elections in Israel saw the virtual collapse of the Likud party (their share of parliamentary seats fell from 32 to just 19) and the subsequent resignation of Netanyahu as leader of the party. The Labour leader Ehud Barak secured a convincing majority and went on to form a coalition government which brought many disparate groups under the Labour wing. Many perceived the election result as a vote in favour of the Peace Process. However, early optimism that Barak would be able to reach a final agreement with the Palestinians, and even Syria, was soon replaced by a more realistic outlook. Initially, negotiations between Israel and Syria looked promising, but by January 2000 they had been broken off. Syria adamantly refused to drop its demands for a complete Israeli withdrawal from the Golan Heights to the pre-1967 lines, while Israel insisted on retaining a narrow strip of land around the Sea of Galilee in order to protect its access to this vital water source. In March 2000, the US President Bill Clinton and President Assad of Syria met in Geneva in an attempt to restart the talks, but without success.

Under intense pressure at home, Barak continued to press ahead regardless with his plans for a unilateral withdrawal from southern Lebanon. Though he had originally pledged that the withdrawal would be completed by July, events for once moved faster than predicted, and by the end of May 2000 the Israeli army had completely withdrawn from their infamous 'security' zone in southern Lebanon, ending 18 years of occupation.

The death of Hafez al-Assad Less than three weeks later, on 10 June 2000, the death of President Hafez al-Assad of Syria was announced. The news reverberated around the world, with words such as 'crisis', 'turmoil', 'power struggle' and 'power vacuum' dominating the headlines. For years observers had speculated on the question of what would happen after Assad's death. Many argued that after so many years of dictatorial rule, Syria had none of the political structures neccessary to cope with a smooth transition of power. A commonly painted scenario predicted an attempt by Sunni Muslim groups, perhaps headed by the Muslim Brotherhood, to put an end to the Alawi dominance of the political hierarchy, with a violent backlash in revenge for the excesses of Assad's long rule. In the event, however, the transition of power has so far proved, on the surface at least, to be almost completely without problems. Nearly 30 years of relative stability and economic growth have created an increasingly affluent society with a sizeable middle class. The vast majority of Syrians, whether they privately detested Assad's regime or not, evidently had no wish to see the country plunged into the chaos and uncertainty which marked its early years of independence. Nor were they keen to see an Islamic revolution along the lines of Iran.

Bashar al-Assad Until his death in a car crash in January 1994, the charismatic Basil al-Assad, Hafez al-Assad's eldest son, had clearly been the *heir apparent*, his poster appearing widely alongside that of his father. Instead, his quieter and more retiring younger brother, Bashar al-Assad was recalled from his studies in London, where he was training to be an eye specialist, and sent to a military acadamy, quickly rising to the position of colonel. He was given responsibility for certain foreign policy issues, including one of the most important: Lebanon. In the months before his father's death, he had been involved in an anti-corruption drive which targetted high-ranking officials in what was seen by many as an attempt to sweep away some of the old guard and establish his own power base in the regime. The military training, foreign policy responsibilities and anti-corruption drive were all clearly part of the grooming process, but when his father died, Bashar was just 34 years old and had held no official position in the state or party heirarchy other than president of the country's computer society. The first thing the Syrian parliament did in the hours following the death of Hafez al-Assad was hurriedly to amend the constitutions, lowering the minimum age of the president from 40 to 34, before nominating Bashar for the post. Equally urgently, it promoted him to the position of Commander in Chief of the armed forces, thereby giving him absolute power over the military. A week later he was elected general secretary of the Ba'ath party. By July 2000 he had been sworn in as president following a referendum in which 97% of voters, predictably enough, had endorsed his candidacy. On New Year's Day 2001, Bashar married the 25 year old Asma Akhras, a British born computer science graduate from a prominent

All change...

Bashar al-Assad's assumption of the presidency in Syria came hot on the heels of the enthronement of King Abdullah II of Jordan in 1999, which in turn came less than a year after young Mohammad VI of Morocco, succeeded his father. They are changes that represent a sweeping away of the 'old order' of Middle Eastern leaders.

There are several still remaining, but it cannot be long before they too give way to a new generation. The 69-year old Yasir Arafat is looking increasingly frail, a trembling lower lip and hands fuelling rumours of Parkinson's disease. In Egypt, President Hosni Mubarak is now 72. In Saudi Arabia, the 77-year old King Fahd is

already seriously ill and barely able to walk since a stroke in 1995. Day to day affairs of state are handled by his heir apparent, Crown Prince Abdullah.

Exactly what the 'new order' of Middle Eastern leaders will bring to the region is impossible to predict, but most observers agree that it is likely to herald a more pragmatic approach to the Arab-Israeli problem, and a concerted drive towards modernization and economic reform. Bashar al-Assad and King Abdullah II of Jordan are both young, western-educated leaders, and are said to have developed an excellent rapport, sharing a keen interest in science and technology.

London based Syrian family. Significantly, Akhras is a Sunni Muslim, thus providing something of a bridge between the minority Alawi background of the Assad family and Syria's predominantly Sunni population.

Bashar's first months in office have thrown up few surprises. Though he is said to be keen to initiate a programme of reforms and modernization similar to that undertaken by King Abdullah II in Jordan, in practice he has moved very slowly and cautiously. His primary objective appears to have been to consolidate his power before doing anything which might antagonize the more conservative elements of the formidable military and secret police, as well as the Ba'ath party. In his inaugural address as president he reaffirmed his father's stance on the Peace Process, insisting that Israel make a full withdrawal from the Golan Heights to the pre-1967 lines. Many observers agree that Hafez al-Assad's death was a major setback for the peace processs. According to this view, only he had the necessary stature and authority to broker a peace deal with Israel which would effectively represent a U-turn on more than half a century of uncompromising opposition to the very existence of the Jewish state.

Recent developments

In any case, events within Israel and the Palestinian territories over the last few months have largely killed off any hope of progress on a peace deal between Syria and Israel for the time being. In May 2000, on the anniversary of what is for Palestinians the *nakba* (literally the 'catastrophe') marking the creation of Israel in 1948, violence exploded across the West Bank. By July, the talks between Ehud Barak and Yasir Arafat, brokered by Bill Clinton at Camp David in a desparate attempt to salvage the Peace Process, finally broke up without an agreement. Evidently, thorny 'final status' issues such as the fate of Jerusalem and the return of Palestinian refugees had proved too great an obstacle.

The visit in September 2000 of the hardline Israeli opposition leader, Ariel Sharon, together with hundreds of armed riot police, to the Haram al-Sharif/Temple Mount was the trigger for a far more dramatic upsurge in violence, dubbed the second *intifada*. Four days of clashes left 27 dead and around 700 wounded. Television images of a 12-year old Palestinian boy cowering next to his father in Gaza before being shot dead by Israeli troops provoked outrage throughout the Arab and Muslim world. Less than two weeks later, two Israeli army reservists were lynched by an angry mob of Palestinians at a police station in Ramallah, in a scene which was likewise captured on film. With the spiral of violence rapidly gathering momentum, an emergency summit in Sharm el-Sheikh (in Egypt's Sinai region) organized by Bill Clinton between Arafat and Barak proved largely ineffectual. By 23 October, Barak formally announced the suspension of the Peace Process.

The resounding victory of Ariel Sharon in the Israeli elections of February 2001, defeating Barak by 62% to 38%, was widely seen as a further blow to any chances of restarting the Peace Process. With suicide bombings, political assassinations, mortar attacks, and airstrikes by helicopter gunships and F-16 fighter jets the order of the day, the prospects for peace were at the time of writing looking increasingly bleak. Some commentators were already referring bluntly to 'civil war'.

Post-independence history of Lebanon

French Mandate & independence (1920-46)

France had played a leading role in forcing the Ottomans to create the province of Mount Lebanon, having long considered itself to be the guardian of the Maronites. In August 1920, under pressure from the Maronite community, the French agreed to enlarge Mount Lebanon by adding Tyre, Sidon, Beirut, Tripoli, the Akkar region, the Bekaa Valley and substantial areas in the south to create what was referred to as **'Grand Liban'** (Greater Lebanon). The Maronites were anxious to carve out for themselves a sufficiently large territory to be able to survive as an independent state, separate from Syria which was predominantly Sunni Muslim. But while the creation of 'Grand Liban' granted them a viable state, it also brought with it a new problem in that the territories which were added were predominantly Muslim (made up of Sunni and Shi'ite Muslims and Druze). Whereas Mount Lebanon had been overwhelmingly Christian (and within this predominantly Maronite), in the new 'Grand Liban' Christians and Muslims were almost equally represented, with Christians being only marginally more numerous, and Maronites a minority of the overall population. Mount Lebanon did at least have a historical basis, giving its claim to autonomy some legitimacy even in pan-Arab eyes (though the Druze of Mount Lebanon might not share the Maronite vision of it as 'unalterably Christian and indivisibly attached to the West'). The new 'Grand Liban' had no such claim to legitimacy, representing a creation of the Maronites and French, in which the newly incorporated Sunni and Shi'ite Muslims and Druze had had no say whatsoever, and which had appropriated some of the best lands of the already truncated 'Greater Syria'. Indeed, it could be argued that the transformation of Mount Lebanon into 'Grand Liban' was the single most significant event in the history of the country and at the root of the terrible troubles which were to follow.

During the Druze revolt of 1925-7 in Syria, Lebanon's Sunni Muslim population petitioned and agitated vigorously for Lebanon, or at least the newly appropriated territories of 'Grand Liban', to be reunited with Syria, but to little effect. In the meantime, the Maronite leader Michel Chiha worked closely with the French to write a constitution. In May 1926, Lebanon was declared a republic, though still under French mandate, and the new constitution put into effect. As a largely symbolic gesture towards the concept of power sharing in the new republic, the French ensured that a Greek Orthodox president was installed, along with a Sunni Muslim prime minister, but in practical terms the Maronites maintained their monopoly over power. Eventually Muslim opposition to this arrangement made it unworkable and the constitution was suspended in 1932. That same year saw the last official census to be carried out in Lebanon in which the Christians were confirmed to be in the majority (although not before various expatriate Christians had been naturalized). In 1936, shortly after a similar treaty had been signed with Syria, a Franco-Lebanese Treaty was signed, committing the French to an eventual complete handover of power. The following year a new constitution was promulgated, though with war in the wider region looming the French refused to ratify it.

During the Second World War Lebanon, like Syria, came under the control of the Vichy government following the surrender of France to Germany in 1940. By November 1941, however, Free French and British troops had landed in Lebanon, the Vichy government had been overthrown and Lebanon formally declared a "sovereign independent state". However, large numbers of French troops and administrators remained in the country and in practice the French still maintained their control. In 1943, with nationalist sentiment gathering momentum, the various Lebanese political-religious factions agreed to the **Lebanese National Covenant** (or National Pact). This unwritten agreement divided power along sectarian lines, ensuring a Maronite president, a Sunni Muslim prime minister and a Shi'ite speaker of the house. Using the 1932 census as a basis, parliamentary seats were divided between Christians and Muslims in a ratio of 6 to 5. In addition, the Maronites were given control over the army. In return for their overall position of power, it was agreed that they should renounce their special relationship with the West and acknowledge Lebanon as an Arab country. In November 1943 the government passed legislation to remove from the constitution all provisions relating to French influence considered to be inconsistent with Lebanese independence. For the French authorities this was a step too far, and they promptly responded by arresting the president, prime minister and most of the cabinet. A widespread outcry within the country along with condemnation internationally forced the French to capitulate, and on 22 November 1943 the president and prime minister formally declared Lebanon an independent state. All the same, the French were more than a little reluctant to transfer complete power to the Lebanese government, in particular control of the Troupes Speciales. Eventually this was achieved in 1945 and in December 1946 the final departure of the last French troops heralded Lebanon's full independence.

Lebanon's early years (1946-58)

In its early years of independence Lebanon struggled hard to make the National Covenant work and forge itself into a truly united nation. However, it faced major economic and political difficulties. In January 1948 France devalued the French franc, to which the Lebanese currency was tied, hitting the economy hard. The Arab-Israeli war of 1948-9, as well as being a heavy economic burden, was a serious blow to pan-Arab aspirations amongst Lebanon's Muslims, triggering disillusionment and resentment towards the Maronite dominated establishment. Finally, the severance of economic ties with Syria in 1950 (partly as a result of conflicting responses to the devaluation of the franc and partly due to disputes over free trade versus protectionism) further damaged the economy.

In 1951 the Sunni prime minister Riad al-Solh was assassinated by Syrian nationalists. By 1952 growing unrest prompted the downfall of the government and resignation of the president, Beshara al-Khoury. While Khoury and Solh were both competent politicians dedicated to the vision of an united independent Lebanon, they had failed to institutionalize the oral understandings of the National Covenant. They had also concentrated on bettering the lot of their own constituencies, the Maronites of Mount Lebanon and the Sunni Muslim business élite of Beirut. Leaders of other constituencies, the Shi'ites of the south, the Druze of the Chouf mountains and the Sunnis of Tripoli and the north also struggled to reap some of the benefits of power, but with less success. To quote SK Aburish, "Greater Lebanon became two countries soon after it gained independence; one led by the Maronites and a collection of Muslim collaborators, leaders who were enamoured with ceremonial positions, and another made up of simple Muslims and Druze, who were relegated to second class citizenship" (Saïd K Aburish, *A Brutal Friendship*).

Background

Civil war of 1958

When Camille Chamoun was installed as the new president in 1952, his first years in office coincided with an Egyptian army coup, the proclamation of Egypt as a republic and the rise to power of Gamal Abdul Nasser in 1954. Chamoun soon proved himself even less sensitive to the needs of Lebanon's non-Maronite population, and more importantly he demonstrated an ardently pro-Western and anti-Arab outlook, effectively betraying the understanding of the National Covenant in this respect. When Nasser nationalized the Suez Canal in 1956, Chamoun declared his support for Israel, France and Britain in the ensuing **Suez Crisis**. At the same time he began to recognize that the US rather than France might be a better ally in protecting Maronite interests against Nasser's pan-Arab nationalism which was then sweeping through the Middle East.

When America began espousing the **Eisenhower Doctrine** in 1957, Chamoun was an eager customer. In July 1957 it was announced that Lebanon would receive around US$15 million in economic and military aid from America. Amongst Lebanon's Muslims, Nasser's pan-Arab nationalist vision was as enormously popular as their president's courting of the US was unpopular. Riots, bombings and assassinations became ever more frequent, while Chamoun became ever more fearful of the prospect of Lebanon being absorbed into some pan-Arab merger. In March 1958 it was officially announced that Lebanon would not join with the United Arab Republic (UAR; Egypt and Syria) or the Arab Federation (Jordan and Iraq), both of which had recently been formed. By May what amounted to civil war between pro-Arab Muslims and the pro-Western Christians had broken out in Tripoli, soon spreading to Beirut, Sidon, Tyre and southern Lebanon. In July Chamoun formally requested the help of the US in quelling the insurrection in Lebanon and preserving its independence. Though initially reluctant to become directly involved, the pro-Nasserist coup in Iraq the same month soon prompted the US to respond.

As Robert Fisk comments, "The 1958 war is remembered not so much for the vicious sectarian battles that occurred in Beirut but for the arrival of the US Marines, who stormed ashore only to find the beaches occupied not by militiamen but by bikini-clad ladies and street urchins who were merely waiting to sell Coca Cola to the country's latest rescuers. The story is true but it has also become part of the myth. For the reality behind the 1958 conflict was the reawakening of the old dispute between pro-Arab nationalism and pro-Western Maronitisme, the same antagonism which had emerged in 1920 when the French created Lebanon." (R Fisk, *Pity the Nation*.)

Peaceful interlude

During the course of the US presence in Lebanon, Chamoun was forced to stand down (he had been attempting to amend the constitution to allow himself to serve a second term). The army Chief of Staff Fouad Chehab, a man seen as acceptable to both sides, was elected as the new president. He invited Rashid Karami, the Sunni Muslim leader of the insurrection in Tripoli, to become prime minister and an agreement was reached whereby the US forces would leave Lebanon by October. Chehab proved to be more sensitive to the urgent need for more even handed rule in Lebanon. He attempted to bring economic development to the country as a whole and redress the enormous social imbalances which were emerging between the Maronites and Sunni élite on one hand and the rest of the country on the other. During his six years in office he achieved some success and his integrity of purpose earned him a great deal of popularity. Despite appeals from the government that he should amend the constitution and stand for a second term, he refused. His successor Charles Helou was less successful. On the surface Lebanon was a thriving country, Beirut already legendary all over the world as the 'playground' or the 'Paris' of the Middle East. To quote Aburish, "Oil money was flowing into the city's 70-odd international banks, and hundreds of thousands of oil-rich Arabs summered there, gambling and chasing blondes. There was a bar for every 140 people and the Casino du Liban claimed it had the biggest and best nightclub show in the world. Glamorous Beirut was Casablanca, Hong Kong and old Havana rolled into one." (ibid.) However, beneath the surface the country was once again becoming polarized, with the Maronites and Sunni élite prospering, while the rest of the country slipped back into economic deprivation and neglect.

Although Lebanon did not participate in the Six Day War of 1967 against Israel, it was to have dramatic repercussions for the country. Soon after the end of the war, southern Lebanon became a base for Palestinian guerrilla attacks on Israel, bringing increasingly frequent Israeli reprisals. Most dramatic perhaps was an Israeli commando attack on Beirut airport in December 1968 which destroyed 13 Lebanese passenger airliners, in retaliation for a Palestinian attack on an El Al airliner at Athens airport. In 1969, following violent clashes between the Lebanese army and Palestinian guerrilla groups, the Cairo Agreement was signed, giving the PLO permission to set up camps in southern Lebanon, provided they situated them away from civilian centres, refrained from using them for military training and only carried out attacks after crossing into Israeli territory. The events of Black September the following year in Jordan resulted in thousands more Palestinians arriving in Lebanon, and finally in the PLO shifting its headquarters to Beirut. By this time there were an estimated 400,000 Palestinians in Lebanon, alongside a Lebanese population of just 3 million. The PLO agenda was clear: to overthrow Israel and reclaim Palestine for the Palestinians, and amongst many of Lebanon's Muslims they found ready support. Lebanon's Christians, however, adopted a far more moderate stance, even starting to view Israel as a potential ally rather than an enemy.

Prelude to war

The demographic balance upon which the National Covenant was based was already being tipped in favour of the Muslims, due to their higher rate of population growth coupled with the higher rate of emigration amongst the Christians, though in the absence of a census since 1932 the Christians continued to dispute this. The arrival of the Palestinians completely upset this balance, as well as exacerbating the pro-Western versus pro-Arab tensions between the Christians and Muslims. With heavily armed Palestinian guerrilla groups operating with almost complete autonomy and scant regard for their Lebanese hosts, what amounted to a Palestinian 'state within a state' was fast emerging. The repeated cycle of Palestinian attacks and Israeli reprisals in the south, meanwhile, was forcing thousands of Shi'ites to flee their homes, the majority winding up in makeshift refugee camps in Beirut's southern suburbs. At the same time, Lebanese society was becoming increasingly factionalized, with various militia groups representing the rival religious/political groups (and within these the rival clans and tribal leaders) being formed.

Suleiman Franjieh, elected to the presidency in 1970, was fiercely militant in his championing of Maronite supremacy, and equally fiercely tribal. To quote Aburish, "His only previous claim to fame had been his involvement in the machine-gunning inside of a church of 22 members of a competing [Christian] Lebanese clan." (ibid.) Around him, the militias flourished. On the Christian side the most important was the **Phalange** (known also as the Lebanese Forces or *Kataeb*), first founded in the 1930s by Pierre Gemayel and now headed by his son Bashir Gemayel. The Phalange developed close ties with the Israelis and received arms and equipment from them to help with the overthrow of the Palestinians. There was also the **Marada**, headed by Suleiman Franjieh's son Tony, the **Tigers**, headed by Camille Chamoun's son Dany, the **Order of Monks**, founded by the Father Cherbel Kasiss, and a host of other smaller ones. On the Muslim side, the Shi'ite leader Mousa al Sadr founded **Amal** (literally 'hope'). The Druze leader Kamal Jumblatt, though initially reluctant, likewise founded his own militia. The Sunni Muslims of Beirut, meanwhile, founded the **Mourabitoun**, and again a host of others thrived.

On both sides there were political as well as military wings, with those on the Muslim side becoming loosely grouped together in what became known as the

National Movement, led by Kamal Jumblatt and closely aligned with the Palestinians, while those on the Christian side at times worked together against the National Movement and the Palestinians and at other times engaged in vicious infighting amongst themselves. All, however, relied increasingly on their militias, with Lebanon as an unified state becoming little more than a pretence. The cycle of violent confrontation continued to escalate, the Lebanese army and Phalange militias clashing with those of the Palestinians and the Muslim National Movement. In May 1973 the Lebanese army even resorted to ground and air strikes against the refugee camps where the Palestinian guerrilla groups were based. Though Lebanon again avoided direct involvement in the Yom Kippur War of 1973, Israeli reprisals against continued Palestinian attacks intensified, as did the clashes between the Palestinians and Phalangists.

The Lebanese Civil War

The spark which ignited full scale civil war in Lebanon came on 13 April 1975. In response to the killing of some Phalange personnel, 27 Palestinians were massacred on a bus travelling through the Beirut suburb of Ain al-Rummaneh. The various militia groups of the National Movement were rapidly drawn into all out war with the Phalangists. In December 1975, after four Christians were found shot dead in a car, the Phalange responded by stopping cars on the ring road around Beirut, checking identity cards and cutting the throats of any Muslims they found. The Muslim militias promptly followed suit and by the end of the day more than 300 people had been massacred by each side in an event which became known as **Black Saturday**. In January 1976 the Phalange and other militias laid siege to the Palestinian refugee camps of Karantina and Tal al-Zatar. The Palestinians, now firmly drawn into the fighting, responded by taking part in an attack on the town of Damour (just to the south of Beirut) and the massacre of the majority of its Christian inhabitants. Beirut meanwhile was plunged into anarchy, the warring factions confronting each other across the infamous 'Green Line' which divided Muslim West Beirut from Christian East Beirut.

Syrian intervention In 1976 Syria's President Assad decided on military intervention to try to end the fighting and by May 1976 there were an estimated 40,000 Syrian troops in Lebanon. Initially, their stated aim was to protect the Palestinians and to curb the activities of their various guerrilla groups. However, after an appeal for help from the Maronite president Suleiman Franjieh, Syria switched sides and instead concentrated its efforts on crushing the PLO. In the course of the civil war Syria was to switch its allegiances many more times. For the moment, however, from Assad's point of view a stabilized Lebanon under a pro-Syrian government would ensure Syria continued influence in the country and counter the rising Israeli influence. In June 1976 Syria launched a full scale invasion and Syria's alignment with the Maronites against the PLO was condemned by the rest of the Arab world. In October a ceasefire was agreed under the auspices of the Arab League and an Arab Deterrent Force (ADF) established to enforce it. Though supposedly a multinational force, this was dominated by Syrian troops. In March 1977 the Druze leader Kamal Jumblatt was assassinated, triggering a wave of revenge killings, but otherwise an uneasy peace was maintained.

1978 Israeli invasion In March 1978 renewed PLO attacks on Israel prompted the Israelis to launch **Operation Litani**, in which they invaded the country as far as the Litani River in southern Lebanon. Following calls by the UN Security Council for a full Israeli withdrawal, the United Nations Interim Force in Lebanon (UNIFIL) was established to 'confirm the withdrawal of Israeli forces and restore international peace'. The Israeli troops did indeed withdraw in June 1978. However, instead of handing over control of the territory they had invaded to UNIFIL, they installed Major Saad Haddad, the leader of an Israeli backed Christian militia, helping him establish the South Lebanese Army (SLA) as a proxy Israeli force in what was later proclaimed 'Free Lebanon'. In July 1978 and again in April 1981 fighting flared up in Beirut between the Syrian troops of the ADF and various right-wing Christian militias. In April 1981 the Syrians, now aligned again with the Palestinians, also besieged the Christian town of Zahle, which had come under the control of the Phalangists. In view of their close links with the Israelis, the arrival of Phalangists in Zahle was seen as a threat to Syria's military presence in the Bekaa Valley. The Israelis, meanwhile, continued to launch frequent raids and air strikes against the Palestinians and in the course of one air strike succeeded in shooting down two Syrian helicopters. The Syrians responded by positioning surface-to-air missiles (SAM) in the Bekaa Valley. For a while the stand off threatened to escalate into full scale war between Syria and Israel. In the event the siege of Zahle was lifted, the Phalangists withdrew from the town and a US brokered ceasefire was agreed.

1982 Israeli invasion

The ceasefire, however, did not last long. Repeated rocket attacks on Israel from PLO camps in southern Lebanon convinced the Israelis that they had to drive the Palestinians from Lebanon once and for all. Following the attempted assassination of the Israeli ambassador in London on 3 June 1982, the Israelis carried out a devastating bombing campaign which largely obliterated parts of Tyre, Sidon, Damour and Nabatiye. On 6 June they launched what was referred to as **Operation Peace for Galilee**, a full scale invasion of Lebanon. By 11 June a ceasefire had been arranged between the Israelis and Syrians (Ariel Sharon, the Israeli Minister of Defence had taken the opportunity to attack the Syrians in the Bekaa Valley, destroying 80 of their fighter aircraft and damaging many of their SAM missiles). By this time, Israeli troops had reached the outskirts of Beirut. Two days later the siege of Beirut began, the Israelis cutting off the water and electricity supply and mounting a relentless bombardment of the city which lasted two months and resulted in an estimated 18,000 dead and 30,000 wounded, the vast majority civilians. Eventually, in August an agreement was reached whereby the PLO would evacuate Lebanon under the supervision of a multinational force. The evacuation of the PLO began on 21 August 1982. Two days later the leader of the Phalange militia Bashir Gemayel was elected president. The multinational force, having overseen the departure of the last Palestinian troops, promptly withdrew. To the Maronites it seemed as though they could finally claim victory.

Sabra & Chatila massacres

Bashir's presidency, however, was brought to an abrupt end three weeks later on 14 September 1982 (before he had even officially assumed office) when he was killed, along with as many as 60 of his supporters, in a bomb attack on the Phalange headquarters. The following day, Israeli troops moved into West Beirut, in direct violation of the terms of the agreement which had led to the PLO withdrawal. The Phalange, meanwhile, eager to avenge the death of their leader, entered the Palestinian refugee camps of **Sabra** and **Chatila** in Beirut's southern suburbs on 18 September and carried out a massacre of their inhabitants. During an extended frenzy of carnage between 1,000 and 2,000 people were brutally murdered. Many were women and children and the vast majority (if not all) were innocent civilians whose only crime was to be Palestinian. The Israelis claimed that they had no part in the massacre, and no knowledge of its occurrence. However, there was strong evidence to suggest that they were fully aware of the massacres and had watched from the sidelines without taking action while it went on. Indeed, it seemed that the Israelis had given the Phalangists permission to enter the camps, and even assisted them, the air force dropping flares to light up the camps during the attack. The

Sabra and Chatila massacres drew international condemnation and prompted massive demonstrations of between 200-400,000 people under the banner of the 'Peace Now' movement within Israel.

On 21 September 1982 Amin Gemayel took over the presidency from his murdered brother. Israel, having withdrawn its troops from Beirut, consolidated its control over southern Lebanon, while Syrian troops remained entrenched in the Bekaa Valley. The government, meanwhile, exerted only nominal control over a small central section of the country. In the Chouf mountains there were frequent clashes between Druze and Christian militias, while in Tripoli fighting raged between pro and anti-Syrian forces.

Multinational force in Lebanon By April 1983 a multi-national peacekeeping force comprised of US, French, British and Italian troops had returned to Lebanon, and on 17 May an agreement was brokered by America whereby the Israelis would withdraw from Lebanon, leaving only a small number of troops to patrol the border alongside the Lebanese army, providing that the Syrians also withdrew from the Bekaa Valley. Syria's refusal to countenance any withdrawal of its troops led to an impasse, but by July popular opinion within Israel forced the Israelis to redeploy their troops to a line south of the Awali River (just north of Sidon).

Their withdrawal from the Chouf mountains resulted in full scale war erupting between the Druze and Christian militias. In southern Lebanon, the Israelis began gradually to reduce their military presence and hand over control to Major Saad Haddad's SLA. At the same time they started arming local militias, irrespective of their religion, in the hope that they would more effectively police their own areas and bring about a reduction in the continuing guerrilla attacks on Israeli personnel.

By September 1983 Yasir Arafat had returned to Lebanon and entrenched himself in Tripoli. The PLO, however, had by this time been split by an internal revolt and Arafat soon found himself and a core of PLO fighters still loyal to him under siege from rival Palestinian factions, supported by Syrian troops and Lebanese Ba'athists. The bombardment of Tripoli continued until December, when a truce was signed and Arafat and his troops evacuated once again from Lebanon under UN protection.

In the meantime, the multinational peacekeeping force in Beirut, whose neutrality had been seriously undermined by the US navy's bombardment of Druze positions in support of Amin Gemayel's Phalange dominated government, was coming under increasing attack. Already, shortly after their arrival in April 1983, the American embassy in Beirut had been blown up, leaving 43 people dead. On 23 October 1983 a far more devastating attack took place, with two suicide bombers driving trucks packed with explosives simultaneously blowing up the US and French military headquarters in Beirut. A total of 265 marines and 56 French soldiers were killed in the attacks. A previously unheard of group calling itself **Islamic Jihad** claimed responsibility.

It later emerged that Islamic Jihad were an armed combat wing of **Hezbollah** (the 'Party of God'), a radical Shi'ite group backed and funded by Iran which rose to prominence following the 1982 Israeli invasion. Historically the most downtrodden of Lebanon's religious/ethnic communities, the Shi'ites suffered heavily from brutal Israeli suppression in the south of the country. In the early 1980s Iranian Revolutionary Guards (the henchmen of Ayatollah Khomeini's revolutionary Iran) stationed themselves in Baalbek in the Bekaa Valley with Syrian compliance. The messages they began to preach calling for the overthrow of 'Western Imperialism' found a particularly receptive audience amongst the Shi'ites and Hezbollah soon began to overtake Amal in importance as the radical champion of the Shi'ite cause. Later, Hezbollah and its various military wings were responsible for the kidnapping and holding of Western hostages in Lebanon in its drive to overthrow 'Western Imperialism' and impose the Iranian model of a Muslim theocratic state on Lebanon.

Ironically, though the Israelis largely succeeded in neutralizing the PLO threat in Lebanon, their occupation of the south of the country played a major role in triggering the rising influence of Hezbollah, which today continues to pose an equal, if not greater, threat to the security of their northern border.

Badly shaken by the suicide bombings and their manifest inability to perform their peacekeeping role, the multinational force left Lebanon in February 1984. By early 1985 the last Israeli soldiers had also withdrawn from most of the country, leaving only a small number to help Haddad's SLA administer a so called 'Security Zone' in the south. In the meantime, against a background of continuing factional fighting, President Amin Gemayel struggled desperately to forge a new 'Government of National Unity' from the leaders of the warring factions, promising equal Muslim-Christian representation and the prospect of further constitutional reforms to reflect the majority status of the Muslims. Though he succeeded briefly, fighting soon broke out again.

War of the Camps

Fighting escalated following the Israeli withdrawal from southern Lebanon, with Phalangists clashing with Druze and Shi'ite militias in and around Sidon. In West Beirut, fighting between Sunni, Shi'ite and Druze militias continued unabated. At the same time, the PLO was beginning to filter back into Lebanon, triggering renewed fighting in the refugee camps around Beirut and in the south. The attacks on the refugee camps were led mostly by Amal, which feared that the return of the PLO would trigger a fresh Israeli invasion and renewed suffering for the Shi'ites of the south. What became known as the 'War of the Camps' dragged on through 1985 and 1986, with numerous truces and ceasefires collapsing almost as soon as they were announced. In June 1986 Syrian forces began to appear in West Beirut, their aim being to help the Lebanese army impose a ceasefire. After an upsurge in fighting in February 1987, about 4,000 Syrian troops were deployed in West Beirut, increasing soon afterwards to around 7,500. An uneasy ceasefire emerged and soon after the Amal siege of the Palestinian refugee camps in the southern suburbs was lifted, though the Syrian army maintained a tight cordon round the camps, Syria being equally opposed to the PLO re-establishing itself in Lebanon. It was not until January 1988 that Nabih Berri (the leader of Amal) formally announced the lifting of the siege of the Palestinian camps (which had continued in southern Lebanon), as a gesture of support towards the Palestinian *intifada* (uprising) which was gathering momentum within Israel. Instead, Amal began to concentrate its efforts against its chief rival Hezbollah.

Western hostages

From 1984 onwards, Westerners living in Beirut began to be abducted and held hostage with increasing frequency. In 1984 the CIA station chief William Buckley was kidnapped (he was tortured and killed); in 1985 the Associated Press journalist Terry Anderson; in 1986 John McCarthy of Worldwide Television; in 1987 Terry Waite, the Archbishop of Canterbury's special envoy in Lebanon. There were many other less well known Westerners who went missing, and hundreds of Lebanese from the different factions. The kidnappings, like the increasingly frequent and indiscriminate use of car bombs, marked a new stage in the war and reflected the tactics of Hezbollah and its various offshoots as it manoeuvred to gain supremacy and achieve its objectives of ridding Lebanon of foreign influences and setting up a theocratic Shi'ite Muslim state.

Constitutional crisis

The expiry of Amin Gemayel's term as president on 23 September 1988 triggered a constitutional crisis in the country. Two attempts to elect a new president failed after an insufficient number of representatives of the National Assembly were able to make it to the temporary parliamentary premises on the Green Line separating East and West Beirut. Only hours before his term in office ended, Gemayel decided to appoint his army Chief of Staff, General Aoun, to head an interim military government. Aoun was renowned for his anti-Syrian stance, making him unacceptable to the Syrians, and also to the Americans who were keen to see the status quo in Lebanon maintained. Aoun's interim government was to be made up of three Christian and three Muslim officers, but in the event the three Muslim officers appointed by Gemayel all refused to take up their posts.

A situation emerged whereby General Aoun headed a Christian government in East Beirut, while Selim al-Hoss, the Muslim prime minister under Gemayel, set up his own rival government in the *Summerland* hotel in West Beirut. For a time it seemed that what many people had long thought inevitable would happen, namely that the country would be partitioned into Muslim and Christian statelets. Indeed, by the end of 1988 the Central Bank was the only government institution which did not have rival Christian and Muslim branches. Unsure of what else it could do in the circumstances, it made funds available to both governments for the maintenance of basic services.

Aoun's war Clashes between the various militias in Beirut in November 1988 were the prelude to a far more violent outbreak of fighting between Christians and Muslims on either side of the Green Line in March 1989. The Christian side, led by General Aoun, was intent on driving the Syrians from Lebanon. The fighting continued, with the usual ceasefires and immediate breakdowns, for most of the year. France, as well as launching various diplomatic initiatives, became involved in supplying humanitarian aid, and although it did so to both sides, the Muslims regarded France's intentions with suspicion, fearing that it would ultimately support the establishment of a Christian dominated government in Lebanon. The conflict gained a more ominous dimension when Iraq began supplying Aoun's forces with arms following the end of the Iran-Iraq war in August 1988, providing Syria and Iraq with a new arena in which to pursue their traditional emnity.

The Taif Accord In the meantime, intensive efforts had been going on in the Arab world to achieve a lasting end to the hostilities. These were conducted primarily by a Tripartite Arab Committee consisting of King Hassan of Morocco, King Fahd of Saudi Arabia and President Chandli of Algeria. On 18 September 1989 the committee announced a new peace plan which envisaged an 'immediate and comprehensive ceasefire' and a meeting of the Lebanese National Assembly to discuss a 'Charter of National Reconciliation'. Crucially, there was no call in the peace plan for a Syrian withdrawal. A ceasefire was duly implemented on 23 September and the Lebanese National Assembly met at Taif in Saudi Arabia to discuss the charter later that month. The Assembly voted to endorse the Charter of National Reconciliation (which subsequently became known as the **Taif Accord**) on 22 October, having made various minor amendments. On 5 November the Assembly formally ratified the Taif Accord and elected René Mouawad as president. A new 'government of national reconciliation' was formed on 13 November, but nine days later and just 17 days after being elected, René Mouawad was assassinated in a car bomb attack. The National Assembly, fearful of a renewed descent into civil war, moved quickly, electing a new president, Elias Hrawi, two days later.

Fighting did indeed break out in early 1990, but it was between General Aoun and other Christian militias opposed to his renegade stance on the Taif Accord. Intra-Christian fighting raged in East Beirut and the Metn region and fighting also erupted between the rival Shi'ite militias, Amal and Hezbollah, first in southern Beirut and then in southern Lebanon. Against this background, and the background of the impending Gulf War, the National Assembly voted on 21 August to amend the constitution to incorporate the reforms outlined in the Taif Accord. In response to Syria's decision to support the US-led international coalition against Iraq in the Gulf War, the US effectively gave Assad permission to use Syrian forces to oust

General Aoun. On 28 September 1990 the Lebanese army imposed an economic blockade on Aoun, who was entrenched in the presidential palace at Baabda. On 13 October Syrian forces launched a full scale offensive against him and by the end of the month he had been defeated. While the south of the country remained volatile, a lasting peace was achieved in the rest of Lebanon for the first time in 15 years.

A fragile peace

In March 1991 the process began of disarming the various militias and extending the army's control over their former fiefdoms. In Beirut, the Green Line separating Muslims and Christians was finally dismantled. In May 1991 Lebanon and Syria signed a Treaty of Brotherhood, Cooperation and Coordination, followed by a Pact of Defence and Security later that year. These formalized Syria's close involvement in Lebanese political, military, security and economic affairs. Five joint councils were established to provide an executive mechanism whereby the "distinctive brotherly relations" referred to in the treaty could be developed and managed.

In the south of the country Israel still occupied its so called 'Security Zone' and through its proxy army, the SLA, maintained its control in certain areas beyond this zone. Palestinian bases also still existed around Sidon, while Hezbollah remained a powerful military force in its own right. The result was that fighting simmered on in the south, sometimes involving raids or *katyusha* rocket attacks on towns in the north of Israel and subsequent Israeli reprisals, and at other times clashes with the SLA or Israeli troops in the occupied 'Security Zone'. Occasionally, more dramatic fighting erupted (though never enough to provoke full scale war), as for example in June 1991 and July 1992. The latter Israeli offensive ('Operation Accountability') was the fiercest since the 1982 invasion and resulted in the displacement of as many as 300,000 civilians from southern Lebanon.

In March 1992 Syrian forces began to withdraw from Beirut, a prelude to their withdrawal to the Bekaa Valley by September 1992 as laid out in the Taif Accord. In the event, however, Syria's withdrawal was only partial and its troops can still be seen today in many parts of the country supposedly under the exclusive control of the Lebanese army. By mid-June the last Western hostages in Lebanon had been released. In August and September 1992 the first parliamentary elections for 20 years were held, although the Christian community largely boycotted them, somewhat undermining Lebanon's attempts to restore national unity.

Rafiq Hariri, a Lebanese born Saudi Arabian entrepreneur and billionaire, was chosen to become prime minister. He also assumed the position of Finance Minister and in 1993 set up the Council for Development and Reconstruction (CDR), charged with the redevelopment and reconstruction of Lebanon's shattered infrastructure and economy. In 1994 Hariri attempted to bring more Christians into the government to redress the imbalance caused by their boycotting of the 1992 elections. In the event he was blocked by President Elias Hrawi and the Syrians, prompting him to resign. After Syrian mediation he was reappointed. In 1995 a similar train of events occurred, with Hariri again resigning and being reappointed. In October 1995 Elias Hrawi's presidency was extended with Syrian approval.

In 1994 Hezbollah's targeting of Israeli troops led to ever more audacious Israeli reprisals, including the abduction of the Shi'ite leader Mustapha al-Dirani from his home in the Bekaa Valley and the assassination of Fuad Mughniya (a senior Hezbollah official and mastermind of the hostage taking campaign of the 1980s) in a bomb attack in south Beirut. Hezbollah rocket attacks and Israeli reprisals continued unabated through 1995. In April 1996, Israel launched **Operation Grapes of Wrath**, which surpassed even Operation Accountability in its range and scope. Though the aim was ostensibly to end Hezbollah's rocket attacks, the operation also targeted Lebanon's economic infrastructure, with air-strikes destroying an electricity generating plant while a blockade of Lebanese ports was mounted. Most infamous, however, was the bombing of an UN refugee camp at

Background

Qana (see page 557). Ironically, the operation failed to curb Hezbollah attacks, though initially at least these were restricted to military targets in accordance with a set of US-brokered agreements between Israel, Lebanon and Syria. More importantly, it earned Israel international condemnation and raised international sympathy for Lebanon's plight. Hariri's standing as a 'national leader' was improved and he was able to secure substantial concessionary aid from Western donors.

Israeli withdrawal

In August 1996, the new right-wing Israeli prime minister Benjamin Netanyahu put forward his **Lebanon First** proposal. This made a full Israeli withdrawal from southern Lebanon conditional on Syria/Lebanon disarming Hezbollah, preventing attacks on Israel from southern Lebanon, and giving amnesty to SLA commanders and troops. From Lebanon's point of view the offer was a good one, but without Syrian consent (and also Syrian cooperation in forcing Hezbollah to disarm), it was powerless to act. Assad rejected the proposal out of hand, and Lebanon meekly followed suit. In the meantime, the usual pattern of low level fighting continued in southern Lebanon. Clearly, however, public opinion in Israel opposing the occupation was steadily gathering momentum.

In April 1998 there was a new development, with Israel signalling its willingness to withdraw from southern Lebanon in accordance with UN Resolution 425 (a resolution dating back to the 1978 Israeli invasion and calling for a complete Israeli withdrawal). Although Israel attached essentially the same conditions as contained in the 'Lebanon First' proposal, the mere fact that it mentioned Resolution 425 represented a major change in Israel's stance. For its part, Hezbollah, scenting victory, simply piled on the pressure. In February 1999 an Israeli colonel and two soldiers were killed in a Hezbollah ambush in southern Lebanon, followed a week later by General Erez Gerstein (the most senior Israeli officer to be killed since the 1982 invasion) and three soldiers. Israel responded by launching Operation Land, Sea and Air. Fighter jets led some 23 air raids against targets in Lebanon, while a gunboat pounded the Nahme Palestinian refugee camp to the south of Beirut, though of the land element of the operation there was no sign.

In the May 1999 elections in Israel, Ehud Barak made it one of his main campaign pledges to effect a withdrawal from Lebanon within one year of taking office. He went on to win a landslide victory, taking office in July of that year. Although peace negotiations with both the Palestinians and Syrians floundered, Barak kept true to his word and by the end of May 2000, more than a month earlier than promised, the Israeli army withdrew from southern Lebanon, ending 18 years of occupation.

Recent developments

The politics of the Israeli withdrawal was complex. Many commentators have argued that, from the Syrian point of view, Hezbollah's war of attrition against the Israelis in southern Lebanon was actually a useful bargaining chip in its own quest for the return of the Golan Heights. Since Syria was widely recognized as having the influence to dictate Hezbollah's actions, Israel would have to negotiate a deal on the Golan Heights in order to be able to withdraw from southern Lebanon without fearing cross-border attacks from Hezbollah. Or so the argument went. In practice, Israel's withdrawal was in the end completely unilateral and it received no guarantees whatsoever as to the security of its northern border. Indeed, Hezbollah promptly filled the vacuum left by their departure, triumphantly raising their flag over former Israeli army bases and patrolling up and down the border in full view of Israeli forces across the fences. Israel was quick to make dire threats, aimed primarily at Syria, but had evidently decided that the cost of staying in southern Lebanon was simply too high.

In what was clearly seen as a Syrian backed move to maintain the legitimacy of Hezbollah's threatening presence in southern Lebanon, the Lebanese laid claim to a hilly tract of land at the foot of Mount Hermon known as Shebaa Farms. This territory had indeed originally belonged to Lebanon, though Syria had been in control of it when Israel captured it in the 1967 war and subsequently annexed it along with the Golan Heights. As Hezbollah made clear, as long as Israel held onto even the smallest bit of Lebanese territory, the 'war of liberation' would continue. Hezbollah's other major objective was to secure the release of Lebanese prisoners held in Israel.

In October 2000 two Palestinians were shot while demonstrating at the Lebanese-Israeli border in sympathy for the new *intifada*, which was by then steadily gathering momentum in the West Bank and Gaza Strip. Almost instantly Hezbollah responded with a daring and clearly long-planned raid into the Shebaa Farms in which they captured three Israeli soldiers, thus giving them the bargaining chip they needed. Since then, with steady worsening of the conflict between Israelis and Palestinians, the Lebanese-Israeli border has remained extremely tense. In April 2001 Israel launched an airstrike on a Syrian rader station in Lebanon, near the Dahr al-Baidar pass on the Beirut-Damascus highway. This was in response to the killing of an Israeli soldier in a cross-border raid, the third to die in this way since the Israeli withdrawal less than a year earlier. It also represented the first deliberate Israeli attack on a Syrian target since their invasion of Lebanon in 1982, and was clearly meant as a warning to Syria to rein in Hezbollah's activities along the border.

Religion

Islam

The word Islam translates roughly as 'submission to God'. The religion's two central tenets are embodied in the creed "There is no god but Allah and Mohammad is his Prophet" (*Lah Illaha illa 'llah Mohammad Rasulu'llah*), which affirms the belief in the oneness of God and recognizes Mohammad as his divinely appointed messenger.

The *Qur'an* (generally referred to as the Koran in English) is Islam's holiest book. The word translates literally as 'recitation' and unlike the Bible, the Qur'an is considered to be the *uncreated* (ie direct) word of God, as revealed to Mohammad through *Jibril* (the angel Gabriel). The text consists of 114 *suras* (chapters). Each sura is classified as Meccan or Medinan, according to whether it was revealed to Mohammad in Mecca or Medina. Most of the text is written in a kind of rhymed prose known as *saj*, and is considered by Muslims to be inimitable. Each chapter of the Qur'an begins with the words *Bismillah al-Rahman al-Rahim* ("In the name of Allah, the Merciful, the Compassionate"), an invocation which is also heard in numerous everyday situations.

In addition to the Qur'an, there is the *Hadith* body of literature, a record of the sayings and doings of Mohammad and his followers, which forms the basis of Islamic laws (*Shariat*), and precepts. Unlike the Qur'an, the Hadiths are recognized to have been written by men, and are therefore potentially flawed and open to interpretation. Thus they are commonly classified into four major categories according to their trustworthiness: *Sahih* (sound, true, authentic), *Hasan* (fair, good); *Da'if* (weak); and *Saqim* (infirm). The two most revered compilations of Hadiths are those by *al-Bukhari* and *Muslim*. It is in the interpretation of the Hadiths that most of the controversy surrounding certain Islamic laws and their application originates.

While Mohammad is recognized as the founder of the Islamic faith and the principal messenger of God, Muslims also regard him as having been the last in a long line of Prophets, starting with Adam and including both Moses and Jesus. They do not, however, accept Jesus as the son of God, but simply another of God's Prophets. Both Jews and Christians are considered *Ahl-e-Kitab* ('People of the Book'), the Torah and the Gospels being seen as forerunners of the Qur'an in Islamic belief.

The Five Pillars of Islam

There are five practices or Akran, known as the Five Pillars of Islam, which are generally accepted as obligatory duties for Muslims.

★ *Shahada: the profession of faith ("There is no god but Allah..."), which also forms the basis of the call to prayer made by the muezzin of the mosque.*

★ *Salat: the ritual of prayers, carried out five times a day at prescribed times; in the early morning before the sun has risen above the horizon, in the early afternoon when the sun has passed its zenith, later when the sun is half-way towards setting, immediately after sunset, and in the evening before retiring to bed. Prayers can be carried out anywhere, and simply involve facing towards the Ka'ba in Mecca and prostrating before God while reciting verses of the Qur'an.*

★ *Zakat: the compulsory payment of alms. In early times this was collected by officials of the Islamic state, and was devoted to the relief of the poor, aid to travellers and other charitable purposes. In many Muslim communities, the fulfilment of this religious obligation is nowadays left to the conscience of the individual.*

★ *Sawm: the 30 days of fasting during the month of Ramadan, the ninth month of the Muslim lunar calendar. It is observed as a fast from sunrise to sunset each day by all Muslims, although there are provisions for special circumstances.*

Hajj: the pilgrimage to Mecca. Every Muslim, circumstances permitting, is obliged to perform this pilgrimage at least once in his lifetime and having accomplished it, may assume the title of Hajji.

Nearly all Muslims accept six basic articles of the Islamic faith: belief in one God; in his angels; in his revealed books; in his Apostles; in the Resurrection and Day of Judgement; and in his predestination of good and evil. Heaven is portrayed in Muslim belief as a paradise filled with sensuous delights and pleasures. Hell, on the other hand, is portrayed as a place of eternal terror and torture, and is seen as the certain fate of all who deny the unity of God.

Islam has no ordained priesthood or clergy. The authority of religious scholars, learned men, imams, judges etc (referred to collectively as the *Ulema*), derives from their authority to interpret the scriptures, rather than from any defined status within the Islamic community. Many Muslims complain that their growing influence interferes with the direct, personal relationship between man and God which Mohammad originally espoused.

Sunnis & Shi'ites Following Mohammad's death, Islam divided into two major sects. Mohammad left no sons and therefore no obvious heir, and gave no instructions as to who should succeed him. There were two main contenders: **Abu Bakr**, the father of Mohammad's wife; and **Ali**, the husband of Mohammad's daughter Fatimah and his cousin. In the event Abu Bakr assumed the title of *caliph* (or vice-regent, from *Khalifat rasul-Allah*, 'Successor to the Apostle of God'). He died two years later in 634 AD and was succeeded by **Umar** who was killed in 644. **Uthman**, a member of the powerful **Umayyad** family, was chosen to succeed him but proved to be a weak leader and was murdered in 656.

At this point the aggrieved Ali managed to assume the title of caliph, thus ousting the Umayyads. However, **Mu'awiya**, the governor of Syria and a member of the Umayyad family, soon rose up in revolt. The two sides met in battle at Siffin on the upper Euphrates, but both eventually agreed to arbitration by delegates from each side. Some members of Ali's camp resented this, seeing such a move as submitting the Will of God to human judgement. Eventually, Ali was murdered by one of his own supporters in 661 and Mu'awiya proclaimed himself caliph. Ali's eldest son **Hassan** set up a rival caliphate in Iraq, but was soon persuaded to

Mohammad, the Holy Prophet of Islam

Mohammad, the founder of the Islamic faith, was born around 570 AD in the city of **Mecca** in present day Saudi Arabia. His family were of noble descent, members of the house of **Hashim**, belonging to the **Abd Manaf** clan and part of the **Quraish** tribal confederacy of Mecca. The Abd Manaf clan had a semi-priestly status, being responsible for certain functions during the annual pilgrimage to the Ka'ba in Mecca (the Ka'ba, the cube shaped stone to which Muslims face when praying, predates Islam; Muslims believe that it was given to Adam when he was driven from Paradise and revere it as a sanctuary where closeness to God can be achieved; more scientific theories suggest that it is a meteorite).

At the age of 40 Mohammad received his first revelations of the Qur'an and began preaching his message. He encountered stiff opposition from the powerful Quraish leaders, the temple guardians and the rich traders, and was eventually forced to flee to **Medina**, known then as Yathrib (this event is known as the Hijra or flight and marks the beginning of the Islamic calendar). There he established himself and achieved a position of power, fighting three major battles with the Meccans before finally returning there in triumph two years before his death in 632 AD.

In his lifetime he had become recognized as a prophet and founded the Islamic faith. Part of his success was in incorporating many aspects of the ancient Arabian religion, such as the pilgrimage to the Ka'ba, as well as aspects of Judaism and Christianity. But his success was not purely in religious. He was also an accomplished statesman who laid the foundations for what would later become a great Islamic empire.

Background

abdicate. All the same, the seeds of the schism in Islam had already been sown: between the Sunnis (those who accepted the legitimacy of the first three caliphs) and the Shi'ites (those who recognized only Ali as the first legitimate caliph). Later, when Mu'awiya died in 680, Ali's second son **Hussein** attempted to revolt against the Umayyads, but was defeated and killed in 681 at Karbala , providing the Shi'ites with their greatest martyr.

Followers of the **Sunni** sect, generally termed 'Orthodox', account for around 74% of the population in Syria, while in Lebanon they account for around 22% of the total population. They base their *Sunna* (path, or practice) on the 'Six Books' of traditions. They are organized into four orthodox schools or rites named after their founders, each having equal standing. The *Hanafi* is the most common in Syria, and the most moderate. The others are the *Shafii*, *Maliki* and *Hanbali*, the latter being the strictest. Many Muslims today prefer to avoid identification with a particular school, preferring to call themselves simply Sunni.

Followers of the **Shi'ite** (or Shia) sect account for only a tiny minority of the population in Syria. In Lebanon, on the other hand, they are now the single largest religious group, accounting for around 35% of the total population. As such, they also now represent the single largest minority in Lebanon, a fact yet to be acknowledged in the country's power-sharing arrangements. At the time of the 1932 census, they represented just 20% of the population. Their rapid rate of population growth, outstripping even that of the Sunnis, is as significant as the overall shift from a Christian to a Muslim majority.

Aside from the dispute over the succession of Mohammad, Sunnis and Shi'ites do not generally differ on fundamental issues since they draw from the same ultimate sources. However, there are important differences of interpretation which partly derive from the practice of *ijtihad* (the exercise of independent judgement) amongst Shi'ites, as opposed to *taqlid* (the following of ancient models) as adhered to by Sunnis. Thus Shi'ites divest far more power in their *imams*, accepting their role as an intermediary between God and man and basing their law and practice on the teachings of the Imams.

The majority of Shi'ites are known as *Ithna asharis* or 'Twelvers', since they recognize a succession of 12 imams. They believe that the last imam, who disappeared in 878 AD, is still alive and will reappear soon before the Day of Judgement as the *Mahdi* (one who is rightly guided), who will rule by divine right.

Ismailis The Ismailis are an offshoot of mainstream Shi'ite Islam. Following the death of the Sixth Shi'ite Imam Ja'far al-Sadiq in 765, there was a dispute as to the rightful heir to the title of Imam, with his eldest son Ismail being passed over by the majority of Shi'ites in favour of his younger son Musa al-Kazim. The Ismailis, however, recognized Ismail as the rightful imam. They are also known as *Sab'iya* or 'Seveners' since, unlike the Twelver Shi'ites, they recognize only seven principal imams after the death of the Prophet Mohammad. The philosophy of the Ismailis is a largely esoteric one, and a further name for them is the *Batiniyya* because of their emphasis on an esoteric (*batin*) interpretation of the Qur'an. Their theology is based on a cyclical theory of history centred around the number seven, which is considered to be of enormous significance. They are less restrictive in their customs and practice, allowing much greater freedom to women. Likewise, prayers are not linked to a specific formula. The mosque is replaced by a *jamat khana* which also serves as a community centre. Their spiritual head is the Agha Khan, who is considered a direct descendant of the Prophet Mohammad through his daughter Fatima.

First founded in the eighth century, they only really began to make their presence felt in North Africa from the beginning of the 10th century, going on to conquer Egypt in 969 and establish the powerful Fatimid Dynasty (named after the Prophet's daughter, Fatima) which flourished for the next two centuries, extending at the height of its power to include Egypt, Syria, North Africa, Sicily, the Red Sea coast of Africa, Yemen and the Hejaz region of Arabia (including the holy cities of Mecca and Medina).

However, under the Fatimids, the radical doctrines of the Ismailis (the source of their initial appeal) were gradually replaced by a more conservative outlook better suited to the responsibilities of such a powerful dynasty. This led to ideological conflicts which culminated in a major internal schism amongst the Ismailis. After the death of the eighth Fatimid caliph Al Mustansir in 1094, there was a dispute over his succession. The conservative elements within the court, led by the Commander of the Armies who had risen to a position of great personal power, installed Al Mustansir's younger and therefore more easily influenced son Al Mustali as caliph, disinheriting his older son Nizar, who was subsequently killed after attempting to revolt.

The followers of Al Mustali became known as *Mustalians* and the followers of Nizar as *Nizaris*. The Fatimid Dynasty, although it continued to rule in Egypt until 1171, was in terminal decline, finally being formally abolished by Salah-ud Din (Saladin) who restored Sunni orthodoxy and went on to establish the Ayyubid Dynasty. After the schism of 1094, the Mustalians (many of whom disowned the declining Fatimid Dynasty) established themselves on the outer peripheries of the Islamic world (notably in Yemen and India, where they are known today as *Boharis*). The Nizaris, meanwhile, began a period of intense political and doctrinal development in Persia, one outcome of which was the formation of the much feared **Assassins**, who established themselves in Syria from the beginning of the 12th century (see the box on page 274). Small numbers of Nizari Ismailis are still found in Syria, in Masyaf, to the west of Hama, and in Salamiyeh, to the southeast.

Alawis The Alawis (or Alawites) are another offshoot of mainstream Shi'ite Islam, although very little is known about their origins, beliefs and practices. They are most numerous in Syria, where they represent nearly 12% of the total population, but are also found in small numbers in Lebanon. They dominate political and military hierarchy in the modern state of Syria (President Bashar al-Assad of Syria is himself an Alawi). For more details on the Alawis, see the box on page 304.

The Druze represent an offshoot of the Ismailis. Their religion developed in the 11th century AD, during the reign of the Cairo based Fatimid caliph Al Hakim (996-1021). Al Hakim allowed himself to be declared a divine representation of God and substituted his own name for that of Allah in mosque services. This blasphemous act, together with heretical decrees such as banning people from fasting during Ramadan or undertaking the pilgrimage to Mecca, earned him the condemnation of mainstream Ismailis of the Fatimid court. Indeed his disappearance in 1021, taken by his followers as an act of divine *ghayba* (concealment) pending his eventual return, was probably the result of a discreet assassination.

Druze

In the meantime one of his closest disciples, Mohammad Ibn Ismail al-Darazi, had left Egypt and began spreading the new faith in Syria (and particularly in the mountains of present day Lebanon), where he found a more receptive audience amongst a people who had already been exposed to various heterodox interpretations of Islam. The term 'Druze' is in fact an Anglicized form of the Arabic word *durzi*, which was in turn derived from this missionary's name. As with the Alawis, very little is known about Druze beliefs or practices. Indeed, even the Druze themselves are divided between the *juhhal* (ignorant) and the *uqqal* (intelligent), with only the latter being fully initiated into the doctrines of the faith. The Druze form an extremely tight-knit community, only ever marrying amongst themselves, and are said to have ceased accepting new members into their religion 20 years after the death of Al Hakim. Mainstream Islam tends to regard the Druze either as a heretical offshoot or else as having nothing whatsoever to do with the Islamic faith.

Historically, the Druze were concentrated in the Lebanon mountains, particularly the Chouf and Metn. However, following the 1860 massacre of as many as 10,000 Maronites at the hands of the Druze and the subsequent French intervention, many of them migrated to Syria, settling primarily in the Hauran. Today they can be found in both countries. In Lebanon they number around 170-200,000 and make up approximately 5% of the population, while in Syria they number around 430,000 but make up just 3% of the population. There are also around 80,000 Druze in Israel, concentrated in the Haifa and Golan regions, and a small number in Jordan.

Sufism is the mystical aspect of Islam, often described as the 'science of the heart'. The word *Sufi* is most probably derived from the Arabic word *suf* meaning 'wool', a reference to the woollen garments worn by the early Sufis. The Sufis do not represent a separate sect of Islam; rather they aspire to transcend sects, emphasizing the importance of personal spiritual development, to be found only through the Qur'an.

Sufis

Nevertheless, various different Sufi orders did emerge, the most famous of them being the *Mawlawiyya* or **Whirling Dervishes**. This Sufi order originated in Turkey, inspired by the 13th-century mystical poet Jalal ud-Din Rumi, and is best known for the whirling dance which forms part of their worship. The dance is performed to music and involves the chanting of the *dhikr*, a kind of litany in which the name of God is repeated over and over again. The Sufis had considerable influence in Syria. The famous Sufi mystic, Mohi ud-Din Ibn al-Arabi, is buried in Damascus (see page 110) and his tomb remains an important pilgrimage site for Sufis. The rooms surrounding the courtyard of the Tekkiyeh as-Suleimaniyeh Mosque in Damascus were originally intended to house Whirling Dervishes before serving as a starting point for the annual pilgrimage to Mecca. Today, some of the more tourist orientated restaurants in Damascus serve meals to the accompaniment of Whirling Dervish dancing, while a Damascus based troupe of Whirling Dervishes have won international acclaim for their performances (though also attracting criticism for reducing what is supposed to be a spiritual act into a spectacle).

Christianity

See box on Maronites, page 652

Christian theology has its roots in Judaism, with its belief in one God, the eternal creator of the universe. Jesus, whom Christians believe was the Messiah or 'Christ' (literally 'Anointed One') and the son of God, was born in the village of Bethlehem, some 20 km south of Jerusalem. Very little is known about his early life except that he was brought up in a devout Jewish family. At the age of 30, he gathered a small group of followers and began to preach in the region between the Dead Sea and the Sea of Galilee. Two years later he was crucified in Jerusalem on the charge that his claim to be the son of God was blasphemous.

The New Testament of the Bible, which, together with the Old Testament, is the text to which Christians refer to as the ultimate scriptural authority, consists of four 'Gospels' (literally 'Good News'), and a series of letters by early Christians outlining the nature of Christian life.

Much of the early development of the Christian church took place within present day Syria and Lebanon. At first, Christians faced persecution within the Roman Empire, but gradually, as the faith spread, it became more widely accepted. In 313 AD the emperor Constantine issued the Edict of Milan, which formerly recognized the right of Christians to practice their faith, and in 380 AD the emperor Theodosius declared it the official religion of the Roman Empire.

Soon afterwards, the Roman Empire was formally divided into East and West, with Constantinople (formerly Byzantium and today Istanbul) becoming the capital of the Eastern Roman Empire, better known as the Byzantine Empire. Under Byzantine rule, Christianity in the Middle East divided into numerous different churches. These different branches of the church arose out of somewhat obscure theological disputes over the nature of Christ, but also reflected the power struggles going on within the empire. Other regional centres of Christianity also developed their own theological doctrines and separate churches.

The orthodox **(Dyophysite)** view was that Christ was of two natures, divine and human, while the alternative view, that of the **Monophysites**, was that he was of one nature – purely divine. This latter interpretation was condemned as a heresy by the Council of Chalcedon in 451. The **Monothelite** doctrine, that Christ had two natures but one will, was seen as something of a compromise, and adopted by the Byzantine emperor Heraclius (610-641) as a means of providing a solution to the Dyophysite versus Monophysite schism which was threatening to tear the church apart. In 680 AD the Sixth Ecumenical Council in turn condemned the Monothelite doctrine as heresy.

In the East, those who adhered to the orthodox (Dyophysite) view became known as **Melkites** (or Melchites), meaning literally 'King's Men', in reference to the fact that they maintained their allegiance to the Byzantine emperor in Constantinople. The Byzantine emperors, meanwhile, regarded themselves as defenders of the **Orthodox** Church. Followers of the Monophysite, Monothelite and other 'heterodox' (as opposed to orthodox) theologies founded their own churches, including: the Antioch based **Syrian** or **Jacobite** church, named after Jacobus Bardaeus, a sixth-century monk responsible for organizing the Monophysites of Syria into a church; the Egyptian **Coptic** church based at Alexandria; the **Armenian (Gregorian)** church; the **Nestorian (Chaldean)** church, founded by Nestorius of Cilicia in the fifth century; and the **Maronite** church which emerged in the seventh century (see box).

To begin with, the Eastern Church of Constantinople and the Catholic (Latin) Church of Rome existed in broad, if at times uneasy, agreement, but over the centuries doctrinal differences intensified, culminating in the great schism of 1054, with the Eastern Church refusing to accept the supremacy of the Pope and recognizing instead the Patriarch of Constantinople as its head. Later, many of the independent churches in the east renounced the doctrines regarded as heretical by the Roman Catholic Church and acknowledged the supremacy of the Pope. They became known as **Uniate** Churches, but were allowed to retain their respective languages, rites and canon law in accordance with the terms of their union. At the same time, the independent churches continued to exist in parallel, with the exception of the Maronite church, which became fully united with the Roman Catholic Church. Thus today, there is in the Middle East the **Greek Orthodox** and **Greek Catholic** church, the **Syrian Orthodox** and **Syrian Catholic** church, and the **Armenian Orthodox** and **Armenian Catholic** church. In addition, the **Roman Catholic** church is itself represented. Later arrivals on the scene were the **Protestant** and **Anglican** churches, which began preaching in the Middle East during the 19th century.

In **Syria**, Christians account for around 10% of the population. The Greek Orthodox and Greek Catholic churches are the most important, although the Armenian Catholic church forms an important and tightly knit community, particularly in the city of Aleppo. There are also small communities of Armenian Orthodox, Syrian Orthodox/Catholics, Maronites, Roman Catholics, Protestants and Anglicans.

Amongst **Lebanon's** Christians, the Maronites represent by far the most significant single group, both historically and numerically, today accounting for around 21% of the total population. Other Christian groups (primarily Greek Orthodox, but also Greek Catholics, Armenian Orthodox/Catholics, Syrian Orthodox/Catholics, Nestorians, Chaldeans, Roman Catholics and Protestants) account for some 14% of the total population.

People

Arabs

The vast majority of the peoples of Syria and Lebanon can be termed Arab, though the term is an extremely broad one, encompassing many different religious and ethnic groups. It is helpful, therefore, to look first at exactly what is meant by the term 'Arab', and how its meaning has evolved over time.

The earliest known use of the word comes from an inscription of the Assyrian king Shamaneser III, which refers to the *Arabi*. Thereafter it appears frequently, either as *Arabi* or *Arabu*, in Assyrian and Babylonian inscriptions. 'Arab' first appears in the Bible (2 Chronicles 17: 11), although it has been suggested that the 'mixed multitude' referred to in Exodus 12: 38 as having accompanied the Israelites into the wilderness could equally be translated as 'Arabs' (in Hebrew, the word for each is *erev* and *arav* respectively, but in their written forms the vowels do not appear). More commonly, however, the Bible makes reference to the Ishmaelites. In Islamic and Hebrew tradition, the Arabs and the Hebrews are both descendants of the prophet Abraham, the Arabs through his son Ishmael and the Hebrews through his son Isaac. The birth of Isaac to Abraham's elderly wife Sarah meant that Ishmael (born to Abraham's concubine Hagar) was superseded as Abraham's natural heir, whose descendants would inherit the Promised Land. Ishmael instead went out into the desert (Genesis 21).

The traditional definition of an Arab, as reflected in the biblical interpretation, was a nomadic inhabitant of the deserts of northern and central Arabia. Indeed, the word 'Arab' is thought to have been derived from a Semitic root related to nomadism, perhaps the word *abhar* (literally 'to move' or 'to pass'), from which the word 'Hebrew' is also probably derived. The settled inhabitants of the rain-fed uplands of present day Yemen could also be termed Arabs, and over the centuries many of the nomadic peoples traditionally recognized as Arabs themselves adopted a settled life based on agriculture and animal husbandry, but the broad definition of an Arab was at this stage fairly clear.

Background

The Maronites in Lebanon

The Maronite church takes its name from a hermit named Marun. The little that is known about this man comes from the writings of Theodoret, Bishop of Cyrrhus (in Syria, northwest of Aleppo), who wrote a book, Religious History, around 440 AD in which he recorded the development of the Christian Church. Although no precise dates are given, it appears that Marun was born in the mid-fourth century AD and died around 410. Theodoret records that Marun lived as a hermit and ascetic in the ruins of an abandoned pagan temple in the vicinity of Cyrrhus, and soon attracted many followers. After his death, his remains were buried somewhere in the Orontes Valley near Hama (the exact location is unknown, although Apamea seems a likely candidate). By the middle of the fifth century, St Marun's burial place had become an important place of pilgrimage and a monastery dedicated to him, had been established on the site.

According to most historical sources, the Maronite church was established at this monastery during the seventh century as a Syrian Monothelite communion: that is, the Maronite church accepted the doctrine that Christ was of two natures (divine and human), but they believed that he had only one will (divine). The significance of this may seem obscure today, but at the time it was of paramount importance. In 680 AD the Sixth Ecumenical Council of Constantinople condemned the Monothelite doctrine as heresy.

The Maronite church disputes that it was ever Monothelite in the first place. It claims rather that after the Sixth Council of Constantinople in 680, the Monothelite Patriarch Macarius was deposed from the see of Antioch and replaced instead by John Marun of Sarum, who was the head of the monastery of St Marun. As Patriarch, Marun and his followers became known as Maronites and thus, they argue, the Maronite church developed from the very beginning as a representative of Roman orthodoxy in the East, to the displeasure of Byzantium.

Interestingly, some Maronite historians claim that Marun of Sarum and his followers were descended from the Mardaites, a tribe from Anatolia and possibly of Armenian origin, who were settled by the Byzantines in the Amanus mountains of northwest Syria and used as a first line of defence against the Umayyads of Damascus. Most historians would reject this view, but its appeal to the Maronites is that it sets them apart as non-Arabs, in the same way as emphasising Lebanon's Phoenician past is seen as a way of distinguishing it from other Arab nations.

Whatever the true picture, the Maronites were driven out of Syria at some point and took refuge in the isolated valleys of Mount Lebanon. According to the conventional Maronite view, they were driven out by repeated Muslim persecutions during the 10th century, although some historians suggest that they were driven out by the Byzantines.

Certainly, by the 11th century they were well established in Mount Lebanon and Bcharre as the seat of their Patriarch. When the first Crusades arrived in the region of Tripoli in 1099, they were welcomed by the Maronites, who advised them as to the safest route along the coast to Jerusalem. It is even claimed that the Maronite Patriarch sent his personal congratulations to the Pope on the capture of Jerusalem, and received gifts in return. Although the relationship between the Maronites and the Crusaders was an ambiguous one,

---

The definition of an Arab became more complicated with the arrival of Islam. The Islamic faith as revealed by the Prophet Mohammad was clearly intended, initially at least, specifically for the nomadic tribes of the Arabian peninsula: ie the Arabs. However, the conquests of the seventh century resulted in the creation of a vast Arab Empire based on the precepts of Islam. Thus, Arab and Muslim identities became very closely intertwined, though the two were never synonymous.

alternating between such displays of friendship and other episodes of hostility and treachery, it was to be of fundamental importance to the later history of the Maronite church, particularly in terms of its relationship with the Roman Catholic church. That friendly relations did exist can be seen in the surnames of some Maronite families which still survive today, most notably that of the Franjieh family (see page 520). Franjieh comes from the colloquial Arabic Franj (itself derived from Frank) meaning literally 'foreigner' or 'Westerner', and hence at the time used to refer to the Crusaders.

In 1180, Maronite representatives met with the Latin Patriarch of Antioch and declared their formal union with the Roman Catholic church, although there were elements amongst the Maronite community which strongly opposed such a union. In 1215 the Maronite Patriarch, Jeremiah of Amchit, was invited by Pope Innocent III to attend the Lateran Council in Rome. The invitation was designed primarily to strengthen the hand of the pro-Uniates, and after his return in 1216 with a papal bull absolving all repentant Maronites of their sins of disobedience to the Roman Catholic church, he was able to rule largely without dissent until his death in 1230. However, with the Crusader presence in the Middle East clearly under threat, there followed a further period of dissension amongst the Maronites, and at one stage there were even two competing Patriarchs, one pro-Uniate, the other anti. After the Crusaders were finally driven out at the end of the 13th century, the Maronites came under Mameluke Islamic rule and contact with Rome faded. Ever adept in securing favourable terms from whoever was ruling them, the Maronites

instead managed to establish special relations with the Mamelukes. With the rise to power of the Sultan Barquq in 1382 they were allowed to govern themselves largely without outside interference, even gaining immunity from certain taxes and endowments for the restoration of many of their monasteries.

Contact with Rome was re-established in 1439, when the Maronite Patriarch John of Jaj, sent a message to the Council of Florence (convened in an attempt to end the schism between the Roman Catholic and Eastern churches), reminding the Pope of the Maronite's allegiance to Rome. The failure of the Council of Florence and the subsequent fall of Constantinople to the Ottomans in 1453 convinced the papal authorities that their best hope of maintaining some sort of foothold in the East lay with the previously ignored and insignificant Maronites. In 1510 Pope Leo X heaped praise on them as defenders of the true (ie Roman Catholic) faith, describing them as a "rose amongst the thorns" in a "field of error". In the following centuries, the Maronites steadily developed their links with Rome and later more specifically with France, their church becoming more Latinized in the process, though still retaining certain distinguishing features. At the same time, from the 16th century onwards they gradually spread from their traditional heartlands around Bcharre southwards into the Metn and Chouf mountains (see page 513).

It was the close relationship between the Maronites and French which lay behind the creation in 1860 of Mount Lebanon as a special province of the Ottoman empire under European protection, and then the decision to create 'Grand Liban' in 1920.

As Kamal Salibi points out: "The Islamic conquests which were undertaken by the Arabs in the name of Islam were depicted as Arab conquests. This, viewed in one perspective, was true. The earlier Islamic conquests, though undertaken in the name of Islam, did result in the actualization of Arab political dominance in areas which had long been predominantly Arab in population – notably Syria and Iraq. It was highly debateable, however, as to whether or not the Islamic Empire of the Umayyad and Abbasid caliphs, which came to extend from the borders of Central Asia and the

Semitic origins

The terms 'Semite' and 'Semitic' are today popularly used to refer to peoples of Jewish origin. Their true meaning, however, is much broader. According to the dictionary definition, a Semite is a member of any of the peoples said (in the Bible, Genesis 10; 21-30) to be descended from Shem, Noah's eldest son: that is, both the Hebrews and

Arabs, and others such as the Aramaens. The terms were in fact first coined by the German historian AL Schlözer in 1781, and used in an exclusively linguistic sense to refer to the family of languages that includes Hebrew, Arabic, Aramaic and certain ancient languages such as Phoenician, Assyrian and Babylonian.

Indian Ocean to the Atlantic, was in fact an Arab Empire. Certainly the caliphate which stood at the head of this empire, though held by Arab Dynasties, was an Islamic rather than an Arab institution, representing an Islamic rather than Arab sovereignty. More important, the imperial civilization which reached its apogée under the Abbasid caliphs of Baghdad was an Islamic rather than Arab civilization, in which non-Arabs as well as Arabs participated. This civilization, in fact, had many of its leading centres outside the Arab world." (Kamal Salibi, *A House of Many Mansions*.) Later, the Arab nature of the Islamic Empire became even more tenuous, with the caliphate passing to the Turkish Ottomans. Kamal Salibi again: "To the early Arab nationalists among the Muslims ... Arab nationalism essentially involved the reclamation of the Islamic caliphate, then held by the Turkish Ottomans, for a caliph of the Arab race."

Even more significantly, although Muslim and Arab identities came to be very closely identified with each other (at least by the Sunni Muslim majority in the region), there existed sizable minorities of Arab Christians (and indeed Jews), who had everything in common with their Muslim counterparts in terms of history, culture and language, but little in terms of religion. Ironically, the Christian Arabs were the first to articulate the concept of Arab nationalism, because they avoided the trap of confusing Arab and Muslim identities. To them: "The Arab nation was amongst the greatest nations in history. It had a civilization prior to Islam, and a much more developed one after Islam. Christians had participated in the development of Arab civilization before and after Islam; and this civilization was not a purely religious one, as the ignorant imagine, but exhibited numerous traits which had no connection with religion whatsoever." (Sati al-Husri, quoted in *A House of Many Mansions*, Kamal Salibi). To the minority Islamic sects of the region, the Shi'ites, Druze, Alawis etc, the idea that Arab history was inseparable from the history of the Sunni Islamic state was equally dubious, since it implied that they would always be relegated to a secondary position and excluded from power within it.

Thus the traditional definition of an Arab, as a nomadic inhabitant of the deserts of northern and central Arabia, was rendered inadequate by the `arabization' of a far larger area, and much of what we today recognize as Arab culture and society has little in common with that of the nomadic desert tribes. Likewise, the tendency of mainstream Sunni Muslims to identify 'Arab' with 'Muslim' is flawed even within the Arab world, given the existence of non-Muslim Arab minorities, and completely untenable when you take into consideration the spread of Islam far beyond the bounds of the Arab world. Today, perhaps the nearest you can get to a definition of 'Arab' is a native speaker of the Arabic language, though this remains a very loose definition, Arabic being the native tongue of around 120 million people across the Middle East and North Africa. As the language of Islam, it is also known to millions more Muslims outside the Arab world.

Lebanon and Phoenicia

Today, many Christian Lebanese seek to emphasize their Phoenician ancestry, claiming that it distinguishes them from the Arab peoples of the rest of the Middle East. In the face of Syrian claims over Lebanon, they cite it as a justification for the creation of Lebanon as an independent state, separate and distinct from Syria. Certainly, the Phoenicians represented a remarkable civilization of sea-farers and traders who achieved unprecedented success in forging commercial links and establishing colonies throughout the Mediterranean and beyond. The Phoenician script probably formed the basis of the alphabet of the ancient Greeks, which in turn was the direct ancestor of the Latin alphabet of western Europe.

However, to quote Kamal Salibi: "...between ancient Phoenicia and the Lebanon of medieval and modern times, there is no demonstrable historical connection.... Yet, the fact remains that most of the Phoenician cities of antiquity did flourish in the coastlands of present day Lebanon, preserving their ancient

Canaanite names in Aramaicized or Arabicized forms to this day.... Like the ancient Phoenicians [the Lebanese] are free-wheeling and rugged merchantilists; adventurous and footloose, yet staunchly attached to home grounds.... What makes modern urban Lebanese so much like the Phoenicians of old is geography, not history. They live in the same cities, along the same Mediterranean shore, and work the same land under the same climate." (Kamal Salibi, A House of Many Mansions.)

The assertion that their Phoenician ancestry, however distant, sets the Lebanese apart from other Arabs is in itself open to question. According to both Herodotus and Strabo, the Phoenicians claimed to have come originally from the Persian Gulf region of the Arabian peninsula, which would mean that they shared a common ancestry with the Arabs. Given that the Phoenicians in all likelihood evolved from the Canaanites, and given that the Canaanites were possibly of Semitic origin, there might be some truth in this claim.

Ethnic minorities

There are several different ethnic minorities within Syria and Lebanon which are specifically non-Arab, though, as pointed out above, there are various ethnic groups which can also be defined as 'Arab'. Likewise, many of the religious groups of the Middle East also see themselves as distinctive ethnic groups. Thus, although more than 90% of Lebanon's population can be defined as Arab, this definition conceals a mosaic of different religious and ethnic groups.

Kurds

The Kurdish people represent the single largest minority group in Syria, accounting for around 9% of the total population. They are concentrated to the north of Aleppo and in the northeastern Jezira region bordering Turkey and Iran. The Kurdish people as a whole form an ethnic group straddling Syria, Turkey, Iraq and Iran. After the first World War, they were denied their promised homeland of Kurdistan and today continue to exist as a 'people without a country'. In Iraq and Turkey they have faced continual persecution as a result of their ongoing struggle for autonomy. Following the Gulf War of 1990/91 Saddam Hussein ruthlessly suppressed Kurdish attempts to overthrow him, while in Turkey what amounts to a civil war continues to rage in the eastern part of the country. In Syria the Kurds have fared somewhat better, although any possibility of freedom of political expression is out of the question.

Armenians

Syria's Armenian population is for the most part descended from the refugees who fled the Armenian genocide in Ottoman Turkey during the First World War. Between one and a half and two million Armenians are thought to have perished as a result of the genocide. In Aleppo many found a safe haven, and today whole quarters of Aleppo are dominated by Armenians who, as in the past, trade in textiles and fabrics, the distinctive Armenian script gracing their shop signs. There are also considerable numbers of Armenians in Deir ez-Zor and Hassakeh (the Jezira region witnessed the massacre of many Armenians at the hands of the Turks). In Lebanon there is a small community of Armenians in Beirut, concentrated in the Bourj Hammoud district in the east of the city. The majority of Armenians in both countries are Christian (Armenian Orthodox or Armenian Catholic).

Palestinians There are substantial numbers of Palestinians in both Syria and Lebanon. In Syria, there are estimated to be more than 378,000, the majority of which are concentrated in and around Damascus. Lebanon, meanwhile, is host to over 373,000 (representing nearly 10% of the total population). The majority are Sunni Muslim and their arrival in Lebanon (in the first instance after the 1947-49 Arab-Israeli War and then in greater numbers during the late 1960s and early 1970s) was a major contributing factor to the increased proportion of Muslims to Christians. Today, the vast majority of Palestinians live in very poor conditions in refugee camps in the south of the country, only a tiny number of them having gained Lebanese citizenship.

Other Syria is also home to small numbers of Circassians (non-Arab Muslim refugees from the Russian Caucasus who came to Syria in the 19th and 20th centuries) and Turks. In addition, there is still a tiny community of **Jews**, numbering less than 100 and concentrated mostly in Damascus, with a few in Aleppo and Qamishle. Before 1948 there were around 30,000 Jews living in Syria, but the majority fled when the state of Israel was created. In 1992 those that remained (around 3,500) were given permission to leave the country if they wished, an offer which the majority took up.

Footnotes

18

658

Footnotes

Useful Arabic words and phrases

Learning just a few basic words and phrases of Arabic is not at all difficult and will make an enormous difference to your travelling experience. Being able to greet people and respond to greetings, point at something in the souks, ask 'how much?' and understand the reply – such simple things are rewarding, enjoyable and of practical benefit. The greatest hurdle most people face is with pronunciation. Arabic employs sounds which simply do not occur in English, so your tongue and mouth have to learn to form new, unfamiliar sounds. With a little patience, though, you can soon pick up the correct pronunciation of most words (or at least good enough to make yourself understood). The following is just a very brief introduction and the Arabic transliterations are simplistic: the bottom line is that there is no substitute for listening to and practicing with a native speaker. Once you are in the Middle East you will have plenty of opportunities to do this. But before you go, language books and tapes can get you started. *Colloquial Arabic (Levantine)*, published by Routledge, is a good package.

It has been observed, perhaps a little unkindly, that the closest most Westerners get to exercising the relevant muscles for intoning Arabic is when they are vomiting!

Greetings and pleasantries

hello (informal 'hi')	*marhaba*
hello ('welcome')	*ahlan wa sahlan* (or just *ahlan*)
hello ('peace be upon you')	*asalaam alaikum*
hello (response)	*wa alaikum as-salaam*
goodbye	*ma'a salaama*
good morning	*subah al-khair*
good morning (response)	*subah an-noor*
good evening	*musa al-khair*
good evening (response)	*musa an-noor*
good night	*tusba allah khair*
good night (response)	*wa inta min ahalu*
How are you?	*kif halak/halik?* or *kifak/kifik* (m/f)
fine, good, well	*qwayees*
please	*min fadlak/fadlik* (m/f)
thankyou	*shukran*
thankyou very much	*shukran jazeelan*
excuse me	*afwan*
sorry	*aassif*
no problem	*mush mushkilay*
Congratulations!	*mabrouk!*
Thank God!	*hamdullilah!*
What is your name?	*shoo ismak/ismik?* (m/f)
My name is....	*ismi...*
Where are you from?	*min wain inta/inti?* (m/f)
I am a tourist	*ana siyaha*

Useful expressions

If God wills it	*inshallah*
yes	*naam/aiwa*
no	*laa*
Where is .....?	*wain...?*
How far?	*kam kilometre?*
Is there/do you have...?	*fi....?*
There is	*fi*
There is not, there's none	*ma fi*
How much?	*bikam/adesh?*

expensive	*ghaali*
cheap	*rakhees*
good	*qwayees*
bad	*mish mnih*
enough, stop	*hallas*
Let's go	*yallah*
I understand	*ana afham*
I don't understand	*la afham*

Getting around

airport	*al matar*
bus station	*mahattat al bas/garagat*
bus	*al bas/autobas*
taxi	*taxi*
service taxi	*servees*
train station	*mahattat al qitar*
car	*sayara*
left	*yasaar*
right	*shimal/yameen*
straight ahead	*ala tuul*
tourist office	*makhtab siyaha*
map	*khareeta*
city centre/old city	*medina*
hotel	*funduq*
restaurant	*mataam/restauran*
museum	*matthaaf*
bank	*masraf/banque*
chemist	*sayidiliya*

Documents

passport office	*makhtab al jawazaat*
passport	*jawas as safar*
visa	*sima*
permit	*tasrih*
name	*ism*
date of birth	*tarikha al mulid*
place of birth	*makan al mulid*
nationality	*jensiya*

Numbers

0	*sifr*	14	*arbaatash*
1	*wahad*	15	*khamastash*
2	*itneen*	16	*sittash*
3	*talaata*	17	*sabbatash*
4	*arba'a*	18	*tamantash*
5	*khamsa*	19	*tissatash*
6	*sitta*	20	*ashreen*
7	*sabba*	21	*wahad wa ashreen*
8	*tamanya*	22	*itneen wa ashreen*
9	*tissa*	30	*talaateen*
10	*ashra*	40	*arbaa'een*
11	*hidaash*	50	*khamseen*
12	*itnash*	60	*sitteen*
13	*talaatash*	70	*sabba'een*

80	*tamanteen*	300	*talaata mia*
90	*tissa'een*	1,000	*alf*
100	*mia*	2,000	*alfein*
200	*miatein*	3,000	*talaata alf*

Days and time

Sunday	*al ahad*	morning	*subah*
Monday	*al itneen*	afternoon	*ba'ad az-zohr*
Tuesday	*at talata*	evening	*musa*
Wednesday	*al arbaa*	day	*yoom*
Thursday	*al khamees*	night	*lail*
Friday	*al juma*	week	*usboo*
Saturday	*as sabts*	year	*sana*
today	*al yoom*	now	*al-aan*
yesterday	*ams*	before	*qabl*
tomorrow	*bukra*	after	*baad*

Footnotes

Glossary

A

ablaq alternating courses of contrasting stone, typical of Mameluke and Ottoman architecture (Arabic)

acanthus a conventionalized representation of a leaf, used especially to decorate Corinthian columns

acropolis fortified part of upper city, usually containing a political, administrative, or religious complex

adyton inner sanctuary of the *cella* of a temple

agora open meeting place or market

amphora Greek or Roman vessel with a narrow neck and two handles, tapering at the base, used for transporting wine or oil

architrave lowest division of an *entablature* or decorated moulding round arch or window

apodyterium changing rooms of a Roman baths complex

apse semi-circular niche; in a Byzantine *basilica* this is always at the eastern end and contains the altar

atrium courtyard of a Roman house or forecourt of a Byzantine church

B

bab gate (Arabic)

barbican an outer defence, usually in the form of a tower, at the entrance to a castle

barrel vault a vault in the shape of a half-cylinder

basilica a Roman building/ Byzantine church of rectangular plan with a central *nave* flanked by two side aisles and usually with an *apse* at one end

bastion strongpoint or fortified tower in fortifcations

beit house (Arabic)

bimaristan hospital, medical school (Arabic)

bir well (Arabic)

birkat pool or reservoir

burj tower (Arabic)

C

caldarium hot room in Roman baths complex

capital crowning feature of a column or pier

caravanserai see *khan* (Arabic)

cardo maximus main street of a Roman city, usually running north-south and lined with colonnades

castrum fortified Roman camp

cavea semi-circular seating in auditorium of Roman theatre

cella the inner sanctuary of a temple

chancel raised area around altar in a church

clerestory upper row of windows providing light to the nave of a church

colonette small, slender *column*

colonnade row of *columns* carrying *entablature,* or arches

column upright member, circular in plan and usually slightly tapering

crenellations battlements

cruciform cross-shaped

cuneiform script consisting of wedge-shaped indentations, usually made into a clay tablet, first developed by the Sumerians

cupola dome

decumanus major east-west cross-street in Roman city, intersecting with the *cardo maximus*

deir monastery (Arabic)

donjon (or *keep*) main fortified tower and last refuge of a castle

diwan see *iwan*

entablature horizontal stone element in Greek/Roman architecture connecting a series of columns, usually decorated with a cornice, frieze and architrave

exedra a recess in a wall or line of columns, usually semi-circular and traditionally lined with benches

forum open meeting place or market

fosse ditch or trench outside fortifications

frieze central section of *entablature* in classical architecture, or more generally any carved relief

frigidarium cold room in Roman baths complex

glacis (or *talus*) smooth sloping surface forming defensive fortification wall

groin vault two intersecting *barrel vaults* forming ceiling over square chamber, also called a cross vault

hammam bath house (Arabic)

haremlek private/family quarters of an Ottoman house (Arabic)

hypogeum underground burial chamber

iconostasis screen decorated with icons separating the *nave* and *chancel* of a Byzantine or Orthodox rite church

iwan (or *diwan/liwan*) open reception area off courtyard with high arched opening (Arabic)

Jami' Masjid Friday congregational mosque (Arabic)

jebel (or *jabal*) hill, mountain (Arabic)

kalybe open-fronted shrine with niches for statuary

keep see *donjon*

khan hostel and warehouse for caravans and traders consisting of walled compound with accommodation, stables/ storage arranged around a central courtyard (Arabic)

kufic early angular form of Arabic script (named after Kufa in southern Iraq)

lintel horizontal beam above doorway supporting surmounting masonry

liwan see *iwan*

loculus (plural *loculi*) shelf-like niche in wall of burial chamber for sarcophogus/ corpse

madrassa Islamic religious school (Arabic)

Mar Saint (Arabic)

maristan see *bimaristan*

masjid mosque (Arabic)

medina old city (Arabic)

mihrab niche, usually semi-circular and vaulted with a semi-dome, indicating direction of prayer (towards Mecca) (Arabic)

minaret tower of mosque

minbar pulpit in mosque for preaching, to right of *mihrab*

muezzin man who recites the call to prayer (Arabic)

narthex entrance hall to *nave* of church

nave the central rectangular hall of basilica/church, usually lined with colonnades to separate it from the side-aisles

necropolis ancient burial ground

noria waterwheel (Arabic)

nymphaeum Roman monumental structure surrounding a fountain (dedicated to nymphs), usually with niches for statue

O

odeon small theatre or concert hall

orchestra paved semi-circular area between stage and *cavea* of Roman theatre

P

pediment triangular, gabled end to a classical building

peristyle colonnaded corridor running around the edges of a courtyard

pier vertical roof support

pilaster engaged pier or column projecting slightly from wall

portico colonnaded porch over outer section of doorway

praetorium Roman governor's residence or barracks

propylaeum monumental entrance to a temple

Q

qadi Muslim judge (Arabic)

qalat castle, fortress (Arabic)

qibla marking direction of prayer, indicated in a mosque by the *mihrab* (Arabic)

qubba dome (Arabic)

R

revetment facing or retaining wall in fortification

ribat Muslim pilgrim hostel or hospice

S

sacristy small room in a church for storing sacred vestments, vessels etc

salemlek area of Ottoman house for receiving guests

sanjak subdivision of an Ottoman *vilayet*

scaenae frons decorated stone façade behind the stage area of Roman theatre

seraya (or *serai*) palace (Arabic)

soffit the underside of a lintel

souk market (Arabic)

stela (plural *stelae*) narrow upright slab of stone, usually inscribed

T

talus see *glacis*

tariq road

tell artificial mound

temenos sacred walled temple enclosure surrounding *cella*

tepidarium warm room of a Roman baths complex

tessera (plural *tesserae*) small square pieces of stone used to form mosaic

tetrapylon arrangement of columns (usually four groups of four) marking major street intersections (eg

between *cardo maximus* and *decumanus*) in Roman city

transept transverse section between nave and apse of church, giving a cruciform (cross) shape instead of basic rectangular shape

triclinium dining room of Roman house

tympanum the space enclosed in a *pediment*, or between a lintel and the arch above

V

via sacra sacred way used by pilgrims to approach shrine etc

vilayet Ottoman adminsistrative province

vomitorium (plural *vomitoria*) entrance/exit to the seating area, or *cavea*, of a Roman theatre

W

wadi valley or watercourse with seasonal stream (Arabic)

Footnotes

Index

Footnotes

Footnotes

Map index

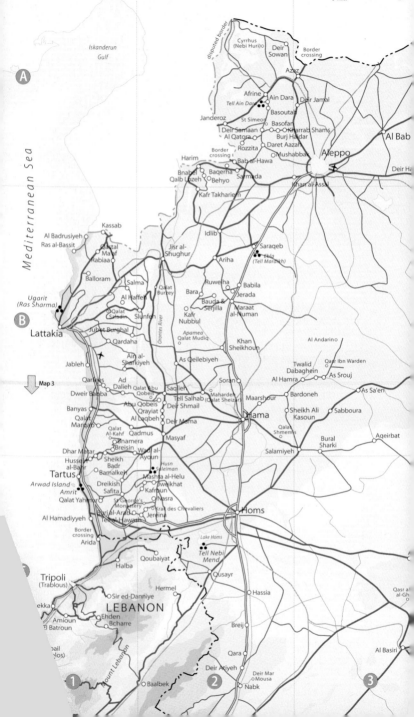

Map 1 Syria

N

TURKEY

0 km   20

0 miles   20

Iskanderun Gulf

A

disputed border

Cyrrhus (Nebi Huri) ○   Deir Sowan   Border crossing

A'zaz

Afrine ○ Ain Dara   Deir Jamal
Tell Ain Dara   Basoutal

Janderoz   St Simeon   Basofan   **Al Bab**
Deir Samaan   Kharrab Shams
Al Qatora   Burj Haidar
Rozzita   Daret Aazah   **Aleppo**
Mushabbak

Mediterranean Sea

Harim   Border crossing   Bab al-Hawa   Khan al-Assal   Deir Ha

Bnabel ○   Baqerha
Qalb Lozeh   Behyo   Salmada
Kafr Takhariem

Kassab

Al Badrusiyeh   Idlib   Saraqeb
Ras al-Bassit   Ehla (Tell Maridikh)

Qastal   Jisr al-   Ariha
Maaf   Shughur   Ruweiha   Babila
Rabiaa   Jerada
Bara   Bauda &   Maraat
Balloram   Serjilla   al-Numan
Salma   Kafr
Al Haffeh   Qalat   Nubbul
Burcey

Ugarit (Ras Sharma)   Qalat   Al Andarino
Saladin   Slunfeh   *Apamea*   Khan
B   Jubet Burghal   Qalat Mudiq   Sheikhoun   Qasr Ibn Warden

Lattakia   Qardaha   As Qeilebiyeh   Twalid   As Srouj
Dabaghein
Jableh ○   Ain al-   Soran   Al Hamra   As Sa'en
Sharkiyeh
↓ Map 3   Qartиез   Saqlieh   Maarshour   Bardoneh   Sabboura
Ad   Qalat Abu   Tell Salhab   Maharden   Sheikh Ali
Dweir Banba   Dalieh   Qobeis   Deir Shmail   (Qalat Sheizar)   Kasoun
Banyas   Abu Qobeis   Deir Mama   **Hama**   Ageirbat
Qalat   Qrayiat
Marqab   Al Laqbeh   Qalat   Bural
Qalat   Qadmus   Masyaf   Shmems   Sharki
Al-Kahf
Dhar Matar   Bnamera   Wadi al-   Salamiyeh
Breisin   Ayoun
Hussein   Sheikh   *Husn
al-Bahr   Badr   Suleiman*
Tartus   Bamalkeh   Mashta al-Helu
Arwad Island   Dreikish   Jwaikhat
Amrit   Safita   Kafroun
Qalat Yahmur   Nasra
St George's   Krak des Chevaliers
Bir al-Arab   Monastery
Al Hamadiyeh   Tellel Hawash   Jereina   **Homs**
Border
crossing   *Lake Homs*   Qasr al
Arida   *Tell Nebi   al-Gh
Mend*
Halba   Qoubaiyat   Qusayr   Hassia

Tripoli
(Trablous)   Hermel   Breij   Al Basiri
Sir ed-Danniye
ekka   **LEBANON**
Amioun   Ehden
el Batroun   Bcharre   Qara   Deir Atiyeh
bail   Deir Mar
os)   **1**   ○ Baalbek   **2**   Mousa   **3**
Nabk

Map 2 Syria

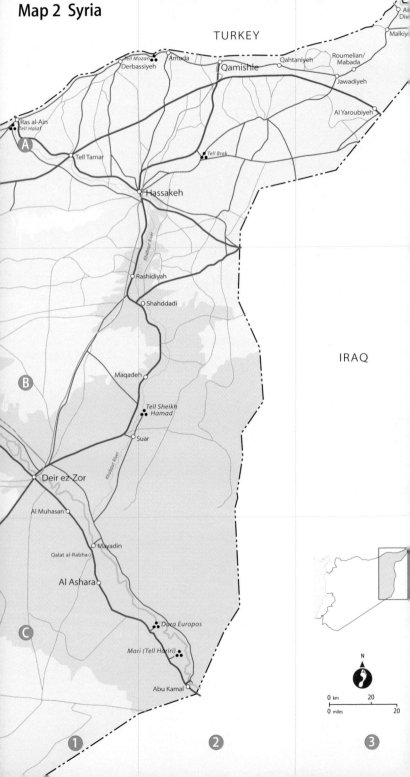

TURKEY

Ail Divi

Malkiy

Tell Mozan
Derbassiyeh
Amuda
Qamishle
Qahtaniyeh
Roumelian/
Mabada

Jawadiyeh

Al Yaroubiyeh

Ras al-Ain
Tell Halaf

A

Tell Tamar

Tell Brak

Hassakeh

Khabour River

Rashidiyah

Shahddadi

IRAQ

B

Maqadeh

Tell Sheikh
Hamad

Suar

Khabour River

Deir ez-Zor

Al Muhasan

Mayadin

Qalat al-Rabha

Al Ashara

C

Dura Europos

Mari (Tell Hariri)

Abu Kamal

N

0 km   20

0 miles   20

1   2   3

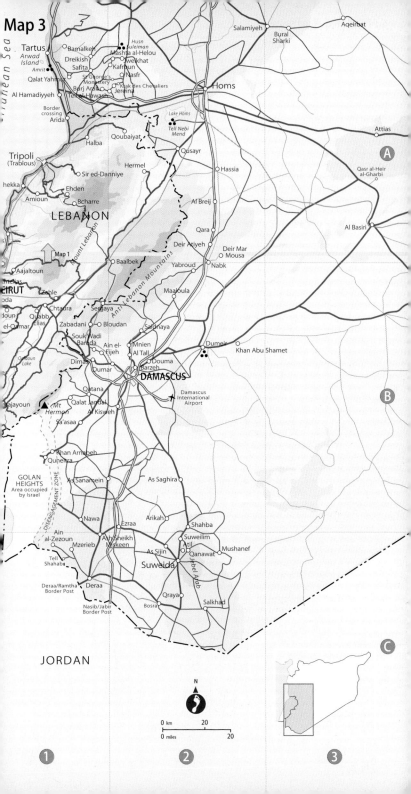

Map 4 Lebanon

Map 5 Lebanon

SYRIA

Mediterranean Sea

Al Hamadiyyen

Border crossing
Aarida

Akkar Plain

El Biré
St Charlita
Aandqet

Qoubaiyat

Jebel Akroum

Halba

Aabdé

Tell Arqa
Roman Temple
Gebrayel
Akkar el-Atiga

Boustane

Jebel Akkar

Mechmech

Hmaire
Fissane

Charbine

El Baddoui
Tripoli
(Trablous)
Jezira
al-Nakhil
Motorway under construction
Jabal Tourbol

Kfar Habou
Bakhoun
Roman Temple
Sfiré

HERMEL

Deir Mar
Maroun
Ain Zarqa
(Springs)
Hermel
Tower

Qalamoun
Majel
Laya
Zghorta
Haqel Azzime
Aassoun
Sir ed-Danniyé

Matl et Thouil

Qornet es Sinan

Orontes River

Enfeh

Balamand

Bsarma

Jebel Jaouz

Jbab el Homr

Mahattet
Ras Baalbek

Chekka

Amioun

Kousba

Touza

Qnat

Horsh Ehden
Nature
Reserve
Ehden

Qornet es-Saouda
(3,083m)

Jebel el Mekmel

Ouyoun
Orogosh

Ras Baalbek

Hamat
Mousayiha
Castle

Bziza

Bcharre
The Cedars
(Al Arz)
Hadath
El-Jobbe
Arz
Tannourine
Bqaa Kafra

Jdaide

El Fakha

Al Ain
Nabi Osmane

Balamand
Hadboun
Bcheale
Doumar
Tartij
Chatine
Tahourine
el-Tahta

Ainata

Labwe

Toufiqiyé

Maifouk
Haqel
Jaj

Tannourine
el-Faouqa
Jebel el Mnaitre

Aaqoura

Yammouné

Deir al-Ahmer

Annaya
(St Charbel's
Monastery)
Jebel el Qaraqit

Jebel
Laqlouq
Laqlouq

Chilfa

Jebel Younine

Ard el Kichek

Ehmej
Qartaba

Majdel
Mugheir

El Ghabat
Lassa

Machnaqa
Adonis
Nahr el-Ibrahim
(Adonis River)
Jebel
Moussa

Mnaitre
Afqa Spring

Younnine

Nahlé

Iaat

Maitouba
Maiteltein

Faraya
Rock Bridge

Temple
Ruins
Kfar
Debiane
Faqra

Faraya Mazaar
(Ouyan es-
Simaan)
Jebel
Kneisse

Hadet
Nabi
Rchade

Baalbek

Qornet el Becha

Krisse
Anjatoun
Banat
Bakich

Douar Bologna

Dhour
Chouer
Mrouj

Baskinta

Zaarour
Jebel Chaoukat
(1,999m)

Jebel Sannine
(2,628m)

Chimstar

Hosn Niha
Rock-cut
Tombs
Niha
el-Faouqa
Osnaba
Temnin

Bednayel

Baabdat
Majdel
Tarchich
Ain
Toura

Furzol

Kamk

Sergaya

Qornet el Becha

Bahr el Baidar
Pass

Zahle

Rayak

Chtaura
Quabb
Elias

Bar Elias

Kfar
Zabad

Zabadani

Aandoun
Ain Dara
Aaba es-Safa
chita

Majdel
Aanjar
Aanjar

Masnaa

SYRIA

arouk
Maasar
ech-Chouf

Dakweh

Jdaide

Map 5

N

Kefraya
Château
Kefraya

Khraizat

Saghbine

Jobb
Janine

Aifa
el-Foukhar

Bakka

Janta

Deir
el-Ashayer

Dimas

Jebel el Mazar

0 km   5
0 miles 5

Qalaoun
Lake

(1)   (2)   (3)

WELCOME TO
CHAM PALACE
DAMASCUS

One Of

The Leading Hotels of the World

And One Of

CHAM
PALACES & HOTELS

The only de luxe chain covering Syria

**Damascus - Aleppo - Lattakia - Palmyra - Hama
Safita - Deir Ezzor - Bosra Cham**

Head office: Maysaloun str. - P.O.Box: 7570 - Damascus
Phone: (963-11) 2232300 - Fax: (963-11) 2226180 - www.chamhotels.com

Acknowledgements

This book could not have been written without the countless people along the way who helped in numerous different ways. It would be impossible to name them all, but a few who deserve particular mention include: Mr Jacques Lemarchand, Deputy Manager, *Chamtour*, Paris; Ms Rawa Batbouta, Tours Manager, *Chamtour*, Damascus; Yaser Alobali, Manager, *WQS Global Village*, Damascus; Kamal Abou Shaar, *American Express Travel Services*, Damascus; all the staff at the *Al Rabie* hotel, Damascus; Khaled As'ad, Director of Antiquities and Museums, Palmyra; Majed Al Bean, Head of Planning and Studies Dept, Project for the Rehabilitation of the Old City of Aleppo; Bader Tonbur, Owner/Manager, *Noria* hotel, Hama; Elie Daniel, Manager, *Daniel* hotel, Tartus; Dr Mohammad Al Russies of Masyaf; Boushra Haffar, Ministry of Tourism, Beirut; Suki Hakimian, National Museum, Beirut; Venise Hobeika, Assistant Manager, *Avis*, Beirut; Elie Nakhal and Catherine Mansour of *Nakhal & Cie*, Beirut; Joelle, *Theatre Monnot*, Beirut; Wadi Chbat, Owner/manager, *Chbat* hotel, Bcharre; Sarkis Khawaja, Horsh Ehden Nature Reserve, Horsh Ehden; Riad Abdallah, Tour Guide, *TLB travel and tourism*, Antelias; Dr Nabil Haddad, Manger, *MAPAS*, Jeita Grotto, Jeita; Nabil Rached, Public Relations, Solidere, Beirut; Jean Daou, Tourism Coordinator, Al Shouf Cedar Reserve, Barouk.

In addition, the help given by the following people for the 1998 *Jordan, Syria & Lebanon Handbook* has remained directly relevant: Anas Tonbur of the *Cairo* hotel, Hama; Bashir Sultan of Hama; Maher Anjari of Hama; Abdul-Hamid Mourad of Hama; Tarek Abd ar-Raman of Mayadin; Nazir Kassoumeh, Customs house, Damascus; Nabil David Younan, tourist information, Hassakeh; Hala Fayçal, Damascus; Ali Badawi, Tyre; Nabil Nasrallah, Beirut Hippodrome, Beirut; Abdallah Jarrah, Lebanon tourist office, London; Khanjar Abdallah in Beirut and Zabadani (Syria).

Special thanks to the artist **Tim Sage** for his excellent line drawings and **Rania Betmouni**, for the Arabic text. **Ben Townsend** produced the fascinating articles on: The rise of the crusading military orders; the Siege of Qalat Marqab; Sultan Baibars and Frankish and Arabic Cultural Exchange. I would also like to thank everyone at Footprint Handbooks whose hard work behind the scenes contributed to this book. Finally, I would particularly like to thank **Klair Allbuary** for her support throughout this project, for her help in proof reading sections of the text so carefully and thoroughly, and for being as wonderful as ever.

The information on health in the region was compiled from information supplied and received from **Dr David Snashall**, Senior Lecturer in Occupational Health at the United Medical Schools of Guy's and St Thomas' Hospitals in London and Chief Medical Adviser to the British Foreign and Commonwealth Office.

Ivan Mannheim

Ivan Mannheim studied Geography at the School of Oriental and African Studies, University of London, finding time in between to travel extensively in Asia and the Middle East. He first became involved with Footprint Handbooks in 1991 when he contributed two chapters to the South Asian Handbook. After a brief spell office-bound, working for a charity, he went on to research and write the *Pakistan Handbook* with Dave Winter in 1995. The 1998 edition of the *Jordan, Syria & Lebanon Handbook*, together with the 2000 Jordan Handbook and now this new edition Syria & Lebanon Handbook, have involved him in extensive travel throughout the Middle East, visiting each of the countries concerned several times in the course of his work. Ivan lives in Dorset and when not writing guidebooks, works as an apprentice organic vegetable grower. In his spare time he pursues his interests in sailing, walking and motorcycles.